THE OXFORD HANDBOOK OF

THE EUROPEAN BRONZE AGE

The Oxford Handbook of the European Bronze Age is a wide-ranging survey of a crucial period in prehistory during which many social, economic, and technological changes took place. Written by expert specialists in the field, the book provides coverage both of the themes that characterize the period, and of the specific developments that took place in the various countries of Europe.

After an introduction and a discussion of chronology, successive chapters deal with settlement studies, burial analysis, hoards and hoarding, monumentality, rock art, cosmology, gender, and trade, as well as a series of articles on specific technologies and crafts (such as transport, metals, glass, salt, textiles, and weighing). The second half of the book covers each country in turn. From Ireland to Russia, Scandinavia to Sicily, every area is considered, and up to date information on important recent finds is discussed in detail.

The book is the first to consider the whole of the European Bronze Age in both geographical and thematic terms, and will be the standard book on the subject for the foreseeable future.

Harry Fokkens is Professor Emeritus of European Prehistory at the University of Leiden.

Anthony Harding is Professor of Archaeology at the University of Exeter.

Praise for *The Oxford Handbook of the European Bronze Age*

'This handbook provides a multitude of voices on, and entry points into, a complex historical epoch we are perhaps only just beginning to understand. It is now the starting point for anyone interested in knowing more about the European Bronze Age.'

Kristian Kristiansen, *Antiquity*

'... an invaluable reference for students and professionals alike, but is also accessible enough for an interested reader to enjoy.'

Polly Heffer, *Current World Archaeology*

'... indispensable ... for anyone seeking to contextualise their Bronze Age findings or research, this volume should be an early port of call.'

Carleton Jones, *Irish Archaeology*

THE OXFORD HANDBOOK OF

THE EUROPEAN BRONZE AGE

Edited by
HARRY FOKKENS
and
ANTHONY HARDING

UNIVERSITY PRESS

Great Clarendon Street, Oxford, OX2 6DP,
United Kingdom

Oxford University Press is a department of the University of Oxford.
It furthers the University's objective of excellence in research, scholarship,
and education by publishing worldwide. Oxford is a registered trade mark of
Oxford University Press in the UK and in certain other countries

© Oxford University Press 2013

The moral rights of the authors have been asserted

First published 2013
First published in paperback 2020

All rights reserved. No part of this publication may be reproduced, stored in
a retrieval system, or transmitted, in any form or by any means, without the
prior permission in writing of Oxford University Press, or as expressly permitted
by law, by licence or under terms agreed with the appropriate reprographics
rights organization. Enquiries concerning reproduction outside the scope of the
above should be sent to the Rights Department, Oxford University Press, at the
address above

You must not circulate this work in any other form
and you must impose this same condition on any acquirer

Published in the United States of America by Oxford University Press
198 Madison Avenue, New York, NY 10016, United States of America

British Library Cataloguing in Publication Data
Data available

Library of Congress Cataloging in Publication Data
Data available

ISBN 978-0-19-957286-1 (Hbk.)
ISBN 978-0-19-885507-1 (Pbk.)

Printed and bound by
CPI Group (UK) Ltd, Croydon, CR0 4YY

Links to third party websites are provided by Oxford in good faith and
for information only. Oxford disclaims any responsibility for the materials
contained in any third party website referenced in this work.

The manufacturer's authorised representative in the EU for product safety is
Oxford University Press España S.A. of El Parque Empresarial San Fernando
de Henares, Avenida de Castilla, 2 – 28830 Madrid (www.oup.es/en or
product.safety@oup.com). OUP España S.A. also acts as importer into Spain of
products made by the manufacturer.

Preface

THIS Handbook in the Oxford series covers an area and period that have produced much spectacular new evidence in recent years. The enormous volume of new publications in all parts of Europe makes it ever harder to keep up with the progress of research, in the Bronze Age as in so many other periods. The authors in this volume, all experts in their field, have provided overviews of the topics assigned them which, it is hoped, will go some way to make it easier for students, specialists, and the interested layperson to get up to date with the latest information in the field.

A range of sources are used for the illustrations. Wherever possible, permission to reproduce copyright material has been obtained from the copyright holder, to whom we offer thanks. In a few cases this was not possible, because the author was dead, the publishing house defunct, or for similar reasons. Every effort has been made to obtain permission in all other cases, but should there be any errors or omissions, we would be pleased to insert the appropriate acknowledgement in any subsequent edition of this publication. Where composite illustrations are involved, making use of many small images, these have been redrawn after the original publication, the source of which is cited.

The authors of Chapter 5 would like to thank Simone Lemmers (University of Leiden) for collecting many of the articles drawn upon therein, Julie Allec for translating a number of papers, and Tim Earle and Marie Louise Sørensen for allowing them to read relevant chapters of their recent volume prior to publication.

Regarding Chapter 10, the Beaker People Project is funded by the UK's Arts and Humanities Research Council. Isotopic analytical work has been undertaken for it at the Max Planck Institute for Evolutionary Anthropology in Leipzig (Germany), the University of Bradford (UK), and the NERC Isotope Geosciences Laboratory in Nottingham (UK). Isotope analyses have involved Mike Richards (Max Planck Institute and Durham University), Maura Pellegrini (Bradford), and Jane Evans (NIGL), as well as the authors.

The authors of Chapter 11 are grateful to Sheila Kohring for suggesting useful references on social complexity and chiefdoms outside the literature on the European Bronze Age, and to Alexander Verpoorte and the editors for many helpful comments on an earlier draft.

The author of Chapter 16 would like to thank Pedro Andres Garzon, Anthony Harding, and Harry Fokkens for valuable suggestions. The translation is by Terry Newenham and Elena Lionnet.

For readily providing them with large amounts of unpublished data, the authors of Chapter 19 give special thanks to Angela Kreuz (Wiesbaden), H. Kroll (Kiel), and Ferenc Gyulai (Gödöllö). Further thanks go to L. Bouby (Montpellier), C. Brombacher (Basel), G. Campbell (Fort Cumberland), F. Green (Lymington), M. Hajnalová (Nitra), A. Hall (York), M. Kohler-Schneider (Vienna), T. Märkle (Gaienhofen), E. Marinova (Leuven), A. M. Mercuri (Modena), A. Mueller-Bieniek (Kraków), G. A. Pashkevich (Kishinev),

G. Pérez Jordà (Valencia), M. Rottoli (Como), L. Sadori (Rome), U. Töchterle (Innsbruck), S. M. Valamoti (Thessaloniki), and M. van der Veen (Leicester).

The author of Chapter 22 would like to thank Professor Albrecht Jockenhövel, who kindly allowed her access to his collection of publications on the topic, read drafts of the text, and made helpful comments.

Thanks are due to the staff at Oxford University Press, in particular Hilary O'Shea (commissioning editor), Taryn Das Neves, and Cathryn Steele, for their help in producing the volume. We also thank Richard Mason for his professional and efficient editing of the manuscript, which has greatly improved the quality and hastened the production of the book. The editors are indebted to Carolien Fokke and Corijanne Neeleman, who formatted the typescripts and checked the bibliographies for each chapter, and to a number of postgraduate students at Exeter University who assisted with improving the translations of articles in languages other than English.

Anthony Harding and Harry Fokkens

May 2012

Table of Contents

List of Illustrations — xviii
List of Tables — xxviii
List of Contributors — xxix

1. Introduction: The Bronze Age of Europe — 1
   HARRY FOKKENS AND ANTHONY HARDING
   - Sources of Information — 3
   - Debates in Bronze Age Archaeology — 7
   - The Way Ahead — 10
   - Conclusion — 11

PART I THEMES IN BRONZE AGE ARCHAEOLOGY

2. Old Father Time: The Bronze Age Chronology of Western Europe — 17
   BENJAMIN W. ROBERTS, MARION UCKELMANN, AND DIRK BRANDHERM
   - Introduction — 17
   - Britain and Ireland — 22
   - The Netherlands, France, and Belgium — 25
   - Iberia — 33
   - Conclusion — 38

3. Europe 2500 to 2200 BC: Between Expiring Ideologies and Emerging Complexity — 47
   VOLKER HEYD
   - Europe at *c.*2500 BC — 47
   - The Period of the 'International Spirit' in the Aegean — 48
   - New Peripheries in the Balkans and Southern Italy — 49
   - Beyond the Peripheries: The Gradual Transmission of New Ideas, Values, and Achievements — 59
   - Meeting the Bell Beaker Network — 62
   - Conflicting World Views Between 2500 and 2200 BC — 64

4. A Little Bit of History Repeating Itself: Theories on the Bell Beaker Phenomenon — 68
   MARC VANDER LINDEN
   - A Sense of *Déjà Vu* — 68

From Beakers to Folk: Culture-History (c.1900–1970s)   70
From Folk to Elites: Processual Approaches
(1970s–early 1990s)   72
From Elites to Phenomenon: The Analytical Age
(late 1990s–Present)   74
A Little Bit of History Repeating Itself   76

5. Bronze Age Settlements   82
   JOANNA BRÜCK AND HARRY FOKKENS

   Introduction   82
   Houses and Households in Anthropological Perspective   83
   Bronze Age House Architecture   84
   Explaining Size Differences Between Houses   87
   The Organization of Household Space   88
   The Bronze Age Farmstead   90
   Bronze Age Villages   91
   Identifying Settlement Hierarchies   93
   The House-Landscapes of Bronze Age Europe   95
   Conclusion   97

6. Burials   102
   MADS KÄHLER HOLST

   Introduction   102
   Bronze Age Burial Traditions   103
   Individuals and their Artefacts   106
   The Burial as Event: Activities, Sequences, and Meetings   109
   Cemeteries, Clusters, and Communities   112
   The Setting of the Burials   114
   Conclusion   117

7. Hoards and the Deposition of Metalwork   121
   RICHARD BRADLEY

   Introduction: The Archbishop's Treasure   121
   Hoards and the Development of Prehistoric Archaeology   122
   Problems of Interpretation   122
   Contexts and Contents   123
   The Role of the Smith   129
   Some Wider Implications   130
   Space and Time   133
   Unfinished Business   135
   Conclusion   137

8. Monuments and Monumentality in Bronze Age Europe   140
   TIMOTHY DARVILL

   Introduction   140
   Late Chambered Tombs   143

Round Barrows, Kurgans, Tumuli, and 'fancy barrows'	144
Standing Stones, Statue Menhirs, and Stelae	146
Pairs and Rows	149
Circles and Ovals	150
Natural Places, Shafts, and Pools	153
Enclosures, Shrines, and Cult Houses	155
Conclusion	157

9. Stonehenge — 159
   MIKE PARKER PEARSON, PETER MARSHALL, JOSH POLLARD,
   COLIN RICHARDS, JULIAN THOMAS, AND KATE WELHAM

Introduction	159
A Short History of Recent Research	160
Previous Chronological Schemes for Stonehenge	161
Before Stonehenge	161
Stonehenge Stage 1 (3015–2935 cal BC)	162
Stonehenge Stage 2 (2620–2480 cal BC)	165
Stonehenge Stage 3 (2480–2280 cal BC)	171
Stonehenge Stage 4 (2270–2020 cal BC)	173
Stonehenge Stage 5 (1630–1520 cal BC)	174

10. The Contribution of Skeletal Isotope Analysis to Understanding the Bronze Age in Europe — 179
    JANET MONTGOMERY AND MANDY JAY

Introduction	179
The Techniques	180
Factors Reflected by the Different Systems	180
Different Skeletal Fractions	181
Isotopic Background	182
Skeletal Data from Animals	184
Migration and Diet Studies	184
Existing Data and Interpretations for the European Bronze Age	187
The Beaker People Project	188
Dietary Studies	189
Limitations and Problems	191
Future Work	192

11. The Myth of the Chief: Prestige Goods, Power, and Personhood in the European Bronze Age — 197
    JOANNA BRÜCK AND DAVID FONTIJN

Introduction	197
Empirical Issues	198
Homo economicus and the Subject-Object Divide	201
Power, Hierarchy, and Personhood	203
Social and Material Relations in the European Bronze Age	204
Conclusion	212

12. Identity, Gender, and Dress in the European Bronze Age — 216
    Marie Louise Stig Sørensen
    - Introduction — 216
    - On Identity and Gender — 217
    - Bronze Age Identities — 218
    - The Evidence for the Dressed Person: Men and Women and Other Identities — 222
    - Changes through the Bronze Age — 226
    - Conclusion — 231

13. Warfare in the European Bronze Age — 234
    Nick Thorpe
    - Introduction — 234
    - Weaponry — 234
    - Art — 238
    - Defended Sites — 239
    - Victims of Violence — 240
    - The Importance of Variability and Future Research — 245

14. Rethinking Bronze Age Cosmology: A North European Perspective — 248
    Joakim Goldhahn
    - Introduction — 248
    - A Brand-New World — 250
    - Cosmology and Bronze Age Landscape Cognition — 253
    - To Get 'something great in exchange for something small' — 255
    - Smiths as Cosmologists — 257
    - Concluding Remarks: Cosmologies in the Making — 263
    - Chapter 14A: The Sky Disc of Nebra — 266

15. Bronze Age Rock Art in Northern Europe: Contexts and Interpretations — 270
    Joakim Goldhahn and Johan Ling
    - Introduction — 270
    - The Images and Interpretative Trends — 272
    - Rock Art Chronology — 274
    - Rock Art and Landscape — 275
    - Rock Art and Seascapes — 277
    - Excavating Rock Art — 282
    - Picturing the Dead — 283
    - Theories about Rock Art, Agency, and Society — 285
    - Rock Art Practice and Cosmology — 286
    - Rock Art as Social Format — 287
    - Conclusion — 288

16. Rock Carvings and Alpine Statue-Menhirs, from the Chalcolithic to the Middle Bronze Age — 291
    Geoffroy de Saulieu

	Introduction	291
	Chrono-Cultural Attributes	293
	The Sites	297
	Factors Affecting the Form and Content of the Art	303
	Iconographic Variations	305
17.	Bronze Age Fields and Land Division	311
	ROBERT JOHNSTON	
	Introduction	311
	Prehistoric Land Division: A Historical Perspective	311
	Classifying Fields	314
	The Chronology and History of Fields	315
	Early Fields on the Edges of Europe	316
	Stone Cairns and Walls in the Western Uplands	318
	Linear Landscapes in Southern Britain	320
	'Celtic Fields' in North-West Europe	322
	Fields, Landscape, and Society	324
18.	Animals in Bronze Age Europe	328
	LÁSZLÓ BARTOSIEWICZ	
	Introduction	328
	Chronological Framework and the Near Eastern Paradigm	329
	Trends in Bronze Age Animal Exploitation	330
	Cattle	331
	Pig	333
	Sheep and Goat	334
	Horse and Ass	335
	Dog	337
	Fowl and Domestic Hen	338
	Hunting	339
	Conclusion	342
19.	Plant Cultivation in the Bronze Age	348
	HANS-PETER STIKA AND ANDREAS G. HEISS	
	Introduction	348
	Methods	348
	Regional Overviews	349
	Individual Cereals, Plants, and Trees	359
	Conclusion	364
20.	Trade and Exchange	370
	ANTHONY HARDING	
	The Meaning of Trade	370
	Sources of Evidence	371
	Objects Found Outside their Place of Manufacture	372
	Conclusion: Connectivity in the Bronze Age	379

21. Seafaring and Riverine Navigation in the Bronze Age of Europe   382
   ROBERT VAN DE NOORT

   Introduction   382
   Mediterranean Europe   383
   Atlantic Europe   387
   Europe's Rivers   390
   Conclusion: Current Debates and Future
   Research Directions   392

22. Land Transport in the Bronze Age   398
   MARION UCKELMANN

   Introduction   398
   Speed of Transport and Loads   400
   Wagons   402
   Roads and Paths   407
   Conclusion   411

23. Copper and Bronze: Bronze Age Metalworking in Context   414
   TOBIAS L. KIENLIN

   Approaches to Prehistoric Metalworking   414
   Prologue: The Beginnings of Metallurgy   415
   Bronze and the Bronze Age   419
   Alpine Copper and Bronze Age Mining Communities   421
   Smelting: Geology-Derived 'Stages' and Prehistoric Reality   425
   Casting and Working: Technological Choice and
   Compositional 'Determinism'   427
   Metalworking and Society   431

24. Bronze Age Copper Mining in Europe   437
   WILLIAM O'BRIEN

   Bronze Age Copper Mines in Europe   438
   The Search for Copper   446
   The Approach to Mining   447
   The Mining Environment   448
   Mining and Metal Production   449
   Mining and Society   450

25. Gold and Gold Working of the Bronze Age   454
   BARBARA ARMBRUSTER

   Introduction   454
   A History of Research   455
   The Find Context   457
   Form and Function   458
   The Chronological Development
   of Goldworking   461
   Methods of Investigation   463

	The Acquisition of Gold	463
	Gold Technology	464
	Beyond the Bronze Age	466
26.	**Craft Production: Ceramics, Textiles, and Bone**	469
	JOANNA SOFAER, LISE BENDER JØRGENSEN, AND ALICE CHOYKE	
	Introduction	469
	Ceramics	469
	Textiles	477
	Worked Bone	482
	Conclusion	487
27.	**Glass and Faience**	492
	JULIAN HENDERSON	
	The Production of Glass and Glassy Materials	493
	Production Zones	494
	Bronze Age Faience/Glass in Northern Italy	496
	Conclusion	498
28.	**Salt Production in the Bronze Age**	501
	ANTHONY HARDING	
	Production Using Briquetage	502
	Coastal and Inland Production in the Mediterranean	502
	Bronze Age Salt Mining at Hallstatt and Other Rock Salt Sources	503
	Bronze Age Salt	505
29.	**Weighing, Commodification, and Money**	508
	CHRISTOPHER PARE	
	Introduction	508
	The Earliest Evidence for Weighing	508
	Developments in the East Mediterranean in the Later Bronze Age	510
	Italy and Central Europe	511
	Weighing in Bronze Age Europe	514
	Weighing and Commodification	522
	Conclusion	524

PART II THE BRONZE AGE BY REGION

30.	**Britain and Ireland in the Bronze Age: Farmers in the Landscape or Heroes on the High Seas?**	531
	BENJAMIN W. ROBERTS	
	Introduction	531
	Monuments, Burials, and Craftsmanship: Mid Third–Early Second Millennium BC	533

Settlements, Cremations, and Hoards: The Mid Second–Early
First Millennium BC 537
Conclusion 543

31. The Bronze Age in the Low Countries 550
    HARRY FOKKENS AND DAVID FONTIJN

    Introduction 550
    The Natural Environment and Palaeogeography 551
    Chronology and Cultural Traditions 552
    Settlements and Architecture 553
    Funerary Archaeology 557
    Treatment of the Dead 558
    Graves and Grave Goods 558
    Metalwork and Hoarding, River Depositions 562
    Conclusion 565

32. The Bronze Age in France 571
    CLAUDE MORDANT

    The Geographical and Cultural Framework 571
    Settlements and the Use of Space 575
    Funerary Practice and Beliefs 581
    Metal Production 585
    Conclusion 590

33. Bronze Age Iberia 594
    VICENTE LULL, RAFAEL MICÓ, CRISTINA RIHUETE HERRADA,
    AND ROBERTO RISCH

    The Early Bronze Age (c.2200–1550 cal BC) 596
    The Late Bronze Age (c.1550–1300 cal BC) 609
    The Final Bronze Age (c.1300–900 cal BC) 611

34. The Bronze Age in the Balearic Islands 617
    VICENTE LULL, RAFAEL MICÓ, CRISTINA RIHUETE HERRADA,
    AND ROBERTO RISCH

    The First Phase of Human Population in Mallorca
    and Menorca (c.2300–1600 cal BC) 619
    The Naviform Group (c.1600–1100/1000 cal BC) 622
    The Proto-Talayotic Period (c.1100/1000–850 cal BC) 628

35. Peninsular Italy 632
    ANNA MARIA BIETTI SESTIERI

    Introduction 632
    The Cultural Sequence 635
    Conclusion 649

36. The Bronze Age in Sicily 653
    ANNA MARIA BIETTI SESTIERI

The Early Bronze Age (*c*.2200–1500 BC)	654
The Middle Bronze Age (*c*.1500–1250 BC)	658
The Late Bronze and Early Iron Ages (*c*.13th–9th Centuries BC)	662
The Final Bronze Age and Early Iron Age in the Aeolian Islands and Sicily (*c*.11th–9th Centuries BC)	664

37. **The Bronze Age in Sardinia** — 668
    FULVIA LO SCHIAVO

    A Large Island: Almost a Continent — 668
    Issues of Chronology — 670
    The Nuragic Civilization — 672
    The 'Nuraghi Golden Age' — 674
    The End of the Bronze Age and Beginning of the Iron Age — 685
    The Coming of the Age of Iron — 687

38. **Northern Italy** — 692
    FRANCO NICOLIS

    Introduction — 692
    Chronology — 693
    Cultural Development — 694
    Funerary Rites — 699
    Ritual, Cult, and Religion — 702
    Conclusion — 703

39. **Switzerland and the Central Alps** — 706
    PHILIPPE DELLA CASA

    Environment, Climate, Settlement — 706
    Chronology and Chorology — 709
    Settlement Topography, Settlement Structures — 713
    Economic Background — 717
    Society and Ideology — 718

40. **Germany in the Bronze Age** — 723
    ALBRECHT JOCKENHÖVEL

    Introduction — 723
    Central and Southern Germany — 725
    Eastern Germany: The Lausitz Culture — 734
    Northern Germany: The Nordic Bronze Age — 735
    Settlement — 738

41. **Scandinavia** — 746
    HENRIK THRANE

    Introduction — 746
    Cultural Development and Diversity — 748
    Chronology and Regional Differentiation — 749
    Settlement — 750

Agriculture and Land Use ... 752
Mounds ... 752
Burials ... 754
Arts and Crafts ... 759
Rock Carvings ... 763
Trade and Transport ... 763
Hoards and Votive Deposits ... 764
Conclusion ... 764

42. The Bronze Age in the Polish Lands ... 767
JANUSZ CZEBRESZUK

Introduction: The Natural Environment ... 767
Historic Regions of Polish Territory ... 768
Cultural Chronology ... 768
The Cultural Sequence ... 770
The Middle Bronze Age ... 772
The Late Bronze Age/Hallstatt Period ... 772
Settlement and Economy ... 773
Burials ... 775
Material Culture ... 776
Industries Based on Other Raw Materials ... 778
Other Aspects of Social Life in the Bronze Age ... 779
Conclusion ... 783

43. The Czech Lands and Austria in the Bronze Age ... 787
LUBOŠ JIRÁŇ, MILAN SALAŠ, AND ALEXANDRA KRENN-LEEB

Introduction: Natural Environment and Landscapes ... 787
Cultural Sequence and Chronology ... 789
Settlement and Settlements ... 791
Funerary Archaeology: Implications
for Society and Identity ... 794
Material Culture ... 799

44. Slovakia and Hungary ... 813
KLÁRA MARKOVÁ WITH GÁBOR ILON

Setting and Natural Conditions ... 813
Chronology ... 814
The Early Bronze Age (c.2500/2300–1500/1450 cal BC) ... 814
The Middle Bronze Age (c.1500/1450–1200/1150 cal BC) ... 825
The Late and Final Bronze Age (c.1250/1150–800/750 cal BC) ... 827
The End of the Bronze Age ... 832

45. The Western Balkans in the Bronze Age ... 837
BIBA TERŽAN, WITH SNJEŽANA KARAVANIĆ

Introduction: Geography and Environment ... 837
Settlements and their Social Implications ... 839

    Burial Rites and their Social Implications   849

46. *Castellieri-Gradine* of the Northern Adriatic   864
    Kristina Mihovilić

    A History of Research   864
    The Characteristics of *Castellieri-Gradine*   867
    Economy   873
    Chronology   873

47. Romania, Moldova, and Bulgaria   877
    Nikolaus Boroffka

    A History of Research   877
    Chronology and Terminology   879
    Cultural Evolution   880
    Metal   891
    Transport and the Symbolic Meaning of Vehicles   894
    Conclusion   895

48. Ukraine and South Russia in the Bronze Age   898
    Hermann Parzinger

    The Foundations of Bronze Age Cultural Development:
    The Eneolithic   899
    Arsenical Bronzes, Wagons, and Domestic Horses:
    The Beginnings of the Bronze Age   901
    Consolidation and Further Development: From the Catacomb Culture
    to the Srubnaya Culture   905
    The Heyday of Bronze Age Cultural Relationships:
    From Sabatinovka to Belozerka   911
    The End of the Bronze Age and Beginnings
    of Horse-Borne Nomadism   914
    Conclusion   915

Index   919

List of Illustrations

1.1	Type table as devised by Oscar Montelius.	5
2.1	Synchronized version of the relevant chronological systems for Western Europe.	18–19
2.2	Synchronized version of the relevant chronological systems for Great Britain and Ireland.	23–24
2.3	Synchronized version of the relevant chronological systems for the Netherlands.	26–27
2.4	Synchronized version of the relevant chronological systems for France, Belgium, and the Netherlands.	28–29
2.5	Synchronized version of the relevant chronological systems for Iberia.	34–35
3.1	Map showing the extent of the circum-Aegean exchange and trade network and its cultural peripheries in the Balkans and central Mediterranean in the formative phase of the Early Bronze Age (*c*.2500–2200 BC).	50
3.2	Chronological correlation of archaeological cultures, groups, and key site stratigraphies for the Balkans in the third millennium BC.	52
3.3	Bulgaria (and Serbia and Sicily): elements of the Lefkandi I-Kastri pottery repertoire, other later third millennium BC pottery imports, and potential imitations.	53
3.4	Former Yugoslavia: heavier gold and silver finds belonging to the second half of the third millennium BC.	56
3.5	Italy: key third millennium BC finds with Aegean, or probable Aegean, connections.	57
3.6	Italy and Greece: later third millennium BC Italian finds of Aegean, or probable Aegean, origin, and comparisons in Greece and Troy.	60
4.1	Distribution map of the Bell Beaker phenomenon.	69
4.2	The changing configurations of interpretative themes regarding the Bell Beaker phenomenon.	77
5.1	Two of the longhouses at Bjerre site 2, north-west Jutland.	85
5.2	House A at Cloghbreedy, County Tipperary, Ireland.	86
5.3	Reconstruction of a house from the tell at Százhalombatta, overlooking the Danube in northern Hungary.	87
5.4	House 13 at Apalle, central Sweden.	89

5.5	Layout of the defended settlement at Fidvár, west central Slovakia, based on geophysical and walkover survey.	94
5.6	Houses, fields, and droveways characterize this highly organized Bronze Age landscape on Chagford Common, Dartmoor, south-west England.	97
6.1	The well-preserved oak-log coffin inhumation burial of Borum Eshøj, Jutland, from 1500–1300 BC and the Hvidegård cremation burial from Sjælland, period III, 1300–1100 BC.	105
6.2	Plan of the Early Bronze Age great barrow of Skelhøj in southern Denmark.	111
6.3	Stratigraphical sequences and gender patterns in the use of the barrows from Early to Late Bronze Age at the Ripdorf cemetery, Lüneburg, Germany.	114
6.4	The development of the Normanton Down barrow group, southern England, with the emergence of linear alignments around 1800–1500 BC.	116
7.1	The relationship between finds of metalwork, Bronze Age settlements, burnt mounds, and freshwater streams at two sites in south-east England.	126
7.2	The siting of two metalwork hoards in south-east England.	127
7.3	The overlapping distributions of Urnfield swords in Austrian rivers and hoards.	132
7.4	The complementary distributions of Mindelheim and Thames swords in rivers and graves.	133
7.5	A model suggesting the spatial and chronological relationships between finds from rivers and graves, and the occurrence of similar artefacts in scrap hoards.	134
8.1	Map of Europe showing the position and extent of the five monument-building zones discussed.	142
8.2	Silbury Hill, Wiltshire, England.	146
8.3	(a) Menhir at Rhos-y-Clegyrn, Pembrokeshire, Wales; (b) Statue menhir at Castel, Guernsey; (c) Stele Torrejón el Rubio II, Ca, Portugal, showing a human figure 0.69 m high and wearing a striking headdress or diadem; Stone rows: (d) Harold's Stones near Trelleck, Monmouthshire, Wales; (e) The Devil's Arrows near Boroughbridge, North Yorkshire, England.	148
8.4	Stone circles: (a) Drombeg, County Cork, Ireland; (b) Stonehenge, Wiltshire, England.	152
9.1	The environs of Stonehenge.	160
9.2	Stage 1 of Stonehenge.	163
9.3	Stage 2 of Stonehenge.	166
9.4	Stage 3 of Stonehenge.	172

9.5	Stage 4 of Stonehenge.	174
9.6	Stage 5 of Stonehenge.	175
10.1	Carbon and nitrogen isotopic ratios for Early Bronze Age and Iron Age humans and terrestrial herbivores (cattle and sheep) from Wetwang and local sites on the East Yorkshire chalk Wolds (UK).	185
10.2	Human enamel data from Neolithic (white symbols) and Bronze Age (black symbols) barrows of the Yorkshire Wolds (UK).	186
11.1	Selective deposition in the last phase of the Late Bronze Age in Belgium, Germany, and the Netherlands. Map showing the location of hoards containing axes and/or ornaments and swords.	199
11.2	Reconstruction of the central burial in the Early Bronze Age Leubingen barrow (eastern Germany).	201
11.3	The lunula from Coolaghmore, County Kilkenny.	210
12.1	Illustrations of a 'lur-blower'.	223
12.2	Examples of Bronze Age clay figurines from the Carpathian Basin.	224
12.3	Illustration of the normative differences between male and female burials at the Early Bronze Age cemetery of Gemainlebarn F, Austria.	227
12.4	Indications of the degree of regional differentiations amongst women in central Europe during the Tumulus culture.	229
12.5	Illustration of the principal structural emphasis of the Middle Bronze Age female body maps in central Europe.	230
13.1	Part of the art panel at Fossum, Bohuslän, Sweden, showing ships and male figures bearing axes, bows, and other weapons.	238
13.2	One of the bone depositions at Velim, Czech Republic, showing partial human skeletons.	241
13.3	Burial pit of Wassenaar, the Netherlands, dated to the Early Bronze Age, with the remains of 12 individuals.	242
13.4	The Tollense Valley, Mecklenburg-Vorpommern, northern Germany: a skull showing major trauma on the cranial vault.	243
14.1	The Bronze Age 'Weltbild' by Karol Schauer.	249
14.2	Iconography on Danish Bronze razors, Late Bronze Age, 1100–500 cal BC.	252
14.3	Bronze Age cosmology and landscape cognition.	254
14.4	The 'workshop' at Hallunda, Stockholm, in Sweden.	259
14.5	Animated tuyères and soapstone moulds from different parts of Scandinavia.	261
14.6	Soapstone quarries with rock art from Krabbestig in Sogn og Fjordane, western Norway.	262
14.A1	The double artefact assemblage found with the Sky Disc. Such groups are also found in Early Bronze Age princely tombs. The shape of the magnificent swords was based on Carpathian prototypes, and the gold wire band on the pommel has Scottish parallels.	267

14.A2	The five phases of development of the Sky Disc imagery. Three types of gold were used for the inlays of the Disc. The horizon arcs and the displaced star (phase II) as well as the boat (phase III) were made of a different type of gold than the original sun, moon and stars. The perforation of the Disc´s rim damaged the earlier inlays. The 'eastern' arc was probably torn off as part of the deposition ritual (phase V).	269
15.1	A very tentative map covering the southern part of Scandinavia, showing the main distribution of the Bronze Age rock-art traditions mentioned in the text.	271
15.2	Realistic ship depictions, humans, animals, feet, and abstract designs from panel Skee 1539 in northern Bohuslän.	273
15.3	The chronological outline of rock-art ships from the Tanum area in northern Bohuslän, Sweden.	276
15.4	The distribution of rock art panels in the Tanum area in western Sweden.	281
15.5	The building sequence of the Sagaholm barrow.	284
16.1	Map of the Po Valley with regions and sites.	292
16.2	Examples of monumental art from northern Italy.	294
16.3	Three examples of art from Foppe di Nadro in Valcamonica, with weapons which can be attributed to the Early Bronze Age.	295
16.4	Left: a geometric figure from the Fontanalba sector in the Mont Bégo region (France). Right: two geometric figures with boxes, from rock 6 from the Luine site in Valcamonica (Italy).	302
16.5	The rock known as 'the man with the zigzag arms', in the Merveilles sector of Mont Bégo (France).	302
16.6	Two examples of discreet art in northern Italy and southern France.	304
17.1	Map of north-west Europe showing the locations of key sites discussed in the chapter.	313
17.2	Simplified plans showing part of the Middle Bronze Age fields and settlement on Leskernick Hill, Bodmin Moor, and the Later Neolithic houses, field boundaries, and clearance cairns at Scord of Brouster, Shetland.	317
17.3	Simplified plans of the co-axial field systems on Horridge Common, Dartmoor, and the Celtic fields at Het Noordse Veld, Zeijen, Drenthe, the Netherlands.	321
18.1	The distribution of 238 Bronze Age archaeozoological assemblages by the percentages of domestic artiodactyls.	331
18.2	Speed ranges of humans, oxen, and horses.	336
18.3	Large and small antler mattocks made from gathered red-deer antler from the Middle Bronze Age Vatya Culture site of Csongrád–Vidre-sziget, Hungary.	341
18.4	The distribution of major animal species by their rates of reproduction and resource mobility.	342

18.5	Bronze Age duck-shaped bronze vessel from an unknown provenance in Hungary.	343
20.1	Distribution of oxhide ingots in the Mediterranean and beyond.	373
20.2	The supposed amber routes linking the Baltic and North Sea with the Mediterranean.	376
21.1	(a) Schematic representation of hull construction using locked mortise-and-tenon joinery of the Uluburun and Cape Gelidonya shipwrecks; (b) Schematic representation of the construction of a sewn-plan boat.	384
21.2	Distribution of logboat 'zones' according to Lanting (1997/8).	391
22.1	The wooden disc wheels from Glum, Ldkr. Oldenburg, Germany.	403
22.2	(a) Cast bronze wheels from Stade, Germany; (b) Schematic drawing of reconstructions of a two-wheeled and a four-wheeled cart.	404
22.3	Bronze cauldron-wagon (*Kesselwagen*) from Acholshausen, Ldr. Würzburg, southern Germany.	408
22.4	Late Bronze Age trackway XII (Le) from a bog near Ockenhausen-Oltmannsfehn, Ldkr. Leer, northern Germany.	409
22.5	Bronze Age trackway 10 from Derryoghil, County Longford, Ireland.	410
23.1	Suggested *chaîne opératoire* for the finishing of Eneolithic/Copper Age hammer-axes and axe-adzes by hot-working.	417
23.2	The earliest copper artefacts known from the north Alpine region of central Europe.	418
23.3	Map indicating the approximate dates of the transition to the use of tin-bronze and the major tin deposits in Europe.	421
23.4	The SAM projects statistical groups, or 'Stammbaum'.	423
23.5	Suggested *chaîne opératoire* for the finishing of Early Bronze Age Saxon-type axes by a cycle of cold-working (bottom), intermediate annealing and final cold-working (top) to increase hardness.	428
23.6	Comparison of the average hardness, minimum and maximum hardness values of various Eneolithic/Copper Age and Bronze Age axe types.	429
24.1	Chalcolithic and Bronze Age copper mines in Europe.	439
24.2	(a) Chalcolithic/Early Bronze Age copper mine at El Aramo, Asturias, Spain; (b) Bronze Age copper mine at the Great Orme, North Wales.	444
25.1	(a) Middle to Late Bronze Age collection of jewellery from Guînes, Pas-de-Calais, France; (b) Forged Early Bronze Age arm ornaments from Lockington, Leicestershire, England.	455
25.2	Gold spirals and a bronze case from Skeldal, Jutland, Denmark.	457
25.3	Gold bowl from Zürich-Altstetten, Zürich, Switzerland.	459
25.4	Arm ornaments cast in lost-wax technique from the Late Bronze Age hoard of Villena, Alicante, Spain.	463

26.1	Early Bronze Age collared urn. Stourhead Collection.	471
26.2	Middle Bronze Age Koszider period bowl, Százhalombatta, Hungary.	472
26.3	An example of the Bronze Age textiles from the salt mines of Hallstatt.	481
26.4	Characteristically simple bone tools from Hungary.	484
26.5	Horse-harness antler fittings produced by part-time specialists, Százhalombatta-Földvár, Hungary.	485
27.1	A highly magnified SEM image of a (turquoise green) faience sample from Hauterive-Champréveyres, Lake Neuchâtel, Switzerland.	493
27.2	The compositional distinction between plant-ash and mixed-alkali Bronze Age glass. Both types have been found in Europe.	495
27.3	Conical faience button found in 2010 at the Parma-Palafitta site, dating to the nineteenth century BC.	497
28.1	Briquetage of Bronze Age date from Britain, Germany, and Poland.	503
28.2	Wooden trough from Băile Figa, Beclean, northern Romania.	505
29.1	Distribution map of weighing equipment (weights and balances) at the time of the Aegean Bronze Age palace civilization (twentieth–thirteenth century BC).	509
29.2	Stone weights of 'Terramare' type: 1. Gaiato; 2. Casinalbo; 3. Montale; 4. Quingento; 5. Lefkandi; 6. Gaggio di Castelfranco Emilia.	511
29.3	1. Copper ring-ingots in bundles in the Ragelsdorf 2 hoard; 2. Copper ring-ingot from the Ragelsdorf 2 hoard; 3. Copper clasp-ingot from St Florian; 4. Miniature copper ingot from Thal.	513
29.4	Distribution map of 1. pure ring-ingot hoards; 2. mixed ring-ingot hoards; 3. clasp-ingot hoards.	515
29.5	Distribution of the weights of the copper ingot fragments in the hoard from Spălnaca II, Transylvania.	516
29.6	Bronze Age weighing equipment.	518
29.7	Final Bronze Age weights from France and Switzerland.	521
30.1	Map of Britain and Ireland showing the sites mentioned in the text.	533
30.2	The Ringlemere gold cup.	537
30.3	The Langdon Bay hoard.	539
30.4	The Dover Boat.	541
30.5	An artistic reconstruction of Springfield Lyons in Essex, showing the Late Bronze Age enclosure with its roundhouse structures.	542
31.1	Map of the Low Countries showing sites mentioned in the text.	552
31.2	The most important house types in the Low Countries.	554
31.3	The Bronze Age cultural landscape at Bovenkarspel-Het Valkje, West Frisia.	556
31.4	A two-period Middle Bronze Age barrow at Oss-Zevenbergen.	559
31.5	The Søgel burial of Drouwen.	560

31.6	The urnfield of Vledder in the northern Netherlands.	562
31.7	Chronological developments in depositional practices for the southern Netherlands and Belgium.	564
32.1a	Bronze Age cultural zones in France in the Early Bronze Age, showing sites mentioned in the text.	572
32.1b	Bronze Age cultural zones in France in the Middle Bronze Age, showing sites mentioned in the text.	573
32.1c	Bronze Age cultural zones in France in the Late Bronze Age, showing sites mentioned in the text.	574
32.2	Bronze Age settlements in east and central France.	577
32.3	Bronze Age settlements in the West of France.	578
32.4	Plan of Late Bronze Age burial at Migennes (burial 298).	584
32.5	Bronze hoards recently discovered in France.	588
32.6	General distribution of Bronze Age hoards in France.	589
33.1	Map of Iberian sites mentioned in the text.	595
33.2	Archaeological groups and artefact styles of the Iberian Peninsula between c.1900 and 1500 BC.	597
33.3	The upland settlement of La Bastida (Murcia).	598
33.4	Ceramic and metal types typical of El Argar.	599
33.5	Settlement patterns in Iberia between c.2200 and 1550 BC.	601
33.6	'Nuclear' area of Cogotas I pottery and its distribution in the Iberian Peninsula.	606
34.1	The Balearic Islands with the principal sites mentioned in the text.	618
34.2	Settlement structures of the second millennium BC.	623
34.3	The main funerary structures of the second millennium BC.	625
34.4	Changes in prehistoric pottery production of Mallorca and Menorca.	626
34.5	Changes in metal production of Mallorca and Menorca.	627
34.6	Digital photogrametric image of the funerary chamber of the cave of Es Càrritx prior to excavation.	628
34.7	Anthropomorphic and zoo-anthropomorphic figures made of olive wood found in the cave of Es Mussol.	629
35.1	Map of Italy showing sites mentioned in the text.	633
35.2	The peninsula of Roca Vecchia (Melendugno, Lecce), on the southern Adriatic coast.	634
35.3	A Bronze Age megalithic tomb from Specchia Artanisi (Ugento, Lecce).	638
35.4	Roca Vecchia, Middle Bronze Age (Apennine) phase. Corridor in the fortification wall.	639
35.5	Santa Palomba, Rome, tomb 6, Early Iron Age cremation burial (adult man): urn and miniature vessels.	645

36.1	Map of Sicily showing sites mentioned in the text.	655
36.2	The basic pottery shapes and decoration of the Early Bronze Age Castelluccio culture, in the area around Mount Etna.	656
36.3	(a) The peninsula of Thapsos, on the eastern coast of Sicily, north of Siracusa; (b) Plan of the Bronze Age settlement of Thapsos.	660
36.4	Some of the most common pottery shapes of the earliest phase of Pantalica.	663
37.1	Map of Sardinia with principal sites mentioned in the text.	669
37.2	Plans of Giants' tombs.	675
37.3	Plans of nuraghi.	677
37.4	Above: Nuraghe Arrubiu (excavated by the author). Below: a reconstruction of the site.	678
37.5	Plans of Nuragic temples.	679
37.6	Metal types of the Recent Bronze Age (RBA).	684
37.7	Bronze statuette of a warrior, the so-called 'Great Bronze' in the Pigorini Museum, Rome.	685
38.1	Map of northern Italy showing places mentioned in the text.	693
38.2	Structures of phase 6 of the pile dwelling settlement of Fiavè (Trentino).	696
38.3	The series of Late Bronze Age smelting furnaces at the Acquafredda site, Passo del Redebus (Trentino).	698
38.4	Details of the swords found in Tomb 31, Tomb 24, and Tomb 410 of the Middle Bronze Age cemetery of Olmo di Nogara (Verona).	701
38.5	The Middle Bronze Age wooden tank of Noceto (Parma) during excavation.	702
39.1	Map of Switzerland showing sites discussed in the text.	707
39.2	Eco-dynamic scenario of Bronze Age settlement expansion into the Inner Alps.	708
39.3	Chronological phases, dates, and events in Switzerland.	712
39.4	Ground plan of the Greifensee-Böschen Late Bronze Age lakeshore settlement near Zürich.	714
39.5	Digital reconstruction of the Friaga Wald early Middle Bronze Age hill fort in Bartholomäberg, Montafon.	716
39.6	Standardized male and female inhumation rituals and grave deposits in the Early Bronze Age for three distinct areas.	720
40.1	Map of Germany showing sites discussed in the text.	724
40.2	The gold disc from Moordorf near Aurich (Lower Saxony).	728
40.3	(a) Wolnzach-Niederlauterbach (Bavaria), tumulus 1, grave 1: male burial of the earlier Tumulus culture; (b) Wolnzach-Niederlauterbach (Bavaria), tumulus 1, grave 2: jewellery of a female burial of the earlier Tumulus culture.	729

40.4	The vessels from the cremation burial at Unterglauheim (Blindheim, Bavaria), dating to the later Urnfield period (Ha B1).	733
40.5	Reconstruction of the Early Bronze Age settlement of Zuchering-Ingolstadt (Bavaria).	739
41.1	Map of Scandinavia, showing sites mentioned in the text.	747
41.2	Bjerre site 2, Jutland.	751
41.3	A row of Bronze Age barrows in Zealand, Denmark.	753
41.4	The oak-coffin burial grave A from the wet core mound Muldbjerg, Hover parish in west Jutland.	755
41.5	Selection of finds from one of the richest Scandinavian Period IV burials, Håga near Uppsala, Sweden.	758
41.6	The Trundholm wagon, Odsherred, north-west Zealand, Denmark.	759
41.7	Selection of finds from Korshøj near Svendborg, Denmark.	761
42.1	(a) Poland: main features of landscape and cultural regions; (b) Finds used to trace the coastal route and the first amber route in the Early Bronze Age.	769
42.2	(a) Plan of the Early Bronze Age settlement at Bruszczewo (Great Poland); (b) Ludgierzowice (Lower Silesia), kurgan of the Tumulus culture; (c) Plan of the barrow cemetery at Łęki Małe (Great Poland), including reconstructed kurgans; (d) Plan of Biskupin (Kuyavia).	771
42.3	Bronze Age/Hallstatt pottery from Poland.	777
43.1	(a) Map showing Bohemian and Moravian sites mentioned in the text; (b) Map showing Austrian sites mentioned in the text.	788
43.2	House constuctions in Austria and the Czech Republic.	793
43.3	Various grave constructions of the Únětice culture (1–3) and the Wieselburg culture (4).	795
43.4	Typical artefacts of the Bronze Age from Bohemia.	800
43.5	Typical artefacts of the Bronze Age from Austria.	801
43.6	Typical artefacts of the Early Bronze Age from Moravia.	802
43.7	Typical artefacts of the Middle Bronze Age (1–12), Late and Final Bronze Age (13–25) from Austria.	803
44.1	Map of Hungary and Slovakia showing sites mentioned in the text.	815
44.2	Koszider-type hoard from the settlement at Včelince–Lászlófala, Slovakia.	819
44.3	Necklaces of bronze spirals, faience, and amber beads from Nižná Myšľa, Slovakia.	823
44.4	Burial pit with human sacrifices from Nižná Myšľa, Slovakia.	824
44.5	The well of the Polgár (Hungary) M3/29 rescue site, showing a vessel *in situ*.	829
44.6	Wound-wire gold ornament from the Várvölgy hoard, Hungary.	831
45.1	Map of the western Balkans, showing sites mentioned in the text.	838

45.2	Feudvar near Mošorin: (a) topographical plan of the settlement with excavated areas; (b) three successive settlement phases with the rectangular plans of buildings along right-angled streets.	842
45.3	Feudvar near Mošorin: (a) reconstruction of a building; (b) reconstruction of the wall stucco.	843
45.4	(a) Ormož: a. topographical plan showing excavated parts of the settlement; (b) plan of the excavated part of the settlement.	848
45.5	(a) Pottery of the Cetina culture (Dalmatia); (b) three-wheeled cult-wagon from Dupljaja (Vojvodina).	850
45.6	Kupreško polje (Bosnia-Hercegovina): (a) Pustopolje, tumulus 16, picture of the excavated mound; (b) the wooden sledge used as a coffin.	851
45.7	Monkodonja, Istria (Croatia): two tombs integrated into the main entrance to the fortified settlement.	852
45.8	Dobova, Pobrežje, Ruše (Slovenia): comparison between the grave goods of the cemeteries.	858
46.1	Map of the *castellieri-gradine* of the northern Adriatic.	865
46.2	Sketch plans of *gradine*.	868
46.3	Monkodonja *gradina*: aerial view and diagrammatic plan of the site.	869
46.4	Monkodonja: detail of the rampart.	870
47.1	Map showing eponymous sites for cultures or groups in Bulgaria, Moldova, and Romania.	878
47.2	Chronological table of the main Bronze Age/Early Iron Age cultures in Romania, Bulgaria, and Moldova.	879
47.3	Evolution of selected pottery types for some important Bronze Age/Early Iron Age cultures in Romania, Bulgaria, and Moldova.	882
47.4	Selected Bronze Age/Early Iron Age burials from Romania, Bulgaria, and Moldova.	885
47.5	Early Bronze Age burial mounds at Meteş, western Transylvania.	886
47.6	Sărata Monteoru, eponymous site of the Monteoru culture.	888
47.7	Outline evolution of clay vehicle models, metal shaft-hole axes, and axes with disc (and spike) in Romania, Bulgaria, and Moldova.	892
48.1	Map showing the extension of the different vegetation zones in Russia and Ukraine.	899
48.2	Yamnaya culture grave and material.	902
48.3	Catacomb Grave culture grave and material.	906
48.4	Sintashta culture sites and material.	908
48.5	Sabatinovka culture material.	912

List of Tables

10.1	Basic Summary of Analytical Fraction, Dietary Input, and Interpretational Aspect Relevant to Each Chemical Element Discussed in the Text.	183
14.1	Relationship Between Bronze Age Sites and Siting in Northern Europe.	254
15.1	Locations of Rock Art in Scandinavia.	272
15.2	The Relationship Between Different Types of Rock Art Images in Areas where BA Rock Art is Present in Scandinavia.	278
16.1	Above: Chronological Chart Showing the Main Cultures. Below: Alternating Timelines for the Sites Belonging to Discreet Art and to Monumental Art According to their Chrono-Stylistic Characteristics (a grey rectangle corresponds to a site, or a set of sites, that cannot be clearly separated).	296
19.1	RI (Representativeness Index) Values of Non-Cereals (Pulses, Oilseeds, and Cultivated Fruit) in the Archaeobotanical Record of Continental and Northern Greece and Southern Bulgaria.	350
19.2	RI Values of Non-Cereals in the Archaeobotanical Record of Central and Northern Italy (outside the Alps).	352
19.3	RI Values of Non-Cereals in the Archaeobotanical Record of Southern France.	353
19.4	RI Values of Non-Cereals in the Archaeobotanical Record of Mediterranean Spain.	354
19.5	RI Values of Non-Cereals in the Archaeobotanical Record of the Pannonian Basin.	355
19.6	RI values of Non-Cereals in the Archaeobotanical Record of the Eastern Alps and their Foreland.	356
19.7	RI Values of Non-Cereals in the Archaeobotanical Record of the Western Alps and their Foreland.	357
19.8	RI Values of Non-Cereals in the Archaeobotanical Record of Western Central Europe (outside the Alps).	358
19.9	RI Values of Non-Cereals in the Archaeobotanical Record of Southern Scandinavia and the North Sea Coast.	359
29.1	Masses of Well-Preserved *Terramare* Weights, and the Suggested Units of $c.6.1$ g/24.4 g.	512
29.2	The Reconstructed Metrological System of the Weights of the Thirteenth Century BC (Bz D) in Central Europe.	519
29.3	Well-Preserved Weights of the Final Bronze Age from France and Switzerland, and the Suggested Units of $c.48.8$ g and $c.104$ g.	522

List of Contributors

Barbara Armbruster UMR 5608 du CNRS–TRACES, Maison de la Recherche, Université de Toulouse le Mirail, Toulouse, France

László Bartosiewicz Osteoarchaeological Research Laboratory, Stockholm University, Stockholm, Sweden

Lise Bender Jørgensen Department of Archaeology and Religious Studies, Norwegian University of Science and Technology, Trondheim, Norway

Anna Maria Bietti Sestieri Dipartimento di Beni Culturali, University of Salento, Lecce, Italy

Nikolaus Boroffka Deutsches Archäologisches Institut, Eurasien-Abteilung, Berlin, Germany

Richard Bradley Department of Archaeology, University of Reading, UK

Dirk Brandherm School of Geography, Archaeology, and Palaeoecology, Queen's University Belfast, UK

Joanna Brück Department of Archaeology and Anthropology, University of Bristol, UK

Alice Choyke Department of Medieval Studies, Central European University, Budapest, Hungary

Janusz Czebreszuk Institute of Prehistory, Adam Mickiewicz University, Poznań, Poland

Timothy Darvill Archaeology Group, School of Applied Sciences, Bournemouth University, UK

Philippe Della Casa Historisches Seminar, Abteilung Ur- und Frühgeschichte, Universität Zürich, Switzerland

Harry Fokkens Faculty of Archaeology, Leiden University, the Netherlands

David Fontijn Faculty of Archaeology, Leiden University, the Netherlands

Joakim Goldhahn School of Cultural Sciences, Linnaeus University, Kalmar, Sweden

Anthony Harding Department of Archaeology, University of Exeter, UK

Andreas G. Heiss Austrian Academy of Sciences (ÖAW), Austrian Archaeological Institute (ÖAI), Vienna, Austria

Julian Henderson Department of Archaeology, University of Nottingham, UK

Volker Heyd Department of Cultures, University of Helsinki, Finland

Mads Kähler Holst Department of Culture and Society, Aarhus University, Denmark

Gábor Ilon Hungarian National Museum, National Heritage Protection Centre, West Transdanubian Region, Szombathely, Hungary

Mandy Jay Department of Archaeology, University of Durham, UK

Luboš Jiráň Archaeological Institute of the Czech Academy of Sciences, Prague, Czech Republic

Albrecht Jockenhövel Abteilung für Ur- und Frühgeschichtliche Archäologie, Westfälische Wilhems-Universität Münster, Germany

Robert Johnston Department of Archaeology, University of Sheffield, UK

Snježana Karavanić Institute of Archaeology, Zagreb, Croatia

Tobias L. Kienlin Institut für Ur- und Frühgeschichte, Universität zu Köln, Germany

Alexandra Krenn-Leeb Institut für Ur- und Frühgeschichte, Universität Wien, Vienna, Austria

Johan Ling Department of Historical Studies, Göteborg University, Sweden

Fulvia Lo Schiavo Istituto per lo studio delle Civiltà dell'Egeo e del Vicino Oriente (ICEVO-CNR), Italy

Vicente Lull Departament de Prehistòria, Universitat Autònoma de Barcelona, Spain

†Klára Marková Archaeological Institute of the Slovak Academy of Sciences, Nitra, Slovakia

Peter Marshall Chronologies, Sheffi eld, UK

Rafael Micó Departament de Prehistòria, Universitat Autònoma de Barcelona, Spain

Kristina Mihovilić Arheološki muzej Istre, Pula, Croatia

Janet Montgomery Department of Archaeology, University of Durham, UK

Claude Mordant UMR 6298 ARTeHIS Archéologie, Terre, Histoire, Sociétés, Université de Bourgogne, Dijon, France

Franco Nicolis Ufficio beni archeologici, Provincia autonoma di Trento, Italy

William O'Brien Department of Archaeology, University College Cork, Ireland

Christopher Pare Institut für Vor- und Frühgeschichte, Johannes Gutenberg-Universität, Mainz, Germany

Mike Parker Pearson Institute of Archaeology, University College, London, UK

Hermann Parzinger Stift ung Preussischer Kulturbesitz, Berlin, Germany

Josh Pollard Department of Archaeology, University of Southampton, UK

Colin Richards Archaeology Institute, University of the Highlands and Islands, UK

Cristina Rihuete Herrada Departament de Prehistòria, Universitat Autònoma de Barcelona, Spain

Roberto Risch Departament de Prehistòria, Universitat Autònoma de Barcelona, Spain

Benjamin W. Roberts Department of Archaeology, University of Durham, UK

Milan Salaš Moravské zemské muzeum, Brno, Czech Republic

Geoffroy de Saulieu UMR 208 IRD/MNHN 'Patrimoines locaux', IRD, France

Joanna Sofaer Department of Archaeology, University of Southampton, UK

Marie Louise Stig Sørensen Division of Archaeology, University of Cambridge, UK

Hans-Peter Stika Institute of Botany, Universität Hohenheim, Stuttgart, Germany

Biba Teržan Department of Archaeology, Philosophical Faculty, University of Ljubljana, Slovenia

Julian Thomas School of Arts, Histories, and Cultures, University of Manchester, UK

Nick Thorpe Department of Archaeology, University of Winchester, UK

Henrik Thrane Department of Culture and Society, Aarhus University, Denmark

Marion Uckelmann Department of Archaeology, University of Durham, UK

Robert Van de Noort University of Reading, UK

Marc Vander Linden Department of Archaeology, University of Cambridge, UK

Kate Welham Archaeology Group, School of Applied Sciences, Bournemouth University, UK

CHAPTER 1

INTRODUCTION: THE BRONZE AGE OF EUROPE

HARRY FOKKENS AND ANTHONY HARDING

WHY a new book on the Bronze Age? When we were invited by Oxford University Press to compile one of their handbooks, covering the Bronze Age of Europe, our first question was: in what ways does this represent a challenge to provide something new? So many books have been written about the prehistory of Europe that we wondered what we could add. In the end it seemed that the challenge lay in producing a book that—while individual elements might not necessarily represent an advance in knowledge—was different in enough respects that it would add significant information to the range of books on the Bronze Age already available.

One of these was Coles and Harding's *The Bronze Age in Europe*, written in the 1970s (Coles and Harding 1979). This has been the textbook for generations of students all over Europe. It summarized the data from all regions and also combined it with the first comprehensive compilation of radiocarbon data. Its approach was above all geographical, treating the data in five separate sections for central, eastern, southern, western, and northern Europe, in two chronological divisions (earlier and later Bronze Age). There was no overarching view of 'the European Bronze Age', merely a short set of concluding remarks that drew out some of the main themes.

A few years earlier Jacques Briard had written a short French-language volume: *L'Age du Bronze en Europe barbare*, in 1979 translated as *The Bronze Age in Barbarian Europe* (a reworked version appeared under a slightly different title in 1997: Briard 1976; 1997). It had a comparable goal: to present a picture of the period to the growing number of students. Briard used a different approach, however. He provided much less data, but described it from a thematic point of view. His chapters have titles like 'Le beau bronze des pays de l'ambre' or 'Les îles cassitérides'. They revealed the European Bronze Age as a wonderful world with many marvels, but there was no coherent view on social processes or processes of change.

These two books held the field for some twenty years. In that period, between 1980 and 2000, the archaeological world changed fundamentally, both through an increase in data and through a new interpretative paradigm. The fall of the Iron Curtain meant that the amount of data accessible on central and eastern Europe grew substantially; and former Eastern bloc scholars started to publish regularly in English and German, which made their work more accessible to other European archaeologists. Another factor that created an increase in data was the beginning of developer-funded archaeology in the latter years of the twentieth century. This was accompanied by a move towards not merely describing the material recovered, but using it to illustrate new models of the past. Especially burial data and the monumental landscapes of (for instance) southern England have been used to illustrate how Bronze Age society became a complex society ruled by elites and chiefs. Perspectives on the past involving the role of material culture in developing power relations, sometimes within a Marxist framework, were especially a hallmark of the work of Kristian Kristiansen (e.g. Kristiansen 1984), while alternative perspectives were provided by authors such as Timothy Earle and Andrew Sherratt (Earle 1987; 1991; Sherratt 1994). Kristiansen stated in 1998 that he was following a modified 'processualist' approach (Kristiansen 1998: 40), but this is mainly evident in his extensive use of models to explain and describe the period. In fact, the theoretical position for which he has become best known, following the seminal work of Friedman and Rowlands (1977), is as an advocate of World Systems and core-periphery thinking (see below), and of the associated search for political institutions, elites, power, and prestige in archaeological data. This was also a major preoccupation of Andrew Sherratt (e.g. Sherratt 1993). Their articles have profoundly changed the way fellow archaeologists view the Bronze Age.

These new interpretations of the past have also led to new kinds of synthesis. In 2000 Harding discarded the format he and John Coles had used twenty years earlier, and wrote a thematic account of the European Bronze Age in *European Societies in the Bronze Age* (Harding 2000). No longer was the geographical approach central, but rather the connections between societies and the way they used material culture. It clearly opposed the World Systems approach that Kristiansen had adopted in his various writings in the 1980s and 1990s, and most recently in *The Rise of Bronze Age Society*, with Thomas Larsson (2005). In the latter book a 'Grand Narrative' of the European Bronze Age has taken shape in a form that is both appealing and controversial. Appealing, because it connects all kinds of developments all over Europe with each other in an intriguing and inspiring manner; controversial, because it follows only one theoretical approach and uses the data in a highly selective manner to accommodate the narrative.

What is interesting in all of these books that summarize the data on a European scale is that in general one or two authors do all the description and synthesizing. That has its advantages and disadvantages. The advantage is that there is one coherent and uniform treatment of the data. The disadvantage, however, is that regional archaeologists tend to shake their heads about (mis)reading or over-interpretation of *their* data. Moreover, most syntheses are viewed from an Anglo-Saxon perspective. That need not in itself be a problem, but on the other hand it is not necessarily how 'continental' and regional archaeologists interpret their data. Here we take a different approach. We have divided the book into two parts: the first written by specialists on various themes and topics (the thematic approach); the second by regional scholars about their particular area of Europe (the geographical approach). We also decided to leave out grand narratives, the World Systems approach, or any other overarching interpretative scheme, but present the data as it is experienced by those who work on particular themes and in particular regions. That may of course be seen as a regrettable omission, but on the other hand this aspect has already received so much attention from the work of

Kristiansen and Larsson that a summary hardly seems necessary. Some chapters do in fact deal with these theoretical issues (power, identity, gender, complexity).

Leading scholars were therefore invited to write a chapter on their topic or region, as they see it. We consider ourselves fortunate in having been able to attract so many of the top scholars in their field to contribute to the volume; and in having (with only a couple of exceptions) used the scholars of the relevant regions to write about their areas, avoiding the common pitfall of inviting a few Anglo-Saxon scholars who could write an acceptable chapter but who would not command the respect of those from the regions in question. Of course, as one will quickly see on reading the book, this leads to very different visions of the past. It also lays bare how different our scholarly traditions are. For instance, typology, chronology, and myriad archaeological cultures are still very much a feature of central and eastern European archaeology. By contrast, in north-western Europe large-scale settlement excavations and surface surveys dominate the record, especially since the introduction of the Valletta Convention and the principle that the developer pays for archaeological fieldwork in advance of construction.

This volume covers Europe outside the Aegean area. The Aegean is not covered because a companion volume in the same series has already appeared; and because for the most part the developments in Bronze Age Greece were on a different level to those in the rest of Europe. Inevitably, of course, it has been necessary to refer to Aegean and east Mediterranean matters in some chapters: in those on trade, for instance (Chapter 20), or on Italy, Sicily, and Sardinia (Chapters 35–7); to some extent also in the discussion of the Copper Age background to the Bronze Age world (Chapter 3). This serves to reinforce the fact that in the Bronze Age there was no barrier to communication between the central and eastern Mediterranean, nor between the Aegean and the rest of the Balkans (or indeed further afield). Greece is part of Europe, but its Bronze Age development was significantly different from that elsewhere: it was much more attuned to developments in the eastern Mediterranean, with which it shares many features.

Not every topic or country receives a chapter to itself, and our authors have interpreted their briefs in somewhat different ways. While we have attempted to provide at least some coverage of all parts of Europe, inevitably there are some areas (e.g. the eastern Baltic, Belorus, Albania, Iceland) that receive little or no attention, whereas others (e.g. Italy) are extensively covered.

In this volume a separate chapter (Chapter 2) is devoted to the chronology of western Europe (Britain and Ireland, France, and Spain); other areas present their own chronological schemes in Part II of the book. A companion chapter to Chapter 2, devoted to central and eastern Europe, was commissioned but unfortunately was not forthcoming. The reader is referred instead to the introductory remarks on chronology in the relevant chapters.

Sources of Information

The sources of information for the Bronze Age are in several ways more informative than those for earlier periods. This implies not only different object types, new materials (metal) and classes of sites (hoards, settlements with farmsteads), but also different traditions of deposition. For instance, the frequent deposition of varied grave goods has enabled archaeologists to make inferences about the status of individuals and the organization of communities in a much more informed manner than was possible in most regions for the Neolithic. The evidence from settlements and farmsteads is also—especially for the Middle Bronze Age onwards—much more extensive and informative than before.

Not only do we have different sources of evidence for the Bronze Age: this book also shows that we have started to use in new ways categories of evidence that have long existed but were previously neglected. Biographies of objects, and their context of use and discard, are now being studied; skeletal material is now analysed for stable isotopes; DNA studies have become possible. The context and meaning of metal deposition is much more a subject of study than previously. These new avenues are partly due to new theoretical approaches to data, but partly too to new methods that are derived from other fields of study. Archaeology has become increasingly a mix of 'alpha' (humanities), 'beta' (physical sciences), and 'gamma' (social sciences) studies (the terminology used in the Netherlands).

One of the most significant sources for Bronze Age archaeology traditionally is represented by the enormous number of copper alloy (hereafter bronze) objects that populate its centuries. These artefacts represent both a challenge and an opportunity: a challenge, because so many thousands of objects, often repetitious in character, can seem to stifle the imagination when it comes to interpretation; an opportunity, because each one of these objects represents a triumph of the craftsman's art, representing decades or centuries of built-up knowledge, and hours of work at extracting the ore, producing the metal, and turning the metal into a finished object. In this sense, every bronze artefact possesses information that could be used to help us interpret the period from which it emanates; the challenge is to work out how to unlock that information.

Traditionally the favoured approach has been to sort these objects into groups (types), based primarily on external appearance (form), aided where possible by contextual information (e.g. stratigraphical position). This was the approach adopted by the great typologists of the nineteenth century, most notably Oscar Montelius and Paul Reinecke, whose studies embraced much of Europe and not only their own home areas. The method was to study closed-find groups (i.e. groups of artefacts that come from the same findspot and are presumed to have been deposited at the same time) and identify which objects occur together within those groups, and which objects occur with more than one set of accompanying artefacts, thus giving the possibility of identifying change through time, both of individual objects and of whole groups of objects (Fig. 1.1). The primary intention was to identify chronological aspects of Bronze Age cultures rather than anything else (e.g. technological, functional), though these other aspects also played a part in some discussions.

The types and sequences identified by these early scholars have stood the test of time remarkably well, even if in some cases they have been extensively modified. Thus we still use a division into Periods I to VI when discussing the Nordic Bronze Age, and on the whole the artefactual contents of each Period are as Montelius suggested. We still divide the south German Bronze Age into a *Bronzezeit* (Bz) with periods A to D and a *Hallstattzeit* (Ha) also with phases A to D, of which the first two (Ha A and B) are recognized as belonging to the Bronze Age whereas the second two (Ha C and D) we now identify as part of the Iron Age; and in both cases, these divisions have been applied to areas far from those where they were initially identified—over most of continental Europe, in fact.

This is not to say, however, that there are no problems arising from this usage. Over the decades, different scholars have interpreted the data originally presented by Reinecke in different

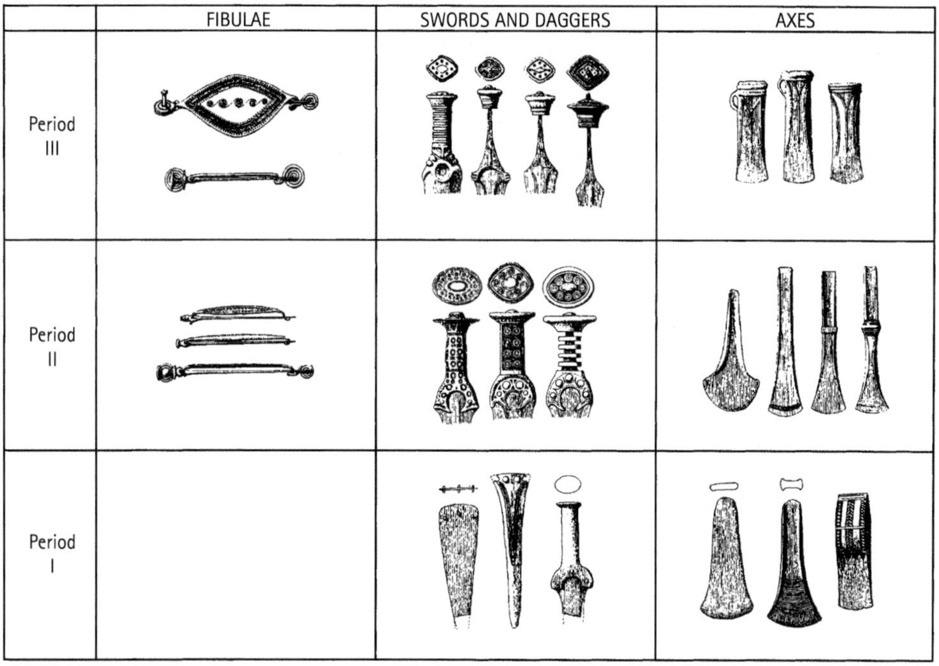

FIG. 1.1 Type table as devised by Oscar Montelius.

Source: adapted from Montelius (1886).

ways, or sorted the objects into different groups or subgroups. Almost all the Reinecke phases have been subdivided, and the existence of some subdivisions has become the subject of controversy (most notably Ha B2, but also within Bz A (e.g. Bz A0 and A3) and Bz B and C.

The source of these disagreements lies in the fact that archaeological depositions did not necessarily follow what we might consider a logical or consistent pattern. Objects of varying date might be collected up and deposited at one time—though this would usually mean that the latest object gave the date of deposition. More difficult is the fact that objects of different function might have been treated differently, so that (for instance) those created specifically for burial with the dead do not occur on settlement sites or in hoards, and vice versa. Such diversity in practice can and does lead to many apparent discrepancies in chronological terms.

Yet another, and more important, reason why chronologies based on metalwork have become of less interest is that the more that becomes known about other classes of data, especially settlements, the more it becomes clear that metal typology is almost useless for types of data other than hoards and burials. Moreover, its value for making inferences about 'normal' social life appears to be limited, or at least one-dimensional. This is also one of the reasons why there is now waning interest in, and increasing criticism of, what was once one of the great and much-praised projects of Bronze Age archaeology: the series of corpora *Prähistorische Bronzefunde* (PBF) that has come to typify the typological approach to artefacts. It was the successor to an altogether more ambitious, if less focused, project, *Inventaria Archaeologica*, a set of cards published by the Union Internationale des Sciences Pré- et Protohistoriques (UISPP), whose stated aim was to publish as many categories of artefacts as possible, of as many periods as possible; perhaps inevitably, funding difficulties and differing national priorities and perceptions have resulted in a very patchy distribution of published card sets, to the extent that they can be used effectively for very few areas and periods. PBF is not the only Bronze Age corpus—another is Aner and Kersten's *Die Funde der älteren Bronzezeit* (Aner and Kersten 1973–2011); nor are such collections confined to the Bronze Age, though inevitably they concentrate in those areas with large numbers of well-preserved objects.

Prähistorische Bronzefunde was conceived during the 1960s, the brainchild of Hermann Müller-Karpe, then at the University of Frankfurt am Main; the first volumes appeared in 1969 (Harbison 1969a, b) and were rapidly followed by a succession of others. Organized into twenty-one 'series' (*Reihe*) according to artefact category (axe, spearhead, sword, etcetera, with two series devoted to specific cultural groups or periods), to date some 165 volumes have been published, and more are in preparation. While the quality of the volumes is variable, the aim of the contributors is always to collect all examples of a given category in a defined geographical area—usually, but not always, a modern country—giving details of each object (dimensions, find context and associations, present location, previous publication details, function, and date) along with a drawing (redrawn to the PBF standard) and distribution maps by type, a chronological chart of the form's development in the area studied, and in some cases drawings of the associated material.

This approach has both benefits and drawbacks. The principal benefit is that all available examples of a given artefact form are presented in visual form with description, along with an indication of their geographical occurrence; thus one can quickly discover what forms occur where and when. This can be particularly useful for tracing the appearance of particular types that may have supra-regional significance or be important in other ways. The principal drawback is that most finds are presented without their associated material, as if they were isolated, individual objects, when in fact the importance of many of them lies in their associations and not simply in their outward appearance.

While some of these objections are serious, we can still agree that the PBF series is immensely valuable as a set of source materials. Some may believe that this type of research—stylistic and oriented towards the individual artefact—has had its day, but this does not mean that what has been done is outdated and useless. It will keep its value, and would become even more valuable if all of the information gathered so far could be made available on the Internet for everyone to use.

New approaches to metals and material culture have now started to produce results. One involves the concept of the biography of objects, as discussed for instance by Kopytoff (1986) and Hoskins (1998). These authors show that objects are not just things, but are often closely interwoven with culturally specific meanings and values (Kopytoff 1986: 68). Objects can be closely tied to persons, become part of their personhood as members of society (Hoskins 1998: 9), especially those objects that were exchanged between official or supernatural entities and persons. David Fontijn (2002), for instance, has shown how the contexts in which objects are discarded or disposed of, and their use, can reveal much about meaning in society (see also Van Gijn 2010) (see Chapter 11). In a different way, the seminal ethnographic work of Olivier Gosselain (2000) and others, on the *chaînes opératoires* of the making of objects, is becoming more and more important because it discusses how apparently self-evident technical procedures are to a large extent culture-specific. This research has also had its impact on pottery analysis, as for instance in the work of Sébastien Manem (2008). This type of work not only tells us about the choices that craftsmen made, but can also provide valuable information about regional styles and identities and about the geographical distribution of style zones. In that respect it is an important new line of study complementing traditional studies.

Distribution maps have always formed the heart of archaeological studies in any period, but especially for the Bronze Age. They used to be an important source for inferences about the distribution of archaeological cultures and the movement of peoples, in the sense in which Gordon Childe used the term. This approach has not yet lost its value in several regions, especially in eastern Europe—as you can read in this book. But the use of maps has changed. Especially for Bronze Age Europe the distribution of specific types of artefacts, in particular bronze artefacts, is of great importance because it shows networks of trade and exchange (Chapter 20). Better than anything else, a distribution map of specific objects or decorative symbols appears to demonstrate contacts between groups of people. A problem, however, is that we are still not very well informed about mechanisms of transport and exchange in Europe. In technological terms these matters are becoming increasingly clear (see Chapters 21–2), but as a social mechanism much remains to be done. The general assumption is that exchange between elites is one of the main mechanisms for the movement of bronzes, but that cannot account for all the metal that was distributed. Moreover, the context of bronze deposition shows that in many cases there is much more symbolism involved than just prestige and status (see Chapter 7). The assumption of a political economy (Earle 2002) as the model for the whole of Bronze Age Europe is also disputed by many scholars (see Chapter 11).

Debates in Bronze Age Archaeology

Chronology

Traditionally the study of Bronze Age archaeology has revolved predominantly around artefacts, mainly pottery and bronzes. The situation varies in different parts of Europe. Where long stratified sequences are available, mainly in the eastern half of the continent (such as tells, or settlement mounds, in Hungary and Bulgaria, or stratified sites in Moldavia), there has been a long-standing tradition of conducting research through the detailed comparison of the contents of the layers of different sites. With bronze artefacts, since the days of Montelius and Reinecke it has been the custom to create chronologies by setting up type sequences and association tables, so that the development of artefacts through time can be charted. One problem has always been that pottery on settlement sites is not often clearly associated with characteristic bronze types, so that two (or more, in the case of funerary assemblages) chronologies have developed side by side. Usually the best way of resolving that issue has been through the use of grave assemblages, since grave goods might include both pots and bronzes. Even here difficulties can arise, though, since the pots put into graves were not necessarily the pots used in domestic life.

In recent decades these preoccupations have become less critical in importance, at least in those parts of Europe where radiocarbon dating is commonly available. It would be wrong to conclude that all chronological problems have been solved, of course. But the way was shown in 1997 when Stuart Needham and colleagues carried out a dating programme on organic material surviving in the sockets of, or otherwise adhering to, bronze implements (Needham et al. 1997). This, for the first time, gave a credible absolute dating sequence for British Bronze Age bronzes—while incidentally confirming the relative sequence, and in outline the previously obtained absolute chronology. Since that time, much has been done to refine the British chronology and bring it into line with those of adjacent countries (Chapter 2).

At around the same time the results of the programme of dendro-dating on oak coffins of the Nordic Bronze Age came to fruition (later summarized in Randsborg and Christensen 2006). This gave a clear indication of the timespan within which graves of Periods II and III fell—again more or less in accordance with predictions based on cross-dating. The particular preservation characteristics of the Nordic coffin graves allowed this development to happen. The other area where an extended dendro sequence has become available is the Alpine zone, mainly Germany and Switzerland. Here, large numbers of excavated sites in wet conditions have produced wood, much of which has been dendro-dated. This remarkable corpus of material suffers only from the disadvantage that there are gaps in occupation: thus there are many sites producing wood from the Early Bronze Age, a number from the earlier Urnfield period, and a large number again from the late Urnfield period. Few sites are dated to the Middle Bronze Age or to the middle part of the Urnfield period.

Most recently a radiocarbon dating programme has been carried out on cremated bone in Nordic burials—which has the advantage that it extends the scope of absolute dating beyond the Nordic Early Bronze Age, when inhumation was the norm, into the Late Bronze Age, when cremation became universal (Olsen et al. 2011). These dating techniques have the potential to put the chronological framework of the Bronze Age beyond doubt (and therefore dispute). Questions of contemporaneity, for instance between objects or motifs apparently of Mycenaean inspiration found in continental Europe, can now be resolved, at least within acceptable limits. Long-standing debates such as the relative chronological positions of the Early Bronze Age of north-west Europe and the Aegean area ('Wessex without Mycenae': Renfrew 1968) can finally be laid to rest. In almost all countries of central and western Europe this is now the case, though some countries in eastern and south-eastern Europe lag behind, partly for resourcing reasons, but partly also through ignorance or scepticism. We can thus look forward to a future where debates over chronology can be set aside, enabling us to consider the implications of the synchronisms defined in social and economic terms.

World Systems

Linked to the question of chronology is that of interconnectedness. How far were different parts of the Bronze Age world linked together, and how far were they separate, like islands in a sea of uninhabited terrain? This is a question that has vexed scholars for many years, with a range of positions being adopted, often increasingly polarized.

In large measure this stems from a debate concerning the extent to which the advanced civilizations of the east Mediterranean were in contact with, or influenced, cultures in the 'barbarian' world. We can trace this debate back as far as Montelius, though it was mainly German scholars in the mid-twentieth century who pointed to the main pieces of evidence, followed in the 1960s by Stuart Piggott and Jan Bouzek. Through the 1970s and 1980s different opinions were expressed, some favouring an extensive range of contacts between the two areas, others adopting a more sceptical position (notably Harding 1984; Bouzek 1985). The publication of parts of a conference held in Aarhus, Denmark, in 1980, at which World Systems Theory (later called core-periphery theory, or similar formulations such as Centre-Periphery relations) was first broached in an archaeological context, was the first major outcome of this approach (Rowlands, Larsen, and Kristiansen 1987); it was followed by the publication of a colloquium held in Mainz, Germany, in 1985, which illustrated more starkly the difference in the positions held (Schauer 1990); here the 'maximalist' position of mainly Danish scholars was clearly articulated. In the following years, it was especially the publications of Kristian Kristiansen that dominated the field, in a series of articles and in two books (Kristiansen 1998; Kristiansen and Larsson 2005). Kristiansen's position is that: a) one can discern a wide range of sites and artefacts in Europe which indicate extensive connections with the Mediterranean world in the Bronze Age, notably though not exclusively Mycenaean Greece; and b) these connections are best viewed within a core-periphery framework, the core drawing in especially raw materials from its periphery and the periphery receiving in return cultural influences that led to technological and social developments, as well as manufactured goods.

In their 2005 work Kristiansen and Larsson went further. While the core-periphery framework remains, they envisaged Europe as a world where travellers moved widely across the continent, bringing with them not only tangible goods (artefacts) but also the more intangible expressions of exotic knowledge, concepts, practices, ideologies, religious symbols, and the like. The authors coupled this with a harsh critique of older artefact-based ideas of 'merely' assessing similarities in material culture, which had led to much of the scepticism expressed by those holding different views. In this manner they built up a narrative in which Europe became a continent linked as much by mental constructs as by material culture.

This is not the place to undertake a full critique of that narrative here, though several have been expressed (e.g. Nordquist and Whittaker 2007), which point out the selective nature of the sources used or even outmoded or erroneous use of factual data. In spite of these criticisms, the book continues to be extensively cited, generally with approval—also by several authors in this volume. Some like the approach based on a 'Grand Narrative'; others prefer to view the Bronze Age through the prism of the detailed analysis of field and artefact data.

The most powerful objection to a World Systems approach for an understanding of the prehistoric past is that it removes much of the autonomy of action of the 'peripheral' societies, who become pawns in the power play of the core. Originally devised by Immanuel Wallerstein as a way of understanding the rise of the capitalist system in the early modern period (Wallerstein 1974), its application to the remote past has always brought with it the danger that we view peripheral societies through the lens of the core. It assigns particular force to notions of power, the supremacy of technological innovation, and the idea that what happened in the core was automatically desirable to those on the periphery—who would then be exploited for their resources (raw materials such as metals), which were crucial to the continuance of the developed societies in the centre. The overtones of modern economic history could not be plainer.

An alternative view would stress the way that local developments in every area proceeded, making use of local power structures and local economic forces. In such a model, it is regional economic systems that are important for the development of such power structures. We have a good idea of how settlement systems worked in several parts of the Bronze Age world (for instance the Low Countries and Scandinavia: Chapters 31 and 41). In some cases there is abundant data on economic life, now subject to sophisticated analyses. We would certainly accept that there was much movement of goods and people across Europe in the Bronze Age, sometimes over long distances, and that an inhabitant of, for example, Britain, could say, like Shelley in his poem 'Ozymandias', 'I met a traveller from an antique land…' who told of wonderful things he had seen.

The Way Ahead

Bronze Age research has a long history of studying metals and metal artefacts. However, as we have seen, much of that research so far has been dedicated to typology/chronology and stylistic comparisons. Metal analysis was important in the 1960s and 1970s with the work of Junghans, Sangmeister, and Schröder, but became less important when it became clear that the more samples were taken, the less clear the provenance of bronzes was in terms of ore sources, especially since bronze tended to be recycled. That does not mean we should belittle these efforts, nor stop doing analyses altogether; lead isotope analysis in particular has proved very useful, if sometimes controversial. Especially in combination with metallurgical research, such analyses can be very informative, as for instance demonstrated in the work of scholars such as Barbara Ottaway, Ernst Pernicka, and Tobias Kienlin (Kienlin and Roberts 2009) (see Chapter 23).

In the future non-destructive analyses will become increasingly important because the rules and scientific ethics for handling metal objects have changed considerably. X-ray fluorescence (XRF) and other methods for studying the composition of metal objects will increase in importance. Here too the biography of artefacts (manufacture—use—discard) will become more important as a line of analysis, as is demonstrated in various articles in Kienlin and Roberts (2009). If we treat the working of metals in the past less as an industrial or a given process and more as a social one, much can be learnt about its embedding in society and the place of the smith in Bronze Age communities. In that respect not much progress has been made since the summarizing work of Michael Rowlands forty years ago (Rowlands 1971). Here much may be gained by recognizing that metal production could have been firmly embedded in local communities and was less connected to elites than is currently assumed. One should also take into account regional and temporal differences, because in the Late Bronze Age the production of weapons, complex ornaments, and other objects was probably organized in a very different way from that in the Early Bronze Age.

Important new sources of information are provided by organic chemistry and biomolecular archaeology. The work of Richard Evershed in Bristol (UK) and Douglas Price in Madison (US) and Edinburgh (UK) especially has shifted the parameters of research. Isotope and lipid analysis are producing new results about mobility and diet on an almost daily basis. While strontium isotopes were at first used only for dietary studies, now mobility of groups of people is measured, or in the case of wool, of sheep or the wool itself (Frei et al. 2009). By measuring the signal in the bones with a control sample, it can be established whether a person or animal was raised locally or somewhere else. Where that somewhere was is generally hard to define, but at least one knows whether or not mobility was an issue. Large projects for determining mobility have now started (see Chapter 10) and we will probably soon see more of this type of research. When data not only about humans but also about animals starts to become more widely available, we will see new levels of interpretation of how the different regions in Bronze Age Europe were connected: proof positive of the Kristiansen hypothesis?

The interpretation of the results, however, is by no means simple. As with the Amesbury Archer (who came from the Alpine region according to oxygen isotope studies: Fitzpatrick 2003), the results may be accepted too fast and too uncritically by archaeologists. We have to be careful that the same does not happen as in the early days of radiocarbon dating: overenthusiastic and uncritical use which led to misreadings of the data. Moreover, interpretation of the results in social terms is not straightforward. We have previously thought of the Bronze Age as a fairly stable society with small-scale communities, some raiding and warfare, and increasingly broad exchange networks. But now it seems people moved all over Europe and settled all parts of it. New migrationist tales are emerging, for instance on continental Bell Beaker prospectors settling in Wessex or Scotland (see Chapter 24). Though this may be part of the explanation, we should not *assume* the social processes without reference to how they work in traditional societies. Isotope studies need a much more careful discussion of Bronze Age mobility and the way it was embedded in society than has happened so far.

The use of mass spectrometers, and especially the laser-induced variants, are now turning out results in other fields of research, notably lipid analysis and phosphate analysis. In Britain experiments have been carried out with intra-site analysis of lipids on pottery (Copley et al. 2005). A great range of comparative research studies can be imagined on the use of pottery and other materials within sites, but also between regions and in different contexts of deposition. Phosphate analyses can be used to study patterns of movement in settlements or cemeteries, if we are able to take and analyse suitable soil samples. DNA studies can also provide many new results, not only from the study of bones but also from soil samples. Careful analysis of soil samples with the aid of these new methods from graves might provide information about the presence of materials that have long decayed.

Conclusion

There are many possible approaches to the Bronze Age, and this volume indicates just some of them. A disjunction between a 'culture'-based approach and one based simply on the available field and laboratory evidence without imposing a mental superstructure onto it is only too apparent; this reflects the research traditions in the different parts of Europe. New approaches are covered in some chapters, as are new interpretations of old material; equally, 'traditional' material is covered to a greater or lesser extent in the regional chapters. We have indicated here some of the ways we expect the subject to develop. While we do not downplay the importance of the culture-based approach, which will always be relevant for setting a framework for study, we expect breakthroughs in understanding in Bronze Age studies to occur mainly with the new analytical and interpretative techniques that have been developed in recent years. Perhaps for resource reasons, these have mostly been applied in the western countries of Europe so far; one challenge will be to enable colleagues in more easterly countries to take part in these developments.

In 1994 the Council of Europe launched its 'European Campaign for Archaeology', with a specific focus on the Bronze Age: 'The first golden age of Europe', encompassing conferences, workshops, and a magnificent closing exhibition that toured several European capitals in

1998–9. More than a decade later, this volume attempts to set out the basis for study to take us into the next period. We hope and believe that what you can read here will set out the framework within which Bronze Age studies will progress in the decades to come.

Bibliography

Aner, E. and Kersten, K. (1973–2011). *Die Funde der älteren Bronzezeit des nordischen Kreises in Dänemark, Schleswig-Holstein und Niedersachsen, I-X, XVII-XVIII*. Copenhagen/Neumünster: Karl Wachholtz.

Bouzek, J. (1985). *The Aegean, Anatolia and Europe: Cultural Interrelations in the Second Millennium BC*. Prague/Göteborg: Academia/Paul Åström.

Briard, J. (1976). *L'Âge du Bronze en Europe barbare. Des mégalithes aux Celtes*. Toulouse: Éditions des Hespérides.

—— (1997). *L'Âge du Bronze en Europe. Économie et société 2000–800 avant J.-C*. Paris: Éditions Errance.

Coles, J. M. and Harding, A. F. (1979). *The Bronze Age in Europe: An Introduction to the Prehistory of Europe c.2000–700 BC*. London: Methuen.

Copley, M. S., Berstan, R., Straker, V., Payne, S., and Evershed, R. P. (2005). 'Dairying in antiquity. II. Evidence from absorbed lipid residues dating to the British Bronze Age', *Journal of Archaeological Science*, 32/4: 505–21.

Earle, T. K. (1987). 'Chiefdoms in archaeological and ethnohistorical perspective', *Annual Review of Anthropology*, 16: 279–308.

—— (ed.) (1991). *Chiefdoms: Power, Economy and Ideology*. Cambridge: Cambridge University Press.

—— (2002). *Bronze Age Economics: The Beginnings of Political Economies*. Boulder/London: Westview Press.

Fitzpatrick, A. P. (2003). 'The Amesbury archer', *Current Archaeology*, 16/184: 146–52.

Fontijn, D. R. (2002). *Sacrificial Landscapes: Cultural Biographies of Persons, Objects and 'Natural' Places in the Bronze Age of the Southern Netherlands, c.2300–600 BC*. Analecta Praehistorica Leidensia 33/34. Leiden: Leiden University Press.

Frei, K. M., Frei, R., Mannering, U., Gleba, M., Nosch, M. L., and Lyngstrøm, H. (2009). 'Provenance of ancient textiles: a pilot study evaluating the strontium isotope system in wool', *Archaeometry*, 45/2 (April 2009), 252–76.

Friedman, J. and Rowlands, M. J. (1977). 'Notes towards an epigenetic model of the evolution of civilisation', in J. Friedman and M. J. Rowlands (eds.), *The Evolution of Social Systems*. London: Duckworth, 201–77.

Gosselain, O. P. (2000). 'Materializing identities: an African perspective', *Journal of Archaeological Method and Theory*, 7: 187–217.

Harbison, P. (1969a). *The Axes of the Early Bronze Age in Ireland*. Prähistorische Bronzefunde. Abt. 9, Bd. 1. Munich: Beck.

—— (1969b). *The Daggers and the Halberds of the Early Bronze Age in Ireland*. Prähistorische Bronzefunde. Abt. 6, Bd. 1. Munich: Beck.

Harding, A. F. (1984). *The Mycenaeans and Europe*. London: Academic Press.

—— (2000). *European Societies in the Bronze Age*. Cambridge: Cambridge University Press.

Hoskins, J. (1998). *Biographical Objects: How Things Tell the Stories of People's Lives*. London: Routledge.

Kienlin, T. and Roberts, B. (eds.) (2009). *Metals and Societies: Studies in Honour of Barbara S. Ottaway*. Universitätsforschungen zur Prähistorischen Archäologie, 169. Bonn: Rudolf Habelt.

Kopytoff, I. (1986). 'The cultural biography of things: commoditization as process', in A. Appadurai (ed.), *The Social Life of Things: Commodities in Cultural Perspective*. Cambridge: Cambridge University Press, 64–91.

Kristiansen, K. (1984). 'Ideology and material culture: an archaeological perspective', in M. Spriggs (ed.), *Marxist Perspectives in Archaeology*. Cambridge: Cambridge University Press, 72–100.

—— (1998). *Europe before History*. Cambridge: Cambridge University Press.

—— and Larsson, T. B. (2005). *The Rise of Bronze Age Society: Travels, Transmissions and Transformations*. Cambridge: Cambridge University Press.

Manem, S. (2008). *Les Fondements technologiques de la culture des Duffaits (Âge du Bronze Moyen)*. Unpublished doctoral dissertation. Paris: Université de Paris X Nanterrre.

Montelius, O. (1886). *Dating in the Bronze Age, with Special Reference to Scandinavia*. Stockholm: Kunglige Vitterhets Historie och Antikvitets Akademien.

Needham, S. P., Bronk Ramsey, C., Coombs, D., Cartwright, C., and Pettitt, P. (1997). 'An independent chronology for British Bronze Age metalwork: the results of the Oxford radiocarbon accelerator programme', *Archaeological Journal*, 154: 55–107.

Nordquist, G. and Whittaker, H. (2007). 'Comments on Kristian Kristiansen and Thomas B. Larsson (2005): the rise of Bronze Age society. Travels, transmissions and transformations. Cambridge University Press, Cambridge', *Norwegian Archaeological Review*, 40: 75–84.

Olsen, J., Hornstrup, K. M., Heinemeier, J., Bennike, P., and Thrane, H. (2011). 'Chronology of the Danish Bronze Age based on ^{14}C dating of cremated bone remains', *Radiocarbon*, 53/2: 261–75.

Randsborg, K. and Christensen, K. (2006). *Bronze Age Oak-Coffin Graves: Archaeology and Dendro-Dating*. Acta Archaeologica 77, Acta Archaeologica, Supplementa VII, Centre of World Archaeology, Publications 3. Copenhagen: Blackwell Munksgaard.

Renfrew, A. C. (1968). 'Wessex without Mycenae', *Annual British School Athens*, 63: 277–85.

Rowlands, M. J. (1971). 'The archaeological interpretation of prehistoric metalworking', *World Archaeology*, 3: 210–23.

——, Larsen, M. and Kristiansen, K. (eds.) (1987). *Centre and Periphery in the Ancient World*. Cambridge: Cambridge University Press.

Schauer, P. (ed.) (1990). *Orientalisch-Ägäische Einflüsse in der Europäischen Bronzezeit*. Römisch-Germanisches Zentralmuseum, Monograph 15. Mainz/Bonn: Habelt.

Sherratt, A. (1993). 'What would a Bronze-Age world system look like? Relations between temperate Europe and the Mediterranean in later prehistory', *Journal of European Archaeology*, 1/2: 1–58.

—— (1994). 'The emergence of elites: earlier Bronze Age Europe, 2500–1300 BC', in B. Cunliffe (ed.), *The Oxford Illustrated Prehistory of Europe*. Oxford: Oxford University Press, 244–76.

Van Gijn, A. L. (2010). *Flint in Focus: Lithic Biographies in the Neolithic and Bronze Age*. Leiden: Sidestone Press.

Wallerstein, I. (1974). *The Modern World-System, vol. I: Capitalist Agriculture and the Origins of the European World-Economy in the Sixteenth Century*. New York/London: Academic Press.

PART I

THEMES IN BRONZE AGE ARCHAEOLOGY

CHAPTER 2

OLD FATHER TIME: THE BRONZE AGE CHRONOLOGY OF WESTERN EUROPE

BENJAMIN W. ROBERTS, MARION UCKELMANN,
AND DIRK BRANDHERM

Introduction

The creation of a chronology that spans the mid third millennium BC to the early first millennium BC and encompasses western Europe—defined here as the modern countries of Spain, Portugal, France, Ireland, Britain, Belgium, and the Netherlands—remains a work in progress rather than a finished product. The absence of any written records has meant that scholars have always had to rely upon distinguishing distinct material or architectural phases at relatively well-excavated and published sites. These sites are then used to build chronological schemes which they would subsequently apply across broader, and less well-studied, regions. The influence of any chronological scheme from the original proposal of a Bronze Age, as distinct from a preceding Stone Age and a subsequent Iron Age, at the Royal Museum of Nordic Antiquities in Denmark by C. J. Thomsen in 1817 (subsequently published in 1836; Rowley-Conwy 2007) onwards has depended on a number of interrelated factors. Any chronology has needed to be at least reasonably reliable and adaptable beyond its original archaeological foundations. Before the advent of radiocarbon dating in the 1950s, this ideally meant developing relative typological chronologies or typo-chronologies based on widely used objects made from ubiquitous and frequently altered materials that survive in the archaeological record, and had been excavated from secure contexts such as graves, settlement layers, and pits. Estimates of calendar date ranges roughly based on written dates from literate states in the eastern Mediterranean would then be applied to each typological phase. However, as the current patchwork of Bronze Age typo-chronological schemes for western Europe, even in the era of radiocarbon dating, currently testifies (Fig. 2.1), reliability and

Date BC	Iberia	France Northwest/Atlantic (Briard)	France Central/Eastern (Hatt)	Central Europe (Reinecke et al)	NL (C14) (Lanting / Van der Plicht)	NL (trad.) (PoNL)	Belgium (De Laet)	Britain (Needham)		Ireland (Eogan)	Date BC
2400	Calcolítico/ Eneolítico (Chalcolithic)	Neolithique final/ Chalcolithique	Neolithique final/ Chalcolithique	Neolithic					Neolithic		2400
2300					Late Neolithic B	Late Neolithic B	Late Neolithic	PERIOD 1	Metal Using Neolithic (Chalcolithic)	Knocknagur	2300
2200											2200
2100	Bronce Inicial (Early Bronze Age)	Br. ancien I	Br. ancien I	Bz A1	Early BA	EBA	EBA	PERIOD 2	MA I/II		2100
2000									MA III	Killaha	2000
1900			Br. ancien II	Bz A2							1900
1800	Bronce Medio (Middle Bronze Age)		Br. ancien III			MBA A	MBA	PERIOD 3 (Wessex I)	MA IV Aylesford	Ballyvally	1800
									MA V Willerby		
1700								PERIOD 4 (WESSEX II)	MA VI Arreton	Derryniggin	1700
1600									EARLY BA		1600

Bronce Antiguo (Earlier Bronze Age)

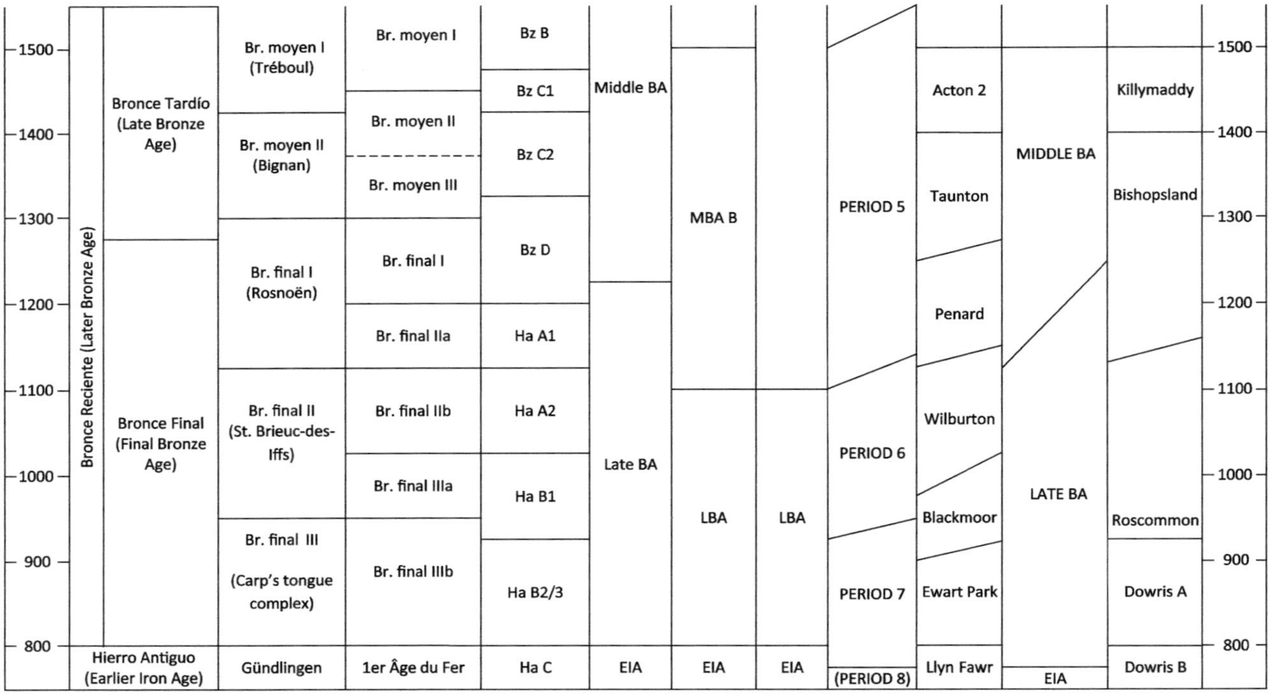

FIG. 2.1 Synchronized version of the relevant chronological systems for Western Europe. – E/M/LBA = Early/Middle/Late Bronze Age; e. = early ; l. = late; MS = Metalwork Stage (after Burgess); Metalwork Assemblage (after Needham). – After: Burgess 1979, 1980, 1988; Needham 1996, Needham et al. 1997, 2010; Lanting/van der Plicht 2001/2002, Gerloff 2007, 2010; Eogan 1984; Waddell 1998; Brindley 2007; Louwe Kooijmans et al. 2005; Arnoldussen/Fontijn 2006; Bourgois/Talon 2009; Carozza/Marcigny/Talon 2009; De Laet 1982.

adaptability were not always enough to secure widespread adoption. The reputation and position of the individual scholar, and the language and country in which they published, could be just as crucial.

The definition of a Bronze Age in western Europe, since its Scandinavian inception in the early nineteenth century and widespread adoption during the mid–late nineteenth century, has rarely experienced consensus or uniform progress, even on apparently fundamental issues. For instance, the recognition of archaeological sites during the mid–late nineteenth century possessing copper but not bronze objects provided a challenge to the Stone Age-Bronze Age continuum. It led to proposals of a distinct Copper, Eneolithic, or Chalcolithic Age, which was adopted in Iberia and southern France but did not find favour in north-west Europe, and still even today continues to be a source of debate (Lichardus 1991; Roberts and Frieman 2012). Inevitably, bronze tools, weapons, and ornaments as well as ceramic vessels were exploited as chronological markers rather than objects in flint and stone, which survived less frequently—and wood, which rarely survived. But it was bronze rather than ceramics that, from the nineteenth century onwards, has tended to be employed in the creation of pan-regional relative chronologies, perhaps due to their often wider distribution as well as the far higher contemporary value placed on metal objects and technology by scholars and collectors. In contrast, relative ceramic chronologies have tended either to be purely regional in scope or, from the early twentieth century, been elevated as fundamental object types within archaeological cultures. These broader temporal and spatial groupings were defined by scholars seeking similarities and differences in the settlement and monument architecture and/or funerary practices. The application of radiocarbon dating has similarly done little to diminish the use of archaeological cultures in chronological schemes where they frequently complement the finer and more specific object typo-chronologies (Roberts and Vander Linden 2012).

The question of how the Bronze Age should be divided has resulted in confusion rather than clarity, perhaps due to the enduring strength of traditional chronological frameworks. Pioneering scholars such as Evans (1881) classified the bronze objects into differing temporal stages, and Fox (1923) in his study on Cambridgeshire introduced the Early-Middle-Late tripartite division for the Bronze Age subsequently institutionalized for Britain and Ireland (Kendrick and Hawkes 1932). Meanwhile, Montelius (1903) in northern Europe and Reinecke (1965) in central Europe developed a more complex system of six phases—Periods I–VI and Bronze A–D and Hallstatt A/B respectively. These typo-chronological schemes, all of which were based on the nineteenth century discoveries of copper and bronze objects, have provided the foundations for *all* subsequent chronological revisions throughout western Europe (see Gerloff 2007 for details of the central European chronology which is referred to in Figs. 2.1, 2.3, and 2.4). The impact of radiocarbon dating in the 1950s and its subsequent calibration in the early 1970s did not, as enthusiastically predicted by several archaeologists, lead to the dismissal of relative chronological frameworks such as typologies or archaeological cultures in favour of absolute dating, free from any baggage accumulated by earlier scholarship. Radiocarbon dating, especially following the calibration by dendrochronology, that corrected artificially younger dates, provided the Bronze Age in western Europe with its first independent and absolute dates (Taylor 1997). Archaeological phases, features, objects, and individuals with sufficient organic remains could now be dated to a calendar year, albeit usually to within a span of 100–250 years. The revisions to previous calendar estimates and relative relationships could be spectacular—the lavish Early Bronze Age burials in Wessex, southern England, and Armorica, north-western France, were traditionally thought to be influenced by earlier graves at Mycenae (e.g. Piggott 1966), but the new radiocarbon dates demonstrated that the Wessex graves were actually several centuries earlier (Needham 2000a). Throughout western Europe, it pushed back the accepted beginning of the Bronze Age from the estimated early–mid second millennium BC to the late third millennium BC, and its end to from the mid to the early first millennium BC (Jacob-Friesen 1981: 641). The new ability to date archaeological sites that did not require any associated metalwork or pottery meant that multi-phase monuments, settlements, and field systems which lacked diagnostic finds could now be dated with far greater precision. In addition, the development of AMS radiocarbon dating during the late 1970s, requiring much smaller samples, allowed archaeologists a far wider choice in their selection of datable material (Taylor 1997). This technique has been especially effective when applied to the dating of cremated bones (Lanting, Aerts-Bijma, and Van der Plicht 2001), which has enabled a much greater resolution as shown in Belgium and north-eastern France during the late second–early first millennium BC (e.g. Peake and Delattre 2005; De Mulder et al. 2007), and Scotland and Ireland during the late third–mid second millennium BC (e.g. Sheridan 2003; 2004; 2007; Brindley 2007).

While this certainly encouraged a shift away from object-based to landscape-based Bronze Age research, a trend that has been most pronounced in Britain and Iberia (e.g. Bradley 2007), it has also complemented and strengthened traditional typo-chronologies as tested and validated using radiocarbon dates (e.g. Needham et al. 1997). The use of dendrochronology in the western European Bronze Age, beyond the calibration of radiocarbon dates, has naturally been restricted to those relatively few sites, usually in wetlands, lakes, or rivers, where sufficient wooden remains have survived (Baillie 1995). It has meant that extremely precise dating can be determined for specific sites, phases, and events, such as the building of the timber circle at Holme-next-the-Sea, Norfolk, eastern England, in spring/early summer 2049 BC (Brennand and Taylor 2003), but it remains difficult to relate these to other activities and finds, even within the same region, which can at best be placed within a given century (Taylor 1997). The application of the Bayesian statistical approach to radiocarbon dates in the last two decades (Bayliss and Bronk Ramsey 2004) has enabled a finer chronological perspective. However, despite being employed relatively widely such as in the Neolithic in southern Britain (e.g. Bayliss et al. 2007), Bayesian statistical methods or alternative approaches such as wiggle matching have only been applied to a few sites and sequences in the western European Bronze Age, such as Early Bronze Age pottery in Ireland (see Brindley 2007; Sheridan and Bayliss 2008).

The current chronologies for the western European Bronze Age (see Fig. 2.1) are therefore a product of over a century of scholarship where frameworks based on relative and absolute dating techniques, frequently relying on different materials and sites, have accumulated but have not always been integrated. Each country has distinct histories and traditions of archaeological research, contrasting archaeological remains, differing regional and national chronological schemes, and a varying enthusiasm for revising or redefining chronologies. For instance, there are relatively frequent chronological revisions on a national scale in the Netherlands (e.g. Lanting and Van der Plicht 2001–2) and Britain (Needham 1996; Needham et al. 1997), but only infrequent proposals in Iberia, and then only at a regional scale (e.g. Castro

Martínez, Lull, and Micó 1996). In devising chronologies that span regional and national boundaries, scholars have tended to address Atlantic Europe, northern Europe, or the western Mediterranean far more than they have synthesized western Europe as defined for the purposes of this paper.

It is therefore only possible to provide an introduction and overview of the current state of knowledge of the Bronze Age in western Europe (see Fig. 2.1). For the purposes of simplicity and space, the chronological framework of each country will be outlined in one of three groups according to proximity and similarity in dating sequences: Britain and Ireland (see Fig. 2.2); Netherlands, Belgium, and France (see Figs. 2.3 and 2.4); and Iberia (see Fig. 2.5). The temporal stages outlined for each group in the text and the figures should not be seen as rigid entities with concrete boundaries. This is not only because there is neither a purely absolute nor a purely relative dating framework, but also because of the many regional variations (Ruiz-Gálvez Priego 1998; Harding 2000) and the potential long-term circulation and duration of objects (e.g. Woodward 2002). The widespread adoption of tin-bronze alloying is not a reliable indicator for the Bronze Age, occurring in Britain and Ireland c.2200–2100 BC but only at c.1500–1300 BC in southern Iberia (Pare 2000; Ottaway and Roberts 2007); the departure point is taken as the Bell Beaker culture (Vander Linden 2006) from the mid third millennium BC, common to all the countries under consideration and pre-dating the earliest bronze in any of them. Similarly, the earliest presence of ironworking in western Europe during the late second millennium BC (Collard, Darvill, and Watts 2006) does not signify the end of the Bronze Age as bronze was still being widely produced, circulated, and used. Though there is not an entirely uniform collapse of bronze across each country, there is certainly a substantial decrease during the early–mid first millennium BC where the Iron Age is traditionally situated, making the early first millennium BC a relatively natural ending to the Bronze Age in our area.

Britain and Ireland

The Bronze Age in Ireland and Britain conventionally spans 2150–800 BC and remains subdivided into Early (2150–1600 BC), Middle (1600–1150 BC), and Late (1150–800/600 BC) periods, following Evans (1881) and Fox (1923) despite a highly prescient proposed scheme by Montelius (1909), which was subsequently influentially rejected (e.g. Abercromby 1912) though not by everyone (e.g. Coffey 1913). However, recent syntheses have preferred to group the Early Bronze Age with the preceding copper-using Late Neolithic/Chalcolithic (2500–2150 BC) and/or integrate the Middle and Late Bronze Age, reflecting continuities in the monument, burial, settlement, and ceramic evidence (e.g. Gibson 2002; Bradley 2007). Though the extensive use of radiocarbon dating on hundreds of new sites and objects throughout Britain and Ireland has contributed immensely to our understanding of the Bronze Age, it has not yet yielded a typo-chronological framework in landscape phenomena equivalent to the pre-existing schemes in ceramics, flint, and gold, and particularly in bronze. Modern excavation techniques together with targeted radiocarbon dating have been very effective at revealing the multi-phase and multi-period nature of the Bronze Age built environment, such as burial mounds (e.g. Woodward and Woodward 2000), field systems (e.g. Johnston 2005), and stone circles (e.g. Sheridan and Bradley 2005), which has strongly discouraged the construction of any general typo-chronologies.

Date BC	Metalwork	Pottery	Britain (Hawkes/Burgess/Gerloff /O'Connor))	Britain	Britain (Needham)			Ireland (Eogan)	Date BC
2500	Use of copper and gold	Beaker	(MS I/II)	Late Neolithic			Late Neolithic	Late Neolithic	2500
2400									2400
2300			Frankford (MS III)		PERIOD 1	MA I / II	Metal Using Neolithic (Chalcolithic)	Knocknagur	2300
2200	Full tin-bronze working								2200
2100		Collared Urns	Migdale/Butterwick (MS IV)	EBA 1	PERIOD 2	MA III Migdale		Killaha	2100
2000									2000
1900	Armorico-British daggers A/B	End Food Vessel Biconical Urns End Beaker	Aylesford (MS V) Bush Barrow Willerby (MS VI)	EBA 2	PERIOD 3 (Wessex I)	MA IV Aylesford	EARLY BA	Ballyvally	1900
1800						MA V Willerby			1800
1700	Armorico-British daggers C Arreton flanged axes Earliest palstaves		Camerton Snowshill Arreton (MS VII)	EBA 3	PERIOD 4 (Wessex II)	MA VI Arreton		Derryniggin	1700
1600									1600

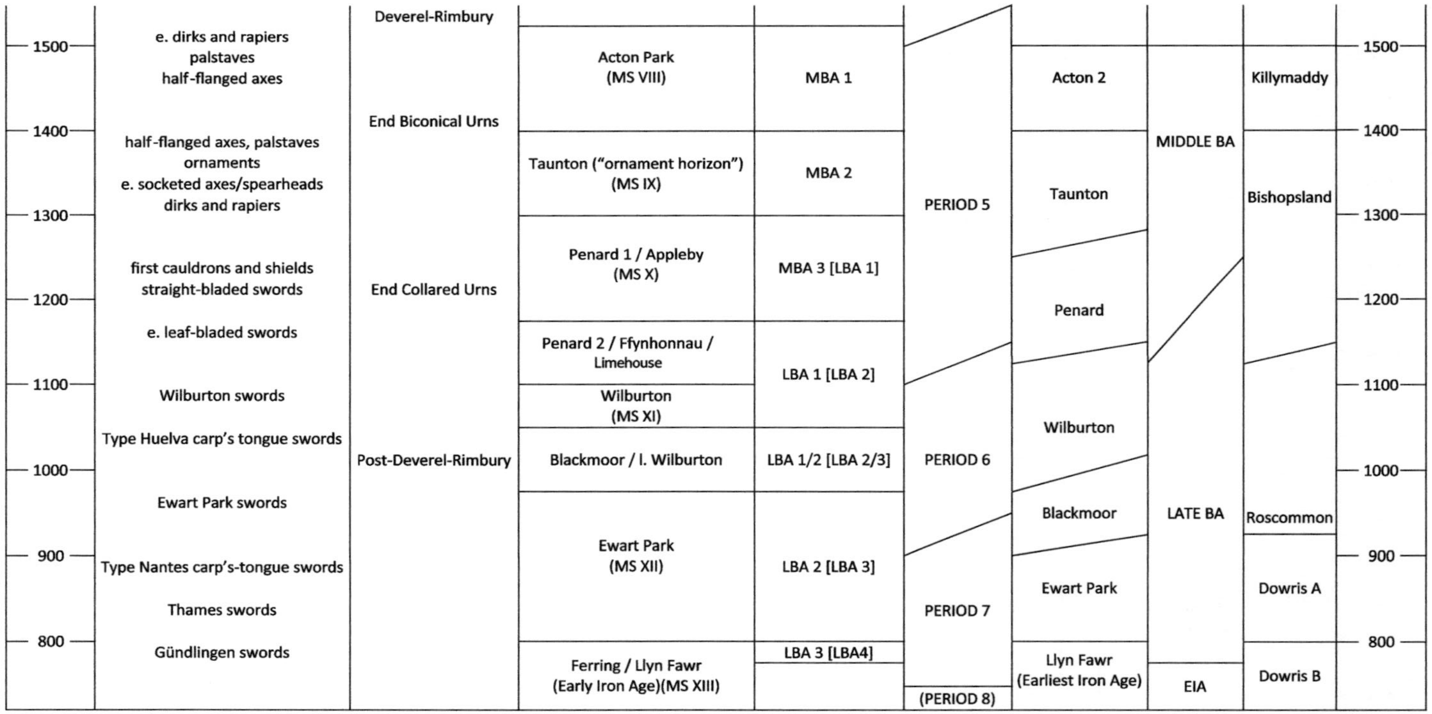

Date	Swords/Metalwork	Ceramic	British MS	Period	British Stage	Metalwork Phase	Irish Stage	Date
1500	e. dirks and rapiers / palstaves / half-flanged axes	Deverel-Rimbury	Acton Park (MS VIII)		Acton 2	MBA 1	Killymaddy	1500
1400	half-flanged axes, palstaves ornaments / e. socketed axes/spearheads / dirks and rapiers	End Biconical Urns	Taunton ("ornament horizon") (MS IX)	PERIOD 5	Taunton	MBA 2		1400
1300	first cauldrons and shields / straight-bladed swords	End Collared Urns	Penard 1 / Appleby (MS X)		Penard	MBA 3 [LBA 1]	Bishopsland	1300
1200	e. leaf-bladed swords		Penard 2 / Ffynhonnau / Limehouse			LBA 1 [LBA 2]		1200
1100	Wilburton swords		Wilburton (MS XI)	PERIOD 6	Wilburton	LBA 1/2 [LBA 2/3]		1100
1000	Type Huelva carp's tongue swords	Post-Deverel-Rimbury	Blackmoor / l. Wilburton		Blackmoor	LBA 2 [LBA 3]	Roscommon	1000
900	Ewart Park swords		Ewart Park (MS XII)	PERIOD 7	Ewart Park		Dowris A	900
800	Type Nantes carp's-tongue swords / Thames swords		Ferring / Llyn Fawr (Early Iron Age)(MS XIII)	(PERIOD 8)	Llyn Fawr (Earliest Iron Age)	LBA 3 [LBA4]	Dowris B	800
	Gündlingen swords					EIA		

FIG. 2.2 Synchronized version of the relevant chronological systems for Great Britain and Ireland. – E/M/LBA = Early/Middle/Late Bronze Age; e. = early; l. = late; MS = Metalwork Stage (after Burgess); Metalwork Assemblage (after Needham). – After: Burgess 1979, 1980, 1988; Needham 1996, Needham et al. 1997, 2010; Lanting/van der Plicht 2001/2002, Gerloff 2007, 2010; Eogan 1984; Waddell 1998; Brindley 2007.

The virtual abandonment of archaeological cultures as valid groupings within Anglo-Irish scholarship has meant that there has been no directed dating programme towards any specific 'culture', with the notable exception of the Bell Beaker culture (c.2500–1700 BC) (Needham 2005; Vander Linden 2006; and papers in Allen, Gardiner, and Sheridan 2012), and to a smaller extent the so-called Wessex culture (Needham 2000a; Needham et al. 2010). It has meant that the establishment of fine chronologies has either been achieved only at a level of the individual site or, on a larger scale, through programmes evaluating and refining several ceramic and metalwork typo-chronologies such as bronze in Britain (Needham et al. 1997) and Early Bronze Age pottery in Scotland (Sheridan 2003; 2004; 2007) and Ireland (Brindley 2007). These complement recently revised typo-chronologies in gold (Eogan 1994; Needham 2000b) and pottery (Gibson 2002), as well as on specific object types such as shields (Ucklemann 2012), cauldrons (Gerloff 2010), and spears (Davis 2012; 2015), which have incorporated new dates. This has meant that metalwork has provided the finest broad divisions during the Bronze Age in Ireland and particularly Britain which are presented in Figure 2.2, following Burgess (1974; 1980; 2012), Eogan (1983), Brindley (1995), Needham (1996), Needham et al. (1997), with slight revisions by Lanting and Van der Plicht (2001–2; see also Brindley 2007: 375–80), O'Connor (2007), and Needham et al. (2010).

The typo-chronological framework for Britain constructed by Hawkes (1960) and Burgess (1974; 1980) comprised *Metalwork Stages* I–XIII as well as sixteen phases named after important sites and hoards. The subsequent revision by Needham (1996) and Needham et al. (1997) used new radiocarbon dates to reorganize this traditional framework into Periods 1–8 spanning c.2500–450 BC including the Early Iron Age (c.750–450 BC). Supplementing these Periods, Needham proposed a new scheme of thirteen *Metalwork Assemblages* instead of *Stages*. These *Assemblages* were based on the interlinked association of certain object groups rather than on rigid temporal sequences (Needham 1996: 123). In Ireland the typo-chronological framework is broadly comparable to that in Britain with variation in specific object types. While the names and date ranges of the eight metalwork stages are different, there has been no programme of systematic evaluation using radiocarbon dates (e.g. Eogan 1983; 1994; Waddell 2000: 2, 124, 180) (see Fig. 2.2). Recent research has produced typo-chronologies in Early Bronze Age ceramics (e.g. Brindley 2007) as well as new dates for monuments and settlements (Brindley 1995; Waddell 2000). The extensive dating programme in Scotland has revealed a significant degree of regional variation, especially when compared to the chronologies that are primarily orientated towards southern England (e.g. Sheridan 2003; 2004; 2007), whilst continental interrelationships continue to stimulate further revisions and refinements (e.g. Gerloff 2007; 2010).

The Netherlands, France, and Belgium

The Netherlands

The Bronze Age in the Netherlands (see Figs. 2.3 and 2.4) conventionally spans c.2000–800 BC with a transitional phase termed Late Neolithic B (c.2500–2025 BC) associated with the Beaker culture (Vander Linden 2006). The first periodization devised specifically for the

Date BC	Scandinavia (Montelius)	Central Europe (Reinecke et al)	NL (C14) (Lanting / van der Plicht)	NL (trad.) (PoNL)	objects	cultures/groups	Date BC
2500	Neolithic	Neolithic				Bell beaker	2500
2400							2400
2300			Late Neolithic B	Late Neolithic B			2300
2200							2200
2100		Bz A1					2100
2000	Late Neolithic I		Early BA	Early BA	low-flanged axes	Barbed wire Beaker	2000
1900		Bz A2					1900
1800	Late Neolithic II				high-flanged axes stopridge axes	Elp / Hilversum (first ring ditches around BA barrows)	1800
1700	Per. IA			Middle BA A			1700
1600							1600

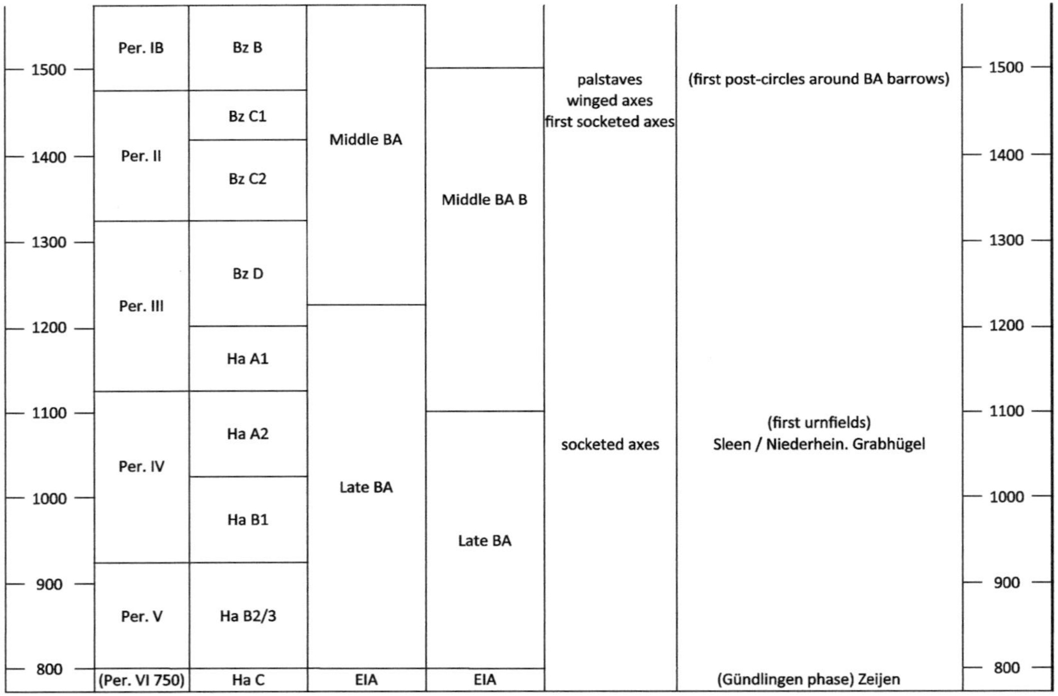

FIG. 2.3 (opposite) Synchronized version of the relevant chronological systems for the Netherlands. All stages are C14 revised (Lanting/van der Plicht 2001/2002. After: Lanting/van der Plicht 2001/2002; (PoNL =) Louwe Kooijmans et al. 2005; Arnoldussen/Fontijn 2006.

Date BC	Northwest/Atlantic (Briard)	France Central/Eastern (Hatt)	(Carozza/Marcigny/Talon)	Central Europe (Reinecke et al)	NL (C14) (Lanting/van der Plicht)	NL (trad.) (PoNL)	Belgium (De Laet)	Date BC
2400	Neolithique final/ Chalcolithique	Neolithique final/ Chalcolithique	Neolithique final	Late Neolithic		Late Neolithic B	Late Neolithic	2400
2300								2300
2200			Br. ancien I		Late Neolithic B			2200
2100		Br. ancien I		Bz A1				2100
2000	Br. ancien I				Early BA	EBA	EBA	2000
1900		Br. ancien II	Br. ancien II	Bz A2				1900
1800								1800
1700		Br. ancien III				MBA A	MBA	1700
1600	Br. moyen I (Tréboul)	Br. moyen I	Br. moyen I	Bz B	Middle BA			1600
1500								1500

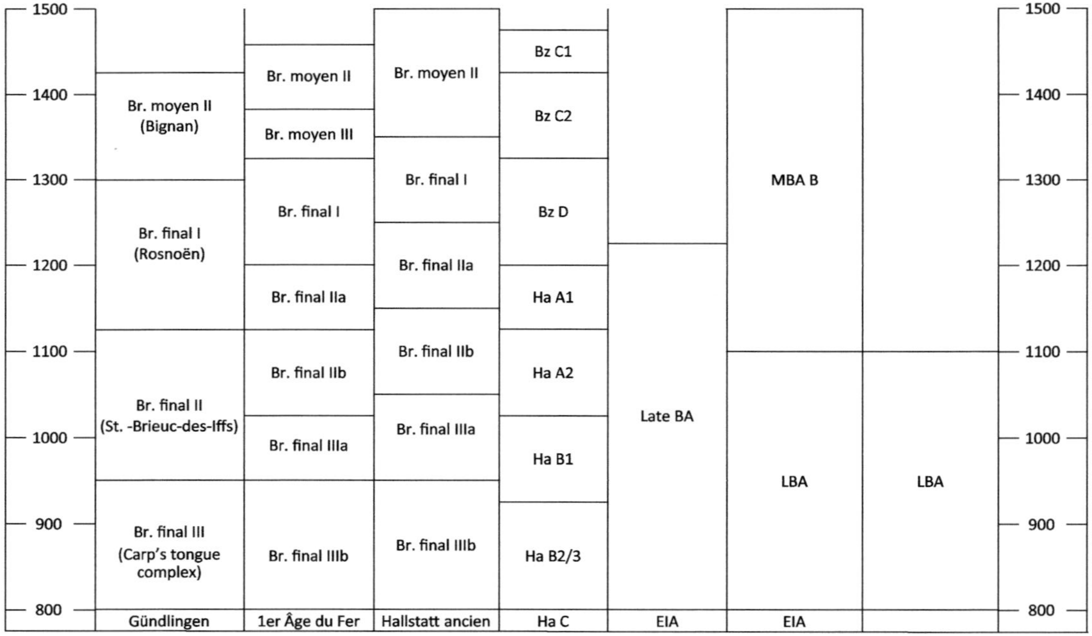

FIG. 2.4 (opposite) Synchronized version of the relevant chronological systems for France, Belgium, and the Netherlands. All stages are C14 revised. – e. = early; l. = late. – After Lanting/van der Plicht 2001/2002; (PoNL=) Louwe Kooijmans et al. 2005; Arnoldussen/Fontijn 2006; Bourgois/Talon 2009; Carozza/Marcigny/ Talon 2009; De Laet 1982.

Bronze Age in the Netherlands was based on a symposium in 1965 (Anonymous 1967), and was subsequently modified by Lanting and Mook (1977; discussion in Fokkens 2001) using the new radiocarbon dates. The divisions followed *Vroege* (Early), *Midden* (Middle) A and B, and *Late* (Late) *Bronstijd* (Bronze Age), though the transitions between these periods often blended into each other with insufficient dates to provide a finer framework, and mainly marking major changes in the material culture, such as pottery or cultural practices, for example at funerary sites. More radiocarbon dates, as well as dendrochronological dating, did not resolve the confusion, though an absolute periodization of the traditional framework was proposed by the National Service for Archaeology in 1992 (see Fokkens 2001), and also used in the *Prehistory of the Netherlands* (Louwe Kooijmans et al. 2005). It is this framework that is widely accepted, and is designed to give a broad outline as to when cultural phenomena appeared, as demonstrated by the extensive continuities between Late Neolithic B and Early Bronze Age. Fokkens (2001) argues that the absence of changes is significant enough to delay the start of a distinctive Bronze Age until $c.1800$ BC, when alterations in settlement, land use, and object deposition mark a genuine shift in practices, and the earliest evidence for Hilversum pottery can be identified. The intensive investigation and dating of recently excavated settlements in the Netherlands has demonstrated unexpected levels of complexity involved in definition, and especially dating, challenging long-held assumptions of contemporaneity and conventional typological frameworks (Arnoldussen and Fokkens 2008). The consequence is that the majority of researchers tend to favour the broader Early-Middle-Late Bronze Age scheme and despite the substantial increase and intensive use of radiocarbon dating, few are proposing finer chronologies beyond metalwork.

However, in a substantial paper Lanting and Van der Plicht (2001–2) have reviewed the impact of new radiocarbon dates on the Bronze Age chronologies of the Netherlands and correlated their results with the neighbouring regional chronologies. They argue that the current framework for the Netherlands is not detailed enough due to the absence of sharp definitions between periods. This is caused by the insufficient dating of transitional sites as well as the inability to relate the chronologies of sites and objects, such as metalwork, to settlement typology. They propose instead that, in the current absence of a better option, the Montelius periods should be used for the northern Netherlands, whereas the Reinecke phases should be used for the southern Netherlands, naturally incorporating all later revisions by dendrochronological and radiocarbon dating (Lanting and Van der Plicht 2001–2: 174). The chronological table (see Fig. 2.4) for the Netherlands shows both approaches, and combines them with some of the main material remains (after Louwe Kooijmans et al. 2005).

Belgium

The Bronze Age in Belgium, as in the Netherlands, spans $c.2000$–800 BC together with a transitional Late Neolithic phase ($c.2500$–2000 BC) which incorporates the Beaker culture (Vander Linden and Salanova 2004). The relatively rare discoveries of bronze objects on land, as opposed to in rivers (see Verlaeckt 1996), created an obstacle to either the complete adoption of the chronological schemes devised by Montelius or Reinecke or the development of a comparable national bronze typo-chronology. Hence, Belgian scholars have tended to employ broad Early, Middle, and Late Bronze Age divisions as well as drawing on the finer Reinecke chronology system because of the relative similarity of finds with those in central Europe (see Fig. 2.3). De Laet (1982) then synchronized each broad division with archaeological cultures in central Europe: thus the Early Bronze Age was linked to the Únětice culture, the Middle Bronze Age with the *Hügelgräberkultur*, or Tumulus culture, and the Late Bronze Age with the Urnfield cultures (De Laet 1982: 414). More recent cultural perspectives have been less clear-cut. For instance, programmes of aerial photography have, in recent decades, revealed a large number of ring ditches throughout northern France, Belgium, and the Netherlands, though few of these have been dated or indeed contain datable material (Bourgeois and Cherretté 2005: 48). It is therefore still difficult to relate the dating of ring ditches, thought to belong to the Early or Middle Bronze Age, to contemporary settlements, which are rarely found, or to the typo-chronological schemes in metalwork or ceramics which are rarely associated with either (Warmenbol 2001). However, more promisingly, for the Late Bronze Age, there have been several programmes dating the cremated bone and associated pottery of the Urnfield burials, which have provided a far finer chronology that can be related to the broader *groupe Rhin-Suisse-France orientale* (western Rhine-Swiss-French group within the Urnfield culture) (De Mulder et al. 2007). As most of the identifiable metalwork that is widespread from the mid second millennium BC comes from rivers rather than burials, the chronology for bronze objects relies instead on inter-regional typologies (Warmenbol 2001). This reflects Belgium's position as bound closely to a network of cultural practices in the surrounding regions, ensuring that any independent chronology for Belgium needs to be coordinated at an international level, whether orientated towards the Atlantic facade or towards central Europe (Bourgeois, Verlaeckt, and Van Strydonck 1996; Bourgeois and Cherretté 2005).

France

The Bronze Age in France conventionally spans 2300/2200–800/750 BC and is preceded by a Chalcolithic in southern and central France and a Late Neolithic in northern France (Carozza and Marcigny 2007; Carozza, Marcigny, and Talon 2009). This difference in terminology and chronology reflects the regional, rather than the national, orientation of both the Bronze Age archaeology and the history of research in France. Chantre's (1873) original three-phase model for the Bronze Age in Burgundy never met with general acceptance in other parts of the country, and it was de Mortillet's coarser twofold distinction between an earlier 'Morgien' and a later 'Larnaudien' that came to provide the chronological framework for French Bronze Age studies during the last quarter of the nineteenth century (see Cartailhac 1875: 374). This simple twofold distinction, however, became obsolete when Montelius (1901), following his seminal work on Nordic Bronze Age chronology, turned his attention to the Bronze Age of France, formulating a model of five distinct periods, based on typologies, primarily of metal objects and funerary sites. It was this model that Déchelette (1910) adapted for use in his influential *Manuel*, reducing by one the number of periods originally proposed by the Swedish scholar.

For the following decades, it was exclusively Déchelette's Periods I–IV that were used to establish temporal coordinates in French Bronze Age studies, and not until the mid twentieth century were any subsequent influential typo-chronologies published. These involved

German scholars such as Kimmig (1951; 1952; 1954) and Müller-Karpe (1959) who, rather than using Déchelette's periodization, extended and revised the Reinecke system; while Sandars (1957) sought to integrate Reinecke, Montelius, and Déchelette and proposed another new scheme of Periods I–V. The French response by Hatt (1958) and Millotte (1970) consolidated the Bronze Age into *ancien* (Early), *moyen* (Middle), and *final* (Late) periods, each subdivided into I–III (see Guilaine 1976 for the contemporary synthesis). Less commonly employed is the concept of a *Bronze récente*, which refers to the earlier part of the *Bronze final*, sometimes including also material from the latest phase of the *Bronze moyen*.

Particularly influential was Hatt's (1961) adaptation of Müller-Karpe's (1959) Urnfield chronology, further subdividing the French *Bronze final* to match the phases established by Müller-Karpe for southern Germany (BF I = Bz D; BF IIa = Ha A1; BF IIb = Ha A2; BF IIIa = Ha B1; BF IIIb = Ha B3), omitting only Müller-Karpe's controversial phase Ha B2. As synchronization between these systems was initially based mainly on bronze types, but definition of the respective phases since then has increasingly come to rely on regional pottery typologies, perception of chronological divides between phases has developed differently in both systems, so that in some cases the corresponding phases can strictly speaking no longer be treated as chronological equivalents.

Further problems have arisen from Briard's (1965) attempt to adapt Hatt's chronology of the central and eastern French *Bronze final*—essentially based on Urnfield grave assemblages—to the Atlantic hoards of Brittany (see Gomez de Soto 1991 for a full discussion), and from the subsequent application of Briard's scheme to other parts of the Atlantic facade. While the Breton hoard chronology can be applied with only minor adjustments to most of Atlantic France north of the Loire (Milcent 2012), further south matters get considerably more complicated, and the unreflective use of this chronological framework for south-western France and even Iberia is more than likely to mask a number of significant temporal offsets between regional assemblages (see e.g. Coffyn 1985).

Southern France also has its own distinct Urnfield group—crossing the border into north-eastern Spain—to which Hatt's chronology is not easily applied, although the same terminology of different *Bronze final* phases is frequently used (Taffanel, Taffanel, and Janin 1998; Giraud et al. 2003). Here also, differences between the material assemblages of distinct cultures and the resulting offsets between chronological divides are masked by uniform terminology, adding another pitfall for the uninitiated.

A radical departure from the established system for subdividing the *Bronze final* was advocated by Brun (1986), who argued that caesuras between BF IIa and IIb as well as between BF IIIa and IIIb in the western Urnfield sphere were much more pronounced than those between the main phases BF I, BF II, BF III, and the following Early Iron Age respectively. He thus proposed an alternative model of three *étapes*, which has found some following but has not met with general acceptance among French Bronze Age specialists (*étape* 1 = BF I + IIa; *étape* 2 = BF IIb + IIIa; *étape* 3 = BF IIIb + *Hallstatt ancien*). Occasionally, the last of those three étapes is referred to as *Bronze tardif*, rather than including it with the *Bronze final*. Some authors, despite the plethora of problems that inevitably come with such an exercise, have not been deterred from trying to apply this chronology also to Atlantic Late Bronze Age hoards (e.g. Quilliec 2007).

If a better understanding of Late Bronze Age chronology in France has thus suffered from repeated attempts to apply a uniform system of rather detailed phases to different cultural domains (Müller-Karpe 1974; 1975 for a general discussion), the same does not necessarily hold true for earlier periods, where differences in Bronze Age archaeology throughout France have encouraged scholars to propose cultural and chronological groupings at a regional, rather than national, scale. In north, north-east, and western France, archaeological cultures are interpreted within an Atlantic Bronze Age, and distinct chronologies have been developed for individual regions, for example Brittany (Gallay 1981; Briard and Onnée 1984). In eastern and central France, archaeological cultures are seen as closely connected to central Europe; and in Mediterranean France, archaeological cultures are discussed in relation to western Switzerland and north-west Italy (e.g. Guilaine and Gascó 1987; Gascó 1990; David-Elbiali 2009). At a more detailed level, a recent study revealed that much of south-east France, including the Early and early Middle Bronze Age, belonged to a north-west Alpine cultural formation, its Danubian and north Italian connections notwithstanding. The authors in this instance used a modified Reinecke system for describing the phases in correlation to the French system (David-Elbiali and David 2009).

With regard to absolute chronology, the initial resistance among French scholars to radiocarbon dating due to its alleged imprecision (Millotte 1970) was eventually abandoned, and over the last few decades an increasing number of chronologies based on radiocarbon dates on objects and sites in France, as well as on typo-chronological links to neighbouring chronologies, have been developed (e.g. Gascó et al. 1996; Lanting and Van der Plicht 2001–2). The current framework for the Bronze Age in France would place the *Bronze ancien* c.2300/1950–1600/1550 BC, the *Bronze moyen* c.1600/1550–1350/1300 BC and the *Bronze final* c.1350/1300–800 BC. The exact dates of these periods as well as those of their various subdivisions can vary slightly with region, as for instance in the Atlantic facade (e.g. Gascó et al. 1996: 235, fig. 8; Lanting and Van der Plicht 2001–2; Carozza, Marcigny, and Talon 2009: 26, fig. 2). For south-eastern France, to name another example, the recent study by David-Elbiali and David (2009) placed the beginning of the Bronze Age (*Bronze ancien* I) at c.2200 BC and the beginning of the Middle Bronze Age (*Bronze moyen* I) at c.1530 BC.

IBERIA

The Bronze Age in the Iberian Peninsula conventionally spans c.2250/2150–850/800 BC and is preceded by a Chalcolithic (c.3200–2200 BC), which from c.2600/2500 BC in most regions is generally associated with the Bell Beaker phenomenon. The earliest attempts at devising a basic chronology for the Iberian Copper and Bronze Ages go back to Simões (1878) and the Siret brothers (1887). While these were mainly concerned with the evidence for defining an Age of Copper in its own right, as distinct from an Age of Bronze, the beginning of the twentieth century saw a number of studies aiming for a definition of more detailed chronological sequences by such prominent scholars as Déchelette (1908; 1909), Schmidt (1909; 1915), and L. Siret (1913). Among those, it was certainly Schmidt's work which, through the influence it exerted on his student Bosch-Gimpera, had the most lasting effects on the development of chronological concepts for Bronze Age Iberia (see Almagro Basch 1959: 163). However, when in the wake of the Spanish Civil War Bosch-Gimpera was exiled, use of his four-phase model for the El Argar culture (Bosch-Gimpera 1944: 101–2) was no longer deemed acceptable within official Spanish archaeology.

Date BC	Iberia							Date BC
	North-west	South-west	Mesetas	South-east	North-east	Metalwork depositions	General	
-2500-	Bell Beakers/ Penha ware	Vila Nova de São Pedro (Monte da Tumba/ Santa Justa)	Bell Beakers	Los Millares	Bell Beakers		Calcolítico/ Eneolithico (Chalcolithic)	-2500-
-2400-								-2400-
-2300-								-2300-
-2200-								-2200-
-2100-	Vilavella-Atios	Bronce del Sudoeste A (Ferradeira)	Ciempozuelos/ Los Pasos/ Dornajos	Bronce del Sudeste A (El Argar A)	Arboli	Finca de la Paloma	Bronce Inicial (Early Bronze Age)	-2100-
-2000-								-2000-
-1900-						Roufeiro		-1900-
-1800-	Caldas de Reyes	Bronce del Sudoeste B/ Bronze do Sudoeste I (Atalaia)	Cogeces (Proto-Cogotas I)/ Manzanares ware	Bronce del Sudeste B (El Argar B)			Bronce Medio (Middle Bronze Age)	-1800-
-1700-						Cuevallusa		-1700-
-1600-								-1600-

Bronce Antíguo (Earlier Bronze Age)

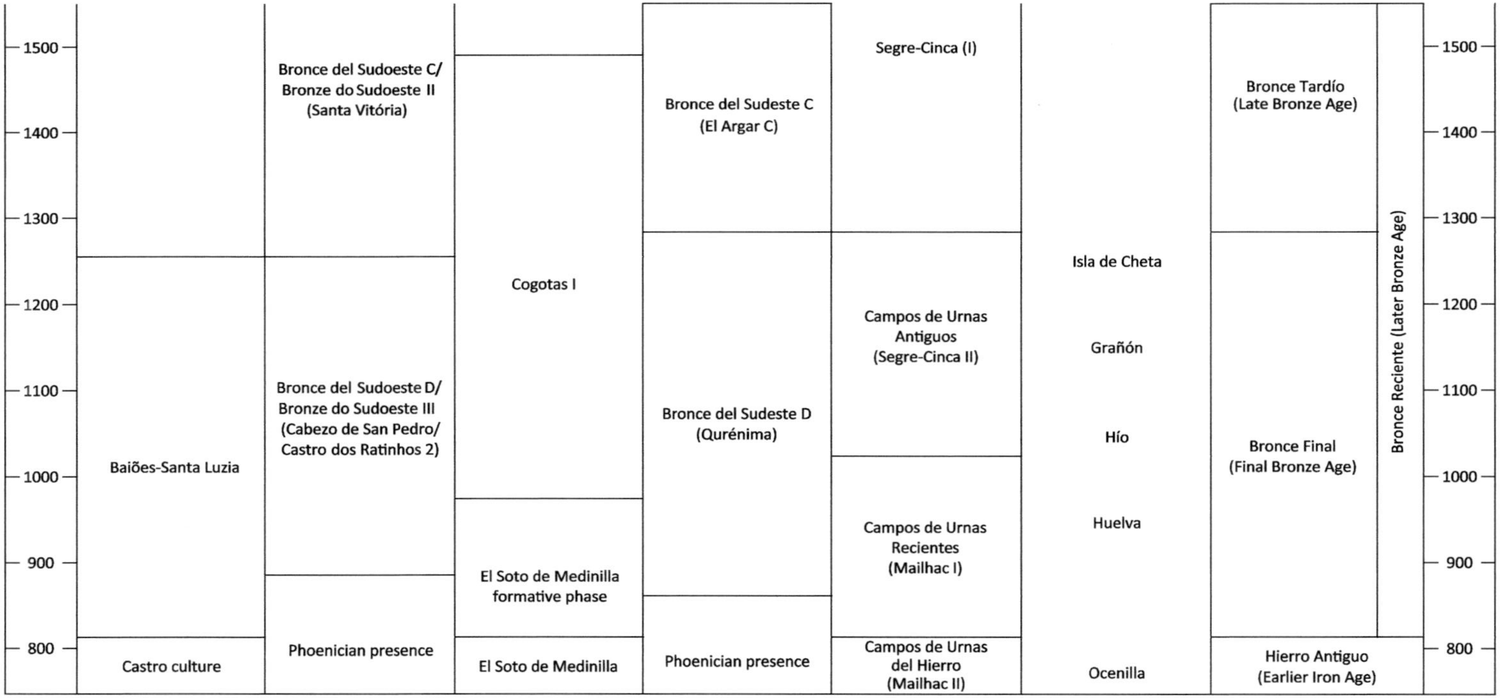

FIG. 2.5 Synchronized version of the relevant chronological systems for Iberia. After: Galán Saulnier 1998; Castro Martínez et al. 1993/94; Castro Martínez, Lull, and Micó 1996; Almagro Gorbea 1997; Pingel 2001; Schubart 1975; Schubart and Arteaga 1978; Molina Gónzalez 1978; Mederos 1997; Mederos 2008; Brandherm 2017.

Instead, it was Martínez Santa-Olalla's (1941: 152–7) formulation of a chronological system based on the definition of four distinct periods which over the following decades was to become the most influential in Iberian Bronze Age studies. His *Bronce I* effectively equals the Chalcolithic of current terminology, while his *Bronce II* corresponds to the El Argar culture, his *Bronce III* covers the Atlantic Late Bronze Age, whereas his *Bronce IV* included everything perceived as Tumulus culture and Urnfield elements. While this may be viewed as a bold first attempt to accommodate remains from all of Iberia and from the entire Bronze Age in one coherent chronological system, even if we are lenient with the very broad brush approach it was hardly based on adequate evidence from stratigraphy or the seriation of closed assemblages. By the early 1970s, even before the impact of radiocarbon dating made itself fully felt, it had become increasingly clear that this system could no longer provide a useful framework for establishing the relative, let alone the absolute, chronology of the Bronze Age south of the Pyrenees. In consequence, relevant data from new fieldwork was mostly cast into regional typo-chronologies, with little attempt made to incorporate these into a larger framework. This seems hardly surprising, given the huge variation in material culture assemblages between the Atlantic and Mediterranean sectors of the Iberian Peninsula.

The ensuing difficulties in building supra-regional chronologies are compounded by a general lack of individual burials and corresponding closed grave assemblages, especially during the later part of the Bronze Age. Furthermore, the burial record from the Earlier Bronze Age remains scanty in many regions, particularly those outside the distribution area of the El Argar culture. Hoards, on the other hand, are almost entirely confined to the western and northern parts of Iberia. As a result, there are considerable uncertainties as to which differences between the two categories of sources have their origin in geographical rather than in temporal distance, making any attempt to align hoard and burial chronologies an even more difficult task. Some well-documented, stratified settlement deposits exist, but the geographical and chronological scope of the respective sequences remains limited, and matching burial, hoard, and settlement chronologies across the Iberian Peninsula continues to be a major challenge. Only very few index fossils straddle the various divides between regions and different categories of context. Diagnostic types of metal objects that occur throughout Iberia and which could provide chronologically sensitive markers remain the exception rather than the rule throughout the Bronze Age. At its very beginning, Beaker pottery provides a meaningful chronological marker for both burial and settlement contexts (Harrison 1988). Later on, some other diagnostic pottery styles such as Cogeces and Cogotas I constitute useful index fossils with a supra-regional distribution, but the chronological intervals defined by these tend to span various centuries and—contrary to the situation in many other parts of Europe—the chronological resolution they offer is more often than not notably lower than that of most science-based dating methods (Galán Saulnier 1998). This state of affairs has contributed to widespread frustration with relative chronologies among Iberian Bronze Age specialists, if not always to the point of advocating their wholesale abandonment in favour of scientific methods of absolute dating (see Castro Martínez et al. 1993–4: 77–84; Castro Martínez, Lull, and Micó 1996: 10–17).

One notable attempt to draw together the various regional chronologies in one overarching framework has been made by Almagro Gorbea (1997), although the absolute dates he uses would now appear rather too low (see Castro Martínez, Lull, and Micó 1996). A somewhat simplified version of his scheme with an updated absolute chronology was introduced by Pingel (2001: table 2). Here we present a slightly revised version of the latter (see Fig. 2.5), incorporating some more regional detail, but maintaining the basic fourfold division into *Bronce Inicial* (Early Bronze Age), *Bronce Medio* (Middle Bronze Age), *Bronce Tardío* (Late Bronze Age), and *Bronce Final* (Final Bronze Age), with an alternative and somewhat coarser twofold distinction between *Bronce Antiguo* (Earlier Bronze Age) and *Bronce Reciente* (Later Bronze Age). It must be pointed out, though, that this terminology was initially developed mostly for the southern half of the Iberian Peninsula, based on specific regional sequences (Schubart 1975: 163–71; Schubart and Arteaga 1978: 36–50; Molina Gónzalez 1978). Thus, with a number of other regional chronologies, the same terms are occasionally applied to different periods, sometimes based on a threefold division into *Bronce Antiguo*, *Bronce Medio* (equalling the *Bronce Tardío* as defined here, rather than used to designate the later part of the *Bronce Antiguo*), and *Bronce Final*. Particularly with regard to north-eastern Iberia, the term *Bronce Reciente* frequently is also used to identify an initial phase of the *Bronce Final*, supposedly equivalent to the Italian *Bronzo recente,* but much less well defined. Among different authors, however, there is little consistency in this. A lack of consistency also plagues the use of the terms *Bronce Inicial* and *Bronce Antiguo*, which are sometimes employed interchangeably, causing no little confusion among non-specialists and sometimes even within the ranks of specialists as well. For some authors, the easy way out has been to apply the blanket term *Bronce Pleno* ('fully developed Bronze Age') to everything post-Beaker and pre-*Bronce Final*. While this may be perfectly acceptable for regions still lacking data which could provide a better chronological resolution, it hardly offers an adequate solution for the problems at hand.

While limitations of space do not permit us to explore regional terminologies in any greater detail, a few alternative proposals for chronological schemes at a supra-regional scale must briefly be mentioned, even though they no longer enjoy any widespread support or have met with general acceptance in the first place. This has particularly been the case with any attempts at aligning Iberian terminology to that employed in the eastern Mediterranean and the Aegean, either by including the Bell Beaker period in the *Bronce Inicial/Bronce Antiguo* (Maluquer 1949; Brandherm 2003: 32–7), thus having the Bronze Age start in the first half of the third millennium BC, or by abandoning the concept of a *Bronce Tardío* in favour of an extended *Bronce Final* beginning in the sixteenth or even seventeenth century cal BC (Mederos 1997; 2008: 37–41).

With regard to the El Argar culture, another proposal to establish chronological subdivisions must be mentioned here. Drawing on the relative frequencies of radiocarbon dates from building timbers, as well as from short-lived organic samples, and based on the assumption that these relate to episodes of building activity and destruction layers respectively, a fivefold subdivision of the Earlier Bronze Age in south-east Spain has been suggested (Castro Martínez, Lull, and Micó 1996: 120–8). While this five-phase model has occasionally been employed as a reference framework by other authors, the nature of both the overall sample and of the respective frequency distribution raises concerns about its validity. Not least due to those issues, the original authors of this proposal have more recently returned to a three-phase model that aligns more closely with previous ideas for structuring the respective sequence (Lull et al. 2011: 389).

In practice, at present it is only through an explicit combination of both relative and absolute dating methods that one can hope to achieve a better understanding of synchroneities and asynchroneities in the development of Iberian Bronze Age societies. A number of well-founded relative-chronological sequences exist at the regional level, based mostly on the stratigraphy from key sites, and it is largely the widespread abandonment of systematic typo-chronological studies on the one hand, and a lack of methodologically sound attempts to draw the existing evidence together at a supra-regional scale on the other, that currently hamper further advances in this field. Even more so than with most other parts of western Europe, the scheme presented here thus very much represents a provisional state of work in progress.

Conclusion

The Bronze Age in western Europe is generally considered in terms of an interconnected Atlantic facade (e.g. Coffyn 1985; Ruiz-Gálvez Priego 1998). The appearance of Bell Beaker material culture and burial practices throughout western Europe during the mid third millennium BC would appear to represent these Atlantic networks, yet this would be to ignore the close relationships with central and northern Europe. Furthermore, when investigated in more detail, the apparent pan-European coherency of the Bell Beaker culture begins to resemble a more regionally orientated phenomenon (Vander Linden 2006). The definition of the Bronze Age in western Europe from the late third millennium BC therefore lies against a background of long-distance communication but also of pronounced regionality. This fundamental pattern defines the archaeological record during the subsequent one and a half millennia until the identification of an Iron Age in the early first millennium BC. This is perhaps most clearly expressed in the definitive material of the Bronze Age—bronze, the alloy of copper and tin. Given the relatively limited sources of tin in western Europe, which beyond the Erzgebirge mountains in central Europe consisted primarily of western Iberia (Meredith 1998) and south-west England (Penhallurick 1986), pan-regional connections would have been required to ensure regular access to tin ore or bronze objects. It might therefore be assumed that this frequent pan-regional interaction would lead to a strong coherency in the technology and form of the bronze objects being used throughout western Europe. Yet the metalwork evidence demonstrates the existence of certain broad patterns, for instance during the late third–early second millennium BC in halberds (e.g. Schuhmacher 2002; Brandherm 2004) or during the late second–early first millennium BC in carp's-tongue swords (e.g. Brandherm and Moskal-del Hoyo 2014). It also demonstrates that pan-regional bronze technologies and forms such as palstave axes during the mid second millennium BC or socketed axes during the late first millennium BC would inevitably also be adapted to local and regional traditions (e.g. O'Connor 1980). It is therefore unsurprising that the Bronze Age communities, whether in settlement architecture and patterns, burial practices, or craft-working, exhibit too much variation to be fitted into one straightforward archaeological scheme or narrative. Nevertheless, there are underlying trends which, with exceptions, can be seen in the evidence. The population of western Europe between the mid third–early first millennium BC relied primarily on arable and pastoral farming. They lived in relatively small settlements in what would be classified today as hamlets or villages in a community of tens and low hundreds rather than thousands. Their material culture, most obviously evidenced in metals, ceramics, and stone, but also in wood and textiles, indicates high levels of sophistication and widespread inter-regional contacts. The increasing diversity and quantity of material culture throughout the period is indicative of greater intensity and complexity of production and consumption, and potentially a larger population underlying this trend (Harding 2000; Bartelheim and Stäuble 2009).

The chronology of the Bronze Age in western Europe remains a patchwork of relative metalwork phases, ceramic traditions, and archaeological cultures whose absolute ranges have been evaluated through radiocarbon and dendrochronological dating. It continues to be a significant challenge merely to understand the different terminologies and sequences and how they relate to one another. This complexity in dating the Bronze Age is due to the historical development stretching over a century of scholarship and debate. It means that the revision of chronology is conducted by relatively few specialists, and their discussions of when can easily overwhelm other fundamental investigations into Bronze Age communities. Ideally, there would be no more relative chronologies encompassing sites and objects throughout western Europe, and researchers would discuss only absolute calendar dates allowing a transparency enjoyed by modern historians, albeit with a resolution of decades rather than days. However, the majority of published objects and sites lack radiocarbon or dendrochronological dates, with the consequence that the best possible dating is an integration of the relative and absolute, especially when attempting to relate broad patterns in objects or sites. This is not an argument for the maintenance of the current situation, as far more typological and scientific dating programmes are required in most regions of western Europe.

It is perhaps time to concentrate on the creation of a comprehensive, coherent, and transparent chronological framework for western Europe that involves using *and* discussing absolute as well as relative dates. This can only be achieved through international collaboration as occurs in the Neolithic (e.g. Arias et al. 2003), easy access to the radiocarbon dates, and dedicated conferences (the last being in 1994—see papers in Randsborg 1996). There would need to be a greater willingness to work across national and regional borders, exploiting the flexibility that accompanies absolute dates in debate, the rapid publication of databases containing dates, and a systematic evaluation of chronological problems and potentials in each region of western Europe. This would need to be integrated closely with material science and material culture theory, discussing how the way objects were used can influence their dating, especially with regards to practices such as curation and recycling. In building on and connecting fine regional chronologies (which remain essential), it would be possible for researchers to devote far more time to understanding the dynamics of Bronze Age material culture and societies at all scales. This would allow more frequent challenges to established interpretations, especially of inter-regional connections and causation, just as in the 1960s and 1970s radiocarbon dating destroyed the prevailing *ex oriente lux* perspective. It would encourage exploration beyond well-worn typo-chronological relationships where they are expected. The means of dating the Bronze Age have yet to be fully exploited—whether the interlinking of environmental and archaeological sequences (e.g. Richard, Magny, and Mordant 2007) or the evaluation of relative object typologies using targeted AMS radiocarbon dating and Bayesian statistics (e.g. Sheridan and Bayliss 2008), which remain relatively rare despite their potential. The divide between object and site chronologies remains substantial, leading to the absurd situation where two or more timelines for the Bronze Age have an uneasy coexistence in every region of western Europe.

Bibliography

Abercromby, J. (1912). *A Study of the Bronze Age Pottery of Great Britain and Ireland and its Associated Grave Goods*. Oxford: Clarendon Press.

Allen, M. J., Gardiner J., and Sheridan, A. (2012). *Is There a British Chalcolithic: People, Place and Polity in the Later 3rd Millennium BC*, Prehistoric Society Monograph, 4. Oxford: Oxbow.

Almagro Basch, M. (1959). 'Elementos para la cronología del Bronce I en la península ibérica', in *Actas e Memorias do I Congresso Nacional de Arqueologia, Lisboa, 15 a 20 de Dezembro de 1958, vol. I*, 161–85. Lisboa: Tipografia Portuguesa.

Almagro Gorbea, M. (1997). 'La Edad del Bronce en la península ibérica: periodización y cronología', *Saguntum*, 30: 217–29.

Anonymous (1967). 'De periodisering van de Nederlandse Prehistorie', *Berichten van de Rijksdienst voor het Oudheidkundig Bodemonderzoek*, 15–16: 7–11.

Arias, P., Burenhult, G., Fano, M. A., Oosterbeek, L., Scarre, C., Schulting, R., Sheridan, A., and Whittle, A. (2003). 'Megalithic chronologies', in G. Burenhult (ed.), *Stones and Bones: Formal Disposal of the Dead in Atlantic Europe during the Mesolithic-Neolithic Interface 6000–3000 BC*. Oxford: Archaeopress, 65–111.

Arnoldussen, S. and Fokkens, H. (eds.) (2008). *Bronze Age Settlements in the Low Countries*. Oxford: Oxbow.

Baillie, M. (1995). *A Slice Through Time: Dendrochronology and Precision Dating*. London: Routledge.

Bartelheim, M. and Stäuble, H. (eds.) (2009). *The Economic Foundations of the European Bronze Age*, Forschungen zur Archäometrie und Altertumswissenschaft, 5. Rahden/Westf.: Leidorf.

Bayliss, A. and Bronk Ramsey, C. (2004). 'Pragmatic Bayesians: a decade integrating radiocarbon dates into chronological models', in E. Buck and A. R. Millard (eds.), *Tools for Constructing Chronologies: Tools for Crossing Disciplinary Boundaries*. London: Springer, 25–41.

——, Bronk Ramsey, C., Van der Plicht, J., and Whittle, A. (2007). 'Bradshaw and Bayes: towards a timetable for the Neolithic', *Cambridge Archaeological Journal*, 17/1: 1–28.

Bosch-Gimpera, P. (1944). *El poblamiento antiguo y la formación de los pueblos de España*. México: Imprenta Universitaria.

Bourgeois, J. and Cherretté, B. (2005). 'L' Âge du Bronze et le premier Âge du Fer dans les Flandres occidentale et orientale (Belgique): un état de la question', in J. Bourgeois and M. Talon (eds.), *L'Âge du Bronze du Nord de la France dans son context européen*. Paris: Comité des Travaux Historiques et Scientifiques/Association pour la Promotion des Recherches sur l'Âge du Bronze, 43–81.

——, Verlaeckt, K., and Van Strydonck, M. (1996). 'Belgian Bronze Age chronology: results and perspectives', *Acta Archeologica*, 67/1: 141–52.

Bradley, R. (2007). *The Prehistory of Britain and Ireland*. Cambridge: Cambridge University Press.

Brandherm, D. (2003). *Die Dolche und Stabdolche der Steinkupfer- und der älteren Bronzezeit auf der Iberischen Halbinsel*. Prähistorische Bronzefunde, VI/12. Stuttgart: Steiner.

—— (2004). 'Porteurs de hallebardes? Überlegungen zur Herkunft, Entwicklung und Funktion der bronzezeitlichen Stabklingen', in H. J. Beier and R. Einicke (eds.), *Varia neolithica III. Beiträge zur Ur- und Frühgeschichte Mitteleuropas*, 37. Langenweissbach: Beier and Beran, 279–334.

—— (2017). 'Von der mittleren zur späten Bronzezeit im Südwesten der Iberischen Halbinsel', in T. Lachenal, C. Mordant, T. Nicolas and C. Veber (eds.), Le Bronze moyen et l'origine du Bronze final en Europe occidentale (XVIIe–XIIIe siècle av. J.-C.). Strasbourg: MAGE, 399–422.

—— and Moskal-del Hoyo, M. (2014). 'Both Sides Now: the carp's-tongue complex revisited', *Antiquaries Journal*, 94: 1–47.

Brennand, M. and Taylor, M. (2003). 'The survey and excavation of a Bronze Age timber circle at Holme-next-the-Sea, Norfolk, 1998–9', *Proceedings of the Prehistoric Society*, 69: 1–84.

Briard, J. (1965). *Les Dépôts bretons et l'Âge du Bronze atlantique*. Rennes: Becdelière.

—— and Onnée, Y. (1984). *Les Tumulus d'Armorique. L'Âge du Bronze en France*, 3. Paris: Picard.

Brindley, A. (1995). 'Radiocarbon, chronology and the Bronze Age', in J. Waddell and E. Shee Twohig (eds.), *Ireland in the Bronze Age*. Dublin: Stationery Office, 4–13.

—— (2007). *Dating of Food Vessels and Urns in Ireland*. Galway: National University of Ireland.

Brun, P. (1986). *La Civilisation des champs d'urnes: étude critique dans le bassin parisien*. Documents d'Archéologie Française, 4. Paris: Maison des Sciences de l'Homme.

Burgess, C. (1974). 'The Bronze Age', in C. Renfrew (ed.), *British Prehistory: A New Outline*. London: Duckworth, 165–221.

—— (1980). *The Age of Stonehenge*. London: J. M. Dent.

—— (2012). 'Alignments: revising the Atlantic Late Bronze Age sequence', *Archaeological Journal*, 169: 127–58.

Carozza, L. and Marcigny, C. (2007). *L'Âge du Bronze en France*. Paris: Editions La Découverte.

——, Marcigny, C., and Talon, M. (2009). 'Ordres et désordres dans l'économie des sociétés durant l'Âge du Bronze en France', in M. Bartelheim and H. Stäuble (eds.), *The Economic Foundations of the European Bronze Age*. Forschungen zur Archäometrie und Altertumswissenschaft, 5. Rahden/Westf.: Leidorf.

Cartailhac, E. (1875). 'Le Congrès et l'exposition de gèographie', *Matériaux pour l'Histoire Primitive et Naturelle de l'Homme*, 6: 372–88.

Castro Martínez, P. V., Lull, L., and Micó, R. (1996). *Cronología de la prehistoria reciente de la península ibérica y Baleares (c.2800–900 cal ANE)*, British Archaeological Reports (International Series), 652. Oxford: Tempus Reparatum.

——, Chapman, R. W., Gili Suriñach, S., Lull, V., Micó Pérez, R., Rihuete Herrada, C., Risch, R., and Sanahuja Yll, M. E. (1993–4). 'Tiempos sociales de los contextos funerarios argáricos', *Anales de Prehistoria y Arqueología*, 9/10: 77–105.

Chantre, E. (1873). 'L'Âge du Bronze dans le bassin du Rhône', in *Congrès international d'anthropologie et d'archéologie préhistoriques. Compte rendu de la cinquième session à Bologne 1871*. Bologna: Fava et Garagnani, 343–55.

Coffey, G. (1913). *The Bronze Age in Ireland*. Dublin: Hodges, Figgis, & Co.

Coffyn A. (1985). *Le Bronze final atlantique dans la péninsule ibérique*. Paris: Centre Pierre Paris.

Collard, M., Darvill, T., and Watts, M. (2006). 'Ironworking in the Bronze Age? Evidence from a 10th century BC settlement at Hartshill Copse, Upper Bucklebury, West Berkshire', *Proceedings of the Prehistoric Society*, 72: 367–423.

David-Elbiali, M. (2009). 'Des Femmes et des hommes dans l'Arc Alpin occidental entre le XIIe et le VIIIe siècle av. J.-C.', in M. J. Lambert-Rouliere, A. Daubigney, P. Y. Milcent, M. Talon, and J. Vital (eds), *De l'Âge du Bronze à l'Âge du Fer en France et en Europe occidentale (Xe–VIIe siècle av. J.-C.) (thème spécialisé); La moyenne vallée du Rhône aux Âges du Fer, actualité de la recherche (thème régional), Actes du XXXe colloque international de la.F.E.A.F., Thème spécialisé co-organisé avec l'A.P.R.A.B., Saint-Romain-en-Gal, 26–28 mai 2006*. Revue Archéologique de l'Est supplément, 27. Dijon: Société Archéologique de l'Est, 343–60.

—— and David, W. (2009). 'À la Suite de Jaques-Pierre Millotte, l'actualité des recherches en typologie sur l'Âge du Bronze. Le Bronze ancien et le début du Bronze moyen: cadre chronologique et liens culturels entre l'Europe nord-alpine occidentale, le monde danubien et l'Italie du Nord', in R. Annick, P. Barral, A. Daubigny, G. Kaenel, C. Mordant, and J.-F. Pinnigre (eds.), *L'Isthme européen Rhin-Saône-Rhône dans la protohistoire. Approches nouvelles en hommage à Jaques-Pierre Millotte*. Actes du colloque de Besançon, 16–18 octobre 2006. Paris: Université de Franche-Comté, 311–40.

Davis, R. (2012). *The Early and Middle Bronze Age Spearheads of Britain*. Prähistorische Bronzefunde V, 5. Stuttgart: Steiner.

—— (2015). *The Late Bronze Age Spearheads of Britain*. Prähistorische Bronzefunde V, 7. Stuttgart: Steiner.

De Laet, S. J. (1982). *La Belgique d'avant les Romains*. Wetteren: Universa.

Déchelette, J. (1908). 'Essai sur la chronologie préhistorique de la péninsule ibérique', *Revue Archéologique*, 12: 219–65 and 390–415.

—— (1909). 'Essai sur la chronologie préhistorique de la péninsule ibérique', *Revue Archéologique*, 13: 15–38 and 219–65.

—— (1910). *Manuel d'archéologie préhistorique, celtique et gallo-romaine II: archéologie celtique ou protohistorique. Première partie: Âge du Bronze*. Paris: Picard.

Eogan, G. (1983). *The Hoards of the Irish Later Bronze Age*. Dublin: University College, Dublin.

—— (1994). *The Accomplished Art: Gold and Gold-Working in Britain and Ireland during the Bronze Age (c.2300–650 bc)*. Oxbow Monograph, 42. Oxford: Oxbow.

Evans, J. (1881). *The Ancient Bronze Implements, Weapons and Ornaments of Great Britain and Ireland*. London: Longmans, Green, & Co.

Fokkens, H. (2001). 'The periodisation of the Dutch Bronze Age: a critical review', in W. H. Metz, B. L. Van Beek, and H. Steegstra (eds.), *Patina: Essays Presented to Jay Jordan Butler on the Occasion of his 80th Birthday*. Groningen and Amsterdam: Metz, Van Beek, and Steegstra, 241–62.

Fox, C. E. (1923). *The Archaeology of the Cambridge Region*. Cambridge: Cambridge University Press.

Galán Saulnier, C. (1998). 'Sobre la cronología de Cogotas I', *Cuadernos de Prehistoria y Arqueología de la Universidad Autónoma de Madrid*, 25/1: 201–43.

Gallay, G. (1981). *Die kupfer- und altbronzezeitlichen Dolche und Stabdolche in Frankreich*. Prähistorische Bronzefunde, VI/5. Munich: Beck.

Gascó, J. (1990). 'La chronologie de l'Âge du Bronze et du Premier Âge du Fer en France méditerranéenne et en Catalogne', *Autour du J. Arnal—Premieres Communautés Paysannes*. Montpellier: Recherches sur les premières communautés paysannes en Méditerranée occidentale, 385–408.

——, Briard, J., Gomez, J., Mordant, C., Vital, J., and Voruz, J.-L. (1996). 'Chronologie de l'Âge du Bronze et du Premier Âge du Fer de la France continentale', *Acta Archaeologica*, 67/1: 227–50.

Gerloff, S. (2007). 'Reinecke's ABC and the chronology of the British Bronze Age', in C. Burgess, P. Topping, and F. Lynch (eds.), *Beyond Stonehenge: Essays on the Bronze Age in Honour of Colin Burgess*. Oxford: Oxbow, 117–61.

—— (2010). *Atlantic Cauldrons and Buckets: Studies in Typology, Origin and Function of Multi-Sheet Vessels of the Late Bronze Age and Early Iron Age in Western Europe.* Prähistorische Bronzefunde II, 18. Stuttgart: Steiner.

Gibson, A. M. (2002). *Prehistoric Pottery in Britain and Ireland.* Stroud: Tempus.

Giraud, J.-P., Pons, F., Janin, T., Carroza, J.-M., Duday, H., Forest, V., Gardeisen, A., Lagarrigue, A., and Roger, J. (2003). *Nécropoles protohistoriques de la région de Castres (Tarn): Le Causse, Gourjade, Le Martinet.* Documents d'Archéologie Méditerranéenne, 7. Paris: Maison des Sciences de l'Homme.

Gomez de Soto, J. (1991). 'Le Fondeur, le trafiquant et les cuisiniers. La broche d'Amathonte de Chypre et la chronologie absolue du Bronze final atlantique', in C. Chevillot and A. Coffyn (eds.), *L'Âge du Bronze atlantique. Ses faciès, de l'Ecosse à l'Andalousie et leurs relations avec le Bronze continental et le Méditerranée.* Actes du 1er Colloque du Parc Archéologique de Beynac. Sarlat: Association des Musées du Sarladais, 369–73.

Guilaine, J. (ed.) (1976). *La Préhistoire française, Vol. 2.* Paris: Centre National de la Recherche Scientifique.

—— and Gascó, J. (1987). 'La Chronologie de l'Âge du Bronze dans le sud de la France', in *Da pré-histoire a historia. Homenagem a Octavio do Veiga Ferrera.* Lisbonne: Delta, 273–85.

Harding, A. (2000). *European Societies in the Bronze Age.* Cambridge: Cambridge University Press.

Harrison, R. J. (1988). 'Bell beakers in Spain and Portugal: working with radiocarbon dates in the 3rd millennium BC', *Antiquity,* 62: 464–72.

Hatt, J.-J. (1958). 'Chronique de protohistoire, IV. Nouveau projet de chronologie pour l'Âge du Bronze en France', *Bulletin de la Société Préhistorique Française,* 55: 304–6.

—— (1961). 'Chronique de protohistoire, V. Une nouvelle chronologie de l'Âge du Bronze final. Exposé critique du système chronologique de H. Müller-Karpe', *Bulletin de la Société Préhistorique Française,* 58: 184–95.

Hawkes, C. F. C. (1960). *A Scheme for the British Bronze Age.* Unpublished CBA conference paper.

Jacob-Friesen, G. (1981). 'Chronologie, Bronzezeit', *Reallexikon der Germanischen Altertumskunde,* 4: 641–8. Berlin/New York: De Gruyter.

Johnston, R. (2005). 'Pattern without a plan: Rethinking the Bronze Age co-axial field systems on Dartmoor, southwest England', *Oxford Journal of Archaeology,* 24: 1–24.

Kendrick, T. D. and Hawkes, C. F. C. (1932). *Archaeology in England and Wales 1914–1931.* London: Methuen & Co.

Kimmig, W. (1951). 'Où en est l'étude de la civilisation des champs d'urnes en France, principalement dans l'Est?', *Revue Archéologique de l'Est et du Centre-Est,* 2: 65–81.

—— (1952). 'Où en est l'étude de la civilisation des champs d'urnes en France, principalement dans l'Est?', *Revue Archéologique de l'Est et du Centre-Est,* 3: 7–19; 137–72.

—— (1954). 'Où en est l'étude de la civilisation des champs d'urnes en France, principalement dans l'Est?', *Revue Archéologique de l'Est et du Centre-Est,* 5: 7–28; 209–32.

Lanting, J. N., Aerts-Bijma, A. T., and Van der Plicht, J. (2001). 'Dating of cremated bones', *Radiocarbon,* 43/2A: 249–54.

—— and Mook, W. G. (1977). *The Pre- and Protohistory of the Netherlands in Terms of Radiocarbon Dates.* Groningen: Published by authors.

—— and Van der Plicht, J. (2001–2). 'De 14C-chronologie van de Nederlandse pre- en protohistorie, IV: bronstijd en vroege ijzertijd', *Palaeohistoria,* 43/44: 117–262.

Lichardus, J. (ed.) (1991). *Die Kupferzeit als historische Epoche*. Bonn: Habelt.
Louwe Kooijmans, L. P., Broeke, P. W. Van den, and Fokkens, H. (eds.) (2005). *The Prehistory of the Netherlands*. Amsterdam: Amsterdam University Press.
Maluquer, J. (1949). 'Concepto y periodización de la Edad del Bronce peninsular', *Ampurias*, 11: 191–5.
Martínez Santa-Olalla, J. (1941). 'Esquema paletnológico de la Península Hispánica', in J. Martínez Santa-Olalla (ed.), *Corona de estudios que la Sociedad Española de Antropología, Etnografía y Prehistória dedica a sus martires*. Madrid: Consejo Superior de Investigaciones Científicas, 141–66.
Mederos, A. (1997). 'Nueva cronología del Bronce Final en el Occidente de Europa', *Complutum*, 8: 73–96.
—— (2008). 'El Bronce Final', in F. García Alonso (ed.), *De Iberia a Hispania*. Barcelona: Ariel, 19–91.
Meredith, C. (1998). *An Archaeometallurgical Survey of Ancient Tin Mines and Smelting Sites in Spain and Portugal*. British Archaeological Reports (International Series), 714. Oxford: Archaeopress.
Milcent, P.-Y. (2012). *Les temps des élites en Gaule atlantique*. Rennes: Presses Universitaires.
Millotte, J. P. (1970). *Précis de proto-histoire européenne*. Paris: Armand Colin.
Molina Gónzalez, F. (1978). 'Definición y sistematización del Bronce tardío y final en el sudeste de la península ibérica', *Cuadernos de Prehistoria de la Universidad de Granada*, 3: 159–232.
Montelius, O. (1901). 'La Chronologie préhistorique en France et en d'autres pays celtiques', *L'Anthropologie*, 12: 609–23.
—— (1903). *Die typologische Methode. Die alteren Kulturperioden im Orient und in Europa 1*. Stockholm: self-published.
—— (1909). 'The chronology of the British Bronze Age', *Archaeologia*, 61: 97–162.
Mulder, G. de, Van Strydonck, M., Mathieu Boudin, M., Leclercq, W., Paridaens, N., and Warmenbol, E. (2007). 'Re-evaluation of the Late Bronze Age and Early Iron Age chronology of the western Belgian urnfields based on 14C dating of cremated bones', *Radiocarbon*, 49: 499–514.
Müller-Karpe, H. (1959). *Beiträge zur Chronologie der Urnenfelderzeit nördlich und südlich der Alpen*. Berlin: De Gruyter.
—— (1974). 'Zur Definition und Benennung chronologischer Stufen der Kupferzeit, Bronzezeit und älteren Eisenzeit', *Jahresbericht des Instituts für Vorgeschichte der Universität Frankfurt am Main*, 1974: 7–18.
—— (1975). 'Zu den Stufenbenennungen der vorgeschichtlichen Metallzeitalter', *Germania*, 53: 24–9.
Needham, S. (1996). 'Chronology and periodisation in the British Bronze Age', Acta *Archaeologica*, 67: 121–40.
—— (2000a). 'Power pulses across a cultural divide: cosmologically driven acquisition between Armorica and Wessex', *Proceedings of the Prehistoric Society*, 66: 151–208.
—— (2000b). 'The development of embossed goldwork in Britain', *Antiquaries Journal*, 80: 27–65.
—— (2005). 'Transforming beaker culture in north-west Europe: processes of fusion and fission', *Proceedings of the Prehistoric Society*, 71: 171–217.
——, Bronk Ramsay, C., Coombs, D., Cartwright, C., and Petitt, P. (1997). 'An independent chronology for British Bronze Age metalwork: the results of the Oxford Radiocarbon Accelerator Programme', *The Archaeology Journal*, 154: 55–107.
——, Parker-Pearson, M., Tyler, A., Richards, M., and Jay, M. (2010). 'A first "Wessex 1" date from Wessex', *Antiquity*, 84/3: 363–73.

O'Connor, B. (1980). *Cross-Channel Relations in the Later Bronze Age*. British Archaeological Reports (International Series), 91. Oxford: British Archaeological Reports.

—— (2007). 'Llyn Fawr metalwork in Britain: a review', in C. Haselgrove and R. Pope (eds.), *The Earlier Iron Age in Britain and the Near Continent*. Oxford: Oxbow, 64–79.

Ottaway, B. and Roberts, B. (2007). 'The emergence of metalworking in Europe', in A. Jones (ed.), *European Prehistory: Theory and Practice*. Oxford: Blackwell, 193–225.

Pare, C. (2000). 'Bronze and the Bronze Age', in C. Pare (ed.), *Metals Make the World Go Round*. Oxford: Oxbow, 1–38.

Peake, R. and Delattre, V. (2005). 'L'Apport des analyses 14C à l'étude de la nécropole de l'Âge du Bronze de "La Croix de la Mission" à Marolles-sur-Seine', *Revue Archéologique du Centre de la France*, 44: 5–25.

Penhallurick, R. D. (1986). *Tin in Antiquity*. London: Institute of Metals.

Piggott, S. (1966). 'Mycenae and Barbarian Europe', *Sborník Národního Muzea v Praze (Historie)*, 20: 117–25.

Pingel, V. (2001). 'Die Bronzezeit im Norden der Iberischen Halbinsel', in M. Blech, M. Koch, and M. Kunst (eds.), *Hispania Antiqua: Denkmäler der Frühzeit*. Mainz: Zabern, 171–92.

Quilliec, B. (2007). *L'épée atlantique: échanges et prestige au Bronze final*. Mémoires de la Société Préhistorique Française, 42. Paris: Société Préhistorique Française.

Randsborg, K. (ed.) (1996). *Absolute Chronology: Archaeological Europe 2500–500 BC*. Acta Archaeologica, 67/1. Copenhagen: Munskgaard.

Reinecke, P. (1965). *Mainzer Aufsätze zur Chronologie der Bronze-und Eisenzeit*. Bonn: Habelt.

Richard, H., Magny, M., and Mordant, C. (2007). *Environnements et cultures à l'Âge du bronze occidentale*. Paris: Comité des Travaux Historiques et Scientifiques.

Roberts, B. W. and Frieman, C. (2012). 'Drawing boundaries and building models: investigating the concept of the "Chalcolithic frontier" in northwest Europe', in M. Allen, J. Gardiner and A. Sheridan, (eds.), *Is There a British Chalcolithic: People, Place and Polity in the Later 3rd Millennium BC*. Oxford: Oxbow.

—— and Vander Linden, M. (eds.) (2011). *Investigating Archaeological Cultures: Material Culture, Variability and Transmission*. New York: Springer.

Rowley-Conwy, P. (2007). *From Genesis to Prehistory: The Archaeological Three Age System and its Contested Reception in Denmark, Britain and Ireland*. Oxford: Oxford University Press.

Ruiz-Gálvez Priego, M. (1998). *La Europa Atlántica en la Edad del Bronce. Un viaje a las raíces de la Europa occidental*. Crítica: Barcelona.

Sandars, N. K. (1957). *Bronze Age Cultures in France: The Later Phases from the Thirteenth to the Seventh Century B.C.* Cambridge: Cambridge University Press.

Schmidt, H. (1909). 'Der Bronzefund von Canena', *Prähistorische Zeitschrift*, 1: 113–39.

—— (1915). 'El origen español de la alabarda y la cronología de los principios de la Edad de los Metales', in H. Schmidt (ed.), *Estudios acerca de los principios de la Edad de los Metales en España*. Memorias de la Comisión de Investigaciones Paleontológicas y Prehistóricas, 8. Madrid: Museo Nacional de Ciencias Naturales, 11–32.

Schubart, H. (1975). *Die Kultur der Bronzezeit im Südwesten der Iberischen Halbinsel*. Madrider Forschungen, 9. Berlin: De Gruyter.

—— and Arteaga, O. (1978). 'Fuente Álamo: Vorbericht über die Grabung 1977 in der bronzezeitlichen Höhensiedlung', *Madrider Mitteilungen*, 19: 23–51.

Schuhmacher, T. (2002). 'Some remarks on the origin and chronology of halberds in Europe', *Oxford Journal of Archaeology*, 21: 263–88.

Sheridan, J. A. (2003). 'New dates for Scottish Bronze Age cinerary urns: results from the National Museums of Scotland "Dating Cremated Bones Project"', in A. Gibson (ed.), *Prehistoric*

Pottery: People, Pattern and Purpose. British Archaeological Reports (International Series), 1,156. Oxford: Archaeopress, 201–26.

—— (2004). 'Scottish food vessel chronology revisited', in A. Gibson and A. Sheridan (eds.), *From Sickles to Circles: Britain and Ireland at the Time of Stonehenge*. Stroud: Tempus, 243–69.

—— (2007). 'Dating the Scottish Bronze Age: "There is clearly much the material can tell us"', in C. Burgess, P. Topping, and F. Lynch (eds.), *Beyond Stonehenge: Essays on the Bronze Age in Honour of Colin Burgess*. Oxford: Oxbow, 162–85.

—— and Bayliss, A. (2008). 'Pots and time in Bronze Age Ireland', *Antiquity*, 82: 204–7.

—— and Bradley, R. (2005). 'Croft Moraig and the chronology of stone circles', *Proceedings of the Prehistoric Society*, 71: 269–81.

Simões, A. F. (1878). *Introdução à archeologia da península ibérica, parte primeira: antigüidades pré-históricas*. Lisbon: Livraria Ferreira.

Siret, H. and Siret, L. (1887). *Les premiers âges du métal dans le sud-est de l'Espagne*. Anvers: self-published.

Siret, L. (1913). *Questions de chronologie et d'ethnographie ibériques: tome I, de la fin du quarternaire a la fin du bronze*. Paris: Paul Geuthner.

Taffanel, O., Taffanel, J., and Janin, T. (1998). *La nécropole du moulin à Mailhac (Aude)*. Lattes: Association pour la Recherche Archéologique en Languedoc Oriental.

Taylor, R. E. (1997). 'Radiocarbon dating', in R. E. Taylor and M. J. Aitken (eds.), *Chronometric Dating in Archaeology*. New York: Plenum, 65–96.

Thomsen, C. J. (1836). *Ledetraad til Nordisk Oldkyndighed udgiven af det kongelige Nordiske Oldskrift-Selskab*. Copenhagen: Det Kongelige Nordiske Oldskriftselskab.

Uckelmann, M. (2012). *Die Schilde der Bronzezeit in Nord-, West- und Zentraleuropa*. Prähistorische Bronzefunde III, 4. Stuttgart: Steiner.

Vander Linden, M. (2006). *Le Phénomène campaniforme dans l'Europe du 3ème millénaire avant notre ère: Synthèse et nouvelles perspectives*. British Archaeological Reports (International Series), 1,470. Oxford: Archaeopress.

—— and Salanova, L. (eds.) (2004). *Le troisième millénaire dans le nord de la France et en Belgique. Actes de la journée d'études SRBAP-SPF, 8 mars 2003, Lille*. Anthropologica et Praehistorica, 115. Paris: Société Préhistorique Française.

Verlaeckt, K. (1996). *Between River and Barrow: A Reappraisal of Bronze Age Metalwork Found in the Province of East Flanders (Belgium)*. British Archaeological Reports (International Series), 632. Oxford: Tempus Reparatum.

Waddell, J. (2000). *The Prehistoric Archaeology of Ireland*. Bray: Wordwell.

Warmenbol, E. (2001). 'L'Âge du Bronze', *Anthropologica et Praehistorica*, 112: 107–19.

Woodward, A. (2002). 'Beads and beakers: heirlooms and relics in the British Early Bronze Age', *Antiquity*, 76: 1,040–7.

—— and Woodward, P. (2000). *British Barrows: A Matter of Life and Death*. Stroud: Tempus.

CHAPTER 3

EUROPE 2500 TO 2200 BC: BETWEEN EXPIRING IDEOLOGIES AND EMERGING COMPLEXITY

VOLKER HEYD

EUROPE AT C.2500 BC

Europe at around 2500 BC can best be described as a chessboard of archaeological entities in different cultural traditions. These traditions can easily be categorized into two blocks: on the one hand there are regionally dispersed archaeological cultures and groups, mostly defined by their respective pottery. These stretch geographically like a belt from the Balkans in the east, over the Carpathian Basin, to Italy and France, including probably also parts of Spain and Portugal in the west. On the other hand there are the supra-regional, expansionistic cultural phenomena, covering wide parts of the continent and connecting, through their respective social, economic, ideological, and material features, regions and landscapes that were previously culturally separated.

During the first half of the third millennium BC, the most prominent of these phenomena is the Corded Ware complex. With all its different regional groupings it stretches from the middle Volga in the east to the Rhine in the west, covering also much of Scandinavia to the north. With the slightly earlier but structurally related Yamnaya (Pit Grave culture) of the north Pontic steppe belt, also including lowland regions west of the Black Sea in their distribution area for a few centuries, much of the continent is covered. But by 2500 BC the Corded Ware has already overcome its peak, and the Yamnaya is on the decline and gradually transforming into the Katakombnaya (Catacomb Grave culture), while retreating to its north Pontic core zone. Also, the regionally dispersed picture of different archaeological cultures and groups in the Balkans and the Carpathian Basin is due to the same process of incorporation into supra-regional cultural phenomena, but a millennium earlier in the form of the Cernavodă III-Boleráz and, from c.3350 BC, the following Baden-Coțofeni complex. In the first half of the third millennium this system has already disintegrated, being transformed through interactions following the Yamnaya infiltration, and more regional aspects prevail, particularly in the pottery. The most up-do-date research into many cultures and groups reflects the situation as it existed in 2500 cal BC.

But Europe at 2500 BC would not be complete without two other cultural developments that are at that time about to dominate the record in Europe for the next centuries: expanding from the west, the Iberian Peninsula, is the Bell Beaker culture as the climax of these ideologically driven cultural phenomena; and from the south-east, the circum-Aegean region, the Early Bronze Age.

The Period of the 'International Spirit' in the Aegean

The starting point for all discussion of the Early Bronze Age is Mesopotamia. From the first centuries of the third millennium BC we see the development of new networks of exchange and trade, reaching its peak in the Sumerian Early Dynastic III and Akkadian periods (Matthews 2003). The centre of this development was in southern Mesopotamia, already urbanized since the fourth millennium BC and by then the most developed region worldwide. However, exchange and trade went far beyond this political and demographic core and, inducing a network structure with regional nuclei, reached as far as central Asia and the Harappa culture of the Indus Valley and north-western India. A new 'Early Dynastic World System', so to speak, arises (e.g. Rahmstorf 2010). On its other north-western side, the Levantine-eastern Mediterranean and Anatolian regions, considered previously as being on the fringe of civilization ('gateway communities'), were also now integrated into this highly complex system of exchange and trade (Primas 2007: 6–7). Here early urban nuclei develop as well, subsequently forming further independent networks and developing their own peripheries. Last to be absorbed was the area around the Aegean of present-day western Turkey and Greece, which was gradually incorporated into this system from c.2700 BC, developing a western nucleus of exchange and trade in the third quarter of the millennium.

Four decades have passed since the discovery of the social, economic, and technical achievements, and the results of wide-ranging communication, exchange, and trade that appear as patterns in the archaeological record of these few centuries, in which the Aegean (and particularly the Cyclades and south and central Greece) was completely incorporated. Colin Renfrew (1972) described the situation very aptly with the term 'International Spirit'. He rightly saw in this concept the origin of a first European 'Civilization'. Since then many new discoveries have been made and insights gained, so that this very period of time—the Early Helladic-Cycladic-Minoan II and particularly its sub-period IIb—may be considered among the best investigated in European prehistory. Without going into too much detail, we may list as perhaps the most important advances: indications of a stratified society, with many prestige and status objects of elites; urbanization and a threefold structured settlement system; quasi-monumental architecture and organized communal works; complex administration and standardized systems of measuring and weighing; economic specialization and mass production such as wheel-made pottery; and fair quantities of copper, gold, and silver, including the first tin bronzes.

This period between c.2450 and 2200 BC seems also to have been one whose climate favoured agricultural production (e.g. Barker 2005: 57–8). This favourable situation leads almost inevitably to a constant growth in population, which we are now able to trace archaeologically through many systematic surveys. In southern and central Greece we see this in the building and enlargement of new urban centres like Manika, Thebes, and many smaller but fortified centres (c.1–4 hectares in extent) often close to the coast (Maran 1998). At the same time this has the effect that large parts of the population, previously working in agriculture, abandon primary food production and move over to crafts, manufacturing, trade, and the service sector in the new centres. Subsistence and, to an increasing extent, some of the wider basic needs of peoples are now covered by barter and trade. Autarchies are therefore lost and dependencies are created.

This boom in barter and trade becomes visible in the records firstly through foreign and exotic objects imported from distant worlds (e.g. Kilian-Dirlmeier 2005). Key finds also include the beams of jewellers' scales and standardized, partly marked stone weights, now known to be in use in the whole Aegean-Anatolian area and copying ultimately a Mesopotamian metronic system (Rahmstorf 2006; 2010). They attest to the particular significance of trade at this time, as do manufactured goods made of metal (such as slotted spearheads and jewellery), of other materials (such as the decorated bone tubes), and not least the new wheel-made pottery of the Lefkandi I-Kastri repertoire. Even if it is difficult to prove this by archaeological means, grain and probably olive oil from surpluses, and preserved foodstuffs such as marine resources from the Aegean, almost certainly also had an important part to play in this short- and long-distance exchange. Consequently, maritime trade gains increased in significance with these products, which are profitable only in quantities as compared with single high-value prestige items. This significance is supported by the proximity of the many newly emerging settlement sites on the coast.

All these achievements and innovations, as well as the inclusion of this area as a further nucleus in the international network of exchange and trade with extensive contacts, naturally increased social complexity to an extent that had never before occurred in Europe, and was not to occur for a long time afterwards. Social hierarchies and elites develop; a society with division of labour is established; systems of redistribution, social storage, and the exchange of prestige goods appear; and daily supplies are obtained through trade. The notions of territory, political control, and even perhaps regional hegemony are born. Although they do not constitute a checklist, it is clear that all these things are also signs of a 'chiefdom' level of culture establishing itself over a wide area. Thus one may accept the assessment of Joseph Maran that culture at this time was 'on the threshold of the birth of state structures' (Maran 1998: 432). Perhaps one can go so far as to accept that for a few hundred years this south-eastern part of Europe took on the features of a developed culture, although writing had not yet appeared, as far as we know. Even if one does not wish to go that far, there may be a consensus that between c.2500 and 2200 BC around the Aegean, in other words partly on European soil, we have a highly complex and dynamic system of communication and exchange that includes everything we would imagine by the term 'Early Bronze Age'.

New Peripheries in the Balkans and Southern Italy

At the time the Aegean was being incorporated as another core area in this international system, neighbouring regions were also reacting, and peripheries advanced further north and west, and entirely new ones came into being (Fig. 3.1). In this process we recognize not only peripheries in the economic sense, as a hinterland with sources of raw materials and a market for finished goods, but also as regions in which elites controlling the available resources participated in these developments, using them as a means of self-promotion. At the same time new social and economic values, information, and innovation, and also probably direct personal contact with people from the core area, now reach regions that had never had access to such resources before. Thus new structures evolve and the level of social complexity rises generally. Therefore the core area was not the only active place, and its peripheries were not the passive recipients, but rather the peripheries developed a dynamic and a life of their own. In this respect, however, each region reacted differently.

Three regions, now entirely within Europe, thus come into much closer contact and direct exchange with this Early Bronze Age Aegean network:

1. The eastern Balkans, with the hinterland of the north Aegean, the European part of Turkey (Turkish Thrace) and Bulgaria, mainly south of the Balkan mountains;
2. The western Balkans, meaning large areas of former Yugoslavia and Albania, particularly the east Adriatic coastal area but also parts of the mountainous hinterland northwards as far as Slavonia and Syrmia (roughly the Sava valley);

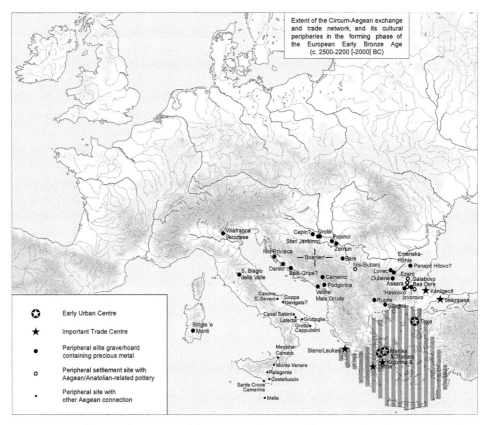

FIG. 3.1 Map showing the extent of the circum-Aegean exchange and trade network and its cultural peripheries in the Balkans and central Mediterranean in the formative phase of the Early Bronze Age (*c.* 2500–2200 BC).

3. The southern central Mediterranean area, particularly Sicily and Malta, but also Apulia.

Whether southern Spain was reached as early as the second half of the third millennium BC as a kind of fourth cultural periphery is a question that cannot yet be answered. The sources for this are ambiguous.

The Eastern Balkans

The greatest progress in terms of new sites, artefacts, and a better understanding about third millennium BC prehistoric archaeology has taken place in this region (Fig. 3.2). The Yamnaya groups in the steppes west of the Black Sea were still the dominant culture in the first half of the third millennium BC, but after the middle of the millennium there is a clear cultural shift towards the south-east and south. In this, the Helladic element is only weakly present, while many finds of north-eastern Aegean and Anatolian provenance show the origin of this cultural current. One key site is Kanlıgeçit in inland Turkish Thrace (Özdoğan 2002); another key site can surely become the Selimpaşa Höyük, a coastal site 50 km west of Istanbul (Heyd, Aydıngün, and Güldoğan 2010).

Large parts of Kanlıgeçit have been excavated since the 1990s. The results are spectacular: not only is there a fortified citadel, a kind of gate-tower, and several large megaron houses with encircling walls built in mud-brick on a stone foundation in the manner of Troy II–III and Küllüoba, but in addition an external settlement of several hectares surrounds this centre. A high proportion of so-called Anatolian red slipware, wheel-made pottery, and elements of the Lefkandi I-Kastri ceramic repertoire, along with typically Anatolian clay idols and signs of a specialized economy, provide more evidence of an Anatolian trading colony in this part of Europe than of a local elite trying to copy the achievements of the south.

Kanlıgeçit is so far the only excavated example of this Anatolian ideal in Europe. However, we have evidence for more of such Anatolian red slipware and/or wheel-made imported pottery from the local, partly fortified late Ezero culture settlements of Michalich-Baa Dere, Assara, and Gŭlŭbovo (which seems to continue till the next chronological watershed of 2200 to c.2000 BC), and from Tell Ezero itself (all in Bulgaria); to top this, we also know of local imitations of the Lefkandi I-Kastri ceramic repertoire (Stefanova 2004; Rahmstorf 2006) (Fig. 3.3a and b). Additional pottery evidence, as yet unpublished, from Altan Tepe, Cherna Gora, and Mudrets demonstrates that we must be dealing with extensive networks of exchange in the upper Thracian plain of Bulgaria (Leshtakov 2006) in this local so-called Early Bronze Age 3 period. The presence of settlers from Anatolia and the persistent cultural current from the south-east clearly cause a dramatic increase in the social complexity of this zone. We see this in the graves of local leaders and elites, their ritual sites, and buried hoards; their adornments of jewellery of gold and silver, new metal fittings for clothing, and equipment such as weapons of a foreign type (e.g. the fenestrated bronze axe from the Haskovo region, the only one of its kind in Europe: Avramova and Todorieva 2005), new alloys, and vessels made of precious metals. The evidence from Rupite in the Struma valley, from Dŭbene and Haskovo in the Thracian plain, and probably also from Izvorovo in the southern Sakar mountains shows this dramatically, but it is probably only the tip of the iceberg. For with the grave of Lovech and the probable hoards from the Emenska Peshtera and Panajot Hitovo (dating yet to be confirmed), we have indications that

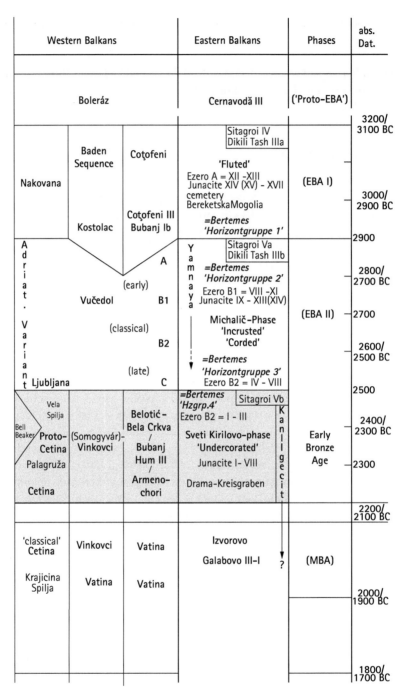

FIG. 3.2 Chronological correlation of archaeological cultures, groups, and key site stratigraphies for the Balkans in the third millennium BC.

this trend succeeded in spreading to the regions north of the Balkan mountains. Finally, Greek Thrace is also included, as demonstrated by the famous stone sceptre in the form of a lion from Sitagroi, amongst other finds and sites.

Thus we have more than a local effect; rather, it is the widespread realization of a 'chiefdom' system based on prestige goods. Nevertheless local terminology speaks nonsensically of the second half of the fourth and the first half of the third millennium BC as an 'Early Bronze Age'—however, one should recognize a structurally defined 'Early Bronze Age' only in relation to this local Early Bronze Age 3, in other words roughly the second half of the third millennium. This is justified through the application of the 'chiefdom' system concept,

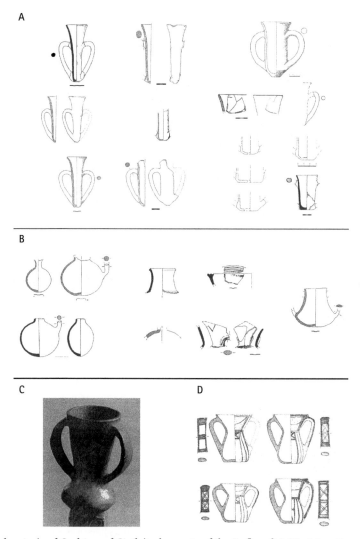

FIG. 3.3 Bulgaria (and Serbia and Sicily): elements of the Lefkandi I-Kastri pottery repertoire, other later third millennium BC pottery imports, and potential imitations: A) *Depas* cups and their imitations from Michalich-Baa Dere, Assara and Gŭlŭbovo; B) Other wheel-made pottery from Gŭlŭbovo; C) Potential imitation of a depas cup from Niš-Bubanj (Serbia); D) Decorated Castelluccio vessels from Santa Croce Camarina (Sicily).

Drawings: author, after various sources.

but also by the advanced economic context, the segmented system of settlement behind it, and the many innovations of the time. Anything else makes no sense in a trans-regional context, and particularly compared with the circum-Aegean regions and Anatolia.

The Western Balkans

As with the eastern Balkans, we see in wide areas of the western Balkans the appearance in the third millennium of larger and more varied gold and silver objects, more prestige goods and exotic finds. We can also detect elites, the way they represented themselves in graves, hoards, and hierarchically structured settlement sites and settlement systems. However, there are clear differences in the structures themselves and particularly in their dating. For if this increase in complexity in Bulgaria and Turkish Thrace occurred suddenly in the local Early Bronze Age 3, then we are dealing with a development as early as 2750 BC or even earlier (Maran 1998; Harrison and Heyd 2007; Primas 2007: 9–10). This is shown by the well-known graves of Mala and Velika Gruda and of Podgorica-Tološi in Montenegro, a Bosnian silver-axe hoard of unknown provenance, as well as the hierarchically structured settlement of Vučedol and similar sites along the Danube and Sava rivers in Croatia and Serbia. The gold dagger weighing 108.8 g from Mala Gruda, silver axes made from supposedly exotic alloys, a knife of tin bronze with 7.3 per cent tin content from Velika Gruda, and a polished rectangular-shaped object with almost exactly the same weight as an Aegean-Near Eastern Mina standard (cf. Rahmstorf 2010: 685, fn. 13)—all are evidence of very early connections through exchange in the eastern Mediterranean area.

In this one cannot overlook the coastal location of many important sites and their direct access to the Adriatic. Clearly in this early exchange connection the contemporary Early Helladic cemetery of Steno on the Ionian island of Levkas is of great importance (Kilian-Dirlmeier 2005; Maran 2007; Primas 2007: 9).

This connection between the Aegean/east Mediterranean and local elites who took part in this system and possibly also controlled it, remains in place during the second half of the third millennium BC, even if the cultural background of the west Balkan area changes markedly. The previously dominant Vučedol complex falls apart shortly after the middle of the millennium, and more regional groups appear—like Vinkovci in Slavonia and Syrmia, Bubanj Hum III and Armenochóri in east Serbia and Macedonia, Belotić-Bela Crkva in central Serbia and Cetina along the Adriatic coast (Maran 1998). The factor connecting them is now largely undecorated pottery, and the dominance of cups and jugs, plates and bowls; a development similarly observed at this time in Bulgaria. However, rich finds of silver and gold from probable and certain graves and hoards clearly demonstrate continuity (Fig. 3.4): the inventory of gold jewellery from a probable burial mound in Nin-Privlaka in Dalmatia; the two axes of cupellated silver, probably Aegean (c.300 g)—along with gold jewellery—from Stari Jankovci (lost); a grave with gold diadem (39.95 g) from Zemun; the gold jewellery from the mound of Bare near Rekovac and the treasure of Orolik (75.56 g of gold in total); probably of the same kind are the chronologically doubtful finds of Cemenci (gold bracelet), Popinci (gold jewellery), and Split-Gripe (gold jewellery, possibly also the uncertain find of Čepin). As far as we know, settlements from this time no longer demonstrate the strict hierarchical divisions found at Vučedol. Nevertheless, alongside regionalization there seem to take shape the beginnings of local centralization processes, as the large tell settlement in the town centre of Vinkovci shows. In addition, a second connecting axis to the Aegean area, via the river systems of the Serbian Morava and Vardar-Axios, also seems to become significant, though this does not emerge clearly from the record. However, a vessel from Niš-Bubanj shows the importance of this connection; the form of this vessel can only be understood if one is familiar with Aegean wheel-made drinking vessels of the *depas* form (see Fig. 3.3c).

Overall, we note a development between the Adriatic, Sava/Danube, and Vardar-Axios similar to the one in the eastern Balkans, in which a 'chiefdom' system based on prestige goods came into being. Exchange and down-the-line trade, particularly along the Adriatic coast, are of prime importance, and it is obvious that the recently discovered Early Bronze Age shipwreck of Kefalonia gives us a clue as to the main means of transport for this connection. Local terminology rightly sees in the cultural changes of the second half of the third millennium the beginnings of the Early Bronze Age in this region. This can also be proven structurally; as is the case later in many other regions of Europe (see below), cultural regionalization, the rather small areas in which cultural identity was established, and the abandonment of decoration on pottery, must be among the fundamental criteria of such a definition. The fact that this occurred in the Vinkovci area together with aspects of centralization, elite graves, and hoards of precious metal, proves the argument is watertight. A second important role in this connection is played by the Cetina group of Dalmatia (e.g. Della Casa 1995): Splitting off from the dissolving Adriatic variant of the Vučedol complex, and at the same time incorporating elements of the Bell Beaker phenomenon (also see below), early Cetina apparently had a quite different social agenda, as shown on the one hand by the conspicuous absence of prestige goods and, on the other, by the group's drive to expand. For not only do we come across Cetina finds on the other side of the Adriatic in Italy, probably from the twenty-fourth century onwards, but also to the south in Albania and later the Peloponnese, where Cetina finds have a particular role in the transition from Early Helladic II to III (around c.2200 BC) (Maran 1998; Nicolis 2005).

The Southern Central Mediterranean Area

The third European region that had direct exchange links with this Early Bronze Age Aegean network is southern mainland Italy and Sicily, along with Malta. Here too knowledge about Early Bronze Age connections with the Aegean is nothing radically new (e.g. Leighton 1999; Cazzella 2003; Maran 2007). But unlike the situation in the Balkans described above, the social background seems different: we find far fewer prestige goods of precious metal, nor do we have direct evidence of local elites. This is partly because of local traditions, particularly burial rituals. In the centre and south of Italy there are mostly communal graves in natural and artificial grottos and caves. In addition there is the problem of relative and absolute chronology, which still causes difficulty today (Maran 1998: 364–5; Maran 2007). This is particularly true of the settlements. Although the beginnings of fortified settlements near the coast, like Coppa Nevigata in Apulia, seem to reach back into the third millennium, we have no other reliable comparison between sites. Thus in the case of many of the relevant small finds made of metal, bone, stone, and clay, the exact time frame cannot always be fixed beyond doubt, especially as some of the most important artefacts have no context (Fig. 3.5).

If we nevertheless try to proceed chronologically, then amongst the earliest finds showing Aegean connections are two stone 'violin idols' found in 1991 and 1996–7 at a Piano Conte site in Camaro outside Messina in Sicily. It is in no way accidental that there are burials at the same site, which interestingly includes an adult burial covered with the sherds of a large

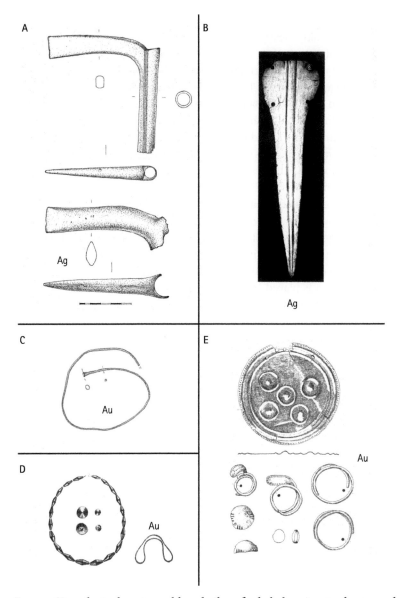

FIG. 3.4 Former Yugoslavia: heavier gold and silver finds belonging to the second half of the third millennium BC: A. Stari Jankovci; B. Hungarian National Museum Budapest; C. Cemenci; D. Nin-Privlaka; E. Orolik.

Drawings: author, after various sources.

pithos (Bacci 1997). There are no others of this kind in Sicily or the entire central Mediterranean area, and indeed the best parallels are found in the Aegean area, where one would place them roughly in the first half of the third millennium BC.

A second watershed from 2500 till about 2200 BC, in other words the peak of Early Helladic IIb, probably provides the chronological background to more finds (Cazzella 2003). To this period belong: a small decorated bone tube, one of which was found in Casone San Severo in

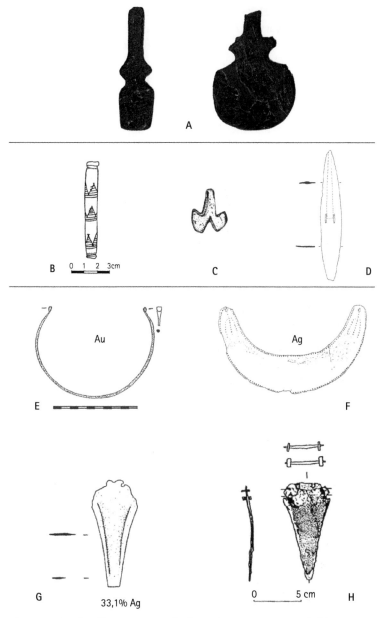

FIG. 3.5 Italy: Key third millennium BC finds with Aegean, or probable Aegean, connections. A. Camaro; B. Casone San Severo; C. Grotta Cappuccini; D. Monte Venere; E. Bingia 'e Monti; F. Villafranca Veronese; G. San Biagio della Valle; H. Palagonia.

Drawings: author, after various sources.

north Apulia, with excellent parallels in the necropolis of Steno in Levkas (grave R4), mentioned above; a small anchor-shaped amulet made of shell, possibly *Spondylus*, found in the Grotta Cappuccini in south Apulia, with clear connections to the Aegaeo-Balkanic clay anchors, and also known from Corfu, Albania, and Malta; the single find of an Aegean-Anatolian slotted spearhead with haft tongue from Monte Venere near Taormina in Sicily (for this item, a date to Early Helladic III, i.e. after c.2200 BC, is also possible); a few copper sheet objects, with a shape varying between elongated rectangular and oval, with two rivets next to each other on one of the short sides, of a kind known from several Italian graves of this period (e.g. from the 'Cavità dei Sassi Neri', Grosseto; Laterza, grave 3, Taranto; Grotta Cappuccini, Lecce), and corresponding best with 'spatulae/scrapers' of Steno and several Cycladic graves, particularly Chalandriani; a neck-ring made of single round-sectioned gold wire from a Bell Beaker context from Bingia è Monti in Sardinia, the best contemporary parallels for which, made of precious metal, come from Eskiyapar, Troy, Poliochni, and perhaps also Steno, graves R4 and R15b (in silver); and finally, various silver finds, among them the two most important graves with silver grave goods, dating from the middle and second half of the third millennium, from Villafranca Veronese in the Veneto (a lunula, 28 cm high, reportedly with 99 per cent silver content) and San Biagio della Valle in Umbria (a riveted dagger of the Guardistallo type with 33.1 per cent silver); as these have not been analysed, it remains uncertain whether they are of cupellated, perhaps Aegean, silver or of local ores, from Sardinia for instance. The geographical distribution would tend to support the latter.

In many of the finds mentioned, the connection with the cemetery of Steno on the Ionian island of Levkas is significant (Kilian-Dirlmeier 2005). Looking at the Steno finds themselves, one is also struck by the typical long and narrow obsidian blades made using a highly specialized pressure-flaking technique, such as are also known from the Grotta Cappuccini, from Laterza itself, and other southern sites. However, further studies are needed to determine whether the technique and material were imported from the Aegean, or rather a local obsidian from Lipari was in use.

The third watershed in the connections between the Aegean and southern Italy may be placed only after c.2200 BC (Maran 2007). From this chronological horizon come the famous bossed bone plaques (*ossi a globuli*), such as those from the Casal Sabini (Bari) and the Grotta del Pipistrello Solitario (Taranto), as well as those found in considerable numbers on Sicily (Leighton 1999). To this period also belong graves and artefacts from the Castelluccio necropolis, eponymous for the Early Bronze Age Castelluccio culture in Sicily. Graves here contain, along with the bossed bone plaques, such outstanding items as what appear to be a scale-beam (grave 22), bronze tweezers (grave 23), and fragments of a bronze vessel, probably a cup (grave 31). There are interesting indications of other imported weapons, like a Sicilian riveted dagger from Palagonia, grave North 5, where the rivets are arranged in a trapeze shape, a feature that otherwise occurs only on Aegean examples. On the other hand, there are perhaps less explicit similarities as for some Castelluccio two-handled jugs, such as those from Santa Croce Camerina, compared with the *depas* cups in the Aegean (see Fig. 3.3d). The same is true for the Balkan connections of asymmetrical handles on other Castelluccio jugs, as well as cups with elbow-formed handles, butted handles, and/or handle-protomes, which came into vogue in a relatively narrow time frame of the Early Bronze Age along the Italian Adriatic coast and in northern Italy. However, their trans-Adriatic connections and the contemporaneity with Bulgarian Early Bronze Age 3 vessels are striking. Finally we must mention Malta, where eastern Mediterranean connections with the Tarxien Cremation Cemetery are evident (the description of the latter seems almost like that of a tumulus).

Overall it seems that the finds and sites listed above are only the proverbial tip of the iceberg of Aegean-Italian connections (Fig. 3.6). The wide spectrum of the finds is revealing, from traded goods to prestige goods to imitations. The significance of the Steno site on the Ionian island of Levkas is also noteworthy in its function as a cultural intermediary, for forms originating in the southern Greek mainland and on the Cyclades, then migrating into the Adriatic and over to

Apulia and Sicily. It also seems clear that these Ionian-Apulian-Sicilian and trans-Adriatic connections—and probably also the presence of peoples from the Aegean and Balkans—have a central significance in the origins of the Early Bronze Age on the Italian Peninsula. Italian scholars also consider that this chronology is not coincidental. The favoured conclusion today sees a progressive development from south to north and from east to west, with a culturally regionalized background and a definition that is still to be standardized: Castelluccio in Sicily is already being influenced by Early Bronze Age culture from the Aegean in the twenty-fifth century BC (Leighton 1999), Apulia, the Marches, and Caput Adriae (Cetina) in the twenty-fourth (Nicolis 2005), and northern Italy (Polada) in the twenty-third (De Marinis 1999); the western half of Italy is similarly included only in the twenty-second century BC.

Even if each region is different and demonstrates its own characteristics, these peripheral areas in the Balkans and in southern Italy are very important in the transmission of Early Bronze Age cultural features in Europe. However, hitherto they have seldom been considered as such.

Beyond the Peripheries: The Gradual Transmission of New Ideas, Values, and Achievements

There seems little transmission of valuable goods to regions beyond these peripheries between 2500 and 2200 BC. This coincides with an absence of hoards containing precious metals, of rich graves distinguished by their lavish provision of grave goods, of objects made of precious metals and other rare and exotic materials, and/or of superior ways of constructing the graves. The few exceptions of over-average individual Bell Beaker graves like those of the Amesbury Archer in Wiltshire, Fuente Olmedo in Castile, Markt in Bavaria, and perhaps Villafranca Veronese in the Veneto cannot alter this picture.

And yet, we observe distinct changes in the pattern of sites and artefacts, first in a wide arc stretching from the lower Danube via the Carpathian Basin as far as northern Italy. These range from innovations in material culture and changes in pottery to shifts in the organization of settlement sites and of regional settlements. Thus the group of objects gradually appears, at first as isolated findspots, that were later to characterize the inventory of the central European Early Bronze Age after 2300 BC (the Bz A0, A1, and A2 periods). These include new elements in weaponry like triangular riveted daggers and halberds. In ornaments and clothing, the composite necklaces, lunulae, and other neck ornaments become important, as do metal diadems, bracelets, and *Noppenringe* (knobbed rings). In burials of the twenty-third century BC the first dress pins made of copper or bone are noteworthy. In general more metal gradually appears in graves and settlements, with different kinds of copper increasingly present, both in terms of alloy and isotopic origin; in addition we find the first tin bronzes (Bertemes and Heyd 2002).

There are also significant changes in pottery. In parts of Romania, as in the entire Carpathian Basin and Italy, there is a general decrease in decoration on pottery. Vessels no longer act as messengers, or symbols indicating affiliation to an identity-group or differentiation from other groups. Instead specific functional aspects of vessels are put in the foreground. At the

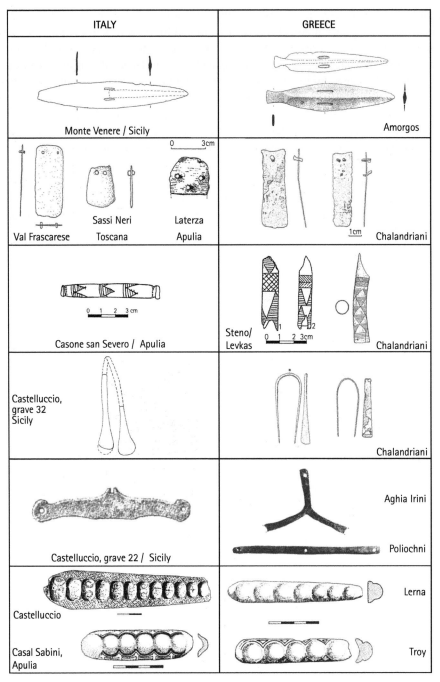

FIG. 3.6 Italy and Greece: later third millennium BC Italian finds of Aegean, or probable Aegean, origin, and comparisons in Greece and Troy.

Drawings: author, after various sources.

same time the repertoire of forms shifts towards a preference for cups and jugs, plates and bowls, that is to say, more personalized drinking vessels with handles and open shapes for eating. In addition they now appear widely in burial rituals. As such, their cups and plates even become a diagnostic criterion for an advanced phase of the central European branch of the Bell Beaker phenomenon, and are introduced into the west of Europe, where they are well-known as the *Begleitkeramik* (accompanying pottery) (see Nicolis 2001).

In looking at the underlying factors behind the abandonment of decoration and alteration to the range of forms, one first notices these changes in the new geographical peripheries described above. However, we would not be wrong to trace the primary cause for these developments back to the Aegean core. Here the initial impulses seem to be given by the appearance of the first wheel-made pottery of the completely undecorated Lefkandi I-Kastri repertoire, with its *depas* cups, tankards, and saucers (Maran 1998; Rahmstorf 2006). Not only does mass production of pottery begin, and pots become goods for trans-regional trade, but there is an increase in the prestige and value of these often high-quality drinking and eating vessels, as shown by the copies of these same vessel shapes made of gold and silver, for instance from the Troy hoards. In the final analysis a factor may be the institution of the 'symposium' originating in the Near East, with its associations of elite image cultivation, hospitality, and dependency relationships (Helwing 2003), which appears in the record as far away as central Europe, though in very attenuated form.

Shifts in the organization of settlements can be seen particularly in the Carpathian Basin. Here we note a gradual return to tell settlements (Gogâltan 2005). Just as settlements are now often preferred in protected locations, this development comes at the beginning of the rise of centralized places and thus probably also the rise of 'segmentary' systems of settlement. This is closely compatible with the changes in regional organization in the Carpathian Basin and its surroundings. While in the second quarter and the middle of the third millennium there were still trans-regional cultural phenomena like Vučedol and Makó/Kosihy-Čaka, we soon detect a more fragmented archaeological cultural pattern with almost a dozen regional cultural units, distinguished from each other in their burial rituals as well as pottery (Maran 1998; Bertemes and Heyd 2002). This process is obviously part of identity creation in smaller areas, possibly a sign of the genesis of tribes. Considered together with the changes in organization of settlements mentioned above, it could also be a sign of the birth of chiefdoms.

Moving further to the north and north-west, in central Europe at the western edge of the Carpathian Basin and also in parts of northern Italy, significant changes occur in the course of the twenty-third century BC (Bz A0), followed by the regions along the upper Danube, Elbe, Oder, and Rhine in the twenty-second century BC (Bz A1). Earlier Bell Beaker cemeteries are now abandoned everywhere, while new ones are established, and these were to be in part maintained for several centuries without interruption, as for instance at Franzhausen in Lower Austria. Alongside continuing regional fragmentation, we also find centralization in the form of the first fortifications on hills, particularly in more southerly areas. At the same time the characteristic longhouses come to predominate both as living places and as the focus of a new form of settlement planning (Bertemes and Heyd 2002).

Similar changes occur at the same time in southern Spain, for instance, where the El Argar culture likewise brings a more regionalized system of influence, with hill forts functioning as a focus. We also see changes on the British Isles, where in the twenty-second and twenty-first centuries BC there is increased circulation of copper, but also there are finds of significant numbers of the first tin bronzes. Following this, the accumulation of wealth and practice of hoarding begins; exotic materials for jewellery like amber, jet, faience, and shells are found in increasing quantities, and are now distributed over an ever-expanding area. This is a trend that stretches right across Europe, a gradual and continuous process involving the intensification of all the cultural subsystems.

The next stage is then reached from $c.2000$ BC when in wide parts of temperate Europe a system of intensified exchange and trade becomes established in Bz A2. Based now on a hierarchically organized society, with many prestige and status objects belonging to elites, and culminating in their lavishly equipped graves (such as Leubingen and Helmsdorf in Germany, Łęki Małe in Poland, Thun-Renzenbühl in Switzerland, Kernonen en Plouvorn and Saint Adrien in Brittany, and Bush and Clandon barrows in Wessex) and the big metal hoards, we also see precious metal vessels, economic specialization, specialized craft production, and widely available tin bronze. No doubt, these are components of a cultural process of the kind that had arrived around the Aegean some five hundred years earlier.

Meeting the Bell Beaker Network

The Bell Beaker phenomenon also pertains, over most of its distribution area, to the period between $c.2500$ and 2100 BC (see Nicolis 2001; Czebreszuk 2003), but by 2000 BC even the very latest beakers, only rudimentarily displaying their original form and decoration, have ceased to be made. As for the beginnings of this development, it is only on the Iberian Peninsula that we have secure radiocarbon evidence for an earlier Bell Beaker formation. This reaches perhaps back as early as $c.2700$ BC, thus bringing it into the chronological range of a Europe-wide transformational horizon that so altered societies in both east and west (Harrison and Heyd 2007).

There is still much speculation in our efforts to understand the origins of the iconic pottery form that the Bell Beaker represents, and of the groups of people producing and using them as their communal symbol in the European west. Safer ground is reached, however, in the evidence that this early Iberian Bell Beaker tradition is apparently confined to parts of the peninsula for over a century. At this early stage, the Bell Beaker phenomenon is not yet fully developed, lacking for example two of its most prominent components, the tanged copper daggers and the wristguards. It was perhaps shortly after 2600 BC when the ideas, expression, values, and ideology behind the Bell Beaker seemingly altered, and an expansionistic drive—almost missionary in its appearance—became the dominant element. This is the moment when the first Bell Beaker vessels, and the people regarding them as their common symbol, were bypassing the Pyrenees along the Atlantic and Mediterranean coastline, reaching for example the mouth of the Rhône in southern France or Brittany in the north-west, perhaps during the later twenty-sixth century BC. From now on, the phenomenon accelerates dramatically, with more people being involved, and seizing the opportunity to promote themselves by adopting the now well-defined assemblage of objects, and with the community of Beaker users growing. At the same time, around 2500 BC, the use of the Bell Beaker expands geographically to encompass more distant regions. By integrating an increasing number of local populations, with their various traditions, the phenomenon was itself being transformed, from being the driver of change to being part of more established regional cultures with their own distinct flavour. This, in turn, shaped the course of developments over the succeeding centuries.

The Bell Beaker phenomenon thus became pan-European in nature (e.g. Nicolis 2001; Czebreszuk 2003), with its centre of gravity located firmly in the western half of the continent. If we take an overview of its distribution, four larger geographical entities can be discerned: an Atlantic domain, a Mediterranean domain, the central European or East Group, and a Beaker tradition in the western part of the north European plain, also including southern Scandinavia. This distribution is the result of an expansion that clearly follows the Mediterranean, Atlantic, and North Sea coasts, and the main river systems such as the Rhône, Rhine, Danube, and Elbe, and their tributaries. However, distinct regional traditions incorporated by the respective new Beaker users are also responsible, and a geographically staggered west-east impulse, resulting in weaker and stronger centres, and secondary and tertiary regions of Beaker expansion. This is particularly evident in Italy where the cultural geography of the underlying cultures is decisive for the Beaker distribution from 2500 BC on (Nicolis 2001). So Remedello societies of the north and Rinaldone in the west were more receptive to Beaker novelties than Conelle and Laterza in the Adriatic Basin, resulting in an uneven distribution of Beaker pots. The same is visible as far south as Sicily, where Bell Beaker users only set foot and established a Beaker core in the Conca d'Oro area, in the west of the island (Leighton 1999). Therefore burial and settlement customs, material culture such as domestic pottery, and economic resources and subsistence economies vary greatly across Europe and in the regions, while the overarching iconic Beaker vessel and the Beaker package act like a glue for the diversity, creating the image of 'similar but different' (Czebreszuk 2003).

Beside these four domains, and their regional networks and distinct cultures, a kind of eastern Bell Beaker periphery has recently come to prominence (Heyd 2007). This is manifested in the form of syncretistic cultures, '... adopting different components of the Bell Beaker ideology and the package in its repertoire ... transforming it together with parts of their own traditional inventory to build a new identity' (Heyd 2007: 102), and located in a zone following a virtual line from central Poland in the north to the heel of the Italian Peninsula in the south (roughly between 15 and 20 degrees of longitude). These syncretistic Beaker/local cultures start about one to two hundred years after the more western regional Beaker cores but are, seen from a different angle, the dominant regional players in the slightly later formation of the Early Bronze Age. Representatives from north to south are the archaeological cultures of Iwno (and partly Trzciniec) in the western Baltic region; Chłopice-Veselé in Little Poland, western Slovakia, and eastern Moravia; Pitvaros/Maros in the south-eastern Carpathian Basin; as well early Cetina in the Adriatic Basin; and the Grotta Cappuccini aspect of the Laterza-Cellino San Marco culture in south-east Italy. It is important to note that the last two concern regions that are among the Early Bronze Age Aegean peripheries described above.

Beyond these ideological peripheries there is even a marginal eastern zone of more remote Bell Beaker traces (Czebreszuk and Szmyt 2003; Heyd 2007). These Bell Beaker margins include parts of eastern Poland, Moldova, and Romania, as well as Malta in the south. Major diagnostic elements are the wristguards, or their imitations in bone and clay. If one includes some early flint dagger types, and there is good reason to think that the dagger idea is propagated in the context of the Beaker phenomenon in the north, these influences even reached the Baltic States, Finland, and Belarus. Surprisingly perhaps, one can argue that these Beaker margins also reached as far as the Early Bronze Age core, Greece, Crete, and the Aegean. This European south-east has only recently come into the focus of Beaker research (Heyd 2007;

Maran 2007). Beside conspicuous pottery evidence mostly from Olympia, it is again the wristguards, and the 'Montgomery toggles' (as on duffle coats), that form the majority of the diagnostic Beaker elements. As a result of this recent interest, more wristguards, both the broader four-holed and the oblong-narrow two-holed, are now known from the Aegean than from the whole of Italy, for example. They almost all date to Early Helladic III levels (as does the pottery evidence from Olympia), thus after 2200 BC in absolute terms. This makes them late Beaker, as compared to the central and western European examples. The best explanation for their relatively late appearance lies with a migratory event, rightly described by Maran (e.g. 1998) as bringing Adriatic Cetina people incrementally to southern Greece for some decades from the transition of Early Helladic II to III. And since early Cetina is one of those syncretistic Bell Beaker cultures of its south-eastern periphery as shown above, this best explains the manifestation of these Bell Beaker elements deep in south-east Europe.

Bell Beaker ideological peripheries and initial Bronze Age cultural, social, and economic peripheries therefore meet from the twenty-fifth century BC in the central Mediterranean, on both sides of the Adriatic Basin including much of the western Balkans as well as southern Italy and Sicily. Here, people from the two directions, and the very different value systems and world views, may have greeted each other. There are even Beaker elements that reached the Early Bronze Age core in the Aegean, if only from 2200 BC. But more decisive for the further course of development are the new cultural, social, and economic ideas and values, ultimately originating in the Aegean, and their materialization and reception, that reached beyond this contact zone, deep into continental Europe—by then regions with Beaker occupation, soon to become the new Early Bronze Age focal points.

Conflicting World Views Between 2500 and 2200 BC

As briefly described in the introduction, the Bell Beaker phenomenon represents the climax of these ideologically driven cultural phenomena, having dominated the course of events on the European continent for almost one and a half millennia. With the Bell Beaker, the western half of the continent is incorporated in these expansionistic phenomena for the first time. The whole became a truly European phenomenon, by virtue of the distribution of influences to the eastern peripheries and adjacent margins, representing more distant parts of the Bell Beaker idea. However, Bell Beakers are not only the climax but also represent the end point of this era, in which what occupies centre stage is more an idea, a message and a particular world view. This fits the aggressive and expansive, almost missionary, outlook well. One also gets the impression that there was an attempt to convert, not always peacefully, as many people as possible for to this newly emerging community. The emblematically decorated Bell Beaker, the symbol, and before that to some extent the Corded Ware beaker, are the ideal communal drinking vessel for such a community: on average enough content so that several persons can consume a special drink from it; a form that forces one to use both hands for drinking; and then to hand it over, again with both hands, in an almost ritual manner, to one's neighbour. However, it was not so much the Bell Beaker itself but two other elements associated with this phenomenon that reached the peripheries and margins more often, and must therefore have been more interesting as innovations for newcomers of any cultural background. These are the dagger, no matter if made of metal or, in southern Scandinavia and along the Baltic Sea, of flint (Sarauw 2008); and archery, materialized in the arrowheads and wristguards (Fokkens, Achterkamp, and Kuijpers 2008). Both were obviously very attractive for distant peoples, who did not hesitate to add these weapons to their own repertoire even if, faraway as they were, these new adherents may not have completely understood the message behind them. But within the wider framework of individualization and internationalization, such daggers were prestigious enough to become highly regarded all over Europe; likewise, the societal acceptance of archery, with the wristguard as its symbol of adherence, brought advantages in hunting and warfare.

The Early Bronze Age, expanding from the south-east at the same time, is fundamentally different. It is a gradual process; more a cultural reorientation than a different ideology. It also has a clear trajectory, ultimately originating in the Aegean, the eastern Mediterranean, and beyond, and then crossing the continent from the south-east to the north-west. For the peoples of the Early Bronze Age, economic and social considerations were at the top of their agenda: production of goods, the exchange of surplus, and the first real trade, as well as the systematic accumulation of possession and wealth; this includes in particular an enhanced role for metals, their exploitation as ores, alloying, manufacturing as finished products, marketing, and hoarding. As such, the Early Bronze Age also stands for a Europe of new values and new symbols of wealth and power; a kind of capitalist world in embryo, so to speak, for the peoples of the time. These begin to witness new categories of weapons, prestigious objects of personal adornment, new dress codes, golden/silver drinking cups, exotica, and so on, in sum a package of ultimately south-eastern innovations. All this makes the Early Bronze Age a Europe of emerging complexity and host to the rise of local elites. Because for most of continental Europe they had previously been Beaker users, in the same way the privileged people of the Beaker period became the new elites of the Early Bronze Age. But geographical positioning and timelines are crucial to this development. For much of Europe the centre of gravity around 2500/2400 BC still lay on the Bell Beaker side, whereas around 2300/2200 BC it shifted towards the new Early Bronze Age agenda. And soon, after 2000 BC, these elites were fully established and so became archaeologically visible in their princely graves, hoarding practices, abundance of weapons and jewellery, and monumental burial places (tumuli), settlements (hill forts), and longhouses. This conflict between two world views therefore also refers to the question of identities, multiple identities, and changing identities over time. Particularly apparent is the development in the central Mediterranean region, and particularly in the Adriatic Basin, where both 'worlds' meet in an early stage of their respective expansions, in the course of the twenty-fifth and twenty-fourth centuries BC, making this area a crossroad for streams of exchange, trade, and peoples.

BIBLIOGRAPHY

Avramova, M. and Todorieva, B. (2005). 'A Bronze Age metalwork hoard from southeastern Bulgaria', in *L'Âge du Bronze en Europe et en Méditerranée. Sessions générales et posters. Éd. Le Secrétariat du Congrès. Actes du XIVème Congrès UISPP, Université de Liège, Belgique, 2–8 septembre 2001*, British Archaeological Reports (International Series), 1,337. Oxford: Archaeopress, 69–73.

Bacci, G. M. (1997). 'Due idoletti di tipo egeo-cicladico da Camaro Sant'Anna presso Messina', in S. Tusa (ed.), *Prima Sicilia alle origini della società siciliana*. Palermo: Ediprint, 295–7.

Barker, G. (2005). 'Agriculture, pastoralism, and Mediterranean landscapes in prehistory', in E. Blake and A. B. Knapp (eds.), *The Archaeology of Mediterranean Prehistory*, Blackwell Studies in Global Archaeology. Malden, Oxford, and Carlton: Blackwell, 46–76.

Bertemes, F. and Heyd, V. (2002). 'Der Übergang Kupferzeit/Frühbronzezeit am Nordwestrand des Karpatenbeckens—kulturgeschichtliche und paläometallurgische Betrachtungen', in M. Bartelheim, R. Krause, and E. Pernicka (eds.), *Die Anfänge der Metallurgie in der Alten Welt. Euroseminar Freiberg/Sachsen, 18.-20. November 1999*. Freiberger Forschung zur Archäometrie und Kulturgeschichte, 1. Rahden/Westf.: Marie Leidorf, 185–228.

Cazzella, A. (2003). 'Conelle di Arcevia nel panorama culturale della preistoria del Mediterraneo centro-orientale e della penisola balcanica tra quarto e terzo millennio', in A. Cazzella, M. Moscoloni, and G. Recchia (eds.), *Conelle di Arcevia, tomo II*. Roma: Università La Sapienza e Rubbettino, 541–68.

Czebreszuk, J. (ed.) (2003). *Similar but Different: Bell Beakers in Europe*. Poznań: Adam Mickiewicz University.

—— and Szmyt, M. (eds.) (2003). *The Northeast Frontier of Bell Beakers: Proceedings of the Symposium Held at the Adam Mickiewicz University, Poznań (Poland), May 26-29 2002*. British Archaeological Reports (International Series), 1,155. Oxford: Archaeopress.

Della Casa, P. (1995). 'The Cetina Group and the transition from Copper to Bronze Age in Dalmatia', *Antiquity*, 69/264: 565–76.

De Marinis, R. C. (1999). 'Towards a relative and absolute chronology of the Bronze Age in northern Italy', *Notizie Archeologiche Bergomensi*, 7: 1–78.

Fokkens, H., Achterkamp, Y., and Kuijpers, M. (2008). 'Bracers or bracelets? About the functionality and meaning of Bell Beaker wrist-guards', *Proceedings of the Prehistoric Society*, 74: 109–40.

Gogâltan, F. (2005). 'Der Beginn der bronzezeitlichen Tellsiedlungen im Karpatenbecken: chronologische Probleme', in B. Horejs, R. Jung, E. Kaiser, and B. Teržan (eds.), *Interpretationsraum Bronzezeit. Bernhard Hänsel von seinen Schülern gewidmet*. Universitätsforschungen zur Prähistorischen Archäologie, 121. Bonn: Habelt, 161–79.

Harrison, R. J. and Heyd, V. (2007). 'The transformation of Europe in the third millennium BC: the example of "Le Petit Chasseur I + III" (Sion, Valais, Switzerland)', *Praehistorische Zeitschrift*, 82/2: 129–214.

Helwing, B. (2003). 'Feasts as a social dynamic in prehistoric western Asia—three case studies from Syria and Anatolia', *Paléorient*, 29/2: 63–85.

Heyd, V. (2007). 'When the West meets the East: the eastern periphery of the Bell Beaker phenomenon and its relation with the Aegean Early Bronze Age', in I. Galanaki, Y. Galanakis, H. Tomas, and R. Laffineur (eds.), *Between the Aegean and Baltic Seas: Prehistory across Borders. Proceedings of the International Conference 'Bronze and Early Iron Age Interconnections and Contemporary Developments between the Aegean and the Regions of the Balkan Peninsula, Central and Northern Europe', University of Zagreb, 10-14 April 2005*, Aegaeum, 27. Liège: Université de Liège, 91–107.

——, Aydıngün, Ş., and Güldoğan, E. (2010). 'Geophysical applications for ITA 2008: the example of the Selimpaşa Höyük', 25, *Arkeometri Sonuçları Toplantısı, XXXI, Uluslararası Kazı, Arastırma ve Arkeometri Sempozyumu, Denizli, 25-29 Mayis 2009*. Ankara: T. C. Kültür ve Turizm Bakanlığı, 553–69.

Kilian-Dirlmeier, I. (2005). *Die bronzezeitlichen Gräber bei Nidri auf Leukas: Ausgrabungen von W. Dörpfeld 1903-13*, Römisch-Germanisches Zentralmuseum Monographien, 62. Bonn: Habelt.

Leighton, R. (1999). *Sicily before History: An Archaeological Survey from the Palaeolithic to the Iron Age*. London: Duckworth.

Leshtakov, K. (2006). 'Bronzovata epocha v gornotrakiiskata nisina', *Godishnik na Sofiiskija Universitet 'Sv. Kliment Ochridski' istorijeski fakultet spezialnost arheologija*, 3: 141–212.

Maran, J. (1998). *Kulturwandel auf dem griechischen Festland und den Kykladen im späten 3. Jahrtausend v. Chr. Studien zu den kulturellen Verhältnissen in Südosteuropa und dem zentralen sowie östlichen Mittelmeerraum in der späten Kupfer- und frühen Bronzezeit*, Universitätsforschungen zur Prähistorischen Archäologie, 53. Bonn: Habelt.

—— (2007). 'Seaborne contacts between the Aegean, the Balkans and the Central Mediterranean in the 3rd millennium BC—the unfolding of the Mediterranean world', in I. Galanaki, Y. Galanakis, H. Tomas, and R. Laffineur (eds.), *Between the Aegean and Baltic Seas: Prehistory across Borders. Proceedings of the International Conference 'Bronze and Early Iron Age Interconnections and Contemporary Developments between the Aegean and the Regions of the Balkan Peninsula, Central and Northern Europe', University of Zagreb, 10–14 April 2005*, Aegaeum, 27. Liège: Université de Liège, 3–21.

Matthews, R. (2003). *The Archaeology of Mesopotamia: Theories and Approaches.* London: Routledge.

Nicolis, F. (ed.) (2001). *Bell Beakers Today: Pottery, People, Culture and Symbols in Prehistoric Europe*, International Colloquium Riva del Garda (Trento, Italy), 11–16 May 1998. Trento: Ufficio Beni Culturali.

—— (2005). 'Long-distance cultural links between northern Italy, the Ionian islands and the Peloponnese in the last centuries of the 3rd millennium BC', in R. Laffineur and E. Greco (eds.), *Emporia—Aegeans in Central and Eastern Mediterranean: Proceedings of the 10th International Aegean Conference at the Italian School of Archaeology, Athens, 14–18 April 2004*, Aegaeum, 25. Liège and Austin: Université de Liège and University of Texas, 527–39.

Özdoğan, M. (2002). 'The Bronze Age in Thrace in relation to the emergence of complex societies in Anatolia and in the Aegean', in Ü. Yalcin (ed.), *Anatolian Metal II*. Bochum: Bergbau-Museum, 67–76.

Primas, M. (2007). 'Innovationstransfer vor 5000 Jahren. Knotenpunkte an Land- und Wasserwegen zwischen Vorderasien und Europa', *Eurasia Antiqua*, 13: 1–19.

Rahmstorf, L. (2006). 'Zur Ausbreitung vorderasiatischer Innovationen in die frühbronzezeitliche Ägäis', *Praehistorische Zeitschrift*, 81/1: 49–96.

—— (2010). 'Die Nutzung von Booten und Schiffen in der bronzezeitlichen Ägäis und die Fernkontakte der Frühbronzezeit', in H. Meller and F. Bertemes (eds.), *Der Griff nach den Sternen. Wie Europas Eliten zu Macht und Reichtum kamen (Reaching for the Stars. How European Elites Attained Power and Wealth), Internationales Symposiums in Halle (Saale), 16.–21. Februar 2005*, Tagungen des Landesmuseums für Vorgeschichte Halle, 5. Halle: Landesmuseums für Vorgeschichte, 675–97.

Renfrew, C. (1972). *The Emergence of Civilisation: The Cyclades and the Aegean in the Third Millennium BC.* London: Methuen.

Sarauw, T. (2008). 'Danish Bell Beaker pottery and flint daggers—the display of social identities?', *European Journal of Archaeology*, 11/1: 23–47.

Stefanova, M. (2004). 'Kontextuelle Probleme der Becher *depas amphikepellon* in Thrakien', in V. Nikolov and K. Bačvarov (eds.), *Von Domica bis Drama. Gedenkschrift für Jan Lichardus*. Sofia: Archäologisches Institut mit Museum der Bulgarischen Akademie der Wissenschaften, 197–201.

CHAPTER 4

A LITTLE BIT OF HISTORY REPEATING ITSELF: THEORIES ON THE BELL BEAKER PHENOMENON

MARC VANDER LINDEN

A Sense of *Déjà Vu*

From its definition in the archaeological literature of the late nineteenth century to a refreshing revival of interest over the last two decades, the Bell Beaker phenomenon (Fig. 4.1) (hereafter Beaker phenomenon) has been subject to various competing interpretations. Yet, as argued here, unquestionable advances thanks to ever-improving analytical and field work have not been matched by a parallel improvement in our understanding of this important period from later European prehistory, lying at the interface between the Neolithic and the Bronze Age. Indeed, older and recent theories of the Beaker phenomenon share several common themes (e.g. they stress social hierarchy and extended human mobility). When read in succession, key publications can thus leave a worrying, bitter taste of déjà vu. This brief review aims at exploring the nature of these ever-repeating themes and their status in the successive stages of research.

This sense of theoretical, interpretative similarity is even more surprising considering that, from the material point of view, the Beaker phenomenon is first and foremost defined through its variation, evidenced by all facets of the archaeological record (for a recent European-scale review, see Vander Linden 2006). Pioneering scholars noted striking similarities in the assemblages from western to central Europe, especially the eponymous S-shaped bell beaker, but also other artefacts (e.g. stone bracers, triangular copper daggers, etcetera) and practices (renewed favour for individual burial, quasi-systematic deposition of a bell beaker in the graves). While this level of uniformity caught—and still catches—the archaeological imagination, there has been at the same time a growing realization that there is no unique pan-European Bell Beaker material culture. Bell Beaker assemblages rather

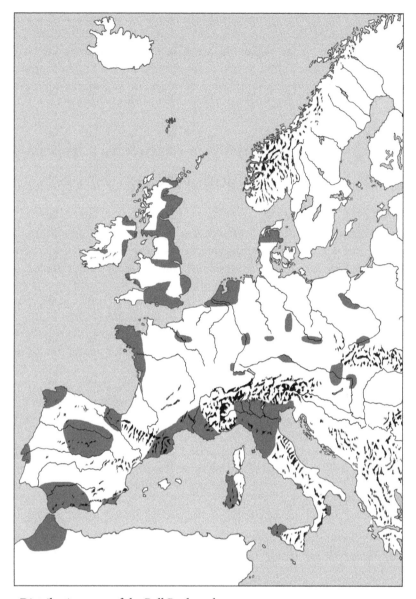

FIG. 4.1 Distribution map of the Bell Beaker phenomenon.

Source: Vander Linden 2006.

exhibit a wide variability from one region to the next, which even led some scholars to question the validity of any global appraisal of the Beaker phenomenon (e.g. Barrett 1994). As a net result, it is fair to state that, all things being equal, limited energy has been spent on a factual description of variations in the Bell Beaker assemblages. The various theories under review here played a key role in this relative disengagement from variation, as they provided interpretative discourses explicitly applied to the entire scale of the Beaker phenomenon, thus enabling either complete avoidance or a sidestepping of descriptive, local issues.

The following presentation is organized according to a traditional, if slightly arbitrary, division of the history of the discipline into successive paradigms (culture-historical, processual, and so on). Each section follows the same layout by investigating a few key themes (chronological questions, mobility of peoples, social hierarchy, causes). This approach allows one to identify the idiosyncrasies of each stage of research, as well as the wide-ranging similarities and recurring problems that criss-cross the entire historiography.

From Beakers to Folk: Culture-History (c.1900–1970s)

As suggested above, this initial phase of the research is instrumental as it saw the definition of the Bell Beaker phenomenon and the constitution of several key research themes. This first section aims at understanding these themes in the context of their emergence.

Lacking any independent way of measuring time in prehistory, culture-historical scholars had to rely upon typology in order to make sense of the material culture at their disposition. The building of any chronological system was thus intricately linked to unravelling typological and geographical patterning in the data. In the Bell Beaker case, the most fundamental research question was to characterize the prototype of the artefacts found throughout Europe, with a particular if not exclusive focus on the bell beaker per se, and to locate where it was first produced. Several candidate regions have been put forward over the years and cover nearly the entire geographical range of the Beaker phenomenon (Iberian Peninsula: Del Castillo Yurrita 1928, Bosch-Gimpera 1940, Sangmeister 1966, Müller and Van Willingen 2001; south-eastern France: Clarke 1970; Sicily: Guilaine 2004; central Europe: Childe 1925; Low Countries: Harrison 1980). Such a 'homeland' would not only have provided the source of the Beaker material culture, but would also have corresponded to the cradle of the Beaker civilization, out of which the so-called 'Beaker Folk' would have sprung to reach eventually the remotest parts of Europe.

The identification of the pan-European distribution of the Beaker phenomenon with a past human group is probably the best-known, most criticized, and most influential contribution of culture-historical scholars to the study of the phenomenon. For instance, as early as 1902, Abercromby pointed out for Britain 'the advent of a new stock, distinguished from the older neolithic inhabitants by taller stature and a moderately brachycephalous head' (Abercromby 1902: 374). The craniological distinctive character of the Beaker people, an argument directly echoing nineteenth-century racial typology, was hardly questioned during this earlier stage of research (see for instance Bryce's comments in Abercromby's own paper: Abercromby 1902: 396) and has since been discussed by several generations of bioanthropologists (e.g. Menk 1979). Nowadays, it appears that other factors are possibly at play in changes in cranial morphology, including a new incoming population (Brodie 1994). Skeletal evidence was, however, not the unique resource deployed by culture-historians in their reconstruction of the migrations of the Beaker folk. In this perspective, the definition of a given homeland was as much, if not more, crucial because it allowed the various movements of the Beaker folk to be traced on the map of prehistory.

One of the difficulties with migrationist scenarios was how to account for the regional variation between the different archaeological assemblages. Some creolization process was generally assumed, with the introduction and progressive dissolution of the new common Beaker elements within the material culture of local groups. Such a view is rooted in pottery typological schemes, which traditionally opposed a supposedly early homogeneous horizon, represented by beakers of the so-called maritime type, with regional later styles (e.g Bosch-Gimpera 1940). The—still scarce—use of radiocarbon dates across the entire Bell Beaker phenomenon has since demonstrated that this binary opposition is only partly valid in few exceptional cases (e.g. south-eastern France: Lemercier 2004): most often maritime beakers are present during the entire sequence (Salanova 2000), or regional styles appear from the earliest stage onwards (e.g. Britain: Kinnes et al. 1991).

The most ambitious and complex attempt to reconcile migrations and material variation is undoubtedly Sangmeister's *Rückstrom* ('reflux', flowing back) theory. This German scholar argued for a two-phase migration of the Beaker folk, with an initial dispersion from the Iberian Peninsula to the rest of Europe, followed by a reflux from central Europe, after extensive mixing with the local Corded Ware culture (Sangmeister 1966; for a strictly typological counter-argument, see Clarke 1970). Not all culture-historical accounts of the Beaker phenomenon by any means took the form of massive human movements. For instance, Gordon Childe considered that the extensive distribution and success of the Beaker phenomenon was due to wandering smiths seeking new copper sources (Childe 1925). This drive for rich copper areas was also at the core of the work of Del Castillo Yurrita, who published one of the earliest authoritative syntheses on the Beaker phenomenon (Del Castillo Yurrita 1928). Since only a restricted number of individuals, rather than entire communities, are the vector of the diffusion, their model provided an easier explanation for the variability of the Beaker phenomenon.

These last two models are also important for they suggest a direct causation between the inception of Beaker traits and the introduction of the earliest metallurgy in several parts of western Europe (see below). In presenting these models, Childe, Castillo Yurrita, and others initiated a still-continuing debate regarding the social structure of the Beaker groups. For them, the advent of metallurgy would have indeed triggered several social and economic changes, for instance long-distance trade (e.g. ores and metal objects: Sangmeister 1960), or possible relationships of patronage between chiefs and smiths (Childe 1925). These would have been accompanied by the development of new, more pyramidal social hierarchies, and reached their full potential during later mature stages of the Bronze Age (Childe 1930). If these discussions on social structure may not be as elaborated as some later ones (see below), there is however no doubt that the Beaker phenomenon was perceived from the first half of the twentieth century onwards as a step forward in the ever-growing social complexity of later European prehistoric communities.

For culture-historians, as for many archaeologists after them, the most distinctive element of the new Beaker social order was without doubt the renewed preference for individual burial. Although this practice is hardly an innovation of the period, it does however offer a striking contrast with the collective burial customs commonly observed for the fourth and early third millennia BC throughout western Europe. This shift from collective to individual burial seems even more impressive in Britain, where hundreds, if not thousands, of round barrows were erected and dotted the landscape during the late third and early second millennia BC (see Childe 1930: 153–4; 161–2). What is noticeable is the underlying suggestion that the individual gets more pre-eminence in the funerary record as a result of its new-favoured central status and role in the society.

All in all, culture-history paves the way for most future research, as it determines not only key research themes but also causal links between them. From the necessity to create a typo-chronological framework for the Beaker phenomenon derives the central importance of defining a 'homeland', itself intimately linked to beliefs about the existence of a migrating Beaker folk. Following Childe and others, the rationale for these large, far-reaching human movements has to be sought in the search for extensive new copper resources. This drive for copper goes hand in hand with the assumption that metallurgy provides an unmatched source of wealth, hence leading to the development of new levels of social complexity.

FROM FOLK TO ELITES: PROCESSUAL APPROACHES (1970S–EARLY 1990S)

Parallel to the general evolution of the discipline, the 1970s are marked by the development of new interpretations of the Beaker phenomenon which openly professed a radical departure from the previous culture-historical theories. Nevertheless, processual scholars still extensively relied upon the themes outlined during the culture-historical period.

Discussions of the typology and chronology of the Beaker phenomenon benefited from the incorporation of absolute radiocarbon dates (e.g. Guilaine 1974). Without doubt, the most significant addition to this debate during the 1970s was the so-called 'Dutch Model' (Lanting and van der Waals 1972, 1976a). In this groundbreaking work, which at first was elaborated as a reaction to Clarke's early hypothesis of multiple invasions of Britain by several continental Beaker groups (Clarke 1970; Lanting and van der Waals 1972), Lanting and van der Waals demonstrated the validity of the typological scheme established two decades earlier by van der Waals and Glasbergen (1955) and definitively demonstrated the existence of a continuous development from the Protruding Foot beakers (nowadays referred to as the Single Grave culture) to the local Bell Beaker group in the Netherlands (a scheme still accepted by Dutch scholars: Drenth and Hogestijn 2001; Fokkens 2005). The advent of a radiocarbon-based chronology thus implied a relative minimization of the role of typology which, albeit remaining a necessary task, became somewhat secondary in the elucidation of the Beaker phenomenon. In turn, the notion of a homeland, a natural correlate to typological studies, also partly fell out of fashion. For instance, Lanting and van der Waals never themselves claimed that the Low Countries were the Bell Beaker homeland, although this step was made on their behalf by others (e.g. Harrison 1980). Typological studies, however, retained a certain global ambition and there was a general assumption that the Dutch typological scheme could be applied throughout the entire Beaker phenomenon (see contributions in Guilaine 1984), as Lanting and van der Waals actually did themselves for Britain and Ireland (Lanting and van der Waals 1972).

At the same time, detailed investigations on the geographical patterning of the Beaker phenomenon in central Europe led Stephen Shennan to discard completely the notion of a single, coherent Bell Beaker archaeological assemblage (Burgess and Shennan 1976; Shennan 1976; 1978). On the contrary, he showed that only a restricted number of artefacts were consistently found in graves, which he labelled the 'Beaker package'. This package comprises the eponymous beaker, barbed and tanged arrowheads, stone wristguards, and, in some cases, copper triangular daggers. Since these artefacts are the sole common link between all regional subgroups, and since they are confined to funerary contexts, Shennan insisted that the Beaker phenomenon did not meet the requirements of an archaeological culture as defined by Childe, and suggested as an alternative that the Beaker phenomenon was to be understood as a set of highly valued objects, circulating amongst emerging elites as a sign of their new power (Shennan 1976). In this schema, the homogeneity of the Beaker phenomenon lies at the uppermost level of society, while the rest of the archaeological assemblage is the mere material expression of each local community. In a way, Shennan's appraisal of the Beaker variation thus reproduces the views of Childe and Del Castillo, as the uniformity of the Beaker phenomenon is confined to the actions of a few individuals rather than entire groups. The main difference between both interpretations lies in the *modus operandi* of these few individuals: migrating copper-seeking smiths on one side, local chiefs exchanging items of power on the other side. David Clarke went further by distinguishing widely distributed—possibly traded—beaker types, such as the maritime type, and locally produced and distributed pots (Clarke 1976). Petrographic analyses done in the 1980s and 1990s have since demonstrated that the vast majority of Beaker pottery in all regions was made using local raw materials (e.g. Rehman, Robinson, and Shennan 1992; Convertini and Querré 1998). Despite this limitation, several variations on the social theme have since been published (reviewed in Brodie 1994).

These various models all agree that the Beaker phenomenon is not a population-based process—there were no migrating Beaker folk—but rather the material translation of a new social order. The Beaker phenomenon would correspond to the introduction of so-called 'prestige goods' and, more fundamentally, to the related social context of use of these items valued by their group. These standard artefacts, deposited in specific funerary contexts, would allow the new elites to distinguish themselves as well as to relate to each other. This goal would be achieved through the common elaboration upon, and reference to, given social categories, for instance a warrior class as evidenced by the emphasis on weapons. This last element also suggests a growing differentiation of gender roles and identities, a theme further developed since (e.g. Shennan 1993; Vandkilde 2001; see below).

Culture-historians did not discuss the new social structures associated with the Beaker phenomenon extensively, but did not doubt the driving role of copper metallurgy in this civilizational change. In a somewhat paradoxical way, processualists spent much energy identifying the Beaker phenomenon with more hierarchical social regimes, but at the same time remained elusive when characterizing the underlying factors responsible for the emergence of these new modes of social power. Shennan seemed to imply that the access to metal probably played a role, although he acknowledged that metal resources only became crucial during later stages of the Bronze Age, when higher quantities of metal were indeed circulating (Shennan 1993). The question of 'why new social systems?' being unanswered, one is left with a bitter taste of implicit evolutionary thought, according to which Beaker communities had to follow an unstoppable movement by reaching a higher level of social evolution.

The 1970s, 1980s, and early 1990s marked a highly influential turn in Beaker studies. The application of radiocarbon dating coupled with less naive analysis of spatial patterns enabled scholars to rely less heavily just on typology and, in turn, led to the rejection of the explanatory value of both 'homeland' and 'migration', at least in the English-language literature.

Continental traditions, especially in central Europe, indeed remained overall more conservative and never entirely dismissed these two concepts (e.g. contributions in Lanting and van der Waals 1976b, Guilaine 1984). For, crucial as this abandonment of the Beaker folk was, it did not lead to any in-depth reassessment of the historical value of the Beaker phenomenon. On the contrary, there was a mere qualitative shift towards its interpretation in social terms, a theme already outlined by culture-historians. While the processual account undeniably exhibits unmatched levels of sophistication, it also corresponds to a certain regression as the causes of this emerging social system were left in the shadows. In this sense, the new 'prestige goods' social order became self-explanatory, being at the same time the cause and the result of the Beaker phenomenon's success in Europe.

From Elites to Phenomenon: The Analytical Age (late 1990s–present)

Throughout the 1980s and early 1990s, variants on the prestige goods model gained wider acceptance. Although this model was originally devised only to account for parts of central Europe, its acceptance generally accompanied the uncritical application of the model to other regions, without any in-depth consideration of local idiosyncrasies. The prestige goods model eventually reached a dominant position as a global explanatory model for the Beaker phenomenon. As a reaction, several researchers from around Europe criticized some of the theoretical tenets of the prestige goods model (especially Brodie 1994; 1997) and took on board the re-description of Beaker material culture at both regional and supra-regional levels (e.g. Benz and van Willingen 1998; Nicolis 2001; Czebreszuk 2004).

Alongside the re-investigation of local chronologies, one can also observe a certain revival of interest in the notion of 'homeland'. The old suggestion of an Iberian origin found new supporters who pointed out the existence of several radiocarbon dates firmly anchored in the first half of the third millennium cal BC (e.g. Kunst 2001; Müller and van Willingen 2001). Three comments must be made, however. First, other regions, such as southern France or the Low Countries, have yielded similarly early dates. Second, chronological precision is limited by the unfavourable shape of the radiocarbon calibration curve in this period (Vander Linden 2006: Chapter 2 and annex I). Third, Iberia lacks an unquestionable ceramic prototype for the beaker type, a major typological weakness especially when compared to the situation in the Low Countries. Alternative homelands have also been proposed (e.g. Sicily: Guilaine 2004). Rather than pursuing this endless quest across Europe for a mythical perfect typological ancestry, there is probably more to gain by considering that no single region contributed all elements of the Bell Beaker material culture.

Similar conclusions have been reached through geographically wide-ranging re-examination of the Bell Beaker material variation. Laure Salanova's work on the *chaîne opératoire* of beaker pottery production showed that beakers not only correspond to a given type, but are also in several examples the outcomes of consistently meaningful technological choices made by the potters (Salanova 2000). On related ground, Marie Besse's typological analysis of the Bell Beaker domestic ceramics has established, within the Bell Beaker domain, the existence of large typologically coherent regional groups (Besse 2003). Similarly, my own survey demonstrated that the variability of Beaker global material corresponds to a suite of areas which appear to be homogeneous when considering several material traits and associated practices (Vander Linden 2006). These three studies, amongst several others (e.g. Prieto Martínez 2008), all point to the fact that the Beaker phenomenon incorporates traits of various origins. Furthermore, each of these traits may not be present throughout the entire area, but their overall distribution seems to be structured along certain lines (Vander Linden 2006).

Another revisited culture-historical theme is the notion of human mobility, which had been ignored during the 1970s and 1980s. This interest was triggered by the development and application of new scientific techniques, namely strontium and—to a lesser extent—oxygen isotope analysis. These techniques identify specific chemical signatures in bone and teeth and allow one to detect whether or not people have changed their location during their lifetime (Price et al. 2004; Evans, Chenery, and Fitzpatrick 2006). Studies undertaken on varying samples in both central and western Europe have systematically indicated a fair degree of mobility within Beaker human populations, in exceptional cases over very long distances (e.g. the 'Amesbury Archer', buried in Wiltshire but probably born in central Europe: Fitzpatrick 2009). So far, there seems to be no clear pattern regarding either age or gender categories. There is thus no reason to consider that there was any large-scale Beaker migration (*contra* Harrison and Heyd 2007). Yet, both isotope and 'traditional' studies indicate that forms of human mobility played a key role in the making of the Beaker phenomenon. Indeed, the structuring of the material variation is impossible to account for without the existence of people moving across Europe and disseminating objects, know-how, and ideas (Vander Linden 2007). Unsurprisingly, several researchers have also revisited Childe's hypothesis of the wandering smiths, especially for the British Isles where the Beaker phenomenon is intimately associated with the onset of copper metallurgy (Sheridan 2008; Fitzpatrick 2009). For all its interest, however, this hypothesis is only of limited use. It is indeed now clear that the link between the Beaker phenomenon and copper metallurgy in the British Isles is only incidental, and that otherwise the phenomenon post-dates copper metallurgy by several centuries in most of its distribution area (Roberts 2008).

The widespread success of the prestige goods model is fundamental to this renewed interest in the Beaker phenomenon. It is therefore not surprising that the model has come under close scrutiny over the last decade or so, yet it has found only limited support. For instance, it is undeniable that some graves stand out in terms of quality and/or quantity of grave goods (e.g. the Amesbury Archer) and could therefore easily be identified as chiefly burials. Likewise, the existence of lavish burials of children in central Europe has been interpreted as a proof of inherited status, itself related to some kind of social hierarchy: it is indeed unlikely that young children had achieved in their short lifespan the sort of richness suggested by the associated grave goods (Heyd 2007). While these two arguments may appear sound, it must be noted that, given the number of known burials for the Beaker period, it is hardly surprising to discover a few outliers characterized by exceptional numbers of artefacts. Furthermore, the simple equation 'higher number of artefacts = higher social role' is of very limited heuristic value. It does not consider other potential factors, especially the symbolic/ideological value attached to the grave goods.

This last question has recently been given much attention. Indeed, while Shennan's 'Beaker package' is rarely encountered in graves outside central Europe (Salanova 2007), its various components are nonetheless found separately in almost every grave: beakers nearly always feature in grave-good assemblages (with a strong preference for the maritime type in western Europe, and for handled beakers in central Europe: Salanova 2000; Besse 2003), as do weapons of various types inside male burials. A growing consensus views this relative standardization of grave goods as the material translation of a given ideology—or 'social context of use', to use Shennan's pioneering expression—broadly shared and constantly reinterpreted by the various human communities composing the Beaker phenomenon (e.g. Vander Linden 2006: Chapter 12). Although there is still no agreement on the precise structure of this ideology, its various components are fairly well outlined. First, the quasi-systematic deposition of beakers most probably echoes their function as vessels for the consumption of (alcoholic) drink and associated communal practices (Sherratt 1987). As suggested by anthropological and ethnoarchaeological work (Dietler 1990), communal drinking practices would have contributed to the elaboration and maintenance of social cohesion within the Beaker communities. At the same time, they would also have provided the possibility for individuals to express given social roles (Vander Linden 2006: Chapters 3 and 12). Second, the long-standing idea that weapons are linked to a form of warfare in this period has gained wider acceptance. Yet several elements actually suggest that warfare played more of an idealized role than a real one. These weapons do not often present wear traces (e.g. Woodward et al. 2006; Fokkens, Achterkamp, and Kuijpers 2008) or were otherwise unsuitable for proper use (e.g. copper daggers: Roberts 2008). In southern France the occurrence of physical injuries on skeletons during the previous Late Neolithic by far outnumbers the limited existing examples for the Beaker period (Guilaine and Zammit 2001). All in all, it seems that the Beaker ideology can be described as a way to ascribe individuals to well-defined, stereotyped categories (i.e. man as warrior and heavy drinker). This particular view does not suppose any particular form of associated social system, although it could have been subject to potential manipulation by ambitious individuals trying to increase their personal social status (Vander Linden 2006: Chapter 12).

Research undertaken over the past two decades has thus greatly improved our analytical knowledge of the Beaker phenomenon, and in particular its global material variability. From an interpretative point of view, these advances have been accompanied by a return to some of the old culture-historical themes, as exhibited by the heated debate on the localization of the homeland, or the new preference for human mobility (e.g. the 'wandering smiths' hypothesis). Likewise, the ideological dimension of the Beaker phenomenon has been explored at length but, at the same time, limited progress has been made regarding the factors responsible for the it. Some researchers have actually identified the Beaker ideology as the main reason for its success (e.g. Strahm 2004), thus reproducing the unfortunate processual confusion between the causes and effects of the Beaker phenomenon.

A Little Bit of History Repeating Itself

A little more than a century since the definition of the Bell Beaker phenomenon, we now arguably have a much-improved documentary knowledge of this key period of later European prehistory. Further work may well be needed on the chronology and geography of local groups, not to mention the challenges raised by new sites excavated as part of

Valletta-related archaeology; still, the analytical achievements remain impressive. Yet there has been no equivalent linear progress from the interpretative point of view, rather a repeating history of intertwined themes and problems (Fig. 4.2).

As we have seen, these themes and the causal relationships linking them together were laid out in the first half of the twentieth century by culture-historical archaeologists. Typologies aimed to classify the already vast body of available evidence, and to position the Beaker phenomenon in time and space. This chronological and spatial anchoring was achieved through the definition of a homeland, the obligatory key to unlock the historical significance of the Beaker phenomenon. From there onwards, it became possible to draw the migrations of the Beaker folk on the map. These copper-seeking wandering smiths not only introduced new items and practices but also some form of social order, with the emergence of new chiefly powers. These various elements eventually form a quadripartite structure 'homeland—human movement—causes—social order', the first three themes being given indisputable prominence by culture historians.

For all their methodological sophistication and theoretical ambition, processual archaeologists never really challenged the core of this structure. Their extensive criticisms of both homeland and migration indeed corresponded to an overemphasis of another element of the structure, namely the role of the new social order. This in turn led to some further imbalance, as evidenced by the limited discussions on the causes of the phenomenon. Recent analytical work, although not following an explicit coherent theoretical agenda, has witnessed another configuration of this quadripartite structure, closer in many ways to the

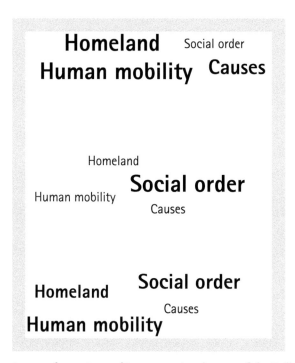

FIG. 4.2 The changing configurations of interpretative themes of the Bell Beaker phenomenon. Upper: culture-historical period; middle: processual period; lower: the contemporary situation.

original culture-historical formulation. The last ten years have thus been marked by a return to the foreground of the issues of both homeland and human mobility, as well as continuity and expansion of the processual take on social order, now expressed less in terms of hierarchies than of ideologies. The causes of the Bell Beaker phenomenon still remain unclear, with either a limited comeback to the role of the onset of copper metallurgy, or further confusion between the identification of the Beaker ideology and the causes of this phenomenon. All in all, the history of Beaker research is thus characterized by the never-ending recombination of the same themes (a process actually observable in other parts of the archaeological discipline: Stozckowski 1994). It is noteworthy that we are dealing here with a real structure rather than a suite of unconnected themes, as the alteration of the properties of one of the elements automatically leads to a reconfiguration of the spatial configuration of the whole.

The goal of this short historiographical essay is not to minimize the fundamental advances made by previous generations, nor the centrality of the interpretative themes mentioned above. I rather wish to point out that the structure described here is so deeply embedded in our discourses that it actually limits, rather than favours, the potential for new hypotheses. Future generations are thus faced with the imperative need to disentangle these different themes—maybe to reconnect them afterwards—as well as to explore a wider range of potential explanatory factors. For instance, population history has so far been limited to mere migrations, so that we only have a very limited understanding of the population structures and demographies of third millennium BC communities. Likewise, we only have glimpses of the relationships between patterns of human mobility, the constant reshaping of the Beaker ideologies, and the material variation of regional archaeological assemblages. Lastly, the older quadripartite structure has all too often been applied solely at the global level. Not that we should abandon once and for all the seductive temptations of a global explanation; but we crucially need a better appraisal of local idiosyncrasies, and of the connections between the various regions composing the Bell Beaker phenomenon.

It would be wrong to end this brief review on a negative or cautionary tone. Quite the contrary, I remain optimistic that future generations will explicitly tackle these issues. Many steps forward have been taken over the course of the twentieth and early twenty-first centuries. What is needed now is a careful exploration of original, unexpected directions.

Bibliography

Abercromby, J. (1902). 'The oldest Bronze Age ceramic type in Britain, its close analogies on the Rhine, its probable origin in central Europe', *Journal of the Royal Anthropological Institute*, 32: 373–97.

Barrett, J. C. (1994). *Fragments of Antiquity: Archaeology of Social Life in Britain, 2900–1200 BC*. Oxford: Blackwell.

Benz, M. and van Willingen, S. (eds.) (1998). *Some New Approaches to the Bell Beaker Phenomenon Lost Paradise...?*, Proceedings of the 2nd meeting of the 'Association Archéologie et Gobelets', Feldberg (Germany), 18–20 April (1997), British Archaeological Reports (International Series), 690. Oxford: Archaeopress.

Besse, M. (2003). 'Les Céramiques communes des Campaniformes européens', *Gallia Préhistoire*, 45: 205–58.

Bosch-Gimpera, P. (1940). 'The types and chronology of West European Beakers', *Man*, 40: 27–35.

Brodie, N. (1994). *The Neolithic-Bronze Age Transition in Britain: A Critical Review of Some Archaeological and Craniological Concepts*, British Archaeological Reports (British Series), 238. Oxford: Archaeopress.

—— (1997). 'New perspectives on the Bell-Beaker Culture', *Oxford Journal of Archaeology*, 16: 297–314.

Burgess, C. and Shennan, S. (1976). 'The beaker phenomenon', in C. Burgess and R. Miket (eds.), *Settlement and Economy in Third and Second Millennia B.C*, British Archaeological Reports (British Series), 33. Oxford: Archaeopress, 309–31.

Castillo, A. del Yurrita (1928). *La cultura del Vaso Campaniforme (su origen i extensión en Europa)*. Barcelona: University of Barcelona.

Childe, V. G. (1925). *The Dawn of European Civilization*. New York: Knopf.

—— (1930). *The Bronze Age*. New York: Biblo and Tannen.

Clarke, D. (1970). *Beaker Pottery of Great Britain and Ireland*. Cambridge: Cambridge University Press.

—— (1976). 'The Beaker network—social and economic models', in J. N. Lanting, and J. D. van der Waals (eds.), *Glockenbecher Symposion Oberried (1974)*. Haarlem: Fibula-Van Dishoeck, 459–77.

Convertini, F. and Querré, G. (1998). 'Apports des études céramologiques en laboratoire à la connaissance du Campaniforme: résultats, bilan et perspectives', *Bulletin de la Société Préhistorique Française*, 95: 333–41.

Czebreszuk, J. (ed.) (2004). *Similar but Different: Bell Beakers in Europe*. Poznan: Adam Mickiewicz University.

Dietler, M. (1990). 'Driven by drink: the role of drinking in the political economy and the case of the early Iron Age France', *Journal of Anthropological Archaeology*, 9: 352–406.

Drenth, E. and Hogestijn, W. J. H. (2001). 'The Bell Beaker culture in the Netherlands: the state of research in (1998)', in F. Nicolis (ed.), *Bell Beakers Today: Pottery, People, Culture, Symbols in Prehistoric Europe. Proceedings of the International Colloquium, Riva del Garda (Trento, Italy), 11–16 May (1998)*. Trento: Ufficio Beni Archeologici, 309–32.

Evans, J., Chenery, C. A., and Fitzpatrick, A. P. (2006). 'Bronze Age childhood migration of individuals near Stonehenge, revealed by strontium and oxygen isotope tooth enamel analysis', *Archaeometry*, 48/2: 309–21.

Fitzpatrick, A. (2009). 'In his hands and in his head: the Amesbury archer as a metalworker', in Clark, P. (ed.), *Bronze Age Connections: Cultural Contact in Prehistoric Europe*. Oxford: Oxbow, 176–88.

Fokkens, H. (2005). 'Late Neolithic, Early and Middle Bronze Age: an introduction', in L. P. Louwe Kooijmans, P. W. van den Broeke, H. Fokkens, and A. L. Van Gijn (eds.), *The Prehistory of the Netherlands*, vol. I. Amsterdam: Amsterdam University Press, 357–69.

——, Achterkamp, Y., and Kuijpers, M. (2008). 'Bracers or bracelets? About the functionality and meaning of Bell Beaker wrist-guards', *Proceedings of the Prehistoric Society*, 74: 109–40.

Guilaine, J. (1974). 'Les Campaniformes pyrénéo-languedociens. Premiers résultats au C14', *Zephyrus*, 25: 107–20.

—— (ed.) (1984). *L'Age du Cuivre européen. Civilisations à vases campaniformes*. Paris: C.N.R.S.

—— (2004). 'Les Campaniformes et la Méditerranée', *Bulletin de la Société Préhistorique Française*, 101: 239–52.

—— and Zammit, J. (2001). *Le Sentier de la guerre. Visages de la violence préhistorique*. Paris: Seuil.

Harrison, R. (1980). *The Beaker Folk*. London: Thames and Hudson.

—— and Heyd, V. (2007). 'The transformation of Europe in the 3rd millennium BC', *Prähistorische Zeitschrift*, 82/2: 129–214.

Heyd, V. (2007). 'Families, prestige goods, warriors and complex societies: Beaker groups and the 3rd millennium cal BC', *Proceedings of the Prehistoric Society*, 73: 327–80.

Kinnes, I., Gibson, A., Boast, R., Ambers, J., Leese, M., and Bowman, S. (1991). 'Radiocarbon dating and British Beakers', *Scottish Archaeological Review*, 8: 35–68.

Kunst, M. (2001). 'Invasion? Fashion? Social rank? Consideration concerning the Bell Beaker phenomenon in Copper Age fortifications of the Iberian Peninsula', in F. Nicolis (ed.), *Bell Beakers Today: Pottery, People, Culture, Symbols in Prehistoric Europe. Proceedings of the International Colloquium, Riva del Garda (Trento, Italy), 11–16 May (1998)*. Trento: Ufficio Beni Archeologici, 81–90.

Lanting, J. N. and van der Waals, J. D. (1972). 'British beakers as seen from the continent. A review article', *Helinium*, 12: 20–46.

—— and van der Waals, J. D. (1976a). 'Beaker culture relations in the Lower Rhine basin', in J. N. Lanting and J. D. van der Waals (eds.), *Glockenbecher Symposion. Oberried (1974)*. Haarlem: Fibula-Van Dishoeck, 2–80.

—— and van der Waals, J. D. (eds.) (1976b). *Glockenbecher Symposion. Oberried (1974)*. Haarlem: Fibula-Van Dishoeck.

Lemercier, O. (2004). 'Explorations, implantations et diffusions: le "phénomène" campaniforme en France méditerranéenne', *Bulletin de la Société Préhistorique Française*, 101: 227–38.

Menk, R. (1979). 'Le Phénomène campaniforme: structures biologiques et intégration historique', *Archives Suisses d'Anthropologie Générale*, 43: 259–84.

Müller, J. and van Willingen, S. (2001). 'New radiocarbon evidence for European Bell Beakers and the consequences for the diffusion of the Bell Beaker phenomenon', in Nicolis F. (ed.), *Bell Beakers Today: Pottery, People, Culture, Symbols in Prehistoric Europe. Proceedings of the International Colloquium, Riva del Garda (Trento, Italy) 11–16 May (1998)*. Trento: Ufficio Beni Archeologici, 59–80.

Nicolis, F. (ed.) (2001). *Bell Beakers Today: Pottery, People, Culture, Symbols in Prehistoric Europe. Proceedings of the International Colloquium, Riva del Garda (Trento, Italy), 11–16 May (1998)*. Trento: Ufficio Beni Archeologici.

Price, T. D., Knipper, C., Grupe, G., and Smrcka, V. (2004). 'Strontium isotopes and prehistoric human migration: the Bell Beaker period in central Europe', *European Journal of Archaeology*, 7/1: 9–40.

Prieto Martínez, M. P. (2008). 'Bell Beaker communities in Thy: the first Bronze Age society in Denmark', *Norwegian Archaeological Review*, 41: 115–58.

Rehman, F., Robinson, V. J., and Shennan, S. J. (1992). 'A neutron activation study of bell beakers and associated pottery from Czechoslovakia and Hungary', *Památky archeologické*, 83: 197–211.

Roberts, B. (2008). 'Creating traditions and shaping technologies: understanding the earliest metal objects and metal production in Western Europe', *World Archaeology*, 40: 354–72.

Salanova, L. (2000). *La Question du Campaniforme en France et dans les îles anglo-normandes. Productions, chronologie et rôles d'un standard céramique*. Paris: C.T.H.S./Société Préhistorique Française.

—— (2007). 'Les Sépultures campaniformes: lecture sociale', in J. Guilaine (ed.), *Le Chalcolithique et la construction des inégalités. Tome I. Le Continent européen. Séminaire du Collège de France*. Paris: Errance, 213–28.

Sangmeister, E. (1960). 'Metalurgia y comercio del cobre en la Europa prehistórica', *Zephyrus*, 11: 131–9.

—— (1966). 'Die Datierung des Rückstroms der Glockenbecher und ihre Auswirkung auf die Chronologie der Kupferzeit in Portugal', *Palaeohistoria*, 12: 195–207.

Shennan, S. J. (1976). 'Bell Beakers and their context in central Europe', in J. N. Lanting and J. D. van der Waals (eds.), *Glockenbecher Symposion. Oberried (1974)*. Haarlem: Fibula-Van Dishoeck, 231–9.

—— (1978). 'Archaeological "cultures": an empirical investigation', in I. Hodder (ed.), *The Spatial Organisation of Culture*. London: Duckworth, 113–40.

—— (1993). 'Settlement and social change in central Europe, 3500–1500 BC', *Journal of World Prehistory*, 7: 121–61.

Sheridan, J. A. (2008). 'Upper Largie and Dutch–Scottish connections during the Beaker period', *Analecta Praehistorica Leidensia*, 40: 240–60.

Sherratt, A. (1987). 'Cups that cheered', in W. H. Waldren and R. C. Kennard (eds.), *Bell Beakers of the Western Mediterranean*, British Archaeological Reports (International Series), 331. Oxford: Archaeopress, 81–114.

Stozckowski, W. (1994). *Anthropologie naïve. Anthropologie savante. De l'origine de l'homme, de l'imagination et des idées reçues*. Paris: C.N.R.S.

Strahm, C. (2004). 'Das Glockenbecher-Phänomen aus der Sicht der Komplementär-Keramik', in J. Czebreszuk (ed.), *Similar but Different: Bell Beakers in Europe*. Poznan: Adam Mickiewicz University.

Vander Linden, M. (2006). *Le Phénomène campaniforme. Synthèse et nouvelles perspectives*, British Archaeological Reports (International Series), 1,470. Oxford: Archaeopress.

—— (2007). 'What linked the Bell Beakers in third millennium BC Europe?', *Antiquity*, 81: 343–52.

van der Waals, J. D. and Glasbergen, W. (1955). 'Beaker types and their distribution in the Netherlands', *Palaeohistoria*, 4: 5–46.

Vandkilde H. (2001). 'Beaker representation in the Danish Late Neolithic', in F. Nicolis (ed.), *Bell Beakers Today: Pottery, People, Culture, Symbols in Prehistoric Europe. Proceedings of the International Colloquium, Riva del Garda (Trento, Italy), 11–16 May (1998)*. Trento: Ufficio Beni Archeologici, 333–60.

Woodward, A., Hunter, J., Ixer, R., Roe, F., Potts, P. J., Webb, P. C., Watson, J. S., and Jones, M. C. (2006). 'Beaker age bracers in England: sources, function and use', *Antiquity*, 80: 530–43.

CHAPTER 5

BRONZE AGE SETTLEMENTS

JOANNA BRÜCK AND HARRY FOKKENS

Introduction

For much of the twentieth century our understanding of the European Bronze Age was dominated by evidence from burials and hoards, and in many regions few settlements were known. As developer-funded archaeology has increased in recent decades, however, our knowledge of the Bronze Age settlement record has dramatically improved. This paper will examine what this evidence can tell us about the social, economic, and material worlds of European Bronze Age communities. Rather than attempting to provide a general overview, it will adopt a thematic and problem-oriented approach, although we will also consider aspects of chronological and regional variation.

Inevitably the character and quality of the dataset is highly variable for a number of reasons. Factors such as differential preservation limit the interpretative potential of sites in certain regions: contrast, for example, the waterlogged lakeside settlements of the Alpine foothills, which have produced large numbers of organic finds, with sites on the North European Plain, where occupation levels and the tops of features such as pits and postholes have often been lost through intensive ploughing. Different research traditions have also had an impact. Some regions, for example Scandinavia, have long histories of research on prehistoric settlement going back to at least the 1930s. Here, and in areas such as the Low Countries, large-scale open-area excavation has long been the norm, but in parts of south-eastern Europe, where deeply stratified tell settlements produce huge volumes of finds from even the smallest trenches, this is rarely feasible and plans for sites of this class are frequently unavailable. In some areas, research priorities remain focused on constructing chronologies and typological frameworks, and little attention is devoted to questions such as the organization of settlement space. Notwithstanding these difficulties, however, the settlement record for the European Bronze Age raises a variety of interesting questions, and this paper will attempt to identify some of the most important ones. Many of the examples that will be discussed in the following pages are from north-west Europe, as that is the region with which we are most familiar, but we believe that the same themes and issues are of relevance to sites in other areas. For reasons of space, we will focus on houses and settlement sites, rather than attempting to discuss regional settlement patterns or models of landscape organization.

Houses and Households in Anthropological Perspective

We will begin by considering the set of ideas and expectations that implicitly influence archaeological approaches to prehistoric settlement. The ideological significance of the home in recent European history undoubtedly affects how we view prehistoric houses. All too rarely are the concepts that we use subjected to critical analysis: we believe we know what a house is, who should live in it, and what should happen there. It is therefore easy for modern Western ideas regarding the character of domestic practice and the domestic domain to be imposed onto the past. However, anthropological research on houses and households calls many of our assumptions into question. Far from being the locus of supposedly 'natural' activities such as reproduction and food consumption—as they are characterized in our own cultural context—houses are a key arena in which social identities and cultural values are constructed, maintained, and transformed (e.g. Parker Pearson and Richards 1994): the homes of middle-class families in Victorian England, for example, gave material form to historically specific forms of gender ideology.

Anthropological studies of houses and households in non-Western contexts demonstrate that not only does domestic architecture vary dramatically across space and time, but so too do the structure and composition of the household group. Houses may be inhabited by one or more families or by groups of unrelated people (such as student houses in contemporary university towns). Families themselves take highly varied forms—they may be nuclear or extended; monogamous, polygamous, or polyandrous; matrilineal or patrilineal; patrilocal or matrilocal. Husbands and wives may live apart, while in some matrilineal societies children reside with their mother's brother rather than with their father.

In the contemporary western world, our homes are spatially distinguished from places of work and of worship, as well as from seats of political power. However, this sharp divide between domestic, ritual, economic, and political practice is not a feature of every society. Elsewhere, particularly in rural communities where little industrialization has taken place, the household is often the primary economic unit, organizing productive activities such as farming and craftwork, and managing the transmission of goods and materials through exchange and inheritance (Netting, Wilk, and Arnould 1984). Where the household plays a significant economic role, it is hardly surprising that it may also form a locus of political action, as did the elite houses of feudal Japan and Medieval Europe. Of course, political and economic activities are sanctioned and safeguarded by ritual practice, and shrines are a feature of houses in places as far apart as Mexico and Bali (e.g. Waterson 1990). Indeed, domestic architecture may embody cosmological referents. For example, the layout of Barasana longhouses in Colombia mirrors the structure of the universe: different architectural elements are identified with the sky, earth, and underworld and with significant geographical feature such as rivers and mountains, so that men, women, ancestors, and outsiders are each assigned their rightful place in the order of things (Hugh-Jones 1996).

Although it may be difficult, if not impossible, to reconstruct aspects of prehistoric societies such as forms of kinship, we must remain sensitive to the fact that Bronze Age houses and households—and the cultural values and beliefs they enshrined—were very different in character and organization to our own homes. On the other hand, as we shall see, there is good evidence that economic, ritual, and political activities were central elements of domestic practice in the European Bronze Age and that the house played a key role in the construction and negotiation of social identities. With these provisos, we will turn now to the archaeological record.

Bronze Age House Architecture

If, as we have argued above, houses are so often central to the construction of identity, it is hardly surprising that the European Bronze Age is characterized by a number of quite distinctive traditions of domestic architecture. Across the lowlands of northern Europe, including southern Scandinavia, longhouses dominate the settlement record (Fig. 5.1). Most buildings of this class are between 15 m and 35 m in length and around 5–8 m wide; typically, they have apsidal ends and are oriented north-west–south-east. In some regions, longhouses provide evidence for internal cattle-stalling after 1500 cal BC.

The houses of central and south-east Europe are also rectangular, but they tend to be shorter in length and smaller in area than the longhouses of the north: the buildings at Tiszaug-Kéménytető in south-central Hungary, for example, were 7–9 m long and 3.5–5 m wide (Csányi and Stanczik 1992). Elsewhere, very different traditions of domestic architecture prevail: in Ireland, Britain, and areas of north-west France such as Normandy, for example, roundhouses of c.8–12 m diameter were the norm (Fig. 5.2; see Brück 1999). Across much of Britain, but also on some parts of the continent, it is during the Bronze Age that houses first become archaeologically visible, replacing megalithic tombs and other forms of ceremonial architecture as the key locus of architectural elaboration. The 'monumentalization' of domestic architecture in the British Isles suggests that the domestic domain was increasingly a focus of ideological concern—a place where key forms of social identity and cultural values were performed and negotiated. This was also the case in parts of lowland north-west Europe; here, as we shall see below, animal stalls were incorporated into the house itself, indicating that cattle meant more to people then just 'meat on legs'.

The significance of these differences in traditions of domestic architecture is difficult to discern. In Britain the barrows and ceremonial enclosures (henges, timber circles, and the like) characteristic of the Late Neolithic and Early Bronze Age were circular in form and it is tempting to suggest that roundhouse architecture was rooted in a set of cosmological principles with an already lengthy history (Bradley 1998, Chapter 7). In other regions, however, for example where Corded Ware cultures developed out of earlier megalithic traditions, house architecture of both the Neolithic and Bronze Age is dominated by rectangular buildings, although contemporary barrows and ceremonial structures were circular. As such, the relationship between domestic and ceremonial architecture, and the cosmological principles embodied in houses and monuments, appear to have been complex and regionally specific.

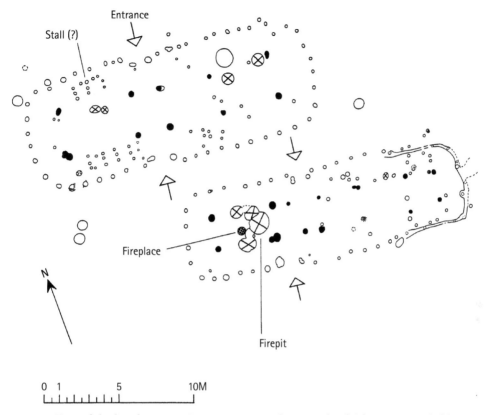

FIG. 5.1 Two of the longhouses at Bjerre site 2, northwest Jutland. They were probably not contemporary but may have been occupied sequentially.

Source: Bech 1997.

In general, Bronze Age houses were post-built structures (Fig. 5.3): in many regions, an open framework of substantial timber posts, usually set in postpits, supported a thatched roof, while the outer walls were normally wattle and daub or comprised contiguous upright wooden planks set in a foundation trench (as at Ochtmissen in north Germany: Gebers 1997); in other areas, the outer walls themselves were load-bearing. In some parts of central Europe, log cabins were constructed: although the timber superstructures of such buildings have not generally survived, the stone footings on which they were laid have been excavated at sites such as Savognin-Padnal in Graubünden, Switzerland (Rageth 1986). Daub caulking used to seal the joints between logs has also been found and this preserves the shape of the original timbers. Elsewhere, other construction materials were employed. In many areas of upland Britain, such as Dartmoor, houses were surrounded by drystone walls (though their roofs were still supported on an internal setting of timber uprights: Fleming 2008), while in parts of south-west France houses of unbaked mud-brick dating to the Late Bronze Age have been identified, for example at Laprade (Billaud 2005). Floors were generally of beaten earth, although examples of stone flagging and timber flooring are also widely known. Occasionally, there is tantalizing evidence that houses may have been painted: for instance, the internal walls of the substantial, centrally placed house at Tiszaug-Kéménytető were decorated with spiral designs (Csányi and Stanczik 1992): we might suspect that only the most socially significant buildings would be considered worthy of this sort of elaboration. Internally, houses were provided with a range of

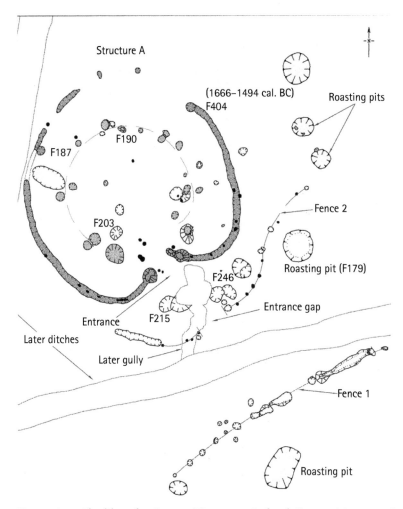

FIG. 5.2 House A at Cloghbreedy, County Tipperary, Ireland. Image: Margaret Gowen & Co. Ltd, courtesy of the National Roads Authority. A load-bearing circular setting of posts supported the roof of this building, while a slot trench defined its outer wall.

Source: McQuade, Molloy, and Moriarty 2009.

fixtures and fittings including drying-racks, storage pits, hearths, ovens (for example, the well-preserved oven at Gandus in the Drôme region of south-east France: Daumas and Laudet 1992), settings for upright weaving looms and benches (for instance the benches around the walls of the roundhouses at La Muculufa, Sicily: McConnell 1992).

The social significance of the house is further indicated by the intimate links—on both a practical and a symbolic level—between the life of the house and that of its inhabitants. In southern England and the Low Countries, for example, houses appear to have been occupied for only a few decades—roughly the length of a single human generation. In these regions, it can be suggested that the creation of a new household group (perhaps on marriage or shortly thereafter) was marked by the construction of a new house; conversely, the death of a senior member of the household may have provided the catalyst for house abandonment (Brück 1999; Gerritsen 2003). In such a context, it is hardly surprising that both house construction and abandonment were sometimes ritualized. In Britain and Ireland, foundation and abandonment deposits were often

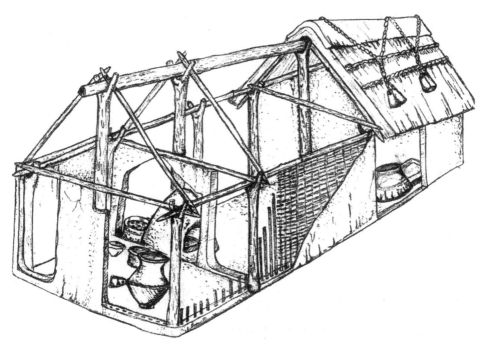

FIG. 5.3 Reconstruction of a house from the tell at Százhalombatta, overlooking the Danube in northern Hungary.

Source: Artursson 2010.

placed in pits, postholes, and ditches; these include animal burials, small bronze objects, and whole and broken quernstones, as well as more unusual items such as the chalk phallus found in one of the porch postholes of house D at Itford Hill in Sussex (Burstow and Holleyman 1957). The metaphorical links between people and houses are perhaps best illustrated by the activities that surrounded house abandonment. In southern England, just as cremation facilitated the fragmentation and burning of human bodies, so too certain houses appear to have been deliberately burnt down, while others were dismantled and buried (Brück 2006). At Trethellan Farm in Cornwall, for example, the roundhouses had their posts removed and the empty postholes sealed with large slabs or deliberately blocked with smaller stones; the buildings were then covered by thick layers of rubble and burnt stone, not unlike the burial cairns in the same region (Nowakowski 1991). Elsewhere in southern England, houses were left standing, their gradually rotting remains acting as visible evidence for particular occupational histories. This variability is interesting as it has implications for the ways in which different places were constituted and maintained in both personal and communal memory.

Explaining Size Differences Between Houses

In many areas, there is a significant degree of variability in house size and this can be interpreted in different ways. It has been suggested that in northern Denmark large houses belonged to local chiefs—men who had access to the resources and connections required for such building projects—so that architecture provided a means of expressing social status. A large house at Legård, for example, with animal stalls in the centre, is interpreted as a chiefly hall for twin rulers because of the two equal-sized rooms at either end of the building (Kristiansen and Larsson 2005: 277–90). However, the problem with this interpretation is that in Drenthe (the Netherlands), for instance, this type of house is the norm, in terms of both size and structure (see Kooi 2008). Moreover, north-west European settlements usually comprise no more than two or three houses together, and provide little other evidence for social stratification.

There are other ways of explaining size differences too. Some larger buildings may have played a special role, for instance as community meeting houses. The ethnographic literature provides many examples of men's and women's houses, and similar structures may have been present in at least some regions of the European Bronze Age: for example, Ernst Lauermann (2003: 479) has suggested that the unusually large house at Šumice in Moravia, which measured 56.6 x 7 m in size, may have been an assembly hall. Factors such as the size and character of the household group were undoubtedly also important: some houses may have been built to accommodate ageing parents or unmarried siblings (see Fokkens 2005). Houses may have been abandoned at different stages in the household life cycle. A newly married couple, with few children or dependent relatives, may have had neither the requirements nor the resources to build a large house; over time, however, their circumstances are likely to have changed. Larger houses may therefore be the result of rebuilding and enlargement (Arnoldussen 2008: 205–12). These may have been extended over time as families increased in size and households reached economic and social maturity: for example, the house at Rodenkirchen-Hahnenknooper Mühle in Lower Saxony was originally 21 m long but was subsequently extended by a further 6 m (Strahl 2005).

In certain regions, the average house size changed over time, although the pattern is far from uniform. In parts of the Alpine foreland, for example, there was an increase in house size over the course of the Bronze Age (David El-Biali 1992), whereas in Scandinavia and the Low Countries houses decreased in size from the Middle to the Late Bronze Age (Bech 1997; Fokkens 1999). The significance of such trends is hard to establish, but they doubtless reflected changes in the character and organization of household activities, the composition of the household group, and the relationship between households and the wider community. For example, there may have been a change from nuclear to extended families or vice versa; activities that were originally undertaken communally, outside the house, may have become the preserve of the individual household, so that both architectural and social boundaries were redrawn. The implications of such changes for concepts of privacy as well as for the control of particular activities and those who carried them out are clearly interesting.

The Organization of Household Space

In continental Europe houses were often internally divided into two or three rooms. In houses 3 and 4 at Croce del Papa, near Nola in southern Italy, internal walls separated the principal living space from a storage area in the apse-shaped north-western end (Livadie et al. 2005). The main room in house 4 was furnished with a central oven surrounded by serving vessels, cups, and quernstones, while in house 3 a large clay grain bin was found to the left of the doorway in the south-eastern corner of the building. Storage vessels were also ranged along the walls of these buildings. At Százhalombatta in north-central Hungary most houses were built as single-room dwellings of approximately 5 x 10 m (Sørensen 2010). They were provided with one or more hearths and ovens, usually located towards the northern (back) wall of the house and away from the probable location of the doorway in the south wall. In some houses, there was also a further centrally placed hearth, suggesting differentiation of tasks relating to food preparation or serving. In some cases a second smaller room to the north is likely to have served as a storage area.

In north-western Europe, houses are not generally as well-preserved, but there are occasional exceptions. The houses of phase 1 at Apalle in southern Sweden were two-roomed and were oriented north-west–south-east (Fig. 5.4; Ullén 1994). The room at the north-west end, which was entered by a door on the south-western side, was floored with clay and produced most of the ceramic, stone, bone, and metal finds. Separated from this by a wooden partition was a second room at the south-eastern end of each house; this had a central hearth but produced few finds. That this division was significant in both symbolic and practical terms is indicated by the deposition of animal bone along the south-western wall of house 13: to the left of the doorway, and marking the edge of the north-western room, the mandibles of cattle were deposited, while to the right of the doorway, sheep mandibles delimited the boundary of the room containing the hearth. As such, depositional practice provided a means of distinguishing spaces, objects, activities and—most importantly—different categories of people, perhaps providing, for example, a way of conceptually dividing public from private space.

Elsewhere in north-west Europe longhouses were sometimes provided with an area specifically for the stalling of cattle. In some cases, houses were divided into three spaces: the

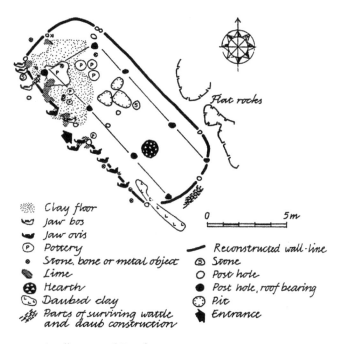

FIG. 5.4 House 13 at Apalle, central Sweden.

Source: Ullén 1994.

central part of the building was the byre, while the living areas were located to either side of this (Kooi 2008). The tripartite house at Trappendal on Jutland, for example, was furnished with two hearths, one placed centrally in each living space (Boysen and Andersen 1983), hinting that the house may have been the dwelling of an extended family, each occupying opposite ends of the building. Such buildings often had two or three doorways and these could be placed in either the long or short sides: the presence of different doorways may indicate a concern to distinguish different activities and people.

On other settlements, for example at Elp and Angelslo in the Netherlands (Kooi 2008), houses were divided into two by opposing doors placed in the long sides: the byre was located to the east or south-east end of this thoroughfare, while the living area was placed at the west or north-west end of the building. The appearance of internal cattle-stalling after *c*.1500 BC has been explained in a variety of ways: it may indicate a change to private ownership of cattle, an increase in raiding, or a change in animal management practices such as more organized collection of manure (Zimmermann 1999). However, it can be argued that cattle-stalling *inside* a house was not necessary for functional reasons, and was probably not even healthy; it can therefore be suggested that internal stalling indicates that cattle acted as a form of 'social capital' during the period (Fokkens 1999; 2005).

It has been suggested that roundhouse architecture in Britain and Ireland was rooted in cosmological principles, reflecting key social distinctions and cultural values. Bronze Age roundhouses were primarily oriented to the east or south-east (see Fig. 5.2; Brück 1999). Although it has been suggested that doorways were placed to face away from the south-westerly winds so prevalent in this region, ideological factors may also have been important. Facing towards the rising sun, the doorway may have been symbolically associated with light, life, and associated concepts of cyclical rebirth. Indeed, roundhouse entrances were often architecturally elaborated; they were usually provided with porches and some were marked out by votive deposits. At Cladh Hallan in western Scotland (Parker Pearson et al. n.d.) the movement of the sun over the course of the day was mapped onto the internal space of three roundhouses, so that the southern halves of these buildings formed a focus for the activities of the living such as food preparation and craft production while the northern halves were associated with sleeping, storage, and the ancestors—several deposits of human remains were found in the northern parts of these houses. It seems likely that such spatial distinctions may have helped to maintain social divisions between, for example, women and men or the young and the old.

THE BRONZE AGE FARMSTEAD

Across most of northern and western Europe scattered farmsteads dominate the archaeological record and nucleated settlement is extremely rare. In northern Denmark and in the Low Countries (see Chapter 31) large-scale surveys have identified farmsteads every few hundred metres and excavated examples suggest that each of these was occupied by a single household group (e.g. Earle and Kolb 2010). Here and elsewhere, the Bronze Age farmhouse was often accompanied by a range of other structures and features including barns, granaries, wells, and waterholes; the preserved wooden wellhead at Zwenkau in north Germany is one such example (Stäuble and Campen 1998).

Pits and hearths are found both inside and outside Bronze Age houses, suggesting a degree of fluidity in areas where activities such as cooking and craft production could be carried out. In some regions there are interesting changes over time in such patterns. In Ireland external hearths are common on Middle Bronze Age settlements (see Fig. 5.2), but in the Late Bronze Age hearths were predominantly located *inside* roundhouses. This may have implications in terms of changing concepts of privacy and suggests an increasing concern to define and control particular activities and the people associated with them—here, perhaps women and the preparation of food. Fenced stock pens have been identified at sites such as Elp in the Netherlands (Waterbolk 1964), while the edges of the farmstead are often defined by banks, ditches, and fence-lines. Votive deposits were frequently placed in boundary features, underscoring their significance in social as well as spatial terms (Brück 1995). At Chancellorsland in County Tipperary, Ireland, for example, part of the skull of a young adult was recovered from the basal fill of one of the ditches that surrounded the settlement (Doody 2008: 331).

It has been argued that the relatively short lifespan of some houses in parts of north-west Europe may have resulted in a pattern of generational movement of farmsteads within a defined 'territory' (Roymans and Fokkens 1991). Recently, however, this model has been challenged (see Arnoldussen 2008: 88–92), and it is clear that some settlements were occupied over longer periods: for example, at Reading Business Park in Berkshire, southern England, roundhouses were rebuilt several times on virtually the same location (Moore and Jennings 1992). Such practices suggest the maintenance of long-term, intimate, and personalized relationships with place that may have—among other things—provided one way of legitimating claims over land.

Of course, while it would be easy to project a familiar picture of rural life drawn from our own recent history onto the Bronze Age, it would be a mistake to do so. As we have seen, ritual activity formed an integral element of the life of Bronze Age farmsteads and it is hardly surprising that at least some of this appears to have been concerned with agricultural fertility. Votive deposits are frequently encountered in wells, waterholes, and storage pits, for example the pierced and shaped roundel of human skull found in a waterhole at Green Park in Berkshire (Boyle 2004). Likewise, even the scattered farmsteads of north-west Europe will on occasion have formed a key locus for inter-group meetings. For instance, a large dump of burnt flint (some 4 x 7.5 m) was found at the Middle Bronze Age settlement at South Lodge Camp in Dorset, southern England (Barrett, Bradley, and Green 1991: 161). This may represent the remains of feasting: it is widely accepted that burnt flint is the by-product of cooking activities and, if so, the size of this deposit suggests the provision of foodstuffs on a large scale. In the Late Bronze Age in the same region, specialized tablewares including decorated fineware cups and bowls appear, suggesting that the entertainment of guests may have been an important component of household activities. As such, settlements doubtless played a significant role in the political life and inter-group negotiations of Bronze Age communities.

Bronze Age Villages

Nucleated settlements are rare in north-west Europe and dispersed single farmsteads are the norm. Bovenkarspel in West Frisia is one of the few examples known in the Netherlands (IJzereef 1988), but even there the number of contemporaneous houses is difficult to estimate and is probably not more than three or four. The large village at Corrstown in Northern Ireland (Conway, Gahan, and Rathbone 2005) is almost exceptional. Here seventy-seven round-houses, the majority of which were contemporary, were ranged along either side of a cobbled roadway. Although settlement is typically dispersed, the nature and organization of inter-settlement interaction in north-west Europe inevitably varied across time and space. In the Low Countries, for example, the single farmsteads characteristic of the Early and Middle Bronze Age were often located near an ancestral barrow (Fokkens and Arnoldussen 2008; Bourgeois and Fontijn 2008), emphasizing the importance of the ancestors for each household group. In the Late Bronze Age, on the other hand, three or four farms shared a single cemetery, suggesting a change in the character and scale of community and/or family identities.

In contrast, in parts of central and south-east Europe substantial villages form a significant element of the settlement pattern and some of these may have housed up to six hundred people. The well-preserved lakeside villages of the Alpine foreland have provided particular insights into this form of settlement (see Chapter 39). Sites such as Cortaillod-Est on the edge of Lake Neuchâtel in Switzerland (Arnold 1992) were surrounded by timber palisades that defined the spatial boundaries of the settlement, giving monumental emphasis to the social distinction between insiders and outsiders. At Siedlung Forschner on the Federsee in Baden-Württemberg, the entrance to the settlement was itself marked out by a substantial gateway structure (Billamboz and Torke 1992). The internal organization of villages such as Unteruhldingen-Stollenwiesen on the north shore of the Bodensee in southern Germany (Schöbel 1996) suggests that these were carefully planned. Rows of closely spaced houses, near-identical in size and shape and oriented in the same direction, flank narrow alleyways. In some cases, as at Cortaillod-Est, houses in the same row share party walls. The layout of such sites suggests that these were tightly knit communities in which architecture was used to create a sense of social cohesion and community identity (David El-Biali 1992). The degree of conformity and order to the layout of such villages is interesting, and suggests a significant degree of social control.

Similar concerns can be seen in the tells of south-east Europe where there is also a considerable degree of intra-site homogeneity in house architecture. On some tell sites, for example at Százhalombatta in northern Hungary, open areas that may have acted as communal gathering places have been identified (Sørensen 2010). In this region too, votive deposits were used to mark out community boundaries: for example, a pit at the base of the inner enclosure ditch surrounding the tell at Jászdósza-Kápolnaholm on the Great Hungarian Plain produced a number of intact animal skulls including brown bear, aurochs, and wild boar (Tárnoki 2003: 146). However, although there are similarities between the tells of south-east Europe and villages further to the north and west, there are also differences. Particularly interesting is the long-lived character of tell settlements. The monumental form of these sites resulted from the repeated rebuilding of houses on the same plots, often over several centuries, for example at Túrkeve-Terehalom in south-east Hungary (Csányi and Tárnoki 2003: 160). Shorter-term house maintenance practices are also visible in the regular replastering of house floors and the renewal of hearths and ovens. Such an interest in the reconstruction of household space is likely to have been linked not only to practical concerns resulting from daily wear and tear but also to the symbolic significance of the house in tell communities. The repair and rebuilding of houses may have been linked to important points in the life cycles of their inhabitants such as birth, marriage, or inter-generational inheritance. Rebuilding a house on the footprint of its predecessor acted as a means of 'sedimenting' memory into settlement space so that the house itself became an ancestral icon, a symbol of the identity of a particular descent group: in this way, the creation of tells suggests long-term attachment to particular places (Bailey 1990). It is therefore hardly surprising that houses on such settlements were foci for ritual practice: the houses on Hungarian Bronze Age tells, for example, frequently produce animal figurines, clay models of wheels and wagons, and bird-shaped ceramic vessels—wheel, wagon, and bird motifs were significant religious symbols in many areas during the Bronze Age.

The scale and organization of villages in central and south-east Europe suggest that these regions were characterized by a greater degree of social complexity than contemporary communities to the north and west. Indeed, over time, there appears to have been an increase in settlement size in some of these areas: Százhalombatta, for example, increased from 2 hectares in size in the Early Bronze Age to 7.5 hectares in the Late Bronze Age (Artursson 2010). Certainly, the intensity of face-to-face interaction implied by the existence of large villages suggests that a range of social regulatory mechanisms must have been in place, perhaps in the form of elites or elders who could control the behaviour of others. Indeed, the regimented layout of such villages may imply the existence of individuals who had the authority to impose both spatial and social order on their communities. Occasionally, there is evidence for possible inter-household differences in status: for example, a hoard buried under a house floor at Jászdósza-Kápolnahalom on the Great Hungarian Plain included thirty-seven gold hair ornaments, amber beads, and a number of other gold and bronze objects (Tárnoki 2003: 146). However, in most Bronze Age villages, it is not possible to identify a house that might have belonged to a village chief or leader. In some cases one or more buildings may be distinguished on the basis of their size, location, or other features, but seldom is it clear that this is a result of their status and other explanations are possible.

Although there may be considerable uniformity in house architecture, social differentiation may be reflected in the layout of settlement space. At Fidvár near Vráble in west-central Slovakia, for example, a combination of detailed geophysical survey and surface collection of finds has illuminated the internal organization of a large, double-ditched enclosure on the bank of the River Žitava (Fig. 5.5; Bátora et al. 2008). Several discrete groups of houses in well-ordered rows have been identified: some of these buildings are located in the centre of the site, others between the inner and outer ditches, while yet further examples were situated outside the enclosed area. Narrow alleyways radiate from the site, and these formed spatial boundaries between clusters of houses. It seems likely that such internal spatial differentiation reflects aspects of social differentiation. At Fuente Álamo in Almería, well-built tower houses, granaries, a water cistern, and rich burials were concentrated on the very top of the hill on which the village is located, while simpler houses were constructed on the surrounding slopes (Schubart, Pingel, and Arteaga 2001).

Identifying Settlement Hierarchies

Having considered the complexity of the evidence for social differentiation *within* individual settlements, we will turn now to address the relationship *between* sites. It has often been argued that the Bronze Age sees the development of settlement hierarchies in many parts of

Europe (e.g. Kristiansen 1998: 111–12). At their apex were sites such as hill forts and other fortified settlements. The scale of some of these sites and their substantial defences mark them out from other settlements in the same regions: the Bullenheimer Berg in northern Bavaria (see Chapter 40), for example, is some 30 hectares in area (Diemer 1995). Hill forts were generally surrounded by one or more ditches and monumental ramparts of stone or of earth revetted by timber posts or planking. Such features represent a substantial investment of both resources and labour: the rampart at the Bullenheimer Berg is some 2.5 km long and it is worth considering whether structures such as this could be built through communal decision-making and

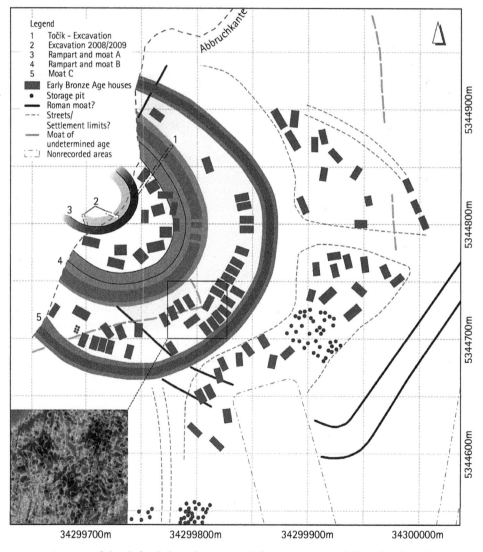

FIG. 5.5 Layout of the defended settlement at Fidvár, west central Slovakia, based on geophysical and walkover survey. Clusters of houses and the tentative location of roadways are shown.

Source: http://www.vfg.uni-wuerzburg.de/forschung/projekte/fidvar_near_vrable/.

reciprocal labour arrangements alone, or whether it implies the existence of an elite who could accumulate the necessary materials and support and mobilize a large workforce.

In addition to their size and form, some fortified sites have produced finds that suggest they controlled access to exotic materials and high-status objects. At Rathgall in County Wicklow over eighty glass beads were found, including a composite bead of gold and glass, along with other objects of gold, amber, and lignite (Raftery 1976). Hilltop settlements such as Crestaulta in Graubünden (Burkhard 1946) were strategically located overlooking rivers, indicating that they may have controlled trade routes, in this case through the Alps. Fortified sites were also often centres of craft production. The workshop area at Rathgall produced several thousand clay mould fragments for the casting of bronze objects such as swords and spearheads, while the large assemblage of pottery wasters excavated in the hill fort at Portal Vielh in Languedoc (Carozza 2000) indicates that the production of ceramics took place at this site. In addition, these sites appear to have played significant roles in other elements of the economy too. For example, the large number of pits at Bruszczewo in west-central Poland suggests centralized storage of agricultural produce (Czebreszuk and Müller 2004).

Together, this evidence can be interpreted in a number of ways. It suggests that hill forts and other fortified sites may have provided a range of specialist economic and defensive functions for their hinterlands, but it may also indicate restricted access to high-status objects and centralized control over both agricultural and craft production. In certain areas the geographical distribution of such sites is also indicative of an emerging tendency towards centralization. In south-west Slovakia, for example, it has been argued that the tributaries flowing into the River Danube each formed the focus for one or two territorial units comprising a hill fort and a large number of open sites; this suggests a settlement hierarchy of at least two tiers (Shennan 1982).

Although models like this are appealing, there is considerable evidence for regional and chronological variability in the size, form, and character of fortified sites. Although hill forts such as Thunau in north-east Austria were densely settled (Karwowski 2006), excavations at other sites, such as at Mooghaun in County Clare, Ireland, have produced few finds and little or no evidence for intensive occupation (Grogan 2005). In many regions fortified sites are entirely lacking. At Cahagnes, an open settlement in Normandy, an unusually large number of four-post structures, interpreted as raised granaries, were found (Jahier 2005), suggesting that centralized storage and control over agricultural production was not a feature of hill forts alone. Elsewhere, evidence for specialized craft activities is not concentrated in central places but is widely distributed, including on open settlements.

The House-Landscapes of Bronze Age Europe

In discussing Bronze Age settlements in Europe, it is clear that the data is regionally variable not only in quality but also in character. The character of settlements differs because of regional traditions in housing (visible in the variation in building materials and techniques as well as spatial layout) due to climate, farming practice, and social organization, among other things. The way communities were organized has a significant impact on the structure and distribution of settlements. We might call regions with similar architectural traditions and forms of settlement organization 'house-landscapes'. One such landscape is certainly constituted by the longhouses of the north-west European lowlands (Scandinavia, Schleswig-Holstein, north-west Germany, the Netherlands, northern Belgium, and the river valleys of north-eastern France) (see Fokkens 2003; 2009). In these regions mixed farming was practised, cattle were kept inside the house during winter and their dung was used to fertilize the fields. How the majority of the dead were treated is not clear everywhere, but some people were buried in barrows. There is much to suggest that monumental barrow structures were constructed to commemorate ancestors—as part of the regional identity of people and their sense of belonging to the land. Hoarding traditions in this area were comparable too: people used rivers, small lakes, bogs, moors, and other natural places to deposit selections of their valuables—probably valuables that they considered as having been gifts from the ancestors or the supernatural (Fontijn 2002).

In Britain, Ireland, and parts of western France a different house-landscape was present. Here, roundhouses dominated the landscape, organized in small groups or dispersed among the fields (Fig. 5.6). Nowhere is the settled Bronze Age landscape preserved in a more impressive way then on Dartmoor in south-west England. Here, preserved drystone field boundaries and hut foundations make the prehistoric landscape visible in a way that is unparalleled elsewhere in Europe (Fleming 2008). Though one may be tempted to think of these coaxial field systems—this goes for Bronze Age field systems elsewhere too—as the first evidence for private property, Andrew Fleming argues that these communities were organized in 'neighbourhood groups', possibly based on extended families who together worked and lived on the land (Fleming 2008: 153). This is comparable to what is visualized for the organization of the longhouse landscape in 'local communities' (Fokkens 1996; Gerritsen 2003)—groups of people who worked the same fields; shared neighbourhood obligations and resources such as harvesting, the building of houses, and the use of teams of oxen; buried their dead in the same cemetery; and honoured gods and ancestors in collective ceremonies at natural places. They did not necessarily live very close to each other, but felt connected through kinship and ancestral bonds.

In other upland areas of western and central Europe settlement patterns are more difficult to grasp for several reasons. In the first place, these areas are less densely occupied today and have not therefore been a focus for large-scale excavation. There are exceptions though, especially in the lake villages of southern Germany, Switzerland, and northern Italy. Here we find aggregated villages, sometimes surrounded by palisades, that have both a different organizational structure and something lacking from most settlements in north-west Europe: defences. This does not mean that warfare and raiding were not an issue in north-west Europe (they certainly were), but they seem to have had less of an impact on the organization of settlements. We might call this the village landscape, though that label may be a bit too general.

In southern and south-eastern Europe, too, fortified and aggregated sites are present. In the Balkans, tell sites exhibit a different type of community organization. Their deep stratigraphy indicates that these villages remained in place for centuries, perhaps because the population of these sites was big enough for continuity to be sustainable. There is a strong sense of social cohesion and community identity visible in the layout and fortification of tell sites, hinting that inter-group warfare may have had a greater influence on the character of settlement in this region than in, say, Britain or Scandinavia. It is far from clear, however, whether tell communities (or indeed the villages of the Alpine foreland) required the leadership of elite individuals; whatever the case, it is evident that the organization of Bronze Age communities in this area was very different to that in western and northern Europe.

FIG. 5.6 Houses, fields, and droveways characterise this highly organised Bronze Age landscape on Chagford Common, Dartmoor, south-west England.

Taken from original source material by permission of English Heritage, NMR.

Conclusion

There have been dramatic improvements in our understanding of Bronze Age settlement over the past two decades, particularly as a result of the increase in developer-funded excavation in advance of construction and infrastructural projects. In some areas there has already been a concerted effort to synthesize and interpret this wealth of new material, although elsewhere much remains unpublished. Nonetheless, both the discovery of new sites and the review and reinterpretation of older excavations continue to contribute important insights into the character and organization of Bronze Age settlements. The variability in architectural styles and settlement layout hints at considerable diversity in forms of kinship as well as in social relations both within and between households, and reminds us that the people, activities, and meanings associated with houses and settlements in the Bronze Age were doubtless very different from our own. Far from being places in which only the most mundane and unimportant tasks were carried out, however, settlements—and the economic, ritual, and political activities that took place in them—were central to the constitution of the Bronze Age social world.

Bibliography

Arnold, B. (1992). 'Villages du Bronze Final sur les rives d Lac de Neuchâtel', in C. Mordant and A. Richard (eds.), *L'Habitat et l'occupation du sol à l'Âge du Bronze en Europe*. Paris: éditions du Comité des Travaux Historiques et Scientifiques, 303–12.

Arnoldussen, S. (2008). *A Living Landscape: Bronze Age Settlements in the Dutch River Area (c.2000–800 BC)*. Leiden: Sidestone Press.

Artursson, M. (2010). 'Settlement structure and organisation', in T. Earle and K. Kristiansen (eds.), *Organizing Bronze Age Societies: The Mediterranean, Central Europe, and Scandanavia Compared*. Cambridge: Cambridge University Press, 87–121.

Bailey, D. W. (1990). 'The living house: signifying continuity', in R. Samson (ed.), *The Social Archaeology of Houses*. Edinburgh: Edinburgh University Press, 19–48.

Barrett, J., Bradley, R., and Green, M. (1991). *Landscape, Monuments, and Society: The Prehistory of Cranborne Chase*. Cambridge: Cambridge University Press.

Bátora, J., Eitel, B., Falkenstein, F., and Rassmann, K. (2008). 'Fidvár bei Vráble: eine befestigte Zentralsiedlung der Frühbronzezeit in der Slowakei', in J. Czebreszuk, S. Kadrow, and J. Müller (eds.), *Defensive Structures from Central Europe to the Aegean in the Third and Second Millennia BC*. Studien zur Archäologie in Ostmitteleuropa, 5. Poznań/Bonn: Wydawnictwo Poznańskie/Habelt, 97–107.

Bech, J.-H. (1997). 'Bronze Age settlements on raised sea-beds at Bjerre, Thy, NW-Jutland', in J. J. Assendorp (ed.), *Forschungen zur bronzezeitlichen Besiedlung in Nord- und Mitteleuropa. Internationales Symposium vom 09.–11. Mai 1996 in Hitzacker*. Internationale Archäologie, 38. Espelkamp: Verlag Marie Leidorf, 3–15.

Billamboz, A. and Torke, W. (1992). 'La Station Forschner dans la bassin du Federsee (Haute Souabe): un habitat palustre fortifié dans les premières phases de l'Âge du Bronze', in C. Mordant and A. Richard (eds.), *L'Habitat et l'occupation du sol à l'Âge du Bronze en Europe*. Paris: éditions du Comité des Travaux Historiques et Scientifiques, 377–82.

Billaud, Y. (2005). 'Traces fugaces et architectures de terre au Bronze final: le cas de Laprade (La Motte-du-Rhône, Vaucluse, TGV Méditerranée)', in O. Buchsenschutz and C. Mordant (eds.), *Architectures protohistoriques en Europe occidentale du Néolithique final à l'Âge du Fer, Actes du colloque de Nancy 2002*. Paris: Comité des Travaux Historiques et Scientifiques, 389–404.

Bourgeois, J. and Fontijn, D. (2008). 'Bronze Age houses and barrows in the Low Countries', in S. Arnoldussen and H. Fokkens (eds.), *Bronze Age Settlements in the Low Countries*. Oxford: Oxbow Books, 41–57.

Boyle, A. (2004). 'Worked bone assemblage', in A. Brossler, R. Early, and C. Allen (eds.), *Green Park (Reading Business Park). Phase 2 Excavations 1995*. Oxford: Oxford Archaeology, 99–100.

Boysen, A. and Andersen, S. W. (1983). 'Trappendal: barrow and house from the Early Bronze Age', *Journal of Danish Archaeology*, 2: 118–26.

Bradley, R. (1998). *The Significance of Monuments: On the Shaping of Human Experience in Neolithic and Bronze Age Europe*. London: Routledge.

Brück, J. (1995). 'A place for the dead: the role of human remains in Late Bronze Age Britain', *Proceedings of the Prehistoric Society*, 61: 245–77.

—— (1999). 'Houses, lifecycles and deposition on Middle Bronze Age settlements in southern England', *Proceedings of the Prehistoric Society*, 65: 145–66.

—— (2006). 'Fragmentation, personhood and the social construction of technology in Middle and Late Bronze Age Britain', *Cambridge Archaeological Journal*, 16/3: 297–315.

Burkhard, W. (1946). *Crestaulta: eine bronzezeitliche Hügelsiedlung bei Surin im Lugnez.* Monographien zur Ur- und Frühgeschichte der Schweiz, 5. Basel: Verlag Birkhäuser.

Burstow, G. P. and Holleyman, G. A. (1957). 'A Late Bronze Age settlement on Itford Hill, Sussex', *Proceedings of the Prehistoric Society*, 23: 167–212.

Carozza, L. (2000). Les Habitats du Bronze Final du Portal Vielh à Vendres, *Bulletin de la Société Préhistorique Française*, 97/4: 573–81.

Conway, M., Gahan, A., and Rathbone, S. (2005). 'Corrstown: a large Middle Bronze Age village', *Current Archaeology*, 195: 120–3.

Csányi, M. and Stanczik, I. (1992). 'Tiszaug-Kéménytető', in W. Meier-Arendt (ed.), *Bronzezeit in Ungarn. Forschungen in Tellsiedlungen an Donau und Theiss*. Frankfurt am Main: Museum für Vor- und Frühgeschichte, 115–19.

Csányi, M. and Tárnoki, J. (2003). 'The Middle Bronze Age population of the Berettyó-Körös region: the Gyulavarsánd culture', in Z. Visy (ed.), *Hungarian Archaeology at the Turn of the Millennium*. Budapest: Ministry of National Cultural Heritage, 145–8.

Czebreszuk, J. and Müller, J. (eds.) (2004). *Bruszczewo 1: Ausgrabungen und Forschungen in einer prähistorischen Siedlungskammer Grosspolens. Forschungsstand—erste Ergebnisse—das östliche Feuchtbodenareal.* Studien zur Archäologie in Ostmitteleuropa, 2. Kiel: Verlag Marie Leidorf.

Daumas, J.-C. and Laudet, R. (1992). 'Les Gandus à Saint-Ferréol-Trente-Pas (Drôme): un habitat de pente original', in C. Mordant and A. Richard (eds.), *L'Habitat et l'occupation du sol à l'Âge du Bronze en Europe*. Paris: éditions du Comité des Travaux Historiques et Scientifiques, 269–78.

David El-Biali, M. (1992). 'L'Habitat à l'âge du Bronze en Suisse: tentative de synthèse', in C. Mordant and A. Richard (eds.), *L'Habitat et l'occupation du sol à l'Âge du Bronze en Europe*. Paris: éditions du Comité des Travaux Historiques et Scientifiques, 359–76.

Diemer, G. (1995). *Der Bullenheimer Berg und seine Stellung im Siedlungsgefüge der Urnenfelderkultur Mainfrankens*. Materialhefte zur Bayerischen Vorgeschichte, A 70. Kallmünz/Opf: M. Lassleben.

Doody, M. (2008). *The Ballyhoura Hills Project*. Bray: Wordwell.

Earle, T. and Kolb, M. (2010). 'Regional settlement patterns', in T. Earle and K. Kristiansen (eds.), *Organizing Bronze Age Societies: The Mediterranean, Central Europe, and Scandinavia Compared*. Cambridge: Cambridge University Press, 57–86.

Fleming, A. (2008). *The Dartmoor Reaves: Investigating Prehistoric Land Divisions*. London: Batsford.

Fokkens, H. (1996). 'The Maaskant project: continuity and change of a regional research project', *Archaeological Dialogues*, 3: 197–215.

—— (1999). 'Cattle and martiality: changing relations between man and landscape in the Late Neolithic and the Bronze Age', in C. Fabech and J. Ringtved (eds.), *Settlement and Landscape: Proceedings of a Conference in Århus, Denmark, May 4-7 1998*. Aarhus: Aarhus University Press/Jutland Archaeological Society, 31–8.

—— (2003). 'The longhouse as a central element in Bronze Age daily life', in J. Bourgeois, I. Bourgeois, and B. Charetté (eds.), *Bronze Age and Iron Age Communities in North-Western Europe*. Brussels: Koninklijke Vlaamse Academie van Belgie voor Wetenschappen en Kunsten, 9–38.

—— (2005). 'Longhouses in unsettled settlements in the Beaker period and Bronze Age', in L. P. Louwe Kooijmans, P. W. v. d. Broeke, H. Fokkens, and A. L. van Gijn (eds.), *The Prehistory of the Netherlands*. Amsterdam: Amsterdam University Press, 407–28.

—— (2009). 'Die Wirtschaft der Nordischen Bronzezeit: mehr als Getreide sähen und Vieh züchten', in M. Bartelheim and H. Staüble (eds.), *Wirtschaftlichen Grundlagen der Bronzezeit Europas*. Rahden/Westf.: Marie Leidorf, 85–104.

—— and Arnoldussen, S. (2008). 'Towards new models', in S. Arnoldussen and H. Fokkens (eds.), *Bronze Age Settlements in the Low Countries*. Oxford: Oxbow Books, 1–16.

Fontijn, D. R. (2002). 'Sacrificial landscapes: cultural biographies of persons, objects and "natural" places in the Bronze Age of the southern Netherlands, c.2300–600 BC', *Analecta Praehistorica Leidensia*, 33/34: 1–392.

Gebers, W. (1997). 'Die jungbronzezeitlichen Häuser von Ochtmissen. Fundstelle 33, Stadt Lüneburg. Bautyp und functionale Aspekte der Innengliederung der Häuser von typ Ochtmissen', in J. J. Assendorp (ed.), *Forschungen zur bronzezeitlichen Besiedlung in Nord- und Mitteleuropa*, Internationale Archäologie, 38. Leopoldshöhe: Marie Leidorf, 60–74.

Gerritsen, F. A. (ed.) (2003). *Local Identities: Landscape and Community in the Late Prehistoric Meuse-Demer-Scheldt Region*, Amsterdam Archaeological Studies. Amsterdam: Amsterdam University Press.

Grogan, E. (2005). *The North Munster Project*, vol. 1. Bray: Wordwell Books.

Hugh-Jones, C. (1996). 'Houses in the Neolithic imagination: an Amazonian example', in T. Darvill and J. Thomas (eds.), *Neolithic Houses in Northwest Europe and Beyond. Neolithic Studies Group Seminar Papers 1*, Oxbow Monographs, 57. Oxford: Oxbow Books, 185–93.

IJzereef, G. F. (1988). 'Boeren in de Bronstijd bij Bovenkarspel', *Spiegel Historiael*, 18: 635–43.

Jahier, I. (2005). 'Le Village de Cahagnes (Calvados)', in C. Marcigny, C. Colonna, E. Ghesquière, and G. Verron (eds.), *La Normandie à l'aube de l'histoire: les découvertes archéologiques de l'âge du Bronze, 2300–800 av J-C*. Paris: Somogy Éditions d'Art, 50–1.

Karwowski, M. (2006). *Thunau am Kamp: eine befestigte Höhensiedlung (Grabung 1965–1990)*. Vienna: Verlag der Österreichischen Akademie der Wissenschaften.

Kooi, P. B. (2008). 'Bronze Age settlements in Drenthe', in S. Arnoldussen and H. Fokkens (eds.), *Bronze Age Settlements in the Low Countries*. Oxford: Oxbow Books, 59–68.

Kristiansen, K. (1998). *Europe before History*. Cambridge: Cambridge University Press.

Kristiansen, K. and Larsson, T. (2005). *The Rise of Bronze Age Society: Travels, Transmissions and Transformations*. Cambridge: Cambridge University Press.

Lauermann, E. (2003). *Studien zur Aunjetitz-Kultur im nördlichen Niederösterreich*. Bonn: Habelt.

Livadie, C. A., Castaldo, E., Castaldo, N., and Vecchio, G. (2005). 'Sur l'Architecture des cabanes du Bronze ancien final de Nola (Naples-Italie)', in O. Buchsenschutz and C. Mordant (eds.), *Architectures protohistoriques en Europe occidentale du Néolithique final à l'Âge du Fer*. Paris: Comité des Travaux Historiques et Scientifiques, 487–512.

McConnell, B. (1992). 'The Early Bronze Age village of La Muculufa and prehistoric hut architecture in Sicily', *American Journal of Archaeology*, 96/1: 23–44.

McQuade, M., Molloy, B., and Moriarty, C. (2009). *In the Shadow of the Galtees: Archaeological Excavations along the N8 Cashel to Mitchelstown Road Scheme*. Dublin: National Roads Authority.

Moore, J. and Jennings, D. (1992). *Reading Business Park: A Bronze Age Landscape*. Oxford: Oxford University Committee for Archaeology/Oxford Archaeological Unit.

Netting, R., Wilk, R., and Arnould, E. (eds.) (1984). *Households: Comparative and Historical Studies of the Domestic Group*. Berkeley: University of California Press.

Nowakowski, J. (1991). 'Trethellan Farm, Newquay: the excavation of a lowland Bronze Age settlement and Iron Age cemetery', *Cornish Archaeology*, 30: 5–242.

Parker Pearson, M., and Richards, C. (1994). 'Ordering the world: perceptions of architecture, space and time', in M. Parker Pearson and C. Richards (eds.), *Architecture and Order: Approaches to Social Space*. London: Routledge, 1–37.

——, Marshall, P., Mulville, J., and Smith, H. (n.d.). *The Prehistoric Village at Cladh Hallan—Part III*. Accessed online 31 August 2011 at http://www.sheffield.ac.uk/archaeology/research/cladh-hallan/cladh-hallan03.html.

Raftery, B. (1976). 'Rathgall and Irish hillfort problems', in D. W. Harding (ed.), *Hillforts: Later Prehistoric Earthworks in Britain and Ireland*. London: Academic Press, 339–57.

Rageth, J. (1986). 'Die wichtigsten Resultate der Ausgrabungen in der bronzezeitlichen Siedlung auf dem Padnal bei Savognin (Oberhalbstein GR)', *Jahrbuch der Schweizerischen Gesellschaft für Ur- und Frühgeschichte*, 69: 63–103.

Roymans, N. and Fokkens, H. (1991). 'Een overzicht van veertig jaar nederzettingsonderzoek', in H. Fokkens and N. Roymans (eds.), *Nederzettingen uit de bronstijd en de vroege ijzertijd in de Lage Landen*. Nederlandse Archaeologische Rapporten, 13. Amersfoort: Rijksdienst voor het Oudheidkundig Bodemonderzoek, 1–20.

Schöbel, G. (1996). *Die Spätbronzezeit am nordwestlichen Bodensee. Taucharchäologische Untersuchungen in Hagnau und Unteruhldingen 1982–1989*. Siedlungsarchäologie im Alpenvorland, IV. Stuttgart: Theiss.

Schubart, H., Pingel, V., and Arteaga, O. (2001). *Fuente Álamo. Teil 1. Die Grabungen von 1977 bis 1991 in einer bronzezeitlichen Höhensiedlung Andalusiens*, Madrider Beiträge, 25. Mainz: Von Zabern.

Shennan, S. (1982). 'From minimal to moderate ranking', in C. Renfrew and S. Shennan (eds.), *Ranking, Resource and Exchange: Aspects of the Archaeology of Early European Society*. Cambridge: Cambridge University Press, 27–31.

Sørensen, M. L. S. (2010). 'Households', in T. Earle and K. Kristiansen (eds.), *Organizing Bronze Age Societies: The Mediterranean, Central Europe, and Scandinavia Compared*. Cambridge: Cambridge University Press, 122–54.

Stäuble, H. and Campen, I. (1998). 'Bronzezeitliche Siedlungsmuster. Die Ausgrabungen im Vorfeld des Braunkohletagebaus Zwenkau, Lkr. Leipziger Land', in B. Hänsel (ed.), *Mensch und Umwelt in der Bronzezeit Europas*. Kiel: Oetker-Voges Verlag, 525–30.

Strahl, E. (2005). 'Die jungbronzezeitliche Siedlung Rodenkirchen-Hahnenknooper Mühle, Ldkr. Wesermarsch—Erste Bauern in der deutschen Marsch', in C. Endlich and P. Kremer (eds.), *Kulturlandschaft Marsch. Natur, Geschichte, Gegenwart*. Schriftenreihe des Landesmuseums für Natur und Mensch, 33. Oldenburg: Landesmuseums für Natur und Mensch: 52–9.

Tárnoki, J. (2003). 'The expansion of the Hatvan culture', in Z. Visy (ed.), *Hungarian Archaeology at the Turn of the Millennium*. Budapest: Ministry of National Cultural Heritage, 145–8.

Ullén, I. (1994). 'The power of case studies: interpretation of a Late Bronze Age settlement in central Sweden', *Journal of European Archaeology*, 2/2: 249–62.

Waterbolk, H. T. (1964). 'The Bronze Age settlement of Elp', *Helinium*, 4: 97–131.

Waterson, R. (1990). *The Living House: An Anthropology of Architecture in South-East Asia*. Oxford: Oxford University Press.

Zimmermann, W. H. (1999). 'Why was cattle-stalling introduced in prehistory? The significance of byre and stable and of outwintering', in C. Fabech and J. Ringtved (eds.), *Settlement and Landscape. Proceedings of a Conference in Århus, Denmark, May 4–7 1998*. Aarhus: Jutland Archaeological Society, 301–18.

CHAPTER 6

BURIALS

MADS KÄHLER HOLST

Introduction

The study of burials has a long and prominent tradition in the research of the European Bronze Age. Barrows and other forms of monumental burial have acquired a particularly central position in early antiquarianism, being easily identifiable in the landscape and reliable providers of artefacts. The significance of burials was furthered by the fact that they provided both closed contexts and stratigraphical observations, which allowed temporal ordering (Worsaae 1843). In this way, the material recovered from burials became the core of early collections, and from the nineteenth century onwards they formed the basis for the definition of the Bronze Age, the development of the first chronological schemes, and the isolation of various cultural traditions.

Since then, there has been an ongoing development in methods, in the corpus of excavated burials, and in theoretical awareness, which has extended the domains of the past where we consider the burials relevant. In this way, burials have over time come to play a central role in the study of demography, kinship structures, social groups and identities, ritual and religion, symbolism, and past comprehensions of history (Parker Pearson 1999). Implied in the thematic extension is the recognition that burials constitute an intricate phenomenon with many interwoven motives and practices. This complexity both complicates the understanding of burials and extends the interpretative possibilities, which has given rise to very varied evaluations of the quality of burials as a source; the differences reflect varying confidence in our ability to disentangle the complexity and convincingly identify the various motives, their effects and relations.

We may distinguish between two main approaches to handling the interpretative problem in the study of burials in recent years. One focuses on the complex burial entities, such as large and detailed investigated monumental burials and groups of burials, often with incorporation of their landscape and settlement setting. Here the complexity of the archaeological context corresponds to the complexity of burial in the past. This allows detailed reconstructions of the sequence of different actions and their relations, which forms the basis for discursive interpretations of the burial events and the motives involved. The other approach focuses on comprehensive records, assumed to be representative, which through classification permit detailed statistical analyses and thereby the revelation of detailed and multivariate structures in the burial record, which may then be related to different domains and motives of the past.

The study of burials has, not least in recent years, benefited from a considerable methodological development. The expanded opportunities offered by the archaeological sciences have offered a new level of detail in the study of individual burials. This applies to the characterization of the buried individual through a range of isotope analyses indicating diet and migrations. Burial practices have also obtained new levels of detail through, for instance, microstratigraphical analyses and scientific soil analysis, while at the same time geophysical prospecting and remote sensing techniques have improved the possibilities of obtaining more complete overviews of the larger burial contexts.

Most European countries have also experienced a transformation in excavation practices, through the introduction of developer-led archaeology. As regards burial research, however, the effects vary considerably. In some regions it has sparked a new focus on burials, and provided comprehensive records with links between settlement and burials, whereas in other areas it appears to have transferred attention away from the burial record.

The expanding material, analytical possibilities, and theoretical approaches, together with the considerable geographical variation in burial and research traditions, have created a multitude of different themes in burial research. Consequently, a coherent research profile does not exist. Still, a common overall awareness appears to have formed, that the burials are not only a reflection of life beyond the burial, but also an expression of a particular part of life. The burials constituted a specific domain in the Bronze Age world. They were social occasions, which provided a scene and an opportunity for the execution of very specific acts within very specific norms. The detailed understanding of this scene in its own right is the precondition for any further interpretations involving the burial record.

Bronze Age Burial Traditions

Bronze Age burials constitute a very varied collection of material. It spans a range from elaborate monuments to an apparently careless disposal of the dead; there are varying degrees of demarcation of the individual; there is a wide range of different accompanying activities; the spatial arrangement of burials varies; and so on (Harding 2000: 73–123). Some of the variation is chronological and geographical. Among this variation a number of large-scale trends can be discerned in the burial record of the European Bronze Age. The most widespread is probably the Tumulus phenomenon, in which barrow burials emerge, re-emerge, or intensify markedly and apparently rather suddenly over large parts of central and northern Europe in the Middle Bronze Age, with possible relations to an older east European tradition. In the Late Bronze Age there develops the spread of the cremation rite, which in many places was accompanied by a new form of cemetery tradition. Other large-scale traditions may be discerned, such as an Early Bronze Age west European barrow tradition, which apparently had very limited connection to the Tumulus culture. To varying degrees these trends in the burial ritual were also accompanied by similarities in the repertoires of artefact depositions in the burials.

Over the years, and first and foremost in the culture-historical research tradition, these trends have been assigned great importance in the formation of the European Bronze Age. They have been seen as the indications of extensive migrations of peoples, spread of religious ideas and social ideology, or establishment of various forms of networks. To some degree these overall trends, and not least the attempts at explaining them, have, however, receded somewhat into the background with a few notable exceptions (e.g. Kristiansen 1998). Part of the reason is a theoretical critique of the grand narratives implied in the focus on overall trends. Another part springs from the increased detail in the excavations, which has demonstrated that when focus is directed beyond the immediate similarity of the general burial form, a considerable variation appears. In mortuary rituals, architecture, use patterns, and spatial organization there are significant regional differences and often also a considerable contemporary variation within the local area. Furthermore, the representativity of the overall trends can be questioned. In most regions fluctuations between periods of relatively standardized burial customs and times of considerable local variation can be recognized. The barrows, for instance, can in some regions be demonstrated to represent short-lived intense bursts of monument construction with a more diverse burial practice outside these periods, and even in the most intense mound-building periods probably only a small segment of the population had a barrow erected over them. Both the burial practice and the social implications of the barrows in this way must have changed significantly over time.

In connection with the cremation tradition, a very gradual adaptation can be demonstrated in many areas, with a slow and successive abandonment of the various characteristics of the preceding inhumation tradition. It can be illustrated by the well-preserved Hvidegård burial from the introduction of the cremation burial tradition in period III (1300–1100 BC) in Zealand, Denmark (Fig. 6.1, right). Here a careful transfer and placement of the burnt bones into a stone coffin and subsequent deposition of artefacts appears to follow in detail the procedures of body treatment observable in the well-preserved log-coffin inhumations of the preceding period II (1500–1300 BC). This gradual transition to the cremation tradition has been seen as an indication of a vaguely defined meaning content and a negotiable ritual practice (Sørensen and Rebay 2007). One may compare this sequence to that of the preceding period II, when inhumation was the norm, as at Borum Eshøj (Fig. 6.1, left).

Beyond the burials, it is also becoming increasingly clear that the overall trends in burial custom extend over very considerable differences in settlement organization, economy, social structure, iconography, and ritual practice. This suggests that the overall burial trends were integrated into very different social and religious contexts, which again causes one to question a unifying interpretation of their meaning and implications.

The overall trends in burial custom in this way appear to represent some very general aspects of practices and meanings adapted to local contexts. There does, however, appear to be an element of correlation over large distances and over some time, which would suggest underlying maintained contacts, and probably supported by a general identification of similarity in the burial custom.

The relation between the overall trends and the underlying variation and dynamics of the burial record may capture another very significant element of Bronze Age burial custom. Often there appears to be a considerable adaptability, where new and foreign elements could be accepted into new contexts, apparently with relative ease. A number of special burial phenomena in this way have very dispersed distributions over areas with otherwise very different burial practices. The ship-setting burials in northern Europe may be an example of this. They are found distributed over large parts of Scandinavia and northern Germany in the Middle to Late

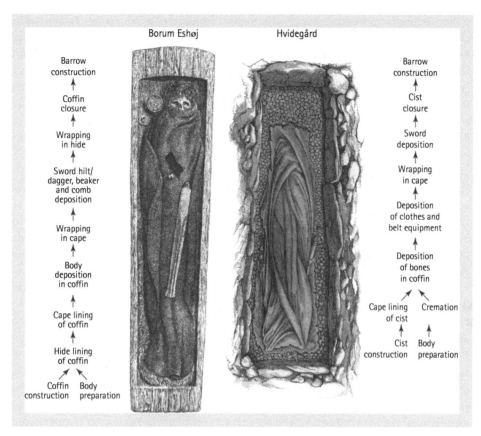

FIG. 6.1 The well-preserved oak-log coffin inhumation burial of Borum Eshøj, Jutland, from 1500–1300 BC and the Hvidegård cremation burial from Sjælland, period III, 1300–1100 BC.

Source: Boye 1896; Herbst 1848.

Bronze Age, but everywhere as a rare occurrence and often combined with burial practices specific to the local region (Artelius 1996; Capelle 1986). Similarly, very specific constructional elements in barrows such as radial posts and wicker constructions have been identified from the great Late Bronze Age barrow at Lusehøj, Denmark, to the Ha C barrow of Magdalenenberg, southern Germany, though apparently in both contexts as an exceptional feature and combined with local barrow-construction practices and patterns of use (Spindler 1972; Thrane 1984). And as a final example, at Hüsby, Schleswig, northern Germany, a 40 m long row of four post structures closely resembling structures found at barrows in Lower Saxony and the Netherlands were uncovered at a fifteenth-century BC barrow, which in every other respect complied closely with the Nordic Bronze Age burial custom (Freudenberg 2009).

These examples convey the impression that the burial practices, at least sometimes, constituted a form of melting pot, where otherwise very distant or exceptional elements, occasionally also from significantly different burial practices, could be integrated within an existing burial ritual. Interestingly enough, it applies both to the structure of rituals as indicated by the Hüsby example, to constructional elements as in the Lusehøj and Magdalenenberg examples, and to elements that are normally assigned significant symbolic meaning, such as the ship setting.

Archaeologically, we are primarily able to identify adaptations of new ideas when they are clearly foreign. Adaptations well represent a process that was even more active at the local level. The burial event, in this way, appears to have been a relatively open forum, which allowed the introduction of foreign elements. This dynamic may also imply that the meaning of specific symbols and actions varied considerably from place to place, depending on the local context into which they were incorporated. There was consequently room for a considerable element of innovation in burial practices. In addition, in most regions there may have been a broad range of alternative practices rather than well-defined prescribed rituals with a clear exposition.

It should be emphasized that the variation and adaptability of the burial custom appear to change considerably over time and from region to region. The Urnfield burials, for instance, generally leave an impression of standardization, which may indicate that both ideas and ritual practice were more conforming than, for example, the inhumation burials in the Middle Bronze Age (Kristiansen 1998: 113). This may point towards differences in the underlying structure of not only the burial activities but also religion in general, with a better-defined and fixed set of conceptions emerging in the Late Bronze Age.

Still, even within the Urnfield tradition, the impression of standardization may in part be due to the obliterating effects of the fire and a widespread norm of limited grave-good deposition beyond a few very elaborate burials. When considered in more detail, indications of variation and regional differences also appear here (Sørensen and Rebay-Salisbury 2008; Roymans and Kortlang 1999). The transition to cremation was not complete, as exemplified in Przeczyce, southern Poland, where about one-sixth of the burials remained inhumations (Szydłowska 1968). At several cemeteries there are also different forms of assumed ritual structure, which suggest varied but elusive rituals in the time before the urn deposition, and detailed analyses of cremation burials also demonstrate larger variation in cremation practices than previously assumed (McKinley 1997). In Scandinavia and the British Isles the large-scale cemetery tradition never caught on, and concentrations of more than thirty burials are a rare occurrence; thus these areas are not generally included in the Urnfield tradition.

In conclusion, geographically widespread burial traditions appear to be a significant characteristic of the Bronze Age when considered from an overall perspective, and these traditions may be one of the primary reasons for studying the burials on a European scale. However, it appears to be equally characteristic that when the individual burials representing these trends are approached in detail, the overall similarities slip away and local variation takes over. The impression of common ideas and cultural rules, and in some respects our understanding of what the overall trends represent, may be said to have become more uncertain and disputed than they appeared just a few decades ago. Thus the overall pan-European burial traditions are perhaps better considered a result of a general relatedness, rather than a common idea.

Individuals and their Artefacts

The identity of the buried individuals is an inevitable issue in burial analyses. The detail with which the identity can be approached varies considerably from burial to burial, depending on both prehistoric differences in burial custom and preservation. Preservation is particularly decisive for the applicability of the ever-growing range of scientific techniques available to reveal various aspects of the life and health of the buried individuals. This applies to the refined anthropological analysis of the skeletal remains, $^{13}C/^{12}C$, $^{15}N/^{14}N$, $^{34}S/^{32}S$, $^{87}Sr/^{86}Sr$ isotope analyses demonstrating diet and mobility, and in the future aDNA may be expected also to come to play a more prominent role. The aspects of the person revealed through these analyses can be considered a relatively unmanipulated imprint of the life of the individual in contrast to the more deliberate expressions in, for instance, the artefact assemblages.

Interpretation of the artefact assemblages in the burials and their references to the dead individual constitute one of the longest-running traditions in Bronze Age burial research. The artefacts have been seen as mirroring a wide range of different properties, from cultural and racial affiliation to social roles and personal histories, including long-distance contact networks reflected in the provenance of imported artefacts, as well as historical references reflected in the biographies of the individual artefacts. The emphasis has generally been on the artefacts as a deliberate expression of some form of identity, which could either be the one perceived by the burying community or by the dead while living, and passed on to the burial by the bereaved. A number of significant reservations about the direct association of the artefacts with a personal identity have, however, been presented over the years, and there is today a widespread awareness that other motives often enter significantly into artefact composition. While the reservations may be generally relevant, they are particularly obvious in some contexts, such as at collective burials, where the identity of the burial community emerges at least as strongly as the identity of the individual. Another example may be the *überausstattete* (over-equipped) burials (Hansen 2005). The term refers to a contrast between the general pattern of composing the artefact assemblages in the individual burial without functional or typological redundancy, and a small group of burials where there is a seemingly almost demonstrative deposition of multiple functionally identical artefacts within a single burial context. The most distinct examples are probably the Early Bronze Age Únětice burials. Here several alternatives to an expression of personal identity are revealed in the reading of the artefact composition (Sørensen 2004).

From an overall perspective the artefact assemblages of the Bronze Age burials are often highly standardized within large regions. In by far the largest number of cases, the artefacts were selected from a limited range of artefact types and functional domains, such as costume accessories, ornaments, toilet equipment, containers, and weapons. When organic matter is preserved, this range obviously extends and there is an increased variation, but still the overall impression of standardization remains. In this respect, there is a strong normativity in the composition of artefact assemblages. The standardization in the burials contrasts with the considerable variation observable in many other aspects of material culture and society, such as mortuary rituals and architecture, settlement organization, and economy. The standardized burial equipment in this way appears first and foremost to express widespread and generalized ideals of overall social roles. Among these roles, gender distinction particularly stands out (Sørensen 1997; Treherne 1995). The way this distinction is expressed varies over time and space, but throughout the Bronze Age it remains a dominant structure in the variation of artefact assemblages throughout the great majority of regions of Europe, and it is also reflected in burial practices and architecture. There are, for instance, often clear differences in the relative proportion of men and women in cremation versus inhumation burials in those periods and regions where both customs were present, and in barrow burials versus flat inhumations. Particularly in the Early Bronze Age, gender is also reflected in large parts of north, east, and central Europe in the orientation of the buried individual, probably as a continuation of a Corded Ware tradition (Häusler 1994).

Variation beyond the gender distinction has been interpreted as an indication of various social roles and capabilities. Some of the interpretations have implied highly institutionalized roles such as hereditary political leaders or chiefs, warriors, craftsmen, and priests (Kristiansen 1984). The identification of these roles primarily relies on a form of emblematic interpretation of the artefacts, where different artefact types or combinations are assumed to represent specific roles, the most obvious example being the sword as indicator of the warrior role. It is, however, worth noticing that the roles rarely stand out as discrete groups in the analyses of artefact combinations. Here fluent transitions between different combinations are revealed, which has led to an alternative interpretation of the artefact variation as some form of more subtle wealth differentiation, either in economic or in social capital (Johansen, Laursen, and Holst 2004).

Burial in a barrow is another element that has been seen as a reflection of a particular form of status and the reuse of the monuments as referring to some form of kinship reckoning, real or postulated. The very considerable fluctuations in intensity in barrow construction, however, mean that there must have been significant redefinitions of the social implications of barrow burial over time.

A different approach to the past perception of the identity of the buried individual refers to the treatment of the dead person's body. There appear to be very varied attitudes towards the integrity of the body through the Bronze Age. The well-preserved oak-log coffins of Denmark and northern Germany are thought to be the result of very deliberate attempts at protecting the integrity of the body (Holst, Breuning-Madsen, and Rasmussen 2001). The carefully layered wrappings of the body in clothes and skins, nested coffins, and occasionally seaweed packings, as well as layered and packed constructions of the covering barrow structure, demonstrate an extensive care for the body, which occasionally entailed a long-term preserving effect (Breuning-Madsen et al. 2003). Cases of mummification have been documented in Scotland (Parker Pearson et al. 2005), and the integration of jar burials in the Early Bronze Age Argaric houses of southern Spain would also appear to reflect some form of deliberate maintenance and association of identity with the remains of the body (Lull 2000).

In contrast, cremation burials and various forms of disarticulated burial constitute a rather efficient obliteration of the body, and occasionally the cremation practices appear to have entailed deliberate dispersals or blending of the bones of several individuals, which have led to the suggestion that they may reflect another form of perception of personhood (Brück 2006).

The studies of the treatment of the dead and the attitude towards the body may in this way provide an alternative approach to the identity of the buried individuals, compared to the studies of artefact assemblages and the various natural scientific analyses of the skeletal material. The treatment of the dead may at first appear to express rather general ideas about death and the perception of the individual, or various forms of collective identities. However, when studied in more detail, the burial practices may provide insight into basic principles of identity formation in the Bronze Age.

The Burial as Event: Activities, Sequences, and Meetings

The burial was generally a collective event, which implied a structured gathering of persons and an organized sequence of activities. There has in recent years been an increasing awareness that the character of these events is essential for the understanding of the burial (Oestigaard and Goldhahn 2006). The assembly of people and the latent cosmological connotations made the forum of the burial an obvious scene for attuning knowledge and ideas about burial. In this way the burial was not only an expression of well-established and fixed conceptions but also a potential place of shaping them. It may even be likely that the burials were the primary forum of maintaining the knowledge associated with death and disposal of the dead, passed on to others through mutual participation in burial activities.

Similarly, the organization of the occasion established a particular social structure, which could both draw on well-established social relations in the world beyond the burial event and elaborate and reshape them in the specific setting of the burial itself (Barrett 1994). The social expressions recognized in the burial context must consequently be considered dependent on the particular character of the burial event, and a consideration of their relation to other domains of the Bronze Age world relies on a detailed understanding of the particular social structure of that event.

The focus upon the event dimension of the burials has also drawn attention to the fact that mortuary rituals may be prolonged and multi-staged. Often there appear to have been comprehensive and repeated ritual activities extending beyond the actual burial. This can be an indication of the complexity of the mortuary practices, but it also reflects that burial areas and monuments occasionally served as focal points for other ritual activities and religious events than just mortuary-related and commemorative practices in a strict sense. In some instances, perhaps most notably in connection with the British henge monuments, the causality appears to be the other way around. Here burials are often incorporated into existing ritual assembly sites (Bradley 1998: 132–46). In both instances, the ancestral link was probably significant, but the connection could also have been more abstract, with previous activities conveying a symbolic significance on the place, which was then maintained and elaborated by further activities developing a complex narrative. The maintaining function may also have applied to knowledge as to the identity of the buried individuals, which would have been particularly relevant at some of the monuments that were used for burials with very long time intervals, and where a practice of remembrance was required, as for instance at some of the barrows.

The study of the burial event presupposes a detailed insight into sequences of activities. As regards methods, this makes the identification of time a primary objective. This applies to the overall chronology of the various identifiable events at a site, which may provide ideas on patterns of use, durability, and possible relations between the different parts of the whole. These patterns may in turn be related to (for instance) different forms of commemorative behaviour and community definition. However, for an understanding of the individual event at a burial, overall chronological dating only very rarely provides sufficient precision. Instead, relative chronological analysis becomes central. Through the identification of stratigraphical relations and various indications of temporal distance, such as vegetation horizons, erosion and soil-forming processes, an impression of the relative sequence of activities can, under fortunate circumstances, be reconstructed in considerable detail.

The identification and interpretation of the relative chronological indications often rely on interdisciplinary cooperation with environmental sciences and soil micromorphology, and presupposes detailed and complex recording. In addition to the altered theoretical focus, the increased attention to the sequence of activities at the burials thus also reflects a methodological development, which has allowed a higher resolution in our reconstruction of burial events.

The excavation of the great barrow of Skelhøj in southern Jutland, Denmark, may exemplify the level of detail obtainable through the relative-chronological analysis of the sequence of activities, and some of the interpretative possibilities. The barrow is dated to the fourteenth century BC and falls within a period of intense barrow construction as a northern branch of the Tumulus culture phenomenon. Like almost all barrows from this period in southern Scandinavia, Skelhøj was constructed of grass sods (turves), which were still recognizable upon excavation. In addition the sods had been procured from different areas with varying soil characteristics. This allowed a detailed reconstruction of the building sequence. The entire barrow had been erected in one complex and continuous sequence, springing from the interment of a male in a coffin covered by a stone packing at the centre of the barrow-to-be. From the onset, the site was radially divided into eight equally sized segments marked by large stones, in what was later to become the kerbstone demarcation of the completed barrow (Fig. 6.2). In this way an eight-spoked wheel structure, with strong references to the cosmological iconography of the period, was laid down over the construction. The partitioning served as a division of the builders into separate work groups, with the sod for each segment being procured in a different part of the landscape, and with small systematic differences in the otherwise very regulated building principles between each radial segment of the barrow. The teams appear to have been strictly separated throughout the construction, each with their own pathways and ramps up into the barrow. However, their actions were parallel and they followed the same overall plan. Through a series of successive enlargements of an initial small domed mound around the burial, the barrow gradually reached its final dimensions of 31 m in diameter and 7 m in height (Holst, Rasmussen, and Breuning-Madsen 2004).

The sequence of construction at Skelhøj points towards a carefully planned and rigidly structured effort. The initial demarcation of the barrow indicates a preconceived clear idea about the size and shape of the completed monument. The implementation of the spoked-wheel structure as organizing principle conveys a symbolic significance onto the entire construction work. It emphasizes the construction of the barrow as an integrated part of the burial ritual, and it suggests a strong moral obligation to comply with the initially established organization of the segregated work group. The strict separation of these groups and their individual building techniques further suggest a reference to groups existing outside the barrow event, and in this way hint at the role of the barrow burial and construction as a form of integrated assembly place within a highly formalized setting.

The focus on the event adds a number of aspects to our understanding of the burials. It entails a shift in attention from the buried individual to the participants in the burial, and by elucidating the scale and particular social structure of the burial event, it qualifies the interpretation of implications behind, for instance, the artefact depositions in the burials. Focus on the event also contributes to a characterization of the rituals, such as their complexity and degree of formalization, as well as possibly providing ideas about the relationship between the preconceived plan and adaptability to new ideas. Finally, the analysis of the sequence of

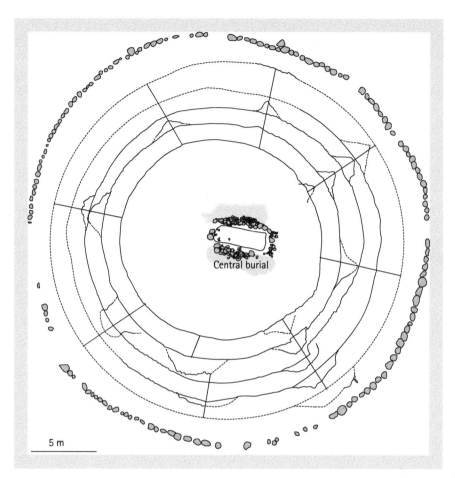

FIG. 6.2 Plan of the Early Bronze Age great barrow Skelhøj in Southern Denmark. The radial lines indicate the segmentary division of the barrow presumably corresponding to different building teams. The concentric circles indicate the building stages in the building sequence, and the irregular bulges on the circles are the approach slopes identified.

Source: author.

activities gives us an idea of the durability both of the individual events and the cemetery or monument context, as well as maybe revealing continuity and discontinuity. This is a basic requirement for understanding the community aspect of the burials and the historicity of the society, among other things.

A final perspective on the burial as a social occasion concerns the large-scale shifts in burial traditions through the Bronze Age. It seems evident that both the character of the event and the mode of social engagement at the burial were significantly transformed. In this respect, the large-scale shifts may be seen as redefinitions of basic principles in the network both of burial participation and knowledge of such events. This may in itself be a significant element in understanding the cause and course of these transformations, in addition to theories about ideological, religious, and other underlying social incentives (Vander Linden 2007).

The desire to obtain detailed insights into the burial event puts demands both on the character of that event and the archaeological record. It requires a complex and coherently preserved whole if analyses are to result in more than simple tautologies. For this reason the study of the burial as activity and event has had a clear focus on the complex and well-investigated monuments that allow the reconstruction of long and composite narratives. This entails a bias towards a particular form of elaborate burial. It is evident that there is a considerable variation in the complexity and the time and effort invested in the individual burials. The largest monuments represented very comprehensive events, which both as regards the size of the assembly and the logistical and constructional challenges had an extraordinary character.

The high demands on the preservation and quality of documentation also means that it has only been possible to obtain a detailed insight into burial events in a relatively limited group of burials. The basis for comparison is consequently limited, and it remains uncertain just how representative the few well-documented examples really are. In some respects the theoretical debate on the significance of different patterns of use, temporalities, and practices may be said still to be more advanced than their demonstration in the archaeological record.

Cemeteries, Clusters, and Communities

Burials often appear together. They may be within the same monument, in well-defined cemeteries, or in clusters in the landscape. When the burials appear together we normally assume that there is some form of relation between the buried individuals. They are seen to represent a community, in a broad sense. However, precisely what sort of community and how it related to various groups in the living society is often open to discussion.

The burial clusters generally accumulated over time. There is consequently a temporal dimension, which figures prominently in the definition of the buried communities. This implies that the population of cemeteries and other burial clusters cannot immediately be taken to represent a contemporaneous living population. The historical dimension may, however, be central to understanding how the buried communities relate to the living ones. The significance of cemeteries and monuments for the formation of social memory has been the subject of several studies, which have drawn attention to the prominent role that reference to earlier burials has in stressing affiliations with earlier generations and interpreting the past (Last 1998). Thereby the earlier burials may support the formation of a particular group identity in the living community. Kinship relations would appear to be an obvious candidate for the type of affiliations being emphasized in the burial patterns. Not least in connection with burial mounds, it has often been suggested that the reuse and new building in relation to existing monuments represents a form of genealogical reckoning or descent construction (Gosden and Lock 1998). The idea is often associated with the perception of a lineage organization of Bronze Age society. The construction of new barrows and the reuse of old ones can then be seen as ways of demonstrating rights of accession. Along these lines, a return to a monument or cemetery after a long gap can be interpreted as an attempt to construct a tradition.

Still, kinship reckoning was not necessarily the only form of relation that was emphasized in cemeteries and burial clusters. Settlement communities form another possible basis for the formation of burial communities. The kind of settlement community that was reflected in the burials would obviously depend on the local settlement pattern, and from the size of cemeteries we can expect that it could be anything from the household, through the village, to the local region. It seems a reasonable assumption that many of the large cemeteries of the Urnfield culture should be interpreted along the lines of either of the two last categories, as over centuries they sometimes represent rather extensive populations of on average up to one hundred contemporary living individuals (Bukowski 1991).

Obviously, the settlement references do not exclude an element of kinship reckoning. The relation between settlement community and kinship reckoning in the cemeteries should in principle define the contours of the marriage locality pattern. Whether we are capable archaeologically of identifying these aspects in sufficient detail to allow considerations of this point is, however, another question.

If we have reason to assume that we have a representative sample of a cemetery or even the complete population, analyses of the burials can be used to characterize that community. Such a characterization may provide a better basis for deciding how the burial community related to the living group, which in turn would make it possible also to transfer the characterization to society beyond the cemetery.

Through the anthropological determinations a demographic profile may be obtained. Several large cemeteries exhibit an age and gender distribution that appears consistent with a representative section of a complete living population. In consequence they have often been used as a demographical proxy for their regions. The analyses have revealed quite varied life expectancies, from 23.9–28.6 years at birth in the Austrian Early Bronze Age sites to as low as 17.6–20.1 years in the south Polish Urnfield communities (Berner 1997; Gedl and Szybowicz 1997; Teschler-Nicola and Prossinger 1997). A discrepancy in the age profiles of males and females in the Early Bronze Age cemetery of Mokrin in Serbia has led to the suggestion of male infanticide or systematic neglect in this community (Rega 1997).

In other contexts, the burials only appear to represent a segment of the population. Here the question of what this segment represents becomes a primary question. Insofar as this can be identified, it may allow a consideration of the development of this group over time, or changes in the principles of group definition. In an analysis of the Ripdorf barrows in the Lüneburg region in northern Germany, it was possible to demonstrate a transformation of gender patterns in the burial practice from Early to Middle Bronze Age. In the Early Bronze Age the primary burials were apparently all male, whereas secondary burials exhibited an even gender distribution. In the Middle Bronze Age, women appear in the primary burials, and there is an emergence of multiple primary burials covered by the same barrow (Fig. 6.3). The pattern may be interpreted as a transformation in the kinship reckoning from a strict patrilineal to some form of bilateral principle (Geschwinde 2000: 151–4).

The cemeteries and burial clusters may in this way contribute significant information in their own right. Often, however, the interpretation of what groups the cemeteries represent, and how the various patterns identified within them are to be understood, require the cemeteries to be related to settlement patterns. There is consequently a considerable, but not easily achieved, interest in integrating cemetery studies with examinations of nearby settlements and landscape.

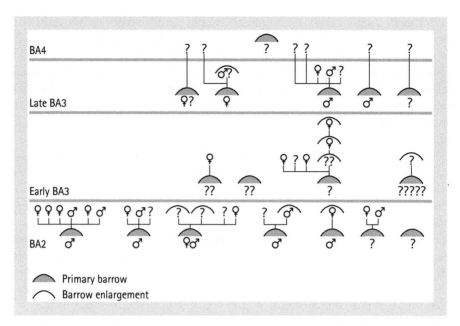

FIG. 6.3 Stratigraphical sequences and gender patterns in the use of the barrows from Early to Late Bronze Age at the Ripdorf cemetery, Lüneburg, Germany.

Source: author, after Geschwinde 2000.

The Setting of the Burials

One of the prominent trends in recent years in the study of burials has been an effort to extend the view from the individual monument or cemetery and to integrate the study of the burials in a broader context, encompassing other nearby monuments, surrounding settlements, various contemporary activity traces, communicative structures, and the landscape in varied senses (Arnoldussen and Fontijn 2006). The approach is generally motivated by a wish to obtain a coherent overall interpretation of landscape and spatial organization, in which the burials constitute one of many components. Some studies of burial settings are, however, also directed more specifically at an understanding of the burials themselves. This applies to how they were experienced in the landscape, how they referred to the surroundings, how they related to each other, and what was the nature of spatial dynamics in burial practices over time. The study of the context of barrows also constitutes a primary basis for interpreting how the social organization of the burial event related to society beyond the burial.

Even if the field has attracted considerable attention in recent years, awareness of the potential of such a contextual approach to the burials is not exactly new. Already in 1904 Sophus Müller examined in detail the distinct linear structures that could sometimes be observed over tens of kilometres in the distribution of barrows in Jutland, Denmark, relating them to hypothetical inland communication corridors based on the physical landscape and potential settlement pattern (Müller 1904). The relation between burials and settlements was also a prominent theme in processual archaeology. But the attention devoted to the context of burials has advanced significantly in the last couple of decades, for several reasons. There has been a theoretical development, where various phenomenological approaches to the monuments and a focus on the relations between burials and the surrounding world have entailed an extension of the interpretative context of the burials. At the same time, the mechanization of excavations and the possibilities of uncovering large areas have made it feasible to achieve more coherent large-scale recording of settlements and their contemporary burials. The extended use of geophysical prospecting and remote sensing techniques, including aerial photography, has contributed further information. Finally, there has been a significant development and increased use of environmental methods in the analysis of the burials, which have provided an insight into their landscape setting. In this connection it has been important that a number of the burial monuments themselves constitute a significant environmental archive. Some of the sod-built burial mounds incorporate a substantial part of the surrounding landscape in their fill, and a careful combination of analyses of the sequence of construction, the soils, the botanical material, and micro-fauna, may contribute to detailed reconstructions of the landscape (Breuning-Madsen and Holst 2003). This may provide an idea abut the relation of burials to other activities in the landscape, such as the degree of integration or separation of the burials, and the ecological impact of monument construction.

The landscape focus entails a challenge in handling the chronological development of burials. The well-dated ones are often only a small minority within a group accumulating over a long period, and the transformations in patterns of use and appearance can be difficult to grasp. The examples where enough dates are available, however, clearly demonstrate perspectives in chronological analysis. An example is the barrow groups of Barrow Hills, Radley, and Normanton Down in southern England, which both exhibit strict linear arrangements of the barrows, with possible orientation towards celestial references (Fig. 6.4). Here the dates have revealed that these alignments were a late occurrence in the history of the barrow groups, emerging at 1800–1500 BC on the background of a long tradition of dispersed barrow construction, and incorporating some of the earlier mounds in the linear structures. The chronological detail in this way indicates the manifestation of a specific, conscious, overall plan for the barrow group, which integrated both history and cosmological references (Garwood 2007).

In connection with their setting, the role of burials as anchors of meaning, and particularly of a historical dimension in the landscape, has often been emphasized (Jones 2006). The burials can be regarded as tangible fixed points for ancestral memory, which grants them a potential central role in the establishment of community identity as well as individual feelings of belonging to a place. The role may be particularly significant in the regions, where the settlement is relatively dynamic and perishable. Insofar as the burials are visible in the landscape, or the memory of their location is maintained, they may over time obtain a stable structuring role in the organization of landscape perception. This would seem an obvious possibility in connection with the kurgans in the eastern European steppe region, assumed to be characterized by an element of nomadic settlement (Kohl 2007: 144–6). It may, however, also be relevant in connection with the north-west European longhouse settlements, which at least for parts of the Bronze Age appear to entail a form of generational durability of the settlement (Fokkens 2005; Bourgeois and Fontijn 2008).

In some cases it appears likely that the burials were perceived as a point of departure for an agency of the ancestors. The indications of meticulous attempts at protecting the dead body, the maintained activities at the burials after the burial event, as well as the suggested antagonistic plunderings and destructions of burials, may all point in this direction (Randsborg 1998).

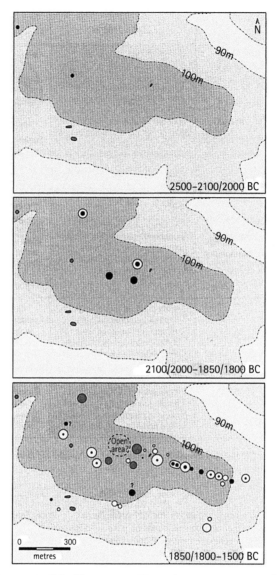

FIG. 6.4 The development of the Normanton Down barrow group, southern England, with the emergence of linear alignments around 1800–1500 BC.

Source: Garwood 2007.

The association of the burials with community identity and feelings of belonging also enter into interpretations of the burials as markers of territorial rights. Considering the location of both cemeteries and individual monuments, one is, however, often left with the impression that the burials are not only marking a delimitation of groups but also represent something connecting and integrating. This applies to the frequently observed concurrence between burial grounds and natural communication corridors or intersections in the landscape, which is consistent with the perception of the large monuments as assembly points for a substantial number of people.

Conclusion

Research into Bronze Age burials entails an ongoing exploration of new themes in the complex life that revolved around the burials. This exploration has been accompanied by a methodological and empirical endeavour to obtain more detail and more complete insights into the activities and contexts of the burials. The still more evident complexity that this process has brought about has led to a critique of previous explanations of the burials as simplistic and uni-causal. This has over time caused considerable shifts in interpretation. To some researchers, the multitude of interwoven motives in the burials even led to considerable scepticism as to our ability to distinguish the operation of different motives in burials. In practice this scepticism implied a dissociation from the burials in archaeological interpretation. Still, the integration of social, religious, domestic, and personal aspects of life have, from a theoretical standpoint, often been emphasized as a general condition, and in this way it applies not only to burials. First and foremost, it became an issue in connection with the burial, because there was an early awareness of the interwoven presence of the different motives inherent in that event. Moreover, detailed studies of individual monuments have revealed still more comprehensive narratives, where the social organization of the event, the symbolic elements, the sequence of activities and aspects of the identity of the buried individuals, have all been accessible within the same context. In these instances, various motives appear to be identifiable, and we can obtain information not only about them separately, but also about the interplay between them. In this respect, burials may still represent one of the contexts where we have some of the best opportunities for approaching the complexity of the past. In this way, one of the major challenges of future burial research would appear to lie in obtaining more complete impressions of the burial event, including as many themes as possible to enable the study of interplay between the various motives.

There may, in this approach, be a justified criticism of a bias towards a particular form of complex burial. It is also necessary to acknowledge that burials refer to particular situations in the past, and the structures we identify there cannot immediately be translated to other domains or even other burials. This problem stands as one of the major challenges of contextual studies where burials are considered in relation to their surroundings. In most regions of Bronze Age Europe, there is a pressing need for a better understanding of the relation between the burials and the rest of life and the surrounding space, and if the few well-preserved and complex burials are to play an increasingly important role, there is also an increasing need to understand how they relate to the rest of the burial record.

The gradual revelation of considerable variation among the burials within and between regions, and the theoretical awareness of the particularity of the individual burial event, have, as mentioned above, contributed to a shift in focus from the overall large-scale trends in the burial record to the study of particular cases and burial patterns in specific regions. That there are overall almost pan-European trends in the Bronze Age burial record is, however, indisputable, and they have also recently played a significant role in various claims about the Bronze Age being instrumental in establishing a form of European large-scale coherency with long-term durability. This leaves unaddressed the question of how we are to perceive and handle the supra-regional structures in the burials. The major challenge would appear to be to approach these structures without relapsing into generalizing models, where everything becomes an expression of the same universal ideas. One approach may be to start with studying the apparently significant role that burial events themselves played in establishing the similarities. The relatively frequent and probably often large-scale assemblies at burials, in combination with a considerable susceptibility to foreign elements in the ritual practices, appear to be important premises for the development of supra-regional similarities. In this respect, burials may provide us with the generative principles of the large-scale trends in the burial record, and possibly even throw light upon an important aspect of how the European Bronze Age was interconnected.

Bibliography

Arnoldussen, S. and Fontijn, D. (2006). 'Towards familiar landscapes? On the nature and origin of Middle Bronze Age landscapes in the Netherlands', *Proceedings of the Prehistoric Society*, 72: 289–317.

Artelius, T. (1996). Långfärd och återkomst. Skeppet i bronsålderns gravar. Arkeologiska undersökningar (skrifter), 17. Stockholm: Göteborgs universitet.

Barrett, J. C. (1994). *Fragments from Antiquity: An Archaeology of Social Life in Britain, 2900–1200 BC*. Oxford: Blackwell.

Berner, M. (1997). 'Demographie des frühbronzezeitlichen Gräberfeldes Franzhaus1 en I, Niederösterreich', in K. Rittershofer (ed.), *Demographie der Bronzezeit. Paläodemographie—Möglichkeiten und Grenzen*. Espelkamp: Verlag Marie Leidorft GmbH, 35–42.

Bourgeois, Q. and Fontijn, D. (2008). 'Houses and barrows in the Low Countries', in S. Arnoldussen and H. Fokkens (eds.), *Bronze Age Settlements in the Low Countries*. Oxford: Oxbow Books, 41–57.

Boye, V. (1896). *Fund af Egekister fra Bronzealderen i Danmark: et monografisk Bidrag til Belysning af Bronzealderens Kultur*. Copenhagen: Høst.

Bradley, R. (1998). *The Significance of Monuments: On the Shaping of Human Experience in Neolithic and Bronze Age Europe*. London: Routledge.

Breuning-Madsen, H. and Holst, M. K. (2003). 'A soil description system for burial mounds—development and application', *Geografisk Tidsskrift. Danish Journal of Geography*, 103/2: 37–45.

——, Holst, M. K., Rasmussen, M., and Elberling, B. (2003). 'Preservation within log coffins before and after barrow construction', *Journal of Archaeological Science*, 30/3: 343–50.

Brück, J. (2006). 'Fragmentation, personhood and the social construction of technology in Middle and Late Bronze Age Britain', *Cambridge Archaeological Journal*, 16/3: 297–315.

Bukowski, Z. (1991). 'Zum Stand der demographischen und siedlungsgeschichtlichen Forschung zur Lausitzer Kultur im Stromgebiet von Oder und Weichsel', *Acta Preahistorica et Archaeologica*, 22, 1990: 85–119.

Capelle, T. (1986). 'Schiffsetzungen', *Praehistorische Zeitschrift*, 61/Heft 1: 1–63.

Fokkens, H. (2005). 'Mixed farming societies: synthesis', in L. P. Louwe Kooijmans, P. W. van den Broeke, H. Fokkens, and A. L. Gijn (eds.), *The Prehistory of the Netherlands*. Amsterdam: Amsterdam University Press, 463–76.

Freudenberg, M. (2009). 'Grab und Kultanlage der älteren Bronzezeit von Hüsby, Kr. Schleswig-Flensburg und erste Überlegungen zu überregionalen Beziehungen', *Archäologie in Schleswig/Arkæologi i Slesvig*, 12: 53–68.

Garwood, P. (2007). 'Before the hills in order stood: chronology, time and history in the interpretation of Early Bronze Age round barrows', in J. Last (ed.), *Beyond the Grave: New Perspectives on Barrows*. Oxford: Oxbow Books, 30–52.

Gedl, M. and Szybowicz, B. (1997). 'Demographische Struktur der Population der Urnenfelderzeit in Südpolen', in K. Rittershofer (ed.), *Demographie der Bronzezeit. Paläodemographie—Möglichkeiten und Grenzen*. Espelkamp: Verlag Marie Leidorft GmbH, 159–71.

Geschwinde, M. (2000). *Die Hügelgräber auf der Grossen Heide bei Ripdorf im Landkreis Uelzen. Archäologische Beobachtungen zu den Bestattungssitten des Spätneolithikums und der Bronzezeit in der Lüneburger Heide*. Neumünster: Wachholz Verlag.

Gosden, C. and Lock, G. (1998). 'Prehistoric histories', *World Archaeology*, 30/1: 2–12.

Hansen, S. (2005). '"Überausstattungen" in Gräbern und Horten der Frühbronzezeit', in J. Müller (ed.), *Vom Endneolithikum zur Frühbronzezeit: Muster sozialen Wandels?* Bonn: Dr Rudolf Habelt GmbH, 151–73.

Harding, A. F. (2000). *European Societies in the Bronze Age*. Cambridge: Cambridge University Press.

Häusler, A. (1994). 'Grab- und Bestattungssitten des Neolithikums und der frühen Bronzezeit in Mitteleuropa', *Zeitschrift für Archäologie*, 28/1: 23–61.

Herbst, C. F. (1848). 'Hvidegårdsfundet', *Annaler for Nordisk Oldkyndighed og Historie*, 336–52.

Holst, M. K., Breuning-Madsen, H., and Rasmussen, M. (2001). 'The south Scandinavian barrows with well-preserved oak-log coffins', *Antiquity*, vol. 75, 287: 126–36.

——, Rasmussen, M., and Breuning-Madsen, H. (2004). 'Skelhøj. Et bygningsværk fra den ældre bronzealder', *Nationalmuseets Arbejdsmark*, 11–25.

Johansen, K. L., Laursen, S. T., and Holst, M. K. (2004). 'Spatial patterns of social organization in the Early Bronze Age of south Scandinavia', *Journal of Anthropological Archaeology*, 23/1: 33–55.

Jones, A. M. (2006). 'Monuments and memories set in stone: a Cornish Bronze Age ceremonial complex in its landscape (on Stannon Down)', *Proceedings of the Prehistoric Society*, 72: 341–65.

Kohl, P. L. (2007). *The Making of Bronze Age Eurasia*. Cambridge: Cambridge University Press.

Kristiansen, K. (1984). 'Krieger und Häuptlinge in der Bronzezeit Dänemarks. Ein Beitrag zur Geschichte des bronzezeitlichen Schwertes', *Jahrbuch des Römisch-Germanisches Zentralmuseums*, 31: 187–208.

—— (1998). *Europe Before History*. Cambridge: Cambridge University Press.

Last, J. (1998). 'Books of life: biography and memory in a Bronze Age barrow', *Oxford Journal of Archaeology*, 17/1: 43–53.

Lull, V. (2000). 'Argaric society: death at home', *Antiquity*, 74/285: 581–90.

McKinley, J. I. (1997). 'Bronze Age "barrows" and funerary rites and rituals of cremation', *Proceedings of the Prehistoric Society*, 63: 129–45.

Müller, S. (1904). 'Vei og Bygd', *Aarbøger for Nordisk Oldkyndighed og Historie*, 1–64.

Oestigaard, T. and Goldhahn, J. (2006). 'From the dead to the living: death as transactions and re-negotiations', *Norwegian Archaeological Review*, 39/1: 27–48.

Parker Pearson, M. (1999). *The Archaeology of Death and Burial*. Phoenix Mill: Sutton Publishing.

——, Chamberlain, A., Craig, O., Marshall, P., Mulville, J., Smith, H., Chenery, C., Collins, M., Cook, G., Craig, G., Evans, J., Hiller, J., Montgomery, J., Schwenninger, J., Taylor, G., and Wess, T. (2005). 'Evidence for mummification in Bronze Age Britain', *Antiquity*, 79/305: 529-46.

Randsborg, K. (1998). 'Plundered Bronze Age graves', *Acta Archaeologica*, 69: 113-38.

Rega, E. (1997). 'Age, gender and biological reality in the Early Bronze Age cemetery at Mokrin', in J. Moore and E. Scott (eds.), *Invisible People and Processes: Writing Gender and Childhood into European Archaeology*. Leicester: Leicester University Press, 229-47.

Roymans, N. and Kortlang, F. (1999). 'Urnfield symbolism, ancestors and the land in the Lower Rhine region', in F. Theuws and N. Roymans (eds.), *Land and Ancestors: Cultural Dynamics in the Urnfield Period and the Middle Ages in the Southern Netherlands*. Amsterdam: Amsterdam University Press, 33-62.

Sørensen, M. S. (1997). 'Reading dress: the construction of social categories and identities in Bronze Age Europe', *Journal of European Archaeology*, 5/1: 93-114.

—— (2004). 'Stating identities: the use of objects in rich Bronze Age graves', in J. Cherry, C. Scarre, and S. Shennan (eds.), *Explaining Social Change: Studies in Honour of Colin Renfrew*. Cambridge: McDonald Institute, 167-76.

—— and Rebay, K. C. (2007). 'Changing social practices of death in later European prehistory', in R. Karl and J. Leskovar (eds.), *Interpretierte Eisenzeiten. Fallstudien, Methoden, Theorie. Tagungsbericht der 2. Linzer Gespräche zur interpretativen Eisenzeitarchäologie*, Studien zur Kulturgeschichte von Oberösterreich, Folge 19. Linz: Oberösterreichisches Landesmuseum, 1-5.

—— and Rebay-Salisbury, K. (2008). 'Landscapes of the body: burials of the Middle Bronze Age in Hungary', *European Journal of Archaeology*, 11/1: 49-74.

Spindler, K. (1972). 'Funde und Befunde organischer Materialen vom Magdalenenberg bei Villingen (Badem-Würtemberg)', *Archäologisches Korrespondenzblatt*, 2: 133-41.

Szydłowska, E. (1968). 'Cmentarzysko kultury hżyckiej w Przeczycach, pow Zawiercie', *Rocznik Muz. Górnośląskiego w Bytomiu, Archeologia*, 5: 7-368.

Teschler-Nicola, M. and Prossinger, H. (1997). 'Aspekte der Paläodemographie anhand der frühbronzezeitlichen Friedhöfe des Unteren Traisentales (Franzhausen I, Franzhausen II, Gemeinlebarn F und Pottenbrunn-Ratzersdorf)', in K. Rittershofer (ed.), *Demographie der Bronzezeit. Paläodemographie—Möglichkeiten und Grenzen*. Espelkamp: Verlag Marie Leidorft GmbH, 43-57.

Thrane, H. (1984). *Lusehøj ved Voldtofte—en sydvestfynsk storhøj fra yngre broncealder*. Odense: Odense Bys Museer.

Treherne, P. (1995). 'The warrior's beauty: the masculine body and self-identity in Bronze Age Europe', *Journal of European Archaeology*, 3/1: 105-45.

Vander Linden, M. (2007). 'For equalities are plural: reassessing the social in Europe during the third millenium BC', *World Archaeology*, 39/2: 177-93.

Worsaae, J. J. A. (1843). *Danmarks Oldtid. Oplyst ved Oldsager og Gravhøje*. Copenhagen: Selskabet for Trykkefrihedens rette Brug.

CHAPTER 7

HOARDS AND THE DEPOSITION OF METALWORK

RICHARD BRADLEY

Introduction: The Archbishop's Treasure

In 2009 divers working in the River Wear beside Durham Cathedral discovered a remarkable collection of metal artefacts. They could be identified as gifts presented to Archbishop Michael Ramsey, who had lived in the vicinity after he retired as head of the Anglican Church. Their sources were very varied. They included a cross presented to him by the leader of the Russian Orthodox Church, a silver trowel given by the Bengal Coal Company when Ramsey laid the foundations of a church in India, a gold coin celebrating the renovation of the Grand Shrine of Ise in Japan, and a series of medals commemorating the second Vatican Council. These finds aroused considerable interest in the press, since it was difficult to decide why some of Ramsey's property had ended up in the river (*The Guardian*, 22 October 2009). Two schools of thought emerged, with widely diverging views. The version favoured by the cathedral authorities was that he had been the victim of a burglary which he had failed to report. The thieves had dumped these items as they would be easy to identify (www.durhamcathedral.co.uk/introduction/news/156). A second view, favoured by some of Ramsey's colleagues, was that he was troubled by owning so many valuables and by the possibility that they would appear on the market after his death. Their special character needed to be protected, and that was why he discarded them. He may even have regarded them as offerings to the deity, for he belonged to the section of the Church of England that approves of this procedure. There was also the argument, put forward by the divers themselves, that the objects had been deposited in small groups, in different places and probably on different occasions. That was not consistent with the behaviour of thieves.

Ramsey died more than twenty years ago and the mystery is unlikely to be solved. It is understandable that deposits of Bronze Age metalwork—some of them found in rivers—have been still more difficult to interpret. Moreover, they form only one part of a much larger body of material which occurs in a series of other contexts. Among the most frequent are the artefacts from hoards of different kinds, but there were also single finds and grave goods. Although the hoards provide the main focus of this chapter, they cannot be discussed in isolation. Some of the problems raised by Archbishop Ramsey's treasure are equally relevant to Bronze Age archaeology.

Hoards and the Development of Prehistoric Archaeology

Hoards can be defined as collections of buried objects that were apparently deposited together on the same occasion. These collections can be used to work out which kinds of artefacts were used concurrently. Seriation of the different groups also allows scholars to place them in sequence. This has been a concern of prehistorians for well over a hundred years. Where traces of organic hafts survive, individual items can be investigated by radiocarbon dating. This method has supported the framework built up by studies of these collections and has established an absolute chronology for Bronze Age metalwork. There are important studies of the hoards of different areas of Europe (examples include Von Brunn 1968 and Maraszek 2006) and some individual collections provide the subject matter for entire monographs (e.g. Coffyn, Gomez de Soto, and Mohen 1981; Needham 1990).

At the same time, the study of hoards has led to the identification of a series of regional traditions of metalworking. This has shed a certain light on patterns of communication, and there have even been attempts to identify local styles of artefacts with specific communities in the past. Thus Colin Burgess (1980) has compared the distributions of particular metal types in Bronze Age Wales with the areas occupied by tribes recorded in the Roman period. Similarly, George Eogan (1974) finds echoes of the historic subdivision of Ireland in the distribution of different kinds of Late Bronze Age metalwork.

Their approach recalls the analytical method followed by Gordon Childe, but instead of using the contents of hoards to identify regional cultures, he employed them to reconstruct the distinctive character of metal production. Following earlier writers, he identified particular combinations of artefacts with different stages in the manufacture and distribution of bronzes. He also emphasized the special status of the smith who, he considered, had been free to move between different communities (Childe 1958: Chapter 10).

If some hoards were associated with the activities of metalworkers, others were interpreted as personal property that had been concealed but not recovered. Peaks in the deposition of these collections were even identified as periods of crisis when valuables were hidden and lost. In this way the evidence of Bronze Age hoards could be used to write a kind of political history. That was especially true where their chronology matched that of hill fort building, since it was often treated as indirect evidence of warfare.

Problems of Interpretation

There are three main problems with traditional approaches of this kind. The first is self-evident. If hoards are regarded as collections of personal valuables, why are their contents virtually restricted to metalwork? The only exceptions appear to be the 'ceramic hoards' of central Europe (Harding 2000: 331–3). Why were other kinds of property excluded from the collections of metal artefacts? And why did the deposition of hoards decline so rapidly when bronze was replaced by iron (Bradley 1998: 159–60)? Perhaps the distinctive character of the raw material was considered to be particularly significant. That would not be surprising since the distributions of copper and tin are so restricted. The same applies to gold.

The second problem is the difficulty of accepting that so many stores of valuables were concealed and never recovered. It seems unlikely in a period when graves were being robbed. There are regions in which the siting of hoards follows such a predictable pattern that these collections can be discovered by archaeologists today. Why was it more difficult in the past when the positions of some of the deposits appear to have been marked?

Thirdly, it is hard to understand why relatively few collections of bronzes are associated with occupation sites which would have provided accessible and convenient locations for collections of valuables—as they obviously were during the Roman period. Instead, the prehistoric metalwork may be found in isolation. Some was buried near settlements, yet there is little overlap between the finds associated with those sites and the objects discovered in hoards. It seems as if metalwork was made and used in the domestic arena, but was separated from other kinds of artefacts when it was placed in the ground (Fontijn 2003).

The medieval English law of Treasure Trove recognized the difficulty of interpreting such finds. It distinguished between collections of valuables meant to be recovered later, and those which were intended to remain in the ground; often they were in graves. The legislation laid down that items which were expected to be retrieved should become the property of the state. The others belonged to the owner of the land in which they were found. The law applied to objects of gold and silver, but the same distinction has been used in Bronze Age studies. Until recently interpretations varied between different parts of Europe, even where the archaeological evidence took exactly the same form. Thus scholars in Germany and Scandinavia considered that most hoards should be identified as votive offerings that were never meant to be recovered. Archaeologists in Britain and France, on the other hand, were more prepared to countenance a 'practical' interpretation in which property was buried for safe keeping and eventually lost (Bradley 1998: 15–17).

Contexts and Contents

It is important to consider the contexts of these deposits together with their contents. Again traditional approaches have been misleading. Hoards have been classified according to at least three separate criteria, which to some extent overlap. Firstly, they might be categorized according to the identity of the people who deposited the artefacts. Thus 'personal hoards' could be recognized by their distinctive composition, so that individual deposits were attributed, without much discussion, to men or women, warriors, craft workers, or ritual specialists. Secondly, those collections associated with smiths were also categorized according to different stages in the production of bronze artefacts. Thus some collections were identified as stores of newly made objects awaiting distribution to the customer, whereas others were interpreted as accumulations of scrap metal that had been brought together for recycling. A good example is Stuart Needham's detailed analysis of the metalwork deposits from Petters Sports Field in the Thames Valley (Needham 1990). 'Merchants' hoards' might include multiples of the same type of object, some of them unfinished or unused. 'Founders' hoards', on the other hand, contained a variety of different kinds of objects, some of which had been broken and were mixed with casting waste. Lastly, the hoards could also be categorized according to the kinds of artefacts being made, so that separate deposits were associated with tools, weapons, and ornaments respectively. These distinctions are sometimes treated as evidence of craft specialization.

Contexts

Collections of metalwork were found in a variety of contexts. At first the most important distinction was between deposits that would have been easy to recover and those where this would have been difficult or impossible to achieve. A fundamental distinction, which also extended to single finds, was between discoveries in dry land and those from watery locations, especially rivers and bogs. It seemed as if artefacts buried in the soil could have been hidden or stored for later retrieval, whereas those deposited in wet places would have been hard to find and equally hard to recover. Such distinctions extended to the composition of the hoards themselves. For the most part tools and metalworking residues were buried on dry land, whereas intact weapons were common finds in rivers (Torbrügge 1971). Groups of ornaments did not conform to this simple scheme, although many were found in bogs. With this exception, it seemed as though deposits of Bronze Age metalwork could be divided into two distinct groups: votive offerings or 'ritual' hoards, which were not meant to be recovered, and 'non-ritual' or 'utilitarian' hoards, which would have remained accessible after they were deposited. The latter group provided most evidence of artefact production (Bradley 1998: 10–14).

A similar distinction was proposed by Janet Levy (1982) in a study of hoards in Bronze Age Denmark, although she paid more attention to the places in which they were found and the character of the artefacts themselves. She also studied the composition of the different hoards, their organization in the ground (where it was recorded), the treatment of the objects found in each collection, and the presence or absence of food remains. Like other writers, she distinguished between sacred and mundane deposits, but Levy placed more weight on ethnographic evidence for the character of votive offerings in traditional societies. This had the advantage of relating the archaeological evidence to thinking in anthropology, but by relying on cross-cultural generalization she moved the discussion away from the specific cultural contexts in which these items were accumulated.

In fact the details of such deposits are too easily overlooked. For example, the dry land hoards come from a variety of completely different locations and do not form a particularly useful category. They are found close to settlement sites, but they may also be associated with more remote places, including hilltops, caves, cliffs, rock fissures, and passes (Wyss 1996). They can be associated with older monuments, including megalithic tombs, round barrows, cairns, and stone circles (Bradley 2000: 156–7). It is true that in some cases these groups of artefacts could have been recovered, but that was not always so. The collections of half-melted artefacts dropped into rock fissures provide an obvious exception. On the other hand, there are examples in which the positions of Bronze Age hoards were marked by an outcrop, a boulder, or a mound. In principle it should have been possible to find them. Their locations may not have been secret, nor were they necessarily forgotten. Perhaps the artefacts remained undisturbed because contact with them was forbidden.

In the same way, the wetland locations are extremely diverse. They include fast-flowing rivers, brackish water, bogs, lakes, pools, streams, and springs. Others are on the coast, and collections of Bronze Age metalwork have even been recovered from the sea. They are usually interpreted as the contents of shipwrecks, but, as Alice Samson (2006) has pointed out, some of them, like those from Langdon Bay or Sotteville-sur Mer, have a similar composition to groups of river finds and dry-land hoards. In fact the contents of the Bronze Age wreck from the Ría de Huelva in southern Spain have been reinterpreted as a votive deposit (Ruiz-Gálvez 2000). Other finds of metalwork are associated with fords, wooden causeways, or bridges like that at Berlin-Spandau (Schwanger 1997), and still more have been found close to heaps of burnt stones in Britain and Ireland, some of which were associated with troughs for heating water. Bronze artefacts have also been discovered inside artificial ponds and wells (Yates and Bradley 2010a). The character of the metal finds reflects some of these distinctions. In central Germany, for instance, finds of weapons are associated with the main river channels, whereas smaller items, especially pins, are found in marshes (Kubach 1979). In the same way, in the English Fenland weapons were deposited in the principal rivers, whereas entire hoards, including groups of ornaments, were placed in still water. Often these deposits consisted of intact objects, but close to the burnt mounds along the edge of the wetlands the same types occurred as fragments mixed with metalworking residues (Yates and Bradley 2010a). Among them was the largest hoard found in Britain, from Isleham in Cambridgeshire.

In this example the distinction between dry land and water finds breaks down. It does so in other cases. Much of the Late Bronze Age metalwork in Belgium comes from an underground river inside a cave, le Trou de Han, yet other items have been found in caves where water is absent (Warmenbol 1996). Similarly, a detailed study of the findspots of metalwork hoards in south-east England shows they were closely associated with the courses of rivers and streams. Here the main association was with fresh rather than salt water, but the objects themselves were buried in the ground nearby. Their locations are particularly revealing. There are finds of metalwork outside settlements identified by field survey (Fig. 7.1). Groups of hoards were deposited along the spring-line, with individual deposits beside the source of the water (Yates and Bradley 2010b). Others were buried near burnt mounds whose distribution follows streams and rivers, or on slight promontories overlooking a confluence (Fig. 7.2). There is even a case in which a hoard from Ditchling Common was associated with a mineral spring, famous in the Victorian period for its medicinal properties.

Such evidence suggests that the distinction between wetland and dry-land hoards is much too simple. Both groups are exceptionally diverse and it is not clear that all the terrestrial finds shared the same chance of recovery. Some places were readily accessible, yet the deposits associated with them remained intact. Other hoards were in remote locations well outside the area settled all year round. In the same way, the collections of metalwork from the wetlands show considerable variation, and it seems likely that different kinds of deposit were associated with different kinds of water. Moreover, the siting of some of the finds from dry land was influenced by the presence of water in the vicinity.

Contents

If the contexts of these finds are more varied than is commonly supposed, the same is true of the treatment of the artefacts themselves.

Some of the most striking patterns were overlooked because the hoards were investigated for evidence of style and chronology. Just as they were studied in museums with little regard for the

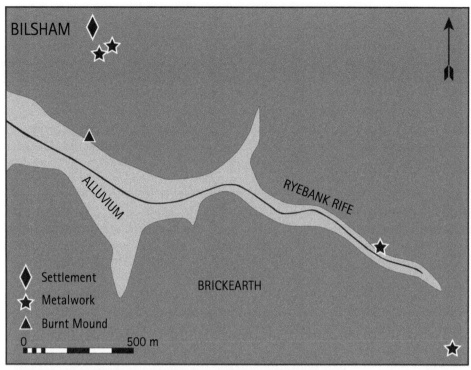
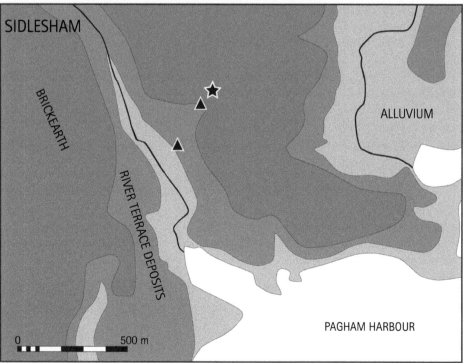

FIG. 7.1 The relationship between finds of metalwork, Bronze Age settlements, burnt mounds, and freshwater streams at two sites in south-east England.

Source: author, after Yates and Bradley.

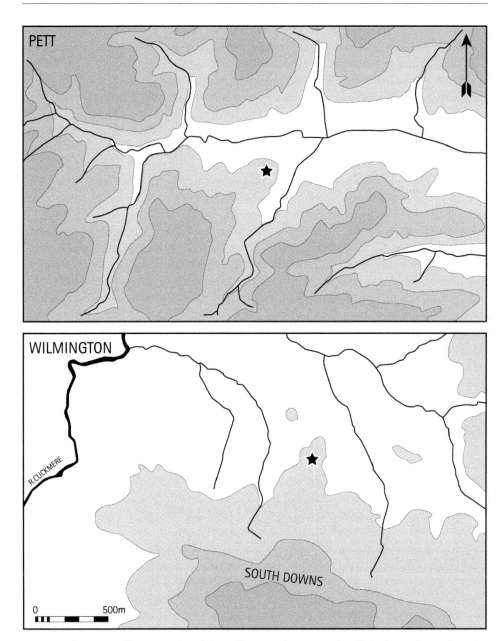

FIG. 7.2 The siting of two metalwork hoards in south-east England. Each was located on the end of a spur of raised ground overlooking freshwater streams.

Source: author, after Yates and Bradley.

distinctive character of the findspots, their components were catalogued with no concern for the biographies of the objects themselves. Only in recent years has more attention been paid to the traces of use-damage and repair on specific artefacts, or to the ways in which they were treated when they were taken out of circulation. On one level metal analysis provided abundant evidence for the recycling of raw materials; on another, hoards of scrap metal were identified in the ground. But there was little connection between these two kinds of research. Rather than investigating the ways in which these groups of artefacts were assembled, specialists lamented that so many of the objects were incomplete, as it made them difficult to classify.

The artefacts found in hoards can be intact or in fragments, and certain collections contain a mixture of both. In some cases it seems as if these items were broken when they were brought together, but there are other instances in which incomplete artefacts were assembled from different sources; classic cases include the French hoard of Vénat (Coffyn, Gomez de Soto, and Mohen 1981). As mentioned earlier, there are numerous hoards which contain freshly made objects and some which had never been finished, but it is clear that these collections also include tools, weapons, and ornaments with a significant history of use and repair. It is important to distinguish between the damage caused in the course of their history and that inflicted when they entered the ground.

This is especially important in the case of collections containing only one kind of artefact, for example sickles in central and eastern Europe (Sommerfeld 1994). Because the same objects are represented so many times, it is tempting to suggest that they were employed as units of metal which may have had prescribed values in exchange. This argument could apply to other artefacts, for example axes (Fontijn 2003: 250–1), but in each case it requires wear analysis to establish whether they had ever been functioning tools (Kienlin and Ottaway 1998). That work is sometimes combined with analysis of their composition, for some axe heads, like those from the latest hoards in north-west France, were probably too soft to be used. Their weights have also been studied. It is possible that common forms of artefact, including axes and sickles, conform to a series of standard weights. The small bronze figurines of Late Bronze Age Scandinavia provide another illustration (Malmer 1992). The sizes and weights of entire hoards have also been considered (Maraszek 2006). A novel approach is to investigate the number of artefacts that were deposited in different collections, for sometimes there seem to be significant patterns (Brandherm 2007). Unfortunately, none of these approaches can show why the hoards were buried. The quantity and weight of the artefacts might have been calculated by the smiths before they made fresh items, but they could also have measured the amount of metal that had to be dedicated to the gods. The deposition of coins at Iron Age and Roman sanctuaries provides a possible analogy.

Many deposits are associated with the by-products of metalworking: casting jets, moulds, crucibles, slag, and ingots. For that reason they have been interpreted by Levy (1982) as 'non-ritual' hoards. This approach makes the unwarranted assumption that the artefacts brought together in these deposits were assembled for practical reasons. They were meant to be melted down in order to make new objects, but it never happened. At first sight the argument is plausible, as the evidence of metal analysis shows that recycling was very common in the Bronze Age. On the other hand, the information provided by the hoards can be taken too literally. This is acknowledged by Claude Mordant (2007) in a new study of the French hoard from Villethierry, which he and his colleagues had originally interpreted in purely functional terms. Now its position on the boundary of two cultural traditions suggests that it played a specialized role.

There are three main problems that need to be addressed. The first is that the evidence of scrap hoards does not correspond with the information provided by metal analysis. It is clear that copper and bronze artefacts were made of recycled material from an early stage, but scrap hoards are most common in the Late Bronze Age. It was not necessary to store these collections in the ground in order to undertake the process, and in any case it still remains uncertain why so much metal was buried and not recovered. On one reading of the evidence scrap metal was used to make new objects throughout the Bronze Age, but only in certain phases did much of this material escape the melting pot. Why it did so has still to be discussed.

Secondly, there is evidence that bronze artefacts were not merely broken to reduce them to a manageable size or weight. In some cases they were reduced to fragments using extraordinary force. It was not easy to break all these objects, and there was little need to do so. Louis Nebelsick (2000), who has drawn attention to this phenomenon, observes that the level of violence with which it was accomplished seems to have varied according to the locations where the hoards are found. Thus in southern Germany metalwork from the domestic landscape received less drastic treatment than artefacts from what he calls 'wild places', such as mountains or cliffs.

Thirdly, a purely practical interpretation of the scrap hoards would not account for some striking regularities in the composition of the collections themselves. They vary along regional lines across different parts of north-west Europe, but there is no reason to believe that these were the only combinations of artefact types available for reuse. Rather, the composition of the hoards—even those containing metalworking residues—seems to have been governed by local conventions, so that all the raw material assembled by the smith cannot have been considered on equal terms (Maraszek 1998; Turner 2010). Clearly, certain combinations of different types were required in hoards. Some were considered appropriate and others evidently were not.

This argument faces the problem that only the artefacts that escaped recycling can be studied today, but what appears to be a difficulty may provide a vital clue. Perhaps a specific selection of the raw material had to be deposited in the ground when other artefacts were melted down. The objects that were actually reused might have been much more diverse. The contents of these hoards need not provide a representative sample of the types in circulation. That is clear from the discovery of moulds for making artefacts of forms that have rarely been found. In the same way, the moulds for making bronze artefacts can appear in quite different frequencies from the objects themselves (Rassmann 1996).

The Role of the Smith

The conventional interpretation of metal hoards was beset by another problem that is being addressed by new research. The argument that certain hoards are 'non-ritual' or 'utilitarian' makes certain assumptions about the roles of the smiths. One reason why this has happened is the influence of Gordon Childe (1958), who thought of them as free agents moving between different communities and marketing their skills on a commercial basis. That conception may be anachronistic and is not consistent with accounts of metalworking in non-western societies, which suggest that the entire process is ritualized and governed by specific protocols (Budd and Taylor 1995). Smiths can enjoy a special position in the community and their unusual skills take on something of the qualities of magic. It may be wrong to think in terms of contemporary notions of manufacture and trade.

A new interpretation of the role of the smith comes from archaeological research in southern Scandinavia. A recent study by Joakim Goldhahn (2007) draws attention to the association between cremation burials and evidence of bronze working. Both can be associated with the same deposits of burnt stone and with a series of specialized buildings that are usually described as 'cult houses'. During the Late Bronze Age human bodies are known to have been burnt to an exceptionally high temperature. According to Goldhahn, this could only have been achieved in a furnace. It might explain why cremation and metal production were sometimes carried out together. For that reason he suggests that in northern Europe the smith was a ritual specialist. Perhaps the strongest evidence comes from Hallunda where a cult house has been identified in association with cremation burials and the largest concentration of metalworking furnaces in Bronze Age Sweden (Goldhahn 2007: 293–306). A comparable but less detailed argument has been put forward by Joanna Brück (2006), who suggests that in Britain and Ireland the fragmentation of the metalwork in Late Bronze Age hoards reflects the treatment of human remains during the same period. It is difficult to take the discussion further, but in southern Germany ingots, weights, copper cake (raw copper fragments), and unfinished objects have been found in Late Bronze Age burials (Winghart 2000).

Such arguments raise the possibility that the transformation of raw metal involved rituals as well as technological procedures. It was a dangerous process in both practical and social terms, so it was often undertaken in special places. Perhaps it was necessary to deposit a prescribed portion of the material as a votive offering. That may be why certain selections of objects were brought together and treated in such a distinctive manner. It may also be why they were buried and never recovered. In this interpretation the link with metalworking remains, but its 'utilitarian' character is questioned. The 'non-ritual hoards' defined by Levy (1982) could have had a more specialized character than is normally supposed. In fact they may result from rituals undertaken by the smiths who were obliged to return to the earth a portion of the material obtained from it.

The social anthropologist Mary Helms suggests this interpretation in a recent paper that draws on evidence from the European Bronze Age:

> Depositional objects like metals…derived from raw materials…believed to be redolent with the cosmological power of the earth that originally generated them. I…posit that Bronze Age people believed, as many traditional cultures have, that if human society takes living, energized material from the world for human use, then human society has the obligation to return life energy to the earth to replenish the store, so that…the renewal and regeneration of all living things may continue (2009: 155).

The distinctive character of Bronze Age hoards has no exact counterpart in the ethnographic record. Helms's interpretation might account for the unusual character of these deposits, but it depends on the same methodology as Levy's scheme. In the end the strongest arguments will always be based on archaeological observations.

Some Wider Implications

If Bronze Age hoards represent a particular kind of votive offering, how were they related to other deposits of metalwork? Should they be considered separately from single finds, and how, if at all, do they compare with the objects in graves? Reassessment of the social and ritual importance of smiths raises some new possibilities, but it brings fresh problems too.

Once it is accepted that the transformation of metals was not just a technological process, it becomes clear that other aspects of hoards and hoarding also need to be considered.

Hoards and Single Finds

The distinction between hoards and single finds reflects the way in which Bronze Age studies have developed. Research on metalwork hoards showed which kinds of artefacts were made and used together, and so this work had priority. By definition, single finds did not lend themselves to the same approach and for that reason they played a secondary role. On the other hand, the objects in these two classes have so much in common that in other respects they can be considered together. Some of those classified as single finds may have formed part of larger collections, but many of them really were isolated discoveries. They share a number of common properties with the contents of hoards. For example, certain of these objects have been broken in exactly the same ways as the artefacts found in those collections; the fragments resemble one another despite their different contexts (Bradley 2005: Chapter 5). There is evidence that a few of the swords deposited in rivers had been burnt. It is not clear whether this happened on a cremation pyre or whether the weapons had been damaged by a smith. What is obvious is that they had been treated rather like the contents of a scrap hoard.

Sometimes it is possible to distinguish between two different stages in the histories of these objects. For example, most of the weapons deposited in the River Thames show signs of duelling scars, resharpening, and repair, but when these artefacts were discarded they were disabled with exceptional force. The proportion of artefacts that were deliberately damaged actually increased over time (York 2002). Again their treatment was comparable to the damage inflicted on objects in dry-land hoards (Nebelsick 2000). There are also cases in which the same types are represented in hoards in one phase and as single finds in the next, suggesting that both kinds of deposit were equivalent to one another (Jensen 1972).

Single Finds, Hoards, and Grave Finds

Single finds of weapons are especially common in rivers and bogs, but complete and fragmentary examples are also represented in hoards (Fig. 7.3). Swords often occur in graves, but, as Walter Torbrügge noted forty years ago, the two kinds of deposit rarely occur together. Either the contexts in which the artefacts were deposited changed over the course of time, or different practices were followed in different parts of Europe (Torbrügge 1971). As a result, grave finds and single finds can have mutually exclusive distributions (Fig. 7.4). This striking pattern has encouraged the idea that weapons were deposited in water in the course of funeral ceremonies. Dry-land hoards containing swords and spears may have been deposited in similar circumstances (Coombs 1975). A good example is the collection from Penard in south Wales.

It is an attractive argument, especially in regions where elaborately furnished burials are rare or absent, but this interpretation presents certain problems. Only a few groups of river finds are accompanied by human remains that can be shown to be contemporary with the metalwork itself. Even then they may not represent a cross section of the Bronze Age population. The remains from the Thames, for example, are mainly skulls, and it is not clear whether entire bodies had once been present or whether unfleshed bones, or even heads, had been deposited in the water after preliminary treatment elsewhere (Bradley and Gordon 1988). At all events such finds have not been recorded from most of the rivers containing Bronze Age artefacts. Thus they represent the exception rather than the norm.

Ornament hoards pose a similar problem, although they are more common in bogs. They have also been found on dry land. In some cases they could represent the personal equipment of one individual. Comparison with grave assemblages suggests that they were probably worn by women (Maraszek 2006: 136–51). Different artefacts show different amounts of wear, implying that they were acquired at separate stages of life, even though they were deposited together on the same occasion. Such ornaments can occur as single finds, but most of them seem to have been discarded as complete sets. Indeed, there are hoards in southern Scandinavia that contain the artefacts associated with as many as five separate people (Levy 1982). A good example is the collection from Skjødstrup in Jutland (Levy 1982: Plate 11 and 152). Similar combinations of objects can be recognized from burials, but again the two groups of material are found in different areas. Although ornament hoards have occasionally been discovered together with bones, it is not always known whether the remains were human.

Both weapons and ornaments can be represented by hoards and single finds in one region and were buried with the dead in another. They could also change their contexts over time, so that they might have been associated with the deceased in one phase and separated from them during a different period (Bradley 1998: Chapter 3). In both cases it is obvious that some of these objects had a lengthy history. They may have enjoyed a special significance too. The high quality and distinctive decoration of the ornaments, which could be made of bronze or gold, suggest that they were not available to everyone; the same may be true of the weapons. It is uncertain whether the more elaborate artefacts were personal possessions or insignia, but their special character would have been threatened if they were treated in the same ways as

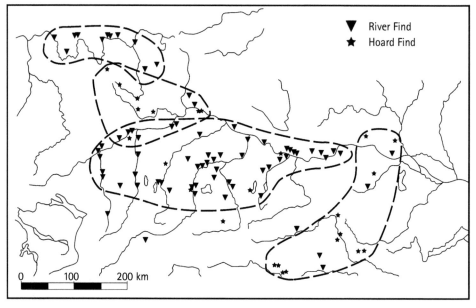

FIG. 7.3 The overlapping distributions of Urnfield swords in Austrian rivers and hoards.

Source: author, after Erbach-Schönberg.

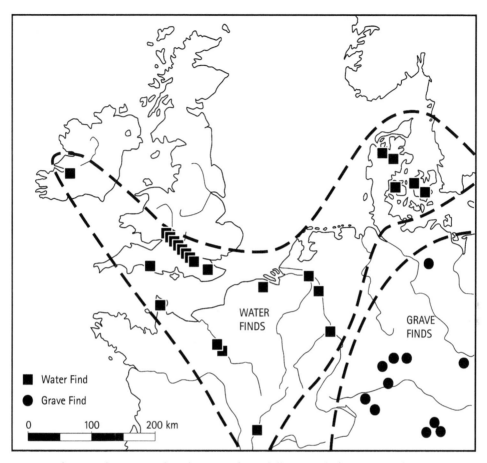

FIG. 7.4 The complementary distributions of Mindelheim and Thames swords in rivers and graves.

Source: author, after Torbrügge.

other valuables when their period of use came to an end. That provides one reason why they were withdrawn from circulation. Perhaps their role as votive offerings protected their special character (Fontijn 2003). The same idea might explain why the gifts presented to Archbishop Ramsey as the head of the Church of England were deposited in the River Wear.

Space and Time

There are difficulties with all these interpretations. If certain objects played such a specialized role that they had to be sacrificed once their use was over, how could the same types of objects have been accumulated and melted down by smiths? And how could ornaments, weapons, and tools have been mixed together as a source of raw material? One possibility is that this process removed these items from circulation as effectively as their deposition in a river. On the other hand, it could suggest that they lost their distinctive character when their outward appearance was transformed (Fig. 7.5).

Another possibility is that these items could be reused precisely because they no longer had their original associations (Mordant 1998; Fontijn 2008). This could happen in at least two ways. Either they had been brought together outside the area in which they carried special connotations or they were made in styles that were becoming obsolete. Both possibilities are suggested by existing studies of hoards, but they are seldom discussed in these terms.

The distribution of metalwork hoards shows two distinctive patterns that have been identified in different parts of Europe. The first concerns the distinction between 'mixed' hoards whose contents combine the conventional categories of tools, weapons, and ornaments, and those in which only one of those classes of artefact is represented. If particular kinds of object had prescribed roles in Bronze Age society, they might have been kept separate in the area where they had a special significance. Similarly, those types would be more likely to appear together outside that region. Such a pattern sometimes can be identified. For example, in the English Middle Bronze Age the main concentration of single-category hoards is bounded by that of mixed deposits (Bradley 1998: 122–3).

A more striking spatial pattern involves hoards and single finds. If the metalwork found in rivers played a specialized role, would it have happened where the same kinds of artefacts were included in hoards of scrap metal? The two types of deposit often have complementary distributions, so that the regions with concentrations of isolated weapons or groups of ornaments are effectively enclosed by deposits in which these objects had been reduced to fragments and mixed with the by-products of metalworking. This phenomenon is clearly

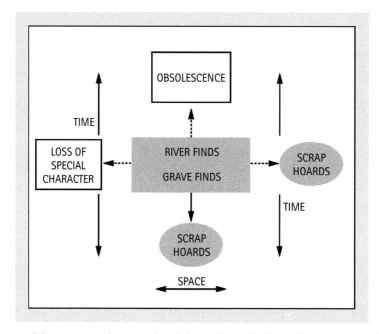

FIG. 7.5 A model suggesting the spatial and chronological relationships between finds from rivers and graves, and the occurrence of similar artefacts in scrap hoards.

Source: author (drawing Elise Fraser).

documented in Britain, Germany, and Denmark (Bradley 1998: 123–7; Mordant 1998). It may be that objects which had travelled outside the areas where they played a restricted role could be treated as a source of raw material. In exactly the same way objects of unfamiliar types entering a region from outside might have been melted down so that they could be replaced by more appropriate forms. Again, that happened towards the edge of their overall distribution. It might explain why so many scrap hoards occur near the coast, for this is where foreign artefacts were most likely to be encountered (Fontijn 2008).

There is yet another possibility to consider. Burgess and Coombs (1979) suggested that metalwork hoards in the British Isles were most frequent towards the ends of the phases to which they are assigned. It is difficult to assess their argument, which is based on artefact typology, but it does raise an interesting possibility. If they are correct—and their hypothesis needs to be verified in other regions—it might suggest that some of the material consigned to the ground was already going of fashion. That is not to endorse their idea that bronze was dumped because it lost its value as iron came into use: an explanation that would not explain the intensity of hoarding in central Europe during Hallstatt A1 (Harding 2000: 356). It seems more likely that certain objects could be recycled because they no longer possessed their original significance. When it happened, a proportion of the material was retained as a votive offering.

This discussion has emphasized three significant points. The first is that hoards should not be investigated without paying equal attention to single finds and the artefacts deposited with the dead. The relationship between these categories helps to identify a number of important issues. Secondly, it is essential to study hoarding in its wider geographical and chronological contexts, as the same forms of artefacts can appear as both hoard finds and single finds. The relationships between them need to be defined in more detail than is possible here. Lastly, it is not enough to catalogue the contents of these deposits, for the treatment paid to the different artefacts provides a vital source of information.

Each of these comments has the same implication. The 'hoard' is an artefact of a particular kind of archaeological analysis. In the past these collections of artefacts did not possess any unifying feature. It is the task of modern research to take this category apart and to investigate its separate components. The collections of artefacts that prehistorians have grouped together as hoards need to be investigated as part of a wider inquiry into the deposition of Bronze Age metalwork.

Unfinished Business

It is too soon to summarize every new development in the study of metalwork deposits, and this account has made no attempt to do so. Instead it has highlighted some of the approaches that appear to be most productive. At the same time, it may be helpful to mention some topics that require more investigation. It is important to emphasize that there is much still to learn. The final section of this chapter suggests a number of ways in which this can be achieved. One set of problems concerns the use of raw materials, and the other relates to the places in which artefacts are found.

A first priority is to consider the roles of hoards and single finds over a longer period than the Bronze Age. The debates that have preoccupied Bronze Age specialists have also taken place in the archaeology of the Iron Age, Roman, and Early Medieval periods, and similar issues have been discussed with little reference to a longer history or a more general body of ideas. It is especially important to consider the earliest deposits of artefacts in wetlands. In northern Europe they pre-date the adoption of farming, but similar practices extended throughout the Neolithic period (Karsten 1994). It would be useful to know more about the ways in which this tradition was modified when metal became available, for copper and bronze must have been thought to possess unusual properties. As mentioned earlier, it is also necessary to investigate the ways in which ritual behaviour changed as bronze was replaced by iron.

If the source of the raw material was an important factor, then it is a priority to investigate hoards and single finds of goldwork in more detail than has happened so far (Morteani and Northover 1993). There are some deposits in which both bronze and gold are found, but it was unusual to use these materials together. To what extent do the patterns suggested for deposits of bronze artefacts apply to those of gold? Were they circulated and consumed according to the same procedures? Were the same people responsible for working both kinds of metal, and were the artefacts themselves deposited in similar places? In many regions that has still to be established.

Objects made of both materials are often represented by fragments. Why did this happen? It implies that the 'missing' parts must have been treated separately, whether or not they were melted down. It seems possible that the circulation of broken objects was a common practice and that it played a role in creating and maintaining relationships between people in the past. In principle, different parts of the same object could have had separate histories, and there may be cases in which the pieces were reunited after an interval. Alternatively, they might have been deposited individually. These questions have been investigated in eastern Europe by John Chapman (Chapman 2000: 112–21), but specialists on the metalwork of other regions show little awareness of this important research.

If these questions need to engage scholars who study metalwork, other observations are more relevant for field archaeologists. There is every reason to believe that certain deposits were appropriate in certain kinds of places. The distinction between river finds and dry-land hoards is only one example of a more general process. It seems as though particular objects or combinations of objects were usually discarded in quite specific locations. Although these relationships could change from one region to another, in some instances they were maintained over a considerable period of time. David Fontijn's work in the southern Netherlands provides the best example of these patterns, for in this case sickles and pins were associated with houses in the settlements; axes, sickles, and spears were deposited in streams and marshes further away; and swords and more elaborate ornaments were confined to the major rivers (Fontijn 2003). In other regions hoards are associated with particular topographical features. In principle it should be possible to predict the future pattern of discovery and to take it into account in the management of the cultural heritage. That has already been achieved in a study of votive offerings in one area near Amsterdam (Kok 2008), and the same methods could be applied in other parts of Europe.

Such work is bound to take place at an extensive geographical scale, but there is scope for other research on the immediate surroundings of hoards and single finds. Too few of these collections are examined while they remain in the ground, and the investigations that do take place can be conducted on too small a scale. In some regions it is clear that hoards were deposited outside settlements of the same date, but only rarely have both been treated together. It is a relationship that can be investigated by sample excavation, fieldwalking, and various forms of remote sensing, and one that should be studied more intensively in the future. That may be easier to achieve now that large areas of ground are investigated by developer-funded fieldwork.

Conclusion

The discovery of Michael Ramsey's treasures in the River Wear posed a difficult problem for the authorities of Durham Cathedral. Had the gifts presented to him during his time as Archbishop of Canterbury been stolen and discarded by the thieves, or had they been deposited by Ramsey himself? Were they taken out of circulation to protect their special character, or could he have intended them as gifts to God? It is quite possible that they fulfilled both roles at the same time.

Deposits of bronze artefacts pose the same problem (among many others), and the ways in which they have been interpreted are equally diverse. Again, there has been a debate between those who see such collections as votive offerings, and scholars who believe that they can be understood in practical terms. If opinion is divided on the character of a deposit which is less than thirty years old, it is hardly surprising that the existence of prehistoric hoards should be so difficult to explain.

Bibliography

Bradley, R. (1998). *The Passage of Arms* (2nd edn). Oxford: Oxbow Books.
—— (2000). *An Archaeology of Natural Places.* London: Routledge.
—— (2005). *Ritual and Domestic Life in Prehistoric Europe.* London: Routledge.
—— and Gordon, K. (1988). 'Human skulls from the River Thames, their dating and significance', *Antiquity,* 62: 503–9.
Brandherm, D. (2007). 'Swords by numbers', in C. Burgess, P. Topping, and F. Lynch (eds.), *Beyond Stonehenge: Essays in Honour of Colin Burgess.* Oxford: Oxbow Books, 288–300.
Brück, J. (2006). 'Fragmentation, personhood and the social construction of technology in Middle and Late Bronze Age Britain', *Cambridge Archaeological Journal,* 16: 297–315.
Brunn, W. von (1968). *Mitteldeutsche Hortfunde der jüngeren Bronzezeit.* Berlin: De Gruyter.
Budd, P. and Taylor, T. (1995). 'The faerie smith meets the bronze industry: magic versus science in the interpretation of prehistoric metal making', *World Archaeology,* 27: 133–43.
Burgess, C. (1980). 'The Bronze Age in Wales', in J. Taylor (ed.), *Culture and Environment in Prehistoric Wales.* Oxford: British Archaeological Reports (British Series), 76: 243–86.
—— and Coombs, D. (1979). 'Preface', in C. Burgess and D. Coombs (eds.), *Bronze Age Hoards: Some Finds Old and New.* Oxford: British Archaeological Reports (British Series), 67: i–vii.
Chapman, J. (2000). *Fragmentation in Archaeology.* London: Routledge.
Childe, V. G. (1958). *The Prehistory of European Society.* Harmondsworth: Penguin.
Coffyn, A., Gomez de Soto, J., and Mohen, J.-P. (1981). *L'Apogée du bronze atlantique (le dépôt de Vénat).* Paris: Picard.

Coombs, D. (1975). 'Bronze Age weapon hoards in Britain', *Archaeologia Atlantica*, 1: 49–81.
Eogan, G. (1974). 'Regionale Gruppierungen in der Spätbronzezeit Irlands', *Archäologisches Korrespondenzblatt*, 4: 319–27.
Erbach-Schönberg, M.-C. zu (1985). 'Bemerkungen zu urnenfelderzeitlichen Deponierungen in Oberösterrreich', *Archäologisches Korrespondenzblatt*, 15: 163–78.
Fontijn, D. (2003). 'Sacrificial landscapes: cultural biographies of persons, objects and "natural" places in the Bronze Age of the southern Netherlands c.2500–600 BC', *Analecta Praehistorica Leidensia*, 33–4: 1–392.
—— (2008). '"Traders' hoards". Revisiting the relationship between trade and permanent deposition: the case of the Dutch Voerhout hoard', in C. Hamon and B. Quilliec (eds.), *Hoards from the Neolithic to the Metal Ages: Technical and Codified Practice*. Oxford: British Archaeological Reports (International Series), 758: 5–17.
Goldhahn, J. (2007). *Dödens hand—en essä om brons- och hällsmed*. Gothenburg: Gothenburg University.
Harding, A. F. (2000). *European Societies in the Bronze Age*. Cambridge: Cambridge University Press.
Helms, M. (2009). 'The master(y) of hard materials: thoughts on technology, materiality and ideology occasioned by the Dover boat', in P. Clark (ed.), *Bronze Age Connections: Cultural Contact in Prehistoric Europe*. Oxford: Oxbow Books, 149–58.
Jensen, J. (1972). 'Ein neues Hallstattschwert aus Dänemark. Beitrag zur Problematik der jungbronzezeitlichen Votivfunde', *Acta Archaeologica*, 43: 115–64.
Karsten, P. (1994). *Att kasta yxan in sjön*. Lund: Acta Archaeologica Lundensia.
Kienlin, T. and Ottaway, B. (1998). 'Flanged axes of the North Alpine region: an assessment of the posibilities of wear analysis on metal artefacts', in C. Mordant, M. Pernot, and V. Rychner (eds.), *L'Atelier du bronzier en Europe. Production, circulation et consummation du bronze*. Paris: Éditions du Comité des Travaux Historiques et Scientifiques, 271–86.
Kok, M. (2008). *The Homecoming of Religious Practice*. Doctoral thesis, University of Amsterdam.
Kubach, W. (1979). 'Deponierung in Mooren der südhessischen Oberrheinebene', *Jahresbericht für Vorgeschichte der Universität Frankfurt a. M*, 198–310.
Levy, J. (1982). *Social and Religious Organisation in Bronze Age Denmark*. Oxford: British Archaeological Reports (International Series), 124.
Malmer, M. (1992). 'Weight systems in the Scandinavian Bronze Age', *Antiquity*, 66: 377–88.
Maraszek, R. (1998), *Spätbronzezeitliche Hortfunde entlang der Oder*. Bonn: R. Habelt.
—— (2006). *Spätbronzezeitliche Hortfundlandschaften in atlantischer und nordischer Metalltradition*. Halle: Landesamt für Denkmalpflege und Archäologie Sachsen-Anhalt.
Mordant, C. (1998). 'Dépôts de bronze et territoires à l'âge du Bronze', in C.Mordant, M. Pernot, and V. Rychner (eds.), *L'Atelier du bronzier en Europe. Production, circulation et consummation du bronze*, Paris: Éditions du Comité des Travaux Historiques et Scientifiques, 185–210.
—— (2007). 'Le Dépôt de Villethierry (Yonne). Un relecture des données', in C. Burgess, P. Topping, and F. Lynch (eds.), *Beyond Stonehenge: Essays in Honour of Colin Burgess*. Oxford: Oxbow Books, 335–43.
Morteani, G. and Northover, J. P. (eds.) (1993). *Prehistoric Gold in Europe: Mines, Metallurgy, Manufacture*. Dordrecht: Kluwer Academic Press.
Nebelsick, L. (2000). '"Rent asunder": ritual violence in Late Bronze Age hoards', in C. Pare (ed.), *Metals Make the World Go Round*. Oxford: Oxbow Books, 160–75.

Needham, S. (1990). *The Petters Late Bronze Age Metalwork*. London: British Museum.

Rassmann, K. (1996). 'Untersuchungen zu spätbronzezeitlichen Hortfunden im nördlichen Schwarzmeergebiet', in C. Huth (ed.), *Archäologische Forschungen zum Kultgeschehen in der jüngeren Bronzezeit und frühen Eisenzeit Alteuropas*. Bonn: Habelt, 535–55.

Ruiz-Gálvez, M. (2000). *Ritos de paso y puntas de paso. La Ría de Huelva en el mundo del Bronze final europeo*. Madrid: Universidad Complutense.

Samson, A. (2006). 'Offshore finds from the Bronze Age in north-western Europe: the shipwreck scenario revisited', *Oxford Journal of Archaeology*, 25: 371–88.

Schwanger, S (1997). '"Wanderer kommst Du nach Spa"—Der Opferplatz von Berlin-Spandau. Ein Heiligtum für Krieger, Händler und Reisende', in A. Hänsel and B. Hänsel (eds.), *Gaben an die Götter*. Berlin: Staatliche Museum zu Berlin–Preussischer Kulturbesitz, 61–6.

Sommerfeld, C. (1994). *Gerätegeld Sichel. Studien zur monetären Struktur bronzezeitlichen Horte im nördlichen Mitteleuropa*. Berlin: De Gruyter.

Torbrügge, W. (1971). 'Vor- und frühgeschichtliche Flussfunde', *Bericht der Römisch-Germanischen Kommission*, 52: 1–146.

Turner, L. (2010). *A Re-interpretation of the Later Bronze Age Metalwork Hoards of Essex and Kent*. Oxford: British Archaeological Reports (British Series), 507.

Warmenbol, E. (1996). 'L'Or, la mort et les Hyperboréens. La Bouche des Enfers ou le Trou de Han à Han-sur-Lesse', in C. Huth (ed.), *Archäologische Forschungen zum Kultgeschehen in der jüngeren Bronzezeit und frühen Eisenzeit Alteuropas*. Bonn: Habelt, 23–34.

Winghart, S. (2000). 'Mining, processing and distribution of bronze: reflections on the organisation of metal supply between the northern Alps and the Danube region', in C. Pare (ed.), *Metals Make the World Go Round*. Oxford: Oxbow Books, 151–9.

Wyss, R. (1996). 'Funde von Pässen, Höhlen, aus Quellen und Gewässern der Zentral- und Westalpen', in C. Huth (ed.), *Archäologische Forschungen zum Kultgeschehen in der jüngeren Bronzezeit und frühen Eisenzeit Alteuropas*. Bonn: Habelt, 417–28.

Yates, D. and Bradley, R. (2010a). 'Still water, hidden depths. The deposition of Bronze Age metalwork in the English Fenland', *Antiquity*, 84: 405–15.

—— (2010b) 'The siting of metalwork hoards in the Bronze Age of south-east England', *The Antiquaries Journal*, 90: 1–32.

York, J. (2002). 'The life cycle of Bronze Age metalwork from the Thames', *Oxford Journal of Archaeology*, 21: 77–92.

CHAPTER 8

MONUMENTS AND MONUMENTALITY IN BRONZE AGE EUROPE

TIMOTHY DARVILL

Introduction

Monuments of many different kinds were constructed in various parts of Europe during Bronze Age times for the celebration, commemoration, remembrance, and forgetting of people, communities, events, festivals, gods, and sacred interventions. Most were overtly concerned with connecting the land of the living with the gardens of the gods or the dominion of the dead. In their design and construction, these monuments mythologize and dramatize a widespread cosmological scheme for the universe in which the gods inhabited three levels—the sky, the earth, and the waters under the earth—each conceived as circular planes that wheel eternally around an *axis mundi* (e.g. Kaul 1998). The living inhabited only the middle plane, while the dead inhabited a fourth dimension accessible through liminal zones and disjunctions at the intersections of sky, earth, and water. In consequence, many Bronze Age monuments are found in situations that variously impinge upon everyday life, as they had in earlier times, of which three are especially common: within or around settlements; in high places with access to the sky; or in watery places beside rivers, lakes, bogs, or the sea. Human burials are associated with many kinds of monument, but one defining characteristic of the Bronze Age across Europe was the development of formal cemeteries with specific relationships to the settlements they served; some such cemeteries were monumentalized.

Although many monuments were certainly massive, physically imposing, larger than life, impressive, sturdy, and enduring, size was not always so important. A broader sense of 'monumentality' is relevant in looking at Bronze Age sites as it is the dramatic content that is critical to their recognition and interpretation; the purposefully constructed ability to communicate elemental emotions through visual and temporal manifestations would prompt discernible psychological effects on those who observed and engaged with the monument. In this sense a single standing stone or timber post may be as powerful in its monumentality as the facade of a great fortified settlement. Nor need monuments be entirely human creations (Bradley 2000). Natural features such as boulders, rock outcrops, springs, waterfalls, pools, caves, shafts, trees, and bushes possess monumentality when identified in some way and imbued with meaning.

Reading meaning is critical to the appreciation of monumentality, but it is not always easy in an archaeological context for two reasons. First, although monuments were generally built of stone, timber, rubble, soil, and turf, the way these materials were viewed as categorical notions in the world by their users is largely lost to us. A little can be glimpsed through the lexicon of reconstructed proto-Indo-European words and the concepts they represent (Mallory and Adams 2006), while patterns of association, context, and materiality provide further clues. From this it is clear that the materials used in monument building were carefully and deliberately chosen for their qualities and meanings. Most were locally sourced, but occasionally only material from distant sources would do. The lithologically diverse pillars collectively known as the 'bluestones' were brought 250 km to the megalithic circles at Stonehenge (Wiltshire), England, and set up in a manner that reflected their physical arrangement at source in the eastern Preseli Hills of north Pembrokeshire in Wales (Darvill 2006: 136–40). It is the kind of process that Tim Insoll has described as 'shrine franchising' and may well have been extensive in Bronze Age Europe. Much of course is missing, especially the organic components that would have added colour, formal designs, motifs, and textures to monuments. And what now appear as foundations once had superstructures that determined the patterns of light and sounds experienced by the users of these sites. Second, archaeologists have been reluctant to think about intangible aspects of the monuments they explore: the animals, people, gods, sights, sounds, smells, beliefs, rituals, and ceremonies; the dancing, chanting, dreaming, and altered consciousness of participants. Ethnographic and anthropological analogies can help illustrate the range of possibilities and lead our thinking away from modern Western value systems and conceptual categories, while within the European context it is increasingly recognized that oral tradition and folklore can sometimes reflect earlier beliefs and views of the world that may help with the interpretation of excavated evidence. As a result of such studies it is now widely accepted that during Bronze Age times the sacred and the profane were fully enmeshed in social practice to the extent that trying to separate them is futile.

The design, construction, purpose, and meaning of monuments changed over time. As one form developed, another declined through processes of social selection, with the result that three successive life-stages can be seen in most traditions: an innovative formative stage; a stable florescent stage; and finally a familiar stage with increasing obsolescence and declining commitments to maintenance and use. Since the introduction of metalworking as the defining indicator of the start of the Bronze Age was generally unrelated to the unfolding trajectories of monumental traditions, it is unsurprising that the formative and/or florescent phase of many monument classes used during the Bronze Age actually date back among Neolithic and Chalcolithic societies. Likewise, some earlier formative ideas, notably for example the use of round barrows, expanded to reach florescence and familiarity during the Bronze Age.

Tensions and fears about the power of monuments already ancient by the Early Bronze Age may have prompted the monumentalization of structured forgetting (Jones 2007: 39–41). In Britain, for example, some earthworks traditionally seen as the boundaries of henge monuments were in fact constructed late in the life of these sites to isolate the structures and contain the legacy of what went on within them. At Durrington Walls (Wiltshire), England, the bank and internal ditch reckoned to represent more than 900,000 person-hours of manual labour were built in the Early Bronze Age around 2500 BC to enclose an area slightly less than 400 m across that included at least five small shrines, a multiple-timber circle, and a large roundhouse.

In this chapter attention is directed towards a selection of structures with a strongly monumental aspect, built or used by bronze-using communities, although the boundaries of what can be covered are slightly arbitrary. Although they have clear monumentalized aspects, space precludes coverage of enclosed or fortified settlements, burnt mounds (Barfield and Hodder 1991), rock-cut tombs, and hypogea (Whitehouse 1972), and the stone towers known as *nuraghi*, *torres*, *talayots*, and *motillas* in Sardinia, Corsica, Mallorca, Menorca, and southwest Spain (Fernández Castro 1995: 106–14). Likewise palaces, semi-urban settlements, and peak-sanctuaries in the Aegean world are also omitted as being geographically beyond the coverage of this volume. Discussion focuses on seven broad monument types that can be found in one or more of five geographical zones extending across peninsular Europe between the Mediterranean and the Atlantic, and eastwards to the rivers Volga and Dvina, effectively linking the Caspian Sea with the White Sea (Fig. 8.1). Some of these monument types are highly restricted in space and time, whereas others are widely distributed and long-lived.

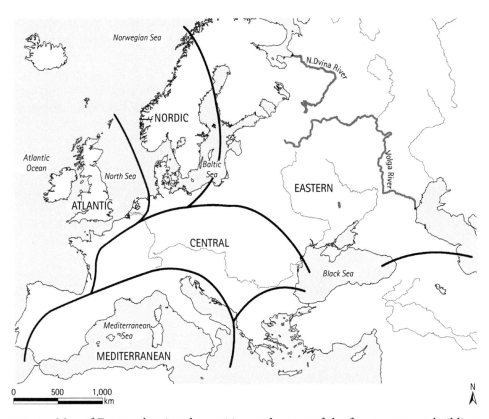

FIG. 8.1 Map of Europe showing the position and extent of the five monument-building zones discussed in this chapter.

Source: author (drawing Vanessa Constant).

Late Chambered Tombs

The earliest European monumental architecture is found in the dolmens, long barrows, and passage graves built in north-western Europe through the fifth, fourth, and early third millennia BC. By the turn of the Bronze Age most of these traditions were long gone, although respect for some earlier structures is shown by the addition of burials. However, in a few geographically restricted areas it seems that a passion for the old ways lived on and fourteen clusters of late chambered tombs can be recognized.

In the Atlantic Zone around fifty Clava Cairns echoing the form of earlier passage graves are known around the Moray Firth in eastern Scotland. Excavations show they were built and used in the period 2200 BC to 1700 BC. South-westwards in Dumfries and Galloway (Scotland) a cluster of 13 Bargrennan Graves also perpetuate the passage-grave tradition well into the early second millennium BC. Further south-west still a group of smaller and simpler Entrance Graves or Scilly-Tramore Tombs lie around the coastlands of the Irish Sea, mainly in Cornwall with outliers in south-east Ireland and the Isle of Man. Across much of Ireland, especially in western counties, more than four hundred wedge-tombs seem to continue the long-barrow tradition with elongated chambers within a trapezoidal or oval mound. And to complete the set, the tradition of building dolmens lived on as Boulder Burials, or Boulder Dolmens, in south-western Ireland where large boulders or thick slabs were placed on three or more low flat-topped orthostats with burials beneath (Ó Nualláin 1978).

In the Mediterranean Zone late passage graves are represented by the tholos-style Millares Tombs of Andalucia (Spain) and southern Portugal, many arranged in cemeteries adjacent to contemporary settlements (Chapman 1990: 74). Dolmens of various kinds are known on Corsica where some have a porthole entrance (Joussaume 1985: 211–15), on Sardinia where some are set within an oval platform (Joussaume 1985: 215–16), on Malta (Evans 1971: 193–8) where small clusters are known, and on the heel of Italy where they are known as Otranto Tombs (Palumbo 1956). Innovative megalithic architecture of the late third and second millennia BC is found eastwards in the Balearic Islands where about thirty *Navetas* each comprise solid stone structures built from large squared blocks, horseshoe-shaped in plan with a small internal chamber accessible through a small opening in the bottom of the facade (Joussaume 1985: 220). On Sardinia, of around 250 *Tombe di Giganti*, usually a rectangular stone-built chamber up to 15 m long is entered through a monumental facade which frames an apsidal or semi-circular forecourt (Whitehouse 1981: 116). Rather similar are the Bari-Taranto Tombs of south-eastern Italy where simple rectangular chambers between 3 and 17 m long lie within oval or rectangular mounds (Joussaume 1985: 223–4).

In the Eastern Zone a cluster of quite unrelated megalithic tombs is known in the mountainous regions of the north-west Caucasus. These Abkhazian Dolmens comprise box-like monuments built from well-fitting stone slabs often with a circular or oval hole in the front. On excavation they are found to contain up to forty interments and are considered to represent long-term family vaults (Markovin 2002).

Round Barrows, Kurgans, Tumuli, and 'Fancy Barrows'

The most widely represented Bronze Age monument in Europe is the round barrow—variously also known as kurgans and tumuli. At its most simple, a round barrow is just a hemispherical mound of turf, soil, and locally quarried bedrock heaped over one or more graves. But even such simple monuments embody physical expressions of deep-seated cosmologies. The visible mound probably represents the vault of the heavens above the earth, while the deceased is placed in a pit cut into the underworld below. Structurally, many are far more complicated with long histories of construction and use and additional symbolism. Concentric rings of stakes or posts below barrows in the British Isles and in the Netherlands, as well as concentric walls below a barrow on the island of Gotland, Sweden, may represent sun-symbolism. Closely connected is the wheel-symbolism represented by a series of radial walls at Hjordkjaer (Jutland), Denmark.

Numerous regional, local, and temporal variations in construction and design can be recognized across Europe, yet all were intended not only to mark the burial place but also to commemorate and celebrate those laid to rest there. Indeed, barrow sites were quite literally performance spaces during funerary rituals, barrow construction, and later commemorative ceremonies. Across Europe many survive as mounds, but where later cultivation has been intense the mounds have often been ploughed away leaving only the surrounding quarry ditches as 'ring-ditches'. Two main seemingly unconnected sources for round barrows can be recognized, one in south-eastern Europe and the other in the north-west.

In the Pontic Steppes of the Eastern Zone kurgan mounds began to be constructed in late Neolithic times, c.3500–3300 BC, often covering richly furnished burials in stone-lined chambers. An early example dated to the mid fourth millennium BC at Maikop (Adygeja), Russia, is 11 m high, 65 m in diameter and covered a spectacularly rich grave (Kohl 2007: 72–3). Yamnaya cultures in the area between the Volga and the Danube developed the kurgan tradition between 3300 and 2300 BC, with the appearance of cemeteries containing more than a dozen mounds becoming fixed ancestral burial grounds for mobile pastoralist communities. During the Middle Bronze Age of the region (*katakombnaya kultura* or Catacomb culture) the fashion for large 'royal kurgans' continued with examples at Sachkere, Bedeni, and Tsnori, in the northern Caucasus, Russia, illustrating the range of styles used at this time. Through the early second millennium BC kurgan cemeteries became more common southwards into Transcaucasia and westwards into the Carpathian Basin (Gimbutas 1965). Throughout the kurgan tradition the construction of the mound was relatively simple with successive layers of turf, soil, and redeposited bedrock. The burials beneath were more elaborate and usually contained within timber-walled or stone-lined chambers that sometimes resembled houses more than graves. As in other parts of Europe it was a tradition that declined through the later second millennium BC to the point where no new examples seem to have been built after about 1200 BC.

A second round-barrow tradition can be traced back to Atlantic Europe, perhaps with inspiration from the Neolithic passage graves of the fifth and early fourth millennia BC. Certainly round barrows covering a variety of timber and stone burial chambers were in use across the British Isles by the mid fourth millennium BC (Leary, Darvill, and Field 2010), and their popularity increased with the uptake of single-grave traditions during the third millennium BC. From this time through to about 1200 BC round barrows formed the dominant burial monument through the Atlantic, Nordic, and Central Zones, the basis of the eponymous 'Tumulus Culture' as a broad cultural tradition of the Early and Middle Bronze Age phases across this vast territory.

Individual barrows witnessed extended and complicated ceremonies and rituals. There were clearly many rules, precedents, and taboos surrounding the way barrows and the burials they contain were created. As well as primary burials at the focus of the monument there are often contemporary satellite burials around about, and secondary and tertiary additions introduced decades or centuries later.

Round barrows are well represented through most of the Atlantic Zone. In Britain more than fifty thousand have been recorded, mainly with simple bowl-shaped mounds surrounded by a ditch that provided material for use in constructing the mound (Woodward 2000). More elaborate examples are generically referred to as 'fancy barrows', with numerous regional expressions definable by differently shaped mounds, the presence of platforms, the use of encircling banks as well as ditches, and the size and position of the mound within the earthwork. Typically, bowl barrows are 10–20 m in diameter and up to 2 m high, but larger examples were often placed in prominent positions, what are sometimes called 'conspicuous' barrows, as with Milston 12 on Silk Hill (Wiltshire), England, at 6 m high and 45 m across.

In Ireland round barrows were often built as stone cairns, especially in the uplands (Waddell 1986). Amongst the largest is Miosgán Meadhbha on Knocknarea Mountain (County Sligo) comprising at least 14,000 cubic metres of local limestone to form a cairn 60 m across and 10 m high. On the continental mainland more than four hundred round barrows have been recorded in Brittany, and while upstanding examples are rare further south and east in France and Belgium, aerial photography is now revealing an abundance of ring-ditches suggesting that this was not always so. As elsewhere, some upstanding barrows are large; Kernonen en Plouvorn (Finistère) is 50 m in diameter and nearly 6 m high. In the Netherlands about two thousand examples have been recorded, mainly in the central part of the country with cemeteries such as that between Toterfout and Halve Mijl (North Brabant) where 40 barrows are spread over a distance of 2 km and include several different forms.

Tumuli are common throughout the Nordic Zone from later Neolithic times through to the start of the late Bronze Age, broadly 2000 BC through to 1100 BC. More than 85,000 *gravhøj* have been recorded in Denmark alone, some as single mounds but often clustered together as cemeteries positioned on hilltops. Most are cupola- or bowl-shaped in profile between 10 and 80 m in diameter and 1 to 12 m high. Excavation shows that many developed and expanded over several phases. At Sagaholm, Sweden, for example, the first barrow was surrounded by a ring of decorated stone slabs before a second rather larger mound encapsulated it. Overall, there is a sense that elite groups built these monuments not only to commemorate themselves and their ancestors but also to maintain authority in a society with some degree of geographical and social mobility. As elsewhere, a few mounds are exceptionally large and prestigious. Eshøj, Denmark, stands out from a cemetery of 40 barrows in being 40 m in diameter and 7 m high. It was built *c.*1351–1345 BC and covered three graves. Formal relationships between settlements and cemeteries have been detected in the Tobø area of Jutland (Denmark) where a cemetery of about 26 round barrows lay north of the River Kongeå, while surveys revealed that the contemporary settlements were to the east and mainly south of the river.

FIG. 8.2 Silbury Hill, Wiltshire, England.

Photo: Timothy Darvill.

In eastern parts of the Central Zone interment under round barrows became the standard burial rite in the Middle Bronze Age after about 1700 BC, although the exact form and structure of these monuments differs from region to region. Over time cremation was favoured over inhumation. Some graves were extremely rich, among them the so-called princely burials of the Únětice area such as Leubingen in Germany, with a mound 35 m in diameter, nearly 9 m high, and estimated to contain about 210 cubic metres of stone.

Round barrows did not always cover burials. At the Buckskin Barrow (Hampshire), England, the mound was raised over the remains of a feasting event, perhaps focused around a totem pole set within a small fenced enclosure. Equally, the exceptionally large mound at Silbury Hill (Wiltshire), England, was built over a round earthwork enclosure at the very start of the local Bronze Age soon after 2400 BC to become what is often claimed as the largest prehistoric mound in Europe (Fig. 8.2): 167 m in diameter, 40 m high, and representing perhaps 18 million person-hours to build (Leary, Darvill, and Field 2010).

STANDING STONES, STATUE MENHIRS, AND STELAE

Single standing stones are a feature of European monument building from at least the sixth millennium BC but they continued to be set up in some areas throughout the Bronze Age. Unadorned examples comprising natural or slightly shaped pillars generally thought to embody phallic imagery are known as menhirs; those modelled on the human form are usually known as statue menhirs, and those employed specifically as grave markers are known as stelae. In reality, however, the boundaries between these categories are blurred, with some menhirs perhaps intended to represent people, and all three types regularly associated with burials even if that was not their original purpose. Dating the erection of such simple monuments is always difficult, but throughout the standing-stone tradition there is a sense that the pillar somehow links the earth with the sky as a representation of the *axis mundi*. Timber monuments probably performed the same role in some areas, but evidence of these is scant. Notwithstanding these difficulties, menhirs, statue menhirs, and stelae appear across Europe from the Atlantic coast to the Pontic steppes (Casini, De Marinis, and Pedrotti 1995).

In the Atlantic Zone menhirs are widely distributed, especially in the west of Britain and Ireland. Most are local stones selected for their shape from nearby outcrops and set up in conspicuous locations. Some may have been erected as markers along routeways into the uplands, or to indicate a traditional campsite visited from time to time by peripatetic communities (Fig. 8.3a). The presence of cremations around standing stones is not uncommon, the stone becoming the marker for a small cemetery. At Stackpole Warren (Pembrokeshire), Wales, a standing stone was surrounded by a trapezoidal setting of over three thousand smaller stones erected sometime after 1870–1460 BC, while a pit dug near the standing stone contained a cremation dated to 1302–902 BC. In northern France at least some of the hundreds of menhirs in Brittany are of Bronze Age date, or were used in Bronze Age times, although the roots of this tradition clearly date back to the fifth millennium BC.

A single possible statute menhir is known from St Mary's in the Isles of Scilly, with two rather better examples on Guernsey in the Channel Islands (Fig. 8.3b), and two more in Brittany. Stelae are only known in the far south of the Atlantic Zone. The earliest, broadly dated to 1800–1300 BC, are the Alentejo stelae found in southern Portugal, which depict axes and weapons carved in relief. Slightly later are four main concentrations on lands surrounding the middle sections of the rivers Guadalquivir, Guadiana, Tagus, and Mondego in the modern Spanish regions of Extremadura and Andalusia and the neighbouring Portuguese provinces of Beira Baixa, Estremadura, and the Alemtejo (Harrison 2004). Dating to the period 1250–750 BC, more than 100 examples are known, the tallest 2.3 m high (Fig. 8.3c). Images representing no fewer than 35 classes of object have been recorded, including arms, body armour, chariots, ornaments and dress fittings, musical instruments, human figures, animals, and wheels. Importantly, the images depict objects known from hoards in the Atlantic Zone and from sites in the Aegean, while motifs match those used on rock-art panels in Scandinavia.

Within the Nordic Zone standing stones are locally numerous in Denmark (Kaul 1998: 44–7) and southern Sweden, but curiously absent from much of the north German plain. At Vadgård (Jutland), Denmark, a large standing-stone carving with a fish motif was the focus of a dense scatter of postholes that must once have supported a cluster of wooden poles west of the stone.

In southern parts of the Central Zone statue menhirs are found in the central Alps in the upper Adige valley, Val Camonica, and the Valellina valley. Males and females are represented and there are also images of carts or ploughs being pulled by oxen much as appear on the rock-art panels in the same regions. At Sion (Valais) on the Swiss side of the Alps two statue menhirs were added to the facade of an earlier long barrow around 2450–2150 BC to form what Harrison and Heyd regard as a wall of ancestors set up to codify a genealogy.

In the Mediterranean Zone, menhirs, statue menhirs, and stelae are concentrated in five areas (Whitehouse 1981: 117). Northern Italy has statue menhirs in north-west Tuscany (the Lunigiana Group) and in the Bologna area (the Filetto Group), where the simple forms focus

FIG. 8.3 (a) Menhir at Rhos-y-Clegyrn, Pembrokeshire, Wales; (b) Statue-menhir at Castel, Guernsey; (c) Stele Torrejón el Rubio II, Ca, Portugal, showing a human figure 0.69 m high wearing a striking headdress or diadem; Stone rows: (d) Harold's Stones near Trelleck, Monmouthshire, Wales; (e) The Devil's Arrows near Boroughbridge, North Yorkshire, England.

Photos: A, B, D, & E: Timothy Darvill; C: Francisco Marco Simon, Universidad de Zaragoza (courtesy Richard Harrison).

on depicting the head and shoulders. In southern Italy more than 150 menhirs (*pietrefitte*), mainly thin pillars of local limestone, are known, together with three or four statue menhirs including one at Castelluccio dei Sauri on the edge of the Tavoliere Plain. On Corsica there are more than 450 menhirs and statue menhirs, mostly in the south. They are mainly of local granite, range in size from 1 to 7 m tall, and are shaped to depict warriors with metal swords, wearing loincloths and helmets. Unusually, there is provision for attaching horns. On adjacent Sardinia about fifty menhirs are scattered across the whole island. Finally, on Malta there are just two convincing menhirs at Kirhop and Kercem, although more may once have existed (Evans 1971: 198–9).

Pairs and Rows

Menhirs were sometimes set up in pairs, although identification is difficult (especially if one is missing) and dating is more often assumed than demonstrated (Burl 1993: 181–202). The greatest concentration occurs in the northern part of the Atlantic Zone where stone pairs are found mainly in Shetland, Orkney, the Hebrides, southern and central Scotland, Ireland, Wales, Cornwall, and Brittany. Wooden versions are very likely represented elsewhere and deserve more recognition. Such pairs of stones or posts seem to mark boundaries between contrasting environments: a terrace edge overlooking a valley floor, or a hilltop where the land changes gradient. As such they might well have formed symbolic doorways or gateways in the landscape, structuring and directing movement while imparting purpose and meaning to those who passed by. Where preservation is good, one of the stones is typically broad with a flattish top while the other is narrow and pointed in a way that suggests sexual symbolism. Rock art in the form of cup-marks is sometimes found, usually on the broader flat-topped (female?) stone.

Rather different in their context and presumed purpose are the linear arrangements of stones or posts found in the Atlantic Zone and occasionally in the Nordic and Mediterranean Zones known simply as stone rows or post rows (Burl 1993). As with so many Bronze Age monuments, the roots of this tradition lay back in Neolithic times, amply demonstrated by the row of 18 pillars including the Grand Menhir Brisé near Carnac (Morbihan) dated to the later fifth millennium BC. In the British Isles short stone rows with anything between three and six pillars over a distance of between 3 and 175 m are known in many western areas, for example at Harold's Stones near Trellech (Monmouthshire), Wales, and the Devil's Arrows near Boroughbridge (North Yorkshire), England (Fig. 8.3d–e). Dating is poor, but at Ardnacross (Mull, Argyll, and Bute), Scotland, a row of three stones had collapsed before 1140–820 BC. Much longer lines are also known, sometimes aligned on stone circles or prominent round barrows as if directing attention to these monuments and structuring processions or movements through the landscape. In lowland Britain the examination of large areas through commercial archaeology has revealed post rows of identical form and size, as for example at Barleycroft Farm (Cambridgeshire), England, where nine rows varying in length from 77 to 129 m were recorded, while three post rows between 11 and 81 m long and with between 16 and 107 posts were found at Hartshill Copse near Bucklebury (West Berkshire), England.

In Ireland stone rows are concentrated in two areas—mid Ulster and south Munster—with a scatter of examples through other counties (Burl 1993). They fall into two main kinds: numerous small stones in lines generally in excess of 30 m and short rows of between 2 and 13 m with relatively few large stones. At Beaghmore (County Tyrone) at least six stone rows were closely associated with stone circles and cairns (Burl 1993: 101–5). Few have been dated, but at Dromatuk (County Kerry), Ireland, the row was probably built around 1740–1520 BC.

Multiple stone rows involving two or more parallel or convergent lines of stones are known only in northern Scotland, south-west England (Dartmoor and Exmoor), and Brittany. The largest are those around Carnac (Morbihan), France; at Kerzerho there are ten rows involving 1,129 stones over a distance of 2.1 km. Investigations at Just, Ille-et-Vilaine, revealed three parallel rows of stones extending over a distance of about 60 m. The tallest stone was over 2 m high, but in the northern row stones were interspersed with timber posts. Although constructed in the fifth millennium BC, their use continued well into the Bronze Age. In the far north-east of Scotland about 25 fan-shaped arrangements of multiple stone rows involve the use of short stumpy stones, which excavations suggest were erected in the second millennium BC (Burl 1993: 123–31).

Northwards in the Nordic Zone stone rows are rare, but one has been excavated at Myrhøj (Jutland), Denmark. Originally it had about 65 stones over a distance of 156 m on a north-west to south-east axis. At Ekaryd (Småland), Sweden, a row of six pillars perhaps with a second row of four pillars parallel to the north were found sealed beneath a round barrow.

In the Mediterranean Zone rows of menhirs and statue menhirs are known at a few sites, for example at Cauria and Palaggiu on Corsica, the latter with more than 250 monoliths.

Circles and Ovals

Probably the most well-known Bronze Age monuments in the Atlantic Zone are the various stone circles and ovals formed of upright stone pillars (Burl 2000); less well-known are the timber versions since these are no longer prominent features of the landscape (Gibson 2005). Dating is difficult as these were long-lived structures, although the tradition seems to have started in the early third millennium BC, if not before, and carried through into the middle of the second millennium BC. In plan, stone and timber circles vary from almost exactly circular through to egg-shaped and elliptical forms, with a number of ovals in the Irish Sea province.

In the British Isles stone and post circles were usually built as free-standing structures, but sometimes they were added to, or formed integral components of, henges and henge enclosures, as at Avebury (Wiltshire), England. Many of the larger circles at least were built at great cost in terms of labour and resources in a way that perpetuated the promotion of local identity through the conspicuous consumption of energy to create enviable structures. Much controversy surrounds the extent to which stone and timber circles include significant lunar, solar, or stellar alignments in their design. Alexander Thom (1967) devised many ingenious and sometime complicated schemes for the layout and design of these circles, but a more pragmatic analysis of the evidence by Clive Ruggles (1999) suggests the verifiable presence of relatively few rather basic astronomical alignments based mainly on the solstices and the lunar cycles. Equally problematic is the question of how they were used, although it is widely accepted that at least part of their role was as performance spaces for ceremony and ritual that perhaps involved music and dancing.

Aubrey Burl (2000) identified three main phases in the history of circle building. Early circles (3370–2670 BC) were moderately large, fairly regular in plan, have closely set stones, and a conspicuous entrance. Examples include Castlerigg, Cumbria, which has a very clear entrance and rock art on the inner face of pillars on the east side. Middle-period circles (2670–1975 BC) are generally large, up to 100 m across, have a range of sometimes elegant shapes, widely spaced stones, and occur in groups. Late-period circles (1975–1200 BC) are generally small rings of varying shapes and sizes, often with regional styles. Examples include the Nine Ladies on Stannon Moor (Derbyshire), England, about 11 m across. Where stones were not available, timber circles were still built instead, as for example at Charnham Lane (West Berkshire), England, where seven posts were arranged in a ring 6 m across. More well known is Seahenge (Norfolk), England, a timber circle comprising 56 half-split oak logs set in a ring 6.8 m across with an entrance on the south-west side built in the spring or early summer of 2049 BC. In the centre of the enclosure was the inverted lower trunk and root plate of a mature oak tree that had been extensively trimmed and worked.

In south-eastern Ireland and north-eastern Scotland a distinctive style of late circles are known as recumbent stone circles. More than two hundred are known and all comprise a ring of pillars graded in height with the two tallest in the south-west quadrant flanking a prostrate block or recumbent stone. Aubrey Burl has convincingly argued that these circles focused on lunar events, particularly the steady procession of the moon across the top of the recumbent stone at certain phases in its cycle. Excavations at Tomnaverie, Aberdeenshire, showed that here the circle was built on top of a round cairn originally constructed in the twenty-fifth century BC. In Cork and Kerry, Ireland, entry into the circle is usually through a pair of matched stones. Drombeg (County Cork) is one of the best examples with 17 close-set pillars and a recumbent stone to the south-west (Fig. 8.4a). It was used through much of the second millennium BC, is orientated so that the midwinter sun sets over the recumbent stone, and lies adjacent to a series of houses and burnt mounds.

Local sources usually provided the raw materials for making stone circles, but at Stenness and Brogar in the Orkney Islands slabs of sandstone were transported 12 km or more from a quarry at Vestra Field on the north-west side of Mainland. By far the greatest achievement in terms of moving stones and creating a truly unique monument can be seen at Stonehenge (Wiltshire), England (Darvill 2006; Fig. 8.4b). Refurbishment of an existing ditched enclosure about 2500 BC included setting up a horseshoe-shaped arrangement of five massive trilithons. Each comprised a pair of close-set uprights joined at the top by a stone lintel. The stones, up to 40 tonnes in weight, were brought from surface outcrops up to 30 km away. The axis of the Trilithon Horseshoe has the open end towards the rising midsummer sun in the north-east, with the Great Trilithon to the south-west straddling a sight-line to the setting midwinter sun. Outside the trilithons was a double Bluestone Circle of 80 bluestone pillars brought to Salisbury Plain from the Preseli Hills of north Pembrokeshire some 250 km to the west. A sandstone block forming the euphemistically named Altar Stone in the centre of the Trilithon Horseshoe was also brought from south Wales, although its exact source is not yet known. Later the monument was restructured. The bluestones were rearranged as an oval setting inside the Trilithon Horseshoe and a circle outside, while a Sarsen Circle of 30 uprights linked by lintels enclosed the central area (see also Chapter 9).

FIG. 8.4 Stone circles: (a) Drombeg, Co. Cork, Ireland; (b) Stonehenge, Wiltshire, England.
Photos: Timothy Darvill.

The use of stones requiring the expenditure of so much effort for their transportation sets Stonehenge apart from other sites. Mike Parker Pearson believes that the stones represent the ancestors of people living in the area during the later third millennium BC, and were therefore passive reminders of their past (Parker Pearson and Ramilisonina 1998). By contrast, Geoffrey Wainwright and Timothy Darvill see the bluestones in particular as active components in the lives of prehistoric people and point to the presence of healing springs around their source in the Preseli Hills as well as long-lived oral traditions attributing healing properties to the stones at Stonehenge. In this theory, transporting the bluestones to Stonehenge effectively franchised the site as a healing centre, reinvigorated it as focus for pilgrimage, and connected the bluestones with the power of the central deities represented by the trilithons (Darvill 2006: 142–6; Darvill and Wainwright 2009).

Closely related to stone circles are the so-called four-posters (Burl 1988): four upright stones in a square formation, typically up to 5 by 6 m, arranged so that the flat faces of the stones mark the circumference of a circle touching the inner edge of each stone. Often set in dramatic locations, around one hundred examples are known in clusters through Scotland, Wales, south-western England, eastern Ireland, and on as far south as Ille-et-Vilaine in France.

More than thirty stone circles are known in northern France, mainly in Finistère and Morbihan. Most take the form of horseshoe settings, but ovals and rectangles are also known and some of the largest are associated with multiple stone rows. Few of the French sites compare well with those commonly found in the British Isles, but exceptions include Béniguet (Côtes-d'Armor), France.

In the Nordic Zone stone and timber circles are rather rare and most visible examples are actually the decayed remains of round barrows. The few authentic examples tend to be small and late in date compared with those in the British Isles. Many continued in use as burial places well into the first millennium BC. Rectangular settings open at one end have been recognized at Disa's Ting at Svarte (Skåne) and a handful of other sites in Sweden. Two concentric rings or stones with an external diameter of 320 m have been identified at Birkendegaard (Kalundborg), Denmark, and interesting comparisons drawn with Stonehenge. Ship-shaped settings common in the Iron Age may also have origins in the later Bronze Age.

Natural Places, Shafts, and Pools

A recurrent interest in natural places, especially rock outcrops, caves, springs, rivers, pools, lakes, and bogs, can be seen in many parts of Europe through the Bronze Age (Bradley 2000). In some cases these features were elaborated or modified in order to draw greater attention to their essential features and their place within a perceived sacred geography or mythical landscape. Sometimes this involved applying rock art. And in still other instances natural places were effectively replicated by new constructions. Certain trees may also have been considered special and singled out for attention, but archaeologically this is hard to detect. Interest in natural places connected with water is especially notable in the later Bronze Age of the Atlantic, Nordic, and Central Zones, with the rise of this interest coincident with increasing use of cremation as the main burial rite and an accompanying decline in round-barrow construction.

Rock Outcrops and Rock art

Rock art of Bronze Age date is found in more than half a dozen clusters across Europe (Bradley, Chippindale, and Helskog 2001) (see Chapters 15 and 16). It was mainly executed by pecking and incising, but originally some of the motifs might have been painted.

In the Eastern Zone the majority of rock art lies around the eastern shores of Lake Onega, in the valley of the River Vyg near the White Sea, and the rocky Kola Peninsula of north-east Russia. The most common motif is the boat, but there are also hunting scenes, swans, reindeer, human figures, and sun-signs.

In the Nordic Zone through Denmark and southern parts of Sweden and Norway natural rock surfaces were selectively decorated with incised and pecked motifs depicting a wide range of ships, animals, people, weapons, tools, wheels, vehicles, ploughs, cup-marks, footprints, circles, and squiggles. Something of the monumental scale of some sites is illustrated by Torsbo near Kville (Bohuslän), Sweden, where a decorated rock surface extends for more than 100 m along a south-facing slope. At least 17 separate panels each 6 to 10 m apart have been recognized, suggesting a degree of composition. Motifs include at least 150 ships, 40 animals, 30 humans, five footprints, five circles or disks, 200 cupmarks, and 120 other squiggles (Coles 2005: Figs. 226–7). Understanding the meaning of these motifs is far from easy, but Richard Bradley (2009, 150–75) has convincingly shown how sometimes there is a link between round barrows, rock art, landscape, and sacred geography. In this we have to envisage a path cutting across the landscape of the living that links two distinct domains: the higher ground where the round barrows celebrated the ancestors, and the seas of the dead to which they had to travel. Foot-sole motifs and ship motifs are consistently orientated downhill from the barrows and lead to the sea.

In the British Isles some Bronze Age monuments include in their construction stones decorated with Galician-style rock art—mainly cup-marks and cup-and-ring-marks (Beckensall 1999). Many of these were probably taken from earlier monuments or broken from outcrops and earth-fast boulders. Often the decoration would have been invisible once the monument was completed, but presumably the images still held meaning and as such served to emphasize a sense of social continuity. Excavations at Torbhlaren (Argyll and Bute), Scotland, show that a stone and clay platform was constructed around a rock outcrop chosen for decoration, followed by periods of activity when quartz hammers were used to cut the motifs in a gradual process of monumentalization. Cist-Grave art was also produced during the Early and Middle Bronze Age, with a range of new motifs including naturalistic human footprints, axes, and daggers. Examples of this style are mainly found on stones used in the construction of burial monuments.

In north-western Spain and northern Portugal the Galician style predominates, with a predominance of cup-marks and cup-and-ring-marks, together with more naturalistic motifs that include weapons, animals, mainly red deer and horses, and occasionally people and wagons.

Through much of eastern Spain and France rock art is seemingly rather rare with no distinctive style, but in southern parts of the Central Zone there are 20–30 recognized clusters of rock-art sites, mostly on the southern side of the Alps. Around Mont Bego, France, over thirty thousand motifs have been recorded in a series of adjacent valleys, mainly lines, figures, and geometric forms, with lesser numbers of ards, weapons, and cattle. At Val Camonica, Italy, between Lake Iseo and the Swiss border, cup-and-ring-marks, perhaps reflecting solar symbolism, cup-marks, wheels, discs with rays attached to them, and linked discs are the dominant motifs, but animal figures, occasional humans, and buildings are also represented along with scenes interpreted as animal sacrifices. Broadly contemporary high-altitude rock art around Carschenna, Switzerland, depicts horsemen together with cup-marks, circles, and wavy line patterns.

Springs, Pools, Wells, and Shafts

Natural springs were widely celebrated and monumentalized. On Sardinia, for example, paved areas with benches were set around springs. More substantial are cases where springs have been elaborated to form pools. At the King's Stables (County Armagh), Ireland, excavations revealed a sunken pool 4 m deep and 25 m across, enclosed by a banked enclosure and used for the deposition of offerings in the form of animal and human remains as well as waste from metalworking.

Water was also the focus of attention at various rock-cut shafts and wells that seem to have become special places. At Swalecliffe (Kent), England, 17 wells with steps and wooden revetments have been dated to the period 1432–1085 BC, while the 30 m deep Wilsford Shaft (Wiltshire), England, remained in use until about 1600–1260 BC. At Gánovce (Poprad), Slovakia, a 2 m deep sacred well was found in the middle of a settlement.

Enclosures, Shrines, and Cult Houses

Monumentalizing space set aside for ceremonial purposes, sometimes including burial, is a recurrent theme of Bronze Age ritual. In part it draws on earlier traditions, but equally important is its legacy for future generations who eventually develop the idea into what might be termed temples. In a very real sense these places were arenas for worship and celebration, and in some cases may be considered the home of the deity or a place where humans and their gods can meet together in one place. There is huge diversity and only a sample of what is known can be mentioned here.

Ring-Cairns and Enclosed Cremation Cemeteries

Relatively small circular enclosed spaces defined by a bank and ditch or a low wall are widespread across northern parts of the Atlantic Zone. Typically about 10 m across, but occasionally up to 25 m, these structures can look quite different according to the materials used in their construction and the way they have decayed. The best preserved are the stone ring-cairns of upland areas, but many of the ring-ditches found in low-lying, predominantly agricultural landscapes performed the same role. Some ring-cairns and ring-ditches were elaborated with posts and stone edging whereas others started as enclosures but were later covered by round barrows, as discussed above. In some the boundary is continuous, so access would have involved stepping over the wall or the ditch; others are pennanular with an entrance gap and/or causeway allowing ready access at any time. These more accessible monuments tend to be called enclosed cremation cemeteries and were most popular in the middle and later second millennium BC as the rate of round-barrow construction slowed (Burgess 1980: 317). In western France enclosed cremation cemeteries, sometimes with a single causewayed entrance to the south, are closely connected with urnfield cemeteries, as for example at Broussy le Grand (Marne), nearly 14 m across.

Ritual Enclosures and Shrines

Aerial photography in many parts of the Central and Eastern Zones are revealing enclosures, usually demarcated by a bank and ditch, some of which were no doubt ceremonial sites. Dating remains a major problem, but excavations are increasingly demonstrating Middle Neolithic origins for structures that initial typological comparisons placed rather later. A variation on the stone-circle theme is represented by the *taula* of Menorca, with an isolated example on Mallorca. At these sites a low stone wall defines a ritual space up to 6 m across within which is a large stone slab set upright in the ground. Excavations revealed large quantities of animal bones suggesting ritual sacrifice or communal feasting. Further afield at Čakovice (Prague), Czech Republic, there is a circular enclosure 17 m across with a single entrance and a sandstone stele off-centre, while monumental structures considered to be shrines or temples have been found in Otomani culture contexts in the Carpathian Basin. At Sălacea (Marghita), Romania, a well-constructed shrine some 8.8 by 5.2 m with a porch at the north-west end and two internal rooms containing fixed altars and a range of cultic paraphernalia has been uncovered by excavation. Hilltop shrines defined by rough stone walls are known at Góry Kościuszki, Ślęża, and Radunia near Sobótka (Wrocław), Poland, closely associated with abundant figurines.

Wetland Shrines

Interest in wetlands was not confined to the deposition of fine metalwork and burials. At Flag Fen (Peterborough), England, raised trackways led from the field systems to a deliberately constructed timber platform supporting a rectangular structure or shrine. Dendrochronology shows that the first post alignments were constructed between 1301 BC and 1257 BC and that the timber platform was built in the second half of the tenth century BC. About 150 bronze tools and weapons were deposited in Flag Fen. Similar sites are beginning to appear on the continent, as for example at St Moritz, Switzerland, where a timber-lined pit used for the deposition of metalwork lay beside a lake. At Bargeroosterveld (Drenthe), Netherlands, a wetland shrine set in a marsh 250 m from the dry land was defined by a ring of stones about 4 m across, in the middle of which was a square timber structure.

Cult Houses

In the Nordic Zone various kinds of cult house (*kulthused*) were constructed adjacent to existing round barrows during the later Bronze Age. They appear in various forms. In northeast Jutland, the 20 or so recorded examples are typically 4 to 5 m square with turf and timber walls associated with postholes that must have held supports for a roof. There is usually a hearth inside the structure. At Sandagergård (Sjadland), Denmark, a cult house with a double-stone foundation 18.5 by 7.5 m was loosely associated with metalworking and had three burials in separate urns beneath the floor. Still larger is the example at Koarum (Skåne), Sweden, at 43 by 44.5 m, lying at the east end of a very extensive cemetery of more than 250 round barrows scattered along a ridge with the great Kivik cairn at the west end. How these cult houses were used is not entirely clear, although their monumental scale and proximity to round barrows suggested to Flemming Kaul (1998: 45) that they were associated with reusing the barrow in a cult of the dead, perhaps for initiation rites.

Conclusion

Many of the monumental traditions of Bronze Age Europe continued practices established in Neolithic and Chalcolithic times, but new forms also evolved and these set the foundations for later developments. Dating is difficult for many classes, but menhirs and round barrows that would have been so familiar to Bronze Age people represent some of the longest-lived monuments known from prehistory. In all cases the use of sites changed over time, and there is much still to learn about how people constructed their world and understood their monuments. It is also increasingly clear that technologies to cope with the unknown and the supernatural come in many shapes and sizes, often with the deliberate and careful selection of materials for their construction. There is now an urgent need to be alert to such possibilities when excavating and surveying sites and landscapes occupied during the Bronze Age.

Bibliography

Barfield, L. and Hodder, M. (eds.) (1991). *Burnt Mounds and Hot-Stone Technology*. West Bromwich: Sandwell Metropolitan Borough Council.
Beckensall, S. (1999). *British Prehistoric Rock Art*. Stroud: Tempus.
Bradley, R. (2000). *An Archaeology of Natural Places*. London: Routledge.
—— (2009). *Image and Audience: Rethinking Prehistoric Art*. Oxford: Oxford University Press.
——, Chippindale, C., and Helskog, K. (2001). 'Post-Palaeolithic Europe', in D. S. Whitley (ed.), *Handbook of Rock Art Sesearch*. Walnut Creek: AltaMira, 482–529.
Burgess, C. (1980). *The Age of Stonehenge*. London: Dent.
Burl, A. (1988). *Four-Posters: Bronze Age Stone Circles of Western Europe*. British Archaeological Reports (British Series), 195. Oxford: Archaeopress.
—— (1993). *From Callanish to Carnac: The Prehistoric Stone Rows and Avenues of Britain, Ireland and Brittany*. New Haven: Yale University Press.
—— (2000). *The Stone Circles of Britain, Ireland and Brittany*. New Haven: Yale University Press.
Casini, S., Marinis, R. C. de, and Pedrotti, A. (eds.) (1995). *Statue-stele e massi incise nell'Europe dell'età del Rame*. Notizie Archeologiche Bergomensi, 3. Bergamo: Civico Museo Archeologico.
Chapman, R. W. (1990). *Emerging Complexity: The Later Prehistory of South-East Spain, Iberia, and the West Mediterranean*. Cambridge: Cambridge University Press.
Coles, J. (2005). *Shadows of a Northern Past: Rock Carvings of Bohuslän and Østfold*. Oxford: Oxbow Books.
Darvill, T. (2006). *Stonehenge: The Biography of a Landscape*. Stroud: Tempus/History Press.
—— and Wainwright, G. (2009). 'Stonehenge excavations 2008', *Antiquaries Journal*, 89: 1-19.
Evans, J. D. (1971). *The Prehistoric Antiquities of the Maltese Islands: A Survey*. London: Athlone Press.
Fernández Castro, M. C. (1995). *Iberia in Prehistory*. Oxford: Blackwell.
Gibson, A. (2005). *Stonehenge and Timber Circles*, 2nd edn. Stroud: Tempus.

Gimbutas, M. (1965). *Bronze Age Cultures in Central and Eastern Europe*. The Hague: Mouton.

Harrison, R. J. (2004). *Symbols and Warriors: Images of the European Bronze Age*. Bristol: Western Academic and Specialist Press.

Jones, A. (2007). *Memory and Material Culture*. Cambridge: Cambridge University Press.

Joussaume, R. (1985). *Dolmens for the Dead*. London: Batsford.

Kaul, F. (1998). *Ships on Bronzes: A Study in Bronze Age Religion and Iconography*. Publications from the National Museum Studies in Archaeology and History, 3. Copenhagen: Nationalmuseet.

Kohl, P. L. (2007). *The Making of Bronze Age Eurasia*. Cambridge: Cambridge University Press.

Leary, J., Darvill, T., and Field, D. (eds.) (2010). *Round Mounds and Monumentality in the British Neolithic and Beyond*. Neolithic Studies Group Seminar Papers, 10. Oxford: Oxbow Books.

Mallory, J. P. and Adams, D. Q. (2006). *The Oxford Introduction to Proto-Indo-European and the Proto-Indo-European World*. Oxford: Oxford University Press.

Markovin, V. I. (2002). 'Western Caucasian dolmens: mysticism, scientific opinions, and perspectives on further study', *Anthropology and Archaeology of Eurasia*, 40/4: 68–88.

Ó Nualláin, S. (1978). 'Boulder-burials', *Proceedings of the Royal Irish Academy*, 78C: 75–100.

Palumbo, G. (1956). 'Inventario dei dolmen di terra d'Otranto', *Rivista di Scienze Preistoriche*, 11: 84–108.

Parker Pearson, M. and Ramilisonina (1998). 'Stonehenge for the ancestors: the stones pass on the message', *Antiquity*, 72: 308–26.

Ruggles, C. L. N. (1999). *Astronomy in Prehistoric Britain and Ireland*. London and New Haven: Yale University Press.

Thom, A. (1967). *Megalithic Sites in Britain*. Oxford: Oxford University Press.

Waddell, J. (1986). *The Bronze Age Burials of Ireland*. Galway: Galway University Press.

Whitehouse, R. (1972). 'The rock-cut tombs of the central Mediterranean', *Antiquity*, 46: 275–81.

—— (1981). 'Megaliths of the central Mediterranean', in J. D. Evans, B. Cunliffe, and C. Renfrew (eds.), *Antiquity and Man: Essays in Honour of Glyn Daniel*. London: Thames and Hudson, 106–27.

Woodward, A. (2000). *British Barrows: A Matter of Life and Death*. Stroud: Tempus.

CHAPTER 9

STONEHENGE

MIKE PARKER PEARSON, PETER MARSHALL,
JOSH POLLARD, COLIN RICHARDS,
JULIAN THOMAS, AND KATE WELHAM

INTRODUCTION

The world's most famous stone circle is located on Salisbury Plain (Wiltshire, in southern England), on a high plateau of Cretaceous chalk (over 100 m above sea level) on a west-facing slope above a dry valley that leads to the River Avon.

Stonehenge was built in five stages over a period of more than a thousand years, 3000 cal BC–1600 cal BC between the Middle Neolithic and the Middle Bronze Age. It is unique as a prehistoric stone circle because of its artificially shaped sarsen stones (blocks of Tertiary sandstone), arranged as lintels on top of uprights, and because of the long-distance origin of its smaller 'bluestones' (igneous and other rocks) from 100–150 miles (160–240 km) away, in south Wales. It is also the largest cemetery of the third millennium cal BC yet found in Britain. The name probably derives from the Saxon 'stan-hengen', 'stone-hanging', or gallows.

Stonehenge sits within one of the densest concentrations of Neolithic and Early Bronze Age monuments in northern Europe. It is one of four large monument complexes on these chalk uplands that include Avebury, Cranborne Chase, Dorchester, and Marden.

Within the Stonehenge environs (Fig. 9.1) there is a wide range of Neolithic and Early Bronze Age monuments: Neolithic long barrows, a causewayed enclosure at Robin Hood's Ball, the Greater Stonehenge Cursus and the Lesser Cursus, the Cuckoo Stone, the Bulford Stone, Coneybury henge, Bluestonehenge at West Amesbury, the Stonehenge Avenue, Woodhenge (and three other timber monuments south of it), Durrington Walls henge, and the Durrington Walls Avenue. There are over four hundred Early Bronze Age round barrows in the Stonehenge environs, on both sides of the River Avon.

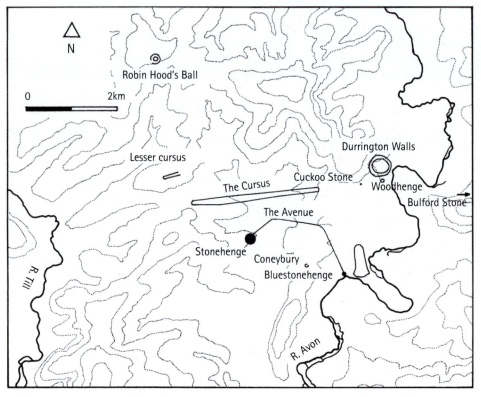

FIG. 9.1 The environs of Stonehenge.

Source: author (drawing: Irene Deluis).

A Short History of Recent Research

Three excavation campaigns were carried out within Stonehenge during the twentieth century: in 1901 by William Gowland, during 1919–26 by William Hawley, and 1950–78 by Richard Atkinson, Stuart Piggott, and J. F. S. Stone (published in 1995 after Atkinson's death by Cleal, Walker, and Montague).

Since the 1960s, Stonehenge has been considered by some to have been a prehistoric calendar or astronomical observatory to predict solar and lunar eclipses (Hawkins 1966). Clive Ruggles has cast doubt on many of these ideas, limiting likely astronomical alignments to midwinter sunset and midsummer sunrise solstices, and particular moonrises and moonsets during midwinter and midsummer (Ruggles 1997; Pollard and Ruggles 2001).

Significant excavations were also carried out at Woodhenge (Cunnington 1929), Durrington Walls (Wainwright and Longworth 1971), and within the Stonehenge Environs Project (Richards 1990).

Between 2003 and 2009, the Stonehenge Riverside Project (SRP) carried out 45 excavations, around and within Stonehenge (Larsson and Parker Pearson 2007; Parker Pearson et al. 2007; 2009). In 2008 Darvill and Wainwright also carried out a small excavation within

Stonehenge (Darvill and Wainwright 2009). Since 2008 English Heritage and others have conducted surveys within and around Stonehenge (e.g. Field et al. 2010).

Previous Chronological Schemes for Stonehenge

In 1956 Richard Atkinson published a sequence for Stonehenge:

Stonehenge I—Heel Stone, ditch and bank, Aubrey Holes.
Stonehenge II—double circle of bluestones (Q & R Holes).
Stonehenge IIIa—sarsen circle and trilithon horseshoe.
Stonehenge IIIb—dressed bluestones and Y & Z Holes.
Stonehenge IIIc—bluestone circle and inner horseshoe.

Atkinson dated Stonehenge I and II to 2125–1575 BC and 1750–1550 BC (1956: 81–2). His theory that carvings of axes and a dagger at Stonehenge were evidence of design by a Mycenaean architect was disputed by Colin Renfrew (1968).

In 1995 Cleal, Walker, and Montague proposed a revised scheme:

Phase 1—ditch and bank, and Aubrey Holes (3015–2935 cal BC).
Phase 2—postholes; then cremation cemetery (2910–2570 cal BC).
Phase 3i/3a—Q & R Holes, Heel Stone, Stonehole 97, four Station Stones (undated).
Phase 3ii/3b—sarsen circle, trilithon horseshoe, Slaughter Stone, Heel Stone ditch, north and south barrows (2850–2100 cal BC).
Phase 3iii—bluestone setting in centre of monument (undated).
Phase 3iv/3c—bluestone circle, bluestone oval, Avenue (2280–2030 cal BC).
Phase 3v—bluestone horseshoe (2270–1930 cal BC).
Phase 3vi—Y & Z Holes (2030–1750 and 1640–1520 cal BC).

Both schemes have been replaced by a new scheme presented below.

Before Stonehenge

The Mesolithic, 8000–4000 cal BC

A line of three pine postholes, a tree hole, and a pit, 200 m north-west of Stonehenge, date to the eighthth millennium cal BC. Mesolithic flintwork has been found 400 m south-west of them, and along the Avon valley.

Monumentality among hunter-gatherers is unusual; the posts have been considered as 'totem poles' or as markers pointing eastwards towards Beacon Hill (204 m ASL). Post-glacial woodland grew more slowly and less densely on the high chalkland, so this area was relatively open (Cleal, Allen, and Newman 2004; French and Scaife pers. comm.).

The Early Neolithic, 4000–3600 cal BC

Earliest evidence of a Neolithic presence is the Coneybury anomaly, a pit filled with feasting refuse from 4040–3640 cal BC (Richards 1990: 40–61). Under Woodhenge, a smaller refuse deposit was buried in a tree-throw hole (Pollard and Robinson 2007). Settlements of this period were probably located in the river valleys.

Middle Neolithic, 3600–3000 cal BC

Long barrows at Netheravon Bake (3710–3350 cal BC) and Amesbury 42 (3520–3350 cal BC) were probably constructed around or after 3600 cal BC.[1] The Greater Cursus (3630–3370 cal BC) and the Lesser Cursus (3500–3340 cal BC) were formed by linear banks and ditches enclosing long, thin areas of land. Cursus monuments are known throughout Britain, and J.F.S. Stone (1947) interpreted the Greater Cursus as a processional route linking the living and the dead. Long barrows are found near the ends of the Stonehenge cursus monuments; the long barrow (Amesbury 42) at the east terminal of the Greater Cursus has the same date as the cursus. Settlements are known from King Barrow Ridge (Richards 1990: 109–23) and Durrington Walls (Wainwright and Longworth 1971).

STONEHENGE STAGE 1 (3015–2935 CAL BC)

Description of Stonehenge Features

Stonehenge's first stage consisted of a circular ditch with an interior bank, about 100 m in diameter, and an outer bank (Fig. 9.2). This earthwork was entered by a main access in the north-east and a smaller entrance in the south. It is not technically a henge, because 'henge' is used to describe earthworks in which the bank is outside the ditch. It was constructed within the period 3015–2935 cal BC (Allen and Bayliss 1995; Bayliss, Bronk Ramsey, and McCormac 1997).

A radiocarbon date of 3030–2880 cal BC from a cremation burial in Aubrey Hole 32 indicates that the 56 Aubrey Holes were probably contemporary with the ditch (Parker Pearson et al. 2009). Some of Stonehenge's other 62 cremation deposits are contemporary with this initial stage of construction.

Re-excavation of Aubrey Hole 7 has produced evidence that the Holes contained bluestone uprights, confirming Colonel Hawley's observation that 'there can be little doubt that they once held small upright stones' (Hawley 1921: 30–1).

Some of the postholes within the central area of Stonehenge pre-date the standing stone settings, so are likely to have been constructed and used in this earliest period. These postholes formed five groups, the southernmost forming a passageway leading from the south entrance

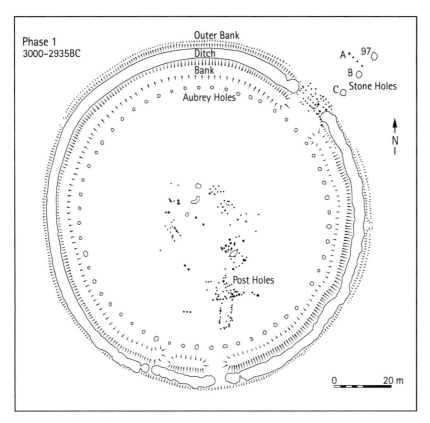

FIG. 9.2 Stage 1 of Stonehenge.

Source: author (drawing: Irene Deluis).

and passing through a post facade towards the centre. The spatial patterning of postholes in the centre suggests a series of rectangular structures, one of them with a sarsen stonehole at its centre.

These may have formed excarnation platforms; over 40 unburnt human bones have been excavated from within Stonehenge, two of them dating to this period (Parker Pearson et al. 2009).

A rectangular post arrangement within the north-east entrance, and a line of posts about 20 m further out, run perpendicular to a line of three equally spaced stoneholes (Stoneholes B, C, and 97). Stonehole 97 sits within a filled, linear depression which may have been a solution hollow, formed beneath a recumbent sarsen (Pitts 1982; 2008).

Another undated feature that could conceivably date to this early stage is a mound within the south-east sector of Stonehenge's central area (Field et al. 2010). This low earthen mound could date to this period or before, although it is more likely to be natural.

Associated Monuments and Features

The Stonehenge Avenue was not built until six hundred years later (Stage 3; see below), but its path from Stonehenge's north-east entrance towards the midsummer solstice sunrise was prefigured by three parallel ridges, each about 5 m wide and 10 m apart. Two of these natural chalk formations were later enhanced as the banks of the avenue. Stonehenge's main (north-east) entrance was positioned at the southern end of these two ridges, running 200 m from the Heel Stone and Stonehole 97. Excavations by the Stonehenge Riverside Project (SRP) found lines of periglacial fissures—gullies formed by freeze-thaw processes—between the two ridges, running parallel with them. Such features are found throughout Salisbury Plain, but those within the two ridges were deeper and wider than those outside the avenue. Their enhanced size is considered to be due to greater periglacial freeze-thaw action between the ridges.

On the Avon riverside, just over 2 km east-south-east of Stonehenge at West Amesbury, a smaller circle of bluestones (about 10 m in diameter) was constructed between 3400 and 2600 cal BC on typological dating of flint 'chisel' arrowheads (Parker Pearson et al. 2010). The bluestones were later removed from this Bluestonehenge within the period 2470–2280 cal BC (Stonehenge Stage 3).

Just over halfway between Stonehenge and Bluestonehenge, a timber post setting was constructed on Coneybury Hill around 3360–2870 cal BC (Richards 1990: 123–58) and enclosed by a henge ditch and bank (3090–2470 cal BC).

No trace of the likely settlement for the builders of Stonehenge Stage 1 has yet been found. Pits and stakeholes on King Barrow Ridge, 1.5 km east of Stonehenge, could date to this period (Richards 1990: 109–23).

Interpretation

The axis of the north-east entrance features is aligned towards the northern limit of the rising moon, especially evident when the moon was full in midwinter (Ruggles 1997; Pollard and Ruggles 2001). However, this axis is not precise (only within 2–3°) and may have been symbolic rather than instrumental.

The recent observation that Stonehenge was constructed at the south-west end of parallel natural features, coincidentally aligned on a solstice axis, raises new issues about its purpose. This axis is oriented north-east towards sunrise on the midsummer solstice and, in the opposite direction, towards sunset on the midwinter solstice. It is possible that this unusual articulation between the movement of the sun and the axis of natural lines in the land may have been considered by Neolithic people (and perhaps even Early Mesolithic people) as part of a supernatural design, an *axis mundi*, which made this location special.

The identification of Stonehenge Stage 1 as a cremation cemetery, as well as a stone circle, invites comparison with similar circular enclosures of the Middle Neolithic elsewhere in Britain. It is one of a dozen that were used as cremation cemeteries, and Stonehenge has the most burials. It is closely comparable to two circles associated with cremations: Llandegai Henge A in north Wales (Lynch and Musson 2004) and Flagstones in Dorchester (Healy 1997).

Of the 63 cremation deposits excavated from Stonehenge, all but four or five were adults, of whom only two were women, and buried over some five hundred years (Parker Pearson et al. 2009). Among the few grave goods were a stone macehead and a ceramic 'incense burner' (Cleal, Walker, and Montague 1995: 360–1, 394), likely symbols of authority. Stonehenge's astronomical alignments, particularly those that are derived from natural features, give it a special status which may have been of greatest significance at midwinter and midsummer.

The inclusion of Welsh bluestones (of spotted dolerite, dolerite, rhyolite, volcanic ash, and sandstone), probably at this stage for both Stonehenge and Bluestonehenge, is another unique feature. Whilst some have argued that these Welsh stones were carried by glaciers to within 80 km of Salisbury Plain (Burl 2006; John 2008; Thorpe et al. 1991), the more generally accepted hypothesis is that they were moved by human agency from quarries in the Preseli hills and other rock outcrops in south Wales, 160–240 km away (Darvill and Wainwright 2009; Green 1997; Scourse 1997). Likely sources of spotted dolerite have been identified at Carn Menyn and Carn Goedog (Thorpe et al. 1991), and of rhyolite at Pont Saeson (Parker Pearson et al. 2011; see also Ixer and Bevins 2010). The Altar Stone and other Stonehenge sandstones do not originate near Milford Haven, as once thought, but may have come from the Brecon Beacons (Ixer and Turner 2006). This, amongst other reasons, argues for a largely land-based route for the bluestones along the Nyfer, Taf, Towy, and Usk valleys, crossing the Severn estuary by boat to Avonmouth and thence along the Somerset Avon and onto Salisbury Plain.

Darvill and Wainwright suggest that the stones were brought to Stonehenge for their supposed healing properties. Another possibility is the ancestral significance of the Preseli area for the Stonehenge builders; the density of Early Neolithic dolmens around Preseli makes this perhaps one of the first places along the Irish Sea settled by immigrant farmers from Brittany (Sheridan 2003; 2004; 2010).

Stonehenge Stage 2 (2620–2480 cal bc)

Description of Stonehenge Features

Around five hundred years after its initial construction, Stonehenge was built in the form it largely takes today (Fig. 9.3). While the deposition of cremated and unburnt human bones continued between Stages 1 and 2 (Parker Pearson et al. 2009), no structural features can be dated to this interval.

The large, shaped sarsen stones were introduced in this period. They stood in a horseshoe-shaped arrangement of five central trilithons (pairs of uprights joined by a stone lintel) and an outer stone circle of uprights with interlinking lintels. Antler picks from packing layers within stoneholes date trilithon 53/54 to 2850–2400 cal bc and the sarsen circle to 2580–2470 cal bc (Cleal, Walker, and Montague 1995: 524; Parker Pearson et al. 2007).

The logistics of construction indicate that the trilithons were probably the first stones to be erected in Stage 2. Their erection was probably followed by a rearrangement of the bluestones from the 56 Aubrey Holes, to form a double arc or circle within the Q and R Holes (Atkinson 1956). Finally, the sarsen circle, enclosing both these elements, was erected.

Atkinson observed that one of the Q Holes in the north-east (Q Hole 4) had been cut by one of the holes for the sarsen circle (Sarsen Stone 3), and thus concluded that the sarsen circle could not have been constructed until the Q and R bluestones had been dismantled (1956: 49–50). Darvill and Wainwright's excavation in 2008, however, cast doubt on Atkinson's conclusion (Darvill and Wainwright 2009). They noted considerable disturbance and recutting within both bluestone and sarsen stoneholes within the last two thousand years and argue that the stonehole for Sarsen Stone 3 was recut in post-prehistoric times. Their argument is

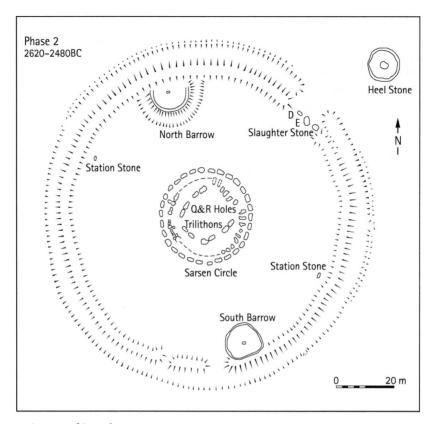

FIG. 9.3 Stage 2 of Stonehenge.

Source: author (drawing: Irene Deluis).

strengthened by the cut for Stone 3 being wider than most other holes of the sarsen circle. Atkinson's argument that the Q and R bluestones were removed before the sarsen circle was erected can no longer be accepted.

Some of the bluestones in the Q and R Holes may have been dressed in Stage 2. Three were topped with tenon projections, two were lintels with pairs of mortise holes, and two had tongue-and-groove jointing. The positions of the two bluestone lintels indicate that they may have framed entrances to the Q and R Hole setting on its north-east and south sides, echoing the two entrances through the enclosure ditch.

The question of whether the Q and R Holes formed a circle or merely an arc is not resolved. Tim Darvill interprets them as a double circle of bluestones, but Atkinson found only a single line of bluestone holes along the south-west (Cleal, Walker, and Montague 1995: 221). Whilst this single line has been ascribed to a later Bluestone Circle (Cleal, Walker, and Montague 1995: 229–31), its earlier stoneholes were recut by later ones; those earlier holes could belong to a first phase of bluestones erected in Stage 2. A more likely option is that the bluestones were arranged in a full circle, with a second, outer arc on its north-eastern side.

The sarsen circle may not have been completed (Ashbee 1998) because no trace survives of stones 13, 17, and 18, on its south-west side. However, Stone 13's stonehole has been excavated, demonstrating that a stone did once stand here. Only six out of 30 sarsen lintels survive within

Stonehenge. It is likely that the missing sarsen uprights and lintels were robbed in historical times, together with around 35 out of an estimated 80 bluestones. The sarsen circle may not have supported lintels all the way around; Stone 11 is too short to have supported lintels, even though the adjacent stones (12 and 10) have tenons to hold lintels. The diminutive Stone 11, however, appears to have lost its top.

Undated features that probably belong to Stage 2 are the four Station Stones, the Slaughter Stone and its two companions (Stoneholes D and E), and the Heel Stone. The ditch may also have been recut during this stage and later deliberately backfilled.

The Station Stones (of which two survive) were positioned just inside the enclosure bank and form a rectangle with astronomical sightlines (Ruggles 1997: 219–20). Their north-east/south-west axis is the same as that of the sarsen circle and great trilithon (the largest of the five trilithons)—towards midsummer solstice sunrise and midwinter solstice sunset. Their north-west/south-east axis is aligned approximately on the major southern moonrise (full in summer) and major northern moonset (full in winter).

The northern and southern Station Stones sat within earthworks—the North Barrow and the South Barrow. Little is known about the North Barrow, but Hawley revealed that the South Barrow covered what can now be interpreted as the floor of a large, roughly D-shaped building positioned inside the enclosure's south entrance. He could not establish whether the stone was inserted into the floor of this building or whether the floor was laid around the stone; if the latter, then the south Station Stone stood in the centre of a non-domestic building. The floor of this structure sealed the top of an Aubrey Hole, therefore post-dating it.

The Slaughter Stone—now fallen—and its two companions (Stoneholes D and E) formed a facade of standing stones immediately inside the enclosure's north-east entrance. Two antler picks were recovered from the fill of Stonehole E. While one dates to 2860–2350 cal BC, the other is later (2490–2200 cal BC; Stage 3).

The Heel Stone stands outside the Stonehenge enclosure, 22 m from the north-east entrance, and is set within its own circular ditch. Viewed from the centre of Stonehenge, it is not positioned precisely on the line of Neolithic midsummer sunrise but slightly east of it. Pitts has suggested that this stone was moved a few metres from its original position in Stonehole 97 (Pitts 2008). Unlike all the other surviving sarsens, the Heel Stone and one of the Station Stones were not dressed. This may mean that these were already present at Stonehenge when the other sarsens arrived in Stage 2.

The ditch's secondary fill was probably recut around 2500 cal BC since it incorporates animal bones dating to 2660–2040 cal BC in an identifiable recut (Cleal, Walker, and Montague 1995: 520–2; Parker Pearson et al. 2009).

The north-east entrance was also modified in this period, with the southern terminal of the enclosure ditch being filled in so that the axis of the enclosure was shifted from its approximate lunar standstill alignment to the solstice alignment. Other sections of the newly recut ditch were also backfilled, presumably by pushing much of the bank material back into the ditch.

Associated Monuments and Features

Within this period, the southern ditch of the Greater Cursus was recut with a series of embayments; recuts along the north ditch may also have been made at this time (Stone 1947;

Richards 1990: 96; Thomas et al. 2009). However, the most significant associated sites in this period are the timber circles at Durrington Walls and Woodhenge, and their associated settlement.

During rescue excavations in 1966–8, Wainwright recovered the plans of two timber circles at Durrington Walls—the larger Southern Circle and the smaller, less well-preserved Northern Circle. The Northern Circle had a square setting of posts at its centre and was approached from the south-west by a timber-lined passageway similar to that of Stonehenge in Stage 1. The Northern Circle's south-east side aligned with midwinter sunrise.

The Southern Circle was constructed in at least two phases. The first was another four-post square setting, similarly aligned on midwinter sunrise, within a single circle of posts and dated to 2630–2460 cal BC. Immediately to the west, a roughly D-shaped building (similar in shape and size to that inside the south entrance to Stonehenge) was constructed with a similar chalk plaster floor (initially interpreted as a midden; Wainwright with Longworth 1971: 38–41). There was no hearth, so this building may have been a gathering space or 'meeting house'.

After the posts of the Southern Circle's first phase had decayed, a large timber monument of six concentric rings of posts was constructed. Its south-east entrance, marked by two posts each over 1 m in diameter, was aligned on midwinter sunrise. Its south-west side was terraced into the hillside. The small postholes of the innermost ring (2F) formed either a circle or an oval. The 10 (or possibly 11) massive postholes of the next ring (2E) were probably set in a horseshoe (with its open end facing south-west; mimicking the trilithon horseshoe at Stonehenge but in the opposite direction). Outside this, ring 2D formed a circle of probably 21 posts. The fourth ring (2C) was a circle of probably 30 posts (equivalent to Stonehenge's sarsen circle of 30 uprights). The two outermost circles (2B and 2A) consisted of small posts, except at its front entrance (south-east) and back (north-west), which were marked with pairs of large posts.

The question of whether the Southern Circle (and the Northern Circle and Woodhenge) was roofed has been resolved by excavations in 2005–6 that suggest it was open to the elements. There was no eavesdrip gully, and no indoor floor surface. Instead, part of its interior had a rough surface of rammed chalk which appears to have formed a route from the south-east entrance into the Circle's centre.

The Southern Circle was linked to the River Avon by an avenue 170 m long, consisting of a 15 m-wide surface of rammed flints bounded on either side by 5 m-wide banks of chalk rubble. This avenue is aligned to the north-west on midsummer solstice sunset (Parker Pearson et al. 2007). At its north-west end, it was identified by Wainwright as a 'platform' (Wainwright and Longworth 1971: 32) where a 5 m-long hearth was positioned immediately outside the Southern Circle's entrance (many of the Grooved Ware pots found here contained dairy residues; Mukherjee 2004).

Woodhenge also consists of six concentric post settings, all oval rather than circular, with the long axis aligned on the midwinter sunset and the midsummer sunrise (Cunnington 1929; Pollard and Robinson 2007). In contrast to Stonehenge, appreciable quantities of Grooved Ware and animal bones were obtained from its postholes. The so-called 'child sacrifice' beneath a flint cairn at its centre is most likely an Early Bronze Age burial with a skull depressed by post-depositional processes rather than human agency (Pollard 1995).

The only Late Neolithic cremation burial within the Durrington Walls complex (from posthole C14 at Woodhenge, dated to 2580–2470 cal BC) is contemporary with Stage 2 at

Stonehenge and with the Southern Circle and avenue at Durrington Walls. The unusual filling of 'posthole' C14—in which the bottom of the pit was partially filled and the upright was extracted rather than allowed to decay (like all the other posts)—raises the possibility that C14 was a stonehole for a bluestone-sized upright.

There are three more timber monuments south of Woodhenge. All have four-post square settings at their centres, one of which is aligned on the midwinter sunrise. Two have the remains of oval posthole rings around them.

Within Durrington Walls, further up the dry valley from the Southern Circle, lie five small henges (David and Payne 1997: Fig. 11, A–E). Two of these Western Enclosures enclose Late Neolithic houses (Thomas 2007). The largest enclosure is 40 m wide, terraced into the hillside, with a south-east-facing entrance. Their square house floors are little different in size (around 5 m across) to the other seven houses excavated at Durrington Walls, but these two houses and their circular palisaded compounds were kept much cleaner. Although fires were maintained in their central hearths, they could have been cult houses or residences for leading families whose compounds were kept clean.

This cleanliness forms a dramatic contrast to the midden debris surrounding the seven houses located either side of the Durrington avenue, south-east of the Southern Circle. Two of these were positioned on the low banks either side of the avenue. Although they had central hearths like the other houses, they were open to the elements on their south-east side. Of the remaining five houses, the largest was associated with a small outhouse; both structures were separated from the other houses by a post-built fence. The large house had slots and postholes from wooden furniture, indicative of box beds, a dresser, and small storage units of the kind built in stone at Skara Brae in Orkney (Childe 1931). In fact, the Durrington Walls house plans are remarkably similar to those of Skara Brae. The other three houses had beam slots, presumably for box beds, but no traces of dressers or similarly elaborate furniture.

The dates for the Durrington Walls settlement and Southern Circle fall within the same period as those for Stonehenge Stage 2, and can be modelled using Bayesian statistics to provide a period of occupation as short as 15–45 years (68 percent probability); beginning in 2525–2470 cal BC and ending in 2480–2440 cal BC, with construction of the Southern Circle in 2490–2455 cal BC.

Previous excavations at Durrington Walls (Farrer 1918; Stone, Piggott, and Booth 1954; Wainwright and Longworth 1971), together with excavations in 2004–7, indicate that the settlement area most likely covered the 17 hectares later enclosed by the henge ditch and bank. Extrapolating from the housing density found within the 2004–7 excavations, this massive settlement could have accommodated up to one thousand dwellings, though the central zone between the Western Enclosures and the Southern Circle may have been open space.

The huge faunal assemblage from Durrington Walls indicates prodigious consumption of pigs and cattle (in a ratio of about 9 to 1; Albarella and Serjeantson 2002). Lack of bone fragmentation indicates that animal carcasses were not exploited to their full nutritional potential; large numbers of people were gathering here to feast extravagantly. Most pigs were culled at nine months and others at 15 months. With farrowing most likely in the spring, these feasts took place in midwinter and midsummer.

The lack of neonates suggests a 'consumer' site where animals were imported rather than raised. Current results indicate that the Durrington Walls village was occupied only seasonally, though a 'caretaker' population may have resided there all year round. Strontium isotopes in cattle tooth enamel demonstrate that cattle were brought long distances across southern Britain (Viner et al. 2010).

Among the lithic assemblage (80,000 flints from 2004–7), there is only one stone axe fragment. This dearth of axes raises the possibility that copper axes were already in use in Britain by 2500 cal BC prior to the arrival of Bell Beakers.

There is no such evidence for large-scale aggregation at Stonehenge itself in this period, where the principal remains are cremation burials and stone-dressing waste; it was not inhabited or used for feasting on any scale. There is also a dearth of occupation debris from Stonehenge's environs in the early–mid third millennium BC, both to the south and east of Stonehenge (Leivers and Moore 2008), and also to its west and north. Durrington Walls provides a marked contrast; the density of worked flint from its occupation surfaces is over twice that of the densest surface scatters within the Stonehenge environs, and eight times that of the average surface scatter density in that area.

Interpretation

Stonehenge has been viewed as primarily an astronomical observatory or calendar, but archaeo-astronomers now emphasize the social embeddedness of astronomy within prehistoric societies, and this is borne out by the evidence from Durrington Walls. Ruggles has identified the only Stonehenge alignments that meet rigorous standards of interpretation as being those of solar rise and set at midwinter and midsummer and of lunar standstill rises and sets at full moon (in midsummer and midwinter). Although lunar alignments have not been identified in the architecture of the timber circles, four of the timber monuments at Durrington Walls are aligned on solstitial directions at midwinter and midsummer. That the two annual solstices were of social and economic significance is supported by evidence for seasonal feasting.

Stonehenge's use as a cemetery continued into Stage 2, with cremation deposits in the ditch in this phase (Parker Pearson et al. 2009). The contrast with the timber monuments and houses at Durrington Walls is striking, where just four loose human bones were found among a faunal assemblage of 80,000 bones. Parker Pearson and Ramilisonina's predictive model of stone for the ancestors and timber for the living (1998) is supported by these results. In that model, the stretch of the River Avon between Durrington Walls and Stonehenge was interpreted as a liminal zone between the living and the dead, a theory supported by the discoveries of an avenue leading to the river at Durrington Walls and of Bluestonehenge stone circle at Stonehenge's riverside (in the place where the Stonehenge avenue [Stage 3] meets the river).

The notion that Durrington Walls and Stonehenge formed two halves of a single complex is further supported by chronology. While Durrington Walls's settlement and Southern Circle date to around or shortly after 2500 cal BC, the dates for the sarsen phase at Stonehenge can be fixed approximately to within the period 2620–2480 cal BC. Whether Durrington Walls was the Stonehenge builders' camp cannot be proved, but it is currently the only candidate.

In one sense, Stonehenge is the greatest example of a Late Neolithic timber circle: its mortise-and-tenon jointing for uprights and lintels, and tongue-and-groove fitting of lintels, are carpentry techniques applied to stone. Its design clearly references timber circular architecture at the levels of both house and monument. The sarsen circle can be paralleled with the palisades surrounding the western enclosures within Durrington Walls, and with the post circles of the Northern Circle and the first phase of the Southern Circle. The horseshoe plan of the five trilithons can also be compared to the D-shaped 'meeting house' at Durrington Walls. Thus Stonehenge's trilithons may represent the uprights or doorways of an 'ancestral' stone 'meeting house'.

Finally, the quarries for the sarsens have not yet been located within the Avebury area of the Marlborough Downs, about 30 km to the north. Whilst Atkinson's favoured route for the sarsens began at Avebury (1956: 111–14), an eastern route is also possible via the large henge enclosure of Marden, where an incline gives access onto the steep northern slope of Salisbury Plain. Wooden rollers would have sunk into the ground under such weights of 20 tons or more; the stones could have been placed on wooden cradles and set on rollers that ran on wooden 'rails'.

Stonehenge Stage 3 (2480–2280 cal bc)

Description of Stonehenge Features

The Stonehenge avenue's parallel ditches and banks were built, stretching over 2.8 km from the sarsen circle to Bluestonehenge on the bank of the River Avon (Fig. 9.4). Bluestonehenge was dismantled and a henge bank and ditch, about 35 m in diameter, were constructed around the position of the former stone circle. It is likely that the stones were brought to Stonehenge, perhaps to be arranged within its centre. An arc of five bluestone holes immediately east of trilithon 57/58 (previously designated as Phase 3iii; Cleal, Walker, and Montague 1995: 206–9, Fig. 109 [WA 3285, 3286, 3700, 3702, and 3402]) has the appropriate spacing and radius for a transplanted Bluestonehenge.

Within Stonehenge, the north-east entrance may have been opened up by removing the stone in Stonehole E (and possibly in Stonehole D too). A large pit, of unknown purpose, was dug to the bottom of the giant trilithon in 2440–2100 cal bc (Parker Pearson et al. 2007).

In 2400–2140 cal bc an inhumation was buried in the ditch, west of the north-east entrance. Known as the Stonehenge Archer, this adult male was shot with arrows at least three times. He has been described as a human sacrifice or a murder victim, but he may have been simply the last of the interments in the Stonehenge cemetery.

Associated Monuments and Features

Henge ditches and banks were constructed around the abandoned village at Durrington Walls (2480–2460 cal bc), and around the timber circle at Woodhenge (2400–2030 cal bc). The Durrington Walls henge had four entrances, of which the northern and the southern were later blocked, perhaps during the period of Stonehenge's Stage 4. Its ditch was preceded by a line of large, ramped postholes that never held posts. The ditch was around 10 m wide and 5.5 m deep, with near-vertical sides. Its scalloped-shaped edges show that it was gang-

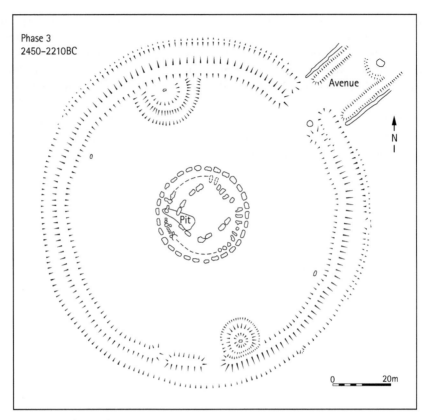

FIG. 9.4 Stage 3 of Stonehenge.

Source: author (drawing: Irene Deluis).

dug in lengths of approximately 40 m. Wainwright's find of 57 antler picks from one of these gives some idea of the numbers of workers involved in each workgang.

After 100–170 years of decay, the Southern Circle's postholes were dug out to deposit pottery, animal bone, flints, and tools (Richards and Thomas 1984; Thomas 2007). Artefacts deposited here included Bell Beaker pottery (containing dairy product residues).

The first Bell Beaker burials date to Stonehenge's Stage 3 and include the Amesbury Archer, 5 km east of Stonehenge (Fitzpatrick 2002). With over one hundred grave goods (including five beakers, three copper knives, and a metalworking cushion stone), the Amesbury Archer is the 'richest' Bell Beaker burial in Europe. Isotopic analysis indicates that the Archer spent his childhood in the Alpine foothills. He had also suffered a disabling knee injury.

Interpretation

This Bell Beaker period was an important transition within Britain. With the sarsen phase of Stonehenge completed by 2480 cal BC and the great henge enclosure of Durrington Walls by 2460 cal BC, relatively few large monuments were now being built. The last of these was the great mound of Silbury Hill near Avebury, built in the decades around 2400 cal BC (Bayliss,

Whittle, and McEvoy 2007). With the end of labour mobilization for large-scale public works, the Bell Beaker arrival may have heralded or coincided with a political system that replaced the autocratic authority of the Stonehenge builders with a more egalitarian, 'big man'-style society.

Discovery of the Amesbury Archer's origins (Evans, Chenery, and Fitzpatrick 2006) has revived the migrationist hypothesis for Bell Beaker people; isotopic analyses of other British Bell Beaker burials indicate that he may have been part of a larger migration from the continent.

Stonehenge Stage 4 (2270–2020 cal bc)

Description of Stonehenge Features

Within this stage, the bluestones were removed from the Q and R Holes and were rearranged as a Bluestone Circle (sitting largely on top of the Q and R Holes; Fig. 9.5). Within the centre, a Bluestone Oval of 24 stones was constructed (possibly from the Bluestonehenge stones) within the period 2280–1940 cal bc. The large hole next to the giant trilithon was filled in, and one of the stones of the Bluestone Oval sat in its fill.

A date of 2460–2040 cal bc from an animal bone in the top of an emptied Q Hole corresponds with construction dates of 2480–2140 cal bc and 2290–2030 cal bc for the Bluestone Circle (Allen and Bayliss 1995: 524).

Associated Monuments and Features

During this period, people began to build round burial mounds (round barrows) throughout Britain, including both sides of the Avon on Salisbury Plain. Most of these were inter-visible either with Durrington Walls or with Stonehenge (Tilley et al. 2007: 203), around which they formed an envelope of visibility (Woodward and Woodward 1996). During this period, bell beakers continued to be used as grave goods but new ceramic forms—food vessels and collared urns—now appeared as grave accompaniments. Cremation had probably continued throughout the period of Bell Beaker inhumations, and it re-emerged significantly at this point (the beginning of the Early Bronze Age), particularly in burials associated with collared urns (such as two found next to the Cuckoo Stone).

Interpretation

Among the few burials across Britain providing indications of status differences at this time, a food vessel cremation at Bulford, east of Durrington Walls, contained over 30 artefacts including a piece of rock crystal. It was not until 'Wessex I' (c.2000–1800 cal bc) that burials in the Stonehenge area (such as Bush Barrow) contained lavish golden grave goods, indicative of major social differentiation.

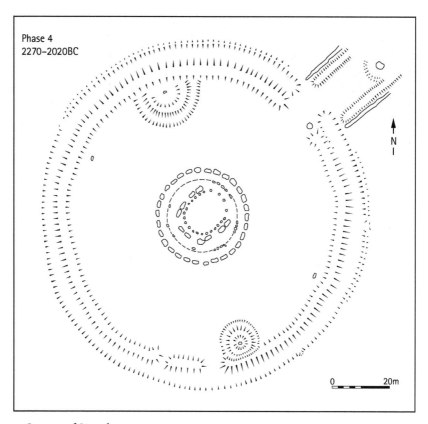

FIG. 9.5 Stage 4 of Stonehenge.

Source: author (drawing: Irene Deluis).

Stonehenge Stage 5 (1630–1520 cal bc)

Description of Stonehenge Features

Two concentric circles of pits, known as the Y and Z Holes, were dug outside the sarsen circle (Fig. 9.6). They were left open and filled with windblown sediments, most likely derived from cultivated areas in the vicinity.

Atkinson suggested that these pits were dug to receive bluestones, to be transferred from within the sarsen circle, and that the task was never completed (1956: 21). The dates from antlers within two of the pit fills are inconsistent, but the latest (1630–1520 cal bc) date to the Middle Bronze Age. They do not provide a date for the digging of the pits, and the possibility remains that the Y and Z Holes formerly held uprights—subsequently removed—in an earlier period.

Associated Monuments and Features

The Stonehenge Palisade Ditch probably dates to around the middle of the second millennium cal bc. This linear earthwork runs west of Stonehenge and intersects with other

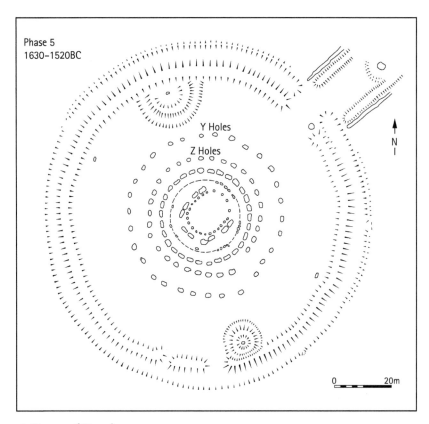

FIG. 9.6 Stage 5 of Stonehenge.

Source: author (drawing: Irene Deluis).

Bronze Age field boundaries. Part of its length was recut as an open ditch in the Late Bronze Age.

Interpretation

The Middle Bronze Age marks a major transition in British prehistory, with the cessation of building of burial monuments and the large-scale construction of land boundaries and coaxial field systems. Whilst activity continued at Stonehenge, revealed by the presence of Bronze Age and Iron Age pottery sherds, the Y and Z Holes mark the end of the Stonehenge constructional sequence as well as a sea change in the wider society.

Note

1. Radiocarbon dates in plain text are simple calibrated results quoted at 95 percent confidence using the calibration dataset (Reimer et al. 2009) and OxCal 4.1 (Bronk Ramsey 2009). Those in italics are *posterior density estimates* derived from mathematical modelling and are quoted at 95 percent probability.

Bibliography

Albarella, U. and Serjeantson, D. (2002). 'A passion for pork: meat consumption at the British Late Neolithic site of Durrington Walls', in P. Miracle and N. Milner (eds.), *Consuming Passions and Patterns of Consumption*. Cambridge: Cambridge University Press, 33–49.

Allen, M. J. and Bayliss, A. (1995). 'Appendix 2: the radiocarbon dating programme', in R. M. J. Cleal, K. E. Walker, and R. Montague (eds.), *Stonehenge in its Landscape: Twentieth-century Excavations*. London: English Heritage, 511–35.

Ashbee, P. (1998). 'Stonehenge: its possible non-completion, slighting and dilapidation', *Wiltshire Archaeological and Natural History Magazine*, 91: 139–42.

Atkinson, R. J. C. (1956). Stonehenge. London: Hamish Hamilton.

Bayliss, A., Bronk Ramsey, C., and McCormac, F. G. (1997). 'Dating Stonehenge', in B. Cunliffe and C. Renfrew (eds.), *Science and Stonehenge*, Proceedings of the British Academy, 92: 39–59.

——, Whittle, A. and McEvoy, F. (2007). 'The world recreated: re-dating Silbury Hill in its monumental landscape', *Antiquity*, 81: 26–53.

Bronk Ramsey, C. (2009). 'Bayesian analysis of radiocarbon dates', *Radiocarbon*, 51: 337–60.

Burl, A. (2006). *Stonehenge: A New History of the World's Greatest Stone Circle*. London: Constable.

Childe, V. G. (1931). *Skara Brae: A Pictish Village in Orkney*. London: Kegan Paul.

Cleal, R. M. J., Allen, M. J., and Newman, C. (2004). 'An archaeological and environmental study of the Neolithic and later prehistoric landscape of the Avon valley and Durrington Walls environs', *Wiltshire Archaeological and Natural History Magazine*, 97: 218–48.

——, Walker, K. E., and Montague, R. (eds.) (1995). *Stonehenge in its Landscape:Twentieth-Century Excavations*. London: English Heritage.

Cunnington, M. E. (1929). *Woodhenge*. Devizes: Simpson.

Darvill, T. and Wainwright, G. J. (2009). 'Stonehenge excavations 2008', *Antiquaries Journal*, 89: 1–19.

David, A. and Payne, A. (1997). 'Geophysical surveys within the Stonehenge landscape: a review of past endeavour and future potential', in B. Cunliffe and C. Renfrew (eds.), *Science and Stonehenge*, Proceedings of the British Academy, 92: 73–113.

Evans, J., Chenery, C. A., and Fitzpatrick, A. P. (2006). 'Bronze Age childhood migration of individuals near Stonehenge, revealed by strontium and oxygen isotope tooth enamel analysis', *Archaeometry*, 48: 309–21.

Farrer, P. (1918). 'Durrington Walls, or Long Walls', *Wiltshire Archaeological and Natural History Magazine*, 40: 95–103.

Field, D., Pearson, T., Barber, M., and Payne, A. (2010). 'Introducing "Stonehenge" (and other curious earthworks)', *British Archaeology*, 111: 32–5.

Fitzpatrick, A. P. (2002). '"The Amesbury archer": a well-furnished Early Bronze Age burial in southern England', *Antiquity*, 76: 629–30.

Green, C. P. (1997). 'The provenance of rocks used in the construction of Stonehenge', in B. Cunliffe and C. Renfrew (eds.), *Science and Stonehenge*, Proceedings of the British Academy, 92: 257–70.

Hawkins, G. S. (1966). *Stonehenge Decoded*. London: Souvenir Press.

Hawley, W. (1921). 'The excavations at Stonehenge', *Antiquaries Journal*, 1: 19–39.

Healy, F. (1997). 'Site 3. Flagstones', in R. J. C. Smith, F. Healy, M. J. Allen, E. L. Morris, I. Barnes, and P. J. Woodward, *Excavations along the Route of the Dorchester By-pass, Dorset, 1986–8* (Report no. 11). Salisbury: Wessex Archaeology, 27–48.

Ixer, R. A. and Bevins, R. E. (2010). 'The petrography, affinity and provenance of lithics from the Cursus Field, Stonehenge', *Wiltshire Archaeological and Natural History Magazine*, 103: 1–15.
——and Turner, P. (2006). 'A detailed re-examination of the petrography of the Altar Stone and other non-sarsen sandstones from Stonehenge as a guide to their provenance', *Wiltshire Archaeological and Natural History Magazine*, 99: 1–9.
John, B. (2008). *The Bluestone Enigma: Stonehenge, Preseli and the Ice Age*. Newport: Greencroft Books.
Larsson, M. and Parker Pearson, M. (eds.) (2007). *From Stonehenge to the Baltic: Cultural Diversity in the Third Millennium BC*, British Archaeological Reports (International Series), 1,692. Oxford: Archaeopress.
Leivers, M. and Moore, C. (2008). *Archaeology on the A303 Stonehenge Improvement*. Salisbury: Wessex Archaeology.
Lynch, F. and Musson, C. (2004). 'A prehistoric and early medieval complex at Llandegai, near Bangor, north Wales', *Archaeologia Cambrensis*, 150: 17–142.
Mukherjee, A. J. (2004). *The Importance of Pigs in the Later British Neolithic: Integrating Stable Isotope Evidence from Lipid Residues in Archaeological Potsherds, Animal Bone, and Modern Animal Tissues*. Unpublished PhD thesis, University of Bristol.
Parker Pearson, M. and Ramilisonina (1998). 'Stonehenge for the ancestors: the stones pass on the message', *Antiquity*, 72: 308–26.
——, Cleal, R., Marshall, P., Needham, S., Pollard, J., Richards, C., Ruggles, C., Sheridan, A., Thomas, J., Tilley, C., Welham, K., Chamberlain, A., Chenery, C., Evans, J., Knüsel, C., Linford N., Martin, L., Montgomery, J., Payne, A., and Richards. M. (2007). 'The age of Stonehenge', *Antiquity*, 81: 617–39.
——, Chamberlain, A., Jay, M., Marshall, P., Pollard, J., Richards, C., Thomas, J., Tilley, C., and Welham, K. (2009). 'Who was buried at Stonehenge?', *Antiquity*, 83: 23–39.
——, Pollard, J., Thomas, J. and Welham, K. (2010). 'Newhenge', *British Archaeology*, 110: 14–21.
——, Pollard, J., Richards, C., Thomas, J., Welham, K., Bevins, R., Ixer, R., Marshall, P., and Chamberlain, A. (2011). 'Stonehenge: controversies of the bluestones', *Journal of Andalusian Prehistory*, 1: 219–50.
Pitts, M. W. (1982). 'On the road to Stonehenge: report on the investigations beside the A344 in 1968, 1979 and 1980', *Proceedings of the Prehistory Society*, 48: 75–132.
——(2008). 'The big dig: Stonehenge', *British Archaeology*, 102: 12–17.
Pollard, J. (1995). 'Inscribing space: formal deposition at the later Neolithic monument of Woodhenge, Wiltshire', *Proceedings of the Prehistoric Society*, 61: 137–56.
——and Robinson, D. (2007). 'A return to Woodhenge: the results and implications of the 2006 excavations', in M. Larsson and M. Parker Pearson (eds.), *From Stonehenge to the Baltic: Living with Cultural Diversity in the Third Millennium BC*, British Archaeological Reports (International Series), 1,692. Oxford: Archaeopress, 159–68.
——and Ruggles, C. (2001). 'Shifting perceptions: spatial order, cosmology, and patterns of deposition at Stonehenge', *Cambridge Archaeological Journal*, 11: 69–90.
Reimer, P. J., Baillie, M. G. L., Bard, E., Bayliss, A., Beck, J. W., Blackwell, P. G., Bronk Ramsey, C., Buck, C. E., Burr, G., Edwards, R. L., Friedrich, M., Grootes, P. M., Guilderson, T. P., Hajdas, I., Heaton, T. J., Hogg, A. G., Hughen, K. A., Kaiser, K. F., Kromer, B., McCormac, F. G., Manning, S. W., Reimer, R. W., Richards, D. A., Southon, J. R., Talamo, S., Turney, C. S. M., Van der Plicht, J., and Weyhenmeyer, C. E. (2009). 'IntCal09 and Marine09 radiocarbon age calibration curves, 0–50,000 years cal BP', *Radiocarbon*, 51:1,111–50.
Renfrew, C. (1968). 'Wessex without Mycenae', *Annual of the British School at Athens*, 63: 277–85.

Richards, C. and Thomas, J. (1984). 'Ritual activity and structured deposition in later Neolithic Wessex', in R. Bradley and J. Gardiner (eds.), *Neolithic Studies: A Review of Some Current Research*, British Archaeological Reports (British Series), 133. Oxford: British Archaeological Reports, 189–218.

Richards, J. C. (1990). *The Stonehenge Environs Project*. London: English Heritage.

Ruggles, C. (1997). 'Astronomy and Stonehenge', in B. Cunliffe and C. Renfrew (eds.), *Science and Stonehenge*, Proceedings of the British Academy, 92: 203–29.

Scourse, J. D. (1997). 'Transport of the Stonehenge Bluestones: Testing the Glacial Hypothesis', in B. Cunliffe and C. Renfrew (eds.), *Science and Stonehenge*, Proceedings of the British Academy, 92: 271–314.

Sheridan, A. (2003). 'French connections I: spreading the marmites thinly', in I. Armit, E. Murphy, E. Nelis, and D. D. A. Simpson (eds.), *Neolithic Settlement in Ireland and Western Britain*. Oxford: Oxbow Books, 3–17.

——(2004). 'Neolithic connections along and across the Irish Sea', in V. Cummings and C. Fowler (eds.), *The Neolithic of the Irish Sea: Materiality and Traditions of Practice*. Oxford: Oxbow Books, 9–21.

——(2010). 'The Neolithization of Britain and Ireland: the "big picture"', in B. Finlayson and G. Warren (eds.), *Landscapes in Transition*. Oxford: Oxbow Books, 89–105.

Stone, J. F. S. (1947). 'The Stonehenge cursus and its affinities', *Archaeological Journal*, 104: 7–19.

——, Piggott, S., and Booth, A. St. J. (1954). 'Durrington Walls, Wiltshire: recent excavations at a ceremonial site of the early second millennium BC', *Antiquaries Journal*, 34: 155–77.

Thomas, J. (2007). 'The internal features at Durrington Walls: investigations in the Southern Circle and Western Enclosures 2005–2006', in L. Larsson and M. Parker Pearson (eds.), *From Stonehenge to the Baltic: Cultural Diversity in the Third Millennium BC*, British Archaeological Reports (International Series), 1,692. Oxford: Archaeopress, 145–57.

——, Marshall, P., Parker Pearson, M., Pollard, J., Richards, C., Tilley, C., and Welham, K. (2009). 'The date of the Stonehenge cursus', *Antiquity*, 83: 40–53.

Thorpe, R. S., Williams-Thorpe, O., Jenkins, D. G., and Watson, J. S. (1991). 'The geological sources and transport of the bluestones of Stonehenge, Wiltshire, UK', *Proceedings of the Prehistoric Society*, 57: 103–57.

Tilley, C., Richards, C., Bennett, W., and Field, D. (2007). 'Stonehenge—its landscape and architecture: a re-analysis', in L. Larsson and M. Parker Pearson (eds.), *From Stonehenge to the Baltic: Cultural Diversity in the Third Millennium BC*, British Archaeological Reports (International Series), 1,692. Oxford: Archaeopress, 183–204.

Viner, S., Evans, J., Albarella, U., and Parker Pearson, M. (2010). 'Cattle mobility in prehistoric Britain: strontium isotope analysis of cattle teeth from Durrington Walls (Wiltshire, Britain)', *Journal of Archaeological Science*, 37: 2,812–20.

Wainwright, G. J. and Longworth, I. H. (1971). *Durrington Walls: Excavations 1966–1968*. London: Society of Antiquaries.

Woodward, A. and Woodward, P. J. (1996). 'The topography of some barrow cemeteries in Bronze Age Wessex', *Proceedings of the Prehistoric Society*, 57: 103–57.

CHAPTER 10

THE CONTRIBUTION OF SKELETAL ISOTOPE ANALYSIS TO UNDERSTANDING THE BRONZE AGE IN EUROPE

JANET MONTGOMERY AND MANDY JAY

Introduction

Isotope analysis of skeletal material has a significant contribution to make to understanding diet and mobility in prehistory. The techniques involve the chemical analysis of bones and teeth, producing data that relate directly to dietary inputs and the environments from which they were obtained, and indirectly to residential mobility, general subsistence, farming and animal management practices. An expanding database is beginning to have a significant effect on our understanding of how groups of people were living in and across landscapes. The larger-scale questions, such as whether populations were mobile across Europe and whether they were utilizing particular forms of dietary resource such as marine products, are complemented by interpretations that relate to individuals, producing 'biographies' at a more personal level. An example of the latter is the 'Amesbury Archer', interpreted from the oxygen isotope data as having been a mobile individual born somewhere in central Europe, but buried with rich Wessex culture accoutrements in southern Britain (Fitzpatrick 2003).

Whilst the Amesbury Archer study may provide a fascinating insight into the life of an individual, such isolated 'biographies' cannot answer the population-scale questions we have about life in prehistory. Those questions require sizeable data-sets, for both humans and animals, and we are still in the relatively early days of producing these. This chapter is intended to reflect on the data available at the moment, how they are shaping up in terms of answering questions, the limitations of the techniques, and what we might expect for the future.

The Techniques

Body tissues are principally formed from foods and liquids ingested, so that the chemical make-up of those dietary constituents will be reflected in the skeleton. The ratios of isotopes found in food and water will show up in bones and teeth in some directly related pattern that can be traced back to the base of the food chain and will reflect local environments and geological backgrounds.

In a generalist paper intended primarily to reflect applications to archaeology, it is not possible to reference the extensive technical research applicable to the techniques referred to here directly, but excellent general summaries and bibliographies can be found in Hedges (2009), Lee-Thorp (2008), Bentley (2006), Montgomery et al. (2010), and Sealy (2001).

The isotope data that is usually associated primarily with mobility studies are from the elements strontium, oxygen, and lead, and these are normally obtained from tooth enamel samples in order to minimize the effects of post-mortem changes. The elements usually associated with dietary studies are carbon and nitrogen, and these are best analysed from collagen extracted from bone and dentine. Sulphur and hydrogen isotope data can also be obtained from organic collagen and these help with both mobility and dietary studies. They are both relatively new in terms of their application to archaeological research and are likely to prove useful in combination with other analyses as the methods develop.

For most of these, two isotopes of each element are measured from a sample, the ratio calculated and then compared with an accepted standard. For the majority of these elements, the resultant value is then shown as a δ value ($\delta^{13}C$, $\delta^{18}O$, $\delta^{15}N$, $\delta^{34}S$, δD [deuterium]), with the unit as 'per mil' or ‰. In the cases of strontium and lead, the values are shown as ratios to a number of decimal places, with strontium traditionally comparing two isotopes (^{87}Sr and ^{86}Sr) and lead often involving different ratios of four isotopes (^{208}Pb, ^{207}Pb, ^{206}Pb, and ^{204}Pb).

Factors Reflected by the Different Systems

The different isotope systems will reflect differing elements of the dietary consumption package (Table 10.1). Strontium concentrations and availability are higher in vegetation than in other dietary sources, so that there is a tendency for the contribution from plants to dominate. Lead is similarly obtained from food and water, but also by inhalation and unintentional ingestion of soil and anthropogenic pollutants, whilst oxygen and hydrogen values are largely related to drinking water. Collagen carbon, nitrogen, and sulphur isotope values reflect dietary protein, although some carbon from whole diet (including carbohydrates and fats) may be present, particularly where dietary protein is in short supply. In contrast to strontium, if animal products are included in the diet these will tend to be disproportionately reflected in the protein isotope data because there tends to be more protein in them than in plants. Carbon from tooth enamel and bone mineral reflects whole diet, rather than just the protein.

In very basic terms, strontium, lead, and probably sulphur tend to reflect the local geology of the place from which dietary resources originated, whilst oxygen and hydrogen reflect drinking water source and are related to climatic regime. For lead, however, the link with geographic location can be severed if the environment is polluted with lead from external sources. In Britain this does not appear to occur in any measurable way in human populations until the widespread extraction of metal ores in the Roman period. Lead does not therefore appear to discriminate between Neolithic societies and the later metal-using societies of the Bronze and Iron Ages at the population level, although this may not be the case for the actual metalworkers. Nitrogen is linked to trophic level, as is hydrogen, and carbon differentiates between C_4 and C_3 plant resources with different photosynthetic pathways (millet versus other plants in the context of prehistoric Europe), whilst nitrogen, carbon, and sulphur will all reflect the consumption of marine and other aquatic resources. Although it is possible to identify the consumption of animal protein using bulk carbon and nitrogen data from collagen, it is not possible to differentiate that signal between meat and/or dairy products.

Most of these systems are significantly more complicated than the basic summary provided here, and will also reflect a wide range of other variables, such as proximity to the coast, aridity, manuring, forest cover, atmospheric carbon dioxide concentrations, temperature, sunlight availability, rainfall levels, cultural and culinary practices, and so on. Whilst it is known that these environmental and cultural factors affect the data to some extent, we are still developing an understanding of the precise mechanisms and effects.

When combining different isotopic data for a study, it is important to take into account the various ways dietary source can be reflected in what we measure and the many factors that may influence the values obtained. Combining strontium and oxygen isotope data constrains the possible geographical area of childhood origin better than using one isotope ratio alone. Adding in additional isotope systems can constrain even further, although differences in formation periods between the tooth enamel and dentine or bone collagen must be borne in mind. Carbon and nitrogen isotopes are nearly always used together for dietary studies, and the inclusion of sulphur and possibly hydrogen data in the future is likely to aid interpretation further. Since the isotopic data for each of the chemical elements provides different information, using more than one for a particular study can allow a much better interpretation of the data.

Different Skeletal Fractions

Tooth enamel, dentine, and bone collagen are formed at different periods during an individual's life, and the time-slice they thus represent (i.e. when and how long) can vary considerably. Deciduous and permanent teeth also form at different times. It is possible, by analysing different fractions of an individual, to compare the situation between childhood and later life. Depending on the teeth chosen, the enamel will be from childhood and infancy and should not alter measurably once fully mineralized, whereas bone collagen will produce a signal that has been averaged over a lifetime of consumption, although probably more skewed to adolescence than to later life. Dentine collagen values will tend to cover a longer childhood period than enamel and reflect the diet of that period, as compared to bone collagen which has a slow molecular turnover during the whole of an individual's life. Dentine collagen does not change in this way, although small amounts of secondary and tertiary dentine do form over a lifetime in the pulp cavity.

The skeletal fraction analysed for a particular chemical element should be chosen carefully, mainly because there are issues for archaeological material relating to diagenesis and contamination in the burial environment, as well as contamination during curation. For strontium, lead, and oxygen, it is generally considered that the best option is to analyse tooth enamel. These elements can be found in the bone mineral, but this is less likely to preserve the *in vivo* signature of the individual, and more likely to reflect diagenetic changes during burial and/or contamination effects. Oxygen isotopes can be measured from either the phosphate or the carbonate fraction of tooth enamel and, if the latter is used, carbon isotope data can also be obtained simultaneously. For carbon, nitrogen, and sulphur, collagen is extracted from bone and dentine samples. Collagen, again, preserves the signal much more reliably than bone mineral. Nitrogen is only available from the protein, so that collagen is the only practical option for that element.

Overall, therefore, the skeletal fraction chosen will have regard to the chemical element being analysed, the issues of diagenesis and contamination, and the desired comparison of different periods in an individual's life.

Isotopic Background

For any isotope analyses, it is important to understand the isotopic background in terms of regional and local geology and environment, both spatially and temporally. For some of the work, this often involves the analysis of animal skeletal material, particularly herbivores, since an animal with a known diet of plants, from the same place and time period as a human burial, will provide a 'baseline' for interpretation. Unfortunately, it is often the case in practice that animal assemblages are rarely found directly associated with human burials.

Obtaining environmental background data for strontium studies is a necessity if the data from a skeleton is to be compared with what is to be expected for the burial location: only rarely is this immediately apparent from an identification of the surface geology. Environmental samples such as soil and water can be used, but these do not always directly reflect the biologically available strontium, so that modern or archaeological animal tooth enamel can be particularly useful, as can archaeological dentine that is in the process of equilibration by absorbing soil-derived strontium during burial. Modern plants have also proved a valid environmental indicator, although the application of modern fertilizers can be a problem if samples are taken from regions of intensive agriculture.

In addition to the comparison with the local signal, if mobility is suspected, an understanding of the values to be expected for possible source regions must also be obtained. This can be, of course, a massive undertaking and is an ongoing feature of this type of research, which will develop as databases become larger and more data are published. It is particularly hampered by the bias in the archaeological skeletal data which, in Europe, derives almost exclusively from soils where bone survives well. As for strontium, the other isotope systems

Table 10.1 Basic Summary of Analytical Fraction, Dietary Input, and Interpretational Aspect Relevant to Each Chemical Element Discussed in the Text

Element	Skeletal fraction best for analysis	Dietary input primarily reflected	Primary interpretational aspect
Sr (strontium)	Tooth enamel. Dentine may be used to establish local baseline values.	Plants, which tend to have higher Sr concentrations and enhanced Sr absorption compared with the rest of the diet.	Mobility (geology and coastal proximity)
O (oxygen)	Tooth enamel, phosphate or carbonate fractions. Dentine apatite and collagen may be used for high-resolution oxygen profiles.	Water	Mobility (climate)
Pb (lead)	Tooth enamel	General diet, water, and by inhalation	Mobility and anthropogenic pollution
C (carbon)	Bone and dentine collagen	Protein	Diet (marine v terrestrial, C_3 v C_4)
	Tooth enamel carbonate	Whole diet (protein, carbohydrate, fat)	Diet (marine v terrestrial, C_3 v C_4)
N (nitrogen)	Bone and dentine collagen	Protein	Diet (trophic level, marine v terrestrial)
S (sulphur)	Bone and dentine collagen	Protein	Mobility (geology and coastal proximity), diet (aquatic v terrestrial)
H/D (hydrogen/deuterium*)	Bone and dentine collagen	Water	Mobility (climate), diet (trophic level)

Note: This table is intended to provided information at a rudimentary level for easy reference. The details given for each element are neither exclusive nor exhaustive, but are only the primary relevant variables in each case, provided to give an entry-level understanding of the material.
* Deuterium is an isotope of hydrogen (^{2}H). δD therefore effectively indicates the stable isotope ratio that would otherwise be shown as δ^{2}H.

will also require an understanding of the environmental background for the time and place being studied. For instance, oxygen isotope data will require an understanding of precipitation data for different regions, and nitrogen interpretations are affected by a variety of localized effects on the environmental background, such as salinity levels and manuring, so that animal samples are usually used to obtain 'baseline' values for comparative purposes.

Without these background data, care must be taken in accepting dietary or mobility interpretations that do not necessarily take into account the level of environmental variation that may occur.

Skeletal Data from Animals

In addition to the importance of data from animals in terms of assessing the isotopic background for a region, they can be useful for answering other questions, some relating to the human data, and some directly relevant to the animals themselves. For instance, if transhumance is suspected, then data from herd animals in addition to those from the humans can aid interpretation, or if it is suspected that a large quantity of animal remains left at a high-status burial site is indicative of a meeting of people from different regions for the funeral, then the animal remains can be analysed to look for the possibility of different source locations (e.g. Towers et al. 2010). Animal data are also particularly required for the interpretation of carbon and nitrogen isotope ratios to put the human data in the context of the overall foodweb, alongside the spatial and temporal environmental context (Fig. 10.1). For instance, discussing the possibility of aquatic inputs in the diet is likely to require the inclusion of data from a number of different faunal species (e.g. Jay 2008).

Migration and Diet Studies

At a very basic level, the two questions archaeologists currently want answered with these techniques are generally 'Were these people mobile and, if so, where did they come from?' and 'What did they eat?'. As data-sets become larger, techniques more advanced, and our understanding of the resolution at which we can discriminate diets and origins improves, more detailed questions can be asked about a whole range of issues such as animal and herd management, transhumance, weaning and breastfeeding, exogamy, agricultural systems, subsistence strategies, and local environments. Notwithstanding such advances in methods and data-sets, such interpretations will ultimately depend on the relationships between human diet, animal diet, and the locality from which food and water were sourced.

Migration studies that involve the analysis of tooth enamel are restricted to a comparison of childhood location with burial location. This is because tooth enamel mineralizes during childhood and 'locks in' the evidence for locale at that time. If an individual, or a group of people, moved from one region to another after childhood formation of tooth enamel, and they were then buried in the destination region, then it may be possible to confirm movement. That will depend, however, on whether the two regions were geologically or

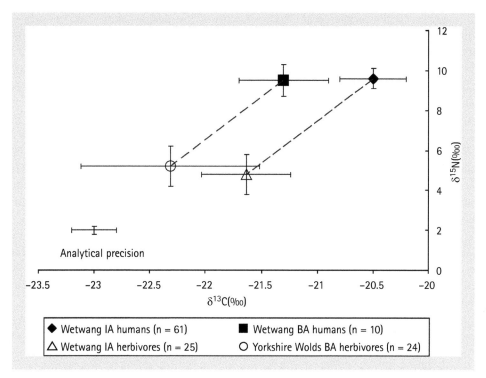

FIG. 10.1 Carbon and nitrogen isotopic ratios for Early Bronze Age and Iron Age humans and terrestrial herbivores (cattle and sheep) from Wetwang and local sites on the East Yorkshire chalk Wolds (UK). The dotted lines connect the humans and herbivores for the two periods. The plot illustrates the species comparisons which allow interpretations of diet. The humans are compared to contemporaneous and local animal protein sources and to the baseline for the local environment inferred from the herbivores. Here, the relationships show that the carbon 'baseline' has changed over time, but usually the primary comparison relates to differences in nitrogen values between regions, or even micro-environments such as fields.

environmentally significantly different, and also on the timing and pattern of movement. Travel between areas that are characterized by the same biosphere isotope ratios, such as when people seek out and settle the same landscapes and soils of their homeland, may leave no detectable trace, and if repeated movement takes place during life, but burial occurs at the same place as childhood was spent, then this movement may not be visible from the skeletal chemistry. Thus, for any group studied, it is likely that mobility will be underestimated.

The link between skeletal values and a specific geological terrain may arise because food and drink were transported to the humans rather than the humans moving to the food. The mechanism may be trade or exchange of foodstuffs, but it may also involve, for instance, choosing to graze animals or grow crops on a different geological terrain to that of the settlement or cemetery site, the inclusion of marine resources such as fish or seaweed into the diet, or freshwater aquatic resources from a river that has drained rocks other than those of the home region. Spring and well waters will reflect the rocks through which they filtered and these may be different to those rocks that crop out at the surface. Rainwater, a major environmental component to soil waters in regions of high rainfall, may also provide drinking water that does not reflect the local geology.

The answer to the question 'Did this person move around during her or his lifetime?' does not, therefore, have a simple 'yes' or 'no' answer, nor is it usually possible to identify, if mobility is indicated, precisely where that childhood was spent. There will be a range of possible provenance areas that must be considered in the particular archaeological and environmental context of the case. The measured skeletal isotope ratio may arise from a mixture of one or more food sources, both of which may be dissimilar to the measured ratio (Fig. 10.2), thus not indicating in any simple manner a specific type of rock (Montgomery 2010).

For dietary patterns, the isotope ratios measured from bone collagen are usually averaged over lifetimes and there are restrictions on the detail available for interpretation. The techniques can distinguish herbivores, high-level carnivores, and omnivores between the two extremes, and can also identify the consumption of marine resources (such as fish), and to some extent freshwater aquatic foods. It is also possible to look at the introduction of C_4 plants into the food chain, in the case of the European Bronze Age the major source being millet. Where infants and young children are available to compare with an adult population, dietary studies can provide information about weaning and breastfeeding behaviour, since the signals seen in the infants are related to their mothers' milk, and thus to the diets of those mothers. More detail than this is usually restricted and will normally only be possible when large datasets are available and a lot is known about overall context, both archaeological and isotopic.

Collagen isotope data can also make some contribution to the discussion of mobility. Nitrogen values can vary spatially for various reasons, and it is sometimes possible to pick out

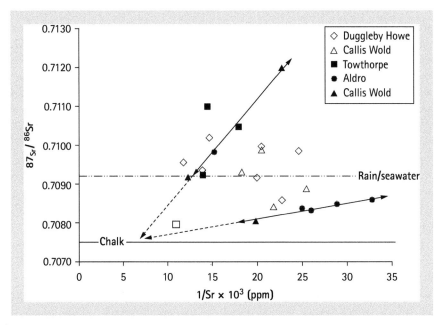

FIG. 10.2 Human enamel data from Neolithic (white symbols) and Bronze Age (black symbols) barrows of the Yorkshire Wolds (UK). This chart illustrates the different data structures seen between the two periods, with the Bronze Age data plotting along mixing lines, whilst the Neolithic data is more widely spread. The horizontal lines indicate possible end-members for the mixing lines: the upper line is seawater and an approximation for rainwater; the lower line on which both mixing lines appear to converge is the value for English Cretaceous Chalk. 2σ errors are within symbol.

an outlier from a group of data that may suggest the possibility of a diet which was sourced from a different region. Sulphur isotopic data are also promising to provide information which is complementary to that obtained from tooth enamel, since these values have a relationship with both geology and a 'sea spray' effect that links into coastal proximity. Comparing data from dentine collagen and bone collagen, these forming at different points during life, can also provide information about mobility between the two periods concerned.

Existing Data and Interpretations for the European Bronze Age

Most of the published and pending mobility data of interest to Bronze Age researchers relate to the late Neolithic, Chalcolithic, or Early Bronze Age, with little currently available for the later period covered by this volume, although examples of dietary studies are available for Middle and later Bronze Age material (e.g. Tafuri, Craig, and Canci 2009 for Italy; Eriksson et al. 2008 for Sweden; Triantaphyllou et al. 2008 for Greece).

Mobility Studies

Existing larger-scale studies of mobility revolve mainly around the strontium isotope work instigated by Price and Grupe on central European Bell Beaker period material (e.g. Price et al. 2004), alongside research undertaken by Janet Montgomery and colleagues in Britain (e.g. Montgomery, Evans, and Cooper 2007) and the British 'Beaker People Project' which, at the time of writing, is coming towards the end of a five-year period looking at 250 individuals from across mainland Britain. The extensive isotope analysis for this project is the brainchild of Parker Pearson, Richards, and Chamberlain (Jay and Richards 2007a; Parker Pearson 2006).

Examples of biographical studies of individuals include the Amesbury Archer and some other material from around the Stonehenge region, an ongoing multi-disciplinary project on 'Gristhorpe Man' from Yorkshire (all of these from Britain) and the Alpine 'Iceman' (Melton et al. 2010; Evans, Chenery, and Fitzpatrick 2006; Fitzpatrick 2003; Müller et al. 2003). Other smaller-scale population studies include work on material from Switzerland, Germany, and Greece (Vika 2009; Haak et al. 2008; Chiaradia, Gallay, and Todt 2003).

One of the 'big questions' for this early transitional period is whether long-distance mobility can be traced amongst the people associated with Beaker cultural material. Isotope studies are ideally employed to see whether this can be tracked in the skeletal record. The existing data suggest that mobility at varying levels for this period can be identified both for individuals and for groups of burials from the same site and that it is probably identifiable both within and across current national boundaries.

In addition to data deriving solely from Bronze Age individuals, there are a growing number of isotope studies from earlier and later prehistoric periods that constitute a growing European database against which to interpret the Bronze Age burials (e.g. Giblin 2009; Nehlich et al. 2009; Richards et al. 2008; Bentley and Knipper 2005). The work done by the Price and Grupe groups has looked at strontium isotope ratios in central European Bell Beaker material, specifically southern Germany, Austria, the Czech Republic, and Hungary

(Price et al. 2004; Grupe et al. 1997). In total they have worked on over 80 burials, the majority from Bavaria, and concluded that a significant proportion of these show evidence for a non-local origin. As they point out in their studies, taking this further involves comparison with other groups in terms of variation in data-sets, possible rates of migration across different time periods, and mapping base data from environmental samples. Examples of smaller-scale studies include Evans, Chenery, and Fitzpatrick (2006) and Chiaradia, Gallay, and Todt (2003). The former used strontium and oxygen to look at five Beaker period adults and two juveniles from the general Stonehenge area (southern England), three of the adults and the children being from an unusual collective grave. They concluded that whereas two of the adults were likely to have spent their lives in this burial area, the three from the mass grave spent their early lives elsewhere and their movement patterns were similar, with travel of at least 150 to 200 km indicated. The juveniles were also not local, although they did not come from the same place as the three adults from the same grave.

The study of Chiaradia, Gallay, and Todt (2003) is diachronic and comprised 12 individuals from the same area. Two were identified as Bell Beaker, whilst the others dated to both before and after, including two Bronze Age. Of the two Beaker period individuals, strontium and lead isotope data identified one of them as being from outside the local region. None of the remaining individuals appeared to have originated from any distance away, but the study did suggest that they had obtained their water and grown their crops in a neighbouring area, with burial occurring in a different place to subsistence activities.

Other projects in progress include collaborative research on Bell Beaker and Early Bronze Age material from Germany, Hungary, and the Pontic steppes involving the University of Bristol (UK), the Universities of Berlin, Halle, and Freiburg (all Germany), as well as the Landesmuseum für Vorgeschichte Sachsen-Anhalt in Halle and the Hungarian Academy of Sciences in Budapest. Most of this work is yet to be published, but will provide valuable data when available.

THE BEAKER PEOPLE PROJECT

The Beaker People Project is a five-year multi-institutional study intended to look at approximately 250 Beaker period burials from across mainland Britain. The project is currently in the final phase and the data are currently being brought together for publication. With two thousand isotopic values to consider, this will be a major contribution to the isotopic database for Britain, particularly since it includes sulphur (for which few archaeological data are currently published), covers a wide geographical area crossing many geological boundaries with varying coastal influences, and includes five isotope systems for each individual, with skeletal fractions that form at different times in life for each one.

Early findings from this project suggest considerable mobility, at least at the regional level, amongst the burials studied, although it is too soon to be clear about the possibility of individuals moving in from the European continent. For instance, a high percentage of the people from the East Yorkshire Wolds appear to have moved to and from the chalk of the Wolds, with approximately 50 per cent apparently moving at least locally and more than 10 per cent moving some quite significant distances. This is in direct contrast to Middle Iron Age people from the same area, who were largely settled on the chalk and for whom isotopic evidence of movement is quite rare (Jay and Richards 2006; authors' unpublished data; Beaker People Project unpublished data). There is also a distinct difference from Middle Neolithic groups for this area in terms of the data structure, with indications that some of the Early Bronze Age people were utilizing two distinct sources of strontium and may have lived and subsisted on a geological terrain some distance to the west or north of the Yorkshire Wolds where they were buried (see Fig. 10.2). This might also involve moving to and from the Wolds regularly or seasonally (hence why individuals from the group display various mixtures of the two dietary sources), or else perhaps a food-procurement strategy with two distinct end members (e.g. animals grazing outside the Wolds or a transhumance pattern) (Montgomery, Cooper, and Evans 2007; Montgomery, Evans, and Cooper 2007). In contrast, whilst the Middle Neolithic people were probably equally mobile, the data structure suggests that this involved opportunistic, more irregular forms of movement with less organization to it, or certainly a less rigid control over dietary sources.

This evidence for the strontium isotope ratios of a group of individuals defining a line between two distinct strontium sources as seen in the Early Bronze Age material from the Yorkshire Wolds, is an example of the absolute strontium isotope value not being directly indicative of location, but an average obtained from ingesting strontium from two different places. It is also seen in a group of individuals from the Hebridean islands of Scotland dating from the Neolithic through to the Norse period, including a Bronze Age individual from Mull in the Inner Hebrides (Montgomery, Evans, and Cooper 2007). A second group of humans and animals exhibit a distinctive strontium composition: marine ratios coupled with concentrations of several hundred ppm, which are anomalously high for mainland Britain. This has been proposed as indicating people who cling to the coast, utilizing coastal resources such as seaweed for fodder and fertilizer, and either directly or indirectly consuming high levels of salt (Montgomery 2010). In terms of diet, it is clear from the Beaker People Project data that these people were not consuming marine fish, even when the burial sites are directly on the coast. No marine consumers have been found. Their diet generally was based on an apparently high level of terrestrial animal protein. Another interesting facet to the data that requires further consideration is a significant shift in $\delta^{13}C$ values when this period is compared with large groups of Middle Iron Age data from the same regions (see Fig. 10.1). This may relate to animal management (as is being suggested by animal data) or environmental factors such as climatic fluctuations and deforestation. Further work is being undertaken to help with understanding this.

Dietary Studies

For dietary matters, one of the main pieces of information coming out of the larger diachronic picture for Europe relates to a switch from a diet containing marine resources to one that is largely terrestrial and apparently excludes marine resources (at least insofar as they can be seen in the isotopic data). This occurs in north-western Europe after the

Mesolithic, usually at the Mesolithic-Neolithic transition, but in some places a bit later, such as the coastal and island communities of Sweden and Norway (Eriksson et al. 2008; Richards, Schulting, and Hedges 2003; Tauber 1986). The interesting factor here appears to be that marine (and possibly freshwater) resources do not come back into the diet in amounts currently visible for isotopic studies, often until Roman influences are starting to spread. This is despite the fact that many of the sites studied for the Bronze Age and Iron Age are located directly on the coast (Jay et al. forthcoming; Jay and Richards 2007b). Even where freshwater fish traps or marine middens appear to be present in the archaeological record, the isotopic data do not appear to be recording a significant presence of fish in the diet (e.g. Eriksson et al. 2008), which might mean that they were being consumed in very low quantities, or might suggest that fish were being caught for purposes other than human consumption (e.g. to feed dogs).

So, overall, Bronze Age people from western Europe do not appear to be eating significant levels of marine fish, although we do find that in eastern Europe through to the Urals there may be evidence for some level of freshwater fish consumption, which is being tracked using elevated $\delta^{15}N$ values and radiocarbon reservoir effects (Hedges 2009; Shishlina et al. 2007). We do not, of course, know why marine, and possibly freshwater, fish and other animals were removed from the range of edible products for a couple of thousand years in many places, but the onset of the use of domesticated resources and agriculture may well have led to a situation in which 'wild' foods were no longer considered to be appropriate constituents of the meal unless circumstances were such that domesticated foods were in short supply and conditions were marginal.

An area of increasing interest for Europe is to identify the point at which millet starts to enter the food chain. There are two basic photosynthetic pathways for plants, C_3 and C_4, and these can be identified using carbon isotope data. The pathway mainly present in temperate European plants is C_3, with C_4 being an adaptation suitable for higher temperatures and lower water availability, but millet is a C_4 plant and its presence is beginning to be identified in late Neolithic and Bronze Age contexts in some parts of Europe, prompting more dietary studies that are looking for this particular plant in the diets of animals and people (e.g. Tafuri, Craig, and Cansi 2009).

Carbon and nitrogen isotope data are available for animals as well as humans. These are not only important in terms of ensuring that the faunal data provide a background for the interpretation of the human data, but also in their own right. As a result of having a better understanding of the animal data, we are beginning to obtain information about domesticated animal-management practices and even funeral rites that involve the suggestion of 'feasting'. For instance, a study of Bronze Age animals from a British estuary suggests the exploitation of coastal and salt-marsh plants in the diet of domesticated herbivores, this supporting archaeological evidence that indicates salt-marsh grazing was a deliberate herding strategy (Britton, Müldner, and Bell 2008). This is important for the whole of north-western Europe, where many areas of coastal salt-marshes were more extensive than they are today and represent a resource that could have been widely exploited. Issues such as the use of seaweed and millet for animal feed, differentiation of aurochsen, and domesticated cattle feeding strategies, and weaning ages in cattle that can help in the discussion of dairying herds, can also be explored, although the small number of data-sets currently published in areas such as these are often not from Europe or from the period under discussion (e.g. Lynch, Hamilton, and Hedges 2008; Copley et al. 2004; Balasse and Tresset 2002).

LIMITATIONS AND PROBLEMS

The potential of isotope analysis to illuminate prehistory is an exciting one but it is vital that users are not seduced into ignoring the limitations and problems involved, both in terms of data quality and in the interpretation of the data.

The isotope data used for identifying mobility cannot firmly identify specific locations as points of origin. They can be used to exclude particular possibilities, but there will remain a range of feasible source domains for any particular data-set. Using a range of isotope data for one individual or group of people will help to constrain the possibilities further, as will including archaeological and other contextual information, but ultimately it is not possible to say that an individual definitely spent her or his childhood at a particular location. Neither is it possible to say, using these techniques, that movement definitely did not occur. All of the isotopic data might well be completely consistent with a local origin, but different locations can look very similar, particularly if the people in question chose to settle on the same soils, geology, topography, and environmental niche, and continued to consume the same diet.

Care must be taken when choosing the skeletal fraction to be analysed for a particular isotope ratio. In some cases, studies have been published using a fraction that might be unsuitable because of diagenesis or contamination issues. For instance, the integrity of strontium in bone and dentine mineral has been shown to be problematic in this respect, and care should be taken in how such data are interpreted; this is also true for carbon from bone mineral. There are publications in the recent literature where the bone or dentine mineral data is compared with the tooth enamel or organic collagen in order to reflect either different signals at different times over an individual's life, or else different dietary components (e.g. Price et al. 2004; Chiaradia, Gallay, and Todt 2003; Grupe et al. 1997). In these circumstances, the enamel and collagen data are likely to be more reliable than data from bone or dentine mineral and the latter must be considered only with care. In some cases the problem may be turned to advantage. For instance, where it is assumed that bone and/or dentine mineral may be contaminated by strontium from the local burial environment and no attempt is made to remove it, then this may provide information about the local 'baseline' with which to compare enamel data from possibly mobile individuals (e.g. Haak et al. 2008; Montgomery, Evans, and Cooper 2007). Probably the most important issue to bear in mind when interpreting isotopic data is understanding the range of variation that can occur in a data-set across space and time for groups with a similar dietary input. Very often interpretation of human data will be severely limited without background or baseline data from non-human samples from the same place or time period.

It has long been known that carbon and nitrogen values from collagen samples will vary significantly according to the local environments in which the plants at the base of the food chain are growing. Dietary components from hot, dry areas will lead to quite different nitrogen values from those from cold, wet environments. Coastal, saline environments will produce values that are different to those inland, and factors such as sunshine hours will have an effect. Most of these influences will vary not just across space (the British coastline will look very different to an African desert), but also across time as climatic and environmental changes occur. For this reason, it is often pointed out in carbon and nitrogen studies that background data from animals (particularly herbivores) are required from the same site and time period as human samples in order to interpret the data properly. Whilst the importance of such analyses is acknowledged, it is often the case that they are not undertaken, or else the data are obtained in such small numbers that they are not particularly helpful. This is usually because animal assemblages are simply not available from the appropriate locations. These kinds of problems will start to lessen as databases for particular regions and time periods become much larger and allow comparisons of different research studies.

Dietary research is currently limited to an estimation of significant levels of quite basic food categories (marine resource protein versus terrestrial protein, plant protein versus animal protein, C_3 plants versus C_4). Attempts have been made, using mixing models, to be precise about the proportions of a diet made up of particular food sources, but we still have a lot to understand, even about the systems we know most about in ecological terms. Precise proportions must be considered with care, and qualitative, rather than quantitative, estimations may still be the best way to approach this issue. For any of the isotopic systems mentioned here, values from single individuals are likely to have severe limitations on interpretation. The complications for any system (dietary resource range, mobility range, agricultural systems, trading and exchange, environmental inputs, etcetera) mean that it is much more productive to have a large group of values, along with animal values and comparative data-sets, which can be looked at together.

Future Work

The development of skeletal isotopic analysis techniques might easily be compared to the development of radiocarbon dating in two respects: first, that the data being obtained have the potential to change our understanding of prehistoric human behaviour, and second, that the development and understanding of the techniques and the interpretation of data in the light of growing databases are subject to evolution over decades and should not be viewed as necessarily definitive at a particular point in time. An element of understanding the developmental nature of this research is important (Hedges 2009). Over the last half a century, techniques for preparing bone for radiocarbon dating have changed significantly, measurement and calibration techniques have increased considerably in precision, and the database of available dates has grown to such an extent that we can interpret dated material in context in a way undreamt of fifty years ago. As the isotopic database grows, our techniques are evolving and our understanding of the science is increasing along with our knowledge of the effective time-resolution available in different biological tissues from different animals. The results of today's analyses form the foundation for future understanding.

This is not to say that we are not gleaning a great deal from the data we have now. A good general picture of worldwide mobility patterns and dietary practice is being built up from isotope data. We are also developing ideas for using the data for more detailed interpretations of behaviour, such as identifying increasing pastoralism, unusual weaning patterns, coastal subsistence, matrilocality, funerary practices, and so on (e.g. Towers et al. 2010; Jay et al. 2008; Montgomery, Evans, and Cooper 2007). It cannot be said that our current interpretations will not be revisited as time goes by, but as databases increase in size, our ability to be more precise in our interpretations of the data will also increase. One of the biggest contributions for future work will be the combination of a number of different isotope systems (e.g. the Beaker People Project). With data from a range of chemical elements, all from the same individuals and populations, we can constrain the possibilities to a much greater extent and be more precise in the picture being built, both of mobility patterns and of diet.

There are several techniques in the early days of their development, which are promising to make significant contributions to this kind of research. These include sulphur and hydrogen analysis of collagen, for which we have small databases for archaeological material and for which our understanding of the systems are more limited than for the strontium, carbon, and nitrogen systems. Lead isotope analysis has been little used to study prehistoric migration, primarily because interpretation is complex and the trace levels present in prehistoric enamel require dedicated clean laboratory facilities, and ultra-pure reagents render it expensive. Biosphere lead isotope ratios in unpolluted environments are perhaps even less understood than those of strontium, but archaeologically important geological terrains such as chalks and limestones are distinctive (Montgomery et al. 2010). For oxygen isotope analysis, one of the urgent questions we need to address is how to make the data produced in different laboratories comparable, and how and if humans can modify the oxygen isotope ratios of the fluids they drink through such processes as brewing, boiling, evaporation during storage, and drinking milk. All of these can increase the oxygen isotope ratio of the water drunk (i.e. make it less negative), and whilst this offers the potential to investigate the consumption of such fluids, until we establish how variable people are from a single family, village, or region, it is difficult to assign an exotic origin with confidence. Another area that shows promise for the future is the analysis of individual amino acids. Collagen is made up of a group of 20 amino acids and our current analytical techniques look at the bulk fraction, averaging the individual values. Each amino acid reflects a different isotope ratio for carbon and nitrogen (only one of them contains sulphur), and this may be particularly interesting when looking at those which are essential (i.e. need to be obtained directly from the diet) and those which are non-essential (i.e. can be manufactured in the body). Although data and direct applications are currently secondary to perfecting the analytical method, this promises to bring more precision to dietary analysis for the future (e.g. Smith et al. 2009).

Bibliography

Balasse, M. and Tresset, A. (2002). 'Early weaning of Neolithic domestic cattle (Bercy, France) revealed by intra-tooth variation in nitrogen isotope ratios', *Journal of Archaeological Science*, 29: 853–9.

Bentley, R. A. (2006). 'Strontium isotopes from the earth to the archaeological skeleton: a review', *Journal of Archaeological Method and Theory*, 13/3: 135–87.

—— and Knipper, C. (2005). 'Geographical patterns in biologically available strontium, carbon and oxygen isotope signatures in prehistoric SW Germany', *Archaeometry*, 47/3: 629–44.

Britton, K., Müldner, G., and Bell, M. (2008). 'Stable isotope evidence for salt-marsh grazing in the Bronze Age Severn Estuary, UK: implications for palaeodietary analysis at coastal sites', *Journal of Archaeological Science*, 35: 2,111–18.

Chiaradia, M., Gallay, A., and Todt, W. (2003). 'Different contamination styles of prehistoric human teeth at a Swiss necropolis (Sion, Valais) inferred from lead and strontium isotopes', *Applied Geochemistry*, 18: 353–70.

Copley, M. S., Jim, S., Jones, V., Rose, P., Clapham, A., Edwards, D. N., Horton, M., Rowley-Conwy, P., and Evershed, R. P. (2004). 'Short- and long-term foraging and foddering strategies of domesticated animals from Qasr Ibrim, Egypt', *Journal of Archaeological Science*, 31: 1,273–86.

Eriksson, G., Linderholm, A., Fornander, E., Kanstrup, M., Schoultz, P., Olofsson, H., and Lidén, K. (2008). 'Same island, different diet: cultural evolution of food practice on Öland, Sweden, from the Mesolithic to the Roman Period', *Journal of Anthropological Archaeology*, 27: 520–43.

Evans, J. A., Chenery, C. A., and Fitzpatrick, A. P. (2006). 'Bronze Age childhood migration of individuals near Stonehenge, revealed by strontium and oxygen isotope tooth enamel analysis', *Archaeometry*, 48/2: 309–21.

Fitzpatrick, A. P. (2003). 'The Amesbury Archer', *Current Archaeology*, 16/184: 146–52.

Giblin, J. I. (2009). 'Strontium isotope analysis of Neolithic and Copper Age populations on the Great Hungarian Plain', *Journal of Archaeological Science*, 36: 491–7.

Grupe, G., Price, T. D., Schröter, P., Söllner, F., Johnson, C. M., and Beard, B. L. (1997). 'Mobility of Bell Beaker people revealed by strontium isotope ratios of tooth and bone: a study of southern Bavarian skeletal remains', *Applied Geochemistry*, 12: 517–25.

Haak, W., Brandt, G., De Jong, H. N., Meyer, C., Ganslmeier, R., Heyd, V., Hawkesworth, C., Pike, A. W. G., Meller, H., and Alt, K. W. (2008). 'Ancient DNA, strontium isotopes, and osteological analyses shed light on social and kinship organization of the later Stone Age', *Proceedings of the National Academy of Sciences of the USA*, 105: 18,226–31.

Hedges, R. (2009). 'Studying human diet', in B. Cunliffe, C. Gosden, and R. A. Joyce (eds.), *The Oxford Handbook of Archaeology*. Oxford: Oxford University Press, 484–516.

Jay, M. (2008). 'Iron Age diet at Glastonbury Lake Village: the isotopic evidence for negligible aquatic resource consumption', *Oxford Journal of Archaeology*, 27/2: 201–16.

—— and Richards, M. P. (2006). 'Diet in the Iron Age cemetery population at Wetwang Slack, East Yorkshire, UK: carbon and nitrogen stable isotope evidence', *Journal of Archaeological Science*, 33: 653–62.

—— and Richards, M. P. (2007a). 'The Beaker People Project: progress and prospects for the carbon, nitrogen and sulphur isotopic analysis of collagen', in M. Larsson and M. Parker Pearson (eds.), *From Stonehenge to the Baltic: Living with Cultural Diversity in the Third Millennium BC*. Oxford: British Archaeological Reports (International series), 1,692. Oxford: Archaeopress, 77–82.

—— and Richards, M. P. (2007b). 'British Iron Age diet: stable isotopes and other evidence', *Proceedings of the Prehistoric Society*, 73: 171–92.

——, Fuller, B. T., Richards, M. P., Knüsel, C. J., and King, S. S. (2008). 'Iron Age breastfeeding practices in Britain: isotopic evidence from Wetwang Slack, East Yorkshire', *American Journal of Physical Anthropology*, 136: 327–37.

——, Parker Pearson, M., Richards, M. P., Nehlich, O., Montgomery, J., Chamberlain, A., and Sheridan, A. (2012). 'The Beaker People Project: an interim report on the progress of the isotopic analysis of the organic skeletal material', in M. J. Allen, A. Sheridan, and D. McOmish (eds.), *The British Chalcolithic: People, Place and Polity in the Later 3rd Millennium*, in *Prehistoric Society Research Paper No. 4*. Oxford: The Prehistoric Society and Oxbow Books, 226–36.

Lee-Thorp, J. A. (2008). 'On isotopes and old bones', *Archaeometry*, 50/6: 925–50.
Lynch, A. H., Hamilton, J., and Hedges, R. E. M. (2008). 'Where the wild things are: aurochs and cattle in England', *Antiquity*, 82: 1,025–39.
Melton, N. D., Montgomery, J., Knüsel, C., Batt, C. M., Needham, S., Parker Pearson, M., Sheridan, A., Heron, C., Horsley, T., Schmidt, A., Evans, A., Carter, E., Edwards, H. G. M., Hargreaves, M. D., Janaway, R., Lynnerup, N., Northover, P., O'Connor, S., Ogden, A. R., Taylor, T., Wastling, V., and Wilson, A. (2010). 'Gristhorpe Man: an Early Bronze Age log-coffin scientifically defined', *Antiquity*, 84/325: 796–815.
Montgomery, J. (2010). 'Passports from the past: investigating human dispersals using strontium isotope analysis of tooth enamel', *Annals of Human Biology*, 37/3: 325–46.
——, Cooper, R. E., and Evans, J. A. (2007). 'Foragers, farmers or foreigners? An assessment of dietary strontium isotope variation in Middle Neolithic and Early Bronze Age East Yorkshire', in M. Larsson and M. Parker Pearson (eds.), *From Stonehenge to the Baltic: Living with Cultural Diversity in the Third Millennium BC*. British Archaeological Reports (International series), 1,692. Oxford: Archaeopress, 65–75.
——, Evans, J. A., and Cooper, R. E. (2007). 'Resolving archaeological populations with Sr-isotope mixing models', *Applied Geochemistry*, 22: 1,502–14.
——, Evans, J. A., Chenery, S. R., Pashley, V., and Killgrove, K. (2010). 'Gleaming, white and deadly: lead exposure and geographic origins in England in the Roman period', in H. Eckardt (ed.), *Roman Diasporas: Archaeological Approaches to Mobility and Diversity in the Roman Empire*. Portsmouth: RI: *Journal of Roman Archaeology*, Supplement 78, 199–226.
Müller, W., Fricke, H., Halliday, A. N., McCulloch, M. T., and Wartho, J.-A. (2003). 'Origin and migration of the Alpine Iceman', *Science*, 302 (31 October): 862–6.
Nehlich, O., Montgomery, J., Evans, J., Schade-Lindig, S., Pichler, S. L., Richards, M. P., and Alt, K. W. (2009). 'Mobility or migration: a case study from the Neolithic settlement of Nieder-Mörlen (Hessen, Germany)', *Journal of Archaeological Science*, 36: 1,791–9.
Parker Pearson, M. (2006). 'The Beaker People Project: mobility and diet in the British Early Bronze Age', *The Archaeologist*, 61: 14–15.
Price, T. D., Knipper, C., Grupe, G., and Smrcka, V. (2004). 'Strontium isotopes and prehistoric human migration: the Bell Beaker period in central Europe', *European Journal of Archaeology*, 7/1: 9–40.
Richards, M. P., Schulting, R. J., and Hedges, R. E. M. (2003). 'Sharp shift in diet at onset of Neolithic', *Nature*, 425: 366.
—— Montgomery, J., Nehlich, O., and Grimes, V. (2008). 'Isotopic analysis of humans and animals from Vedrovice', *Anthropologie*, 46: 185–94.
Sealy, J. (2001). 'Body tissue chemistry and palaeodiet', in D. R. Brothwell and A. M. Pollard (eds.), *Handbook of Archaeological Sciences*. Chichester: John Wiley & Sons, 269–79.
Shishlina, N. I., Van der Plicht, J., Hedges, R. E. M., Zazovskaya, E. P., Sevastyanov, V. S., and Chichagova, O. A. (2007). 'The catacomb cultures of the north-west Caspian Steppe: ^{14}C chronology, reservoir effect, and paleodiet', *Radiocarbon*, 49/2: 713–26.
Smith, C. I., Fuller, B. T., Choy, K., and Richards, M. P. (2009). 'A three-phase liquid chromatographic method for δ^{13}C analysis of amino acids from biological protein hydrolysates using liquid chromatography-isotope ratio mass spectrometry', *Analytical Biochemistry*, 390: 165–72.
Tafuri, M. A., Craig, O. E., and Canci, A. (2009). 'Stable isotope evidence for the consumption of millet and other plants in Bronze Age Italy', *American Journal of Physical Anthropology*, 139: 146–53.

Tauber, H. (1986). 'Analysis of stable isotopes in prehistoric populations', in B. Herrmann (ed.), *Innovative Trends in Prehistoric Anthropology*. Göttingen: Mitteilungen der Berliner Gesellschaft für Anthropologie, Ethnologie und Urgeschichte, 31–8.

Towers, J., Montgomery, J., Evans, J., Jay, M., and Parker Pearson, M. (2010). 'An investigation of the origins of the cattle and aurochs deposited in the Early Bronze Age barrows at Gayhurst and Irthlingborough', *Journal of Archaeological Science*, 37: 508–15.

Triantaphyllou, S., Richards, M. P., Zerner, C., and Voutsaki, S. (2008). 'Isotopic dietary reconstruction of humans from Middle Bronze Age Lerna, Argolid, Greece', *Journal of Archaeological Science*, 35: 3,028–34.

Vika, E. (2009). 'Strangers in the grave? Investigating local provenance in a Greek Bronze Age mass burial using $\delta^{34}S$ analysis', *Journal of Archaeological Science*, 36: 2,024–8.

CHAPTER 11

THE MYTH OF THE CHIEF: PRESTIGE GOODS, POWER, AND PERSONHOOD IN THE EUROPEAN BRONZE AGE

JOANNA BRÜCK AND DAVID FONTIJN

Introduction

The emergence of social complexity is widely seen as one of the defining characteristics of the European Bronze Age. The development of the so-called 'palace civilizations' of Minoan Crete and Mycenaean Greece may be the best-known examples, but social change was not restricted to the eastern Mediterranean. South of the Carpathians, we find a zone of often fortified settlements in Hungary and Slovakia, some of which were of an unprecedented size. In temperate Europe large, village-like settlements are generally rare, but the occurrence of 'wealthy' graves and of hill forts producing exotic imports have been seen as an indication that here also the egalitarian relations of the Neolithic made way for more hierarchical ones.

Lacking the features of eastern Mediterranean communities such as a developed administrative system and written records, the social organization of Bronze Age societies in other European regions is generally considered to have been of a different—read: less advanced—nature. Originally labelled with phrases of ambiguous meaning like 'petty princes' or 'warrior aristocracies', European Bronze Age societies beyond the eastern Mediterranean are now generally conceptualized as chiefdoms (Kristiansen 1998). These are ranked, centralized societies led by chiefs and they are often seen as an evolutionary bridge between egalitarian societies and bureaucratic states (Earle 2002: 42).

The adoption of bronze has long been seen as the key factor in the emergence of social stratification during the late third and second millennia BC. Many objects were now made of bronze, yet the ores of its main constituents, copper and tin, are unevenly distributed over Europe. According to influential scholars like Gordon Childe (1930), this created networks of dependency between metal-producing and metal-importing societies on a scale previously unseen. As bronze is generally considered to have been vital to the needs of Bronze Age societies (Earle 2002: 294–6), control of the bronze supply has often been seen as one of the most important sources of power in this period.

Whereas it was originally thought that bronzes were primarily appreciated as superior implements, it is now generally accepted that they were first and foremost viewed as prestige goods. A particular form of 'wealth finance' is seen to have emerged in which entrepreneurial male individuals came to power by controlling the supply of bronzes. Bronze objects acted as a form of capital that could be accumulated and converted into the labour of vassals, the reproductive capacity of wives, or the military support of neighbouring chiefs (e.g. Rowlands 1980; Kristiansen and Larsson 2005: 35).

However, control over exchange networks and over sources of copper and tin may have been hard to maintain in the long term, and the chiefdoms of the European Bronze Age are thought to have been characterized by a considerable degree of competition and political instability. According to Earle (1997: 106), one consequence of this was the prevalence of warfare. Finely crafted swords and body armour have been interpreted as prestige items, and it is widely accepted that such artefacts were integral to the expression and maintenance of chiefly power. As such, the 'warrior chief' has become the central character of Bronze Age literature: he (and it is always a 'he') assumes a dominant position at the apex of the political hierarchy, commanding the resources of his vassals and engaging alternately in acts of exchange and violence with chiefly competitors in neighbouring regions.

Overall, then, prevailing visions of the Bronze Age paint a picture of centralized and stratified societies in which power was vested in individualistic and self-interested warrior elites who competed for political dominance by controlling exchange. However, as we shall see, there are both theoretical and empirical problems to the established interpretation of these communities as 'chiefdoms'.

Empirical Issues

We will begin by discussing aspects of the archaeological evidence that render the chiefdom model problematic.

Selective Deposition

As set out above, it is generally assumed that bronze was valuable because it was—in many regions—an exotic and scarce material. Since bronze can be recycled, a process mastered by Bronze Age communities in most non-metalliferous parts of Europe, we must ask why so much bronze was deposited—for example in hoards—and never retrieved? Such a seemingly 'wasteful' attitude is explained by the prestige goods model as a form of wealth management. The deliberate sacrifice—often labelled as 'consumption'—of metal, notably votive deposition in watery places, is argued to have maintained the value of bronze by removing it from circulation (Levy 1982: 102). However, this view seems hard to reconcile with one of the most conspicuous aspects of the evidence. Numerous regional studies—ranging from Ireland to the Caucasus—have shown that the deposition of metalwork was highly structured and selective (Needham 1989; Vandkilde 1996; Fontijn 2002). All across Europe, specific kinds of objects were deposited in particular contexts only. For example, in the southern Netherlands, Belgium, and western Germany, swords—to pick an object that is often seen as an archetypical symbol of male chiefly power—were rarely deposited in burial mounds during the Middle Bronze Age. However, they are known to have been deposited in large quantities in major rivers like the Meuse and the Rhine (Fig. 11.1). If we consider that in a barrow-rich country like large parts of the Netherlands, some 50 percent of known Bronze Age barrows have been excavated by archaeologists, we seem to be dealing with a truly representative pattern. A review of studies of deposition from all over Europe shows that the contexts in which particular objects were deposited differed from region to region and changed over time, but the principle of selective deposition did not vary. It seems that right across Europe, certain types of objects were supposed to end their lifepaths by being deliberately deposited in a particular context. If deposition or 'consumption' of metalwork was purely a means of enhancing its prestigious character by ensuring its scarcity, how then are we to explain the *selective* nature of metalwork deposition?

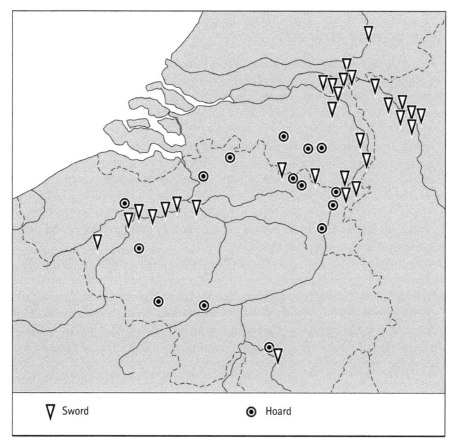

FIG. 11.1 Selective deposition in the last phase of the Late Bronze Age in Belgium, Germany, and the Netherlands. Map showing the location of hoards containing axes and/or ornaments and swords. As can be seen, swords are mainly known from riverine contexts and absent in hoards, even when hoards are situated close to the river. Most of the large ornaments in those hoards, on the other hand, are absent from rivers.

Source: authors (Fontijn 2002: fig. 8.22).

Such patterning extends even to the contents and composition of scrap hoards—finds usually seen as indicating that the accumulation and exchange of wealth in the form of metal was central to the acquisition of economic and political power. Richard Bradley (2005: 152–3), for example, has observed that in many parts of Europe scrap hoards contain an unexpectedly high proportion of fragments from the sockets of axes and the hafts of swords in comparison to their blades. In a similar way, the many Late Bronze Age Plainseau 'trade' or 'scrap' hoards found from northern France to the River Rhine often contain objects that are lacking in other depositional contexts: for example, bracelets with everted terminals are found in considerable numbers in such hoards, but are rare or absent from major rivers and contemporary burials in this region (Fontijn 2002: 243–4). Together, these observations suggest that metalwork in graves, hoards, and elsewhere should not be interpreted solely as 'wealth'—something that is expressed in quantity and can be converted into something else. Rather they hint that the particular meanings ascribed to an object governed how it was used and ultimately how it was deposited.

Chiefly Warrior Graves?

This also holds true for 'wealthy' warrior graves. An almost paradigmatic example is the impressive 'princely' burial of the so-called Únětice culture at Leubingen, central Germany. Inside a large Early Bronze Age barrow, there was a wooden tent-like structure (Fig. 11.2; Höfer 1906). On its floor two bodies were arranged, one across the other, along with a variety of objects including metalworking tools, a bronze halberd, daggers, chisels, axes, and gold jewellery. This has always been interpreted as a 'princely' grave because it differs markedly in equipment and monumentality from the many other 'poorer' contemporary graves in the area. However, other types of 'high-status' objects from the same region are found in very different contexts. For example, elaborate composite necklaces with amber pendants, such as that from Halle-Queis, were deposited in hoards, not graves (Breuer and Meller 2004). Again, this suggests that factors other than the economic or prestige value of objects influenced where and how they were deposited.

An interpretation of the grave goods from Leubingen purely as indicators of wealth and status also fails to explain the finer details of depositional practice within this mortuary context. As Marie Louise Sørensen (2004) has discussed, the mourners carefully grouped the objects and placed them in particular locations relative to the body of the adult male inhumation. These included a group of gold ornaments by his right arm and a stone pickaxe and whetstone to the right of his feet. In addition, some of these items were laid parallel to one another, whereas others were positioned on top of and more or less at right angles to each other, mimicking the position of the two human bodies. The careful selection, juxtaposition, and arrangement of items in the grave go beyond the simple communication of personal prestige and suggest that the objects were employed to convey other sorts of meanings. By taking such a position, it may be possible to generate a more inclusive narrative that allows us to make sense of the sorts of 'low-status' grave goods that so often get overlooked in studies of Bronze Age mortuary rites, for example small items of clay, bone, and stone.

If we accept that certain paraphernalia signalled a particular 'status' or social role, then there is another empirical observation that is difficult to explain. As we have seen, only certain objects were deposited with the dead: many others formed part of

FIG. 11.2 Reconstruction of the central burial in the Early Bronze Age Leubingen barrow (eastern Germany), based on information in Höfer 1906. Note the careful positioning of both grave gifts and the dead. Reconstruction drawing: authors, after Piggott 1965.

permanent deposits in hoards or as single finds, for example in watery places. If swords were a widely shared symbol of chiefly status, as is generally assumed, how are we to explain why swords and other 'warrior' items were permanently deposited in rivers and hoards in many parts of north-west Europe during the Middle and Late Bronze Age (see Harding 2007: 125–7)? After all, if weapons signal warrior identities, here we are dealing with situations where the symbols of warriorhood were deliberately surrendered. This suggests that 'chiefly warrior identities' might have been less fixed or institutionalized than established views would have it.

HOMO ECONOMICUS AND THE SUBJECT-OBJECT DIVIDE

We now wish to address the conceptual framework that underpins the chiefdom model in the European Bronze Age. It has long been recognized that the idea of the 'chiefdom' is firmly rooted in social evolutionary narratives which can be traced back to the nineteenth century and beyond. Much of the allure of these models derives from an implicit desire to legitimate the 'achievements' of modern, Western society by setting it at one end of an evolutionary spectrum. Although possessing a certain heuristic value, terms such as 'chiefdom' have been jettisoned by social anthropologists who recognize the complex, multilinear, and historically contingent character of social change. Indeed, it is now recognized that the chiefdoms of eighteenth- and nineteenth-century Africa and Oceania on which classic anthropological models were based must themselves be understood as a product of colonial contact and the requirements of mercantile capitalism, as European powers sought to control land and people by creating defined territories and formalizing contested indigenous hierarchies (McIntosh 1999: 2–3).

These important, general points have been discussed at length elsewhere and we do not wish to consider them further here. Instead, we will focus on a set of problems made evident by the material itself. Although based on substantivist approaches to the ancient economy, the chiefdom model in fact imposes significant elements of modern capitalist economics onto the past. As we have seen, bronze objects are primarily viewed as a form of capital. Even where objects are recognized as symbols of power, this is often little more than a superficial gloss over their core economic value. The Bronze Age is often thought to have seen a dramatic increase in the *exploitation* of natural resources, *competition* over trade routes, and *maximization* of agricultural productivity (e.g. Earle 2002) to finance elite political ambitions; as such, much of the literature retains a distinctly rational-economist tone. This explanatory framework extends even to ritual practices: as we have seen, the deposition of bronze objects in wet places, for example, is explained as a means of removing excess metal from circulation so that its value is maintained. Behaviour that seems economically irrational at first sight thus becomes economic in the end. This focus on economic gain and the accumulation of wealth means that capitalist values, priorities, and attitudes become projected into the past. Yet, as we have argued above, the deposition of bronzes in contexts such as hoards and burials strongly suggests that the meanings ascribed to these and other objects at particular stages in their life histories were more important than their economic value.

This view of Bronze Age economics is based on an underlying assumption that a categorical distinction can be drawn between prehistoric people as active subjects and passive, inanimate objects. In discussions of Bronze Age exchange, objects are acquired, accumulated, and disposed of at will by prestigious individuals who wield power over their ultimate fate. Like money in a capitalist economy, they become undifferentiated and anonymous: their quantity and economic potential is prioritized over their qualities and social efficacy. This view can be critiqued from a number of different perspectives.

First, the distinction between subject and object, characteristic of modern, Western thinking, must be understood as the outcome of a particular set of historical conditions (e.g. Thomas 2004) and should not be projected into the past. During the eighteenth and nineteenth centuries, the development of a discourse that drew a distinction between the thinking (male) subject and the natural world of objects (including a feminized landscape) provided a means of vesting power in particular social groups by creating an objectified 'other' that could be mapped, measured, explored, and exploited. As we will argue below, however, there is good evidence that a sharp division between people and objects was not recognized in the Bronze Age.

Second, it is widely accepted that gift exchange was an important element of the Bronze Age 'economy'. Anthropological studies of gift exchange cast objects in a very different light to the way they are viewed within capitalist economics (e.g. Mauss 1990). According to these perspectives, artefacts play an active role in the constitution of the person. Networks of exchange link human and artefactual biographies so that people do not simply make objects: objects too can be said to make people. Objects are inalienable because they cannot be cleft from their histories nor severed from the claims of former owners; as such, memory and identity cannot be disentangled from their material components. Because artefacts can be seen as creating—indeed animating—particular types of person, they are frequently considered to be active agents with their own intrinsic social, practical, and ritual potency. In such contexts, a sharp distinction between people and objects is not drawn.

Moreover, in the context of acts of gift exchange, the character of the objects given is crucial. A woman's identity and worth are made evident by the gifts she is offered: their particular qualities and attributes both reflect and constitute the self. The gifts given by others at crucial points in the life cycle mark out the relationships that together construct the person (e.g. Battaglia 1990). As such, identity must be seen as an inherently relational quality constituted (in part) by the interaction between people and objects.

These points have a number of significant implications. In particular, the *meanings* that are ascribed to objects are almost always more important than their economic worth. The form and character of a gift reflect the cultural values that are central to the relationship being created; this can help us make sense of the phenomenon of selective deposition. It is precisely because such objects were inalienable—because they had particular cultural biographies—that they were treated in specific ways. This suggests that the quantitative calculations it is so tempting to make to estimate the relative status of different burials (for example, comparing the number or weight of bronze artefacts) are problematic. It was the histories of particular artefacts that made them suitable choices for deposition, so that quality rather than quantity was central to the construction of value.

Power, Hierarchy, and Personhood

The distinction between subject and object also underpins accepted models of power, agency, and the self in the European Bronze Age, in particular dominant images of the warrior chief. This androcentric preoccupation with 'male' qualities and values means that warfare and other forms of competitive individualism are considered the primary factors in social change. Conventional accounts of the transformations that occurred during the second millennium BC focus on 'warrior' graves, so that particular objects, notably swords, are singled out at the expense of others. However, although swords are found in association with gold hair rings and razors, graves with the latter two categories are also known without swords (Warmenbol 1988: 252–6); strangely, there are no terms for such weaponless graves. This signals a flaw in our interpretations that is perhaps most conspicuous in the case of the well-studied group of 'richly' furnished female graves of the German Middle Bronze Age (Wels-Weyrauch 1989). Despite the large number of substantial bronze ornaments with which their bodies were adorned, these women are not considered to have held positions of political power nor to have played prominent roles within their communities. Rather, they figure only passively in models of Bronze Age society as the objects of (marriage partner) exchanges (see Kristiansen 1998: 398).

We would argue that the image of the Bronze Age warrior chief embodies qualities characteristic of the idealized individual in the modern, Western world. Post-Enlightenment concepts of the individual construct the person as a rational and autonomous subject situated outside and above the natural world (e.g. Fowler 2004)—a bounded, stable locus of agency who wields absolute power over an objectified 'other'. This self is implicitly gendered male, and the pursuit of power and prestige through competitive self-aggrandizement is one of his key characteristics. A self-interested desire to exert dominance over the natural world in the pursuit of economic gain is legitimized by an ideology that distinguishes subject from object and culture from nature. Over the past two centuries, this model of the individual has underpinned a series of major social, economic, and political transformations, including the development of institutionalized class divisions, mercantile capitalism, and imperial expansion. It is hardly surprising, then, that the uncritical imposition of this model onto the Bronze Age has had a particular impact on our understanding of economic and political organization in the past.

Just as anthropological studies have critiqued the distinction between subject and object, so too the analogous division between self and other can be called into question. Studies of personhood in non-Western societies demonstrate that the self is often constructed as an unbounded amalgam of elements, substances, and relationships (e.g. Strathern 1988). Here, the self is an ongoing project to which the contributions of others are central. As such, identity should not be thought of as fixed or categorical, but as fluid and relational. Such sociocentric conceptions of the person are given material form through the circulation of objects that contribute to the construction, transformation, and dissolution of personhood (Battaglia 1990). So, too, as we shall discuss below, interpersonal relationships became literally *embodied* through the deposition of objects with particular histories of exchange in Bronze Age burials.

In such contexts, power must also be construed in relational terms. Although the circulation of objects can, in certain circumstances, generate prestige, this is rarely lasting. The inalienable character of gifts reminds us that people are always subject to the demands of others. Power is socially sanctioned and those in positions of power derive this from their interpersonal links. In other words, power is not a *thing* that is held or owned by particular people. Instead, it is a property of interpersonal relationships, enacted—and hence created—within the context of specific events, practices, and performances. This is because agency (the power to act or to have an effect on the world) is a product of relationships; one's relationships with others (both people and things) open up particular possibilities for action while others are foreclosed. In turn, relationships themselves require performance, in the course of which social categories and social boundaries emerge: identity itself must therefore be considered a cultural construct. As such, power is not an *a priori* given, but must be constantly negotiated and maintained in the face of shifting social and material conditions. It should be viewed not as static or vested in a single person or group, but as fluid, dispersed, and contextually specific (see McIntosh 1999).

Social and Material Relations in the European Bronze Age

As we have seen, dominant narratives of the European Bronze Age conjure an image of centralized and hierarchical chiefdom societies in which political power was vested in those who controlled the circulation of metal, with metal standing for 'wealth' and 'prestige'. We argued that this view not only leaves a number of empirical patterns unexplained, but also stems from an anachronistic understanding of the self that projects the modern, Western distinction between subject and object onto the Bronze Age. We will now explore alternative ways of interpreting the material.

Selective Deposition: Objects as Inalienable Items

As we have discussed, the idea that bronze objects and other so-called 'prestige goods' were principally valued as forms of wealth and for their ability to mark social status is challenged by patterns of selective deposition. Such patterns indicate that metal artefacts (and other objects too) were imbued with meanings derived from particular histories of circulation. Objects may have invoked different and perhaps even conflicting cultural values. In many regions, there are distinctive patterns of association and exclusion between objects in hoards and grave assemblages. During the Bell Beaker period, for example, copper daggers and gold ornaments repeatedly figure in graves in both northern Europe and Britain, but we rarely find copper axes and halberds in such contexts—instead, these objects appear to have been deposited in other places (Vandkilde 1996: 267–8). Such patterning makes sense only if we see objects not as alienable metal wealth or prestige goods, but as inalienable objects, inextricably linked to specific cultural values, identities, and biographies.

There is much to suggest that the histories of particular metal objects had a significant impact on the manner of their deposition. This is illustrated by the identification of two joining fragments of a single sword from Staffordshire in the English Midlands. These were deposited as isolated finds on two hilltops; the hilltops themselves were intervisible and lay some 3 km apart on either side of the River Trent (Bradley and Ford 2004). One of these pieces was more heavily worn than the other, suggesting different histories of use. Nonetheless, their depositional contexts were so similar that we can suggest that the history and original relationships of the pieces were known, even at the end of their lives. Often, bronze objects that repeatedly occur in certain contexts show signs of specific use-histories. This suggests that—for example—swords were not selected to be thrown into rivers solely because of their form, but also because they had particular kinds of life-paths (use in battle, certain histories of circulation, etcetera) that made them acceptable for deposition in such liminal places (Fontijn 2002).

These points remind us that just as the subject-object divide is problematic, so too is the analogous distinction between nature and culture so often implicit in writings on the Bronze Age. Not only were objects invested with specific meanings and qualities; so too were particular features of the landscape—landscape was not solely an economic resource. Hence, the widely shared tendency to deposit swords in major rivers in western Europe, for example, suggests that both these objects and the rivers into which they were thrown had particular meanings—meanings that may have been linked to the location of rivers in the Bronze Age cultural and conceptual landscape. Certain kinds of rivers were seen as appropriate receptacles for swords, and there are indications that such preferences relate both to the histories of these rivers (most have long traditions of use as multiple-deposition zones) and also to particular visual characteristics that they possessed (Fontijn 2002).

Objects Make Persons

One of the results of the strict selections made during depositional practices in the Bronze Age is that specific sets of objects seem to have been used to create particular appearances: individuals in graves were portrayed with the imagery of certain social and religious identities so that objects worked to make them into particular kinds of persons. The Early Bronze Age Leubingen burial set, for example, is highly unusual amongst the large numbers of contemporary graves of the Únětice groups in central Europe. However, it finds a curious parallel in the burial at Helmsdorf in the same region which dates to a century later, as well as in two graves some 350 km away in Great Poland, Łęki Małe A and B, each of which contains a very similar set of artefacts (Kowiańska-Piaszykowa 2008). The rarity of these burial kits and the temporal and spatial distances between them make it unlikely that we are dealing with a ruling class or aristocracy here. Instead, these graves suggest that Early Bronze Age communities in different regions and in exceptional circumstances chose to portray particular people in a way that gave material form to widely shared understandings and beliefs; as such, the key concern in these 'princely' burials may have been to express dominant cultural values rather than wealth and status.

This is something for which we find evidence in the later Bronze Age as well (Harding 2007: 141–4). Gold hair rings and toilet articles like razors and tweezers regularly occur in Middle and Late Bronze Age 'warrior' graves, suggesting that certain ideas about personal appearance were widely shared, as were understandings of the objects and bodily transformations required to adopt a role as a sword-bearing 'warrior'. However, this does not mean that 'warriorhood' can be seen as a Europe-wide social institution. The frequency with which we find evidence of sword burials, for example, differs enormously. In some parts of Denmark, some 25 per cent of burials contain swords. In northern Germany and the north of the Netherlands these frequencies are much lower. In the latter region, only 3 per cent of all Middle Bronze Age barrows contain weapons. Remarkably enough, the 'richest' grave of the group of north European 'Sögel' warrior graves, the burial from Drouwen, is situated precisely in that region (see Harding 2007: 125–33, for further examples from other regions). So in spite of similarities in appearances, the social meaning of sword graves must have differed considerably from region to region.

Objects and Relational Identity

If artefacts were so central to the construction of identity, it is hardly surprising that the Bronze Age mortuary data challenge us to rethink the categorical distinction between subject and object. Inalienable objects appear to have been especially important in funerary rites of the period. Many of the artefacts deposited in the grave appear to have been made and used by others over the course of their lives. For example, in the British Early Bronze Age, fragments of jet and amber necklaces that were already old on deposition can be interpreted as heirlooms (e.g. Woodward 2002); deposition of these objects in the mortuary context located the deceased in a complex and historically constructed network of social relations. Other objects, too, may have been gifts from the mourners rather than the possessions of the deceased (Brück 2004); as such, they gave material form to interpersonal relationships central to the constitution of the self. The relational character of identity is also suggested by the removal of objects from the mortuary context: some items appear to have been deliberately broken during the funerary rite, so that part of these could be deposited in the grave and other elements retained as tokens of the dead by the living. For instance, the bone pommel from burial H at Bedd Branwen on Anglesey had been carefully snapped in two; one half of this object was deposited in the grave but the other piece, along with the blade of the dagger to which it was once attached, is missing (Lynch 1971).

Elsewhere, the dead were accompanied by accoutrements that may have been employed in the funeral rite. For example, the ten flint objects that accompanied the cremation of an adult female from Roxton in Bedfordshire (Taylor and Woodward 1985) had been struck from a single nodule, suggesting that these were made specifically for use in the mortuary rite. Deposition of these objects in the grave highlighted the place of particular people in the life of the deceased; certain members of the family may have been ascribed particular roles during the funeral—roles given material form through artefacts. As such, the objects given by mourners at the graveside or employed in the mortuary rite spoke of the significance of interpersonal relationships, constructing narratives of identity not only for the deceased but also for those who prepared the body, shared the funerary feast, or placed objects in the grave (Brück 2004).

It is hardly surprising, therefore, that there is such good evidence for the careful arrangement of artefacts in the grave itself, as we have already seen at Leubingen. If objects gave material form to interpersonal links, then this acted as a way of mapping out those relationships onto and around the body. The location of artefacts—for example at the head or the feet, or on the right or left side of the body—may have said something specific about the relationship between the deceased and those who had placed these items in the grave (see Fig. 11.2). If, as in many societies, the human body acted as an image of the body politic (e.g. Douglas 1973), then particular identities and relationships may have been constituted in spatial terms in the micro-topography of the mortuary context.

Together, such evidence suggests that Bronze Age identities were relational rather than categorical; identity was constructed in sociocentric rather than individual terms. Our observations suggest that even the abundance of objects that is so characteristic for Early Bronze Age 'chiefly' graves in Europe need not simply reflect the material wealth of the deceased. For example, in the Early Bronze Age 'princely graves' of Brittany, burials were accompanied by between 4 and 12 daggers (Hansen 2001: table 4). It is remarkable that only particular categories of objects in a grave set appear in large numbers. It is possible that multiples may not have been the possessions of the deceased but were gifts from the mourners. As such, rather than a display of prestige through abundance, the principle of redundancy may have been a means of emphasizing the significance of particular forms of interpersonal relationship and associated cultural values (see Hansen 2001: 167).

Objects as Persons

There is, then, evidence for intimate personalized relationships between people and objects. The selective and patterned use of items in depositional practices can only be understood if they were regarded as inalienable objects that played a key role in the construction of identities and were inextricably linked with particular cultural values. As many of those objects, especially bronzes, appear to have had a (long) history of circulation and were deposited in a worn and fragmentary condition, they are likely to have acquired meaning as a result of their previous life-paths or cultural biographies (Kopytoff 1986). However, it is not simply the case that objects make persons. Anthropological discussions of exchange indicate that the generative power of inalienable objects is such that they are often themselves regarded as persons (Mauss 1990).

In the European Bronze Age people and objects were frequently treated in similar ways, challenging the distinction archaeologists so often draw between these categories. For instance, we have already seen that in the grave at Leubingen there is an interesting parallel between the arrangement of the bodies of the dead and the positioning of some of the grave goods. At Nebra in Saxony-Anhalt the famous sky disc appears to have been placed in a small cist-like setting of stones—although the details of its depositional context are uncertain because it was found by metal detectorists. Although it is almost three hundred years younger than the Leubingen burial, it was accompanied by a similar array of equipment (Meller 2004). Here, a unique, ceremonial item replaced a human body.

In other regions, too, there is evidence that calls into question the division between people and things. In the British Middle and Late Bronze Age both human bodies and a variety of objects (including pottery, quernstones, and bronzes) were burnt and broken at the end of their life cycles (Brück 2006). Just as the normative mortuary rites of the period (cremation and excarnation) resulted in the fragmentation of the human body on death, so too the abandonment of settlements was marked by the deliberate destruction of ceramics and other artefacts associated with the life of the site. At Broom Quarry in Bedfordshire (Mortimer and McFadyen 1999), a substantial assemblage of pottery was deposited in two pits at the edge of a roundhouse late in the life of this structure. This comprised large, freshly broken sherds and included vessels of different shapes and sizes, suggesting that the household's inventory of pottery may have been deliberately broken as a leave-taking deposit to mark the 'death' of this house.

The deposition of token cremations at sites such as the ring cairn at Moel Goedog, Gwynedd, north Wales (Lynch 1984), hints that fragments of human bodies may—like artefacts—have been retained as heirlooms by the participants in funerary rites (Brück 2006). At Green Park in Berkshire a piece of unburnt human skull was recovered from a waterhole (Boyle 2004: 99). Although no longer complete, this had originally been shaped into a roundel with a roughly central piercing; the perforation of this object was worn, suggesting that it may have been used and handled over a considerable period of time. As such, we can argue that both the bodies of the dead and the objects with which they were associated during life were circulated for use in a variety of non-mortuary contexts, highlighting the significance of particular interpersonal and familial relationships. Finally, after possibly lengthy histories of circulation, the remains of both people and objects were often deposited in similar places, for example the entrances to settlements (Brück 2006). For instance, at Knocksaggart, County Clare, in the west of Ireland, three of the porch postholes in roundhouse B contained deposits of cremated human bone (Hanley 2002), while at Ballybrowney, County Cork, a saddle quern was recovered from one of the two large postholes that marked the entrance to roundhouse B (Cleary 2006).

There is further evidence to suggest that ancestral fragments of various sorts were considered animate objects. As we have seen, bronzes, human remains, and other artefacts were often deposited in contexts of social and spatial transformation such as rivers, bogs, and settlement entrances. Such acts may have been associated with rites of passage or with moments of significance in the histories of particular places. This hints that for Bronze Age communities, the lives of people, objects, and places were seen as a series of social cycles, with ritual acts—including particular depositional practices—marking movement from one state (or one place) to another. This concept of temporality is visible in some of the key technological practices of the period: both metallurgy and pottery production, for example, involved the recycling of older artefacts—artefacts that themselves may have had specific histories (Brück 2006). As such, ancestral objects, including the remains of the dead, may themselves have been seen as possessing generative potential: they both marked and made possible new life and new relationships.

The Transformation of Identities: Deposition as Dissolution

If, as we have argued above, objects constituted persons in relational terms, then it follows that social and political identities were not fixed but were contextually specific. There was no categorical distinction between self and other; instead, power relations must be seen as a product of fluid and transformative encounters between people, objects, and places. This conjures a very different vision of Bronze Age society to the defined and circumscribed roles and ranks envisaged in the chiefdom model. A variety of archaeological evidence points in this direction.

Artefacts (including fragments of human bone) central to the constitution of personhood were not only worn and used but were also surrendered in places such as bogs and rivers. These were acts that effected the dissolution of identity, suggesting that identities were often temporary and context-specific. Examples include groups of objects that may once have formed the components of particular costumes, such as a pair of sun discs, two wrist bracers, and some jet beads found in a wooden box in Corran Bog, northern Ireland (Case 1977: 21). Across western Europe, objects such as swords were often removed from society in this way; the marked contrast between the 'non-martial' identities that prevail in most Middle and Late Bronze Age graves in this region and the weaponry found in large quantities in rivers suggests that different and perhaps even conflicting kinds of identities were current in one and the same society, but differently contextualized. This implies that weapons—and the notion of violence and warrior identities they evoked—were not relevant to or even at odds with the cultural values and social identities that were emphasized by the mourners during burial.

Social identities were doubtless transformed over the course of the human life cycle. For instance, the deliberate destruction of grave goods symbolized the changing relationships between the living and the dead and reminds us that death must often have resulted in a profound restructuring of social identities: the handle was deliberately torn from the dagger that accompanied the cremation burial of an adult female at Reardnogy More, County Tipperary (Waddell 1969), for example. There may also have been more transitory forms of identity adapted to the needs of certain occasions. One might think here of ceremonial roles specific to particular events or social gatherings. Ethnographic examples demonstrate that the special paraphernalia used in the construction of such temporary identities are often removed from society afterwards by deliberate acts of destruction (Harrison 1995). In a Bronze Age context, there is evidence that Irish gold lunulae were repeatedly folded and unfolded prior to final deposition (Fig. 11.3): this suggests that they were temporarily removed from use before being retrieved for the duration of specific ceremonies (Becker 2008: 14).

Although Bronze Age mortuary evidence suggests that there may have been an attempt to 'fix' an image of the deceased by the structured arrangement of objects in the grave, this does not mean that the identities constructed in the grave were static and uncontested. Evidence

FIG. 11.3 The lunula from Coolaghmore, County Kilkenny. This object has been repeatedly rolled and/or folded, and has also had its ends cut off in a final act of decommissioning.

Source: National Museum of Ireland by kind permission.

for the reopening of burials and the removal and rearrangement of ancestral relics (including both bones and objects) at sites such as Barrow Hills in Oxfordshire (Boyle and Harman 1999: 59) indicates that the dead continued to be drawn into practices of identity construction amongst the living. Such practices suggest that we must reject the imposition of modern, Western concepts of the individual onto the past. Today, we are concerned to retain the integrity of the human body; in contrast, the fragmentation, rearrangement, and circulation of elements of human bone in the Bronze Age indicates that the self was not considered a bounded or immutable entity but was constituted within the ebb and flow of social transactions: mortuary rites provided a context in which relational identities were dissolved, transformed, and reconfigured in the changing social contexts brought about by death.

Bronze Age Economics

One may object that most of the patterns outlined above describe objects that were deliberately removed from society and as such must represent the more exceptional cultural biographies of artefacts. Particularly in non-metalliferous Europe, the dominant biography of bronzes must have ended in recycling. From the Early Bronze Age on, there are many finds of what seem to be standardized units of metal or ingots, like *Ösenringe*, that tend to figure in large one-type hoards in central Europe. In Late Bronze Age western Europe hoards comprising substantial deposits of scrap metal or large numbers of axes are widely known (Maraszek 2006: 160, 248–61). Such finds seem to defy an interpretation of bronzes as meaningful, inalienable items, and it has often been argued that they reflect a trade in metal that was commodified to a considerable degree (Huth 1997). Accepting this would mean that in the Bronze Age we have a dominant 'short-term' economic sphere in which items are alienable commodities or 'things' on the one hand, separated from a minor but significant 'long-term' sphere on the other, in which metal figures in the form of inalienable, meaningful objects that express important cultural values (see Bloch and Parry 1989). However, this conceptual duality is more apparent than real.

It is evident, for example, that many of the finds that are seen as evidence for commodity exchange actually represent items that were deliberately taken out of circulation for the purpose of deliberate deposition. Hoards of *Ösenringe* on settlements are traditionally interpreted as temporary stores of metal (Lenerz-de Wilde 2002), but why were such 'commodities' never recovered? Other *Ösenring* hoards were deposited in natural places such as lakes and lake shores, presumably as votive offerings (Lenerz-de Wilde 2002). The large scrap hoards of north-west Europe raise similar questions. For example, the Middle Bronze Age hoard at Voorhout on the Dutch coast is generally seen as a classic example of trade stock temporarily hidden for safekeeping (Butler and Steegstra 1997–8). This hoard consisted of scrap bronze of British and French origin. However, it was deposited in a bog, which makes it highly unlikely that it represents a cache of material that was simply not retrieved. Elsewhere the principle of selective deposition appears to extend to scrap hoards. Together, these examples suggest that items such as *Ösenringe* and broken bronze objects did not just have an economic value.

There are several ways of interpreting such evidence. It is possible that objects moved in and out of the commodity state at different points in their life cycles (Vandkilde 2003), much as today a wedding ring must be bought before it can be given as a gift on marriage. In the Bronze Age a portion of the material acquired via commodity exchange may have been donated to gods or spirits in order to make it morally acceptable for such items to play a specialized role as valuables (Bloch and Parry 1989). However, inalienable valuables and alienable commodities are inextricably linked in practice (Strathern and Stewart 2005: 242). On modern money, we still print references to the supernatural ('in God we trust'); it is the price of something like a Gucci bag that gives it meaning, while the more 'priceless' an object is considered to be in cultural terms (for example a Van Gogh painting), the higher its price is likely to be. Certainly, anthropological studies suggest that all forms of exchange are inherently social (Gudeman 2005): modern, Western commodity exchange is constituted within a particular ideological framework and is entangled with specific forms of social and political relationships. This suggests that the distinction between 'value' (economic) and 'values' (moral/social/cultural) must be questioned.

In the Early Bronze Age metal ingots like *Ösenringe* refer in their shape to body ornaments that—as we have seen—may have played an important role in the construction of particular identities. As a matter of fact, there are cases where *Ösenringe* were used to adorn the bodies of the dead, for example in grave 322 at Franzhausen 1 grave 322, lower Austria (Vandkilde 2003: 271). In the Low Countries and western Germany there are indications that metal often circulated in the form of axes (Huth 1997). However, used axes were frequently sacrificed in watery contexts such as streams and bogs (Fontijn 2002: Chapter 13). In other words, material often interpreted as trade stock also figured in long-term exchanges as sacrifices, suggesting that objects may have circulated as gifts and commodities at different points in their life cycles.

We can perhaps take these arguments further. The 'accumulation' of objects such as complete axes and *Ösenringe* in hoards need not indicate commodification. Items of standard form may be amassed for special-purpose social transactions: quantities of gold discs, porcelain plates, and shell armlets have traditionally formed parts of marriage and funerary prestations in some areas of Indonesia (Clamagirand 1980). Moreover, our observations regarding the possible significance of fragmentary objects in burials have implications for our interpretation of scrap hoards. The presence of broken bronzes in hoards is usually seen as indicating that these objects have lost their original significance and are now reducible to their raw material value. In contrast, we have argued above that the presence of broken artefacts in graves indicates the significance of relational forms of identity constituted through the circulation of meaningful objects—forms of 'object-relations' very different to those characteristic of capitalist economics. It can therefore be suggested that the broken artefacts in scrap hoards *were* socially meaningful precisely because of their fragmentary state: they symbolically referenced states of transformation and rebirth, the significance of genealogical links, and the relational character of identity. Collections of broken objects might therefore have been considered suitable votive deposits in particular spatial or ritual contexts.

To sum up, purported evidence for the commodification of metal in the Bronze Age can be interpreted in other ways. At the very least, there are indications that there was no rigid distinction between alienable commodities and inalienable valuables: instead, the qualities and values conveyed by objects at particular points in their life cycles informed how and why they were circulated.

Conclusion

In this paper we have argued that it is time to rethink the forms of institutionalized, male-dominated hierarchies so often envisaged in the literature on Bronze Age Europe. Discussions that focus on power and status cannot explain the form that particular acts—including acts of deposition—took. Of course, the meanings ascribed to the objects deposited in graves, wet places, and elsewhere could be drawn on to uphold or to undermine particular value systems—value systems that maintained certain forms of authority. Problems arise, however, when we assume that status (and social identity) was circumscribed and when we impose onto the past concepts of the 'individual' that are a product of the modern, Western world. Although power differentials were doubtless a feature of Bronze Age communities, they were not their sole interest. Instead, the material we have discussed from graves, hoards, and other deposits speaks of wider concerns regarding the reproduction of the cosmos and the location of people, animals, and places within it.

There is much to suggest that forms of social identity changed over the human life cycle (and from context to context) and that identity was considered a relational rather than an intrinsic property. Power could be made to reside—temporarily at least—in particular people and objects, but this required ongoing work as their location in networks of interdependency shifted. Whether at the graveside or as a sword was thrown into a river, power was socially conferred: the objects that defined a person's position were themselves once the gifts of others and had histories that linked them to other people, events, and places. As we have seen, the archaeological evidence indicates that the division between subject and object that underpins modern conceptual frameworks may not have been made in the Bronze Age. If this is so, it is no longer possible to envisage chiefly overlords whose ability to accumulate and control inanimate objects gave them absolute authority. Instead, by re-empowering the objectified 'other'—be it bronze axes, women, or the bodies of dead ancestors—we can construct more nuanced histories in which the productive interactions between people, places, and things together created the communities of Bronze Age Europe.

Bibliography

Battaglia, D. (1990). *On the Bones of the Serpent: Person, Memory and Mortality in Sabarl Island Society.* Chicago: University of Chicago Press.
Becker, K. (2008). 'Left but not lost', *Archaeology Ireland*, 22/1: 12–15.
Bloch, M. and Parry, J. (1989). 'Introduction: money and the morality of exchange', in J. Parry and M. Bloch (eds.), *Money & the Morality of Exchange.* Cambridge: Cambridge University Press, 1–31.
Boyle, A. (2004). 'Worked bone assemblage', in A. Brossler, R. Early, and C. Allen (eds.), *Green Park (Reading Business Park). Phase 2 Excavations 1995.* Oxford: Oxford Archaeology, 99–100.
—— and Harman, M. (1999). 'Human remains', in A. Barclay and C. Halpin, *Excavations at Barrow Hills, Radley, Oxfordshire. Vol. 1: The Neolithic and Bronze Age Monument Complex.* Oxford: Oxbow Books, 59.
Bradley, R. (2005). *Ritual and Domestic Life.* London: Routledge.
—— and Ford, D. (2004). 'A long-distance connection in the Bronze Age: joining fragments of a Ewart Park sword from two sites in England', in H. Roche, E. Grogan, J. Bradley, J. Coles, and B. Raftery (eds.), *From Megaliths to Metals: Essays in Honour of George Eogan.* Oxford: Oxbow Books, 174–7.
Breuer, H. and Meller, H. (2004). 'Tränen der Götter', in H. Meller (ed.), *Der geschmiedete Himmel. Die weite Welt im Herzen Europas vor 3600 Jahren.* Stuttgart: Konrad Theiss Verlag, 104–7.
Brück, J. (2004). 'Material metaphors: the relational construction of identity in Early Bronze Age burials in Ireland and Britain', *Journal of Social Archaeology*, 4: 7–33.
—— (2006). 'Fragmentation, personhood and the social construction of technology in Middle and Late Bronze Age Britain', *Cambridge Archaeological Journal*, 16/2: 297–315.
Butler, J. J. and Steegstra, J. (1997–8). 'Bronze Age metal and amber in the Netherlands (II:2). Catalogue of the Palstaves', *Palaeohistoria*, 39/40: 163–275.
Case, H. (1977). 'The Beaker culture in Britain and Ireland', in R. Mercer (ed.), *Beakers in Britain and Europe.* British Archaeological Reports (Supplementary Series), 26. Oxford: British Archaeological Reports, 71–101.
Childe, V. G. (1930). *The Bronze Age.* London: Cambridge University Press.
Clamagirand, B. (1980). 'The social organisation of the Ema of Timor', in J. J. Fox (ed.), *The Flow of Life: Essays on Eastern Indonesia.* Cambridge, MA: Harvard University Press, 134–51.

Cleary, K. (2006). 'Intriguing discoveries at Ballybrowney, County Cork', *PAST*, 53: 12–14.
Douglas, M. (1973). *Natural Symbols: Explorations in Cosmology*. London: Barrie and Jenkins.
Earle, T. (1997). *How Chiefs Come to Power: The Political Economy in Prehistory*. Stanford: Stanford University Press.
—— (2002). *Bronze Age Economics: The Beginnings of Political Economies*. Oxford: Westview Press.
Fontijn, D. R. (2002). 'Sacrificial landscapes. Cultural biographies of persons, objects and "natural" places in the Bronze Age of the southern Netherlands, c.2300–600 BC', *Analecta Praehistorica Leidensia*, 33/34: 1–392.
Fowler, C. (2004). *The Archaeology of Personhood: An Anthropological Approach*. London: Routledge.
Gudeman, S. (2005). 'Community and economy: economy's base', in J. Carrier (ed.), *A Handbook of Economic Anthropology*. Northampton/Cheltenham: Edward Elgar Publishing, 94–106.
Hanley, K. (2002). 'AR 85/86 Knocksaggart', in I. Bennett (ed.), *Excavations 2000*. Bray: Wordwell, 32–3.
Hansen, S. (2001). '"Überaustattungen" in Gräbern und Horten der Frühbronzezeit', in J. Müller (ed.), *Vom Endneolithikum zur Frühbronzezeit: Muster sozialen Wandels?*, Universitätsforschungen zur prähistorischen Archäologie, 90. Bonn: Habelt, 151–74.
Harding, A. (2007). *Warriors and Weapons in Bronze Age Europe*. Budapest: Archaeolingua.
Harrison, S. (1995). 'Transformations of identity in Sepik warfare', in M. Strathern (ed.), *Shifting Contexts: Transformations in Anthropological Knowledge*. London and New York: Routledge, 81–97.
Höfer, P. (1906). 'Der Leubinger Grabhügel', *Jahresschrift für Vorgeschichte der sächsisch-thüringischen Länder*, 5: 1–99.
Huth, C. (1997). *Westeuropäische Horte der Spätbronzezeit. Fundbild und Funktion*. Regensburger Beiträge zur prähistorischen Archäologie, III. Regensburg: Universitätsverlag.
Kopytoff, I. (1986). 'The cultural biography of things: commoditisation as process', in A. Appadurai (ed.), *The Social life of Things*. Cambridge: Cambridge University Press, 64–91.
Kowiańska-Piaszykowa, M. (2008). *Cmentarzysko kurhanowe z wczesnej epoki brązu w Łękach Małych w Wielkopolsce*. Poznań: Archaeological Museum.
Kristiansen, K. (1998). *Europe before History*. Cambridge: Cambridge University Press.
—— and Larsson, T. (2005). *The Rise of Bronze Age Society: Travels, Transmissions and Transformations*. Cambridge: Cambridge University Press.
Lenerz-de Wilde, M. (2002). 'Bronzezeitliche Zahlungsmittel', *Mitteilungen der Anthropologischen Gesellschaft in Wien*, 132: 1–23.
Levy, J. E. (1982). *Social and Religious Organization in Bronze Age Denmark*, British Archaeological Reports (International Series), 124. Oxford: Archaeopress.
Lynch, F. (1971). 'Report on the re-excavation of two Bronze Age cairns in Anglesey: Bedd Branwen and Treiorwerth', *Archaeologia* Cambresis, 120: 11–83.
—— (1984). 'Moel Goedog circle 1: a complex ring cairn near Harlech', *Archaeologia Cambrensis*, 133: 8–50.

Maraszek, R. (2006). 'Spätbronzezeitliche Hortfundlandschaften in atlantischer und nordischer Metalltradition', *Veröffentlichungen des Landesamtes für Denkmalpflege und Archäologie Sachsen-Anhalt*. Halle (Saale): Landesmuseum für Vorgeschichte.

Mauss, M. (1990). *The Gift: The Form and Reason for Exchange in Human Societies*. London: Routledge.

McIntosh, S. K. (1999). 'Pathways to complexity: an African perspective', in S. K. McIntosh (ed.), *Beyond Chiefdoms: Pathways to Complexity in Africa*. Cambridge: Cambridge University Press, 1–30.

Meller, H. (2004). 'Der Körper des Königs', in H. Meller (ed.), *Der geschmiedete Himmel. Die weite Welt im Herzen Europas vor 3600 Jahren*. Stuttgart: Konrad Theiss Verlag, 94–7.

Mortimer, R. and McFadyen, L. (1999). *Investigation of the Archaeological Landscape at Broom, Bedfordshire: Phase 4*, Cambridge Archaeological Unit Report, 320. Cambridge: Cambridge Archaeological Unit.

Needham, S. (1989). 'Selective deposition in the British Early Bronze Age', *World Archaeology*, 20: 229–48.

Piggott, S. (1965) *Ancient Europe, from the Beginnings of Agriculture to Classical Antiquity*. Edinburgh: Edinburg University Press.

Rowlands, M. (1980). 'Kinship, alliance and exchange in the European Bronze Age', in J. C. Barrett and R. J. Bradley (eds.), *Settlement and Society in the British Later Bronze Age*, British Archaeological Reports (British Series), 83. Oxford: British Archaeological Reports, 59–72.

Sørensen, M. L. S. (2004). 'Stating identities: the use of objects in rich Bronze Age graves', in J. Cherry, C. Scarre, and S. Shennan (eds.), *Explaining Social Change: Studies in Honour of Colin Renfrew*. Cambridge: McDonald Institute for Archaeological Research, 167–76.

Strathern, M. (1988). *The Gender of the Gift: Problems with Women and Problems with Society in Melanesia*. Berkeley: University of California Press.

Strathern, A. and Stewart, P. J. (2005). 'Ceremonial exchange', in J. Carrier (ed.), *A Handbook of Economic Anthropology*. Northampton/Cheltenham: Edward Elgar Publishing, 230–45.

Taylor, A. and Woodward, P. (1985). 'A Bronze Age barrow cemetery, and associated settlement at Roxton, Bedfordshire', *Archaeological Journal*, 142: 73–149.

Thomas, J. (2004). *Archaeology and Modernity*. London: Routledge.

Vandkilde, H. (1996). *From Stone to Bronze, the Metalwork of the Late Neolithic and Earliest Bronze Age in Denmark*, Jutland Archaeological Society Publications, XXXII. Moesgard. Aarhus: Jutland Archaeological Society.

—— (2003). 'A biographical perspective on Osenringe from the Early Bronze Age', in T. Kienlin (ed.), *Die Dinge als Zeichen: Kulturelles Wissen und materieller Kultur*. Bonn: Habelt, 263–81.

Waddell, J. (1969) 'Two Bronze Age burials from Reardnogy More, County Tipperary', *North Munster Antiquarian Journal*, 12: 3–5.

Warmenbol, E. (1988). 'Broken bronzes and burned bones. The transition from Bronze to Iron Age in the Low Countries', *Helinium*, XXVIII: 244–70.

Wels-Weyrauch, U. (1989). 'Mittelbronzezeitliche Frauentrachten in Süddeutschland', in *Dynamique du Bronze moyen en Europe occidentale. Actes du 113e congrès national des sociétés savantes*, Strasbourg 1988. Paris: Commission de Pré- et Protohistoire, 117–34.

Woodward, A. (2002). 'Beads and Beakers: heirlooms and relics in the British Early Bronze Age', *Antiquity*, 76: 1,040–7.

CHAPTER 12

IDENTITY, GENDER, AND DRESS IN THE EUROPEAN BRONZE AGE

MARIE LOUISE STIG SØRENSEN

INTRODUCTION

In Bronze Age literature the word 'identity' has been used to refer both to cultural groups and, especially over recent decades, to individuals. Here it is the latter, the question of identity in terms of differences and similarities between people, that will be considered. This level of identity is especially pertinent for the European Bronze Age as there is little evidence about people as social personae. In response, evidence of dress from large cemetery assemblages that allow comparisons between individuals has been subject to detailed analyses, as have the examples of well-preserved pieces of clothing.

Before considering such evidence in greater detail, however, it is worth explaining why identity is such a seminal concern within Bronze Age studies. The reasons are to be found in the substantial differences in the expression of identity between the Bronze Age and earlier periods, raising core questions about whether and how the constitution of the individual changed. At a general level, the change represents the transformation of tribal societies into chiefdoms, with the consequential increase in social differentiation together with other influences on the relationships between people. Meanwhile, irrespective of theoretical frameworks it is generally agreed that in the Bronze Age, people began to be differentiated in new ways and treated in manners that stress them as individuals. It is most likely that this was not a sudden shift but rather a gradual transformation of social relations and of fundamental aspects of societal organization; a transformation that unfolded in the course of the Bronze Age and seemingly progressed through stages. Thus, we may argue that during the third millennium BC, and in particular the Bell Beaker cultures and the Early Bronze Age groups, we see a change from the former emphasis on the individual as an incorporated member of the community, which included the ancestors as part of the communal corpus, to one that treated individuals primarily in terms of them being the same kind of people as others; they are members of categories (for a discussion of the concept of categories of people with regard to the Bronze Age see Blake 1999; Sørensen 1997: 93–5). These categories, as discussed below, were primarily based on gender. By the late Early Bronze Age, burial evidence suggests this was changing and each person was now recognized in terms of more complex social variables, which included gender, age, kin, regional identities, and also some recognition of social status. This perception of the individual characterizes, for instance, the Tumulus culture and the Nordic Bronze Age periods II–III. By the middle of the second millennium BC, with the spread of the Urnfield culture, the burial practices changed again and there was generally much less emphasis on the display of individuals and their differences. Around this time the perception of the individual became more complex and multilayered, including the ability to differentiate between identity in life and in death. It is therefore feasible that the individualized person, in other words people perceived as distinct separate human beings rather than connected individuals, first appeared with the Urnfield culture and other Late Bronze Age groups. Why this happened during the Bronze Age is not clear; but maybe the intensity of contacts between groups and the mobility of individuals had a dramatic disruptive influence on the earlier group-societies. The character and reasons for such movements are not yet clearly understood, but in many cases the foreign individuals never became fully integrated in the area where they finally lived. Together with increased social differentiation, the presence of such peoples is likely to have challenged the presumption of shared identity or incorporality that had underwritten earlier societies.

The explicit emphasis on the outward expression of identity, and gender identity in particular, during the Bronze Age can therefore be associated with the particular transformation of the perception and role of the individual that seems to have begun during the third millennium BC and which can be followed through the Bronze Age. The three elements considered here (identity, gender, and dress) are accordingly closely intertwined in Bronze Age studies whether by assumption or as an explicitly formulated question. With little else to link discussions of identity to gender, appearance and the roles of people are the most fruitful lines of inquiry.

On Identity and Gender

Identity has been widely debated in archaeology since the 1990s, and there are different ways of arguing for what identity is and how it is acquired. Nonetheless, most authors agree that identity is not given but continuously constituted and performed, and that it is multivarious. Identity is accordingly emphasized as a self-conscious awareness of the self, contextualized within social relationships. Identity, even individual identity, is therefore not just about the personal, as it is also always about relationships and about others—both persons and groups. The multivarious nature of identity means that different aspects of the person are joined up and mutually affect each other in the formation, expression, and experience of identity within different settings. Amongst the multiple identities, gender is particularly interesting as it is so fundamental to society: it is always there and always part of how social relationships are conceptualized and negotiated.

The challenge to archaeology is how we turn such theoretical arguments into concrete analyses of how identity is constructed within particular cultural contexts. There are many ways of doing this. This chapter focuses on the manner in which material culture becomes implicated in the construction of identity. That means the concern is with how gender, through material engagement and performance, becomes externalized and encounterable as distinct and separate from sex. Objects can, for example, be used to stress and signal differences and similarities; they can express affinities and provide a means of identifying sameness and likeness. They can also, as I have argued elsewhere (Sørensen 2000), be used subversively and as a means of defiance and opposition. Of particular interest are elements of dress since these objects are used directly on the individual person and can be used to visualize (and in turn be part of constructing) aspects of the person's identity. In the fabrication of different ways of appearing, individuals as well as groups are able to articulate notions of identity as well as making clear the possibility of 'identifying with'. Such articulations, of course, happen within a context, including those provided by already existing social groups.

Evidence of the formation and importance of different identities is always difficult to extract from proxies. This is also the case for the Bronze Age. Evidence of production, settlement, and hoards provides little direct evidence about people, and mainly tends to lend support to arguments about group identities, including some tentative reflections about the basic social unit of the family (Fokkens 2003). The evidence for dress thus provides the best opportunities.

Bronze Age Identities

The rich and often striking material culture of the Bronze Age has commonly led to more or less colourful speculation about, and analysis of, identities. Amongst the most consistently conjured ones we find the identities associated with special roles or status, such as smiths and warriors, and others referring to more generic social identities based around age-sets and leadership roles, either within the kin group or within a community. Gender is, of course, implicated in all of these roles and identities insofar as the exclusion or inclusion, or even lack of relevance, of particular genders within certain specialized activities or particular sectors of society are formed around culturally specific understandings of gender, including the norms and values that are attached to gender ideologies. The acknowledgment of gender as an important basic social variable, and the recognition of the need to investigate the nature of gender relations during the Bronze Age, have nonetheless varied. Explicit concern with and attempts at problematizing and investigating gender relations, rather than merely treating them as familiar and known, only emerged in the 1980s as gender archaeology began to be formed as a specialist subject within archaeology. This has been followed by increased recognition of gender as a fundamental structural aspect of Bronze Age societies. Gender is now widely recognized within syntheses of the Bronze Age (e.g. Harding 2000) as well as in research specifically aiming to locate and dissect its specific forms (e.g. Brück 2009; Sofaer Derevenski 2000; Sørensen 1997).

Among the distinct specialist identities that have been proposed for Bronze Age societies, the smith, the priest, and the warrior are worth particular attention. This is because these positions (in whatever form and however organized) were probably significant within Bronze Age societies at least at some sociopolitical levels; it is also noteworthy that these roles are often implicitly gendered in our descriptions, although the basis for this is rarely discussed.

The Smith

It is presumed that the bronzesmith was a highly valued person of special status and that this role was occupied by men. This view tends to be held irrespective of how the role of the smith is otherwise understood and whether 'he' is thought to have been integrated in the community, working for local leaders, or a travelling craftperson (for an overview of different explanations see Levy 1991). The notion of the male smith is probably partly rooted in the nineteenth-century fascination with bronze objects and the assumptions of the technical skills needed for their production, and partly legitimated by historic and ethnographic observations that show smithing as an exclusively male activity. Although only a few graves exist that may arguably be those of smiths (see Harding 2000: 226–7, 239), and despite evidence that metalworking was generally widespread, with much of it at a modest scale and many objects less technologically demanding than previously assumed, this view still holds sway, despite attempts to consider its basis critically (e.g. Kuijpers 2008). It is therefore important to question what is known about the role and status of the bronzesmith; indeed, we need to consider whether it is correct to single this out as a special identity during the Bronze Age, and on what basis this specialist craft may be assumed to be a gendered activity. It is immediately obvious that there is little factual evidence linking any specific gender group to metalworking. More significantly, metalworking refers to not just one activity but to a range of linked practices, from procurement of ores to the final decoration of the objects, and different people may have been involved at different stages. This raises questions about the nature of labour—its control and organization—within Bronze Age communities: could metalworking, or at least part of the process, be done by most people within the communities, was it fitted in between other domestic and subsistence activities, or was it a craft that became increasingly dependent on skills that could only be acquired through apprenticeships and time-consuming experimentation? We know too little about the links between metalworking and people to be able to answer such questions, and it is therefore exceedingly complicated to argue that metalworking was a gender-based activity (see also Harding 2000: 239). It is worth noting, therefore, that the burials which have been 'identified' as smiths have been done so on the basis that they contain tools interpreted to be for metalworking. There are no suggestions that smiths were in other ways—either through special burials or through particular dress elements—separated out from the rest of the community.

The Warrior

Another important question about social roles and identities in the Bronze Age relates to the presence of the warrior and the very identity of this position (for an extensive discussion of the warrior see Harding 2000: 271–307; 2007; Kristiansen and Larsson 2005: 246–50). Apart from fortifications, attack and defensive weapons developed during the Bronze Age—the sword appeared towards the end of the Early Bronze Age as a new object dedicated to face-to-face combat between two opponents—making it relevant to question when the warrior emerged as a distinct identity, and what the characteristics of this identity were. It is commonly assumed that there were warriors in the Bronze Age and that they were men; and there is some evidence to support this even if the nature of the warrior identity may not be self-evident (*contra* Treherne 1995). There is substantial evidence for the use and development of weapons, including body armour, and weapons are found routinely in graves as well as hoards (e.g. Schauer 1990; Born and Hansen 2001). Nonetheless, one can question how many of the graves fit the description of 'weapon graves', rather than rich graves with weapons, and the exact identity and roles of the 'warrior' seem unclear. Basically, we must ask whether the mere presence of a weapon signals a warrior, or whether more is needed. Kristian Kristiansen has used wear analysis and typological differences amongst swords to argue that warriors constituted one of two power structures of the Bronze Age, with the second being the religious leaders (Kristiansen and Larsson 2005). Others have looked at the number of swords overall to gain an impressions of their importance (Harding 2000: 279–80), whereas some have been interested in the combination of different weapon types to detail the outfit of the warrior (Born and Hansen 2001).

A different approach is to use the characteristics of weapons, including their technological features and the ways they are used within graves. This in turn may help to clarify how the weapons may have been involved in the construction of identities, rather than just signalling them. During the Early Bronze Age daggers became the significant object, replacing the emphasis on the bow and arrow in the Bell Beaker cultures and the axe in the Corded Ware. At this time daggers possibly began to be able to assign status or special identity to the people possessing them, and they were in many areas closely, although not exclusively, associated with men. Daggers are typically found on the body, together with other objects and with a similar relationship to the body as the other objects: placed on or very near to the part of the body where they would have been worn. The regular use of the dagger, together with its close relationship with the single, and usually male, individual makes it difficult to establish whether it was used as a kind of signifier of a male, or a warrior, or both. The signifying role of weapons in terms of the warrior identity appears clearer in the Middle Bronze Age when swords replaced the dagger as the weapon par excellence. One of the striking differences, apart from the function and appearance of the objects themselves, is the change in how the distinct character of the object was stressed. This is partly seen technologically through the high quality of many swords and the rapid development of their form, which has led to detailed sword typologies, setting the sword apart from other weapons and in particular from contemporary tools. More strikingly, it can also be observed through changes in how the sword was embodied and related to the body in a distinct manner. This is best observed in well-preserved graves, such as some of those in Denmark. In many of these, the sword was treated differently form the other objects associated with the deceased, as it was placed on top of the body (in some cases even outside the wrapping of the body) or parallel to it, rather than at the hip, where it would normally have been: it is accompanying the body rather than worn by it (Sørensen 2010). For the sword, this may mean that the object per se was empowering. It assigns identity rather than merely reflecting it; it has symbolic value.

This still leaves the question of whether we can characterize this identity more fully, including its gender dimension. Skeletal remains in themselves have so far not been able to identify a warring group on the basis of battle-induced traumas or similar clues. The evidence has not been systematically assessed; nonetheless it seems that the frequency of such traumas may be low and their geographical distribution uneven. The limited number of so-called weapon graves, in the form of rich graves where the assemblage is dominated by or exclusively consists of a repetitive combination of weapons, is puzzling. There are too few of these graves (in contrast to graves with a sword along with other things) to suggest that they represent a special social identity, but the fact they exist indicates the possibility of thinking about and equipping the deceased in terms of a warrior theme. The lack of consistency undermines arguments that the 'warrior' identity was shared widely and was integral to the nature of Middle and Late Bronze Age society (Kristiansen and Larsson 2005). Thus, whereas 'warrior' was clearly a kind of identity in the Bronze Age, it remains unclear to what extent it had become a permanent and fixed attachment of individual people, rather than a more fluid, temporally performed identity of great symbolic and social importance, but without practical everyday significance. For most Bronze Age communities, it may be that no one was full-time and only a warrior, while most men sometimes acted as if they were. Burials, supplemented by the more ambiguous evidence provided by rock carvings and figurines, do, however, firmly suggest that those who had weapons were dominantly male, and that carrying a weapon may have become a signifier for male gender. This does not mean that there are not some exceptions; but these are few and may easily be understood as examples of individual women who within their community had taken on a role usually linked to men. Meanwhile, the carrying of weapons, irrespective of the actual roles of the warrior, became part of the ways in which men and women appeared as different.

The Priest and the Shaman

There is a scarcity of direct evidence about Bronze Age religious life and rituals, but some objects force us to face questions about ceremonies and from these emerge others about the possible presence of priests, religious leaders, the ones who guard sacred knowledge or everyday cosmological beliefs or understand healing. Studies of these roles and identities have varied enormously in their links to actual evidence and many appear as speculations. There is, however, some extremely suggestive evidence that even the most sceptical must consider. Some of these, such as lurs (large trumpet-like musical instruments commonly found in matching pairs, manufactured to be played together, and distinctive of the Nordic Bronze Age), conjure up images of elaborate Bronze Age ceremonies, the outlines of which may be sketched from depictions on rock art (Fig. 12.1). The discovery of the Nebra sky-disc in 1999 (Meller 2004) strengthened our understanding of this aspect of the Bronze Age considerably. With its depictions of cosmological elements and apparently a calendar, the disc suggests shared system of beliefs over a very large area. It also suggests that there were members of communities who held special knowledge, similar maybe to the priestly roles suggested by Kristiansen and Larsson (2005). A famous but enigmatic image that possibly shows such people are the figures drawn on the stone slabs enclosing the burial chamber in the large barrow at Kivik, Sweden (Harding 2000: 343; Randsborg 1993). On two of the slabs human-like figures are seen engaged in activities that are presumably ceremonial. These figures have often been interpreted as priests, although their beak-like faces may also suggest a human-animal transform and thus a shamanistic reference (e.g. Randsborg 1993). Suggestions of shamanism are otherwise largely absent from the Bronze Age and clear human-animal hybrids are very rare. The figurative decoration on the bronze razors from Scandinavia, which has been used by Kaul (1998) to reconstruct the narrative elements of a cosmology, clearly treats animals and humans as different; they work together and are in that sense interrelated but do not merge. There are, however, a few grave assemblages that suggest the deceased was a special person. One of these is the well-known grave from Hvidegård, Denmark, which contained a leather bag with various oddities including bones and teeth from several animals, birds, and reptiles (Harding 2000: 321). It is, however, equally likely that these were healers, wise men and women, rather than assuming they had the specific identity of a shaman. There is thus clear, although indirect, evidence for priests, healers, and maybe shamans, and probably various combinations of the roles and activities we associate with each of these. But the evidence is usually unclear in terms of how we may link it to individual people (e.g. Harding 2000). Nor are there any indications of these people being dressed differently, although it has been proposed that the so-called gold cones may have been hats used by ritual leaders (Gerloff 1995), and Kristiansen and Larsson interpret several dress elements as being from the costumes of priestesses (2005: 150–3). The elements of dress that set them apart may, of course, have been perishable. Lacking links to individual persons, it is curious that we nonetheless routinely assume they were all men. This is especially striking since both historical and ethnographic sources show that these roles are often taken by women. Kristiansen and Larsson, using the similarities between Minoan figurines and decorative elements found widely in central and northern Europe, are amongst the few to have explicitly proposed that there were also priestesses, but in their interpretations they link them to 'the institutionalized role of high-ranking women in rituals of fertility'. The reasons for the common male bias are not entirely clear, but they may simply reflect the extent to which we have allowed ourselves to think non-discursively about the Bronze Age as male and in masculine terms. The solution is not, of course, to insist that these roles and identities were female ones, but it is important to free this part of Bronze Age research from gender-stereotypical assumptions.

The Evidence for the Dressed Person: Men and Women and Other Identities

In contrast to these specialists, there are also elements in our description of the Bronze Age that are coloured by expectations about gender and other identities of a more generic social type. These are often influenced by unstated assumptions about differences between the sexes and the presumption of direct correspondence between such differences and gender systems, and also by the expectations that the Bronze Age had familiar marriage systems and family organizations. These assumptions have both coloured and in subtle ways become reinforced by the settlement evidence, which seems to conform to the expectation of a core family unit, and by the data from cemeteries, which often seems to reflect an emphasis on gendered individuals and family groups. Although there are substantial geographical variations and distinct regional traditions in how people dressed, it is possible to extract some underlying principles, and to see how they were transformed over time, in order to sketch a history of the Bronze Age based on gender and dress.

FIG. 12.1 Illustrations of a 'lur-blower'.

Source: author (drawing M. Sapwell, based on Probst 1996).

There has been a long-standing interest in textiles and clothing technology from the Bronze Age, in part fuelled by work on the superbly preserved pieces of clothing from Denmark. The earliest work (e.g. Broholm and Hald 1935–40) was mainly concerned with investigations of textile technologies; differences between male and female clothing were recorded, but there was little attention directed towards the impact of clothing, and how it can be used as a means of self-identification and of identifying social conventions.

The relationship between identity and dress is, however, often close, as well as revealing of societal norms, including its regulative mechanisms. Contemporary experiences, as well as historical and ethnographic documentation, demonstrate this. With the increased intellectual focus on the individual, for which various theoretical approaches, including gender studies, have argued from the 1980s onwards, this relationship has been recognized and explored. Within archaeology, the interest in investigating gender as a construction of difference focused early on dress as a medium for the social performance of such differences (e.g. Sørensen 1997; 2000). Dress, it was argued, could be used as evidence about how people appeared to themselves and others, and this in turn meant it could be used to investigate identities, including gender. The importance of appearance is now widely recognized, and has led to increased recognition that the appearance or the impression of the dressed person is due not only to the items used to dress and adorn the body, but also to the manner in which such elements were used, including the movement and animation of the body. The concept of the technology of the body has been used to argue for the constructed nature of the social body and to focus on the practical and material dimension of how the body is understood. For the Bronze Age, this argument has been explored by Paul Treherne in his proposal of a Bronze Age warrior ideology focused on the 'beautiful body' (1995).

It is important to stress that the cultural appearance of a person is a complex signifier, and some of the decoding is probably dependent on an insider understanding rather than freely available for scrutiny by just any outsider, including the archaeologist. The embroidered patterns on womens' skirts in northern Transylvania were, for instance, until recently immediately readable for local women in terms of which valley a woman came from (Nona Palincaş, pers. comm.), whereas for others these details appear as mere pretty decorations. Such observations are relevant for appreciating the codes that may have been present within the few Bronze Age depictions that seem to show dress (Fig. 12.2).

For the Bronze Age, evidence about the dressed person is simultaneously very rich and very one-sided. Most of it comes from objects that were connected to people's costumes, supplemented by rarer fragments of well-preserved pieces of clothing. This data is evidentially burdened by their discoveries in graves, which some argue means they were part of funerary clothing that do not provide insights into how people dressed in life, and therefore how dress was actually used in the performance of identity. This problem is due to the paucity of complementary sources, and also our lack of a comprehensive insight into what death meant during the period. This is in contrast to periods for which written documents help to clarify how objects in graves relate to and compare with those used in everyday life. It is, however, possible to counter the scepticism about the evidential value of objects from Bronze Age burials in a number of

FIG. 12.2 Examples of Bronze Age clay figurines from the Carpathian Basin; their decorations suggest dress accessories and decorations.

Source: author (drawing M. Sapwell, after Schumacher-Matthäus 1985).

ways. First, although most of the dress accessories are found in graves, there is also a considerable number from hoards and even some from settlements, and these in general show a similar range of types despite differences in the contexts of deposition; this is especially the case for the Early and Middle Bronze Age. Secondly, the bronze ornaments and dress accessories commonly show wear patterns which demonstrate that they had been used prior to their inclusion in the grave and were thus not produced specifically for funerary use. Thirdly, although depictions are rare, those that do exist, such as the small bronze figurines from Scandinavia, tend to indicate similar costumes to those found in graves, and provide no hints of other types of garment. Finally, it is reasonable to propose that even if these are funerary costumes, their elements and underlying structures were probably based on the clothing of the living; in other words an explicit funerary costume would have semantic similarities with the costumes of the living, as these would provide the model for how costumes were being thought about.

In terms of the actual evidence, we have both pieces of clothing and the ornaments used to adorn the person. The evidence of the latter is numerous as there are many thousands of ornaments from Bronze Age graves and hoards. They are, however, unevenly distributed over both time and space. The volume of finds from late Early and Middle Bronze Age burials is particularly high, whereas for the Late Bronze Age most ornaments, and in particular the most spectacular ones, come from hoards, as the inclusion of objects in graves declines dramatically with the spread of cremation. Geographically the evidence is also uneven. There are, for instance, comparatively few ornaments from the British Bronze Age (Roberts 2007), whereas southern Scandinavia is very rich. The limitations of any generalized portrayal of dress fashions during the Bronze Age should therefore be recognized. At the same time such efforts will help to determine whether there was a shared body ethos and what its temporal and geographical limits were.

In order to explore such questions in a manner that is sensitive to how identity is constructed, how it emerges from a range of distinct decisions, and how the resultant appearance as well as its different elements are used as a means of communication, some years ago I developed two analytical principles. These aimed to investigate the stages of decision making, the 'discursive pathways', in the construction of appearance. The aim was to develop an approach that would make it possible to locate and investigate the actual construction of appearance rather than taking the totality of the dressed person as a natural given (Sørensen 1997). These principles suggested a differentiation between cloth, clothing, and costumes, with the second line of analysis being concerned with compositional choices regarding the elements that affect the costumes.

Cloth refers to the base material out of which many different pieces of clothing can be made, including pieces for different gender and social groups or items with special connotations. For the Bronze Age this was usually wool or linen; leather and various fibres may also have been used although probably to a limited extent. It is noteworthy that textiles changed through the period, becoming more refined and in themselves gradually becoming a means of expressing distinctions. This is seen in the development of dyes, the use of embroideries, and more advanced weaving patterns (see Chapter 26); there are also distinct geographical differences (Bender Jørgensen 1991). As yet there are no indications of gender differentiation affecting this level of production (i.e. there was no gender differentiation built into the production of the cloth), although amongst the well-preserved clothing there are some production techniques that are only used in the making of garments for women (hairnets) or men (caps).

The clothing entails sets of decisions about design and outcome, which include considerations about what kind of pieces are made from the cloth, for whom, and with what functions in mind. This aspect of appearance is interesting in that it may provide distinctions between basic elements of clothing, such as between trousers and skirts, which are visually distinct and noticeable, and can be observed at a distance. The difference they expressed is, moreover, performed routinely, and they are, so to speak, one's social skin. Clothing is, therefore, an obvious medium for the communication of identities such as gender, age, or status that are part of everyday routine encounters, and their uses are often subject to explicit social strictures and regulations (Sørensen 2000). It is therefore interesting that where we have good preservation, such as the Early Bronze Age oak coffins from Denmark, distinctly different pieces of clothing have been found, and that they are associated with different gender groups: the trousers, capes, and special types of caps/hats are found with men, and skirts and blouses, with hairnets or bonnets, are found with women (see Chapter 26). This suggests that gender distinction was built into the construction of differences in people's appearance already at this fundamental level; different pieces of clothing were being produced for men and for women.

The final element, the costume, refers to the combination of clothing, dress fittings, and ornaments of different kinds, but it adds to these the second analytical principle concerned with the distinction between objects per se, the ways in which they are combined, and the compositional themes they are partners to (Sørensen 1997: 98). To this we should add the culturation of the body's movement and stature: the elements that together make up the impression of the whole.

Recently I have added another dimension to this analytical framework, exploring the idea of 'body maps and coordinates' (Sørensen 2010). I argue that attitudes to the body are a fundamental characterizing aspect of any society. The body is something that we have to live in and with, but is also a matter we try to comprehend. To do this we formulate narrative tropes about the body, which enable us to engage discursively with it in terms of, for example, what is right and wrong, what are the needs of the deceased, what is beauty, and what are the differences between bodies and the allowances that follow such differences. I have therefore proposed that the relationship between people and objects that are being exercised in the construction of costumes can be further scrutinized by focusing on the different qualities of objects. Basically, I propose that we pay greater attention to the different kinds of possibilities (or kinds of agency) that objects have as they become elements of the costumes.

With these points in mind we can now turn to the material from the Bronze Age in pursuit of evidence about what kind of differences were important to people and how these were being expressed.

Changes through the Bronze Age

During the Early Bronze Age the body is treated as a discrete and intact entity that carries meaning through its tangible characteristics; differences between people are therefore articulated through the manipulation of the material body. The positioning of the deceased's body during burials, with men and women all placed in crouched positions but with the head in opposite directions, is decisive for claims about the body's identity (Fig. 12.3). The body's sexual identity is its prime identifying feature. Depending on the body's sex, it is treated as one or another category of person, and this difference is used explicitly, overriding other potential differences such as age and kin. In almost all cemeteries of central Europe this is the overwhelming pattern, although there is often a small number of graves that do not fit, as the sex and orientation of the body do not match the norm. There are even a few examples of some graves orientated totally differently from other graves. In the former case it may of course be a matter of erroneous sex determination. There are also, however, instances where the gender association of objects does not correspond to what would be expected based on the orientation of the grave. In the early stages of gender archaeology, such instances would have tended to be interpreted as a third gender. This, rather than exploring what exceptions may be about, tends to explain it in terms of a rather static understanding of gender that misses the important role of the exceptions. The fact that such graves exist, even though few in number, suggests we need to understand how within the rigid gender system it was also possible to express alternative identities, represented for example by outsiders or people with severe handicaps, as is the case in the Early Bronze Age cemetery of Gemeinlebarn F, Austria (Appleby 2010; Neugebauer 1991).

In addition to the different treatment of the deceased body, some objects (differing depending on region) also show clear gender associations, whereas others may be used by either gender. This is not solely a question of weapons versus ornaments but also instances of some pin types being associated with women and others with men, or of men and women having different numbers of pins. This suggests a nuanced gender differentiation that might have included apparently minor details of how the costume was worn.

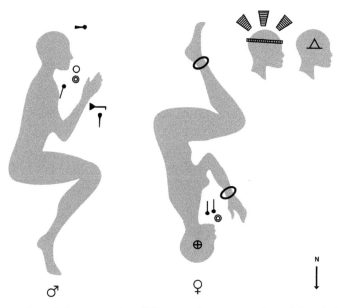

FIG. 12.3 Illustration of the normative differences between male and female burials at the Early Bronze Age cemetery of Gemeinlebarn F, Austria. Male and female bodies have opposite orientation but face the same direction. Objects associated with the dead accentuate the fundamental body based gender differentiation.

Source: author (drawing M. Sapwell, based on information in Neugebauer 1991).

This does not mean, however, that other identities were not visualized as well, as the Early Bronze Age is the period during which we begin to see distinct social differentiation, and also the importance of age (e.g. Appleby 2010; Rega 1997; Sofaer Derevenski 2000). Some have discussed these overall trends in terms of the emergence of modest ranking (e.g. Shennan 1975), but they can also be interpreted as the first stage in the transition towards an individualizing society as people are now presented through categorical identities.

It is not easy, however, to arrive at any sense of whether a particular value or esteem was granted to any particular group. Such assessment needs very thorough analysis of sizeable cemeteries to make comparison between people in terms of many different variables, including ones relating to lifestyle and life cycles. Among the sites that have enabled such comparison is the cemetery of Gemeinlebarn F, Austria. Here it seems that age gradients may have introduced several stages of increased status, but there are also indicators that this worked differently for men and women, with women possibly losing status or social visibility if they reached very high ages (Appleby 2010; Neugebauer 1991; Sørensen 2004).

In terms of appearance and body tropes (Sørensen 2010), we can now attempt to characterize the Early Bronze Age through the principles outlined above. Cloth was simple and did not by itself give rise to visual differences. Although textiles were not a new material, it is unclear whether all people would have been wearing cloth or whether some were still using skins and fur, or cloth made from various plant fibres; this may have been a source of major visual differences between people or regions. We have hardly any evidence about the clothing itself, although indirect evidence such as the decline in the use of buttons and the increase in pins may suggest new pieces of clothing, or at the least new ways of wearing it. We therefore know most about the costumes from the accessories and ornaments used. These were in the main attachments, such as beads and metal pendants: objects that were either sewn onto garments or combined in neck ornaments. There were also smaller decorative objects used in the hair and for the ears.

Overall, there were probably many visual similarities between the appearance of men and women, particularly in terms of the basic material used and the kind of clothing worn, but also in terms of the schemes used to decorate the costumes and the body. Women's clothing, and in particular their heads, may often have been more richly decorated than men's, but the differences between men's and women's appearance probably declined with age.

By the end of the Early Bronze Age in central Europe, burial traditions began to shift. The body remained the focus in burial rites, but it is now presented extended on its back and often elaborately dressed, and many resources are invested in the construction of the burial mounds. Ornaments and weapons had developed from the previous period, and they were now both more numerous, more sizeable, and more elaborate, and there was also a wider range of types than before. Many ornaments also became regionally distinct, suggesting there were particular local habits or codes of dress, such as those represented by the rich female outfits from the Lüneburg area of northern Germany (e.g. Laux 1981), and the ones from the Nordic Bronze Age, as well as the regional distinct costumes that Ulrike Wels-Weyrauch (1988) has shown characterized large stretches of central Europe (Fig. 12.4). The treatment of the body itself was not differentiated on the basis of sex, and gender differentiation is now primarily expressed in terms of the dress of the person and the type of accompanying objects in the graves. Differences in burial constructions may at times also have had gender connotations, but it seems that the construction of the graves was more directed towards making statements about kin and social relations, including for the mourners. As men and women were dressed in distinctly different manners and employed objects differently on their bodies, it is difficult to compare them directly and argue for systematic differences in the social roles and ranking of the different genders. Where several burials are found beneath one barrow it is often the case that the central grave was for a male, with women's graves in secondary and more peripheral positions; there are, however, also examples of rich female burials in central graves. Caution is therefore needed in making sweeping generalizations about the value systems that might have underwritten the clear differentiation between men and women in these burials.

Despite ongoing research and a gradual increase in the data, it is still difficult to determine in detail the progression and change in cloth production, but it is clear that it gradually became more elaborate in terms of weaving patterns and the use of dyes, as well as in the deliberate exploration of natural colour differences in the wool (Bender Jørgensen 1991). Studies of the bone material from Százhalombatta, Hungary, shows that in this region there was a dramatic change towards an almost total dominance of sheep at the end of the Early Bronze Age/Nagyrév Phase (Vretemark 2010), suggesting that textile production became a major craft activity. Using such indirect evidence together with the preserved pieces of clothing, it seems very likely that cloth became both more common and also more elaborate in the Middle Bronze Age. There is still no suggestion of gender differentiation at the level of cloth production; the well-preserved clothing from Denmark, for instance, shows that male and female clothing was made from similar pieces. Differences in the weave and the use of dyes may, however, have resulted in different pieces of cloth having particular values and thus being able to add connotation to the assembled costume. Where evidence exists, it seems that distinctly different pieces of clothing were now made for men and women, and trousers may have appeared in some areas. This gender differentiation was in most areas of Europe further exaggerated by the ways in which objects were used to compose costumes. The most radical difference from the previous period is that objects were now produced to be used on particular parts of the body, such as the neck, the upper arm, or the ankle. The body is being

FIG. 12.4 Indications of the degree of regional differentiations amongst women in central Europe during the Tumulus culture.

Source: author (drawing M. Sapwell, based on Sørensen 1997 and Probst 1996).

annotated and its different parts are being stressed; using multiple objects (such as several arm-rings), sets of objects (such as matching arm-spirals for each arm), and symmetrical arrangements, the body is used as a surface for display (Fig. 12.5). In addition to age, status, kin, and regional differences, gender was now presented as profoundly different.

At this time we also begin to see some major differences in the body tropes characterizing different Bronze Age meta-regions. Western Europe in particular does not follow this shift from using small pendants, attachments, and beads to large plate-based ornaments designed for different parts of the body. In the Middle Bronze Age people in different parts of Europe probably began to look distinctly different in their appearance: some used wool and others linen, but some were also adorned with large shiny bronze objects including pins that were up to 50 cm long, arm-rings in the form of spirals that encircled the entire length of the arm, and large bronze plates attached to the belt, whereas others would wear ornaments made out of strings of black jet beads.

The spread of cremation was introduced in the Late Bronze Age and with it there were changes in the way the body is emphasized and in what evidence survives about how people

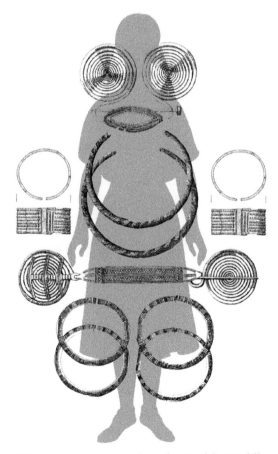

FIG. 12.5 Illustration of the principle structural emphasis of the Middle Bronze Age female body maps in central Europe.

Source: author (drawing M. Sapwell, after Sørensen 2010).

dressed. The cremation ritual appears curiously egalitarian, and as the practice became fully adopted it resulted in little visual differentiation among people in death. There are generally few meaningful indicators of emphasis on any aspect of identity, with the strongest one probably being the tendency for clusters within cremation cemeteries, usually interpreted as representing kin groups. Gender is generally not an obvious concern in the burial of the cremated remains. This is curious, as settlement evidence suggests society had become more stratified. Contemporary hoards also show that elaborate ornaments were still being made and used, but neither these nor the weapons are generally included in the burials. We can only conclude that social differentiation and identities were expressed within other spheres.

This also means that we know less about how Late Bronze Age people dressed than we do about their predecessors. Considering the quality and elaborate characteristics of Early Iron Age textiles it is, however, highly likely that cloth in itself had by now become a sophisticated medium and that differences in cloth (such as colour or weaving type) might have been associated with particular social groups; we do not know, however, whether gender constituted such a group. Similarly, as regards the clothing being produced, we can only attempt to triangulate between Middle Bronze Age and Iron Age garments and suggest that different pieces of clothing were made for men and women and, probably, also for particular social groups; gender and social status may have both been dominant visual messages. The large eye-catching ornaments also continued to be used, and in some areas, such as the Nordic Bronze Age, they reached their peak in terms of exaggeration of forms and decoration at the end of the Bronze Age. In other areas we may, however, detect a gradual shift from the emphasis and decoration of the body and its parts to an interest in new kinds of objects, such as finger-rings and the use of precious stones; new body tropes were probably being formulated.

Conclusion

In linking dress, identity, and gender it is not sufficient to observe differences between men and women. Of far greater interest is the question of how these differences are constructed and performed, how bodies are made to appear not just biologically but also culturally different. These questions have come to the fore over recent decades and in attempting to answer them we have developed new ways of investigating the archaeological evidence. This has led to increased attention on how objects were used. In particular, the potential and affects of objects and the manner in which they may have become intertwined with the life cycles of people, in a partnership of mutually making each other, have become important angles for analysis.

In addition, developments in archaeological science are providing new kinds of data. Isotope analysis and DNA are giving us new ways of discussing mobility, biological relations, or differences in lifestyles, and are providing new means of sex determination and characterization of the individual. These methods are not free from problems and biases, but they are interesting in the ways they supplement existing data and challenge interpretations. Gradually the individuals of the Bronze Age may become clearer to us, rather than—as at present—just seen in odd fragments.

Bibliography

Appleby, J. (2010). 'Ageing as fragmentation and disintegration', in K. Rebay-Sainsbury, M. L. S. Sørensen, and J. Hughes (eds.), *Body Parts and Bodies Whole: Changing Relations and Meaning*. Oxford: Oxbow, 46–53.

Bender Jørgensen, L. (1991). *North European Textiles until AD 1000*. Aarhus: Aarhus University Press.

Blake, E. (1999). 'Identity mapping in the Sardinian Bronze Age', *European Journal of Archaeology*, 2/1: 35–55.

Born, H. and Hansen, S. (2001). *Helme und Waffen Alteuropas*. Berlin: Verlag Phillipp von Zabern.

Broholm, H. C. and Hald, M. (1935–40). *Costumes of the Bronze Age in Denmark*. Copenhagen: Arnold Busck.

Brück, J. (2009). 'Women, death and social change in the British Bronze Age', *Norwegian Archaeological Review*, 42/1: 1–23.

Fokkens, H. (2003). 'The longhouse as a central element in Bronze Age daily life', in J. Bourgeois, I. Bourgeois, and B. Charetté (eds.), *Bronze Age and Iron Age Communities in North-Western Europe*. Brussels: Vlaams Kennis—en Kultuurforum, 9–38.

Gerloff, S. (1995). 'Bronzezeitliche Goldblechkronen aus Westeuropa. Betrachtungen zur Funktion der Goldblechkegel vom Typ Schifferstadt und der atlantischen "Goldschalen" der Form Devel's Bit und Atroxi', in A. Jockenhövel (ed.), *Festschrift für Hermann Müller-Karpe zum 70. Geburtstag*. Bonn: Rudolf Habelt, 153–94.

Harding, A. F. (2000). *European Societies in the Bronze Age*. Cambridge: Cambridge University Press.

—— (2007). *Warriors and Weapons in Bronze Age Europe*. Budapest: Archaeolingua (Series Minor 25).

Kaul, F. (1998). *Ships on Bronzes: A Study in Bronze Age Religion and Iconography*. Copenhagen: The National Museum of Denmark.

Kristiansen, K. and Larsson, T. (2005). *The Rise of Bronze Age Society: Travels, Transmissions and Transformations*. Cambridge: Cambridge University Press.

Kuijpers, M. H. G. (2008). *Bronze Age Metalworking in the Netherlands (c. 2000–800 BC): A Research into the Preservation of Metallurgy-Related Artefacts and the Social Position of the Smith*. Leiden: Sidestone Press.

Laux, F. (1981). 'Bemerkungen zu den mittelbronzezeitlichen Lüneburger Frauentrachten vom typ Deutsch Evern', in H. Lorenz (ed.), *Studien zur Bronzezeit. Festschrift für Wilhelm Albert v. Brunn*. Mainz: von Zabern, 251–75.

Levy, J. E. (1991). 'Metalworking technology and craft specialization in Bronze Age Denmark', *Archaeomaterials*, 5: 55–74.

Meller, H. (ed.) (2004). *Der Geschmiedete Himmel. Die weite Welt im Herzen Europas vor 3600 Jahren*. Stuttgart: Theiss.

Neugebauer, J.-W. (1991). *Die Nekropole F von Gemeinlebarn, Niederösterreich. Untersuchungen zu den Bestattungssitten und zum Grabraub in der ausgehenden Frühbronzezeit in Niederösterreich südlich der Donau zwischen Enns und Wienerwald*. Römisch-Germanische Forschungen, 49. Mainz: Philipp von Zabern.

Probst, E. (1996). *Deutschland in der Bronzezeit*. Munich: C. Bertelsmann.

Randsborg, K. (1993). 'Kivik: archaeology and iconography', *Acta Archaeologica*, 64/1: 1–147.

Rega, E. (1997). 'Age, gender and biological reality in the Early Bronze Age cemetery at Mokrin', in J. Moore and E. Scott (eds.), *Invisible People and Processes*. London: Leicester University Press, 229–47.

Roberts, B. W. (2007). 'Adorning the living but not the dead: a reassessment of Middle Bronze Age ornaments in Britain', *Proceedings of the Prehistoric Society*, 73: 135–67.

Schauer, P. (1990). 'Schutz- und Angriffswaffen bronzezeitlicher Krieger im Spiegel ausgewählter Grabfunde Mitteleuropas', in V. Furmánek and F. Horst (eds.), *Beiträge zur Geschichte und Kultur der mitteleuropäischen Bronzezeit*. Berlin: Akademie der Wissenschaften der DDR, 381–410.

Schumacher-Matthäus, G. (1985). *Studien zu bronzezeitlichen Schmucktrachten im Karpatenbecken. Ein Beitrag zur deutung der Hortfunde im Karpatenbecken*. Mainz: Philipp Von Zabern.

Shennan, S. (1975). 'The social organization at Branč', *Antiquity*, 49: 279–88.

Sofaer Derevenski, J. (2000). 'Rings of life; the role of early metalwork in mediating the gendered life course', *World Archaeology*, 31/3: 389–406.

Sørensen, M. L. S. (1997). 'Reading dress: the construction of social categories and identities in Bronze Age Europe', *Journal of European Archaeology*, 5/1: 93–114.

—— (2000). *Gender Archaeology*. Cambridge: Polity Press.

—— (2004). 'The interconnection of age and gender: a Bronze Age perspective', in R. Struwe and S. Owen (eds.), *Von der Geburt bis zum Tode. Individuelle und gesellschaftliche Dimensionen von Alter und Geschlecht in der Urgeschichte, Ethnographisch-Archäologische Zeitschrift*, 45/Heft 2: 327–38.

—— (2010). 'Bronze Age bodiness—maps and coordinates', in K. Rebay-Sainsbury, M. L. S. Sørensen, and J. Hughes (eds.), *Body Parts and Bodies Whole: Changing Relations and Meaning*. Oxford: Oxbow Books, 54–63.

Treherne, P. (1995). 'The warrior's beauty: the masculine body and self-identity in Bronze Age Europe', *Journal of European Archaeology*, 3/1: 105–44.

Vretemark, M. (2010). 'Subsistence strategies', in T. Earle and K. Kristiansen (eds.), *Organizing Bronze Age Societies: The Mediterranean, Central Europe & Scandinavia Compared*. Cambridge: Cambridge University Press, 155–84.

Wels-Weyrauch, U. (1988). 'Mittelbronzezeitliche Frauentrachten in Süddeutschland, Beziehungen zur Hagenauer Gruppierung', in *Dynamique du Bronze moyen en Europe occidentale. Actes du 113éme congrès national des sociétés savantes, Strasbourg 1988*. Paris: Commission de Prè- et Protohistoire, 117–34.

CHAPTER 13

WARFARE IN THE EUROPEAN BRONZE AGE

NICK THORPE

INTRODUCTION

In recent years there has been a significant volume of literature relating to warfare in the European Bronze Age, from general works on prehistoric conflict such as Otto, Thrane, and Vandkilde (2006), Parker Pearson and Thorpe (2005), and Peter-Röcher (2007), to works specifically concerned with the Bronze Age such as Harding (2007). Whether this is a response to the 'pacification of the past' identified by Keeley (1996) is uncertain, given the continuing tradition of studies of weaponry, burials, and defensive sites in Bronze Age Europe. A heightening of interest in the study of European war in general may also be in part a reaction to the re-emergence of violent conflict in the Balkans in the 1990s. In the specific case of the Bronze Age, the prominence given to conflict and warfare in the literature is more a factor of the long-standing interest in the notion of the emergence of 'the warrior' as a distinct social identity during this period (see Chapter 12).

The topic can be discussed using the five major types of evidence—weaponry (offensive and defensive); warrior burials; art; defended sites; and palaeopathology. Each of these has its own particular difficulties, but one general problem is that even in the best syntheses the categories are rarely brought together to develop an overall picture. When they are, some interesting and perhaps unexpected patterns seem to be emerging.

WEAPONRY

In terms of weaponry, that employed during the Bronze Age is a mixture of items already in use in earlier periods, such as the wooden or stone club, the stone macehead, the stone or bone arrowhead fired from a bow, and those of bronze which appear at this time. These new items consist of the halberd, the dagger, the dirk, the rapier, the spearhead, and above all the sword, as offensive equipment, countered by the shield, the helmet, and the cuirass. Naturally, most discussion relates to the new items of weaponry, and to the wider question of the military effectiveness of these innovations and the question of a Bronze Age 'arms race'.

Since the halberd is undoubtedly an unwieldy-looking object, there have long been suggestions that it was a ceremonial item rather than a practical weapon. However, frequent use damage to the back of the hafting plate suggests that halberds may have been used in a similar way to medieval pole arms, in other words mostly using the wooden staff and only striking with the metal head to deliver a *coup de grâce*. Although this is a plausible explanation, it still remains the case that skeletal injuries which might have been caused by halberds are extremely rare across Europe.

Despite the widespread adoption of the idea that daggers were weapons (e.g. Keeley 1996: 50), the evidence supporting this is actually far less clear-cut than is often assumed. In the Únětice culture, daggers are worn, often resharpened, and with damaged rivets or broken tangs. However, in Britain there are few traces of combat on the daggers, except for examples from the River Thames. Some British daggers also seem inappropriate as weapons, as they are too small, have highly polished and unworn blades, very wide blades, or rounded tips (Mercer 2006). It is also the case that in some regions of Europe, for example Spain and Denmark, daggers are often found with the burials of women, such as the elderly woman from the Argaric culture site of Cerro de le Encina. In other cases, daggers are found as grave goods with children (Harding 2007: 59).

Such evidence has led to daggers being differentiated from mainstream weaponry. Not surprisingly, alternative interpretations of their use have been put forward, such as cleaning the flesh from dead people during mortuary rituals, or for sacrificing animals (Mercer 2006).

Spearheads of the Later Bronze Age have generally been divided into lighter throwing spears and heavier thrusting spears. The development of hollow-cast spearheads may have been to lighten them so that larger examples could be thrown. At Dorchester-on-Thames in England, Over Vindinge in Denmark, and Hernádkak in Hungary, in each case a spearhead broke off in the victim's pelvis as it was being pulled out, suggesting the use of great force (Osgood 1998). Significantly, the Tormarton individuals (see below) were stabbed with small spears, suggesting that some functional divisions may exist primarily in the minds of archaeologists.

The value of shields as defensive weapons has been the subject of some discussion relating to Britain. The damage to shields has been considered by Richard Osgood (1998: 8–11), who argues that it was mostly ritual in nature rather than due to traces of use in conflicts. Some shields do seem to be stabbed or slashed, which could be the result of combat incidents, but the recent discovery from South Cadbury in south-west England does not fit this scenario. Three holes were punched through the shield, probably with a sharpened stake, after it was laid down in an enclosure ditch. This looks much more like ritual violence than combat, although as Osgood notes (1998: 9) the specific form taken by one may have been influenced by the other.

Moreover, it seems to be the case that the most common British shield type (the Yetholm type) is too thin to resist a determined blow, although recent experimental work suggests that this may not always be the case. There are only two examples of the thicker Nipperwiese type known from Britain.

Helmets are relatively rare finds, but they do seem to have been used in actual conflict, for example that from Hajdúböszörmény in Hungary, which has suffered a range of damage inflicted by several different weapons (Kristiansen 2002).

Dirks and especially rapiers are longer and thus have more serious potential as weapons than the daggers from which they developed, with dirks for stabbing and rapiers for thrusting. However, 'the extreme length, narrowness and general fragility of many rapier blades, especially of the longer and finer... examples... combined with the inherent weakness of the butt attachment method, leaves little doubt that such weapons could not have been successfully used in combat' (Burgess and Gerloff 1981: 5). Not surprisingly, there have been questions raised about why Bronze Age warriors persisted with the rapier for centuries (Harding 1999; Fontijn 2005). Despite this, 86 percent of the dirks and rapiers from the River Thames in England show signs of use in the form of edge damage, while torn rivet-holes suggest that rapiers were used as slashing weapons. However, Parker Pearson (2005) has argued that the rapier was designed to stab the opponent in the face, throat, or groin, either above or below the protection of a shield. The situation is still unclear.

Anthony Harding suggests that Bronze Age swords would have been ineffective in a slashing role, producing only bruising, and were much more suited to stabbing (1999: 166). Both Harding and Osgood (1998) stress that we are not dealing with medieval-style hand-to-hand combat or modern fencing, with the sword used as much to parry the opponent's blows as to land them oneself, as the shortness of the Later Bronze Age swords would mean that warriors were very close to each other (Harding 1999: 166). Osgood (1998: 13) is right to urge a degree of caution, but the level of edge damage recorded in many areas seems excessive for misuse (Thorpe 2006; Thrane 2006), and certainly cannot be attributed to finders 'trying out' their discoveries (see Kristiansen 2002). The social importance of swords seen in later periods (with swords being named and magical powers attributed to them) also makes it likely that they were highly valued in the Bronze Age as well (Kristiansen 2002).

Sword distribution is extremely variable (Harding 2006; 2007: Chapter 7), with the density of swords ranging from less than one per 1,000 km^2 in former Yugoslavia to over seven per 1,000 km^2 in Ireland. However, this may have as much to do with patterns of deposition, which can vary even within a single country, as with the actual numbers of swords present in the Bronze Age (Harding 2006). What is abundantly clear is that there is no straightforward pan-European pattern of production or distribution.

This is also connected with the apparent function of swords, as solid-hilted swords (*Vollgriffschwerter*) from Scandinavia show much less evidence for edge damage than flange-hilted (organic-hilted) swords (*Griffzungenschwerter*), and were thus interpreted by Kristian Kristiansen as the swords of chiefs and warriors respectively. This has more recently been claimed to be a general phenomenon for the whole of northern and central Europe. However, as Harding (2006) notes, in Denmark and northern Germany the numbers of the two types are roughly equal, but in Britain the solid-hilted swords are really quite rare, and in Ireland they are absent altogether (but over six hundred of the organic-hilted type are known). If any such division did exist, then it clearly could not apply everywhere, and even in Scandinavia it seems unlikely, as here there would be too many chiefs and not enough Indians. It is also worth noting that analyses of Austrian swords suggest that solid-hilted swords there were often damaged. This observation points to the need for detailed studies across Europe to be able to assess the full range of regional diversity.

Similarly, bronze arrowheads are relatively common in Mediterranean Europe, with several hundred finds from Spain, for example, and in central Europe, where a middle-aged adult (probably male) was found with ten of them at Worms-Herrnsheim in Germany. In contrast, they are rare in western Europe, especially Britain, where there are only some 25 examples known in total (Parker Pearson 2005).

Sets of weapons have been located with some burials in central Europe, such as sword and spear, or sword and arrowheads (Harding 2007: 144–7). The only proposed equipment set for 'a small regional army' comes from Smørumovre in Denmark, interpreted as the weaponry for a force of 10 commanders with spears and axes, and 40 common warriors with axes: perhaps two boatloads. Klavs Randsborg (2006) also identifies a bronze hoard from Torsted in Denmark as the weaponry of a militia force or small army of seven commanders with spears and axes, and 33 common warriors with spears and a bronze hoard from Frøjk in Denmark as the weaponry of 'an elite force' (Randsborg 2006: 43), with one commander (with a battleaxe, dagger, and spear), four men in a personal retinue (with spears and axes), and ten ordinary fighters (with just axes). The difficulties with translating such deposits into army units are obvious; Harding (2007: 165–8) expresses an appropriate degree of caution.

The 'warrior' as a social category has frequently been identified with the beauty of the male warrior and the importance of the warrior look and body culture (Kristiansen and Larsson 2005: 228). As these authors put it (213), with the widespread appearance of swords and spears across Europe 'the professional warrior, well trained and organized, was introduced'. However, we should remember the berserker tradition, in which the warrior fights without the aid of armour, but with the benefit of animal transformative power. This can be seen as the opposite extreme to the fully armoured and protected warrior, gaining renown by scorning such artificial devices. Berserkers are most famous from the Viking world, for example the bear-warrior Bodvar Bjarki, but it has been argued that their origins lie in the Bronze Age.

In identifying Bronze Age warriors, the assumption has usually been that burials with weapons are those of warriors, and that they are male. While this is often confidently stated, in practice the rarity of reliable skeletal identifications means that only a tiny minority of weapon burials can be confirmed as those of males, while possible female examples tend to pass without comment, as in the case of recent studies on Bavaria and Moravia. Where they have been noted, there have been attempts to explain them away, as in the case of burials in Denmark. Thus in the late nineteenth century Sophus Müller argued that daggers found in female graves such as Borum Eshøj were for defence, whereas swords and daggers found in male graves were for offensive purposes (Bergerbrant 2007 for commentary). The tradition continues, as here by Randsborg (2006: 32, 34): 'The dagger of some women, found in both poor and rich graves, may refer to a sword-bearing husband.... Thus, women were not "official" fighters, but certain females carried the junior trappings of such, likely to signal their rank, or even their marital status as married women (wives of sword bearers).'

Attempts have been made to pass the problem of the large number of female dagger burials on the north bank of the Elbe in Germany back to Scandinavian archaeologists, by suggesting that these women were immigrants or imported marriage partners. As Sophie Bergerbrant (2007: 96–8) notes, this ignores the evidence that several of these women were accompanied by typical local ornaments.

However, it has to be noted that these are mostly burials of women with daggers, and doubts have been expressed as to the identification of daggers as weapons (see above), although there may well be an element of circular reasoning involved here. Despite this, local and chronological variations in the presence of female burials with daggers are surely worth pursuing, as Bergerbrant (2007: 100–1) has done for southern Scandinavia.

There are, however, some weapon burials with more elaborate mortuary rites where the warrior identity is held to be more certain, for example those in 'death houses' at the Nitra culture site of Mýtna Nová Ves, interpreted as high-ranking warriors or war-chiefs (Hårde 2006). A number of these individuals had peri-mortem traumatic injuries (Hårde 2006).

Art

Scandinavian rock art, together with engravings on bronzes, features chariots (although mostly without riders), weaponry, including swords, axes, shields, and helmets, and apparent scenes of combat, often in pairs—sometimes interpreted as champions conducting a duel (Fig. 13.1). Attempts have been made to analyse the rock carvings and bronze engravings in terms of boat crews (e.g. Randsborg 2006). However, others have concluded from an analysis of the rock carvings at Kville in Sweden that the very large numbers of crew shown on boats in scenes of conflict implied that the pictures of violence, including those of single combat, were highly idealized.

Galician rock art frequently depicts weapons, and in many cases these are the sole images in specific carvings. The weapons are argued to be in an active position, with the blades fac-

FIG. 13.1 Part of the art panel at Fossum, Bohuslän, Sweden, showing ships and male figures bearing axes, bows, and other weapons.

Photo: A. Harding.

ing upwards, suggested to be the weaponry of warrior-champions, and argued to have supported claims to territory and position. However, the actual weapons are extremely rare as grave goods.

The better-known south-west Iberian stelae (with over one hundred known) of the later Bronze Age are usually interpreted as funerary markers (e.g. Garcia Sanjuán 2006). They depict a range of weapons—swords, shields, daggers, spears, bows and arrows, and axes, often arrayed around a single human figure—which are again rare in actual burial contexts. The difference from the Argaric culture of south-east Spain is significant—here the weapons are common but depictions of them are rare (e.g. Garcia Sanjuán 2006). So perhaps in the south-west and Galicia actual coercive power was possible to claim in art, but more difficult to achieve in practice.

The Nuragic bronze figurines of Sardinia are shown with weaponry in about eighty cases. Weapons represented are heavy sticks/clubs, bows and arrows, daggers, swords, helmets, and various forms of body armour. As in Spain, there is a difference between the art and the artefactual record, with bows and arrows prominent in the art but absent from burials and hoards.

Overall, the art may well tend to present one view of warfare in the Bronze Age. As Vandkilde (2006: 488) puts it: 'It is highly likely that the rock carvings—like the poems of heroes and war in early history—overemphasize the ideals of war combat and aristocratic companionship, and consequently underrate another much more violent face of war.'

DEFENDED SITES

Perhaps the most famous of the defended sites of the Bronze Age are the *nuraghi* of Sardinia, surviving in their thousands today. The first examples appear at the beginning of the Bronze Age, though many are much later in date and become extremely elaborate over time as additional features including more towers were added. The towers were up to 15 m tall, with three storeys. Complex *nuraghi* have enclosing walls set with towers with an inner courtyard and the central taller tower, with the 'proto-castles' such as Su Nuraxi di Barumini having further outer walls. Outside the defences are large numbers of smaller huts. Although their appearance is undoubtedly defensive, and there is some evidence for destruction by burning, as at Su Nuraxi di Barumini, in general there is little trace that they came under attack, and arrowheads (the most likely offensive weapons against stone defences) are rare in the Nuragic Bronze Age. It is also unclear why such large numbers of *nuraghi* were constructed, but competitive display within a climate of uncertainty must be a factor.

The picture in the Iberian Peninsula is rather mixed for the Early Bronze Age. The famous Chalcolithic fort sites in south-east Spain (e.g. Los Millares) are abandoned, replaced by hilltop settlements with a small walled area or defended 'acropolis' of the Argaric culture, but similar sites in Andalucía continue to be occupied, while in southern Portugal the Chalcolithic forts (e.g. Zambujal) are replaced by undefended villages (Barcelo 1999). Many of the Argaric centres are later abandoned, some after episodes of destruction (Barcelo 1999). The central Spanish Meseta has a similar sequence to southern Portugal, with the large ditched enclosures of the Chalcolithic not being replaced by new defended sites. Here hill forts emerge in the Late Bronze Age, although their numbers are not clearly established. In Valencia small hilltop fortifications are created.

In La Mancha fortified sites are built on hills, while the better-known *motillas* (consisting of concentric stone walls with a central stone tower up to 11 m tall) are constructed on riverbanks and in marshes. The most intensively investigated example is Motilla del Azuer. Here there were two concentric walls enclosing a courtyard with a deep well, grain storage pits, and the central rectangular tower. Located outside the defended area, in a manner reminiscent of the *nuraghi*, were small houses and a cemetery. Evidence of violence can be seen on the skeletons of the dead, including several healed depressed fractures on the cranium, parry fractures, and a highly unusual broken (and healed) hyoid bone, which could be the result of strangulation or a fall (Jiménez-Brobeil 2011).

Hill forts as defended settlements appear widely across Europe during the Bronze Age, especially in the Urnfield period. They appear in the Lausitz culture after about 1000 BC, continuing down into the Iron Age as at Biskupin in central Poland. As settlements increase in size some become fortified, although there are frequent traces of destruction, so the success of fortification is not certain. In central Europe many are known (Osgood 1998: 67–73), both with wooden palisades and stone walls. Sites such as Spišský Štvrtok in Slovakia still have visible defensive walls. Some do show signs of attack, such as the Heunischenburg near Kronach in Bavaria, where in one phase the substantial stone wall and wooden gateway was burnt down. Associated with this were a large number of bronze arrowheads, some of them burnt, and fragments of swords, spearheads, and possibly armour. The site of Velim in the Czech Republic is considered below. Control of trade may be one factor in the appearance of these sites.

In Britain it is now well established that the earliest hill forts are of Bronze Age date. These appear to be defended settlements with substantial earthen banks and timber ramparts. There are examples with clear dating evidence in the form of radiocarbon dates or artefact assemblages from ramparts and ditches in England, Wales, and Ireland (Thorpe 2006).

However, the only later Bronze Age hill fort with possible direct evidence of conflict is Dinorben in Wales, with defences radiocarbon-dated to around 800 BC. According to the excavators, there were three fragmentary male skeletons in the bottom of the ditch, one with its skull cut in two. This need not, of course, represent an episode of conflict between groups. Many of these hill forts appear to have relatively slight defences, at least compared with Iron Age hill forts, but this need not mean that their wall-and-fill ramparts were of negligible defensive value, and of course lack of evidence for successful assaults may mean such hill forts were successful in deterring attacks.

Victims of Violence

The Velim site in the Czech Republic provides a significant insight into the debates surrounding the recognition, and interpretation, of claimed repeated acts of violence in the Bronze Age. Here, large numbers of skeletons, and parts of skeletons, have been excavated in both the enclosure ditches and internal pits (Fig. 13.2). These human remains have been variously interpreted either as the result of the operation of the standard burial practice of the period and place (Peter-Röcher 2007), or as the end product of repeated acts of ritual sacrifice and cannibalism, or as the consequence of a violent attack or sequence of attacks on the inhabitants of the enclosure (Harding et al. 2007). Despite the detailed publication of the excavations (Harding et al. 2007), some continue to argue that the burials are not the result of warfare, on the basis of the lack of settlement remains in the interior, the evidence of successive deposition, the presence of some grave goods, and the lack of knowledge of normative burial rites in the region. However, the majority of the area inside the enclosure has been too disturbed for excavation to be worthwhile, and in any case a defended site may be resorted to in times of trouble. It is clear from the excavation report (Harding et al. 2007) that there are successive burials and mass burials, the latter lacking grave goods and lying in such a way that dumping of bodies and hasty covering over is the most plausible interpretation of the stratigraphy. If this is the standard local burial rite then it would be entirely unlike anything known elsewhere in central Europe and would require a specific explanation. The anthropological analysis of the skeletal remains (Knüsel and Outram 2007) does note the presence of broken bones, but does not attribute these to cannibalism. Instead, it is pointed out that the treatment of the human bones is quite different to that of the animal bones—a similarity in processing human and animal bone being one of the standard criteria used to argue for cannibalism. In any case, the destruction of the site in a massive fire, the presence of large numbers of bronze arrowheads in the ditches and pits, and the high frequency of traumatic injuries on the human bones all indicate conflict on a large scale. As Harding (2007: 88) puts it, 'the overall impression is that the occupants of Velim in the late Middle Bronze Age were the subject of a violent attack or attacks which left many people dead'.

At Sund in Norway 22 people, half of them children, were found on the Bronze Age buried ground-surface pit together with some animal bones (Fyllingen 2006); of the adults, nearly all were over 40 years old at the time of their death, and several had sword, axe, or spear wounds. In most cases these had healed some time before death, but there were also a few

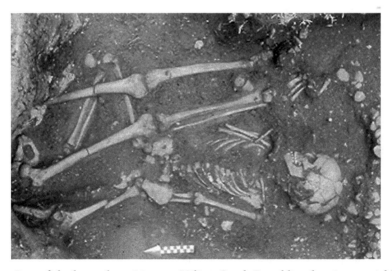

FIG. 13.2 One of the bone depositions at Velim, Czech Republic, showing partial human skeletons.

Photo: A. Harding.

peri-mortem injuries, some apparently inflicted from behind. The osteological analysis also suggested that the dead came from a community in poor general health.

In terms of the age at death of victims, it is also worth noting that the man from Over Vindinge with the spearhead tip stuck in his left hip bone was at least 50–60 years old at the time of his death and accordingly described by Randsborg (2006: 36) as 'hardly an ordinary fighter'.

In Holland, at Wassenaar (Louwe Kooijmans 1993) 12 individuals had been buried in a pit dated *c*.1700 BC (Fig. 13.3). They were mostly adult males (predominantly aged 30–40), with just one definite and one possible woman, two adolescents, and two young children. A flint arrowhead found between the ribs of No. 10 (a young man) represented a clear indication of violence; there were impact fractures at the tip of the arrowhead. Three injuries to the head

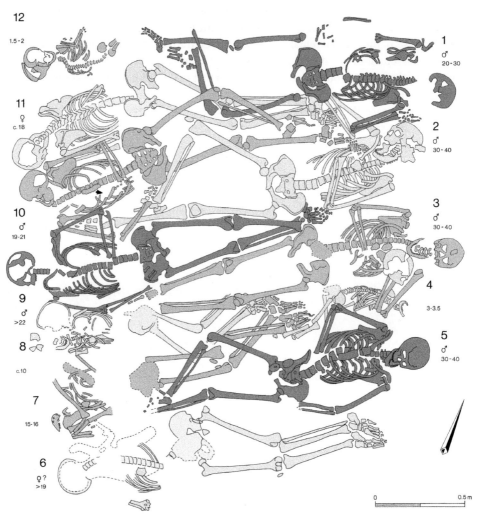

FIG. 13.3 Burial pit of Wassenaar, the Netherlands, dated to the Early Bronze Age, with the remains of 12 individuals. Probably all individuals were killed in an armed conflict. Indications are gashes in the lower jaw of individual No 2, in the right upper arm of No 3, and in the skull of No 5. Individual No 10 had a flint arrowhead embedded in the chest.

Source: Louwe Kooijmans 2005: 459.

could be seen, all without traces of healing, on the lower jaw of No. 2, on the right humerus of No. 3, and on the skull of No. 5.

The most direct evidence of mass violent death in Britain comes from Tormarton, Gloucestershire, where two young adult males had been killed from behind in a spear attack. One had fragments of later Bronze Age spearpoints in the vertebrae and pelvis and had also suffered a blow to the head. The other had a spear wound in the pelvis. Recent re-excavation of the site (Osgood 2006) demonstrated that the bodies (along with three others without visible wounds) had been thrown into a boundary ditch which was then swiftly backfilled. The location of the bodies in one of the boundary ditches, which become widespread at this time and are generally believed to relate to control over resources, is significant.

In Mecklenburg, northern Germany, the recently investigated site at the bottom of the valley of the Tollense river (Jantzen et al. 2011) dates to the end of the Early Bronze Age *c*.1200 BC. Both human remains and weaponry (including arrowheads and spear-points, a dagger blade, and a fragment of a sword) have been found by dredging over a number of years. Then in the 1990s finds of an upper arm with an embedded flint arrowhead and a fractured skull pointed to a role for violence in the formation of this deposit (Fig. 13.4). Recent excavations and analysis of earlier finds have added to this picture. Some one hundred individuals at least are now known to have been deposited in the river, with subsequent movement dispersing the bodies over a distance of about 1.5 km, so that in many cases only the skull now survives. These people were mostly young men, with only a few young women and children present. There are several further injuries that have been identified, inflicted by axes, clubs, and arrowheads, some healed but many peri-mortem. Two wooden clubs have been found preserved in the peat, which may have caused some of the fatal wounds. Crucially, despite the large number of skeletal remains and the variety of injuries present, none seems to have been caused by edged bronze weapons such as swords. Of course, these massacres, although significant as events, do not inform us of the more general patterns of violence across Bronze Age Europe.

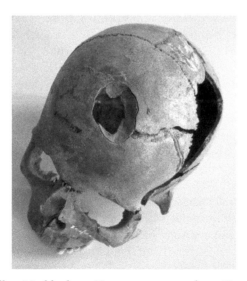

FIG. 13.4 Tollense Valley, Mecklenburg-Vorpommern, northern Germany: a skull showing major trauma on the cranial vault.

Photo: Landesamt für Kultur und Denkmalpflege, Schwerin.

Some more general assessments of the frequency of violence in different regions of Europe have been made. In Iberia a small number of fatal blunt-force and penetrating injuries have been recorded—it is noteworthy that they amount to fewer than half the cases in the preceding Chalcolithic. However, the smaller-scale studies of the Argaric culture and the Granadan Bronze Age suggest that healed cranial and post-cranial injuries were more common in the Early Bronze Age than the Chalcolithic. The majority of victims were men, often over 40 years old at the time of death, but there were also injuries to women (mostly parry fractures).

In the Nitra and Únětice culture sites in Slovakia and Moravia, burials with traumatic injuries are relatively common, with 22 cranial fractures, 15 on arms or legs, and 3 fatal arrowhead wounds. Most of the victims (21 individuals) are adult males (mostly of older age), but women (11 cases) and children (5 instances) also suffered attack (Hårde 2005; 2006). Surprisingly, but in line with the findings so far from the Tollense river site, the cranial fractures were mostly blunt-force traumas inflicted by stone or wooden clubs, even though weapon burials from the same sites have metal daggers, knives, and arrowheads rather than stone clubs (Hårde 2005; 2006). In Britain and Ireland, however, the numbers for the earlier Bronze Age are far lower, even though there is a plentiful skeletal record for this period (Thorpe 2006).

The largest area examined in a single analysis is in the work of Heidi Peter-Röcher (2007), who covers central Europe in her sample but includes most of Europe north of the Alps in her catalogue. She suggests that the level of violence seen in skeletal trauma is less in the Bronze Age (especially the Early Bronze Age) than in either the Neolithic or the Iron Age (Peter-Röcher 2007: Table 40a), and is indeed very rare. The victims of violence are nearly all men. Although this is a very useful tabulation of evidence, it is by no means comprehensive, for example only two British sites are mentioned out of about ten instances known (Thorpe 2006), and several more sites are included in Hårde's (2005; 2006) list of Nitra and Únětice culture sites in Slovakia and Moravia than in Peter-Röcher's catalogue. There are also some major sites that are not included, for example Velim in Bohemia, which is interpreted as a normal burial site, a view rejected by the excavators on good grounds (Harding et al. 2007), as seen above.

Finally, there are a number of cases involving the multiple burial of individuals who may not have been the direct victims of warfare in the form of enemy action, but may have met their death as a result of being identified as 'the enemy within'. This could be the result of the climate of fear engendered by the threat of external attack. The majority of the identified instances are in eastern Europe (see Hårde 2006 for a listing), but they may well be underestimated.

These multiple burials follow no clear pattern in terms of the age and sex of those interred, except that they are usually a mix of ages. For example, at Kettlasbrunn in Austria, three adults (the two oldest—a man and an elderly woman—killed by sharp blows to the neck and stabs to the heart) and a young child were buried in a pit, but only after long exposure to the elements (evidenced by both weathering and rodent gnawing). The man had recently suffered a broken jaw and a stabbing wound at the top of the thigh, and cuts to the chest. Also in Austria, at the fortified site of Stillfried, mass burials in pits from the very end of the Bronze Age include adults and children, some with peri-mortem injuries and others with disabilities and evidence of starvation (Hellerschmid 2006). One pit containing 15 individuals has been suggested to be the result of a 'palace revolution'. Within the settlement at Blučina in Moravia a pit contained burnt and broken bones from about a dozen individuals, mostly small children. At Nižna Myšľa in Slovakia a pit on the edge of the settlement area inside a fortification contained five burials—two children, an adolescent, and two adult women, the adults with their heads twisted round, perhaps to cut their throats. One of the children's skulls appeared to have been boiled.

The Importance of Variability and Future Research

It is clear that the various sources of evidence (artefactual, skeletal, pictorial, and excavational) do not co-vary in any systematic way, as we have already seen in Iberia with regard to images of weapons and weaponry as grave goods.

In Scandinavia, for example, there is a lack of either defended settlements or forts of any kind, but no shortage of weapons (Thrane 2006), with over 2,500 swords from southern Sweden, Denmark, and the northernmost part of Germany. On the other hand, in the eastern Baltic region there are several fortified sites, but weaponry (apart from bone arrowheads) is very scarce. Indeed, it may be that in some cases one form of evidence may preclude another. It must be significant too that there are also variations through time in the evidence from a single area (Bergerbrant 2007: 94–5). The difficulty with this kind of analysis, however, is that the more precisely drawn the chronological and geographical parameters of a sample become, the smaller the sample size. Thus chance variation becomes an ever more likely occurrence.

The identity of 'warriors' also needs to be rethought to allow for a serious consideration of women and older men as active participants in conflict at some times and in some places. Undoubtedly, variations in the age and sex of those buried with weapons need to be considered more systematically. Here, new excavations (and re-analysis of surviving well-documented museum collections) should provide better-quality data. Until variations of all kinds in the evidence are addressed in a more systematic fashion, discussions of the causes of European Bronze Age warfare are likely to be confined largely to speculation when attempting to encompass a wider picture.

Finally, we should not forget the victims of Bronze Age warfare, especially those of the massacres at places such as Sund, the Tollense valley, and Wassenaar. Some of the evidence at these sites implies killing after surrender (clubbing to death and stabbing in the back). Also, that violent death in warfare was not just the fate of the (assumed) young male professional warriors is clear from both Sund, where half the victims were children and nearly all the adults were aged over 40, and Wassenaar, where two of the victims were children. When we consider the beauty of Bronze Age warriors and their weapons, we must not forget the terror of the victims and the destructive effects of warfare on their communities.

Bibliography

Barcelo, J. A. (1999). 'Patriarchs, bandits and warriors. An analysis of social interaction in Bronze Age south-western Iberian peninsula', in C. Clausing and M. Egg (eds.), *Eliten in der Bronzezeit*, Monographien des Römisch-Germanischen Zentralmuseums, 43. Mainz: Verlag des Römisch-Germanischen Zentralmuseums, 223–43.

Bergerbrant, S. (2007). *Bronze Age Identities: Costume, Conflict and Contact in Northern Europe 1600–1300 BC*, Studies in Archaeology, 43. Stockholm: Bricoleur.

Burgess, C. B. and Gerloff, S. (1981). *The Dirks and Rapiers of Great Britain and Ireland*, Prähistorische Bronzefunde IV, 7. Munich: Beck.

Fontijn, D. (2005). 'Giving up weapons', in M. Parker Pearson and I. J. N. Thorpe (eds.), *Warfare, Violence and Slavery in Prehistory*, British Archaeological Reports (International Series), 1,374. Oxford: Archaeopress, 145–54.

Fyllingen, H. (2006). 'Society and the structure of violence: a story told by Middle Bronze Age human remains from central Norway', in T. Otto, H. Thrane, and H. Vandkilde (eds.), *Warfare and Society: Archaeological and Social Anthropological Perspectives*. Aarhus: Aarhus University Press, 319–29.

Garcia Sanjuán, L. (2006). 'Funerary ideology and social inequality in the Late Prehistory of the Iberian South-West (c.3300–850 cal BC)', in P. Díaz del Río and L. García Sanjuán (eds.), *Social Inequality in Iberian Late Prehistory*, British Archaeological Reports (International Series), 1,525. Oxford: Archaeopress, 149–69.

Hårde, A. (2005). 'The emergence of warfare in the Early Bronze Age: the Nitra group in Slovakia and Moravia, 2200–1800 BC', in M. Parker Pearson and I. J. N. Thorpe (eds.), *Warfare, Violence and Slavery in Prehistory*, British Archaeological Reports (International Series), 1,374. Oxford: Archaeopress, 87–105.

—— (2006). 'Funerary rituals and warfare in the Early Bronze Age Nitra Culture of Slovakia and Moravia', in T. Otto, H. Thrane, and H. Vandkilde (eds.), *Warfare and Society: Archaeological and Social Anthropological Perspectives*. Aarhus: Aarhus University Press, 341–82.

Harding, A. F. (1999). 'Warfare: a defining characteristic of Bronze Age Europe?', in J. Carman and A. Harding (eds.), *Ancient Warfare*. Stroud: Sutton, 157–73.

—— (2006). 'What does the context of deposition and frequency of Bronze Age weaponry tell us about the function of weapons?', in T. Otto, H. Thrane, and H. Vandkilde (eds.), *Warfare and Society: Archaeological and Social Anthropological Perspectives*. Aarhus: Aarhus University Press, 505–13.

—— (2007). *Warriors and Weapons in Bronze Age Europe*, Archaeolingua Series Minor, 25. Budapest: Archaeolingua.

——, Šumberová, R., Knüsel, C., and Outram, A. (2007). *Velim: Violence and Death in Bronze Age Bohemia. The Results of Fieldwork 1992–95, with a Consideration of Peri-mortem Trauma and Deposition in the Bronze Age*. Prague: Archeologický Ústav.

Hellerschmid, I. (2006). *Die urnenfelder/hallstattzeitliche Wallanlage von Stillfried an der March*. Mitteilungen der Prähistorischen Kommission, 63. Vienna: Verlag der Österreichischen Akademie der Wissenschaften.

Jantzen, D., Brinker, U., Orschiedt, J., Heinemeier, J., Piek, J., Hauerstein, K.-H., Krüger, J., Lidke, G., Lübke, H., Lampe, R., Lorenz, S., Schult, M., and Terberger, T. (2011). 'A Bronze Age battlefield? Weapons and trauma in the Tollense Valley, north-eastern Germany', *Antiquity*, 85: 417–33.

Jiménez-Brobeil, S. A. (2011). 'An example of a severe neck injury with survival seen in a Bronze Age burial', *International Journal of Osteoarchaeology*, 21: 247–52.

Keeley, L. H. (1996). *War Before Civilization: The Myth of the Peaceful Savage*. Oxford: Oxford University Press.

Knüsel, C. and Outram, A. (2007). 'A comparison of human and animal deposition at Velim-Skalka through an integrated approach', in A. F. Harding, R. Šumberová, C. Knüsel, and

A. Outram, *Velim: Violence and Death in Bronze Age Bohemia. The Results of Fieldwork 1992-95, with a Consideration of Peri-mortem Trauma and Deposition in the Bronze Age*. Prague: Archeologický Ústav, 97-136.

Kristiansen, K. (2002). 'The tale of the sword—swords and swordfighters in Bronze Age Europe', *Oxford Journal of Archaeology*, 21: 319-32.

——and Larsson, T. B. (2005). *The Rise of Bronze Age Society*. Cambridge: Cambridge University Press.

Louwe Kooijmans, L. P. (1993). 'An Early/Middle Bronze Age multiple burial at Wassenaar, the Netherlands', *Analecta Praehistorica Leidensia*, 26: 1-20.

——(2005). 'Bronze Age war—A collective burial at Wassenaar', in L. P. Louwe Kooijmans, P. W. van den Broeke, H. Fokkens, and A. L. van Gijn (eds.), *The Prehistory of the Netherlands*, vol. I. Amsterdam: Amsterdam University Press, 459-62.

Mercer, R. (2006). 'By other means: the development of warfare in the British Isles 3000-500 B.C.', *Journal of Conflict Archaeology*, 2: 119-51.

Osgood, R. (1998). *Warfare in the Late Bronze Age of North Europe*, British Archaeological Reports (International Series), 694. Oxford: Archaeopress.

——(2006). 'The dead of Tormarton: Bronze Age combat victims?', in T. Otto, H. Thrane, and H. Vandkilde (eds.), *Warfare and Society: Archaeological and Social Anthropological Perspectives*. Aarhus: Aarhus University Press, 331-40.

Otto, T., Thrane, H., and Vandkilde, H. (eds.) (2006). *Warfare and Society: Archaeological and Anthropological Perspectives*. Aarhus: Aarhus University Press.

Parker Pearson, M. (2005). 'Warfare, violence and slavery in later prehistory: an introduction', in M. Parker Pearson and I. J. N. Thorpe (eds.), *Warfare, Violence and Slavery in Prehistory*, British Archaeological Reports (International Series), 1,374. Oxford: Archaeopress: 19-33.

——and Thorpe, I. J. N. (eds.) (2005). *Warfare, Violence and Slavery in Prehistory*, British Archaeological Reports (International Series), 1,374. Oxford: Archaeopress.

Peter-Röcher, H. (2007). *Gewalt und Kreig im prähistorischen Europa*, Universitätsforschungen zur prähistorischen Archäologie, 143. Bonn: Habelt.

Randsborg, K. (2006). 'Opening the oak coffins. New dates—new perspectives', *Acta Archaeologia*, 77: 1-162.

Thorpe, N. (2006). 'Fighting and feuding in Neolithic and Bronze Age Britain and Ireland', in T. Otto, H. Thrane, and H. Vandkilde (eds.), *Warfare and Society: Archaeological and Social Anthropological Perspectives*. Aarhus: Aarhus University Press, 141-65.

Thrane, H. (2006). 'Swords and other weapons in the Nordic Bronze Age: technology, treatment, and contexts', in T. Otto, H. Thrane, and H. Vandkilde (eds.), *Warfare and Society: Archaeological and Social Anthropological Perspectives*. Aarhus: Aarhus University Press, 491-504.

Vandkilde, H. (2006). 'Warriors and warrior institutions in Copper Age Europe', in T. Otto, H. Thrane, and H. Vandkilde (eds.), *Warfare and Society: Archaeological and Social Anthropological Perspectives*. Aarhus: Aarhus University Press, 393-422.

CHAPTER 14

RETHINKING BRONZE AGE COSMOLOGY: A NORTH EUROPEAN PERSPECTIVE

JOAKIM GOLDHAHN

INTRODUCTION

Generally there are four fundamental questions that human beings have contemplated since the dawn of time:

- How and why was the world created?
- How and why were human beings created?
- How should we live a righteous life?
- What happens to us after death?

The answers to these persistent questions have varied from time to time, and from religion to religion, but they also depend on the place from where the world is perceived. Life-worlds in the European Bronze Age were undoubtedly different from ours (Fig. 14.1) and people obviously did things differently then. The answers to these fundamental questions were likewise formulated in different ways from ours, a fact that raises both problems and possibilities for our ability to gain knowledge about those life-worlds (Insoll 2007). Despite that, our futile questions meet and conjoin in a common venture and wonder over life's inevitable end.

During traditional and processual archaeology, issues like those above were considered too unfathomable even to be raised. Christopher Hawkes (1954) expressed it memorably with his often-quoted archaeological 'ladder of inference'. The bottom rung represents ancient societies' technology and economy, spheres that archaeologists often consider convenient to handle. Knowledge about these fields of prehistoric societies is within reach and possible to gain, according to Hawkes. Higher up the ladder, however, things become trickier and he explicitly warned us of increasing vertigo. It may be possible to study the social organization of ancient societies under certain specific conditions, while religious thoughts

FIG. 14.1 The Bronze Age 'Weltbild' by Karol Schauer. Reproduced here by kind permission of the artist and Landesamt für Denkmalpflege und Archaeologie Sachsen-Anhalt.

Source: State Office for Heritage Management and Archaeology Saxony-Anhalt.

and actions were considered to be more or less inaccessible (e.g. Binford 1972). They were simply beyond our perception.

Today we know better. We are also better equipped to tackle such issues. This is partly because our knowledge of ancient societies has improved significantly since the 1950s and 1960s, but also because we have learned more about how pre-literary societies were constituted and how their life-worlds were composed.

In short, there are two basic premises for the study of human life-worlds by archaeological means. The first is that people's immaterial world is not essentially different from their experienced world (Insoll 2004). The second premise is based on the first and is that not only were these immaterial worlds expressed through oral accounts and rituals, which tend to be very difficult for archaeologists to study, but that people's life-worlds were also expressed, mediated, and materialized through a conscious use and reuse of material culture. It is through the material culture and its contexts that we archaeologists can trace different acts and practices in the past (Tilley 2006).

With a distinctly holistic approach, we might then go on to explore how different fields of social and ritualized practices in these societies were related to each other. From there we can go further and attempt informed interpretations of how the life-worlds of these societies might have been constituted. In this respect, a simple piece of ceramic can be as important for our understanding as more spectacular, eye-catching finds about which we shall soon learn more.

Before such an understanding can be reached, we need to make a somewhat closer scrutiny of our own and former colleagues' theoretical starting points. An outspoken ideal and norm in traditional and normative processual archaeology was to study prehistoric material cultures in a 'substantialist' manner (e.g. Bourdieu 1994: Chapter 1). The analysis of prehistoric culture was divided after specific constituent materials, which were more or less explicitly thought to reflect cultural and historical reality. In short: stone experts studied stone artefacts, ceramic specialists studied ceramics, and metal objects were entrusted to metallurgy specialists. A good example is the larger-than-life project manifested in the countless volumes of *Prähistorische Bronzefunde*. In most cases this meant that objects which were found together in a specific context were divided up among various experts. All too often this has meant that contemporary objects from the same archaeological context have ended up in different parts of a museum's collection. Every now and then, reassembling a given excavated context can be just as difficult as it was to dig up the site in the first place.

This substantialism also anticipated that each separate field of prehistoric practice that could be identified—houses, settlements, burials, economy, farming, transport and contacts, metals, crafts, warfare, religion and ritual, hoards and hoarding, social organization, and cosmology, for example—could and should be studied and understood independently of other defined practices. A serious criticism of this procedure, which still lingers in contemporary archaeology, is that our joint pursuit of a deeper knowledge of prehistoric contexts and conditions tends to be waylaid by separate, decontextualized analyses, formed and nourished by our increasingly specialized archaeological interests. The present structure of the archaeological field is then implicitly recreated in our interpretations and our enigmatic striving to understand and deconstruct the past. In short: the present is mirrored in the past.

An alternative to this rather naive approach is to acknowledge that different fields of practice were related to each other and must therefore be studied in relation to each other, not least since they constituted part of one another in the first place (e.g. Bourdieu 1977; 1994). In communities that we label, for want of better notions, 'traditional', 'cold', 'oral' or, even worse, 'low-technological', these fields of practice were interwoven and connected with ritualized life-worlds where 'technology' was inseparable from 'cosmology', and vice versa (Barth 1987; Bell 1992; Insoll 2004). Therefore, if we as archaeologists hope to reach an understanding of the life-worlds of past societies, we must admit that besides trying to broaden our understanding of how different fields of practice were formed and constituted, we must try to figure out *whether, how,* and *why* these fields were related to each other (e.g. Goldhahn 2007). No other era of prehistory is perhaps better suited for such a task than the Bronze Age.

In the following I will present two influential ways of reconstructing past life-worlds in relation to recent research concerning the cosmology of the Bronze Age in northern Europe. The discussion will include some current views about how this cosmology was constituted and reflected in landscape cognition. Thereafter I will scrutinize whether, how, and why these fields might be related to each other and try to present a tentative path for an alternative perception of Bronze Age cosmology.

A Brand-New World

As will be evident from reading the individual chapters of this handbook, one of the biggest changes in the prehistory of northern Europe occurs in the transition between the Early and the Middle Bronze Age, at approximately 1600 cal. BC (e.g. Kristiansen 1998; Harding 2000; Vandkilde 2007). A brand-new world was born. This change is evident in a variety of fields. Contacts between regions became more intense. The economy grew more diverse and specialized. A more than 2000-year-old tradition of building houses with two aisles gave way fairly quickly to a new, three-aisle design. Prestige goods of flint, such as the enigmatic flint daggers from Scandinavia, were replaced by shining bronze artefacts. Bronze tools and weapons were standardized (Vandkilde 1996). Warriors were armed, admired, and killed (Otto, Thrane, and Vandkilde 2006; Harding 2007). Ornaments expressing gender, status, rank, identity, and ethnicity became a vital part of social displays and renegotiations. Enormous burial monuments were created and ceremonies were held to commemorate and celebrate prominent chiefs and warriors (Goldhahn 2008). And, not least, bronze artefacts acquired motifs of cosmological significance (Kaul 1998); depictions of the sun and moon, fish motifs, axes, mushroom-shaped symbols, snakes, and ships (see Chapter 15). The changes are so radical and profound that they ought to be understood as one of the major transformations in European prehistory (e.g. Jensen 1982; Kristiansen 1998; Vandkilde 1996; Kaul 1998; 2005).

Two of Europe's best-known archaeological finds originate from this formative era—the bronze discs from Trundholm and Nebra. Both are of the utmost importance for our understanding of these changes in general and changes in Bronze Age cosmology in particular. The first was found on northern Zealand in Denmark in the early twentieth century and the second at Nebra, 60 km west of Leipzig in Germany, in the 1990s. Both bronze discs had been decorated with thin foils of gold, apparently to reflect a cosmology concerning the sun's daily and annual rebirth—the mythological journey of the sun. For all we know, they are both unique ritual paraphernalia and both have a find story that is as evocative and fascinating as the finds themselves.

The sun disc from Trundholm, dated to Montelius Period II (1500–1300 cal BC), was found in 1902 in a bog (see Fig. 41.6). The farmer who made the discovery gave it to his young daughter, who used it for some time as a toy. Only fortunate circumstances, such as the child's careful handling, allowed the disc to survive to our day (Müller 1903).

This sun disc, 26 cm in diameter, is mounted on a six-wheeled wagon drawn by a horse (a string or a bronze chain connected the horse's throat to the front edge of the disc). However, when it was found the cultic gear was in a disjointed state (Müller 1903). One side of the disc is covered with thin gold foil decorated with concentric circles and spirals. This side, interpreted as a 'day side', stands in contrast to the other side, which consists of bronze only and is not decorated in the same flashy style. It is also ornamented differently, with patterns that bear some resemblance to stylized axe motifs (with connotations to the moon and the underworld). Over time, this side of the disc would turn dark, and is accordingly interpreted as a 'night side'.

The disc from Nebra, 32 cm in diameter, is decorated with symbols made of thin gold foil (see Chapter 40); it was found in 1999 by metal detectorists. The three main symbols depict the sun, the moon, and a curved design that can be interpreted as a ship. In addition, the bronze disc is decorated with numerous small golden dots that can be interpreted as stars. Some of them seem to depict the Pleiades, which nowadays appear in the sky around mid August. On the disc's edges are two arcs made of gold foil. Each of them covers 82 degrees of the disc, which exactly reproduces the angular distance between sunrise and sunset at the solstice at the latitude where the Nebra disc was deposited 3,600 years ago. After the disc had been created it was used for a considerable period and was reworked several times before it got its current appearance (Meller 2004).

Following Flemming Kaul, both these precious finds reflect the basic components of a tripartite cosmology that gained significance fairly rapidly in northern Europe around 1600 cal BC. The discs may have been used in various rituals that aimed to reflect and demonstrate this new cosmology. The sun and the ship were—without doubt—the new era's two major symbols. In the north, the sun was accompanied by a mythological horse throughout the Bronze Age

(Kaul 2005). From this point of view, the changes described above ought to be regarded as a major religious transformation that affected the fundamental structure of Bronze Age societies in northern Europe, manifested and materialized in the two bronze discs.

According to Kaul (2005), this cosmology was relatively intact up to the end of the Bronze Age. This is evident from his seminal analysis of the iconography of Late Bronze Age razors from Denmark (here 1100–500 cal BC) (Fig. 14.2). The day/night dichotomy that seems to govern the discs from Trundholm and Nebra is also manifested in the iconography of the razors (Kaul 1998). An analysis of more than eight hundred ship depictions reveals that the ship sailing from left to right, just like the sun's daily journey over the sky in this part of the world, is related to an iconography where sun symbols are placed in 'the sky' over the ships' hulls. Kaul interprets them as 'day ships' (Kaul 2005: 140, Fig. 3). Ships travelling in the opposite direction do not seem to have the same clear connection with sun symbols, and are accordingly interpreted as 'night ships'. Sun symbols do occur in connection with night ships but

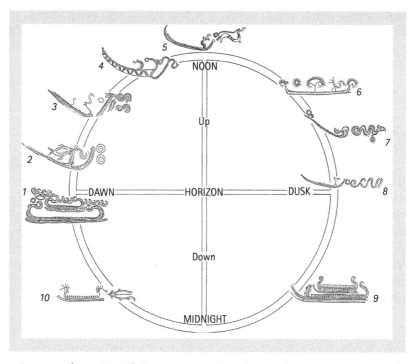

FIG. 14.2 Iconography on Danish Bronze razors, Late Bronze Age, 1100–500 cal BC, showing different points of the cyclical movement of the sun. 1. Sunrise. The fish pulls the rising sun up from the night-ship to the morning ship; 2. For a while, the fish was allowed to sail on with the ship; 3. The fish is to be devoured by a bird of prey. Stylized sun-horses (S-figures) are ready to fetch the sun; 4. Two sun-horses are about to pull the sun from the ship; 5. At noon the sun-horse has collected the sun from the ship; 6. In the afternoon the sun-horse lands with the sun on the sun-ship; 7. Some time after the sun-horse has landed, the sun is taken over by the snake from the afternoon-ship; 8. The snake is concealing the sun in its spiral curls. It will soon lead the sun down under the horizon; 9. Two night-ships sailing towards the left. The sun is not visible, extinguished and dark on its voyage through the underworld; 10. A night ship followed by a fish swimming to the left. The fish is ready to fulfil its task at sunrise.

Source: reworked after Kaul 2005.

they are attached to the ships' hulls. Kaul views these night ships as a mythological vessel for the sun on its nightly voyage, now travelling from west to east through the underworld—the land of death—so that the sun could be reborn again in the morning (Kaul 2005: 141; Fig. 4).

Several mythological beings accompany the sun on its mythological journey; besides the horse there are snakes, birds, fish, and so on. Moreover, Kaul (2005: 138) argues that a certain order can be observed in this iconography: 'as the pictures show that the fish could not bring the sun to the horse, and the horse could not bring the sun to the snake. Always, the ship has to be in between the other mythological agents of the sun on its voyage, being the divine mediator of the heavens and the underworld.' Kaul then uses this order to present a picture of Bronze Age cosmology in general and of the sun's mythological journey in particular.

Kaul's analysis also includes other ritual paraphernalia from the Bronze Age, not least the enigmatic rock art from southern Scandinavia. The same iconography is sometimes detected in this medium but, as Kaul (2005) argues, the rock art rather seems to reflect certain aspects of Bronze Age ritual life and cult practices, while the iconography of razors is more a reflection of Bronze Age cosmology (see Chapter 15).

COSMOLOGY AND BRONZE AGE LANDSCAPE COGNITION

As Richard Bradley (2005) has so sensitively shown, rituals and cosmology are never far removed from human thoughts and actions. These phenomena permeate people's everyday lives and act both as the outcome and as a medium for their being in the world (e.g. Bourdieu 1977). An illustration of this assumption is the locations and relations between Bronze Age settlements and ancient monuments in northern Europe, which often seem to be established in reconcilable, well-known patterns (Kristiansen 1998; Harding 2000; Fontijn 2003; Kristiansen and Larsson 2005). The placing of burials on heights and prominent places in the landscape is well attested, as is that of settlements on well-drained land. The same goes for ritual deposits on dry lands and in wetlands (Bradley 1998), such as bogs, moors (ornaments), and rivers (weapons). Figurative rock art was located in various places but often within sight of the shore (see Chapter 15). Heaps of fire-cracked stones (in south-east Scandinavia only) are found at settlements (Larsson 1986) or cemeteries (Goldhahn 2007). These patterns seem to comply with common standards and regulations, as shown in Table 14.1.

This idealistic landscape model was presented to illuminate the Bronze Age situation in the Mälar Valley in Sweden, but it has also been acknowledged—with some notable variations—not only in other parts of Sweden (Bradley 2009) but also in other areas of northern Europe (see Kristiansen and Larsson 2005). These include the Netherlands (Fontijn 2003), Germany (*passim*), Denmark (Frost 2008), and Norway (Myhre 2004). The placing of these phenomena in the Bronze Age landscape appears to be meaningful and significant, and it is usually interpreted as mirroring Bronze Age cosmology (Fig. 14.3).

My purpose here is not to embrace or verify these tentative pictures of the placement of prehistoric remains in the landscape and link them to Bronze Age mythology and cosmology. Instead, I would take the opportunity to argue that such interpretations must be based on an explicit notion of *specific social and ritual practices* that make these phenomena *meaningful*. Looking at Kaul's seminal study of Late Bronze Age razors, for example, it is not

Table 14.1 Relationship Between Bronze Age Sites and Siting in Northern Europe

	Ancient site	Placing	Connotation
High			Upper World
	Burial monuments	Mountains, heights	
	Settlements	Sand, moraine	Middle Earth
	Rock art	Clay soils	
	Ritual deposits/offerings	Bogs, moors, rivers	
Low			Underworld

clear how this particular iconography is related to any form of social or religious practice per se. What I think is missing from the picture is how this particular cosmology was played out, negotiated, and renegotiated in the context in which these artefacts were made and used, and subsequently found; in this case in relation to different cremation rituals and the burial contexts of these razors (see Goldhahn and Oestigaard 2008). For instance, some of the razors depicted in Figure 14.2 are to be considered as stray finds, others were retrieved from cremation burials (Kaul 1998). Some but not all were evidently found together with other objects. Who were the people with whom these razors were found? Were they tall or short? Old or young? Why were these razors not cremated with their owners? In what way was the Bronze Age cosmology involved in these contexts?

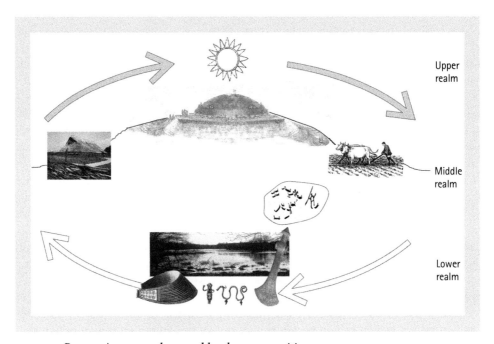

FIG. 14.3 Bronze Age cosmology and landscape cognition.

Source: Kristiansen and Larsson 2005.

The point here is that our perception of the bronze discs from Trundholm and Nebra, as well as of the Danish bronze razors, is often—but not always—coloured by a 'substantialistic' perception of form. Whether this is implicit or explicit, the outcome is that archaeologists tend to perceive these ritual paraphernalia as rather passive ritual icons reflecting Bronze Age cosmology. The same goes for the cognitive model in Figure 14.3. It may well describe the ideal placement of different prehistoric remains in the landscape, but as any deeper and more sincere analysis will show, this representation is highly idealistic (e.g. Fontijn 2003). The past is more unpredictable, varied, and diverse.

Another criticism of this idealistic picture of Bronze Age life-worlds is that most analyses of this phenomenon tend to end where they ought to start. Looking again at Figure 14.3, it does not contain much information about *whether, how,* or *why* the different practices depicted there were related to each other. What kind of social and ritual practices bound them together? How? And why? What are evidently missing in the pictures presented are past people and their actions, the social and ritual contexts, and some explicit interpretations of how the fields distinguished might relate to Bronze Age cosmology. If, for instance, the recurrent placing of prehistoric remains in the landscape is taken more as a starting point than a conclusion, we might be able to reverse this argument and identify the events and actions that linked these and other ritualized practices together.

Such an analysis cannot, of course, be contained in a single paper such as this; nevertheless, some tentative thoughts should be presented on how this information and knowledge could be gained and perceived. My point of departure here is the relationship between bronzesmiths and 'rock-smiths' in southern Scandinavia. As we shall see in the following, this also has some consequences for our interpretation of the bronze discs from Trundholm and Nebra.

To Get 'something great in exchange for something small'

The substantialist approach that embodies our sense of Bronze Age life-worlds is never as evident as in our perception of one of the most significant social and ritual institutions in northern Europe—the bronze and rock smiths (e.g. Goldhahn 2007). First and foremost, we seldom reflect on these social personas, yet we are constantly using the outcome of their work to explore every corner of Bronze Age societies (e.g. every rung on Hawkes's ladder).

In order to get closer to being able to put different ritualized practices into a new and more relational perspective, and thus deepen the relationship between 'different' ritualized spheres during this era (see Fig. 14.3), our view of Bronze Age societies must be examined in more detail. Most researchers agree that these communities were governed by a prestige-goods system where local products, such as amber, cattle, women, hides, slaves, and salt, were used to gain access to more exotic objects of bronze (copper/tin) and gold (e.g. Vandkilde 1996; Harding 2000; Pare 2000; Earle 2002; Kristiansen and Larsson 2005).

These prestige-goods systems were characterized by the performance of particular types of transaction and alliances built on exotic goods with limited access. Lotte Hedeager has stressed that prestige-goods systems in northern Europe were built on gifts and counter-gifts at a personal level: 'they could not be bought but had to be obtained through personal relationships and connections; either when the elite received them from far away or when the elite undertook their local redistribution' (Hedeager 1992: 89; also Earle 2002; Kristiansen and Larsson 2005).

In this context, it is easy to imagine that smiths were an important node in a similar prestige-goods system, where locally produced and exotic objects were charged with symbolism and an iconography with mythological and cosmological significance; objects that were used to create and recreate alliances, social positions, rank, gender, and, ultimately, cosmology itself (see Fig. 14.3).

These perceptions of form all build on Marcel Mauss and his seminal work *Essai sur le Don*, first published in 1925 (here 1969) (see Chapter 16). Similar prestige-goods systems were characterized by three principles according to Mauss (1969: 10–12; 37–41): the obligation to give and receive, to give further, and to repatriate the gift. Essential for this thinking was the *mana* associated with different material cultures among Maoris on New Zealand: the magical, religious, and spiritual power that came through the *hau* of gifts (Mauss 1969: 8–9).

Mauss argues that: 'Whatever it is, food, possessions, women, children or ritual, it retains a magical and religious hold over the recipient. The thing given is not inert. It is alive and often personified, and strives to bring to its original clan and homeland some equivalent to take its place' (Mauss 1969: 10). To hand over a gift was thus equivalent to giving away a piece of the giver herself. It was the *hau* of gifts that made it possible to present a gift while keeping it (Godelier 1999). Moreover, according to Mauss, gifts are a 'total social phenomenon' because they bring with them both personal, economic, social, legal, political, aesthetic, and ideological dimensions. As a global social phenomenon, gifts are essential as an integral part of individuals' *rites de passage*; at birth and naming, in sickness, when boys and girls are initiated into adulthood or to another social persona (e.g. smiths, warriors, potters), at weddings and divorces, in connection with peace and war, and at death (Goldhahn 2008).

Mauss also stressed that although these gifts negotiated and renegotiated relationships on a 'voluntary' personal level, this should be understood as a forceful social and cultural phenomenon that created and recreated social and cultural values, ideals, and norms (Mauss 1969: 3; also Bourdieu 1977). A gift should not unreservedly be understood as the exchange of material things, for it (often) involved a 'total prestation' that also included:

> ...courtesies, entertainments, ritual, military assistance, women, children, dances, and feasts; and fairs in which the market is but one element and the circulation of wealth but one part of a wide and enduring contract. Finally, although the prestations and counter-prestations take place under a voluntary guise they are in essence strictly obligatory, and their sanction is private or open warfare. We propose to call this the system of *total prestations*.... Furthermore, the obligation is expressed in myth and imagery, symbolically and collectively; it takes the form of interest in the objects exchanged; the objects are never completely separated from the men who exchange them; the communion and alliance they establish are well-nigh indissoluble (Mauss 1969: 3, 31, italics in original).

In his thought-provoking book *The Enigma of the Gift*, Maurice Godelier (1999) has scrutinized Mauss's classical work and developed his ideas about the gift as a total social and cultural phenomenon. It is mainly Mauss's strong emphasis on gifts as interpersonal phenomena that Godelier wants to alter and change: 'By excluding sacred objects from his field of analysis, Mauss may have unintentionally created the illusion that exchange was the be-all and end-all of social life' (Godelier 1999: 69). He then goes on to argue that the gift's three principles should be extended with a fourth—often neglected—obligation: gifts and counter-gifts to ancestors, spirits and gods, or other immaterial forces (Godelier 1999: 29–36). In brief, the tangible and intangible possessions that were given by different immaterial forces could not be passed on and exchanged, but despite that, they still were governed by the dialectic principles of the gift that Mauss presented and advocated. Although the sacred character of these objects meant that they could not be given away, they still had to be returned in an appropriate way. Moreover, Godelier shows that it is through an inaugural gift from specific immaterial powers that more ordinary gift-giving is able to work among mortals (Godelier 1999: 72).

One consequence of this is that, to quote Mauss (1969: 13), 'the exchanges and contracts concern not only men and things but also the sacred beings that are associated with them'. For Mauss, the reciprocal exchange between humans and their immaterial powers was the main reason for the complex nature of gift-giving documented in various parts of the world: 'It is not simply to show power and wealth and unselfishness that man puts slaves to death, burns his precious oil, throws coppers into the sea, and sets his house on fire... for the gods who give and repay are there to give something great in exchange for something small' (Mauss 1969: 14–15).

Smiths as Cosmologists

Returning to the Bronze Age of northern Europe, the thoughts of Mauss and Godelier have some profound consequences for our understanding of its life-worlds, not least if we want to avoid the substantialist preconceptions and their consequences, discussed above.

For the prestige goods of the Bronze Age to be able to work among mortals, the negotiation and renegotiation with the powers of immortals were necessary, even unavoidable. The exchange among mortals was built and constituted on gifts between humans and the immortal, immaterial forces that inhabited their life-worlds, which might explain the profound cosmological connotations that we find depicted on different bronze items and ritual paraphernalia. The razors discussed by Kaul, for instance, are all individual 'art works'. They most certainly belonged to specific 'owners', and could not be traded in the same way as axes, swords, and other bronze items. For instance, razors are never found in hoards and could not be cremated together with the deceased owner. Kaul interprets the razors as a ritual sign that the owner had been initiated into esoteric cosmological knowledge (Kaul 1998; 2005). Maybe these razors were understood as a sacralized gift from the immaterial powers and mythological beings that are depicted on them, which could explain both the fact that they could not be given away or re-melted, and their cosmological significance.

Moreover, this perception might also explain the profound offering practice that is so well documented in the archaeological record. It also puts a lot more emphasis on those who created these items that enabled the negotiations and renegotiations associated with Bronze Age prestige-goods systems to take place in general, in particular the initiations and esoteric knowledge associated with the razors, suggesting that the social and ritual practice of smiths ought to be reconsidered.

Of course, it is generally advocated that the works of smiths were used to express status, gender, rank, and identity during the Bronze Age, and that the created objects sometimes were sacrificed in bogs, moors, and rivers (Larsson 1986; Bradley 1998; Harding 2000; Earle 2002; Fontijn 2003). Traditionally, these phenomena were explained in 'neutral terms', such as 'production, distribution, and consumption' (e.g. Rowlands 1976; Larsson 1986; Kristiansen 1998), and nowadays through increasingly worn-out and muddy concepts such as 'rituals' and 'cosmology'. Although these perspectives certainly have validity, I believe they are partially blinded by their own spotlight, not least because this maintains a profound distinction between technology and cosmology, as described by Hawkes in the 1950s.

In another context, I have argued that neither 'bronze smith' nor 'rock smith' are apt terms for understanding these social and ritual personas and practices (Goldhahn 2007). The absence of smiths in Bronze Age burials in Scandinavia, for instance, is real. I interpret this as indicating that neither the bronze smith nor the rock smith was distinguished as a specific social and ideological category, and consequently that these crafts were performed through other forms of social and ritual institutions. This is underlined by the fact that it is not possible to distinguish specific production sites for different 'crafts' from one another during the Bronze Age; instead they seem to be integrated and coincide in time and space. Where bronze artefacts were created, other 'specialized' crafts such as pottery and stone crafts were also practised.

Contextual analysis of archaeological sites also makes it clear that 'different' ritual spheres were connected to each other during the Bronze Age. Basically the same material culture is found at different places that were used for ritual matters: fire-cracked stones, charcoal, soot, fragmented pottery, burnt bones of animals and humans, cup marks, grinding tools, crushed flint and quartz, and traces of 'metallurgical operations' (Goldhahn 2007). The 'different ritual contexts' all seem to be linked to the 'smiths' as ritual specialists, and to their specific capability to transform clay and quartz into moulds, crucibles, and ceramics; copper and tin into bronze, and bronze into symbolically and cosmologically charged objects. The deposits of crucibles and moulds sometimes occur in front of rock art panels. Sometimes rock art was produced at places where the smiths worked. These 'workshops' were sited with the greatest discretion, often in confidential places associated with death and transformation, such as burial grounds, cult houses, and/or behind tall wooden palisades. Both rock art and bronze objects were produced as an integrated part of death ceremonies and rituals (Goldhahn and Oestigaard 2008).

An illuminating example of these intricate relationships is the so-called cult house, found in Denmark and Sweden and apparently associated with initiation rituals, cremations, rock art, and bronze casting (Goldhahn 2007). The Sandagergård cult house from Zealand, with four decorated stones depicting hand motifs, is widely known and often discussed (e.g. Kaul 1998; see Harding 2000; Bradley 2005). Another important case that seems to have been forgotten in this context is the cult houses at Hallunda, from Stockholm in Sweden. Here, one of Scandinavia's largest 'workshops' for bronze production has been excavated, with 13 well-preserved furnaces. No fewer than six of them were situated in a cult house, and the others just outside a similar feature (Fig. 14.4). From the same spot we also have some of the best evidence of extensive and specialized ceramic production in northern Europe. This complex was surrounded by 30–40 cremation burials, many of them with traces of metal production and even rock art in their structure, situated on a small hill just above a large settlement. All these practices seem to be related to the 'smith as transformer' and performed in an exclusive area separated from 'ordinary life' (Goldhahn 2007: Chapter 9; Goldhahn and Oestigaard 2008). Seen from the perspective presented above, Bronze Age ritual practices seem to coalesce into a unit where the sum was greater than the individual parts, technology merged with cosmology, and vice versa. The smith was an all-inclusive cosmologist.

FIG. 14.4 The 'workshop' at Hallunda, Stockholm in Sweden. Note the furnaces and the stone structure that has been interpreted as walls from a cult house.

Photo: Swedish National Board, adapted by the author.

This interpretation finds some support in anthropological and ethnological studies, where the smith is often regarded as a dangerous, strange figure (Eliade 1962; Helms 1993; Blakely 2006). In Norse saga, for instance, the smith was attributed supernatural forces. Smiths played an active role in the creation myths and, accordingly, the objects created by smiths were often loaded with symbolic and cosmological significance. For example, it is significant that in Norse mythology the creation of Asgård was associated with the smith's furnace, as expressed in *Voluspå* and in Snorre Sturlason's *Edda*. This is also evident in Finland's national epic, *Kalevala*, where the master-smith Ilmarinen, 'the chief blacksmith among blacksmiths', held a similar position. Ilmarinen was renowned for creating the heaven above without leaving any trace of his magic act, indeed an act of mythological creation. The role of the smith during the Iron Age was likewise connected with ritual and mythological spheres (Haaland 2004).

This is also highlighted in anthropological studies, where smiths often occupy an ambiguous position. Travelling smiths, tradesmen, attached specialists, and artisans, often implicated in traditional Bronze Age research (e.g. Childe 1930; see Kristiansen 1998; Harding 2000; Earle 2002, etcetera), are rare or even absent (Rowlands 1971: 214). The social position of smiths varied considerably. The smith was feared in some societies, privileged in others; sometimes he was an outcast and despised. In some societies the smith had a high social position, in other contexts he belonged to the lowest castes (Goldhahn 2007: 101).

Regardless of the smith's social status and position, there is a significant structural similarity between the contexts in which smiths worked, namely that they played a central role in the ritual, mythological, and cosmological realms (Eliade 1962; Helms 1993; Blakely 2006).

Eugenia Herbert summarizes this as follows in her seminal study of traditional copper smiths in Africa:

> Smiths have traditionally been viewed as a people set apart from the rest of mankind by the nature of their work and the common practice of endogamy, or at least marriage within prescribed groups.... True, the smith occupies a clearly inferior position among some people.... Often, too, the smiths are ethnically different or at least regarded as 'others'.... In the agricultural or mixed-farming societies that predominate south of the desert, this inferiority is decidedly rare. On the contrary the smith plays a central and powerful role in both the natural and supernatural spheres. In fact, the distinction itself is false, since the roles are intimately connected and since such dualism is alien to African thought. The smith functions as priest, artist, shaman, magician, initiator precisely because his work demands not merely manual skills but esoteric knowledge to manipulate the dangerous forces at play in the extraction of ores and in their transformation into finished objects (Herbert 1984: 23).

The technological know-how was usually dressed in a mythological and cosmological disguise. For smiths in western Mexico, for example, the colour of the copper ore and its sound were of the utmost importance, and both of these characteristics embodied cosmological meanings. While these characteristics were critical to what Hawkes and Binford would describe as 'the technological quality of the ore', they also expressed fundamental religious and cosmological beliefs that were embedded in, and perpetuated through, the technology and its products (Hosler 1995: 113).

From this we can learn that metallurgy and mythology, technology and cosmology, are Western concepts that are seldom relevant outside this cultural space. In traditional societies technology was inseparable from ideology; technological know-how could not be separated from either its social context or its mythological and cosmological embodiment (cf Hawkes 1954). The creation of metal and metal items was connected with social and ritual taboos, and uninitiated persons, particularly women and children, were held at a safe distance. The technological knowledge was loaded with cosmological and sexual metaphors. In eastern Africa, for example, the forge was thought of as a woman in disguise—the smith's bride—and accordingly attributed with breast and vulva (Haaland 2004; Blakeley 2006). To share the smith's esoteric knowledge was synonymous with sharing society's norms and ideals on sexuality, birth, and death, and how these aspects were linked to society's mythology and cosmology.

Similar findings of mythologically materialized furnaces are, as far as I know, not known from the Bronze Age in northern Europe, but nevertheless there are zoomorphic tuyères in the shape of horse-heads and anthropomorphic moulds made out of soapstone (Fig. 14.5). In view of the horse's role and function in society's mythology and cosmology (Kaul 2005; see Fig. 14.2), it is reasonable to interpret this as Bronze Age smiths, like their African brothers, dressing their esoteric knowledge in a mythological and cosmological disguise (Goldhahn 2007). The smith was a transformer, a ritual specialist, a mediator between worlds, a cosmologist.

What may be worth noting in this context is the profound knowledge of the world that Bronze Age smiths needed to possess in order to perform their enigmatic practices. Besides the most obvious—having the technological know-how about where to extract copper, tin, bronze, and gold, and process them into finished objects, which probably required extensive knowledge of exotic places in different parts of Europe—there are several other more local ingredients with which smiths had to be acquainted, not least beekeeping and producing wax for casting bronze with *cire perdue* technology.

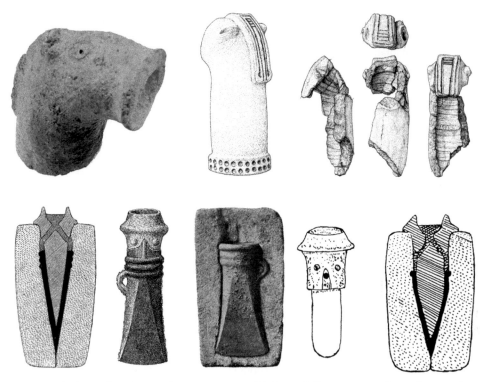

FIG. 14.5 Animated tuyères and soapstone moulds from different parts of Scandinavia that indicate that the esoteric knowledge of smiths was dressed in a mythological disguise.

Source: author (Goldhahn 2007).

Another important raw material for the smith in northern Europe was soapstone (Goldhahn 2007: Chapter 5). This metamorphic rock, composed in general of the minerals talc and magnesium, is not 'democratically' distributed on the Scandinavian Peninsula; despite this, intermediate products and finished moulds have been found far away from the areas where soapstone occurs, including Denmark and northern Germany. Several of the known Bronze Age soapstone quarries in Scandinavia are decorated with rock art. Based on the chronology of the depicted ship images (following the chronology of Kaul 1998), it is clear that people used these places for generations, sometimes up to 600–800 years (Fig. 14.6). Some soapstone moulds exhibit anthropomorphic traits and careful handling, suggesting that they were connected with mythological beliefs and taboos (see Fig. 14.5). For all we know, soapstone may have been a mythologically loaded 'raw material' during the Bronze Age, both where it was 'born' at remote, inaccessible sites, and during its 'life', 'death', and 'burial' (see Goldhahn 2007: Chapter 5).

Another essential raw material, with a much more democratic distribution, was quartz (see Goldhahn 2007: Chapter 6). This mineral could be used as a flux in the production of copper from copper sulphides. It was also essential as a temper in crucibles and moulds for creating bronze artefacts. Local clays in northern Europe start to decompose at around 700° C, copper starts to melt at 1,083°, and the melting point of bronze varies between 830 and 1,000°, depending on the amount of tin. In contrast, quartz does not melt below 1,470–1,756°, depending on its composition. This shows that a temper is needed for moulds and crucibles in order to create bronze objects with *cire perdue* technology. Bronze Age moulds usually contain over 60 per cent quartz, which makes them very porous and explains why such finds are so rare. Without quartz, there would not have been a Bronze Age.

Saying that, quartz is one of the world's most common minerals, accessible to some extent more or less everywhere. Still, it seems to have been quarried at rock art sites, and vice versa: rock art was made at places where quartz was quarried. Sometimes this was done at the same places as where ceramic and bronze items were produced, which shows that these practices were related and were performed by the same social and ritual institutions. Quartz was also used in other related fields during the Bronze Age. It has been found deposited in front of rock art panels, as well as in their cracks and crevices. At some rock art sites, the pecked images integrate with natural veins of quartz. Sometimes, quartz veins are even a direct and an important part of specific rock art images.

Moreover, quartz is frequently found during excavations of ancient monuments with ritual elements from the Bronze Age, such as burials and ritual deposits. Often the quartz from the ritual contexts seems to have been deliberately crushed, without any explicit purpose of producing objects or tools. Possibly this was done as an audiovisual performative act in rituals and ceremonies. Quartz has also been found in so-called 'medicine bags' or 'shaman bags', like Maglehøj from Zealand in Denmark, which shows that this rather common mineral was associated with different realms of ritual and ceremonial life during the Bronze Age in northern Europe (see Goldhahn 2007: Chapter 6).

In this context one should not underestimate the need of good clay for making moulds and crucibles. Knowledge of where such clay was to be found, which qualities were preferred for different purposes, and so on, was no doubt an esoteric possession.

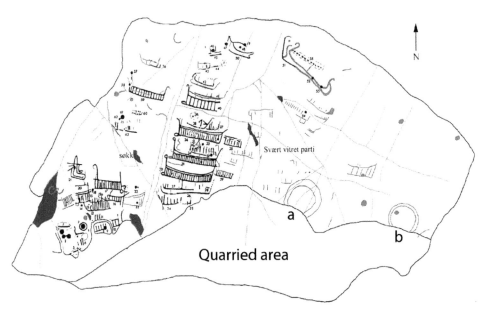

FIG. 14.6 Soapstone quarries with rock art from Krabbestig in Sogn og Fjordane, western Norway. Documentation by Trond Linge and Melanie Wrigglesworth.

Source: author (Goldhahn 2007).

Concluding Remarks: Cosmologies in the Making

From the discussion above it is clear that the craft of smiths during the Bronze Age was connected with cosmology. We also found some strong reasons for changing our perception of this matter. Cosmology was not a free-floating phenomenon, reflected in these issues in a passive way, but an active act, grounded and embodied in people's everyday lives and their ritualized dealings with their life-worlds. Moreover, Mauss's and Godelier's seminal thoughts on the gift as 'total prestation' enable us to link and conjoin different ritual spheres. For gifts and counter-gifts to function in Bronze Age prestige-goods systems, it was essential to have some inaugural gift from the immaterial powers to more mortal beings. More importantly, like all other gifts that circulated during this era, those gifts had to be returned. So by adding people and their ritualized actions to the picture (see Fig. 14.3), we might arrive at a new perception and understanding of Bronze Age life-worlds.

Under these circumstances I think it is important to acknowledge that when Bronze Age people was born, the world they came to know and embrace was already there, present, vivid and animated, sacralized, and inhabited by both material and immaterial forces. Altering or changing this given world amounted to changing the order that had been laid down by those immaterial forces. Quarrying per se is an act that alters the sacralized world, and in doing so puts the primordial order at stake. The act of creating pictures on rocks at soapstone or quartz quarries, or of making offerings at places where clay was gathered for ceramics, moulds, and crucibles, could be understood from that perspective. Moreover, these 'gifts' were essential for the smiths to be able to perform their tasks, not least for making the prestige-goods economy of the Bronze Age function. In this context I want to suggest that the rock art and offerings found at these places could be seen as counter-gifts, a reordering and recreation of the sacralized world—an act of emplacement (Goldhahn 2010).

The perspective presented here does not suggest that enigmatic objects such as bronze razors or bronze discs, for instance those from Trundholm and Nebra, were made 'to think with'; instead, it rather highlights the act of creating these ritual paraphernalia in the first place. Objects like these, overloaded with cosmological connotations, were not primarily made to contemplate the world, and making them was not an act that reflected the mythological journey of the sun per se. These acts were imbued with esoteric knowledge and were themselves a mythological and cosmological act, a recreation of the cosmos, and an act of emplacement.

Here it is worth noting that bronze items are known to have been melted down and remade (Bradley 1998; Barber 2003), and rock art re-pecked (Wahlgren 2004), time and time again. The same is true of the Nebra disc, which has been reworked several times, as well as the disjointed paraphernalia from Trundholm, which seems to have been reassembled each time it was used. This shows that the cosmology, or rather the cosmologies, of the Bronze Age lifeworld were grounded in pragmatic ritualized practices that were repeated and recreated at certain times and occasions, over and over again. This was literally not a world fixed in stone but a fluid, transparent, and alterable cosmology mastered by ritual specialists only—'smiths'. As the examples of Nebra and Trundholm show, it was a world view in constant flux, negotiated and renegotiated, melted and remelted, shaping life-worlds where the cosmologies were in the making.

Bibliography

Barber, M. (2003). *Bronze and the Bronze Age: Metalwork and Society in Britain c.2500–800 BC*. Stroud: Tempus.

Barth, F. (1987). *Cosmologies in the Making: A Generative Approach to Cultural Variation in Inner New Guinea*. Cambridge: Cambridge University Press.

Bell, C. M. (1992). *Ritual Theory, Ritual Practice*. New York: Oxford University Press.

Binford, L. R. (1972). *An Archaeological Perspective*. New York: Seminar Press.

Blakely, S. (2006). *Myth, Ritual and Metallurgy in Ancient Greece and Recent Africa*. Cambridge: Cambridge University Press.

Bourdieu, P. (1977). *Outline of a Theory of Practice*. Cambridge: Cambridge University Press.

—— (1994). *Raisons pratiques: sur la théorie de l'action*. Paris: Seuil.

Bradley, R. (1998). *The Passage of Arms: An Archaeological Analysis of Prehistoric Hoard and Votive Deposits*, 2nd edn. Oxford: Oxbow Books.

—— (2005). *Ritual and Domestic Life in Prehistoric Europe*. London: Routledge.

—— (2009). *Image and Audience: Rethinking Prehistoric Art*. Oxford: Oxford University Press.

Childe, V. G. (1930). *The Bronze Age*. Cambridge: Cambridge University Press.

Earle, T. (2002). *Bronze Age Economics: The Beginnings of Political Economies*. Cambridge, MA: Westview Press.

Eliade, M. (1962). *The Forge and the Crucible*. Chicago: University of Chicago Press.

Fontijn, D. F. (2003). *Sacrificial Landscapes: Cultural Biographies of Persons, Objects and 'Natural' Places in the Bronze Age of the Southern Netherlands, c.2300–600 BC*, Analecta Praehistorica Leidensia, 33/34. Leiden: Leiden University, Faculty of Archaeology.

Frost, L. (2008). *Himmerland's Late Bronze Age Hoard Finds in a Landscape Archaeological Perspective*. Aarhus: Aarhus University, Department of Anthropology, Archaeology, and Linguistics.

Godelier, M. (1999). *The Enigma of the Gift*. Chicago: University of Chicago Press.

Goldhahn, J. (2007). *Dödens hand—en essä om brons- och hällsmed*, Gotarc Serie C. (Arkeologiska Skrifter), 65. Göteborg: Göteborg University.

—— (2008). 'From monuments in landscape to landscapes in monument: death and landscape in Early Bronze Age Scandinavia', in A. Jones (ed.), *Prehistoric Europe: Theory and Practice*. Oxford and New York: Blackwell Studies in Global Archaeology, 56–85.

—— (2010). 'Emplacement and the hau of rock art', in J. Goldhahn, I. Fuglestvedt, and A. Jones (eds.), *Changing Pictures: Rock Art Traditions and Visions in Northern Europe*. Oxbow and Oakville: Oxbow Books, 106–26.

—— and Oestigaard, T. (2008). 'Smith and death: cremations in furnaces in Bronze and Iron Age Scandinavia', in K. Childis, J. Lund, and C. Prescott (eds.), *Facets of Archaeology: Essays in Honour of Lotte Hedeager on her 60th Birthday*, Oslo Arkeologiske Serie, 10. Oslo: Oslo Academic Press, 215–41.

Haaland, R. (2004). 'Technology, transformation and symbolism: ethnographic perspectives on European iron working', *Norwegian Archaeological Review*, 37/1: 1–19.

Harding, A. (2000). *European Societies in the Bronze Age*. Cambridge: Cambridge University Press.

—— (2007). *Warriors and Weapons in Bronze Age Europe*. Budapest: Archaeolingua.

Hawkes, C. F. (1954). 'Archaeology theory and method: some suggestions from the Old World', *American Anthropologist*, 56: 155–68.

Hedeager, L. (1992). *Iron-Age Societies: From Tribe to State in Northern Europe, 500 BC to AD 700*. Oxford: Blackwell Publishing.

Helms, M. J. (1993). *Craft and the Kingly Ideal: Art, Trade, and Power*. Austin: University of Texas Press.

Herbert, E. W. (1984). *Red Gold of Africa: Copper in Precolonial History and Culture*. Wisconsin: University of Wisconsin Press.

Hosler, D. (1995). 'Sound, colour and meaning in the metallurgy of ancient West Mexico', *World Archaeology*, 27: 100-15.

Insoll, T. (2004). *Archaeology, Ritual, Religion*. London: Routledge.

—— (2007). *Archaeology: The Conceptual Challenge*. London: Duckworth.

Jensen, J. (1982). *The Prehistory of Denmark*. London: Methuen.

Kaul, F. (1998). *Ships on Bronzes: A Study in Bronze Age Religion and Iconography*, Publications from the National Museum (Studies in Archaeology and History), 3/1-2. Copenhagen: National Museum of Denmark.

—— (2005). 'Bronze Age tripartite cosmologies', *Praehistorische Zeitschrift*, 80/2: 135-48.

Kristiansen, K. (1998). *Europe before History*. Cambridge: Cambridge University Press.

—— and Larsson, Th. B. (2005). *The Rise of Bronze Age Society: Travels, Transmissions and Transformations*. Cambridge: Cambridge University Press.

Larsson, Th. B. (1986). *The Bronze Age Metalwork in Southern Sweden: Aspects of Social and Spatial Organization 1800-500 B.C*, Archaeology and Environment, 6. Umeå: University of Umeå, Department of Archaeology.

Mauss, M. (1969). *The Gift: Forms and Functions of Exchange in Archaic Societies*, 3rd edn. London: Cohen and West Ltd.

Meller, H. (ed.) 2004. *Der geschmiedete Himmel. Die weite Welt im Herzen Europas vor 3600 Jahren*, Ausstellungskatalog. Stuttgart: Theiss-Verlag.

Müller, S. (1903). *Solbilledet fra Trundholm*, Nordiske Fortidsminder, 1/6. Copenhagen: Gyldendal.

Myhre, L. N. (2004). *Trialectic Archaeology: Monuments and Space in Southwest Norway 1700-500 BC*, AmS-Skrifter, 18. Stavanger: Arkeologisk museum i Stavanger.

Otto, T., Thrane, H., and Vandkilde, H. (eds.) (2006). *Warfare and Society: Archaeological and Social Anthropological Perspectives*. Aarhus: Aarhus University Press.

Pare, C. (ed.) (2000). *Metals Make the World Go Round: The Supply and Circulation of Metals in Bronze Age Europe*, Proceedings of a Conference Held at the University of Birmingham in June 1997. Oxford: Oxbow Books.

Rowlands, M. J. (1971). 'The archaeological interpretation of prehistoric metal working', *World Archaeology*, 3/2: 210-24.

—— (1976). *The Production and Distribution of Metalwork in the Middle Bronze Age in Southern Britain*, British Archaeological Reports, 31. Oxford: Archaeopress.

Tilley, C. (ed.) (2006). *Handbook of Material Culture*. London: Sage.

Vandkilde, H. (1996). *From Stone to Bronze: The Metalwork of the Late Neolithic and Earliest Bronze Age in Denmark*, Jysk Arkæologisk Selskabs Skrifter, 32. Aarhus: Aarhus University Press.

—— (2007). *Culture and Change in Central European Prehistory: 6th to 1st millennium BC*. Aarhus: Aarhus University Press.

Wahlgren, K. H. (2004). 'Switching images on and off: rock-carving practice and meaning in the Bronze Age life-world', in G. Milstreu and H. Prøhl (eds.), *Prehistoric Pictures as Archaeological Source/Förhistoriska bilder som arkeologisk källa*. Gotarc Serie C (Arkeologiska Skrifter), 50. Göteborg: Göteborg University, 149-65; 209-11.

CHAPTER 14A

THE SKY DISC OF NEBRA

HARALD MELLER

THE Nebra Sky Disc is one of archaeology's prime finds because its cosmological iconography offers a unique insight into the mental processes of Bronze Age people. It was discovered and looted by unlicensed metal detectorists on the summit of the Mittelberg hill, near the village of Nebra, Sachsen-Anhalt, in 1999. The disc was part of a hoard find which included two superbly crafted swords, two flanged axes, two spiral bracelets, and a chisel (Fig. 14.A1).

According to the looters, the Sky Disc was standing upright in the ground and formed a backdrop to the swords and axes which lay across each other. The finders' statements about the find spot and integrity of the hoard were checked by state archaeologists and confirmed both archaeologically and scientifically. The associated finds date the deposition of the Sky Disc to the very end of the central European Early Bronze Age, around 1600 BC.

It is, however, highly likely that the Disc itself had been manufactured some 100 to 200 years earlier. From technical observations, as well as the analysis of the gold inlays, the following five-phase reconstruction of the development of the imagery on the Disc seems the likeliest sequence for the Disc's development (Fig. 14.A2). In the oldest version, an elaborately encoded image reflects a sophisticated command of astronomical knowledge. In subsequent stages this is forgotten and replaced by traditional knowledge, focused on the interaction of the heavenly bodies and the horizon; and finally knowledge gives way to mythology.

PHASE I

The initial image on the Sky Disc was crafted by inlaying gold in the lustrous surface of the disc. It consisted of 32 stars, a crescent moon, and the full moon/sun, and is at first glance a deceptively simple composition. The stars are evenly distributed over the disc to represent the firmament. A cluster of seven stars which represent the Pleiades are the exception. These were already known in antiquity as calendar stars. They disappear on 10 March each year and re-emerge on 17 October, making it possible to calibrate the solar year.

A far more significant event was probably the conjunction between their springtime disappearance and the 4.5 day-old crescent moon shown on the Disc. If this happened, the specialists

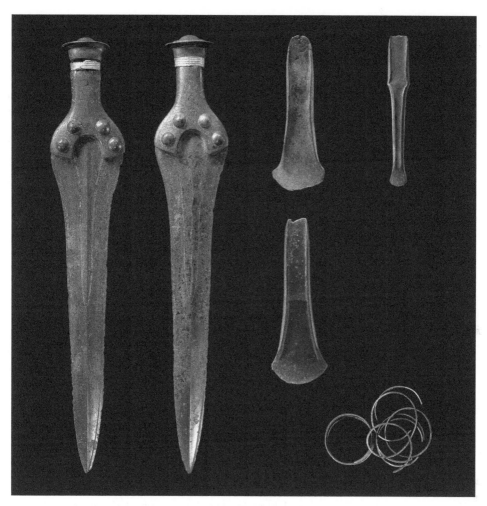

FIG. 14.A1 The double artefact assemblage found with the Sky Disc. Such groups are also found in Early Bronze Age princely tombs. The shape of the magnificent swords was based on Carpathian prototypes, and the gold wire band on the pommel has Scottish parallels. © Landesamt für Denkmalpflege und Archäologie, Sachsen-Anhalt, and Juraj Lipták.

who maintained the type of luni-solar calendar that was then current in the Near East inserted a leap month in order to adjust the shorter lunar to the longer solar year. Moreover, if the course of the moon runs above the Pleiades rather than, as usual, below, a lunar eclipse could be predicted in eight days time, something of no inconsiderable value for prehistoric people.

The 32 stars probably stand for the 32 days which elapsed from the first light of the previous month and the conjunction of Pleiades and crescent moon. The sophistication necessary to design and understand the Disc's initial imagery was the result of widespread commercial and ideological contacts, and the emergence of a central European elite at the beginning of the Bronze Age. The patron who commissioned the Disc, and those who understood its meaning, must have belonged to the topmost group of this elite, who were buried in ostentatious barrows such as those in nearby Leubingen and Helmsdorf. The East Alpine copper used to make the Disc became available in the mid-eighteenth century BC, thus indicating the earliest period during which the Disc could have been created.

Phase II

The Sky Disc fell into new hands and the original image was altered. Its new owners removed two stars and displaced another, while placing two horizon arcs on opposite edges of the disc. The size of the two arcs corresponds to the 82.5° of the horizon traversed by the sun between the summer and winter solstices. The slight shift of the arcs towards the top of the disc allows us to identify the upper rim as north and the lower as south. Thus the crescent lies in the west, and the firmament is shown as if one was looking upwards, as in modern star maps. All of this points to the existence of the concept of the heaven as a hemispherical dome more than a millennium before Thales of Miletus.

Phase III

A feathered sky ship is fitted to the lower rim of the Disc. Such ships appeared as a religious symbol in the Scandinavian Bronze Age around 1600 BC. Its appearance on the Disc alludes to a new mythology which envisaged a boat transporting the sun by day and night. This iconographic shift indicates a radical change in the role of the Disc. It stopped being the bearer of knowledge and instead became an emblem of a new religion. It may be that the Sky Disc was now viewed by a larger public, but the owner who transformed its iconography must have belonged to the ruling elite.

Phase IV

The entire rim of the Disc was crudely perforated, damaging both the boat and the horizon arcs. The perforations were used to mount the Disc on an organic backing, possibly a standard, partially covering the motifs at the edge of the Disc, thus making them unreadable. The new religion had failed, and the Disc now served simply as a solar disc, a motif known in the whole of Bronze Age central Europe. It is probable that like the standards shown on Bronze Age Scandinavian rock art the sun disc standard was paraded in public.

Phase V

In a final ceremonial act, the Disc was irrevocably removed from circulation and deposited in the earth on the summit of the Mittelberg hill. During this process the left horizon arc was ripped off making the Disc unusable. The precious double weapon assemblage which accompanied the Disc is a typical feature of local princely tombs (Fig 14.A2). Thus the Sky Disc represents the absent body of its last princely owner.

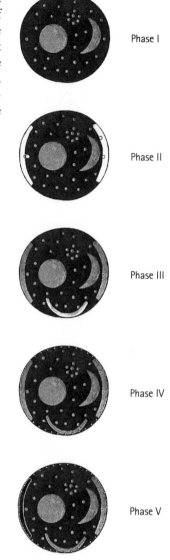

FIG. 14.A2 The five phases of development of the Sky Disc imagery. Three types of gold were used for the inlays of the Disc. The horizon arcs and the displaced star (phase II) as well as the boat (phase III) were made of a different type of gold than the original sun, moon, and stars. The perforation of the Disc's rim damaged the earlier inlays. The 'eastern' arc was probably torn off as part of the deposition ritual (phase V). © Landesamt für Denkmalpflege und Archäologie, Sachsen-Anhalt.

Bibliography

Maraszek, R. 2009. *The Nebra Sky-Disc*. Kleine Reihe zu den Himmelswegen, 2. Halle: Landesamt für Denkmalpflege und Archäologie Sachsen-Anhalt.

Meller, H. 2002. Die Himmelsscheibe von Nebra—ein frühbronzezeitlicher Fund von außergewöhnlicher Bedeutung. *Archäologie in Sachsen-Anhalt* 1: 7–20.

Meller, H. (ed.) 2004. *Der geschmiedete Himmel. Die weite Welt im Herzen Europas vor 3600 Jahren. Begleitband zur Sonderausstellung*. Halle/Stuttgart: Landesamt für Denkmalpflege und Archäologie Sachsen-Anhalt / Konrad Theiss Verlag.

Meller, H. and Bertemes, F. (eds.) 2010. *Der Griff nach den Sternen. Wie Europas Eliten zu Macht und Reichtum kamen. Internationales Symposium in Halle (Saale) 16–21. February 2005*. Tagungen des Landesmuseums für Vorgeschichte Halle (Saale), 5. Halle: Landesamt für Denkmalpflege und Archäologie Sachsen-Anhalt.

CHAPTER 15

BRONZE AGE ROCK ART IN NORTHERN EUROPE: CONTEXTS AND INTERPRETATIONS

JOAKIM GOLDHAHN AND JOHAN LING

Introduction

Scandinavia has the largest concentration of Bronze Age rock art in Europe. There are about thirty thousand registered sites. Approximately 20 per cent of them show figurative art, the rest of them represent abstract and non-figurative images such as cup marks and cupules. As far as we know, most of the figurative art was made from the Middle Bronze Age to the Pre-Roman Iron Age, here 1600–300 cal BC. However, some axe and ship depictions might be a little older. Cup marks seem to belong to an older tradition and have been found in archaeological contexts from the Middle Neolithic B in Scandinavia, at least from 2800 cal BC an onwards. Cup marks were also frequently made after the figurative art went out of fashion, at least to AD 550 (Goldhahn, Fuglestvedt, and Jones 2010a; Lødøen and Mandt 2010).

In this context it is worth mentioning that rock art associated with Mesolithic and Neolithic hunter-gatherers in the middle and northern parts of Scandinavia preceded the Bronze Age traditions. These northern traditions mostly depict prey animals, often in a quite naturalistic fashion, but also boats, humans, and abstract designs (Lødøen and Mandt 2010). It is interesting to note that depictions of boats, the most prominent Bronze Age rock art motif in northern Europe, were frequently made from the Late Mesolithic within the northern traditions, which suggests that this feature and format was first articulated within hunter-gatherer communities in the northernmost part of Europe (Goldhahn 2008a; Goldhahn, Fuglestvedt, and Jones 2010a; Lødøen and Mandt 2010, cf Malmer 1981; Kristiansen and Larsson 2005). This praxis was then transmitted to southern Scandinavia during the second millennium BC where it was evidently expressed in a quite different way (Cornell and Ling 2010: 65). The area of Trøndelag in mid Norway is here of greatest importance because both the northern and southern rock art traditions seem to have been articulated on the same panels in this area. Or rather, this is the best area where in a concrete way you can see how the northern traditions inspired and triggered the southern ones (Sognnes 2008; Goldhahn, Fuglestvedt, and Jones 2010a).

The southern Bronze Age traditions became more occupied with culturally created features, such as ships, weapons, and wagons, or anthropomorphic beings in different social or ritual positions. Still, the format and action of making images on rocks could be seen as a general feature for the Middle and Late Bronze Age societies in the whole of southern Scandinavia (approximately 1600–500 cal BC); from Nordland in Norway in the north to northern Germany in the south, from the Norwegian coast in the west to the Baltic island of Gotland in the east (Fig. 15.1).

Generally speaking, there are at least two different but related customs and memory practices that we can associate with Bronze Age rock art format in southern Scandinavia. First we find areas where rock art was made on open-air panels in the landscape. Then we find areas where rock art was made on portable slabs and incorporated in burial monuments in the form of barrows (see Fig. 15.5). The former areas consist of the coastal area of the southern

FIG. 15.1 A very tentative map covering the southern part of Scandinavia, showing the main distribution of the Bronze Age rock art traditions mentioned in the text: Light grey – 'barrow-and-slab-areas'; grey – 'cairn and open-air rock art areas'; dark grey – mixed areas.

Source: authors.

Table 15.1 Locations of Rock Art in Scandinavia

	Barrows	Cairns
Depictions on bronze items	+	–
Rock art on open-air panels	–	+
Rock art on portable slabs	+	–
Ritual deposits of bronze artefacts	+	–

and middle parts of present-day Norway, as well as Dalsland, Bohuslän, northern Halland, Blekinge, Småland, western Östergötland, Gotland, Södermanland, Uppland, and Västmanland in Sweden; the latter areas consist of Denmark and northern Germany, as well as Scania, the southern parts of Halland, Västergötland, and eastern Östergötland in present-day Sweden (see Fig. 15.1). In the latter areas rock art designs, motifs, and images are frequently found depicted on different bronze items (e.g. Kaul 1998, 2004). Hoards are common. The opposite goes for the areas where rock art was created on open-air sites; here the cairn was the most common monumental burial expression. In the contact zones between these cultural areas, such as Rogaland and Lista in Norway, south-eastern Scania in Sweden, and the Danish island of Bornholm, expressions of both these customs have been found. Exceptions confirm the rule (Goldhahn 2007: 208–9) (Table 15.1).

The Images and Interpretative Trends

Taçon and Chippindale (1998) have suggested that there are two distinctive but related means of gaining an understanding of different rock art traditions, their meaning and significance, which they label the *informed* and *formal methods*. The informed methods are based on anthropological and historical sources, *texts*, while formal methods consist of the information that can be gained by 'simple dirt archaeology', *contexts* (Goldhahn, Fuglestvedt, and Jones 2010a, cf Malmer 1981). For Bronze Age societies in northern Europe, anthropological or historical sources are lacking, and as a consequence the information that we have about the rock-art traditions in this part of the world has to be provided by formal methods and without informants (Bradley 2002, cf Kristiansen and Larsson 2005). This information is based on two foundations, the images themselves, and the different kinds of context with which the rock art is associated. Let us consider the first.

As the saying goes, 'a picture is worth a thousand words'. Still, the highly innovative expression and aesthetic artistry of the Scandinavian Bronze Age rock art are hard to put into words (Fig. 15.2). The images have been hammered out in stone with the emphasis on place, motion, light, form, style, and content. They are performed so concretely that they tend to both trigger and blur our perceptions of them. Another paradox with the figurative rock art is that although the images are fixed in stone, they are full of life, vivid and mobile. They convey motion as often as immobility and this contradiction is so stimulating that one never tires of looking at the panels. Ideals of communication, landscape, and motion seem to have been mixed with highly ritualized symbols. Broadly speaking, the rock art may be described as a selection of images that represent ideal social actions, social positions, and abstract ritual features and matters. Some compositions may be regarded as episodic, others rhapsodic, performed in a repeated but varied and ambiguous way (Ling 2008).

In the following we have tried to make a broad distinction between the different kinds of image that have been depicted on rock in Bronze Age northern Europe (reworked after Ling 2008: 178–9):

- *Mobile wooden devices*: ships, wagons, and chariots
- *Portable items and tools*: weapons, tools, ards (light ploughs), instruments, and other objects made of bronze, wood, stone, or textiles
- *Anthropomorphic beings*: warriors, acrobats, adorants, lur-blowers, or anthropomorphized beings with bodily anomalies such as a beaked face, wings, or enlarged hands or feet
- *Animals*: bulls, cattle, horses, aquatic birds, deer, dogs, wolves, goats, sheep
- *Specific abstract images*: cup marks, sun-wheels or crosses, concentric circles
- *Depictions of social actions, positions and performances*: maritime positions and performances, actions or interactions on or in connections with ships; scenes that represent farming, hunting, fishing, or herding
- *Depictions of antagonism and sex*: combat scenes, intercourse between anthropomorphic beings and between anthropomorphic beings and animals
- *Animals with specific gear or in specific action*: horses, bulls, and horses attached to circular designs, ships, ards

FIG. 15.2 Realistic ship depictions, humans, animals, feet, and abstract designs from panel Skee 1539 in northern Bohuslän. Scale is 1 m.

Source: authors (Ling 2008).

The figurative rock art belonging to these traditions is extremely evocative, and it is hardly surprising that over the years the medium has inspired such a wide range of interpretations. Show a rock art image to five researchers and you end up with at least half a dozen interpretations. Consequently, over the years, the rock art has been subject to many different interpretations, at least as many and innovative and varied as the depictions themselves (see Goldhahn 2008a; Goldhahn, Fuglestvedt, and Jones 2010a; Lødøen and Mandt 2010). It would be neither meaningful nor possible to give an account of all of these different interpretations or trends here. Instead we have tried to list some of the major themes in the perception of this format:

- *Historical events* (Hildebrand 1869)
- *Religious declarations* (Kristiansen and Larsson 2005)
- *Magico-religious incantations* (Almgren 1934; Bengtsson 2010)
- *Cult and cultic action* (Almgren 1934; Kaul 1998; 2004)
- *Eschatology* (Goldhahn 1999; Kaul 2004)
- *Socio-ritual initiations or celebrations of seasons, actions, genders* (Yates 1993; Kristiansen 2004; Wahlgren 2002; Coles 2005; Goldhahn 2007)
- *Social positions and antagonism* (Bertilsson 1987; Sognnes 2001; Vogt 2012)
- *Communicative and spatial aspects of landscape* (Nordbladh 1980; Bertilsson 1987; Sognnes 2001; Myhre 2004; Coles 2005; Nord 2009)
- *Semiotic approaches* (Nordbladh 1980; Fredell 2003; Vogt 2012)
- *Landscape, rituals, and cosmology* (Sognnes 2001; Wahlgren 2002; Goldhahn 2007; Bradley 2009)
- *Landscape phenomenology* (Tilley 2004)
- *Rock art, social praxis, and landscapes/seascapes* (Coles 2000; 2005; Sognnes 2001; Myhre 2004; Goldhahn 2007; Ling 2008; Goldhahn, Fuglestvedt, and Jones 2010b)
- and so on…

Rock Art Chronology

Since the latter part of the nineteenth century the dating of the southern Scandinavian rock art has been related to the Bronze Age and this notion has been confirmed by later research. The first Bronze Age dating of the rock art was proposed by Bror Emil Hildebrand (1869), whose main contribution was a stylistic comparison between typologically determined swords and copies of rock art sword images made out of plaster. Hildebrand's comparative chronological method was accepted as a dating norm by other researchers (Kaul 1998; 2004; Sognnes 2001; Myhre 2004; Vogt 2006; Ling 2008).

Thus the comparative chronological approach put forward by Hildebrand has been advocated and developed over the years, and two main directions can be distinguished. One trend focuses on just a few qualitative elements and mainly uses and compares ship renderings on bronze items or from burials to determine the chronology of ship images on the rocks (e.g. Glob 1969). The most recent contribution of this trend is Flemming Kaul's comparative study of 'Ships on bronzes' (Kaul 1998; 2004). His comprehensive approach has been cited and advocated by a number of scholars for its method as well as its outcome (Fredell 2003; Coles 2005; Ling 2008). Other scholars have criticized these attempts and argued that the taxonomies simply confirm the Montelius typology, where the bronze items determine the chronological order of the rock art (e.g. Nordbladh 1980, also Goldhahn 1999; Sognnes 2001; Wahlgren 2002; Myhre 2004).

The other 'comparative' school tends to rely more on typological and/or quantitative records of styles and techniques, such as single-lined, double-lined, contour-lined, pecked or entirely pecked ship hulls, etcetera (Malmer 1981; Mandt 1991), but also to some extent on shore displacement to determine the age of the open-air ship images (e.g. Sognnes 2001; 2003). In our opinion these taxonomies are extremely complicated, sometimes to a tiresome degree, with far too many classes and subclasses of ship renderings (e.g. Malmer 1981, cf Kaul 1998: 76).

Recently two independent approaches to dating rock art—shore displacement and comparative chronology—have been applied to the same rock art material in northern Bohuslän, Sweden, by Johan Ling (2008). This study broadly confirms Kaul's comparative study of 'Ships on bronzes', graves, and rock art (Fig. 15.3). Recent analogous research on the rock art from Uppland, situated in the Mälar valley in Sweden (Coles 2000), seems to confirm previous results, and it is encouraging to note that these different yet independent methods have a similar outcome (Ling forthcoming).

In the following we will highlight some of the most prominent contexts in which rock art has been created during the Bronze Age. Thereafter we will try to draw attention to some current theoretical and interpretative trends within Bronze Age rock art research in northern Europe.

Rock Art and Landscape

When working with rock art in northern Europe, it is important to remember shore displacement and land uplift. It is, however, difficult to grasp the fact that the ice sheet once covered the whole of the Scandinavian Penninsula, and that some areas, like the ones in the northern Baltic sea, were subjected to greater pressure of the ice sheet and therefore a more rapid rebound and shore displacement than others. In short, some areas with rock art have had less shore displacement than others.

However, during most of the twentieth century many scholars have tended to ignore this fact and the outcome of these studies has therefore been rather misleading (e.g. Almgren 1934; Bertilsson 1987; Fredell 2003; Vogt 2012). Recent research that has accounted for these facts in Scandinavia clearly demonstrates a maritime location of the figurative rock art sites in the prehistoric landscape. This goes for both the northern and the southern traditions (Coles 2000, 2005; Sognnes 2001, 2003; Myhre 2004; Ling 2008). Still, the practice of making rock art in Bronze Age landscapes probably had numerous dimensions and intentions.

Even if shore displacement and altered landscapes have not been the main issue for rock art research in northern Europe, other approaches to landscape were introduced quite early.

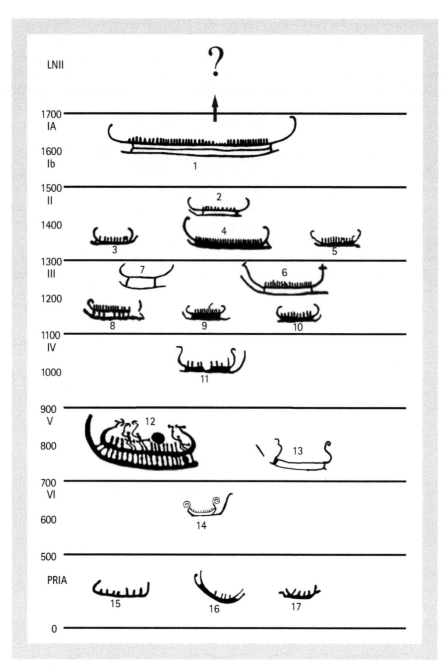

FIG. 15.3 The chronological outline of rock art ships from the Tanum area in northern Bohuslän, Sweden. Ship images with inward-turned prows dominate during the Middle Bronze Age, about 1600–1100 cal BC. During the Late Bronze Age, 1100–500 cal BC, the ship images were made with outward-turned prows ending up in animal heads. During the Early Iron Age, 500–300 cal BC, the ship images were made with a symmetrical shape.

Source: authors (Ling 2008).

For instance, researchers such as Gro Mandt (1991), Jarl Nordbladh (1980), and Kalle Sognnes (2001) stressed various approaches to do with location, visibility, social communication, and accessibility in the landscape. The notion of seascape was first introduced by John Coles, who has discussed many aspects of south Scandinavian rock art and stressed the conscious choice of making rock art by the shore (Coles 2005). This concept has been furthered elaborated by scholars such as Lise Myhre (2004), Ling (2008; forthcoming), and Richard Bradley (2009). Many Scandinavian archaeologists have been inspired by the 'new landscape archaeology': for instance, Bradley's influential work (1997; 2009) has stimulated many later attempts in Scandinavia (Sognnes 2001; Myhre 2004, see Goldhahn 2008a). In the meantime, Chris Tilley has explored the phenomenology of rock art landscapes (Tilley 2004). Moreover, the works on rock art as a social and ritual action in the landscape have contributed on many levels (e.g. Goldhahn 1999; 2007; Sognnes 2001; Wahlgren 2002), and some of these aspects will be discussed later in this essay.

Rock Art and Seascapes

In order to understand the original setting of the rock art in areas that have been subjected to extensive shore displacements in northern Europe since the Bronze Age, it may help to look at rock art from areas where shore displacement has been less extensive. All these studies highlight the fact that similar societal norms appear to have governed the spatial choice of making rock art in a maritime context during the Bronze Age. Thus the shore or coast seems to have been the major feature towards which the rock art was deliberately oriented, a relationship that is far more frequent and substantial than agricultural features or settlements (Coles 2000; 2005; Myhre 2004; Ling 2008). The sea was present and affected the location and making of the numerous and varied configurations of ship depictions on the rocks, and indicates a general social announcement or transition towards the maritime realm (Table 15.2).

A good example to demonstrate this maritime location is the rock art from the Norwegian west coast. Here the shore displacement has been very moderate, and the relationship between sea and rock art is still very obvious (Mandt 1991; Myhre 2004). At Unneset and Leirvåg in the Sogn and Fjordane districts, a complex of rock art panels, along with several cairns of various shapes and forms, is situated just a few metres above today's shoreline, typically around 3 to 5 m (Mandt 1991). This is interesting because some scholars claim that at the beginning of the Bronze Age the surface of the sea was about 5 m higher than at present and then descended to 3 m above sea level by the end of the period, indicating that most of the rock art was originally placed near the shoreline (Sognnes 2003). The sea is everywhere present and was undoubtedly the major consideration behind the placing of rock art.

Gro Mandt argues that the archaeological material from this area reveals an intentional and horizontal subdivision of the landscape that reflects different activities as well as identity and cosmology (Mandt 1991). Rock art and burial monuments in the form of cairns are located in an outer zone on islands and isthmuses, and settlements in an inner and a middle zone represented by the fjords. From this, Mandt concludes that the outer 'liminal' zone, where the maritime rock art is to be found, may have reproduced seasonal activity of an

Table 15.2 The Relationship Between Different Types of Rock Art Images in Areas where BA Rock Art is Present in Scandinavia (after Goldhahn et al. 2010a)

Area	Cup marks	Ship	Human	Animal	Feet	Sun/circle	Other
Bornholm	3523	78	3		20	26	13
S-E Scania	2762	167	51	35	233	60	96
Östergötland	5619	1558	275	544	334	204	394
Västergötland	2060	73	7	6	281	51	7
Uppland	19000	1665	190	185	309	128	612
Bohuslän	27338	7721	3556	1522	533	610	1795
Sogn og Fjordane	2484	165	5	4	2	13	21
Trøndelag	2475	517	57	254	561	316	94

economic, socio-political, and socio-religious character (Mandt 1991: 39). Rock art also occurs in the inner and middle zone, but is then located on higher ground, such as the rock art site at Bakke in the Hardanger district or Bruteigsteinen in the Etne district (Lødøen and Mandt 2010). The rock art in these places is often more varied and structured, and it includes more arranged and abstract features than the maritime ones, such as concentric circles, sun symbols, humans, processions, ships, animals, trees, etcetera. This suggests that rock art locations situated closer to settlement areas were related to a different ritual sphere and praxis.

Similar relationship between rock art and sea, sometimes in close connection with burials, can be demonstrated in the Stavanger area, about 200 km south of the Sogn and Fjordarne districts, an area renowned for its numerous Bronze Age remains (Myhre 2004). In addition to the rock art, barrows, and bronze items, it has one of the largest numbers of flint daggers from the Late Neolithic and Early Bronze Age. In her dissertation, Lise Myhre emphasizes the close relationship between the Bronze Age remains and the sea (Myhre 2004). Almost all of the complex rock art sites in the Stavanger area have a maritime location, on islands, isthmuses, and straits. The ship is the dominant but by no means the only image.

We need to remember, however, that this pattern is also evident in other areas of Scandinavia where the shore displacement has been less significant. One of these is the Simrishamn area in south-east Scania, Sweden. In addition to the figurative rock art, the area has yielded some of the most numerous finds and monuments related to the Bronze Age, among them the famous Bredarör cairn on Kivik with its elaborated rock art (Randsborg 1993; Goldhahn 2009). On lower ground, close to the sea, ships and axes are the main iconic features, and on higher ground, especially on the great site of Järrestad, feet (footsoles) are the most represented image along with humans, animals, abstract design, and sun symbols. The altitude of the rock art in the shore area ranges in general from about 7 to 15 m above sea level. This is rather interesting because some scholars claim that at the beginning of the Bronze Age the sea level was about 2–3 m higher than at present, and that it had fallen back to 1 m above sea level by the end of the period. However that may be, even if the shore displacement had not affected the area so much, the sea's presence at the rock art sites would still be very obvious (Ling 2008). From this it is clear that the rock art in this area was created in succession from the higher ground down towards the sea, or vice versa. And as the Norwegian case above, the images from the different areas seem to reflect its placing in a very pragmatic way.

Turning now to the rock art areas that have been more exposed to the shore displacement phenomena, such as Østfold in south-east Norway and northern Bohuslän on the west coast of Sweden, we find both problems and possibilities. This is the area where Oscar Almgren did his ground-breaking work on rock art and cultic praxis. His 'terrestrial' theories shaped the rock art discourse in northern Europe for the major part of the twentieth century. Almgren was seduced by the contemporary connection between rock art and agrarian fields in the landscape, basically because he had poor and erroneous facts about shore displacement. According to Almgren, the ships on the rocks were not depicting real ships but rather 'terrestrial cult ships' that could be connected to Indo-European-influenced fertility rites in the landscape (Almgren 1934). However, recent studies have shown that Almgren's theory of an agrarian connection with rock art is wrong, and they demonstrated its maritime location (Coles 2005; Ling 2008, cf Fredell 2003; Vogt 2012).

At the moment, the only area where a profound rock art study has been made in relation to the shore displacement is the Tanum area in northern Bohuslän, Sweden, an area that has been on the UNESCO World Heritage list since 1994. Here Ling has conducted extensive empirical investigations (Ling 2008). By measuring the altitude of a large number of rock art sites, it could be shown that the pattern discussed above also seems to hold true for northern Bohuslän (Fig. 15.4).

According to these studies of the shore displacement phenomena in this part of the world, the sea level was about 16–18 m higher at the beginning of the Middle Bronze Age, c.1600 cal BC, and about 10–12 m higher at the end, c.500 cal BC (Ling 2008). About 70 per cent of the rock art is found within 100 m of the sea. There are also many rock art sites, about 30 per cent, on higher ground closer to areas suitable for agriculture. Once again the figurative art preferred in the different parts of the landscape seems rather to be selected in a pragmatic way. For instance, the largest figurative rock art sites dominated by ship images were located close to the shore, while rock art sites with large human figures, as well as most of the cup-mark sites, were placed on higher ground (see Fig. 15.4).

In this context it is notable that the rock art in general seems to have been sited on the perimeter of the inner skerries in rather sheltered places, close to or on the shore of rather large inlets, bays, lagoons, or natural harbours, or at strikes, isthmuses, peninsulas, and small islands. Moreover, a majority of the rock art was made on panels oriented towards the seascape (Coles 2005; Ling 2008). In this communicative maritime location of rock art in northern Bohuslän, the domination of ship depictions on the panels is evident (see Table 15.2). Consequently, the high numbers of rock-art sites in northern Bohuslän might be interpreted as traces of a kind of seasonal meeting ground—'a third space'; a maritime space for different social, economic, and ritual interactions, transactions, and initiations, used by both a domestic and a non-domestic public, preferably on a seasonal basis (Kaul 1998; Kristiansen 2004; Coles 2005; Ling 2008).

Similar societal norms appear to have governed the spatial choice of making rock art in the south Scandinavian landscape during the Bronze Age. These norms reflect both ideal social actions and positions in the landscape, as well as highly ritualized performances, scenes, and cosmologies. The combination of rock art and an expanse of water seem to be a common theme in northern Europe. Indeed, the element of water appears to be common to rock art in general; for instance, the ship-dominated rock art panels in south-west Uppland were seemingly made successively from the water's edge up to the shore (Coles 2000; Ling forthcoming). Thus the shore or coast seems to have been the major feature towards which the rock art was deliberately oriented, a relationship that is far more frequent and substantial than agricultural features or settlements (Ling 2008).

The sea was very present in some of these landscapes and this affected the location and making of the numerous and varied configurations of ship depictions on the rocks, and indicates a general social announcement or transition towards the maritime realm (see Table 15.2, Figs. 15.2 and 15.4). In this context it seems that the places with maritime-dominated images on the rocks may be traces of different forms of maritime movements, actions, initiations, reflections, rules, and norms. We suggest that the rock art was made before, during, or after different ritualized maritime practices, such as trade and communications, warfare, maritime ceremonies and initiations, and even boat-building (e.g. Ling 2008: 220–30).

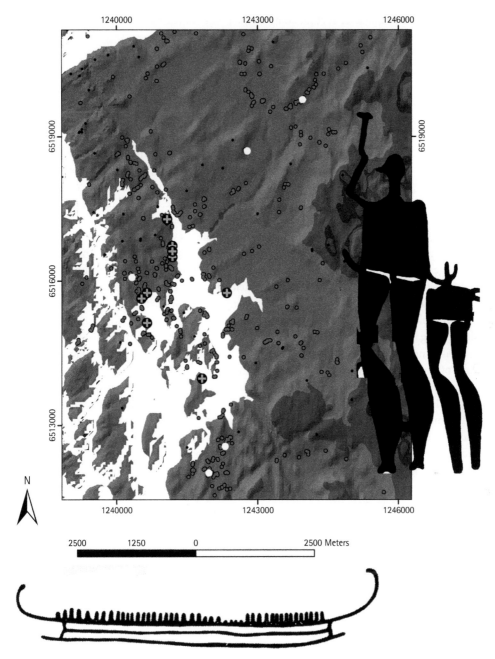

FIG. 15.4 The distribution of rock art panels in the Tanum area in western Sweden (grey dots) showing oversized human images located on higher ground (white dots) and shore-connected panels that include most ship depictions (crosses).

Source: authors (Ling 2008).

This leads us to consider further some of the other contexts where rock art was created during the Bronze Age.

Excavating Rock Art

Traditionally, most focus has been directed towards the rock art images and their connotations, and less emphasis has been placed on clarifying the nature and chronology of the action at the panels. Instead of interpreting or connecting the images to broad cosmological, political, religious or mythological notions, some excavation results may broaden our understanding of rock art's socio-ritual role in the landscape (Goldhahn 2007; 2008a; Bengtsson and Ling 2007; Bengtsson 2010). Thus whereas some sites have displayed numerous artefacts and features both ritual and domestic in character, others have shown little or no activity.

The general outcome of these excavations is that comparatively small and less complex rock art sites located on higher ground have yielded a large number of prehistoric finds and features that correspond to the typological dating of the rock art images, while larger and more complex rock art sites turn out to be more or less 'empty' (Bengtsson 2010). For example, investigations at three less complex rock art sites on higher ground in Tossene parish on Sotenäset, northern Bohuslän, have uncovered a spectacular number of artefacts and features of both ritual and practical character (Bengtsson and Ling 2007); stone pavements, hearths, postholes, and heaps of fire-cracked stones have been recorded just beside the rock art panels. Traces of metallurgical activity, such as fragments of tuyères, furnace linings, crucibles, and moulds have also been found by the panels. Moreover, radiocarbon dating of the finds has demonstrated a clear chronological connection between the prehistoric activity and the images on the rocks, with dates that mostly range from about 1500 to 300 cal BC (Bengtsson and Ling 2007), thus corresponding to the period when most of the rock art in this region was made (Ling 2008). In contrast, excavations at larger, monumental rock art sites with more communicative locations in the landscape, have yielded very sparse finds and no concrete prehistoric features (Bengtsson 2010).

Interesting finds and features have also been recorded in the rock on the Danish island of Bornholm. Extensive areas have been excavated at a major rock-art site located on higher ground at Madsebakke on the island. Similar features and finds to those recorded in Bohuslän, such as stone pavements, quartz, pottery, and flint, have turned up just in front of the panels. Moreover, observations of large postholes in a row on the adjacent arable land, which can be stratigraphically dated to the Bronze Age, suggest that the art panels could have been framed by some kind of wooden henge. The fencing of the rock art at Madsebakke clearly suggests that the knowledge and memory practice associated with the rock art was esoteric and restricted (e.g. Goldhahn 2007). There is, however, no direct dating of the postholes yet to confirm their contemporaneity with the rock art.

The results from these excavations at rock art sites is to a large extent in line with those of more than 25 years of large-scale contract archaeology in Sweden. The most well-investigated area in Sweden, and indeed among the most well-investigated Bronze Age regions in northern Europe, is Norrköping, located at the estuary of the Motala river in eastern Östergötland. Here, settlements, rock art, and burial grounds are found within sight of each other (Wahlgren 2002; Nilsson 2010). Heaps of fire-cracked stone, hearths, and house structures have been recorded close to the panels. However, none of these features seems to correspond chronologically to the rock art: most of the art here dates to the Middle and Late Bronze Age, and these features are either earlier or later than this. Nevertheless, just about 500–1,000 m from the more complex panels, a large domestic area including about fifty contemporary house structures has been excavated (Wahlgren 2002; Nilsson 2010).

Results from contract archaeology in other areas in Scandinavia appear to confirm these patterns. It has, for instance, been possible to link cup-mark sites to contemporary Bronze Age settlements, but so far figurative images or complex panels are absent. The latter seem to occur some 400–800 m from contemporary settlements (Goldhahn 2008a; Ling 2008).

Seen from this perspective, the patterns described from 'dirt archaeology' at rock art sites can be interpreted as reflections of different kinds of social and ritual praxis. At settlements, or nearby, different cup-marks were used for smaller offerings and rituals, leaving traces of pots, burnt clay, and so on, but at larger, more complex sites the production and reproduction of rock art images were the main reasons for attending these places (Wahlgren 2002). Maybe the latter more complex figurative sites, such as Madsebakke, were associated with some kind of ancestral knowledge, though they either seem to be managed and kept clean or, sometimes, even fenced off by wooden constructions. Perhaps these panels were associated with esoteric knowledge and bounded by a taboo against leaving traces from more deadly human beings, only to be visited at certain times, and in the context of specific ceremonies and rituals (Goldhahn 2007; 2008a). In short, on the less complex sites making rock art was a means to other ends, whereas on the complex sites making rock art seems to have been an end in itself—the medium was the message.

Picturing the Dead

The placing of art in the landscape is indeed vital for our understanding of its meaning and significance, yet it is hard to relate the images to their original social and ritual context. As a result, our interpretation of the contexts where the rock art was made and used tends to becomes as ambiguous and varied as the images themselves. The exception to this rule is represented by the rare cases where rock art is found in association with, or incorporated into, different kinds of burial monument (Randsborg 1993; Goldhahn 1999; Myhre 2004). Many of these examples of burial rock art have been found to be 'freshly made' when they were discovered. Sometimes even the hammer-stone that was used for making the art has been found deposited in the same context, suggesting that the art was created as an integral part of various death rituals (Goldhahn 2007). Altogether there are about 350 examples of rock art known from different kinds of burial context in Scandinavia. As with the more ordinary rock art on 'open-air panels' in the landscape, most of them consist of cup-marks. Once again, at least two distinct traditions can be distinguished, one associated with abstract art, for example, cup-marks, the other with figurative art. The former has a longer tradition than the latter. The oldest find of cup-marks in burial contexts dates to the Middle Neolithic B, about 2800–2350 cal BC, while the later figurative art is associated with the Middle and Late Bronze Age, here 1600–500 cal BC.

The five major finds of rock art from burial monuments have all been revisited in the last few years, including the Bredarör cairn at Kivik, the Sagaholm barrow, the Hjortekorg cairn, and the rock art from Ör in Sweden, as well as Mjeltehaugen in western Norway (see Randsborg 1993; Kaul 1998; 2004; Goldhahn 1999; 2007; 2008b; 2009; Lødøen and Mandt 2010; Skoglund 2010). Besides these case studies, Myhre (2004) has analysed the portable burial slabs from Rogaland, while Kaul (2004) has discussed the finds that have turned up in Denmark since Peter Glob's (1969) indispensable survey.

The relationship between rock art and burials is also very evident in the landscape (see Nordbladh 1980). In contemporary Sweden about 18 per cent of the rock art sites are situated within 15 m of prehistoric remains that are interpreted as grave structures (Goldhahn 2008a). The same pattern is noticeable in Bohuslän (Ling 2008) and western Norway (Mandt 1991; Lødøen and Mandt 2010), and can also be demonstrated in other rock art areas.

As mentioned above, most of the rock art that has been documented in burial contexts in Scandinavia seems to be made explicitly for the burial ritual itself. Sometimes this has demanded careful planning and the gathering of large numbers of people. The enormous Bredarör cairn required more than 15,000 working days to complete, which equals 43 persons working full time for a year (Goldhahn 2008b; 2009). Another example is the slabs from Mjeltehaugen from Sunnmøre in western Norway, which were quarried in Trøndelag some 250 km to the north-east (Goldhahn 2008b; Lødøen and Mandt 2010).

The most informative burial context in this respect is the fascinating Sagaholm barrow from the middle part of southern Sweden (Goldhahn 1999). The mound, 22–24 m in diameter and 4 m high, probably dates to Period II or III, 1500–1100 cal BC (Fig. 15.5). The art was found on the outside of the middle kerb, made of specifically selected red sandstone that was quarried some 30 km north of the barrow. The mound was badly damaged at the time and about half was destroyed. The remaining kerb consisted of 46 slabs of which one third were decorated with art images, altogether 31 horses, nine ships, four human beings, two cup-marks, and some abstract designs of unknown connotation (Goldhahn 1999).

After the burial ritual came to an end and the creation of the monument was complete, the rock art was incorporated into the barrow, never to be seen again, which shows that it was not made with the purpose of being admired by the descendents of the deceased. Because of the intricate building sequence of the barrow, it has been possible to link the time depth of the monument to the time rhythm of the burial ritual, where the very act of making the rock

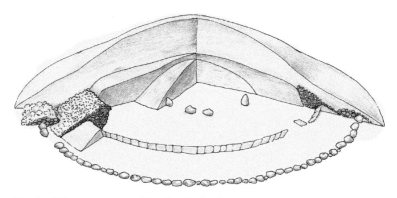

FIG. 15.5 The building sequence of the Sagaholm barrow.

Source: authors (Goldhahn 2007).

art seems to be linked to the transitional phase of the burial ritual (Goldhahn 1999; 2008b). After this phase was finished, the rock art was covered with a plain layer of sand and a thin stone packing layer, before the art was sealed from the world.

The rock art images in Sagaholm, with an overwhelming emphasis on horses and ships, seem to relate the eschatology of the deceased to the cosmology of the Bronze Age (e.g. Goldhahn 1999; Kaul 2004).

Theories about Rock Art, Agency, and Society

It has been the custom to argue that the rock art seems to display norms of social inequality, and this has been taken to indicate that it was a symbolic tool of the elite (Fredell 2003; Kristiansen and Larsson 2005; Vogt 2006). For instance, some scholars have suggested that less complex sites were associated with 'common people' and offerings conducted at their settlements, whereas complex sites were associated with the 'elite'—in other words chiefs and/or warriors (Bertilsson 1987; Vogt 2006). There is, however, much that contradicts this view. First and foremost, it is hard to link the more complex sites to any settlement or any other context that supports this interpretation (Ling and Cornell 2010). Second, if we take the prevailing notions of Bronze Age elites and chiefs as advocated by many scholars (Kristiansen and Larsson 2005), such as strict control of society's political, religious, and economic means of power, we would expect both the amount and the expression of rock art to be more normative and placed at more inaccessible locations in the landscape. However, the opposite seems to have been the case: most of the rock art has an open, communicative location and a varied figurative expression. There are other monuments, features, or items, such as cairns, stone settings, barrows, ritual paraphernalia made of bronze, such as lurs, shields, helmets, and so on, that seem to come closer to 'chiefly' demands of closeness, control, and privacy.

There are, however, other rules of conduct that favour a more confined agency regarding the production and consumption of rock art. About 90–95 per cent of the human images demonstrate masculine traits (Nordbladh 1989: 325). In this light, Timothy Yates (1993) suggests that the rock art may demonstrate male pubertal rites: the stylistic awareness of the male body and typical male warrior's equipment point to the production of the rock art being closely connected with masculine agencies. However, the general maritime location and content of the Bronze Age rock art may rather reveal the agency of a special task-oriented group. A tempting assumption in line with these observations is that rock art may have been produced in accordance with maritime, martial 'pubertal' or 'initiation' rites (into esoteric societies or into knowledge and skills), that is, rites for maritime tasks such as sea ventures, long-distance travel, or maritime warfare (Ling 2008).

Another concrete suggestion around rock art and agency has been put forward by one of us in another context (Goldhahn 2007). The argument here is that the metalsmith and the 'rock-smith' could have been related to the same social institution as ritual specialists. There is, in fact, much in favour of this hypothesis on those sites where clear traces of metallurgy have been found adjacent to rock art sites (Goldhahn 2007). For example, there is evidence for rock art been made on obvious soapstone quarries that were used by smiths for making moulds for bronze objects (Chapter 14). Among other things, this might explain the strong resemblance between the images made on rocks and those on bronze items (see Malmer 1981; Kaul 1998).

Moreover, based on the so-called feet (footsole) images, it has been suggested that these were related to life-course rituals. Large 'adult' feet do occur, but many of those depicted are small, often only 15 to 26 cm in length. If they resemble 'real' feet these depictions would correspond to shoe sizes 23–38, which are usually found on children, young teenagers, or women. This is a rather widespread pattern that has been demonstrated through three independent studies from different rock art areas of Scandinavia, such as Östergötland and Kronoberg in Sweden, and Trøndelag in Norway. Maybe the foot images were pecked as a confirmation of the initiates' newly achived status and as insignia of their insight into the esoteric knowledge that was associated with these places and media (Goldhahn; 2008a). The placing of rock art away from settled areas might be another indication that these places were used for transmitting and transforming different kinds of esoteric knowledge. This hypothesis can hardly be proved, but if we accept it as a starting point the rock art could be interpreted as a trace of different initiation ceremonies when young people started their journey to adolescence and/or adulthood. Moreover, it stresses the importance of and need for studying *how* similar restricted information was formulated and transformed, rather than concentrating our minds, efforts, and interpretations in the meagre hunt for *finding out the 'original' meaning and content* of different rock art images (e.g. Nordbladh 1980; Goldhahn 2007; Ling 2008).

Rock Art Practice and Cosmology

Several scholars have highlighted the religious and symbolic aspects of the rock art images, and there is no doubt that these images, especially those depicting certain ritual elements, should be considered in terms of a more symbolic intention (Kaul 1998; 2004). But if, for instance, the ship was such a strong religious symbol during the Bronze Age in northern Europe (see Table 15.2), why was it not dispersed more evenly over the Scandinavian Peninsula? The same argument could apply to the rock art depictions of armed humans, in other words warriors, claimed by some scholars to represent gods (e.g. Fredell 2003; Kristiansen and Larsson 2005). If these features were meant to represent general religious icons and gods during the Bronze Age in northern Europe, why were they not depicted on open-air panels, boulders, or rocks in areas such as southern Halland, Scania, Västergötland, Tjust, and Kronoberg in Sweden, or on Jutland, Zealand, and Bornholm in Denmark?

What is clear is that areas with numerous rock art ships are generally located close to the present or former shores of the sea, lakes, or other waterways (Kaul 1998; Ling 2008). In this context the rock art could be regarded as an intentionally active medium connected to certain praxis in the landscape, not merely as depictions of an abstract cosmology in the hands of the higher strata of society. Could such socio-ritual actions, described by anthropologists as 'magic' or 'magical rituals', be connected to the action behind rock art? According to scholars such as Bronislaw Malinowski (1922), magic is an active social process, mediating between society's ideological 'structure' and pragmatic 'individual' action in the landscape.

Thus, magic, in contrast to religious rituals, is intended to alter and transform social positions in the landscape, and to bring about some desired practical result without the interference of supernatural beings (Malinowski 1922: 105). Magic can then be said to denote the belief in the individual's own powers, while religion shows a belief in immaterial powers. Following this distinction, it is clear that Bronze Age rock art in Scandinavia is more in line with a magical than a religious perception of form (Ling and Cornell 2010).

Moreover, following from this, it seems more interesting to highlight specific local or regional traits and thereby discuss the differences, nuances, and articulations between the regions in northern Europe than to state a general 'system' of religion and cosmology (Wahlgren 2002; Myhre 2004, see Kristiansen and Larsson 2005). Certain elements and aspects from these actions seem to have been common to the whole of northern Europe, albeit articulated and performed with different material, monumental, or figurative content and structure (Goldhahn 2007; Bradley 2009). The 'maritime' location of the cairns and rock art versus the 'terrestrial' location of the earthen barrows and bronze items is one example (see Fig. 15.1). Here, if we may speculate a little more, these differences may have important implications. Burying the dead in the agrarian landscape, in earthen barrows, may be an important statement. But, in the same way, burying the dead overlooking the sea inside stone cairns, occasionally even on small islands, is an altogether different statement (Goldhahn 2008b). The agrarian connection may point to a connection between the land and the ancestors; the maritime cairn indicates a relation between the dead, the animated world of stones, and the sea (Bradley 2009). Certain elements and practices seem to have been common to the whole of southern Scandinavia, but for us it is evident that these similarities must be viewed against the pronounced and articulated differences.

Rock Art as Social Format

As we have seen, interesting ideas have been proposed regarding rock art and its connection to ritual, religion, and cosmology. However, what tends to be forgotten when using all these different concepts and ideas when explaining the art is the rock art medium itself (Cornell and Ling 2010). Thus, the making of rock art establishes a particular format, a particular sphere of social action, which cannot be reduced to broad notions such as 'cosmology', 'oral tradition', or 'ideology'. In itself, the interaction with the raw material, the stone, is of key significance (see Chapter 14). For instance, the average ship depiction takes about 10 to 12 hours to produce (Ling 2008: 165). Thus the technological and material prerequisites for the making of the images imply the existence of certain skills and knowledge about the nature of the rock, such as its composition, hardness, reaction, and reflection. Moreover, the highly elaborate images call for an 'aesthetic' knowledge and insight regarding perspectives, conduct, space, form, composition, and content (Coles 2005: 9). And, of greatest importance, the surface pecked into the stone was hard to alter and could remain relatively stable over centuries.

This suggests that rock art can be conceived as a particular format of communication, which was certainly affected by other formats, but also had a direct effect through the media it was exploring and communicating with—stone. The surface cut in stone could well have been the point of departure for a communication, not only the passive result of verbal communication. There was of course an oral discourse regarding the production and consumption of rock art. However, rock art should not simply be regarded as a sub-product of oral discourses. Oral discourse may have been one important source of inspiration; but there are more sources of inspiration that need to be included such as materiality, audiovisual experience, and social action (e.g. Goldhahn 2002). Rock art, materialized images in the rock, persistent and stable, has unquestionably functioned far more as a source and producer of social information than as a passive reflection of an 'oral' model. For instance, in many 'oral' societies the transmission of information, knowledge, and ideology is, in fact, one of a material or gestural nature (Cornell and Ling 2010; Ling and Cornell 2010).

Conclusion

It is hard and maybe erroneous to try to connect the making and use of rock art in northern Europe during the Bronze Age to some general notions about cosmology or religion. If that were the case, the rock art images from northern Europe, their expressions, aesthetic content, and geographical distribution, would be more homogeneous. The rock art material discussed here seems too diverse, manifold, and ambiguous for such conclusions. Instead we find that this format was grounded and formed in specific regional and even local traditions, sometimes embodied in specific places and their distinguishing attributes and qualities. Cosmology was indeed a necessary guiding light in the understanding of the world during the Bronze Age, but these specific world views were very seldom reflected or expressed directly through the use of stone media. Rock art seems not to be made to contemplate the world itself; it was rather made and associated with distinct ritualized practices such as maritime actions, performance, and positions, death rituals, quarrying, or initiation rituals.

It follows from this that in future we should be more concerned with discovering these and other ritualized practices and examining how they engendered the life-course for different people during the Bronze Age—the craftsmen, the warriors, the children and adolescents, those who travelled to exchange gifts, treasures, and stocks, the ritual specialists, and so on. In short, we should focus on how the rock art medium enabled people to undertake and change their journey through life, and through death.

Bibliography

Almgren, O. (1934). *Nordische Felszeichnungen als Religiöse Urkunden*. Frankfurt am Main: Verlag Moritz Diesterweg.

Bengtsson, L. (2010). 'To excavate images: some results from the Tanum Rock Art project 1997–2004', in Å. Fredell, K. Kristiansen, and F. Criado Boado (eds), *Representations and Communications: creating an Archaeological Matrix of late prehistoric Rock Art*. Oxford: Oxbow Books, [116]-131.

Bengtsson, L. and Ling, J. (2007). 'Scandinavia's most finds associated rock art site', *Adoranten*, 40–50.

Bertilsson, U. (1987). *The Rock Carvings of Northern Bohuslän: Spatial Structures and Social Symbols*. Stockholm Studies in Archaeology 7. Stockholm: Stockholm University.

Bradley, R. (1997). *Rock Art and the Prehistory of Atlantic Europe: Signing the Land.* London: Routledge.

—— (2002). *Working Without Informants: Field Studies of Rock Art in Later Prehistory Europe.* Canberra: Centre of Archaeological Research, The Australian National Museum.

—— (2009). *Image and Audience: Rethinking Prehistoric Art.* Oxford: Oxford University Press.

Coles, J. M. (2000). *Patterns in a Rocky Land: Rock Carvings in South-West Uppland, Sweden.* AUN, 27. Uppsala: Uppsala University.

—— (2005). *Shadows of a Northern Past: Rock Carvings of Bohuslän and Østfold.* Oxford: Oxbow Books.

Cornell, P. and Ling, J. (2010). 'Rock art as social format', in J. Goldhahn, I. Fuglestvedt, and A. Jones, A. (eds.), *Changing Pictures: Rock Art Traditions and Visions in Northern Europe.* Oxford: Oxbow Books, 73–87.

Fredell, Å. (2003). *Bildbroar. Figurativ bildkommunikation av ideologi och kosmologi under sydskandinavisk bronsålder och förromersk järnålder*, Gotarc Serie B (Gothenburg Archaeological Theses), 25. Göteborg: Göteborg University.

Glob, P. V. 1969. *Danmarks helleristningar*, Jysk Arkeæologisk Selskabs Skrifter, VII. Aarhus: Jutland Archaeological Society.

Goldhahn, J. (1999). *Sagaholm—hällristningar och gravritual*, Studia Archaeologica Universitatis Umensis 11. Umeå: Umeå University.

—— (2002). 'Roaring rocks—an audio-visual perspective on hunther-gatherer engravings in Northern Sweden and Scandinavia', *Norwegian Archaeological Review*, 35/1: 29–61.

—— (2007). *Dödens hand—en essä om brons- och hällsmed.* Gotarc Serie C (Gothenburg Archaeological Theses), 65. Göteborg: Göteborg University.

—— (2008a). 'Rock art research in northernmost Europe, 2000–2004', in P. Bahn, N. Franklin, and M. Strecker (eds.), *Rock Art Studies: News of the World*, III. Oxford: Oxbow Books, 16–36.

—— (2008b). 'From monuments in landscape to landscapes in monument: death and landscape in Early Bronze Age Scandinavia', in A. Jones (ed.), *Prehistoric Europe: Theory and Practice.* Oxford and New York: Blackwell Studies in Global Archaeology, 56–85.

—— (2009). 'Bredarör on Kivik: a monumental cairn and the history of its interpretation', *Antiquity*, 83: 359–71.

—— Fuglestvedt, I., and Jones, A. (eds.) (2010a). 'Changing pictures: an introduction', in J. Goldhahn, I. Fuglestvedt, and A. Jones (eds.), *Changing Pictures: Rock Art Traditions and Visions in Northern Europe.* Oxford: Oxbow Books, 1–22.

—— Fuglestvedt, I., and Jones, A. (eds.) (2010b). *Changing Pictures: Rock Art Traditions and Visions in Northern Europe.* Oxford: Oxbow Books.

Hildebrand, B.-E. (1869). 'Till hvilken tid och hvilket folk böra de Svenska Hällristningarne hänföras?', *Antiqvarisk Tidskrift för Sverige*, II: 417–32.

Kaul, F. (1998). *Ships on Bronzes: A Study in Bronze Age Religion and Iconography*, Publications from the National Museum, Studies in Archaeology and History, 3:1/2. Copenhagen: National Museum of Denmark.

—— (2004). *Bronzealderens religion*, Nordiske Fortisminder (Serie B), 22. Copenhagen: Det Kongelige Nordiske Oldskriftselskab.

Kristiansen, K. (2004). 'Seafaring voyages and rock art ships', in P. Clark (ed.), *The Dover Boat in Context: Society and Water Transport in Prehistoric Europe.* Oxford: Oxbow Books, 111–21.

—— and Larsson, Th. B. (2005). *The Rise of Bronze Age Society: Travels, Transmissions and Transformations.* Cambridge: Cambridge University Press.

Ling, J. (2008). *Elevated Rock Art: Towards a Maritime Understanding of Rock Art in Northern Bohuslän, Sweden*, Gotarc Serie B (Gothenburg Archaeological Theses), 49. Göteborg: Göteborg University.

—— (in prep). *Rock Art and Seascapes in Uppland, Sweden*, Oxford: Oxbow Books.

—— and Cornell, P. (2010). Rock art as secondary agent? society and agency in Bronze Age Bohuslän. *Norwegian Archaeological Review*, 43 (1), 26–43.

Lødøen, T. and Mandt, G. (2010). *The Rock Art of Norway*. Oxford: Windgather Press.

Malinowski, B. (1922). *Argonauts of the Western Pacific: An Account of Native Enterprise and Adventure in the Archipelagoes of Melanesian New Guinea*. London: Routledge and Kegan Paul.

Malmer, M. P. (1981). *A Chorological Study of North European Rock Art*, Kungl. Vitterhets Historie och Antikvitets Akademien (Antikvariska Serien), 32. Stockholm: The Royal Swedish Academy of Letters, History, and Antiquities.

Mandt, G. (1991). *Vestnorske ristninger i tid og rom*, I–II. Bergen: Bergen University.

Myhre, L. N. (2004). *Trialectic Archaeology: Monuments and Space in Southwest Norway 1700–500 BC*. AmS-Skrifter, 18. Stavanger: Arkeologisk Museum i Stavanger.

Nilsson, P. (2010). 'Reused rock art: Iron Age activities at Bronze Age rock art sites', in J. Goldhahn, I. Fuglestvedt, and A. Jones (eds.), *Changing Pictures: Rock Art Traditions and Visions in Northern Europe*. Oxford: Oxbow Books, 155–68.

Nord, J. (2009). *Changing Landscapes and Persistent Places: An Exploration of the Bjäre Peninsula*, Acta Archaeologica Lundensia (Series in prima 4°), 29. Lund: Lund University.

Nordbladh, J. (1980). *Glyfer och rum kring hällristningar i Kville*. Gothenburg: Department of Archaeology, Gothenburg University.

—— (1989). 'Armour and fighting in the south Scandinavian Bronze Age, especially in view of rock art representations', in T. B. Larsson and H. Lundmark (eds.), *Approaches to Swedish Prehistory: A Spectrum of Problems and Perspectives in Contemporary Research*, British Archaeological Reports (International Series), 500. Oxford: Archaeopress, 323–33.

Randsborg, K. (1993). *Kivik: Archaeology and Iconography*, in Acta Archaeologica, 64. Copenhagen: Munksgaard.

Skoglund. P. (2010). 'Cosmology and performance: narrative perspectives on Scandinavian rock art', in J. Goldhahn, I. Fuglestvedt, and A. Jones (eds), *Changing Pictures: Rock Art Traditions and Visions in Northern Europe*. Oxford: Oxbow Books, 127–38.

Sognnes, K. (2001). *Prehistoric Imagery and Landscapes: Rock Art in Stjørdal, Trøndelag, Norway*, British Archaeological Reports (International Series), 998. Oxford: Archaeopress.

—— (2003). 'On shoreline dating of rock art', *Acta Archaeologica*, 74: 189–209.

—— (2008). 'Stability and change in Scandinavian rock art: the case of Bardal in Trøndelag, Norway', *Acta Archaeologica*, 79: 230–45.

Taçon, P. S. C. and Chippindale, C. (1998). 'An archaeology of rock-art through informed methods and formal methods', in C. Chippindale and P. S. C. Taçon (eds.), *The Archaeology of Rock-Art*. Cambridge: Cambridge University Press, 1–10.

Tilley, C. Y. (2004). *The Materiality of Stone: Explorations in Landscape Phenomenology*. Oxford: Berg.

Vogt, D. (2012). Rock *Carvings in Østfold and Bohuslän, South Scandinavia. An Interpretation of Political and Economic Landscapes*. Oslo: Novus Press.

Wahlgren, K. H. (2002). *Bilder av betydelse. Hällristningar och bronsålderslandskap i nordöstra Östergötland*, Stockholm Studies in Archaeology, 23. Stockholm: Stockholm University.

Yates, T. (1993). 'Frameworks for an archaeology of the body', in C. Tilley (ed.), *Interpretative Archaeology*. Oxford: Berg, 31–72.

CHAPTER 16

ROCK CARVINGS AND ALPINE STATUE-MENHIRS, FROM THE CHALCOLITHIC TO THE MIDDLE BRONZE AGE

GEOFFROY DE SAULIEU

Introduction

The number of Alpine rock carvings multiplies dramatically between the Chalcolithic (Final Neolithic) and Bronze Age, roughly between 3000 and 2000 BC. Large rock-art sites develop at the same time as megalithic statues appear. There are well over thirty thousand carvings in France in the Mont Bégo region, as well as thousands in northern Italy (Valcamonica), and over a hundred statue-menhirs or stelae in the whole Alpine region (including the southern fringe of the Po Valley), often monumental in nature.

The Alpine region is very diverse and fragmented geographically. In addition, the mountain range forms an arc that envelops the Po Valley along the length of its northern and western borders (Fig. 16.1). Towards the south, the Alps become maritime as they approach the Mediterranean and soon give way to the Apennines, mountains that complete the encirclement of the Po Valley at the south-western corner, from where the Italian Peninsula begins. It is obvious that the Po Valley was a crossroads for the prehistoric Alpine peoples who created the different carvings. Indeed, not only is it the geographical centre of gravity of this Alpine-Apennine arc, but it is a necessary route between cave sites to both north and south that show striking similarities. The Po Valley was in fact a central region in this regard.

The images discussed here highlight the extremely diverse terminology used: rock carvings (on rocks in the open air), monuments, statue-menhirs, statue-stelae, and compositions. Many regions are involved (see Fig. 16.1): the Alpes-Maritimes, the upper Ubaye Valley (France), Valais, Vaud (Switzerland), Val d'Aosta, Valcamonica-Valtellina, Trentino-Alto Adige, Veneto, and Lunigiana in Liguria (Italy). Each grouping reveals signs of strong originality, and its own artistic conventions. However, some groups share an undeniable family

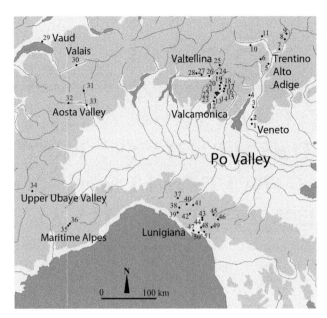

FIG. 16.1 Map of the Po valley with regions and sites. 1 and 2 Veneto, 3 to 11 Trentino Alto Adige, 12 to 23 Valcamonica, 24 to 28 Valtellina, 29 and 30 Vaud and Valais, 31 to 33 Aosta Valley; 34 Upper Ubaye Valley, 35 and 36 Mont Bégo region (Merveilles and Fontanalba sectors), 37 to 51 Lunigiana.

Map: author.

resemblance, such as in Trentino-Alto Adige and in the Valcamonica-Valtellina group, or the megalithic sites of Petit-Chasseur in Sion (Valais, Switzerland) and St Martin de Corléans (Val d'Aosta, Italy).

What is striking about the phenomenon of the Alpine carvings is that they involve megaliths as well as natural rocks. Yet it is precisely this aspect that has eluded research until recently. Indeed, the study of these examples of rock art has long been the preserve of two intellectual positions, which either try to 'decode' the carvings in the literal sense or make them 'fit', so to speak, rudimentary evolutionary assumptions (i.e. from the simple to the elaborate). These two schools of thought, as old as archaeology itself and concerned with affiliations and justifications, sought continuity at any price, either with the European Palaeolithic or the Near East, perceived as the cradle of all cultural manifestations of agricultural societies. But in recent years other trends have emerged: from excavation of the Petit-Chasseur site. Alain Gallay (1995a) has shown that certain carvings were experiencing 'life cycles', going from building to demolition and reuse, suggesting a much more complex status than would be considered by a direct interpretation of the images alone. Based on this site, Gallay (1995b) put forward comparisons with known social types from social anthropology, such as chiefdoms, ranked societies, or big-men societies. From this information, it was possible to suggest new social scenarios for the origin of the Alpine megalithic phenomenon (Moinat and Gallay 1998). Meanwhile Testart (2000) wondered whether megalithism is not a sign of ostentation, like the Kula and the Potlatch in short (and borrowing from the terminology of Mauss 1950), whether the megalithic phenomenon does not constitute traces of *total prestation of agonistic type* (Mauss's formulation). In a nutshell, the presence of Alpine-type carvings on megaliths opens the door to a new understanding of the phenomenon as a whole.

My approach follows the latter course. In this context I consider that the media used for the images and their context are as significant as the simple identification of symbolic schemes. That the carvings represent the traces of an intense social life, expressed through the objects selected, seems obvious, but their appearance—largely dependent on the medium used—marks them as fundamentally different, and indicates opposing choices. Specifically, I base my argument on four aspects:

- the chronological order of the carvings
- analysis of the evolution of the themes
- analysis of the different types of rock face (artificial/natural)
- consideration of the different types of visual imagery in the landscape.

It is with these criteria in mind that I consider the correlation between time periods, the types of media used, imagery, and iconographic content. I thus propose a social interpretation of the phenomenon, based on the different power and wealth practices adopted by these societies.

Chrono-Cultural Attributes

Before continuing, it is necessary to revert to the problem of the chrono-cultural content of the carvings. This exercise is more difficult than it appears, but it is fundamental. Three criteria are available to the researcher to attain this objective: archaeological context, imagery of weaponry, and relative chronology.

Archaeological Context

The archaeological context, such as it is, provides an initial basis for building a chronology. I should at this point stress the importance of the site of Petit-Chasseur as constituting one of the longest Alpine cultural stratigraphies for the Chalcolithic and Bronze Age (Gallay 1995b). It is also one of the sites that provides some of the more reliable chrono-cultural characteristics in the carvings of the region.

Carvings of Weapons

The main weapons known are daggers, axes, and halberds. This assemblage is typical of the Chalcolithic and Early Bronze Age: no true swords are known before the Middle Bronze Age; at most, very elongated daggers can be found but without the proportions to qualify as swords. Similarly, the halberd is a weapon that appears in the Chalcolithic, only to disappear at the end of the Early Bronze Age. Finally, metal spearheads, like proper swords, are only known from the start of the Middle Bronze Age. This first summary already provides an understanding of the importance of weapon imagery in the carvings, but one can go a little further. Indeed, in the Chalcolithic period it is possible to distinguish two major groups of weapon carvings: one group is connected to the second phase of the Remedello culture between 2900/2800 and 2500/2400 BC (Table 16.1), with daggers of the Remedello type as shown on various stelae (Fig. 16.2); and a later group that could be from the Bell Beaker culture, between 2500/2400 and 2300/2200 BC. Very little is known about weapons from the beginning of the Bronze Age in this region, but they appear to be very diverse. It should be noted that at a later stage of the Early Bronze Age halberds still existed, but new types of dagger appear, often referred to as solid-hilted (*Vollgriffdolche*, i.e. all metal, *poignard à manche massif*): the base of the blade is often rounded and fixed by multiple rivets. Also at the end of the Early Bronze Age new forms of axe appear: spatula axes, characterized by a rounded or circular cutting edge (Fig. 16.3, extreme right). This unique form is a good chronological marker in rock art for the end of the Early Bronze Age and start of the Middle Bronze Age.

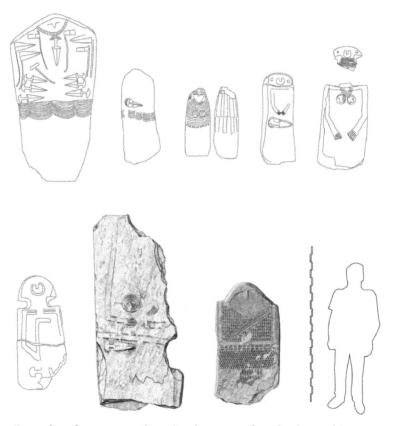

FIG. 16.2 Examples of monumental art (in the sense of reading): menhir-statues, stelae-statues from Arco 1, Lagundo Arco 4 (Trentino Alto Adige), Pontevecchio 8, Sorano 2 (fragment), Filetto 3 (headless fragment), Minucciano 3 (Lunigiana), the stele on the west wall of the dolmen MI, the stele reused as a wall from the adventitious cyst on dolmen MXI. The 1.80 m high figure gives an idea of the scale and shows how monumental art grabs the attention of the visitor. The monumental art emphasizes the motifs symbolizing social status: metal weapons, ornaments and clothing.

Source: author, except bottom middle and right: Sébastien Favre.

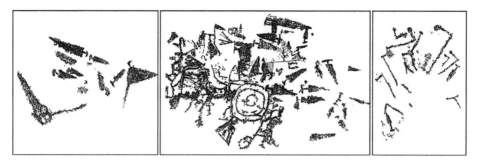

FIG. 16.3 At the beginning of the Bronze Age, we can see a tendency for weapons to accumulate as engravings on slabs of natural rock. They are found in the area of Merveilles in the Mont Bégo region (France), in the Aosta Valley, in Valtellina, and in Valcamonica (Italy). Here, we see three examples from Foppe di Nadro in Valcamonica, with weapons which can be attributed to the Early Bronze Age (in particular the halberds, left and centre, rock 4 of Foppe di Nadro) and Middle (on the right, spatula axes, rock 23 of Foppe di Nadro).

Drawings: G. de Saulieu from photographs.

Superimposition of Carvings

The relative order of some superimposed images can be linked with specific types of weapon or archaeological context. In the Valtellina-Valcamonica group, the images of well-dated weapons, and the careful study of styles and superimposition, helped to define phases within the Copper Age (periods IIIA1 and IIIA2), thus enabling a closer identification of earlier and later periods of use (De Marinis 1994; 1997). At Mont Bégo a similar attempt was made, still inadequate so far, to find chronological contrasts between the two major sectors of the site (Fontanalba and Merveilles) (Saulieu 2004; Saulieu and Serres 2006).

Limitations of the Method

The dating of carvings should be more flexible than that of archaeological cultures. One is naturally inclined to think of periods of long duration, but there is no evidence to support this, and a study of traditional societies does not see human groups as static, experiencing no change or evolution. On the contrary, one often has the impression of exploring short periods of carving, or even stylistic schools of carvings. From a methodological point of view the chronology is relative (upper or lower) rather than absolute. Thus:

- Recognizing that a carving is of a Remedello-type dagger does not allow us to say it was carved in 2800 BC. The dagger might have been carved at the very end of the Remedello II period. This question arises every time carvings continue to exist at the same time as later weapon types appear;
- Superimpositions can certainly help us, but this is often insufficient: firstly, they are meaningless unless correlated to clearly identified weapon types; secondly, the chronological priority of one carving overlain by another does not rule out the possibility that they belong to the same cultural period, although several years may separate them.

Table 16.1 Above: Chronological Chart Showing the Main Cultures. Below: Alternating Timelines for the Sites Belonging to Discreet Art and to Monumental Art According to their Chrono–Stylistic Characteristics (a grey rectangle corresponds to a site, or a set of sites, that cannot be clearly separated)

Chronological phase	3400/3300 BC Copper Age I (Remedello Culture) 2900/2800 BC	2900/2800 BC Copper Age II (Remedello Culture) 2500/2400 BC	2500/2400 BC Copper Age III (Bell Beaker) 2300/2200 BC	2300/2200 BC Early Bronze Age (La Polada) 1800/1700 BC
Chronostylistic attribution	Copper Age, prior or contemporary to Copper Age II, but prior to the Remedello-type dagger carvings	Copper Age II	Copper Age III	Early Bronze Age and beginning of Middle Bronze Age
Monumental art				
Discreet art				

Some carvings date most probably prior to, or contemporary with, Remedello-type dagger images (which does not mean they are from Copper I or II, since the end of Remedello represents the *terminus ante quem*), whereas others are rather more likely to be contemporary or later (*terminus post quem*). In practice this means identifying those carvings that are earlier than the mid third millennium, and those that are later. In the light of the evidence mentioned above, I propose the correlation shown in Table 16.1 (the two first lines).

The Sites

Venice Region

Two very similar statue-stelae have been recorded in the Veneto and in Verona province: Sassina di Prun and Spiazzo di Cerna. They are very small and simple: the head is circular, the eyes are holes, and in Sassina di Prun a T shape represents the face.

Trentino-Alto Adige

The region of Trentino has 18 statue-menhirs, 17 of which form the 'Trentino group'. Three types of statue are distinguished: male, female, and of indeterminate gender.

The male statues, numbering 11, are tall (1 to 2 m). Among the iconographic themes are scalloped belts and weapons (daggers, axes, and halberds). These last indicate two periods: one illustrated by a triangular dagger blade of Remedello type (see Fig. 16.2: Arco and Lagundo), the other with very different daggers, with globular pommel and a longer blade with sheath (Tötschling and Tanzgasse). Four female statues have been identified because of the presence of breasts (see Fig. 16.2: Arco 4). The principal iconographic themes are jewellery and decorated textiles. The asexual statues are smaller than 60 cm and the facial T is barely formed.

Valcamonica and Valtellina

The two great Italian Alpine valleys, Valcamonica (Brescia province) and Valtellina (Sondrio province) stretch over tens of kilometres and constitute the richest collection of rock carvings in the Alps, and cover the longest time; they are together known as 'Camunian' rock art. For protohistory, two main periods are recognized with certainty: period IV, attributed to the Iron Age, and period III, belonging to the Copper and Bronze Ages. Period IV is characterized by representations of animals, people involved in fighting, or ploughing scenes. Among the weapons are swords, spears, and shields. We can identify horses, sometimes ridden by warriors, sometimes harnessed to ploughs or to four-wheeled wagons. The chrono-cultural attribution is certain as, archaeologically speaking, swords, spears, shields, and ridden or draught horses do not seem to be common before the end of the Bronze Age.

Often covered by carvings of period IV, other carvings are attributed to the Copper and Bronze Ages (period III). Period IIIA belongs to the Copper Age, while IIIB and IIIC represent different periods of the Bronze Age. As the distinction between periods IIIB and IIIC differs from one researcher to another, it is better not use these two labels; instead, I use the expression 'carving later than period IIIA' and give details about most important 'type-fossils': 'with/without swords', 'with/without halberd', 'with/without spatula axe'. In the Valcamonica-Valtellina group, we find monumental compositions (on vertical rocks and megaliths) and rock carvings (on horizontal or sloping rock surfaces). Thanks to the typology of the weapons, the representations can easily be dated, following the chronology of period III.

The monumental compositions (carved ensembles on vertical surfaces) have two different phases of carvings during the Chalcolithic, as was shown in the 1980s by Raffaele de Marinis (1994): IIIA1 for Copper Age II and IIIA2 for Copper Age III. The representations are visually organized following different stages or levels (upper, middle, and lower), in some cases recalling the structure of the statue-stele or statue-menhir. The monumental compositions concentrate in two areas of Valcamonica, near Capo di Ponte and on the plateau of Ossimo-Borno. More than 30 monuments have been found, often only a few hundred metres distant from each other. In Valtellina there are a dozen decorated rocks near Teglio, and just one in Tirano. From a chronological point of view, it is possible to distinguish the separate phases IIIA1 and IIIA2, each characterized by weapons and different decorative themes.

These two phases often overlap. The first (IIIA1) is recognizable by daggers assignable to the Remedello culture, especially those with a triangular blade ending in a crescent or half-moon-shaped pommel. These daggers look contemporaneous to halberds, with a blade in the shape of a laurel leaf. There are also representations of stone and metal axes. Other motifs include animals (cervids, suids, canids, and some bovids), geometrical figures (circles, fringed rectangles, figures known as 'topographics'), small human figures, composite anthropomorphs, carts, ornaments (double-spiral pendants, necklaces, scalloped belts), and representations of the sun.

On certain rocks some carvings are covered by others, attributed to phase IIIA2. Daggers with triangular blades and convex bases, with a globular pommel that can be compared to the find from Santa Cristina di Fiesse, attributed to the Bell Beaker culture, characterize this style. These daggers appear near various halberds, identified as the Villafranca-Tivoli or Gambara types, which are also attributed to the end of the Copper Age (Copper Age III). The range of motifs is even less diverse: the human figures have triangular bodies, with legs like a V and arms most often stretched out horizontally, the head sometimes encircled by a disc with rays coming from it.

One should stress that on certain rocks the carvings of phase IIIA cover geometrical motives of an earlier period (Borno 1 face B, Bagnolo 1, Ossimo 8). In other monumental compositions, different geometrical figures are an integral part of the composition (Borno 1 face D, Ossimo 3, Valgella 3, Vangione 1, Vangione 2, Vangione 3). Yet these geometrical figures, earlier than or contemporary with the monumental compositions of period IIIA, can be found in the rock art of the region, while other types can be found only in rock art characterized by the presence of Bronze Age weapons. We can thus distinguish sites that do not have representations of weapons but have many geometrical figures.

There are also rock carvings with Remedello-type daggers, the oldest chronological marker, and halberds, characteristic of the Chalcolithic, but these are relatively few in number. By contrast, the depiction of weapons seems to increase during the Early and Middle Bronze Age (especially axes with a flattened and circular blade edge). The sites of Luine, Foppe di Nardo (see Fig. 16.3), where several hundred images are present, are important. The themes are less clearly differentiated: we find mostly representations of weapons on large rock surfaces, accompanied during the Early Bronze Age by rectangular grid figures. During the Middle Bronze Age the phenomenon becomes more prevalent, as shown by the site of Tresivio where several daggers with massive handles and axes with a circular edge are carved. At the end of the Middle

Bronze Age and in the Final Bronze Age another set of themes is added (or renewed, because they had been employed before): small stereotyped characters (*personages*), the upper and lower limbs symmetrically opposed. They are often called by analogy 'praying figures' or 'figures in the praying position'. This motif sometimes appears together with another, less frequent, consisting in a circle with four rays. This motif, the 'little wheel' (*rouelle*), continues the Copper Age tradition of solar representations, but at the same time it corresponds to other representations of the period that seem to prefigure certain aspects of early European mythologies.

Val d'Aosta

The region of Val d'Aosta has statue-stelae at the megalithic site of St-Martin-de-Corléans (found in 1969) and rock carvings at Montjovet and Valtournenche.

At St-Martin-de-Corléans the stelae are mostly large, around 2 m high. Around 40 have been found. There are two styles: style I has daggers with a triangular blade and a semicircular pommel like Remedello, double-spiral pendants, belts, and hands. Style II is characterized by the presence of elaborate geometrical decoration representing clothing ornaments, bows, arrows, arms, and schematic faces suggested by a facial T. This site, with its two styles, looks very much like Petit-Chasseur (see below).

Two sites of rock carvings are also known from the Val d'Aosta. The first, Montjovet-Chenal, a low-altitude site, is very eroded; there are axe figures, double-spiral pendants, geometrical motifs, and non-figurative representations. The presence of double-spiral pendants indicates a period close in time to period IIIA1 in Valcamonica, style 1 of St-Martin-de-Corléans and type A at Petit-Chasseur. This shelter of Vatournenche-la-Barma, situated at 1,600 m above sea level, has lines, spatula axes, a Rhodanian dagger, and cup-marks. The axes can be attributed to the Early or Middle Bronze Age.

Switzerland

Switzerland has many sites, including Lutry, Petit-Chasseur, Chemin des Collines, and St-Léonard. The Lutry stele belongs to an alignment discovered in 1984, composed of elements the height of which diminishes symmetrically on one side, with a monumental central block. Only one stele still bears some carvings, no. 14. One can distinguish two crossed shoulder straps, five circles, and a mysterious object, which looks like the '*pendeloques*' features on the statue of Rouergue, in the South of France.

The Sion group, discovered in 1961 on the megalithic site of Petit-Chasseur, has been excavated and fully published. The 29 stelae thus have a good archaeological context. Many were found lying on the ground near a cist or dolmen, but more often they were reused in a funerary monument. They have two morphological and stylistic variants: A and B, recalling styles I and II of St-Martin-de-Corléans. The stelae nearly always represent male figures, as shown by the presence of weapons (dagger, bows, and arrows). Ornaments are also represented, along with clothes richly decorated with geometrical motifs. The stelae of group A, the decoration of which is characterized by several daggers with triangular blades of Remedello type, and of a pendant made of two circles, one inside the other, are found in the monuments of the early and middle periods (see Fig. 16.2: Sion M XI). The stelae of type B are later, because they appear either in the middle period, or in cists and rebuilding of later periods, going down to the beginning of the Early Bronze Age. Type B is more profusely decorated than A: the ornamentation of clothes is very detailed, but the Remedello-type daggers have disappeared in favour of representations of bows and arrows (see Fig. 16.2: Sion M XI).

In the immediate vicinity of the Petit-Chasseur site the menhir alignment in the Chemin des Collines has a statue-menhir with several carvings, and another bearing the representation of an anthropomorph.

The rock carvings of St-Léonard have four successive periods: in the first there are concentric circles, small anthropomorphs in the praying position, very much like those of Chemin des Collines. The second period is more varied: one can recognize various maeander-like figures (linear figures forming maeanders or labyrinths), rectangular figures, zigzags, 'arboriforms' (vertical figures with a number of descending branches), and U-shaped figures. The third is characterized by a praying figure surrounded by dots and vertical rectangular shapes, the upper part of which is shaped like an arch. Finally, the fourth period has a number of rectangular dotted areas, some with appendages (an identical motif can be found in the Fontanalba valley at Mont Bégo), lines, and anthropomorphic figures.

Ubaye Valley

A carved panel at Saint-Paul-sur-Ubaye (Alpes-de-Haute-Provence), in the high valley of the Ubaye, bears a composition with two Remedello-type daggers, and a male anthropomorph with discoidal head. The carvings cover several painted images that recall the schematic paintings of the south of France.

Lunigiana

The region called Lunigiana, in the east of Liguria, has about 50 statue-menhirs in sandstone dated to the Copper Age. Two types can be identified. The first, the Pontevecchio type, is characterized by a rectangular or trapezoidal body, a head without a neck directly stuck on the trunk, a face suggested by a carved U (see Fig. 16.2: Pontevecchio 8). Twelve figures are known, which can be divided into armed statues, female statues, and statues without features. The armed statues are the taller, while those without features are the smaller. The only known weapons are daggers with triangular blades of Remedello type. The female statues have breasts and sometimes representations of clothing. The second type, Filetto-Malgarte, is characterized by the presence of a neck (see Fig. 16.2: Sorano, Filetto 3, and Minucciano). Eight female figures with breasts and sometimes a necklace are known, and ten figures armed with daggers or axes.

Mont Bégo

Mont Bégo is situated in the southernmost part of the Alps closest to the sea, in the south-eastern part of the Mercantour massif. About thirty thousand carvings are spread over four large valleys: Merveilles, Fontanalba, Valaurette, and the Valmasque. There are also smaller peripheral areas such as Ste Marie, Col du Sabion, and Vei del Bouc. In total the site extends over 1,700 hectares.

The carvings do not tell stories, nor are they disposed randomly; on the contrary, four parameters are involved: few themes, different density of carvings according to area, different distribution of carvings by theme, and repetitive associations. The exhaustive study of the site enabled Henri de Lumley to establish a classification of the carvings (Lumley et al. 1995). While the non-figurative representations are more numerous, it is possible to discern 13 main families of figurative representations. The most frequent are:

- horned figures (*corniformes*): these are animal representations, probably of domestic bovines, because they are found with representations of harnessing. The outline is always the same: a central part (linear, rectangular, trapezoidal, or round) representing the body of the animal; and two appendages starting from the upper part of the body, thought to be horns. Those can have one or more segments, curved or angular, sometimes in zigzag form. Some appendages can lie on the edge of the body: for instance, legs on either side, tail, ears, and a small appendage linking the body and the horns.
- geometric net-like figures, or reticules (*réticulés*, from Latin *reticulum*, 'net'): geometrical figures, polygonal or curved, their inner space divided into irregular squares. They recall some of the Valcamonica figures (Fig. 16.4, right).
- geometric composed figures: this group is defined by a basic design in which a rectangular area is linked with one or more lines. The best-known type has a rectangular space to which one or several arcs of a circle are attached, its inner space filled with small areas of cup-marks (Fig. 16.4, left). These geometrical figures often have lines that connect them to the others, forming a web. Like the previous examples, these images are also found at Valcamonica-Valtellina.
- weapons: mainly represented by daggers (their size is varied, but the blade is rarely more than four times the width), halberds, and axes. These images correspond to a type of weapon known only during the Chalcolithic and Early Bronze Age.
- harness: this group has horned animals with yoke. Certain harness depictions are shown alone; others, more numerous, draw a plough, a wagon with small wheels, or rectangular or triangular objects without wheels, possibly sledges.
- anthropomorphs: they are divided into two types, the complex anthropomorphs that are represented only once ('anthropomorph with zigzag arms', as in Figure 16.5, and the simple anthropomorphs, represented in a repetitive way and always composed of horned figures and recalling the 'praying figures' of Valcamonica-Valtellina.
- human figures (*personages*): human representations showing the main parts of the body (trunk, legs, arms, head, sometimes sex, and feet).

Of a total of 3,700 rocks studied in 2001, 31.1 per cent of the carved rocks of Mont Bégo have only one sign. The rocks with up to three signs constitute 60.7 per cent of the whole site. It seems, however, that 13.2 per cent of the rocks have more than ten carvings (Serres 2001).

The density of carvings and the associations between the different thematic groups are very different from one area to another. It is thus important to understand how the carvings are concentrated in order to comprehend the structure of the site. The two richest sectors and with the most types are Merveilles and Fontanalba, which each have nearly the same number of carvings (sixteen thousand and fifteen thousand). On the basis of a 1994 count, while the number of carvings is larger in the Merveilles, the density, 26 carvings per hectare, is lower than that of Fontanalba, which is 34 per hectare. The other sectors are negligible by comparison, and similar in style to one or the other of the two big sectors. The latter are

FIG. 16.4 Left: a geometric figure from the Fontanalba sector in the Mont Bégo region (France). This motif appears in sites attributed to the Copper Age. Right: two geometric figures with boxes, from rock 6 from the Luine site in Valcamonica (Italy). The latticed motif appears in sites more commonly attributed to the Bronze Age, particularly in France in the Merveilles sector of Mont Bégo.

Photo: G. de Saulieu.

FIG. 16.5 The rock known as 'the man with the zig-zag arms', is located in the Merveilles sector of Mont Bégo (France). Large ordered compositions, composed of different motifs, are rare in discreet art and tend to highlight exceptional figures. This anthropomorphic figure, with its discoid head, probably refers to the celestial and solar world.

Photos: G. de Saulieu.

characterized by themes and associations, an inventory of which has been made by Thierry Serres (1997). He locates 56 repetitive associations, which are geographically distributed with a logic that has nothing to do with chance but are linked not only to the themes but also to the limited choices of the carver. Certain associations can be found only in particular spots, whereas other associations are found widely.

Factors Affecting the Form and Content of the Art

Carving Visibility

Visibility can be considered from two aspects: the orientation of the carved face and its geographical position. By orientation I mean the incline of the panel bearing the carvings: a vertical panel is a far more visible sign than a tilted or horizontal panel, and is indicative of a display intended to attract the attention of the passer-by. The geographical position is an indication of whether the images were visible at all times, or only at certain times of the year: carvings high in the Alps are accessible only for three months of the year after the thaw, which is obviously not the case with valley carvings. A site at high altitude with the carvings on inclined or horizontal faces is not the same as carvings found near a village, on a vertical panel, whether natural or artificial. The artist's intentions cannot have been the same.

These findings are confirmed by the fact that the organization of the carvings is very different from one type of rock face to another, and that there are certain correlations between the themes and the type of carved surface. From the available data, it can be seen that vertical rock faces often have faults, ridges, or crevices that limit the space for carving. On the other hand, when the face is inclined or horizontal, we are dealing with natural rock, either in blocks or slabs—geological outcrops—where the space for carving is ample, and at times huge (Fig. 16.6; on the left a huge carved rock in Luine site). The limitations and inclination of the rock face do not lend themselves easily to the same types of organization for the carvings: the space available requires the carver to prioritize the drawings according to what he wishes the visitor to see. The human eye can quickly and easily take in a global picture of an organized composition that is displayed on a vertical surface with well-defined contours; however, the same does not apply to a horizontal surface covered with carvings. Prehistoric people took these factors into account: the great majority of compositions are found on limited vertical surfaces (and very few on inclined surfaces), but accumulations of carvings are found on non-vertical natural rock. It is therefore clear that a dagger in a composition on a vertical surface is not perceived in the same way as one on natural stone. This difference in perception is as important and as significant as the fact that a dagger is being represented rather than, say, a sandal.

Rock Faces (Support Structures)

There are two kinds of rock face or support structure: natural and artificial. The natural materials include blocks, natural walls, and rock outcrops. The artificial materials can be

FIG. 16.6 Two examples of discreet art: on the left, slab 34 from the Luine site (Valcamonica, Italy); the figure is 1.80 m tall; on the right, a rock from group II, zone XIX, located in the Fontanalba sector, in the Mont Bégo region (France). Discreet art is an art that fits and blends into the landscape. It may even be forgotten and covered over by vegetation.

Photo: G. de Saulieu.

recovered blocks, megaliths, but also isolated stelae of even thickness (see Fig. 16.2). The vast majority of natural faces are on an incline or horizontal, whereas all artificial faces are (or were) vertical. Not only did the artificial faces, sometimes accompanied by or integrated with other architectural structures, require organized teamwork, but, as mentioned above, because of their verticality they had the advantage of displaying sets of structured carvings in an environment accessible all year round.

Symbolic Strategies

To summarize, there are two ways of appraising the carvings in the Alps between the Chalcolithic and the Early Bronze Age. They depend on the nature of the rock face and the context. These constraints determine the type of organization of symbols, and how the visitor perceives them. Either the image is displayed on a vertical face, which is almost always artificial, in an environment habitable throughout the year: it then becomes an image intended 'to be seen', whether on a statue-menhir, a statue-stele, or a monumental composition. The human figure plays an important role: it can be explicitly represented or merely suggested by the objects that usually accompany it, such as waist or breast ornaments. Or else the image is carved on a natural rock face, occasionally vertical, to blend into a landscape. The fact that this landscape is spectacular is certainly a meaningful choice on the part of the carvers, but it does not make this art a spectacular art. Indeed, as they are carved on natural rocks, the carvings are often hard to spot, and one must examine the rocks closely in order to make them out.

There are thus two strategies represented in the archaeological record: an art that is to be seen, in other words *monumental* (like the stelae of Fig. 16.2), and an art whose role is not principally to be seen by the visitor, namely *discreet* art—which does not, however, mean that it is secret (e.g. the natural rocks shown in Fig. 16.6). The carvings from this period are either monumental or discreet (see Table 16.1). These two art types are therefore different, even opposing, but related in some way because they occupy the same areas, and especially because they use a large number of common symbols. Correlations between certain themes and types of rock face should be stressed, however: for example, monumental art has a monopoly on wild animals, depictions of ornaments, and clothing.

Iconographic Variations

Overall Trends

Study of the carvings shows that on both local and regional scales there is an undeniable family resemblance between the two types of art, as much in the choice of topics as in the shapes, patterns, and structures of the carvings (Saulieu 2003; 2004; 2007). Themes of the plough led by a human figure, carvings of weapons, geometric figures, and so on appear on very similar natural sites from widely separated regions. It thus seems legitimate to try to identify common trends across the timeline.

First one may distinguish an evolutionary element: there are fewer carvings of weapons on sites attributed to the Copper Age (first half of the third millennium BC) than on the sites attributed to the Bronze Age (late third and early second millennium), where there are accumulations of carvings of weapons over large slabs of rock (see Fig. 16.3). The best example is the Mont Bégo region: the Fontanalba sector contains mostly halberds and very few daggers, while the Merveilles area has many more weapons, including most of the dagger carvings and rocks with accumulations of weapons (such as a slab called 'the altar'). But, as Figure 16.3 shows, this phenomenon occurs in the Valcamonica-Valtellina groups too. In the same period right across the Alps, there is a change in geometric figures, which firstly focuses on carvings of rectangular shape linked by lines (see Fig. 16.4 left), then gives way to openwork carvings (i.e. circular shapes and figures with squares), and finally only the geometric figures with multiple squares (see Fig. 16.4 right). At the start of the sequence, the geometrical figures are synonymous with links (the geometrical figures form webs); afterwards they are synonymous with separation, with fragmentation of space (they are separated, without any bond joining them). At the same time, it appears that the carvings are progressively more schematic. The people become worshippers (geometric figures holding their forearms upwards), carvings of animals in profile from Valcamonica are replaced by rare corniform carvings, and at Mont Bégo the very neat corniforms of Fontanalba (small rectangular figures topped by two small horns, with very small appendage) are replaced in Merveilles by much coarser corniforms. Solar imagery also experiences a distinct evolution: absent from the earliest sites, it appears in the periods featuring monumental art. The sun is then a dominant figure in carved compositions: at times it dominates a series of ordered motifs, or it is a halo for a central figure, or it replaces the head of the central figure—a dominant figure in every sense of the word. With the return of discreet art during the Bronze Age, after the final abandonment of monumental art, the sun becomes a composite being, far removed from the human figure, but retaining a unique and also dominant appearance (see Fig. 16.5).

Correlation Between Form and Content

Despite these frequent and sometimes unnerving similarities between remote sites across the Alps, some thematic families are excluded from monumental art or discreet art. Thus, only monumental art shows wild animals in hunting scenes and large predators (ibex, chamois, wild boar, deer, wolf, fox) as well as domestic animals (cattle, dogs), with carvings of ornaments and textiles (e.g. the female statue with collar, and males with clothes, as in Fig. 16.2). One cannot explain this just because monumental art emphasizes the human figure in megalithic statuary. Indeed, in Valcamonica, for instance, the monumental compositions, where the human figure is not even implicit, still contain carvings of copper ornaments and probable textiles; on the other hand Camunian rock art on natural rocks, which is contemporary with the monumental compositions, has no carvings of this type. So it is an art that stands out as being based on carvings implying the imprint of the type of society that created it. Discreet art never represents ornaments, just domestic animals, and contains geometric figures based on rectangular figures and latticework, which are not found in the monumental art.

Chronological Alternation Between the Two Types of Art

Table 16.1 suggests the different conclusions it is possible to draw after examining each group (monumental and discreet art). Discreet art is present almost continuously over the period, albeit at times markedly more intense than at others. In contrast, monumental art is confined to certain well-defined periods: what is really remarkable is the 'monumental wave' throughout the Alps and northern Italy where there are successively and exclusively Remedello and then Bell Beaker-type daggers (column Copper II and III in Table 16.1). This period has minimal discreet art, making it appear as if the two types alternated. The sequence therefore functions as if the two types of art were potential competitors. Unfortunately it is impossible to say anything about the existence of such a contrast for carvings attributed to the Middle Neolithic, which are few in number and whose features are imprecise. The alternation between a period that emphasizes the monumental and two periods with only discreet carvings is an important factor in this interpretation: I assume that social phenomena at the beginning of the two types of art are an indication of two different social projects.

Monumental Art and the Emergence of Ostentation

The contrast between monumental and discreet art is evident in the archaeological material, and necessarily leads to the question of social context: what is it that would make one prefer an art form that is visible to everyone, a collective effort that demonstrates a kind of self-advertisement, that is often individualistic (since megalithic sculpture is clearly dominant), to an art without architecture, in a secluded place, with few anthropoid elements and difficult to see? The former reveals a link between a contribution from the community and the promotion of a dominant image; whereas what is evident in the latter is an act that involves no communal action at all, and is within a site that was already structured. To emphasize this, we could say, in an anachronistic way, that monumental art has an 'aristocratic' aspect (individualism, solar imagery, jewellery and clothing, hunting animals); and that discreet art seems more concerned about community (ploughs, fields, livestock). The contrast, even rivalry, between discreet and monumental art suggests there is a factor in group organization that allows one type of art to exist rather than another.

What seems striking is the ostentatious character of monumental art. Ostentation consists in making a public demonstration of superiority, thereby deriving prestige, intended to dazzle the passer-by). It is therefore a practice specific to societies where social inequalities are present. But it is not enough to be an upstart or the son of a prominent family; the individual must also prove his own ability to deserve the prestige. This is a practice where the individual image plays a part. There is, therefore, a connotation of *agon* (in the Greek sense) in ostentation: superiority over others must be demonstrated and shown in a more striking manner than that of any predecessors. Ostentation has to be visible; it is a spectacle, which is offered up or even imposed, such as a castle in a landscape, or a gymnasium in a Greek city. It is an unavoidable practice in the sense that one is obliged to meet the challenge or risk losing status: the act of receiving a gift during a ceremony involves giving a reciprocal gift of equal or greater value, otherwise there is an implicit recognition of weakness, inferiority, and therefore submission. The element of demonstration, the display, is fundamental. Ostentation determines hierarchy: there are first the giver and the recipients; then there is the manner of the action, since one does not give just anything to just anyone; wealth is not paraded carelessly. One must be better than others, without becoming ridiculous. One must maintain rank without departing from tradition. In short, ostentation is a carefully considered and well-prepared process.

In the same way, one does not practise ostentation with just anything. It involves weighing up the available materials and the scale of their worth. Finally, ostentation is not mere arrogance; it serves to gain prestige, in other words wielding social power. In short, ostentation expresses deep tendencies in society: the importance of gifts in creating dependants, the importance of being the first citizen in the city in order to gain a higher position, or the importance of showing the unassailability of a social position by not hesitating to remove a large share of wealth from one's heirs. The ostentation is therefore a cornerstone of what Marcel Mauss (1950) calls the *prestation totale de type agonistique*.

Why do we think monumental art looks ostentatious? Firstly, it demonstrates the element of display, which is characteristic of ostentation. It is visible all the time. Besides, by its vertical position and the fact that it is often incorporated into architectural structures, monumental art becomes a veritable advertisement: it draws the attention of the passer-by, unlike the images on natural rocks (see Figs. 16.2 and 16.6). Next, monumental art selects and prioritizes themes, since they can be either monumental compositions or statues. This hierarchical content in the carvings therefore results in the enhancement of a solar figure or a human figure, or both. Thus monumental art presents an individual character as an example of ostentation: it projects the dominant figure, assumed to represent the donor in one way or another. Finally, the inherent themes themselves suggest a search for marks of prestige: the presence of carvings of metal weapons is particularly noticeable, both in the compositions and on the statues (bearing in mind this occurs at the dawn of metallurgy in the area, and weapons only appear in certain graves and never in the context of simple rubbish), as well as ornaments and clothing. Monumental art also betrays ostentation for another reason: it is an art that is used over and over again. Many stelae were pulled down and reused. Once the prestige of the sponsor has been reassessed, for example following his death, the image no longer fulfils the role it previously had: demolition therefore becomes a possibility.

Discreet art goes against this dramatic representation and the bringing of symbols to life. There are no carvings of ornaments or clothing here. This form of art, which does not suggest a collective act by a number of individuals, is spread over a number of geographical sites where the carver follows a succession of previous carvers without challenging them (see Fig. 16.3). There is no question of showing off to the passer-by, or of demolishing and reusing previous images, but rather of contributing to building them up. Discreet art therefore lacks an ostentatious character; on the contrary, it rejects such display in order to allow the carvings to be one with an indestructible landscape.

Ostentation as a Social Marker

In traditional societies before the emergence of city-states, relationships between individuals were not expressed solely in terms of family relationships, or in symbolic terms, but also in political and economic terms. More particularly, these last two factors can also constitute markers for social tendencies, since more than in other fields they can represent contradictions and asymmetries, and even point to their own self-appraisal (Balandier 1967). In this context ostentation—the ultimate consequence of power and wealth—does not take on the same forms, nor aspire to the same goals according to their role in society.

In my view, the spectacular nature of the statue-menhirs, the fact that they were commonly reused, their short life cycle, and the importance given to motifs seen as insignia (weapons and ornaments), make this form of ostentation typical of societies where access to power is open to competition, and where wealth circulates rather than accumulates. Indeed, in these societies prestige is acquired not only through the deeds of warriors or lineal descent, but also through offering grand and sumptuous feasts, or by paying out exorbitant social benefits (such as bride price). These were societies where goods were distributed voluntarily: they circulated freely within the world of the living and played a role in structuring social relations, but were rarely invested on a massive scale in grave goods.

It seems to me that the temporal nature of monumental art is a reflection of the temporary nature of power. At this point one should note that there are no lavish funerary deposits at the time of monumental art, nor religious deposits; these appear instead along with discreet art in the Bronze Age. The Remedello cemetery and Bell Beaker tombs in the region show the existence of funerary finds which, though not insignificant, remain limited: a few daggers, maybe one or two halberds, some stone tools (knife blades, arrowheads), an archer's wristguard, and some pottery. Multiple graves are atypical. We are far from finding in the graves everything that appears on the statues. We are equally far from the princely tombs of other regions and other times. Following this line of thought, one can better understand the nature of discreet art, where there are no carvings of ornaments and clothing. In this form of art, which was perhaps merely the result of private initiative, different ways of organizing symbols from that of monumental art occur: the importance of discreet art lies in associating one theme with another, carving certain themes or certain associations in certain sectors and not in others. In this way, the carver slips discreetly and anonymously into a tradition that he does not challenge. It is for this reason that exceptional compositions are so rare in discreet art. Moreover, they seem to be reserved for the representation of myths, such as the 'Rock of the Tribe Chief' or the composition of the 'Hominoid with zigzag arms' (see Fig. 16.5) in the Mont Bégo region. What is striking here is the impression that the carvers wanted to give their creations the ability to be at one with an eternal landscape through which one could dream of a social system that would be unchangeable.

If one considers the origins of the oscillation between discreet and monumental art during the thousand years separating the Copper and Bronze Ages in the Po Valley, one turns naturally to the development of copper and bronze metallurgy that marked this period. Social anthropology can again provide many instances of societies faced with radical technological change. Maurice Godelier (1996: 271), for example, remarked that the Baruya of New Guinea did not raise as many pigs when they had no steel axes; the expansion of pig production is linked to the arrival of those axes. The introduction of new goods therefore pushed the Baruya into an economic cycle of production that was foreign to them. Another example could be the Island of Nias in Indonesia, where the rise of megalith building seems very recent and sudden: it could relate to the widespread presence of the slave trade and contact with merchants. This contact triggered an economic race in order to acquire luxury goods (especially iron) in exchange for captured slaves, and contributed to the creation of a ranked society complete with megaliths (Guillaud, Forestier, and Simanjuntak 2008). To return to the Alps for a moment, the copper boom and then the production of the first bronze objects may have altered social relations in a comparable way. Rock art, through these changing trends in carving, could therefore be one of the symptoms of the phenomenon, indicating change in social and economic parameters.

In this context one may recall other factors that seem to correlate with the milestones in the development of rock art. Since metallurgy existed in this region from the late fourth millennium BC, a period that can be placed alongside the birth of the first forms of discreet art, the development of metallurgy in the Copper II period, illustrated by the introduction of the first metal (Remedello culture), still fairly limited, corresponds to the emergence of monumental art as marked by megalithic statuary. The re-emergence of discreet art, and the disappearance of monumental art, characterized by an unequalled peak in weapon carvings (concentrated on large rocks, such as large symbolic or votive deposits; Fossati 1997), correspond to the development of bronze metallurgy and the production of even more important metal assemblages than those of Copper II. While at this time there is no funerary data from the Po Valley, probably due to the nature of the practices involved, votive deposits of metal objects emerge, in other words deposits that take wealth out of circulation.

Bibliography

Balandier, G. (1967). *Anthropologie politique*. Paris: Presses Universitaires de France.
De Marinis, R. C. (1994). 'Problème de chronologie de l'art rupestre du Valcamonica', *Notizie Archeologiche Bergomensi*, 3: 99–120.
—— (1997). 'The Eneolithic cemetery of Remedello Sotto (BS) and the relative and absolute chronology of the Copper Age in Northern Italy', *Notizie Archeologiche Bergomensi*, 5: 33–51.
Fossati, A. (1997). 'Weapons in Bronze Age rock art: votive hoards and initiation rites in the Alps. Ideas for preliminary discussion',*Tracce*, 9: 36–7.
Gallay, A. (ed.) (1995a). *Dans les Alpes, à l'aube du métal. Archéologie et bande dessinée*. Sion: Musées cantonaux du Valais.
—— (1995b). 'Mégalithisme et chefferies: approche transculturelle', in A. Gallay (ed.), *Dans les Alpes à l'aube du métal. Archéologie et bande dessinée*. Sion: Musées Cantonaux du Valais, 163–71.

Godelier, M. (1996). *La Production des grands hommes*, 2nd edn. Paris: Flammarion.
Guillaud, D., Forestier, H., and Simanjuntak, H. T. (2008). 'Insular models of technical change: Sumatra, Nias and Siberut (Indonesia)', in J. Conolly and M. Campbell (eds.), *Comparative Island Archaeology*, British Archaeological Reports (International Series), 1,829. Oxford: Archaeopress, 31–45.
Lumley, H. de, Begin-Ducornet, J., Echassoux, A., Fournier, A., Giusto-Magnardi, N., Lavigne, G., Lumley, M. A. de, Machu, P., Mano, L., Meslin, L., Park, Y. H., Rey, M., Romain, O., Romain, S., Saguez, S., Serres, T., and Villain-Rinieri, F. (1995). *Le Grandiôse et le Sacré. Gravures rupestres protohistoriques et historiques de la région du Mont Bégo*. Aix-en-Provence: Edisud.
Mauss M. (1950). *Sociologie et anthropologie*. Paris: Presses Universitaires de France.
Moinat, P. and Gallay, A. (1998). 'Les Tombes de type Chamblandes et l'origine du mégalithisme alpin', *Archäologie der Schweiz*, 21: 2–12.
Saulieu, G. de (2003). 'Comparaison structurale et spatiale de deux compositions rupestres alpines (Valcamonica et Mont Bégo) attribuées au Chalcolithique et au début de l'Âge du Bronze ancien', in R. Desbrosse and A. Thévenin (eds.), *Actes des Congrès Nationaux des Sociétés Historiques et Scientifiques*, 125ᵉ Lille, 2000, Préhistoire de l'Europe. Des Origines à l'Age du Bronze. Paris: Éditions du Comité des Travaux Historiques et Scientifiques, 151–67.
—— (2004). *Gravures rupestres et statues-menhirs dans les Alpes. Des pierres et des pouvoirs (3000–2000 av. J.-C.)*. Paris: Errance.
—— (2007). 'Hiérarchisation sociale et art rupestre dans les Alpes: la figure solaire dans l'art gravé du Chalcolithique et du début de l'Âge du Bronze', in J. Guilaine (ed.), *Le Chalcolithique et la construction des inégalités*, tome I. Le continent européen, Séminaire du Collège de France. Paris: Errance, 125–50.
—— and Serres, T. (2006). 'Les Représentations de tractions animales dans la région du Mont Bégo (Alpes-Maritime, France)', in P. Pétrequin, R. M. Arbogast, A. M. Pétrequin, S. van Willigen, and M. Bailly (eds.), *Premiers Chariots, premiers araires. La diffusion de la traction animale en Europe pendant les IVe et IIIe millénaires avant notre ère*. CRA-Monographies, 29. Paris: Centre National de la Recherche Scientifique Éditions, 73–86.
Serres, T. (1997). 'Vers la compréhension d'un langage symbolique, étude des gravures protohistoriques de la région du mont Bégo, Tende, Alpes Maritimes', *Bulletin d'Études Préhistoriques et Archéologiques Alpines*, VII–VIII: 83–95.
—— (2001). *Les Associations de gravures protohistoriques de la region du Mont Bégo. Etude et interprétation*. Thèse de doctorat du Muséum National d'Histoire Naturelle, Paris.
Testart, A. (2000). 'Que peut dire aujourd'hui l'anthropologie sociale des chasseurs-cueilleurs d'hier?', in C. Cupillard and A. Richard (eds.), *Les Derniers Chasseurs-Cueilleurs d'Europe occidentale*, Actes du Colloque International de Besançon, octobre 1998. Besançon: Presses Universitaires Franc-Comtoises, 343–9.

CHAPTER 17

BRONZE AGE FIELDS AND LAND DIVISION

ROBERT JOHNSTON

INTRODUCTION

This chapter introduces the archaeology of field systems and land boundaries in Bronze Age Europe. It begins by offering a historical overview of research on ancient fields. This is followed by a discussion of the interpretative issues affecting the study of prehistoric land division, focusing on terminology, classification, and chronology. The majority of the chapter provides an overview of the evidence for Bronze Age fields in north-west Europe. This is ordered chronologically, and trends eastwards, beginning on the edges of Europe, in Ireland and northern Scotland, and finishing in the Netherlands. Land division is an important source for researching changes in the organization and technology of agriculture, and in some regions it is a key element in explanations of social and political transformations during the second and first millennia BC.

PREHISTORIC LAND DIVISION: A HISTORICAL PERSPECTIVE

Ancient fields were recognized by antiquarian and topographic writers from the late Middle Ages: a sixteenth-century document described 'a long conger of stones called Le Rowe Rew' on Dartmoor, south-west England, which was later recognized as one of the long Bronze Age boundaries known as 'reaves' (Fleming 2008). In the mid seventeenth century the Reverend Johan Picardt described *legerplaatsen* (settlements or camps) on the heathland of Drenthe, Netherlands, which were subsequently recognized to be later prehistoric field systems (Brongers 1976). These written descriptions demonstrate that antiquarians recognized that the field systems were cultural landscapes, yet they rarely understood their significance. Picardt, for instance, interpreted the grid-like arrangements of earthen banks as settlement enclosures, and nineteenth-century antiquarians took their function to be in some way related to mortuary rituals because of their proximity to barrows. The long-distance boundaries on Dartmoor, although initially categorized as boundaries, were later reinterpreted as trackways, and this misunderstanding was not corrected until the 1970s, nor was their prehistoric date appreciated.

The accurate survey of prehistoric fields began in the later nineteenth century, and it was during the 1920s and 1930s that sustained investigation of fields and boundaries led to the wider recognition of their significance. Pioneers in the study of ancient fields included A. E. van Giffen in the Netherlands, Gudmund Hatt in Denmark, O. G. S. Crawford, and Eliot and Cecil Curwen in England. The development of field archaeology into a mature and sophisticated craft had an important impact on the understanding of fields. The surveys of earthwork field systems completed on the Sussex downland provided a reasoned interpretation of the date, function, and formation processes of the fields (Curwen and Curwen 1923). In parallel, aerial photography provided a wider perspective, allowing Crawford, for instance, to identify large areas of field systems as earthworks and to trace their cropmarks in modern arable land (Crawford 1923).

Ancient fields were incorporated into the culture-historical frameworks that prevailed in the first half of the twentieth century. In Britain, morphological differences in the fields were used to distinguish between systems that were ethnically Celtic or Saxon origin. In the Netherlands, the debate was between whether the fields were Germanic or Roman, although it was the term 'Celtic fields' that gradually took on the widest acceptance. Fields were one amongst a package of innovations that were introduced by Celtic invaders who arrived in Britain in the mid first millennium BC (Crawford 1923). This was not a dry label; 'Celtic' carried political meanings, indicating a way of life that was supplanted in England following the early medieval colonizations but survived in the western 'fringes' of Ireland, Wales, and Scotland (Wickstead 2008).

The popularity of landscape and economic archaeology from the 1950s onwards brought a renewed purpose and rigour to the study of prehistoric fields. Michael Müller-Wille's (1965) corpus compared the morphology, chronology, and environmental context of prehistoric fields in the North Sea region, including Germany, the Netherlands, and Denmark. In Britain, Collin Bowen (1961) reviewed the state of knowledge in the face of the widespread destruction of earthworks by modern agriculture. In parallel with these reviews, a number of detailed landscape studies were undertaken, which investigated field systems at a variety of scales. Ayolt Brongers's (1976) aerial mapping of fields in Drenthe in the northern Netherlands and excavations at Vaassen are an example. This fieldwork established a longer chronology for the field systems, revealing the limitations of using the label 'Celtic': field systems were founded at different times in separate parts of Europe.

The scale of fieldwork has significantly increased in most areas of north-west Europe during the last thirty years. In Britain, aerial and ground surveys have been employed to considerable effect in mapping and interpreting the land divisions. While new methods of remote sensing, such as airborne laser scanning, are proving effective in regions where earthworks are ephemeral or are obscured by vegetation, elsewhere, where earthworks have not survived, the application of area excavation has proven very effective at revealing ancient fields, for instance in the Thames Valley and East Anglian Fenland of England. One challenge is to synthesize and interpret this increasingly large body of research, particularly when

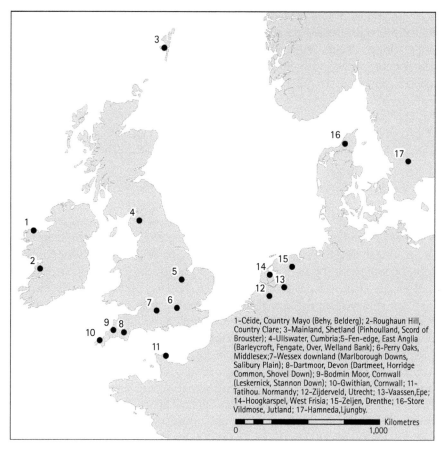

FIG. 17.1 Map of north-west Europe showing the locations of key sites discussed in the chapter.

Basemap: copyright 2010 DeLorme, reproduced by permission.

commercially funded excavations result in a fragmented and unevenly published record. The potential of this resource is, however, very significant as illustrated by David Yates's recent synthesis (2007).

In parallel with the increase in field-based investigations, there have been important changes in the ways that land division and agriculture have been integrated into accounts of social change during the Bronze Age. This has involved a move away from using fields solely to reconstruct subsistence strategies, and instead relating enclosure to particular forms of social order, as a precondition for, or an outcome of, political change. The development of field systems has been explained as the outcome of an intensification in the production of agricultural resources in order to sustain competitive political networks (Yates 2007). If field systems were in some ways related to social organization, then it follows that social organization can be interpreted on the basis of the spatial patterning of the fields. In his research on the boundaries on Dartmoor, Andrew Fleming (2008) argued that the different levels of land enclosure—from small subdivided fields to large territories—mapped onto varied scales of social organization, ranging from individual farms to valley-based communities within which labour and land were pooled cooperatively. Some of the most recent research has questioned this equivalence between the organization of boundaries and society. In her study of Dartmoor's fields, Helen Wickstead (2008) interpreted tenure as a constituent of people's identities, and as with other aspects of identity it was defined through a person's wider networks of relations with people, things, and landscapes.

Classifying Fields

Terms such as 'field', 'field system', and 'land division' encompass a wide variety of archaeological structures. At its simplest, the term 'field' is applied to a cultivated area of ground, whether or not it is defined by a boundary. A field may also be a small and often bounded area of pasture. Terms such as 'plot' and 'garden', in turn, describe hand-dug areas either close to domestic buildings or as part of shifting horticulture. The identification of prehistoric fields need not depend on the presence of physical boundaries. A variety of processes connected with the creation of fields will impact on the material qualities of the land, including the clearance of stone, cultivation, and soil improvement through manuring. Fieldstone was sometimes piled into small cairns, dumped along the edges of fields, placed against features such as earthfast boulders and abandoned houses. The transformation of soils through cultivation and manuring is detectable in a variety of ways. The marks left by both ards and spades have been recognized in excavation, geochemical analysis can detect the effects of manuring, and unstable sediments may erode from the surfaces of fields and accumulate against barriers such as fences and ditches.

Fields may be organized into wider patterns of land allotment, which are described as 'field systems'. Field systems need not require the construction of physical boundaries, as the patterns may have emerged through processes of stone clearance and the build-up or erosion of sediments forming baulks and lynchets. On the other hand, there are many examples of prehistoric field systems that were defined by constructed boundaries: fences, walls, hedges, ditches, and earth banks were all used, creating fields of varying degrees of regularity. Such 'systems' may be small (a hectare or two) or very extensive (up to 3,000 hectares), and exhibiting varying degrees of integration with the existing landscape.

The morphologies of field systems have served as one of the main means by which archaeologists have ordered the evidence. The most enduring attempts at doing this have distinguished different classes of systems on the basis of the relative regularity of the relationships between their components. Richard Bradley (1978) marked a contrast between aggregate and cohesive field systems. The term 'co-axial' has in turn been widely adopted to describe systems where a single cardinal alignment structures the layout of the boundaries. Yet there are other distinctions that cut across these classifications, one being the materials from which boundaries are constructed, distinguishing between the stone-walled fields predominating in western Britain and Scandinavia, and the boundaries defined by earthen banks, ditches, and sandy ridges mainly known from south-eastern Britain, Netherlands, Denmark, and Germany (Spek *et al.* 2003). There are also forms of land division that cannot be described as 'fields' because they represent a significantly larger scale of landscape organization: boundaries have been traced for distances of a few hundred metres up to 10 km across the landscape. In some cases these were organized into well-defined 'territories', which overlay earlier networks of co-axial fields, and on other occasions their purpose remains enigmatic, as with pit and post alignments.

The Chronology and History of Fields

The various types of land division introduced in the last section are all known from the European Bronze Age, although the chronologies can be difficult to reconstruct and are frequently insecure. Where the chronological sequences of field systems have been established, these are often based on the investigation of the boundaries themselves rather than the fields that they enclose. This is partly because the boundaries are the most commonly surviving structural evidence of the fields. Boundaries are also important because they provide 'traps' for cultural material, such as pottery, which has eroded from the surfaces of the fields.

This is not to say that field surfaces are archaeologically invisible. They were cleared, manured, or used for various activities. Unfortunately, these surfaces are often lost through the impact of later agriculture or as the result of soil formation processes. This is not uniformly the case, and some exceptional examples have illustrated the value of excavating the field surface as well as the boundaries, as in the pioneering projects in Store Vildmose, northern Denmark, and Gwithian, south-west England (Nielsen 1986; Nowakowski 2009).

In spite of these examples, it is more commonly the character and the physical relationships between boundaries and other features in the landscape that remain some of the key ways in which a chronology is assigned to field systems. This landscape stratigraphy was critical to early identifications of prehistoric fields and it continues to play an important part in the reconstruction of landscape histories. The earthwork field systems on Salisbury Plain, southern England, for instance, are dated to the Middle Bronze Age principally on the basis of their physical relationships with settlement enclosures and Late Bronze Age linear ditches (McOmish, Field, and Brown 2002).

These relative chronologies are refined and made absolute through a variety of techniques. Artefacts, particularly ceramics, have an important role in dating boundaries. For instance, the Beaker pottery recovered from the ditches at Sutton Hoo provides the only means of assigning a date to the field system (Carver 2005). One important difficulty with using artefacts to date fields is that the boundaries can accumulate material culture that is residual from earlier occupations or subsequent to the boundary going out of use. Radiocarbon dating can also be extremely valuable in spite of the difficulties with recovering samples from 'event contexts' associated with field systems. The approach taken by Stephen Carter in Moray, north-east Scotland, was to cross-correlate multiple dates obtained from charcoal recovered from buried soils beneath boundaries (Carter 1993). The analysis identified a phase of Early Bronze Age stone clearance followed by the laying out of co-axial boundaries in the late second millennium BC. A similar strategy, although on a much larger scale, was employed in a study of clearance cairns in Hamneda, southern Sweden, showing that clearance began in the study area during the early first millennium AD (Lagerås and Bartholin 2003).

Other methods have been adopted in order to overcome the difficulty of recovering datable samples. Optical Stimulated Luminescence dating has been used to date boundaries, for instance in Småland, southern Sweden (Häggström et al. 2004), while at Perry Oaks, a construction date of 1800–1700 BC was argued for on the basis that hedgerow pollen was recovered from datable sediments within waterholes that were adjacent to the boundary ditches (Framework Archaeology 2006). One of the more unusual techniques for establishing the chronology of a field system comes from Carlton Jones's (1998) fieldwork in the Burren, County Clare, Ireland. Jones used the relative depths of limestone bedrock preserved beneath the stone banks to argue that the boundaries dated from the Early Bronze Age.

The challenges in establishing the chronologies of prehistoric land division are a reflection of the complexities of large and extensive structures that may remain important features in the landscape for millennia. While some boundaries may be short-lived, most were reworked over many generations: walls were periodically repaired, ditches were recut, earth banks and lynchets accumulated sediments and accompanying material culture at varying rates. These processes serve to underscore the idea that prehistoric fields were lived-in landscapes with long histories, which may have begun to develop in the Bronze Age but often continued to be inhabited for many centuries afterwards.

Early Fields on the Edges of Europe

The earliest land division in Europe pre-dates the Bronze Age. Seamus Caulfield's remarkable discovery of stone boundary walls enclosing over one thousand hectares of land on the northern coast of County Mayo, Ireland, is the earliest and also one of the most geographically marginal field systems in Europe (Caulfied, O'Donnell, and Mitchell 1998). It is even more extraordinary when it is considered that the stone walls are buried beneath deep accumulations of peat. There are several groups of land divisions around Céide, and they have different morphologies, and may be of a variety of dates. The earliest fields, at Behy, are organized into distinctive north-south aligned strips, each of which is further subdivided into rectangular fields up to 7 hectares in area. They were laid out and used during the middle to later centuries of the fourth millennium BC. There is some evidence for settlement within the fields in the form of small enclosures, and in one case excavations have revealed a circular structure, perhaps a building. The relatively large size of the fields led the excavator to suggest they were primarily constructed to manage pasture for cattle, although the evidence of both cereal pollen and ard marks within some of the excavated areas show that cultivation was also practised.

Although the fourth millennium BC date of the boundaries at Behy has attracted most of the academic interest, there is evidence that some of the field systems in County Mayo were reused in the Early Bronze Age, while other parts of the landscape may have been organized into new field systems at around the same time. At Belderg, the fields are smaller and more irregular in shape than the co-axial boundaries to the east. There is also evidence that the stone walls were reinforced with wooden fences in the Early Bronze Age, and the peaty soil within the fields was cultivated.

Another example of an Early Bronze Age enclosed landscape in west Ireland is Roughaun Hill, County Clare. Here, the survival of the stone walls is the physical inverse of the situation at Céide: they stand broad on pedestals of limestone, with the surrounding field surfaces and bedrock having eroded to a lower level (Jones 1998). The large network of fields is fragmentary in many places, although it is possible to distinguish small irregular plots close to settlements and a few longer, axial boundaries, including the distinctive double banks of trackways, towards the periphery. The settlements at Roughaun Hill all seem to have been located within roughly oval stone-built enclosures, up to 50–70 m in size, within which there were some fragmentary remains of stone structures, although these did not form definable dwellings.

The fields at Roughaun Hill can be compared with those surveyed and excavated on Shetland, the northernmost group of Scottish islands. At Scord of Brouster, on the west side of Mainland, a group of oval houses were occupied in the early and middle centuries of the third millennium BC (Whittle 1986) (Fig.17.2). They were set within a group of fields, and amongst a large number of clearance cairns. Settlements, similarly comprising houses and small enclosures or fields, are known from elsewhere in the surrounding landscape. The intervening areas between the settlements were divided by stone boundary walls, marking out a much larger, fragmentary system of land apportionment.

These examples illustrate that land enclosure was a feature of both Neolithic and Early Bronze Age landscapes. There was considerable variety in the morphology of these field

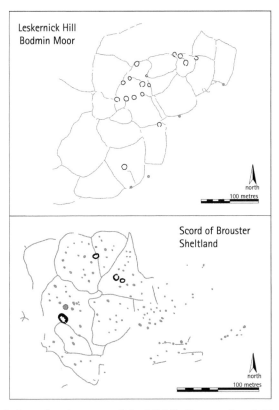

FIG. 17.2 Simplified plans showing part of the Middle Bronze Age fields and settlement on Leskernick Hill, Bodmin Moor, and the Later Neolithic houses, field boundaries, and clearance cairns at Scord of Brouster, Shetland. Buildings are depicted in black, boundaries and cairns in grey, and structured cairns are marked with a dashed black outline.

Source: author, based on Johnson and Rose 1994, Whittle 1986.

systems, which presumably reflected land-use practices, and the social and historical conditions in which they were formed. There was evidently not an evolutionary development from small-scale, more 'organic' fields to large-scale and regular land division. Equally, the morphology of field systems cannot be said to be chronologically sensitive. The distribution of these field systems on the geographical margins of Europe is likely to be a factor of the exceptional environmental circumstances in which they are preserved: either buried beneath deep accumulations of peat, or in landscapes that have seen little subsequent intensive agriculture.

STONE CAIRNS AND WALLS IN THE WESTERN UPLANDS

The evidence for fields dating to the second and first millennia BC is substantially more common than the rare instances surviving from the fourth and third millennia BC, although again the history of later land use has a significant impact on its visibility. This is evident in zones of the landscape where medieval and later agriculture has not altered the land surface and relatively subtle above-ground features have therefore survived. In many cases, the signatures of prehistoric agriculture are durable because they are primarily constituted of stone, whether cairns or walls, and there has been relatively limited intensive land use in subsequent millennia. Some of the best-studied examples that date from the Bronze Age lie in the west and north of Britain, and this region will form the primary focus for this section.

By far the simplest evidence of agricultural fields in highland areas is provided by 'clearance cairns', which were created when fieldstone was dug out to improve the soil, gathered and placed into small mounds. These structures are not uniquely prehistoric: they continue to be created in modern landscapes throughout the world. Yet field survey demonstrates that prehistoric clearance cairns survive as 'tidemarks' across the uplands at altitudes above the limits of later agriculture. Studies in southern Scotland have shown the cairns are distributed on southerly facing slopes and at altitudes above modern enclosed land (Yates 1984). The cairns are invariably found in groups, termed 'cairnfields'. Sometimes these might comprise no more than four or five mounds, while in other cases there can be hundreds of cairns in a cairnfield covering many hectares, with some of the largest examples known from Cumbria, north-west England.

The interpretation of cairnfields has focused on the land use, technologies, and environmental context of their formation. The long-standing orthodoxy is that the clearance of stone into cairns occurred when the uplands were 'colonized' during a period of warmer climate and increasing pressure on resources during the early and mid second millennium BC. Suitable areas were cultivated intensively although for a short period of time, until the soils became impoverished and the deteriorating climate made agriculture unsustainable. More recent research has argued against this model, pointing instead to evidence for long-term, non-intensive management of the uplands during the Bronze Age. In their research in Cumbria, drawing on evidence from excavations and palaeo-environmental studies, Hoaen and Loney (2007) have suggested the cairnfields expanded with frequent shifts in the locations of cultivation plots, along with medium to long fallow periods and the maintenance of clearings as pasture. Willy Kitchen (2001) has argued that cairnfields were created by relatively mobile communities whose attachments to the places that they cultivated and where their animals grazed may only have lasted a season. The cairns provided a practical means of disposing of stone as well as being social markers of groups' temporary uses of a plot.

Fieldstone was also cleared to the edges of cultivated plots, where it formed loose banks or it was used to build low walls. The walls may have served a variety of functions including controlling livestock. Stone banks also, on occasions, accumulated around the exterior of roundhouses or on top of the foundations of abandoned buildings. The result of these clearance practices were patterns of land use and settlement that were visibly more organized than the cairnfields. The archaeological surveys on Bodmin Moor, south-west England, have provided a large number of examples of field systems and associated roundhouses that seem to have formed in this way (Johnson and Rose 1994) (see Fig.17.2). This 'peak' of activity during the second millennium BC is supported by palaeo-environmental evidence, which indicates the widespread clearance of woodland at various times during the second millennium BC and the maintenance of an open, grazed landscape until the later first millennium BC (Gearey, Charman, and Kent 2000).

The field walls and houses of the Bronze Age settlement on Leskernick Hill, Bodmin Moor, were built amongst a dense area of natural surface stone. Some of the plots may have been cultivated, but the stoniness of the ground and the presence of double-banked trackways would suggest that livestock were likely to have been more important. The archaeological team that undertook the most recent fieldwork at Leskernick have proposed that the cultural identities of people living on the moor during the Bronze Age were constituted by the 'stone worlds' that they inhabited (Bender, Hamilton, and Tilley 2007). They argue that rather than imagining these as marginal landscapes, which were perhaps seasonally occupied, they were settled year-round by Bronze Age communities who had strong economic and cultural attachments to the land.

There are similarities between this interpretation and that of the Bronze Age coastal settlements in south-west England, where there is strong evidence that communities, perhaps constituted from extended families, lived in small settlements of roundhouses with associated fields and garden plots. At Gwithian, a long-lived Bronze Age settlement and its fields were uncovered beneath sand dunes on the north coast of Cornwall (Nowakowski 2009). During 1500–1200 BC the inhabitants of the settlement had to contend with windblown sand and managing thin, unstable soils. In spite of these challenges, they continued to live on and work the land, employing practical measures such as creating physical barriers to control erosion and using manure to make the soils cultivable. One reason why people laboured to make these difficult places inhabitable might be found in the presence of cremated human remains placed in pits along the edges of fields, perhaps hinting at strong social and probably emotional attachments between communities and land.

The well-preserved evidence for agriculture and small-scale field systems shows the intensity with which landscapes were inhabited, and the different ways in which people established connections with places, organized land around their dwellings, and managed crops and animals. Cairnfields were perhaps located in places of long-term significance but which were only cultivated periodically and potentially with access negotiated amongst a large community. The aggregated field systems, organized around settlements, were formed under varied land-use regimes, although they seem to reflect longer-term attachments between small communities and the land. This bond was marked physically by the association of houses with fields, and the use of permanent boundaries to mark out the edges of gardens, stock enclosures, and cultivation plots.

Linear Landscapes in Southern Britain

To the east and south of Britain, Bronze Age land divisions were laid out on a much grander scale and according to distinctive, linear patterns. These have variously been termed 'co-axial', 'rectilinear', 'cohesive', and 'linear' field systems, because the basic framework comprises long boundaries laid parallel with one another and following a common axis. In a recent synthesis of the evidence from Britain, Yates (2007) demonstrated that the co-axial fields were common in lowland southern England during the middle and later centuries of the second millennium BC.

One region that has dominated the study of co-axial fields is Dartmoor, an area of high moorland in Devon, south-west England (Fig.17.3). The co-axial field systems survive best around the southern and eastern sides of the moor, where they enclose thousands of hectares of land. Andrew Fleming's research on these moorland co-axial boundaries has shown that they form a series of distinct and internally coherent systems, some of which are very large (enclosing up to 3,000 hectares) (Fleming 2008). Commonly the enclosed strips are subdivided and terminate at a single boundary that is topographically higher and serves to distinguish between lower-lying, enclosed land and unenclosed upland. This basic pattern seems to have developed in different ways. Some systems are relatively small, and are keyed into much larger subdivided moorland blocks, as on Shovel Down. Others were built on a truly grand scale, and the basic form is followed for up to 6 km over hills and valleys, notably Dartmeet, on the eastern side of the moor. Palaeo-environmental studies show that the landscape was becoming significantly less wooded during the middle of the second millennium BC, around the same time that the boundaries were built, and pasture was the predominant form of land use on the moor (e.g. Fyfe et al. 2008).

Comparisons have frequently been made between the systems of Bronze Age boundaries on Dartmoor and the field systems on the chalk uplands to the east on the Marlborough Downs, Salisbury Plain, and the South Downs. Some of these field systems also share a common axis, as on Dartmoor, but the patterns are variable and the means by which they were formed were different. The downland fields survive as earthworks, rather than stone walls, either as low banks or as lynchets. The lynchets were formed as cultivated soils accumulated downslope against barriers such as lines of stones, fences, or hedge banks, or where cultivation eroded the land surface on the downslope side of a boundary. On the Marlborough Downs, Wiltshire, the boundaries may initially have been arranged in axial strips. But the fields were later subdivided and infilled, forming a mixture of small square and larger rectangular enclosures, up to 2 hectares in size. A similarly complex pattern exists on Salisbury Plain, where early and sometimes very extensive co-axial field systems were in use, probably discontinuously, until at least the first millennium AD (McOmish, Field, and Brown 2002).

The survey of field systems in the uplands enables extensive areas of the boundaries to be mapped and for elements of landscape stratigraphy to be recognized. Large-area excavation, usually in lowland settings, offers a more concentrated look at small parts of the landscape. On

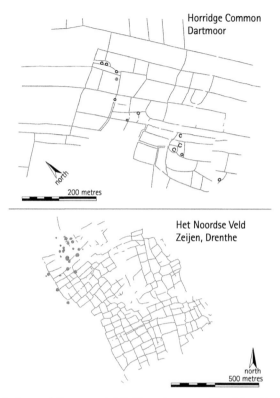

FIG. 17.3 Simplified plans of the co-axial field systems on Horridge Common, Dartmoor, and the Celtic fields at Het Noordse Veld, Zeijen, Drenthe. Buildings are depicted in black, boundaries and cairns/barrows in grey, and structured cairns/barrows are marked with a dashed black outline.

Source: author, based on Butler 1991, Spek et al. 2003.

the negative side, these are landscapes that have been heavily disturbed by later agriculture and development, and so the Bronze Age features are often poorly preserved. At Perry Oaks, Middlesex, in the Thames Valley, the excavations uncovered over 20 hectares of a Bronze Age co-axial field system (Framework Archaeology 2006). The fields were formed by hedge and ditch boundaries arranged north-south and defined at regular intervals by trackways. The earliest north-south boundaries were probably built sometime during 1800–1600 BC, and care was taken to avoid the silted ditches of Neolithic monuments. The areas between the axial boundaries were subsequently subdivided by ditches that cut across the grain of the earlier monuments. This process may have taken some time, as analysis seems to indicate spatial variations in the proportions of Middle and Late Bronze Age ceramics across what the excavators termed 'landholdings', reflecting use of the fields stretching over one thousand years.

The fields at Perry Oaks were in a low-lying landscape, but one that was relatively high, at 23 m above sea level, in comparison to the topography of the fen-edge of East Anglia. There, some of the excavated Bronze Age surfaces, although inland, now lie below sea level and are preserved beneath up to 4 m of peat or alluvium. The excavations at Fengate, Over, Barleycroft, Welland Bank Quarry, and most recently at Bradley Fen, are a selection of the many examples of Bronze Age field systems in this region (Yates 2007). The boundaries at Fengate, Peterborough, were excavated in the 1970s and have since received the most attention because they were the first lowland Bronze Age fields to be uncovered on a large scale (Pryor 1998). The boundaries were defined by ditches and banks, probably topped with hedges. They formed a co-axial pattern, with the axis defined by droveways, which in the case of the Fengate fields led eastwards from dry ground to the seasonal pasture on the fenland. Francis Pryor has argued that the Fengate droveways formed part of a system of paddocks for managing sheep, with each community having its own group of stockyards. At Welland Bank, to the north of Fengate, the fields seem to have been in use later than those at Fengate, they were not arranged co-axially, there were fewer droveways, and the scale of the ditches has led the excavation team to suggest they served to control cattle (Pryor 1998).

It is possible to conceive of these landscapes in wholly economic terms, as an efficient and exploitative use of the environment. Nevertheless, as with Gwithian, discussed in the previous section, there is recurring evidence for social conditions that structured the formation of the fields. At Over and Barleycroft, Cambridgeshire, excavations on either side of the River Ouse have identified extensive areas of co-axial boundaries (Evans and Knight 2000). The boundaries at Barleycroft followed a variety of alignments and in a couple of instances were closely associated with earlier ring-ditches. The relationship between the ring-ditches and field boundaries at Barleycroft and Over would seem to indicate that the monuments were important nodes in organizing the landscape. They were probably all earlier than the boundaries, although in some cases they remained a focus for the deposition of burials when the field system was in use. Barrows were also located at critical locations and respected by boundaries in other landscapes that have already been discussed, notably on Salisbury Plain and on Dartmoor. It is possible that the barrows served as convenient landmarks, but in some cases they were still active places in the landscape where burials had recently been placed.

The 'linear' field systems appear to mark a widespread and relatively abrupt transformation in the organization of landscapes in southern Britain. The similarities in the layout of the field systems is striking, and the chronological evidence shows that many of them originated during 1600–1150 BC. This has led prehistorians to interpret the fields as the outcome of related phases of land enclosure, which formed a particular historical process. In some explanations, this process was driven by a need to intensify the production of agricultural resources in order to sustain competitive exchange networks (e.g. Yates 2007). The field systems were therefore a technological innovation that enabled more resources to be produced from the land. Other researchers have instead emphasized a change in the relationship between people and land that came about in the context of a fragmentation of corporate groups into small, family-based units, and with this an increasing concern to control domestic spaces and the productive resources of the household (e.g. Brück 2000).

'Celtic Fields' in North-West Europe

The themes of economic and social change also apply to the Late Bronze Age and Iron Age of north-west continental Europe, when, as in southern Britain in the Middle Bronze Age, there was a phase of land division during which large areas of the landscape were enclosed in a regular pattern of 'Celtic fields'. The chronology of this land enclosure is imprecisely understood, although the earliest extensive fields systems were probably built during 1100–500 BC.

There are a few examples of field systems that pre-date this more widespread phase of land enclosure. In West Frisia, the northern Netherlands, the Middle Bronze Age settlements were associated with networks of field ditches. At Hoogkarspel, these extended across at least 20 hectares of land, with evidence for units or landholdings, which were further subdivided into small plots (Bakker et al. 1977). The ditches around the fields were periodically redug, seemingly after the field had lain fallow for some time. This re-established the boundaries as physical barriers and may have served as a means of affirming rights of access to an area of land for the duration of its cultivation. The Middle Bronze Age settlement at Zijderveld, Utrecht, in the southern Netherlands, also produced evidence of field boundaries although of a different character to those in the north (Hulst 1991). Here a complex palimpsest of fencelines marked the shifting edges of enclosed land lying beyond the core settlement area.

These early examples of field systems are rare survivals. The majority of evidence for later prehistoric land division in the Netherlands—and to the north and east, in Belgium, Germany, Denmark, and Sweden—dates from the first millennium BC and later. Some of the earliest and best preserved of these systems are found on the sandy uplands of the northern and central Netherlands. The fields form a grid-like pattern, which in some cases extends over 100 hectares. A recent survey in the central Netherlands estimated that up to 4,500 hectares had been enclosed in this way (Kooistra and Maas 2008). The fields are square or rectangular in shape, roughly 20–50 m in length, and defined by low, broad banks (see Fig.17.3). In excavation, the banks of the earthwork fields at Vaassen, Epe, comprised earth and stone cleared from the interior of the enclosures (Brongers 1976). The banks had been laid out on an already cultivated landscape, and there was evidence of both houses and granaries pre-dating the cultivation of the fields. In a more recent excavation of a field near Zeijen, Drenthe, the study of the banks and field surfaces has shown that initially the fields were unenclosed or bounded by temporary structures such as fences (Spek et al. 2003). Turf and stones were then dug up from the field surfaces and used to create ridges along the field edges. During the later first millennium BC, these ridges were widened with sand and manure and then cultivated; the 'interior' of the field was then abandoned, depleted of nutrients and organic matter.

The settlement and environmental evidence recovered in association with the Celtic fields indicates a mixed farming system. For instance, ard marks are visible in the excavated surfaces of fields, and the botanical remains recovered from settlements includes emmer wheat, hulled and naked barley, and millet (Brinkkemper and Van Wijngaarden-Bakker 2005). The preservation of faunal remains is poor from the settlements on the sandy soils across which the Celtic fields are distributed. Nonetheless, there is evidence for manuring of fields, and longhouses include stalls for cattle, which gives the impression of a relatively stable farming system. However, there is a case for interpreting a more dynamic pattern of settlement in which farmsteads moved after a generation of intensive use of a block of fields (Gerritsen 2003). New areas of fields were then cultivated, and the old enclosed land was left fallow and used as pasture.

Explanations of why the Celtic fields developed in such a regular fashion have tended to focus on the technologies through which they were formed: particularly the possibility of using ox-drawn ards, the convenience of parcelling land so that one plot could be cultivated or harvested by one person in one day, and the requirements of different manuring practices. Tenure and the social organization of land within the field systems has also been discussed by some authors (e.g. Brongers 1976; Gerritsen 2003). A recurrent idea in these discussions is that land was held by a community rather than forming the private property of individuals. It was therefore the group, rather than specific families, that laid claim to the territory defined by the fields. Tenure, or the rights of access to cultivate the fields, was shared, although it may have remained stable for the duration of a family's occupation of a farmstead. The enclosed land was therefore one means by which a community defined itself, while rights to short-term tenure over parcels of land provided individuals and families with a means of identifying themselves within the community.

Fields, Landscape, and Society

This chapter has offered an overview of the ways in which land division transformed the landscapes in several regions of Europe during the Bronze Age. The focus has been on the evidence for enclosure, where physical boundaries around fields were deliberately constructed or they were formed through the gradual accumulation of material such as soil or stone. The earliest examples of field systems pre-date the Bronze Age and are known from the edges of Europe, in western Ireland and northern Scotland. Subsequent 'phases' of enclosure followed in southern Britain in the Middle Bronze Age and on the near continent from the Late Bronze Age. Many more examples of prehistoric fields are dated to the later first millennium BC, including areas of central and northern Europe.

The current distribution of Bronze Age fields cannot be taken as an unproblematic reflection of their original extent. Landscape formation processes have played a key role in preserving the remains of ancient land divisions, such as when processes of sedimentation sealed old land surfaces, as in the peat-covered walls of western Ireland or the accumulation of turf and manure on the banks of Dutch fields. Equally, the distribution of many prehistoric fields is often limited to land that is now agriculturally marginal, which reflects the impact of three millennia of land use. The heavily truncated ditches of co-axial field systems in the Thames Valley revealed through large-area excavations indicate the narrow margins between preservation and destruction.

These same excavations also highlight the role played by traditions of archaeological fieldwork in forming our knowledge of Bronze Age fields. It is for this reason and the variability of preservation that there is potential for the geographical distribution of Bronze Age land enclosure to be extended and for the time-depth of known systems to be lengthened. For instance, excavations are now expanding the distribution of Bronze Age field systems to northern France, as on the island of Tatihou, Normandy (Marcigny and Ghesquière 2003), while in the Baltic region, where most fossil fields are dated to the Iron Age, the case has been made that some may be earlier (e.g. Lang 1994).

The distribution of prehistoric field systems may be conditioned by formation processes and research traditions, but land enclosure was not ubiquitous across Europe nor were episodes of land enclosure historically contiguous. There were times and places, such as western Ireland in the late fourth millennium BC and southern Britain in the mid second millennium

BC, when land division served as a large-scale organizing structure in the landscape. These systems enclosed many hectares of pasture and arable, provided mechanisms for controlling production, social relations, and the environment. At other times and in other places, fields were an extension of a household's domestic space, with plots and houses drawing a more localized order in the landscape. Field systems therefore developed under particular social and historical conditions, and they will then have served to structure societies' inhabitation of their land.

The social dynamics and economy of land enclosure have been explored separately by scholars in each region, although there are common themes. One of these is the proposition that the construction of land boundaries was conditional upon a more settled and intensive occupation of the landscape. The terms 'settled' and 'intensive' have a spectrum of meanings within these models. The 'settled' inhabitation of places ranges from the permanent and long-term, to shifting and 'wandering' farmsteads that were relocated on generational or more frequent timescales. Intensive agriculture includes both the careful maintenance of the same small area of land by a family and the large-scale management of crops or animals by a community in order to generate a surplus of resources to sustain competitive political networks. These ways of living with and working the land are generally treated as part of broader transformations within the environment and society. A pressure on food and agricultural resources more generally is frequently suggested as a driver for change. This pressure is brought about through a combination of climatic change, over-exploitation of the environment, and demographic expansion. Political changes, notably the emergence of hierarchical social networks founded on the exchange of high-status goods, are also presented as an explanation for the need to exploit the environment more intensively.

These 'grand narratives' offer an assured explanation of land enclosure. On the other hand, they rely upon causal relationships between rather coarsely defined processes such as demographic or environmental change and the emergence of new forms of human-land relations. The detailed studies of particular regions and landscapes offer alternative and quite varied and contingent histories with a much more complex entanglement of economic, environmental, and social processes. The challenge remains for prehistorians to work effectively between these scales, from the social practices and land-use histories amongst the fields to the wider social structures and traditions of human-land relations that those same practices generated and sustained.

Bibliography

Bakker, J. A., Brandt, R. W., Van Geel, B., Jansma, M. J., Kuijper, W. J., Van Mensch, P. J. A., Pals, J. P., and IJzereef, G. F. (1977). 'Hoogkarspel—Watertoren: towards a reconstruction of ecology and archaeology of an agrarian settlement in 1000 BC', in B. L. van Beek, R. W. Brandt, and W. Groenman-van Waateringe (eds.), *Ex Horreo*. Amsterdam: University of Amsterdam, 187–225.

Bender, B., Hamilton, S., and Tilley, C. (2007). *Stone Worlds: Narrative and Reflexivity in Landscape Archaeology*. Walnut Creek, CA: Left Coast Press.

Bowen, H. C. (1961). *Ancient Fields: A Tentative Analysis of Vanishing Earthworks and Landscapes*. London: British Association for the Advancement of Science.

Bradley, R. (1978). 'Prehistoric field systems in Britain and north-west Europe: a review of recent work', *World Archaeology*, 9: 265–80.

Brongers, J. A. (1976). *Air Photography and Celtic Field Research in the Netherlands*. Amersfoort: Rijksdienst voor het Oudheidkundig Bodemonderzoek.

Brück, J. (2000). 'Settlement, landscape and social identity: the Early–Middle Bronze Age transition in Wessex, Sussex and the Thames Valley', *Oxford Journal of Archaeology*, 19/3: 273–300.

Butler, J. (1991). *Dartmoor Atlas of Antiquities: volume 1. The East*. Exeter: Devon Books.

Carter, S. T. (1993). 'Tulloch Wood, Forres, Moray: the survey and dating of a fragment of prehistoric landscape', *Proceedings of the Society of Antiquaries of Scotland*, 23: 215–33.

Carver, M. (2005). *Sutton Hoo: A Seventh-Century Princely Burial Ground and its Context*. London: British Museum Press.

Caulfield, S., O'Donnell, R. G., and Mitchell, P. I. (1998). '^{14}C dating of a Neolithic field system at Céide Fields, County Mayo, Ireland', *Radiocarbon*, 40/2: 629–40.

Crawford, O. G. S. (1923). 'Air survey and archaeology', *Geographical Journal*, 61/5: 342–66.

Curwen, E. and Curwen, E. C. (1923). 'Sussex lynchets and their associated fieldways', *Sussex Archaeological Collections*, 64: 1–65.

Evans, C. and Knight, M. (2000). 'A Fenland delta: later prehistoric land-use in the lower Ouse Reaches', in M. Dawson (ed.), *Prehistoric, Roman and Post-Roman Landscapes of the Great Ouse Valley*, Council for British Archaeology (Research Report), 119. London: CBA Publishing, 89–106.

Fleming, A. (2008). *The Dartmoor Reaves: Investigating Prehistoric Land divisions*, 2nd edn. Oxford: Windgather Press.

Framework Archaeology (2006). *Landscape Evolution in the Middle Thames Valley: Heathrow Terminal 5 Excavations: Volume 1. Perry Oaks*. Oxford/Salisbury: Framework Archaeology.

Fyfe, R., Brück, J., Johnston, R., Lewis, H., Roland, T., and Wickstead, H. (2008). 'Historical context and chronology of Bronze Age land enclosure on Dartmoor, UK', *Journal of Archaeological Science*, 35: 2,250–61.

Gearey, B. R., Charman, D. J., and Kent, M. (2000). 'Palaeoecological evidence for the prehistoric settlement of Bodmin Moor, Cornwall, southwest England. Part II: land use changes from the Neolithic to the present', *Journal of Archaeological Science*, 27: 493–508.

Gerritsen, F. (2003). *Local Identities: Landscape and Community in the Later Prehistoric Meuse-Demer-Scheldt Region*. Amsterdam: Amsterdam University Press.

Häggström, L., Baran, J., Ericsson, A., and Murray, A. (2004). 'The dating and interpretation of a field wall in Öggestorp', *Current Swedish Archaeology*, 12: 43–60.

Hoaen, A. W. and Loney, H. L. (2007). 'Cairnfields: understanding economic and ecological practice during the Bronze Age of central Britain', in P. J. Cherry (ed.), *Studies in Northern Prehistory: Essays in Memory of Clare Fell*. Kendal: Cumberland and Westmoreland Antiquarian and Archaeological Society.

Hulst, R. S. (1991). 'Nederzettingen uit de midden-bronstijd in het rivierengebied: Zijderveld en Dodewaard', in H. Fokkens and N. Roymans (eds.), *Nederzettingen uit de Bronstijd en de Vroege IJzertijd in de Lage Landen*. Amersfoort: Rijksdienst voor het Oudheidkundig Bodemonderzoek, 53–9.

Johnson, N. and Rose, P. (1994). *Bodmin Moor: An Archaeological Survey: Volume 1. The Human Landscape to c.1800*. London: English Heritage.

Jones, C. (1998). 'The discovery and dating of the prehistoric landscape of Roughan Hill in Co. Clare', *Journal of Irish Archaeology*, 9: 27–44.

Kitchen, W. (2001). 'Tenure and territoriality in the British Bronze Age', in J. Brück (ed.), *Bronze Age Landscapes: Tradition and Transformation*. Oxford: Oxbow Books, 110–20.

Kooistra, M. J. and Maas, G. J. (2008). 'The widespread occurrence of Celtic field systems in the central part of the Netherlands', *Journal of Archaeological Science*, 35/8: 2,318–28.

Lagerås, P. and Bartholin, T. (2003). 'Fire and stone clearance in Iron Age agriculture: new insights inferred from the analysis of terrestrial macroscopic charcoal in clearance cairns in Hamneda, southern Sweden', *Vegetation History and Archaeobotany*, 12: 83–92.

Lang, V. (1994). 'Celtic and Baltic fields in north Estonia: fossil field systems of the Late Bronze Age and pre-Roman Iron Age at Saha-Loo and Proosa', *Acta Archaeologica*, 65: 203–19.

Marcigny, C. and Ghesquière, E. (2003). *L'Île de Tatihou à l'Âge du Bronze (Manche). Habitat et occupation du sol*. Paris: Éditions de la Maison des Sciences de l'Homme.

McOmish, D., Field, D., and Brown, G. (2002). *The Field Archaeology of the Salisbury Plain Training Area*. Swindon: English Heritage.

Müller-Wille, M. (1965). *Eisenzeitliche Fluren in den Fëstlandischen Nordseegebeiten*. Münster: Geographischen Kommission für Westfalen.

Nielsen, V. (1986). 'Ploughing in the Iron Age: plough marks in the Store Vildmose, North Jutland', *Journal of Danish Archaeology*, 5: 189–208.

Nowakowski, J. A. (2009). 'Living in the sands: Bronze Age Gwithian, Cornwall, revisited', in M. J. Allen, N. Sharples, and T. O'Connor (eds.), *Land and People: Papers in Memory of John G Evans*. Oxford: The Prehistoric Society and Oxbow Books, 115–25.

Pryor, F. (1998). *Farmers in Prehistoric Britain*. Stroud: Tempus.

Spek, T., Groenman-van Waateringe, W., Kooistra, M., and Bakker, L. (2003). 'Formation and land-use history of Celtic fields in north-west Europe: an interdisciplinary case study at Zeijen, The Netherlands', *European Journal of Archaeology*, 6/2: 141–73.

Whittle, A. W. R. (1986). *Scord of Brouster: An Early Agricultural Settlement on Shetland*. Oxford: Oxford Committee for Archaeology.

Wickstead, H. (2008). *Theorising Tenure: Land Division and Identity in Later Prehistoric Dartmoor, South-West Britain*. Oxford: Archaeopress.

Wijngaarden-Bakker, L. van and Brinkkemper, O. (2005). 'All-round farming: food production in the Bronze Age and Iron Age', in L. P. Louwe Kooijmans, P. W. v. d. Broeke, H. Fokkens, and A. L. van Gijn (eds.), *The Prehistory of the Netherlands*. Amsterdam: Amsterdam University Press, 491–512.

Yates, D. T. (2007). *Land, Power and Prestige: Bronze Age Field Systems in Southern England*. Oxford: Oxbow Books.

Yates, M. J. (1984). 'Groups of Small Cairns in Northern Britain: A view from SW Scotland', *Proceedings of the Society of Antiquaries of Scotland*, 114: 217–34.

CHAPTER 18

ANIMALS IN BRONZE AGE EUROPE

LÁSZLÓ BARTOSIEWICZ

INTRODUCTION

When Christian Jørgensen Thomsen (1788–1865) coined the term 'Bronze Age' as part of his Three Age System, he focused on a single aspect of material culture, the raw material of artefacts, to aid the classification of collections at the National Museum of Denmark. Archaeozoological remains must also be considered artefacts on two different levels. Firstly, domesticates are human constructs, reflecting needs and aspirations as much as any other man-made object. Moreover, the way animals were processed after death mirrors idiosyncratic cultural behaviour. A metaphoric language of 'ancient herding' developed in processual archaeology, especially in the economic school of archaeozoology during the 1960s. However, animal remains offer evidence only of consumption or the state of certain animals; bone fragments are but loosely correlated with strategic aspects of animal keeping such as stocking rates and kill-off patterns, far less tangible than previously thought. Meanwhile the critical evaluation of archaeozoological data has refined the interpretation of consumption patterns through better understanding the taphonomic process, in other words the formation of animal-bone deposits.

Animal exploitation has never been driven exclusively by practical considerations: the symbolism inherent to animals from direct acquisition by eating to mortuary sacrifices or abstract, artistic representation is culture-specific. In the Near East and Greece, Bronze Age documentary sources reveal the roles of animals. Such sources are not available in mainland Europe where interpretations remain empirical, based on bone remains and equipment relevant to husbandry. A special source is rock art, providing information on animal use rather than the physiognomy of animals themselves. Topics depicted range from hunting scenes in Norway (Trøndelag, Tykamvatn) through naturalistic depictions in Sweden (Bohuslän county) to representations of draught animals in northern Italy (Val Camonica).

Depending on the research tradition, osteological information concerning Bronze Age animals varies between countries. In south-east Europe tells flourished during the Late

Neolithic and Copper Age (also referred to as 'Eneolithic' or 'Chalcolithic') as well as the Bronze Age. These artificial mounds have been seen as extensions of similar features in the Near East and studied using comparable methods. Hill forts represent another form of settlement whose animal-bone finds have been studied. Fortified central settlements may be seen as chiefly residences in stratified societies, inhabited by elites and specialists, rather than larger groups of commons. Rulers in these societies tried to exercise hands-on control over production in a spatially well-defined setting.

Terramare are late Neolithic and Bronze Age pile-structures in the plains of northern Italy dating to the Middle Bronze Age and Late Bronze Age (*c*.1700–1150 BC), named after the marl of which most are composed. They were typically surrounded by a rampart within which the villages were arranged in a limited space.

Artificial settlement mounds called *terpen* ('village') are distributed in the coastal areas of the Netherlands, southern Denmark, and Germany as an adaptation to tides and river floods. Terpen began in the local Bronze Age around 500 BC and lasted to *c*.AD 1200. Similarly to the *terramare*, they were settlements of wooden huts erected on piles on regularly inundated land. A feature shared between these Bronze Age settlement types is a prominent central area where part of the human population was concentrated and where the keeping of animals, especially large stock, was probably limited.

In parts of western and northern Europe, Early and Middle Bronze Age ploughmarks (Thrane 1990; Tegtmeier 1993) were instrumental in reconstructing landscapes (Harding 2000: 126). After 1500 BC evidence of manuring is available in northern Europe (De Hingh 2000; Robinson 2003), indicative of a mixed farming economy (Wijngaarden-Bakker and Brinkkemper 2005: 496). Integrating faunal and agricultural data has been best achieved at lakeshore settlements in central Europe where animal and plant remains were preserved in waterlogged pile dwellings. It was at such sites in Switzerland where the study of animal remains began (Rütimeyer 1861). That research followed principles espoused by Charles Darwin, who praised Ludwig Rütimeyer's work as 'the most important contribution on domestic races ever published' (Darwin 1861).

CHRONOLOGICAL FRAMEWORK AND THE NEAR EASTERN PARADIGM

In cultural terms, the Bronze Age in Europe—dated to approximately between the mid third and early first millennium BC—post-dates the emergence of agriculture, but pre-dates written history. By this time most innovation in animal husbandry had taken place: all common livestock were known and the 'secondary products revolution' (Sherratt 1983) was over. This latter includes forms of exploitation aimed at gaining products from live domesticates in addition to the primary use of meat, fat, bones, and hide that may also be procured by hunting. With increasingly early dates for various secondary products, it became clear that the invention of dairying, draught-animal exploitation, and wool shearing was a complex of protracted processes that varied both by species and between regions.

Bronze Age animal husbandry was not only well established in most areas, but mixed-herd farming offered sufficient flexibility in buffering effects in varied natural and social environments from Scotland to Sicily, Iberia to Siberia. Technical innovation, indicators of status and redistribution, are thus worth considering within the context of Bronze Age animal exploitation.

Generations of archaeologists grew up with the legacy of Gordon Childe, who studied prehistoric connections between Europe and the Near East in an effort to understand ancient western cultures (Childe 1925). Although a direct diffusion of Bronze Age cultures to Europe would be a spurious assumption, better-understood phenomena in the Near East have often inspired the interpretation of Bronze Age finds in Europe. However, local environments, both natural and social, cause many deviations from the main tendencies seen in the Near East.

The Late Chalcolithic and Early Bronze Age transition in the Near East is marked by a shift to large-scale sheep and/or goat (caprine) herding, provisioning emerging urban centres (Clason and Buitenhuis 1998). Palaces and temples are seen as foci of power that ruled populations over large areas. Urban settlements, often fortified, were divided into different quarters, including areas of manufacturing and habitation. Deforestation is another phenomenon across that region as agricultural production increased along with population density in sometimes precarious natural environments. These changes have valid parallels in the Balkans, but they seem less clear-cut in the rest of Europe. Bronze Age phenomena apparent in the eastern Mediterranean Basin seem to taper away toward the north-west in Europe. The tentative absolute dates used in subdividing the Bronze Age into early (Early Bronze Age: late third/early second millennium to 1600 BC), middle (Middle Bronze Age: 1600–1300 BC), and late (Late Bronze Age: 1300–800 BC) phases in central Europe are likewise subject to change within a broader geographical context.

Trends in Bronze Age Animal Exploitation

Given the heterogeneity of Bronze Age archaeozoological data in the literature, a general picture needs to be drafted first. A fundamental methodological problem is that faunal lists are frequently published in percentual terms, the original numbers of identifiable bones being available at best in individual site reports. Percentages are misleading when assemblages of different sizes are compared. They also preclude the use of parametric statistics by masking the distributions of the original variables. Nevertheless, by relying on a substantial body of data we may compensate for this source of intangible bias in reviewing the literature.

Figure 18.1 shows the distribution of 238 Bronze Age assemblages by the contributions of cattle, caprines, and pig in major areas of Europe based on data published by Matolcsi (1982), Choyke (1984), Benecke (1994), Hüster-Plogmann and Schibler (1997), De Grossi Mazzorin and Riedel (1997), Schibler and Studer (1998), as well as Choyke and Bartosiewicz (1999; 2000; 2009), Choyke (2000), Harding (2000), and Bartosiewicz (2012).

Even without in-depth statistical analyses it is clear that assemblages in Figure 18.1 were more or less normally distributed in terms of beef: many contained 30–60 per cent (on average 44 per cent) cattle bones. Extremes were relatively few. Bones from either pig or caprines, on the other hand, rarely reached 50 per cent; the curves fitted to both distributions show a positive skew. Among the 238 assemblages, caprine remains averaged 27.3 per cent, while the

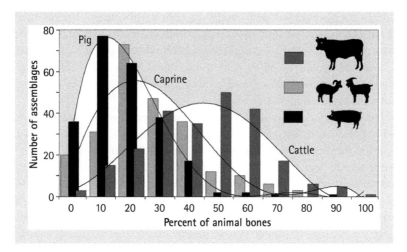

FIG. 18.1 The distribution of 238 Bronze Age archaeozoological assemblages by the percentages of domestic artiodactyls. Note the symmetry, showing a near-normal distribution for cattle, and that small numbers of pig bones tend to occur in low proportions at many sites. Caprine remains are intermediate from this point of view.

average site contained only 17.9 per cent of pig bones. Allowing an average 10–20 per cent for the remains of other animals (horse, dog, and game), half of the bones at a typical settlement would be of cattle, while a quarter would originate from caprines, and one fifth from pig.

Cattle

There has been a consensus that beef played a major role in Bronze Age diets, cattle usually making up 30–60 per cent of the number of identifiable bones. This holds true during most of the Bronze Age, especially in the central plains (Germany and Poland). In Middle Bronze Age northern Europe mixed farming was based on cattle husbandry and cereal cultivation forming a single system, animals providing traction and dung (Louwe Kooijmans 2005: 701). At Bovenkarspel (IJzereef 1981), Dodewaard, and Zijderveld (Louwe Kooijmans 1985: 72) in the Netherlands, as well as Bjerre in Denmark (Bech 1997: 7), cattle contributed 75–80 per cent of the animal remains.

Cattle, however, are often over-represented in assemblages due to the intensive butchering and natural fragmentation of large bones. They are, therefore, difficult to compare to the remains of pig or sheep/goat, similar in size and with bone fragmentation properties that are far more comparable to each other. Since cattle are uniparous, large, slowly maturing, and multi-purpose, they represented special value as they do today in many herding communities: when slaughtered, their replacement was slower than that of small stock. Training working oxen was a tedious task taking well over a year, thereby contributing to the animals' high value, resulting in longevity (Bartosiewicz et al. 1997: 85). Moreover, masses of meat provided by a single individual had to be consumed by larger groups, sometimes through feasting, unless techniques of meat preservation were in place. Cattle were also traded over longer or shorter distances. Towers et al. (2010) employed strontium isotope ratio analysis on teeth from 15 cattle and 1 aurochs from Early Bronze Age round barrows in England, at Irthlingborough, Northamptonshire, and Gayhurst, Buckinghamshire. While strontium results show that most cattle and the aurochs included in their study were of local origin, one animal from each barrow was born remotely, most likely in western Britain.

Sándor Bökönyi (1974: 116) quoted the first appearances of hornless specimens in Copper Age Germany, Poland, and Switzerland. However, Veniamin Iosifovich Zalkin's (1964: 26) theory that hornless forms became widely spread by the Late Bronze Age in Europe is based on negative evidence, the scarcity of horn core finds (0.06–0.65 per cent among cattle bones), rather than the discovery of de facto polled skulls. Overall, increasing variability in Bronze Age horn shapes and body size is evident. This diversity is also characteristic of localized populations, not simply a product of our synthetic view of the entire continent. The rich repertoire of forms and colours is clearly illustrated by iconographic evidence of bull games from Crete.

A withers height decrease of about 10 cm from the Neolithic to the Bronze Age was reported by Boessneck (1958) in southern Germany, although in neighbouring Switzerland tall cattle measuring 150 cm were identified during the Early Bronze Age (Hüster-Plogmann and Schibler 1997: 67). Tall individuals are thought to have been castrates, whose large frames are a desirable trait in draught work (Bartosiewicz et al. 1997: 85); early castration interferes with the endocrine control of bone growth, prolonged in the absence of testosterone. While the resulting elongated bones are typical of oxen, cows and late castrates (physically more reminiscent of bulls) must also have been regularly put to work in many areas.

Cattle traction was firmly established by the Bronze Age. Massive wooden wheels found in waterlogged Late Neolithic deposits (Pétrequin et al. 2006: 102; Fig. 16) are indicative of large and slow vehicles that could only have been moved by powerful oxen. Another type of rarely preserved wooden artefact relevant to cattle exploitation is the sporadically occurring yoke, found at extreme ends of the European continent such as Catalonia, northern Italy, Switzerland, and Scotland (Harding 2000: 129; Pétrequin et al. 2006: 26, 142). These discoveries are supported by the iconographic record: ploughing is shown in rock art at a number of sites.

Overworking is manifested in the diachronically increasing incidence of pathological lesions, especially in the hind limb, a consequence of abnormal dynamic loading posed by traction (Pétrequin et al. 2006: 262; Fig. 8). This trend is evident at several settlements in Spain. Only two arthrotic specimens were identified among the 14.1 per cent cattle remains in the 51,417 bones at the large Copper/Early Bronze Age assemblage from Cerro de la Virgen, Granada (Von den Driesch 1972: 168, Abb. 22). The 33,550 bones from Bronze Age (2000–1000 BC) Cabezo Redondo in Villena, Alicante (Von den Driesch and Boessneck 1969: Taf. 7/1), yielded a single pathological specimen among the meagre set of 7 per cent cattle bones. Smaller assemblages of three to five thousand bones dated to the El Argar culture (1800–1500 BC) in Granada, originating from Cerro de la Encina, Monachil (Friesch 1987: 24), Terrera de Reloj, and Castellón Alto (Milz 1986: 26), also contained only 10–22.5 per cent cattle bones. Some, however, consistently showed potentially work-related symptoms. These suggest that in spite of the small local importance of beef, cattle were used in traction and slaughtered at the end of their working lives. Meanwhile, the Early Bronze Age site of West Row Fen (Suffolk, England) yielded three pathologically modified specimens among 31,451 bone finds whose 39 per cent was made up of cattle (Olsen 1994: 145, Fig. 21): the higher percentual contribution of beef to the diet probably enhanced the manifestation of articular disorders. Horn core deformations are often interpreted as resulting from horn-yokes attached to the heads of the animals.

Most bones originate from mature cattle, implying that beef must have originated from retired working animals or dairy cows. Milking cattle was well known by the Bronze Age.

Pig

Remains of these single-purpose meat animals appear easy to interpret. Throughout European prehistory, wild pigs were available for back-crossing with domestic populations or even for local domestication. Similarly to wolf packs, wild pigs form small groups whose natural hierarchy may easily be controlled by humans, making them amenable to domestication.

In contrast to cattle, pigs are small and prolific (a single litter may contain four to six piglets, sometimes twice a year). The easily renewable nature of pig stocks is shown by the frequent occurrence of bones from young animals in archaeological deposits. For example, at the fortified settlement of Ridala, Estonia (eighth–seventh century BC), over half of the pigs were slaughtered during the first year, and 80 per cent during the first 18 months (Maldre 2008: 269). Rapid reproduction, and the fact that pigs thrive on domestic refuse and even human faeces, has made them ideal for the household economy. However, the emergence of pork prohibition by biblical times may be linked to increasing socio-economic complexity that began at Bronze Age urban settlements in the Near East. Dwelling on the 'impurity' of these animals, their keeping may have been banned by central authorities as a form of independent, family-level meat production, since sizeable sheep herds were far easier to control in terms of taxing and redistribution (Diener and Robkin 1978). There is, however, no material trace of similar regulations during the European Bronze Age. A radical decline in Bronze Age pork consumption is evident in the Levant and lowland areas towards the east. This decrease is less marked in the hills of Anatolia, and pigs were in use all over Bronze Age Europe, gaining importance towards the end of this period (Harding 2000: 134). The overall contribution of pork to the diet is complementary to that of mutton: the emphasis on either sheep or pig in small-scale meat production may have been chiefly influenced by local environmental conditions. This is yet another narrow aspect of the European Bronze Age in which, in spite of increasing social complexity, paradigmatic trends observed in the eastern Mediterranean do not hold.

During the central European Bronze Age, Bökönyi (1974: 212) noted a size decrease in comparison with Neolithic domestic pig and a shortening of the facial skull, a sign of advanced domestication. He explained this in part by the declining genetic influence of wild pig on domestic stocks. The rapid reproduction of pigs results in great morphological plasticity (Hüster-Plogmann and Schibler 1997: 75); forms have strongly varied through time and between regions. Size estimations of this animal, however, may be biased by the mixed-age structure represented in food refuse: other domesticates with well-established secondary forms of exploitation have tended to be slaughtered more consistently at a mature age at the end of their working lives. Certain bone fragments of subadult and mature pigs, however, cannot be accurately distinguished, resulting in the inadvertent inclusion of smaller young individuals in size estimations.

Sheep and Goat

While bones of these two species are not easily distinguished, their numerical dominance at major Bronze Age sites in the Near East seems to be a sign of centralization, as their large stocks could be more easily managed and taxed than those of pig or even cattle. Forms of secondary exploitation include milk (especially goat, a very efficient dairy animal) and wool (mostly in the case of sheep; woolly goats are a late innovation). Although twin lambing tends to be a modern phenomenon, small-bodied sheep and goat reproduce more rapidly than cows whose calving interval exceeds one year. Consequently, the lactation timetables of the three bovid species are complementary to each other. When identifiable to species, sheep bones tend to outnumber those of goat in most archaeozoological assemblages in Europe (Bartosiewicz and Greenfield 1999).

Both domestic sheep and goat originate from the Near East: their introduction to Europe took place at the beginning of the Neolithic. By the Bronze Age, they may be seen as naturalized animals. In addition to Greece, not discussed in detail here, caprines gained in importance in the semi-arid environments of Iberia as well as in the southern section of the Apennine Peninsula, recently reviewed within the context of evaluating Bronze Age animal exploitation at Morgantina, Sicily (eleventh–eighth century BC; Bartosiewicz 2012). Large published assemblages, numbering thousands of identifiable bones such as at Tufariello, Buccino (end of the third millennium BC), Coppa Nevigata, Puglia (Early, Middle, and Late Bronze Age), Broglio di Trebisacce, Calabria (Late Bronze Age), Termitito, Basilicata (thirteenth century BC), show 30–50 per cent contributions largely by sheep and to some extent goat to the Number of Identifiable Specimens (NISP). A few notable exceptions include the assemblage from Torre Mordillo, Calabria (1600 BC), comparable to ninth–eighth century BC Monte Maranfusa in Sicily where the contribution of caprines is suppressed by the higher combined percentage of pig and cervid bones. However, sheep and goat would dominate over the remains of pig even in northern Mediterranean regions such as the 1400–1100 BC *terramare* settlements located in the central-western Po Valley summarized by De Grossi Mazzorin and Riedel (1997). Caprines were also best suited to semi-arid areas in Iberia, for example at the sites in Granada where only small contributions of cattle bone have been recorded.

In most of temperate Europe, the balance between the consumption of mutton and pork is upset only under environmental pressures or special sociocultural circumstances. In Switzerland, for example the contribution of remains from these two species has increased from around 20 per cent to 30–40 per cent between the Early Bronze Age and Late Bronze Age at pile-dwelling sites where pig keeping and hunting were significant. The contribution by sheep and goat, however, was much higher at dry, inland settlements, ranging constantly between 30–70 per cent (Schibler and Studer 1998: 182, Abb. 72). A similar, mosaic-like distribution of sheep frequencies was observed complementing the representation of pigs at Bronze Age sites in the Carpathian Basin, although pigs seemed less important here.

In contrast to similarities in body size and meat output, caprines are far more mobile than pigs. This introduces dynamism in the false homeostasis suggested by the pig/caprine mosaic. Ruminants need good graze, and caprine transhumance probably played a key role in the centralization of food production and redistribution in the Near East where tentative archaeological evidence of early transhumance is often cited as a form of adaptation to social complexity.

In geographically diverse Europe, marked summer droughts in many lowlands are followed by cold winters within relatively short distances in hilly areas where herders have adapted to the seasonal availability of good pastures over millennia. This, however, would have meant simple opportunistic herd movements between lowland and highland areas to offset variation in seasonal water and pasturage availability. It would not have required the presence of sedentary core communities, permanent routes, specialist herders, and merchandising networks for meat and preserved dairy products, all documented for ethnographic examples of transhumance. Osteological evidence is difficult to obtain, as much of the discussion revolves around the complementary nature of highland/lowland age profiles for herds, a discussion that has turned out to be flawed as is any herd reconstruction relying merely on the analysis of excavated food refuse. Estimations of the seasonality of death based upon the age-at-death of the various species at several sites tend to indicate year-round occupation, as a high-resolution stratigraphic study of the cumulative archaeological data is seldom possible.

Both sheep and goat originate from semi-arid areas of the Near East, so their dominance in Mediterranean archaeozoological assemblages is unsurprising. Wool, however, is the likely reason behind the emergence of sheep keeping in northern areas of Bronze Age Europe. Sheep offer one of the most plausible proofs that domesticates are true artefacts. Their wild ancestors live in hilly habitats in Asia and have coarse hair—no better developed than that of deer. Domestication resulted in the massive increase of the fine undercoat, a mutation recognized and promoted by early farmers who thus invented wool shearing. During the first three to four millennia of sheep breeding from the Neolithic to the Bronze Age, this animal became adapted to harsh climates not only as a result of the ever-evolving fleece, but also by a selection for forms that survived in cold habitats. Understandably, it was in these areas where the human need for high-quality animal fibre was also the greatest. While less significant in the Bronze Age of the Ural piedmont area (Matolcsi 1982: 81), sheep often contributed over half (remarkably) of the animal remains in numerous assemblages from Estonia (Maldre 2008: 265) through Scandinavia (Lepiksaar 1969; Ullén 1996) to the Netherlands (IJzereef 1981) and the British Isles (Harding 2000) towards the end of the Bronze Age. Fashioning sheep for cold and humid climates was a major cultural achievement, rarely given credit in the archaeological literature.

Horse and Ass

Domestic horses are of extreme importance in Bronze Age Europe. As surplus contributed to the maintenance of increasingly sophisticated social stratification in which power relations had to be constantly renegotiated both within and sometimes in relation to a hostile outer world, horses developed into an indispensable high-status military device.

For the first time in prehistory, convincing artefactual evidence of horseback riding is available in the form of horse gear such as bridle cheek-pieces and harness elements. Light chariots are also known. While cattle were a powerful, steadfast, but slow-working companion, the reining of horses accelerated the movement of people, goods, and information (Fig. 18.2), and by expressing status it provided a new, imposing medium for self-representation (Olsen, Littauer, and Rea 2006: 175).

Similarly to that of cattle, the horse's reproduction is slow. Given the cultural importance of these animals, therefore, their meat may have been rather a luxury than a staple in the diet of some communities.

Wild horses once roamed the entire Eurasian steppe belt. Masses of horse bone in the food refuse of Copper and Early Bronze Age strata of settlements from the fourth millennium BC onwards, such as Dereivka (southern Ukraine) or Botai (northern Kazakhstan), however, indicate a turning point in domestication. The recent identification of mare's milk residue on c.3500 BC pot sherds confirms that at least some of the mares at Botai were domesticated (Outram et al. 2009: 1334). Moreover, these finds prove the early secondary exploitation of horse. One may thus hypothesize that as the northward spread of Near Eastern metallurgy reached the southern distribution zone of the wild ancestor, the scene was set for horse domestication.

In the territory of modern-day Russia (somewhat similarly to northern Europe) the dominance of domesticates in the 'Neolithic package' (cattle, caprines, pig, and the omnipresent dog) was somewhat delayed in comparison with south-eastern and central Europe. Domestic horse, on the other hand, appeared relatively early here, thereby narrowing the chronological gap between the adoption of other livestock and horse itself. Horse remains of the Katakombnaya kultura (Catacomb Grave culture, 2500–1200 BC) provide the earliest evidence of the importance of these animals during the Bronze Age. In the lower Volga region, skulls of 40 horses were deposited in a single burial (Anthony 1997). It remains a question, however, to what extent horses may have been used in combat at this early time.

The Andronovo culture is a collective term for local Bronze Age cultures during the period 2300–1000 BC in western Siberia and the adjacent west Asiatic steppe. Its animal husbandry was largely based on the exploitation of cattle, caprines, and horses. The Sintashta fortified

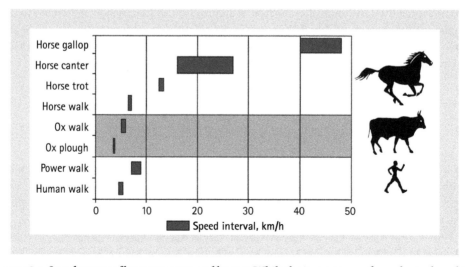

FIG. 18.2 Speed ranges of humans, oxen, and horses. While the importance of oxen lay in draught power rather than speed, horses at least tripled the velocity of human communication.

settlement in the southern Ural Mountains (c.2000–1600 BC) is considered the very beginning of urbanization in Siberia. The horses buried at this settlement had their legs arranged so as to imitate galloping. Remains of six two-wheeled chariots dating to c.1700–1500 BC were also found at Sintashta (Parzinger 2006: 251–7). In fact, the Andronovo culture has been tentatively credited with the invention of spoke-wheeled chariots around 2000 BC (Anthony and Vinogradov 1995). On its western border, the Andronovo culture is succeeded by the Srubnaya kultura (Timber-Grave culture). The earliest peoples with written histories in this area are the Cimmerians and Saka/Scythians, little-known equestrian pastoralists mentioned in Assyrian records. They had originally inhabited the region north of the Caucasus and the Black Sea and migrated into Europe through the territory of Ukraine from the ninth century BC onwards. The first mounted troops identified as Cimmerians appeared when a new type of bridle cheek-piece became common between central Europe and the Caucasus (Olsen, Littauer, and Rea 2006: 157). It remains a question how much influence Cimmerians had beyond eastern Europe, since aside from the circulation of luxury artefacts (weapons, horse tackle, and jewellery), their movements into the Carpathian Basin cannot be confirmed (Metzner-Nebelsick 2000: 165).

The first deposits of domestic horse bone in the Carpathian Basin are associated with the Early Bronze Age Bell Beaker culture (Bökönyi 1974: 242). An increase in horse remains around 2600 BC at Zürich-Mozartstrasse in Switzerland may also be explained by the occurrence of domestic horses, especially as by this time hunting had in general decreased at pile-dwelling sites (Hüster-Plogmann and Schibler 1997: 112). These finds, however, offer only evidence of meat exploitation. The possibility of local domestication versus diffusion from the eastern steppe region is hotly debated in central Europe. Much of the discussion revolves around indirect evidence. DNA studies as well as strontium isotope measurements would be indispensable in assessing the origins and mobility of Bronze Age horse stocks within Europe.

In Greece, the first domestic horses appeared around 1900–1570 BC (Bökönyi 1974: 240). In the south, the occurrence of ass among the domesticates at Termitito in southern Italy (Late Bronze Age, 1200s BC; Bökönyi 2010: 5) is a noteworthy development. This find, along with the asses of the Late Bronze Age phase of Coppa Nevigata (Bökönyi and Siracusano 1987: 707), is the earliest evidence for domestic ass in Europe. As regards their origins, asses may have arrived directly from Egypt (where their domestication probably took place), or from Greece where they first occurred at the Middle Bronze Age settlement of Kastanas (Becker 1986: 72).

Dog

Seldom considered a primary source of meat, scavenging dogs were probably often tolerated rather than kept. In such cases dog may be considered a commensal species, simply adapted to human habitats. Dogs, however, defend the territory shared with humans and have some natural capacity for serving as hunting and herding companions.

'Man's best friend' seems to have served as a source of meat in some prehistoric communities, especially those engaged in intensive hunting (Bartosiewicz 2005: 54, Fig. 6.3). From the Bronze Age onwards, the remains of this animal become relatively rare in the food refuse, its rather consistent presence being indicated mostly by gnawing on the bones of other animals.

Dog skulls found cracked open at the Middle Bronze Age site of Tószeg–Laposhalom in Hungary and a number of pile dwellings in Switzerland led Bökönyi (1974: 320) to speculate about dog brains having been a special delicacy at the time. While this possibility cannot be ruled out, due to a lack of consistent evidence it cannot be generalized. 'Cynophagy' has been a complex, emotionally charged phenomenon in Western culture, a part of dietary tradition that did not end in the Bronze Age, for example north of the Alps where it continued into the Iron Age.

The evidence of dog burials and amulets made from the teeth and metapodia of these animals show their special, more than utilitarian status during the Bronze Age. The question also arises whether emerging social stratification that increased demand for domestic animals serving as a means of self-representation also resulted in breeds or at least functional types of dogs that would have reflected human specialization in society. A recent study comparing Chalcolithic and Bronze Age dogs from pile dwellings in the Ljubljana Marsh (Slovenia) and their counterparts in Switzerland, however, shows little diversity. Most remains bear a striking resemblance to not only the classical 'turbary dog' (*Torfspitz*) described by Ludwig Rütimeyer (1861), but also to non-distinct, medium-size traditional sheep dogs (withers height: 30–40 cm) as well as pariah dogs. It has been hypothesized that such uniform phenotypes were not created and cultivated by conscious breeding but result with the greatest statistical probability from a panmixis (random mating) of dogs best adapted to the human environment (Bartosiewicz 2002: 87). Although greater samples would be needed to test this hypothesis, cranial and long-bone measurements of a primitive dog found at the Copper Age site of Volosovo near the Oka river in Russia were nearly identical to the averages calculated for turbary dogs from bone remains brought to light at Lake Biel in Switzerland (Matolcsi 1982: 301). Both Bökönyi (1974: 329) and (Benecke 1994: 142) mention increasing dog size as well as a greater range of variability by the end of the Bronze Age in central Europe within the context of improved animal breeding. There is no evidence, however, that beyond their possible sacrificial function, live dogs would have been a medium for reasserting social status or expressing individual tastes. Sampling bias must also be reckoned with: aside from turbary dogs, there are no rich Bronze Age dog-bone assemblages.

Fowl and Domestic Hen

Bones of small animals such as hare, wild birds, and fish tend to be little known from Bronze Ages sites, largely because of the lack of water-sieving at most excavations. These animals, however, were at hand in many environments and may have been preyed upon opportunistically as a colouring element of the diet or for special resources such as decorative plumage. If information on large mammals is inconsistent over the continent, gathering comparable data on birds or fish is completely out of the question.

Altogether 23 avian taxa were identified from 27 settlements in a recent systematic survey of Bronze Age bird remains from Hungary and western Romania (Transylvania; Gál, forthcoming). The 20 species identified are mainly waterfowl and wading birds, but also include raptors as well as some terrestrial birds. The main trends fall in line with those in the far better-known Neolithic and Chalcolithic of the central and lower Danube Valley (Gál 2007). The numbers of Bronze Age bird finds range between 1 and 19 per site, resulting in relatively low taxonomic diversity in comparison with earlier sites, an evident product of small sample sizes. Of the Swiss pile dwellings an unusually rich assemblage is available from the Late Bronze Age site of Hauterive-Champréveyres on Lake Neuchâtel. Six of the identified species were waterfowl (especially mallard), making up 84 per cent of the bones (Schibler and Studer 1998: 191). Citing Bronze Age iconographic evidence, Vasić and Vasić (2003: 186) concluded that ducks may have been domesticated in the central Balkans. This statement would be difficult to confirm using osteological data, although the cognitive importance of these birds is beyond doubt. Benecke (1998: 61) refers to the possible Bronze Age local domestication of greylag goose. Morphometric distinctions between the wild and domestic forms, however, are usually impossible. The complexity of this question has recently been highlighted by Dale Serjeantson (2009: 292–3).

The domestic status of hen of south-east Asiatic origin poses no such problems: the wild ancestor is not available in Europe; therefore the confusing problems of local domestication do not arise. Domestic hen occurred in south-eastern Europe already towards the end of the second millennium, then spread to the Pontic region as well as to the western Mediterranean before reaching central Europe (Benecke 1998: 61). The skeleton of a female from Ostrov-Zápy in Prague and remains from the site of Rubín (Czech Republic) show that hen was possibly present already during the Late Bronze Age Hallstatt B3 Period (Kyselý 2008: 64).

Most evidence of fowling is typical of opportunistic wild-bird consumption at Bronze Age settlements in the aquatic environments of central Europe. The research potential of investigating the exploitation of marine avifauna as well as fowling in the broad variety of natural habitats cannot be overestimated. Recent investigations at the 900–500 BC Late Bronze Age settlement of Asva on Saaremaa Island (Estonia) are indicative of coastal water-fowling (Lõugas, Wojtal, and Tomek 2008: 141).

Hunting

Most works on Bronze Age animals in Europe emphasize the near absence of wild animal remains. In the south, Kristian Kristiansen (1998: 393) refers to a clear 40 to 20 per cent decline of wild-animal bones between the Early Bronze Age and Late Bronze Age at Pitigliano in Etruria, Italy. In the Netherlands the decreasing contribution of game by the Middle Bronze Age (Clason 1970; 1980) was explained by the dwindling interest in exploiting wild resources, the inadequacy of game in feeding the rapidly expanding human population, and deforestation that had converted prime wild habitats into plough-land and pasture (Louwe Kooijmans 2005: 705–6).

On the other hand, the diachronic trend shown by 22 Swiss pile dwellings dated to between 1600 and 830 BC quoted by Norbert Benecke (1998: 71) is far less straightforward. Although on average a 0.05 per cent annual decrease took place in the contribution of wild animal remains to Bronze Age assemblages within these eight centuries (totalling almost 40 per cent), about one-third of the sites consistently yielded high percentages of wild-animal remains throughout this entire period. Similarly, a comparison of Neolithic to Late Bronze Age assemblages representing another hilly region, 18 Carpathian sites in Romania (Becker 1999: 98–9, Table 4), showed a less clear-cut decrease in the reliance on wild animals. Although the overwhelming importance of domesticates (90–95 per cent of identifiable bones) was evident by the Bronze

Age, some of these sites also showed a remarkable diversity within the relatively small contingent of wild animals.

Interpreting the majority of common archaeozoological finds as food remains means that wild animals did not have to be extinct to be missing from the dietary record. Preferring the meat from domesticates may have had a number of practical or sociocultural reasons that have all led to their dominance in Bronze Age assemblages. But some people may have resorted to opportunistic hunting for the same number of complex cultural reasons.

Within the small portion of wild animals, bones of Late Bronze Age aurochs have been reported throughout the continent from Galloway, Scotland, where a skull was dated to c.1300 BC (Kitchener, Bonsall, and Bartosiewicz 2004: 75), to the Greek rural sanctuary of Metaponto in southern Italy (600–250 BC; Bökönyi 2010: 6). Remains of aurochsen may also be under-represented, for even when occasionally hunted many of the large bones may have been left behind at kill sites. By the time of the Bronze Age, bones of two other large ungulates, bison and elk (moose), tend to occur even more sporadically in forested areas of central Europe, such as mountainous habitats in the proximity of lakeshore settlements in the Alpine region (Schibler and Studer 1998: 149). Sporadic elk remains were also recovered at the Early Bronze Age (c.2400 BC) settlement of Poiana in the hilly Carpathian region of Romania (Becker 1999: 94, Table 2). Because they were ubiquitous, elk remained understandably important in Scandinavia, the Baltic, and the northern territories of Russia. Although by the second millennium BC domestic animals gained in importance west of the Ural mountains, 75 per cent of the sites assigned to the c.1600–1400 BC Khazan and Chirkovo-Seyma cultures contained elk remains (Matolcsi 1982: 301).

Lions offer a good example of how a dangerous vermin and royal prey item of little food value but focal cultural interest became eradicated in Bronze Age Europe. Lions occurred throughout the Balkans and the Carpathian Basin during the Copper Age. While some of their remains—especially teeth—must have been circulated as trophies or high-status personal items, bones from butchered body parts are indicative of local hunting. According to a recent review (Bartosiewicz 2009), in addition to various Late Copper Age lion bones, a robust Late Bronze Age lion mandible was recovered at the tell settlement of Durankulak, Bulgaria. All other Bronze Age lion finds originate from the territory of Greece. They include a calcaneus recovered from the Mycenaean Grave 67 (c.1230 BC) at Tiryns and six additional postcranial bones offering evidence that lions lived in the Peloponnese in the Late Bronze Age. At the tell site of Kastanas in Greek Macedonia, layers spanning the transition to the Iron Age (1100–800 BC) yielded a variety of lion bones (Becker 1986). The other large carnivore, brown bear, was decimated and driven to mountain refuges by habitat loss to arable land.

The variable, non-linear trend of human intrusion into the natural environment is clearly shown by the case of red deer. Antler is shed in annual cycles and may thus be collected, accumulated, and traded regardless of hunting. While hunting red deer was unquestionably practised in several areas, in some publications an unspecified ratio of deer remains may originate from shed antler, contributing to the impression that 'especially deer, still played a role in the economy well into the Early and Middle Bronze Age...probably also to supply antler' (Kristiansen 1998: 394). Commonly occurring Middle Bronze Age antler mattocks showing the naturally separated antler rose, for example from the Po river Valley in Italy or the Great Hungarian Plain (Fig. 18.3), prove that deer were regularly exploited for antler, even if few bone finds indicate the consumption of venison. Gathering antler corresponds to 'secondary exploitation', to use the analogy of domesticates: the stag does not have to be killed for the product; moreover collecting antler did not require the cooperative effort of skilled hunters, although it probably also lacked the high-status aspect of killing large game: these alternative ways of procuring the same raw material had different if not opposite social implications.

While red deer thrive all over Europe today, residual populations of Pleistocene fallow-deer in the Mediterranean seem to have become extinct as late as the Bronze or Early Iron Ages (Bartosiewicz 2012). Early Bronze Age finds are reported from the Carpathian site of Poiana in Romania. The northernmost occurrences include those from the Bronze Age tell of Feudvar along the Danube in Serbia and the site of Ripač in the Dinaric Alps, Croatia (Becker 1999: 94–101, Table 2, Fig. 7).

New investigations at the 900–500 BC Late Bronze Age settlement of Asva on Saaremaa Island in Estonia (Lõugas, Wojtal, and Tomek 2008: 141), as well as from the eighth–seventh century BC fort of Ridala in Estonia, revealed bones of grey seal, harp seal, ringed seal, and harbour seal of all ages that made up 19 per cent of the bones from the latter site, while the remains of terrestrial game contributed only 3 per cent (Maldre 2008: 271). Marine resources, including fish, have been consistently exploited by coastal communities along the edges of Europe.

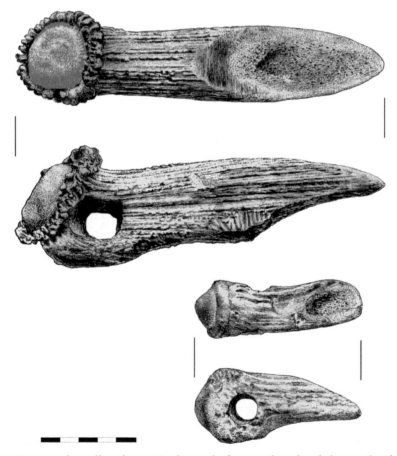

FIG. 18.3 Large and small antler mattocks made from gathered red deer antler from the Middle Bronze Age Vatya culture site of Csongrád–Vidre-sziget, Hungary.

Source: Choyke 1998, by permission of Archaeolingua Publishers.

Conclusion

The biological, economic, and cultural traits of Bronze Age animals may be best compared in terms of rates of reproduction and resource mobility. In the first case, there is an inverse relationship between body size and the number of offspring expected from a dam. On the other hand, resource mobility is rather a cultural concept showing how much an animal would be characteristic of an agrarian versus pastoral way of life. Figure 18.4 shows how the most important species are distributed within the plane defined by these two dimensions. Primary exploitation is polarized between meat-purpose pig, characteristic of sedentary household economies, and horse—highly mobile, rarely eaten. Domestic ruminants occupy transitional positions in the graph. Early Bronze Age cattle were moved around in local trade within Britain (Towers et al. 2010). Meanwhile the numbers of sheep expanded spectacularly across northern Europe.

Animals not fitting this model include red deer (often represented by unspecified numbers of shed antler fragments), a localized wild resource; domestic hen, whose bones would be difficult to recover consistently without water-sieving but is known to have travelled long

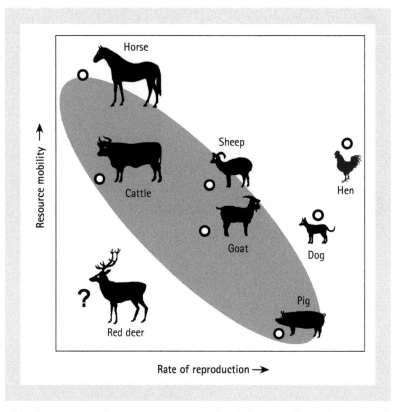

FIG. 18.4 The distribution of major animal species by their rates of reproduction and resource mobility. The main trend of meat consumption is marked by shading. Pig and game animals characterize more localized lifeways. Mobile pastoralism is dominated by less prolific, large ungulates.

FIG. 18.5 Bronze Age duck-shaped bronze vessel from an unknown provenance in Hungary.
Source: Hampel 1886.

distances; and dog, following humans but not regularly exploited for meat, in other words poorly represented in most Bronze Age deposits.

Even mundane meat consumption had social and psychological implications both in relation to the animal and between members of the community. Such phenomena are difficult to study as they may become visible only through the high-resolution analysis of contexts within sites (e.g. spatial patterns of body-part distributions indicative of feasting). Given the negligible practical importance of hunting, remains of game may also indicate symbolic relations to nature or reiterate archaic lifestyles, in other words in an effort at connecting with the past. Comparing osteological and iconographic sources may also reveal the cognitive significance of animals rarely killed or under-represented for taphonomic reasons. For example, birds admired for their plumage and possibly envied for the ability to fly are frequently depicted in Bronze Age art (Fig. 18.5).

Bibliography

Anthony, D. W. (1997). 'Let them eat horses', *Newsletter—Institute for Ancient Equestrian Studies*, 4/Summer 1997.

—— and Vinogradov, N. (1995). 'Birth of the chariot', *Archaeology*, 48/2: 36–41.

Bartosiewicz, L. (2002). 'Dogs from the Ig pile dwellings in the National Museum of Slovenia', *Arheološki Vestnik*, 53: 77–89.

—— (2005). 'Plain talk: animals, environment and culture in the Neolithic of the Carpathian Basin and adjacent areas', in D. Bailey and A. Whittle (eds.), *(Un)settling the Neolithic*. Oxford: Oxbow Books, 51–63.

—— (2009). 'Lion's share of attention: archaeozoology and the historical record', *Acta Archaeologica Academiae Scientiarum Hungariae*, 59: 759–73.

—— (2012). 'Faunal remains (part 2, section 17)', in R. Leighton (ed.), *The Archaeology of Houses at Morgantina, Sicily: Excavations of Later Prehistoric Contexts on the Cittadella (1989–2004)*. London: Accordia Research Institute, University of London.

—— and Greenfield, H. J. (eds.) (1999). *Transhumant Pastoralism in Southern Europe*. Budapest: Archaeolingua Kiadó.

——, van Neer, W., Lentacker, A., and Fabiš, M. (1997). 'Draught cattle: their osteological identification and history', *Koninklijk Museum voor Midden-Afrika, Annalen, Zoologische Wetenschappen*, 281.

Bech, J.-H. (1997). 'Bronze Age settlements on raised sea-beds at Bjerre, Thy, NW Jutland', in J. J. Assendorp (ed.), *Forschungen zur bronzezeitlichen Besiedlung in Nord- und Mitteleuropa*. Leopoldshöhe: Internationale Archäologie, 38: 3–15.

Becker, C. (1986). *Kastanas. Ausgrabungen in einem Siedlungshügel der Bronze- und Eisenzeit Makedoniens 1975-1979. Die Tierknochenfunde*, Prähistorische Archäologie in Südosteuropa, 5. Berlin: Wissenschaftsverlag Volker Spiess.

—— (1999). 'Domesticated and wild animals as evidenced in the Eneolithic-Bronze Age cultures Coțofeni and Monteoru, Romania', in N. Benecke (ed.), *The Holocene History of the European Vertebrate Fauna*, Archäologie in Eurasien, 6. Rahden/Westfalen: Marie Leidorf, 91–105.

Benecke, N. (1994). *Archäozoologische Studien zur Entwicklung der Haustierhaltung in Mitteleuropa und Südskandinavien von den Anfängen bis zum ausgehenden Mittelalter*, Schriften zur Ur- und Frühgeschichte, 46. Berlin: Akademiae Verlag.

—— (1998). 'Haustierhaltung, Jagd und Kult mit Tieren im bronzezeitlichen Mitteleuropa', in B. Hänsel (ed.), *Mensch und Umwelt in der Bronzezeit Europas*. Kiel: Oetker-Voges Verlag, 61–75.

Boessneck, J. (1958). *Zur Entwicklung vor- und frühgeschichtlicher Haus- und Wildtiere Bayerns im Rahmen der gleichzeitlichen Tierwelt Mitteleuropas*, Studien an vor- und frühgeschichtlichen Tierresten Bayerns, II. Munich: Tieranatomisches Institut der Universität München.

Bökönyi, S. (1974). *History of Domestic Mammals in Central and Eastern Europe*. Budapest: Akadémiai Kiadó.

—— (2010). 'Animal husbandry from the Late Neolithic through the Roman period', in L. Bartosiewicz (ed), *The Chora of Metaponto 2. Archaeozoology at Pantanello and Five Other Sites*. Austin: The University of Texas Press, 1–31.

—— and Siracusano, G. (1987). 'Reperti faunistici dell'età del bronzo del sito di Coppa Nevigata: un commento preliminare', in S. M. Cassano, A. Cazzella, A. Manfredini, and M. Moscoloni (eds.), *Coppa Nevigata e il suo territorio. Testimonianze archeologiche dal VII al II millennio a. C.* Rome: Edizioni Quasar, 205–10.

Childe, V. G. (1925). *The Dawn of European Civilisation*. London: Kegan Paul.

Choyke, A. M. (1984). 'An analysis of bone, antler and tooth tools from Bronze Age Hungary', *Mitteilungen des Archäologischen Instituts der Ungarischen Akademie der Wissenschaften*, 12/13: 13–57.

—— (1988). 'Bronze Age red deer: case studies from the Great Hungarian Plain', in P. Anreiter, L. Bartosiewicz, E. Jerem, and W. Meid (eds.), *Man and the Animal World. Studies in Memoriam Sándor Bökönyi*. Budapest: Archaeolingua, 157–78.

—— (2000). 'Refuse and modified bone from Százhalombatta–Földvár. Some preliminary observations', in I. Poroszlai and M. Vicze (eds.), *SAX: Százhalombatta Archaeological Expedition. Annual Report 1–Field Season 1998*. Százhalombatta: Matrica Museum, 97–102.

—— and Bartosiewicz, L. (1999). 'Bronze Age animal keeping in Western Hungary', in E. Jerem and I. Poroszlai (eds.), *Archaeology of the Bronze Age and Iron Age: Experimental Archaeology, Environmental Archaeology, Archaeological Parks*, Proceedings of the International Archaeological Conference, Százhalombatta, 3–7 October 1996. Archaeolingua Series Major. Budapest: Archaeolingua, 239–49.

—— and Bartosiewicz, L. (2000). 'Bronze Age animal exploitation in the Central Great Hungarian Plain', *Acta Archaeologica Academiae Scientiarum Hungaricae*, 51: 43–70.

—— and Bartosiewicz, L. (2009). 'Telltale tools from a tell: bone and antler manufacturing at Bronze Age Jászdózsa-Kápolnahalom, Hungary', *Tisicum*, XX: 357-76.

Clason, A. T. (1970). 'De dierenwereld van het terpenland', in J. W. Boersma (ed.), *Terpen, mens en milieu*. Haren: Knoop & Niemeijer, 54-73.

—— (1980). 'Jager, visser, veehouder, vogellijmer', in M. Chamalaun and H. T. Waterbolk (eds.), *Voltooid verleden tijd? Een hedendaagse kijk op de prehistorie*. Amsterdam: Intermediair, 131-46.

—— and Buitenhuis, H. (1998). 'Patterns in animal food resources in the Bronze Age in the Orient', in H. Buitenhuis, L. Bartosiewicz, and A. M. Choyke (eds.), *Archaeozoology of the Near East III*, Proceedings of the Third International Symposium on the Archaeozoology of Southwestern Asia and Adjacent Areas. Groningen: Centre for Archeological Research and Consultancy, 233-42.

Darwin, C. R. (1861). Letter 3339—*Darwin, C. R. to Rütimeyer, K. L., 5 Dec [1861]* [online]. Cambridge: The Darwin Correspondence Project. Available at: http://www.darwinproject.ac.uk/darwinletters/calendar/entry-3339.html [accessed 23 November 2010].

De Grossi Mazzorin, J. and A. Riedel (1997). 'La fauna delle terramare', in M. Bernabò Brea, A. Cardarelli, and M. Cremaschi (eds.), *Le Terramare. La più antica civiltà padana*. Milan: Electa, 475-80.

Diener, P. and Robkin, E. E. (1978). 'Ecology, evolution and the search for cultural origins: the question of Islamic pig prohibition', *Current Anthropology*, 19/3: 493-540.

Driesch, A. von den (1972). *Osteoarchäologische Untersuchungen auf der Iberischen Halbinsel*. Studien über frühe Tierknochenfunde von der Iberischen Halbinsel, 3. Munich: Institut für Palaeoanatomie, Domestikationsforschung und Geschichte der Tiermedizin der Universität München—Deutsches Archäologisches Institut, Abteilung Madrid.

—— and Boessneck, J. (1969). *Die Fauna des 'Cabezo Redondo' bei Villena (Prov. Alicante)*. Studien über frühe Tierknochenfunde von der Iberischen Halbinsel, 1. Munich: Institut für Palaeoanatomie, Domestikationsforschung und Geschichte der Tiermedizin der Universität München—Deutsches Archäologisches Institut, Abteilung Madrid, 45-106.

Friesch, K. (1987). *Die Tierknochenfunde von Cerro de la Encina von Monachil, Provinz Granada (Grabungen 1977-1984)*. Studien über frühe Tierknochenfunde von der Iberischen Halbinsel, 11. Munich: Institut für Palaeoanatomie, Domestikationsforschung und Geschichte der Tiermedizin der Universität München—Deutsches Archäologisches Institut, Abteilung Madrid.

Gál, E. (2007). *Fowling in Lowlands: Neolithic and Copper Age Bird Bone Remains from the Great Hungarian Plain and South-East Romania*, Archaeolingua Series Minor, 24. Budapest: Archaeolingua.

—— (unpublished). *Bird Bone Remains from Bronze Age Settlements in the Carpathian Basin*. Budapest: Archaeological Institute of the Hungarian Academy of Sciences.

Harding, A. F. (2000). *European Societies in the Bronze Age*. Cambridge: Cambridge University Press.

Hingh, A. E. de (2000). *Food Production and Food Procurement in the Bronze Age and Early Iron Age (2000-500 BC)*, Archaeological Studies, Leiden University, 7. Leiden: Leiden University.

Hüster-Plogmann, H.-M. and Schibler, J. (1997). 'Archäozoologie', in *Ökonomie und Ökologie neolithischer und bronzezeitlicher Ufersiedlungen am Zürchersee*, Monographien der Kantonsarchäologie Zürich, 20. Zürich: Egg, 40-121.

IJzereef, G. F. (1981). *Bronze Age Animal Bones from Bovenkarspel: The Excavation at Het Valkje*, Nederlandse Oudheden, 10. Amersfoort: Rijksdienst voor het Oudheidkundig Bodemonderzoek.

Kitchener, A., Bonsall, C., and Bartosiewicz, L. (2004). 'Missing mammals from Mesolithic middens: a comparison of the fossil and archaeological records from Scotland', in A. Saville (ed.), *Mesolithic Scotland and its Neighbours*. Edinburgh: Society of Antiquaries of Scotland, 73–82.

Kristiansen, K. (1998). *Europe Before History*, New Studies in Archaeology. Cambridge: Cambridge University Press.

Kyselý, R. (2008). 'New pre-La Tène evidence from the Czech Republic for domestic fowl (*Gallus gallus* f. *domestica*) in its European context', in D. Makowiecki, R. Ablamowicz, D. Ablamowicz, K. Smiarowski, and M. Makohonienko (eds.), *Badania archeologiczne w Polsce I: Europie Środowo-Wschodniej. Materialy—metody—interpretacje*, Third Symposium of Environmental Archaeology, 26–29 November 2008, Katowice-Koszęcin. Poznań: Wydawnictwo Naukowe, 64.

Lepiksaar, J. (1969). 'Knochenfunde aus den bronzezeitlichen Siedlungen von Hötofta', in B. Stjernquist, *Beiträge zum Studium von bronzezeitlichen Siedlungen*, Acta Archaeologica Lundensia 80/8. Stockholm: Almqvist and Wiksell International, 174–207.

Lõugas, L., Wojtal, P., and Tomek, T. (2008). 'New zooarchaeological data of the Late Bronze Age Asva site (Saaremaa Island, Estonia)', in D. Makowiecki, R. Ablamowicz, D. Ablamowicz, K. Smiarowski, and M. Makohonienko (eds.), *Badania archeologiczne w Polsce I: Europie Środowo-Wschodniej. Materialy—metody—interpretacje*, Third Symposium of Environmental Archaeology, 2008, Katowice-Koszęcin. Poznań: Wydawnictwo Naukowe, 141–2.

Louwe Kooijmans, L. P. (1985). *Sporen in het land. De Nederlandse delta in de prehistorie*. Amsterdam: Meulenhoff Informatief.

—— (2005). 'The Netherlands in prehistory: retrospect', in L. P. Louwe Kooijmans, P. W. van den Broeke, H. Fokkens, and A. L. van Gijn (eds.), *The Prehistory of the Netherlands*, vol. 2. Amsterdam: Amsterdam University Press, 695–720.

Maldre, L. (2008). 'Karjakasvatusest Ridala pronksiaja asulas [Animal husbandry in the Bronze Age settlement of Ridala]', *Muinasaja teadus*, 17: 263–76.

Matolcsi, J. (1982). *Állattartás őseink korában* [Animal keeping in the time of our ancestors]. Budapest: Gondolat.

Metzner-Nebelsick, C. (2000). 'Early Iron Age pastoral nomadism in the Great Hungarian Plain—migration or assimilation? The Thraco-Cimmerian problem revisited', in J. Davis-Kimball et al., *Kurgans, Ritual Sites and Settlements: Eurasian Bronze and Iron Age*, British Archaeological Reports (International Series), 890. Oxford: Archaeopress, 160–84.

Milz, H. (1986). *Die Tierknochenfunde aus drei agrarzeitlichen Siedlungen in der Provinz Granada (Spanien)*, Studien über frühe Tierknochenfunde von der Iberischen Halbinsel, 10. Munich: Institut für Palaeoanatomie, Domestikationsforschung und Geschichte der Tiermedizin/Deutsches Archäologisches Institut—Deutsches Archäologisches Institut, Abteilung Madrid.

Olsen, S. (1994). 'Exploitation of mammals at the Early Bronze Age site of West Row Fen (Mildenhall 165), Suffolk, England', *Annals of Carnegie Museum*, 63/2: 115–53.

——, Littauer, M. A., and Rea, I. (eds.) (2006). *Horses and Humans: The Evolution of Human-Equine Relationships*, British Archaeological Reports (International Series), 1,560. Oxford: Archaeopress.

Outram, A. K., Stear, N. A., Bendrey, R., Olsen, S., Kasparov, A., Zaibert, V., Thorpe, N., and Evershed, R. P. (2009). 'The earliest horse harnessing and milking', *Science*, 323/6 March: 1,332–5.

Parzinger, H. (2006). *Die frühen Völker Eurasiens. Vom Neolithikum bis zum Mittelalter*, Historische Bibliothek der Gerda-Henkel-Stiftung, Band 1. Munich: Beck.

Pétrequin, P., Arbogast, R.-M., Pétrequin, A.-M., Van Willigen, S., and Bailly, M. (eds.) (2006). *Premiers Chariots, premiers araires. La diffusion de la traction animale en Europe pendant les IVe et IIIe millénaires avant notre ère*, CRA Monographies, 29. Paris: CNRS éditions, 107–20.

Robinson, D. E. (2003). 'Neolithic and Bronze Age agriculture in southern Scandinavia—recent archaeobotanical evidence from Denmark', *Environmental Archaeology*, 8: 145–65.

Rütimeyer, L. (1861). *Die Fauna der Pfahlbauten der Schweiz*, Neue Denkschrift der Allgemeine Schweizerische Gesellschaft der ges. Zurich: Naturwissenschaft, 19.

Schibler, J. and Studer, J. (1998). 'Haustierhaltung und Jagd während der Bronzezeit in der Schweiz', in S. Hochuli, U. Niffeler, and V. Rychner (eds.), *Die Schweiz vom Paläolithikum bis zum frühen Mittelalter. Bronzezeit*. Basel: Verlag Schweizerische Gesellschaft für Ur- und Frühgeschichte, 171–91.

Serjeantson, D. (2009). *Birds*, Cambridge Manuals in Archaeology. Cambridge: Cambridge University Press.

Sherratt, A. (1983). 'The secondary products revolution of animals in the Old World', *World Archaeology*, 15: 90–104.

Tegtmeier, U. (1993). *Neolithische und bronzezeitliche Pflugspuren in Norddeutschland und den Niederlanden*, Archäologische Berichte, 3. Bonn: Holos.

Thrane, H. (1990). 'Bronzezeitlicher Ackerbau—Beispiel Dänemark', in *Beiträge zur Geschichte und Kultur der mitteleuropäischen Bronzezeit. In memoriam Fritz Horst*. Berlin—Nitra: Zentralinstitut für Alte Geschichte und Archäologie der Akademie der Wissenschaften der DDR—Archeologický ústav Slovenskej akadémie vied, 483–93.

Towers, J., Montgomery, J., Evans, J., Jay, M., and Parker Pearson, M. (2010). 'An investigation of the origins of cattle and aurochs deposited in the Early Bronze Age barrows at Gayhurst and Irthlingborough', *Journal of Archaeological Science*, 37: 508–15.

Ullén, I. (1996). 'Food ethics, domestication and togetherness. A close-up study of the relation of horse and dog to man in the Bronze Age settlement of Apalle', *Current Swedish Archaeology*, 4: 171–84.

Vasić, R. and Vasić, V. (2003). 'Bronzezeitliche und eisenzeitliche Vogeldarstellungen im Zentralbalkan', *Praehistorische Zeitschrift*, 78/2: 156–89.

Wijngaarden-Bakker, L. H. van and Brinkkemper, O. (2005). 'All-round farming. Food production in the Bronze Age and the Iron Age', in L. P. Louwe Kooijmans, P. W. van den Broeke, H. Fokkens, and A. L. van Gijn (eds.), *The Prehistory of the Netherlands*, vol. 2. Amsterdam: Amsterdam University Press, 491–512.

Zalkin, V. I. (1964). 'Some Results of Studying the Bone Remains of Animals from the Excavations of Archaeological Monuments of the Late Bronze Age', *(Russian) Academy of Sciences of the USSR—Short Communications of the Institute of Archaeology*, 101: 24–30.

CHAPTER 19

PLANT CULTIVATION IN THE BRONZE AGE

HANS-PETER STIKA AND ANDREAS G. HEISS

Introduction

For millennia, cultivated (or, to be more precise, domesticated) plants have been the main foundation of human nutrition. In Europe, this is true since the Neolithic introduction of a set of several cultivated crops from the 'Fertile Crescent' in the Near East and the accompanying cultural techniques involved in their cultivation, processing, and consumption.

Investigating these present and past interactions of domesticated crop plants with environmental and cultural factors is one of the central questions when researching human history and prehistory. Several compilations on crop cultivation and plant use as staple food exist for different regions of Bronze Age Europe. Of the supraregional studies, one especially well-known publication should be emphasized: *Progress in Old World Palaeoethnobotany: A Retrospective View on the Occasion of 20 Years of International Work Group for Palaeoethnobotany* (Van Zeist, Wasylikowa, and Behre 1991). Twenty years later, we are trying to face the same challenge of compiling data on crop cultivation. Apart from basing ourselves on updated knowledge in archaeobotany, the main difference between the current study and the approach followed in Van Zeist et al. is the use of a semi-quantitative approach, in contrast to mere presence-absence data or a coarse estimation of dominance. Another important change is the referral to site representativeness and thus to the reliability of the conclusions drawn. Our goal, however, is to assess both the regional dominance and the general importance of certain crops in Bronze Age Europe, and to assess the representativeness of the extant data used in the study.

Methods

A problem with the term 'Bronze Age' in an overview of Europe is that it is used in different ways for different parts of the period across Europe, with different durations and varying subdivisions. Therefore we have limited ourselves to rough regional classifications of Early,

Middle, and Late Bronze Age following the chronology compiled in Von Schnurbein (2009: 240). A handicap is that although large numbers of publications are available for most regions in Europe, the habit of publishing tables containing raw data is clearly still not mandatory in archaeobotany. Thus, several regions of Europe either could not be included in our synopsis, or are represented by weaker supporting data than the intensive research carried out by local colleagues would suggest, or could otherwise enable. In total, the data from 229 sites have been integrated into our study. (On the full record of literature used, see Note)

The spectrum of plants included in the current study primarily covers the three main groups of cultivated crops most important for nutrition: 1. cereals; 2. legumes and pulses; 3. oilseeds. Cereals (grasses of the Poaceae family) are the main contributors to human daily calorie intake. Legumes or pulses (Fabaceae family) also provide, apart from their calorie content, essential amino acids. Oilseeds, from different plant families, provide essential fatty acids crucial for human metabolism and hormonal balance. The most important ones in prehistory were flax (*Linum usitatissimum*), hemp (*Cannabis sativa*), gold-of-pleasure (*Camelina sativa*), and opium poppy (*Papaver somniferum*). Apart from their use as a source of vegetable fat, many of these oilseeds are also multifunctional plants used, for example, in fibres (flax, hemp) or as narcotics (hemp, poppy). In addition to these three main groups, cultivated fruit were also included, as past studies (e.g. Kroll 1991a: 166) have shown that the beginnings of the cultivation of these plants lie in the Bronze Age.

In devising a means of data evaluation, the question was how to deal with the different archaeological contexts, and the different states of preservation of plant remains, and how to maintain comparability across all these data. We decided to evaluate all available sites in a region with a weighted, semi-quantitative approach that respects both the presence of a taxon and its relative quantity per site (i.e. dominance), the total quantity of plant material recovered from a site, and the number of samples analysed. In this way the representativeness of the dominances observed in particular sites could be assessed.

Occurrences of cultivated plants were extracted from the extant archaeobotanical and archaeological literature from across Europe. Only publications with raw data were included in the survey. Seed/fruit counts of charred, subfossil, and mineralized finds of seeds or fruits of cultivated taxa were recorded per site. (For further details about the way in which the data were evaluated see Note.)

REGIONAL OVERVIEWS

Continental and Northern Greece, and Southern Bulgaria

In this overview we have combined the data from northern Greece and southern Bulgaria because these regions show a comparable agricultural development and are ecologically close. In spite of the fact that the data available to us from this region only covers 15 sites, the *Representativeness Index* (RI) reaches the highest levels in our study, both for cereals and non-cereals. The mainly diachronic tell sites were excavated with large series of samples producing high numbers of finds. Earlier regional compilations of archaeobotanical results (e.g. Kroll 1991a: 166) already pointed out a certain continuity of the Late Neolithic

Table 19.1 RI (Representativeness Index) Values of Non-Cereals (Pulses, Oilseeds, and Cultivated Fruit) in the Archaeobotanical Record of Continental and Northern Greece and Southern Bulgaria

Plant species		EBA	MBA	LBA
Cicer arietinum	chickpea	10	6	1
Lathyrus sativus/cicera	grass pea	13	11	6
Lens culinaris	lentil	39	21	11
Pisum sativum	garden pea	10	6	6
Vicia ervilia	bitter vetch	78	22	29
Vicia faba	field bean	26	11	7
Camelina sativa	gold-of-pleasure	10	5	26
Carthamus tinctorius	safflower	1		
Lallemantia sp.	lallemantia	13	5	8
Linum usitatissimum	flax	28	6	5
Papaver somniferum s.l.	opium poppy	14	6	10
Cucumis melo	melon		1	
Ficus carica	fig	49	15	16
Olea europaea (undiff.)	olive	1	2	2
Punica granatum	pomegranate		1	
Vitis vinifera (undiff.)	grapevine	25	12	12

agricultural system up to the Middle Bronze Age, while changes become noticeable in the Late Bronze Age.

The main cereal during the Early and Middle Bronze Age was barley (*Hordeum vulgare*). Most remains have been identified as hulled barley (*Hordeum vulgare* var. *vulgare*), and only a few derived from naked barley (*Hordeum vulgare* var. *nudum*). Besides hulled barley, emmer (*Triticum dicoccum*) and einkorn (*T. monococcum*) were subdominant. Spelt (*T. spelta*), free-threshing wheat (*T. aestivum/durum/turgidum*), broomcorn millet (*Panicum miliaceum*), and oats (*Avena* sp.) were recorded, but of minor importance, or in the case of oats of no importance in cultivation terms. From the Neolithic onwards, there are hints of another cereal in Greece: a 'new type' of glume wheat with uncertain taxonomic affiliation, probably closely related to *Triticum timopheevi* Zhuk. (Jones, Valamoti, and Charles 2000: 140–2). During the Middle Bronze Age species percentages are generally comparable to the Early Bronze Age, although seed counts (and thus representativeness) are noticeably lower.

Intensively investigated Late Bronze Age finds document a change in cereal cultivation observable in a marked decrease in barley and a smaller one in emmer, in favour of increasing values of broomcorn millet and spelt.

As with the cereals, the non-cereals records for northern Greece and southern Bulgaria exceed all other regions covered in our study in terms of find numbers, diversity, and representativeness (Table 19.1). For the Early Bronze Age the Representativeness Index of non-cereals (RI = 317) is even higher than that of cereals (RI = 248). This clearly indicates the importance of non-cereals in cultivation and consumption, mainly deriving from finds of pulses (RI = 176). The same is true for the Middle and Late Bronze Age, with the importance of cereals slightly rising towards the Late Bronze Age. The dominant pulses are bitter vetch (*Vicia ervilia*) and lentil (*Lens culinaris*), followed by field bean (*Vicia faba*). Grass pea (*Lathyrus sativus/cicera*), garden pea (*Pisum sativum*), and chickpea (*Cicer arietinum*) are of less importance. However, the spectrum of pulses does not display any clearly detectable shift between the different Bronze Age periods.

Oilseeds are also very diverse. For the Early and Middle Bronze Age, flax/linseed, opium poppy, lallemantia (*Lallemantia* sp.; s.; Jones and Valamoti 2005), gold-of-pleasure, and a single find of safflower (*Carthamus tinctorius*) are recorded. Towards the Late Bronze Age, gold-of-pleasure rises in importance whereas the others decrease (or go missing altogether, as in safflower). Remains of cultivated fruit are dominated by woody plants: fig (*Ficus carica*) is dominant, while grape (*Vitis vinifera*) is subdominant, and a few finds of olive (*Olea europaea*) occur. Also single records of pomegranate (*Punica granatum*) and melon (*Cucumis melo*) from Tiryns (Kroll 1982: 470, Table 1) are displayed in Table 19.1. In accordance with prior investigations, it seems indeed that fruit (mainly fruit tree) cultivation rose during the Bronze Age in the eastern Mediterranean (Zohary and Hopf 2000: 142–5). Certain aspects, such as oil production from olives, seem however to have been introduced to Europe, and even to the Aegean, after the Bronze Age (Riehl 1999: 62–3). The earliest evidence for the production of olive oil comes from a non-European site: Early Bronze Age Tel Yarmouth, Israel, in the Levant (Salavert 2008: 59–60).

Central and Northern Italy (South of the Alps)

In a former compilation of crops for Italy (Hopf 1991: 243–50), emmer was judged as being prevalent, and naked wheat as almost equally frequent. In the current compilation for the Early and Middle Bronze Age, emmer is still the dominant cereal. But barley is subdominant, together with free-threshing wheat and einkorn. However, this change may result mainly from new archaeobotanical research in the region carried out over the last 20 years, and the vastly increased amount of data provided by the research centres in Como, Modena, Florence, and Rome. The representativeness for cereal remains is, however, still low for the Early Bronze Age (RI = 14), moderate for the Middle Bronze Age (RI = 125), and low for the Late Bronze Age (RI = 62). The presence of broomcorn millet and foxtail millet (*Setaria italica*) is reported, and spelt is represented by the weakest count (RI = 1) for the region.

During the Late Bronze Age, the dominance of emmer persists, as well as the subdominance of barley. Einkorn decreases and free-threshing wheat is replaced mainly by broomcorn millet. Central and northern Italy (excluding the Alps and their foreland) was clearly a 'non-spelt' area, but rather an emmer region, following the main trend of increased millet cultivation in the Late Bronze Age observed in most other regions.

A few words need to be said about Sardinia, which is not included in our regional evaluation, and where a compilation by Bakels (2002) covers the Nuragic culture. Here it seems that the replacement of naked barley by hulled barley took place very late, during the Early Bronze Age, and from the Middle Bronze Age onwards only hulled barley is recorded. Emmer and free-threshing wheat are reported as well, the latter presumably a tetraploid wheat (such as durum wheat) as suggested by the identified rachis fragments (Bakels 2002: 5).

Table 19.2 RI Values of Non-Cereals in the Archaeobotanical Record of Central and Northern Italy (outside the Alps)

Plant species		EBA	MBA	LBA
Cicer arietinum	chickpea		1	1
Lathyrus sativus/cicera	grass pea			2
Lens culinaris	lentil		1	2
Pisum sativum	garden pea		2	6
Vicia ervilia	bitter vetch			4
Vicia faba	field bean		28	14
Vicia sativa	common vetch		2	1
Linum usitatissimum	flax		1	
Ficus carica	fig		1	
Juglans regia	walnut		2	
Olea europaea (undiff.)	olive	1	1	
Prunus domestica subsp. insititia	plum			1
Prunus dulcis	almond	1		
Sorbus domestica	service tree		2	
Vitis vinifera (undiff.)	grapevine	1	17	9

In the non-cereals, crop diversity is high in Italy, but only two species are well-represented: field bean and grape both in the Early/Middle Bronze Age and the Late Bronze Age. The beginning of grape cultivation for the regions of Tuscany and Emilia-Romagna during the Bronze Age has been discussed, but so far there is no confirmation for this hypothesis (Bellini *et al.* 2008: 108–9). Other pulses are recorded at low counts: garden pea, bitter vetch, lentil, grass pea, and chickpea. Bitter vetch, grass pea, and chickpea were found in the Late Bronze Age but are missing in the earlier periods. Linseed is only represented by two seeds (from Castellaro del Vhò: Rottoli 1997) from the Middle Bronze Age. Apart from grapes, fruit trees are weakly represented by olive, fig, and almond (*Prunus dulcis*) during the Early and Middle Bronze Age (Table 19.2). For the Late Bronze Age, plum (*Prunus domestica* subsp. *insititia*) is documented.

Southern France

Eleven sites in this region contribute to the evaluation of crop finds. Sites from the Early Bronze Age are absent, and the Middle Bronze Age is weakly documented (RI = 38). The Late Bronze Age again shows moderate representativeness (RI = 115). During the Middle Bronze Age, barley and free-threshing wheat are dominant at comparably high levels, and emmer and einkorn are subdominant. Other cereals are missing. In the Middle Bronze Age, the shift from naked barley to hulled barley is nearly complete in this region, with naked barley finds absent during the Late Bronze Age. In contrast to the continuously dominant hulled barley and subdominant emmer and einkorn during the Late Bronze Age, free-threshing wheat decreases from dominant to subdominant in this period. Spelt and oats as well as broomcorn

Table 19.3 RI Values of Non-Cereals in the Archaeobotanical Record of Southern France

Plant species		EBA	MBA	LBA
Lathyrus sativus/cicera	grass pea		1	11
Vicia ervilia	bitter vetch			2
Vicia faba	field bean		1	10
Linum usitatissimum	flax			2
Papaver somniferum s.l.	opium poppy			6
Olea europaea (undiff.)	olive		1	
Vitis vinifera (undiff.)	grapevine			1

millet and foxtail millet appear in the Late Bronze Age. Their high representativeness values are mainly based on two sites (Bouby, Fages, and Treffort 2005): one at Baume Layrou, Gard, was a storage find mainly consisting of hulled barley, spelt, and broomcorn millet, while Balme Gontran resulted in two nearly pure finds of stored spelt and broomcorn millet. For non-cereals the Middle Bronze Age sites were not productive; only single counts for the pulses field bean and grass pea and the fruit tree olive were noted.

During the Late Bronze Age, non-cereals are better represented both by grass pea and field bean, and in addition some bitter vetch (Table 19.3). Few counts of the oil seeds, poppy, and linseed, as well as grape are reported from Late Bronze Age contexts. General trends are pointed out by the available publications, but the data basis is still weak for this region.

Mediterranean Spain

The 15 sites that have entered our evaluation mainly cover the Middle Bronze Age (RI = 196) and the Late Bronze Age (RI = 106) with high and moderate representativeness indices, while the Early Bronze Age (RI = 36) is only weakly represented. Across the whole Bronze Age, barley remains the main cereal. A remarkable observation is that about half of the counts derive from naked barley and half from hulled barley. Consequently, the shift from naked to hulled barley, noticeable in most other regions, seems not to have taken place in Mediterranean Spain. In the Early and Middle Bronze Age, free-threshing wheat is subdominant whereas emmer, einkorn, broomcorn millet, and (most probably non-cultivated) oats appear with few or single counts. Indicated by few but well-preserved rachis fragments from Fuente Álamo (Stika 2001: 271–2), both tetraploid and hexaploid free-threshing wheats are documented for southern Spain.

Towards the Late Bronze Age, free-threshing wheat decreases while emmer increases; our study does not show any increase of millets as observed in most other regions. However, the site of Masada de Ratón (Fraga, Baix Cinca), situated inland in north-eastern Spain, must be mentioned before reaching conclusions. The site was not included in our evaluation because the relevant samples are ambiguously dated as Middle/Late Bronze Age (Alonso i Martínez 1999: 109–14). Yet in Masada de Ratón both foxtail millet and broomcorn millet are reported—foxtail millet with 485 finds (RI = 2) and broomcorn millet with 66 finds (RI = 1). So the evidence

Table 19.4 RI Values of Non-Cereals in the Archaeobotanical Record of Mediterranean Spain

Plant species		EBA	MBA	LBA
Lens culinaris	lentil		3	
Pisum sativum	garden pea		8	4
Vicia ervilia	bitter vetch	1		
Vicia faba	field bean	3	11	10
Linum usitatissimum	flax	4	8	5
Papaver somniferum s.l.	opium poppy	2		4
Castanea sativa	sweet chestnut			1
Ficus carica	fig	4	10	30
Olea europaea (undiff.)	olive	1	9	5
Phoenix dactylifera	date			1
Vitis vinifera (undiff.)	grapevine		8	6

seems to show a dramatically delayed spread of millets to the Iberian Peninsula in the Bronze Age by comparison with other regions in Europe (continental Greece and southern Bulgaria, the Pannonian Plains, Italy, the Alps, and western central Europe). Spelt arrived even later (several authors cited in Buxó i Capdevila 1997: 104).

The non-cereals from Mediterranean Spain (Table 19.4) display a high diversity. During the Early and Middle Bronze Age, field bean dominates the pulses, followed by garden pea, lentil, and bitter vetch. Oil plants are represented by finds of linseed and opium poppy, whereas among fruit trees fig, olive, and grape are recorded. Towards the Late Bronze Age, the pulse spectrum is reduced to field bean and pea. Again, linseed and poppy are found. Records of fig increase while olive and grape remain at the same level. For two sites in the province of Almería in Andalucía (Gatas and Fuente Álamo) there are unpublished data with further finds of grape pips (Stika 1996a; 2003), which are not included in the recent study. So the question when fruit-tree cultivation started in Spain is still unanswered. Rodríguez-Ariza and Montes Moya (2005) reviewed the origin and domestication of *Olea europaea* L. (olive) in Andalucía, Spain, by assessing charcoal and fruit data. For Mesomediterranean altitudes it seems to be clear that cultivation appeared no earlier than the Roman period. But at the Thermomediterranean level, where several sites included in our study are situated, the possible use of wild olive or even its cultivation during the Bronze Age still needs assessment.

Pannonian Basin

An earlier compilation (Wasylikowa et al. 1991: 214–17) covered the Pannonian Basin and gave a first impression about Bronze Age cereal cultivation, with einkorn, emmer, and hulled barley as the most important cereals in 25 analysed sites. For our new compilation, 46 sites were evaluated. Representativeness of archaeobotanical data is low for the Early Bronze Age (RI = 60), very high for the Middle Bronze Age (RI = 548), and high for the Late Bronze Age (RI = 264).

In accordance with the study by Wasylikowa et al. (1991: 215), the current data show that during the Early and Middle Bronze Age the three main cereals are hulled barley, einkorn, and emmer. Barley is also documented in its free-threshing (naked) variety, but to a low extent. Free-threshing wheat appears in some sites, more precisely identified as club wheat (*T. compactum*), and therefore subsumed in *Triticum aestivum* s.l. in the diagrams presented online, and spelt and broomcorn millet were recorded with few counts. The taxa rye (*Secale cereale*) and oats, most probably still non-domesticated, appeared with single counts. For the Late Bronze Age we recognize a change to four main cereals: broomcorn millet, hulled barley, emmer, and einkorn. While barley and einkorn decrease, broomcorn millet increases remarkably towards the Late Bronze Age. Spelt increases slightly, and free-threshing wheat keeps approximately the same proportion in the spectrum of cultivated crops. Foxtail millet was introduced to the area but was of low importance. For the Bronze Age Pannonian Basin, the 'new type' glume wheat is reported (Kohler-Schneider 2001: 116–25; Stika and Berzsényi forthcoming). No calculation of the importance of this taxon on the basis of grains can yet be given because identification criteria for the grains are still not available (and they have to remain unidentifiable for the moment)—in contrast to the glume bases/spikelet forks which are well-identifiable since the articles by Glynis Jones et al. (2000: 134–6) and Marianne Kohler-Schneider (2001: 116–25). For Stillfried an der March (Kohler-Schneider 2001: 180), it was possible to successfully identify rye brome (*Bromus secalinus*) grains as an important component in a porridge-like cereal preparation ('Hirsotto').

The diversity of pulses and oil plants is high in the region (Table 19.5). In the Early Bronze Age and Middle Bronze Age, lentil and pea are the main pulses, while subdominant ones are bitter vetch and field bean. Grass pea and common vetch (*Vicia sativa*) are recorded but are of less importance. Towards the Late Bronze Age conditions are similar, with slightly increased amounts of bitter vetch, but common vetch is now missing. In Early Bronze Age and Middle Bronze Age contexts, gold-of-pleasure, safflower, poppy, and linseed are documented, while

Table 19.5 RI Values of Non-Cereals in the Archaeobotanical Record of the Pannonian Basin

Plant species		EBA	MBA	LBA
Lathyrus sativus/cicera	grass pea		4	1
Lens culinaris	lentil	2	50	14
Pisum sativum	garden pea	2	40	12
Vicia ervilia	bitter vetch		20	14
Vicia faba	field bean	1	10	4
Vicia sativa	common vetch		1	
Camelina sativa	gold-of-pleasure	1	16	6
Carthamus tinctorius	safflower		11	
Linum usitatissimum	flax		14	
Papaver somniferum s.l.	opium poppy		5	4
Cucumis sativus	cucumber			1
Vitis vinifera (undiff.)	grapevine		2	7

the Late Bronze Age saw a reduction in gold-of-pleasure and poppy. Fruit trees are represented by finds of grape pips which might have been collected from the wild stands in the floodplains of the Danube.

Eastern Alps and their Foreland

This region is limited to the west by an imaginary line formed by the Alpine part of the River Rhine, the Splügen pass, and Lake Como. Twenty-seven sites are in our compilation, producing a well-balanced representativeness for the three main Bronze Age phases: Early Bronze Age (RI = 101), Middle Bronze Age (RI = 135), and Late Bronze Age (RI = 279). During the Early Bronze Age and Middle Bronze Age, barley was the dominant cereal mainly represented by its hulled variety, but free-threshing barley is recorded as well. Emmer and spelt are subdominant, followed by einkorn and free-threshing wheat. Broomcorn millet, rye, and oats are listed with only a few counts. Towards the Late Bronze Age, broomcorn millet increases remarkably while barley decreases. An earlier investigation (Küster 1991: 183) claimed that a complete change of the spectrum of cultural plants for this period could be detected. Our study, however, suggests otherwise: for the Late Bronze Age, barley, emmer, and broomcorn millet are recorded as the main cereals, with subdominant spelt and einkorn. On current data, the main changes refer to only two cereal taxa: parts of the barley production are replaced by broomcorn millet. A mixed find of mainly stored emmer and rye brome grains, along with low numbers of other weed finds, at the mountain site of Kulm, Trofaiach (Stika 2000: 165–7), suggests the cultivation of rye brome for its grains at higher elevations.

For the non-cereals (Table 19.6), pulses are important and are recorded with moderate representativeness especially for the Late Bronze Age (RI = 90), with low scores for the Early and Middle Bronze Age (RI = 44). In the Early/Middle Bronze Age, garden pea is dominant with few counts for field bean and lentil. Towards the Late Bronze Age, pulses become even more important with garden pea still being dominant, but now with a subdominance of field bean and lentil. Additionally, there are a few counts of bitter vetch. The oil plants poppy, gold-of-pleasure, and linseed are present with single counts, as is grape.

Table 19.6 RI Values of Non-Cereals in the Archaeobotanical Record of the Eastern Alps and their Foreland

Plant species		EBA	MBA	LBA
Lens culinaris	lentil		4	26
Pisum sativum	garden pea	12	24	33
Vicia ervilia	bitter vetch			6
Vicia faba	field bean	1	3	25
Camelina sativa	gold-of-pleasure			2
Linum usitatissimum	flax			1
Papaver somniferum s.l.	opium poppy	2	2	2
Vitis vinifera (undiff.)	grapevine	3		

Table 19.7 RI Values of Non-Cereals in the Archaeobotanical Record of the Western Alps and their Foreland

Plant species		EBA	MBA	LBA
Lathyrus sativus/cicera	grass pea			2
Lens culinaris	lentil			32
Pisum sativum	garden pea	4	1	15
Vicia faba	field bean	2	8	37
Camelina sativa	gold-of-pleasure			10
Linum usitatissimum	flax	5	2	24
Papaver somniferum s.l.	opium poppy	1		52
Castanea sativa	sweet chestnut			1
Vitis vinifera (undiff.)	grapevine			1

Western Alps and their Foreland

This region is extremely well represented for the Late Bronze Age, especially due to the well-investigated lakeside settlements with huge quantities of plant finds: Early Bronze Age (RI = 88), Middle Bronze Age (RI = 157), and Late Bronze Age (RI = 556). Twenty-four sites were evaluated in total. For the Early/Middle Bronze Age, three main cereals are reported: barley being dominant, emmer, and spelt subdominant. Free-threshing wheat and einkorn are frequently reported but of little importance. For broomcorn millet and oats only few counts and a single count for rye are given. In the Late Bronze Age, broomcorn millet increased and foxtail millet becomes important, arriving at its highest representativeness for all evaluated regions in this study. Barley and emmer decrease during the Late Bronze Age. Free-threshing wheat is still frequently represented, both tetraploid and hexaploid naked wheats being determined from rachis fragments (e.g. Jacomet and Karg 1996: 235). In Zug-Sumpf, spelt is quite important with 19 storage finds (a total of 68 storage finds from that site), but nevertheless hulled barley is the dominant cereal there (Jacomet and Karg 1996: 228–9). At the Late Bronze Age lakeside settlement of Hagnau-Burg on Lake Constance (Rösch 1996: Tab.le 1), three spikelets of oats were found and determined as common (i.e. cultivated) oats (*Avena sativa*).

For the Early/Middle Bronze Age the non-cereals (Table 19.7) are represented mainly by pulses, with a dominance of field bean and a subdominance of garden pea, and finds of linseed and opium poppy. Towards the Late Bronze Age, the representativeness rises considerably with field bean and lentil being dominant and garden pea being subdominant. Grass pea is represented with two counts only. The increased counts of oilseeds (RI = 86) during the Late Bronze Age are dominated by opium poppy with a subdominance of linseed and several counts for gold-of-pleasure. The latter is considered a weed in flax fields (Jacomet and Karg 1996: 249). The lakeside settlements, with both carbonized and waterlogged preservation conditions, reflect crop cultivation quite well, for both cereals and non-cereals.

West-Central Europe (Outside the Alps)

This region is quite diverse in terms of environmental setting. The sites are mainly located in Baden-Württemberg and Hesse in Germany, and Lorraine in France. The lower Rhine region,

Luxemburg, Bavaria as well as parts of northern Germany (but away from the North Sea) are included too, so we end up with quite a mixed group. Even allowing for that, the representativeness for the earlier phases is in general rather low: Early Bronze Age (RI = 65), Middle Bronze Age (RI = 35). The Late Bronze Age (RI = 284) is, however, well represented.

For the Early/Middle Bronze Age the dominance of barley is documented, mainly relying on its hulled variety. Emmer and spelt are subdominant. Einkorn and broomcorn millet are frequently reported but without any importance as far as the main crops are concerned. Free-threshing wheat, foxtail millet, and rye are reported with single counts. The Late Bronze Age results display an increase in broomcorn millet and a decrease in barley. In spite of an increase in scores of spelt in our evaluation, its percentage decreases towards the Late Bronze Age. A publication by Karl-Heinz Knörzer (1972: 399–401) reports several finds of grains of oats at the Urnfield site of Langweiler. In addition, spikelet bases were also found, both from common wild oats (*A. fatua*) and common (cultivated) oats. Langweiler, located on the Aldenhovener Platte in the westernmost part of North Rhine-Westphalia, thus hints at the presence of domesticated oats.

For non-cereals (Table 19.8), several taxa of pulses were found. In the Early/Middle Bronze Age, only a few counts were recorded of garden pea, field bean, lentil, and bitter vetch. Towards the Late Bronze Age, the representativeness of pulses rises (RI = 55): lentil and garden pea are dominant followed by some counts for field bean and single counts for bitter vetch and common vetch. The low counts of gold-of-pleasure in the Early/Middle Bronze Age are complemented by opium poppy and linseed in the Late Bronze Age.

For eastern central Europe we have not found enough data to arrive at an acceptable representativeness for the three phases of the Early, Middle, and Late Bronze Age. Research is ongoing at the well-known site of Bruszczewo in Poland. In the earlier period, barley and emmer are dominant. In the later period, there is a broad spectrum of cereals, with barley, emmer, spelt, free-threshing wheat, and broomcorn millet, as well as pulses with lentil, garden pea, bitter vetch, and field bean being present (pers. comm. H. Kroll). For the Czech Republic, a compilation was published very recently, containing valuable information that we were unable to include in this article (Kočár and Dreslerová 2010): 20 sites from the Early Bronze Age, 9 from the Middle Bronze Age, and 49 from the Late Bronze Age, indicating a clear dominance of emmer during the Early Bronze Age, with einkorn subdominant. Amounts of barley increase,

Table 19.8 RI Values of Non-Cereals in the Archaeobotanical Record of Western Central Europe (outside the Alps)

Plant species		EBA	MBA	LBA
Lens culinaris	lentil	2	1	24
Pisum sativum	garden pea	6		20
Vicia ervilia	bitter vetch		1	2
Vicia faba	field bean	2	1	8
Vicia sativa	common vetch			1
Camelina sativa	gold-of-pleasure	2	1	8
Linum usitatissimum	flax			3
Papaver somniferum s.l.	opium poppy			5
Vitis vinifera subsp. sylvestris	grapevine			1

Table 19.9 RI Values of Non-Cereals in the Archaeobotanical Record of Southern Scandinavia and the North Sea Coast

Plant species		EBA	MBA	LBA
Vicia faba	field bean			5
Camelina sativa	gold-of-pleasure			25
Linum usitatissimum	flax	1	1	22

and local flax cultivation begins. Millet cultivation is indicated from the Middle Bronze Age onwards. In the Late Bronze Age, the importance of einkorn decreases, leading to approximately equal proportions of four main cereals: emmer, barley, millet, and spelt. This is also the period when the cultivation of naked wheat begins in the region.

Southern Scandinavia and North Sea Coast

The data used for this region originate mainly from two recent compilations (Robinson 2003; Kučan 2007). The total of 26 sites, however, produced only weak representativeness for the Early Bronze Age (RI = 57) and Middle Bronze Age (RI = 27) and moderate values for the Late Bronze Age (RI = 177). Nevertheless, the data available for the North Sea coast and southern Scandinavia have greatly increased compared with what was available to previous researchers (Bakels 1991: 286–8; Jensen 1991: 337–8).

For cereals, the region is dominated by barley with a subdominance of emmer. Barley is represented with both its varieties, the free-threshing form and the hulled form. Spelt, free-threshing wheat, einkorn, and broomcorn millet are reported with few counts. In the Late Bronze Age site of Rodenkirchen in the marshlands of the River Weser (Kučan 2007: 40), aside from spikelets of wild oats, one grain within its spikelet and one spikelet basis were identified with certainty as common oats. There is no change detectable in the percentage of cereal counts towards the Late Bronze Age. Non-cereals are represented by linseed and gold-of-pleasure (Table 19.9).

On a coarse scale, not much change is visible during the Bronze Age. But when focusing on sub-regions, some changes seem to be detectable. In Thy, northern Jutland, from the Early to the Late Bronze Age barley and emmer persisted as the main crops (Stika and Henriksen 2010). No shift is visible from free-threshing to hulled barley as a main crop. In this region the change took place in the Iron Age around AD 100. In eastern Denmark and southern Sweden (Gustafsson 1998), the shift is observable one thousand years earlier in the Late Bronze Age.

Individual Cereals, Plants, and Trees

Barley

During the Early and Middle Bronze Age, barley is the dominant cereal in all regions of Europe evaluated in our analysis. In most regions the replacement of naked (free-threshing) barley by hulled barley took place already before the Bronze Age, in Greece and southern

Bulgaria, the Pannonian Basin, the eastern and western Alps, western central Europe, and southern France. Nevertheless, free-threshing barley is still recorded for these regions at low levels. In Mediterranean Spain as well as in southern Scandinavia and the North Sea coast, both for the Early/Middle Bronze Age and the Late Bronze Age, the record of free-threshing barley versus hulled barley remained balanced between both varieties. In some regions a slight decrease of barley is detectable from the Early/Middle Bronze Age towards the Late Bronze Age: Greece and southern Bulgaria, the Pannonian Basin, and in the eastern and western Alps. However, in all regions barley remains an important crop.

Wheat

The tetraploid hulled wheat species of emmer is among the main crops in all regions. In southern Spain its importance is somewhat less than in the other regions of Europe. The semi-arid south-west of Spain, from which the records for the Early/Middle Bronze Age in Mediterranean Spain are mainly derived, was probably too dry for emmer cultivation. In ecological terms, the Atlantic area of northern Spain, a region not included in our evaluation, is more suitable for emmer cultivation; emmer is still grown today in that region (Peña-Chocarro 1996: 131–3). In central and northern Italy (without the Alps and their foreland), emmer is the predominant cereal for the Early/Middle Bronze Age and Late Bronze Age. In a few regions, specifically Greece and southern Bulgaria, and in the western Alps, emmer slightly decreases towards the Late Bronze Age.

The diploid hulled wheat einkorn is an important cereal of Greece and southern Bulgaria, and in the Pannonian Basin, with slightly less dominance in central and northern Italy and southern France. In the other regions einkorn is listed frequently but with low counts. The Bronze Age finds, as well as recently cultivated einkorn in the Archaeological Park at Százhalombatta, have well developed grains, and cultivation seems to be productive in this region, as we can attest from our own experience. Generally there is a slight decrease in einkorn towards the Late Bronze Age in many regions.

The hexaploid hulled wheat species spelt tells another story. In contrast to einkorn and emmer, both deriving from wild ancestors in the Fertile Crescent and domesticated there (Zohary and Hopf 2000: 19–51), no wild-growing ancestor exists there for spelt; it evolved under cultivation. Apart from some 'Asian' spelt appearing early in Transcaucasia (see Zohary and Hopf 2000: 57), there seems to be a 'European' spelt of different origins, probably based on an introgression of a tetraploid hulled wheat (emmer) into free-threshing hexaploid wheat (bread wheat) as discussed by Örni Akeret (2005: 284 for discussion and further references). He dates the beginning of spelt cultivation in the northern Alpine foreland of Switzerland between 2400 and 2200 BC. There are even older hints of a 'European' spelt from south-western Germany and areas further north (cited in Körber-Grohne 1987: 72). One may conclude that the 'European' spelt possibly originated somewhere north of the Alps prior to the Bronze Age, and spread from there in the period transitional to the Early Bronze Age. This hypothesis is well displayed in our online diagrams: for the Early/Middle Bronze Age onwards, spelt is a dominant cereal in western central Europe, the western and the eastern Alps, and their respective forelands. From there it seems that spelt cultivation spread north to the North Sea coast and southern Scandinavia, south-west to southern France, and east and south-east to the Pannonian

Basin and Greece (with southern Bulgaria). The rise of spelt cultivation in Late Bronze Age Greece is remarkable. During the Bronze Age spelt was introduced neither to the Iberian Peninsula nor to Italy south of the Po.

Since Jones, Valamoti and Charles (2000) and Kohler-Schneider (2001: 116–25) have introduced the archaeobotanical community to a 'new' glume wheat, basing their belief on identifications from northern Greece and from eastern Austria ('emmer-like spelt wheat'), several researchers have found a new type of glume wheat which might be related to the tetraploid Timopheev's wheat (*Triticum timopheevi*). The identification can, however, only be carried out on well-preserved spikelet forks. In our experience the 'new type' glume wheat is present in archaeological samples from Turkey via the Balkans to Germany, and from the early Neolithic through to Early Iron Age layers. From the available literature, at the moment we cannot draw a reliable map of its distribution during the Bronze Age. In our evaluation we used the grain finds to describe the proportions of the different cereals in cultivation and use. The grains that might be connected to the spikelet forks of the 'new type' glume wheat can still not be identified with certainty, however, and the importance of this cereal is still largely unknown.

In free-threshing wheat, it is impossible to distinguish with certainty between tetraploid (*Triticum durum/turgidum*) and hexaploid (*T. aestivum* s.l.) species by grain morphology alone. There are quite globular grains that might be determined as hexaploid club wheat (*T. compactum*), a taxon mostly treated as a subspecies of *Triticum aestivum* s.l. (the wheat taxonomy in this paper follows the classification accepted by archaeobotanists, but which is not the latest nomenclature in systematic botany: see Jacomet 2006). Only if well-preserved rachis fragments are found in archaeobotanical samples can a more detailed classification be given. For Fuente Alamo in Spain (Stika 2001: 272) and Zug-Sumpf in Switzerland (Jacomet and Karg 1996: 235), both tetraploid and hexaploid free-threshing wheats are reported from the same sites and layers. Free-threshing wheat was dominant in Mediterranean Spain, in southern France, and central and northern Italy. In these three regions free-threshing wheat increased from the Early/Middle Bronze Age towards the Late Bronze Age. In all other evaluated regions free-threshing wheat is recorded but not of great importance in cultivation and use, either for the Early/Middle Bronze Age or the Late Bronze Age.

Due to identification problems with archaeobotanical finds, the reliability of the proportions within recorded finds of wheat species is far from satisfactory.

Millets

In prehistoric Europe, two species of millet (i.e. small-grained cereals) are cultivated: broomcorn millet and foxtail millet. Both species are first recorded from the seventh–sixth millennia BC in the Yellow River Valley and other regions in northern China. Broomcorn millet appeared almost synchronously in eastern Europe and the Caucasus, while the appearance of foxtail millet in Europe (fifth–fourth millennia BC) was delayed (Hunt et al. 2008: 5). Both millet species were widespread in the European Neolithic as well as the Early and Middle Bronze Age (Zohary and Hopf 2000: 83–8), though not grown as main crops. As our compilation clearly shows, the transformation of millets from minor to major (or even main) crops took place in the transition from Middle to Late Bronze Age in Europe. Broomcorn millet became important in many of the evaluated regions (Greece and southern Bulgaria, the Pannonian Basin, the Alps and their foreland, western central Europe, and in Italy). In the Bronze Age of the Iberian Peninsula, southern France, the North Sea coast and southern Scandinavia, millets are reported but of minor importance. During the Late Bronze Age foxtail millet became an important crop only in the western Alps and its foreland. Later, especially in medieval times, broomcorn and foxtail millet became the main crops on sandy soils in several parts of Europe (Körber-Grohne 1987: 332–6).

Oats

In the pre-Roman Iron Age settlement of Rullstorf on the lower terrace of the Elbe Valley close to Lüneburg, the currently oldest storage find of oats was discovered, and determined as cultivated common oats by their well-preserved glume bases (Behre 1990: 148–50). In contrast, during the Bronze Age only single finds of common oats are reported. In the regions we have evaluated one grain within its spikelet and one separate spikelet basis of common oats were identified with certainty in the Early Bronze Age site of Rodenkirchen in the Weser marshlands (Kučan 2007: 40). Later, from the Urnfield site of Langweiler on the Aldenhovener Platte in the westernmost part of Germany, several finds of spikelet bases of common (cultivated) oats are reported (Knörzer 1972: 399–401). At both sites, apart from common oats, common wild oats are also reported. *A. fatua* is, together with *A. sterilis*, one of the probable wild progenitors of common (i.e. cultivated) oats (Zohary and Hopf 2000: 78–82). The three spikelets of common oats from the Late Bronze Age lakeside settlement of Hagnau-Burg on Lake Constance (Rösch 1996: Table 1) are reported with no finds of wild oats species. This might suggest that the domestication of common oats happened in the transition phase between the Bronze and Iron Age somewhere in northern Germany or neighbouring areas. The cultivation of common oats spread in the Roman Iron Age along the North Sea coast, and later on the species became a main crop especially in the northern European countries (Körber-Grohne 1987: 64–5).

Rye

In several evaluated regions we have records of rye grains (e.g. the Pannonian Basin, the Alps and their foreland, western central Europe, and the North Sea coast and southern Scandinavia). Rye migrated to Europe as a weed among other cereals, with single finds from the Neolithic and increasing numbers during the Bronze and Iron Ages (Behre 1992). The start of rye as a crop in its own right is estimated by Karl-Ernst Behre (1992) to have taken place independently by acculturation in different areas during the pre-Roman Iron Age and Roman period. The further spread of cultivated rye happened during the early Middle Ages. It is usual to assign the few Bronze Age finds of rye in Europe the status of a weed.

Legumes/Pulses

There are several species of legume of great importance in Bronze Age Europe. This is not only due to the use of their seeds in human nutrition, but additionally for their ability to fix atmospheric nitrogen in symbiosis with root-associated rhizobium bacteria (*Rhizobium* s.l.).

Crop rotation involving pulses following cereal cultivation can therefore help to maintain higher levels of soil fertility (Zohary and Hopf 2000: 92). In the Bronze Age the main legume crops are field bean, lentil, and garden pea. Of more regional importance are bitter vetch, grass pea, common vetch, and chickpea. Their wild ancestors are mainly distributed in the eastern Mediterranean basin and the Near East, or are of unknown origin, as in the case of field beans. In Bronze Age Europe the domestication process was over and the cultivation of pulses was already widespread. For Greece and southern Bulgaria, Italy, the Pannonian Basin, and the eastern Alps and their foreland, both diversity and representativeness of the pulses are high. There is a trend towards an increase in pulse cultivation during the Late Bronze Age in some regions, such as central western Europe, the Alps and their foreland, and Italy.

Oil Plants

In diversity and representativeness it is again the region of Greece and southern Bulgaria that display the highest values in this group. However, for all the other evaluated regions, the record of oil plants is low, or at best rather unbalanced. Oilseeds are generally under-represented in sites where only charred material is preserved; they are easily destroyed when they are in contact with fire. Where waterlogged preservation conditions exist, the representativeness of oil plants is therefore much higher, as seen in the western Alps and their foreland as well as the North Sea Coast and southern Scandinavia. In contrast, in Italy, Mediterranean Spain, and southern France values are low by comparison.

Linseed and opium poppy are old domesticates that spread throughout Europe from the Neolithic on. During the Bronze Age lallemantia and safflower are regionally limited to the south-eastern part of Europe in their use and distribution. Gold-of-pleasure is a secondary crop and was acculturated from its weed ancestor growing in linseed fields, and used in its cultivar form from the Bronze Age onwards (Zohary and Hopf 2000: 138–9). The Late Bronze Age pure storage find of gold-of-pleasure from Kastanas, filling a whole vessel, is proof of the intentional use of this oil plant (Kroll 1983: 58–9). Likewise, a large quantity (> 8 kg) of crop-processing by-product of gold-of-pleasure from the North Sea coast Late Bronze Age settlement of Rodenkirchen clearly demonstrates its cultivation and use in this region (Kučan 2007: 41–3). As gold-of-pleasure is a salt-tolerant plant, it is suitable for cultivation in these marshland areas sometimes affected by storm tides.

Fruit Trees (and Other Cultivated Fruit)

In our evaluation fruit trees are recorded with remarkable scores for three regions: Greece and Bulgaria, central and northern Italy, and Mediterranean Spain. For southern France only single scores are reported, which might relate to the weaker data basis of the region. Fig, olive, and grape are the species involved, but their domestication status during the Bronze Age is still a matter of debate. For the Pannonian Basin as well as the eastern Alps and their foreland, grape is reported, but located in the range of the natural distribution of wild grape. Additionally, there are reports from Italy of almond and plum, and from Greece of pomegranate and melon as a herbaceous cultivated fruit. The probable use of all these species is undoubted, in contrast to the status of their domestication. Perhaps agreement can be found that during the Bronze Age the Mediterranean area was the starting point of European fruit-tree cultivation, and probably of the first stages of their domestication.

Conclusion

Before concluding, we need to decide how much the observed (or supposed) patterns of Bronze Age crop cultivation as evaluated in this study (see Tables 19.1–19.9) follow natural and social environmental conditions. Natural factors limiting crop cultivation influence marginal regions, like Mediterranean Iberia with its semi-arid conditions, or the North Sea coast and southern Scandinavia with their cold, wet, and frequently salt-influenced situation, or the Alps at higher altitudes (Primas 2009: 193–6). Consequently, these regions display some significant differences in their crop systems, such as the cultivation of salt-tolerant crops (field bean, gold-of-pleasure, and barley) in the North Sea coastal area.

In other regions the cultivation of cereals, pulses, and oil plants probably follows social factors that determined a preferred food system. Millets, for example, are completely different from large-grained cereals in their ecology and therefore their cultivation demands, their processing, and their consumption. How easily wheats can be used for baking bread, as another example, separates the wheat species from all other cereals cultivated during the Bronze Age. The influence on crop choices of bread-baking and other food preparation methods on the one hand, and their influence on crop representation in the archaeobotanical record on the other, is still a difficult issue, as demonstrated by recent research on porridge/bread remains (Hansson 1994; Heiss 2008: 26–30, 131–7; Valamoti et al. 2008), or on beer/malt (Stika 1996b). The beer topic is among many others discussed in Van Zeist (1991: 118–21), Kroll (1991b), and Procopiou and Treuil (2002).

At all events, the shift to millet, spelt, and hulled barley together with an increase in pulse cultivation that is observed in some regions towards the Late Bronze Age, reflects a change in subsistence strategies, and changes in the agrarian system in general. These may have happened because of the growth of local populations, the building of settlements in new landscapes with different natural conditions, or the acquisition of new techniques. Changes in the agrarian system, for example, are indicated in the Nordic Bronze Age by the switch from the two-aisled house to three-aisled farms with the byre included (most recently Fokkens 2009: 91), introducing the possibility of manuring with cattle dung, now readily available. There are hints at manuring described by Helmut Kroll (1987: 107–9) for the North Sea island of Sylt, which might explain the formation of 'Celtic field' systems (Fokkens 2009: 94). Numerous other indications of the beginning of manuring are given by Bakels (1997), De Hingh (2000: 159–62), Robinson (2003: 163), Brinkkemper and van Wijngaarden-Bakker (2005: 496), and in Stika and Henriksen (2010). As visible in the Nordic Bronze Age, the mixed-farming economy using cattle traction (see Chapter 18) for ploughing permanent fields with an ard (Fokkens 2009: 90) changed and intensified the agrarian system. Lists of ard finds and traces of ploughing, as well as field systems of Bronze Age date, are given by Tegtmeier (1993) and Fries (1995).

Another feature, much more difficult to grasp, is represented by the cultural aspects of plant cultivation, their processing and consumption—for instance, fostering esteem or disregard of certain crops, maybe even their tabooization. Field beans, for instance, were strongly connected to death and the underworld in Hellenistic Greece (Hanelt 1972: 209; Ciarialdi 1999), and in Egypt, according to Herodotus, they were even considered unclean and taboo for certain social groups, such as priests (*Histories* II, 37; Macaulay 1890). Such beliefs may have seriously affected the choice or avoidance of certain crops (Hansson and Heiss forthcoming).

Even if this short chapter can only scratch the surface of what actually might have taken place during the centuries of the European Bronze Age, a few clear trends have been highlighted and discussed. Archaeobotany has already contributed significantly to the knowledge of prehistoric agricultural systems, and thanks to the ever-increasing data basis, we believe it will do so even more in the future.

Note

A longer version of this chapter with additional illustrative and tabular material is available online on the Oxford Handbooks website.

Bibliography

Akeret, Ö. (2005). 'Plant remains from a Bell Beaker site in Switzerland, and the beginnings of *Triticum spelta* (spelt) cultivation in Europe', *Vegetation History and Archaeobotany*, 14/4: 279–86.

Alonso i Martínez, N. (1999). *De la Llavor a la Farina. Els Processos Arícoles Protohistòrics a la Catalunya Occidental*, Monographies d'Archéologie Méditerranéenne. Lattes: CNRS Éditions.

Bakels, C. C. (1991). 'Western continental Europe', in W. van Zeist, K. Wasylikowa, and K.-E. Behre (eds.), *Progress in Old World Palaeoethnobotany: A Retrospective View on the Occasion of 20 Years of the International Work Group for Palaeoethnobotany*. Rotterdam/Brookfield: A. A. Balkema, 279–98.

—— (1997). 'Fields and their manuring', *Antiquity*, 71/272: 442.

—— (2002). 'Plant remains from Sardinia, Italy, with notes on barley and grape', *Vegetation History and Archaeobotany*, 11: 3–8.

Behre, K.-E. (1990). 'Kulturpflanzen und Unkräuter der vorrömischen Eisenzeit aus der Siedlung Rullstorf, Ldkr. Lüneburg', *Nachrichten aus Niedersachsens Urgeschichte*, 59: 141–65.

—— (1992). 'The history of rye cultivation in Europe', *Vegetation History and Archaeobotany*, 1/3: 141–56.

Bellini, C., Mariotti-Lippi, M., Mori Secci, M., Aranguren, B., and Perazzi, P. (2008). 'Plant gathering and cultivation in prehistoric Tuscany (Italy)', *Vegetation History and Archaeobotany*, 17/Supplement 1: 103–12.

Bouby, L., Fages, G., and Treffort, J. M. (2005). 'Food storage in two Late Bronze Age caves of southern France: palaeoethnobotanical and social implications', *Vegetation History and Archaeobotany*, 14: 313–28.

——, Terral, J.-F., Ivorrah, S., Marinval, P., Pradat, B., and Ruas, M.-P. (2006). 'Vers une Approche bio-archéologique de l'histoire de la vigne cultivée et de la viticulture: problématique, choix méthodologiques et premiers résultats', *Archéologie du Midi médiéval*, 23–24/2005–6: 61–74.

Brinkkemper, O. and Wijngaarden-Bakker, L. van (2005). 'All-round farming. Food production in the Bronze Age and the Iron Age', in L. P. Louwe Kooijmans and P. W. van den Broeke, H. Fokkens, and A. van Gijn (eds.), *The Prehistory of the Netherlands*. Amsterdam: Amsterdam University Press, 491–512.

Buxó i Capdevila, R. (1997). *Arqueología de las Plantas. La Exploitación económica de las semillas y los frutos en el marco mediterráneo de Península Ibérica*. Barcelona: Crítica.

Ciarialdi, M. (1999). 'Food offerings at the Archaic/Hellenistic sanctuary of Demeter and Persephone at Monte Papalucio (Oria, Apulia, southern Italy)', *Accordia Research Papers*, 7 (1997–8): 75–91.

Fokkens, H. (2009). 'Die Wirtschaft der Nordischen Bronzezeit: mehr als Getreide säen und Vieh züchten', in M. Bartelheim and H. Stäuble (eds.), *Die wirtschaftlichen Grundlagen der Bronzezeit Europas* [*The Economic Foundations of the European Bronze Age*], Forschungen zur Archäometrie und Altertumswissenschaft, 4. Rahden: Verlag Marie Leidorf, 85–104.

Fries, J. C. (1995). *Vor- und frühgeschichtliche Agrartechnik auf den Britischen Inseln und dem Kontinent. Eine vergleichende Studie*, Internationale Archäologie. Espelkamp: Verlag Marie Leidorf.

Gustafsson, S. (1998). 'The farming economy in South and Central Sweden during the Bronze Age. A study based on carbonised botanical evidence', *Current Swedish Archaeology*, 6: 63–71.

Hanelt, P. (1972). 'Zur Geschichte des Anbaues von *Vicia faba* L. und ihrer verschiedenen Formen', *Die Kulturpflanze*, 20: 209–23.

Hansson, A.-M. (1994). 'Grain-paste, porridge and bread. Ancient cereal-based food', *Laborativ Arkeologi*, 7: 5–20.

—— and Heiss, A. G. (forthcoming). 'Plants used in ritual and festive contexts', in A. Chevalier, E. Marinova, and L. Peña-Chocarro (eds.), *Plants and People: Choices and Diversity through Time*, ESF EARTH Monograph, 1. Oxford: Oxbow Books.

Heiss, A. G. (2008). *Weizen, Linsen, Opferbrote—Archäobotanische Analysen bronze- und eisenzeitlicher Brandopferplätze im mittleren Alpenraum*. Saarbrücken: Südwestdeutscher Verlag für Hochschulschriften.

Hingh, A. E. de (2000). *Food Production and Food Procurement in the Bronze Age and Early Iron Age (2000–500 BC): The Organisation of a Diversified and Intensified Agrarian System in the Meuse-Demer-Scheldt Region (The Netherlands and Belgium) and the Region of the River Moselle (Luxemburg and France)*, Archaeological Studies, Leiden University, 7. Leiden: Leiden University Press.

Hopf, M. (1991). 'South and Southwest Europe', in W. van Zeist, K. Wasylikowa, and K.-E. Behre (eds.), *Progress in Old World Palaeoethnobotany: A Retrospective View on the Occasion of 20 Years of the International Work Group for Palaeoethnobotany*. Rotterdam/Brookfield: A. A. Balkema, 241–77.

Hunt, H. V., Vander Linden, M., Liu, X., Motuzaite-Matuzeviciute, G., Colledge, S., and Jones, M. K. (2008). 'Millets across Eurasia: chronology and context of early records of the genera *Panicum* and *Setaria* from archaeological sites in the Old World', *Vegetation History and Archaeobotany*, 17/Supplement 1: 5–18.

Jacomet, S. (2006). *Identification of Cereal Remains from Archaeological Sites*, 2nd edn. Basel: Universität Basel.

—— and Karg, S. (1996). 'Ackerbau und Umwelt der Seeufersiedlungen von Zug-Sumpf im Rahmen der mitteleuropäischen Spätbronzezeit', in *Die spätbronzezeitlichen Ufersiedlungen von Zug-Sumpf., Band 1. Die Dorfgeschichte*. Zug: Kantonales Museum für Urgeschichte Zug, 198–303.

Jensen, H. A. (1991). 'The Nordic countries', in W. van Zeist, K. Wasylikowa, and K.-E. Behre (eds.), *Progress in Old World Palaeoethnobotany: A Retrospective View on the Occasion of 20 Years of the International Work Group for Palaeoethnobotany*. Rotterdam/Brookfield: A. A. Balkema, 335–50.

Jones, G. E. M., and Valamoti, S. M. (2005). '*Lallemantia*, an imported or introduced oil plant in Bronze Age northern Greece', *Vegetation History and Archaeobotany*, 14: 571–7.

——, Valamoti, S. M., and Charles, M. (2000). 'Early crop diversity: a "new" glume wheat from northern Greece', *Vegetation History and Archaeobotany*, 9: 133–46.

Knörzer, K.-H. (1972). 'Subfossile Pflanzenreste aus der bandkeramischen Siedlung Langweiler 3 und 6, Kreis Jülich, und ein urnenfelderzeitlicher Getreidefund innerhalb dieser Siedlung', *Bonner Jahrbücher*, 172: 395–403.

Kočár, P., and Dreslerová, D. (2010). 'Archeobotanické nálezy pěstovaných rostlin v pravěku České republiky' ['Archaeobotanical finds of cultivated plants in the prehistory of the Czech Republic'], *Památky Archeologické*, 101: 203–42.

Kohler-Schneider, M. (2001). *Verkohlte Kultur- und Wildpflanzenreste aus Stillfried an der March als Spiegel spätbronzezeitlicher Landwirtschaft im Weinviertel, Niederösterreich*, Mitteilungen der Prähistorischen Kommission, 37. Vienna: Verlag der Österreichischen Akademie der Wissenschaften.

Körber-Grohne, U. (1987). *Nutzpflanzen in Deutschland. Kulturgeschichte und Biologie*. Stuttgart: Verlag Konrad Theiss.

Kroll, H. (1982). 'Kulturpflanzen von Tiryns', *Archäologischer Anzeiger*, 1982: 467–85.

—— (1983). *Kastanas. Ausgrabungen in einem Siedlungshügel der Bronze- und Eisenzeit Makedoniens 1975–1979. Die Pflanzenfunde*, in B. Hänsel (ed.), Prähistorische Archäologie in Südosteuropa, 2. Berlin: Verlag Volker Spiess.

—— (1987). 'Vor- und frühgeschichtlicher Ackerbau in Archsum auf Sylt', in G. Kossack, F.-R. Averdieck, H.-P. Blume, O. Harck, D. Hoffmann, H. J. Kroll, and J. Reichstein (eds.), *Archsum auf Sylt, Teil 2. Landwirtschaft und Umwelt in vor- und frühgeschichtlicher Zeit*, Römisch-Germanische Forschungen, 44. Mainz: Philipp von Zabern, 51–158.

—— (1991a). 'Südosteuropa', in W. van Zeist, K. Wasylikowa, and K.-E. Behre (eds.), *Progress in Old World Palaeoethnobotany: A Retrospective View on the Occasion of 20 Years of the International Work Group for Palaeoethnobotany*. Rotterdam/Brookfield: A. A. Balkema, 161–77.

—— (1991b). 'Bier oder Wein?', in B. Hänsel and P. Medović (eds.), *Vorbericht über die jugoslawisch-deutschen Ausgrabungen in der Siedlung von Feudvar bei Mosorin (Gem. Titel, Vojvodina) von 1986–1990: Bronzezeit—Vorrömische Eisenzeit*, Berichte der Römisch-germanischen Kommission, 72. Mainz: Philipp von Zabern, 165–71.

Kučan, D. (2007). 'Archäobotanische Untersuchung zu Umwelt und Landwirtschaft jungbronzezeitlicher Flussmarschbewohner der Siedlung Rodenkirchen-Hahnenknooper Mühle, Ldkr. Wesermarsch', *Probleme der Küstenforschung im südlichen Nordseegebiet*, 3: 17–83.

Küster, H. (1991). 'Central Europe south of the Danube', in W. van Zeist, K. Wasylikowa, and K.-E. Behre (eds.), *Progress in Old World Palaeoethnobotany. A Retrospective View on the Occasion of 20 Years of the International Work Group for Palaeoethnobotany*. Rotterdam/Brookfield: A. A. Balkema, 179–87.

Macaulay, G. C. (1890). *The History of Herodotus*, Project Gutenberg e-book, 2707. Accessed online 1 March 2011 at http://www.gutenberg.org/ebooks/2707.

Peña-Chocarro, L. (1996). '*In situ* conservation of hulled wheat species: the case of Spain', in S. Padulosi, K. Hammer, and J. Heller (eds.), *Hulled Wheat*. 'Promoting the conservation and use of underutilized and neglected crops', 4. Rome: International Plant Genetic Resources Institute.

—— and Zapata Peña, L. (1999). 'History and traditional cultivation of *Lathyrus sativus* L. and *Lathyrus cicera* L. in the Iberian Peninsula', *Vegetation History and Archaeobotany*, 8: 49–52.

Primas, M. (2009). 'Nicht nur Kupfer und Salz: Die Alpen im wirtschaftlichen und sozialen Umfeld des 2. Jahrtausends', in M. Bartelheim and H. Stäuble (eds.), *Die wirtschaftlichen Grundlagen der Bronzezeit Europas* [*The Economic Foundations of the European Bronze Age*], Forschungen zur Archäometrie und Altertumswissenschaft, 4. Rahden: Verlag Marie Leidorf, 189–211.

Procopiou, H., and Treuil, R. (eds.) (2002). *Moudre et broyer. L'interprétation fonctionnelle de l'outillage de mouture et de broyage dans la préhistoire et l'Antiquité*. Paris: Éditions CTHS.

Riehl, S. (1999). *Bronze Age Environment and Economy in the Troad: The Archaeobotany of Kumtepe and Troy*, BioArchaeologica, 2. Tübingen: Mo Vince Verlag.

Robinson, D. E. (2003). 'Neolithic and Bronze Age agriculture in southern Scandinavia—Recent Archaeobotanical Evidence from Denmark', *Environmental Archaeology*, 8: 145–65.

Rodríguez-Ariza, M. O., and Montes Moya, E. (2005), 'On the origin and domestication of *Olea europaea* L. (olive) in Andalucía, Spain, based on the biogeographical distribution of its finds', *Vegetation History and Archaeobotany*, 14: 551–61.

Rösch, M. (1996). 'Archäobotanische Untersuchungen im Bereich der spätbronzezeitlichen Ufersiedlung Hagnau-Burg (Bodenseekreis)', in G. Schöbel (ed.), *Siedlungsarchäologie im Alpenvorland IV: Die Spätbronzezeit am nordwestlichen Bodensee. Taucharchäologische Untersuchungen in Hagnau und Unteruhldingen 1982–1989*, Forschungen und Berichte zur Vor- und Frühgeschichte in Baden-Württemberg, 47. Stuttgart: Verlag Konrad Theiss, 239–312.

Rottoli, M. (1997), 'I resti botanici', in P. Frontini (ed.), *Castellaro del Vhò. Campagna di scavo 1995. Scavi delle civiche raccolte archeologiche di Milano*. Milan: Comune di Milano, 141–58.

Salavert, A. (2008). 'Olive cultivation and oil production in Palestine during the early Bronze Age (3500–2000 B.C.): the case of Tel Yarmouth, Israel', *Vegetation History and Archaeobotany*, 17/Supplement 1: 53–61.

Schnurbein, S. von (ed.) (2009). *Atlas der Vorgeschichte*. Stuttgart: Verlag Konrad Theiss.

Stika, H.-P. (1996a). *Archäobotanische Ergebnisse der Grabungskampagne 1996 in Fuente Álamo. Arbeitsbericht für das DAI Madrid* (unpublished report).

—— (1996b). 'Traces of a possible Celtic brewery in Eberdingen-Hochdorf, Kreis Ludwigsburg, southwest Germany', *Vegetation History and Archaeobotany*, 5: 81–8.

—— (2000). 'Pflanzenreste aus der Höhensiedlung der späten Urnenfelderzeit am Kulm bei Trofaiach', *Fundberichte aus Österreich*, 38/1999: 163–8.

—— (2001). 'Archäobotanische Ergebnisse der Grabungskampagne 1988 in Fuente Álamo', in H. Schubart, V. Pingel, and O. Arteaga (eds.), *Fuente Álamo Teil 1, Die Grabungen von 1977 bis 1991 in einer bronzezeitlichen Höhensiedlung Andalusiens*, Madrider Beiträge, 25. Mainz: Philipp von Zabern, 263–336.

—— (2003). *Verkohlte Pflanzenreste aus der bronzezeitlichen Höhensiedlung Gatas, Turre, Almería* (unpublished report).

—— and Berzsényi, B. (forthcoming). *Agriculture and Crop Processing in the Bronze Age Tell Site of Százhalombatta, Hungary*.

—— and Henriksen, P. S. (2010). 'Southern Scandinavia—Archaeobotanical case study', contributions in M. Vretemark, '6. Subsistence Strategies', 155–84, in K. Kristiansen and T. Earle (eds.), *The Emergence of European Communities*. Cambridge: Cambridge University Press, 159–64.

Tegtmeier, U. (1993). *Neolithische und bronzezeitliche Pflugspuren in Norddeutschland und den Niederlanden*, Archäologische Berichte, 3. Bonn: Holos.

Valamoti, S.-M., Samuel, D., Bayram, M., and Marinova, E. (2008). 'Prehistoric cereal foods from Greece and Bulgaria: investigation of starch microstructure in experimental and archaeological charred remains', *Vegetation History and Archaeobotany*, 17/Supplement 1: 265–76.

Wasylikowa, K., Cârciumaru, M., Hajnalová, E., Hartyányi, B. P., Pashkevich, G. A., and Yanushevich, Z. V. (1991). 'East-Central Europe', in W. Van Zeist, K. Wasylikowa, and K.-E. Behre (eds.), *Progress in Old World Palaeoethnobotany: A Retrospective View on the Occasion of 20 Years of the International Work Group for Palaeoethnobotany*. Rotterdam/Brookfield: A. A. Balkema, 207–39.

Zeist, W. van (1991). 'Economic aspects', in W. van Zeist, K. Wasylikowa, and K.-E. Behre (eds.), *Progress in Old World Palaeoethnobotany: A Retrospective View on the Occasion of 20 Years of the International Work Group for Palaeoethnobotany*. Rotterdam/Brookfield: A. A. Balkema, 109–30.

——, Wasylikowa, K., and Behre, K.-E (eds.) (1991). *Progress in Old World Palaeoethnobotany: A Retrospective View on the Occasion of 20 Years of the International Work Group for Palaeoethnobotany*. Rotterdam/Brookfield: A. A. Balkema.

Zohary, D., and Hopf, M. (2000). *Domestication of Plants in the Old World: The Origin of Cultivated Plants in West Asia, Europe and the Nile Valley*, 3rd edn. Oxford: Oxford University Press.

CHAPTER 20

TRADE AND EXCHANGE

ANTHONY HARDING

Much has changed in the last 30 years in our knowledge of Bronze Age trade and exchange. A series of remarkable new finds, allied to new interpretative and analytical models, has revolutionized the picture that prevailed as recently as 1980. Some of these finds will be mentioned here, but in general the aim of this contribution is to consider the broader picture of what we may call trade in Bronze Age Europe.

THE MEANING OF TRADE

In a prehistoric context the use of the word 'trade' is not very appropriate, since it implies an economic system in which markets or even money were in use. In the great cities of the Near East, it is true that the economy involved a set of measures and values encapsulated by balance weights used for measuring out commodities, probably corresponding to named units of value, such as shekels (see Chapter 29). These economies were not monetary, in the sense that they did not use coinage or other fixed exchange tokens, but they involved markets of some kind, traders as a class, and widely recognized value systems that could be understood over a considerable area.

In the Aegean we have insufficient information to be certain whether such systems were present there too, but there are some signs that Near Eastern value systems were operating in such matters as the metals trade, as the evidence of the Uluburun and Cape Gelidonya ships show. In Europe beyond Greece, however, we have no information about any such arrangements, even if there is evidence for systems of weights and measures that may have existed across large parts of the continent (see Chapter 29). It is highly unlikely that markets as such existed; on the other hand, there is plenty of room for speculation that there were merchants who specialized in the acquisition and distribution of particular commodities, transporting them long or short distances, and delivering them to those groups or individuals who wanted them. Thus it will be possible to talk about a supplier-client relationship, though not one based on money. We can assume that scales of value existed, and that those engaging in exchange knew the values involved. (For comparison, we may mention *Iliad*, Book VI, 234–6, where Glaukos exchanges gold armour worth one hundred head of cattle for bronze, worth nine; or other values in terms of oxen, for instance *Iliad* XXIII, 700–5, where a tripod for the winner of the wrestling contest is worth 12 oxen, whereas a skilled woman for the loser is valued at four. The *Iliad* admittedly relates to an Early Iron Age context in Greece and is of uncertain value for the Bronze Age, even though it is probably contemporary with the later stages of the Bronze Age in 'barbarian' Europe.)

Sources of Evidence

The main sources of evidence are those where goods (raw materials, finished or half-finished goods) are found in places removed from where they were extracted or manufactured. The most telling of these is represented by shipwrecks, since one can hardly doubt that a ship full of goods was on the move from one place to another, presumably engaged in mercantile activity. It is less easy to identify such movement over land: collections of objects (i.e. hoards) can have many explanations, which may have little or nothing to do with trade (see Chapter 7). In a few cases it seems reasonable, however, to see such collections as representing goods for exchange on the move.

Shipwrecks

The number of Bronze Age shipwrecks known has increased markedly in recent years. Most of these lie in Mediterranean waters, but a couple of notable examples come from the English Channel—though strictly speaking these are cargoes rather than shipwrecks, and may even represent deliberately dumped goods. Remarkably, in view of the importance of water in Scandinavia for contact and movement, and the abundance of ship representations on Nordic rock art, no actual ships of this date have yet been found in northern waters (see Chapter 21).

Of all the wrecks known from Bronze Age contexts, there can be no question that the most spectacular is that from Uluburun off the south Turkish coast, found in 1982 and the subject of study and speculation ever since (most recently Yalcin, Pulak, and Slotta 2005). Although its location puts it outside the area covered by this volume, the wreck nevertheless deserves mention because of its contents: as well as large numbers of copper and tin ingots, these included a wide range of personal and other objects with far-flung origins or connections. Apart from pottery of Near Eastern or Aegean manufacture, and objects of Syrian and Egyptian provenance, we may mention swords and daggers that appear to have their closest parallels in Italy, beads of amber of Baltic origin, and a stone sceptre whose closest parallels are in Bulgaria, Romania, and Moldova. Add to this the fact that ox-hide ingots of the type found on the ship, and widely distributed in the eastern and central Mediterranean, have now turned up in Bulgaria in some numbers, and it is evident that the Uluburun ship testifies to wide-reaching trading connections with Europe beyond the Aegean.

Other cargoes have been found in the Aegean, off the south coast of France, and in the mouth of the Odiel river at Huelva in Spain, but perhaps the most intriguing are those that have been found in the waters off the southern coast of England, at Dover at one end of the Channel and

Salcombe (Devon) at the other. The material from Langdon Bay near Dover, still not fully published, includes a large number of palstaves, socketed and winged axes, sword, rapier, and spearhead fragments, and other objects, at least some of continental types. The material from the waters off Salcombe has turned up in a series of finds made over a number of years, most recently in 2009 (http://www.artfund.org/artwork/11559/salcombe-hoard). It stems from more than one phase of the Late Bronze Age, and may thus either represent successive wrecks, or collections of curated material eventually included in a movement of metal for remelting. As well as bronze objects there are also some of gold; at present it is not known what the origin of the gold is, but since gold occurs in Cornwall it could be of local rather than Irish origin. Most spectacular are a number of tin ingots, which would seem to confirm the extraction and movement of tin from Devon and Cornwall, presumably across the Channel to France and beyond. A hook-tanged sword found in earlier years is of central European type.

One may speculate what this metalwork was doing in cargoes lost offshore in southern English waters. Most authorities have assumed that this was metal on the move, and since all these finds include bronzes that are very obviously continental in origin, it seems highly likely that the metal was being imported into Britain for industrial purposes. Indeed, the work of Peter Northover (1982) has shown that much Late Bronze Age metalwork in Britain came from continental, perhaps Alpine, sources.

Objects Found Outside their Place of Manufacture

Raw Materials

Copper

While sources of copper are abundant in Europe, not every area possesses them, nor were they all readily accessible to Bronze Age technology. Sources typically occur in hard-rock areas and are absent on plains with glacially derived or steppe soils like much of the north European plain or the Hungarian plain. In mountainous areas with suitable geologies, such as many parts of the Alps, there are numerous small sources that may have been exploited in ancient times but are now totally worked out, or only survive as such small deposits that modern mining is not economically viable. In Britain and Ireland, for instance, most copper is found in the west and north of Britain and in the south-west of Ireland, where indeed it was commercially exploited as late as the nineteenth century. In much of lowland Britain, particularly southern England where the Wessex culture is situated, there are no copper deposits; all metal must have been imported from elsewhere. The same is true for the rich cultures of Denmark and northern Germany, the Hungarian Plain, and many parts of Russia and Ukraine.

In terms of volume, however, some sources stand out. While Cyprus lies beyond the scope of this article, it was highly important for the whole of the East Mediterranean, probably the largest producer in that area and supplying many, if not all, of the great cities of the Near East and Aegean; analytical evidence (though disputed) suggests that Cypriot copper in the form of oxhide ingots reached the central Mediterranean, Sardinia in particular (Buchholz 1959; Lo Schiavo 1998; Lo Schiavo et al. 2009) (Fig. 20.1). There are even fragments of such an ingot in a hoard in south-west Germany (Primas and Pernicka 1998). There are other important copper sources in the countries to the north of the Mediterranean, notably in Etruria (Italy), Sardinia, and various parts of Spain, but with the exception of the latter it is quite uncertain whether they supplied any significant quantities of copper to the Bronze Age world. In continental Europe the sources of Transylvania, Slovakia, the Alps, the Harz Mountains, and southern France are likely to have been important, but we can really only specify the sources of the eastern Alps, particularly Austria, as having been dominant. It has often been suggested that the Stora Kopparberget, the large copper source at Falun in central Sweden, one of the largest producers in Europe in the early modern period, might have been exploited in prehistory and supplied the rich Bronze Age cultures of the Nordic area, but there is so far no indication of prehistoric working, and analytical evidence seems to exclude it.

The mining area of the Mitterberg in Salzburg province was probably the most important of these (see Chapter 24), but many other sources in the area were also exploited. For present purposes it is the distribution of the metal from source to consumer that is at issue. It is believed, given the number of smelting sites in the vicinity of the sources, that the ore was smelted (and roasted, if a sulphide) on the spot, and transported from the mountains in ingot form. Most ingots in Bronze Age Europe were of the 'plano-convex' form, that is, rounded on

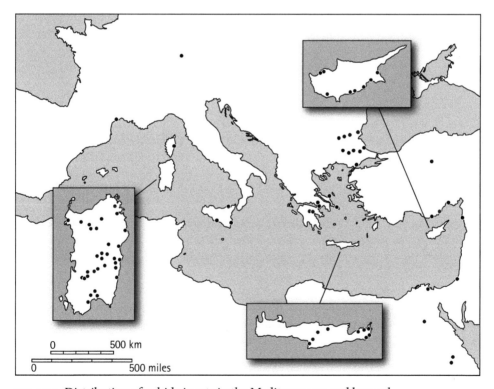

FIG. 20.1 Distribution of oxhide ingots in the Mediterranean and beyond.

Compiled by the author from various sources (drawing: Seán Goddard, University of Exeter).

the bottom and flat on the top, as the molten metal settled into a bowl-like cavity at the bottom of the furnace. In central Europe, however, and specifically north of the Alps into Bavaria, Austria, and the Czech Republic (with occasional finds further north), a characteristic pair of forms was developed: the ring and rib ingots (in shape these are bars, the first bent round into a ring shape, the second only slightly concave, both forms having an eyelet termination) (Bath-Bílková 1973; Menke 1982). While these objects must originally have been intended as neck-rings, the number and simplicity of them makes this impossible in most instances (i.e. other than in graves), and it is virtually certain that they are a means of transporting metal to the consumer, or at least to the smith operating in the consumption area.

One would expect that metal analysis would have been able to indicate from precisely which source ingots emanated, but there have been numerous problems with such analysis. Normal spectrographic analysis has produced ambiguous results, sometimes nonsensical in archaeological terms; new programmes of research are addressing these problems, though definitive results are not yet widely available (see Chapter 23). Over the last 30 years much hope has been placed in the results of lead isotope analysis of copper ores (lead appears as a trace element in many ores, its isotopic composition relating to its geological age and thus its geographical location), but though many results seem logical and conclusive, there has also been controversy about the validity of these interpretations. A programme of lead isotope analysis applied to British ores was inconclusive (Rohl and Needham 1998).

In spite of these difficulties, some success has been achieved using spectrographic methods. The work of Northover, for instance, has shown that different metal types were in use at different periods of the British Bronze Age, with a move from local sources (initially Irish, later Welsh and others in Britain) to continental sources, specifically those from the Alps (Northover's 'S' metal) (Northover 1982).

Tin

Tin was needed by metalworkers to add to copper to make bronze (Muhly 1973). Copper alloyed with between 8 and 15 per cent tin is harder and more durable than it is on its own, a fact that Bronze Age metallurgists discovered some time around 2000 BC (though copper had already been worked for over two thousand years by that point). As a consequence, bronzesmiths required access to tin, and in large quantities. Given the many tonnes of bronze artefacts which survive in the archaeological record, and bearing in mind that many more must have been destroyed (or have not yet been found), the volume of tin used was very considerable. But European sources of tin are few, and even where it does occur it may not have been accessible to Bronze Age technology—as is the case with the sources in the Erzgebirge on the German-Czech border. The main sources are those in the West (south-west England, Brittany, parts of Iberia, Etruria); there are apparently small sources in western Serbia and Romania (see Chapter 47). There is little direct evidence for prehistoric exploitation at any of these places, however; usually the evidence is circumstantial (Bronze Age sites in areas with tin sources, or artefacts found in tin-streaming locations). In a few cases it may have been possible to mine tin ore (usually cassiterite) directly, where it occurs near the surface in deposits with other minerals, but it is thought that in many cases 'placer mining' would have been necessary, with streams running down hillsides and bringing lumps of ore with them, to places where they could be collected. This technique was common in south-west England in the medieval period and probably too in the Roman and prehistoric eras as well; one can still see the signs of this alluvial working at many places in Devon and Cornwall (Penhallurick 1986).

There were tin ingots on the Uluburun ship, though the origin of the tin is not known. If the ship was sailing around the east Mediterranean, and had visited Levantine ports, then the tin may have come from eastern sources, in which case Afghanistan is a possibility, there being significant deposits in the west of that country. Tablets in the great archives of Mari on the Euphrates and other Near Eastern cities speak of an extensive trade in a material called *anāku,* which is widely believed to be tin, transported in caravans from some origin point to the east (Muhly 1973: 243).

It seems improbable that south-west England could have supplied all of Europe with tin in ancient times, not least because of the transport issues involved. The discovery of the cargo off Salcombe, containing a number of tin ingots as well as other Bronze Age objects (finished objects as well as copper ingots), indicates that such views may be more pessimistic than is warranted. The find surely dispels any doubt that the tin sources of Devon and Cornwall were exploited in the Bronze Age and exported to continental Europe.

Amber

Amber represents one of the most informative and remarkable substances to have been used in the Bronze Age. Since the sources of amber are few, and there is an analytical technique that is generally agreed to be able to distinguish between them, it has been possible to work out in some detail where the amber in archaeological finds originated. This usually means the sources called 'Baltic', and indeed the largest occurrences of amber are found on or near the shores of the Baltic, particularly in present-day Poland, Kaliningrad, and Lithuania, but also off the coast of Jutland. In addition, 'Baltic' amber occurs naturally in a number of areas in northern Germany, Poland, and as far south as Ukraine; all this comes from fossil pine trees of the same geological age as amber found on Baltic coasts, and cannot be distinguished analytically from it. While other sources may well have been used as well, notably those in Romania and Sicily, in practice it is likely that it was Baltic amber that supplied much of Europe in the Bronze Age—as in later periods. It is much the most prolific, and can be acquired on beaches or reached through simple digging.

If this is the case, and the amber found in Italy and Greece in Bronze Age contexts comes from the Baltic, the remarkable implication is that it was transported over long distances. These 'amber routes' have been the subject of discussion and speculation for nearly 90 years (De Navarro 1925) (Fig. 20.2). It is generally thought that they followed the great rivers of the north European plain, notably the Vistula, Oder, and Elbe, all of which lead into the heart of Europe. One route, the more westerly, might have left the Elbe north of Prague and followed the Vltava southwards to southern Bohemia; from there it is a short step to the Danube at Linz, allowing access both east to Austria and Hungary, and west to Germany and Switzerland. The more easterly routes would come down through Poland along the Oder and Vistula, after which a crossing of the northern Carpathian ring would be needed to access the Hungarian Plain; or an easy traverse south-eastwards to the Dniester, Siret, and Prut, from where it is a simple route to the Black Sea. All of the westerly routes would involve crossing the Alps at some point in order to get to Italy or the head of the Adriatic; once there, sea transport would be possible and perhaps preferable.

An alternative might have consisted of sea travel all the way from the Baltic, round Jutland, along the coast of the North Sea, through the English Channel, and along the coasts of France, Spain, and

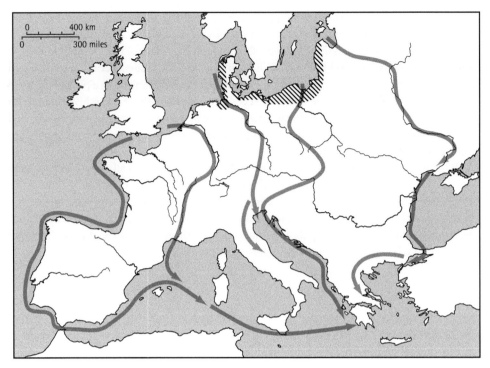

FIG. 20.2 The supposed amber routes linking the Baltic and North Sea with the Mediterranean.

Source: author, adapted from De Navarro 1925; Czebreszuk 2010.

Portugal, going through the Straits of Gibraltar and into the Mediterranean. This lengthy journey might seem beyond the technological capabilities of Bronze Age craft and indeed cannot be demonstrated with any certainty; but as we shall see, there are some apparently transported goods that link the far north-west with the south and south-east.

Amber was made into beads, usually spherical or annular, but sometimes formed into special shapes, of which the most notable is the 'spacer-plate', a flat bead typically around 4 x 3 cm, perforated with transverse borings in various patterns. These borings were intended to keep the threads of a necklace apart, the necklace having a crescentic form and consisting of multiple strings of beads. The crescentic form is repeated in Britain and Ireland in other media, notably gold (lunulae; see Chapter 25) and jet (Harding 1993); the amber crescentic necklaces in these countries seem to have been an English (mainly southern English) version of a prestige ornament widely found through the islands.

Of great interest and importance is the fact that these spacer-plates are found in a number of discrete areas of Europe: parts of southern Germany and adjacent areas, southern France, and—remarkably—parts of Greece. But the pattern of borings varies from area to area. The so-called 'basic pattern', with transverse borings and V-shaped borings at the edges, is found in Britain, in southern Germany, and in Greece—but not, so it was believed until recently, in France. Since V-perforations are a 'northern' trick, common since the Neolithic and especially in the Beaker period, the conclusion seems inescapable that the beads found in Greece were made in central or north-western Europe and transported there, by one of the routes discussed above (Harding 1984: 74).

In any case, a good number of sites in Greece in the Late Bronze Age, especially in the early Mycenaean period (c.1600–1400 BC), were found to have amber; some of the Shaft Graves of Mycenae had surprisingly large quantities of the substance (several hundred beads in some cases) (Harding and Hughes-Brock 1974). Most of what has been analysed has turned out to be Baltic and thus brought to Greece from distant northern shores. We may speculate on the nature of that movement: was it part of a larger exchange process? Who conducted it? As mentioned already, there were beads of amber on the Uluburun ship, moving around the east Mediterranean (we do not know whether these were the personal possessions of a member of the crew, or trade goods in their own right). Amber is a light substance and the beads are not bulky; it has been pointed out that all the amber known in Bronze Age Greece could have fitted into one rucksack, and while that is perhaps unlikely, we do not need to imagine many repeated journeys to account for its appearance in Greece. Nevertheless, it represents one of the few commodities whose movement over long distances can be demonstrated beyond doubt, and it raises many interesting questions about the mechanisms—social, economic, technological—by which the movement took place.

Gold

As Chapter 25 makes clear, the main sources of gold used in the European Bronze Age are those of the Balkan-Danubian area, especially Transylvania, of Iberia, and of eastern Ireland. Smaller sources are present in many other areas, however, and may have supplied local needs: thus gold in Cornwall and Wales may have supplied southern Britain in the Early Bronze Age. All this gold must have been obtained from gold-bearing streams and other placer deposits, not mining. Since considerable quantities of gold artefacts occur in Scandinavia and north Germany, where no local sources are known, the industry must have been significant and the volume of trade in raw gold considerable; the same must be true for the movement of gold from Transylvania into Hungary.

Salt

A commodity that is not often thought of when trade and exchange are discussed is salt, yet salt was a substance of immense importance to ancient people as to modern, while its sources are unevenly distributed across the continent (Nenquin 1961) (see Chapter 28). Although those living on the sea could, and did, obtain salt from the sea, by evaporating seawater in the coarse ceramic vessels known as briquetage, in inland areas people relied either on rock salt where it outcropped on the earth's surface, or on brine springs. But whereas salt is widespread in some parts of Europe, for instance in Germany, Poland, and Romania, in other areas it is absent, for instance in Hungary or large parts of the Balkans. Since humans and animals all need a certain intake of salt to maintain normal health, the corollary is that salt must have been moved from salt-rich to salt-poor areas.

The means by which salt was thus transported is not known in Bronze Age contexts (though there is relevant Iron Age evidence from both Britain and the Netherlands), but it seems unlikely that it was in durable containers. From ethnography we know that salt is moved in cakes or sheets, wrapped in textile or basketry, and in Africa is transported in camel caravans from the Sahara down the Niger to the coast. There is no reason why something similar could not have occurred in the Bronze Age.

A case has been made for a number of different production types, depending on the consumer for whom the product was made. This production by briquetage was arguably small in scale and intended for domestic consumption, whereas the great wooden installations and troughs of Romania were producing salt on what we might term an industrial scale. The volume thus produced would have been far in excess of local needs, and must have been destined for export. That from Transylvania probably went to salt-less Hungary; that from Moldavia arguably went to what is now Ukraine. By this means, salt was an integral part of the exchange economy of Bronze Age Europe.

Finished Goods

Raw materials were not the only commodities that were moved about in the Bronze Age: finished objects moved too. Since such objects had a place of manufacture, in other words a cultural and technological context, it is of interest and importance to establish the point of origin, and to consider how and why they ended up where they did.

In this connection, it is evident that different types of exchange were in operation, involving different types of object. There is a clear difference between the movement of personal items, such as ornaments or clothing attachments, weapons (swords, daggers), and tools (axes, sickles). The first group has been studied by scholars such as Albrecht Jockenhövel (see Chapter 40), in the context of the movement of women in marriage, as shown by specific ornament forms appearing outside their 'home' area (Jockenhövel 1991). There are many such instances; perusal of the distribution maps of volumes of the *Prähistorische Bronzefunde* series shows that even on a cursory inspection many such items moved, very possibly with their owner or wearer.

Weapons too may have moved with the person who used them. The finding of Mycenaean swords in Albania, Macedonia, and Bulgaria, for instance, is plausibly to be connected with the movement of individual warriors northwards beyond the 'Mycenaean frontier'—or to the movement of a prestige weapon passed down an exchange line to join the panoply of a warrior beyond the Mycenaean world. Other individual sword types spread far and wide: an Alpine sword turns up in a hoard from the Sava Valley, for instance, or another from a hoard in Slovakia (Rimavská Sobota). Special swords of continental type have turned up in Britain, as with antenna swords from Lincolnshire contexts. In the Early Bronze Age, the finding of west European daggers in graves at Singen near Lake Constance is also notable (Krause 1988: 56ff.).

Tools occasionally moved as well, as for instance with a sickle of Transylvanian type turning up in a Slovakian hoard (Blatnica). Continental axes have been found in Britain, for instance on Horridge Common on Dartmoor, as well as on the cargoes from Langdon Bay and Salcombe; in the opposite direction, Irish flat axes travelled to the continent in the Early Bronze Age. Axes are tools, but they evidently had a significance beyond their mere function; many cultures of the Old World seem to have regarded them as bearing a symbolic load—which is probably why they appear on carvings or depictions in a variety of contexts, and why they were carried into battle even when they were not effective weapons.

Pottery was probably moved less frequently than bronzework, it being fragile and easily made in local contexts. There are notable exceptions to this. The most obvious is perhaps the movement of Mycenaean pottery to the central Mediterranean, from the early Mycenaean period onwards; it concentrates in southern Italy and Sicily, but occurs also in the north and in Sardinia. Isolated instances further afield, for instance in Spain, probably reflect local circulation systems rather than any direct trade with the East Mediterranean. In Italy, however, the import of Aegean pottery is directly related to the commercial systems operating in the East Mediterranean, as evidenced by the Uluburun ship and the abundant textual evidence. We cannot be sure that Italy was a form of Magna Graecia in the Bronze Age, in other words a land of extensive Greek settlement; whether it was or not, it is clear that ships from the Aegean reached the central Mediterranean on a regular basis. The pottery was partly moved for its contents, particularly where closed forms are involved (e.g. 'stirrup-jars', probably containing oil or perfumes), and partly for its intrinsic value as prestige tableware, such as elites would have dined from. Sardinian and Maltese pottery is found on Sicily, albeit in small quantities. Individual pots outside their presumed production area occur sporadically in contexts in continental Europe as well, usually in graves.

Prestige goods are another matter. From the Early Bronze Age, special bronzes travelled over long distances: the weaponry of Scandinavia in Period I is intensely influenced by that from the Carpathian Basin, and some objects (e.g. swords) seem to be actual imports. This movement of special goods to Scandinavia continued into later periods, as the cult 'sun drum' from Balkåkra in Sweden indicates—its closest parallels are in Hungary, which is where it was manufactured (Knape and Nordström 1994). It seems to be a Bronze Age forerunner of the famous Gundestrup cauldron, which was manufactured in an east Balkan workshop and exported to the North in the Iron Age.

A scatter of goods apparently of Aegean manufacture is found across Europe, mainly in the Middle and Late Bronze Age. These have often been discussed, usually without any conclusive results, because the objects are in all cases isolated finds without proper context, or not clearly imports. In the latter case, for instance, a group of rapiers in Romania and Bulgaria are often called 'Mycenaean', though they are clearly not of Greek manufacture, but at most local imitations. Other objects are more convincing, however, if hardly understandable: a number of spearheads or daggers of Cypriot type occur in central Europe, France, and Britain; double-axes of Mycenaean type occur sporadically; and isolated objects of clear Aegean manufacture, such as the bronze cup from Dohnsen, district Celle, northern Germany (Sprockhoff 1961), have been found. These objects, if genuine imports in antiquity, must represent some kind of exchange across long distances, reflecting the inherent symbolic value of the objects involved, and imparting prestige to the owner. The same is no doubt true of the amber objects discussed above. It seems wise, however, to remain sceptical about the genuineness of the amber beads from Bernstorf, Bavaria, inscribed with what appear to be Linear B signs, given the uncertain find circumstances and the lack of any such objects in the Aegean (Gebhart and Rieder 2002).

Conclusion: Connectivity in the Bronze Age

What does this evidence for contact and exchange signify? Granted that there was extensive connectivity in the Bronze Age European world, can we envisage regular and long-distance movement of traders across the continent, bearing goods of various kinds? Or do we rather imagine that individual travellers moved, bringing with them tales of far-off places, and carrying objects to impress hosts, as has been suggested a number of times in the literature?

In considering these points, we inevitably come across questions of wider significance, for instance the existence of a 'world system' that applied to the Bronze Age, in which distant places were linked by a network of exchange that had specific implications for the economy of producer and receiver. These questions are discussed in the Introduction to this volume and are mentioned here only in order to set the question of trade and exchange in context.

As Chapter 10 has shown, in the Bronze Age people moved about as well as the goods and materials that I have discussed so far. Isotope evidence has shown that (for instance) the richly equipped Beaker man known as the Amesbury Archer, found near Stonehenge, grew up in an environment with a quite different geology, probably in central Europe; and that a teenage boy in the same area, found in 2010, was born and brought up in a Mediterranean environment, while a significant number of the Bell Beaker people studied in southern Germany came from a different area (see Chapter 10). These important new results have shed entirely new light on the question of Bronze Age mobility (some would say they have confirmed long-standing views), and raised anew the whole question of connectivity between different parts of the Bronze Age world.

In technological terms there is nothing strange or implausible in this. Chapters 21 and 22 discuss transport on water and land respectively; from this it is quite clear that the technology for the movement of both people and goods was not merely in existence but in regular use. Thus while we have no examples of Scandinavian Bronze Age boats, the number of depictions of them—as well as simple logic—makes it obvious that boat transport was commonplace. Over land, even without wheeled transport human and animal feet could and surely did cover large distances. Most of the objects discussed here are not bulky or heavy; the exception is metal in ingot form, which would have been extremely cumbersome to transport without the aid of vehicles and pack animals.

One can approach the question of linkage and connectivity in the Bronze Age world in a number of different ways, with models based on the core-periphery approach competing with those seeing Europe as a series of independent entities. What is clear is that few parts of the continent were immune from the all-pervading nature of the connectedness of the period. One can debate the origins of this or that object, and especially its significance, but one cannot doubt that goods and materials were extensively exchanged, sometimes over long distances, throughout the European Bronze Age.

Bibliography

Bath-Bílková, B. (1973). 'K problému původu hřiven'. *Památky Archeologické*, 64: 24–41.
Buchholz, H.-G. (1959). 'Keftiubarren und Erzhandel im zweiten vorchristlichen Jahrtausend', *Prähistorische Zeitschrift*, 37: 1–40.
Czebreszuk, J. (2011). *Bursztyn w kulturze mykeńskiej. Zarys problematyki badawczej*. Poznań: Wydawnictwo Poznańskie.
De Navarro, J. M. (1925). 'Prehistoric routes between northern Europe and Italy defined by the amber trade', *Geographical Journal*, 66: 481–504.
Gebhart, R. and Rieder, K. H. 2002. 'Zwei bronzezeitliche Bernsteinobkjekte mit Bild- und Schriftzeichen aus Bernstorf (Ldkr. Freising)', *Germania*, 80: 115–33.
Harding, A. (1984). *The Mycenaeans and Europe*. London: Academic Press.

—— (1993). 'British amber spacer-plate necklaces and their relatives in gold and stone', in C. W. Beck, J. Bouzek, and D. Dreslerová (eds.), *Amber in Archaeology*. Prague: Institute of Archaeology, 53–8.

—— and Hughes-Brock, H. (1974). 'Amber in the Mycenaean world', *Annual of the British School of Archaeology at Athens*, 69: 145–72.

Jockenhövel, A. (1991). 'Räumliche Mobilität von Personen in der mittleren Bronzezeit des westlichen Mitteleuropa', *Germania*, 69: 49–62.

Knape, A. and Nordström, H.-Å. (1994). *Der Kultgegenstand von Balkåkra*, Museum of National Antiquities, Stockholm, Monographs 3. Stockholm: Statens Historiska Museum.

Krause, R. (1988). *Die endneolithischen und frühbronzezeitlichen Grabfunde auf der Nordstadtterrasse von Singen am Hohentwiel*, Forschungen und Berichte zur Vor- und Frühgeschichte in Baden-Württemberg, 32. Stuttgart: Konrad Theiss Verlag.

Lo Schiavo, F. (1998). 'Sardinian oxhide ingots 1998', *Der Anschnitt*, Beiheft 8: 99–112.

——, Muhly, J. D., Maddin, R., and Giumlia-Mair, A. (eds.) (2009). *Oxhide Ingots in the Central Mediterranean*, Biblioteca di Antichità Cipriote, 8. Rome: A. G. Leventis Foundation; CNR— Istituto di Studi sulle Civiltà dell'Egeo e del Vicino Oriente.

Menke, M. (1982). 'Studien zu den frühbronzezeitlichen Metalldepots Bayerns', *Jahresbericht der Bayerischen Bodendenkmalpflege*, 19–20: 5–305.

Muhly, J. D. (1973). 'Copper and tin. The distribution of mineral resources and the nature of the metals trade in the Bronze Age', *Transactions Connecticut Academy of Arts and Sciences*, 43: 155–535 (with Supplement, vol. 46, 1976: 77–136).

Nenquin, J. (1961). *Salt: A Study in Economic Prehistory*, Dissertationes Archaeologicae Gandenses, 6. Brugge: De Tempel.

Northover, J. P. (1982). 'The exploration of the long-distance movement of bronze in Bronze and Early Iron Age Europe', *Bulletin Institute Archaeology London*, 19: 45–72.

Penhallurick, R. D. (1986). *Tin in Antiquity*. London: Institute of Metals.

Primas, M. and Pernicka, E. (1998). 'Der Depotfund von Oberwilflingen. Neue Ergebnisse zur Zirkulation von Metallbarren', *Germania*, 76/1: 25–65.

Rohl, B. and Needham, S. (1998). *The Circulation of Metal in the British Bronze Age: The Application of Lead Isotope Analysis*, British Museum Occasional Paper, 102. London: British Museum.

Sprockhoff, E. (1961). 'Eine mykenische Bronzetasse von Dohnsen, Kr. Celle', *Germania*, 39: 11–22.

Yalcin, Ü., Pulak, C., and Slotta, R. (eds.) (2005). *Das Schiff von Uluburun—Welthandel vor 3000 Jahren. Katalog zur Ausstellung*. Bochum: Deutsches Bergbaumuseum.

CHAPTER 21

SEAFARING AND RIVERINE NAVIGATION IN THE BRONZE AGE OF EUROPE

ROBERT VAN DE NOORT

INTRODUCTION

A key feature of the European Bronze Age is the connectedness of the whole continent, expressed archaeologically in the distribution of such objects as bronze tools and weapons, certain pottery types, and jewellery of gold, amber, faience, and other materials, traded and exchanged over long distances. The origin of this connectedness lies in the later Neolithic. It involved, at least to begin with, principally the upper echelons of society. As yet, there is no evidence that this connectedness included migrations or other forms of large-scale movement of people—overland or across seas—but it is beyond doubt that individuals engaged in long-distance travel, with the Amesbury Archer presenting an excellent example of this phenomenon (Fitzpatrick 2002). Because of the limited natural availability of the ores that were required for the fabrication of metal tools and weapons, it seems probable that the demand for gold, copper, tin, and bronze provided a major stimulus for the development of trade and exchange networks in the Copper and Bronze Ages of Europe (Pare 2000).

Other chapters in this handbook provide details on the archaeological evidence for trade and exchange in the Bronze Age, but the role of seafaring and riverine navigation is often a matter of inference. For example, the geographical distribution of the various Beaker types in coastal regions and alongside major rivers—the Maritime Bell Beaker offering the most evocative example—suggests ships and boats played a significant role in establishing and maintaining contacts between regions with abundant Beaker burials (Harrison 1980; Vander Linden 2004). However, clear evidence that seafaring played a role in maintaining these networks exists only in the case of the links between the British Isles and Ireland and continental Europe (e.g. Van de Noort 2006).

This chapter provides an outline of the state of knowledge of seafaring and riverine navigation for the Bronze Age of Europe. Direct evidence is provided by a relatively small number of wrecks, a much larger body of iconographic representations of boats and ships—including miniature models, graffiti on pottery and bronze swords and razors, rock carvings—and stone settings resembling the outline of boats surrounding interments. The aim is to give an overview of these available sources, and to consider aspects of boat and ship construction, seafaring, and riverine navigation in three geographical regions: the Mediterranean, Atlantic Europe, and the rivers of Europe. In the conclusion, current debates and future developments in maritime archaeology will be considered.

Mediterranean Europe

Evidence for communication, trade, and exchange in the Mediterranean—in the form of the distribution of materials or artefacts with known origins—leaves no doubt that long before the beginning of the Bronze Age, the Mediterranean was traversed by seafarers. The earliest evidence for seafaring activity in the Mediterranean is, famously, claimed for the case of obsidian from the island of Melos in the Franchthi Cave on mainland Greece in a context dated to c.9000 BC (Cherry 1990). The colonization of Cyprus is dated to the middle of the eighth millennium BC, and of Crete to the fifth millennium BC. Malta was settled by humans around 5000 BC (Trump 2002), and the temples on this island were constructed during the period from c.3600 to 2050 BC (Rainbird 2007: 71).

For the Bronze Age, there is ample evidence for trade and exchange. This is especially the case for the eastern part of the Mediterranean where the focus for many of these activities was Egypt, and later Crete, the Cyclades, the Greek mainland, and the Levant (e.g. Sherratt and Sherratt 1991; Meijer and Van Nijf 1992; Cline 1999; Davies and Schofield 1995). During the third millennium BC, there is both archaeological and documentary material relating to Egyptian contacts with the coasts of the eastern Mediterranean; these were clearly not always of a peaceful nature. Inter-island trade and travel is also shown in the distribution of pottery, copper, bronze, and gold and silver ornaments and jewellery. For example, Cretan goods have been found on the Aegean coast of Turkey whilst Cycladic pottery has been found as far away as Sicily (Bass 1997: 269). In the first half of the second millennium BC the Minoans appear to have become the principal maritime power, and the Athenian historian Thucydides famously notes that King Minos of Crete had a navy (Haggis 1999; Niemeier 2004). The effectiveness of the maritime defence of Crete from piracy and raiding is thought to explain the unfortified nature of Middle Minoan cities and palaces. From about 1600 BC the power in the eastern Mediterranean shifted to the Mycenaeans, and Mycenaean goods have been found throughout the Aegean, including the Aegean coast of Turkey, and in the west in Italy and Sardinia (Bass 1972: 22).

Against this wealth of evidence for seafaring activity based on the products of trade and exchange stands a modest collection of shipwreck evidence. In fact, only two shipwrecks dated to the Bronze Age have been discovered to date in the Mediterranean: the Uluburun wreck near Kaş, and the Cape Gelidonya wreck near Finike, both on the south coast of modern Turkey. A third shipwreck site dated to around 1200 BC, at Point Iria in the Gulf of Argos is known for its cargo of pottery only (Phelps, Lolos, and Vichos 1999).

The Uluburun shipwreck, excavated between 1983 and 1994, has been dated to 1320–1295 BC based on a combination of dendrochronological evidence and artefacts linked to Egyptian chronologies (Bass et al. 1989). The ship itself was very poorly preserved, with only fragments surviving. Nevertheless, this ship is believed to have been *about* 16 m long and made largely from cedar planks. The Uluburun wreck represents the earliest example of the use of small oak mortises and tenons, fixed to each plank by a small treenail, as the principal manner in which the hull of the craft is constructed (Fig. 21.1a). The Egyptian technique of hull construction already used mortise-and-tenon joints, but these were not locked by means of treenails, as in the Uluburun wreck (McGrail 2001: 125). The Uluburun ship was a 'shell-first' plank construction. The cargo, or at least the non-organic part of the cargo, survived better

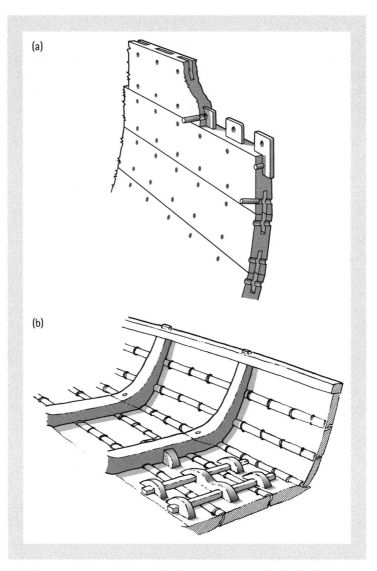

FIG. 21.1 (a) Schematic representation of hull construction using locked mortise-and-tenon joinery of the Uluburun and Cape Gelidonya shipwrecks; (b) Schematic representation of the construction of a sewn-plan boat.

Drawings: Mike Rouillard, University of Exeter.

than the ship itself, and provides a picture of the dynamic character of trade in the Late Bronze Age Mediterranean: it contained artefacts from 11 different (modern) countries around the Mediterranean, including 10 tonnes of copper 'ox-hide' ingots and 1 tonne of tin ingots, 145 Canaanite amphorae containing terebinth resin, probably used as incense, and 135 Cypriot pottery vessels, as well as raw glass, ivory of elephant and hippopotamus, African blackwood or 'ebony', cedarwood, and ostrich eggshells (Bass, Frey, and Pulak 1984). This craft is believed to be of Canaanite or Cypriot origin.

The Cape Gelidonya shipwreck was excavated in 1960. The wreck was dated by a combination of radiocarbon and artefact analysis to c.1200 BC. Little of the ship itself survived, but the excavator George Bass noted (1967) that its construction utilized the locked mortise-and-tenon joinery present in the Uluburun ship, and was an estimated 9 m in length. A significant amount of brushwood dunnage lined the hull, and this has been linked to the final chore of the mythical hero Odysseus in building his boat, as recounted in Homer's *Odyssey*. The cargo of the ship when it sank included 34 copper and bronze ingots, about 20 kg in weight each, a large number of different metalworking tools, and hundreds of other tools and weapons including picks, hoes, double-axes, chisels, awls, and spearheads. This ship, too, is believed to have had its port of origin in Cyprus or Syria.

No other wrecks of Bronze Age date are known from the Mediterranean. Evidence for the types of craft used in seafaring in the Mediterranean before the later second millennium BC comes from incised 'graffiti' on so-called Cycladic 'frying pans', as models in lead or clay, on a fresco, and painted on vases.

Graffiti or incised depictions of boats on 'frying pans'—circular objects with projecting handles made of terracotta, stone, or bronze—from the Cycladic islands, central Greek mainland, and southern Anatolia, have been dated to the third millennium BC (Broodbank 1989). The images of craft on some of these objects are remarkably similar, and comprise two parallel lines representing the 'gunwale' and keel line. These are closed off at one end with a line at right angles with a horizontal protrusion, and at the other with a large upward extension of the two parallel lines, topped by a fish ensign and a 'tassel'. Sometimes the area between the two parallel lines, presumed to be the hull of the ship, is infilled with lines or zigzag decoration. Simple lines are shown both above the gunwale and below the keel, and are taken to represent oars or paddles on either side of the boat. In many cases the number of oars or paddles exceeds 20 pairs, which seems large for the Early Bronze Age. Cyprian Broodbank (1989, 1993) has argued that these images depict long boats with large crews, which were symbols of prestige and power rather than being employed for trade, utilizing on special occasions the manpower resources from whole islands. Seán McGrail (2001: 111) believes that the images represent planked boats.

Further evidence for the types of boats used in the third millennium BC is available in the form of four lead models of boats from Naxos (Renfrew 1967; Basch 1987; Broodbank 1989), and Early Minoan clay models from Palaikastro and Mochlos on Crete (Basch 1987; Wachsmann 1998). The lead models are made from three strips of metal, with the middle one upturned at the bow, and with a fitted transom at the stern. McGrail (2001: 106) calculated that the Naxos models represent a long boat of 12.5 m length and 1 m wide, with room for a crew of up to 18 for warfare and piracy. Alternatively, when such craft were used for trade or the early colonization of islands in the Mediterranean, they could have carried a crew of eight alongside a significant cargo, including some animals. The Palaikastro clay model includes two cross-beams or thwarts and has a 'forefoot' protruding from the hull. The clay model from Mochlos has 'forefoots' at both ends, and bow and stern are turned up. This model includes clay protrusions that have been interpreted as tholepins for attaching oars.

Iconographic evidence for seafaring and boat construction dated to the first half of the second millennium BC is available from engraved gemstones or seals from Crete (Casson 1971; Wachsmann 1998; Schoep 2004), and from the frescoes of the West House in Akrotiri on Thera (e.g. Marinatos 1984; Morgan 1988; McGrail 2001: 113–22). The ships engraved on gems are, inevitably, very small and lacking in detail. In outline, these ships appear very similar to those of the third millennium BC, with one end extended upwards and the other end much lower, but importantly these ships include masts, square sails, and rigging, whilst oars were still being used. The frescoes from Akrotiri include maritime themes, which as yet provide the greatest detail on the operation of ships in the Mediterranean. Dated to $c.1650$ BC, the West House is believed to have been destroyed by earthquakes and then covered by pumice and ash by the Thera volcanic eruption. The house was excavated in 1972 (Marinatos 1974), and the maritime scenes on the south and north friezes have received much attention ever since. The south frieze has been interpreted as the portrayal of a procession of 11 ships in a ritual ceremony. The larger craft have extended bows; nearly all carry a small structure on deck near the stern of the boat, presumably to provide 'officials' with cover from the sun, whilst larger tent-like structures are positioned in the middle of the ships. Two ships are propelled by oars, another by a square-rigged sail. All have a steersman towards the stern, using steering oars, and one ship has two steersmen. The ships have rounded bottoms, with a triangular-shaped object projecting from the stern, possibly a stabilizer of some sort. The north frieze was not as well preserved, and alongside the depiction of nine additional ships, the presence of people diving or drowning has received the most attention.

For the second half of the second millennium BC ships painted on vases of Geometric type add to our knowledge of seafaring. These painted ships have a near-vertical bow and a high curving stern. They have platforms or raised decks fore and aft, respectively for a lookout and for the helmsman who is seen using a rudder with tiller. A slight protrusion of the keel could be interpreted as a proto-ram. These ships all have square-rigged sails. Continuing an ancient practice, some of the painted ships have a fish ensign on the bow. This could indicate that the ships of the third millennium BC, as represented by the depictions of boats on the 'frying pans', had upward extended bows and lower sterns. Finally, several models of boats are known for this period, including a terracotta model from Phylakopi, which has *oculi* near the bow and painted stripes across the inside that could represent framing (Wachsmann 1998: 149). Two models from Tanagra have painted decoration, and one from Argos has a mast step.

When these various sources of evidence are brought together, the development of seafaring ships for the Mediterranean in the Bronze Age can be reconstructed. The craft of the third millennium BC were presumably plank boats that were paddled or rowed. One end was considerable higher than the other. Whether the long boats accommodated crews of 20 or more, or whether this is an exaggeration, remains a matter of some debate. Larger and wider craft with rounded bottoms, and fitted with square-rigged sails, were introduced early in the second millennium BC. The rudder with tiller was introduced in the second half of the second millennium BC, replacing the steering oar. The plank boats of the later second millennium BC were connected using mortise-and-tenon constructions, which were fixed by treenails. The origin of this method of building 'shell-first' ships lay with Egyptian boat-building practices.

Atlantic Europe

Atlantic Europe, which includes here the connected waters of the North Sea and the Baltic alongside the Atlantic coasts of Norway, Ireland, Britain, France, Spain, and Portugal, offers greater riches of archaeological evidence for the type of craft that could have been used for seafaring in the Bronze Age. These include a number of Bronze Age wrecks from Britain, rock carvings from Sweden and Norway, graffiti or etchings of ships on bronze swords and razors from Denmark, and a number of burials with stone settings in the shape of boats in the Baltic region.

In the broadest of outlines, two distinctive phases of intensity of seafaring can be distinguished during the Bronze Age in Atlantic Europe. The first phase, coinciding with the second half of the third millennium and the first half of the second millennium BC, was characterized by the long-distance trade or exchange of copper and bronze artefacts, alongside a range of objects understood as having esoteric value, or giving prestige to their owner or wearer—especially distinctive pottery types, gold, amber, faience, jet, and shale (e.g. Rowlands 1980; Clarke, Cowie, and Foxon 1985). The distribution of these 'prestige goods' has been widely accepted as representing exchange between elite groups. This exchange had its origin in the late Neolithic and connected elite groups in Atlantic Europe with those in central Europe and the Mediterranean (e.g. Harding 1984; 1993).

In the second phase, beginning around 1500 cal BC, trade and exchange appear to have gained in intensity, at the same time losing much of their long-distance character. Exchanges involved bronze in great quantities, sometimes as scrap metal (e.g. Needham and Dean 1987). The archaeological evidence implies a diminished role for prestige goods in this phase. It has been argued that increased availability of bronze and bronze-casting skills was largely responsible for the differences observed between the two phases (e.g. Pare 2000).

The Bronze Age sewn-plank boats from England and Wales are the oldest archaeologically known plank boats from Atlantic Europe, with the earliest example, Ferriby-3 from the Humber estuary in England, dated to 2030–1780 cal BC (Wright *et al.* 2001). The planks of this boat had been hewn or carved from oak trees, given bevelled edges for a close fit, and, in the absence of nails and treenails, were stitched or sewn together using yew withies. An integral system of cleats, through which transverse timbers were positioned, together with thwarts, provided integrity to the hull (Fig. 21.1b). Stitching or sewing of planks in boat construction is not unique to these Bronze Age boats, but they form a distinct class in spatial and temporal terms (Crumlin-Pedersen 2009). It seems probable that the concept of sewing or stitching planks together, and the use of an internal frame to give stiffness to the hull, may have been inspired by the sewing or stitching of hides or skins in a type of craft for which there is no archaeological evidence, but where ethnographic research offers many parallels (McGrail 2001). If this is indeed the case, then the reason for switching from hides to planks may have been to build bigger boats, and this may reflect the increased importance and sophistication of early seafaring activities. In seafaring the size of the boat relative to the size of the waves is an important factor in the boat's ability to 'ride the waves', especially when fitted with a rounded bilge. Furthermore, larger boats are less easily foundered—that is when the waves overtop the gunwale, filling the hull with water—than smaller boats. Thus, the innovation represented by the sewn-plank boats could be explained as a reflection of the increased importance of seafaring and the development and maintenance of the elite networks established in the late Neolithic (Van de Noort 2006).

To date, the remains of ten such sewn-plank boats have been discovered. All craft are from coastal or estuarine locations in England and Wales and date between c.2000 cal BC and 800 cal BC (see Wright et al. 2001 for an overview of the latest dates; Van de Noort 2006; Van de Noort 2009 for an overview of their composition and contexts). Whilst these craft share a number of technological aspects—such as the bevelled edges of the oak planking, the stitching or sewing, and the use of integral cleats for the internal frame—each boat also has certain unique design characteristics. For example, whereas Ferriby-2 has its two keel planks joined amidships, the Dover boat's seam was formed by two planks joined by an upstanding longitudinal cleat rail (Marsden 2004). However, one aspect of boat design variability appears more significant. McGrail (2001: 190; 2004) has argued for the existence of two subgroups: an older group from c.2000 cal BC to 1500 cal BC, characterized by the use of individual stitches or lashings through relatively big holes to fasten the planks together, and a younger group dated after c.1500 cal BC, in which planks were joined together by continuous stitching through small holes set close together. Several finds of paddles on the North Ferriby foreshore, and the absence of any structural elements such as mast steps or keels that could indicate the use of sails, imply that these sewn-plank boats were paddled craft, requiring crews of up to 20 to provide the propulsion necessary for a journey across the North Sea, the Irish Sea, or the English Channel (Van de Noort 2006).

Three Bronze Age shipwreck sites in British waters are known from their cargo. The Langdon Bay wreck site, east of Dover harbour, contained over four hundred bronze tools and weapons, many of French types, dated to the thirteenth century BC. It is widely understood that this was 'scrap' material, to be recycled somewhere in England (Muckelroy 1981; Northover 1982; Needham and Dean 1987). At Moor Sands near Salcombe, in Devon, the cargos of at least two ships have been found by divers of the South West Maritime Archaeological Group. The most recent finds remain, as yet, unpublished, but the older of the two wrecks dates to around 1200 BC, the younger to c.900 BC. Alongside tools and weapons, a large number of tin ingots (presumably from the Cornish sources) have been recovered from this site.

There are no other shipwrecks of Bronze Age date in Atlantic Europe, but the rock carvings in Norway's Østfold and Sweden's Bohuslän and Uppland regions have inspired a number of archaeologists to consider the significance of seafaring in Bronze Age Scandinavia. Over ten thousand rock carvings of boats are known from these regions (Coles 2000; 2005: 18), dated to the Bronze Age and early Iron Age, c.1500–300 cal BC. Whilst these boats on the rocks sometimes appear in isolation, the overwhelming majority are found incorporated into composite displays that also include cup-marks, people, discs, animals, animal-drawn vehicles, and feet or footprints (footsoles). The context of these panels, when reconstructing the Bronze Age coastline at 13–15 m above present-day sea levels, reveals that their contemporary setting was one overlooking marine inlets. John Coles (2005, 100–19; see Chapter 15) has argued that this is no coincidence and it may even be the case that some of these panels were meant to be viewed from the water. Richard Bradley (2000) has suggested that the boats symbolized marine inlets, and were carved onto the rocks to maintain the impression of water and preserve the ritual isolation of the burial grounds that had originally been located on islands.

In nearly all cases the boats on the rocks consist of two parallel lines, the upper representing the gunwale and the lower the keel line. The two lines are closed off or joined at the stem and stern, and at their terminals the keel line is turned upwards, with an upward bow clearly distinguishable from an enlarged stabilizer at the stern. The gunwale terminals are frequently turned into S and reversed S-shapes. The debate on what type of craft is depicted on the rocks of Østfold, Bohuslän, and Uppland is ongoing. The earlier inclination for interpreting the carvings as depictions of hide-covered boats (e.g. Marstrander 1963; Glob 1969; Johnstone 1972; Malmer 1981; see Coles 1993: 27) has given way, in more recent years, towards an understanding that these pictures are of plank boats (Kaul 2002; 2004; Kaul and Valbjørn 2003; Crumlin-Pedersen and Trakadas 2003). However, alternatives are being pursued, for example by Sven Österholm (2002), who has argued that the carvings represent logboats with (multiple) outriggers; the seaworthiness of such craft has been tested through experimental trials. Flemming Kaul (1998) has developed a framework for the dating of these boats. Using the iconography of ships etched on bronze razors, axes, and swords as a proxy, he allocates the majority of these ships to six chronological phases from 1700 to 500 BC. In this typology the plainer versions with stems turned inwards are dated to the early part of the Scandinavian Bronze Age, and the more elaborate variants with stem adornments or outward-turned stems to later parts. None of these pictures of ships includes sails, but there are plenty of images that depict crews with paddles.

In his analysis of the rock carvings from Østfold, Bohuslän, and Uppland, and the boats on bronzes from Denmark and southern Sweden, Kaul (1998) has considered the cosmological message that was conveyed through these (see Chapter 14). He concludes that these ships are shown in various stages of the cyclical movement of the sun, usually represented as a wheel-cross. Animals are involved in this daily journey, for example the horse that pulls the sun or sun-chariot in the day time, or the fish and snake that accompany the journey during the sunrise and sunset respectively. Furthermore, the ship was a platform for ceremonies and rituals, shown by human figures playing lures, carrying ceremonial axes, and performing acrobatics, sometimes leaping backwards over the ships.

There are no known Bronze Age rock carvings on the Atlantic coast of Britain, Ireland, or France, but a single example of a rock carving depicting a ship has been found at Auga dos Cebros, near Santa Maria de Osia in Spanish Galicia (Costas Goberna et al. 1999). The carving depicts a craft comprising two parallel lines representing the gunwale and keel, which are connected by a series of vertical lines. The stem appears to be shaped as an indeterminate animal head, whilst the stern is shown as a looped line or ring. The carving clearly shows a mast and elementary rigging, and additional lines appear to represent the crew or cargo. The ship represented in this carving belongs to the Mediterranean tradition of shipbuilding.

The final evidence for Bronze Age seafaring in Atlantic Europe is provided by the so-called Baltic 'stone ships'. These funerary monuments, comprising alignments of stones forming boat outlines, are dated to the period 1300–700 cal BC. Early Bronze Age examples include Dömmestorp and Serlingsholm on the coast of Halland, and Oeversee and Thumby on the Baltic coast of Schleswig-Holstein (Aner and Kersten 1978; Lundborg 1974, Strömberg 1961; see Capelle 1995). Late Bronze Age stone ships come mainly from Gotland (13 sites), Halland (3), Latvia (2), Scania (2), and Småland (1). The stone ships are made of natural erratic blocks, or limestone on Gotland, with the smooth side typically facing inwards. The stem and stern were accentuated with the highest stones. Torsten Capelle (1995: 74) has pointed out that none of the Bronze Age stone ships has any indication of a mast step, and the craft that were represented in the stone ships were probably paddled, although the higher stones that can be found amidships in some Bronze Age examples have been interpreted as representing the tholepins of rowed boats. The stone ships vary in length from 2 to 16 m, but two stone ships at Gnisvärd in Gotland were 33 and 45 m long, and are considered to be 'oversized' for

Bronze Age ships (Capelle 1995: 71). Where rock carvings occur in these stone settings, they are found on the stone representing the stem or stern, or in a few cases on the midship stones.

Taking an overview of the archaeological evidence for seafaring craft in the Bronze Age of Atlantic Europe, we can be sufficiently confident that these craft were plank boats. The boats were paddled; there is no evidence for the use of sails or oars. In the absence of nails and treenails for most of the Atlantic Bronze Age—the first occurrence of them in Atlantic Europe is in the logboat from Appleby, Lincolnshire, dated to *c.*1100 cal BC (McGrail 1978: 147–9)—sewing or stitching of the planks appears to have been the basic technique of boat construction. The significance of Bronze Age seafaring in Atlantic Europe clearly went beyond its function as a vehicle for trade and exchange, as illustrated by the use of stone ships in funerary behaviour and by the depiction of ships on rocks and bronzes. In this context we are reminded of Kaul's (2004: 132) observation that the ship in the Nordic Bronze Age not only represented the cosmology of the sun but 'became the paramount symbol of everything powerful, and an important vehicle in all spheres'.

Europe's Rivers

There is no doubting that the earliest boats in Europe were built for use on rivers and lakes, and that the types of craft that enabled riverine traffic included hide- and skin-covered boats and logboats (McGrail 2001). No archaeological evidence for hide- and skin-covered boats for the Bronze Age exists (with the possible exception of the Caergwrle Bowl from Wales; Denford and Farrell 1980), but it seems more than likely that this type of craft would have been a fairly common sight on rivers and lakes, and would have been used for communication, trade and exchange, and fishing. The more robust and more readily preserved logboats, however, provide a rich source of information on the role of inland waterbodies as arteries for communication. It is not surprising that the craft used on Europe's rivers share few characteristics with the craft used in the Mediterranean or the Atlantic. After all, riverine and lacustrine craft do not have to cope with waves or swell, and when caught by unanticipated storms, riverine craft could simply be pulled onto the nearest bank where the boatmen would await more clement weather.

Logboats are, by definition, made from single logs, although these may have been used in pairs for greater stability and capacity (e.g. Weski 2009). Most logboats from the rivers and lakes of continental Europe have rounded bows and sterns carved from the log, but the use of fitted transoms at the stern of some very large Bronze Age craft appears a characteristic of logboats from the British Isles. One of the very largest logboats is the *c.*1000 BC Brigg logboat from the River Ancholme in Lincolnshire, over 15 m long and with a diameter of 1.9 m (McGrail 1978: 166–72). Such boats were too large for use by a single family; it seems more likely that such a craft was used for longer-distance trade and exchange, conducted by specialist boatmen on behalf of their community. There is no evidence for the use of sails or oars on Bronze Age logboats on Europe's rivers, and it is likely that these were paddled craft.

Among the several thousand monoxylous logboats discovered to date, about one thousand have been absolutely dated through radiocarbon or dendrochronological essay. These have been used by Jan Lanting (1997/8) to provide a remarkable insight into the origin of logboats in Europe. Lanting's groupings of logboats by country reveal a number of distinct chronological patterns (Fig. 21.2). The earliest logboats can be found in a 'Continental Zone 1', consisting of Denmark, north-west Germany, the Netherlands, Belgium, and north-western France. The oldest logboats in this Zone date to before 7500 cal BC, and these craft were in use throughout the Mesolithic, Neolithic, Bronze Age, and Iron Age, and continued into the Roman period and Middle Ages. A 'Continental Zone 2' encompasses the rest of Germany and France, Poland, the Czech Republic, Austria, and Switzerland, and possibly the Baltic States. Within this zone, logboats appear relatively early in the Rhine-Saône-Rhône corridor (from c.4350 cal BC), and the southern shore of the Baltic Sea (from c.3800 cal BC). In other parts within Zone 2, logboats are introduced later still. For example, the earliest logboats in Bavaria are of Late Bronze Age date (see also Weski 2009), despite this region—with access to the Rhine and

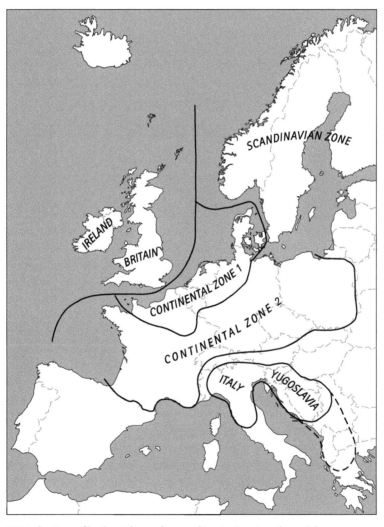

FIG. 21.2 Distribution of logboat 'zones' according to Lanting (1997/8).

Drawing: Mike Rouillard, University of Exeter.

Danube—having close connections with distant lands, as evidenced by its material culture. The oldest logboats in Ireland are dated to the early Neolithic (from *c*.3500 cal BC), and the earliest in Britain are of Bronze Age date (from *c*.2200 cal BC). As these boats come from the west side of Britain, it is not improbable that the British logboats may have developed from Irish forerunners. In Scandinavia, Late Bronze Age logboats are known from southern Sweden (from *c*.800 cal BC), but those from the rest of Sweden, Norway, and Finland are of significantly later date. Logboats are relatively rare from the rivers of Spain, Italy, Greece, and the former Yugoslavia, but the few radiocarbon dates available for boats from these countries suggest their early, albeit sporadic, use here during the Bronze Age.

It has been claimed that log-coffins used in burials covered by mounds at Loose Howe and Gristhorpe in Yorkshire, Shap in Cumbria, and Disgwylfa Fawr in Ceredigion, Wales, were reused logboats. However, Leslie Grinsell (1940: 375) observed correctly that these were not logboats, but log-coffins with shapes that resemble logboats. One of the three wooden vessels found within the burial mound of Loose Howe admittedly includes striking boat-like details, notably a triangular-shaped 'keel' and a 'stem' carved from solid wood (Elgee and Elgee 1949), but McGrail (e.g. 2001: 193) has argued that Bronze Age logboats had neither a keel nor a stem. The inclusion of a keel in any type of craft would imply the use of sails, for which no evidence exists, and it is highly unlikely that these log-coffins were either reused craft or log-coffins modelled on ships.

Conclusion: Current Debates and Future Research Directions

In the last 50 years significant progress has been made in the study of seafaring and navigation in the Bronze Age of Europe. The importance of the study of shipwrecks, such as the Uluburun wreck in the Mediterranean or the Dover boat in Atlantic Europe, is difficult to overstate. However, the number of shipwrecks securely dated to the Bronze Age remains small, and any opportunity to extend this knowledge through the study of newly discovered wrecks must be awarded the highest priority, especially so in the Mediterranean where direct evidence of seafaring activity before *c*.1500 BC remains particularly scarce. The absolute dating of shipwrecks is essential for their potential to be fully realized, and for the further development and refinement of our understanding of the origin and adoption of innovations of boat building and seafaring. However, it will be evident that shipwrecks alone cannot give us a full understanding of the significance of seafaring, inland navigation, trade, and exchange in Bronze Age Europe, and the integrated study of the *products* of trade and exchange with that of the *practice* of trading and exchanging goods is the only sensible way forward for maritime archaeologists.

The short overviews of seafaring and inland navigation presented in this chapter clearly show that distinct boat-building traditions existed during the Bronze Age in the Mediterranean, Atlantic Europe, and the rivers of Europe. Undoubtedly, the separation of these traditions was closely linked to the very different environmental conditions encountered by the crews in these three regions. Nevertheless, in view of the clear material evidence for high levels of connectedness of Europe in the Bronze Age, the geographically restricted use of certain shipbuilding techniques is surprising, most notably in the non-adoption of treenails and mortise-and-tenon techniques in Atlantic Europe and for the craft on the rivers of Europe.

Admittedly somewhat arbitrarily, current debates on seafaring and inland navigation can be divided into three parts. The first concerns the technological aspects of boat building. In the Mediterranean the complete lack of shipwrecks dated to before *c*.1500 BC continues to stimulate a vigorous debate, especially for the third millennium BC when the iconographic evidence is equivocal. The role of Egyptian craft, and their influence on Mediterranean shipwrights, plays an important part in this debate. In Atlantic Europe current debates are ongoing on the origin and seaworthiness of the sewn-plank boats, the type of craft represented by the rock carvings and the boats etched on the bronzes, and the potential role of hide-covered boats in the Bronze Age. The latter issue remains lively, despite the absence of such craft from the archaeological record, stimulated by the Roman descriptions of rawhide covered boats used by the Britons, as found in Caesar's *Bello Civili* (1.54) and Pliny the Elder's *Historia Naturalis* (4.104), and of hide-boats used on the Iberian Atlantic coast in Strabo's *Geography* (3.3.7). The debate on the introduction of sailing in the Atlantic region remains unresolved, but is further stimulated by Roman sources such as Caesar's *de Bello Gallico* (3.8–15), which notes that sailing skills were well developed on the Atlantic coast, for example in the case of the Veneti, who inhabited the southern part of Brittany. For the rivers of Europe, current debates include the use of rafts as alternatives to logboats, the origin of logboat construction in the different regions of Europe, and the ways in which boat-building innovations were adopted by boat builders in different river catchments. A growing interest in the importance of portages—overland transport between two ports—may in time extend to include the Bronze Age.

The second debate centres on issues of pilotage and navigation skills. This debate has been reinvigorated following the discovery of the Nebra Sky Disc (Meller 2002), which challenged the consensus that navigational skills—including the reading of the stars—were insufficiently developed in the Bronze Age for anything other than coastal seafaring. The discovery of the Nebra disc also raises questions of whether navigators were key individuals in the development of trade and exchange, whether they formed a distinct group of people in the Bronze Age, and what their status may have been. Additionally, if people in the Bronze Age could navigate by the stars, then this contributes to an understanding of the link between ships and cosmological concepts, expressed for example in the rock carvings in Østfold, Bohuslän, and Uppland. This challenge to the consensus that voyages were limited to coastal seafaring is beginning to produce an appreciation of the opportunities that existed for environmental navigation on journeys directly across the North Sea and other large waterbodies. Sightings of seabirds might have been used, for example, or observations of the ways in which sediment-rich rivers gave texture to the sea.

The third debate goes beyond the discussions focused solely on boats and seafaring. Following the publication of Mary Helms's (1988) *Ulysses' Sail: An Ethnographic Odyssey of Power, Knowledge, and Geographical Fistance*, a new momentum was given to the study of the significance of geographical distance and travel in prehistory. Examples of research influenced by Helms's book include the Bronze Age studies by Beck and Shennan (1991), Needham (2000), Van de Noort (2003; 2011), and Kristiansen and Larsson (2005); and for the Mediterranean notably the work of Broodbank (1993). These studies are significant in that they make the connection between research into the products of long-distance trade and exchange—which has a long tradition in archaeology—and research into the practice and sociopolitical implications of travel, which prior to these studies had been largely ignored.

Bibliography

Aner, E. and Kersten, K. (1978). *Die Funde der älteren Bronzezeit der Nordischen Kreises in Dänemark, Schleswig-Holstein under Niedersachsen IV*. Neumünster: Wachholz.

Basch, L. (1987). *Le Musée imaginaire de la marine antique*. Athens: Institut Hellénique pour la Préservation de la Tradition Nautique.

Bass, G. F. (1967). 'Cape Gelidonya: A Bronze Age shipwreck', *Transactions of the American Phililogical Society, New Series*, 57/8.

—— (1972). *History of Seafaring*. London: Thames and Hudson.

—— (1997). 'Mediterranean sea', in J. P. Delgado (ed.), *Encyclopaedia of Underwater and Maritime Archaeology*. London: British Museum, 268–74.

—— Frey, D. A., and Pulak, C. (1984). 'A Late Bronze Age shipwreck at Kaş, Turkey', *International Journal of Nautical Archaeology*, 13: 271–9.

—— Pulak, C., Collon, D, and Weinstein, J. (1989). 'The Bronze Age shipwreck at Ulu Burun', *American Journal of Archaeology*, 93: 1–29.

Beck, C. and Shennan, S. (1991). *Amber in Prehistoric Britain*. Oxford: Oxbow Books.

Bockius, R. (ed.) (2009). *Between the Seas: Transfer and Exchange in Nautical Technology*, Proceedings of the Eleventh International Symposium on Boat and Ship Archaeology, Mains 2006. ISBSA 11. Mainz: Römisch-Germanischen Zentralmuseums.

Bradley, R. (2000). *An Archaeology of Natural Places*. London: Routledge.

Broodbank, C. (1989). 'Longboat and society in the Cyclades in the Keros-Syros culture', *American Journal of Archaeology*, 93: 319–37.

—— (1993). 'Ulysses without sails: trade, distance, knowledge and power in the early Cyclades', *World Archaeology*, 24: 315–31.

—— (2000). *An Island Archaeology of the Early Cyclades*. Cambridge: Cambridge University Press.

Capelle, T. (1995). 'Bronze-Age stone ships', in Crumlin-Pedersen and Thye (eds.), *The Ship as Symbol in Prehistoric and Medieval Scandinavia*, Papers from an international research seminar at the Danish National Museum, Copenhagen, 5–7 May 1994, eds. Ole Crumlin-Pedersen and Birgitte Munch Thye, 1995. Copenhagen: Nationalmuseet, 71–6.

Casson, L. (1971). *Ships and Seamanship in the Ancient World*. Princeton: Princeton University Press.

Chaniotis, A. (ed.) (1999). *From Minoan Farmers to Roman Traders: Sidelights on the Economy of Ancient Crete*. Stuttgart: Franz Steiner.

Cherry, J. F. (1990). 'First colonization of the Mediterranean islands: a review of recent research', *Journal of Mediterranean Archaeology*, 3: 145–221.

Christakis, K. (2004). 'Palatial economy and storage in Late Bronze Age Knossos', in G. Cadogan, E. Hatzaki, and A. Vasilkis (eds.), *Knossos: Palace, City, State*. London: The British School in Athens, 299–310.

Clark, P. (ed.) (2004). *The Dover Bronze Age Boat in Context: Society and Water Transport in Prehistoric Europe*. Oxford: Oxbow Books.

Clarke, D. V., Cowie, T. G., and Foxon, A. (1985). *Symbols of Power at the Time of Stonehenge*. Edinburgh: National Museum of Antiquities of Scotland.

Cline, E. (1994). *Sailing the Wine Dark Sea: International Trade and the Late Bronze Age Aegean*. Oxford: Archaeopress.

—— (1999). 'The nature of the economic relations of Crete with Egypt and the Near East during the Late Bronze Age', in A. Chaniotis (ed.), *From Minoan Farmers to Roman Traders: Sidelights on the Economy of Ancient Crete*. Stuttgart: Franz Steiner, 115–44.

Coles, J. M. (1993). 'Boats on the rocks', in J. Coles, T. Wright, V. Fenwick, and G. Hutchinson (eds.), *A Spirit of Enquiry: Essays for Ted Wright, 1993*. Exeter: Wetland Archaeology Research Project, 23–31.

—— (2000). *Patterns in a Rocky Land: Rock Carvings in South-West Uppland, Sweden*. Uppsala: Department of Archaeology and Ancient History.

—— (2005). *Shadows of a Northern Past: Rock Carvings of Bohuslän and Østfold*. Oxford: Oxbow Books.

Costas Goberna, F. J., Hidalgo Cuñarro, J. M., and De la Peña Santos, A. (1999). *Arte Rupestre no Sur da Ría de Vigo*. Vigo: Instituto de Estudios Vigueses.

Crumlin-Pedersen, O. (2009). 'Plank boat—a problematic term for prehistoric vessels? Archaeological evidence for the impact of logboat techniques on the concepts of early built boats', in R. Bockius (ed.), *Between the Seas: Transfer and Exchange in Nautical Technology*, Proceedings of the Eleventh International Symposium on Boat and Ship Archaeology, Mainz 2006. Mainz: Römisch-Germanisches Zentralmuseum, 387–98.

—— and Trakadas, A. (2003). *Hjortspring: A Pre-Roman Iron-Age Warship in Context*. Roskilde: Viking Ship Museum.

Davies, W. and Schofield, L. (1995). *Egypt, the Aegean and the Levant: Interconnections in the Second Millennium BC*. London: British Museum.

Denford, G. T. and Farrell, A. W. (1980). 'The Caergwrle Bowl—a possible prehistoric boat model', *International Journal of Nautical Archaeology*, 9: 183–92.

Elgee, F. and Elgee, H. W. (1949). 'An Early Bronze Age burial in a boat-shaped wooden coffin from north-east Yorkshire', *Proceedings of the Prehistoric Society*, 15: 87–106.

Fitzpatrick, A. P. (2002). '"The Amesbury Archer": a well-furnished Early Bronze Age burial in southern England', *Antiquity*, 76: 629–30.

Gale, N. H. (ed.) (1991). *Bronze Age Trade in the Mediterranean*. Götenborg: Åström.

Glob, P. V. (1969). *Helleristninger i Danmark*. Aarhus: Jysk Arkæologisk Selskabs Skrifter VII.

Grinsell, L. V. (1940). 'The boat of the dead in the Bronze Age', *Antiquity*, 14: 360–9.

Haggis, D. (1999). 'Staple finance, peak sanctuaries and economic complexity in late Prepalatial Crete', in A. Chaniotis (ed.), *From Minoan Farmers to Roman Traders: Sidelights on the Economy of Ancient Crete, 1999*. Stuttgart: Franz Steiner, 53–86.

Hammer, C. U., Clausen, H. B., Friedrich, W. L., and Tauber, H. 1987. 'The Minoan eruption of Santorini in Greece dated to 1645 BC?', *Nature*, 328: 517–19.

Harding, A. F. (1984). *The Mycenaeans and Europe*. London: Academic Press.

—— (1993). 'British amber spacer-plate necklaces and their relatives in gold and stone', in C. W. Beck and J. Bouzek, with D. Dreslerová (eds.), *Amber in Archaeology*. Prague: Institute of Archaeology, 53–8.

Harrison, R. (1980). *The Beaker Folk: Copper Age Archaeology in Western Europe*. London: Thames and Hudson.

Helms, M. W. (1988). *Ulysses' Sail: An Ethnographic Odyssey of Power, Knowledge, and Geographical Distance*. Princeton: Princeton University Press.

Johnstone, P. (1972). 'Bronze Age sea trials', *Antiquity*, 46: 269–74.

Kaul, F. (1998). *Ships on Bronzes: A Study in Bronze Age Religion and Iconography*. Copenhagen: National Museum of Denmark.

—— (2002). 'The oldest war-ship sails again', in A. Nørgård Jørgensen, J. Pind, L. Jørgensen, and B. Clausen (eds.), *Maritime Warfare in Northern Europe*. Papers from an International Research Seminar at the Danish National Museum, Copenhagen, 3–5 May 2000. Copenhagen: National Museum of Denmark (Studies in Archaeology and History 6), 7–19.

—— (2004). 'Social and religious perceptions of the ship in Bronze Age Europe', in P. Clark (ed.), *The Dover Bronze Age Boat in Context: Society and Water Transport in Prehistoric Europe*. Oxford: Oxbow Books, 122–37.

—— and Valbjørn, K. V. (2003). *The Hjortspring Find: A Pre-Roman Iron Age Warship in Context*, Ships and Boats of the North, 6. Roskilde: Viking Ship Museum.

Kristiansen, K. and Larsson, T. B. (2005). *The Rise of Bronze Age Society: Travels, Transmissions and Transformations*. Cambridge: Cambridge University Press.

Lanting, J. N. (1997/8). 'Dates for the origin and diffusion of the European logboat', *Palaeohistoria*, 39/40: 627–50.

Lundborg, L. (1974). *Lugnarohögen*, Svenska Fornminnesplatser, 5. Stockholm: Almqvist & Wiksell.

McGrail, S. (1978). *Logboats of England and Wales*, British Archaeological Reports (British Series), 51. Oxford: British Archaeological Reports.

—— (2001). *Boats of the World*. Oxford: Oxford University Press.

—— (2004). 'North-west European seagoing boats before AD 4000', in P. Clark (ed.), *The Dover Bronze Age Boat in Context: Society and Water Transport in Prehistoric Europe*. Oxford: Oxbow Books, 51–66.

Malmer, M. P. (1981). *A Chorological Study of North European Rock Art*. Stockholm: Almquist and Wiksell.

Marinatos, N. (1984). *Art and Religion in Thera*. Athens: D. and I. Mathioulakis.

Marinatos, S. (1974). *Excavations at Thera VI (1972 Season)*. Athens: Ekdotiki Hellados.

Marsden, P. (2004). 'Description of the boat', in P. Clark (ed.), *The Dover Bronze Age Boat*. London: English Heritage, 32–95.

Marstrander, S. (1963). *Østfolds Jordbruksristninger, Skedbjerg*: Oslo: University of Oslo.

Meijer, F., and Van Nijf, O. (1992). *Trade, Transport, and Society in the Ancient World*. London and New York: Routledge.

Meller, H. (2002). 'Die Himmelscheibe von Nebra', *Archäologie in Sachsen-Anhalt*, 1: 7–20.

Morgan, L. (1988). *Miniature Wall Paintings of Thera: Study in Aegean Culture and Iconography*. Cambridge: Cambridge University Press.

Muckelroy, K. (1981). Middle Bronze Age trade between Britain and Europe, *Proceedings of the Prehistoric Society*, 47: 275–97.

Needham, S. J. (2000). 'Power pulses across a cultural divide: Armorica and Wessex', *Proceedings of the Prehistoric Society*, 66: 151–94.

—— and Dean, M. (1987). 'La Cargaison de Langdon Bay à Douvre; la signification pour les échanges à travers la manche', in C. Mordant and A. Richard (eds.), *Les Relations entre la continent et les îles Britanniques à l'âge du Bronze*. Amiens: Revue archéologique de Picardie, 119–24.

Niemeier, W. (2004). 'When Minos ruled the waves: Knossian power overseas', in G. Cadogan, E. Hatzaki, and A. Vasilakis (eds.), *Knossos: Palace, City, State*. Proceedings of the Conference in Herakleion organized by the British School at Athens and the 23rd Ephoreia of Prehistorical and Classical Antiquities of Herakleion, in November 2000, for the Centenary of Sir Arthur Evans's Excavations at Knossos. British School at Athens Studies, 12. London: British School at Athens, 393–8.

Northover, J. P. (1982). 'The exploration of the long-distance movement of bronze in Bronze and Early Iron Age Europe', *Bulletin of the University of London Institute of Archaeology*, 19: 45–72.

Österholm, S. (2002). 'Boats in prehistory—report on an archaeological experiment', in G. Burenhult (ed.), *Remote Sensing, Volume II: Archaeological Investigations, Remote-Sensing*

Case Studies and Osteo-Anthropological Studies. Stockholm: Stockholm University theses and papers in North-European archaeology, 13b, 232–42.
Pare, C. (2000). 'Bronze and the Bronze Age', in C. Pare (ed.), *Metals Make the World Go Round: The Supply and Circulation of Metals in Bronze Age Europe*. Oxford: Oxbow Books, 1–38.
Phelps, W., Lolos, Y., and Vichos, Y. (eds.) (1999). *The Point Iria Wreck: Interconnections in the Mediterranean ca. 1200 BC*, Proceedings of the International Conference, Island of Spetses, 19 September 1998. Athens: Hellenic Institute of Marine Archaeology.
Rainbird, P. (2007). *The Archaeology of Islands*. Cambridge: Cambridge University Press.
Renfrew, C. (1967). 'Cycladic metallurgy and the Aegean Bronze Age', *American Journal of Archaeology*, 71: 1–20.
Rowlands, M. (1980). 'Kinship, alliance and exchange in the European Bronze Age', in J. Barrett and R. Bradley (eds.), *Settlement and Society in the British Later Bronze Age*. Oxford: BAR (British Series 83), 15–55.
Schoep, I. (2004). 'The socio-economic context of seal use and administration at Knossos', in G. Cadogan, E. Hatzaki, and A. Vasilakis, eds., *Knossos: Palace, City, State*, Proceedings of the Conference in Herakleion Organised by the British School at Athens and the 23rd Ephoreia of Prehistoric and Classical Antiquities of Herakleion, in November 2000, for the centenary of Sir Arthur Evans's excavations at Knossos. London: British School at Athens, 2004 (British School at Athens Studies 12), 283–94.
Sherratt, S. and Sherratt, A. (1991). 'From luxuries to commodities: the nature of Mediterranean Bronze Age trading systems', in N. H. Gale (ed.), *Bronze Age Trade in the Mediterranean*, Studies in Mediterranean Archaeology, XC. Jonsered: Paul Åströms Förlag, 351–86.
Stos-Gale, Z. and Macdonald, C. (1991). 'Sources of metals and trade in the Bronze Age Aegean', in N. H. Gale (ed.), *Bronze Age Trade in the Mediterranean*, Studies in Mediterranean Archaeology, XC. Jonsered: Paul Åströms Förlag, 249–88.
Strömberg, M. (1961). *Die bronzezeitlichen Schiffsetzungen im Norden*. Lund: Meddelanden.
Trump, D. (2002). *Malta: Prehistory and Temples*. Valletta: Midsea.
Van de Noort, R. (2003). 'An ancient seascape: the social context of seafaring in the Early Bronze Age', *World Archaeology*, 35: 404–15.
—— (2006). 'Argonauts of the North Sea—a social maritime archaeology for the 2nd millennium BC', *Proceedings of the Prehistoric Society*, 72: 267–88.
—— (2009). 'Exploring the ritual of travel in prehistoric Europe: the Bronze Age sewn-plank boats in context', in P. Clark (ed.), *Bronze Age Connections: Cultural Contact in Prehistoric Europe*. Oxford: Oxbow Books, 159–75.
—— (2011). *North Sea Archaeologies: A Maritime Biography, 10,000 BC–AD 1500*. Oxford: University of Oxford Press.
Vander Linden, M. (2004). 'What linked the Bell Beakers in third millennium BC Europe?', *Antiquity*, 81: 343–52.
Wachsmann, S. (1998). *Seagoing Ships and Seamanship in the Bronze Age Levant*. College Station: Texas A&M University Press.
Weski, T. (2009). 'Logboats and local boats in Bavaria, Germany—a summary of current research', in R. Bockius (ed.), *Between the Seas: Transfer and Exchange in Nautical Technology*, Proceedings of the Eleventh International Symposium on Boat and Ship Archaeology, Mains 2006. ISBSA 11. Mainz: Römisch-Germanischen Zentralmuseums, 123–32.
Wright, E. V., Hedges, R., Bayliss, A., and Van de Noort, R. (2001). 'New AMS dates for the Ferriby boats: a contribution to the origin of seafaring', *Antiquity*, 75: 726–34.

CHAPTER 22

LAND TRANSPORT IN THE BRONZE AGE

MARION UCKELMANN

INTRODUCTION

From the Neolithic on there was a gradual change in large parts of Europe towards a settled form of life, but this did not mean that people were all tied to one place. A small part of the population, at least, was still mobile, and occasionally there were migrations by entire groups. There was no cessation in the exploration of surrounding areas, or in contact and exchange with people and communities both near and far. The motives for human mobility can be many and varied, as is still the case today: the exchange of news, knowledge, and goods; the search for resources; marriage partners; craftsmen, who were both absorbing and passing on knowledge; refugees; expelled persons; adventurers; traders; explorers; and messengers (e.g. of a religious or military nature).

Attesting to this mobility are, on the one hand, foreign objects, whether raw materials or finished goods, and on the other, the means of transport and the routes that are, however, only rarely found. In rare cases 'foreign people' can be recognized in archaeological finds, for example as bearers of objects not known locally in that form (e.g. 'foreign women'; Jockenhövel 1991), and also through scientific methods (including DNA and strontium isotope analysis). One of the best-known examples is probably the Early Bronze Age 'Amesbury Archer' who grew up in central Europe or Scandinavia, more probably in an Alpine region, and was buried with a rich set of grave goods of the Beaker culture in the vicinity of Stonehenge (Fitzpatrick 2009: 177) (see Chapter 10).

From the large numbers of bronzes one can detect a lively exchange between different regions of Europe and beyond, into the Mediterranean, North Africa, Asia Minor, and the Eurasian Steppes. Only those transported objects that are not perishable survive, such as metal, stone, and ceramic objects, and raw materials. The term 'imported goods' describes objects and raw materials that are unusual or absent in the area where they were found (e.g. Primas 2008: 149). The quantities of material are sometimes too large and heavy to have been carried by humans, although considerable quantities could have been carried by trained porters (see below).

From as early as the Neolithic, depictions show bovids first drawing a plough, and later a cart. It can be assumed that they were also used as pack animals during this time. Horses appear frequently in Bronze Age settlements, but there is still wide disagreement whether, as with other domestic animals, they were used for meat and/or milk, and only later as draught and ridden animals. Certainly evidence for the latter is only attested for the Late Bronze Age.

Simple wagons or carts are known from the Late Neolithic, but their development is difficult to trace. At present, on the grounds of new finds and improved dating techniques, there are various approaches, monocentric or polycentric. It is generally accepted that the wagon is found in various regions of Europe, Asia, and the Near East from the middle of the fourth millennium BC (see essays and discussions in Fansa and Burmeister 2004).

These vehicles are simple carts with two or four wooden disc wheels (Fig. 22.2b). In the course of the Bronze Age lighter wheels with perforations and a replaceable hub appear. It is possible that spoked wheels developed from these in order to be used in both four-wheeled wagons and two-wheeled chariots, whilst simple carts with disc wheels continued to be used. The evidence for vehicles in the Bronze Age consists of individual elements, mostly wooden and hence preserved only in special conditions, such as bogs. In the course of the Bronze Age more elaborate chariots were constructed, frequently with bronze components and fittings. These are often found as grave goods and objects in hoards. In addition there are many pictorial representations, even in regions where the original objects have not yet been found, as well as a great number of miniature chariots in graves that were probably used in a ritual context (Vosteen 1999).

Amongst the most important innovations of the Bronze Age are the spoked wheel; the exchangeable hub; the steering function of the front axle; and the use of the horse as a draught animal. The spoked wheel brought a considerable reduction in weight. Horses as draught animals can cover long distances in a short time if the terrain and subsoil are favourable.

Sledges and slide-cars (travois), drawn by man or beast, were probably used earlier than wheeled vehicles, but are difficult to attest as they seldom survive and only rarely appear in images.

Means of Transport: Humans, Oxen, Horses

To calculate the speed and loads of the various means of transport, a multiplicity of variables must be considered. To give greater precision to this investigation, GIS analyses were used by various projects in which least-cost-path and cost-surface analysis were carried out in order to understand which of the possible paths required the least effort for humans.

A recent study (Murrieta-Flores 2010) attempts to assemble all the possible determining factors, for instance:

- terrain, but also the differences caused by the changing seasons (e.g. rivers in flood, snowed-up mountain passes, drought-affected areas);
- territorial boundaries (rarely identifiable by archaeological means);
- human factors (based on human physiology);
- identifying which paths are still suitable from gradient or subsoil, i.e. which require the least effort;
- the 'intrinsic' will of humans (the role of human agency) as individual or community;

- geographical features (hills, river valleys, places of special importance) rather than the shortest distance;
- the need for provisioning, essential in the case of long-distance journeys (e.g. whether supplies needed to be brought along, or hunted and prepared *en route*—a time-consuming process—and whether water was readily available, an essential requirement for draught and pack animals).

Only if one attempts to include all these factors can more precise models be created. The same process would then need to be applied for vehicles drawn by horses and cattle.

Speed of Transport and Loads

Humans as Bearers

Until recently such models have been relatively rare, but for humans the following values have been established: men between 20 and 60 years old have an average walking speed of 4.9 km/hour and women 4.4 km/hour (Murrieta-Flores 2010: 7). It is difficult to provide data for prehistoric people as the available studies derive from medicine and ethnography, yet if one were to give merely indicative values and not a precise model, it would be realistic to posit *c*.20 km (3.8 km/hour, *c*.5 hours actual walking) for one day's travel distance (depending on terrain and weather), with a load of *c*.20–35 kg. In the case of trained bearers higher values may be proposed, as emerges from ethnographic and historic evidence, such as for Mayan and Aztec bearers (Murrieta-Flores 2010).

The evidence for the effects on humans of transporting loads can be established in European prehistory only where there is good preservation of skeletal material, and so far it is sparse. For instance, from an examination of part of the skeletal material from the Hallstatt cemetery it was found that men and women probably shared heavy labour in the Iron Age salt mine. The muscle marks indicate that the men mainly mined the salt and the women carried heavy loads (Pany 2008: 139). This is admittedly only one regionally specific indication of how labour was divided, but it may nevertheless have a wider significance. In the future, examination of skeletons will perhaps be able to discern several kinds of division of labour, and show signs that bearers served as transport workers, in other words not just traders in the traditional or modern sense.

A wide variety of items, mostly made of organic material, may have served as transport equipment and containers, such as are still used today. Among these are woven or leather sacks, bags and pouches, woven baskets, wooden crates, bark containers, and much besides, but smaller receptacles made of clay and bronze are also possible. Unfortunately these finds have only rarely been preserved, as in the Hallstatt salt mine where five backpacks were found, all efficiently designed for carrying and emptying out mined salt blocks (Reschreiter and Kowarik 2008: 60). These make it likely that elaborate carrying equipment was used to carry the maximum load possible, and to make the work as easy as possible.

Animals as a Means of Transport

Animals drawing simple carts or wagons to carry heavy loads are known from the Neolithic, and their use increased during the Bronze Age. The walking speed of ox teams was around 1.8–2.5 km/hour, and of horses around 3.2–4.3 km/hour. The latter could reach higher speeds on traversable ground, and depending on their build and condition up to 38 km/hour over short distances, as is attested by reconstructed Egyptian war chariots. With alternating walking and cantering one may assume $c.$10 km per 45 minutes for a pair of horses. The horse thus significantly increased the speed of transport of humans and wagons, as cattle teams reached a maximum speed of 3.7 km/hour, or, as recent comparisons show, ox-drawn covered wagons around 24–28 km per day (Piggott 1983: 89). A modern riding horse can carry about one fifth of its own weight, thus a horse weighing 350 kg can carry 70 kg, of rider and/or baggage. A horse with a good harness on good terrain can pull about double its own weight; on rough ground or steep inclines it can only pull its own weight (Schwindt 1995). A bullock/ox of $c.$500 kg weight can, however, pull only about 150 kg, at a speed of 3 km/hour (http://www.payer.de/entwicklung/entw081.htm#2.2, viewed 17.8.2010), or possibly a slightly faster 3.7 km/hour (Piggott 1983: 89). Riding horses or using them as draught animals requires long training and is a costly undertaking. The animals must also work together as a team and must therefore be matched in size, condition, and character.

Wagons drawn by draught animals, particularly cattle, are often found on Bronze Age rock art (Larsson 2004). Representations of laden pack animals are seldom found, but they occur for instance in the rock art at Carschenna (Canton Grisons, Switzerland). Harnessed horses are attested through representations, but also through the remains of bits. There are three-dimensional representations, as on the famous sun chariot from Trundholm, Denmark, although the horse is on wheels, like the chariot. There are snaffle and bar bits for two horses on the four-wheeled wagons of Poing type (ceremonial chariots). Reliable evidence for the use of horses carrying humans, in other words as ridden animals, are found only in the Late Bronze Age.

The development of the horse harness is another source of evidence in the study of the use of horses as draught and ridden animals. How the horse harness was developed and used is fiercely debated, as it relates to when the riding of horses started. In order to use the animals to pull carts or to be ridden, and to achieve better steering, reins were required. There are two different kinds: the nose rein, with a ring or bolt through the nasal septum, which was used mainly with bovids but also with equids, and reins fastened to the head, which was mainly used with equids and is still used today. The latter could be made entirely of organic material or partly also of metal (for early reins and the effect on steering see Dietz 2011). The first indications of harnessing are found from the end of the third millennium BC in two different regions, the Carpathian Basin and the Eurasian steppe. On these so-called snaffle-bits the side or cheek-pieces were used to stop the mouth-pieces from shifting, thus making it easier to control and direct the animals; with cattle this is not necessary. These bits were made of antler, bone, or bronze. Two types are developed in the two regions. In the steppes mainly disc-shaped and for a short period flat cheek-pieces were in use. In the Mediterranean and Carpathian area bar cheek-pieces were most common, made initially from antler and, from the end of the second millennium BC, of bronze. These bar pieces were increasingly used in western and central Europe, and became the preferred form by the end of the Bronze Age (Hüttel 1981; Boroffka 2004b; Dietz 2011).

Wagons

From the time of its Neolithic invention, the wooden disc wheel was used on heavy carts drawn by cattle. These agricultural vehicles were used until the Late Bronze Age, as many wheels found in the marsh and lakeside settlements of the Alpine foothills show, and they have continued in use until relatively recent times (Pare 2004; Züchner 2004). Whether the simple carts and the more elaborate wagons were pulled over long distances or whether they were just used for short local journeys cannot be said for certain. In the following, a sketch of the development first of the wheels, from wooden disc to wooden spoked and metal spoked wheels, and then of wagons, two- and four-wheeled is given.

Disc Wheels

The wheels that survive show that various kinds of wood were used: maple, ash, birch, beech, oak, alder, elm—in other words a wide variety. An innovation added to Neolithic wheels was the replaceable hub. The wheel and the hub were made of two different pieces; frequently the hub was made of softer wood than the wheel. The wood grain of the hub ran at right angles to that of the wheel and was thus significantly more durable and could support a greater weight. The disc wheels with diameters of $c.70-90$ cm are slightly larger than their Neolithic predecessors, as are the spoked wheels that emerged during the course of the Bronze Age (Vosteen 1999; Burmeister 2004: 330). Well-preserved examples are the four wooden wheels with inserted hubs from Glum (Oldenburg, Germany: Fig. 22.1).

Representations in the form of clay wheel models are known from the Late Neolithic in central Europe (Seregély 2004), and the many small Bronze Age clay discs, perforated and thicker in the middle, may also have been wheel models.

An innovation over Neolithic wheels was composite construction out of several wooden boards, some of which have crescent-shaped cut-outs to make them lighter, which points the way to the spoked wheel. These are attested in northern Italy, through southern and northern Germany to Ireland in the west, and are evidence of communication and the relatively fast transfer of technology. A wheel of this kind was discovered in good condition in the excavation of the Late Bronze Age Wasserburg at Bad Buchau (Germany). Such wheels were probably used mainly with simple single or double-axle wagons to transport goods, while the newer spoked wheels of the Bronze Age were used more for religious and prestige purposes, or for warfare.

A hybrid of the disc and the spoked wheel is the strutted or cross-bar wheel. Instead of spokes oriented to the centre, it has struts across the diameter. These wheels were not as widely distributed and are used in the period $c.1300-900$ BC, particularly in southern Europe.

Spoked Wheels

Spoked wheels on two- and four-wheeled wagons are attested in actual finds, bronze or clay models, and representations on pottery and rock art. They are lighter but also significantly more fragile than disc wheels. Horse-drawn, manoeuvrable, and fast, war chariots with

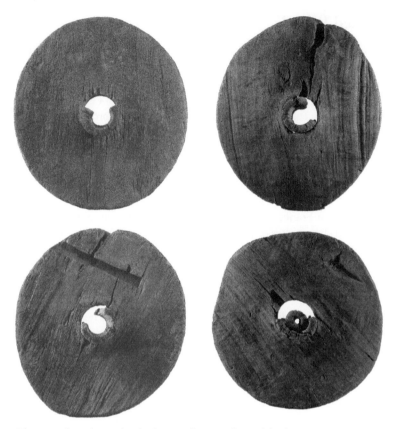

FIG. 22.1 The wooden disc-wheels from Glum, Ldkr. Oldenburg, Germany, made from alder with inserted bushes made from birch; Dm. 75 cm.

Photo: Landesmuseum für Natur und Mensch Oldenburg.

spoked wheels were an intimidating and efficient means of combat at the beginning of the second millennium BC in Asia Minor and later in Mycenae and Egypt. The first spoked wheels to appear in central Europe in the Middle Bronze Age (see below, Veľké Raškovce and Trundholm) were mostly unsuited to their 'primary function', the transport of humans and heavy loads, owing to the often small number of spokes. Thus it is not surprising that spoked wheels are found almost exclusively as funerary or votive objects.

In Europe, the earliest finds of actual spoked wheels date from the twelfth century BC (a fragment of a rim from the Barnstorfer Moor, Landkreis Diepholz, Germany: Burmeister 2004: 333). By contrast, they are attested in clay models in eastern and southern Europe from the Early to Middle Bronze Ages. Also from the Middle Bronze Age are the first Danish spoked wheels, for example on the famous six-wheeled Trundholm sun chariot, drawn by a horse and bearing a disc with one side covered in gold sheet (see Fig. 41.6). There is still no explanation for the gap in time and space between this and the finds from central Europe, but it may be the result of delays in transmission. The number of spokes varies, but four spokes are most frequently depicted, though five or six spokes do occur; yet there are no finds of wooden four-spoked wheels. A wooden wheel from the Barnstorfer Moor even has ten spokes, and a wheel like this could certainly have been used in transporting heavy loads (Vosteen 1999).

Metal Spoked Wheels

Of special note are the bronze spoked wheels, made through a sophisticated, single casting process. They are the most ambitious craft endeavour of all Bronze Age bronze objects and required many kilograms of casting metal; for instance, those from Stade, Germany, have around 12 kg per wheel (see Fig. 22.2a). Even if the casting was not always perfect, the pieces were finished and used. They reflect the wider development of bronze wheels at the end of the Urnfield and beginning of the Hallstatt period. Such finds of the so-called Stade/Hassloch/Fa/Coulon type are found from the ninth-eighth centuries BC in the Pyrennean foothills to the lower Elbe, have a diameter of 50–60 cm, and exhibit a wooden running surface studded with bronze nails. They were components of four-wheeled vehicles. The occurrence of such wheels together with an Early Iron Age situla in the French grave site of La Côte-Saint-André (southern France) shows that this was a ceremonial vehicle. The wheels each have six spokes and show traces of wood in the groove of the rim, but at the hub there were no signs of friction, which makes it likely that the vehicle was made only for funerary purposes (Vosteen 1999). The large bronze bucket standing on the wagon suggests a cult procession, in which libation rites may have played a part, as is also suggested by the miniature chariots considered below.

The everyday use of these vehicles for transporting goods and heavy loads is thought to have been rare owing to the brittleness and low strength of the wheels, so they were probably mostly used in a votive context. The four bronze wheels from Hassloch (Germany), each with five spokes, their wooden rims studded with bronze nails, are presumably from a simi-

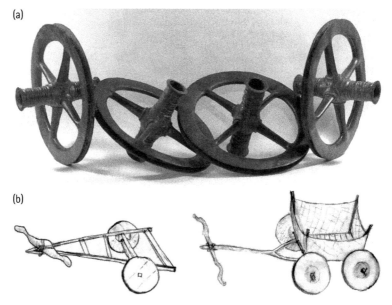

FIG. 22.2 (a) The cast bronze wheels from Stade, Germany; Dm. 58 cm; (b) Schematic drawing of reconstructions of a two-wheeled and a four-wheeled cart.

(A. Photo: Schwedenspeicher Museum, Stade; B. drawing A. Sherratt, © Landesmuseum für Natur und Mensch Oldenburg).

lar votive context. The small number of spokes, at least eight in the case of later vehicles, is an indication of their use in religious ceremonies rather than for carrying loads (Vosteen 1999).

Two-Wheeled Chariots

Currently the oldest two-wheeled chariots with spoked wheels come from Eurasia and were placed in graves of the West Siberian Sintashta culture. These light chariots were drawn by two horses. Parts of the harness are also found in the graves. They date from the late third and early second millennia BC (Epimakhov and Koryakova 2004). Other chariots are found in the Aegean from the seventeenth–sixteenth centuries BC, but survive almost exclusively in images (Crouwel 2004: 341). In Egypt under Ramesses II they finally acquired the reputation as a dangerous weapon that could decide the outcome of a conflict (as at the Battle of Kadesh, thirteenth century BC). In central and north-west Europe there are few indications of two-wheeled chariots, the earliest dating to the Middle Bronze Age. Among them is the incised depiction on a Middle Bronze Age pot from Vel'ké Raškovce, Slovakia, which shows a two-wheeled chariot with spoked wheels, each with four spokes, with a half-round chariot body on which a figure is drawn. It is pulled by two animals, presumably horses (Boroffka 2004a: 351). Wagons and carts occur also frequently in Nordic rock art. The two-wheeled chariots depicted there are each drawn by two horses; in rare but impressive cases a charioteer is shown in outline standing on the wheel or on the wagon body. There are examples in the art at Frännarp, for instance, and in the famous grave of Kivik, both in Scania, Sweden.

From their find contexts, two-wheeled chariots in graves can very probably be connected with an elite, and must be considered as status symbols. These vehicles were probably not used for transporting loads, but rather for rapid transport and as prestige items. Whether they were also used as war chariots in battles in these regions of Europe remains highly debatable (Pare 2004).

In south-west European rock-art depictions of two-wheeled vehicles can also be found, presumably with disc wheels, with a rather triangular chariot body, quite similar to the sledges and slide-cars that are also depicted. Here it is more likely that they are carts for transporting loads (Züchner 2004). In the Late Bronze Age in the Iberian Peninsula there are chariots depicted on so-called warrior stelae. These are mostly two-wheeled chariots that are interpreted as the prestige vehicles of the warrior (Harrison 2004).

Four-Wheeled Wagons

Evidence for four-wheeled vehicles with disc wheels are found early in the Bronze Age. They are in the tradition of Late Neolithic wagons, and survive as clay models, known especially from the Carpathian Basin. These show wagons with high sides and four wheels, the early ones with disc wheels and the later ones with spoked wheels (Boroffka 2004a: 347). In the rock art of southern Scandinavia four-wheeled wagons mostly have disc wheels, more rarely four-spoked wheels, and almost always have cattle as draught animals (Larsson 2004: 392). An important innovation is the possibility of steering with a swivelling front axle, which is attested by Late Bronze Age finds, for example in northern Germany (Burmeister 2004: 333).

In the course of the Bronze Age the four-wheeled vehicles are found more and more often in votive or religious contexts. Wagons certainly continued to be used to transport heavy loads, but from the thirteenth century BC there emerged an elaborate four-wheeled wagon construction whose body and other parts were often adorned with bronze fittings and appear frequently as funerary goods in rich burials. Two traditions of construction can be distinguished; one is from north of the Alps and the other in the eastern Carpathian Basin. The tradition north of the Alps is particularly visible in the wagon burials of the thirteenth–twelfth centuries BC at the beginning of the Urnfield period. After an apparent gap in finds during the following Urnfield period, they reappear in increased numbers at the end of the Urnfield period, and then make a further, more widespread appearance in the Hallstatt period (from c.800 BC onwards). As cremation predominated in the Urnfield culture, and often the funerary gifts were burnt along with the body on the pyre, only the bronze parts of the wagons have survived. The various finds permit the reconstruction of a four-wheeled vehicle, with the wheels mostly having four spokes. The hub is usually conical with bronze fittings, and sometimes the spokes and rims also have bronze fittings. Such a wagon was drawn by two horses, which is demonstrated by bits or components of bits in these graves. The wagon body is rectangular and richly adorned in part with bronze fittings. Frequently the fittings have horn-like or bird-like extensions and elements of a rail at the edge of the body. The very few finds of wagon body fittings show that the elaborated four-wheeled wagons spread to large parts of northern and western Europe (Pare 2004: 358).

The eastern tradition is less well represented in the finds and is distinguished by its cast hub fittings. As only isolated pieces are known from hoards or single finds, it remains unclear what the vehicle body looked like and whether the vehicles had two or four wheels.

The Functions of Wagons and Wheels

The vehicles used for everyday transport only rarely survive because they were made of organic materials. Two-wheeled chariots were used as vehicles in Greece but also in the rest of Europe, but more to convey the warrior into battle or to participate in prestige processions, and less to be used as a weapon in conflict, as happened in the Near East (Crouwel 2004).

The significance of the four-wheeled vehicle with spoked wheels in the Bronze Age in central Europe is shown by a series of cremation graves from the early Urnfield period (thirteenth–twelfth centuries BC), particularly in the Alpine foothills and on the central Swiss plateau. In these graves were found the deformed remains of the bronze components of four-wheeled vehicles. Axle caps, axle nails, hubs, and wheel fittings from graves and hoards are easily recognized as vehicle components; what remains problematic is the unambiguous identification of the function of the numerous bar-shaped objects, socket-like attachments, handles, decorative panels, and fittings.

The vehicles were luxury and prestige items of a social elite as well as ceremonial wagons used for cult purposes. Finds of weapons, tableware, and metal vessels demonstrate the prominent position of the buried individual, whilst wagon adornments with the character of amulets or bird figures point to the religous sphere.

The rich grave found in 1956 at Hart an der Alz (Upper Bavaria, Germany), with numerous bronze parts of a four-wheeled vehicle, was the first of this group to be discovered. Today about a dozen such graves are known. The best known of them, aside from Hart an der Alz, are the graves of Mengen, Königsbronn (both in southern Germany), Kaisten, St Sulpice (both in western Switzerland), and the most recent discovery in Poing (Upper Bavaria). The graves, all of them male cremations in sometimes huge burial chambers or cists, are mostly richly equipped, with weapons and/or bronze objects, as well as many clay vessels arranged as a table service.

The four-wheeled vehicle from Poing was probably pulled by two horses, as there were two horse bits among the grave goods. As there were no bones in any of the graves, the horses were clearly not buried with the deceased—as happened in the Middle Ages—but rather only the bit was included as *pars pro toto*.

The final function of these vehicles was as a hearse. On the rectangular body of the wagon the dead person was laid out and taken to the place of cremation, in a manner possibly comparable to the ancient Greek custom of *ekphora* (driving out). In the imagination, this drive continued into the realm of the dead. It is very doubtful that these vehicles had previously been used for everyday transport. They were probably used in cult processions or were the exclusive prestige vehicles of their 'rich' owners, who in addition to their secular function as warriors and chiefs, may also have carried out priestly roles in their community (as so-called priest-chieftains). At the same time, owing to their many metal parts, the vehicles functioned as displays of wealth.

The wagon as a funerary gift for a prominent social class declined in significance over the centuries, but in the Hallstatt period it was revived over a wide geographical area in central and western Europe. The everyday cart of the Urnfield period continued as an all wooden vehicle with disc wheels (Pare 1992; 2004).

There is evidence of the dominance of the vehicles among the symbols and cult practices of the Bronze Age in central Europe not only in grave finds but also in the multiplicity of model chariots and wagons. At the end of the Urnfield period (tenth–ninth centuries BC) the Lausitz culture, in the area from Brandenburg to Silesia (north-east Germany to west Poland), has produced small two- or three-wheeled chariots fitted with a socket, adorned with birds, bulls, or 'hybrid creatures', all stylized to a greater or lesser degree. One may safely assume these chariots served as an ornament: perhaps as the finial of a shaft of a normal chariot or mounted on the top of a staff used in cult processions.

Also ornamented with depictions of birds are a few vessels on wheels, the so-called cauldron-wagons (*Kesselwagen*). The largest example, found in Peckatel (Mecklenburg, Germany), has a height of almost 40 cm. These cauldrons could be connected with rain magic through their similarity to depictions on coins from the Thessalian city of Krannon from the fourth century BC. The cauldron wagons that survive whole come without exception from rich graves, for example Milavče, Peckatel, and Acholshausen (Fig. 22.3), which, like the chariot graves, have clear warrior elements like swords and spearheads as grave goods.

Roads and Paths

The extent to which the vehicles described above were used for actual everyday transportation of heavy loads cannot be determined with certainty. Presumably the simpler carts and wagons, few of which survive, were used primarily to transport products at the local level, such as harvested grain. For wagons especially, relatively firm ground and, ideally, a paved or levelled path is required. Currently there is no archaeological evidence of an inter-regional

FIG. 22.3 Bronze cauldron-wagon (*Kesselwagen*) from Acholshausen, Ldr. Würzburg, southern Germany; Height 12 cm.

Photo: E. Hahn, Veitshöchheim.

system of roads connecting large parts of Europe, which is a pre-condition for the intensive use of animal-drawn vehicles in the exchange of raw materials and finished goods.

Many stretches were very probably travelled by waterways (see Chapter 21). For the Bronze Age it is possible to point directly or indirectly to a number of routeways. These sometimes very impressive monuments lie far from each other and do not constitute a connected inter-regional network. Finds from the bog areas of north-west Europe show the existence of prehistoric traffic networks. In recent decades the focus of research has been in England in the Somerset Levels (Coles, Caseldine, and Morgan 1982) and East Anglia (Flag Fen: Pryor 2005); Ireland (Raftery 1990); Holland (Casparie 1984); in parts of Jutland, Denmark (Schou Jørgensen 1993); and in north-west Germany (Hayen 1989; Burmeister 2004).

In Flag Fen, lying in the fenland south-east of Peterborough, eastern England, a large area was excavated. Amongst other features, a Late Bronze Age raised causeway was found, connecting two dry areas and extending on one side into a large wooden platform. The exact purpose of this construction has not yet been idenitfied, but numerous finds—weapons, tools, and ornaments—from the area around the platform and on the south-west side of the path indicate the sacrificing of votive gifts in large numbers. The dendrological dates of the wood extend from the thirteenth to the tenth century BC. However, the finds reflect a much longer use of the place, which extends up to the Iron Age and the early Roman period (Pryor 2005). These excavations throw new light on the discussion about whether the paths led through the bog or only into it in order to procure resources (e.g. hunting and fishing; flint), or exclusively for votive purposes (see Vosteen 1999). The more finds that are discovered, the more it seems probable that it was a network to connect dry areas in the fen (see Burmeister 2004).

In north-west Germany prehistoric wooden trackways are known in the Weser-Ems region in Lower Saxony. So far more than 300 built trackways have been found, and in the adjoining Netherlands there are 40 more. In this region an extensive system of plank- and log-paved roads, bridging impassable bogs, had existed since the Neolithic. There are both narrow footpaths and broad carriageways. The Bronze Age trackways consist of oak planks

FIG. 22.4 Late Bronze Age trackway XII (Le) from a bog near Ockenhausen-Oltmannsfehn, Ldkr. Leer, Northern Germany.

Photo: Landesmuseum für Natur und Mensch Oldenburg.

with holes at each end; vertical pegs in the holes prevented the planks shifting with the constant movement of the bog(Fig. 22.4). Because of the small turning circles of the vehicles they are only 2.5 m wide in contrast to the Neolithic paths that had a breadth of up to 4 m. The trackways were maintained constantly. Numerous discarded parts of vehicles at the edge of the path indicate the actual use of the tracks as well as breakdowns (Burmeister 2004: 334). In several areas it has been possible to prove the planning of a network of paths and infrastructure works. An example is a tree cut into planks, which was used in construction sites 75 km from each other. They date from the end of the eighth century BC and attest an extensive planned road network. Paving with planks required a large quantity of building wood, and Bronze Age metal axes undoubtedly facilitated timber procurement, and were instrumental in making works of this magnitude possible (Hayen 1989).

Trackways have also survived in bogs in Ireland where a large number of the excavated paths date to the Bronze Age. Here there was greater use of thinner wood, bundles of twigs and thicker branches (brushwood) with planks being used only for exceptional purposes. The bundles of twigs were firmly tied together and pressed lengthways into the bog-floor and secured against shifting by lateral branches. Well-attested examples are the paths in the Corlea and Derryoghil bogs (Fig. 22.5), dating to the beginning of the Late Bronze Age (Raftery 1990). The trackways in the Somerset Levels were built in a similar fashion and also suggest links between the drier areas by either side of the bog (Coles, Caseldine, and Morgan 1982).

Constructions along the routes of the trackways, such as bridges over rivers and fords, are known, but they are not often found. Examples are the approaches to the Bronze Age lake settlements of Forschner in southern Germany and Biskupin in Poland. The entry ways to the gates of Bronze Age fortifications indicate that paths existed, at least in the areas close to the fortification.

FIG. 22.5 Bronze Age trackway 10 from Derryoghil, Co. Longford, Ireland.

Photo: B. Raftery.

Paved paths apart from bog paths are very seldom found, and if they are they tend to be small areas paved with stone or rubble. In Cham-Oberwil, Switzerland, ruts were discovered under this paving, so that it may be assumed that this part of the road was very frequently used and paved in order to give vehicles a better surface (Vosteen 1999: 72).

Further evidence of Bronze Age routes is given indirectly by other finds. Thus notable finds at mountain and upland passes, for example in the Alps, show that these natural thoroughfares were used as early as the Bronze Age (Wyss 1970).

From lines of burial mounds one may assume the existence of paths along which the mounds were placed, perhaps leading between two settlements or to one particular settlement or monument. Naturally the existence of such paths can only be confirmed by large-scale excavation. A good example is in the Bronze Age barrow cemetery of Warendorf-Neuwarendorf (Germany), where a broad clearing is perceptible between the graves, and wheel-tracks can even be made out. The later megalithic *Langbetten* are also arranged in such a way as to flank the track on either side (Grünewald 2008).

There are numerous indications of more recent routeways, which may in part have already been used in the Bronze Age, but evidence for this is scarce, as most of the ways were probably not improved by means of built constructions and have left no datable traces. It is risky to assume the existence of routes on the basis of distribution maps of Bronze Age objects. The sites (particularly the find-places of hoards) are merely the places where the objects were deposited, and these are more likely special places in the landscape than points on traffic routes.

CONCLUSION

There are numerous indications of extensive transport connections and human mobility in the Bronze Age, mainly based on the distribution of artefacts. In addition, many discoveries, direct and indirect, point to the existence of transport technologies—cattle, horses, and vehicle parts. However, on present knowledge, there would not have been an extensive wagon-based traffic over long distances across Europe, as the ground in many parts would simply not be suited for this, because of the damp climate. Paved and stabilized paths did exist, as one can recognize particularly in boggy areas, where such trackways served mainly to link drier settlement areas.

The everyday vehicle consisted of a simple cart drawn by cattle with two or four disc wheels, later perforated disc wheels, by means of which goods were transported probably only over short distances. For longer distances, pack animals and more likely human bearers were probably used as carriers. For really long distances it is very probable that waterways, along rivers and coasts, were used. The first vehicles drawn by horses are thought to be chariots, used in combat or to gain prestige, and only later, probably at the end of the Bronze Age, with better routeways and improved use of reins, were they harnessed as draught animals for transport. The more elaborate vehicles of the Urnfield period, ornamented with bronze fittings, were not suited to transport over land; at best they were used over short stretches at low speed. They were used mainly in burial ritual.

The wagon and the wheel had a many-layered significance in the Bronze Age, as is shown by the different finds and contexts that extend well beyond transport, and to some degree reflect the fascination that they exercised on humans, not only as a status symbol and religious cult object but also as a symbol of mobility.

BIBLIOGRAPHY

Boroffka, N. (2004a). 'Bronzezeitliche Wagenmodelle im Karpatenbecken', in M. Fansa and S. Burmeister (eds.), *Rad und Wagen. Der Ursprung einer Innovation. Wagen im Vorderen Orient und Europa*. Mainz: Von Zabern, 347–54.

—— (2004b). 'Nutzung der tierischen Kraft und Entwicklung der Anschirrung', in M. Fansa and S. Burmeister (eds.), *Rad und Wagen. Der Ursprung einer Innovation. Wagen im Vorderen Orient und Europa*. Mainz: Von Zabern, 467–80.

Burmeister, S. (2004). 'Neolithische und bronzezeitliche Moorfunde aus den Niederlanden, Nordwestdeutschland und Dänemark', in M. Fansa and S. Burmeister (eds.), *Rad und Wagen. Der Ursprung einer Innovation. Wagen im Vorderen Orient und Europa*. Mainz: Von Zabern, 321–40.

Casparie, W. A. (1984). 'The three Bronze Age footpaths XVI (Bou), XVII (Bou) and XVIII (Bou) in the raised bog of Southeast Drenthe (the Netherlands)', *Palaeohistoria*, 26: 41–94.

Coles, J. M., Caseldine, A. E., and Morgan, R. A. (1982). 'The Eclipse Track 1980', *Somerset Level Papers*, 8: 26–39.

Crouwel, J. (2004). 'Bronzezeitliche Wagen in Griechenland', in M. Fansa and S. Burmeister (eds.), *Rad und Wagen. Der Ursprung einer Innovation. Wagen im Vorderen Orient und Europa*. Mainz: Von Zabern, 341–6.

Dietz, U. L. (2011). 'Zäumungen: Material und Funktion', in A. Jockenhövel and U. L. Dietz (eds.), *Bronzen im Spannungsfeld zwischen praktischer Nutzung und symbolischer Bedeutung. Prähistorische Bronzefunde Kolloquium Oktober 2008, XX*, Prähistorische Bronzefunde. Munich: Beck, 55–69.

Epimakhov, A. V. and Koryakova, L. N. (2004). 'Streitwagen der eurasischen Steppe in der Bronzezeit: Das Wolga-Uralgebirge und Kasachstan', in M. Fansa and S. Burmeister (eds.), *Rad und Wagen. Der Ursprung einer Innovation. Wagen im Vorderen Orient und Europa*. Mainz: Von Zabern, 221–36.

Fansa, M. and Burmeister, S. (eds.) (2004). *Rad und Wagen. Der Ursprung einer Innovation. Wagen im Vorderen Orient und Europa*. Mainz: Von Zabern.

Fitzpatrick, A. P. (2009). 'In his hands and in his head: the Amesbury Archer as a metalworker', in P. Clark (ed.), *Bronze Age Connections: Cultural Contact in Prehistoric Europe*, 176–88. Oxford and Oakville: Oxbow Books.

Grünewald, C. (2008). '"Infrastruktur" in der Bronzezeit Westfalens? Indizien für Wege und Verkehr', in D. Bérenger and C. Grünewald (eds.), *Westfalen in der Bronzezeit*. Münster/Westf.: Landschaftsverband Westfalen-Lippe, 100–1.

Harrison, R. J. (2004). *Symbols and Warriors*. Bristol: Western Academic & Specialist Press.

Hayen, H. (1989). 'Bau und Funktion der hölzernen Moorwege: einige Fakten und Folgerungen', in H. Jankuhn and E. Ebel (eds.), *Untersuchungen zu Handel und Verkehr vor- und frühgeschichtlicher Zeit in Mittel- und Nordeuropa*, 5. Göttingen: Vandenhoeck & Ruprecht, 11–82.

Hüttel, H.-G. (1981). *Bronzezeitliche Trensen in Mittel- und Osteuropa. Prähistorische Bronzefunde*, XVI, 2. Munich: Beck.

Jockenhövel, A. (1991). 'Räumliche Mobilität von Personen in der mittleren Bronzezeit im westlichen Mitteleuropa', *Germania*, 69: 49–62.

—— and Dietz, U. L. (eds.) (2011). *Bronzen im Spannungsfeld zwischen praktischer Nutzung und symbolischer Bedeutung. Prähistorische Bronzefunde Kolloquium Oktober 2008, XX*, Prähistorische Bronzefunde. Munich: Beck.

Larsson, T. B. (2004). 'Streitwagen, Karren und Wagen in der bronzezeitlichen Felskunst Skandinaviens', in M. Fansa and S. Burmeister (eds.), *Rad und Wagen. Der Ursprung einer Innovation. Wagen im Vorderen Orient und Europa*. Mainz: Von Zabern, 381–98.

Madel, S. (2001). 'Kapitel 8: Tierische Produktion. 1. Rinder', in M. Payer (ed.), *Entwicklungsländerstudien. Teil I. Grundegegebenheiten*. Accessed online 17 August 2010 at http://www.payer.de/entwicklung/entwo81.htm.

Murrieta-Flores, P. (2010). 'Travelling in a prehistoric landscape: exploring the influences that shaped human movement', in B. Frischer, J. Webb Crawford, and D. Koller (eds.), *Making History Interactive: Computer Applications and Quantitative Methods in Archaeology (CAA)*. Proceedings of the 37th International Conference, Williamsburg, Virginia, USA, 22–26 March 2009. British Archaeological Reports (International Series), 2079. London: Oxbow Books, 258–76.

Pany, D. (2008). 'Muskelmarken', in A. Kern, K. Kowarik, A. W. Rausch, and H. Reschreiter (eds.), *Salz-Reich. 7000 Jahre Hallstatt*. Vienna: Naturhistorisches Museum Wien, 139–41.

Pare, C. F. E. (1992). *Wagons and Wagon-Graves of the Early Iron Age in Central Europe*. Oxford: Oxford University Committee for Archaeology.

—— (2004). 'Die Wagen der Bronzezeit in Mitteleuropa,' in M. Fansa and S. Burmeister (eds.), *Rad und Wagen. Der Ursprung einer Innovation. Wagen im Vorderen Orient und Europa*. Mainz: Von Zabern, 355–72.

Piggott, S. (1983). *The Earliest Wheeled Transport from the Atlantic Coast to the Caspian Sea*. London: Thames and Hudson.

Primas, M. (2008). *Bronzezeit zwischen Elbe und Po. Strukturwandel in Zentraleuropa, 2200–800 v. Chr*. Bonn: Rudolf Habelt.

Pryor, F. (2005). *Flag Fen: Life and Death of a Prehistoric Landscape*. Stroud: Tempus.

Raftery, B. (1990) *Trackways through Time: Archaeological Investigations on Irish Bog Roads, 1985–1989*. Dublin: Headline Publishing.

Rehschreiter, H. and Kowarik, K. (2008). 'Die Tragesäcke—strikte Arbeitsteilung und höchste Effizienz', in A. Kern, K. Kowarik, A. W. Rausch, and H. Reschreiter (eds.), *Salz-Reich. 7000 Jahre Hallstatt*. Vienna: Naturhistorisches Museum Wien, 60–1.

Schwindt, G. (1995). *Fahren mit Pferd*. Stuttgart: Franck-Kosmos.

Schou Jørgensen, M. (1993). 'Roads', in S. Hvass and B. Storgaard (eds.), *Digging into the Past: 25 Years of Archaeology in Denmark*. Aarhus: Jutland Archaeological Society, 144.

Seregély, T. (2004). 'Radmodell und Votivaxt, aussergewöhnliche Funde der Kultur mit Schnurkeramik von der Nördlichen Frankenalb', in M. Fansa and S. Burmeister (eds.), *Rad und Wagen. Der Ursprung einer Innovation. Wagen im Vorderen Orient und Europa*. Mainz: Von Zabern, 315–20.

Vosteen, M. U. (1999). *Urgeschichtliche Wagen in Mitteleuropa. Eine archäologische und religionswissenschaftliche Untersuchung neolithischer bis hallstattzeitlicher Befunde*, Freiburger Archäologische Studien, Bd. 3. Rahden/Westf.: Marie Leidorf.

Wyss, R. (1970). 'Alpenpässe', in *Reallexikon der Germanischen Altertumskunde*, Bd. 1. Berlin/New York: De Gruyter, 191–4.

Züchner, C. (2004). 'Frühbronzezeitliche Wagen und Transportmittel in der Felskunst Süd- und Südwesteuropas', in M. Fansa and S. Burmeister (eds.), *Rad und Wagen. Der Ursprung einer Innovation. Wagen im Vorderen Orient und Europa*. Mainz: Von Zabern, 399–408.

CHAPTER 23

COPPER AND BRONZE: BRONZE AGE METALWORKING IN CONTEXT

TOBIAS L. KIENLIN

APPROACHES TO PREHISTORIC METALWORKING

Research in the early history of metallurgy reaches back almost to the beginnings of archaeology as an academic discipline and it soon became entangled in the wider methodological and intellectual development of prehistoric archaeology. As early as 1836 C. J. Thomsen used the succession of stone, bronze, and iron implements to establish our tripartite system of European prehistory, which increasingly came to draw upon notions of technological progress and its supposed effects on the wider domains of culture and society. Somewhat later it was realized that at least in some parts of Europe copper was in fact the first metal widely used, not bronze. This finding added complexity on the terminological side, for early metalworking communities could now be designated (Late) Neolithic, Eneolithic, Chalcolithic, Copper Age, or (Early) Bronze Age, depending on regional context and archaeological tradition. Some of the earliest analyses of prehistoric copper and bronze objects were carried out with chronological questions in mind, such as the use of copper before bronze. Ever since, the application of scientific methods—the sub-discipline of archaeometallurgy—has played an important part in the study of early metalworking in prehistoric Europe. Large-scale projects were carried out with thousands of analyses, typically focusing on composition as a guide to provenance and often with inconclusive results. Less often attention is paid to the knowledge gained by prehistoric metalworkers of the properties of the different types of copper and copper alloys they were working, and the development of methods of casting and forging.

Science, however, is similar to archaeology in that analyses or data are in need of interpretation. This tends to be concealed by the application of ever more sophisticated analytical methods, which is also why specialist studies focusing on technological aspects tend to dominate the field, resulting in a failure to integrate scientific perspectives with wider culture-historical concerns. In particular, there are interpretative problems with the notion of technological 'progress' and the increasingly better understanding of nature. The early evidence for copper mining and smelting is discussed in terms of evolution, and the succession of different types of copper and copper alloys is interpreted as an improvement in operational and functional terms. The field of craft specialization is another area that might profit from a true integration of the science-based reconstruction of metalworking processes and technological choices with an anthropologically informed discussion of its social and ideological contexts. Typically, however, this still takes the form of evolutionist grand narratives linking perceived technological progress to the emergence of hierarchical society (e.g. Kristiansen and Larsson 2005). Finally, of course, the origins of metallurgy are hotly debated. Some opt for single invention in the East (e.g. Roberts, Thornton, and Pigott 2009), whereas others hold that the autonomous invention of metallurgy is an open question (e.g. Parzinger 1993). A number of recent syntheses integrate the evidence at hand into a coherent culture-historical picture, which typically involves the spread of metallurgy ultimately from the Near East via south-eastern to central and northern Europe (e.g. Pernicka 1990; Krause 2003), whereas others try to provide scientific evidence for an independent development in the Balkans (Radivojević et al. 2010).

The aim of this chapter, therefore, is twofold: first, starting in the Eneolithic or Copper Age but focusing mainly on the Bronze Age, to review the early evidence for the mining of copper ores, smelting, metalworking, and the succession of different types of copper and copper alloys, with particular emphasis on the situation in central and south-eastern Europe. Bronze Age metallurgy, in particular, is thought to have rapidly developed in scale and complexity. It supposedly necessitated exchange and specialized production, triggered social hierarchization and invited attempts by higher-ranking individuals to increase the efficiency and stability of their power. Hence, the second aim is to challenge evolutionist assumptions in our notions of technological 'progress' and to try to deconstruct some commonly held perceptions of the social context of early metallurgy. It will become clear that previously clear-cut technological stages tend to become blurred by new discoveries. We cannot any more rely on inevitable 'progress' and/or geological conditions as a guide to the development of early metallurgy. The early use of copper and the subsequent development of metallurgy was the result of technological choices drawing upon and embedded in the cultural and social textures of groups. These choices were taken by actors firmly integrated within networks of communication and decision-taking. They were determined in their action neither by the laws of chemistry or physics alone, nor by any 'political' authority manipulating the production and circulation of 'prestigious' metal objects.

Prologue: The Beginnings of Metallurgy

Bronze Age metallurgy cannot be understood without an awareness of the much longer history of the early use of copper and copper minerals. In fact, *Early* Bronze Age metallurgy did not differ significantly from its Late Neolithic, Eneolithic, or Copper Age predecessors—both in terms of technology and scale. It was only in the course of the Bronze Age that the techniques applied saw a diversification, and the scale of metallurgy-related activities increased significantly.

In the Carpathian Basin and the Balkans the earliest artefacts made of native copper and copper minerals such as beads, fish-hooks, and awls are known from the Early to Middle Neolithic (e.g. from Starčevo/Criş contexts; Pernicka 1990; Parzinger 1993). These finds predate proper metallurgy, which apart from working native copper (and copper minerals) should include the deliberate production of metal, in other words mining, smelting, and casting—a somewhat later development. Instead, the earliest interest in native copper and copper minerals falls into the wider domain of Neolithic communities' involvement with their natural surroundings and their attempts at the manipulation of materials. It must not be seen as purposeful experimentation leading up to the science of metallurgy but may rather reflect broader aesthetic values and symbolic concerns expressed and negotiated through material culture.

A significant increase in the number of such finds and an expansion of the copper artefact types in use occurred during the early fifth millennium BC in the Late Neolithic (Eneolithic) Vinča culture in the north-central Balkans (Vinča-Gradac and Pločnik phases). From the settlements of this group, in particular from Belovode, there is also the first reliable evidence of smelting in south-eastern Europe and the working of copper produced from its ores (Radivojević et al. 2010). In addition, recent radiocarbon dating shows that the mining site of Rudna Glava in Serbia was most likely exploited from at least 5400 cal BC, in other words right from the beginning of the Vinča culture, until its end around 4600 cal BC (Borić 2009). It is apparent that during the late Neolithic—in the Vinča culture and adjacent groups—the potential for a proper metallurgy was gradually building up in south-eastern Europe.

In the course of time larger amounts of copper became available and with the introduction of casting there was a shift in aesthetic values and the perception of materials. The earlier concern, which also motivated the beginnings of mining at Rudna Glava, had been with the colour of native copper or copper minerals, hammered and annealed into ornaments or used as pigments. Now there occurred an increase in the size and variety of shapes that copper objects could take. We enter the domain of what Douglass Bailey (2000, 209–39) aptly called 'expressive material culture'. These objects also had the characteristic shine or 'bling' of earlier (native) copper ornaments. But there certainly was an added potential of symbolic expression in the sometimes massive copper implements of the period. Among them there is a variety of different types of shaft-hole hammer-axes (e.g. Pločnik and Vidra types) and axe-adzes (e.g. Jászladány type), flat axes, and chisels. All of these forms are made of pure copper. They were cast, most likely in closed moulds, and finished by hot-working (Fig. 23.1; Kienlin 2010). Hence their hardness was low and their potential for practical use was limited when compared to contemporary stone or flint implements. By their sheer size and weight some shaft-hole axes were obviously beyond use. But it should also be noted that at least some of them bear traces of use wear. Use in this sense may include occasional conflict. It certainly was of limited intensity and restricted just to certain practical activities that need not correspond to that of modern steel axes. But it is likely that such implements were present in people's daily life on a more regular basis than our interest in their use in formalized social display, ceremonies, and burial ritual implies. Rather than focusing on their conspicuous deposition during burial ceremonies and the like, it is likely that it was precisely their presence in more mundane situations and activities that substantiated the axes' suitability as markers of (male) *habitus* and/or as an expression of a person's given role or position.

In the north Alpine region of central Europe there was only a weak reflection of the early development of Copper Age metallurgy in the Carpathian Basin and the Balkans. From

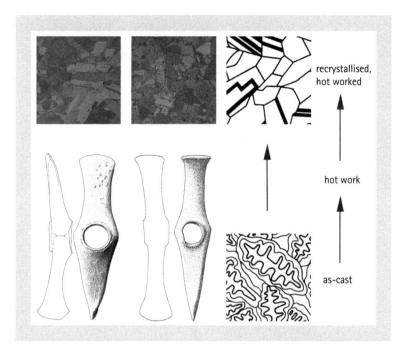

FIG. 23.1 Suggested *chaîne opératoire* for the finishing of Eneolithic/Copper Age hammer-axes and axe-adzes by hot working.

Source: author (Kienlin 2010).

Neolithic contexts of the late fifth and the early fourth millennium BC only about 10 to 20 copper objects are known. Among them there are the well-known disc from the lakeside settlement of Hornstaad-Hörnle on Lake Constance, two shaft-hole axes and one flat axe from Linz-St Peter, Austria, and Überlingen on Lake Constance, awls as well as some small copper beads and rings (Fig. 23.2). Until the recent discovery of smelting slag supposedly dating to this horizon at Brixlegg in Austria (c.4500–3900 cal BC; Bartelheim et al.2002), these early copper finds were thought to be imported from south-east Europe. This would make up for a rapid spread of smelting from south-east to central Europe, and/or roughly contemporaneous local experimentation. There is a problem, however, with the dating of the metallurgical remains from Brixlegg, which might belong to a later horizon on the site (Gleirscher 2007). For the time being it may be safer to maintain that copper came from the east, for the shaft-hole axes clearly originate from the Carpathian Basin. Even if some experimentation with smelting was going on at Brixlegg, and despite the obvious cultural contacts with the east, it is quite clear that neither process resulted immediately in the widespread use of copper objects or the practice of metallurgy.

It is only somewhat later after about 3800 cal BC with the Late Neolithic (*Jungneolithikum*) Cortaillod, Pfyn, Altheim, and Mondsee groups that the number of copper artefacts increases. There are numerous flat axes, daggers, awls, and ornaments such as spirals and beads mainly from the wetland sites along the Alpine foothills (Krause 2003). In this context there is also good evidence of metalworking with numerous crucibles and copper prills related to the casting process (Matuschik 1998). Extractive metallurgy, on the other hand,

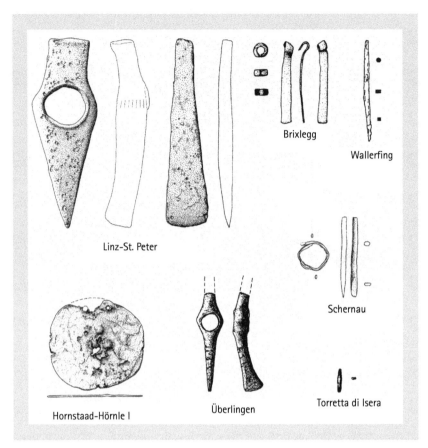

FIG. 23.2 The earliest copper artefacts known from the north Alpine region of central Europe.

Drawing: author (various sources).

has been suggested but is still not proven beyond doubt. Hence copper is thought either to have been derived from nearby Alpine ore deposits and/or to have been imported from south-east Europe. In particular, the east Alpine mining district is thought to have been exploited by the population of the Mondsee group, although related evidence of extractive metallurgy (smelting) from the Götschenberg settlement in the Alpine Salzach Valley is disputed (Bartelheim et al. 2002). Copper composition may point towards ongoing exchange with the Carpathian Basin instead and indicate the exploitation of ore deposits in the Slovakian Ore Mountains (Schreiner 2007).

Interestingly, neither the Eneolithic/Copper Age metallurgy of south-east Europe, nor its western counterpart during the local Late Neolithic, developed continuously into the Bronze Age. Rather, progress—if such was represented by metallurgy—turned out to be reversible: with the end of Kodžadermen-Gumelnița-Karanovo VI in Bulgaria, and somewhat later of Bodrogkeresztúr and related groups in the Carpathian Basin, there was change in many aspects of this culture system. Metallurgy—in particular the production of heavy copper implements—lost much of its attraction in Late Eneolithic/Copper Age

Baden times. Similarly, although the existence of at least some crucibles indicates that knowledge of metallurgy was not entirely lost, after the Pfyn, Altheim, and Mondsee groups there is a significant decrease in the intensity of metalworking during the subsequent Horgen culture and related groups of the local Late Neolithic (*Spätneolithikum*). Traditionally this is explained by the exhaustion of oxide ore deposits exploited at this early stage, in other words by technological incapability vis-à-vis changing external parameters. However, since there is increasing evidence for the early use of sulphidic copper ores it is more likely that we witness culture change and a shift in the role of material culture in the social reproduction of these 'hiatus' or 'transition period' communities.

Bronze and the Bronze Age

Similar to the different usages of 'Eneolithic' and 'Copper Age', the term 'Early Bronze Age' that encompasses the subsequent development throughout south-east and central Europe denotes quite different phenomena. Typically it is culturally defined rather than metallurgically, for in its earliest stages it refers to groups that did not yet use tin bronze. This is most marked in the Balkans and the Carpathian Basin where groups like Ezero (from c.3100/3000 cal BC), late Vučedol, and Makó (from c.2600/2400 cal BC) in local terminology constitute the beginnings of the Bronze Age. There is culture change to justify this view since these groups mark the end of the Eneolithic hiatus and there was a renewed rise in metallurgy after 3000/2800 cal BC. However, this was based on arsenical copper, which was used for new types of axe (e.g. Baniabic and Fajsz; Bátora 2003) and dagger, and new types of precious metal ornament were introduced (also axes and daggers in silver and gold: Velika and Mala Gruda in Montenegro; Primas 1996).

In central Europe the re-emergence of metallurgy is linked to various regional groups of the Corded Ware and Bell Beaker cultures (the local Final Neolithic or *Endneolithikum*) that were later replaced by Únětice and the communities of the north Alpine Early Bronze Age. In the Carpathian Basin, Makó gave way to a variety of Early Bronze Age II/III and Middle Bronze Age groups such as Nagyrév, Hatvan, or Maros. Hence, with Únětice in north-eastern central Europe and the north Alpine Early Bronze Age, there are three large culture areas of the Early Bronze Age divided by differences in artefact spectrum, burial customs, and settlement patterns. Drawing on earlier beginnings in the Beaker period, all of them are distinctly 'metal age' because copper artefacts became increasingly widespread in burial ritual and hoarding. In some areas at least, mining and metal production became of some importance. The precise way, however, in which tin bronze entered this system is subject to debate.

Tin was most likely won from alluvial stream deposits carrying tin-oxide minerals. These might have been used directly to produce bronze by co-smelting with copper ores or by adding tin oxide to molten copper under reduced conditions. This process might account for highly variable tin contents at the beginning of the Bronze Age. But later, when tin contents stabilized in the 8–12 per cent range (the 10 per cent typically cited in the literature is an idealized value, hardly achieved in practice), it is more likely that metallic tin was produced and added to the liquid copper (Pernicka 1998). Metallic tin is apt to decompose at low temperatures and this is why very few tin artefacts or ingots are known from prehistoric Europe. Notable exceptions are, for example, the tin ingots from the Uluburun shipwreck.

Unlike arsenical copper, tin-bronze with tin contents in excess of about 2–3 per cent is a proper alloy because in the Old World there are few occurences of both copper and tin minerals that on co-smelting could have produced an unintentional copper-tin 'alloy' (among the few exceptions are Iberia and central Asia). In fact copper-ore deposits are far more common than occurrences of tin, the most well known of which are located in Cornwall and in the German-Czech and Slovak Ore Mountains (Erzgebirge). Additional ones are known from the Iberian Peninsula, Brittany and the French Massif Central, Tuscany, and Sardinia, but their prehistoric exploitation is even more controversial than that of Cornwall and the Erzgebirge (Muhly 1985; Bartelheim and Niederschlag 1998).

Thus many debates about Bronze Age trade go back to the question of tin supply for what was to become the standard alloy of this period, and to the amazing fact that the earliest tin bronzes after 3000 cal BC appeared in northern Mesopotamia and Anatolia—an area devoid of tin sources. Only somewhat later, by the middle of the third millennium BC, did a more regular use of bronze in the Near East and the Aegean occur, typically at first for prestigious objects. Traditionally, the ancient civilizations of this area were thought to have drawn upon tin deposits either in Britain or in the German Ore Mountains (Erzgebirge). Radiocarbon dating necessitated a review of these far-ranging contacts and resulted in a more nuanced picture of pre-Bronze Age and Early Bronze Age exchange systems, extending along the Danube and/or the Adriatic and across the Balkans towards the Carpathian Basin and central Europe (Maran 1998) (Fig. 23.3). Interestingly, while authors working in this area consider western tin sources one of the possible causes of contact and exchange, lead isotope analyses show that at least the mid third millennium BC increase in Aegean tin-bronze metallurgy was most likely supported by copper and tin ultimately imported from as far east as central Asia (e.g. Parzinger 2002).

This finding might explain why apart from some early finds such as Velika Gruda the regular use of tin-bronze in south-eastern Europe is a relatively late phenomenon (Liversage 1994; Pare 2000). Since there is better evidence for early low-tin bronzes in Bell Beaker contexts than in local Early Bronze Age ones, it has been suggested that this technology might reflect western influences instead of transfer along the Danube route (see Fig. 23.3). In Bulgaria, Romania, and the former Yugoslavia regular use of high-tin bronze is only attested from the local Middle to Late Bronze Age (after 1700/1600 cal BC). Similarly, in the Carpathian Basin in early cemeteries such as Mokrin or Branč, there is little evidence for the use of tin-bronze prior to 1900/1800 cal BC. In the Slovak cemetery of Jelšovce it is only in the later graves that tin-bronze became the standard alloy and the same is true for the north Alpine region where bronze was widely used only in Bz A2 after about 1900/1800 cal BC. Thus, in central and south-eastern Europe the move to tin-bronze was a gradual process that only came to an end well into the second millennium cal BC. In western Europe, on the other hand, tin-bronze is well attested somewhat earlier at about 2200–2000 cal BC, and its introduction took place in a rather short period of time, drawing on local placer deposits in south-west England. Given the evidence of early contact between the British Isles and the continent, it is possible that the knowledge of tin-bronze was in fact a western European innovation which subsequently spread east—perhaps to an area where it met eastern influences, reflecting the longer tradition of tin-bronze in the Near East and the Aegean.

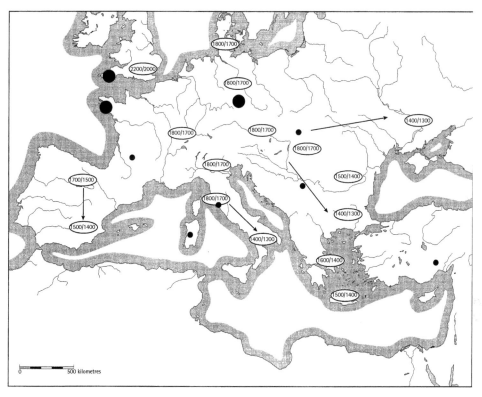

FIG. 23.3 Map indicating the approximate dates of the transition to the use of tin bronze and the major tin deposits in Europe; note the early occurrence of bronzes on the British Isles.

Source: author, after Pare 2000.

Alpine Copper and Bronze Age Mining Communities

Early Bronze Age metallurgy in central Europe is characterized not only by the incipient use of tin-bronze but by a shift in copper production from oxide to sulphidic ores that yielded a variety of new copper types. In the broadest terms, this sequence reflects the structure of ore deposits with oxide ores on top and sulphidic ones underneath (but see below). Unlike western Europe, however, with its well-attested exploitation of mining districts such as Ross Island, Mount Gabriel, or the Great Orme in the British Isles and Cabrières in southern France, in central Europe the evidence of third and early second millennium BC copper mining and production is for the most part circumstantial. Apart from a number of smaller copper sources, the Alps as well as the German and Slovak Ore Mountains have traditionally received most attention because of their substantial copper ore deposits, known to have been exploited in medieval and early modern times. Early Bronze Age groups, rich in copper and bronze objects to a greater or lesser extent, are situated in both the Alpine foreland and in the vicinity of the Ore Mountains. This coincidence has been taken to imply both the Bronze Age exploitation of adjacent ore deposits as well as the derivation of wealth and power from metallurgy and the control of exchange of its products. In addition, at some stage for each of these mining areas analytical evidence of Bronze Age exploitation has been claimed, but not universally accepted. Otto and Witter (1952), for example, drew attention to the so-called fahlore-type copper (*Fahlerz*), their *Leitlegierungsgruppe* IV, which they claimed was mined in the German Erzgebirge and distributed throughout Bronze Age central Europe. A comparable approach relating copper objects and ore deposits was conducted by Richard Pittioni (1957) and Ernst Preuschen (1967). In their case, however, it was the Bronze Age exploitation of east Alpine copper sources, especially those in the Mitterberg area, that they thought could be proven.

A substantial increase in the number of analyses—still mainly on the artefact side—was achieved by the *Studien zu den Anfängen der Metallurgie* (SAM) project (Junghans, Sangmeister, and Schröder 1968) (Fig. 23.4). The collaborators in this project were somewhat more careful about the question of relating artefacts to specific mining areas, relying instead on the mapping of different types of copper, based on the assumption that spatial patterning would emerge and hint at the origin of the copper types used in the Neolithic and Bronze Age. For the Early Bronze Age, two large groups of fahlore metal were distinguished according to whether nickel is present among the characteristic trace elements or not, and the differences in their distributions were noted. In the debate that followed, the nickel-containing variant was named *Singen copper* after the eponymous Bz A1 cemetery (*c*.2200–2000 cal BC), close to the western part of Lake Constance that produced numerous artefacts of this type of (mostly unalloyed) fahlore copper. Fahlore copper with little or no nickel, on the other hand, was frequently found in neck-rings (*Ösenringe*) and rib ingots (*Spangenbarren*) from large hoards in Bavaria and further east. It became known as *Ösenringkupfer* (Butler 1978).

It was only in the 1990s, with a statistical re-evaluation of the older SAM groups and an increasing number of analyses from eastern central Europe, that it became possible to differentiate truly north Alpine Singen copper from similar fahlore-type copper that was circulating in the area of the Únětice culture. We are dealing with closely related copper types that originated from the exploitation of similar ore deposits in different mining areas, and by the use of a comparable smelting technique (Krause 2003). Such issues are now being re-examined by large-scale lead-isotope analysis projects. But systematic work on ore deposits was long neglected, and we still lack sufficient chemical and lead-isotope data from the Alpine deposits as well as from the German and Slovak Erzgebirge. Most attempts, therefore, at provenancing the different types of fahlore copper may still be seen as informed guesses based mainly on the distribution of various types of copper artefacts (see, however, recent studies, for example by Höppner et al. 2005; Schreiner 2007).

Much the same is true for the organization of copper mining and the distribution of copper, which are often modelled along modernist notions of managerial elites, craft specialization, and trade in valuable or prestigious copper objects. This situation differs markedly from research into Neolithic mining and its social organization, which tends to draw on anthropological approaches and often favours seasonal mining activities. By contrast, in Bronze Age research there is a tendency to see the European Bronze Age as a historically unique development. Consequently, Bronze Age society and—in the present context—the organization of its metallurgical activities are conceptualized as somehow distinct both from what anthropology tells us about technology in traditional societies and from the evidence of earlier, Neolithic, societies. Mining and metallurgy are seen as an exceedingly complex undertaking discussed in the context of full-time craft specialization and emerging social hierarchies.

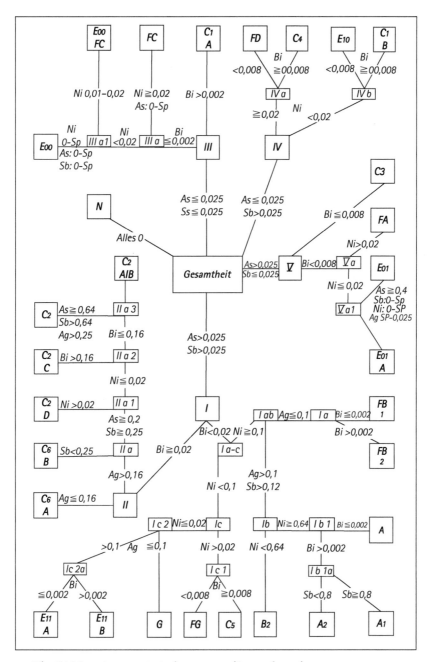

FIG. 23.4 The SAM projects statistical groups or 'Stammbaum'.

Source: Junghans, Sangmeister, and Schröder 1968.

The information on early mining and copper production in the western and the eastern Alps is not equally good, and the most unequivocal evidence of extractive metallurgy comes from somewhat later times. In Switzerland, for example, there is so far no evidence at all of Bronze Age copper mining or smelting furnaces, and radiocarbon-dated slag heaps relate to Late Bronze Age and Iron Age activity. The same is still true of the Alpine Rhine Valley and Montafon area in Austria, where the search for Bronze Age mines has recently been intensified. In the eastern Alps, on the other hand, there are the famous Mitterberg and Paltental mining areas, with extensive evidence of Middle to Late Bronze Age mining. Elaborate deep mining and surface shaft working (*Pingenbau*) were practised, typically exploiting sulphidic chalcopyrite copper ores—resulting in the so-called east Alpine copper (*ostalpines Kupfer*) that from the second half of the Early Bronze Age onwards replaced the earlier fahlore-type copper.

The evidence of Early Bronze Age mining and metallurgy, on the other hand, is much less clear and typically comes from the earliest settlements established towards the end of the Early Bronze Age and during the early Middle Bronze Age, after c.1800/1700 cal BC, when permanent settlement started to extend well into the Alps. The well-known site of St Veit-Klinglberg in the inner-Alpine part of the Salzach Valley is one of these (Shennan 1995). Other examples include the Buchberg near Wiesing in the lower Tyrolean Inn Valley, Savognin-Padnal and Savognin-Rudnal in the western Alps in the Graubünden (Switzerland), and—the most recent excavations—the Bartholomäberg in the central Alpine Montafon region (Krause 2005). In organizational terms, metallurgy—both copper production and working—was still practised in the settlements or their immediate surroundings, unlike the situation later on.

Typically, these sites are rather small, situated on hilltops, and some of them show signs of fortification. In addition, some but by no means all were drawing on neighbouring ore deposits, for example St Veit-Klinglberg where there is evidence of food brought in from outside to support a mining population. For this reason, in the standard model of Early Bronze Age settlement such sites are interpreted as central places in control of smaller neighbouring sites, in what is conceived of as a hierarchical settlement system (Krause 2005). Although there is no evidence of metallurgical activities from the Bartholomäberg, for instance, it is supposed that power was derived from control of the exploitation of copper ore deposits in the vicinity and the exchange of copper. Early mining and metal production, in this perspective, is a complex technology that required organization and control exercised by emergent Bronze Age elites. The move into the Alps itself is seen as a consequence of the growing need for copper.

An alternative approach was suggested in Stephen Shennan's (1995) study on St Veit-Klinglberg, conceptualized as a mining settlement operating largely autonomously without centralized control. From a formalist perspective this usefully deconstructs the controversial emphasis on elites and metallurgy of the standard model—Shennan's (1993: 59) 'myth of control'. It is unclear, however, whether the notion that mining offered hitherto unknown potential for individual ambition and ways to break through traditional social boundaries by acquiring metal and wealth in fact applies to traditional (prehistoric) society. Instead, we should ask whether copper was really the main economic reason for the colonization of the Alps. A review of the earliest settlement evidence suggests a much more nuanced picture, and most likely different Alpine areas and valleys followed different trajectories in early mining and metal production (Kienlin and Stöllner 2009).

Right from the start of the Early Bronze Age (c.2200 cal BC) there is a marked discrepancy between the lack of Alpine settlement and the use of (Singen-type) fahlore copper that is thought to have been mined somewhere in mining districts along the Alpine valley of the Rhine and its tributaries. It is likely that we are dealing with small-scale activities organized on a seasonal basis, expeditions to copper ore deposits carried out in connection with pastoral activities. Direct evidence of this kind of approach to mining is difficult to obtain. But there is variability in compositional and lead-isotope data to support the notion of a decentralized approach to mining that may well have been organized in a communal or kinship-based mode of operation. Copper production was more complex than just 'down-the-line' from specific mining centres to the lowlands, and it was regionally specific. We should not subsume this under a model of elite-driven mining and metallurgy. Rather there is evidence that the expansion into the Alps was driven forward by lowland communities with a subsistence-based economy initially drawing only limited advantage from alternative resources such as the Alpine copper deposits.

Only during the first half of the second millennium BC is there evidence that in some areas this system evolved to comprise communities practising mining and metallurgy on a larger scale. At this point, small communities chose arable areas that lay on medium-altitude terraces to establish permanent settlements based on agriculture. Certainly the choice of hilltops for settlement might indicate rivalry with neighbouring groups, but one should not underestimate the need for cooperation in a new environment such as the Alps, and we are entitled to ask what kind of hierarchy may be inferred for the small-scale communities who settled on these sites. Much too often a link is drawn between mining, metallurgy, and power, whereas ethnography clearly shows that in decentralized tribal societies a large workforce can be mobilized by drawing on kinship ties and other obligations. Working cooperatively on a communal, consensus-driven basis, great quarrying works can be accomplished and the production shared, without individuals manipulating this process and acquiring undue wealth. In the Alps, in some cases such groups continued exploiting copper ore deposits by seasonal or sporadic visits. In other areas mining apparently had to be abandoned due to the increasing efforts involved in agriculture and cattle breeding. Not all communities were in a position to intensify their attempts to benefit from the additional economic opportunities offered by mining and metallurgy, and in the long run this turned out to be a viable adaptation only in those areas with more abundant and sustainable ore deposits. This may be the reason why only in some potential mining areas could communities establish intensive copper production as we know it from the Middle Bronze Age Mitterberg area in the sixteenth to fourteenth centuries BC.

SMELTING: GEOLOGY-DERIVED 'STAGES' AND PREHISTORIC REALITY

At the beginning of metallurgy high-purity copper was used that derived from either native copper or the smelting of oxidic copper ores (copper-carbonate minerals). Later on this *Reinkupfer* was increasingly replaced by arsenical copper, which is not an alloy but typically has rather low arsenic contents (up to about 2 per cent), derived from the smelting of copper ores associated with arsenic-bearing minerals. As far as central Europe is concerned it is only during the Early Bronze Age that arsenical copper was replaced—on a large scale—by fahl-ore copper and other copper varieties derived from sulphidic ores. This sequence is interpreted in terms of geology and technological progress, since the earliest miners and smelters are thought to have worked the upper, oxidized regions of their mines with relatively simple technology, whereas the exploitation of the deeper, sulphidic ore bodies required advances both in mining and smelting techniques.

This standard model is derived from a simplified geological view of the ore bodies in question, and from early modern sources such as Agricola's description of the smelting of sulphidic copper ores in a multi-stage process that involved the roasting of the ore prior to smelting. It is this process we encounter in the Late Bronze Age eastern Alps. Copper production in substantial furnaces was increasingly standardized, resulting in the specific eastern Alpine tradition of multi-stage roasting and smelting already mentioned (the Mitterberg process). There is evidence of this process from a large number of Middle to Late Bronze Age copper production sites in the eastern Alps, often situated in the vicinity of potential ore outcrops. From the Early Bronze Age site at Buchberg, on the other hand, there is evidence of on-site smelting of fahlore minerals from neighbouring ore deposits in a one-step process without roasting. Apparently smelting was carried out in open hearths that left behind little archaeological trace apart from some slag (Martinek and Sydow 2004). This might explain why from some other sites evidence of smelting is controversial and not easily distinguished from the remains of casting and metalworking that is also attested in some of the settlements. However, at least in the eastern Alps smelting slag was widely used as a temper in pottery, thus providing indirect evidence of extractive metallurgy. In technological terms the processes involved were simple and had not yet reached the standardization apparent somewhat later in the Middle and Late Bronze Age.

So during the Bronze Age there was undoubtedly some kind of progress in smelting technique, and organizational patterns changed. Nonetheless, the standard model is rather simplistic, and there is increasing evidence for a more nuanced picture with the earliest working of sulphidic ores reaching back far into the Eneolithic. Early Bronze Age fahlore copper typically has high impurity levels, indicating the use of this specific type of sulphidic ore, and compositional data implies the early use of such copper prior to the Early Bronze Age in some parts of central Europe (e.g. 'diluted' fahlore copper in the Late/Final Neolithic of east-central Germany; Krause 2003). Furthermore, although sulphur is not routinely analysed for in many projects, it can be shown by metallography that Eneolithic/Copper Age objects occasionaly contain sulphide inclusions that point towards the early use of sulphidic and mixed oxidic/sulphidic ores.

From 5000 cal BC onwards, there is evidence of smelting in south-eastern Europe (Radivojević et al. 2010). The approach taken relied on the careful selection and processing of specific copper-oxide ores rich in manganese, which facilitated reduction and the formation of slag. Previously, from other Vinča sites evidence of thermally altered copper-carbonate minerals or 'slags' had been reported that were also thought to relate to smelting activities. Typically these are small pieces of slag whose interpretation as residues of smelting rather than slags from casting copper and forging activities is rather controversial (e.g. Bartelheim et al. 2002 on the Selevac evidence). But with the Belovode evidence it is quite clear that smelting could be carried out in ephemeral installations that leave little archaeological traces—an approach to early smelting found throughout the Old World that relies on highly concentrated, self-fluxing ores to produce small copper prills embedded in a matrix of partially smelted ore and slag (Hauptmann 2007). By a combination of metallography and the analysis of refractory ceramics this crucible-type smelting technique can be shown to have worked equally well on sulphidic copper ores as early as the second half of the fifth millennium BC in the Bulgarian Gumelnitsa and Varna groups (Ryndina, Indenbaum, and Kolosova 1999). At about the same time in the Münchhöfen culture (c.4500–3900 cal BC) from the site of Brixlegg, what is thought to be the earliest evidence of smelting in the north Alpine region is recorded (Bartelheim et al. 2002). There may be problems with such an early date (see above). Yet even if the metallurgical activities observed in fact belong to the somewhat younger Pfyn, Altheim, and Mondsee horizon, it is remarkable that at Brixlegg as well, drawing on nearby fahlore deposits, sulphidic copper ore was used already at an early stage.

Smelting evidence from the (late) fifth and fourth millennium BC tends to be problematic because of the poor archaeological visibility of the processes and installations involved. But early experimentation with both oxidic and sulphidic ores clearly has to be taken into consideration, and the smelting of the two types of ore does not represent two clear-cut technological stages. Hardly any mine follows the ideal of oxide ores on top and sulphidic underneath. This is why early miners found different types of copper minerals that typically—but by no means universally—could have been distinguished and sorted by colour and the like. Experimental work shows why this did not pose fundamental problems for subsequent smelting: it is just because early oxide ore smelting was 'primitive', using rather oxidizing conditions, that sulphidic ores could be incorporated without causing the failure of the entire process (Timberlake 2007; Hauptmann 2007).

Casting and Working: Technological Choice and Compositional 'Determinism'

Information on the basic production parameters of metal artefacts can be obtained from metallographic analyses, in other words from the examination of an object's microstructure under the optical microscope and by relating these findings to composition. In a long-term perspective there is clear patterning and the development of methods of casting and forging can be outlined. Thus it has been shown that the earliest Neolithic artefacts of native copper were hammered to shape and annealed to restore deformability. Much later, casting was introduced and there is circumstantial evidence that from an early stage heavy shaft-hole implements from the south-eastern European Eneolithic/Copper Age were cast in closed moulds. Some centuries later, with the Late Neolithic Altheim-type flat axes of the north Alpine region, there is unequivocal evidence for this casting method (Kienlin 2008b).

In general terms one would expect the production of copper-based weapons or tools to involve the following steps: casting—cold-working the as-cast object—annealing—final cold-hammering (Fig. 23.5). This procedure has a twofold aim: some degree of deformation is required to finish the as-cast object, a smooth surface is to be achieved and feeders or castings seams may need to be removed, which is done by hammering and subsequent grinding and polishing. If a stronger deformation is required, such as for shaping an axe's body or blade, this may necessitate more than one annealing process. Final cold-working, on the other hand, increases hardness and adds to the strength and durability of a weapon or tool. Late Neolithic Altheim-type axes and related forms clearly follow this procedure and their microstructures show traces of cold-working of the as-cast object, followed by annealing and final cold-hammering. Their producers fell short of recognizing the differential work-hardening of pure copper and arsenical copper. But they clearly operated on the basis of an empirically gained knowledge of the cold-working properties of their copper with low arsenic contents, and they certainly were interested in the hardness of their axes (Kienlin

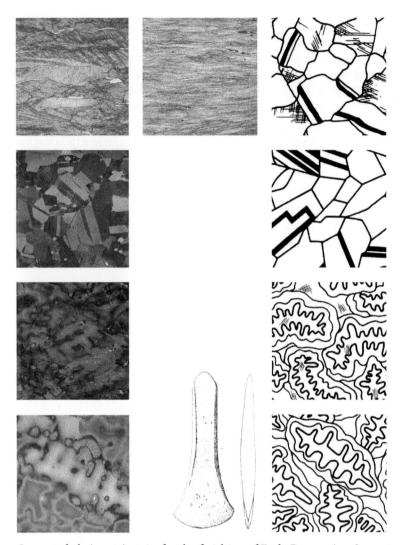

FIG. 23.5 Suggested *chaîne opératoire* for the finishing of Early Bronze Age Saxon type axes by a cycle of cold-working (bottom), intermediate annealing, and final cold-working (top) to increase hardness.

Drawing: author.

2008b). The tradition they established can be traced right up to the Early Bronze Age, when a two-step working of flanged axes is the rule (Kienlin 2008a). Profiting from the new fahlore-type copper and tin-bronze, at this stage a considerable increase in hardness was achieved by a rather strong final cold-work (Fig. 23.6).

Metallography, however, combined with compositional data may also be used to examine the knowledge of raw materials gained by prehistoric metalworkers and to deconstruct some modernist assumptions on the properties of the different types of copper and copper alloys they were working. Tin-bronze, for example, is thought to be superior to copper for a number of reasons: among them its lower casting temperature, its better casting properties,

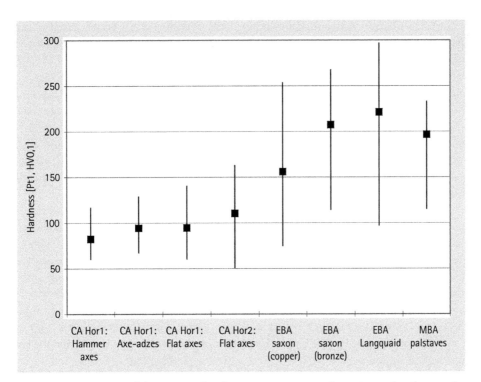

FIG. 23.6 Comparison of the average hardness, minimum, and maximum hardness values of various Eneolithic/Copper Age and Bronze Age axe types. Note the comparable increase in hardness achieved by the cold-working of Early Bronze Age fahlore copper (EBA: Saxon type copper) and tin bronze (all other Bronze Age forms).

Drawing: author.

and its higher hardness both in the as-cast state and after working. However, often such arguments fall short of the actual compositions used or the approach to metalworking taken. There are strong evolutionist notions involved in our conception of technological progress and the interpretation of changing compositional patterns. Thus, early low-tin bronzes in the 2–6 per cent range tend to be seen as a result of poor initial control over the alloying process or problems with access to tin, but the overall direction is thought obvious and directed towards the superior alloy—high-tin bronze. This certainly is true in retrospect, and eventually tin-bronze became the standard alloy of the Bronze Age. But in many parts of the Old World bronze did not replace copper for a considerable period of time, indicating that its adoption was 'a cultural choice, not a product of technological determinism' (Pare 2000: 25). In particular this is true wherever arsenical or fahlore copper was in widespread use, offering a serious alternative to tin-bronze, for example in parts of central Europe, but also in the Aegean or Iran, where arsenical copper and bronze coexisted for a long time. The British Isles, where tin-bronze replaced arsenical copper rather quickly, provide an example to the contrary (Needham et al. 1989). These are technological choices informed, on the one hand, by the rapid spread of metallurgical knowledge among metalworkers in a wider area and depending on the availability of different sorts of copper and tin. But they were taken against a local or regional background that needs to be understood in cultural terms and must not be subsumed to our modern knowledge of long-term trends in Copper to Bronze Age metallurgy.

Starting with the first step in metalworking, namely casting, it has been argued that along the sequence from pure copper via arsenical copper to fahlore copper and tin-bronze the presence of trace elements and the addition of tin allows for a reduction of the casting temperature. This is the first in a series of modernist assumptions related to the properties of different types of copper and copper alloys used in prehistory, and it is easily refuted by a look at the actual evidence (Kienlin 2008a): copper containing 'impurities' such as arsenic or tin solidifies over a wider temperature range between the so-called liquidus and solidus lines of the phase diagram. But for this interval to drop significantly below the melting point of pure copper (1,084°C), impurity contents in the plus 10 per cent range are required. Such concentrations are rarely found in Neolithic/Copper Age arsenical copper. Most of the earliest bronzes remain well below 10 per cent tin, so that during the early stages of metallurgy composition would have had little effect on casting temperature in the way suggested by many reviews of early metalworking. Moreover, even with higher trace-element contents in Early Bronze Age fahlore copper, and the advent of high-tin bronze in the second half of the Early Bronze Age, casting temperature did not drop. There are copper-sulphide inclusions in many objects that solidified at around 1,100 °C which provide evidence that casting still took place at high temperatures—which at this stage meant superheating the molten copper with beneficial effects on the success of the casting process. Our interest in lower casting temperatures clearly does not adequately reflect the concerns of prehistoric metalworkers.

A related point concerns the supposed effect of impurities, such as arsenic and the alloying element tin, on porosity and oxide content. It is possible that the wider solidification interval of impure or alloyed copper facilitated the casting of more complex objects because part of the molten copper remained liquid somewhat longer, and a complete fill of the casting mould was more easily achieved. This may apply, for example, to some Early Bronze Age pins and solid-hilted daggers, and requires a differentiated approach to the production of different kinds of ornaments and weapons or tools. It is not, however, an argument in favour of tin-bronze alone, since much Early Bronze Age fahlore copper would have offered the same advantage. Complex objects, however, are also known in rather pure copper. It is quite obvious that complex shapes such as Copper Age shaft-hole axes could be cast to a high standard using pure copper. Generally speaking, the success of casting was not dependent on composition alone but upon the care taken and the expertise acquired in various steps of the casting process.

As far as weapons and tools are concerned, during the Copper and Bronze Ages it is likely that advantages of new types of copper and copper alloys would have been most obvious and most readily taken up in the wider field of mechanical properties. But again, we must be wary of transferring our knowledge derived from a reading of modern materials science to traditional prehistoric metalworking. The presence of arsenic and even more of tin increases the as-cast hardness of the resulting (natural or artificial) copper alloy by a mechanism called solid-solution hardening. But with arsenic contents up to around 3–4 per cent this effect is limited (~ 60–70 HV), and even for tin contents of around 10 per cent are required for an increase in hardness to twice the value of pure copper at 50 HV (Lechtman 1996). A minor increase in hardness and strength at lower concentrations may or may not have been noticed. It may have been relevant in the production of copper objects such as ornaments that could not be cold-worked, or whenever mechanical properties were of little interest. In the case of ornaments (or prestigious weaponry), colour also has to be taken into consideration to account for the presence of trace and alloying elements. But for all weapons proper and tools it is a modernist misconception that prehistoric metalworkers should have relied on manipulating as-cast hardness via composition: from the Late Neolithic onwards hardness was a function of both composition and at times substantial cold-working. As-cast hardness (i.e. solid-solution hardening) was certainly a concept familiar to the metalworkers themselves in this period. But whenever an axe or other bronze object entered the sphere of exchange and use, its mechanical properties were determined by previous cold-working and would have been attributed to the effort involved in forging and the expertise of the smith.

Here, too, composition is thought to play an important role and different types of copper and copper alloy are aligned in terms of progress and improvement because of (assumed) differences in deformability and work-hardening of arsenical copper and tin-bronze in particular. These differences, however, are comparatively slight when viewed in the light of more recent experimental data. Often they occur under circumstances not directly relevant to prehistoric metalworking: arsenical copper, for example, is clearly more ductile than pure copper and can be worked to a very high reduction in thickness and a considerable increase in hardness. Bronze may achieve even higher hardness values, but this requires tin concentrations in excess of 10 per cent, not reached in a majority of early tin-bronzes. In addition, unrealistically high deformation rates are involved from a Copper or Bronze Age perspective: metallographic analyses show that cold-work typically was in the 20–50 per cent range of reduction in thickness, and working was not done with the highest possible hardness of the respective copper or copper alloy in mind. Rather, it was carried out to profit from the strong initial increase in hardness at lower deformation, which for different concentrations of arsenic and tin is very similar. Because of this initial closeness and parallelism in cold-working behaviour, arsenical copper, fahlore copper, and tin-bronzes reached comparable hardness values (see Fig. 23.6). For the same reason the alleged brittleness of copper compared with arsenical copper or tin-bronze may not have been as relevant as modern expectations have us believe. Irrespective of composition, working was simply not powerful enough to cause unacceptable embrittlement.

Metalworking and Society

The production of weapons or tools is, of course, just one domain in which Bronze Age metalworkers excelled, and in the course of time an amazing array of quite sophisticated techniques became available for the production of elaborately crafted and lavishly decorated metal objects (see Chapter 25). The Nebra disc comes to mind in this context and inlays of copper, gold, and silver may also be found on late Early Bronze Apa swords from the Carpathian Basin or on the famous daggers recovered from the Late Bronze Age Shaft Graves of Mycenae. The Late Bronze Age also saw the production of vessels of bronze or precious metals, and both weapons and defensive armour, such as highly decorated shields, placed great demands on the skills of their producers.

At some later stage there was obviously a two-tier system of metalworking, for it is unlikely that every metalworker was able to apply all techniques known or to work both in copper and gold, nor was there a demand for such objects in every community. Surprisingly little is known, however, about the actual organization of metalworking, and maybe it is in consequence of the sheer impressiveness of some of its more elaborate remains that metallurgy tends to become so readily enmeshed in narratives of elite control over production and exchange. We are confronted with a highly elaborate material culture, which we cannot imagine 'ordinary' people were capable of crafting, nor can we imagine why anyone should have bothered without aggrandizement in mind or having pressure put upon him. We tend to be concerned with elites and their display of wealth, when in fact during most of the Bronze Age and in most areas we are dealing with a segmentary society very much in a Neolithic tradition and depending mainly on agriculture and animal husbandry. There is a centralization bias in our approaches to Bronze Age society and we should consider the possibility that hereditary elites and institutionalized social ranking were less stable and not as common across Bronze Age Europe as we tend to expect. We are entitled then to ask by what mechanisms other than elite control the practice of metallurgy and the transmission of metallurgical knowledge from one generation to the next may have been organized.

An alternative model may refer to the essentially kinship-based organization of traditional society. Apart from structuring traditional groups as a whole, kinship is of particular importance for any kind of specialized tasks extending beyond everyday household-based production. For the right and the ability to carry out such activities often depend on affiliation to a particular segment of society. One does not become a founder or smith in the same way one decides to study archaeology, but by descent from a particular lineage. The individual is not only taught the knowledge and practical skills required for his future 'profession' but picks up the norms and values, the *habitus*, of his descent group. By socialization he (or she) becomes not only a metalworker but finds his position in a particular kinship group and in society as a whole (Costin 1991; Kuijpers 2008).

The ethnographic evidence of craft specialization was reviewed many years ago by Michael Rowlands (1971), and in such kinship-based groups there is great variability with regard to craft specialization, organization of production, social position of (metal-)craftsmen, the activities carried out and objects produced. We find specialized full-time metalworkers attached to an elite, alongside those producing for a village community that derives most of its living from agriculture, the metalworkers being firmly integrated in local groups in spite of ethnic differences and high mobility, both smiths held in high esteem and those who were the subject of superstition and segregation. Clearly, metallurgy cannot be said in any way to be connected exclusively to elites. Part-time metalworkers may be able to produce the most complex objects and the communication of metallurgical knowledge does not have to rely on the presence of strong leadership and political control to be efficient. More likely it was 'self-organizing' in some manner, among segments of Bronze Age society familiar with the practice of metallurgy, and part of wider kinship-based networks of information exchange.

It is suggested that the practice of metallurgy was passed along kinship lines, and command of such (ritually framed?) knowledge set apart those involved from their neighbours, and from others. This is true to the extent that—ethnographically—in oral societies some kind of 'secrecy' seems to be a precondition for the transmission and stability of such 'special' knowledge and related practical skills. It should not be taken to imply, however, that metallurgists were foreigners to their supporting communities, the notorious 'itinerant craftsmen'. Ethnography implies that metalworkers operating in a foreign cultural context are rare. Typically mobility, if any, is restricted to an area with some kind of previously established contact and affinity in terms of communication, exchange, and/or a broadly similar sociocultural background. We should expect, then, that metalworkers were conceived as more or less firmly integrated within local communities (see Kuijpers 2008 on the problem of 'detribalization'). Demand initially was low, the amount of copper won and worked was small, and metal only gradually replaced other materials such as flint or stone in the large-scale production of weapons and implements. This implies some kind of part-time specialization and parallel involvement of metalworkers in subsistence activities. Thus, metalworkers were not that much 'special' or foreign, and pressure put on local communities to support metallurgy would have been low. It is another matter whether mining and/or smelting were communal events or involved 'secret' knowledge, and whether attempts were made to restrict access to such activities. The latter has been suggested, for example, for stone and copper mining in the British Isles and smelting in the Bronze Age Aegean (e.g. O'Brien 2007). In any case, people may not have been working *for* their metallurgist or have been obliged to keep the provision of a valued commodity going, but they may have been engaging *with* him (her?) in some communally sanctioned raw-material procurement acitivity.

This means that the casting and working of copper should be seen more in the context of already existing 'technologies' and intra-community 'specialization': it is thought likely that the knowledge and skills involved were 'special' or complex enough to be handed down in particular families, lineages, or clans. So not every community member was able to cast and work copper, and possibly metalworkers' knowledge of and ties with segments of far-off communities were closer than was normally the case, particularly so if they themselves had to procure copper from abroad. But to some extent this may reflect the situation of working other materials such as stone, flint, wood, or bone, some of which were also obtained from abroad, and also provide early indications of intra-community 'specialization'. So initially metalworking may have been just one 'specialization' or preference among others, albeit one that developed into a firm tradition with a long-term tendency towards increasing scale, and increasingly becoming a full-time occupation.

Bibliography

Bailey, D. W. (2000). *Balkan Prehistory*. London: Routledge.

Bartelheim, M., Eckstein, K., Huijsmans, M., Krauss, R., and Pernicka, E. (2002). 'Kupferzeitliche Metallgewinnung in Brixlegg, Österreich', in M. Bartelheim, E. Pernicka, and R. Krause (eds.), *Die Anfänge der Metallurgie in der Alten Welt. Forschungen zur Archäometrie und Altertumswissenschaft 1*. Rahden/Westf.: Verlag Marie Leidorf GmbH, 33–82.

—— and Niederschlag, E. (1998). 'Untersuchungen zur Buntmetallurgie, insbesondere des Kupfers und Zinns, im sächsisch-böhmischen Erzgebirge und dessen Umland', *Arbeits- und Forschungsberichte zur sächsischen Bodendenkmalpflege*, 4: 8–87.

Bátora, J. (2003). 'Kupferne Schaftlochäxte in Mittel-, Ost- und Südosteuropa (Zu Kulturkontakten und Datierung—Äneolithikum/Frühbronzezeit)', *Slovenská Archeológia*, 51: 1–38.

Borić, D. (2009). 'Absolute dating of metallurgical innovations in the Vinča culture of the Balkans', in T. L. Kienlin and B. Roberts (eds.), *Metals and Societies: Studies in Honour of Barbara S. Ottaway*, Universitätsforschungen zur prähistorischen Archäologie, 169. Bonn: Habelt, 191–245.

Butler, J. J. (1978). 'Rings and ribs: the copper types of the "Ingot Hoards" of the Central European Early Bronze Age', in M. Ryan (ed.), *The Origins of Metallurgy in Atlantic Europe*, Proceedings of the Fifth Atlantic Colloquium Dublin, 1978. Dublin: Stationery Office, 345–62.

Costin, C. L. (1991). 'Craft specialization: issues in defining, documenting, and explaining the organization of production', in M. B. Schiffer (ed.), *Archaeological Method and Theory*, 3. Tucson: University of Arizona Press, 1–56.

Gleirscher, P. (2007). 'Frühes Kupfer und früher Kupferbergbau im und um den Ostalpenraum', in M. Blečić, M. Črešnar, B. Hänsel, A. Hellmuth, E. Kaiser, and C. Metzner-Nebelsick (eds.), *Scripta praehistorica in honorem Biba Teržan*, Situla, 44. Ljubljana: Narodni Muzej Slovenije, 93–110.

Hänsel, B. and Medović, P. (2004). 'Eine Bronzegießerwerkstatt der frühen Bronzezeit in Feudvar bei Mošorin in der Vojvodina', in B. Hänsel (ed.), *Parerga Praehistorica. Jubiläumsschrift zur Prähistorischen Archäologie. 15 Jahre UPA*, Universitätsforschungen zur prähistorischen Archäologie, 100. Bonn: Habelt, 83–111.

Hauptmann, A. (2007). 'Alten Berg- und Hüttenleuten auf die Finger geschaut: Zur Entschlüsselung berg- und hüttenmännischer Techniken', in G. A. Wagner (ed.), *Einführung in die Archäometrie*. Berlin: Springer, 115–37.

Höppner, B., Bartelheim, M., Huijsmans, M., Krauss, R., Martinek, K.-P., Pernicka, E., and Schwab, R. (2005). 'Prehistoric copper production in the Inn Valley (Austria), and the earliest copper in Central Europe', *Archaeometry*, 47: 293–315.

Junghans, S., Sangmeister, E., and Schröder, M. (1968). *Kupfer und Bronze in der frühen Metallzeit Europas. Die Materialgruppen beim Stand von 12000 Analysen*, Studien zu den Anfängen der Metallurgie, Band 2. Berlin: Mann.

Kienlin, T. L. (2008a). *Frühes Metall im nordalpinen Raum. Eine Untersuchung zu technologischen und kognitiven Aspekten früher Metallurgie anhand der Gefüge frühbronzezeitlicher Beile*. Universitätsforschungen zur prähistorischen Archäologie, 162. Bonn: Habelt.

—— (2008b). 'Tradition and innovation in Copper Age metallurgy: results of a metallographic examination of flat axes from Eastern Central Europe and the Carpathian Basin', *Proceedings of the Prehistoric Society*, 74: 79–107.

—— (2010). *Traditions and Transformations: Approaches to Eneolithic (Copper Age) and Bronze Age Metalworking and Society in Eastern Central Europe and the Carpathian Basin*, British Archaeological Reports (International Series), 2,184. Oxford: Archaeopress.

—— and Stöllner, T. (2009). 'Singen copper, Alpine settlement and Early Bronze Age mining: is there a need for elites and strongholds?', in T. L. Kienlin and B. W. Roberts (eds.), *Metals and Societies: Studies in Honour of Barbara S. Ottaway*, Universitätsforschungen zur prähistorischen Archäologie, 169. Bonn: Habelt, 67–104.

Krause, R. (2003). *Studien zur kupfer- und frühbronzezeitlichen Metallurgie zwischen Karpatenbecken und Ostsee*, Vorgeschichtliche Forschungen, 24. Rahden/Westf.: Verlag Marie Leidorf GmbH.

—— (2005). 'Bronzezeitliche Burgen in den Alpen. Befestigte Siedlungen der frühen bis mittleren Bronzezeit', in B. Horejs, R. Jung, E. Kaiser, and B. Teržan (eds.), *Interpretationsraum Bronzezeit. Bernhard Hänsel von seinen Schülern gewidmet*, Universitätsforschungen zur prähistorischen Archäologie, 121. Bonn: Habelt, 389–413.

Kristiansen, K. and Larsson, T. B. (2005). *The Rise of Bronze Age Society: Travels, Transmissions and Transformations*. Cambridge: Cambridge University Press.

Kuijpers, M. H. G. (2008). *Bronze Age Metalworking in the Netherlands (c.2000–800 BC): A Research into the Preservation of Metallurgy-Related Artefacts and the Social Position of the Smith*. Leiden: Sidestone Press.

Lechtman, H. (1996). 'Arsenic bronze: dirty copper or chosen alloy? a view from the Americas', *Journal of Field Archaeology*, 23: 477–514.

Liversage, D. (1994). 'Interpreting composition patterns in ancient bronze: the Carpathian Basin', *Acta Archaeologica*, 65: 57–134.

Maran, J. (1998). *Kulturwandel auf dem griechischen Festland und den Kykladen im späten 3. Jahrtausend v. Chr. Studien zu den kulturellen Verhältnissen in Südosteuropa und dem zentralen sowie östlichen Mittelmeerraum in der späten Kupfer- und frühen Bronzezeit*. 2 Bände, Universitätsforschungen zur prähistorischen Archäologie, 53. Bonn: Habelt.

Martinek, K.-P. and Sydow, W. (2004). 'Frühbronzezeitliche Kupfermetallurgie im Unterinntal (Nordtirol). Rohstoffbasis, archäologische und archäometallurgische Befunde', in G. Weisgerber and G. Goldenberg (eds.), *Alpenkupfer—Rame delle Alpi. Der Anschnitt, Beiheft 17*. Bochum: Deutsches Bergbau-Museum, 199–211.

Matuschik, I. (1998). 'Kupferfunde und Metallurgie-Belege, zugleich ein Beitrag zur Geschichte der kupferzeitlichen Dolche Mittel-, Ost- und Südosteuropas', in M. Mainberger, *Das Moordorf von Reute. Archäologische Untersuchungen in der jungneolithischen Siedlung Reute-Schorrenried*. Staufen i. Br.: Teraqua, 207–61.

Muhly, J. D. (1985). 'Sources of tin and the beginnings of bronze metallurgy', *American Journal of Archaeology*, 89: 275–91.

Needham, S. P., Leese, M. N., Hook, D. R., and Hughes, M. J. (1989). 'Developments in the Early Bronze Age metallurgy of southern Britain', *World Archaeology*, 20: 383–402.

O'Brien, W. (2007). 'Miners and farmers: local settlement contexts for Bronze Age mining', in C. Burgess, P. Topping, and F. Lynch (eds.), *Beyond Stonehenge: Essays on the Bronze Age in Honour of Colin Burgess*. Oxford: Oxbow Books, 20–30.

Otto, H. and Witter, W. (1952). *Handbuch der ältesten vorgeschichtlichen Metallurgie in Mitteleuropa*. Leipzig: Barth.

Pare, C. F. E. (2000). 'Bronze and the Bronze Age', in C. F. E. Pare, *Metals Make the World Go Round: The Supply and Circulation of Metals in Bronze Age Europe*. Proceedings of a Conference held at the University of Birmingham in June 1997. Oxford: Oxbow Books, 1–38.

Parzinger, H. (1993). *Studien zur Chronologie und Kulturgeschichte der Jungstein-, Kupfer- und Frühbronzezeit zwischen Karpaten und Mittlerem Taurus*, Römisch-Germanische Forschungen, 52. Mainz: Von Zabern.

—— (2002). 'Das Zinn in der Bronzezeit Eurasiens', in Ü. Yalçin (ed.), *Anatolian Metal II. Der Anschnitt, Beiheft 15*. Bochum: Deutsches Bergbau-Museum, 159–77.

Pernicka, E. (1990). 'Gewinnung und Verbreitung der Metalle in prähistorischer Zeit', *Jahrbuch des Römisch-Germanischen Zentralmuseums Mainz*, 37: 21–129.

—— (1998). 'Die Ausbreitung der Zinnbronze im 3. Jahrtausend', in B. Hänsel (ed.), *Mensch und Umwelt in der Bronzezeit Europas. Abschlusstagung der Kampagne des Europarates 'Die Bronzezeit: das erste goldene Zeitalter Europas' an der Freien Universität Berlin, 17.–19. März 1997*. Kiel: Oetker-Voges, 135–47.

Pittioni, R. (1957). *Urzeitlicher Bergbau auf Kupfererz und Spurenanalyse. Beiträge zum Problem der Relation Lagerstätte-Fertigobjekt. Archaeologia Austriaca, Beiheft 1*. Vienna: F. Deuticke.

Preuschen, E. (1967). *Urzeitlicher Kupfererzbergbau in den österreichischen Alpen*, Leobener Grüne Hefte, 104. Vienna: Montan-Verlag.

Primas, M. (1996). *Velika Gruda I. Hügelgräber des frühen 3. Jahrtausends v. Chr. im Adriagebiet—Velika Gruda, Mala Gruda und ihr Kontext*, Universitätsforschungen zur prähistorischen Archäologie, 32. Bonn: Habelt.

Radivojević, M., Rehren, T., Pernicka, E., Šljivar, D., Brauns, M., and Borić, D. (2010). 'On the origins of extractive metallurgy: new evidence from Europe', *Journal of Archaeological Science*, 37: 2,775–87.

Roberts, B. W., Thornton, C. P., and Pigott, V. C. (2009). 'Development of metallurgy in Eurasia', *Antiquity*, 83: 1,012–22.

Rowlands, M. J. (1971). 'The archaeological interpretation of prehistoric metalworking', *World Archaeology*, 3: 210–24.

Ryndina, N., Indenbaum, G., and Kolosova, V. (1999). 'Copper production from polymetallic sulphide ores in the northeastern Balkan Eneolithic culture', *Journal of Archaeological Science*, 26: 1,059–68.

Schreiner, M. (2007). *Erzlagerstätten im Hrontal, Slowakei. Genese und prähistorische Nutzung*, Forschungen zur Archäometrie und Altertumswissenschaft, 3. Rahden/Westf.: Verlag Marie Leidorf GmbH.

Shennan, S. (1993). 'Commodities, transactions, and growth in the Central European Early Bronze Age', *Journal of European Archaeology*, 1.2: 59–72.

—— (1995). *Bronze Age Copper Producers of the Eastern Alps: Excavations at St. Veit-Klinglberg*, Universitätsforschungen zur prähistorischen Archäologie, 27. Bonn: Rudolf Habelt.

Timberlake, S. (2007). 'The use of experimental archaeology/archaeometallurgy for the understanding and reconstruction of Early Bronze Age mining and smelting technologies', in S. La Niece, D. Hook, and P. Craddock (eds.), *Metals and Mines*. London: Archetype Publications and The British Museum, 27–36.

CHAPTER 24

BRONZE AGE COPPER MINING IN EUROPE

WILLIAM O'BRIEN

The many thousands of copper, bronze, and gold objects known from the Bronze Age in Europe reflect the growing dependency on metal in this period. This was preceded by the use of copper and gold during the Chalcolithic, which occurred in different regions between the fifth and third millennia BC. Technical advances and an increasing demand for metal led to the widespread adoption of bronze by 2000 BC, or shortly afterwards. This was made possible by the discovery of copper and tin sources in many regions. The metal from these mines was supplied to areas lacking their own resources, creating trade networks and economic opportunities for individuals and groups that had wider social repercussions. A striking feature of the Bronze Age is the way that many regions were able to develop bronzeworking to a sophisticated level without becoming directly involved in mining or metal production.

Over the past one hundred years Bronze Age copper mines have been identified in many parts of Europe, with major research projects ongoing in Russia, Cyprus, Austria, France, Spain, Britain, and Ireland. This reflects the widespread geological occurrence and surface exposure of copper deposits. These, however, are not evenly distributed across Europe, which partly explains why it took three millennia or so for metallurgy to spread throughout the continent. It would not have been possible to exploit all of these copper deposits in the Bronze Age, as many occur at great depth, have a low metal content and complex composition that requires advanced treatment. Conversely, many locations where copper was extracted in the Bronze Age were not economically viable in historic times, which can contribute to the survival of such mines. The distribution of mines also reflects the efforts of some source regions to control metal supply by limiting the spread of mining expertise and metallurgical knowledge.

The selection of a particular copper deposit for mining was determined by several factors. These include the geological environment and topographic setting, the nature and concentration of the mineralization, and the available technology. Various sociocultural factors are also relevant, such as the perceived 'ownership' of the resource, the motivation to invest time and energy to exploit it and the broader significance of the resulting metal. Not all regions with copper deposits responded in the same way to the opportunities presented by the new technology. Some were less receptive to the spread of the new technology due perhaps to their cultural outlook, other economic priorities, or an inability or reluctance to mobilize resources. Others chose not to engage in copper mining or primary metal production, opting instead to obtain supplies through trade, as did those areas with no natural resources. Some regions exploited metal resources at a low level, while for others copper mining was a key economic activity over many centuries that shaped the development of their societies. Different regions had their own mining traditions, which were both historically and environmentally contingent, as well as being determined by cultural choices and economic circumstances.

Bronze Age Copper Mines in Europe

Research in many regions began with the discovery of 'old man's workings' during metal mining carried out in recent centuries. Early explorations in Austria provided the first major insight into Bronze Age copper mining (Zschocke and Preuschen 1932). In recent decades there have been numerous programmes of geo-archaeological research and radiocarbon dating at early mine sites across Europe.

The archaeology of Bronze Age copper mining is distinctive to this activity and its physical environment. Much depends on the time and energy commitment to mining at a given location. This involved some measure of rock extraction, and so most mines comprise one or more surface openings that may lead into underground workings. These can vary in size and form depending on the geological setting, the approach to mining, and the scale of operation. They include shallow and deep surface pitting and trenches, vertical or inclined shafts, and tunnels, which are generally accompanied by surface dumps of broken rock spoil. Many of these mines contained work camps where hut shelters, hearths and cooking areas, equipment and fuel stores were located, as well as places where copper ore was smelted to metal in furnaces.

The following is a brief survey of the main centres of Bronze Age copper mining presently known in Europe (Fig. 24.1).

East Mediterranean

Cyprus was a significant source of metal in the Bronze Age, with the very name of this island derived from the Greek word for copper. The earliest mining dates to the fourth millennium BC, with the extraction of native copper and oxidized ores. This was followed in the Bronze Age by mining of copper ores at Apliki and elsewhere in the Troodos Mountains of central and western Cyprus (Gale 2001). From 1600 to 1200 BC Cyprus became a major supplier of copper in the east Mediterranean, with trade extending into the Near East and Egypt, and as far west as Sardinia and Sicily. This is confirmed by lead-isotope studies and by the discovery of the Uluburun shipwreck off the coast of Turkey. Dating to the fourteenth century BC, this ship contained a cargo with some 11 tons of oxhide ingots probably of Cypriot copper. There were numerous other copper sources in the east Mediterranean, with lead-isotope studies pointing to possible early mining in the Laurion region in Attica, the islands of Siphnos, Kythnos, Seriphos, and Syros (all Greece), as well as in Sardinia. In most cases the mine sites have not been identified with any certainty, though there is evidence of early mining in many

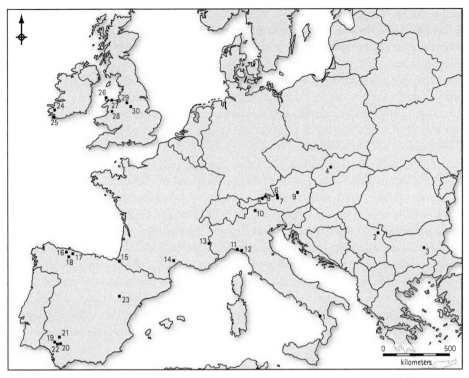

FIG. 24.1 Chalcolithic and Bronze Age copper mines in Europe. 1. Grotta della Monaca; 2. Rudna Glava; 3. Aibunar; 4. Špania Dolina; 5. Schwarz-Brixlegg; 6. Mitterberg, Bischofshofen; 7. St Veit; 8. Glemmtal; 9. Eisenerz; 10. Trentino; 11. Libiola; 12. Monte Loreto; 13. St Véran; 14. Cabrières; 15. Causiat; 16. El Aramo; 17. El Milagro; 18. La Profunda; 19. Cuchillares; 20. La Loba; 21. Berrocal; 22. Chinflón; 23. Loma de la Tejeria; 24. Ross Island; 25. Mount Gabriel; 26. Parys Mountain; 27. Great Orme; 28. Cwm Ystwyth; 29. Alderley Edge; 30. Ecton.

Source: author.

locations. An unusual copper mine has been investigated at Grotta della Monaca, a natural limestone cave located 740 metres above sea level in Calabria, Italy. Mining began during the Palaeolithic with the removal of goethite, and was followed in the fourth millennium BC by extraction of copper-carbonate minerals using stone hammers and bone tools, which continued into the Middle Bronze Age.

South-East/Eastern Europe

The south-eastern part of Europe is highly metalliferous, with rich deposits of copper and other metals in the west Carpathian and Transylvanian mountain belts. This region has the oldest evidence of copper metallurgy in Europe, with copper finds dating to the sixth millennium BC. While there was some early use of native copper, the discovery of mines and smelting sites confirms that copper ores were processed in this region during the fifth millennium BC. One of the best-known copper mines is the site of Rudna Glava near Majdanpek in eastern Serbia, discovered during modern exploitation of an open-cast iron mine. Archaeological excavations in the 1970s revealed prehistoric shafts worked by firesetting, stone hammers, antler picks, and bone tools (Jovanović 1979). These mines followed vertical veins of copper ore to a depth of up to 20 m from platforms cut into the hillside. The discovery of Vinča culture pottery and recent radiocarbon analyses date this mine to the later fifth or early fourth millennium BC.

Early copper production is also recorded in Bulgaria where a Chalcolithic mine contemporary with Rudna Glava was excavated at Ai Bunar in the Sredna Gora mountains. The miners used similar techniques to work narrow open trenches to a depth of 20 m along parallel veins of copper ore in the dolomitized limestone geology (Cernych 1978). The analysis of early copper objects indicates that Ai Bunar and Rudna Glava were not the only early sources for copper ore in the Balkans. Another possible early copper mine has been identified at Mali Sturac, a site in the Rudnik mountain range in central Serbia.

Copper metallurgy was established in eastern Europe by the fourth millennium BC. This was also probably based on the discovery of local copper sources in mountain areas such as the Slovak Erzgebirge. Though research is lacking, there is evidence of early copper mining at Špania Dolina and Slovinsky in central Slovakia, where pottery of Chalcolithic and Late Bronze Age date was found in mine spoil containing stone hammers. It is also evident that copper was already being exchanged over long distances, with some supply from eastern or central Europe reaching as far north as Denmark in the fourth millennium BC. Copper may even have been obtained from mines in Eurasia, with the most notable in the Kargaly district in the southern Urals of Russia. Mining commenced there in the later fourth and early third millennium BC, reaching a peak in the second millennium BC when there were many thousands of individual mine operations (Chernych 1998). The copper-bearing sandstone geology was mined for malachite and azurite ore, using opencasts, shafts, drifts,and underground tunnelling to depths of up to 40 m. The amount of copper from these mines was enormous, with some estimates suggesting that up to 2 million tonnes of copper ore were extracted during the Bronze Age.

Central Europe and the Eastern Alps

Copper was widely used in central Europe during the late fifth, fourth, and third millennia BC. Artefact analysis confirms that much of this early copper, the so-called Singen type (see Chapter 23), contained arsenic, antimony, silver, and nickel, derived from the processing of fahlores (*Fahlerzen*, grey ores) of the tennantite-tetrahedrite series. This older metallurgical tradition was to continue into the Early Bronze Age, c.2300–2000 BC, with the widespread adoption of tin bronze made with fahlore copper. The mines that provided this copper have not all been identified, with possible sources in the Harz and Erzgebirge mountain ranges, and the mountains of central-west Germany. There is some evidence for fahlore smelting in Austria in the early fourth millennium BC, from Brixlegg in the north Tyrol and the Götschenberg hilltop settlement near Bischofshofen, south of Salzburg. The discovery of thousands of *Ösenringe* (ring-ingots) in central Europe, with characteristic arsenic/antimony compositions, reveals an extensive use of fahlore in the Early Bronze Age. This was largely based on the use of Alpine ores, from mines in the Inn Valley and other locations in Austria, which achieved an industrial scale of production by the Late Bronze Age.

The use of *Ösenring* copper, c.1800–1600 BC, overlapped with a new type of copper in central Europe towards the end of the Early Bronze Age. This had a higher purity and was probably smelted from copper-iron sulphide (chalcopyrite) ore. The most likely source was the eastern Alps, specifically Austria where copper production is recorded from several mining districts. Actual mine workings are known in some cases, but often their existence must be inferred from the discovery of smelting sites that presumably utilized local ores. The focus of this mining was a belt of Palaeozoic sedimentary rocks ('greywacke zone') crossing the Austrian Alps. The most important copper sources were in the Salzach Valley, including both the Mitterberg mountain area west of Bischofshofen, the St Veit area to the south, and the Glemmtal area to the west (Goldenberg 1998). Farther west, Bronze Age mining was undertaken in the Kelchalm and Schwaz-Brixlegg areas of north Tyrol, and the Matrei area of east Tyrol. Bronze Age smelting sites have also been identified in eastern Austria, notably at Eisenerz in Obersteiermark. Mining also extended into the southern Alps in northern Italy, with Chalcolithic and Late Bronze Age copper smelting recorded in the Trentino district of south Tyrol. These were presumably based on the many occurrences of copper ore in this region, with workings of possible Bronze Age date identified at Vetriolo near Levico.

Radiocarbon dating and other evidence indicate that copper mining began in Austria around 1800 BC, and intensified from 1500–1000 BC in the transition from the Middle to Late Bronze Age, continuing into the Iron Age to around 400 BC (Stöllner 2009). The emphasis in mining up to 1200 BC was on the chalcopyrite deposits of the Mitterberg, with the fahlore deposits of Schwaz-Brixlegg in northern Tyrol being actively exploited from 1200 to 700 BC. Research in the Mitterberg mining district provides much detail on the organization and technology of this mining. The focus was a series of large quartz-sulphide veins containing chalcopyrite ore, which crossed the mountain ridges over many kilometres. Surface workings, or *Pingen*, of varying depth have been identified at numerous locations along these veins. The deepest workings are 190 m deep and are best exposed in the Arthurstollen adit as a complex network of tunnels and galleries. There was an extraordinary preservation of wooden mine equipment in these workings (Pittioni 1951).

The production of copper in the eastern Alps developed from a small-scale activity associated with seasonal pastoralism in the Early Bronze Age to a mining-based economy in the Middle and Late Bronze Age. There is evidence of permanent mining communities in the Alpine zone by 1600 BC. This is reflected in the establishment of hill forts associated with the production and supply of copper, sites like the Götschenberg at Bishofshofen or the Klinglberg at St Veit. The scale of the Austrian copper mines is impressive, with evidence of an industrial level of copper production by 1500 BC, employing an advanced shaft-furnace technology. Estimates from the Mitterberg suggest that as much as 18,000 tonnes of raw copper were extracted there during the Bronze Age. This copper was exchanged over a wide area, as evidenced by discoveries of large quantities of copper ingots along river valleys in the north Alpine lowland leading into southern Bavaria, lower Austria, and Moravia. By the Late Bronze Age the circulation of east Alpine copper would have been widespread across Europe, reaching even Britain and Ireland.

France and the Western Alps

The oldest known copper mines in western Europe have been identified in the mountainous region of Liguria, north-west Italy. Early shaft mines discovered at Libiola in the nineteenth century are now dated to the later fourth millennium BC, while those at Monte Loreto were worked *c.*3500–2500 BC (Maggi and Pearce 2005). There is no evidence that these mines continued to be worked in the Bronze Age, but recent lead-isotope analysis has identified potential ore sources in the west Italian Alps.

Farther west, evidence of early copper mining has been uncovered at St Véran in the French Alps, close to the Italian border. The copper-iron sulphide, bornite, was mined there c.2400–1800 BC, and possibly later in the Bronze Age. Narrow galleries were worked along exposed veins at an altitude of 2,300 m. Excavation at Clausis uncovered an ore treatment site 350 m below these mines, with evidence for an advanced smelting of bornite ore in the Late Chalcolithic/Early Bronze Age. Indirect evidence of Bronze Age mining has been discovered in the Grandes Rousses massif, where metal pollution in glacial varves points to local production of copper c.2200–1650 BC.

The earliest evidence of copper mining and metallurgy in France comes from the south-east part of the Languedoc in the third millennium BC. It is possible to distinguish an early phase of copper metallurgy, c.3100–2500 BC, influenced by Alpine/Italian traditions, separate from production c.2500–2100 BC associated with Beaker pottery cultures with Iberian links. This centred on the small mining district of Cabrières-Peret (Hérault), where a series of copper workings and production sites have been identified (Ambert 1995). These occur on three small massifs, namely at Vallarade (the mines of Les Neuf Bouches and Le Petit-Bois), Pioch-Farrus, and La Roussignole.

Excavation at the mining site of Les Neuf Bouches identified evidence of Chalcolithic mining dated 2900–2500 BC. The mine is near the settlement of La Capitelle du Broum, dated 3100–2800 BC, where stone-walled houses and Late Neolithic pottery, as well as evidence of copper smelting and ingot production, was found. This is confirmed by investigations at Pioch Farrus site 448, where pottery, stone-mining tools, crucibles, and metallurgical products were recovered in contexts that are radiocarbon dated 3100–2900 BC. Excavations at Pioch-Farrus mine IV revealed firesetting extraction and use of stone hammers dated 2500–2200 BC. The nearby production site of Roque-Fenestre has evidence of copper production from 2600–2000 BC, involving stages of crushing and washing copper ore to separate out the metal-bearing minerals, followed by roasting, smelting, and slag treatment to extract copper prills. The ore used was tetrahedrite, a type of fahlore, which is naturally rich in copper, antimony, and silver. This antimonial copper has been identified in over half of the metal tools from the third millennium BC identified in the Languedoc.

Copper production at Cabrières continued into the Bronze Age. Excavation of a small mine working at La Vierge recovered stone-mining tools and a pottery vessel of the Early Bronze Age. Evidence of firesetting extraction dated 1740–1120 BC has been identified at Vallarade. There is also evidence of Late Bronze Age mining at Les Neuf Bouches dated 850–740 BC. Other early copper mines have been identified along the south-western end of the Massif Central in southern France. These include mines at Bouco-Payrol in Aveyron, and possibly in the district of Seronais between St Girons and Foix in the south. The Bouco-Payoll mines comprise a series of workings connected to natural caverns in karstified limestone. While the deeper workings are of Roman date, there is evidence of narrow tunnels and shafts closer to the surface where stone hammers were found with Early Bronze Age pottery.

Iberia

The Iberian Peninsula is one the most mineralized regions in Europe, with a long history of metal mining from prehistoric to Roman, medieval, and modern times. The earliest evidence for early copper metallurgy dates to the fifth millennium BC, with strong regional metalworking traditions emerging during the Chalcolithic and Bronze Age. These were based on local exploitation of copper and tin ores, though evidence of mining is often lacking and must be inferred from the discovery of smelting sites or copper ores in settlements.

The earliest copper mines have been identified in the Cantabrian mountains in northern Spain, and in south-western Iberia. Copper was extracted in the Asturian mines of El Aramo and El Milagro, and at La Profunda in León, from the third millennium BC into the early centuries of the Bronze Age. At El Aramo inclined shafts up to 30 m deep accessed a series of underground tunnels and connecting chambers extending 150 m in length (Fig. 24.2a); De Blas Cortina 2005). At El Milagro irregular inclined shafts were worked to a depth of 10 m or more (De Blas Cortina 2008). In these karstic environments oxidized copper minerals were extracted using deer-antler picks and rilled stone hammers, with some use of firesetting. The miners left rock columns to support these tunnels, a practice that was certainly warranted as human remains were found in both mines.

The largest concentration of prehistoric copper mines in Spain occurs in the south-west, in Huelva and surrounding provinces. Some 115 sites with primitive workings and stone hammers have been identified, with associated copper smelting at many locations (Hunt Ortiz 2003). Examples include the mines at Cuchillares in Huelva, Potosí and Aznalcóllar in Seville, La Loba in Córdoba, and Berrocal in Badajoz. The majority of these were for the extraction of copper carbonates, malachite and azurite. While several were identified as 'Chalcolithic' on the basis of the primitive technology (Rothenberg and Blanco-Freijeiro 1981), few have been scientifically dated. Many are likely to be Bronze Age, including Chinflón mine in Huelva where excavation has identified Late Bronze Age trench workings up to 1 m wide and 20 m deep, associated with the use of grooved stone hammers.

An early copper mine has been identified at Loma de la Tejería, Albarracín, Teruel, in eastern Spain. The discovery of Beaker pottery and other ceramics in this mine points to the extraction of oxidized copper ores in the late Chalcolithic/Early Bronze Age. No dated early copper mines have been recorded in south-east Spain, even though this is a highly mineralized region, with a strong metalworking tradition associated with Millaran, Beaker, and Argaric cultures from the fourth to the second millennia BC. The same is true for Portugal, where primitive workings with stone hammers are recorded in Faro, Beja, and other regions. Further research is likely to identify Bronze Age copper mines in these and in other parts of Iberia.

Ireland and Britain

Beaker pottery cultures had an important role in the spread of copper metallurgy across north-west Europe in the mid third millennium BC. This included the transfer of mining expertise along Atlantic coastal connections stretching from northern Spain and southern France to Ireland. The latter was to emerge as an important centre of early copper production, with mines identified at 12 locations in the south-west region of Cork and Kerry (O'Brien 1996). These include the Chalcolithic/Early Bronze Age mine of Ross Island, Killarney, Kerry, where copper mining was undertaken c.2400–1800 BC by a group using Beaker pottery (O'Brien 2004). The tennantite fahlore from this mine was smelted using a low temperature, non-slagging technology to produce a low-arsenic copper. This distinctive metal was widely used in Ireland to produce copper axeheads, dagger, and halberds, some of which were exchanged into Britain.

The decline of the Ross Island mine was immediately followed by the initiation of copper mining in the peninsulas of west Cork c.1800–1400 BC. This involved the extraction of

FIG. 24.2 (a) Chalcolithic/Early Bronze Age copper mine at El Aramo, Asturias, Spain; (b) Bronze Age copper mine at the Great Orme, North Wales.

Photos: author.

low-grade oxidized ore, principally malachite, from small drift mines located on exposures of sedimentary copper-beds. The largest concentration is located along the eastern slopes of Mount Gabriel, County Cork, where some 32 surface workings are associated with firesetting and stone-hammer technology (O'Brien 1994). The preservation of these mines in a blanket bog environment, almost entirely free of later mining disturbance, represents one of the most intact Bronze Age mining landscapes in Europe. Similar Bronze Age workings have been identified at Boulysallagh, Callaros Oughter, and Carrigacat in the Goleen area, and at Tooreen, Canshanavoe, Crumpane, and Reentrusk in the Beara Peninsula of County Cork. Finally, trench mines of Middle to Late Bronze Age date are recorded at Derrycarhoon to the east of Mount Gabriel.

Britain was both a major producer and consumer of copper in the Bronze Age. The earliest copper used $c.2500-2100$ BC was arsenical metal sourced through Beaker culture exchanges with the continental mainland and Ireland. The mining of local copper deposits began $c.2100-2000$ BC, at a time when bronze metallurgy was being developed using tin sources discovered in Cornwall. Recent research has identified intense copper-mining activity in mid and north Wales, and in north-west England, $c.2100-1400$ BC (Timberlake 2003a).

Bronze Age mining began along the north Wales coastline around 2000 BC, with workings at Parys Mountain on Anglesey and on the Great Orme, a limestone headland near Llandudno. The latter is one of the largest copper mines in Bronze Age Europe, worked more or less continuously from $c.1800$ to 600 BC (Lewis 1998). This mining took the form of opencasts and trenches on exposures of oxidized mineralization in rotted dolomitized limestone (Fig. 24.2b). These surface workings continued underground to form an elaborate complex of tunnels extending some 6 km and up to 65 m in depth. Stone hammers and bone gouges were used to tunnel the softer limestone, with firesetting used on harder rock.

A number of Bronze Age copper mines have been identified in the mountains of central Wales, in the area north of the Rheidol and on either side of the Dyfi estuary. These include Cwmystwyth where mining commenced around 2100 BC at an altitude of 420 m, and continued for the next four hundred years or so with open-trench extraction of oxidized chalcopyrite ores to a depth of about 12 m (Timberlake 2003b). This required the use of firesetting, stone hammers, antler picks, and wooden tools. Other copper mines of Early to Middle Bronze Age date have been investigated at Nantyreira, Nantyrickets, Llancynfelin, Nantyrarian, Tyn y fron, Ogof Wyddon, and Erglodd, all connected to the use of stone hammers.

Bronze Age workings have been identified at two historic copper mines in England. Antiquarian and recent investigations at Alderley Edge near Manchester reveal a series of surface pits that extracted oxidized copper ore from soft Triassic sandstones using firesetting and stone-hammer techniques. Bronze Age mining has recently been identified at Ecton mine in the Peak District of Staffordshire.

In addition to radiocarbon-dated sites, stone hammers possibly linked to Bronze Age mining have been found in south Wales near Llandovery and on the Gower Peninsula near Swansea. They are also recorded in other mining districts, for example in Scotland, the northern Pennines, and the Isle of Man, but no conclusive evidence of Bronze Age mining has been identified in those areas. The absence of early copper mines from south-west England is notable, as this metal was extensively mined in Cornwall in the early modern era. The explanation may be that this region could easily obtain copper by trade with Wales, Ireland, or other mining areas dependent on Cornish tin to make bronze.

Copper Supply in Prehistoric Europe

In summary, it is possible to distinguish three major cycles of copper mining in Chalcolithic and Bronze Age Europe, based on the type of ore resources exploited and the prevailing technology. The earliest mining of copper ore involved the extraction of secondary minerals, such as malachite and azurite, from surface zones of oxidation. These minerals are rich in copper and easy to smelt using a primitive hearth or crucible technology. They were first used in the Chalcolithic, and where locally available continued to be exploited throughout the Bronze Age, in mines such as Chinflon, Mount Gabriel, and the Great Orme.

The second mining tradition involved the use of fahlore (from German *Fahlerz*), namely copper sulpharsenides of the tennantite-tetrahedrite series. These were rich in copper, and like the oxidized ores could be smelted using a low temperature, non-slagging technology. Fahlore mining probably commenced in central Europe in the fourth millennium BC, and is particularly associated with the spread of Beaker culture metallurgy in western Europe in the third millennium BC. Relevant mining sites include El Aramo, Cabrières, and Ross Island. The use of fahlore declined significantly with the adoption of tin bronze around 2000 BC, but was developed further in central Europe during the Late Bronze Age, at mines such as Brixlegg and Mauk in north Tyrol.

The final copper-mining tradition in Europe centred on the extraction of sulphide ores, particularly copper-iron sulphides such as bornite and chalcopyrite. Their earliest exploitation is not well dated, possibly beginning in the late Chalcolithic/Early Bronze Age at mines such as St Véran in the French Alps. Many mines once thought to have processed sulphide ore, for example the mines of central Wales, are now believed to have used oxidized minerals. While sulphide ores can be reduced with primitive processes, the efficient recovery of metal requires an advanced furnace technology, which may have been first developed in Austria in the Middle and Late Bronze Age.

These mining traditions may have overlapped significantly in individual mining districts. This would have occurred where separate mines were contemporaneously worked using different smelting technology, and even in the same mine operation where different ore types were encountered. It should also be noted that the circulation of bronze always included both primary copper smelted directly from a mine source and secondary metal recycled from scrap over time, as well as mixtures of both types.

THE SEARCH FOR COPPER

Though occasionally found in a pure or 'native' form, copper most commonly occurs as a mineral ore, where the metal is mineralogically and chemically combined with other elements. The concept of 'ore' is an economic one that relates the cost of mining a mineral deposit against the real or perceived benefits to a society. While modern cost-benefit concepts of 'ore' may be inappropriate, there is no doubt that early mining groups operated some type of threshold below which it was not 'profitable' or physically possible to extract metal.

Bronze Age miners targeted highly accessible deposits of surface ore where the copper minerals were present in a sufficient concentration to be extracted and smelted. This was only possible in bedrock deposits as copper, unlike tin or gold, does not occur in concentrated form in secondary drift or alluvial deposits. Prospecting in the Bronze Age involved a careful search in areas of favourable geology, looking for rock outcrops stained with the vivid green and blue colours of oxidized copper minerals. This reliance on surface exposures explains why most Bronze Age mines are found in coastal or mountainous areas of high bedrock exposure.

Copper ores can be very complex in their geological setting, mineralogy, and chemistry. Bronze Age mining was heavily influenced by these geological controls and by the surface expression of an ore deposit. There is a distinction between mining carried out on sources of concentrated mineralization, such as quartz-sulphide veins, and that where the ore is dispersed through a particular rock stratum. The mine record reveals an empirical understanding of geological controls on the mineralization, which could only be gained by many hours at the mine face. The miners learned to adapt to variability within an ore-body, selecting those copper ores that could be extracted and processed with the prevailing technology.

The Approach to Mining

The ability to mine metal ore from the Earth's surface has a background in many thousands of years of rock extraction in the Stone Age. In some cases the discovery of copper sources was connected to an earlier search by Neolithic farmers for hard rocks to make stone tools. The technology in early copper mines was essentially 'Stone Age', involving the use of fire in combination with stone hammers, wooden and bone tools, with only a limited use of metal implements. The basic techniques can be paralleled in the quarries and flint mines of the Neolithic, though there are important differences such as the use of firesetting.

Bronze Age mines are usually surface workings in the form of open-casts and surface pits, narrow trench cuttings, and inclined drifts, which often accessed extensive underground workings of varying shape and size. Some operations involved a proliferation of small surface workings, moving from one mineralized outcrop to the next. The Mount Gabriel mines are a good example of small-scale mining across an entire landscape. Other mines, such as the Great Orme, represent a concentration of effort on a rich ore deposit over a long period. Mining generally began directly on the mineralized exposure, and followed the visible ore underground to depths of to 20 m, and occasionally more. The Great Orme reached a remarkable 70 m at its deepest, with a complex network of tunnels extending some 6 km. Those copper miners took advantage of natural tunnels and caves in karstic limestone to access copper ore, a phenomenon also recorded at the Grotte du Broum in Cabrières, at El Aramo and El Milagro in Spain, and the Grotta della Monaca in Italy.

Bronze Age miners worked in many different geological environments where the ease of extraction depended not just on rock type, but on the degree of surface weathering, the influence of rock structures, and the oxidation of sulphide ores. There is an important distinction between mining in hard rocks and in softer more friable types. Calcareous rock types such as limestone and dolomite occur in the mines at Ai Bunar, Rudna Glava, Cabrières, Bouche Payrol, Ross Island, and the Great Orme. Mines in non-calcareous geology include those in sedimentary rocks such as sandstones, mudrocks, and slates (Alderley Edge, Cwmystwyth,

Mount Gabriel, and the Mitterberg), and those working igneous rocks (Parys Mountain). These rock types have a different ground-water chemistry, which affects the hardness of the county rock, and the type and richness of ore mineralization. The mining of the softer calcareous rocks tends to produce more extensive workings, such as the extensive underground tunnels of the Great Orme mine. This influenced the type of tools used, with pick-like implements often used in softer geologies, as opposed to the use of firesetting in hard-rock geology.

Early mining was usually marked by an economy of effort, where only rock that contained ore minerals was extracted. These miners had the ability to tunnel at will, but many Bronze Age workings are essentially emptied ore channels, where the geology largely determined their form. Development in the modern sense of exploratory or service shafts and adits was unknown, but there was obviously considerable skill in these early mine operations. Large underground mines like the Great Orme were not carefully planned from the outset, but instead developed over many centuries of slow systematic working.

The Mining Environment

A remarkably similar range of techniques was used to mine copper across Europe in the Bronze Age. These represent similar cultural adaptations in similar environments to the challenges posed by early rock extraction and ore treatment. Firesetting was one of the most commonly used techniques in early metal mining. It involved the burning of wood-fuelled fires against a rock face, causing it to weaken and fracture, occasionally assisted by sudden water quenching. Rock was removed by direct thermal exfoliation or by pounding the fire-cracked face with stone hammers. The effectiveness of this method depended very much on the geology, as it was particularly suitable for hard siliceous rocks and less so for calcareous geology. The use of firesetting was constrained by local availability of wood, consuming large amounts of fuel from local woodland.

The miners exploited any structural weakness in the rock, such as cleavage or other fracture planes, using pick-like implements and fingers to prise out the rock. Pointed wooden sticks, picks, and wedges used for this purpose were discovered on Mount Gabriel. There is evidence for the use of antler picks in Chalcolithic mines at Rudna Glava, Ai Bunar, El Aramo, and El Milagro, and in Bronze Age mining at Cwmystwyth. Miners at the Great Orme, and possibly at Potosi in Spain, used pointed animal bones to gouge out copper minerals from the rotten dolomite. These have left their mark on the mine walls, which also show traces of pounding with stone hammers. Bronze picks are recorded in the Mitterberg mines, with two copper axe-hammers discovered in the Chalcolithic mine at Ai Bunar. The metal tools used were mostly limited to axeheads and blades used in wood collection and for domestic purposes, rarely discarded in these sites. Copper axes are recorded in primitive workings in Portugal, while stone axeheads are known from Ross Island and Ballyrisode in Ireland.

Broken rock extract and charcoal residues from these mines would have been removed to the surface for sorting, using shovels and containers of some kind. In the case of deeper mines like the Orme, there is evidence of underground sorting and stacking of 'deads' or waste rock in abandoned tunnels in a very organized fashion. The use of wooden shovels is known from the Mitterberg mines, Alderley Edge, and Mount Gabriel. Cattle shoulder-blade bones were used at Ross Island as scoops or shovels and like the antler picks have parallels in Neolithic flint mining. While containers have only been rarely identified in Bronze Age mines, baskets, sacks, or wooden equivalents were necessary to move rock extract and ore concentrate, with examples recorded at Cwmystwyth, as well as wooden troughs at the Mitterberg and El Aramo. Vertical workings may have required ropes, but there are no recorded examples from these mines (twisted withies found at Mount Gabriel and Cwmystwyth are probably connected to either basketry or stone-hammer handles). Notched tree-trunk ladders have been discovered in the Mitterberg mines, at Chinflon and at Derrycarhoon.

Some provision also had to be made for ventilation in deeper mines. The underground workings in the Great Orme had numerous connections to the surface for this purpose and there is some evidence for stacking of rock waste to control air-flow for fires lit at depths of at least 30 m. There is also a suggestion that controlled firesetting in inclined workings at the Mitterberg ventilated those mines in a systematic way (Pittioni 1951). In many operations the workings were vacated while the fires were lit underground.

The miners may have used animal-fat lamps, but the only recorded find is a small clay example at Chinflon. Charred splints of pine, used individually or bundled as torches, were found at the Mitterberg, St Véran, and Mount Gabriel. Like their counterparts in historic times, Bronze Age miners had much to fear from roof collapse and flooding. There are few recorded instances of the former, partly because the mining process did not disturb the rock strata as significantly as modern explosives. Firesetting tends to create workings with smooth load-bearing walls, which partly explains why support timbering is rare in these mines, with examples known from deeper workings at the Mitterberg. There is little evidence for fatalities in Bronze Age copper mines. The discovery of human leg bones at Ross Island and Chinflon may be connected to accidents similar to the fate of the 'Copper Man', a mummified corpse from the Chuquicamata prehistoric mine in northern Chile. Two undated skeletons were found with stone hammers in a collapsed copper mine at Penaflor, Seville province. Mining was always a dangerous activity, yet surprisingly there is little evidence of mine rituals and superstitions from the Bronze Age.

Flooding was undoubtedly a concern, particularly in any mine that used firesetting. Many workings are permanently flooded today, however this may have been less of a problem in Bronze Age times if the climate was marked by lower rainfall. To limit water seepage into open workings, the miners may have confined their operations to the drier months. Once operations began, mining may have been continuous to minimize flooding, using animal skins or some such container where hand-bailing was necessary. Evidence for drainage equipment comes from excavations at Cwmystwyth where a wooden launder was uncovered leading out from a Bronze Age working. The use of pottery was restricted to either domestic activity in mining camps, as at Ross Island, or as ritual deposits (e.g. Rudna Glava and possibly La Vierge).

Mining and Metal Production

Once mineralized rock was extracted, the miners faced the task of removing barren rock matrix to prepare an ore concentrate for smelting. Modern mines achieve this by exploiting some physical or chemical property of the metal ore through water flotation or chemical treatment. While the methods were more basic, there is evidence of a multi-stage approach to the concentration of copper ore in Bronze Age mines. This began with the crushing of rock extract that was already highly broken by firesetting, using stone hammers and anvil stones, with continuous hand-sorting of visibly mineralized fragments. Though laborious, the efficiency of this approach may be seen in the absence of visible mineralization in many Bronze Age mine dumps. While it is difficult to obtain archaeological evidence where carried out in streams, the use of washing in ore concentration and slag processing is attested in the Austrian mines.

The final stage of copper production involved the smelting of ore concentrates to metal in a furnace operation. This was undertaken either at the mine or in the general vicinity. Examples of the former are known in south-west Spain, in sites such as Chinflon and Cuchillares where smelting slag is found close to the mine workings. Bronze Age smelting in Austria was often carried out a short distance downslope from the mines and close to streams. The chalcopyrite ore was initially roasted in open beds, before being smelted in stone-built furnaces with slag-tapping features. Smelting was undertaken close to the mines, as many of the Austrian examples and at Ross Island, or in nearby settlements, such as the Chalcolithic site of La Capitelle du Broum in the Cabrières mining district.

The discovery of copper-smelting sites depends very much on the nature of the process, and specifically whether the main surface indicator, slag, was created. This was partly determined by the types of copper ore, as the smelting of oxidized minerals or rich fahlore may produce little or no slag, certainly in comparison to the treatment of copper-iron sulphides. A reliance on oxidized ores is the main reason why virtually no Bronze Age smelting sites have been discovered in Britain or Ireland. There is no evidence that bronze casting was ever undertaken at mining sites. The fabrication of artefacts was typically carried out in parent settlements to the mine or in those receiving down-the-line exchange of metal.

The production of copper ore during the Bronze Age had certain consequences for the environment, which depended on the intensity and duration of mining and smelting at different locations. The consumption of enormous amounts of wood in mine firesetting, and the use of charcoal as a smelting fuel, did impact on local woodland. Palynological studies reveal a complicated picture, ranging from a sharp reduction of tree growth after mining commenced to some form of woodland management to maintain fuel supply (e.g. Mighall et al. 2002). Geochemical analysis of lake and bog sediments often indicates a rise in heavy-metal concentrations in these same environments, which can be a useful proxy indicator of local mining and smelting activities.

Mining and Society

The mining of copper and other metals in the Bronze Age demanded considerable organization, both in terms of the activity itself and its impact on the wider economy. The logistics of a mine operation could be considerable, involving the mobilization of a workforce, the preparation of equipment, and the supply of food and fuel. The scale of operations ranged from short-lived, seasonal activity involving miner/farmers, to specialized mining communities working on a permanent basis. The duration and intensity of mining is often unclear, which makes estimating the metal production from any particular mine difficult. In some instances, production was far in excess of local requirements, with the metal traded in the form of ingots or finished artefacts over long distances. The destination of the metal is often uncertain; for example, the Great Orme mine may have produced several hundred tonnes of copper in the Bronze Age, but very little of this can be identified in contemporary metalwork in Britain. While some mines produced massive amounts of copper, smaller operations like those at Mount Gabriel often produced only enough to meet local needs with some regional exchange.

Copper mining had far-reaching implications for the Bronze Age societies involved in this activity. Control over the supply of metal is widely viewed as critical to the exercise of social power in this period. The value of metal, whether in the form of prestige objects or commodities, contributed to the aggrandizement of certain individuals and groups, as expressed in lavish funerary display or metal hoarding. These material benefits did not necessarily pass down to the miners themselves, whose work in some instances may have been controlled and exploited by other groups. Many miners, including children, may have spent long periods underground, working in confined and dangerous conditions. Whether this was done voluntarily, or required the use of slave labour, is unclear.

Historical and ethnographic sources confirm the distinctive character of mining communities the world over. There is an important distinction between groups engaged in mining on a permanent basis, on a large or small scale, and those that came together specifically for this purpose, often with loose social ties, and subsequently disbanded. The former is more likely to apply to Bronze Age groups who generally undertook mining within their own social territory, in close contact with parent agricultural settlements. These miners tend to be invisible as a distinct social group, with the absence of distinctive funerary rituals and settlement contexts making it difficult to examine their standing in Bronze Age societies.

Mining was not just a technological process, but was also about the making and reproduction of social relations, identities, and cultural ontologies. It was structured by particular societal values and circumstances, and woven into a complex web of social relations and work routines. There is an increasing emphasis on understanding the social dynamics of Bronze Age mining and its role in social reproduction (e.g. Wager 2002). This requires some consideration of how kinship and other social relations shaped the composition of a workforce, as well as leadership structures, the division of labour, and task specialization. Many of these social questions are not easily amenable to archaeological enquiry, but they must be to the forefront of future research to gain more insights into these Bronze Age mining communities. This requires a broader approach that considers the operation of these mines and the flow of the metal within contemporary settlement landscapes and social contexts.

Bibliography

Ambert, P. (1995). 'Les Mines préhistoriques de Cabrières (Hérault): quinze ans de recherches. État de la question', *Bulletin de la Société Préhistorique Française*, 92/4: 499–508.

Blas Cortina, M. A. de (2005). 'Un Témoignage probant de l'exploitation préhistorique du cuivre dans le nord de la Péninsule Iberique: le complexe minier d'El Aramo (Asturies)', in P. Ambert and J. Vaquer (eds.), *La Première Métallurgie en France et dans les Pays Limitrophes*. Carcassonne: Mémoire 37 de la Société Préhistorique Française, 195–206.

—— (2008). 'Minería prehistórica del cobre en el reborde septentrional de los picos de Europa: Las olvidadas labores de El Milagro (Onís, Asturias)', *Veleia*, 24–5: 723–53.

Chernych, E. N. (1978). 'Aibunar, a Balkan copper mine of the fourth millennium BC', *Proceedings of the Prehistoric Society*, 44: 203–17.

—— (1998). 'Kargaly: le plus grand ancien complexe minier et de métallurgie à la frontière de l'Europe et de l'Asie', in M.-C. Frère-Sautot (ed.), *Paléomètallurgie des Cuivres*. Montagnac: éditions Monique Mergoil, 71–6.

Gale, N. (2001). 'Archaeology, science-based archaeology and the Mediterranean Bronze Age metals trade: a contribution to the debate', *European Journal of Archaeology*, 4: 113.

Goldenberg, G. (1998). 'L'Exploitation du cuivre dans les Alpes autrichiennes à l'âge du Bronze', in C. Mordant, M. Pernot, and V. Rychner (eds.), *L'Atelier du Bronzier en Europe du XX au VIII siècle avant notre ère*, Actes du Colloque International Bronze '96. Neuchâtel et Dijon, Paris, Tome II: 9–23.

Hunt Ortiz, M. (2003). *Prehistoric Mining and Metallurgy in the South-West Iberian Peninsula*, British Archaeological Reports (International Series), 1,188. Oxford: Archaeopress.

Jovanović, B. (1979). 'The technology of primary copper mining in south-east Europe', *Proceedings of the Prehistoric Society*, 45: 103–10.

Lewis, C. A. (1998). 'The Bronze Age mines of the Great Orme and other sites in the British Isles and Ireland', in C. Mordant, M. Pernot, and V. Rychner (eds.), *L'Atelier du Bronzier en Europe du XX au VIII siècle avant notre ère*, Actes du Colloque International Bronze '96. Neuchâtel et Dijon, Paris, Tome II: 45–58.

Maggi, R. and Pearce, M. (2005). 'Mid fourth millennium copper mining in Liguria, north-west Italy: the earliest known copper mines in western Europe', *Antiquity*, 79: 66–77.

Mighall, T., Timberlake, S., Clark, S. and Caseldine, A. 2002. 'A palaeoenvironmental investigation of mine sediments from Copa Hill, Cwmystwyth, mid-Wales', *Journal of Archaeological Science*, 29 (10), 1,161–88.

O'Brien, W. (1994). *Mount Gabriel: Bronze Age Mining in Ireland*, Bronze Age Studies, 3. Galway: Galway University Press.

—— (1996). *Bronze Age Copper Mining in Britain and Ireland*. Princes Risborough: Shire Publications.

—— (2004). *Ross Island: Mining, Metal and Society in Early Ireland*, Bronze Age Studies, 6. Galway: National University of Ireland Galway.

Pittioni, R. (1951). 'Prehistoric copper mining in Austria: problems and facts', *Seventh Annual Report—Institute of Archaeology, University of London*: 17–40.

Rothenberg, B. and Blanco-Freijeiro, A. (1981). *Studies in Ancient Mining and Metallurgy in South-West Spain*. London: Institute of Archaeology.

Stöllner, T. (2009). 'Die zeitliche Einordnung der prähistorischen Montanreviere in den Ost- und Südalpen: Anmerkungen zu einem Forschungsstand', in K. Oeggl and M. Prast (eds.), *Die Geschichte des Bergbaus in Tirol und seinen angrenzenden Gebieten*. Innsbruck: Innsbruck University Press.

Timberlake, S. (2003a). 'Early mining research in Britain: the developments of the last ten years', in P. Craddock and J. Lang (eds.), *Mining and Metal Production through the Ages*. London: British Museum, 21–42.

—— (2003b). *Excavations on Copa Hill, Cwmystwyth (1986–1999)*, British Archaeological Reports (British Series), 348. Oxford: Archaeopress.

Wager, E. (2002). 'Mining as social process: a case study from the Great Orme, North Wales', in B. Ottaway and E. Wager (eds.), *Metals and Society*, British Archaeological Reports, S1061. Oxford: Archaeopress, 32–48.

Zschocke, K. and Preuschen, E. (1932). *Das urzeitliche Bergbaugebiet von Mühlbach-Bischofshofen*, Materialien zur Urgeschichte Österreichs, 6. Vienna: Anthropologische Gesellschaft in Wien.

CHAPTER 25

GOLD AND GOLD WORKING OF THE BRONZE AGE

BARBARA ARMBRUSTER

Introduction

Gold is a rare metal, whose magical power derives from its shining, sunlike colour and its resistance to corrosion. The noble metal plays an important role in all cultures in art, religion, trade, and society. The Bronze Age is a period exceptionally rich in gold, and produced heavy pieces of jewellery weighing up to 2500 g (Guînes, Pas-de-Calais, France, Fig. 25.1a), vessels up to 900 g (Zürich-Altstetten, Switzerland, Fig. 25.3), and impressive large objects in gold sheet (golden cones; the Mold 'cape'). A considerable number of gold artefacts are known, owing to the custom of depositing valuable objects in graves and hoards, in the ground, or in rivers and bogs. Even so, a precise estimate of the actual occurrence of gold is problematic, since our knowledge of early gold production is partial. The craft of goldworking was anchored religiously, socially, and economically in Bronze Age society. The objects produced testify to a specialized craft with a high technical and aesthetic standard. The goldsmith, who knew how to work with valuable materials and whose task was to make important prestige goods and ritual objects, can therefore be seen as a prominent figure in Bronze Age society. Richly furnished graves of the Late Copper and Early Bronze Age, like that of the Amesbury Archer in Wiltshire in southern England, or the 'princely grave' at Leubingen, Thuringia, containing gold and bronze finds as well as stone metalworking tools, indicate the high social esteem in which early metallurgists were held (Fitzpatrick 2009; Meller 2004).

The first indications of the use of gold as a material go back to the Neolithic. The rich Copper Age grave finds at the Varna cemetery in Bulgaria, dating from the fifth millennium BC, are the earliest evidence of goldworking in Europe. It is no accident that the first appearance of gold artefacts accompanies early hierarchically structured societies. Across Europe, early finds occur first in the Bell Beaker culture, which extended into Britain in the Early Bronze Age. Goldwork of the Aegean Bronze Age naturally differs from eastern European, Nordic, or even Atlantic Bronze Age goldwork. Yet in the European area as a whole there

FIG. 25.1 (a) Middle to Late Bronze Age collection of jewellery from Guînes, Pas-de-Calais, France; (b) Forged Early Bronze Age arm ornaments from Lockington, Leicestershire, England.

Photos: Armbruster.

are indications of inter-relationships and a common approach in geographically distant regions, not only with regard to the custom of depositing valuable luxury goods, but also as far as their morphological and technological characteristics are concerned (Springer 2003; Meller 2004). Despite quite independent regional developments, signs of non-European influences, above all from the eastern Mediterranean, the Middle East, and Egypt, can also be detected in the objects.

A History of Research

Goldwork has played an increasingly important part in Bronze Age research since the nineteenth century. Significant gold finds were published early on in individual studies and regional overviews. From the 1980s these finds received much attention in exhibitions, both permanent and special (Clarke, Cowie, and Foxon 1985; Springer 2003;

Meller 2004). Questions of Bronze Age production technique and the analysis of precious metal finds have been part of research since the 1940s. The first attempts to consider prehistoric gold from a Europe-wide perspective go back to the ambitious analytical project *Studien zu den Anfängen der Metallurgie* (SAM) [*Studies on the Beginnings of Metallurgy*] by the Württemberg Landesmuseum in Stuttgart (Hartmann 1982). These spectrographic analyses are only valuable up to a point, however, since they do not include trace elements as a means of establishing source, nor were they accompanied by technical investigation. In Spain a survey of analyses involving problems of origin is currently being compiled in the *Proyecto-Au* (Perea, Montero, and Garcia Vuelta 2004: 139–146).

Since the 1990s prehistoric gold has been the topic of a number of scientific conferences (Morteani and Northover 1995; Springer 2003; Perea, Montero, and Garcia Vuelta 2004). From the second half of the twentieth century the study of prehistoric goldworking has developed into an interdisciplinary research field, which, besides typological and historico-cultural studies, also includes scientific analysis, experimental and technological investigations, and the obtaining of raw materials (Perea and Armbruster 2008). The knowledge that the aesthetic and typological features of an artefact are directly related both to its function and cultural milieu and to the production process is also important. In today's research, therefore, the aesthetics of spectacular gold finds is not our foremost concern; what matters is their potential for providing information for historico-cultural, technological, and socio-political contexts.

In recent years the Bronze Age research landscape has been enriched by many new finds, a process to which building activity and the use of metal detectors have contributed considerably. Among such finds are exceptional pieces that have changed our view of the Bronze Age. Thus extensive connections with Danubian and Mycenaean cultures were demonstrated by the Early Bronze Age find at Bernstorf, Bavaria. New Early Bronze Age finds in Britain, like the bracelets from the gold hoard at Lockington in Leicestershire (Fig. 25.1b), or the handled cup from Ringlemere, Kent, provided the impetus for new interdisciplinary studies of prestige items (Hughes 2000; Needham, Parfitt, and Varndell 2006). Further recent discoveries from the south of England and northern France are the gold hoards of Milton Keynes, Buckinghamshire, Guînes (see Fig. 25.1a), and Balinghem, both in the Pas-de-Calais (Armbruster and Louboutin 2004). In 2003 the British Museum and the Musée d'Archéologie Nationale in St-Germain-en-Laye independently exhibited these three exceptional finds, all of them comprising solid gold necklaces and bracelets. Since these new finds reveal parallels in hoard composition and aspects of craft production and technique, a common cultural history and close contacts between the two sides of the Channel can be inferred. Moreover, because of their considerable total weight (*c.*6,800 g) these hoards have changed opinions about the volume of gold that was in circulation and that was deposited in the northern French/southern English area during the Bronze Age. The unexpected find of two Late Bronze Age bar-torcs with conical ends, which came to light in a fishing net in the Channel, definitely proves sea traffic between southern England and the continent. This zone of culture contact between the south of England and north-west France can be shown to have existed since the Early Bronze Age Wessex culture, and is reflected among other things in precious-metal working (Clarke, Cowie, and Foxon 1985).

The Find Context

When metallurgy begins in the Copper and Early Bronze Age, gold is found in burial contexts, predominantly in male graves. The custom of depositing the gold of important persons in their graves disappears in the Middle Bronze Age. Substantial gold hoards are typical of the advanced phases of the Bronze Age, with heavy solid-gold artefacts indicating the presence of a considerable amount of gold in western Europe. The accumulation of precious metal in hoards is interpreted on the one hand as a cultural practice and on the other as the wealth of a community, with votive hoards, grave deposits, and stored raw material all being possible interpretations.

Only a small number of the Bronze Age gold finds known today come from archaeological excavations with detailed information on find context. The majority are objects that had already reached museums and collections in the nineteenth century. Quite a number were melted down immediately after their discovery for their intrinsic value and thus lost to archaeology. This way of dealing with prehistoric gold has been proved only in isolated cases, however, like that of the Spanish gold hoard of Caldas de Reyes, Pontevedra. The hoard, originally weighing approximately 28 kg, was discovered in 1940 during farm work, and divided between the two finders. One half was immediately melted down by a goldsmith, so we can only assess the remaining half, which comprises three heavy handled cups, a large number of ring bars, and a comb (Armbruster 2000: 128–35, pl. 38–40).

Several gold objects were deposited in sealable jewellery boxes, indicating experience in the storage of valuable metal objects. In the case of the find at Skeldal, Jutland, two gold-wire spirals were preserved in a small bronze vessel (Fig. 25.2). While the hive-shaped vessel and the spirals can be ascribed to the Early Bronze Age Únětice culture, the bronze bracelets and

FIG. 25.2 Gold spirals and bronze case from Skeldal, Jutland, Denmark.

Photo: B. Armbruster.

a necklace in the hoard are clearly of local manufacture and, according to Danish chronology, Late Neolithic (Jørgensen and Petersen 1998: 39). The wooden container of a bronze razor with gold inlay from Vester Skerninge, south-west Fyn, is also preserved. In another example, the dress-fastener from Killymoon, County Tyrone, was likewise kept in a wooden container with a lid (Eogan 1994: pl. 17).

Other gold objects were obviously deformed deliberately for deposition so that they would fit neatly into a container. This kind of deformation is proved for numerous gold torcs, which were rolled into spirals, as with the Crow Down hoard, West Berkshire. Sometimes the deliberate destruction of gold objects may be inferred, perhaps to divest them of their magical powers. Thus numerous Early Bronze Age lunulae were found obviously rolled. On the other hand, beside the marks of use there are also examples of repairs, which indicate long usage. In some hoards of several items made in pottery or bronze containers a careful order can be observed. The 66 objects of the Late Bronze Age precious-metal hoard of Villena, Alicante, were closely layered together in a large pottery vessel (Perea 1991: 61–73; Armbruster 2000: 142–63). This hoard find is of particular significance, not only for the quantity of precious metal, but also for the assemblage of 28 cast bracelets, 11 gold bowls, and two gold flasks, together with three silver flasks, and the first iron objects, a bracelet and a hemispherical decorative object in gold leaf, in a Late Bronze Age context. In the south German Unterglauheim hoard, two gold beakers, each placed in bronze bowls, were put into a bronze bucket (Springer 2003: 133–41). A similar rare assemblage of gold and bronze vessels is the Mariesminde hoard from Denmark, in which 11 gold vessels were stowed in a large sheet-bronze container (*situla*) (Jørgensen and Petersen 1998: 101). Another remarkable finding is that the gold beakers from Unterglauheim served as containers for cremated remains. This makes them comparable with the two gold vessels from Alberdorf in Schleswig-Holstein, which likewise served as cremation urns.

Gold objects in the typical metal hoards of the Middle and Late Bronze Age are only rarely associated with bronze objects or pottery. Absolute dating is often difficult, since organic materials are rarely present. Radiocarbon dating has sometimes been possible, as in the case of a necklace from the Irish gold hoard at Derrinboy, County Offaly, made of a leather strap wound round with gold wire (dated between 1740 and 1450 cal BC; Cahill 2002).

Form and Function

The main categories of Bronze Age gold are jewellery, ornamental objects, and ritual objects, which include vessels and weapons. There are also gold ingots, pre-products, and scrap metal. Most Bronze Age gold comes under the category of jewellery. The following are distinguished: 1. wire spirals (loop rings, spirals, spiral coils); 2. ornamental sheet and discs for attaching to fabric or leather; 3. head and hair jewellery (diadems, hair-rings, hair-spirals, pins, spheres); 4. neck ornaments (chokers, lunulae, pendants, beads, torcs, collars, gorgets); 5. jewellery worn on clothing (pins, brooches); 6. arm or wrist jewellery (ring- and cuff-shaped); 7. small rings (for fingers, ears, or nose); 8. jewellery worn on the ear (pendant earrings, ear plugs). Among these, personal jewellery can be distinguished from jewellery with a ritual function, pieces worn on elaborate ceremonial robes, and those purely for burials. Jewellery was worn on the body or placed on figurines. Grave jewellery with no evidence of wear indicates it might have been made specifically for burial. Gold objects found in two burials in the mound at Hüsby, Schleswig-Holstein, are interpreted as ornaments for the dead.

By ornamental pieces are meant those objects that have no independent function, but are rather for decorating furniture, weapon hilts, or sceptres. Among the ritual objects are gold discs, ceremonial hats (cones), or the Mold cape, and also single bronze or gold objects, for example, the Nebra sky disc, the Trundholm sun chariot, or the Hagendrup (Zealand) headpiece (Meller 2004; Jørgensen and Petersen 1998). Miniature objects, like the collection of over one hundred little golden boats from Nors in north-west Jutland, also belong in this category.

The large group of gold vessels belong to the category of ritual objects. Many of the Bronze Age gold vessels have been ascribed a function not only in religious practices but also as prestige objects for feasts (Springer 2003). From Mycenaean Greece, through Romania, to the British Isles, Scandinavia, and the Iberian Peninsula, the most diverse forms—beakers, cups, bowls, pots, and flasks—are known. More than 60 vessels have survived from the Nordic Bronze Age alone (Jørgensen and Petersen 1998). For many years the largest piece known has been the Late Bronze Age bowl from Zürich-Altstetten (Fig. 25.3). Significant hoards with numerous precious-metal vessels can be mentioned: first and foremost, the Spanish hoard of Villena (16 vessels), the Danish boards of Mariesminde (11) and Borgbjerg (6), and the Eberswalde hoard in Germany (8) (Springer 2003). The production of precious vessels, hats, and capes was achieved by plastic shaping techniques, such as stamping and chasing. The only exception with cast specimens comes from the hoard of Caldas de Reyes (Armbruster 2000: 132, pl. 38). Besides gold vessels, there were also silver, amber, and jet vessels in the Early Bronze Age (Needham, Parfitt, and Varndell 2006).

Also classed as ceremonial tools or insignia of power are solid-gold weapons, which, unlike weapons of bronze, because of the material properties of the metal, fulfilled no practical purpose. Here, only the gold axe from the 'princely grave' at Dieskau in the former district of

FIG. 25.3 Gold bowl from Zürich-Altstetten, Kanton Zürich, Switzerland.

Photo: B. Armbruster.

Saalkreis in eastern Germany, the Perşinari assemblage in southern Romania, with one dagger and 11 halberds, and the dagger from a grave at Mala Gruda in Montenegro (Morteani and Northover 1995: 77–93), would belong in this category. Apart from these gold blades, there are also ceremonial weapons that were made of bronze and then decorated with gold sheet or gold wire. Early Bronze Age dagger hilts were sometimes decorated with gold sheet *appliqué*, like the Nebra swords or certain Scottish daggers (Meller 2004: 23, 176–7). Besides ceremonial axes and the numerous gold-inlaid sword hilts of the Nordic Bronze Age, individual pieces like the flanged axe from Thun-Renzenbühl, Bern, and an Early Bronze Age dagger with pointillée work from Priziac (Morbihan, Brittany) have gold inlay (Clarke, Cowie, and Foxon 1985). Especially remarkable among the decorated weapons are the well-known bronze daggers from Armorica and Wessex, whose handles are richly embellished with tiny gold pins. Well-preserved specimens come from Bush Barrow in southern England and Kernonen in Brittany.

Among the inlaid objects of the Bronze Age, the Nebra sky disc with its inlaid gold sheet is a unique piece from the early period in central Europe. Bronze objects that had been decorated with gold sheet or gold-thread inlay are recorded in considerable numbers from the Nordic Bronze Age. Included in this group of Nordic gold pieces, besides weapons and ritual objects, are pieces of jewellery such as fibulae, pins, or buttons (Jørgensen and Petersen 1998). Rare examples of bicoloured precious-metal objects in the east are heavy gold bracelets with bull-head terminals from Hungary, decorated with inlaid silver thread. Also bicoloured are small rings of the 'hair-ring' group, in which both natural yellow gold and electrum, a very light gold alloy with a high concentration of silver, were used.

Another group of gold objects includes items of jewellery where it is unclear what function they served and how they were worn. Thus it has not yet been possible to resolve how the large piece of jewellery from the Guînes hoard was worn (see Fig. 25.1a). How the Late Bronze Age gorgets, found only in Ireland, were worn is likewise a matter of debate. In addition, there are several examples of completely impractical prestige objects that imitate in gold functional objects of bronze, wood, or stone. The Early Bronze Age wristguard from Vila Nova da Cerveira in Portugal is non-functional, not only because it is made from gold sheet rather than stone but also because of the four purely decorative studs that imitate the functional metal rivets of a real wristguard (Armbruster 2000: pl. 105). Other gold objects that are unusable in practice are the heavy golden comb imitating a wooden comb found in the Middle Bronze Age hoard of Caldas de Reyes (Armbruster 2000: 131, Fig. 72), or the gold tweezers from the burial mound at Lyshøj on the island of Zealand, Denmark, from the later Nordic Bronze Age. Dating from the Late Bronze Age in Ireland are large numbers of so-called dress- or sleeve-fasteners, whose usage is unclear. They include two inordinately large and heavy specimens from Clones, County Monaghan, and Castlekelly, County Galway, which together weigh as much as 1,300 g and can be considered purely prestige objects (Eogan 1994; Cahill 2002: Fig. 3). Another group of puzzling gold objects is formed by the so-called lock-rings that occur widely in the British Isles and also, more rarely, in northern France. These are concave spindle-shaped pieces of jewellery that frequently appear in pairs. Worthy of note is the new find made by a metal detectorist at Berwick-upon-Tweed, Northumberland. Together with 36 bronze objects, there were three complete lock-rings, and fragments of others, made of fine gold sheet, in which a spacing material, a mixture of wax and wood, had been preserved. Small box- and spindle-shaped gold sheet pieces from Ireland have recently been identified as earplugs. In the long-standing debate over the function of the gold cones, the general interpretation is that they served as ceremonial hats.

Bronze Age goldwork probably never had a purely decorative or pre-monetary material character; above all, it had a ritual and social function, as a symbol of status and power. For the elite, gold objects served to represent, legitimize, and preserve their power, authority, and identity (Clarke, Cowie, and Foxon 1985). As in many traditional cultures even today, gold objects were enveloped in a system of symbols, coded sign language, and religious or social values, which were conveyed through their ownership, accumulation, categorization, or exchange. In prehistory gold was symbolic of the life-dispensing sun and thus embodied fertility, well-being, and permanence, as well as an apotropaic quality. Numerous exhibitions in recent decades have presented the astonishing gold wealth of the Bronze Age under the banner of cult, magic, and power.

Gold grave goods had a social and religious function. Burial gifts of vessels, bowls, or diadems are interpreted as a reference to the ritual items used by priests or shamans in sacrifices and cult practices. The Early Bronze Age grave assembly from Quinta da Agua Branca, Portugal, contains a diadem and gold rings together with a long bronze dagger. The unique Mold 'cape' from North Wales is also among the few ritual objects to come from a grave (Needham 2000). The Early Bronze Age handled cup from Rillaton, Cornwall, which was found—amongst others—with a bronze dagger and a pottery vessel, is one of the rare examples of gold vessels in a definite burial context (Needham, Parfitt, and Varndell 2006: 84–7). Other early precious-metal vessels are supposed to have come from Breton burial mounds, but only fragments of two silver cups are preserved. Three other male burials from the earlier Nordic Bronze Age are connected with cultic items. At Gönnebek, Schleswig-Holstein, a burial mound contained a bowl, a bracelet, and spirals of gold wire, as well as a sword and other bronze objects (Springer 2003: 286). Large discs of thin gold sheet are known from earlier Bronze Age barrows at Glüsing, Schleswig-Holstein, and Jægerborg Hogn, Copenhagen.

Crescent-shaped lunulae, discs, and vessels are clearly symbolic of Bronze Age belief systems. However, sun and moon symbolism also occurs in the detail of the decoration. Concentric circles, rays, and wheels are symbols that refer to the heavenly bodies and probably reflect a Bronze Age sun cult. Moreover, the arrangement and number of ornamental motifs on some objects, like the gold cones from Schifferstadt, Enzelsdorf, 'Berlin', and Avanton, which are interpreted as ceremonial hats, are regarded as representations of the solar and lunar cycles and thus as astronomical calendars (Eluère 1982; Springer 2003). Evidently astronomy and calendrical systems were already developed in the Early Bronze Age. The most remarkable evidence of the astronomical knowledge of that time is the Nebra sky disc, with what is the first concrete representation of the constellations (Meller 2004).

THE CHRONOLOGICAL DEVELOPMENT OF GOLDWORKING

The craft of goldworking changed over time and space from the beginnings of gold metallurgy to the advent of iron, as its products, unlike tools, were affected by a steady alteration of style and advances in production techniques. During the Bronze Age developments in form and technique occurred neither simultaneously nor along the same lines over the European continent. Thus goldworking begins considerably later in the north than in eastern Europe or the Mediterranean region.

The potential of prehistoric gold objects to provide information on the artistic and technical level of the society that produced them lies in a combination of typology and technology. Consequently the diachronic study of Bronze Age goldworking can give us an insight into social structures, societal change, and cultural contacts. On the one hand, the limited spread of certain types and techniques indicates a regionally specific form. On the other, cross-regional forms show wide contacts as well as shared expressions of belief and symbolic language. Indigenous innovations and exogenous influences through contacts with other cultures are important for the introduction of new styles. In this way it has been possible to show that cultural changes are reflected in the development of goldworking in the Iberian Peninsula. In the transitional phase between the Late Bronze Age and the Early Iron Age there was interaction between local goldsmiths of the Atlantic tradition and eastern Mediterranean craftsmen. This cultural contact on several levels led to profound changes in the identity of the population, something that is apparent in the prestige objects (Armbruster and Perea 2007). The exchange of technical knowledge and a gradual adaptation to the many forms of Mediterranean and Middle Eastern origin can both be observed, as well as specific production methods. Imitations sometimes point to contacts where there was no direct exchange of technical knowledge between craftsmen, since it was the form of an object, not the way it was made, that was passed on.

Universally typical of the beginning of the Early Bronze Age are gold-wire spirals and flat, two-dimensional objects made of gold sheet. From east to west, diadems and discs are a pan-European phenomenon. Discs, lunulae, and basket earrings are spread across the entire Atlantic region from Ireland to Portugal. During the Early Bronze Age three-dimensionally conceived hollow objects, such as handled cups or cylindrical bracelets, appear in Atlantic Europe. This development has its origin in the British Isles. The Wessex culture, however, developed a unique style, with gold-sheet objects and daggers featuring hilts decorated with minute gold pins, found only in southern England and Brittany (Needham 2000; Taylor 1980).

In the Middle and Late Bronze Age heavy, solid necklaces and bracelets, as well as bar-torcs, are typical cross-regional jewellery forms in the Atlantic region, while gold bowls predominate in continental Europe. Certain regional characteristics, however, develop in parallel. Independent Late Bronze Age gold forms develop in Ireland, with gold-sheet objects, such as gorgets and earplugs, on the one hand, and cast gold dress-fasteners on the other (Cahill 2002). Typical of Ireland, Britain, and north-west France are the so-called lock-rings and hair-rings, which also appear in Belgium. On the Iberian Peninsula another development occurs, with heavy cast bracelets that were produced using the lathe and the lost-wax process (Fig. 25.4). After an early phase when objects were made of gold wire and gold sheet, the Nordic region produces remarkable cast pieces, in particular heavy bracelets (Jørgensen and Petersen 1998). Also in northern Europe the very many gold vessels are proof of a developed goldworking technique. In the eastern European region there are likewise simple gold-wire and gold-sheet objects such as beads at the start, which are then followed by personal jewellery—hair ornaments and convex discs. Hair-rings, heavy bracelets, wire necklaces, convex discs, and vessels are typical of the Late Bronze Age in the Danubian and Carpathian areas.

FIG. 25.4 Arm ornaments cast in lost-wax technique from the Late Bronze Age hoard of Villena, Alicante, Spain.

Photo: B. Armbruster.

METHODS OF INVESTIGATION

In the Homeric epics gold was a means by which conflict between elites could be resolved, it being used in the exchange of political or hospitality gifts. Gold vessels were also used in sacrifices or in feasts for those of high rank. Written sources and pictorial representations giving detailed information about gold in the European Bronze Age are, however, rare. Therefore our knowledge relies mainly on the study of the archaeological artefacts themselves, their find circumstances and their sociocultural context. Interpretations are also based on functional analogies and modern analysis. The interdisciplinary methods available to the archaeologist today for studying the history of goldworking are diverse. The study of style—typology of form, decoration, and function—remains fundamental, together with visual examination of tool marks and thus of the implements and workshops involved. Analogies drawn from ethnography, experimental archaeology, visual images, and ancient written sources help us develop explanatory models. Lastly, a range of analytical approaches have greatly aided research on gold artefacts (Perea and Armbruster 2008). Among the scientific methods that can yield information about the composition and properties of the material are various techniques for determining alloys, X-ray fluorescence (XRF), scanning electron microscopy, particle-induced X-ray emission (PIXE), laser-ablation inductively coupled plasma mass spectrometry (LA-ICP-MS), and synchrotron radiation. Radiography makes it possible to see inside the object and can show the thickness of material, tool marks, and repairs. Electron microscopy, besides allowing non-destructive analysis, also enables detailed observation of the topography of an object.

THE ACQUISITION OF GOLD

Hitherto it has been difficult to establish the origin of the raw material used in Bronze Age goldworking, not least because it has been assumed that the metal would have been rapidly recycled. Lead-isotope studies and analyses of platinum inclusions in gold using LA-ICP-MS have produced highly promising results in the field of provenance studies (Schlosser et al. 2009). At the same time, analyses of archaeological artefacts need to be compared with ore samples from potential sources.

On current knowledge, Bronze Age gold was mainly river gold recovered from alluvial deposits. As yet, apart from a goldfield recently discovered in Georgia, there has been no Bronze Age evidence for the mining of primary gold deposits in Europe. Small particles of gold were presumably washed from the sands of gold-bearing riverbeds or placer deposits of old riverbeds. The most important Bronze Age gold sources are the Balkan and Danube areas (especially Transylvania), Ireland, and the Iberian Peninsula. Other regions, like Scandinavia, with no noteworthy deposits of their own, must therefore have had to obtain the raw material for jewellery and religious objects from other regions. In this case, amber might have served as the reciprocal trade good. Gold could be traded in the form of gold dust, bars (ingots), or finished products. Whether acquired in exchange, taken as tribute, received as hospitality or political gifts, seized as war booty or in plundering raids, gold was always a valuable commodity that only certain persons could possess.

Gold Technology

Direct proof of goldworking is exceedingly rare for the Bronze Age, because of the absence of any features that would identify workshops. Enough tools and tool marks on gold products are recorded, however, to indicate indirectly what equipment was used in gold workshops and how the production process operated (Armbruster 2000). Traces of gold on tools, such as the small anvil at Lichfield, Staffordshire, or the gold touchstone at Choisy-au-Bac, Oise, are clear indications of the working of precious metals. Apart from touchstones for establishing the quality of gold, most of the equipment could have been used equally by goldsmiths and bronzesmiths. There are grindstones, ingot-casting moulds, hammers and anvils, and punches and chisels. Other pieces of equipment, such as the lathe, can only be inferred from tool marks. Besides tools, ingots, primary products, and unfinished goldwork may also indicate the presence of workshops.

Because of its exceptional material properties, gold is highly suitable for the manufacture of jewellery, ornamentation, and vessels by means of casting or plastic deformation techniques. Its melting point is around 1,000° C. To reach this temperature the charcoal furnace must be fitted with a bellows. Gold is very malleable and can be burnished to a high lustre. It hardens in cold-working by forging, chiselling, punching, bending, or torsion. To avoid cracking or breaking, precious metals are annealed at around 750° C. Annealing recrystallizes the metal structure after it hardens and becomes brittle during plastic deformation. Except for the melting, casting, soldering, and firing, goldworking is done in a cooled state. As gold is resistant to most chemical influences, its shining colour stays unchanged, even after millennia.

Before a piece of gold work is begun, an idea of the form, decoration, and technical realization of the desired object must be developed. This shaping concept can be a model in another material, a sketch, or simply an idea. The quantity of metal is then measured using weights and scales, and, if the composition is not known, the gold content is checked. To do this, special dark, fine-grained, gold touchstones were already in use in the Bronze Age.

Smelting, Alloying, and Casting

Every gold object is produced from a cast primary product. The cast was made in moulds of stone, metal, or clay. For this the gold had to be melted in a furnace in a clay crucible, possibly alloyed with silver or copper, and then poured into the mould. Native gold is always a natural alloy with a tiny proportion of copper and, depending on the deposit, up to 50 per cent of silver. Deliberately made gold alloys first appear in circulation at the end of the Bronze Age. These alloys are used to join together several metals. Analyses have shown that in western Europe in the Late Bronze Age a metallic gold solder was in use, the melting point lower than that of the base metals. Tiny particles of solder are placed in position, melt during heating, and join the separate parts together.

Two casting methods are relevant to prehistoric goldworking: bar (or ingot) casting and the lost-wax technique. Usually a gold-bar cast in an open ingot mould would be transformed by hammering into rods, sheets, or wire. A casting mould from the Isle of Man served to cast bars for making rods, necklaces, bracelets, and round plates for the manufacture of vessels or discs. By contrast, in the lost-wax technique a model of the desired object is made of wax. The wax model is coated in clay that is applied in several layers. After drying, the mould is heated to melt the wax. The hollow space that remains is then filled with molten gold. Following casting the clay mould is destroyed to release the cast piece. The unfinished cast must be chiselled free from the casting jets and the upper surface smoothed by grinding. The lost-wax technique was already being used in the earlier Nordic Bronze Age to cast decorated bracelets. In the west it occurs for the first time in the Middle Bronze Age hoard of Caldas de Reyes. Cast gold objects differ from forged in their greater weight and the thickness of the material. A particular variant of lost-wax casting, in which the wax model is worked using a lathe, is typical of Late Bronze Age goldworking of the Iberian Peninsula (Morteani and Northover 1995: 399–423). There is also the so-called casting-on technique, by which two or more parts are joined or added together by casting. For this, a connecting part made of wax is added to a metal object and then coated in clay as described above, the wax melted, and the hollow space filled.

Plastic Deformation

The technique of forging sheets, rods, and wire from a gold bar was mastered from the outset. Some of the oldest Bronze Age gold-sheet objects are small decorated sheets, diadems, discs, and crescent-shaped neck ornaments (lunulae). In sheet- and wiremaking, the cross section of a gold bar undergoes a radical change through plastic deformation using hammer and anvil. Repeated heating prevented the gold from becoming brittle during forging. Most forged objects show traces of the forging, small flattened patches left by the hammer. Hammers and anvils were made of stone or bronze, and wooden tongs were used as well as bronze chisels and punches. The complex process used to produce vessels or other three-dimensional hollow shapes is another of the forging techniques.

Sheets and wires were made exclusively by hand using a hammer and anvil. Wire as fine as a millimetre in diameter was achieved. Very fine threads, used in filigree, are rolled from small strips of gold sheet or fine squared wires. Such rolled filigree wires have been found in the British Isles from the Late Bronze Age. Even in the Early Bronze Age twisted wire pins were used to decorate the hilts of daggers.

Decorative Techniques

Cast decoration was prepared in the wax model and transferred directly to metal in the casting. Like all cast objects they require afterwork. Among the plastic decorative techniques are torsion of square-section bars, bending, for instance of spiral wire, stamping (punch-marking), and chasing. In stamping, a repeated pattern is hammered into the gold surface with the aid of chisels and decorating punches. In chasing, by contrast, numerous blows are repeatedly struck with different punches whose imprints combine, producing linear patterns or plastic relief decoration. In stamping and chasing, the piece is positioned on a base, usually of chasing putty. Both techniques are also suitable for finishing off cast objects. Gold discs and lunulae are simple chased objects, while the Mold cape and the gold vessels show a complex application of this decorative technique. Filigree and granulation are ornamental techniques based on application of fine wire or granules to gold sheet. The ornamental parts are positioned individually, then soldered to the surface of the gold object. Both techniques reach a high standard in the Mediterranean region as early as the Bronze Age. In temperate Europe granulation and filigree only appear at the end of the Late Bronze Age. In this context it is interesting that, in western Europe, jewellery pieces with filigree and granulation first appear in Ireland and Britain with the so-called lock-rings and *bullae*, even before the first signs of this new technology from the Mediterranean are found on the Iberian Peninsula. Since engraving with a graver, which cuts filings out of the metal surface, is only possible with tempered iron tools, this technique can be ruled out in the Bronze Age. Joining techniques for gold working, besides soldering and casting-on, are riveting and seaming, and also sewing with gold thread. Among the polychrome decorative techniques of the Bronze Age are damascening and ornamental riveting. Damascening is a method of inlaying a different coloured metal into another metal surface. The depths of the metal inlays were produced either at casting or were worked with punches and chisels. The metal for inlaying is then hammered into the background using the plastic deformation technique. Wire, punch, and flat inlay occur in the Bronze Age.

Finishing

The final cleaning removes oxide layers with chemical agents, such as acids. Sandstones, ash, sand, or even silica-rich plants like horsetail were used in the finishing process to sand and polish objects.

Beyond the Bronze Age

In the Early Iron Age, the Bronze Age craft of goldworking was superseded in different ways in different parts of Europe. Gold objects once more occur mainly in elite graves. Except at the beginning of the Iron Age, north-west and northern Europe were poor in gold, while in south-western Europe the orientalizing goldwork from Tartessos developed, and in its wake came precious metalwork that used granulation and filigree techniques, strongly influenced by the east Mediterranean. In other regions in the late Hallstatt period, new Iron Age styles and techniques come to the fore, appearing above all in assemblages of richly decorated gold sheet objects such as necklaces and bracelets, fibulae, and bowls, together with bronze vessels and other prestige goods.

Bibliography

Armbruster, B. R. (2000). *Goldschmiedekunst und Bronzetechnik. Studien zum Metallhandwerk der Atlantischen Bronzezeit auf der Iberischen Halbinsel*, Monographies Instrumentum, 15. Monique Mergoil: Montagnac.

——and Louboutin, C. (2004). 'Parures en or de l'Âge du Bronze de Balinghem et Guînes (Pas-de-Calais): les aspects technologiques', *Antiquités Nationales*, 36: 133–46.

——and Perea, A. (2007). 'Change and persistence: the Mediterranean contribution on Atlantic metalwork in Late Bronze Age Iberia', in C. Burgess, P. Topping, and F. Lynch (eds.), *Beyond Stonehenge: Essays in Honour of Colin Burgess*. Oxford: Oxbow Books, 97–106.

Cahill, M. (2002). 'Before the Celts: treasures in gold and bronze', in P. F. Wallace and R. O Floinn (eds.), *Treasures of the National Museum of Ireland: Irish Antiquities*. Dublin: Gill & Macmilan, 86–124.

Clarke, D. V., Cowie, T. G., and Foxon, A. (1985). *Symbols of Power at the Time of Stonehenge*. Edinburgh: National Museum of Antiquities of Scotland.

Eluère, C. (1982). *Les Ors préhistoriques*, L'Age du Bronze en France, 2. Paris: Picard.

Eogan, G. (1994). *The Accomplished Art: Gold and Gold-Working in Britain and Ireland during the Bronze Age (c.2300–650 bc)*, Oxford Monograph, 42. Oxford: Oxbow Books.

Fitzpatrick, A. (2009). 'In his hands and in his head: the Amesbury Archer as a metalworker', in P. Clark (ed.), *Bronze Age Connections: Cultural Contact in Prehistoric Europe*. Oxford: Oxbow Books, 176–88.

Hartmann, A. (1982). *Prähistorische Goldfunde aus Europa II. Spektralanalytische Untersuchungen und deren Auswertung*, Studien zu den Anfängen der Metallurgie (SAM), 5. Berlin: Mann.

Hughes, G. (ed.) (2000). *The Lockington Gold Hoard: An Early Bronze Age Barrow Cemetry at Lockington, Leicestershire*. Oxford: Oxbow Books.

Jørgensen, L. and Petersen, P. V. (1998). *Guld, magt og tro [Gold, Power and Belief]. Danske guldskatte fra oldtid og middelalder*. Copenhagen: Thaning & Appel.

Meller, H. (ed.) (2004). *Der geschmiedete Himmel. Die Welt im Herzen Europas vor 3600 Jahren*. Stuttgart: Theiss.

Morteani, G. and Northover, P. (1995). *Prehistoric Gold in Europe: Mines, Metallurgy and Manufacture*. Amsterdam: Kluwer.

Needham, S. (2000). 'The development of embossed goldwork in Bronze Age Europe', *The Antiquaries Journal*, 80: 27–65.

——, Parfitt, K., and Varndell, G. (eds.) (2006). *The Ringlemere Cup: Precious Cups and the Beginning of the Chanel Bronze Age*, British Museum Research Publications, 163. London: The British Museum.

Perea, A. (1991). *Orfebrería prerromana*, Arqueología del Oro. Madrid: Caja de Madrid & Communidad de Madrid.

——and Armbruster, B. R. (2008). L'Archéologie de l'or en Europe, in *Perspectives*, 1: 29–48.

——, Montero, I., and Garcia Vuelta, O. (eds.) (2004). *Tecnología del oro antiguo: Europa y América. [Ancient Gold Technology: America and Europe.]* Anejos de Archivo Español de Arqueología, 32. Madrid: CSIC.

Schlosser, S., Kovacs, R., Pernicka, E., Günther, D., and Tellenbach, M. (2009). 'Fingerprints in gold', in M. Reindel and G. Wagner (eds.), *New Technologies for Archaeology: Multidisciplinary Investigations in Palpa and Nasca, Peru*. Heidelberg: Springer, 409–36.

Springer, T. (ed.) (2003). *Gold und Kult der Bronzezeit*. Nuremberg: Germanisches Nationalmuseum Nürnberg.

Taylor, J. J. (1980). *Bronze Age Goldwork of the British Isles*. Cambridge: Cambridge University Press.

CHAPTER 26

CRAFT PRODUCTION: CERAMICS, TEXTILES, AND BONE

JOANNA SOFAER, LISE BENDER JØRGENSEN, AND ALICE CHOYKE

Introduction

The Bronze Age witnessed an unprecedented flowering of craft activity. Throughout the period there were developments in decorative motifs, techniques, and skill with distinctive emphasis on the pleasing aesthetic through intricately elaborated objects made of a wide range of contrasting materials. These include metal, clay, bone, textiles, wood, bark, horn, antler, ivory, hide, amber, jet, stone, flint, reeds, shell, glass, and faience, either alone or in combination. Yet this period precedes the development of the state and urbanism, in which the creation of art became recognized as a distinct activity.

Although the Bronze Age was a period of common cultural values across Europe, crafts were performed in regionally specific ways leading to diversity of practice. Local developments in metalworking are well understood, but a frequent emphasis on metalworking has often been to the detriment of other crafts, some of which played a major role in everyday life. This chapter examines craft production in three contrasting materials that would have been widespread in the Bronze Age: ceramics, textiles, and bone. These were used throughout Europe, although they were differently articulated over time and space in ways that exploited the different properties and potentials of the individual materials to different degrees, and that responded to the varying needs of local communities.

Ceramics

Ceramics are the most prevalent of all Bronze Age craft items in archaeological contexts. Clay was a familiar medium in the Bronze Age (Michelaki 2008; Sofaer 2006) and there is an enormous range of objects made from fired clay. These reveal the use of a wide range of resources, manufacturing techniques, and decoration, reflecting the complexity and dynamism of Bronze Age ceramic craftsmanship.

Types of Objects and Contexts of Use

The majority of ceramics are vessels used for serving food, drinking, storage, or food preparation, but there is also a range of other objects including spoons, loom-weights, spindle-whorls, roof-weights, portable ovens, perforated clay slabs, briquetage and other ceramics related to salt production, anthropomorphic and zoomorphic objects, abstract shapes including stars or crescents, models such as carts or house urns, as well as miniature replica vessels (thought of variously as toys, practice pieces, or votive objects). There are also clay objects used in metalworking such as tuyères and crucibles, as well as clay moulds for casting metal objects, although many of the latter were probably fired through the heat produced in pouring metal.

In the majority of locations in Europe, pottery is found in both settlement and cemetery contexts. In only a few cases, such as in the Early Bronze Age of the Rhine Valley, is it restricted to the domestic domain. In many areas, however, the relationship between settlement and cemetery material is poorly understood, as ceramics have traditionally been analysed on a site by site basis and comparative work is lacking. Nonetheless, cross-over between domestic and mortuary forms has frequently been observed. In some places domestic vessels may be reused in mortuary contexts, including making offerings to the deceased as observed at Pitten in Austria (Sørensen and Rebay 2008). In other contexts, however, specific forms or soft, low-fired facsimiles may have been made specifically for deposition in graves, such as at Dunaújváros-Kosziderpadlás in Hungary (Budden 2008).

In settlements ceramic vessels were used for storage, preparation, cooking and serving of food and drink. In some regions they were also deployed as prestige items used in display or in cult activities. In several Middle Bronze Age groups in the Carpathian Basin, fine-ware bowls with motifs on their base were designed to be hung on walls, indicating the value placed on ceramic craftsmanship (Sofaer 2006; 2010). It has been suggested that the increased elaboration of pottery represents the transfer of a prestige ideology from metal to ceramics (Vicze 2001). By contrast, in other regions, such as Iberia, the predominantly plain pottery has been seen as a deliberate attempt to hide otherwise well-established social inequalities (Diaz-Andreu 1994).

Regional and Temporal Variation

From the Early to Late Bronze Age there is a great deal of temporal and regional variation in ceramic forms and prevalence. This enormous variability has been used to develop chronologies and distinguish local and regional cultural groups. A strong typological emphasis and focus on understanding local chronological sequences means, however, that comparative work on pottery is relatively under-developed. National traditions sometimes insist upon different names for what may, in some cases, be rather similar pottery types crossing modern borders. Furthermore, in many parts of Europe a historical emphasis on the analysis of pottery from graves (which is frequently more complete than material from settlements) has guided the development of local and regional typologies and has led to problems of terminology. For example, the term 'urn' suggests a vessel found in burial contexts used to hold cremated bone, but typologically similar storage vessels found on settlement sites can also be called urns.

In general, the range of ceramic objects increases in a north-west to south-east gradient across the continent. Thus in north-west Europe, Scandinavia, and Iberia the range of ceramic forms is rather restricted compared to central, southern, and eastern Europe. In Britain and Ireland, Early Bronze Age forms are simple bipartite and tripartite vases and bowls often known as Food Vessels, as well as a variety of urn forms showing regional trends (Gibson 2002) (Fig. 26.1). Middle Bronze Age forms are dominated by urns of bucket, barrel, and globular form, with a few smaller vessels such as cups. In the Late Bronze Age some areas, in particular Ireland and Wales, are almost aceramic, but in southern England the range of vessels increases, including tall jars and bowls. In Scandinavia the quantity of pottery increased considerably from the earlier to later Bronze Age, although this change in abundance may reflect changes in disposal patterns (Sofaer 2010). The range of vessel types remained rather narrow and relatively consistent throughout the Bronze Age. Forms include biconical or cylinder-necked urns of various sizes and different domestic vessels, including storage and cooking vessels, with a few strainers and pot lids added late in the Bronze Age. There are also some small bowls and drinking cups, found more frequently in burials. There are no plates, although large open forms

FIG. 26.1 Early Bronze Age collared urn. Stourhead Collection.

Photo: Wiltshire Heritage Museum, Devizes.

sometimes occur in the Late Bronze Age as vessel shape categories became more distinct. In Iberia pottery forms are generally rather simple throughout the period, with carinated bowls, shallow open dishes, cups, and baggy storage vessels of various sizes, although more technically difficult forms are represented by *pithoi* (large jars) and chalice-shaped vessels such as those found in the El Argar B burials. In the Late Bronze Age of north-east Spain, cylinder-necked urns and other forms relating to the urnfields of southern France are known.

In central and eastern Europe there is much greater development in ceramic types through the course of the Bronze Age. Early Bronze Age forms are initially relatively simple with one-handled cups and polypod bowls, such as at Straubing, Bavaria. In general, vessels change from globular shapes to more angular conical and carinated forms at the height of the Early Bronze Age, a typical example being the Únětice 'hour-glass' cup. Other forms include jugs, small shallow bowls, storage vessels, sieves or strainers, and hanging vessels. Middle Bronze Age Tumulus culture pottery is marked by a range of complex very fine wares including vessels with globular bellies and cylindrical or conical necks, related urn forms, jugs, and pedestalled bowls, expressed as many local forms. The widespread Urnfield pottery of the Late Bronze Age includes the urn itself—often with a biconical body, cylindrical neck, and everted rim—cups, low conical bowls, and sometimes plates. These general forms are also interpreted in local ways and become more complex and angular over time.

Developments in the Carpathian Basin and east to the Black Sea show a tendency to extraordinary elaboration and exaggeration of forms, some of which are very angular or highly stylized (Fig. 26.2). The range of vessel types is wide and varied, representing the work of accomplished potters capable of producing a range of technically complex forms. Basic Early Bronze Age types include cups, bowls, jugs, hanging vessels, pedestalled vessels, and storage vessels as the core of the assemblage. At the transition from the Early to Middle Bronze Age the range of forms within individual vessel types increases and new types are

FIG. 26.2 Middle Bronze Age Koszider period bowl, Százhalombatta, Hungary.

Photo: Matrica Museum, Százhalombatta.

introduced, resulting in a wide assemblage that includes small cups, sieves, fish-dishes, deep domestic bowls, small domestic bowls, cooking jars, storage vessels, fine-ware bowls, jugs, globular and biconical urns, and ember covers. The range of vessel forms contracts at the end of the Middle Bronze Age, but there is noticeable embellishment and exaggeration of existing shapes; shared basic forms were explored within a proliferation of local potting traditions. In the Carpathian Basin, Late Bronze Age vessels are less abundant and have been comparatively little studied. There are new fine-ware shapes with everted rims and high strap handles, bucket and cylindrical neck urns, as well as a marked distinction between the coarse and fine-ware repertoires, which seem to mark a break from previous traditions. In some parts of the region there is an increase in large storage jars, while other areas display local variations on the Urnfield pottery.

Similarities between the pottery of the north Italian *terramare* and that found on Hungarian tells, in particular the exaggerated 'horned' handles of fine-ware jugs and cups, has frequently been observed (Pearce 1998). The abundant and elaborate pottery of the Apennine culture, found through much of the Italian Peninsula, displays a wide variety of shapes, although these are remarkably homogeneous throughout the region, with well-defined size ranges (Lukesh and Howe 1978). The *capeduncola* (one-handled cup or bowl) is particularly common, while other types include cheese strainers and milk boilers.

Materials Selection and Manufacturing Processes

Although ceramic production was guided by the availability of local resources, potters' technical decisions were not confined to the environment, raw materials, and tools, but were also socially and culturally defined. Throughout the production process, from procurement of clay through to firing, Bronze Age pottery represents a wide range of technological choices. In many places, however, potting techniques were not substantially altered over the course of the Bronze Age. Instead established techniques were deployed in new ways, combinations, and with changes in technical skill, resulting in contrasting ways of designing objects, surface treatments, and decoration.

Treatment of clays is complex and highly variable, with a full range of deliberately added tempers that frequently cluster in temporal and spatial groups. These include grog, small pebbles, crushed flint, granite, limestone, shell, and sand, either on their own or in combination. Compared to earlier periods there is relatively little evidence for organic tempers. Very fine wares made from well-prepared clay and no added inclusions are also found. Despite the emphasis of modern ceramic studies on the functional reasons for the addition of tempers to clays, in particular their role in modulating the thermal dynamics of vessels, this does not always appear to be the case for Bronze Age vessels. For example, the deliberate inclusion of quartz pebbles in Early Bronze Age pottery in Denmark risks such vessels cracking during firing. Middle Bronze Age cooking and storage vessels from Hungary are tempered with grog but in smaller quantities than required to benefit the thermodynamics of the vessel. Here pottery of the same colour and fabric as the new vessel may have been targeted for reuse as grog, suggesting that the making of pottery may have been imbued with symbolic significance (Kreiter 2007).

Throughout the continent the vast majority of ceramics are handmade. They were constructed using a range of vessel-forming techniques including coiling, slab and ring-building, pinching, and paddle and anvil techniques. There is little evidence for the use of moulds, although some very fine wares, such as those of the Szeremle group straddling Hungary and Croatia, have walls only 2–5 mm thick. In some regions, such as northern Poland, vessel-forming techniques appear to have remained the same throughout the Bronze Age despite changes in vessel form, and to have been locally specific; vessels that look the same were made in different local traditions (Dąbrowski 2004). In other regions, such as in the Carpathian Basin, vessel-forming techniques were deployed in expedient combinations depending on vessel size and shape (Budden and Sofaer 2009). In central and south-east Europe, particularly in the Late Bronze Age, modelling techniques were used to create innovative and complex shapes such as the zoomorphic vessels of the Lausitz group, Urnfield vessels resembling boots in Lower Austria and Hungary, or the model chariot from Dupljaja in Serbia (see Fig. 45.5b). Representational modelling declines the further west one goes; it is rare in Scandinavia (although there are a few anthropomorphic urns), and is absent in Britain. In the Late Bronze Age the potter's wheel was adopted in southern Italy and Iberia. In the former this is associated with Mycenaean influence, while in the latter there is some evidence for an independent local tradition of wheel-turned ceramics prior to Phoenician colonization (Almagro-Gorbea and Fontes 1997; Tanasi 2005).

There is a wide range of decorations and surface finishes, ranging from technically very simple to highly complex and elaborate, that may cover all, part, or none of the vessel. As with variation in ceramic types, there is a north-west to south-east gradient in the elaboration of ceramic vessels, with greater use of the vessel surface towards the south-east. This may reflect differential emphasis on pottery as a creative medium. An exception to this distribution is the pottery of the British Early Bronze Age where decoration is technically simple but can be ornate, with abstract geometric patterns made up of lozenges, hatching, zigzags, and herringbone designs made by twisted cord and comb impressions, stab, stab-and-drag, and false-relief techniques (Gibson 2002). In Scandinavia, few vessels were decorated and decoration was rather simple with incised lines, criss-cross lines, parallel stripes, and, in the Later Bronze Age, occasional horizontal cordons. In earlier Bronze Age Jutland clay was deliberately and unevenly applied to some vessel exteriors in a form of rustication that shares traits with the Middle Bronze Age ceramics of the Netherlands (Bakker et al. 1977). Tempering with small pebbles visible on the vessel surface may have acted as a decorative medium. In Iberia, much of the pottery is plain or has limited decoration. Argaric ceramics, for example, are burnished but rarely decorated except for finger impressions on the rims and applied buttons. Where pottery is decorated this is frequently linked to high-quality surfaces, and may indicate a marked difference between luxury vessels, perhaps with ceremonial significance, and coarser domestic ones (López-Astilleros 2000). A notable exception to the lack of decoration is the Las Cogotas pottery of the Meseta, which displays various combinations of decorative techniques, including incised, impressed, stabbed, *Kerbschnitt* (incised decoration resembling lattice work), and so-called 'boquique technique' (a series of small interrupted marks impressed on a continuous incised line).

In central, southern, and eastern Europe, in the Middle and Late Bronze Age in particular, certain classes of pottery, such as fine wares, are particularly striking in their visual qualities and appeal, requiring great technical skill for successful production, and significant investment of time. Exaggerated embellishments and elaborately decorated surfaces combined a variety of finishes and decorative techniques. In some areas, such as in the Otomani group, this resulted in a 'baroque' effect. Complex surface designs may be applied to the vessel, sometimes over its entire surface or in specific zones, including swirls, lines, circles, or triangles. Applied decorations such as bosses and cordons resulted in three-dimensional vessel surfaces. The Tumulus phase in central Europe is marked by the development of rich and complex decoration applied to a range of fine-ware jugs, urns, and pedestalled bowls. *Kerbschnitt* decoration is a particular feature. The black, burnished ware of the Apennine culture pottery is also very striking, being decorated with incised spirals, meanders, dots, and bands of dots. The rilled or fluted decoration on vessel bodies and 'turban decoration' on the rim that is characteristic of Urnfield pottery throughout large parts of Europe also has the effect of creating a three-dimensional surface that draws the eye across the surface of the pot. Significantly, despite the widespread nature of this decorative device, not all vessels are decorated; decoration varies in its positioning on the pot and in execution. Thus, while general principles of decoration were adhered to, a general notion of aesthetics may have been important rather than faithful copying.

Colour may also be deployed to create effects. In the Transdanubian Encrusted Pottery culture and Gîrla Mare culture, a striking feature is the use of white inlay on a black (or occasionally red/brown) vessel body. The inlays are made from calcareous and, intriguingly, bone mixtures (Roberts, Sofaer, and Kiss 2008). The application of metal to ceramic, while relatively rare, also creates distinctive surface colour contrasts seen, for example, in the Late Bronze Age vessels decorated with thin tin strips from the settlement site of Hauterive-Champréveyres in Switzerland. In contrast to developments in the Aegean, painting was rarely used, although graphite-coated pottery is known from the end of the Late Bronze Age in, for example, the Swiss lake villages and the eastern Iberian Peninsula.

The emphasis on surface qualities and finish is also reflected in some regions in the use of distinct colour effects achieved through control over firing. The black burnished wares of the Tumulus, Terramare, and Vatya cultures were produced through complete reduction of the clay, a process requiring great skill and knowledge of fuel and firesettings. This may have been assisted through the use of kilns enabling air regulation during firing such as those found at the sites of Basilicanova, Italy (Cattani 1997), and Herzogenburg, Austria (Willvonseder 1937: 338–41, Taf. 13–15; Neugebauer 1994: 159, Taf. 92, 4–9). However, compared with the quantity of Bronze Age ceramics, excavations of kilns are relatively rare and their use was probably confined to particular regions. Even where kilns were in use, other firing strategies may also have been deployed for specific kinds of pots; large storage vessels or urns are too big to have been fired in the excavated kilns and may have been pit-fired, while coarse wares may have been bonfire-fired. In the rest of the continent almost all pottery conforms to the characteristics of bonfire firing, displaying smudging and colour variation in cross-section. The majority of European Bronze Age ceramics were fired at relatively low temperatures (600–800° C) (see Dąbrowski 2004; Gibson 2002; Maniatis and Tite 1981).

Organization of Production

Despite the ubiquity of pottery, direct evidence for its production is relatively rare. Interpretations are based largely upon the qualities of pottery itself and correlations of these with ethnographic studies. The latter have shown a range of production modes and the potential complexity of Bronze Age pottery production strategies has been both highlighted and subject to scrutiny (Hamilton 2002). In general, however, simple coarse wares made from local materials are considered to be the products of non-specialist household production, whereas high-quality fine wares with complex form and decoration are considered more likely to be the product of specialists. Based on this distinction, production strategies can be considered to vary across Europe following the north-west to south-east gradient in form and decoration described above. Thus in Britain, for example, pottery production is generally thought to have taken place within the domestic domain for local use, although particular fine- ware forms may have been made in workshops or by part-time specialists on a seasonal basis (Gibson 2002; Hamilton 2002). By contrast, in the Carpathian Basin the role of specialist potters may have been more prominent, although here too a mixture of different production strategies may be identified with both specialist and non-specialist potters at work (Budden 2008). In those few areas where the wheel was adopted in the Late Bronze Age, this has been associated with the development of craft specialization linked to elites, although recent work on the adoption of the wheel in the Aegean hints that the picture may be more subtle and complex (Berg 2007).

More recently, studies of skill in Bronze Age pottery production have emphasized the learned nature of pottery making and have aimed to explore general assumptions about pottery production in more detail (Michelaki 2008; Budden and Sofaer 2009). At the Vatya tell settlement of Százhalombatta in Hungary the most technically complex vessels (fine wares and urns) show the least technical error, those that are moderately difficult to make (domestic vessels) show modest error, and those that are technically easiest (cups) show the most faults. In a system of casual household production where potters are not specialists, one might expect more complex vessels to be most error-prone and simplest forms to suffer least. The pattern at Százhalombatta, however, indicates a range in potting proficiency associated with a structure of apprenticeship and lower tolerance for faults in more elaborate forms; less skilled potters learned on easier pieces before progressing to more complex forms produced by experts (Budden 2008; Budden and Sofaer 2009). At Százhalombatta the consistently high quality of firing compared to the execution of other technical variables suggests that there may have been specialists in this aspect of production. Vessels may therefore have been the product of multiple authors, something that has also been suggested for British Collared Urns on the basis of a detailed study of their decoration (Law 2008).

Links to Other Crafts

Bronze Age ceramics from across the continent have frequently been linked to other crafts through skeuomorphism (the sharing of the formal qualities of objects in order to deliberately evoke an object made in one material in another). Most commonly skeuomorphism has been identified between pottery vessels and objects made out of metal and basketry. The exaggerated 'horn' handles and high surface sheen of the black burnished wares of central Europe and north Italy have been considered imitative of metal forms and surface finish (Sofaer 2006), while some British Bronze Age vessels have been identified as basketry skeuomorphs (Hurcombe 2008). In the case of the latter, recent experimental work has shown that rather than being true to one particular type of basket, pottery skeuomorphs were generalized rather than specific renditions (Hurcombe 2008). The influence of leather and wood objects on ceramics has also been identified (Manby 1995).

In some places, rather than deliberate imitation, decorative motifs on ceramic objects seem to have drawn inspiration from other materials. Some of the intricate and elaborately decorated inlaid vessels found in Croatia may have been inspired by stitching or embroidery patterns in textiles. Similar inspiration has been suggested for the decoration on Cogotas

I pottery in Iberia (López-Astilleros 2000). Some ceramics also appear to borrow decorative techniques from other materials. For example, *Kerbschnitt* decoration is reminiscent of wood-carving. Decorative designs may also be shared between materials, such as the sun motif that is found on both pottery and metal objects.

Cross-fertilization between crafts is also evident in some technical elements of ceramic manufacture that may involve the use of tools or techniques drawn from other crafts. This can include the use of bone tools for incising and impressing decoration, twisted cord for decorative impressions, and textile wrappings to support thin wet clay during the building up of the pot or thinning of the wall. In the case of the latter, textile impressions may also act as a deliberate symbolic visual reference to other materials (Hurcombe 2008), and have been observed in a range of Bronze Age ceramics including the Lausitz and Trzciniec cultures in Poland (Klosinska 1991; Dąbrowski 2004). Very rarely imprints of bronze objects have been observed on ceramics (Dąbrowski 2004). Such observations imply either exchange between craftspeople or multi-skilled potters who are able to work competently in more than a single craft (Sofaer 2010). In some cases technical solutions may be shared between potters and other craftspeople. For example, in the Nagyrév and Vatya cultures of Hungary the method of attaching handles to ceramic vessels using a kind of peg joint echoes rivets in metal and mortice and tenon joints in wood (Sofaer 2006). In the Iberian Late Bronze Age the use of the lathe and the drill in metalworking and jewellery manufacture may have been influential in the development of a local wheel-turning tradition (Almagro-Gorbea and Fontes 1997). This transfer of know-how from one medium to another requires direct familiarity with other craft practices and the development of social networks among craftspeople (Sofaer 2006, 2010).

Textiles

Textiles, and the making of them, were important aspects of Bronze Age life. In the form of clothing, soft furnishings, and other household textiles, tents, sacking, and animal trappings, textiles served a wide range of practical as well as symbolic functions. Colours, texture, and decoration of textile items contributed to inform observers of the owner's rank, wealth, and identity. The manufacturing process involved many stages, different skills, and considerable consumption of time in every household, and played an important role in the organization of society. Textiles are, however, organic materials and decompose easily. Major archaeological finds are therefore rare. The main bodies of Bronze Age textiles in Europe derive from sources with freak conditions of preservation: the oak coffins of Denmark, the alkaline lakes in the Alpine region, and the salt mines of Austria. Samples, chiefly in the form of textile fragments, have been found in most parts of Europe. They derive from graves, depositions (particularly in wetlands), or as impressions in pottery. Textile tools (where they can be properly identified) form another important source that help in establishing an overview of textile crafts in the European Bronze Age.

Types of Objects and Contexts of Use

The most conspicuous items of Bronze Age textiles are the complete sets of clothing recovered from oak coffins in Denmark (Broholm and Hald 1940; for a recent overview see

Bergerbrant 2007). Four male and three female costumes are on display in the National Museum of Denmark. Whether they represent only the ritual dress of an elite or also the daily wear of an average Bronze Age man and woman is an open question, but they certainly offer us some very welcome and vivid glimpses of Bronze Age clothing. The men were laid to rest in wrap-around kilts of various lengths, large oval or kidney-shaped cloaks, footwear consisting of simple hide shoes, strips of cloth, and in one case a cloth shoe with the sole sewn on. Headwear obviously was an important item and appears in two different forms: a semi-globular, piled hat made of several layers of cloth and finely sewn, and a simpler, taller version, sewn from a single layer of cloth without decoration. Some graves contained both types, indicating that they held a different meaning. In addition, a few further items of male clothing have been found in other graves. A tongue-shaped piece of cloth found with a collection of objects for magical purposes bears close resemblance to loin coverings depicted on figurines, presumably ritual garments. An oak coffin in southern Jutland contained a complete, as yet unidentified garment. Rectangular, 97 cm long and 9.5 cm wide, it is a strap rather than a belt, and may, perhaps, represent another ritual garment.

The women were buried wearing blouses of almost identical form, with elbow-length sleeves. All three females also wore belts, long bands of woven material ending in a fringed tassel. Two of the women were wrapped in large pieces of cloth sewn together to form a tube, interpreted in a variety of ways: as a long skirt, as a draped garment covering the body in different ways, or simply as a burial shroud. The young woman in the Egtved oak coffin wore a short skirt constructed from cords that caused quite a sensation when it was found in 1921. It was worn hanging on the hips, some 20 cm below the blouse; similar corded skirts depicted on figurines indicate that they were sometimes worn as sole garments, presumably in ritual contexts. Several graves have been found to contain rows of bronze tubes as decoration for corded skirts. Producing jingling sounds and flashes of golden metal as the wearer moved, this added to the garment's symbolic significance. The blouse of the Skrydstrup woman is decorated with embroideries. Fragments of similar decoration in several other graves show that this was not a unique feature. Headgear also formed an important part of women's attire, in various forms such as bands, hairnets, and a quite elaborate 'bonnet'. Footwear appears in the same forms as in the male graves.

The salt mines of Hallstatt in Austria form the second major source of Bronze Age textiles in Europe (Grömer 2007). The roughly 250 items recovered so far are fragments, presumed to be mostly the remains of clothing. Some have been put to secondary uses as working clothing, mats or knee-pads; some show repairs after heavy use, or have been used as patches. Some, however, are interpreted as the remains of carrier sacks for salt, and represent primary uses. The textiles from the salt mines offer limited information on the types of object they represent; instead, they form a rich source for the study of textile craftsmanship, design, and technology in Bronze Age Europe.

Regional and Temporal Variability

The Bronze Age brought a series of textile innovations, but also regional and chronological variations (Bender Jørgensen 1986, 1992; Rast-Eicher 2005). Differences are reflected in fibre, yarn, weave, density, textile, and various forms of decoration. The bast fibres and basketry techniques of twining, coiling, netting, and knotless netting that formed the staple of Neolithic textile traditions were replaced by flax, wool, and woven fabrics. Flax was introduced to south and central Europe during the sixth millennium BC, while wool does not seem to have been an aspect of sheep husbandry before c.2800 BC. Both fibres, however, remained relatively marginal until the Middle Bronze Age.

The main variable of Bronze Age textiles is yarn types. Yarn may be twisted clockwise (z) or counter-clockwise (s), and appear as single yarns or as plied. Further, different yarns may be used for warp and weft, or even within one of these systems. Fibre, weave, density, finishing processes, dyeing, and other forms of decoration add further variability.

In Scandinavia and the north European lowlands, almost all Bronze Age textiles are made of relatively thick wool yarns. They show a preference for s-spun warp and z-spun weft in the Early Bronze Age; this changed with Period III towards using s-spun yarns in both systems. Most are woven in tabby or plain-weave in rather coarse qualities (2–6 threads/cm). Bands and belts appear in tabby variations such as repp. Some of the garments seem to have been subject to fulling; decoration is seen in the form of embroidery, elaborate tassels, long pile on fabrics intended for cloaks, stripes obtained by yarn spun in different directions, and applied bronze decoration. Patterns could also be created by combining wools of various natural colours; evidence of dyeing has not yet been found in the north. A single example of twill is dated to Montelius Period VI. Evidence of textiles made from vegetable fibres is almost non-existent, but this is presumably due to adverse conditions of preservation. A fine fabric of nettle cloth from the princely grave of Lusehøj on Funen (Period V) is as yet the main example.

In west and central Europe, linen tabbies made from plied yarns seem to remain standard throughout the Bronze Age, although a series of changes in loom-weights, spindle-whorls, and sheep bones suggest that another fibre—presumably wool—had also become important (Rast-Eicher 2005). In Britain and the Iberian Peninsula, z-plied yarns were common, whereas central Europe seems to have preferred s-ply. In east-central Europe, wool fabrics gained importance with the beginning of the Middle Bronze Age, and were increasingly made from single, s-spun yarns.

Twill first makes an appearance in the Middle Bronze Age (Grömer 2007). It is especially suited for wool, enhancing properties like insulation and flexibility, and also offered a series of entirely new options for Bronze Age weavers in the form of textures, woven patterns such as chevrons and rhomboids, and specific effects when combined with different spun or coloured yarns. Basket weave appeared in the Urnfield period, offering further variables. To these may be added applied decoration such as different forms of needlework, including patterns created from sewn-on seeds.

Materials Selection and Manufacturing Processes

Textile production consists of a long series of work processes, starting with the procurement and preparation of raw materials, primarily flax and wool. Hemp is first found in Hallstatt period contexts. Gold makes a first appearance as a textile material in an Austrian grave of the Urnfield period. Each fibre requires separate processes of procurement. Flax needs to be grown in well-fertilized soils; when ready, the plant is pulled out of the ground, dried and rippled to remove the pod. Then retting, drying, breaking or pounding, scotching and heckling follow, to extract and prepare the fibres for spinning. Wool is obtained from sheep. Bronze Age sheep had a double coat, with long, coarse hairs and fine bottom wool, and was harvested by plucking or rooing. Afterwards the wool was sorted into categories, cleaned, teased, combed, and drawn into slivers or rovings before spinning. Shearing was first introduced in the La Tène period.

Spinning and weaving are the next steps in the process of textile production. Spindle and distaff were the main spinning tools, applicable for flax as well as wool fibres, although spinners usually employed different variants for each fibre, as well as for warp and weft yarns. Spindle-whorls indicate that the drop spindle was commonly used in most parts of Europe. Their weights offer further information on the range of yarn types, as heavy whorls were used for thick yarns and lightweight whorls for thin yarns. In Scandinavia, few or no Bronze Age spindle-whorls have been found, suggesting that spinning was carried out on spindles without whorls, perhaps made entirely out of wood. Often z-spinning is associated with the drop spindle, s-spinning with supported spinning or by rolling the spindle down the spinner's thigh; most spindles can, however, be twisted in both directions, although one of them seems to have served as a norm in most societies. This remains the case even today, as s-spun yarns for weaving are very difficult to acquire!

Weaving required a loom. Loom-weights and details such as starting borders in extant textiles indicate that the warp-weighted loom was the most common type in Bronze Age Europe. Again, little evidence is available from Scandinavia, suggesting that a different loom may have been used here. Several alternatives such as the back-strap loom, the ground loom or the two-beam loom are possible. Tools for weaving also comprise weaving swords and weaving combs (Bazzanella et al. 2003). Tabby is the main Bronze Age weave, with variations such as repp, where the yarns of one system are so dense that they cover the other. The Middle Bronze Age saw the introduction of twill. It appears in several varieties and requires the addition of sheds to the loom. This may be done by adding one or two heddle rods (rods to which cord loops or 'heddles' are attached, separating the warp threads and making a path for the weft), or by manipulating continuous heddle loops. Rather than a different loom, twill weaving demanded more technical skill, as did the introduction of woven and applied decoration. Woven decoration is constricted by the basic framework of the two yarn systems, favouring simple geometric patterns like stripes and checks, but the skilled weaver can create a rich variety of these, including forms that appear rhomboid or curvilinear. The insertion of pattern wefts or band techniques such as tablet weaving may produce almost any type of motif, while embroidery and other forms of stitching offer no restrictions at all.

The art of dyeing was introduced to Europe during the Bronze Age. A richly decorated fabric from Pfäffikon-Irgenhausen in Switzerland, dated to the transition from Early to Middle Bronze Age, is one of the earliest. Further evidence derives from the salt mines of Hallstatt where analyses have shown dyeing with woad (*Isatis tinctoria*), weld (*Reseda luteola*), tannins, some unidentified yellows, and a red dye, possibly of the madderworth family (*Rubiaceae*). One of these textiles was piece-dyed, the others presumably in the fleece (Grömer 2007).

FIG. 26.3 An example of the Bronze Age textiles from the salt mines of Hallstatt.

Photo: Natural History Museum Vienna.

Organization of Production

Written sources from Mycenaean Greece, early second millennium BC Anatolia and Mesopotamia, and Pharaonic Egypt show highly specialized textile production, workshops, and division of labour (Trolle-Larsen 1987; Kemp and Vogelsang-Eastwood 2001; Killen 2007). Infrastructures in northern and central Europe hardly allowed such organization, but evidence for contacts across the continent, such as Baltic amber found in Greece, indicates some reciprocal knowledge. At first glance, the coarse woollen textiles of the north European Bronze Age do not appear to bear any evidence of specialized production. On the contrary, irregularities due to uneven warp tension and weaving faults give the impression that weavers were far from professionals. Still, the texture of these textiles remains homogeneous throughout the Bronze Age, suggesting that this was in fact how they were designed. Details like the piled hats, embroideries, and tassels prove that Bronze Age textile craftspeople did not lack skill. Since context as well as the peculiar nature of some of the items suggest that they served ritual purposes, we may, perhaps, see them as the products of specialists at the household level. The Bronze Age textiles from Hallstatt show a similar mixture of skilled and less skilled work, but with much more variety and reflecting primary uses along with recirculation (Fig. 26.3). They may reflect household production on a scale beyond the needs of the producers.

Links to Other Crafts

A patterned textile from Molina di Ledro has a close parallels in anthropomorphic stelae found in the Alpine region, indicating that the stelae are indeed statues of clothed people, displaying fashions at the transition to the Bronze Age (Rast-Eicher 2005). As described above, several links can be found between items of clothing from the Danish oak coffins and bronze figurines. At the end of the Bronze Age we find depictions of textile work on pottery as well as bronzes.

Worked Bone

People remained reliant on bone tools to carry out many day-to-day tasks until well into the Late Bronze Age in most of Europe. Although social networks must have ranged well beyond the confines of the household, the bone tools suggest that individual settlements still remained an important frame of reference. At the same time, the worked osseous material was implicated in far-flung trade connections. These bone tools probably spread rapidly with horsemen across broad areas of Europe, and so the Middle and Late Bronze Age is also characterized by the production of decorative antler objects produced with a variety of metal tools by semi-specialists. Two contradictory social tendencies are thus expressed in the worked osseous materials: technical conservatism at the household level and production of new, sophisticated objects, largely meant for display of rank and social position.

Types of Objects and Contexts of Use

Many bone tool types from the earlier periods continue to be made throughout the Bronze Age. Some new types were introduced including certain leather-working tools, elaborate projectile points, and paired skates, as well as ornamented antler objects. Ordinary household bone tools were conceived in a less complex fashion, enabling rapid, self-sufficient production from food refuse. This simplification does not mean the tools were not curated or that the crafts where they were used were less important, only that the attention given to their production became less formalized.

The two most important types of equipment in Bronze Age households were awls and bevel-ended tools (Fig. 26.4). Until the Late Bronze Age both were made from animal bone waste extracted during food processing or, like ribs or whole bones, selected at the time of primary butchering. Compared to Neolithic bone tool production, these bone objects tend to be based on spiral fractures that occurred when long bones were broken for their marrow. The classic prehistoric awl based on metapodials, grooved along the diaphysis and split, was still made but was generally quite rare in Middle and Late Bronze Age bone tool assemblages. The know-how still existed to make them but was only infrequently employed.

Recent use-wear analyses on Middle and Late Bronze Age tools from tell sites in northern Greece and Albania provide hints on how these pointed tools and bevel-edged tools may have functioned in small-scale household crafts (Christidou 2008). More than half of the points from the Middle Bronze Age Albanian site of Sovjan seem to have been used in piercing hides and leather. The remainder of the pointed tools, especially needles, display wear commensurate with contact with plant-based materials for sewing, weaving, and coiled basketry. Bevel-edged tools based on fractured long bones of large ungulates were often used for splitting wood or as bark-peelers and cutters, as were many of the rose and beam-based heavy-duty antler tools with a bevelled active end (Christidou 2008) (see Fig. 26.4). There is evidence that tools from fractured long bones and complete ribs were also used to extract ore in mines (Antipina 2001).

From the Balkans up into the Hungarian Plain, one group of caprine tibia-based bevel-edged tools were certainly used as hide scrapers. Rib-based scrapers with a defined edge at their distal end also characterize bone tool assemblages of the period in the same region. The macro-wear analyses on these rib tools mostly suggest use on soft pliant animal materials (Choyke 1984,

2000; Christidou 2008). Rib scrapers are also found in Late Bronze Age levels at Biskupin (Drzewicz 2004). Some rib tools worked along the distal and medio-lateral sides but without sharp defined edges may have been used to smooth large clay surfaces in Middle to Late Bronze Age contexts in northern Greece and Albania (Christidou, pers. comm.). Similar rib tools have been found in some Early Bronze Age Bell Beaker and Makó culture contexts in Hungary.

Finally, the Neolithic tradition of using split boar tusks as scrapers remains widespread across Europe until the end of the Middle Bronze Age, with only the size and shape of these tools varying somewhat between regions. Use-wear studies of such objects from the final Neolithic of France at the site of Chalain in the French Jura show they were used to scrape wood and peel bark (Maigrot 2005). 'Smoothers' made from phalanges and/or astragali with abraded flat surfaces, made from caprines, cattle, red and roe deer, and horse (depending on availability), may be found on Middle and Late Bronze Age sites in Hungary, the Balkans, and within the *Terramare* material as well (see Fig. 26.4). Whether these are actually gaming pieces, or burnishers of some kind, or both, is unclear.

Some simple tools, probably for leather-working, appear for the first time in Bronze Age contexts. Based on use-wear studies (Olsen 2001), leather thong-smoothers from the Early Bronze Age (c.2800–2500 BC) were first identified on Early Bronze Age sites in Kazakhstan. Made from horse mandibles, they were notched around the area of the third molar. Similar objects from slightly later Early Bronze Age contexts in Slovenia and Middle Bell Beaker contexts have been studied by Alice Choyke (1984), and examples have been reported from the Czech Republic (Kyselý, pers. comm.). Probable thong smoothers, this time with polished, rounded wear on the oral portion of the cattle mandible, were produced in Early Bronze Age, Bell Beaker Csepel group and Makó culture settlements in Hungary. Caprine mandibles were used to manufacture the same type in the Middle Bronze Age in the Carpathian Basin.

Another specialized tool, often incorrectly published as skates (Gerškovič 1999), spread rapidly over large areas of central and eastern Europe at the end of the Middle Bronze Age. Such tools are even found in Late Bronze Age Biskupin in Poland (Drzewicz 2004). Made exclusively from complete radii of red deer, wild and domestic cattle, horse, or even roe deer, domestic pig and caprines, they have a facet running down the length of the dorsal surface of the radius and may be perforated in a medial-lateral direction above the distal epiphysis.

Where red-deer antler was not in good supply as in the Baltic region, certain bone-based objects were carefully manufactured—more in the manner of antler tools and ornaments elsewhere. In Estonia, some barbed and tanged arrowheads with a triangular cross-section, a type widespread at the beginning of the Late Bronze Age in Europe, were mostly made from bone as opposed to the more usual antler. Socketed spearheads in neighbouring Lithuania were made carefully, exclusively from caprine and pig-tibia diaphyses (Luik and Maldre 2007).

The best-documented class of antler tools are perforated, heavy objects incorporating the burr and beam of the antler rack (see Fig. 18.3). The rose portion often displays some kind of battering while the other end may be bevelled in an axe or adze-like manner. Although it has been assumed that these tools were used in agricultural activities, use-wear studies suggest that such items functioned rather to split wood (Maigrot 2005; Christidou 2008). Another rose and beam tool that co-occurs with the axe/adze over wide areas of Europe in the Bronze Age was used as a sleeve with a hole for a separate blade at the end opposite the rose. Red deer antler tines were frequently made into a variety of small picks or handles. These sleeves, although mostly simple, can also be ornamented and polished on Middle Bronze Age Hungarian sites.

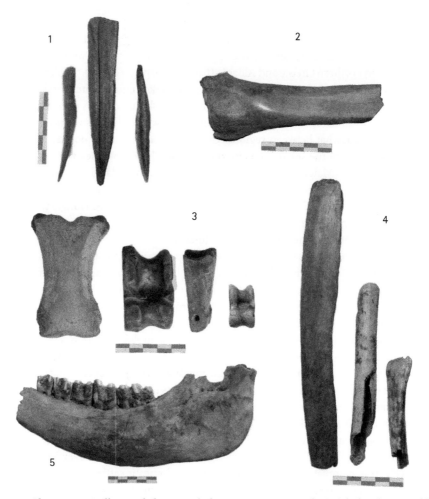

FIG. 26.4 Characteristically simple bone tools from Hungary: 1. Awls, Százhalombatta-Földvár. 2. late Middle Bronze-early Late Bronze Age radius-based faceted tool, Százhalombatta-Földvár; 3. Assorted faceted phalanges and astragali, Jászdozsa-Kápolnahalom; 4. Bevel-ended tools, Jászdozsa-Kápolnahalom; 5. Mandible with facet on buccal surface along long axis, Jászdozsa-Kápolnahalom.

Photos: A. Choyke or K. Kozma on behalf of A. Choyke.

From the Middle Bronze Age, special purpose objects, often part of complex multi-media artifacts, begin to be widely made from antler. They include single-point harpoons, projectile points, line guides perhaps for netting, polished and decorated handles, buttons, toggles, pins and pin-heads, various bridle fittings (Fig. 26.5), and decorative boxes.

Animal canines, most notably bear, wild pig, and dog or wolf, were drilled through the root and used as ornaments. Plaques of drilled boar's tusk either for suspension or with multiple holes—possibly for some kind of decorative helmet armour—appear in small numbers but in many different places. They represent a widespread type associated in coeval sites in Anatolia with helmet or armour decoration and reinforcement. There is little use of shell compared to previous periods.

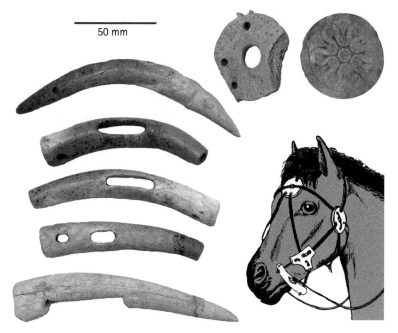

FIG. 26.5 Horse harness antler fittings produced by part-time specialists, Százhalombatta-Földvár.

Photos: A. Choyke, reconstruction drawing: L. Bartosiewicz, after: Choyke 2009.

Regional and Temporal Variability

It is difficult to compare Bronze Age worked osseous materials on a Europe-wide basis. Besides chronological disconnects, far too little work has been published and many of the older works contain little detailed information on raw materials and details of the production sequence. What data does exist, however, suggests that bone tools tend to be less well made than objects in other materials, with production geared towards speed rather than slower, cognitively more complex, multi-stage work with strongly selected raw materials.

Red deer antler becomes the material of choice for producing rose and beam wood-working tools and elaborate ornamental objects from the Middle Bronze Age onwards throughout most of Europe and the Balkans. In the Baltic area, Late Bronze Age antler is apparently less available and bone is often substituted for the production of spearheads, pins, buttons, and decorated handles (Luik and Maldre 2007). Conversely, Noelle Provenzano (2001) reports that 70 per cent of the worked osseous material in the *Terramare* derives from antler, mostly worked with a full range of bronze tools. Antler-working had an especially strong and long-lasting tradition in the *Terramare*.

Hungary lies somewhere in between these two extremes of production, with red deer antler being unevenly available across the area. Antler may even have been traded between regions. Despite clear evidence that antler was sectioned using bronze axes in the Hungarian and Balkan material, access to metal knives, saws, chisels, and awls was limited to part-time specialists until the Late Bronze Age in this region. Thus, availability of red deer antler and access to a full range of metal objects also affected the sophistication of antler objects present in a given assemblage.

The manufacture of a variety of projectile points in antler and more rarely in bone, while hardly new, is a special, widespread marker of tool manufacture from the end of the Middle Bronze Age. Paired skates, with binding holes produced by a metal awl and cut into shaped metapodials from small equids, appear on Urnfield sites throughout Transdanubia (Hungary) for the first time. The elaborate, decorated antler objects represent more of a real innovation. Antler inlay in dagger hilts and pinning to hold box bases in place is part of this trend. Examples are known from Hungary and north Italian *Terramare*, although such materials surely appear elsewhere as well.

Materials Selection and Manufacturing Processes

Local and regional continuity in raw material choice for certain simple household objects is evident in the archaeological record across Europe, demonstrating that while sociopolitical systems were transformed, life and rules of the production of goods at the household level remained fairly constant. Identification of regional manufacturing trends depend on species and skeletal element selection, the degree and manner in which abrasion and scraping with stone tools was employed, as well as recognition of when metal tools were employed to work osseous materials at a given settlement.

After the Final Neolithic there is a striking diminution in the amount of energy and time put into the production of most household equipment (Choyke 1984; Luik and Maldre 2007; Provenzano 2001; 2003). These simplified local rules of household production for bone tools, made mostly from domestic species, depend on the species availability, physical characteristics of particular skeletal elements, food processing traditions, and culturally ascribed qualities (Birtalan 2003).

While most points and bevelled-edged tools in the *Terramare* material from the Po Valley were quickly made, mostly from the bone refuse after food processing, metal tools are often used even in bone tool manufacturing, suggesting that such tools were widely available within the population (Provenzano 2003). In Hungary and the Balkans, while antler was sectioned using bronze axes, the remainder of the worked osseous objects in households were still made using flint and abrasive stone technologies until the Late Bronze Age. Bone objects from Estonia in the Late Bronze Age continued to rely heavily on the flint and abrasive stone of earlier times due to the difficulty of obtaining metal (Luik and Maldre 2007). For the most part, however, it is patterned selection by species and skeletal element, and the choices of how to process bone using the old Neolithic technologies, that differ by region.

The refined appearance of the new classes of antler-based decorative objects is in stark contrast to the household tools, suggesting that in many places they were manufactured for an emerging elite by part-time artisans with specialized technological knowledge and access to a range of metal tools beyond simple axes. The four- and six-spoke wheel pinheads of the *Terramare*, for example, were made by people with specialist knowledge in the use of bronze axes and chisels to shape the rough-outs and blanks of these objects from the pedicle and beam of hunted red deer, and then create the fine polished surfaces and delicate, incised decoration found on some of them. Chisels were needed to establish a small, deep notch in the antler surface, which could then be widened to create the spaces between the spokes (Provenzano 2001).

Within the Carpathian Basin, stretching south into the Balkans, and in Late Bronze Age Estonia, traditions of bone and antler manufacturing in the household continued directly from the Neolithic and Chalcolithic periods into the Bronze Age with few modifications in technique. Flaked stone tools and abrasion were sometimes still used in household production well into the Late Bronze Age (Luik and Maldre 2007). The apparent widespread access to metal tools among the people at the *Terramare* is much less typical of Bronze Age technologies elsewhere in Europe, where bronze only becomes important in manufacturing patterns of simple bone and antler objects from the beginning of the Late Bronze Age (Provenzano 2001; 2003; Christidou 2008; Drzewicz 2004).

Organization of Production

While bone tools and the heavy-duty rose- and beam-based antler tools are certainly the products of household-based crafts on Hungarian and Balkan sites, the refined and beautiful antler pieces from Hungarian and *Terramare* assemblages were made using a variety of metal tools and required talented, individual *savoir faire* to produce. The most beautiful pieces were surely made by part-time specialists. There may even have been functioning workshops on *Terramare* sites (Provenzano 2003).

Links to Other Crafts

Bone tools were made for a variety of craft activities especially related to hide, basketry, and clay-product production. Many decorative objects were used in conjunction with other materials such as wood, leather, cloth, and metal in complex objects. Imitation of bronze ornamental types such as buttons and clothing pins in antler and bone is not only related to scarcity of bronze. Bone and antler may have been valued in their own right, not only for their white colour (contrasting nicely as fittings on dark clothing) but also for the attributes ascribed to the animals from which they derived. The wheel and disc heads of pins from the *Terramare* began to be copied from antler into bronze (Provenzano 2003) as a way to enhance their basic message, which must have been closely intertwined with the raw material coming from the pedicle and beam of the antler rack of hunted red deer stags.

Conclusion

In the Age of Bronze, ceramics, textiles, and bone objects were a vital part of daily life throughout Europe. They literally created the fabric of existence by bringing shape, colour, and texture to Bronze Age lives. Nonetheless, the spatial and temporal variability evident in the expression of each craft reflects a differential emphasis and investment placed on them by different communities. Regional attitudes to innovation in form, manufacturing techniques, and decoration are visible in developments for each material, with contrasting attempts to explore these reflecting both conservatism and experimentation in craft production in all three media. Relationships between crafts evident in all three materials suggest that Bronze Age craftspeople were potentially open to a range of influences, as well as influencing the work of other craftspeople. Furthermore, not only was the production of craft objects in regional styles part of the construction of local identities, but ceramic, textile, and bone objects were important in articulating other social values, including prestige, through their everyday use and display.

We have some insights into the developing role of specialists and different models of production in different media, but who these craftspeople were remains something of an open question. Were they, for example, young or old? Women or men? New research on skill and learning in craft production is adding another dimension to our understanding of the social dynamics of craft production (Michelaki 2008; Budden and Sofaer 2009), while further recent work highlights that even in societies where craft production is highly gendered, it involves negotiation and cooperation between gender and age groups (Sørensen 1996; Sofaer and Sørensen 2002). Assumptions regarding the roles of women and men in prehistoric craft production that see ceramic and textile production as predominantly female, and bone tool production as predominantly male, may therefore benefit from re-examination.

Bibliography

Almagro-Gorbea, M. and Fontes, F. (1997). 'The introduction of wheel-made pottery in the Iberian Peninsula: Mycenaeans or pre-orientalizing contacts?', *Oxford Journal of Archaeology*, 16/3: 345–61.

Antipina, Y. (2001). 'Bone tools and wares from the site of Gorny (1690–1410) in the Kargaly mining complex in the south Ural part of the East European steppe', in A. M. Choyke and L. Bartosiewicz (eds.), *Crafting Bone: Skeletal Technologies through Time and Space*. Proceedings of the 2nd meeting of the (ICAZ) Worked Bone Research Group Budapest, 31 August–5 September 1999. British Archaeological Reports (International Series), 937. Oxford: Archaeopress, 171–8.

Bakker, J. A., Brandt, R. W., Van Geel, B., Jansma, M. J., Kuijper, W. J., Van Mensch, P. J. A., Pals, J. P., and IJzereef, G. F. (1977). 'Hoogkarspel-Watertoren: towards a reconstruction of ecology and archaeology of an agrarian settlement of 1000 BC', *Ex horreo* (Festschrift W. A. Glasbergen. Cingula, 4). Amsterdam: Universiteit van Amsterdam, 187–225.

Bazzanella, M., Mayr, A., Moser, L., and Rast-Eichter, A. (2003). *Textiles: intrecci e tessuti dalla preistoria europea. Catalogo della mostra tenutasi a Riva del Garda dal 24 maggio al 19 ottobre 2003*. Trento, Esperia.

Bender Jørgensen, L. (1986). *Forhistoriske textiler i Skandinavien—Prehistoric Scandinavian Textiles*. Nordiske Fortidsminder Ser B., vol. 9. Copenhagen: Det Kongelige Nordiske Oldskriftselskab.

—— (1992). *North European Textiles until AD 1000*. Aarhus: Aarhus University Press.

Berg, I. (2007). 'Meaning in the making: the potter's wheel at Phylakopi, Melos (Greece)', *Journal of Anthropological Archaeology*, 26/2: 234–52.

Bergerbrant, S. (2007). *Bronze Age Identities: Costume, Conflict and Contact in Northern Europe 1600–1300 BC*, Stockholm Studies in Archaeology, 43. Stockholm: Stockholm University.

Birtalan, Á. (2003). 'Ritualistic use of livestock bones in the Mongolian belief system and customs', in A. Sárközi and A. Rákos (eds.), *Altaica Budapestinensia*. MMII, Proceedings of the 45th Permanent International Altaistic Conference (PIAC), Budapest, Hungary, 23–28 June 2002. Budapest: Hungarian Academy of Sciences, 34–62.

Brohol, H. C. and Hald, M. (1940). *Costumes of the Bronze Age in Denmark*. Copenhagen: Nyt Nordisk Forlag Arnold Busck.

Budden, S. (2008). 'Skill amongst the sherds: understanding the role of skill in the Early to Late Middle Bronze Age in Hungary', in I. Berg (ed.), *Breaking the Mould: Challenging the Past through Pottery*. Oxford: Archaeopress, 1–17.

—— and Sofaer, J. (2009). 'Non-discursive knowledge and the construction of identity: potters, potting and performance at the Bronze Age tell of Szazhalombatta, Hungary', *Cambridge Archaeological Journal*, 19/2: 203–20.

Cattani, M. (1997). 'Una fornace per ceramica nelle terramare', in M. Bernabò Brea, A. Cardarelli, and M. Cremaschi (eds.), *Le Terramare. La più antica civiltà padana*. Modena: Foro Boario, 507–15.

Choyke, A. M. (1984). 'An analysis of bone, antler and tooth tools from Bronze Age Hungary', *Mitteilungen des Archäeologischen Instituts der Ungarischen Akademie der Wissenschaften*, 12/13: 13–57.

—— (2000). 'Refuse and modified bone from Százhalombatta-Földvár. Some preliminary observations', in I. Poroszlai and M. Vicze (eds.), *SAX: Százhalombatta Archaeological Expedition. Annual Report 1—Field Season 1998*. Százhalombatta: Matrica Museum, 97–102.

Christidou, R. (2008). 'The use of metal tools in the production of bone artifacts at two Bronze Age sites of the southwestern Balkans: a preliminary assessment', in L. Longo, and N. Skakun (eds.), *'Prehistoric Technology' 40 Years Later: Functional Studies and the Russian Legacy*, Proceedings of the International Congress, Verona (Italy), 20–23 April 2005. British Archaeological Reports (International Series), 1,783. Oxford: Archaeopress, 253–64.

Dąbrowski, J. (2004). *Ältere Bronzezeit in Polen. (Starsza epoka brązu w Polsce)*. Warsaw: Instytut Archeologii i Etnologii Polskiej Akademii Nauk.

Diaz-Andreu, M. (1994). *La Edad del Bronce en la provincia de Cuenca*. Cuenca: Diputación Provincial de Cuenca. Serie Arqueología Conquense, XIII.

Drzewicz, A. (2004). *Wyroby z kości i poroża z osiedla obronnego ludności kultury łużyckiej w Biskupinie*, Warsaw: Wydawnictwo Naukowe 'Semper'.

Gerškovič, J. P. (1999). *Studien zur spätbronzezeitlichen Sabatinovka-Kultur am unteren Dnepr und an der Westküste des Azov'schen Meeres*, Archäologie in Eurasien, 7. Rahden/Westfalen: Verlag Marie Leidorf GmbH.

Gibson, A. (2002). *Prehistoric Pottery in Britain and Ireland*. Stroud: Tempus.

Grömer, K. (2007). *Bronzezeitliche Gewebefunde aus Hallstatt—Ihr Kontext in der Textilkunde Mitteleuropas und die Entwicklung der Textiltechnologie zur Eisenzeit*. Doctoral dissertation, Vienna: Vienna University.

Hamilton, S. (2002). 'Between ritual and routine: interpreting British prehistoric pottery production and distribution', in A. Woodward and J. D. Hill (eds.), *Prehistoric Britain: The Ceramic Basis*, Prehistoric Ceramics Research Group Occasional Publication, 3. Oxford: Oxbow Books, 38–53.

Hurcombe, L. (2008). 'Organics from inorganics: using experimental archaeology as a research tool for studying perishable material culture', *World Archaeology*, 40/1: 83–115.

Kemp, B. J. and Vogelsang-Eastwood, G. (2001). *The Ancient Textile Industry at Amarna*. London: Egypt Exploration Society.

Killen, J. T. (2007). 'Cloth production in Late Bronze Age Greece: the documentary evidence', in C. Gillis and M.-L. Nosch (eds.), *Ancient Textiles: Production, Craft and Society*. Oxford: Oxbow Books, 50–8.

Klosinska, E. (1991). 'Early phase of Lusatian culture barrow burial ground in Lower Silesia at Mikowice, Opole Voivodship site 1', *Antiquity*, 65: 651–61.

Kreiter, A. (2007). *Technological Choices and Material Meanings in Early and Middle Bronze Age Hungary: Understanding the Active Role of Material Culture through Ceramic Analysis*, British Archaeological Reports (International Series), 1,604. Oxford: Archaeopress.

Law, R. (2008). *The Development and Perpetuation of a Ceramic Tradition: The Significance of Collared Urns in Early Bronze Age Social Life*. Cambridge: University of Cambridge (unpublished PhD thesis).

López-Astilleros, K. M. (2000). 'The Tagus middle basin (Iberian Peninsula) from the Neolithic to the Iron Age (V-I millenium cal BC): the long way to social complexity', *Oxford Journal of Archaeology*, 19/3: 241–72.

Luik, H. and Maldre, L. (2007). 'Bronze Age bone artefacts from Narkunai, Nevieriske and Kereliai fortified settlements: raw materials and manufacturing technology', *Archaeologia Lituana*, 8: 5–39.

Lukesh, S. N. and Howe, S. (1978). 'Protoappenine vs. Subappenine: mathematical distinction between two ceramic phases', *Journal of Field Archaeology*, 5/3: 339–47.

Maigrot, Y. (2005). 'Ivory, bone and antler tools production systems at Chalin 4 (Hura, France: late Neolitic site 3rd millennium)', in H. Luik, A. Choyke, C. Batey, and L. Lõugas (eds.), *From Hooves to Horns, from Mollusc to Mammoth: Manufacture and Use of Bone Artifacts from Prehistoric Times to the Present*, Proceedings of the 4th meeting of the (ICAZ) Worked Bone Research Group, Muiasaja Teadus, 15. Tallinn Book Printers.

Manby, T. G. (1995). 'Skeuomorphism: some reflections of leather, wood and basketry in Early Bronze Age pottery', in I. Kinnes and G. Varndell (eds.), *Unbaked Urns of Rudely Shape*. Oxford: Oxbow Books, 81–8.

Maniatis, Y. and Tite, M. S. (1981). 'Technological examination of Neolithic–Bronze Age pottery from Central and Southeast Europe and from the Near East', *Journal of Archaeological Science*, 8: 59–76.

Michelaki, K. (2008). 'Making pots and potters in the Bronze Age Maros villages of Kiszombor-Új-Élet and Klárafalva-Hajdova', *Cambridge Archaeological Journal*, 18/3: 355–80.

Neugebauer, J.-W. (1994). *Bronzezeit in Ostösterreich*, Wissenschaftliche Schriftenreihe Niederösterreich, 98/99/100/101. St Pölten. Vienna: Verlag Niederösterreichisches Pressehaus.

Olsen, S. L. (2001). 'The importance of thong-smoothers at Botai, Kazakhstan', in A. Choyke and L. Bartosiewicz (eds.), *Crafting Bone: Skeletal Technologies through Time and Space*, British Archaeological Reports (International Series), 937. Oxford: Archaeopress, 197–206.

Pearce, M. (1998). 'New research on the *terramare* of northern Italy', *Antiquity*, 72: 743–6.

Provenzano, N. (2001). 'Worked bone assemblages in northern Italy Terremares: a technological approach', in A. M. Choyke and L. Bartosiewicz (eds.), *Crafting Bone: Skeletal Technologies through Time and Space*, Proceedings of the 2nd meeting of the (ICAZ) Worked Bone Research Group Budapest, 31 August–5 September 1999. British Archaeological Reports (International Series), 937. Oxford: Archaeopress, 93–103.

—— (2003). 'Interactions entre hierarchisation sociale et spécialisation artisanale dans l'âge du Bronze d'Italie septentrionale', in P. Brun and P. de Miroschedji (eds.), *Thème transversal no. 2: Évolution des structures et dynamiques sociales: Les moyens d'action sur les hommes*. Cahier des Thèmes Transversaux ArScAn, MAE-Nanterre. Accessed online 10 May 2011 at http://www.mae.u-paris10.fr/arscan/Theme-Transversal-II-Evolution-des.html.

Rast-Eicher, A. (2005). 'Bast before wool: the first textiles', in P. Bichler, K. Grömer, R. Hofmann de Keijzer, A. Kern, and H. Reschreiter (eds.), *Hallstatt Textiles: Technical Analysis, Scientific Investigation and Experiment on Iron Age Textiles*, British Archaeological Reports (International Series), 1,351. Oxford: Archaeopress, 117–31.

Roberts, S., Sofaer, J., and Kiss, V. (2008). 'Characterization and textural analysis of Middle Bronze Age Transdanubian inlaid wares of the Encrusted Pottery Culture, Hungary: a preliminary study', *Journal of Archaeological Science*, 35/2: 322–30.

Sofaer, J. (2006). 'Pots, houses and metal: technological relations at the Bronze Age tell at Százhalombatta, Hungary', *Oxford Journal of Archaeology*, 25/2: 127–47.

—— and Sørensen, M. L. S. (2002). 'Becoming cultural: society and the incorporation of bronze', in B. Ottaway and E. C. Wager (eds.), *Metals and Society*, Papers from a session held at the European Association of Archaeologists sixth annual meeting in Lisbon 2000, British Archaeological Reports (International Series), 1,061. Oxford: Archaeopress, 117–21.

—— with contributions by Bech, J.-H., Budden, S., Choyke, A., Eriksen, B. V., Horváth, T., Kovács, G., Kreiter, A., Mühlenbock, C., and Stika, H.-P. (2010), 'Technology and craft', in T. Earle and K. Kristiansen (eds.), *Organizing Bronze Age Societies: The Mediterranean, Central Europe and Scandinavia Compared*. Cambridge: Cambridge University Press, 183–215.

Sørensen, M. L. S. (1996). 'Women as/and metalworkers', in A. Devonshire and B. Wood (eds.), *Women in Industry and Technology from Prehistory to the Present Day*. London: Museum of London, 45–51.

—— and Rebay, K. (2008). 'Interpreting the body: burial practices at the Middle Bronze Age cemetery at Pitten, Austria', *Archaeologia Austriaca*, 89: 153–76.

Tanasi, D. (2005). 'Mycenaean pottery imports and local imitations: Sicily vs southern Italy', in R. Laffineur and E. Greco (eds.), *Emporia: Aegeans in Central and Eastern Mediterranean*, Acts of the 10th International Aegean Conference at the Italian School of Archaeology in Athens, Athens 14–18 April 2004 (Aegaeum 25). Liège: Université de Liège, 561–9.

Trolle-Larsen, M. (1987). 'Commercial networks in the Ancient Near East', in M. Rowlands, M. T. Larsen, and K. Kristiansen (eds.), *Centre and Periphery in the Ancient World*. Cambridge: Cambridge University Press, 47–56.

Vicze, M. (2001). *Dunaújváros-Dunadűlő: The Early and Middle Bronze Age Cemetery of Dunaújváros-Kosziderpadlás*, PhD thesis. Budapest: Eötvös Loránd University.

Willvonseder, K. (1937). *Die mittlere Bronzezeit in Österreich*. Vienna: Anton Schroll/Leipzig: Heinrich Keller.

CHAPTER 27

GLASS AND FAIENCE

JULIAN HENDERSON

GLASS is unlike pottery and metal: it is often translucent and generally does not contain crystals. Faience on the other hand is a mixture of silica crystals and a glassy material. In Bronze Age Europe glass and faience were used to make beads. Faience occurs in the Near East earlier than in Europe (from about the fourth millennium BC) and Stone and Thomas (1936) suggested a Near Eastern origin as being the most likely for European faience; subsequent research has changed this view. The evidence, such as it is, for the occurrence of the earliest glass indicates that it was made in Mesopotamia (Moorey 1994). In Europe the earliest sporadic occurrences of glass dates to the Early and Middle Bronze Age, with the material becoming somewhat more common in the Late Bronze Age. Glass and faience have been found all over Europe in a variety of archaeological contexts (Harding 2000: 141). For example, one of the few surveys of Bronze Age glass and faience objects in Europe (Venclová 1990: Table 1) listed 291 separate objects found in Bohemia. In another, Peggy Guido (1978) noted 26 beads of Bronze Age or possible Bronze Age date in her survey of prehistoric glass beads from Britain and Ireland. Examples of archaeological sites that have produced glass and faience are a possible Early Bronze Age cremation deposit at Knackyboy, Isles of Scilly, many more Early Bronze Age burials in central Europe, the Late Bronze Age Swiss Lake Villages such as Hauterive-Champréveyres on Lake Neuchâtel, the Late Bronze Age entrepôt of Frattesina in northern Italy, and the eighth century BC ritual site of Rathgall in Ireland. It is only by the Late Bronze Age that glass appears in any quantity, with the largest amount deriving from the industrial site of Frattesina in northern Italy, along with evidence for other industries, including metal, amber, and bone working.

Even the large amount of glass found at Frattesina is still on a relatively small scale compared to the amount found at thirteenth century BC Ugarit in the Levant or the amount found on board the thirteenth century BC shipwreck of Ulu Burun off the south coast of Turkey. Rebecca Ingram (2005) has noted that about 75,000 faience beads and about 9,500 glass beads were found on the Uluburun wreck, so this puts the scale of the European finds into perspective. Although glass was introduced later than faience, faience continued in use in Europe, with faience still being used in the Late Bronze Age. In one of the latest Late Bronze Age contexts in which beads have been found, at eighth century BC Rathgall, one of the translucent turquoise beads had a collar of gold attached (Raftery 1987), showing that glass was highly prized at the time in Ireland.

THE PRODUCTION OF GLASS AND GLASSY MATERIALS

Bronze Age faience has a glassy matrix and contains sand or crushed quartz. It is not to be confused with the stonepaste ceramic that was manufactured in Italy from the fifteenth century (termed *faenza*) and which spread to other European production centres (Henderson 2000: 181–2). Unlike faience, glass often contains few, if any, crystals, partly because it was heated to higher temperatures so that the crystals dissolve. Opaque glass, on the other hand, is deliberately rendered opaque (and coloured) by the addition of crystals. Because faience was introduced earlier than glass, several researchers have pointed out that it must have contributed to the emergence of the earliest glass. However, a high proportion of faience and the earliest glass is of a turquoise green colour (Fig. 27.1) due to the presence of copper oxide, and this certainly suggests that copper production also influenced the manufacture of the earliest glass. Moreover, the production of metals and glass had many characteristics in common, including the construction of furnaces that achieved sufficiently high temperatures and the fuel that would have been used to produce both materials. Another possible influence on the manufacture of the earliest glass would have been a substance produced during the smelting of metals: a glassy slag is often formed from the combination of fuel ash and silica in, for example, crucible walls. This brilliant and lustrous glassy material that reflected and refracted the light, and which may have been a red colour from the presence of copper, possibly provided one of the impetuses for the deliberate production of glass.

Relatively recent research has revealed that some examples of what was once termed faience are better termed 'glassy faience' because it contains a significantly higher proportion of

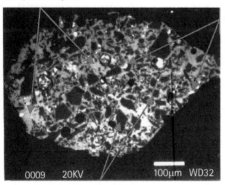

FIG. 27.1 A highly magnified SEM image of a (turquoise green) faience sample from Hauterive-Champréveyres, Lake Neuchâtel, Switzerland.

Photo: author.

glass. Therefore purely in terms of materials (rather than the social factors that affect production) there would seem to be a progression from faience to vitreous faience to glass. All three materials have been found in Middle and Late Bronze Age Italy.

Glass, and the glassy component of faience, would have been made from a combination of two raw materials. Silica in the form of sand or crushed quartz would have been mixed with plant ashes to act as a flux. Silica melts at $c.1,700°C$, which was an excessively high temperature for Bronze Age artisans to have achieved. The addition of a flux would have reduced the glass-melting temperature to between $c.1,100°$ C and $1,200°$ C. A furnace would still have been necessary to melt the ingredients fully—and they would probably have been contained in a crucible. However, no indisputable archaeological evidence has been found for the manufacture of faience or glass in Bronze Age Europe, as discussed below.

Bronze Age glass in Europe is of two compositional types that reflect the use of different types of raw materials. Both were made using silica, but it is the type of flux used that was clearly different. Some European Bronze Age glass is of the typical 'plant-ash' type, and some of a 'mixed-alkali' composition. The alkali introduced in plants is the same as that still used for making soap in some parts of the Near East today—it is the alkali that makes soap feel slippery. Indeed, the same plants were used for making Bronze Age glass. They are termed 'halophytic' (salt-loving) because they can tolerate highly alkaline soils. They grew and still grow in semi-desert, maritime, and evaporitic environments. Once ashed, these plants are thought to provide both the flux and the third key component in glass, calcium. The latter makes the glass durable (Barkoudah and Henderson 2006). Once fused, this glass is characterized by elevated levels of magnesium and potassium oxide (Sayre and Smith 1961; Henderson 1988a and 1988b), both of which are introduced in the ash (Fig. 27.2). The same ratio of these oxides is found in Bronze Age glass and in ashed plants of the genus *Salsola*. It is therefore likely that such plants were used in the manufacture of the glass (Barkoudah and Henderson 2006).

The alkali found in the second kind of Bronze Age glass, 'mixed-alkali' glass, appears to result from a mixture of two alkalis, both possibly of a mineral origin because they lack the elements that would be associated with the use of an organic (plant ash) origin. The other characteristic of mixed-alkali glass is that it contains low levels of calcium and relatively high levels of silica. Some examples of Middle Bronze Age 'glasses' from Italy contain a relatively high proportion of silica grains that make them semi-opaque (Angelini et al. 2005: 33), so they can be regarded as glassy faience. Thus far no examples of mixed-alkali glass beads have been found in the Near East and only a small number have been found in Greece (Nikita and Henderson 2006). Most mixed-alkali glass has been found in Europe.

Production Zones

Faience

Faience was first manufactured in the Near East during the fourth millennium BC. Its earliest occurrence in Europe is on Crete and dates to the third millennium BC. Thousands of faience *shabti* figurines were manufactured in Egypt—and these formed an important part of ritual life there. By *c*.2000 cal BC Anthony Harding (2000: 266) has noted that faience beads were

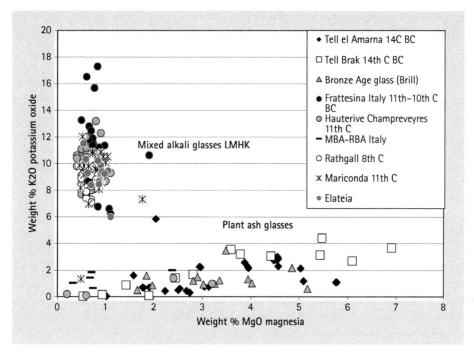

FIG. 27.2 The compositional distinction between plant-ash and mixed-alkali Bronze Age glass. Both types have been found in Europe.

Source: author.

found quite widely across Europe. Stone and Thomas (1956) suggested that faience beads found in Europe had a Near Eastern origin. Subsequent (scientific) research has provided convincing evidence that faience was made in several separate production zones in Europe stretching from Scotland to Poland (Newton and Renfrew 1970; Harding and Warren 1973; Robinson, Baczyńska, and Polańska 2004). It is therefore clear that by c.2000–1500 BC different communities across Europe were manufacturing faience in their own right. Whether a transfer of technology occurred between the Near East and Europe is open to question. An alternative explanation is that faience was invented independently in Europe.

Glass

It is with good reason that the Near East has been suggested as the earliest area where glass was fused from raw materials. Nevertheless it is only recently that primary archaeological evidence for its manufacture has been found there in thirteenth century BC Egypt (Rehren and Pusch 2005). There is also now scientific evidence for independent *primary production* of Late Bronze Age glass in both Egypt and Mesopotamia (Henderson, Evans, and Nikita 2010). We therefore still await the discovery of the first *archaeological* evidence of primary glass making in Mesopotamia. It appears that primary production occurred in the elite context of Bronze Age palatial economies and a small amount of this same plant-ash glass, in the form of beads, found its way to Europe. It is however, worth noting that there is a possibility that some Bronze Age raw or ingot glass was imported to Europe from the Near East where it was shaped into beads (*secondary production*). Suitable plants for making such glass do grow in European maritime environments, but the present evidence indicates that it is unlikely it was made in Europe during the Bronze Age.

The evidence for the manufacture of Bronze Age mixed-alkali glass and glassy faience in Europe is much stronger. Although there is no archaeological evidence for this, the presence of diagnostic compositional subgroups (one of which correlates to a specific artefact type) *within* the general compositional type suggests the existence of a localized production centre (see below). From the Middle Bronze Age (c.1500 BC) there is no question that glassy faience and glass occur with increasing frequency in Italy. There is also no doubt that by the Late Bronze Age mixed-alkali glass beads were being used in Europe. By far the largest concentration of prehistoric glass in Europe that includes evidence of glass-working has been discovered during excavations and fieldwalking at Frattesina in northern Italy (Bietti Sestieri 1996; Bellintani 1997). The fact that, until now, no examples of mixed-alkali glass have been found in the Near East suggests strongly that its manufacture from raw materials was invented in Europe. As noted above, the increase in the amount of mixed-alkali glass, including the very significant concentration at the entrepôt site of Frattesina, happened c.1100 BC when the Bronze Age palatial economies in the Mediterranean were in a state of collapse (Henderson 1988a). Therefore it would appear that the production of large quantities of mixed-alkali glass filled a lacuna when the palace economies collapsed.

Mixed-alkali glass has been found in Late Bronze Age archaeological contexts in Italy, Switzerland, France, Germany, England, and Ireland. Most is Late Bronze Age in date, although it is claimed that some glass/glassy faience found in France dates to as early as 2000 BC or earlier (Gratuze, Louboutin, and Billaud 1998). If the dating is indeed correct for the material, then its presence could suggest that the first manufacture of such glass/glassy faience in Europe occurred in France. Unfortunately the archaeological contexts for the French beads could be more secure, but we should be alert to the possibility that its invention may have occurred there. After all, since there are very few examples of the earliest plant-ash glass in the Near East, one would not necessarily expect to find large numbers of glass objects in either area following its first production: it would depend on how quickly the innovation was adopted in society. In trying to decide on where mixed-alkali glass was first invented, a lot depends on a small number of occurrences. It is the quality of the archaeological contexts and the associations of glass with other objects that are important here. Presumably it is only a matter of time before more well-dated third millennium BC glass is found in the Near East—and possibly also in Europe.

Bronze Age Faience/Glass in Northern Italy

Lawrence Barfield's (1978: 153) study of conical faience buttons (Fig. 27.3) showed that they were mainly concentrated in northern Italy and the southern Alps; he argued that they were made locally. Subsequently further archaeological (Bellintani 2000; Bellintani, Angelini, and Barnabò Brea 2010) and scientific work by Angelini et al. (2005) has shown that these early Middle Bronze Age conical buttons found in the northern Italian *Terremare* had a distinctive chemical composition. The distinctive characteristic is the high sodium oxide relative to the potassium oxide levels in the glassy phase of what is better termed 'glassy faience'. Thus not only does the concentration of this distinctive artefact type suggest that they were made in northern Italy, but the chemical composition of the glassy phase in the faience supports this. There is no guarantee that variation in artefact type is necessarily correlated with chemical composition, but in this case it is.

In a later part of the Bronze Age, Frattesina near Fratta Polesine in northern Italy was founded on a branch of the River Po. The site dates to between $c.1100$ BC and some time in the tenth century BC. Excavation and field walking have produced the largest concentration of glass from any site in prehistoric Europe. It is especially important because the finds from the site include definite evidence for the manufacture of glass objects. Not only that, but there is evidence that the site was involved in long-distance trade, as is indicated by the presence of, for example, amber beads of so-called Tiryns type. The site has also produced evidence for metal smelting and amber working, with recent archaeological evidence suggesting that the latter occurred on a very large scale.

The evidence for the glass industry at Frattesina consists of several artefact types that have not been found elsewhere in prehistoric Europe. Several crucibles with different glass colours (e.g. white and red) adhering to the inside and small trays on which glass was reheated and worked have been found. A number of complete or broken disc-shaped glass ingots in cobalt blue and opaque red glass have also been found; the 'red' glass has a core of translucent turquoise glass in the centre and a layer of red glass on the surface. The presence of malformed and conjoined beads shows that these were the main products on the site. However, perhaps the only example of a fragment of glazed pottery from prehistoric Europe has also been found there, suggesting that pottery glazing was another activity on site. The evidence from the artefacts therefore shows that glass working took place at Frattesina.

Inevitably there are still a number of unanswered questions. One is whether the glass ingots were made on the site or whether they were imported. If they were imported, it is difficult to establish where they might have come from. The currently available archaeological evidence suggests that they were made at Frattesina, though naturally this could change as a result of

FIG. 27.3 Faience conical button found in 2010 at the Parma – Palafitta site, dating to the 19th century BC (Bellintani, Angelini, and Bernabò Brea 2010).

Photo: Ministero per i Beni a le Attivitá Culturali – Soprintendenza per i Beni Archeologici dell'Emilia Romagna, by kind permission.

new discoveries. Another question that remains to be answered is whether glass was fused from primary raw materials on the site. Thus far no glass-making furnaces have been found. Possible semi-fused raw materials have been found but the evidence is uncertain. Given the large concentration of glass at the site it is tempting to suggest that it was made there, but only further archaeological excavation and scientific research can provide the proof.

Scientific analysis of the glass from Frattesina has shown it to be of the mixed-alkali chemical composition, with a small number of high-potassium glasses (Fig. 27.2). The mixed-alkali glasses contain a mixture of sodium and potassium oxides; the only other major component is silica. Some of the silica is present in both kinds of glass as crystals but the proportion is too low for it to be labelled faience. Whereas sand and crushed quartz would be available locally, the source and type of the alkaline raw material used is yet to be identified. Some of the impurities associated with plant ashes used to make glass in the Bronze Age Near East are present, but only at low levels in the mixed-alkali glasses, so plant ashes can be ruled out as a source of the alkali. This alone suggests that the type of alkali used is a mineral one, but apart from the use of 'night soil' that Robert Brill has suggested it is difficult to be sure. One thing is not in question, however: the glass found at Frattesina is most unlikely to have been imported from the Near East. It appears that this type of glass, and the compositionally related glassy faience and faience, were European inventions. Amazingly there are other, somewhat later, examples of high-potassium glasses with very similar compositions, dating to the early Warring States and Warring States periods (500–300 BC), from Henan and Hubei provinces as well as southern China (Gan Fuxi, Cheng Huansheng, and Li Quighui 2006). The European examples are earlier and this could suggest that they travelled along the Silk Road to China. Alternatively perhaps high-potassium glass was made independently in both Europe and China.

Conclusion

Although relatively small amounts of faience and glass occur in Bronze Age Europe, from the Early Bronze Age onwards, what there is must have had a relatively high social value: it was mainly used as jewellery and must have been regarded as an exotic rarity in northern Europe. Scientific evidence shows that the glass was of two different types, one made from silica and plant ashes, probably imported (however indirectly) from the Near East, and the other from silica and a mixed alkali almost certainly made in Europe and possibly in northern Italy (see Fig. 27.2). The most comprehensive evidence for the manufacture of glass in prehistoric Europe has been found at the Late Bronze Age site of Frattesina in northern Italy. It is surely only a matter of time before further evidence for other glass-production centres are found in Europe, but at present the evidence from northern Italy is unique and it must be related to the presence of other industrial activities feeding trade from the site. The production of faience, glassy faience, and glass of the 'Frattesina' mixed-alkali type was almost certainly a European invention. Although there is scientific evidence for the production of faience in several separate locations in northern Europe, currently this evidence is missing for glass.

Future research may answer the question as to whether high-potassium glass originated in Europe or in south-east Asia, or whether it was exported along the Silk Road.

Bibliography

Angelini, I., Artioli, G., Bellintani, P., and Polla, A. (2005). *Protohistoric Vitreous Materials of Italy: From Early Faience to Final Bronze Age Glasses.* 16e Congrès de l'Association Internationale pour l'Histoire du Verre, London 2003. Nottingham: l'Association Internationale pour l'Histoire du Verre, 32–6.

Barfield, L. H. (1978). 'North Italian faience buttons', *Antiquity*, 52: 150–3.

Barkoudah, Y. and Henderson, J. (2006). 'Plant ashes from Syria and the manufacture of ancient glass: ethnographic and scientific aspects', *Journal of Glass Studies*, 48: 297–321.

Bellintani, P. (1997). 'Frattesina, l'ambre e la prudozione vitrea nel contesto delle relazioni transalpine', in L. Endrizzi and F. Marzatico (eds.), *Ori Delle Alpi*, Quaderni della Archeologica del Castello del Buonconsiglio, 6. Provincia autonoma di Tento: Servizio Beni Culturali, 117–33.

—— (2000). 'I bottoni conici ed altri materiali vetrosi delle fasi non avanzate della media età del Bronzo dell'Italia settenrionale e centrale', *Padusa*, XXXVI: 95–110.

——, Angelini, I., and Bernabò Brea, M. (2010). 'Bottoni conici in glassy faience dell'età del bronzo: nuovi rinvenimenti dall'Emilia e inquadramento nella tematica dei materiali vetrosi della Protostoria italiana'. Poster presented at *Preistoria e Protostoria dell'Emilia-Romagna*, XLV Riunione Scientifica IIPP in Emilia Romagna, Modena, 27–31 October 2010.

Bietti-Sestieri, A. M. (1996). *Protostoria, teoria e pratica.* Rome: Nuova Italia Scientifica.

Gratuze, B., Louboutin, C., and Billaud, Y. (1998). 'Les Perles protohistoriques en verre du Musées des Antiquités Nationales', *Antiquités Nationales*, 30: 11–24.

Gan Fuxi, Cheng Huansheng, and Li Quinghui (2006). 'Origin of Chinese ancient glasses—study on the earliest Chinese ancient glasses', *Science in China Series E: Technological Sciences*, 49/6: 701–13.

Guido, C. M. (1978). *The Glass Beads of the Prehistoric and Roman Periods in Britain and Ireland*, Society of Antiquaries of London Research Report, XXXV. London: The Society of Antiquaries.

Harding, A. F. (2000). *European Societies in the Bronze Age.* Cambridge: Cambridge University Press.

—— and Warren, S. E. (1973). 'Early Bronze Age faience beads from Central Europe', *Antiquity*, XLVII: 64–6.

Henderson, J. (1988a). 'Glass production and Bronze Age Europe', *Antiquity*, 62: 435–51.

—— (1988b). 'Electron probe microanalysis of mixed-alkali glasses', *Archaeometry*, 30/1: 77–91.

—— (2000). *The Science and Archaeology of Materials.* London and New York: Routledge.

——, Evans, J., and Nikita, K. (2010). 'Isotopic evidence for the primary production, provenance and trade in late Bronze Age glass in the Mediterranean', *Mediterranean Archaeology and Archaeometry*, 10/1: 1–24.

Ingram, R. S. (2005). *Faience and Glass Beads from the Late Bronze Age Shipwreck at Uluburun*, unpublished MA thesis, Texas: A&M University.

Moorey, P. R. S. (1994). *Ancient Mesopotamian Materials and Industries: The Archaeological Evidence.* Oxford: The Clarendon Press.

Newton, R. and Renfrew, C. (1970). 'British faience beads reconsidered', *Antiquity*, XLIV: 199–206.

Nikita, K. and Henderson, J. (2006). 'Glass analyses from Mycenae, Thebes and Elateia: compositional evidence for a Mycenaean glass industry', *Journal of Glass Studies*, 48: 71–120.

Raftery, B. (1987). 'Some glass beads of the later Bronze Age in Ireland', in *Glasperlen der Verromischen Eisenziet II*, Marburger Sudien zur Vor- und Frühgeschichte, 9. Mainz: Phillip von Zabern, 39–48.

Rehren, T. and Pusch, E. B. (2005). 'Late Bronze Age glass production at Qantir-Piramesses, Egypt', *Science*, 308: 1,756–8.

Robinson, C., Baczyńska, B., and Polańska, M. (2004). 'The origins of faience in Poland', *Sprawozdania Archeologiczne*, 56: 79–121.

Sayre, E. V. and Smith, R. W. (1961). 'Compositional categories of ancient glass', *Science*, 133: 1,824–6.

Stone, J. F. S. and Thomas, L. C. (1956). 'The use and distribution of faience in the ancient Near East and Europe', *Proceedings of the Prehistoric Society*, 22: 37–84.

Venclová, N. (1990). *Prehistoric Glass in Bohemia*. Prague: The Archaeological Institute of the Czechoslovak Academy of Science.

CHAPTER 28

SALT PRODUCTION IN THE BRONZE AGE

ANTHONY HARDING

It is well known that salt represents one of the most important commodities for daily life. Humans and animals all need a certain daily intake of salt, though the amount stated to be essential for health varies, while its uses in the preservation of foodstuffs make it a highly important element of life in many peasant societies—especially at those times of the year when ice cannot be made and stored. In addition, at the present day salt is commonly used in a range of curative treatments such as lung disorders or rheumatism, and is also used as a disinfectant for wounds, especially on animals. It has uses in a range of industrial processes, some of which (e.g. tanning) were important in ancient times as well as modern.

In a Bronze Age context, information on how salt was produced has traditionally been restricted to a few well-known areas of Europe where the coarse ceramic known as briquetage has been found. These vessels and other forms have long been known from the area around Halle (Saale) in Sachsen-Anhalt in Germany (Riehm 1954; Matthias 1961; 1976), and from the Seille Valley in Lorraine in eastern France (Bertaux 1976). The former seems to have been particularly important in the Bronze Age, as in later periods; the latter has abundant evidence for both Bronze and Iron Age exploitation. Other areas that produced briquetage of Bronze Age date were hardly known until quite recently, and restricted to a small number of findspots. This evidence was reviewed by Jacques Nenquin (1961), and again by Thomas Saile (2000).

Over the last 30 years the situation has changed in a number of ways. First, the number of sites producing briquetage has greatly increased, with many new findspots now known in Britain, France, Germany, Italy, Spain, and elsewhere. Second, it has become clear, through a series of remarkable discoveries of well-preserved wooden objects, that the briquetage technique (see below) was by no means the only one utilized in the Bronze Age. It has also become clear that there was a significant Neolithic salt production industry, usually but not always using briquetage. Such evidence, barely known to Nenquin, certainly comes from Romania, Poland, and France, and is probably present elsewhere.

Apart from the technologies to be described below, it is highly likely that in warmer parts of Europe, notably the Mediterranean, salt was produced in coastal lagoons simply through solar evaporation and the collection of the crystals thus formed. This was the technique known to the Romans (as described by Pliny the Elder in his *Natural History*) and surely used for centuries or millennia before that; but it would leave little or no archaeological trace. The other source of salt is rock salt, also used in antiquity. Deposits of rock salt vary greatly in composition and purity; only the purest are suitable for grinding up for human consumption, while less pure ones would need to be sorted manually after extraction (and perhaps dissolved in water for evaporation) or fed to animals as licks.

Production Using Briquetage

The briquetage technique essentially involves heating salt water in clay containers so that the water boils off and the salt crystals can be collected. The salt water could come straight from the sea or it could come from inland salt springs. Seawater contains a number of undesirable elements that produce a bitter taste, so dissolving the crystals in fresh water and reheating is likely to have occurred. Brine springs vary greatly in their composition, but the crystals obtained can sometimes be used without further purification.

A number of different briquetage forms regularly occur, including trays, pedestals, and a range of chalice-like pots. Unlike the situation in the Iron Age, where many production sites have been excavated, producing abundant evidence for the form of the furnaces that heated the brine, little is known about the details of Bronze Age briquetage use. It is presumed that the brine was poured into trays which were placed over the pedestals, with hot coals (charcoal) underneath. As the crystals formed, they would be removed by hand and placed in the chalices for washing with fresh water and reheating; in this way, a chalice of pure salt crystals might be produced.

As well as the abundant finds around Halle, good examples of briquetage can be seen in a coastal site such as Brean Down in Somerset, south-west England (Bell 1990) and other areas, in France, Germany, and Poland—the latter occurring in graves of the Lausitz culture (Kadrow 2003) (Fig. 28.1).

Coastal and Inland Production in the Mediterranean

The shores of Italy, both Tyrrhenian and Adriatic, have produced evidence of salt production (Di Fraia 2006). Near Nettuno large collections of sherds were found in a deposit with concentrations of burnt tufa (Nijboer et al. 2005–6), while further north at Isola di Coltano large quantities of briquetage were found in the Bronze Age settlement, and there are strong suggestions of other similar sites along the shores of Tuscany (Pasquinucci and Menchelli 2002). There are sites with briquetage of Bronze Age date on the Trieste karst and around the Caput Adriae (Montagnari Kokelj 2007).

Various areas of Spain have produced actual or potential evidence of Bronze Age salt exploitation, usually in the form of ceramics interpreted as briquetage (Morère 2002). While

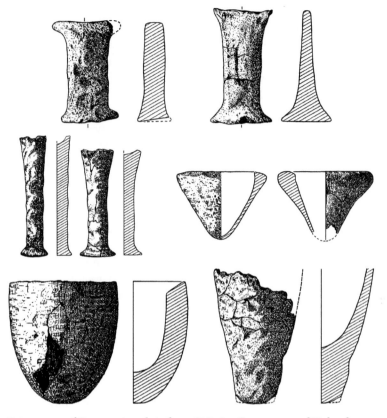

FIG. 28.1 Briquetage of Bronze Age date from Britain, Germany, and Poland.

Source: various.

there is circumstantial evidence for Neolithic exploitation of the 'Salt Mountain' at Cardona in Catalonia, there is much more definite evidence from the salt lagoons at Villafáfila in the Zamora district, where hearths and ovens have been recovered along with large quantities of briquetage (Delibes de Castro et al. 2007; Abarquero Moras et al. 2010). Other areas of Spain with possible evidence for Bronze Age exploitation include the valleys of the Jarama and Tajo rivers south of Madrid, and potentially the Murcia region, known to have been important in classical times for salt production.

Bronze Age Salt Mining at Hallstatt and Other Rock Salt Sources

Hallstatt is of course best known as an Iron Age site, its rich cemeteries believed to have derived their wealth from control of the salt source in the mountain on which the site sits. It is less well known that there is also extensive Bronze Age evidence for salt mining at Hallstatt, though this work goes back some years and has been the subject of both radiocarbon dating and dendrochronology (Barth 1998; Kern et al. 2009: 48ff.). The Bronze Age mining was concentrated on the so-called 'North group' of shafts, with three shafts having been extensively investigated. Remarkable preservation of organic artefacts is present, particularly in the Christian von Tuschwerk group of shafts, including bast ropes, woollen fabrics, and leather objects. Most spectacular, however, are the implements and constructions used in the mines: shovels, picks with their wooden hafts (and broken hafts), troughs for transporting the rock, lighting tapers, skin carry-packs, and most remarkable of all, a wooden staircase, beautifully preserved. While Iron Age mining may have been more extensive than Bronze Age, given the much larger surface area and greater depth reached, nevertheless the extent of Bronze Age mining is impressive, starting in the sixteenth/fifteenth centuries BC and concluding in the thirteenth (there are no objects dated later than 1245 BC).

Hallstatt is the only large-scale Bronze Age mine where rock salt was extracted that has been systematically investigated, but there were surely others, given the prevalence of outcrops in several parts of Europe. The problem for archaeologists is that the exploitation of such outcrops is likely to leave little trace, and to have been systematically destroyed by later working (Roman, medieval, and modern). Thus the great mines of southern Poland (Wieliczka, Bochnia), where Neolithic exploitation is assured, were very likely also worked in the Bronze Age, though this cannot be demonstrated. The same is no doubt also true for other areas of Europe.

Salt Production in Wooden Troughs

A remarkable discovery in 1977 in a salt stream in northern Romania (first published in 1988) has led the way in reassessing how salt was produced in the prolific deposits of Transylvania and adjacent areas (Chintăuan and Rusu 1988; Chintăuan 2005). This took the form of a wooden trough, over 3 m long and shaped like a dug-out canoe, with a series of holes in the base, filled with wooden pegs that were themselves perforated, the perforations being filled with twisted cord (Fig. 28.2). The find came from Băile Figa near Beclean on the Someș river; on investigation the findspot proved to be host to many hundreds of wooden posts and other installations, the majority of the radiocarbon determinations falling in the Bronze Age (Harding and Kavruk 2010). At least three further troughs have been discovered in excavation, along with evidence for ancient digging down to the rock-salt surface, which lies a few metres below the present-day surface.

These troughs join a number of others that have been found over the years, most in Transylvania but at least one north of the River Tisza in what is now Ukraine (Maxim 1971; Harding 2011). These finds have been the subject of much speculation over the years since they were first brought to the attention of the scientific world in the late nineteenth century; it is now clear they were involved in salt production on a quasi-industrial scale. The method by which they worked is not entirely certain but seems to have involved running fresh water into the troughs and letting it drip slowly onto a rock-salt surface. Over a few hours depressions are formed in the rock, which enables it to be broken up more easily and the pieces removed for further processing. At the same time, brine was concentrated in ponds that were reveted with wattle walls, and during the summer crystals could be collected on the edges and surface. While much remains to be elucidated about production techniques at Figa and similar sites, it seems clear that the technology involved was elaborate and, to judge from the

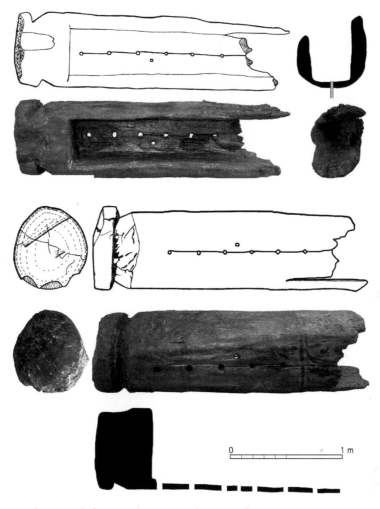

FIG. 28.2 Wooden trough from Băile Figa, Beclean, northern Romania.

Source: Harding and Kavruk 2010.

timescale and geographical area over which it was adopted, successful. Exploitation continued into the Iron Age and beyond, but the techniques seem to have been rather different.

Bronze Age Salt

In spite of the progress of research, which has brought to light many new finds and sites where salt production took place, we still do not have a unified or systematic picture of the situation across Europe: many gaps remain where there is no evidence in spite of the presence of salt deposits, as well as bigger gaps where there is neither evidence nor salt. In this case we have to consider the possibility that salt was transported from where it was produced to areas without salt where it was consumed. One obvious area is modern Hungary, which today has no salt of its own. The western part (Transdanubia) might have imported salt from the Austrian Alps or Slovakia; the eastern part (the Great Hungarian Plain) is much more likely to have obtained it from the Carpathian sources or Transylvania. How the salt moved is unknown in a Bronze Age context (see Chapter 20), but the needs of everyday life must mean that it surely was transported, perhaps in organic containers or in cake form.

Only one find of actual salt is known from Bronze Age sites, from Zakro in Crete (Kopaka and Chaniotakis 2003), where it is thought to have been deposited as part of a ritual performance. The solubility of salt means that usually no traces are left, either as salt crystals or as residues on artefacts. Future work may be able to solve this problem, which is a serious drawback in any consideration of salt production and exchange.

One may speculate on the identity of those who carried out production work. For some of the tasks physical strength was needed, particularly breaking up rock salt; even modern iron sledgehammers find it hard-going to fracture the rock. The carpentry skills evident on the Romanian sites and at Hallstatt might also have required considerable strength, as well as long experience. These tasks might have been undertaken by men, whereas most of the other tasks could have been divided equally between men and women: making briquetage, for instance, along with the related activites involved in it, and the collection of salt crystals or gathering up of broken lumps of rock salt, could have been undertaken by either sex. Mining has often been seen as a quintessentially male activity, but given the type of work involved in salt extraction, this was not necessarily the case.

The map of Bronze Age salt production in Europe has filled up remarkably in recent years. While many gaps remain in both our understanding of how it operated and in what was done in salt-less areas, one can be confident that the progress of research will solve many of these problems in the years to come.

Bibliography

Abarquero Moras, F. J., Guerra Doce, E., Delibes de Castro, G., Palomino Lázaro, A. L., and Val Recio, J. D. (2010). 'Excavaciones en los "cocederos" de sal prehistóricos de Molino Sanchón II y Santioste (Villafáfila, Zamora)', in F. J. Abarquero Moras and E. Guerra Doce (eds.), *Los yacimientos de Villafáfila (Zamora) en el marco de las explotaciones salineras de la prehistoria europea*. Valladolid: Junta de Castilla y León, Consejería de Cultura y Turismo, 85–118.

Barth, F. E. (1998). 'Bronzezeitliche Salzgewinnung in Hallstatt', in B. Hänsel (ed.), *Mensch und Umwelt in der Bronzezeit Europas*. Kiel: Oetger-Voges, 123–8.

Bell, M. (1990). *Brean Down Excavations 1983–1987*, English Heritage Archaeological Report 15. London: English Heritage.

Bertaux, J.-P. (1976). 'L'archéologie du sel en Lorraine, "Le briquetage de la Seille" (état actuel des recherches)', in J.-P. Millotte, A. Thévenin, and B. Chertier (eds.), *Livret-Guide de l'excursion A7, Champagne, Lorraine, Alsace, Franche-Comté, UISPP IXe Congrès Nice 1976*, 64–79.

Chințăuan, I. (2005). 'Pan used for salt extraction from brines', *Studii și Cercetări, Geologie-Geografie*, 10: 75–8.

Chințăuan, I. and Rusu, I. I. (1988). 'Considerații cu privire la utilizarea sării și apelor sărate din nord-estul Transilvaniei', *File de Istorie*, 5: 238–77.

Delibes de Castro, G., García Rozas, R., Larrén Izquierdo, H., and Rodriguez Rodriguez, E. (2007). 'Cuarenta siglos de explotación de sal en las lagunas de Villafáfila (Zamora) de la

Edad del Bronce al Medioevo', in A. Figuls and O. Weller (eds.), *La Trobada internacional d'arqueologia envers l'explotació de la sal a la prehistòria i protohistòria, Cardona, 6–8 de desembre del 2003*. Cardona: Institut de Recerques envers la Cultura (IREC), 111–43.

Di Fraia, T. (2006). 'Produzione, circolazione e consumo del sale nella protostoria italiana: dati archeologici e ipotesi di lavoro', *Atti XXXVII Riunione Scientifica I.I.P.P., 'Materie prime e scambi nella preistoria italiana'*, III: 1,639–49.

Harding, A. (2011). 'Evidence for salt production rediscovered in the Hungarian Central Mining Museum', *The Antiquaries Journal*, 91: 1–23.

Harding, A. and Kavruk, V. (2010). 'A prehistoric salt production site at Băile Figa, Romania', *Eurasia Antiqua*, 16: 131–67.

Kadrow, S. (ed.) (2003). *Kraków-Bieżanów, stanowisko 27 i Kraków-Rząka, stanowisko 1, osada kultury łużyckiej*, Via Archaeologica. Źródła z badań wykopaliskowych na trasie autostrady A4 w Małopolsce. Cracow: Krakowski Zespół do Badań Autostrad.

Kern, A., Kowarik, K., Rausch, A. W., and Reschreiter, H. (eds.) (2009). *Kingdom of Salt: 7000 years of Hallstatt*, Veröffentlichungen der prähistorischen Abteilung, 3. Vienna: Naturhistorisches Museum.

Kopaka, K. and Chaniotakis, N. (2003). 'Just taste additive? Bronze Age salt from Zakros, Crete', *Oxford Journal of Archaeology*, 22/1: 53–66.

Matthias, W. (1961). 'Das mitteldeutsche Briquetage—Formen, Verbreitung und Verwendung', *Jahresschrift für mitteldeutsche Vorgeschichte*, 45: 119–225.

—— (1976). 'Die Salzproduktion—ein bedeutender Faktor in der Wirtschaft der frühbronzezeitlichen Bevölkerung an der mittleren Saale', *Jahresschrift für mitteldeutsche Vorgeschichte*, 60: 373–94.

Maxim, I. A. (1971). 'Un depozit de unelte dacice pentru exploatarea sării', *Acta Musei Napocensis*, 8: 457–63.

Montagnari Kokelj, E. (2007). 'Salt and the Trieste karst (north-eastern Italy)', in D. Monah, G. Dumitroaia, O. Weller, and J. Chapman (eds.), *L'Exploitation du sel à travers le temps*. Piatra-Neamţ: Editura Constantin Matasă, 161–89.

Morère, N. (2002). 'À propos du sel hispanique', in O. Weller (ed.), *Archéologie du sel: techniques et sociétés dans la pré- et protohistoire européenne/Salzarchäologie. Techniken und Gesellschaft in der Vor- und Frühgeschichte Europas*, Internationale Archäologie: Arbeitsgemeinschaft, Symposium, Tagung, Kongress, Band 3. Rahden/Westf.: Verlag Marie Leidorf, 183–8.

Nenquin, J. (1961). *Salt: A Study in Economic Prehistory*, Dissertationes Archaeologicae Gandenses, 6. Gent: De Tempel.

Nijboer, A. J., Attema, P. A. J., and Van Oortmerssen, G. J. M. (2005–6). 'Ceramics from a Late Bronze Age saltern on the coast near Nettuno (Rome, Italy)', *Palaeohistoria*, 47/48: 141–205.

Pasquinucci, M. and Menchelli, S. (2002). 'The Isola di Coltano Bronze Age village and the salt production in north coastal Tuscany (Italy)', in O. Weller (ed.), *Archéologie du sel: techniques et sociétés dans la pré- et protohistoire européenne/Salzarchäologie. Techniken und Gesellschaft in der Vor- und Frühgeschichte Europas*, Internationale Archäologie, 3. Rahden/Westf.: Verlag Marie Leidorf, 177–82.

Riehm, K. (1954). 'Vorgeschichtliche Salzgewinnung an Saale und Seille', *Jahresschrift für mitteldeutsche Vorgeschichte*, 38: 112–56.

Saile, T. (2000). 'Salz im ur- und frühgeschichtlichen Mitteleuropa—eine Bestandsaufnahme', *Bericht der Römisch-Germanischen Kommission*, 81: 129–234.

CHAPTER 29

WEIGHING, COMMODIFICATION, AND MONEY

CHRISTOPHER PARE

INTRODUCTION

In Europe evidence for the use of new techniques for measuring commodities, particularly by weighing, begins in the Bronze Age (Fig. 29.1). As a general principle, measurement by weight or volume is useful for the quantification of materials that cannot otherwise be 'counted'. These are homogeneous, infinitely divisible materials such as liquids, powders, or undifferentiated masses. Archaeological and written sources show that during the Bronze Age a wide range of things were weighed at some time or another, including raw materials (e.g. metals, precious stones), foodstuffs (grain), and other products (e.g. wool). Archaeological finds can sometimes provide hints about the purpose of weighing: for example, large weights and scales were presumably used for bulk goods, whereas sensitive balances and fine weights, for precision weighing, indicate valuable materials measured out in small quantities.

In the following some of the main evidence for weights, weighing, and metrological systems will be briefly described. In the discussion, the close relationship of weighing with commodification and monetization will be highlighted. The treatment focuses on weighing equipment (balances and weights), and it is important to stress that only a sample of a much larger and more complex range of material is presented here.

THE EARLIEST EVIDENCE FOR WEIGHING

Precision weighing with the equal-arm balance began in the first half of the third millennium BC in Mesopotamia, Syria, and Egypt. The earliest securely dated weights are from Early Dynastic III contexts in Mesopotamia and Fourth Dynasty Egypt. Already at this early

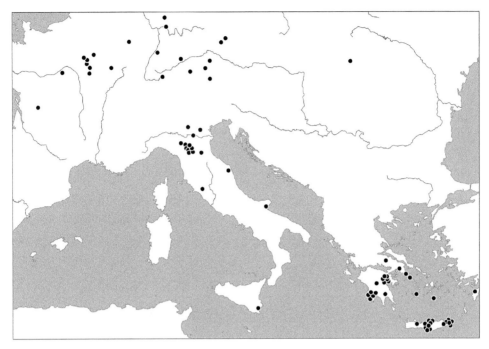

FIG. 29.1 Distribution map of weighing equipment (weights and balances) at the time of the Aegean Bronze Age palace civilization (twentieth-thirteenth century BC).

Map: author.

stage there is evidence for the widespread use of weight standards: the deben of 13.6–13.9 g in Egypt and the shekels of c.8.3 g and c.9.4 g in Mesopotamia and Syria. At this time we also see the origin of characteristic materials and shapes for weights, such as the sphendonoid (slingshot) made of haematite. Cuneiform texts mention the weighing of metals (e.g. silver, gold, and tin), wool, ivory, lapis lazuli, and coral (Rahmstorf 2006a; Ratnagar 2003; for the weighing of lapis lazuli at Ebla: Ascalone and Peyronel 2006: 53).

Precision weighing was adopted in the Aegean in the twenty-seventh or twenty-sixth century BC along with a range of other new elements of 'international' culture, such as stamp and cylinder seals or the *depas amphikypellon* (two-handled drinking cup). Lorenz Rahmstorf has recently identified a large number of spool-shaped stone weights in the Early Bronze Age Aegean, which were mainly based on the 'Syrian' shekel of c.9.4 g and the 50-shekel mina of c.470 g (Rahmstorf 2003; 2006b).

By the middle of the third millennium precise weighing was practised in a vast area between the Aegean, Egypt, Anatolia, Syria, Mesopotamia, and the Indus Valley. Rahmstorf notes the relationship between weighing practices and the development of complex metalworking: 'With the widespread trade and usage of precious metals like gold, silver and tin not only did the manufacture of these materials reach new levels, but the metals themselves had become standards of value, which could be measured exactly by their mass' (Rahmstorf 2006a: 38). The most important standard of value in the Near East was silver, which gradually adopted the functions of money, as a weighed metal currency.

As most of these materials had been known in the Near East for millennia, it seems logical to suggest that the main cause for the introduction of weighing and weight standards was the need for quantification and commodification. Commodification is an important and much-discussed process, which is useful not only for trade but also for economic administration (for a discussion of commodification, see Gregory 1982; Hart 1982; Van Binsbergen 2005). Furthermore, the process is intimately related to monetization, because money allows commensuration of different commodity values by giving them a 'money-price' (Aristotle, *Nicomachean Ethics* 5, 5, 10–16; Marx 1990: part I, for important discussions of commodification and commensuration). Theoretically, there are various different ways in which commensuration could have come about: the relative value of the commodities could have been dictated by law, established by custom or by the practice of barter and trading. Corresponding to these different reasons for introducing money, the functions of money can be differentiated: unit of account, means of payment, and medium of exchange (Ingham 2000; for a brief introduction to the question of the origins of money, see Grierson 2001). The introduction of weighing can only be understood in relation to the nexus of commodification and commensuration.

Developments in the East Mediterranean in the Later Bronze Age

During the Middle and Late Bronze Age, the main weight unit used for trade in the East Mediterranean remained the shekel of 9.3–9.4 g, as finds from the Ulu Burun and Gelidonya shipwrecks indicate (Pulak 2000). However, another metrological system was developed by the Minoan palaces; as Crete had particularly close relations with Egypt in the early second millennium BC, it is likely that the Minoan weight system was linked to the Egyptian deben unit. Exactly when the Minoan system originated is uncertain, although the earliest securely dated weights belong to the nineteenth or eighteenth century BC (Middle Minoan IB–II). The Minoan weights were mainly lead and stone discs, based on a talent of $c.29$ kg and a mina of $c.488$ g; the mina was divided into eight units of $c.61$ g, the basic unit for fine measurement (Petruso 1992). The best evidence for Minoan weighing comes from contexts of Late Minoan I–II, for example from the sites of Ayia Irini (Chios) and Akrotiri (Thera). At Akrotiri more than one hundred disc-shaped weights found in all parts of the settlement were clearly not used in barter or trade, but in the administration of the intensive and specialized production of textiles and metals (Alberti 2003b: 613).

Sadly, our knowledge of Mycenaean weighing systems is much poorer. Although the Linear B texts suggest that there was no fundamental difference between Minoan and Mycenaean weighing systems, there are some indications, from Athens, Mycenae, and Thebes, that new metrological standards may have been introduced in Late Helladic III (fourteenth–thirteenth century BC), probably to facilitate exchange with Anatolia and the Levant (Petruso 2003; Alberti 2003b). At this time precision weighing using weights of small or minimal mass became more important, and the weights reflect intense contact with the East Mediterranean. Sphendonoids now came into use, based on oriental weight units (*qedet, shekel*), in particular the values 'e' of 9.7–10.4 g, 'k' of 19.4–20.8 g, and 'x' of 58–62 g (Alberti 2003a; 2003b; 2009). Alongside settlement material, weighing equipment has been found in about 45 graves of the Aegean Late Bronze Age, generally relatively rich tholos and chamber tombs. A study by Maria Emanuela Alberti has shown that the balances in the graves were generally small, most of the examples having scale-pans between 5.0 and 8.4 cm in diameter, and suitable for weighing masses up to the unit 'x' of $c.58$–62 g (Alberti 2003a).

Italy and Central Europe

The earliest evidence for weighing in Italy seems to be the 8.5-cm-long bronze balance beam from Castelluccio grave 22 in Sicily (Fig. 29.6, 1), found together with possible remnants of the scale pans and a bronze sphere (Cardarelli, Pacciarelli, and Pallante 2001: 36, Fig. 9.7). However, this tomb can only be roughly dated to the first half of the second millennium BC. A series of about 30 globular, roughly pear-shaped polished stone weights with a perforation through the projecting upper part ('*pesi con appiccagnolo*') are of greater importance (Fig. 29.2). They are mainly known from the *Terramare* settlements of the Po Valley, although examples are found further south, for example from Grotta Nuova (Prov. Viterbo), Coppa Nevigata (Prov. Foggia), and four from Moscosi di Cingoli (Prov. Macerata). Most of the weights seem to date to the fifteenth–thirteenth century BC. For example, a weight from Gaggio (Castelfranco Emilia, Prov. Modena) is dated to Bronzo medio 2, a piece from Grotta

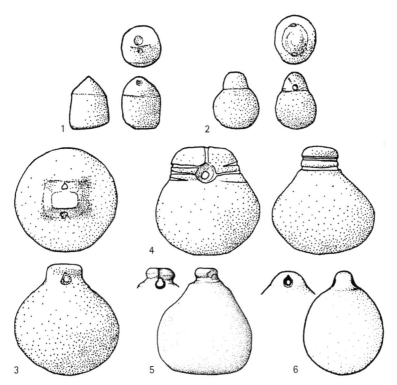

FIG. 29.2 Stone weights of '*Terramare*' type: 1. Gaiato; 2. Casinalbo; 3. Montale; 4. Quingento; 5. Lefkandi; 6. Gaggio di Castelfranco Emilia. Not to scale.

Drawings: author, after Cardarelli, Pacciarelli, and Palante 2001, Balista *et al.* 2008, Evely 2006.

Nuova cannot be dated later than Bronzo medio 3, and weights from Moscosi date to Bronzo recente 2 (for Gaggio, see Balista et al. 2008; for Moscosi, see Picener 1999: 189, cat. no. 42–45). The published examples weigh between 36.5 g and c.842 g; however, as no more than 15 are well preserved, the basis for metrological analysis is rather slight. Cardarelli, Pacciarelli, and Pallante (2001) suggest an underlying unit of c.6.1 g (or its multiples) for the *Terramare* system; indeed the two lightest pieces with very similar masses of 36.5 g and 36.6 g surely indicate a common unit. The masses of these stone weights form clusters at 36.5–36.6 g, 340–351 g, c.392 g, 417–420 g, and c.453 g. The resulting denominations (Table 29.1) give rise to a rather unwieldy set of weights, suggesting either that the metrological reconstruction is incorrect (perhaps more than one metrological standard was used), or that the weights were mainly used for a specialized purpose requiring precise weighing in the 300–500 g range. Despite this uncertainty, it is important to note the relationship of the proposed *Terramare* unit of c.6.1 g or 24.4 g (4 x 6.1 g) with the Aegean or Minoan unit '*x*' of around 61 g (10 x 6.1 g). This could indicate that the Italian weighing technology was introduced from the Aegean around the middle of the second millennium BC.

Systematic research on weight norms has been conducted by Majolie Lenerz-de Wilde (1995; 2002) for the Copper and Early Bronze Age in central Europe. She believes she has demonstrated the existence of 'primitive money' based on a rough weight system, suggesting that neck-rings ('ring-money') appeared as means of payment and store of value in the Early Bronze Age, and were gradually replaced during the later part of the period by ever smaller and eventually miniature forms.

The ring-ingots (*Ösenringbarren*) are often found in large hoards consisting exclusively of this form of raw copper. The ingots were often tied together in bundles of five (Fig. 29.3; 1).

Table 29.1 Masses of Well-Preserved *Terramare* Weights, and the Suggested Units of c.6.1 g/24.4 g

Provenance	Well-preserved weights	Proposed units
Gaiato	36.5 g	6 x 6.08 g
Casinalbo	36.6 g	6 x 6.10 g
Montale	c.43.2 g	?
Montale	295 g	12 x 24.58 g
Quingento	340 g	14 x 24.29 g
Servirolo S. Polo	340(-) g	14 x 24.29(-) g
M. Barello	348 g	14 x 24.86 g
Moscosi	350.8 g	14 x 25.06 g
Peschiera	376 g	15 x 25.07 g
Gorzano	390(-) g	16 x 24.38(-) g
Montale	392 g	16 x 24.50 g
Peschiera (lead)	417 g	17 x 24.53 g
Tosc. Imolese	420 g	17 x 24.71 g
Moscosi	447(-) g	18 x 24.83(-) g
Grotta Nuova	453 g	18 x 25.27 g

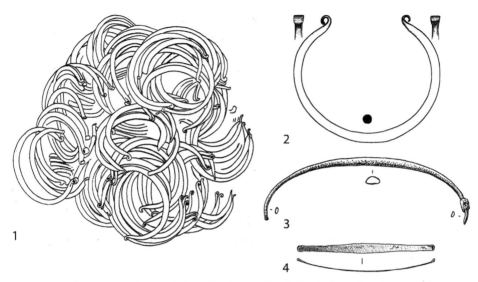

FIG. 29.3 1. Copper ring-ingots in bundles in the Ragelsdorf 2 hoard. 2. Copper ring-ingot from the Ragelsdorf 2 hoard. 3. Copper clasp-ingot from St Florian. 4. Miniature copper ingot from Thal. 1. not to scale; 2.-4. scale 1:4.

Drawings: author, after Lenerz-de Wilde 1995 and Neugebauer 2002.

For example, the hoard of Piding (Kr. Berchtesgadener Land) contained 60 ingots, many of which were bound together in bundles of five with cords made from tree-bark fibres. Evidence for the weight system posited by Majolie Lenerz-de Wilde is provided, for example, by a hoard from Ragelsdorf in Lower Austria, in which the distribution of ingot weights has two modes (180–190 g and 370–380 g) with a ratio of c.1:2. The development described by Lenerz-de Wilde can be summarized as follows:

1. Bz A1a: looped neck-rings used as jewellery
2. Bz A1b: looped ring-ingots with roughly standardized weights used as a form of currency ('ring-money') (Fig. 29.3, 2)
3. Bz A2a–b: ingots in smaller units of weight became common (clasp-ingots and miniature forms) (Fig. 29.3, 3-4)
4. Bz A2c/B(?): hoards with very light miniature ingots and ingot fragments mark the transition to a different form of currency
5. Bz A2c/B: use of 'ring-money' and 'token-money' ceases; instead fragmented raw and scrap metal appears in hoards. This new system lasts till the end of the Bronze Age.

In the data collected by Lenerz-de Wilde it is possible to recognize certain concentrations of weight, for example around 45–50 g, 85–100 g, 175–200 g, and 881–994 g. Regional differences are also noticeable, for example between south-east Bavaria/Salzburg/western Upper Austria on the one hand, and Lower Austria/Moravia on the other. However, the histograms published by Lenerz-de Wilde make it perfectly clear that the ingots were not precisely weighed.

They functioned as *aes formatum* (utensil-money or ring-money), where the form of the ingots ensured rough quantitative equivalences. Rather than a strict metrological system, we seem to be dealing with quantities of size and weight established by custom and not by a standardized metrological system. If the ingots were generally exchanged in large quantities, as the bundled ingots from Ragelsdorf (Lower Austria), Bernhaupten, and Valley (Bavaria) suggest, then the individual ingots would not have needed to be standardized exactly. However, in the course of the first centuries of the second millennium BC, increasing precision in the exchange of metal was achieved by the introduction of lighter ingots, eventually weighing as little as *c*.5 g.

Lenerz-de Wilde's interpretation of the ring- and clasp-ingots as a form of money has been reinforced by metallurgical analyses. Junk, Krause, and Pernicka (2001) and Liversage (2001) showed that most of the ingots consist of a characteristic copper, rich in trace elements (arsenic, antimony, silver) but without nickel and tin. By contrast, the majority of contemporary artefacts are made from a different kind of copper: 'Hence, the *Ösenring* is possibly not an ingot at all, but instead a distinctive kind of copper in a specific form denoting a certain value, and used for monetary purposes' (Junk, Krause, and Pernicka 2001: 356). According to these results, we are dealing not with commodity-money, but with token-money.

In specialist works a distinction is often made between 'primitive valuables' and 'primitive money', the distinguishing feature being that 'primitive money' can be used as a unit of account. 'Primitive money' has a number of distinguishing features, including attributes such as uniformity in appearance and fungibility (Dalton 1965; 1982; for the principle of fungibility, see Simmel 1922: 92; 'money is "interchangeability personified"—each quantum can be replaced without distinction by any other'). While marine shells served as money in many small-scale societies around the world, the ethnographic record reveals a vast range of other possible forms, including raw materials such as salt and gold-dust. Sometimes 'primitive money' has both use-value and exchange-value (commodity money), sometimes only exchange-value (token money).

Weighing in Bronze Age Europe

At the start of the Bronze Age in Europe the huge increase in metal production together with the restricted occurrence of copper ores led to a new level of spatial specialization. As a corollary, external exchange relationships and new mechanisms of exchange gained a much more important role than previously in the Neolithic. For this period around 600 kg of raw copper in the form of ring- and clasp-ingots have been registered in the Alpine foothills around the German-Austrian border. Within a well-defined ecumene between South Bavaria, Bohemia, Moravia, and Lower Austria (Fig. 29.4) it seems that metal became 'fetishized' and was exchanged as token-money, for a certain span of time having 'prime value', in the sense outlined by Colin Renfrew (1986).

The Early Bronze Age use of token-money was probably disrupted and rendered obsolete by the regular practice of tin alloying since the eighteenth century BC (Bz A2b), requiring a much greater scale of exchange in order to supply copper and tin to all parts of central, western, and northern Europe (Pare 2000). Finally, around the seventeenth or sixteenth century BC the Early Bronze Age system was replaced by the use of scrap and raw metal in the

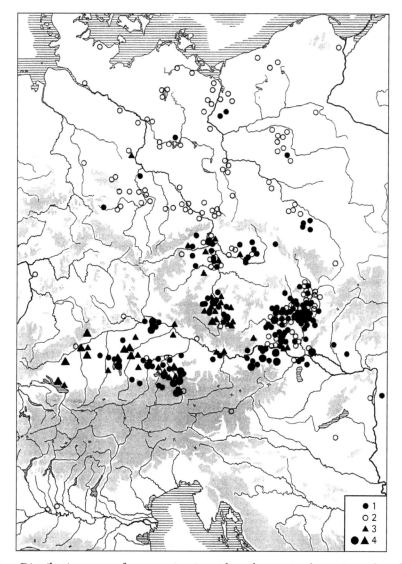

FIG. 29.4 Distribution map of 1. pure ring-ingot hoards; 2. mixed ring-ingot hoards; and 3. clasp-ingot hoards. Hoards with more than 50 ingots are marked with a large symbol (4).

Source: Innerhofer 1997 (photo: Klaus Göke).

exchange process. Margarita Primas describes this process as follows (1997: 123): 'The centuries following the Early Bronze Age are now seen to be a period of fundamental change. The pattern of hoard contents was modified drastically.... Scrap metal and ingots of various shapes began to circulate regularly on an interregional scale. Gold was now available in considerable quantities. These features speak for the widespread use of weighed metal as a means of payment.' This argument was supported by a detailed study of bronze sickles and their state of fragmentation, in which Primas showed that these tools were often intentionally broken into small pieces. In the hoard from Sigmaringen, for example, an incomplete sickle(73 g) was broken into four pieces of 45 g, 14 g, 7 g, and 7 g, showing that it had repeatedly been snapped into smaller fragments. The purpose of this practice was clearly to produce smaller pieces of metal which, she argued, could then be used as a kind of currency (Primas 1986: 37–40). Furthermore, Primas noted that in hoards and settlements the fragments are often from sickles of foreign types, which led her to put forward a model of wide-ranging scrap-bronze circulation in which the weighed metal scrap served as a 'substantialization of value' (i.e. a form of money). A similar degree of fragmentation is found in many hoards of the Middle and Late Bronze Age: in the Transylvanian hoard of Şpălnaca II, for example, copper ingots were fragmented to a minimum mass of 7 g (Fig. 29.5); more precise weighing of copper and bronze was presumably unnecessary. The suggestion by some authors (e.g. Sommerfeld 1994; Peroni 1998) that fragments of scrap metal, ingots, and casting cakes were intentionally broken into fragments corresponding to weight-measurement units seems unlikely, and has not yet been demonstrated convincingly.

Primas's arguments are plausible, suggesting fundamental changes in the form of metallic currency around the transition from the Early to the Middle Bronze Age (c.seventeenth–sixteenth century BC): in Latin terms this is the transition from *aes formatum* (ring-money/

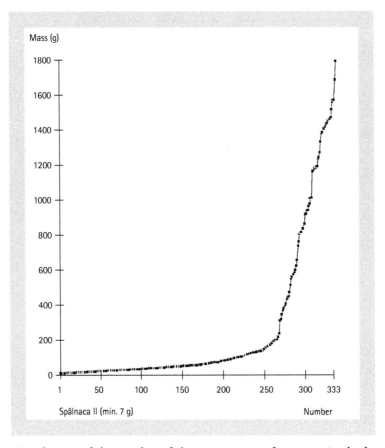

FIG. 29.5 Distribution of the weights of the copper ingot fragments in the hoard from Şpălnaca II, Transylvania.

Source: Primas and Pernicka 1998.

utensil-money) to *aes rude*. In the new exchange system raw metal was the standard of value. According to the level of fragmentation in Middle and Late Bronze Age hoards, an accuracy much finer than 10 g was not required in the weighing of copper or bronze. This kind of use of weighed copper/bronze as a means of exchange (*per aes et libram*) is described by Pliny the Elder (*Natural History* 33, 13) for the time before Servius, and it was probably widely used before the introduction of coinage both in Italy and Greece (Kroll 2008). Indeed, Linear B tablets from Pylos and Knossos show that in the Mycenaean palace economy, while grain was the basic unit of account (*numéraire*), weighed bronze was the main means of payment (Sacconi 2005: 73). Although the use of weighed metal in the Bronze Age seems plausible, the proposed system can hardly have functioned without standard weights. Suitable weights are, however, not documented in central Europe until the end of the second millennium BC. Even then they are so rare that it is difficult to imagine their use in a pan-European system of metal exchange. The use of weighed bronze as commodity-money therefore remains hypothetical, even if the theory is attractive.

Exactly when precision weighing was introduced in Italy and temperate Europe is uncertain. As we have seen, an early date is indicated by the balance-beam from Castelluccio in Sicily (Fig. 29.6; 1), and the so-called *Terramare* weights were introduced by the fifteenth century BC. Further north there are further weights and scales possibly dating to the Middle Bronze Age, although the balance-beam from the Grotte des Perrats near Agris (length 9.3 cm) is the only reliably dated example (Fig. 29.6; 2). Clear evidence for precision weights and weighing becomes frequent in the thirteenth century BC (Bz D). The distribution map (see Fig. 29.1) suggests that the weighing technology originated in the Aegean and then spread via Italy to central Europe.

In contrast to Italy, weighing equipment from north of the Alps is mainly known from graves. Late Bronze Age bone scale-beams have, however, been excavated in settlement pits from Bordjoš (Serbia) and Mannheim-Wallstadt (Germany), and three caves in Charente (France): Agris 'Grotte des Perrats', Vilhonneur, Bois du Roc 'Grotte de la Cave Chaude', and Chazelles 'Grotte du Quéroy' (Fig. 29.6; 2 and 5; Medović 1995; Görner 2003: 256, Fig. 71.3; Gomez de Soto 2001). Copper-alloy weights are known from settlement contexts in Flintsbach and Singen in south Germany and from the hoards of Tiszabecs in Hungary and Larnaud in France (Pare 1999). Otherwise our evidence comes from at least 14 graves with weights and balances, almost all of which date to Bz D. It is these grave finds of the thirteenth century BC that provide most information, and which will be discussed in more detail.

In a few graves, the weighing equipment was found inside a boxlike container complete with bronze fittings from a closing mechanism. In Marolles-sur-Seine (Seine-et-Marne), 'Gours-aux-Lions', cremation grave 5 was situated inside a circular ditched enclosure. The grave pit contained an urn, a lid, and six accessory vessels. A collection of 19 unburnt objects was found in the remains of a rectangular wooden receptacle (Pare 1999: 450, Fig. 20). Apart from a bronze dagger, bronze tweezers, a bronze awl, three fragments of gold, an oval amber object, a miniature polished stone axe, a whetstone, and two bronze fish-hooks, the contents included the bone beam of an equal-arm balance. The centre of the beam is perforated and holds a bronze-wire suspension loop. The ends of the bone beam are incomplete, but the original length must have been 11–13 cm (Fig. 29.6; 3). A similar grave was uncovered at Étigny 'Le Brassot' (Yonne). In this case the rectangular receptacle contained an awl and tweezers of bronze, along with a bone balance-beam (length *c*.11.5 cm) and at least eight copper-alloy weights. A similar grave has recently been excavated at Migennes, 'Le Petit Moulin' (Yonne), again with a rectangular receptacle containing an antler balance-beam (length 10.1 cm), about

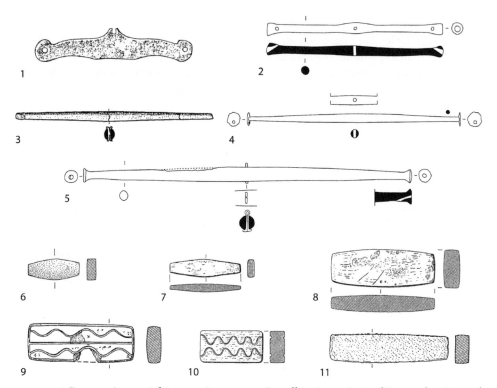

FIG. 29.6 Bronze Age weighing equipment: 1. Castelluccio 2. Agris, 'Grotte des Perrats' 3. Marolles-sur-Seine, 'Gours aux Lions', grave 5 4. Marolles-sur-Seine, 'La Croix de la Mission', grave 13 5. Vilhonneur, 'Cave Chaude' 6. Flintsbach, 'Rachelburg' 7. Steinfurth. 8. Gondelsheim 9. 'Sologne' 10. Richemont-Pépinville 11. Poing, grave 1. Scale 1:2.

Drawings: author, after various sources.

20 weights, 14 fragments of gold, a bronze awl, and an assortment of other small objects (Étigny and Migennes: Delor, Muller, and Roscio 2009). A probable balance-beam from Richemont-Pépinville (Moselle) is exceptional, being made of bronze and slightly longer than the more common bone and antler examples (preserved length: 12.8 cm). In no case have balance-pans survived, indicating that they were made of an organic material such as horn.

The weights are made of copper alloy and are mainly rectangular or sub-rectangular in shape. The sizes of the objects vary widely, from tiny examples with a mass of less than 3 g to the largest weighing more than 60 g. The shapes also vary, including oval or angular amygdaloid blocks with flat rectangular cross section (Fig. 29.6; 6–8), rectangular blocks with flat rectangular cross section and inlaid copper wavelike designs (Fig. 29.6; 9–10), and rectangular blocks with rectangular, square, or trapezoidal cross section (Fig. 29.6; 11). The weights are often made from a tin-rich alloy, with values of 16–25 per cent Sn being recorded; the high tin content lends these weights a greyish colour.

In some cases, relationships between the masses of the weights are obvious. In the grave of Gondelsheim, the masses of the two rectangular weights, 7.45 g and 60.65 g, have a ratio of c.1:8. In the case of Pépinville, two of the rectangular weights have similar masses (39.27 g and 41.00 g) and presumably represent the same metrological value; a third example of 19.89 g has roughly half the mass. However, a more detailed analysis is difficult, partly because some

Table 29.2 The Reconstructed Metrological System of the Weights of the Thirteenth Century BC (Bz D) in Central Europe

Reconstructed metrological system	Hypothetical value	Well-preserved weights	Provenance
1 Unit	(61.3 g)	60.65 g	Gondelsheim
2/3 Unit	(40.9 g)	39.27 g, 41 g, 43 g	Pépinville, Königsbronn
1/3 Unit	(20.4 g)	19.89 g, 21.40 g	Pépinville, Horušany
1/4 Unit	(15.3 g)	15.01 g	Milavče
1/6 Unit	(10.2 g)	10.00 g	Flintsbach
1/8 Unit	(7.7 g)	7.45 g, 7.86 g	Gondelsheim, Pépinville
1/9 Unit	(6.8 g)	6.50 g, 6.70 g	Horušany, Poing
1/16 Unit	(3.8 g)	c.3.86 g	Courtavant

of the weights are poorly preserved, and partly because other weights clearly had different shapes (spherical, cylindrical, fusiform), making a clear identification difficult. For this purpose, statistical methods have been useful, in particular the Quantal Analysis developed by David Kendall. A detailed study resulted in the reconstruction of a fundamental metrological unit of c.61.3 g (for details, see Pare 1999). Table 29.2 shows a reconstruction of the weight system for a selection of well-preserved rectangular weights.

This system consists of a tertiary (1/9, 1/6, 1/3, 2/3) and a binary (1/16, 1/8, 1/4) series of fractions; significantly, the two series converge at a value of c.61.3 g, which presumably represents a fundamental unit within the metrological system. This is very interesting in view of the correspondence with the Aegean unit 'x' for fine weighing of c.61 g. It emerges from this discussion that a special kind of technology specifically for precision weighing is represented by these grave finds. In central Europe the balances were small, with beams averaging around 10–13 cm in length; likewise, apart from a few exceptions (tholos tombs from Pylos, Thorikos, and Vapheio), the graves of the Late Bronze Age in the Aegean also had weights and balances for fine weighing, presumably using fractions of the precision-weighing unit of c.61 g. As mentioned above, most of the balances had scale-pans 5.0–8.4 cm in diameter, suitable for use with small weights. The only grave with weighing equipment so far published from Italy, Castelluccio grave 22, once again has a short balance-beam (length 8.5 cm) clearly for use in weighing small quantities of material (Fig. 29.6; 1).

It is difficult to avoid the conclusion that the fine-weighing equipment found in these high-status graves between the Aegean and central Europe had a specific and related function. That the technology spread from the Aegean is indicated by the 'Minoan' metrological system of some of the central European weights, and also by the shape of some of the weights (the oval or angular amygdaloid blocks resemble the sphendonoids that became frequent in the Aegean in LH IIIA–B). Exactly what was being weighed is uncertain: a wide range of materials (e.g. amber, pigments, spices) is conceivable. However, precious metals (gold, also silver in the Aegean) are the most likely candidates. Weighed gold could have served as an inter-regional or international currency, used in exchange between trade partners in a wide area between the east Mediterranean, the Aegean, the central Mediterranean, and central Europe. The scraps of gold in the graves from Marolles-sur-Seine and Migennes can be mentioned in support of this suggestion. And the tiny weights from Étigny and Migennes, capable of weighing fractions of a gram, can only be understood in connection with the 14 scraps of gold found in the latter grave, weighing between 0.01 g and 1.23 g. Delor, Muller, and Roscio (2009: 29) conclude as follows: 'The study of the weights from Migennes and Étigny proves that this weighing equipment was functional and indicates a well-established system of numeration. Such objects attest the existence of individuals having the capacity to control weights and measures, as well as the exchange of precious metals' (my translation).

These important new discoveries indicate clearly how extremely valuable gold was for the inhabitants of the Yonne region during the thirteenth century BC. The Uluburun shipwreck has produced further evidence. Cemal Pulak, in his discussion of the sphendonoids used for fine weighing, writes: 'Precious metals are represented on the Uluburun ship by pieces of finished and scrap jewellery of gold and silver, and by others that had been melted down into lumps. Pieces or sections have been cut from some of the gold and silver objects, indicating that they were used as bullion in trade transactions, and the sphendonoid weights would have been ideal for weighing these valuable metals' (Pulak 1996: 279–80). The relatively large number of burials with precision-weighing equipment in the Aegean and in central Europe makes it likely that precious metals were in use as a widely accepted form of commodity-money, used in transactions concerning a range of goods, such as copper, tin, and amber.

In central Europe this precision-weighing equipment is often found in high-status graves. It is very interesting that it was carried, along with other utensils such as tweezers and awls, in a boxlike receptacle, perhaps hanging from a belt. This implies that the balance and weights were used by these individuals for relatively frequent exchange transactions. The use of weighed metal as commodity-money (*Gewichtsgeldwirtschaft*) is well known, for example from late Roman and Merovingian Austrasia, the Viking period around the Baltic Sea, or among the Akan-speaking peoples of Ghana and the Ivory Coast following the establishment of trans-Saharan trade (Steuer 2004; Werner 1954; Garrard 1980). These comparisons are perhaps unsuitable, because in the examples mentioned the practice of weighing metals as currency arose on the periphery of economies using coinages of precious-metals. Nevertheless, this could be understood as an analogy for the position of central Europe at the periphery of a trade network in the central and east Mediterranean. The distribution of Mycenaean pottery reached up the Adriatic in Late Helladic IIIB-C, and it is plausible that exchange networks in the Po Valley were linked to those north of the Alps, a scenario that must be envisaged to explain the widespread adoption of weighing over such a large geographical area (for Mycenaean pottery at Moscosi di Cingoli and other sites in the Marche, see Vagnetti et al. 2006). Furthermore, a link between Italian and Aegean weighing practices is indicated by a stone weight of the *Terramare* type (*peso con appicagnolo*) from Lefkandi, dated to Late Helladic IIIC (see Fig. 29.2; 5; see Evely 2006: 52, no. 47; 276).

In the Final Bronze Age, between the twelfth and ninth century BC, evidence for weights and weighing becomes more frequent, but at the same time more complicated. The evidence no longer comes from graves, but instead from settlements and hoard finds. The largest collection of weights is from the region north-west of the Alps, mainly from the riverside and lakeside settlements dating from the mid eleventh to the end of the ninth century BC (an example has recently been published from north-west France: Charnier et al. 1999: 574, Fig. 5, 35). These weights are generally made of stone or lead, and a single exception from Cortaillod is of bronze. The piriform shape of the stone examples is similar to the earlier *Terramare* examples, and again they are perforated at the top for suspension (see Fig. 29.2; Fig. 29.7). Analysis of the masses of these weights suggests the existence of weight standards (Table 29.3).

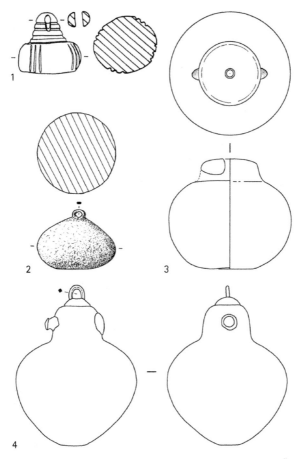

FIG. 29.7 Final Bronze Age weights from France and Switzerland: 1. Mörigen. 2. Saint-Léonard-des-Boix. 3. Bragny, from the Saône. 4. Ouroux, from the Saône. Scale 1:2.

Drawings: author, after Pare 1999: Charnier et al. 1999.

Whereas 11 of the weights seem to be organized around a unit of c.48.8 g (or 6.1 g/12.2 g/61 g), the remaining nine most likely correspond to a system based on a unit of c.104 g. The unit of c.48.8 g must surely be related to the 'Minoan' metrology (unit of c.61 g for fine weighing, mina of c.488 g), which has been suggested for both the fifteenth–thirteenth centuries in Italy (see Table 29.1) and the fourteenth–thirteenth centuries in central Europe (see Table 29.2). It is therefore likely that this metrological system was used continuously in regions north of the Alps for half a millennium. The second unit of c.104 g presumably represents a new unit, perhaps introduced during the twelfth or eleventh century BC. Sadly, the precise find-contexts of these weights is not known, and it is impossible to be sure what they were used for. Although they are clearly too heavy to have been used for weighing precious metals, there is a wide range of other conceivable commodities, including base metals such as copper, bronze, tin, or lead.

Table 29.3 Well-Preserved Weights of the Final Bronze Age from France and Switzerland, and the Suggested Units of c.48.8 g and c.104 g

Provenance	Mass	Unit of c.48.8 g	Unit of c.104 g
Mörigen	98.3 g	2 x 49.15 g	
Concise	102 g		1 x 102 g
Tessin	195(-) g	4 x 48.75(-) g	
Cortaillod	210 g		2 x 105 g
Columbier	385.98(-) g	8 x 48.25(-) g	
Vallamand	389(-) g	8 x 48.63(-) g	
Port	530(-) g		5 x 106(-) g
Onnens	613.77(-) g		6 x 102.30(-) g
Wollishofen	727 g	15 x 48.47 g	
Auvernier	730(?) g	15 x 48.67(?) g	
Auvernier	731.7 g	15 x 48.78 g	
Wollishofen	735 g	15 x 49 g	
Wollishofen	735(-) g	15 x 49(-) g	
Ouroux	741 g	15 x 49.40 g	
Bragny	770(-) g	16 x 48.13(-) g	
Mörigen	848 g		8 x 106 g
Orpund	935.8(-) g		9 x 103.98(-) g
Corcelettes	920 g		9 x 102.22 g
Auvernier	940 g		9 x 104.44 g
Strasbourg	1052(-) g		10 x 105.2 g

WEIGHING AND COMMODIFICATION

An interesting aspect of the introduction of weighing, and its practice during the Bronze Age, is the intimate relationship with the process of commodification; as mentioned above, weights and measures are necessary for the commodification of non-countable wares. But commodification entails the problem of commensurability: how are relations of equivalence (exchange values) possible when the things themselves (use values, for example shoes, beds, houses) are different, and which common standard can be used to express the exchange values? The problem was solved by the mechanism of money-price. Exactly in which form or forms money evolved in the Old World is uncertain; nevertheless, metals were certainly of fundamental importance in the periods for which we have information from written records.

Although the relationship between weighing, commodification, and monetization seems plausible, the origin of this 'nexus' is by no means clear. In discussing the origins of money, some authors emphasize non-economic factors, with money starting as a unit of account (an abstract *numéraire*, or token), for example as a means of payment or compensation imposed by social regulation. Others believe that money emerged as a medium of exchange 'naturally' out of barter, originally being the most favoured object in customary barter transactions (Ingham 2004: 6; Schumpeter's 'Claim Theory' and 'Commodity Theory'). However, the Substantivist school of Karl Polanyi and his followers has argued that barter had only peripheral importance in small-scale societies, and that markets and money emerged in the course of interaction with external spheres of transaction or long-distance trade (Polanyi 1944: 58; Sahlins 1974: 280). For example, as Caroline Humphrey (1985: 49) notes: 'we know from the accumulated evidence of ethnography that barter was indeed very rare as a system dominating primitive economies'. Similarly, Karl Marx sought the origins of commodification in communities' external relationships of 'reciprocal isolation and foreignness' (Marx 1990: 182). Against this background it seems unlikely that weighing and money emerged 'naturally' from barter, but a range of other possibilities can be envisaged for the Bronze Age. Three mechanisms will be discussed for the central European cases discussed above:

- For the precision balances and the rectangular weights mainly found in high-status graves of the thirteenth century BC a derivation from Italy and/or the Aegean is very likely. This is suggested not only by the related weight metrology and the shapes of some of the weights, but also by the practice of providing fine-weighing equipment as grave goods both in the Aegean and in central Europe. In both areas high-status groups regularly weighed material in the 3–60 g range using similar equipment. It seems likely that these weights and balances were carried and used specifically for use with one particular material, the only obvious candidates being precious metals: in central Europe gold, in the Aegean gold and silver. Gold could then have been introduced and used as a widely recognized money form (commodity-money) for the articulation of long-distance trade in a range of other commodities such as copper, tin, and amber. The cut fragments of gold in the graves from Marolles-sur-Seine and Migennes (Delor, Muller, and Roscio 2009; Pare 1999: 450, Fig. 20.10–12; 459, Fig. 27.6) can be best interpreted in this way. Furthermore, in the fourteenth-century BC deposition from Bernstorf (Kr. Freising), analysis has shown that the gold is so pure that it was probably purified by a technique (parting by salt cementation) unknown in central Europe at that time (Gebhard 1999: 9–10), suggesting that the gold had come from the eastern Mediterranean. This illustrates the possibility that gold was circulated very widely in the fourteenth and thirteenth centuries BC, and the graves from the Yonne region show how it could have been exchanged in raw or fragmented form.
- The copper ring-ingots and later the clasp-ingots and miniature forms were not weighed using balances or standard weights. They can best be understood as a form of *aes formatum*. In excavated hoards the ingots are often found in bundles of five, recalling the use of the well-known Greek utensil-money, the iron spits of the Late Geometric period (*oboloi*), which were exchanged in handfuls (*drachmae*) of six (Teržan 2004). Metallurgical analysis has shown that the metal of the ring- and clasp-ingots was generally not used for making artefacts, suggesting an interpretation as token-money. It is impossible to be sure how the ring-ingots were used, but a non-economic interpretation as unit of account, for example in the payment of social or religious obligations, at least seems feasible.

- For the deliberately fragmented scrap and raw metal found in hoards since the end of the Early Bronze Age, interpretation must again remain hypothetical. The use of weighed metal as a form of money (*aes rude*) is well known in the Ancient World, for example in pre-coinage Italy and in the Mycenaean palaces, and an analogous use is possible in central Europe, considering the crucial role of the supply and exchange of copper and tin for the reproduction of Bronze Age society. Although it is difficult to imagine how the copper and tin supply functioned without weighing or some other form of commodification, suitable weights have not yet been found in most of Europe, important exceptions being the so-called *Terramare* weights and the examples from the riverside and lakeside settlements north-west of the Alps (see Figs. 29.2 and 29.7). It is equally uncertain to what extent European spheres of metal circulation were linked together, although it has often been speculated that north-west European tin may have reached the palaces of the Aegean. However, clear evidence for such wide-ranging exchange of copper is rare; the oxhide-ingot fragments from the hoard of Oberwilflingen in Germany are an important exception (Primas and Pernicka 1998).

CONCLUSION

The reasons for the introduction of precise weighing are by no means obvious, requiring thought about a range of processes including quantification, number, commodification, and commensuration. In the Old World the introduction of weighing seems to be related to the development of complex metalworking (Rahmstorf 2006a: 38), perhaps also the control of metal circulation and provisioning. In contrast with many parts of the world, in which a wide variety of money forms are known (most frequently marine shells), in the Near East, the Mediterranean, and Europe metals (particularly weighed metals, but also *aes formatum*) appear to have been the main form of currency.

BIBLIOGRAPHY

Alberti, M. E. (2003a). 'Weighing and dying between East and West. Weighing materials from LBA Aegean funerary contexts', in K. P. Foster and R. Laffineur (eds.), *METRON: Measuring the Aegean Bronze Age*, Aegaeum, 24. Liège: Université de Liège, 277–83.
—— (2003b). 'I sistemi ponderali dell'Egeo nell'Età del Bronzo. Studi, storia, pratica e contatti', *Annuario della Scuola Archeologica di Atene*, 81: 597–640.
—— (2009). 'Pesi e traffici: influenze orientali nei sistemi ponderali egei nel corso dell'età del bronzo', in F. Camia and S. Privitera (eds.), *Obeloi. Contatti, scambi e valori nel Mediterraneo antico. Studi offerti a Nicola Parise*. Athens: Scuola Archeologica Italiana di Atene, 13–40.
Ascalone, E. and Peyronel, L. (2006). 'Early Bronze IVA weights at Tell Mardikh-Elba. Archaeological associations and contexts', in *Weights in Context: Bronze Age Weighing Systems of the Eastern Mediterranean*. Proceedings of the International Colloquium, Rome 2004. Rome: Istituto Italiano di Numismatica, 49–70.

Balista, C., Bondavalli, F., Cardarelli, A., Labate, D., Mazzoni, C., and Steffè, G. (2008). 'Dati preliminari sullo scavo della Terramara di Gaggio di Castelfranco Emilia (Modena): scavi 2001-2004', in M. Barnabò Brea and R. Valloni (eds.), *Archeologia ad alta velocità in Emilia. Indagini geologiche e archeologiche lungo il tracciato ferroviario.* Atti del Convegno, Parma 2003. Quaderni di Archeologia dell'Emilia Romagna, 22. Bologna: All'insegna del giglio, 113-38.

Binsbergen, W. van (2005). 'Commodification. Things, agency, and identities: introduction', in W. van Binsbergen and P. Geschiere (eds.), *Commodification: Things, Agency and Identities: The Social Life of Things Revisited.* Berlin and Münster: LIT Verlag, 9-52.

Cardarelli, A., Pacciarelli, M., and Pallante, P. (2001). 'Pesi e bilance dell'Età del Bronzo Italiana', in C. Corti and N. Giordani (eds.), *Pondera. Pesi e Misura nell'Antichità.* Modena: Libra, 33-58.

Charnier, J.-F., Briard, J., Bouvet, J.-P., Bourhis, J.-R., and Poulain, H. (1999). 'Le Dépôt de Saint-Léonard-des-Bois, "Grand Champ du Veau d'Or" (Sarthe), un nouveau témoignage de relations atlantiques/continentales au Bronze final', *Bulletin de la Société Préhistorique Française,* 96: 569-79.

Dalton, G. (1965). 'Primitive money', *American Anthropologist,* 67: 44-65.

—— (1982). 'Barter', *Journal of Economic Issues,* 16/1: 181-90.

Delor, J.-P., Muller, F., and Roscio, M. (2009). 'L'Exceptionelle Sépulture d'un orfèvre de l'Âge du Bronze à Migennes', *L'Echo de Joigny. Bulletin de l'Association Culturelle et d'Études de Joigny,* 69: 7-30.

Evely, R. D. G. (ed.) (2006). *Lefkandi IV: The LH IIIC Settlement at Xeropoli.* Athens: British School at Athens.

Garrard, T. F. (1980). *Akan Weights and the Gold Trade.* London and New York: Longman.

Gebhard, R. (1999). 'Der Goldfund von Bernstorf', *Bayerische Vorgeschichtsblätter,* 64: 1-18.

Gomez de Soto, J. (2001). 'Un Nouveau Locus du Bronze final au Bois du Roc à Vilhonneur (Charente): le réseau de la Cave Chaude', *Bulletin de la Société Préhistorique Française,* 98: 115-22.

Görner, I. (2003). 'Die Mittel- und Spätbronzezeit zwischen Mannheim und Karlsruhe', *Fundberichte aus Baden-Württemberg,* 27: 79-279.

Gregory, C. A. (1982). *Gifts and Commodities.* London: Academic Press.

Grierson, P. (2001). 'The origins of money', in P. Grierson, *Scritti Storici e Numismatici,* Centro Italiano di Studi sull'Alto Medioevo, Collectana 15. Spoleto: Centro Italiano di Studi sull'Alto Medioevo, 70-106.

Hart, K. (1982). 'On commoditization', in E. Goody (ed.), *From Craft to Industry.* Cambridge: Cambridge University Press.

Humphrey, C. (1985). 'Barter and economic disintegration', *Man,* 20/1: 48-72.

Ingham, G. (2000). '"Babylonian madness": on the historical and sociological origins of money', in J. Smithin (ed.), *What is Money?* London: Routledge, 16-41.

—— (2004). *The Nature of Money.* Cambridge: Polity Press.

Innerhofer, F. (1997). 'Frühbronzezeitliche Barrenhortfunde—Die Schätze aus dem Boden kehren zurück', in A. Hänsel and B. Hänsel (eds.), *Gaben an die Götter. Schätze der Bronzezeit Europas.* Berlin: Museum für Vor- und Frühgeschichte, 53-9.

Junk, M., Krause, R., and Pernicka, E. (2001). 'Ösenringbarren and the classical Ösenring copper', in W. H. Metz, B. L. van Beek, and H. Steegstra (eds.), *Patina: Essays Presented to J. J. Butler on the Occasion of his 80th Birthday.* Groningen: Metz, Van Beek, and Steegstra, 353-66.

Kroll, J. H. (2008). 'The monetary use of weighed currency in Archaic Greece', in W. V. Harris (ed.), *The Monetary System of the Greeks and Romans*. Oxford: Oxford University Press, 12–37.

Lenerz-de Wilde, M. (1995). 'Prämonetäre Zahlungsmittel in der Kupfer- und Bronzezeit Mitteleuropas', *Fundberichte aus Baden-Württemberg*, 20: 229–327.

—— (2002). 'Bronzezeitliche Zahlungsmittel', *Mitteilungen der Anthropologischen Gesellschaft in Wien*, 132: 1–23.

Liversage, D. (2001). 'Riddle of the ribs', in W. H. Metz, B. L. van Beek, and H. Steegstra (eds.), *Patina: Essays Presented to J. J. Butler on the Occasion of his 80th Birthday*. Groningen: Metz, Van Beek, and Steegstra, 377–98.

Marx, K. (1990). *Das Capital*, Book 1. London: Penguin.

Medović, P. (1995). 'Die Waage aus der frühhallstattzeitlichen Siedlung Bordjoš (Borjas) bei Novi Bečej (Banat)', in B. Hänsel (ed.), *Handel, Tausch und Verkehr im bronze- und früheisenzeitlichen Südosteuropa*. Berlin: Seminar für Ur- und Frühgeschichte der FU Berlin, 209–18.

Neugebauer, J.-W. (2002). 'Die Metalldepots der Unterwölbinger Kulturgruppe Ragelsdorf 2 und Unterradelberg 1 und 2', *Mitteilungen der Anthropologischen Gesellschaft in Wien*, 132: 25–40.

Pare, C. F. E. (1999). 'Weights and weighing in Bronze Age Central Europe', in *Eliten in der Bronzezeit. Ergebnisse zweier Kolloquien in Mainz und Athen*, Monographien des Römisch-Germanischen Zentralmuseums Mainz, 43. Mainz: Römisch-Germanisches Zentralmuseum, 421–514.

—— (2000). 'Bronze and the Bronze Age', in C. F. E. Pare (ed.), *Metals Make the World Go Round*. Proceedings of a conference held at the University of Birmingham in June 1997. Oxford: Oxbow Books, 1–38.

Peake, R., Delattre, V. and Pihuit, P. (1999). 'La Nécropole de l'Âge du Bronze de "La Croix de la Mission" à Marolles-sur-Seine (Seine-et-Marne)', *Bulletin de la Société Préhistorique Française*, 96: 581–605.

—— Séguier, J.-M., and Gomez de Soto, J. (1999). 'Trois Exemples de fléaux de balances en os de l'Âge du Bronze', *Bulletin de la Société Préhistorique Française*, 96: 643–4.

Peroni, R. (1998). 'Bronzezeitliche Gewichtssysteme im Metallhandel zwischen Mittelmeer und Ostsee', in B. Hänsel (ed.), *Mensch und Umwelt in der Bronzezeit Europas*. Kiel: Oetker-Voges, 217–24.

Petruso, K. M. (1992). *Ayia Irini. The Balance Weights: An Analysis of Weight Measurement in Prehistoric Crete and the Cycladic Islands*, Keos, 8. Mainz: Phillip von Zabern.

—— (2003). 'Quantal analysis of some Mycenaean balance weights', in K. P. Foster and R. Laffineur (eds.), *METRON: Measuring the Aegean Bronze Age*, Aegaeum, 24. Liège: Université de Liège, 285–91.

Picener (1999). *Die Picener. Ein Volk Europas*, exhibition catalogue, Schirn Kunsthalle, Frankfurt. Rome: De Luca.

Polanyi, K. (1944). *The Great Transformation*. Boston: Beacon Press.

Primas, M. (1986). *Die Sicheln in Mitteleuropa I (Österreich, Schweiz, Süddeutschland)*, Prähistorische Bronzefunde, XVIII/2. Munich: Beck.

—— (1997). 'Bronze Age economy and ideology: Central Europe in focus', *Journal of European Archaeology*, 5/1: 115–30.

—— and Pernicka, E. (1998). 'Der Depotfund von Oberwilflingen. Neue Ergebnisse zur Zirkulation von Metallbarren', *Germania*, 76: 25–65.

Pulak, C. M. (1996). *Analysis of the Weight Assemblages from the Late Bronze Age Shipwrecks at Uluburun and Cape Gelidonya, Turkey.* Texas: A&M University (unpublished dissertation).

—— (2000). 'The balance weights from the Late Bronze Age shipwreck at Uluburun', in C. F. E. Pare (ed.), *Metals Make the World Go Round: The Supply and Circulation of Metals in Bronze Age Europe*. Proceedings of a conference held at the University of Birmingham, June 1997. Oxford: Oxbow Books, 247–66.

Rahmstorf, L. (2003). 'The identification of Early Helladic weights and their wider implications', in K. P. Foster and R. Laffineur (eds.), *METRON: Measuring the Aegean Bronze Age*, Aegaeum, 24. Liège: Université de Liège, 293–9.

—— (2006a). 'In search of the earliest balance weights, scales and weighing systems from the East Mediterranean, the Near and Middle East', *Weights in Context: Bronze Age Weighing Systems of the Eastern Mediterranean*, Proceedings of the International Colloquium, Rome 2004. Rome: Istituto Italiano di Numismatica, 9–45.

—— (2006b). 'Zur Ausbreitung vorderasiatischer Innovationen in die frühbronzezeitliche Ägäis', *Prähistorische Zeitschrift*, 81: 49–96.

Ratnagar, S. (2003). 'Theorizing Bronze-Age intercultural trade: the evidence of the weights', *Paléorient*, 29: 79–92.

Renfrew, C. (1986). 'Varna and the emergence of wealth in prehistoric Europe', in A. Appadurai (ed.), *The Social Life of Things*. Cambridge: Cambridge University Press, 141–68.

Sacconi, A. (2005). 'La "Monnaie" dans l'économie mycénienne. Le témoignage des textes', in R. Laffineur and E. Greco (eds.), *Emporia: Aegeans in the Central and Eastern Mediterranean*, vol. 1, Aegaeum, 25. Liège: Université de Liège, 69–74.

Sahlins, M. (1974). *Stone Age Economics*. London: Tavistock.

Simmel, G. (1922). *Philosophie des Geldes*. Munich and Leipzig: Duncker & Humblot.

Sommerfeld, C. (1994). *Gerätegeld Sichel. Studien zur monetären Struktur bronzezeitlicher Horte im nördlichen Mitteleuropa*, Vorgeschichtliche Forschungen, 19. Berlin and New York: De Gruyter.

Steuer, H. (2004). 'Die Ostsee als Kernraum des 10. Jahrhunderts und ihre Peripherien', *Siedlungsforschung*, 22: 59–88.

Teržan, B. (2004). 'Obolos—mediterrane Vorbilder einer prämonetären "Währung" der Hallstattzeit?', in B. Hänsel (ed.), *Parerga Praehistorica*, Universitätsforschungen zur prähistorischen Archäologie, 100. Bonn: Rudolf Habelt, 161–202.

Vagnetti, L., Percossi, E., Silvestrini, M., Sabbatini, T., Jones, R. E., and Levi, S. T. (2006). 'Ceramiche egeo-micenee dalle Marche: Indagini Archeometriche ed inquadramento iniziale dei dati', in *Atti della XXXIX Riunione Scientifica dell'Istituto di Preistoria e Protostoria, Florence 2004*, II: 1,159–72.

Werner, J. (1954). *Waage und Geld in der Merowingerzeit*, Sitzungsberichte der Bayerischen Akademie der Wissenschaften, Philosophisch-historische Klasse, 1954/Heft 1. Munich: Bayerische Akademie der Wissenschaften.

PART II

THE BRONZE AGE BY REGION

CHAPTER 30

BRITAIN AND IRELAND IN THE BRONZE AGE: FARMERS IN THE LANDSCAPE OR HEROES ON THE HIGH SEAS?

BENJAMIN W. ROBERTS

INTRODUCTION

The Bronze Age in Britain and Ireland spans at least 17 centuries, from *c*.2500 BC to *c*.800/600 BC. This encompasses a short copper-using 'Chalcolithic' period (*c*.2500–2150 BC), which pre-dates the rapid and widespread adoption of tin-bronze (see papers in Allen et al. 2012). The distinction of prehistoric periods by the appearance and disappearance of a metal has long been lamented as a nineteenth-century anachronism but is now immovably institutionalized in the discipline. Similarly, the broad chronological division into Early (*c*.2150–1600 BC), Middle (*c*.1500–1150 BC), and Late (*c*.1150–800/600 BC) Bronze Ages in both countries reflects early scholarly preoccupations supported by later dating techniques rather than an up-to-date or subtle understanding of past activities (see Chapter 2). Both Britain and Ireland enjoy a long and rich tradition of archaeological discovery, fieldwork, and scholarship that has been fundamental in shaping the present perception of their prehistory. The vast expansion in developer-funded fieldwork in Britain and Ireland (e.g. 19,000 field evaluations in England alone between 1990 and the end of 2007, of which 20 per cent produced evidence of prehistoric activity) over the last two decades has produced hundreds of new Bronze Age sites which are only now starting to be incorporated into broader prehistoric narratives (e.g. Bradley 2007; Darvill 2010). Unfortunately, the Bronze Ages in both Britain and Ireland still lack any up-to-date, dedicated, and detailed syntheses (although a recent exception is the Scottish Archaeological Research Framework).

What has been excavated is not only naturally influenced by where development has taken place but also by the legal regulations relating to archaeological fieldwork, which vary from country to country (see Bradley et al. 2012). For instance, the legal requirement to excavate comprehensively *all* archaeological sites encountered during development in the Republic of

Ireland can be contrasted with the strategies of sample excavations and preservation by record employed throughout Britain. The consequence of the former legislation together with a vast programme of road-building in the Republic of Ireland can be seen in the eight monographs currently published by the National Roads Authority (NRA). The problem that this apparent golden age of archaeological survey and fieldwork has generated on both sides of the Irish Sea is the lack of publication or public access to the majority of these new sites, leaving them to languish as 'grey literature'. This is partially addressed by annual volumes providing very short summaries of all national archaeological fieldwork, such as *Discovery and Excavation in Scotland*, *Excavations Bulletin: Summary Accounts of Archaeological Excavations in Ireland* and *Archaeology in Wales*. No comparable publications exist for England, which has experienced the highest concentrations of fieldwork, although there are recently published *Regional Research Frameworks* which provide regional syntheses, albeit of varying quality. The recording of objects found by metal detectorists and members of the public in England and Wales since 1996 under the *Treasure Act* and *Portable Antiquities Scheme* on a nationwide database (www.finds.org.uk) has been extremely successful and has yielded thousands of new Bronze Age artefacts, most visibly in gold or bronze, whose implications are only now being appreciated (e.g. Yates and Bradley 2010). Where the scheme does not exist as in Scotland, or where metal-detecting remains illegal as in the Republic of Ireland, there has been no comparable increase in new finds in any material. It is perhaps too early to state whether this flood of new information will radically or only partially revise the current interpretations of the period. However, what is now clear is that the main challenge facing all Bronze Age archaeologists is the analysis of ever-increasing quantities of data.

The island landscapes of Britain and Ireland would naturally have shaped the activities of their Bronze Age inhabitants (Fig. 30.1). Although the surrounding seas may well have contributed to an insular distinctiveness that is frequently highlighted in narratives of prehistory, deep connections to the continent are also revealed in the same archaeological record—whether down the coasts of the Atlantic facade or along the rivers of mainland Europe. Excavations on the smaller offshore islands such as South Uist off the coast of western Scotland (e.g. Parker Pearson, Sharples, and Symonds 2004), surrounding the larger mainlands, have revealed similarly broader connections as well as insular practices. The landscape topography of mainland Britain and Ireland is dominated by long coastlines, but they differ substantially from one another further inland. The traditional tendency to divide Britain into agriculturally desirable southern and eastern lowlands and more challenging northern and western uplands is far too simplistic. Nonetheless, it still influences many scholars, ignoring areas such as eastern Scotland and south Wales with sheltered valleys, well-drained soils, and a suitable environment for farming. In Ireland, the coastline is frequently flanked by higher ground, which in turn encloses central lowlands. The agricultural potential is generally higher towards the south and the east of the island, though there are fertile coastal strips and river valleys in the north and the west (Bradley 2007: 1–25). The natural resources of the islands that are known to have been widely exploited during the Bronze Age include the copper ore sources in southern Ireland and Wales (Timberlake 2009), the gold sources of eastern Ireland and Wales (Eogan 1994), and very probably the tin sources of south-west England (Bray 2012). Flint sources in northern Ireland, Scotland, southern and eastern England continued to be exploited (Edmonds 1995), as did jet from north-east England (Sheridan and Davis 1998; 2002). The exploitation of stone (e.g. Edmonds 1995), timber (e.g. Coles, Heal, and Orme 1978), clay (e.g. Gibson 2002), and wild-animal and plant resources, which were far more extensively drawn upon by Bronze Age communities, are far harder, if not impossible, to provenance and, if organic, survive only in certain environments. The apparent absence of any faunal or isotopic evidence for fish and shellfish consumption remains puzzling given the extensive navigation of seas and rivers.

MONUMENTS, BURIALS, AND CRAFTSMANSHIP: MID THIRD–EARLY SECOND MILLENNIUM BC

At *c*.2500/2400 BC the earliest copper objects in Britain and Ireland appear nearly a millennium later than in northern France. This is not necessarily due to the inaccessibility of the copper objects and metallurgy, but probably more due to their irrelevance in the material world of the islands during the late fourth–early third millennium BC (Roberts 2008; Roberts

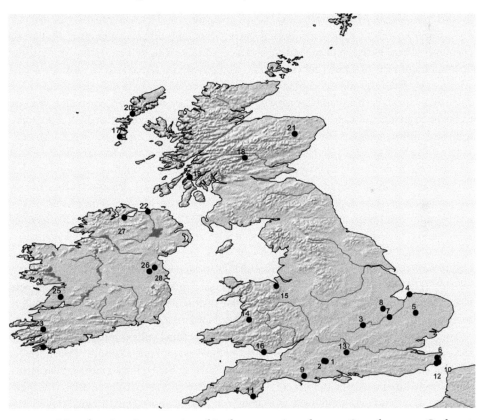

FIG. 30.1 Map showing sites mentioned in the text. 1. Amesbury, 2. Stonehenge, 3. Gayhurst, 4. Holme-next-the-Sea, 5. Grimes Graves, 6. Ringlemere, 7. Barley Croft Farm, 8. Flag Fen, 9. Bestwall Quarry, 10. Langdon Bay, 11. Salcombe, 12. Dover, 13. Hartshill Copse, 14. Great Orme, 15. Mold, 16.Llanmaes, 17. Cladh Hallan, 18. Croft Moraig, 19. Kilmartin valley, 20. Northton, 21. Tomnavernie, 22. Corrstown, 23. Ross Island, 24. Mount Gabriel, 25. Roughan Hill, 26. Mound of the Hostages, 27. Gransha, 28. Newgrange.

and Frieman 2102). The explanation for the westward presence of copper as well as gold objects seems to lie in the contemporary appearance of a distinct material assemblage from continental Europe that included Beaker pottery, stone wristguards, flint barbed and tanged arrowheads, as well as copper daggers and gold basket ornaments (Needham 2005; Vander Linden 2006; Carlin and Brück 2012; O'Brien 2012). Yet the adoption of these novel objects and technologies varied considerably. In Britain all elements were employed in a novel individual Beaker burial rite as exemplified by the Amesbury Archer in southern England (Fitzpatrick 2011), though fragments of Beaker pottery are also found at the few known contemporary settlements and with older monuments (Gibson 2002; Needham 2005). In Ireland, the Beaker funerary rituals did not include any individual burials but did involve the placing of Beaker pottery and occasionally other elements at older monuments, as well as contemporary burnt mounds and settlements as at Newgrange (O'Brien 1999; Waddell 1998, 114–23; O'Brien 2012; Carlin and Brück 2012). The discovery of Beaker pottery sherds at the copper mine of Ross Island, south-west Ireland, which dates from c.2400 BC (Timberlake 2009; O'Brien 2012), as well as the application of strontium isotope analysis to Beaker burials in Britain (such as the Amesbury Archer from southern England: Fitzpatrick 2011), has reignited older debates of a 'Beaker' people sailing from continental Europe bringing new objects, technologies, and ideas.

Any new arrivals to Britain and Ireland during the mid third millennium BC would have encountered established communities constructing and gathering at increasingly large circular or oval monuments of earth, timber, or stone, and pits with internal architectures of varying complexity—famously and misleadingly exemplified by Stonehenge (Bradley 2007: 122–42; see Allen et al. 2012). Each monument appears to have been carefully sited, whether at physical routes through the landscape, in association with older monuments, or in visually or topographically striking locations. Avenues in timber and stone emphasized the approach at certain monuments whilst high wooden palisades excluded external viewers at others. The carving of rock art into outcrops in northern Britain and Ireland during the third millennium BC appears to relate to the creation of these monumental landscapes (e.g. Beckensall 1999). The construction of burial mounds or barrows for Beaker burials in Britain (Woodward 2000) and megalithic wedge-tombs for the dead as in western and northern Ireland (O'Brien 1999) contributed to this ritual topography. The scale of these circular or oval monuments varied regionally, with larger structures being found in southern and north-east England, central Scotland, east Ireland and Orkney, and smaller ones in eastern and central England and northern Scotland (Bradley 2007: 122–42). The closest parallels are frequently found in geographically distant regions throughout Britain and Ireland, a pattern reflected in the wide distribution of associated material culture such as Grooved Ware pottery, which originally developed in Orkney (Gibson 2002).

The archaeological evidence for the second half of the third millennium BC in Britain and Ireland remains dominated by the internment of the dead and the buildings of the devoted. The settlement evidence tends to be restricted to fairly ephemeral oval and circular structures formed by postholes and hearths, although more substantial sites exist in northern Scotland as at Northton on the Isle of Harris (e.g. Doody 2000; Darvill 2010: 174–6). The majority of settlement sites have limited archaeological visibility, reflecting a pattern that continues even into the early second millennium BC (e.g. Brück 1999a; Doody 2000; Ashmore 2001). The evidence for subsistence is similarly fragmentary and consists primarily of animal bone depositions and small quantities of charred seeds in pits at burial or ceremonial sites which cannot be assumed to be representative of the broader farming or consumption patterns. The prevalence of cattle in ceremonial pits and funerary practices as during the early second millennium BC at Gayhurst and Irthlingborough in central England (Towers et al. 2010) has led to suggestions of a mobile pastoral agricultural regime in certain regions rather than one based on sedentary arable farming of wheat and barley (e.g. Lawson 2007). It is perfectly possible, as Francis Pryor (1998) suggests, that small plots of land could have been cultivated without the need for ploughing; this would then be very hard to detect in the archaeological record. The occasional survival of upland field systems such as at Roughan Hill, western Ireland (Jones 1998), relies on relatively rare circumstances of preservation, and these remain exceptions rather than the rule. The excavation burnt mounds, or *fulacht fiadh*, throughout Britain and especially Ireland dating from the late third millennium BC onwards has led to numerous explanations, though their interpretation as the remains of multiple episodes of heating food and water seems the most likely (Waddell 2011, 181–5). Wild plants and animals continue to be exploited, though there remains very little evidence for any exploitation of fish or shellfish despite the coastal and riverine geography of Britain and Ireland and the ability to navigate these waterways, as demonstrated by similarities in architecture and artefacts (e.g. Parker Pearson 2003).

In the relative absence of settlements and subsistence practices, the late third–early second millennium BC is dominated by discussions of the evidence for and interpretation of burial practices, the associated material culture, and, to a lesser extent, hoards of bronze metalwork. Traditionally, it has been inhumations in clusters of burial mounds or barrows with visually striking objects in exotic materials such as gold, amber, and faience that have dominated interpretations, contributing to the pervasive influence of the model of the Wessex culture for regions far beyond southern England (Needham 2000; Lawson 2007). Yet there is a distinct diversity in funerary practices with evidence of cave burials in northern England (Barnatt and Edmonds 2002); bog burials in eastern England (Healy and Housley 1992); burials in stone cists and pits with no commemorative mound in flat cemeteries over large areas of western Scotland and Ireland (Waddell 1990; Brück 2004); the reuse of wedge-tombs in western Ireland (O'Brien 1999), as well as old and specially constructed large mounds in Ireland (Waddell 1990; Eogan 2004). There is also regional variation in the objects placed with the dead, such as jet spacer-plate necklaces in northern Britain (with female burials), amber spacer-plate necklaces in southern Britain, and bronze and flint daggers in differing regions within Britain but rarely in Ireland. In whatever context the dead were placed, inhumation and cremation frequently overlap in the treatment of the body and, from the beginning of the second millennium BC, cremation rather than inhumation appears to have been the dominant funerary practice. The multiple reuse of funerary sites over several centuries, whether interring the newly deceased in close proximity to, or together with, the ancestors, appears to have been widespread. The location of the dead close to older monuments continued in regions such as southern England and north-east Scotland, but also occurred on very high ground in regions such as north Wales and north-east England (Waddell 2011: 5–72; Lynch, Aldhouse-Green, and Davies 2000: 121–8; Bradley 2007: 158–68).

The placing of the dead was not necessarily distinguished from the everyday life of the living, as has been demonstrated at Roughan Hill, western Ireland, where wedge-tombs were interspersed with field walls (Jones 1998). Similarly, the rituals of the dead naturally overlap with the rituals of the living, as demonstrated by the extensive stone monuments constructed and reworked throughout Britain and Ireland during the late third–early second millennium BC. These are often in regionally specific architectural forms as exemplified by recumbent stone circles in north-east Scotland such as Tomnaverie, frequently associated with inhumations, cremations, and round barrows, and occasionally can be demonstrated to orientate towards the sun or moon (Bradley 2007: 168–75). These include ring-cairns found throughout upland south-west and northern England, Wales, and Scotland; small stone circles throughout upland Britain and Ireland, and standing stones concentrated in south-west England and Wales. Any overly neat definitions of these stone monuments are rapidly undermined by their excavation: there are numerous phases of construction that integrate forms such as stone circles, standing stones, ring-cairns, and settlements (Waddell 2011: 175–81; Lynch, Aldhouse-Green, and Davies 2001: 128–36; Bradley 2007: 168–75).

The material culture placed with the dead, together with the bronze axes and halberds deposited in the landscape as hoards, has overwhelmingly influenced the current understanding of the material world in the late third–early second millennium BC. At a broader level, it also influences the very perception of time through the fine chronological frameworks of the Bronze Age in Britain and Ireland (see Chapter 2). The traditional classification of the funerary world in Ireland is even based on pottery types, with a Bowl Tradition mainly in the north and east; a Vase Tradition with concentrations in the east, north, and west; a Cordoned Urn Tradition mainly in the north-east extending through to southern and eastern Scotland; and a Collared Urn Tradition along the coast of eastern Ireland that covers Britain with the exception of north-west Scotland (Waddell 1990; 2011: 50–62; Brindley 2007). Though the world of rituals and the dead can be assumed to have a close relationship with the world of the living, gaps between the two can certainly be demonstrated. The excavation of a preserved timber circle at Holme-next-the-Sea, eastern England, dating to 2049 BC, allowed a rare opportunity to examine woodworking tools and techniques from this time. Despite bronze axes representing one of the most thoroughly researched contemporary artefacts, none of the marks on the timber could be matched to any known bronze-axe type (Brennand and Taylor 2003). It is evident that the bronze axes that were deliberately placed in the ground (and only rarely with the dead) may not reflect those that were in circulation and general use. This problem of archaeological representation is by no means confined to metalwork, as by any demographic estimate the vast majority of the population were not included in the burial rites. The underlying reasons for the potentially narrow selection of certain objects and individuals for interment is generally thought to relate to their specific biography as well as the desires of the broader community involved.

The mainly funerary and hoard evidence reveals a relatively rapid expansion in the scale, diversity, and sophistication of craftsmanship in metal, ceramics, flint, stone, and exotic inorganic materials such as amber, jet, faience, and shale during the late third–early second millennium BC.

The subsequent widespread and rapid adoption of tin-bronze in Britain and Ireland in the late third millennium BC (Bray 2012) led to a flourishing, rather than a decline, in flint and stone working, with elaborate ground and chipped axes, edge-ground knives, plano-convex knives and arrowheads being made alongside stone-perforated maceheads, axe-hammers, battle-axes, wristguards, whetstones, and moulds for metal objects (Clarke, Foxon, and Cowie 1985; Edmonds 1995). Jet spacer-plate necklaces, disk bead necklaces, V-perforated buttons and belt rings (Sheridan and Davis 1998; 2002), amber spacer-plate necklaces, V-perforated buttons and beads (Clarke, Foxon, and Cowie 1985; Beck and Shennan 1991), and faience beads and pendants (Sheridan and Shortland 2004) were placed with the dead in varying combinations in what Alison Sheridan has termed 'supernatural power dressing'. Flint mines such as Grimes Graves, eastern England (Longworth et al. 2011), record high levels of activity from the mid third millennium BC which only begin to recede several centuries later when copper mines such as the Great Orme, north-west Wales, and Mount Gabriel, south-west Ireland (Timberlake 2009; O'Brien 2012), using a similar mining technology, begin extracting ore. The copper metal was alloyed with tin, very probably tin ores from south-west England, to create objects such as flat axes, halberds, daggers, and latterly spears, which were recycled or placed in graves or hoards (Bray 2012; see Chapter 2). Goldworking is represented in a far broader repertoire than before: the lunulae, discs, and basket ornaments of the mid–late third millennium BC give way to embossed capes such as from Mold, north Wales, cups such as that from Ringlemere, south-east England (Fig. 30.2), bracelets from Lockington, central England, as well as a range of smaller adornments such as plaques, pendants, beads, and button covers (Eogan 1994; Needham 2009). Beaker and Grooved Ware ceramic vessels were joined and subsequently supplanted by Food Vessels, Collared Urns, Cordoned Urns, and Irish Bowls and Vases, amongst others (Gibson 2002; Brindley 2007; see Chapter 2).

Settlements, Cremations, and Hoards: The Mid Second–Early First Millennium BC

The mid second millennium BC sees fundamental changes throughout Britain and Ireland and, as a consequence, provides a convenient division for many recent syntheses that distinguish between an Earlier and Later Bronze Age (e.g. Waddell 2011; Bradley 2007). Whilst not denying the underlying validity of the broad interpretation, it is worth emphasizing that the changes are perhaps most acute in southern and eastern England where, perhaps not entirely coincidentally, there has been a far greater intensity of fieldwork and research. None of the changes is genuinely without precedent, and earlier traditions were actively continued in many regions. In contrast to previous centuries, it is the settlement and subsistence evidence

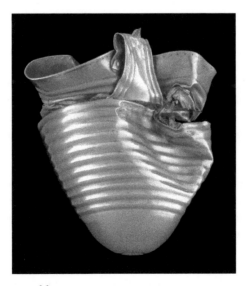

FIG. 30.2 The Ringlemere gold cup.

Photo: Trustees of the British Museum.

that is abundant, the monumental and funerary evidence that is fragmentary, and the craft-working evidence that, rather than encompassing a broad material spectrum, is mainly restricted to metal and ceramics. In the landscape, the change is especially visible in the widespread construction of circular settlements or roundhouses (e.g. Brück 1999b) and, in southern and eastern England, the building of rectilinear field systems especially in river valleys, coastal lowlands, and the edges of wetlands (e.g. Yates 2007). The assumption that the settlements and the fields were constructed in parallel by communities is not borne out by the evidence. Where it is possible to identify a sequence, as at Barleycroft Farm, eastern England (Knight and Evans 2001), it appears that the fields pre-date the settlements, and the spatial integration of the settlements with the field systems is irregular at best. The labour involved in building the fields and therefore reshaping entire landscapes encompassed the digging of ditches, erection of hedges and fences, building of gates, and placing of trackways (Yates 2007). Careful excavation and dating has revealed the piecemeal nature of their creation, even with the largest field systems on Dartmoor, south-west England (Johnston 2005). However, the existence of similar orientations and patterns in their organization seems to imply a common sense of purpose, making the overall scale and undertaking comparable to the erection of earlier monuments.

This investment in the creation of fields is generally thought to represent an arable and pastoral intensification from the mid second millennium BC, yet there is relatively little evidence for field systems dating to this period beyond southern and eastern England, despite numerous contemporary roundhouses throughout Britain and Ireland. This absence of fields could well be the result of a number of factors: a problem of preservation, especially due to destruction by later agriculture; the difficulty of obtaining independent dates for ditch systems; or the absence of large-scale systematic survey. However, as David Yates (2007) has argued, development archaeology in several fertile river valleys in central England did not reveal the field-systems encountered further south. It is certainly possible therefore that the differences in southern and eastern England reflected a distinctive practice that set the region apart from areas further north and west. Explanations relating to the agricultural purpose of the fields have been stimulated by excavations in the environs of Flag Fen, eastern England, which revealed extensive fields, pens, and droveways that, on analogy with modern farming, would have involved the management of several thousand animals—flocks of sheep rather than herds of cattle (Pryor 1998). The ability to sink supported shafts into the ground allowed the introduction of wells, ensuring a regular supply of water to areas where it would previously have been inaccessible. In arable agriculture, there is also a change in crop species during this period with emmer wheat giving way to spelt wheat, naked varieties of barley to hulled types, and beans and rye being introduced (Yates 2007). In contrast to the earlier centuries, there is little evidence for the exploitation of wild foods and animals.

The circular settlements or roundhouses were constructed of timber or stone with a roof probably made from turf or rushes. Architectural variation can be seen in the presence or absence of ditches, banks, and porches, but there were very few sites that exhibit extensive ancillary buildings for animals beyond small structures potentially associated with grain storage (Brück 1999b; Doody 2000). Nor is there substantial evidence for the concentration of settlements into villages beyond a few sites such as Corrstown in Northern Ireland, where excavations revealed over 70 roundhouses linked by individual tracks and a metalled roadway (Ginn and Rathbone 2011). It is far more usual to find sequences of settlement abandonment as at Bestwall Quarry, south-west England, where a settlement was formally closed with a burnt mound, probably used for cooking. This pattern of abandonment is frequently accompanied by the rebuilding of new settlements nearby (Ladle and Woodward 2009). The placing of special deposits such as human bones, quernstone fragments, and bronze metalwork, especially during the foundation and abandonment of roundhouses, and in their entrances, has revealed an important ritual dimension to these seemingly domestic structures (e.g. Brück 1999b; Cleary 2005).

There is a material transformation during the mid second millennium BC that sees the widespread decline in stone, flint, and exotic organic and inorganic craftsmanship, and their replacement with gold and bronze. Ceramic vessels continue to be made, though they tend to be in large quantities that do not exhibit earlier distinctive and varying styles. Throughout Britain and Ireland decorated and plain Barrel and Bucket urns, often in regionally specific forms such as Deverel-Rimbury in England, coexist with the continuation of certain earlier forms such as Biconical and Cordoned urns (Gibson 2002: 104–8; Ladle and Woodward 2009). Similarly, flint and stone continued to be widely used though the quality of the objects being produced declined substantially. The rapid increase in archaeologically visible bronze and gold consumption from the mid second millennium BC sees a far more extensive quantity and diversity of metal tools, weapons, and ornaments in circulation, which is strangely paralleled by the virtual cessation of copper ore mining in Britain and Ireland, with the exception of the Great Orme, north Wales (Timberlake 2009). Whilst it has always been suspected that the tin ore sources in south-west England were exploited from the late third millennium BC onwards, there are no reliably dated mining or smelting sites and very few tin objects. Similarly, there are no dated gold mines, possibly because gold nuggets were panned from streams, but the quest to provenance objects to the rich and probable sources of eastern Ireland and Wales remains unresolved.

Whilst it is highly probable that recycling of earlier objects was involved, the evidence from the metalwork found along the coast such as at Langdon Bay, south-east England (Fig. 30.3),

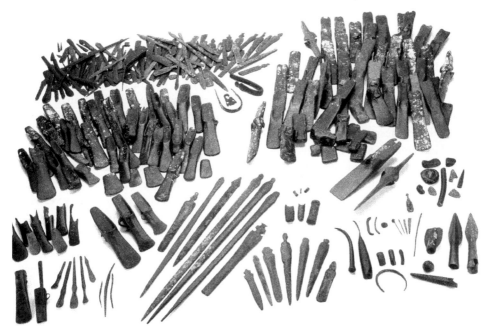

FIG. 30.3 The Langdon Bay hoard.

Photo: Trustees of the British Museum.

and Salcombe, south-west England (Needham, Parham, and Frieman forthcoming), implies the importation of bronze objects from the continent that could be converted into new forms. The rare excavation of shipwrecks such as the Dover Boat, south-east England (Clark 2009b) (Fig. 30.4), certainly demonstrates that vessels of sufficient size existed when cross-channel connections were established in the early second millennium BC (Needham 2009). The location of the actual metalworking is hard to define due to the potentially sparse evidence left behind by smelting, melting, or casting, and is usually manifested in stone or clay mould fragments, with sand moulds leaving no potential trace (see O'Faoláin 2004). Whether the metal was being imported or locally sourced in Britain and Ireland, theoretically it could all have been re-melted and recycled and therefore be largely undetected in the archaeological record. The reason that there appears to be such a vast increase in the quantity of bronze and gold lies in the widespread deliberate deposition of thousands of metal objects from the mid second millennium BC in pits, caves, wells, rivers, lakes, and, to a lesser extent, in fields and settlements. It is possible to discern broad patterns such as the placing of shields in rivers and bogs; spears and swords in rivers, river valleys, and along the edges of wetlands (e.g. Bourke 2001; Yates and Bradley 2010); ornaments and tools, usually in distinct hoards, in the landscape; as well as a deliberate separation of gold and bronze (e.g. Roberts 2007). It is also possible to identify specific places where metalwork was being deposited, such as the Thames and Shannon rivers as well as specific locations within broader landscapes, as recently demonstrated in south-east England (e.g. Yates and Bradley 2010). The bronze objects being deposited provide a fine typo-chronological sequence, as there are widespread changes in object form approximately every two centuries (see Chapter 2). The mid second millennium BC sees common object types such as bronze palstaves, spears, pins, torcs, dirks, and rapiers giving way during the late second–early first millennium BC to socketed axes, swords, spears, pins, razors, horse gear, flesh-hooks, chisels (e.g. Lynch, Aldhouse-Green, and Davies 2000: 180–6; Waddell 2011: 7–13; see Chapter 2). In gold during the same period, there is a shift away from the earlier decorated sheet-working towards casting and manipulating more substantial solid forms to produce twisted torcs, penannular bracelets, and composite rings in far greater quantities (Eogan 1994).

The relative wealth of evidence concerning the living is contrasted with the fragmentary, yet regionally diverse, remains of the dead. There is a widespread adoption of the cremation of the body and the burial of the dead in flat cemeteries close to settlements, frequently only accompanied by pottery, through many regions of England during the mid second millennium BC (e.g. Bradley 2007: 197–9). In Ireland there is a continuation of cremation burial with Cordoned Urns as well as the construction of burial mounds or barrows, the latter continuing into the first millennium BC. The older practices gradually give way to the deposition of cremated remains accompanied by plain coarse pottery vessels in a diverse range of contexts, such as enclosed and unenclosed pit cemeteries, barrows, ring ditches, and settlements (e.g. Cleary 2005; Cooney and Grogan 1994: 126–33). The presence of token cremations has been found at many sites such as the enclosed cemetery at Gransha, Northern Ireland, where charred grain, especially barley, featured in large quantities in the rock-cut cists (Chapple 2010). In Scotland the cremated dead were frequently placed at older monuments, and the reuse of these monuments belies the idea that they were uniformly abandoned, especially with the recent dating of Croft Moraig and others, demonstrating that monument construction probably occurred even towards the end of

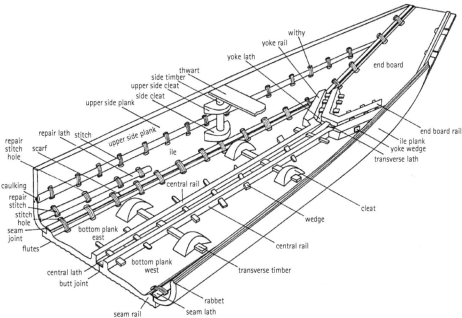

FIG. 30.4 The Dover boat.

Photo: © Canterbury Archaeological Trust.

the second millennium BC in Britain and Ireland (Bradley and Sheridan 2005). The early first millennium BC sees the evidence of the dead restricted further to small quantities of cremated human bone found in settlements, fields, and enclosure ditches (e.g. Brück 1995; Cooney and Grogan 1994: 144–8). This archaeological disappearance of the dead does not necessarily mean that the ancestors ceased to have a role in society but rather that the

FIG. 30.5 An artistic reconstruction of Springfield Lyons in Essex, showing the Late Bronze Age enclosure with its roundhouse structures.

Source: Essex County Council.

performance of funerary rites may well have had greater importance than the deposition of the human remains.

The influence of the colder temperatures and wetter conditions during the late second–early first millennium BC on the inhabitants of Britain and Ireland is not well understood. A consequence would be the shortening of the growing season and an increased pressure on subsistence, especially in upland areas that became increasingly acidic and poorly drained (Bradley 2007: 183–4). It is possible to detect a reduction in upland settlements in northern Britain during the early first millennium BC, but relating this to any environmental change remains under discussion (e.g. Tipping et al. 2008). A far more visible trend is the widespread construction of settlements surrounded by banks, ditches, and wooden palisades in prominent places in the landscape (e.g. Springfield Lyons, Essex, eastern England: Fig. 30.5). This includes the building of settlements known as crannogs on artificial islands in lakes in Scotland and Ireland, settlements enclosed by earth banks and frequently palisades known as ring-works in eastern and central England, ditched or walled enclosures throughout Ireland and enclosed hilltop settlements in Wales, western England, and Scotland (Waddell 2011: 3: Lynch, Aldhouse-Green, and Davies 2000: 144–54; Bradley 2007: 204–22). The frequently high concentration of production evidence at many of these enclosed settlements has been frequently highlighted as evidence for their role as production centres, though as a survey of the evidence for contemporary metal production in Ireland demonstrates, there is no clear case of centralized control (O'Faoláin 2004). Smaller roundhouse settlements continued to be built throughout Britain and Ireland (e.g. Brück 2007), leading to interpretations of new settlement hierarchies (e.g. Waddell 2011: 31–2).

Whilst certain field systems were abandoned, long linear earthworks, potentially acting as new boundaries in the landscape, have been identified in England as on Salisbury Plain and east Yorkshire (Bradley 2007: 240–52). Beyond the varying evidence of primary arable and pastoral farming it is possible that broader changes in subsistence can be seen in the potentially increased consumption of dairy products, inferred from the decreased size and age ranges of sheep during the late second millennium BC (Serjeantson 2007), and the lipid analysis of ceramics as demonstrated at sites such as Cladh Hallan, north-west Scotland (e.g. Parker Pearson, Sharples, and Symonds 2004). The evidence for the production of salt from boiling seawater dramatically increases along the coastal and wetland areas of eastern England (e.g. Lane and Morris 2001). Not only would this have been essential for the preservation and storage of meat, it created new possibilities in the exchange of salt, meat, butter, and cheese (see Chapter 28). The evidence for widespread food consumption in the landscape can be seen in the dating of the majority of burnt mounds, which are thought to have been cooking places, to this period. More spectacularly are the large accumulations of food consumption, animal management, and craft production in middens in southern Britain as at Llanmaes, south Wales, during the early first millennium BC (Gwilt and Lodwick 2008). The dating of the creation of these middens overlaps with the peak intensity of bronze deposition throughout Britain and Ireland which abruptly collapses c.800 BC (Needham 2007; see Chapter 2). There is relatively little evidence for iron objects, though ironworking is known from Hartshill, southern England, c.1000 BC (Collard, Darvill, and Watts 2006). Whether circulation of the new material had a destabilizing effect on the practice of bronze production, circulation, and deposition is hard to evaluate—especially given the problems with radiocarbon dating during this period. The apparent abandonment of bronze has tended to dominate the debate, yet this may be merely one of the most visible aspects of broader societal change (Haselgrove and Pope 2007).

Conclusion

The Bronze Age in Britain and Ireland spans around seventy generations of communities (assuming 25 years a generation) who, following their Neolithic ancestors, relied primarily on arable and pastoral agriculture rather than hunting, gathering, or fishing for their food. Though there is no accurate way to estimate the number of people alive at any one time (usually assumed to be a few hundred thousand), the far greater visibility of farming and settlement practices together with the sheer quantity of material being recovered towards the end of the period relative to its beginning would seem to imply at least a gradual population increase. Yet, where it exists, the settlement evidence indicates a dispersed population living in small communities, potentially not larger than a few extended families. Even the idea of a Bronze Age 'village', potentially comprising a few hundred individuals, exists only at a few sites. Any general model concerning the social organization of Bronze Age communities is immediately undermined by the changing and contrasting nature of the archaeological data. For instance, the funerary evidence which starts with the burial of a select few, is transformed into widespread cremation, and finishes with the virtual disappearance of the dead from the archaeological record. The challenges of interpretation from the dead are matched by those of the living, as the settlement evidence is exceptionally sparse until around a millennium into the period and, although this evidence is relatively abundant thereafter, problems such as the puzzling absence of field systems beyond southern and eastern England, or of surviving animal bone throughout much of Scotland, mean that there can be no easy assumptions. Similarly, the evidence of ritual sees the construction of burial and ceremonial monuments at prominent places; the landscape gradually gives way to the widespread, but far less visible, votive deposition of bronze and gold objects, as well as the deliberate placing of objects and human remains in roundhouses and ditches. The headline transition from stone to metal technology does not appear to be the cause of major social changes, especially when it can be demonstrated that flint is being finely worked until well into the second millennium BC, and continued to be used throughout the whole period. Finally, there is the problem of fieldwork distribution and archaeological preservation, which has meant that societal models have tended to be based on the evidence in the Thames Valley or Wessex in southern England, and any debate on trade and exchange is dominated by bronze and gold rather than livestock or textiles.

In proposing interpretations for Bronze Age communities, virtually all scholars have sought to identify a small minority who wield a form of political and/or religious power over the majority. They are generally termed 'chiefs', or more recently in recognition of the complexity of social possibilities, 'elites'. They are frequently thought to be connected to individuals or groups with special expertise in areas such as astronomy, monumental architecture, exotic travel, metalworking, warfare, and trade. The underlying majority have traditionally been characterized by individual 'cultures' or 'groups' on the basis of broad patterns in object and site types but more recently tend to be referred to by the generic but relatively neutral term of 'community'. This is not only due to new theoretical understandings of material culture, but also the shift from object-based to landscape-based research in British and Irish prehistory over the last three decades. The consequence is that rather than the majority of the population being presented as an undifferentiated yet mobile mass, the emphasis is instead on using the fine detail of modern excavation techniques to explore the small-scale and communal activities that shaped daily life during the Bronze Age. This has served to demonstrate the multiple phasing in the creation and reworking of monuments, burials, field-systems, and roundhouses, which contradict many earlier interpretations of large single-phase construction projects involving a substantial labour force. The problem is that this landscape-orientated vision of Bronze Age society, crudely titled in this chapter 'farmers in the landscape', is hard to relate to the object-oriented vision, equally crudely labelled 'heroes on the high seas'.

The interpretation of relatively isolated and self-sufficient agrarian extended families gradually and peacefully reshaping their homes and local landscape can be challenged by the patterns revealed in the production, movement, and consumption of surviving materials and objects. For instance, the current typo-chronology of the Bronze Age in Britain and Ireland exists because the characteristics of the bronze objects in circulation through the islands changes around every two centuries, and these changes are mainly, but not always, minor innovations on bronze forms and technologies deriving from continental Europe (see Chapter 2). The implication is that the farming communities were consistently well connected *and* receptive to networks of bronze distribution, whether the metal was imported from continental Europe, from the mines in western Britain or south-west Ireland, or recycled from existing objects. Nor should bronze be regarded as a special case; it is simply the best preserved and studied material. The distribution of particular object types can reveal profound and close inter-regional connections, especially when integrated with the funerary evidence, which demonstrate that communication and exchange were not evenly spread. These regions cross water as well as modern political boundaries, as shown by the artefacts and burial practices in northern Ireland and southern Scotland (exemplified by burials in the Kilmartin Valley, Argyllshire, or in southern England and northern France during the early second millennium BC: Needham 2009; Waddell 2011: 50–62). The presence of exotic objects and materials, especially in these burials, has stimulated extensive debate on the status and role of individuals with distant origins or connections. If this was not sufficient, then the growing evidence from isotope analysis is starting to identify the actual movement of individuals rather than simply objects or practices. These include the early Beaker burial of the Amesbury Archer, who was probably born in central Europe but was buried in southern England with several of the earliest dated gold and copper objects in Britain, and is thought to have brought knowledge of working metal to the island (e.g. Fitzpatrick 2011). The idea of migrating or mobile elites spreading new technologies and ideas from east to west, thereby initially major changes in the existing communities, is deeply embedded in Bronze Age scholarship. In contrast to the peaceful continuities implied by the 'farmers in the landscape' perspective, it implies a far greater scope for conflict resulting from the clashes of two different cultural worlds. Old debates on the nature and extent of warriors and warfare in the Bronze Age have recently been reinvigorated by the systematic examination of bronze weaponry and defensive armour which has demonstrated frequently extensive use in combat (Uckelmann and Mödlinger 2011). Taken together with the presence of thousands of bronze weapons, such as rapiers, spears, and swords found in Britain and Ireland from the mid second millennium BC, and the appearance of apparently fortified enclosures during the late second–early first millennium BC, widespread cooperation and extensive communication appear to have coexisted with significant evidence for conflict.

The 'farmers in the landscape' and the 'heroes on the high seas' models present two apparently opposing perspectives for communities in Britain and Ireland during the Bronze Age that tend to be based on different strands of evidence. Yet they are not incompatible. Many regions in Britain, Ireland, and the near continent can be shown to be culturally interconnected during the Bronze Age yet maintain, or even deliberately develop, differences in material culture, food production, architecture, or the treatment of the dead. Similarly, the timescale over which any changes unfold could easily have covered several generations but appears in the archaeological record as almost instantaneous. Partial resolution is being achieved by the increasing refinement of our methodologies, which contributes to a dataset that is a closer reflection of the real Bronze Age sequence. However, further resolution will only be achieved by the ability to access freely and analyse systematically *all* available data, rather than simply constructing interpretations on the basis of a few case studies.

Bibliography

Allen, M., Gardiner, J., and Sheridan, A. (eds.) (2012). *Is There a British Chalcolithic? People, Place and Polity in the Later 3rd Millennium* BC. Oxford: Oxbow Books.

Ashmore, P. (2001). 'Settlement in Scotland during the second millennium BC', in J. Brück (ed.), *Bronze Age Landscapes: Tradition and Transformation*. Oxford: Oxbow Books, 1–8.

Barnatt, J. and Edmonds, M. (2002). 'Places apart? Caves and monuments in Neolithic and Earlier Bronze Age Britain', *Cambridge Archaeological Journal*, 12: 113–29.

Beck, C. and Shennan, S. (1991). *Amber in Prehistoric Britain*. Oxford: Oxbow Books.

Beckensall, S. (1999). *British Prehistoric Rock Art*. Stroud: Tempus.

Bourke, L. (2001). *Crossing the Rubicon: Bronze Age Metalwork from Irish Rivers*. Galway: Galway University Press.

Bradley, R. (2007). *The Prehistory of Britain and Ireland*. Cambridge: Cambridge University Press.

—— and Sheridan, A. (2005). 'Croft Moraig and the chronology of stone circles', *Proceedings of the Prehistoric Society*, 71: 269–81.

—— Haselgrove, C., Vander Linden, M., and Webley, L. (2012). *Development-led Archaeology in North-West Europe*. Oxford: Oxbow.

Bray, P. (2012). 'When 14Cu became copper', in M. Allen, J. Gardiner, and A. Sheridan (eds.) (2012), *Is There a British Chalcolithic? People, Place and Polity in the Later third Millennium BC*. Oxford: Oxbow Books, 56–70.

Brennand, M. and Taylor, M. (2003). 'The survey and excavation of a Bronze Age timber circle at Holme-next-the-Sea, Norfolk, 1998–9', *Proceedings of the Prehistoric Society*, 69: 1–84.

Brindley, A. (2007). *Dating of Food Vessels and Urns in Ireland*. Galway: National University of Ireland.

Brück, J. (1995). 'A place for the dead. The role of human remains in Late Bronze Age Britain', *Proceedings of the Prehistoric Society*, 61: 245–77.

—— (1999a). 'What's in a settlement? Domestic practice and residential mobility in early Bronze Age southern England', in J. Brück and M. Goodman (eds.), *Making Places in the Prehistoric World: Themes in Settlement Archaeology*. London: Routledge, 52–75.

—— (1999b). 'Houses, life cycles and deposition on Middle Bronze Age settlements in southern England', *Proceedings of the Prehistoric Society*, 65: 1–22.

—— (ed.) (2001). *Bronze Age Landscapes: Tradition and Transformation*. Oxford: Oxbow Books.

—— (2004). 'Bronze Age burial practices in Scotland and beyond: differences and similarities', in I. Shepherd and G. Barclay (eds.), *Scotland in Ancient Europe: The Neolithic and Early Bronze Age of Scotland in their European Context*. Edinburgh: Society of Antiquaries of Scotland, 179–88.

——— (2007). 'The character of Late Bronze Age settlement in southern Britain', in C. Haselgrove and R. Pope (eds.), *The Earlier Iron Age in Britain and the Near Continent*. Oxford: Oxbow Books, 24–38.

Carlin, N. and Brück, J. (2012). 'Searching for the Chalcolithic: continuity and change in the Irish Final Neolithic/Early Bronze Age', in M. Allen, J. Gardiner, and A. Sheridan (eds.) (2012), *Is There a British Chalcolithic? People, Place and Polity in the Later third Millennium BC*. Oxford: Oxbow Books, 193–210.

Chapple, R. M. (2010). *The Excavation of an Enclosed Middle Bronze Age Cemetery at Gransha, Co. Londonderry, Northern Ireland*, British Archaeological Reports (British Series), 521. Oxford: Archaeopress.

Clark, P. (ed.) (2009a). *Bronze Age Connections: Cultural Contact in Prehistoric Europe*. Oxford: Oxbow Books.

—— (2009b). 'Building new connections', in P. Clark (ed.), *Bronze Age Connections: Cultural Contact in Prehistoric Europe*. Oxford: Oxbow Books, 1–11.

Clarke, D., Foxon, A., and Cowie, T. (1985). *Symbols of Power at the Time of Stonehenge*. Edinburgh: HMSO.

Cleary, K. (2005). 'Skeletons in the closet: the dead among the living on Irish Bronze Age settlements', *Journal of Irish Archaeology*, 14: 23–42.
Coles, J., Heal, S., and Orme, B. (1978). 'The use and character of wood in prehistoric Britain and Ireland', *Proceedings of the Prehistoric Society*, 44: 1–47.
Collard, M., Darvill, T., and Watts, M. (2006). 'Ironworking in the Bronze Age? Evidence from a 10th century BC settlement at Hartshill Copse, Upper Bucklebury, West Berkshire', *Proceedings of the Prehistoric Society*, 72: 367–423.
Cooney, G. and Grogan, E. (1994). *Irish Prehistory: A Social Perspective*. Dublin: Wordwell.
Darvill, T. (2010). *Prehistoric Britain*, 2nd edn. Abingdon: Routledge.
Doody, M. (2000). 'Bronze Age houses in Ireland', in A. Desmond, G. Johnson, and M. McCarthy (eds.), *New Agendas in Irish Prehistory: Papers in Commemoration of Liz Anderson*. Bray: Wordwell, 135–60.
Edmonds, M. (1995). *Stone Tools and Society. Working Stone in Neolithic and Bronze Age Britain*. London: Batsford.
Eogan, G. (1994). *The Accomplished Art: Gold and Gold-Working in Britain and Ireland during the Bronze Age (c.2300–650 BC)*. Oxford: Oxbow Books.
Eogan, J. (2004). 'The construction of funerary monuments in the Irish Early Bronze Age: a review of the evidence,' in H. Roche, E. Grogan, J. Bradley, J. Coles, and B. Raftery (eds.), *From Megaliths to Metals*. Oxford: Oxbow Books, 56–60.
Fitzpatrick, A.P. (2011). *The Amesbury Archer and the Boscombe Bowmen: Bell Beaker burials at Boscombe Down, Amesbury, Wiltshire, Great Britain*. Salisbury: Wessex Archaeological Report 27.
Gibson, A. (2002). *Prehistoric Pottery in Britain and Ireland*. Stroud: Tempus.
Ginn, V. and Rathbone, S. (2011). *Corrstown: A Coastal Community. Excavations of a Bronze Age Village in Northern Ireland*. Oxford: Oxbow.
Gwilt, A. and Lodwick, M. (2008). Recent fieldwork at Llanmaes, *Archaeology in Wales*, 48: 67–69.
Haselgrove, C. and Pope, R. (eds.) (2007). *The Earlier Iron Age in Britain and the Near Continent*. Oxford: Oxbow Books.
Healy, F. and Housley, R. (1992). 'Nancy was not alone: human skeletons from the Early Bronze Age from the Norfolk peat fen', *Antiquity*, 66: 948–55.
Johnston, R. (2005). 'Pattern without a plan. Rethinking the Bronze Age co-axial field systems on Dartmoor, south-west England', *Oxford Journal of Archaeology*, 24: 1–24.
Jones, C. (1998). 'The discovery and dating of the prehistoric landscape of Roughan Hill in Co. Clare', *The Journal of Irish Archaeology*, 9: 27–43.
Knight, M. and Evans, C. (2001). 'The "community of builders": the Barleycroft post alignments', in J. Brück (ed.), *Bronze Age Landscapes: Tradition and Transformation*. Oxford: Oxbow Books, 83–98.
Ladle, L., and Woodward, A. (2009). *Excavations at Bestwall Quarry, Wareham 1992–2005. Volume 1: The Prehistoric Landscape*. Dorchester: Dorset Natural History and Archaeological Society.
Lane, T. and Morris, E. (eds.) (2001). *A Millennium of Saltmaking: Prehistoric and Romano-British Salt Production in the Fens*, Lincolnshire Archaeology and Heritage Reports, 4. Heckington: The Heritage Trust of Lincolnshire.
Lawson, A. (2007). *Chalkland: An Archaeology of Stonehenge and its Region*. Salisbury: Hobnob Press.

Longworth, I., Varndell, G., and Lech, J. (2012). Excavations at Grimes Graves, *Norfolk, 1972-1976. Fascicule 6: Exploration and excavation beyond the deep mines*. London: British Museum Press.
Lynch, F., Aldhouse-Green, S., and Davies, J. (2000). *Prehistoric Wales*. Stroud: Tempus.
Needham, S. (2000). 'Power pulses across a cultural divide. Cosmologically driven acquisition between Armorica and Wessex', *Proceedings of the Prehistoric Society*, 66: 151–208.
—— (2005). 'Transforming Beaker culture in north-west Europe. Processes of fusion and fission', *Proceedings of the Prehistoric Society*, 71: 171–217.
—— (2007). '800 BC: The great divide', in C. Haselgrove and R. Pope (eds.), *The Earlier Iron Age in Britain and the Near Continent*. Oxford: Oxbow Books, 39–63.
—— (2009). 'Encompassing the sea: "Maritories" and Bronze Age maritime interactions', in P. Clark (ed.), *Bronze Age Connections: Cultural Contact in Prehistoric Europe*. Oxford: Oxbow Books, 94–121.
Needham, S., Parham, D., and Frieman, C. (forthcoming). *Claimed by the Sea: Salcombe, Langdon Bay and other marine finds of the Bronze Age*. Swindon: English Heritage.
O'Brien, W. (1999). *Sacred Ground: Megalithic Tombs in Coastal South-West Ireland*. Galway: Galway University Press.
—— (2012). 'The Chalcolithic in Ireland: a chronological and cultural framework', in M. Allen, J. Gardiner, and A. Sheridan (eds.) (2012). *Is There a British Chalcolithic? People, Place and Polity in the Later third Millennium BC*. Oxford: Oxbow Books, 211–25.
O'Faoláin, S. (2004). *Bronze Age Artefact Production in Late Bronze Age Ireland: A Survey*, British Archaeological Reports (British Series), 382. Oxford: British Archaeological Reports.
Parker Pearson, M. (2003). *Food, Culture and Identity in the Neolithic and Early Bronze Age*, British Archaeological Reports (International Series), 1,117. Oxford: Archaeopress.
——, Sharples, N., and Symonds, J. (2004). *South Uist: Archaeology and History of a Hebridean Island*. Stroud: Tempus.
Pryor, F. (1998). *Prehistoric Farmers in Britain*. Stroud: Tempus.
Roberts, B. W. (2007). 'Adorning the living but not the dead. Understanding ornaments in Britain c.1400–1100 BC', *Proceedings of the Prehistoric Society*, 73: 137–70.
—— (2008). 'Creating traditions and shaping technologies: understanding the emergence of metallurgy in Western Europe c.3500–2000 BC', *World Archaeology*, 40/3: 354–72.
—— and Frieman, C. (2012). 'Drawing boundaries and building models: investigating the concept of the "Chalcolithic frontier" in north-west Europe', in M. Allen, J. Gardiner, and A. Sheridan (eds.) (2012). *Is There a British Chalcolithic? People, Place and Polity in the Later third Millennium BC*. Oxford: Oxbow Books, 27–39.
Serjeantson, D. (2007). 'Intensification of animal husbandry in the Late Bronze Age? The contribution of sheep and pigs', in C. Haselgrove and R. Pope (eds.) *The Earlier Iron Age in Britain and the Near Continent*. Oxford: Oxbow Books, 80–93.
Shepherd, I. and Barclay, G. (eds.) (2004). *Scotland in Ancient Europe: The Neolithic and Early Bronze Age of Scotland in their European Context*. Edinburgh: Society of Antiquaries of Scotland.
Sheridan, J. A. and Davis, M. (1998). 'The Welsh "jet set" in prehistory. A case of keeping up with the Joneses?', in A. Gibson and D. Simpson (eds.), *Prehistoric Ritual and Religion*. Stroud: Tempus, 148–62.
—— and Davis, M. (2002). 'Investigating jet and jet-like artefacts from prehistoric Scotland. The National Museums of Scotland project', *Antiquity*, 76: 812–25.
—— and Shortland, A. (2004). '…beads which have given rise to so much dogmatism, controversy and rash speculation: faience in Early Bronze Age Britain and Ireland', in

I. Shepherd and G. Barclay (eds.), *Scotland in Ancient Europe: The Neolithic and Early Bronze Age of Scotland in their European Context*. Edinburgh: Society of Antiquaries, 263–82.

Timberlake, S. (2009). 'Copper mining and production at the beginning of the British Bronze Age: new evidence for Beaker/EBA prospecting and some ideas on scale, exchange, and early smelting technologies', in P. Clark (ed.), *Bronze Age Connections: Cultural Contact in Prehistoric Europe*. Oxford: Oxbow Books, 94–121.

Tipping, R., Davies, A., McCulloch, R., and Tisdall, E. (2008). 'Response to Late Bronze Age climate change of farming communities in north-east Scotland', *Journal of Archaeological Science*, 35: 2,379–86.

Towers, J., Montgomery, J., Evans, J., Jay, M., and Parker Pearson, M. (2010). 'An investigation of the origins of cattle and aurochs deposited in the Early Bronze Age barrows at Gayhurst and Irthlingborough', *Journal of Archaeological Science*, 37/3: 508–15.

Uckelmann, M. and Mödlinger, M. (2011). *Warfare in Bronze Age Europe: Manufacture and Use of Weaponry*, British Archaeological Reports (International Series, S2255). Oxford: Archaeopress.

Vander Linden, M. (2006). *Le Phénomène campaniforme dans l'Europe du 3ème millénaire avant notre ère. Synthèse et nouvelles perspectives*, British Archaeological Reports (International Series), 1,470. Oxford: Archaeopress.

Waddell, J. (1990). *The Bronze Age Burials of Ireland*. Galway: Galway University Press.

—— (2011). *The Archaeology of Prehistoric Ireland*. Dublin: Wordwell.

Woodward, A. (2000). *British Barrows: A Matter of Life and Death*. Stroud: Tempus.

Yates, D. (2007). *Land, Power and Prestige: Bronze Age Field Systems in Southern England*. Oxford: Oxbow Books.

—— and Bradley, R. (2010). 'The siting of metalwork hoards in the Bronze Age of south-east England', *The Antiquaries Journal*, 90: 41–72.

CHAPTER 31

THE BRONZE AGE IN THE LOW COUNTRIES

HARRY FOKKENS AND DAVID FONTIJN

Introduction

The Low Countries occupy a special place in the Bronze Age of north-west Europe, for several reasons. First, the Rhine-Meuse delta constitutes a border zone between three major Bronze Age exchange networks or spheres of influence: Nordic, Atlantic, and continental. Second, extensive settlement research in combination with data on burials and hoards enable us to undertake well-informed analyses of the way the cultural landscape was structured, and how that structure changed over time.

As in many parts of Europe, the archaeology of the Low Countries has been determined first by research on visible monuments, notably burial mounds from the Late Neolithic and the Bronze Age. It was especially A. E. van Giffen, the founding father of scientific Dutch archaeology, who determined research agendas and methods for a large part of the twentieth century. His quadrant method for the excavation of barrows is applied as standard all over north-west Europe. His barrow research, and that of his students (Tjalling Waterbolk, Willem Glasbergen, Pieter Modderman), and in Belgium of M.-E. Mariën, has provided us with a fund of high-quality data. Since the Monuments Law was introduced in 1961, virtually no burial mounds have been excavated in the Netherlands. Only in the last few years has Leiden University started a new research project under the direction of David Fontijn.

In Belgian Flanders data on burials were still virtually absent until the 1980s. An aerial-photography programme initiated by the University of Ghent, however, demonstrated that this absence was the result of gaps in research, and now more than a thousand barrows are known through photography and field research (see Ampe et al. 1996; Cherreté and Bourgeois 2005).

In the 1960s, when large-scale housing and industrial estates began to be developed, large-scale settlement research also started, especially in the Netherlands. At Bovenkarspel, Angelso, Ekkersrijt, and Oss, for instance, dozens of hectares with Bronze and Iron Age settlement remains have been excavated. In the last two decades in Belgium too, developer-led commercial archaeology undertaken following the Valletta Convention has greatly increased the amount of data obtained.

The Natural Environment and Palaeogeography

The Low Countries are known for their large river systems, polders, and dikes. But in fact the region is divided over, broadly, three kinds of physical environment: the Holocene coastal and riverine zones, the higher Pleistocene (sandy) uplands and loess plateaux, and the tertiary limestone plateaux of the Ardennes. In order to understand Bronze Age cultural developments in the Low Countries, the palaeogeography of the landscape is of crucial importance because it explains to a large extent the cultural differences that existed in the region (and in fact had done from an early part of the Neolithic). Two general divisions are visible in this respect: first a distinction between riverine and coastal lowlands and Pleistocene uplands, and second a distinction between the regions north and south of the large river systems of the Rhine and Meuse (Fig. 31.1). The Ardennes were in most periods more oriented towards continental cultural developments. For details we refer to the next section, but here we will discuss the palaeogeography in more detail.

Apart from the south-eastern Ardennes, the whole region was formed in the Quaternary, the uplands during the last Ice Ages and the lowlands in the Holocene. In the Pleistocene the North Sea Basin was dry, and parts of the Netherlands were covered by thick ice sheets that pushed up several of the northern, eastern, and middle regions. The land-ice determined the present flow of the Rhine and Meuse and created the low parts of the Low Countries. During the last Ice Age the boulder clay eroded, cover sands and river dunes originated, and in the south, aeolian deposits originating in the North Sea Basin formed the loess region.

During the Holocene, the North Sea and the lower basins filled with peat and clay deposits and the shoreline withdrew to around its present location. In the Bronze Age the coast was formed by a number of coastal barriers, and behind it evolved the large estuaries of the Scheldt, the Meuse, and the Rhine, and in the North the IJssel. In the estuaries and wide river areas, Bronze Age farmers found good settlement land on sandy outcrops, silt deposits, and silted-up break-through channels. In particular the region of West Frisia is known for its well-preserved Bronze Age cultural landscapes. In the sand regions conditions for farming may have been more difficult since the sandy soils are poor in terms of fertility, but nevertheless there is evidence for dense settlement patterns, and from the Late Bronze Age onwards also for elaborate 'Celtic' field systems.

Few people realize that in the Late Neolithic and the Bronze Age the wide river areas of the Rhine, Meuse, and IJssel constituted a border zone between two large cultural networks: the Nordic network to the north and east, and the Atlantic network to the south. The limestone plateaux of south-eastern Belgium connected with the third major network, the 'continental' exchange network.

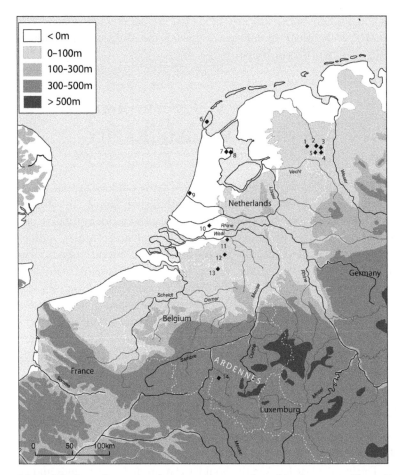

FIG. 31.1 Map of the Low Countries showing sites mentioned in the text: 1. Elp, 2. Drouwen, 3. Exloo, 4. Bargeroosterveld, 5. Angelslo-Emmerhout, 6. Den Burg (Texel), 7. Enkhuizen, 8. Bovenkarspel (West Frisia), 9. Noordwijk, 10. Zijderveld, 11. Oss, 12. Son en Bruegel-Ekkersrijt, 13. Weelde, 14. Han-sur-Lesse.

Map: authors.

Chronology and Cultural Traditions

These varied ecological zones, each with its own characteristics, formed the background for differences in cultural identities throughout the ages. Since the Neolithic, the river deltas of the Rhine, Meuse, and Scheldt have been inhabited by cultural groups that distinguished themselves from the occupants of the adjacent Pleistocene sandy soils, and in the south from those of the loess soils north of the Ardennes. In the Early Neolithic the loess soils were inhabited by farmers of the *Linearbandkeramik* and related culture groups, while the delta was occupied by farmer-hunter-fishers of first the Swifterbant and later the Vlaardingen groups (see Louwe Kooijmans 1976). The Pleistocene uplands north of the Rhine were occupied by the people of the Funnel Beaker (TRB) and later the Single Grave culture. It is clear that the 'lowland' groups had regular contact with farmers of the uplands, but they kept their own identity both in material culture and settlement traditions and burial rites.

In the Late Neolithic the situation became more complex, partly because of our definitions of the different culture groups between 3000 and 2000 cal BC. Roughly speaking, until 2500 cal BC the late Vlaardingen culture is situated in the lowlands and the Stein group in the Meuse region down to the present-day Belgian borders. Until 2500 cal BC the Single Grave culture is distributed on the higher Pleistocene soils of the central, northern, and eastern Netherlands as a successor to the Funnel Beaker culture. This diversity seems to end between 2600 and 2500 cal BC. From then onwards, in principle all eco-zones appear to be occupied by one culture group, even down to the Ardennes in the south: the Bell Beaker culture. This may be more apparent than real, however. The Bell Beaker culture and the Early Bronze Age Barbed Wire Beaker culture *appear* to be one coherent group, but there is almost no settlement evidence from this period and the homogeneity is most probably caused by similarities in Bell Beakers from barrows. In reality the cultural division that was always there probably persisted.

That regionality did not disappear is also clear from the fact that in the Middle Bronze Age several regional traditions again existed. These traditions become visible at the end of the Early Bronze Age, characterized by late Beaker pottery with Barbed Wire decoration (Lanting 1973), which is found in all of the Low Countries except for the Ardennes. Around 1850 cal BC different pottery traditions develop in the north-east, west, and south. North and east of the rivers IJssel and Vecht the Elp tradition is distinguished, using plain, undecorated pottery tempered with broken quartz. This finish prompted German colleagues to call it *Kummerkeramik* ('sorrow-pottery'). Nowadays it is called Elp pottery after the first site where it was found in a settlement context (Fokkens 2005b).

South of the IJssel the Hilversum tradition developed, which shows connections with both southern England and north-west France (Fokkens 2005b). The traditional style (Early Hilversum pottery) with cord-decorated necks and very marked rim-profiles only occurs in the early phase (between 1850 and 1600 cal BC). After 1600 the neck decoration disappears and only decoration with fingernail-impressed cordons (traditionally called Drakenstein pottery) remains. In the western Netherlands after 1600 BC yet another regional style developed, called the Hoogkarspel style (Brandt 1988).

After 1200 cal BC Urnfield pottery showed many more diverse forms. North and east of the IJssel the Urnfield pottery style of the Ems group developed (see Kooi 1979; Verlinde 1987). The southern regions are under the influence of what is still called the Lower Rhine Urnfield culture (*Niederrheinische Grabhügelkultur*: Kersten 1948), though that concept is badly in need of redefinition. In the south of Belgium in the Late Bronze Age the pottery styles follow the Rhin-Suisse-France Oriental tradition (RSFO), with its marked forms and incised decoration (see Chapter 32; De Mulder, LeClerq, and Van Strydonck 2008).

Settlements and Architecture

General Trends

The Low Countries are famous for their well-preserved and well-structured longhouses, some with evidence of cattle-stalling (Fig. 31.2). Though this is thought to have been *the* Bronze Age farm, it is now clear that that type of house is both regionally and temporally

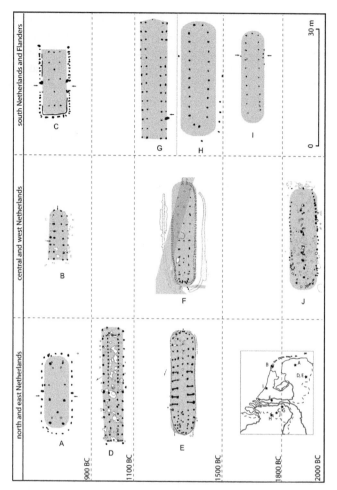

FIG. 31.2 The most important house types in the Low Countries: A. Een, B. Texel-Den Burg, C. Oss, D. Elp, E. Emmerhout, F. Zijderveld, G. Oss, H. Weelde, I. Ekkersrijt, J. Noordwijk.

Source: authors.

restricted in occurrence. The development of house plans depicted in Figure 31.2 is therefore based on evidence spread unevenly in time and space.

From the Late Neolithic we know a few house plans from the Vlaardingen culture in the western Netherlands and from West Frisia. These are two-aisled and rather small, not unlike their Scandinavian counterparts (Boas 1997). In the Early Bronze Age this tradition continues, but in fact only two clear examples are known from the Netherlands and Belgium, one of which is the Noordwijk farm, dated to c.1850 cal BC (Van de Velde 2008; Fig. 31.2, J).

Of the following first part of the Middle Bronze Age we have even less data. In this period the well-known three-aisled Bronze Age longhouses must have developed, but for unknown reasons they are not yet visible archaeologically. However, after 1500 cal BC this is 'suddenly' the dominant type in a very large distribution area from Scandinavia down to France (see Bourgeois and Arnoldussen 2006; Fokkens 2005a; Arnoldussen 2008). The longhouse apparently developed in the lower regions of north-west Europe, because there is no evidence for this type in the loess zone, or in the higher and mountainous regions of Belgium, France, and Germany. We suggest that this is related to the type of mixed farming practised in the lowlands, probably also combined with cattle-stalling and the collecting of manure (see Fokkens 2005a; see Chapter 18).

The Middle Bronze Age longhouse is present everywhere in the low-lying areas, but regional styles are visible. The farms of the north and east reveal, like in some instances in Denmark, clear evidence of cattle-stalling in the house. In the south and west of the Low Countries stall partitions are invisible, but we nevertheless assume that cattle may have been stalled inside. This practice clearly developed in the Early Bronze Age and first part of the Middle Bronze Age, but becomes visible only after 1500 cal BC. By then cattle-stalling has become an integral part of the farming system, in essence continuing until today. One interpretation is that in the Bronze Age cattle became important as social capital (exchange networks) and therefore became, so to speak, an integral part of the household (see Fokkens 1999; see also Zimmermann 1999).

All reliable plans show a very clear structure and a very regular placement of posts (Arnoldussen and Fokkens 2008: 30). The best-known examples are the houses of Elp and Emmerhout-Angelslo, but they are in fact only typical for the northern regions, including also Denmark. Figure 31.2 shows that in the river area and the western Netherlands house walls are demarcated by thin stakes, probably hurdles, possibly also combined with sods (IJzereef and Van Regteren Altena 1991). The southern parts of the Low Countries show another variant again, while in the hilly areas of the south-east any evidence of settlement is so far absent.

In the first half of the Late Bronze Age (between 1000 and 800 cal BC) the longhouse disappears and is replaced by smaller farms with a different structure (see below). In this period of replacement, at the end of the Late Bronze Age, there is again an under-representation of house plans (Fokkens 2008). The new developed type, abundantly present in the Early Iron Age, is systematically smaller then Bronze Age plans and of a different construction (see Fig. 31.2).

The reason for this change is so far unclear. Harry Fokkens (1999; 2005a) has pointed out that the Middle Bronze Age longhouse, with its large living floor-space (often 5 x 10–15 m), may have been inhabited by extended families. The smaller houses of the later period then would have been inhabited by single families, which would indicate a dissolution of the traditional Bronze Age social structure into single family groups. A similar development may be visible in the transition from barrows to urnfields, though different interpretations may be possible as well (see Gerritsen 2003; Bourgeois and Fontijn 2008).

Settlement Structure

Although large coherent areas have been excavated in many parts of the Low Countries, it is still difficult to get a clear image of settlement structure (see Arnoldussen 2008; Bourgeois, Cheretté, and Bourgeois 2003). It is clear that in West Frisia the situation is different from other regions. Here houses appear to cluster in small settlements (Fig. 31.3). Elsewhere there is evidence for repeated use of the same settlement area, even if there are also periods of abandonment (see Bourgeois and Verlaeckt 2001; Arnoldussen and Fokkens 2008). The impression is that in general one or two dispersed farmsteads formed a small local community. The solitary character probably also explains the low visibility of Bronze Age sites.

The organization of the farmsteads does not show clear patterns either. Larger pits and wells are constant features, as are four- or six-post outbuildings. These are generally interpreted as

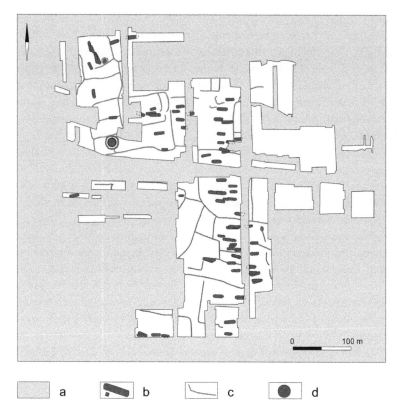

FIG. 31.3 The Bronze Age cultural landscape at Bovenkarspel-Het Valkje, West Frisia. A. not excavated, B. Bronze Age farms (not all contemporary), C. Bronze Age ditches, D. Bronze Age barrow.

Source: authors (Fokkens and Arnoldussen 2008).

granaries and reconstructed with the floor above the ground as a protection against vermin. These outbuildings are absent in West Frisia, however. There, pit circles and circular ditches appear to have functioned as grain-storage facilities (see Buurman 1979). Similar structures appear also in the low-lying areas of Denmark (e.g. Bech 1997).

Agriculture

From the evidence of the house plans, stratigraphy, and from plant remains (Bakels 1997; De Hingh 2000), it is clear that in the Middle Bronze Age manuring was or became a structural part of farming practices in the Low Countries and adjacent regions. For the 'Celtic' field systems that developed from the Middle and Late Bronze onwards, this is also evidenced by phosphate analysis (see Zimmermann 1976). In this respect the Bronze economy of the Low Countries can be characterized as a mixed-farming economy where stock rearing and arable farming were practised in close association and in support of each other.

Plough marks, or rather traces of criss-cross ploughing with an ard, have been discovered in many places. The layout of the fields, however, only becomes visible when 'Celtic' fields start to develop. Research using aerial photographs (Brongers 1976) and now using LIDAR-based altimetry has revealed many very large complexes, especially in the northern and central Netherlands. Though dating is very difficult, the development of 'Celtic' fields is now placed in the latest part of the Middle Bronze Age, and was certainly in full swing by the Late Bronze Age. Whether this means that already by then large continuous fields were present around farms is doubtful. The layout that we can see nowadays is very much a product of the Iron Age and Roman periods (see Zimmermann 1976). Since phosphate samples always show high concentrations around the 'Celtic' fields, it is probable that manuring was part of the new system. One explanation for the wide banks around the fields might for instance be that they arose from a practice of mixing depleted topsoil from the fields every five years or so with dung from stables (compostation), and then bringing the enriched soil back onto the field (see Kroll 1987 for a description of this practice; Fokkens 1998: 119–20). This practice is of course difficult to apply in clays and silts, which may be one of the reasons why the 'Celtic' field system seems to be absent in West Frisia.

Funerary Archaeology

The evidence for barrows and cemeteries is of a different character in the different regions of the Netherlands. Late Neolithic and Bronze Age barrows are known in the Netherlands in abundance, especially on the sandy uplands of the northern, eastern, central, and southern Netherlands. In Belgian Flanders, due to different reclamation and cultivation strategies, barrows have almost all been completely levelled. As a result now over a thousand are known, of which a few have been tested by excavation (see Cherette and Bourgeois 2005). For urnfields the situation is more comparable: Late Bronze Age and Early Iron Age urnfields are known from all regions of the Low Countries, though regional traditions are discernible (see Kooi 1979; Verlinde 1987; Roymans and Kortlang 1999). The Belgian Ardennes were actually part of a different tradition, related to what in France is called Rhin-Suisse-France Oriental (RSFO) (see Chapter 32), which covers a wide area from the Paris Basin to the Rhine and incorporates the tributary valleys of the Rhône and Seine. The same pottery is also found in the Belgian Ardennes. In the Ardennes, for instance at Han, caves have been used for funerary purposes (inhumations), especially in the Late Bronze Age, the Bronze Final II and III (see Warmenbol 1988; 1996).

The tradition of building barrows started in large parts of the Low Countries around 2900 cal BC in the areas where the Single Grave culture replaced the earlier megalithic tradition. To the north-west and south of the Meuse, where Single Grave/Early Bell Beaker elements only developed after 2600 cal BC, only scanty burial evidence for the Vlaardingen culture is present. In a large part of the Low Countries including northern Belgium, the tradition of building monumental barrows started only in full after 2600 BC, or even after 2000 cal BC, and lasted until *c.*1400 BC (Bourgeois and Arnoldussen 2006). After 1200 cal BC the urnfield tradition started. Older Bronze Age barrows often became the focus of larger urnfield cemeteries. In the Low Countries the urnfield traditions last longer then elsewhere, continuing right until the end of the Early Iron Age.

These different regional developments demonstrate once more the cultural 'division' between the Nordic and the Atlantic exchange networks mentioned above. In the north and the east Middle Bronze Age traditions are slightly different, and this situation persists in the Late Bronze and Early Iron Age. Differences are visible, for instance in the treatment of the dead, in grave gifts, grave forms, and ceramic traditions.

Treatment of the Dead

In many regions of Europe the Tumulus or *Hügelgräber* 'culture' is associated with inhumation of the dead, the Urnfield period with cremation. In most regions there is a rather distinct change between the two periods in this respect. This also applies to the north and east of the Low Countries where there is a marked preference for inhumation until $c.$1200 cal BC. From the Middle Bronze Age ($c.$1850 cal BC) onwards the dead are laid out stretched on their back, sometimes accompanied by grave gifts, rarely by bronzes and pottery. After 1200 cal BC cremation becomes the dominant treatment of the dead and urnfields develop. Pottery then becomes one of the prominent features in cemeteries because it was used as containers for the dead.

South of the Meuse, however, the tradition of cremation had already started in the Late Neolithic (Bell Beaker period) and became dominant in the Middle Bronze Age, from $c.$1850 BC onwards (see Theunissen 1999). This also means that in the south we are rather well informed about pottery traditions, because here too pottery was used as urns.

In the western Netherlands, especially in West Frisia, the situation is different again. Here after 1600 BC barrows are totally absent; there are not even any urnfields. Considering the vast areas that have been excavated in this region, this absence is not merely due to a gap in research but must be related to regionally specific traditions that developed here and so far have remained archaeologically invisible.

Graves and Grave Goods

Compared to the barrows of the Nordic Bronze Age, Bronze Age barrows of the Low Countries are modest in size and low in height. They rarely measure more than 15 m across and their surviving height is not more than 1.5 m. Several studies show that there are no clear relations between the size of a barrow and status of the deceased (see Lohof 1991); nor can a connection between the structures surrounding barrows and the status of the dead be demonstrated. There are big differences in how the burial area is delimited. Sometimes large numbers of wooden posts were set around the grave or the barrow, almost forming a physical boundary for access to the dead. On other occasions this boundary only has the form of a more or less shallow ditch, a wide post-setting, or a combination of these (Fig. 31.4). Though there are a few structure types that are specific for the south (see Theunissen 1999), recent research has shown there is so much variability that regional traditions in these barrow structures are hard to substantiate (Bourgeois forthcoming).

It is clear however, that the burial ritual is far more complex than has been assumed. We tend to interpret burials of the Middle Bronze Age from a modern Western viewpoint: as mere interments of loved members of society. But it is clear that in the Bronze Age not everyone was entitled to a barrow burial. Sometimes decades, even centuries, may have passed between two burial events in one barrow group. Though this is generally interpreted as an indication that only members of the elite were buried under barrows, there is much evidence that this interpretation is too simple and modern (see Fontijn 2002; Fokkens 1999; see

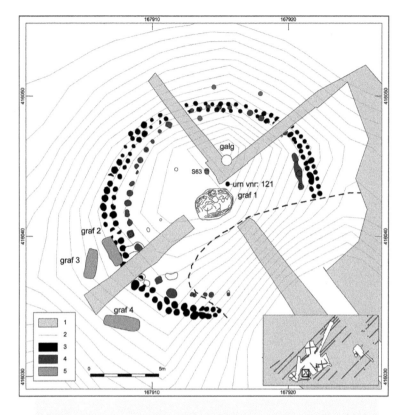

FIG. 31.4 A two-period Middle Bronze Age barrow at Oss-Zevenbergen. The double post circle is typical for the region. The central grave underneath the barrow appeared to be empty, a cenotaph completely filled with sods. In the Early Iron Age an urn was inserted in the top (indicated as urn) and in the twelfth Century AD a gallows was erected on top of the barrow (indicated as *galg*), and the three executed persons were buried just outside the barrow (*graf* 2, 3, 4).

Source: authors.

Chapter 6). For instance, barrows south of the Meuse hardly ever contain bronzes or other signs of this supposed elite status, nor is there much difference in size or structure. North of the Rhine and in the north-west of the Netherlands, where inhumation was the dominant tradition, we find the dead laid stretched out on their back, sometimes with several bronzes. Typical for the few male burials that we can identify are a rapier, a nicked flanged axe, sometimes a spearhead, arm-rings or hair-rings, tweezers, a razor, and arrowheads. One of the

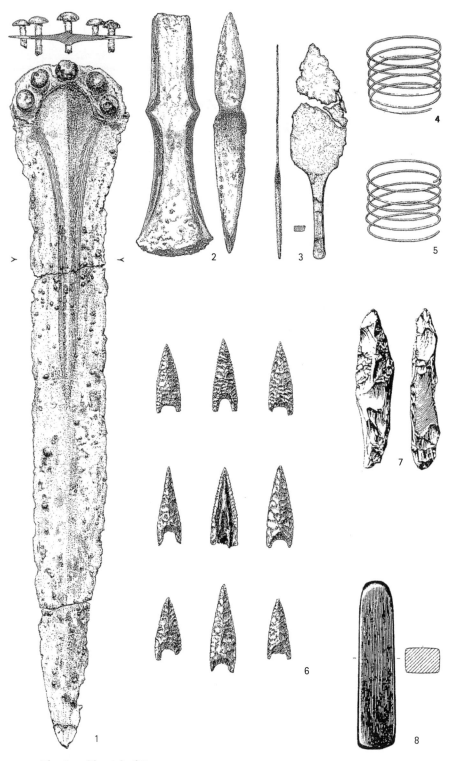

FIG. 31.5 The Søgel burial of Drouwen.

Source: Butler 1990.

most famous of these, and among the richest because of the gold-spiral arm-rings, is the Sögel-type grave at Drouwen (Fig. 31.5). Burials like this have been called chieftains' burials time and again. Though this is not the right place to dispute those claims, one can question why these 'chieftains' always have a more or less standardized set of grave goods; so standardized that such a burial can immediately be classified typologically. It has been suggested that this 'standardization' can be interpreted in part as an idealized way to bury important ancestors. Standard sets of weapons and tools and of ornaments and tools may relate to values that were of crucial importance to Bronze Age society (Fokkens 1999; Fontijn 2002). These avenues of interpretation are still open to new research.

Though Late Neolithic and Bronze Age barrows are often painted as solitary elements in the settled landscape, sometimes related to settlements proper, the real situation is far more complex. Indeed, for instance at Elp and Bovenkarspel, solitary barrows appear to be located in the vicinity of the settlement (see Waterbolk 1966; IJzereef 1988). But over the years it has become clear that these barrows were older than the settlements. Nowadays we interpret these barrows as indicative of the importance of ancestral presences rather than cemeteries associated with contemporary settlements (Bourgeois and Fontijn 2008; Fokkens 2005a).

Recent barrow research has demonstrated that these tendencies are present in the burial landscape as well (see Bourgeois and Fontijn 2008; Bourgeois forthcoming; Fokkens, Van Wijk, and Jansen 2009). For example, recent research has shown that warrior graves tend to be built on older barrows as part of a new barrow-building period. This underlines the significance of ancestral links (Fontijn 2010). In several regions barrows from different periods cluster together, and often also constitute the core of a later urnfield. It appears that these barrow groups had long traditions of (intermittent) use. As well as living in the vicinity of the ancestors, being buried among them—even if they were often very distant and unknown to the mourners—appears to have been important to Bronze Age people (see Bourgeois and Fontijn 2008: 48).

In the Late Bronze Age, from $c.1200-800$ cal BC, the practice of burying only a selection of the dead changes dramatically. Urnfields develop, first in the form of monumental long barrows (Fig. 31.6), often related to an older barrow. After 1000 cal BC all urnfield barrows become generally of the same form: a small barrow surrounded by a shallow ditch, often with a causeway in the south-east. Though the urnfield tradition appears to be much more egalitarian than earlier Bronze Age burial traditions, this is probably only how it appears and the reality was different (Fokkens 1997). Here too, in size and form differences are visible, though they more difficult to interpret. As Roymans and Kortlang (1999) have pointed out, urnfields seem to emphasize the identity of local communities as important units in society, rather than individual ancestors. Though very large urnfields exist, the majority—if one calculates population size using the Ascadi and Nemeskéri formula (1970)—are only small and contain some three to four families, which implies that these communities consisted of three to four farmsteads.

Since from the Late Bronze Age more people are buried visibly and urns are conspicuous containers, we know far more about urnfield pottery than we do about earlier Bronze Age pottery. Moreover, both in the north and east and in the southern part of the Low Countries, the variability in forms increases dramatically. Also in settlements there is much more variation. Consequently, pottery typology has a prominent place in dating urnfield phenomena. Traditionally two larger traditions have been distinguished: a northern and eastern Ems tradition (Verlinde 1987), and a southern tradition still indicated as the *Niederrheinische Grabhügelkultur*, though this concept has lost its original meaning. In fact it indicates a wider network of exchange relations that becomes visible in similar pot forms and similar decoration.

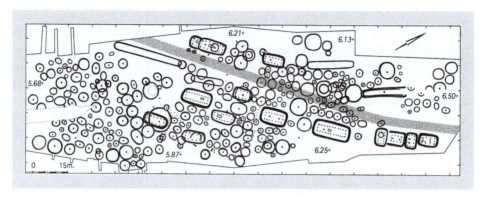

FIG. 31.6 The urnfield of Vledder in the Northern Netherlands.

Source: Kooi 1979.

METALWORK AND HOARDING, RIVER DEPOSITIONS

Metal in the Low Countries

The Low Countries are far removed from the metalliferous areas: essentially, all copper, tin, and gold had to be imported over vast distances. For that reason, it is all the more conspicuous that metal was relatively rapidly introduced, for example by replacing stone as the dominant material for the production of axes in the south of the Low Countries from the later Bell Baker period onwards. Although metal may have occasionally circulated among Neolithic communities in the northern Netherlands (Butler and Van der Waals 1966: 76), the earliest indications for the use of metal in the Low Countries date to a late phase of the Bell Beaker culture (2300–2000 BC; Fontijn 2002: Chapter 5). These are multi-impurity copper-tanged daggers and needles, and gold ornaments, in Bell Beaker graves, as well as single deposits of flat axes, halberds, and a gold lunula. There is evidence for local production of copper alloys and/or gold for this same period in the Dutch river area and to its north, evidenced by metalworking implements found in Bell Beaker graves such as cushion stones. Regional production of axes has been attested for the Early Bronze Age (Butler 1996). Finds of moulds, and the evidence of at least one true production site (Oss-Horzak: Fontijn, Fokkens, and Jansen 2002; see Chapter 5), indicate that axes, spearheads, arrowheads, knives, and ornaments were locally made in most parts of the Low Countries from the Middle Bronze Age onwards (Kuijpers 2008). There is no evidence, however, for more elaborate metalworking techniques, like production of sheet-metal vessels or composite figurines. Whether swords were produced here remains a matter of debate. Ingots like the central European *Ösenringe* or *Rippenbarren* (ring and rib ingots) are unknown, but finds like the Middle Bronze Age scrap axe hoard of Voorhout suggest that regional bronze production thrived on recycling of metal (Butler 1990; Fontijn 2008). Throughout the Bronze Age, flint remained in use, for example as scrapers and knives (Van Gijn 2010: Chapter 8).

For the Bell Beaker phase, we are mainly dealing with multi-impurity coppers, including the so-called Bell Beaker and Singen metal (Butler and Van der Waals 1966). For later phases, we lack representative studies on metal composition. Available studies demonstrate trends that neatly fit with what is known from adjacent western Germany and northern France. The first tin bronzes are attested for the period between 2000 and 1800 BC, and probably become dominant after that period (Bourgeois, Verlaeckt, and Van Strydonck 1996; Verlaeckt 1996), whereas lead becomes a deliberate addition to the alloy from around the thirteenth century BC (Bronze final I/Bz D-Ha A1). Late regional non-functional axes of the Geistingen type (dating to the transition to the Early Iron Age) show a conspicuous variety in metal types used to manufacture what were essentially strikingly similar items (Postma et al. 2005). Iron replaced bronze relatively rapidly during the earliest phase of Ha C, the first half of the eighth century cal BC, when iron versions of Gündlingen swords came to figure in river depositions in the Scheldt (Fontijn and Fokkens 2007: 365). The find of an iron pin on a trackway through the peat bog near Bargeroosterveld in Drenthe, however, demonstrates that iron was already known around 1350 BC (Van den Broeke 2005: 606).

Networks

Situated along the Channel and the North Sea, and shaped as the delta of three major European rivers (Rhine, Meuse, and Scheldt), the Low Countries seem to have an almost natural predisposition for functioning as a transitory zone between different European contact and exchange networks. Indeed, this is reflected in the provenance of imported bronzes in each region. The Scheldt Valley and the Belgian-Dutch area to the east of it, up to the Rhine, is characterized by continental and Atlantic imports and regional items, in frequencies varying from place to place and time to time. Nordic imports are practically absent.

North of the Rhine, the situation is different. Both along the coast and in the north-eastern Netherlands certain object types, like winged axes and bronze sickles, are hardly known or rare, and occasionally we find Nordic imports. There has long been a strong tendency to see the Low Countries as an area that was in close contact with Britain (Butler 1963). Later analyses, however, play down the role of British imports, to emphasize the significance of importation of Atlantic-style French bronzes and imports from central Europe (O'Connor 1980; Fontijn 2009). Maritime connections are now more likely to reflect coastal seafaring, linking the French-Belgian coastal areas to the Dutch, north German, and Danish ones (see Butler 1990). When one looks at the provenance of bronzes, it is clear that they sometimes result not so much from natural links with a hinterland, but rather reflect historically contingent developments in the orientation of circulation networks. The north-eastern Netherlands (particularly the province of Drenthe) are far removed from any larger river and do not lie near the sea. Still, this region has extraordinary imports from the Atlantic zone, like the composite Wessex-type necklace of Exloo (with tin, faience, amber, and bronze beads; Haveman and Sheridan 2006). Through time, we also see remarkable shifts between the frequency of continental and Atlantic-style imports in one region, like the marked upsurge of the latter in the Scheldt Valley during the last century of the Late Bronze Age. This seems to reflect a profound reorientation of the networks of metalwork circulation that would again be drastically reversed only one century later with the rise of Ha C networks (Verlaeckt 1996: Fig. 13; Fontijn and Fokkens 2007: 365–6).

Metalwork Deposition

Several studies have shown that most bronzes found in the Low Countries were deliberately deposited (Essink and Hielkema 1997; Fontijn 2002; Van Impe 1994; Verlaeckt 1996;

Warmenbol 1996). Research by David Fontijn demonstrated that deposition was selective: particular types of objects were only deposited in specific kinds of places (Fig. 31.7). Although deposited bronzes now dominate our knowledge of Bronze Age metalwork, it has been calculated that by far the largest amount of metal must have been recycled and only a small part was taken out to be permanently deposited. Frequencies vary through time and per region, but even when the deposition rate was highest (last phase of the Late Bronze Age), in the southern Netherlands-northern Belgium, on average one deposition was made per annum in this region (Fontijn 2002: 214–15).

Deposited items like axes and weapons generally show signs of a use-life and many must have circulated across considerable distances. This suggests that the life-path of the object—its cultural biography—was relevant to its selection for deposition. Throughout the Bronze Age there was a marked tendency to deposit bronzes in unaltered 'natural', usually watery places like rivers, streams, peat bogs, fords in streams, or rivers flowing out of caves in southern Belgium (Fontijn 2002; Warmenbol 1996). Bronzes were only rarely left on settlement sites and are also rare in graves.

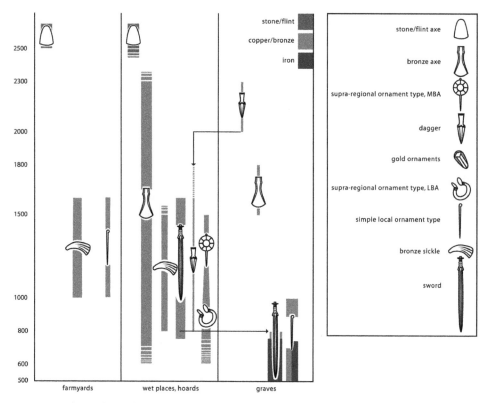

FIG. 31.7 Chronological developments in depositional practices for the southern Netherlands and Belgium. For each period, specific types of objects tend to be deposited in specific kinds of places only (settlements-wet places/hoards-graves). Note that there is a shift from graves to wet-place and hoard deposition around 2000 BC, and from wet places/ hoards to graves during the eighth century BC.

Source: authors (Fontijn 2002).

We are mostly dealing with single depositions. Cases where more than one object was put into the ground (hoards) are clearly exceptions and this also comes to the fore in the differences between items in single deposits and in hoards—the latter often consisting of imports of exceptional types. It is possible that some river finds represent material that was deposited in one go. A conspicuous trait is that deposited items tend not to be transformed (broken, burnt). Rather, there is evidence that many items were sharpened before deposition.

Research has demonstrated that we are dealing with selective deposition: specific items end up in specific kinds of places only. An important preference, as mentioned, is that for watery natural places. Axes, and weapons like spears and swords, are extremely rare in burial contexts. With one exception, weapon graves are only known north of the Rhine, like in the monumental Sögel-type warrior grave of Drouwen, and even then such weapon graves represent only 3 per cent of all Middle Bronze Age graves (Fontijn 2010). The dominance of weapons, particularly south of the Rhine, and the presence of ceremonial versions of swords and spears, underlines the social significance of martial values. They are mainly known to us, however, from situations in which weaponry was deposited. Swords (slightly fewer than one hundred examples known) seem to have been preferentially deposited in major rivers like the Meuse or the Scheldt. Axes and spears are also known from smaller bogs and streams in the near vicinity of settlements. On farms, however, bronzes were only rarely deposited. For the Dutch region south of the Rhine, the only bronze items that are repeatedly found on settlements are bronze sickles. Even in the Late Bronze Age, when hundreds of graves are known from urnfields, bronzes are rare as grave goods (15 per cent or less), and weapons and axes are again absent. Items selected for funerals are mainly local ornaments like pins.

South of the Rhine, in particular, often kilometre-long stretches of the major rivers are the most important deposition sites. They can be seen as multiple-deposition zones, with a long history of use for a particular type of deposition (for example, near the Maas-Roer confluence). In the north-eastern Netherlands, certain peat bogs seem to have been used in the same way. The peat bog near Bargeroosterveld has been used for deposition from the Middle Neolithic onwards. Apart from a trackway leading to the centre of the bog, people also constructed a remarkable building here, the so-called 'Temple' of Bargeroosterveld (Waterbolk and Van Zeist 1961). This is also the only region where several Late Bronze Age hoards are situated (probably in a barrow group fronting the bog; Butler 1961). In south-east Belgium, at Han-sur-Lesse, bronzes and many gold ornaments were deposited in a river just where it emerges from the cave. Finds of human bones indicate a direct link with funerary rites (Warmenbol 1996).

Deposition of metalwork in natural places decreases dramatically at the transition to the Early Iron Age, although the practice does not entirely cease to exist. At that period deposition of valuables in so-called 'Hallstatt chieftains' graves' becomes the most conspicuous context (see Fontijn and Fokkens 2007).

Conclusion

The Low Countries have a rich and varied archaeological record. Due to good preservation conditions in the wetlands, and a tradition of large-scale excavation of settlements and cemeteries, the data allow the creation of well-informed models for the settled landscape. The

Early Bronze Age (Barbed Wire Beaker culture) still shows a continuation of burial, housing, and hoarding traditions from the Bell Beaker period. A period of change sets in after *c*.1850 cal BC. Different burial traditions are introduced and the structure of the farms changes, though we have very little concrete evidence for this. The only evidence is that after 1500 cal BC the situation seems to have changed completely, at least in settlement structure. Large farms occur with stalls, indicating that cattle are important, not only as providers of meat, milk, hides, and draught power, but also as social factors.

The settlements appear to lie dispersed in the landscape in groups of two or three, possibly inhabited by extended families. They buried most of their dead in a manner unknown to us; only a small selection of men, women, and children are buried under and in barrows (in secondary position). We have no indication that these people were elites or rich and powerful, though they were undoubtedly important within the community. In any case these people were considered important as ancestors and the monuments created for them were probably meant to last for ever.

That the ancestral presence was important is demonstrated by the fact that both settlements and urnfield cemeteries are associated with older barrows. In West Frisia, for instance, centuries-old barrows were incorporated into the farmyard and into arable land, and this occurs in other regions as well. Farmyards themselves are less stable elements in the landscape. After a period of habitation of maybe just a few generations, the yard would be abandoned and a new farm would be erected on another yard. This may have been close by, so when large areas are excavated, as at Ekkersrijt (De Jong and Beumer 2011), Enkuizen, or Angelso, dozens of house plans can sometimes be identified, but they still only represent two or three contemporary farms (see Fig. 31.3).

In the Late Bronze Age farm buildings become considerably shorter, but still have cattle stalls. For the period between 1000 and 800 BC we have very little settlement evidence, though urnfields are abundant. 'Celtic' fields develop, and after 800 cal BC we see small clusters of farms, three to five, forming a local community that used one complex of arable fields, one cemetery (an urnfield), and probably had their own natural places for deposition and ritual. As in the Middle Bronze Age, cemeteries were the most stable elements in the landscape and probably important for marking out the identity of those small communities.

Bibliography

Ampe, C., Bourgeois, J., Crombé, P., Fockedey, L., Langohr, R., Meganck, M., Semey, J., Van Strydonck, M., and Verlaeckt, K. (1996). 'The circular view. Aerial photography and the discovery of Bronze Age funerary monuments in East- and West-Flanders (Belgium)', *Germania*, 74/1: 45–94.

Arnoldussen, S. (2008). *A Living Landscape: Bronze Age Settlement Sites in the Dutch River Area (c.2000–800 BC)*. Leiden: Sidestone Press.

—— and Fokkens, H. (eds.) (2008). *Bronze Age Settlements in the Low Countries*. Oxford: Oxbow Books.

Ascadi, G. and Nemeskéri, J. (1970). *History of Human Life Span and Mortality*. Budapest: Akadémiai Kiadó.

Bakels, C. C. (1997). 'The beginnings of manuring in western Europe', *Antiquity*, 71: 442–5.

Bech, J.-H. (1997). 'Bronze Age settlements on raised sea-beds at Bjerre, Thy, NW Jutland', in J. J. Assendorp (ed.), *Forschungen zur bronzezeitlichen Besiedlung in Nord- und Mitteleuropa*. Espelkamp: Marie Leidorf Verlag, 3–15.

Boas, N. A. (1997). 'Settlements and fields covered by sand drift in the Bronze Age, Djursland, East Jutland', in J. J. Assendorp (ed.), *Forschungen zur bronzezeitlichen Besiedlung in Nord- und Mitteleuropa*, Internationale Archäologie, 38. Leopoldshöhe: Marie Leidorf Verlag, 16-28.

Bourgeois, I., Cheretté, B., and Bourgeois, J. (2003). 'Bronze Age and Iron Age settlements in Belgium. An overview', in J. Bourgeois, I. Bourgeois, and B. Cheretté (eds.), *Bronze Age and Iron Age Communities in North-Western Europe*. Brussels: Koninklijke Vlaamse Academie van België voor wetenschappen en kunsten, 175-90.

Bourgeois, J. and Verlaeckt, K. (2001). 'The Bronze Age and Early Iron Age in Western Flanders (Belgium): shifting occupation patterns', in M. Lodewijckx (ed.), *Belgian Archaeology in a European Setting: Album Amicorum Joseph Remi Mertens*, vol. II. Leuven: Universitaire Pers Leuven, 13-22.

——, Verlaeckt, K., and Van Strydonck, M. (1996). 'Belgian Bronze Age chronology: results and perspectives', *Acta Archaeologica*, 67: 141-52.

Bourgeois, Q. P. J. (forthcoming). *The Genesis and Histories of Barrow Groups*. Leiden: Sidestone Press.

—— and Arnoldussen, S. (2006). 'Expressing monumentality: some observations on the dating of Dutch Bronze Age barrows and houses', *Lunula*, 14: 13-25.

—— and Fontijn, D. (2008). 'Bronze Age houses and barrows in the Low Countries', in S. Arnoldussen and H. Fokkens (eds.), *Bronze Age Settlements in the Low Countries*. Oxford: Oxbow Books, 41-58.

Brandt, R. W. (1988). 'Aardewerk uit enkele Bronstijd-nederzettingen in West-Friesland', in J. H. F. Bloemers (ed.), *Archeologie en Oecologie in Holland tussen Rijn en Vlie*. Assen: Von Gorcum, 206-20.

Broeke, P. W. van den (2005). 'IJzersmeden en pottenbaksters, materiële cultuur en technologie', in L. P. Louwe Kooijmans, P. W. van den Broeke, H. Fokkens, and A. L. van Gijn (eds.), *De Prehistorie van Nederland*. Amsterdam: Bert Bakker, 603-26.

Brongers, J. A. (1976). *Air Photography and Celtic Field Research in the Netherlands*, Nederlandse Oudheden, 6. Amersfoort: Rijksdienst voor het oudheidkundig Bodemonderzoek.

Butler, J. J. (1961). 'A Bronze Age concentration at Bargeroosterveld', *Palaeohistoria*, 7: 101-26.

—— (1963). *Bronze Age Connections across the North Sea: A Study in Prehistoric Trade and Industrial Relations between the British Isles, The Netherlands, North Germany and Scandinavia, c.1700-700 BC*, in *Palaeohistoria*, 9. Groningen: Biologisch Archeologisch Instituut.

—— (1990). 'Bronze Age metal and amber in the Netherlands (I)', *Palaeohistoria*, 32: 47-110.

—— (1996). 'Bronze Age metal and amber in the Netherlands (II:1)', *Palaeohistoria*, 37/38: 159-243.

—— and Waals, J. D. van der (1966). 'Bell Beakers and early metal-working in the Netherlands', *Palaeohistoria*, 12: 44-139.

Buurman, J. (1979). 'Cereals in circles. Crop-processing activities in Bronze Age Bovenkarspel (the Netherlands)', in U. Körber-Grohne (ed.), *Festschrift Maria Hopf*, Archaeo-Physika, 8. Bonn: Habelt, 21-37.

Cheretté, B. and Bourgeois, J. (2005). 'Circles for the dead. From aerial photography to excavation of a Bronze Age cemetery in Oedelem (West-Flanders, Belgium)', in J. Bourgeois and M. Meganck (eds.), *Aerial Photography and Archaeology 2003: A Century of Information*. Gent: Academia Press, 255-65.

De Mulder, G., LeClerq, W., and Strydonck, M. van (2008). 'Influence from the "group Rhin-Suisse-France orientale" on the pottery from the Late Bronze Age urnfields in western Belgium. A confrontation between pottery-forming technology, 14C dates and typochronology', in I. Berg (ed.), *Breaking the Mould: Challenging the Past through Pottery*.

Prehistoric Ceramics Research Group: Occasional Paper 6. British Archaeological Reports (International Series), 1,861. Oxford: Archaeopress, 105–15.

Drenth, E. and Lohof, E. (2005). 'Mounds for the dead. Funeray and burial ritual in Beaker period, Early and Middle Bronze Age', in L. P. Louwe Kooijmans, P. W. van den Broeke, H. Fokkens, and A. L. van Gijn (eds.), *The Prehistory of the Netherlands*. Amsterdam: Amsterdam University Press, 433–54.

Essink, M. and Hielkema, J. (1997). 'Rituele depositie van bronzen voorwerpen in Noord-Nederland', *Palaeohistoria*, 39: 277–321.

Fokkens, H. (1997). 'The genesis of urnfields: economic crisis or ideological change?', *Antiquity*, 71: 360–73.

—— (1998). *Drowned Landscape: The Occupation of the Western Part of the Frisian-Drenthian Plateau, 4400 BC–AD 500*. Assen (PhD thesis): Van Gorcum.

—— (1999). 'Cattle and martiality. Changing relations between man and landscape in the Late Neolithic and the Bronze Age', in C. Fabech and J. Ringtved (eds.), *Settlement and Landscape*. Proceedings of a conference in Aarhus, Denmark, 4–7 May 1998. Aarhus: Jutland Archaeological Society, 31–8.

—— (2005a). 'Longhouses in unsettled settlements settlements in the Beaker period and Bronze Age', in L. P. Louwe Kooijmans, P. W. van den Broeke, H. Fokkens, and A. L. van Gijn (eds.), *The Prehistory of the Netherlands*. Amsterdam: Amsterdam University Press, 407–28.

—— (2005b). 'Le Début de l'Âge du Bronze aux Pays-Bas et l'horizon de Hilversum Ancien', in J. Bourgeois and M. Talon (eds.), *L'Âge du Bronze du Nord de la France dans son contexte européen*. Paris: Comité des Travaux Historiques et Scientifiques, 11–33.

—— (2008). 'The temporality of culture changes', in H. Fokkens, B. Coles, A. L. van Gijn, J. P. Kleijne, H. H. Ponjee, and C. G. Slappendel (eds.), *Between Foraging and Farming: An Extended Broad Spectrum of Papers Presented to Leendert Louwe Kooijmans*, Analecta Praehistorica Leidensia, 50. Leiden: Faculty of Archaeology, 15–24.

—— and Arnoldussen, S. (2008). 'Towards new models', in S. Arnoldussen and H. Fokkens (eds.), *Bronze Age Settlements in the Low Countries*. Oxford: Oxbow Books, 1–16.

——, Wijk, I. van, and Jansen, R. (2009). 'Monumenten en herinnering: het grafveld Oss-Zevenbergen in samenhang', in H. Fokkens, I. van Wijk, and R. Jansen (eds.), *Het grafveld Oss-Zevenbergen. Een prehistorisch grafveld ontleed*, Archol Rapport, 50. Leiden: Archol B.V., 209–24.

Fontijn, D. R. (2002). *Sacrificial Landscapes: Cultural Biographies of Persons, Objects and 'Natural' Places in the Bronze Age of the Southern Netherlands, c.2300–600 BC*, Analecta Praehistorica Leidensia, 33/34. Leiden: Leiden University, Institute of Prehistory.

—— (2008). '"Traders' hoards". Reviewing the relationship between trade and permanent deposition: the case of the Dutch Voorhout hoard', in C. Hamon and B. Quillec (eds.), *Hoards from the Neolithic to the Metal Ages in Europe: Technical and Codified Practices*, British Archaeological Reports (International Series), 1,758. Oxford: Archaeopress, 5–17.

—— (2009). 'Land at the other end of the sea? Metalwork circulation, geographical knowledge and the significance of British/Irish imports in the Bronze Age of the Low Countries', in P. Clark (ed.), *Bronze Age Connections: Cultural Contact in Prehistoric Europe*. Oxford: Oxbow Books, 130–49.

—— (2010). 'Mittelbronzezeitliche Kriegergraeber und Waffendeponierungen in Nordbelgien und den Niederlanden', in A. Krenn-Leeb, B. H.-J. Beier, E. F. Klassen, F. Falkenstein, and S. Schwenzer (eds.), *Mobilität, Migration und Kommunikation während des Neolithikums und der Bronzezeit*, Beiträge zur Ur- und Frühgeschichte Mitteleuropas, 53. Langenweissbach: Beier & Beran, 161–9.

—— and Fokkens, H. (2007). 'The emergence of Early Iron Age "chieftains' graves" in the southern Netherlands. Reconsidering transformations in burial and depositional practices', in C. Haselgrove and R. Pope (eds.), *The Early Iron Age in North-West Europe*. Oxford: Oxbow Books, 354–73.

——, Fokkens, H., and Jansen, R. (2002). 'De gietmal van Oss-Horzak en de inheemse bronsproductie in de Midden-bronstijd. Enkele voorlopige resultaten', in H. Fokkens and R. Jansen (eds.), *2000 Jaar bewoningsdynamiek. Brons- en ijzertijdbewoning in het Maas-Demer-Scheldegebied*. Leiden: Faculty of Archaeology, 63–72.

Gerritsen, F. (2003). *Local Identities: Landscape and Community in the Late Prehistoric Meuse-Demer-Scheldt Region*, Amsterdam Archaeological Studies, 9. Amsterdam: Amsterdam University Press.

Gijn, A. L. van (2010). *Flint in Focus: Lithic Biographies in the Neolithic and the Bronze Age*. Leiden: Sidestone Press.

Haveman, E. and Sheridan, J. A. (2006). 'The Exloo necklace: new light on an old find', *Palaeohistoria*, 47/48: 101–39.

Hingh, A. E. de (2000). *Food Production and Food Procurement in the Bronze Age and Early Iron Age (2000–500 BC)*, Archaeological Studies, Leiden University. Leiden: Leiden University Press.

IJzereef, G. F. (1988). 'Boeren in de Bronstijd bij Bovenkarspel', *Spiegel Historiael*, 18: 635–43.

—— and Van Regteren Altena, J. F. (1991). 'Nederzettingen uit de midden- en late bronstijd bij Andijk en Bovenkarspel', in N. Roymans and H. Fokkens (eds.), *Nederzettingen uit de Bronstijd en Vroege IJzertijd in de Lage Landen*, Nederlandse Archeologische Rapporten, 13. Amersfoort: Rijksdienst voor het Oudheidkundig Bodemonderzoek, 61–82.

Impe, L. van (1994). 'Een depot met kokerbijlen uit de Plainseau-cultuur (late Bronstijd) te Heppeneert-Wayerveld (Maaseik, provincie Limburg)', *Archeologie in Vlaanderen*, 4: 7–38.

Jong, T. P. de and Beumer, S. (2011). *Opgraving knooppunt Ekkersrijt-IKEA, gemeente Son en Breugel. Deel II: Prehistorische bewoning in Ekkersrijt*, Archeologisch Centrum Eindhoven Rapport, 52. Eindhoven: Afdeling Archeologie gemeente Eindhoven.

Kersten, W. (1948). 'Die Niederrheinische Grabhügelkultur', *Bonner Jahrbücher*, 148: 5–81.

Kooi, P. B. (1979). *Pre-Roman Urnfields in the North of the Netherlands*. Groningen: Groningen University.

Kroll, H. J. (1987). 'Vor- und frühgeschichtlicher Ackerbau in Archsum auf Sylt, eine botanische Großrestenanalyse', in G. Kossack, O. Harck, and J. Reichstein (eds.), *Archsum auf Sylt, II: Landwirtschaft und Umwelt in vor- und frühgeschichtlicher Zeit*. Mainz am Rhein: Römisch-Germanische Forschungen, 51–158.

Kuijpers, M. H. G. (2008). *Bronze Age Metalworking in the Netherlands (c.2000–800 BC): A Research into the Preservation of Metallurgy-Related Artefacts and the Social Position of the Smith*. Leiden: Sidestone Press.

Lanting, J. N. (1973). 'Laat Neolithicum en Vroege Bronstijd in Nederland en N.W. Duitsland: Continue ontwikkelingen', *Palaeohistoria*, 15: 215–312.

Lohof, E. (1991). *Grafritueel en sociale verandering in de bronstijd van Noordoost-Nederland*. Amsterdam: University of Amsterdam, Albert Egges van Giffen Instituut voor Prae- en Protohistorie.

Louwe Kooijmans, L. P. (1976). 'Local developments in a borderland: a survey of the Neolithic at the Lower Rhine', *Oudheidkundige Mededelingen van het Rijksmuseum van Oudheden te Leiden*, 57: 227–97.

O'Connor, B. (1980). 'Discussion', in B. O'Connor (ed.), *Cross-Channel Relations in the Later Bronze Age: Relations between Britain, North-Eastern France and the Low Countries during the Later Bronze Age and the Early Iron Age, with Particular Reference to the Metalwork*, British Archaeological Reports (International Series), 91. Oxford: Archaeopress, 269–310.

Postma, H., Fontijn, D. R., Schillebeeckx, P., Perego, R. C., and Butler, J. J. (2005). 'Neutron resonance capture analysis of Geistingen axes', *Lunula*, 13: 41–6.

Roymans, N. and Kortlang, F. (1999). 'Urnfield symbolism, ancestors and the land in the Lower Rhine Region', in F. Theuws and N. Roymans (eds.), *Land and Ancestors: Cultural Dynamics in the Urnfield Period and the Middle Ages in the Southern Netherlands*, Amsterdam Archaeological Studies, 4. Amsterdam: Amsterdam University Press, 33–62.

Theunissen, E. M. (1999). *Midden-bronstijdsamenlevingen in het zuiden van de Lage Landen. Een evaluatie van het begrip 'Hilversum-cultuur'*. Leiden: Leiden University, Faculty of Archaeology.

Velde, H. M. van de (2008). 'The Early Bronze Age farmstead of Noordwijk', in S. Arnoldussen and H. Fokkens (eds.), *Bronze Age Settlements in the Low Countries*. Oxford: Oxbow Books, 167–74.

Verlaeckt, K. (1996). *Between River and Barrow: A Reappraisal of Bronze Age Metalwork Found in the Province of East-Flanders (Belgium)*, British Archaeological Reports (International Series), 632. Oxford: Archaeopress.

Verlinde, A. D. (1987). *Die Gräber und Grabfunde der späten Bronzezeit und frühen Eisenzeit in Overijssel*. Leiden: Leiden University, Faculty of Archaeology.

Warmenbol, E. (1988). 'Le Groupe Rhin-Suisse-France orientale et les grottes sépulcrales du Bronze final en Haute Belgique', in P. Brun and C. Mordant (eds.), *Le Groupe Rhin-Suisse-France oriëntale et la notion de la civilisation des Champs d'Urnes*, Mémoires du Musée de Préhistoire d'île-de-France, 1. Nemours: éditions A.P.R.A.I.F., 153–8.

—— (1996). 'L'Or, la mort et les Hyperboréens. La Bouche des Enfers ou le Trou de Han à Han-sur-Lesse', in *Archäologische Forschungen zum Kultgeschehen in der jüngeren Bronzezeit und frühen Eisenzeit Alteuropas. Ergebnisse eines Kolloquiums in Regensburg 4.-7. Oktober 1993*. Bonn: Rudolf Habelt GmbH, 203–35.

Waterbolk, H. T. (1966). 'The Bronze Age settlement of Elp', *Helinium*, 6: 97–131.

—— and Zeist, W. van (1961). 'A Bronze Age sanctuary in the raised bog at Bargeroosterveld (Dr)', *Helinium*, 1: 5–19.

Zimmermann, W. H. (1976). 'Die eisenzeitlichen Ackerfluren—Typ "Celtic Field"—von Flögeln-Haselhörn, Kreis-Wesermünde', *Probleme der Küstenforschung im südlichen Nordseegebiet*, 11: 79–90.

—— (1999). 'Why was cattle-stalling introduced in prehistory? The significance of byre and stable and of outwintering', in C. Fabech and J. Ringtved (eds.), *Settlement and Landscape. Proceedings of a conference in Aarhus, Denmark, 4–7 May 1998*. Aarhus: Jutland Archaeological Society, 301–18.

CHAPTER 32

THE BRONZE AGE IN FRANCE

CLAUDE MORDANT

The Geographical and Cultural Framework

The geographical and cultural region of Bronze Age France is made up of three areas. The first of these provinces is made up of the west-facing Atlantic coast, closely linked to the British Isles, the North Sea countries, and the Iberian Peninsula to the south. The Paris Basin and eastern France are located in the North Alpine area, and southern France has significant links with the Italian world, the Iberian Peninsula (as mentioned), and, more widely, the whole of the western Mediterranean.

The time frame considered here follows the generally accepted French chronology, with the Bronze Age lasting about 15 centuries in total, from 2300 to 800 BC. A classic three-part division of this period will be followed: Early Bronze (2300–1650 BC), Middle Bronze (1650–1350 BC), and Late Bronze (1350–800 BC). The Early Bronze and Middle Bronze Age are each commonly divided into two sub-periods, while the Late Bronze Age is usually split into three.

During the Early Bronze Age (Fig. 32.1a), Armorica (Brittany) and the surrounding area were characterized by a hierarchical society, illustrated by classic groups of burial mounds in the image of the innovative Wessex or Únětice cultures of the European Early Bronze Age. The direct impact of this society might be measured in the Paris Basin and by the limited distribution of metal 'Armorican' products beyond Normandy (Briard 1984). However, in north-western France a great number of tumuli are known from aerial prospection or rescue excavations, and although some of them are of considerable size, more than 40 m in diameter, they do not contain rich burial goods. The circulation of status symbols such as daggers, halberds, and axes is attested by river or isolated finds. So these data suggest also a hierarchical society but with differences in funerary practices and the social consumption of bronze. This zone, Britain and Belgium, and the Netherlands up as far as the Rhine estuary, does not seem to be the driving force behind the invention of metallurgy. Its influences can be seen in domestic architecture (large houses), in funeral monuments and customs (cremations), and in pottery (Bourgeois and Talon 2005).

The Rhône culture, in its strictest sense, occupies the Franche-Comté, eastern Burgundy, the northern Alps close to the Swiss Plateau, and the Valais, but a wider definition of this entity could be said to cover the whole of the Rhône Valley, extending even beyond part of the Massif Central (Gallay 1996). The fact remains that certain types of metallurgy or

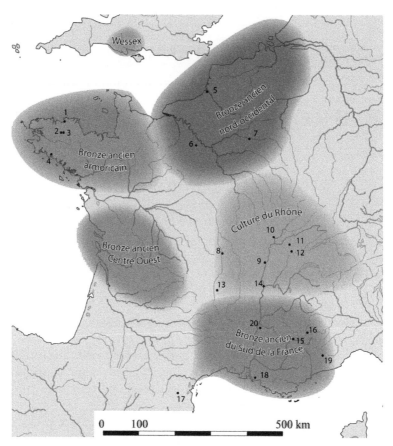

FIG. 32.1.a Bronze Age cultural zones in France in the Early Bronze Age, showing sites mentioned in the text: 1. Lannion, La Motta, 2. Plouvorn, 3. Bourbriac, 4. Quimperlé, 5. Saint-Valéry-sur-Somme; 6. Sorel-Moussel, Fort Harrouard, 7. Bucy / Missy-sur-Aisne, 8. Bègues, 9. Berzé, 10. Genlis et Izier, 11. La Chapelle-sous-Furieuse, Salins, 12. Doucier, Chalain, 13. Dallet, 14. Lyon Vaise, 15. Taburles-en-Avançon, 16. Saint-Véran, 17. Montou, 18. Camp de Laure, 19. Mont-Bégo, 20. Roynac, Le Serre.

Source: after Mordant 2010, fig. 2; Garcia and Vital 2006, fig. 1 (D.A.O. B. Baudoin UMR 55 94 Dijon).

particular characteristics of pottery thought of as 'Rhodanian' spread right across eastern and central France and the Rhône corridor. This highlights the significant impact of metal production, which used metal resources from the western Alps during the late part of the Early Bronze Age. The Italian influence during this early part of the Bronze Age is considered crucial in the evolution of the Early Bronze Age in the south-east of France.

During the Middle Bronze Age (Fig. 32.1b) the metalwork industry sees an increase in large-scale production and witnesses a real qualitative and quantitative leap forward. It is the time of the palstave but also of the invention of first the rapier and then the sword. Technical innovation and manufacture reach areas such as the Seine Valley, the Saône Valley, and the middle Loire, which are lacking in natural resources but are at the heart of trading networks in raw materials.

In western France different metallurgical horizons are based on major bronze hoards. For the first stage of the Middle Bronze Age, these horizons are named after finds at Tréboul,

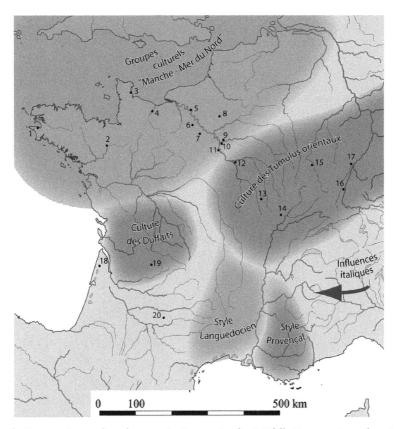

FIG. 32.1.b Bronze Age cultural zones in France in the Middle Bronze Age, showing sites mentioned in the text: 1. Tréboul-en-Douarnenez, 2. Bignan, 3. Tatihou, 4. Nonant, 5. Muids, 6. La Chapelle du Bois-de-Faulx, 7. Sorel-Moussel, Fort Harrouard, 8. Bailleul-sur-Thérain, 9. Bussy-Saint-Georges, 10. Sucy-en-Brie 11. Videlles, 12. Misy-sur-Yonne, 13. Granges-sous-Grignon, 14. Couchey La Rente Neuve, 15. Crévéchamps, 16. Appenwihr, 17. Haguenau, 18. La-Lède-du-Gurp, 19. Les Duffaits La Rochette, 20. Le Noyer.

Muids, and Bailleul, and then for second stage, palstaves, rapiers, and massive bracelets (Bignan type) are typical (Briard 1965). The west coast of France falls within the extensive cultural province referred to as 'Channel-North Sea', which also incorporates the south of England and Flanders. It acquires characteristics of the distribution area of Deverel-Rimbury-type pottery (Marcigny and Ghesquière 2003: Fig. 146).

In the east, indications of the eastern Tumulus culture (pottery with excised decoration, pins, leg-rings) spread to the Paris Basin and the Loire Valley, demonstrating a significant expansion of this cultural group (*Dynamique du Bronze moyen* 1989). Within this cultural process we may include the Duffaits culture, which extended from the Charente region to the Middle Loire and also incorporated Atlantic features (Gomez 1995).

In the south-east, the local Rhodanian element develops, with some northern Alpine influences from the eastern Tumulus culture. Italian influences are clearly visible from Provence to Languedoc (Vital 1999), and slowly filter through from the Languedoc to the Auvergne. Regional characteristics are defined from Quercy to the Pyrenees through the

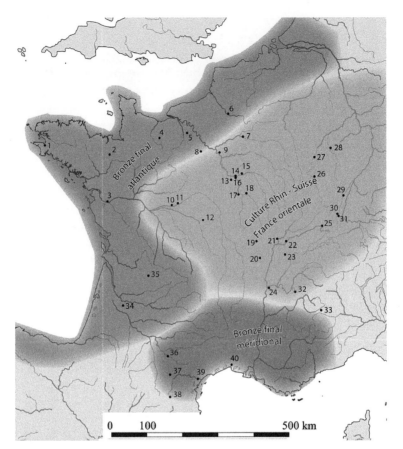

FIG. 32.1.c Bronze Age cultural zones in France in the Late Bronze Age, showing sites mentioned in the text: 1. Rosnoën, 2. Saint-Brieuc-des-Iffs, 3. Nantes, 4. Bernières-d'Ailly, 5. Malleville-sur-le-Bec, 6. Amiens-Le Plainseau, 7. Choisy-au-Bac, 8. Sorel-Moussel, Fort-Harrouard, 9. Paris, 10. Amboise, 11. Onzain, 12. Neuvy-sous-Barangeon, 13. Villethierry, 14. Marolles-sur-Seine, 15. Barbuise-Courtavant/La Saulsotte/La Villeneuve-au-Châtelot, 16. Barbey, 17. Champlay-La Colombine, 18. Migennes, 19. Blanot, 20. Génelard, 21. Chalon-sur-Saône, 22. Evans, 23. Larnaud, 24. Saint-Priest, 25. Dampierre-sur-le-Doubs, 26. Rosières-les-Salines, 27. Maizières-les-Metz, 28. Vaudrevanges, 29. Colmar, 30. Ensisheim, 31. Rixheim, 32. Le Bourget, 33. Sollières, 34. Saint-Denis-de-Pile, 35. Rancogne, 36. Gourjade, 37. Carsac, 38. Llo-Ladre, 39. Mailhac, 40. Tonnerre.

production of polypod vases. Cultural links are also established with the other side of the Pyrenees, from Catalonia to the Basque country.

In southern France, metallurgical production, which was still strong at the start of the Middle Bronze Age (flanged axes), seems to weaken by comparison with productions from the north-western or eastern zones.

With the fourteenth century BC and the transition to the Late Bronze Age (Fig. 32.1c), an east-west cultural divide is established. The Atlantic world witnesses new areas of metalwork (Rosnoën, St Brieuc-des-Iffs, Carp's Tongue swords/Vénat) alongside their English counterparts (Penard, Wilburton, Carp's Tongue swords/Ewart Park) (Briard 1965). This rich body of metal is also found in eastern France in a number of bronze hoards from both dry-land and wet places. Hierarchical societies of the Late Bronze Age in northern France therefore saw abundant metal production, and social consumption of metal placed great emphasis on bronze hoards.

In eastern France the first stage of the Late Bronze Age, which was dependent on the cultural dynamics of the advanced Middle Bronze Age, demonstrates an increase in the importance of cremation in its funeral customs alongside more traditional methods of burial (for example, burials in cists). A good indicator of this period is rilled-ware pottery, which expands widely into eastern cultures within France. Along the Saône-Rhône axis, these ceramic shapes along with rilled decoration come into contact with styles that are very similar but of different origin, and can be compared with the Late Bronze Age in northern Italy.

The Atlantic Bronze Age achieves its maximum visibility during the middle and later stages of the Late Bronze Age (eleventh–twelfth century BC), while the Rhine-Switzerland-eastern France culture (Rhin-Suisse-France orientale, or RSFO) establishes itself over a wide area, from the Paris Basin to the Rhine. This culture is characterized in particular by the systematic practice of cremation ('urnfields') but also by fine incised and combed decorated pottery. The impact of this RSFO culture (or of some of its products) is also strongly felt in the Rhône Valley and the Languedoc, where regional development continues on the basis of the previous Italian and Languedoc influences (Guilaine 1972). This wide distribution of 'RSFO type-fossils' should not be interpreted using the obsolete Urnfield diffusionist perspective, but put in the context of trading and competition between regional cultures (Brun and Mordant 1988). On the north-west coast of France strong links continue between the provinces bordered by the Channel, and they develop in the form of structural continuity in the Channel-North Sea cultural complex. At the end of this period, during the ninth century BC, smaller cultural groups begin to establish themselves on a national scale. A 'central France' group, extending from Savoie to the Charente, marks a southerly shift in cultural dynamics, until then strongly focused along the east-west axis.

The dual cultural nature of northern France, containing elements of both the Atlantic and the northern Alps cultural identities, is now well established, but our current understanding of cultural dynamics in the south is rather weak; in fact, the importance of Italian connections (and Pyrenean ones) needs further explanation. By contrast, the Mailhacien culture, and its extension to the south-west (and also the south-east), gives a good picture of the dynamism of the cultures of the south at the end of the Late Bronze Age and the transition to the Iron Age (Janin 2009).

Settlements and the Use of Space

The Early Bronze Age is rather warm and dry compared to the Middle Bronze Age, which is cooler and damper. The start of the Late Bronze Age remains similar, but there is a drier period during the middle stage before the significant deterioration of conditions during the ninth century BC. These variations affected people's lives, especially those living in susceptible areas such as lakeshores, low-lying alluvial or coastal plains, and mid-altitude mountains (Magny and Peyron 2008). For the lake dwellings of the Early and Late Bronze Age, the cycles of occupation are closely linked to these climatic shifts, but cultural choice is also involved. During the Middle Bronze Age new subsistence strategies developed, focused more on livestock, in response to these climatic factors in the mid-altitude Basque mountains or in Forez (Carozza and Galop 2008). The extent of relocation of the population caused by these climate changes is difficult to assess, but all coastal and lakeside areas would have been permanently deserted during the second half of the ninth century BC.

We know of settlements on the banks of the Jura lakes (Chalain, Clairvaux) and of the Savoie lakes (Léman, Bourget, Annecy) (Billaud and Marguet 2009). These types of settlement also appear on the banks of lagoons in the Languedoc like Maugio and Thau. Similar settlements are established on riverbanks, such as on the Saône at Chalon-Gué-des-Piles or Ouroux (Bonnamour 2000), the Seine in Paris (Port-St Bernard), and the Hérault in Agde (Moyat, Dumont, and Mariotti 2005).

Wood and Earth Constructions

These constructions dominated in their societies but they are very unevenly preserved, except in certain exceptional wetland sites; so it is usually only postholes that survive. Stone constructions are not widely known and there are only a few at this time, even in limestone areas. There are constructions of ellipsoid plan in the Chalcolithic tradition from the very start of the Early Bronze Age in Provence at Simiane-Collongue (Bouches-du-Rhône), and even from the very end of the Late Bronze Age at Malvieu (Hérault), with stone walls and houses.

The recent excavation of Laprade in the Vaucluse has revealed the use of mud-brick and clay in the construction of rectangular houses with apsidal ends (measuring 5 x 10 m maximum), from the middle phase of the Late Bronze Age (Fig. 32.2c). More widely, the recent excavations of Languedoc settlements show an area marked out with simple rectangular buildings, formed of structural posts and earth (Burrens-Carroza, Carozza, and De Chazelles 2005).

Domestic buildings also use a system of raised and levelled soleplate construction (Catenoy, Choisy-au Bac). On the whole, this technique is more susceptible to erosion and remains under-reported.

In the eastern area, these numerous post buildings are of modest size (40 to 60 m^2 surface area) and are most frequently rectangular (length 6–10 m, width 4–5 m: Mordant 2008). These simple one-storey constructions have roofing either in two sections or with a rounded top, or even an apse. The unusual nature of some house plans adds weight to the theory that they had an upper storey (Rosières-les-Salines, Meurthe-et-Moselle). Large buildings with apses from the Early Bronze Age in Genlis-Izier (Côte-d'Or, eastern Burgundy) (length 26 m) remain exceptional (Fig. 32.2a). In the western region, recent finds show a widespread use of typically British circular constructions between 6 and 10 m in diameter (Cahagnes; Malleville-sur-le-Bec), but quadrangular layouts also exist (e.g. Nonant: Marcigny and Ghesquière 2008) (Fig. 32.3).

The Arrangement of the Settlement: From Farm to Village

The isolated farmstead is in keeping with the recurrent model of the Bronze Age in France. In its classic structure the fragmented farm is made up of one building for residential use plus annexes: raised attics or small barns, and some storage facilities (and sometimes wells, in Alsace and Lorraine). These farms were most commonly unenclosed, but on the Atlantic coast they were sometimes enclosed and integrated into networks of criss-crossing ditches surrounding farm plots. From the Early/Middle Bronze Age onwards it would therefore be easy to reconstruct a picture of partitioned and hedged farmland in the west, in contrast to the more open plains and plateaus of eastern France. The large houses of Genlis-Yzier might

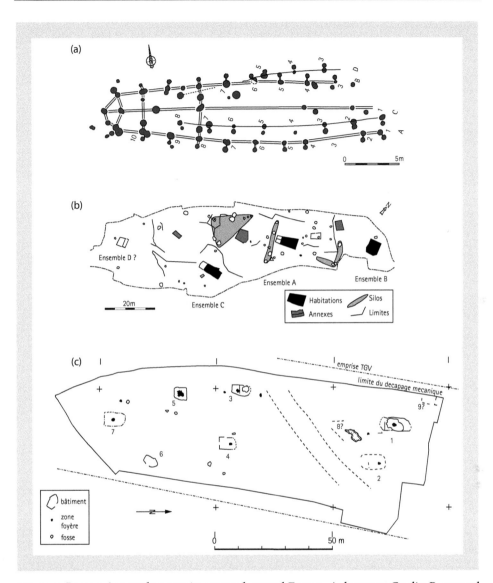

FIG. 32.2 Bronze Age settlements in east and central France. A. house at Genlis; B. general plan of the Early Bronze Age settlement of Lyon-Périphérique Nord; C. general plan of the Late Bronze Age settlement of Laprade.

Drawings: author, after Dartevelle 1996, Vital 2008 and Billaud 2005.

suggest a type of 'block' farm that is rare in France, with long buildings housing both livestock and people, on the lines of those often seen from Flanders to Scandinavia.

The hamlet, the first stage of grouped settlement, is formed by the aggregation of several contemporary elements but, as sites consist of scatters of postholes, demonstrating the actual coexistence of different buildings is often problematical. This model is attested in some cases during the Early Bronze Age (Lyon or Roynac-le Serre: Vital 2008: Figs. 2–3, 7) and is more common during the Late Bronze Age (second and third stages).

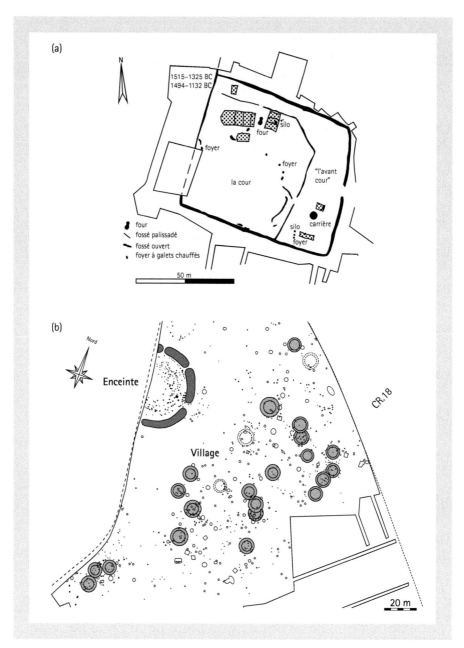

FIG. 32.3 Bronze Age settlements in the West of France. A. plan of the Middle Bronze Age farm of Nonant; B. plan of the Final Bronze Age village of Malleville-sur-le-Bec.

Drawings: author, after Marcigny and Ghesquière 2008, Marcigny et al. 2005.

The well-known village of Dampierre-sur-Doubs (Doubs) is best seen as a palimpsest of several phases of hamlets, more or less superimposed on each other. In the western area, where there was a different architectural tradition of circular houses, the groups of houses around a ring-fort at Malleville-sur-le Bec, or at Cahagnes, might also be interpreted as hamlets (Marcigny and Ghesquière 2008: Fig. 8) or villages (see Fig. 32.3).

The organized village, the most complex type, is only easily reconstructed in lakeshore sites where wood conservation allows the use of dendrochronology. These sites have been discovered on the banks of Lake Léman (Chens/Tougues), Lake Annecy (Sévrier), and Lake Bourget (Grésine), but also in the lagoon environment of the Languedoc (Thau and Maugio pools).

The settlements of Gué-des-Piles in Chalon-sur-Saône (Bonnamour 2000), Ouroux (Saône-et-Loire), and Choisy-au-Bac (Blanchet 1984: Figs. 241–3) are similar to the model. These settlements on riverbanks, with quadrangular houses in rows, close to a ford or a river confluence, highlight the strategic importance of a watercourse for their establishment. This would also demonstrate a major similarity between settlements on the banks of rivers and those on the shores of lakes. For these organized villages, trade and the need for access to fresh food supplies, wood, and metal, seem to be the driving force behind the decision to live in larger communities. A stronger social control is imperative for this way of life as compared to the contemporary isolated hamlets or farms. This higher level of organization does not seem to be standard in all agriculturally exploited areas (e.g. the Paris Basin).

Upland Settlements

Argilo-limestone environments, or *cuestas*, encourage the creation of fortified upland settlements, such as *éperons barrés* (spurs or ridges with cross-dykes) and protected hills. Some of these excavated sites date mainly to the Late Bronze Age, for example Etaules-le-Châtelet or Vitteaux-Myard (Côte-d'Or, eastern Burgundy). The Laure settlement at Rove (Bouches-du-Rhône), featuring a wall with tower and protected entrance, has been attributed to the early years of the Early Bronze Age.

Clearly identifiable but often not well dated, upland settlements are regarded as central sites in the pattern of land occupation. This is true of sites such as Fort-Harrouard on the Eure, or St-Pierre-en-Chastres, at the confluence of the Oise and the Aisne, Carsac on the Aude, and Camp Allaric on the Clain. However, in a region favourable to this type of settlement, like eastern France, not all such sites can be put into this category. For many, it is necessary rather to think of an adaptation of agricultural activity to a dry plateau environment, so that such sites can be compared instead with farms or hamlets. Excavations have shed much light on the ramparts, the first of which are established during the Middle Neolithic, with successive rebuilding taking place during the Late Neolithic, the Early Bronze Age, the Late Bronze Age, and finally the Iron Age. Etaules is a good example of such a sequence, with houses built for the most part along the inside of the wall.

The enclosed area varies from a few hectares to 20 hectares, as does the strength of the ramparts. The population density seems to vary from site to site. Dense occupation can be seen, for example at Catenoy (Oise) at the edge of the corniche (Blanchet 1984: Fig. 199), and at Fort-Harouard near the rampart (Mohen and Bailloud 1987), but we might ask whether we could extrapolate this density of occupation for the whole surface area of such plateaux in all cases.

These naturally protected, upland sites are often linked to periods of crisis and insecurity. Their frequency in the ninth century BC may be linked to the sociocultural changes that paved the way for the Iron Age.

Controlled Land and Territories

The recent discoveries of moated systems and 'boundaries' from the Bronze Age in Normandy (Val de Saire, île de Tatihou; Marcigny and Ghesquière 2003) allow useful comparisons to be made with 'reaves' in southern England, particularly in Devon. On the continent this system, established from the start of the Middle Bronze Age, implies structured social land management by the elite for its successful implementation and upkeep. Beyond this Atlantic fringe such linear organization is lacking, and the demarcation of farmed and controlled areas proves more difficult. There is very little information relating to the 'fields' of the Bronze Age, such as the traces of 'ridge' cultivation in Lède-du-Gurp (Gironde) from the Middle Bronze Age, or the carved schematic representations at Mont Bégo or the Camonica Valley.

The 'dikes' of the Cotentin Peninsula in La Hague (Manche), or those within the meander of the Seine at Jumièges (Seine-Maritime), form huge enclosed areas protected by a rampart: 3,500 hectares at La Hague and 1,300 hectares at Jumièges. This strategy for laying out territories with natural borders appears now for the first time in France, but had previously been seen across the Channel and in Ireland.

Domestic farms used restricted territories (from 100 to 300 hectares) in a different way in the Late Bronze Age (and probably well before), both on plateaux (e.g. the regional airport of Lorraine and western Gâtinais) and in valleys (for example, Ferme-d'Île, Grisy-sur-Seine). During the tenth century BC the appearance of more stable hamlets within these areas exerts real demographic pressure on the available space; the focus changes to the use of land by one or more families.

Residences of an upper class are hardly perceptible in such a dispersed settlement model, and hypotheses about the extent of territories controlled by the elite are often based on the geography of cemeteries. Spatial analysis of the burial mounds of Early Bronze Age chiefdoms in Brittany suggests burial areas on a modest scale, with a radius of only 5 to 20 km despite the notable prestige of the people buried there (Brun 1998: Fig. 7). Other reconstructions of Late Bronze Age cemeteries in western Burgundy at the confluence of the Seine/Aube/Yonne suggest similar settlement scales, with a radius of approximately 20 km (Mordant 2008).

Joel Vital suggests that in the Early Bronze Age in the Rhône Valley some territorial units should be recognized around tributaries of the Rhône, such as the Drôme or the Roubion. These areas contain several types of pastoral unit potentially farmed by the same human groups. The scale of these territories reaches about 2,000 km². The same author proposes that indispensable complementary resources were to be found in the high Alps, like the copper sources of Oisans or transhumance routes and summer pastures (Vital 2008: Fig. 9). Carsac is located in a similar strategic position with respect to different ecological zones in the Aude Valley, in a centrally located position (Guilaine et al. 1986).

Indications of bronze manufacture (such as furnaces, cast bronze objects, or casting debris), which might indicate the importance of certain sites, are very rare. Fort Harrouard is one of them. The recently discovered 'aristocratic' residence at Villiers-sur-Seine (Seine-et-Marne), dated to the very end of the period, has given some indications of bronze casting (R. Peake in Mordant 2008).

The farming of complementary ecosystems in the lower plains and the mountains requires specific sites such as sheepfold-caves or pasture sheds. The long occupation of these sites, which for some began in the Neolithic Age, continued during the Bronze Age. Sollières-Sardières, Maurienne, and Montou in the eastern Pyrenees are good examples of this. Transhumance enables people to integrate their territory on a seasonal basis over a scale that exceeds the few dozen kilometres occupied by sedentary populations in the plains. It is vital to take this into account for all lower and middle parts of the Massif Central, and for the Mediterranean, Alpine, and Pyrenean periphery, particularly during the Middle Bronze Age when investment in livestock becomes more prominent (Carozza and Galop 2008).

The continued use of caves during the Bronze Age is a recurrent feature and their use by the population ranges from stopovers (occasional or regular) to places of refuge, but also for cult and funerary practices (Manem 2010).

Funerary Practice and Beliefs

Diversity of Practices by Period and Area

The large burial mounds of Early Bronze Age Armorica (Brittany), the most spectacular of which are 40 to 50 m wide and up to 5 to 6 m in height (for example Kernonen-en-Plouvorn, Bourbriac, Côtes-d'Armor), and the very size and the richness of their grave goods (daggers, axes, halberds, gold or silver, amber, faience, as seen for example at St Adrien, Plouvorn), represent a peak in hierarchical society. These monuments are reserved for the burial of a single individual, usually a man, carefully placed in the middle of large built chambers (Kernonen-en-Plouvorn) which sometimes incorporate megalithic elements in the construction of sealed cists (Lannion, La Motta). The few instances of privileged childrens' tombs (e.g. Kersaint-Plabannec) are perhaps to be seen as sign of the hereditary transmission of power. This funerary and social custom develops in the Armorican Massif and on the border with Normandy from around 2000 to 1500 BC, with a decline in these structures and offerings over time (Briard 1984). North-western France is also characterized by burial mounds, but often only their outer ditch has survived erosion (e.g. Bucy-Le-Long/Missy-sur-Aisne). Burials and cremations are present in these monuments but funeral offerings are either very limited or absent, however the diameter of the circular enclosures can reach spectacular dimensions of up to 100 m. Funerary urns, which are sometimes large, are similar to those from southern England or Flanders (see Bourgeois and Talon 2005). Cremation cemeteries that house urns or contain organic matter are also present throughout the whole of the western area (in Picardy and Île-de-France in particular).

In the eastern area small burial mounds from the Early Rhodanian Bronze Age (6–8 m in diameter, 1 m in height) are found in Franche-Comté (Champagnole, La Rivière-Drugeon), and in eastern Burgundy (Berzé). Certain cists and megalithic monuments remain in use during the first part of the Early Bronze Age, from Burgundy to the Grands Causses, like caves, which continue to be used for funerary purposes.

In eastern Burgundy (Précy-le-Sec, Côte-d'Or) or the eastern Languedoc (Beaucaire-Canteperdix) individual burial was practised, either in pits adapted for the purpose or in individual cists, either laid flat, semi-flexed, or in very contracted positions. Often found alone or in small numbers, these tombs are concentrated in large cemeteries, each housing several dozen individuals, for instance in Marchal-Dallet or in Chantemerle-Gerzat (Puy-de-Dôme).

On the whole, during the Early Bronze Age, metal grave goods remain few but are representative of the gender and status of individuals: daggers, axes, pins for men, and jewellery only for women.

Middle Bronze Age burial practices in the Armorican region remain largely unknown after the abandonment of burial mounds in these regions. In the north-west, cremation cemeteries continue to be used with similar austerity in grave goods, at the most a funeral vase, and no metal (e.g. Bussy-St Georges) (Mordant et Depierre 2005). In eastern France the burial mound becomes commonplace. It houses several tombs, mainly inhumations but also cremations, which become more common towards the end of the period. Accompanying ornaments are abundant, with obvious gender distinctions: weapons (daggers, axes, arrowheads) for men, and jewellery (pins, bracelets, beads, pendants) for women. There is an abundance of Baltic amber beads and pendants whose presence highlights the establishment of trading networks from far afield. The cemeteries in the Forêt de Haguenau are the archetypal funerary sites of this period. Their construction took place over a long period of time, from the Early to the Late Bronze Age, but with a marked development during the Middle Bronze Age, on the lines of what is seen in southern Germany during this period (*Dynamique du Bronze moyen* 1989). This model is adopted in Lorraine, eastern Burgundy, and the Franche-Comté.

During the Late Bronze Age a clear shift towards cremation can be seen across the whole of north-eastern France, but in the west considerable continuity is maintained, with the same rules, and extremely poor grave goods: few or no urns, and very occasionally small bronze items such as the peculiar Atlantic-style 'hair-rings' (Billand and Talon 2007), made out of bronze or sometimes gold-plated, which appear from the middle period onwards. While this cremation practice is introduced at this time in the eastern area (1150–950 BC), it was established throughout the course of the fourteenth and thirteenth centuries BC alongside burials in various styles in the south of the île-de-France and in the contact zone between the Atlantic and north Alps regions. It is within this context that cemeteries with highly contracted cists are established, such as those in Marolles-les Gours-aux-Lions (Seine-et-Marne) (Mordant and Mordant 1970), Barbey-Les Cent Arpents (Seine-et-Marne), or Barbuise-La Saulsotte (Aube). The creation of burial mounds is reserved for important people, often men, who were richly provided for and sometimes accompanied by a sword (Courtavant, 'Morel grave'), but also, in some cases, by precision weighing equipment (assay balance, small weights) (see Chapter 29). Other remarkable objects of this type have been found with burials without such ostentatious funeral monuments, as at Migennes (Yonne) (Fig. 32.4).

In the eastern area the consistent appearance of cremation during the middle period constitutes a defining characteristic of the Rhine-Switzerland-eastern France culture, in line with the diffusionist 'Urnfield' model. Since the Nemours conference of 1986, these concepts have been abandoned in France, except to illustrate the specific, even dominant place that cremation occupies in Late Bronze Age funeral practice. During this period, the standardization of the funeral rite is accompanied by a move away from metal grave goods and an abandonment of monuments. Any variation is in the presence or absence of urns, and the number of pots provided.

The ninth century BC sees the reappearance of burials in the eastern zone, with, in some instances, newly raised mounds, certain of which, such as that found in St-Romain-de-Jalionas (Isère), at the foot of Camp Larina, are very imposing (50 m in diameter, 5 m in height). Its central male burial chamber, complete with sword and a rich display of bronze tableware (situla, goblet, cup), marks the final stages of the Late Bronze Age, around 800 BC. Smaller monuments, around 10 m wide, exist in eastern France with central or peripheral burials and cremations.

In western Languedoc the arrival of the Mailhacien culture goes hand in hand with the development of huge cremation cemeteries like the recently published examples of Mailhac or Castres (Giraud, Pons, and Janin 2003). These highly structured sites often include small funeral monuments (mounds and/or enclosures), genuine 'familial' burial plots with spaces between them to allow movement. Cemeteries develop, with concentrated tomb areas becoming displaced from the ninth through to the sixth century BC.

In southern France the funerary use of caves continues throughout the Bronze Age, with inhumations and cremations featuring a more or less structured deposition, as is indicated by collective family graves like that at Sindou (Lot), belonging to the Late Bronze Age.

Thus, while individual graves are as a rule the most common in Bronze Age France, there is also evidence of simultaneous or successive multiple burials throughout the whole period. The increase in bioarchaeological studies of cremations frequently also indicates the presence of the remains of several individuals in the same urn, as one cremation followed another (adults, children) (Mordant et Depierre 2005).

Sanctuaries and Ritualized Cult Practices

The topic of sanctuaries and other places of worship has not been widely explored in France. Some large, ditched, rectangular monuments are built within cemeteries at the end of the period: at Acy-Romance (Ardennes), Aulnay-aux-Planches (Marne), and La Villeneuve-aux-Châtelot (Aube), for example. The architecture of these *Langgraben* (long ditched graves) recalls several examples in the Lower Rhine area and Westphalia where they are interpreted as founders' burials. In France they are often considered as sanctuaries because no graves exist inside the monuments, and hoards of high-quality pottery are frequently discovered in the bottom of the ditches, as at La Villeneuve-au-Châtelot.

Recent discoveries of numerous metal artefacts also support a cult interpretation of these finds. A good example, dating to the fourteenth century BC, is provided by the dozens of bronze fragments (axes, ingots, weapons, pins) found in the Salins Valley (Jura). These were discovered in 'unusual' locations (in the cracks of rocks, at the foot of cliffs, in *lapiaz*, or grooved limestone surfaces in karst regions: Piningre and Grut 2009). This situation mirrors the abandonment of functional objects in the fords of large rivers (Seine, Loire, Vilaine) and in springs and marsh areas (Bonnamour 2000). These observations lend credibility to the identification of contemporary ritual practices in connection with the gods or spirits of the area, without the architecturally impressive structures of sanctuaries.

Spatial research into hoards also supports the theory that both artefacts and funerary monuments were used to demarcate territory, as a recent theory about central Brittany suggests (Fily 2008). The existence of territorially significant places (related to water, to landscape, to *lieux de mémoire*) reflects people's hidden identity principles.

Recent research into the occupation of the karst caves in La Rochefoucault in the Charente region during the Middle Bronze Age also favours such cult interpretations of how groups of people come together, in contrast to interpretations that see such places as domestic or places of refuge (Manem 2010).

Alpine sites with engravings, including the famous Early Bronze Age Mont Bégo, also fall into this category of sacred places. The themes depicted consist of weapons (daggers, axes, and halberds) as well as representations of cattle, other quadrupeds, and in rare cases even humans (De Lumley 1995) (see Chapter 16).

At the end of the Late Bronze Age, from the centre-west to Languedoc, pictograms that are more or less understandable, and made by incision or by means of the application of thin strips of tin, appear in the decoration of certain types of plate, bowl, and urn: zigzags, sun motifs, quadrupeds, humans, and chariots. These surely reflect the recording of scenes and ritual practices. The Iberian-style figurative stele found in Buoux in the Vaucluse underlines

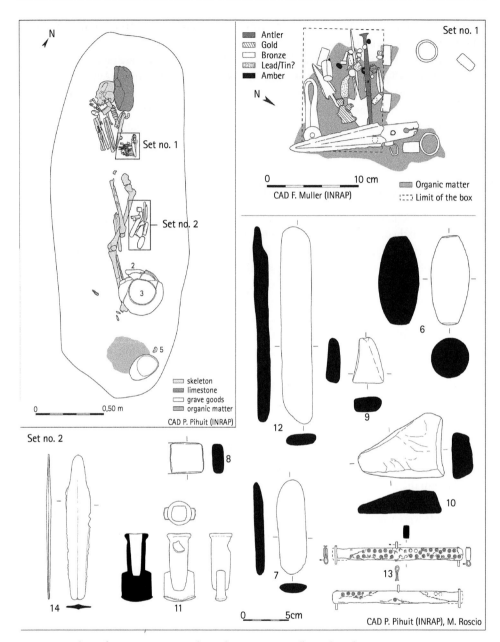

FIG. 32.4 Plan of Late Bronze Age burial at Migennes (burial 298).

Drawing: author, after Muller *et al.* 2007.

not only the enlargement of the role of the warrior, his heroization even, but also the impact of Iberian influences in Provence.

Stefan Wirth has recently provided an explanation of the theme of the *Vogelsonnenbark* (sun-boat decorated with birds), seen on Hajdúböszörmény-style situlae. This symbol of Late Bronze Age pan-European mythology can be found in France on breastplates from Fillinges and on situlae from St Romains-de-Jalionas. Protomes of swans or aquatic birds are often used by bronze craftsmen (Wirth 2006).

Metal Production

Metalliferous Resources

In France knowledge of early Chalcolithic metallurgy of the third millennium BC has progressed significantly with studies of the Cabrières (Hérault) mining district, which has allowed the metal production of this region to be placed in the context of its Iberian and Mediterranean contemporaries (Guilaine 2007). During the Early Bronze Age the possible areas of copper mining are primarily in the Alps (see Chapter 24). In the south this includes the mines at St-Véran (Hautes-Alpes), which were in use at various points between 2200 and 1700 BC. In the north mines dating back to between the nineteenth and seventeenth centuries BC have recently been discovered at high altitude (2,500–2,800 m) in Oisans (Vital 2009). This confirmation of the importance of the western Alps raises again the question of relations or competition with the Valais during the time of the first metal production in the Early Rhodanian Bronze Age.

The direct dating of mining remains difficult, but recent palaeo-environmental studies of peat stratigraphies have clearly identified indications of metallic palaeo-pollutants, mainly those linked to lead. The most revealing works can be seen in the Morvan around Bibracte, which were in use from the Early Bronze Age and then at the start of the Late Bronze Age (fourteenth century BC: Monna et al. 2004a), and in the Basque country (Quinto Réal) during the Late Bronze Age (Monna et al. 2004b). In this context, the old question of the copper sources of the Armorican Massif resurfaces, because geologically the possibilities are the same.

As for tin, reference is always made to the classic deposits in Finistère, Morbihan, and the Atlantic Loire, mirroring those in Cornwall, which also supplied the continent. It is also important to remember the possibilities offered by the Limousin in the Creuse and the Morvan in the Autun area (Saône-et-Loire), where extensive mining work has recently been shown to have taken place in antiquity.

These new data suggest a greater potential for access to metallurgical innovations thanks to the variety of local resources. However, several regions rely heavily on external sources, particularly sedimentary basins. Even if all these recent findings enable a better appreciation of areas suitable for mining, they do not reveal anything about the processes of ore reduction and ingot production. No indications of large operations like those in the Austrian Alps or the Trentino survive. Different technologies using direct-reduction furnaces of modest size are suggested by the findings from excavation (for example, Cabrières, St-Véran) and from experiments.

Ingots and Semi-Finished Products

Some 'semi-finished products' are specific, such as the miniature examples from Montalivet with very flat edges from Late Neolithic/Early Bronze Age Médoc, or the 'semi-finished axes' in the Granges style (Burgundy) that originate in the Languedoc region and are distributed along the Rhône corridor at the start of the Middle Bronze Age. Most flat axes are still poorly dated and their cultural attribution is uncertain.

The extent of copper-trading networks is well illustrated by the Cap Hornu hoard from north of St-Valéry-sur-Somme (Somme), where 71 bar ingots in the form of basket handles (*Spangenbarren*) confirm that distribution originated in centres in the northern Alpine periphery. This new find indicates also the wide influence of the Únětician culture in areas far to its west.

The most common ingot type, plano-convex, found from the Middle to the Late Bronze Age, is often said to be of eastern origin, from the eastern Alps in the Carpathian area. The heavy double-axe from the Late Bronze Age hoard in Larnaud (Jura) suggests Italian connections originating from the southern Alpine foothills.

Bronze Production

There is limited information available about the sites where bronze production took place: Fort-Harrouard remains the only example cited regularly, with its remarkable collection of Late Bronze Age clay moulds, tuyère fragments, and hearths. A new set of clay moulds for lozenge-shaped scabbards from the middle stage of the Late Bronze Age has been recovered from the unenclosed site of Aubervilliers in the suburbs of Paris. These show a fine mastery of fine core-based casting during this period.

Tools for metallurgy are found in hoards such as Génelard (Saône-et-Loire) or Larnaud (Jura), but the spatial organization of the craftsman's workshop remains speculative. A new interest has recently developed in the stone tools of metalworkers (hammers, cushion stones, anvils). A remarkable collection originates from burial 298 at Laroche-Migennes (Yonne), including a bronze-handled hammer, a cushion stone or anvil in the shape of a barrel, four small metal plates, and a long 'abrader' made of fine stoneware. These were found in a young man's grave together with weighing equipment (see Fig. 32.4).

The distinction between objects moved over long distances and local copies has recently been addressed using morphometric analysis combined with statistical and chemical analysis (Gabillot et al. 2009). This new method, tested on Norman and Breton palstaves from the hoard in Sermizelles (Yonne), lends credibility to the theory of regional production of 'western' palstaves, echoing the signs of palaeo-pollution identified in Morvan relating to the fourteenth century BC (see above, Monna et al. 2004a).

Elementary chemical analysis conducted on entire hoards like Farébersviller leads to the identification of specific alloy formulae, an extension of the studies of Valentin Rychner. Eastern and Atlantic forms are distinct in their tin and lead content, and in their impurity patterns. This analysis also provides information about the organization of the casting, through evidence of different types of 'composition twins' in ingots, crucibles, and castings of identical and different types of object (Veber 2009).

All these metallurgical findings indicate the great mastery of the smith in the creation of massive metal objects, from the simplest (axes) to the most complex, using cores (wheels and chariot pieces: Coulon, Onzain) but also in the fine core-based casting of the Late Bronze Age, as with the lozenge-shaped scabbards at Aubervilliers in the suburbs of Paris, or the large bracelets and ankle-rings in the Vaudrevanges style.

Technical observations confirm the regular use of the lost-wax process, especially for pieces of jewellery or weaponry. Evidence of the use of the wax-turning technique in the creation of trial versions of some pins with large globular heads is clearly identified in the Villethierry hoard (Mordant and Prampart 1976).

Work carried out using plastic deformation during the Late Bronze Age leads to the creation of exceptional pieces such as helmets (Bernières d'Ailly, Pont-à-Mousson, Chalon-sur-Saône), armour (Marmesse, St-Germain-du-Plain, Fillinges), and vessels (Evans). There are issues in identifying production centres for these remarkable products, because even though it is possible to recognize some examples of cauldrons (with cross-shaped handles) or cups in the Kirkendrup style as imports (e.g. Blanot, Evans), the difficult distinction between local products and imitations reopens the question of the mobility of craftsmen and the spread of technology. The remarkable discoveries at Evans (Jura) and neighbouring assemblages reinforce the theory of the Val de Saône as an active area in the production of these luxury goods.

Hoards

The overall distribution of hoard finds in France provides a general picture, but there are certain valleys where there is a greater concentration of finds, such as the Seine, Somme, Saône, and Loire, and even smaller regions that have been intensively prospected and controlled, such as the Salins area in the Jura (Piningre and Grut 2009), and central Brittany (Fily 2008). Although the picture is highly dependent on survey conditions and recording, as these two examples show, the picture supports the idea of systematic hoarding, not only in regions that are rich in metal sources, such as the Alps, but also the Paris Basin, which is completely lacking in such resources. A general presence of this phenomenon can also be seen to a lesser extent in the south, even if certain areas of the Rhône Basin weaken this assertion. The distribution map also highlights the main lines of movement of manufactured objects and of trade, along the major axial lines of the Seine, the Loire, and the Saône-Rhône corridor.

In France today there is a tendency to consider any discovery of artefacts, whether isolated or grouped, in the ground or in water, as a hoard. This broad recognition emphasizes the variety of practices seen in individual items, which range from status goods such as swords or defensive equipment found in rivers, to modest collections of miscellaneous fragments, often called 'foundry' pieces.

Another type of interpretation is linked to size, identifying small and large hoards and estimating the volume of bronze in circulation, and therefore the amount being hoarded. A recent overall estimation of the volume of bronze from all known hoards has suggested a figure of at least six tonnes (Pennors 2005).

French hoards of the Early Bronze Age are modest in relation to their Únětician counterparts, and while the scale of burial mounds or the richness of certain funerary offerings can rival those of central Germany, hoards often consist of individual pieces found in rivers or small collections of axes, either on their own (Bègues/Allier) or found together with daggers (La Bâtie-Neuve-Les Tarbules/Hautes-Alpes).

During the Middle Bronze Age the notion of large-scale production is clearly illustrated by hoards: they reflect this change in the scale of production and the technical success of foundry workers. Palstaves are found in large numbers (sometimes up to several hundred) in hoards in Brittany and Normandy (Gabillot 2003), as are collections of bracelets (Bignan, Île-de-France, Vinols). The Médoc phenomenon, with its homogeneous collection of flanged axes, highlights the success and originality of the Gironde region, completely lacking in resources but at the centre of long-distance trade networks—perhaps maritime? The typological particularity of this production also raises questions in an Atlantic context where the palstave model dominates. It is from this time that hoards of gold objects appear, some of which are unique, such as the Avanton gold cone (Vienne), the Villeneuve St-Vistre vessels (Marne), or the Rongères Cup (Allier) (Eluère 1983).

FIG. 32.5 Bronze hoards recently discovered in France. A. detail of female jewellery and ornaments deposited in a pot at Mathay. Photo: J. F. Piningre; B. bronze and amber jewellery of the 'dépôt de La Motte à Agde' found in the river Hérault.

Photo: Philippe Moyat.

During the Late Bronze Age the fragmentation of bronze objects is systematically practised in western areas, but less so in the east. This area is characterized by 'personalized' hoards with very 'feminine' offerings, such as those from Blanot in the Late Bronze Age (Thevenot 1991) where jewellery and luxury vessels are prevalent, or those with 'masculine' offerings such as those in Neuvy-sous-Barangeon/Petit-Village, Venarey-les Laumes, Vaudrevanges, where swords are prevalent.

In the recently discovered Mathay hoard (Doubs) a single vase was found containing an extraordinary linked belt, a set of bracelets and pendants, hundreds of glass and bronze beads, and small gold-plated beads: this is a collection of female jewellery belonging to the Blanot tradition (Fig. 32.5).

These fine collections of female jewellery (linked belts and pendants, bracelets, torcs) are also characteristic of hoards from the middle stage of the Late Bronze Age in the southern Alps (St-André-de Méouilles, Bénévent-en-Champsaur, Réallon, Moriez). The exceptional hoard at Agde, with its assortment of bronze, amber, and glass female jewellery, confirms that this practice is still current in the populations of the final stages of the Late Bronze Age and the early stages of the First Iron Age (Moyat, Dumont, and Mariotti 2005) (Fig. 32.5). The large quantity of new jewellery (pins, fibulae, bracelets, rings) stored in a vase in the Villethierry hoard should no longer be considered as a jeweller's stock, in the process of being traded, but rather as a collective votive offering.

When evaluating the social standing of warriors one also needs to explain the spectacular hoards of armour. These include the extraordinary set of nine Late Bronze Age cuirasses (breastplates) from Marmesse (Haute-Marne), or the nine helmets from Berniéres-d'Ailly (Calvados).

A peak in the value and technical complexity of jewellery is reached in collections of gold jewellery found recently, again in northern France. In Guînes in particular the 'belt' with three twisted rings has no contemporary regional equivalent, and the techniques employed reflect those from the British Isles and as far away as the Iberian Peninsula (see Chapter 25).

Hoards of fragmented objects are also linked to the recurrent question of recycling. More generally, hoards are also affected by the social control of metal in circulation through selective and focused hoarding. This systematic diversion of metal from its natural life cycle leads to a significant stagnation in production, which is well known and well documented. This affects all areas, whether rich in or lacking metal resources: it can be said therefore to be a major cultural and social feature of societies of Bronze Age France.

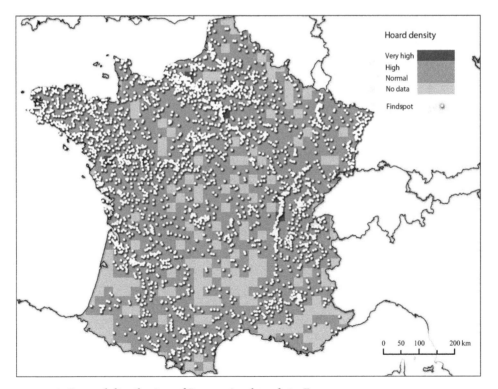

FIG. 32.6 General distribution of Bronze Age hoards in France.

Source: Saligny et al. 2008; D.A.O.E. Gauthier, Archaedyn Project

The general distribution map, however, highlights areas with an uneven distribution of hoards. From the Middle Bronze Age onwards, for example, this applies to large areas of south-east and south-west France that nonetheless have plentiful sources nearby (southern Alps, Montagne Noire, Corbières, and the Pyrénées) (Fig. 32.6). Conversely, Normandy or Île-de-France, which do not have any metal-bearing potential, have an unusually high concentration of hoards (Saligny et al. 2008, Figs. 2–4; Fig. 6).

This observation suggests that different cultural areas of France reacted to the needs of managing and controlling metal differently over time. In the northern Alpine and western area it is commonplace throughout the Bronze Age for societies to hoard metal systematically in funerary contexts, sometimes with marked differences between east and west but always in hoards of varying type, size, and complexity. The southern area breaks more or less entirely from this model, especially from the second part of the Middle Bronze Age and the Late Bronze Age, when hoards are rare or even absent. As the use of bronze cannot have disappeared in these regions, and ore is found close by, it is more appropriate to look at the management of metal when trying to understand the reason for this difference. Bronze was constantly in circulation in these areas among the living, with active recycling taking place. This use of the 'just-in-time' principle obviously means there is less stagnation in production and a greater difficulty in identifying and estimating the nature of these regional metal items. In this case we can ask: Is the scarcity of bronze hoards an indication of the shortage of resources, a blockage in trade networks, a decline in innovation and therefore a crisis, or simply a reflection of different social consumption of bronze in different regions of France? These considerations require more study.

Conclusion

Present-day France reveals itself to be diverse throughout the Bronze Age, with an evolving mosaic of cultural entities whose fertile contact areas generate and stimulate technological transfer and social and cultural innovation. These interfaces fluctuate over time between the centre of the Paris Basin and along the Rhône Valley. They illustrate the dynamic of the influences exerted on a country that is open at its Atlantic, North Sea, and Mediterranean coasts but enclosed in the east by continental Europe.

The 15 centuries of the Bronze Age witness technical success and the general adoption of bronze metallurgy, which caused essential trading networks to expand. Even though recent investigations have revealed a greater diversity of regional metal sources, France remains dependent on external resources to sustain this rise in the demand for metal. Copper and tin from the British Isles, Iberian copper, copper from the eastern Alps and the Carpathian region, all converged on French soil, especially from the Middle Bronze Age onwards. However, the potential for technical innovation is not linked to these external resources; the originality of 'French' production techniques confirms the 'creative' independence of Bronze Age craftsmen who are, nevertheless, closely linked to technologies being developed across continental Europe as a whole. This is why there is an ongoing debate about the mobility of Bronze Age craftsmen and their place in the hierarchical society of the period.

Metal proves to be essential as an indicator in recognizing differences in the type and status of individuals, and more broadly in the reconstruction of social and economic structures. Bronze also reveals a society that creates its own indicators of regional identity (jewellery in particular) but also long-distance contacts and alliances between the elite (for example, Nordic swords from the Neuvy-sous-Barangeon hoard, or Hungarian cauldrons from Blanot).

The current cultural approach favours a view that sees evolution occurring in one place over the medium term: the definition of the Rhine-Switzerland-eastern France culture, focused on eastern France, has rendered the diffusionist 'Urnfield' model obsolete, but the spatial expansion of the 'eastern Tumulus culture' still remains well placed to explain the dynamic of the Middle Bronze Age. The birth of the Channel-North Sea group, from the Middle Bronze Age onwards, represents a significant step towards a new understanding of the cultural dynamics of the western coast. A similar question should be asked for the southern area, with its long-term sharing of Italian and Iberian roots.

Bibliography

Billand, G. and Talon, M. (2007). 'Apport du Bronze Age Studies Group au vieillissement des "hair-rings" dans le Nord de la France', in C. Burgess, P. Topping, and F. Lynch (ed.), *Beyond Stonehenge: Essays on the Bronze Age in Honour of Colin Burgess*. Oxford: Oxbow Books, 345–53.

Billaud, Y. and Marguet, A. (2009). 'Structures et vestiges de la fin de l'âge du Bronze et du Fer sur les rives des lacs savoyards: récentes données de terrain', in M. J. Lambert, A. Daubigney, P.-Y. Milcent, M. Talon, and J. Vital (eds.), *De l'âge du Bronze à l'âge du Fer en France et en Europe occidentale (Xe–VIIe s. av. J.C.)*, Actes du Colloque International de l'Association Française pour l'Étude de l'Âge du Fer, St Romain-en-Gal, 26–28 Mai 2006. Supplément à la Revue archéologique de l'Est, 27. Dijon: Societé Archéologique de l'Est, 361–72.

Blanchet, J.-C. (1984). *Les Premiers Métallurgistes en Picardie et dans le Nord de la France*, Mémoire de la Société Préhistorique Française, 17. Paris: Société Préhistorique Française.

Bonnamour, L. (ed.) (2000). *Archéologie des fleuves et des rivières*. Paris: Errance.

Bourgeois, J. and Talon, M. (ed.) (2005). *L'Âge du Bronze du Nord de la France dans son contexte européen*, Actes du Colloque de Lille, 2000. Paris: Comité des Travaux Historiques et Scientifiques.

Briard, J. (1965). *Les Dépôts bretons et l'Âge du Bronze armoricain*. Rennes: Travaux du Laboratoire d'Anthropologie Préhistorique de la Faculté des Sciences de Rennes.

—— (1984). *Les Tumulus d'Armorique*, L'Âge du Bronze en France, 3. Paris: Picard.

Brun, P. (1998). 'Le Complexe culturel atlantique: entre le cristal et la fumée', in S. Jorge (ed.), *Existe uma Idade do Bronze Atlântico*, Actes du Colloque de Porto, Octobre 1995. Trabalhos de Arqueologia, 10. Lisbon: Institute Portuges de Arqueologia, 40–51.

—— and Mordant, C. (eds.) (1988). *Le Groupe Rhin-Suisse-France orientale et la notion de civilisation des Champs d'Urnes*, Actes du Colloque International de Nemours, 1986. Mémoire du Musée de Préhistoire d'Île-de-France, 1. Nemours: Association pour la Promotion de la Recherche Archéologique en Île-de-France.

Burrens-Carozza, A., Carozza, L., and Chazelles, C. A. de (2005). 'Les Maisons en Languedoc de la fin du Néolithique à la fin de l'Âge du Fer', in O. Buchsenschutz and C. Mordant (eds.), *Architectures protohistoriques en Europe occidentale du Néolithique final à l'Âge du Fer*, Actes du Colloque de Nancy, 2002. Paris: Comité des Travaux Historiques et Scientifiques, 429–61.

Carozza, L. and Galop, D. (2008). 'Le Dynamisme des marges. Peuplement et exploitation des espaces de montagne durant l'Âge du Bronze', in J. Guilaine (ed.), *Villes, villages, campagnes de l'Âge du Bronze*. Séminaire du Collège de France, 2007. Paris: Errance, 224–53.

De Lumley H. (1995). *Le Grandiose et le Sacré: gravures rupestres protohistoriques et historiques de la région du Mont Bégo*. Aix-en Provence: Edisud.

Dynamique du Bronze moyen (1989). Actes du 113ème Congrès National des Sociétés Savantes, Strasbourg, 1988. Paris: Comité des Travaux Historiques et Scientifiques.

Eluère, C. (1983). *Les Ors préhistoriques*. L'Âge du Bronze en France, 2. Paris: Picard.

Fily, M. (2008). *Les Monuments funéraires et les dépôts métalliques dans le paysage rituel de l'Âge du Bronze: l'exemple du centre-ouest de la Bretagne et du Finistère littoral (France)*. Thèse de doctorat. Rennes: Université de Rennes 1.

Gabillot, M. (2003). *Dépôts et production métallique du Bronze moyen en France nord-occidentale*, British Archaeological Reports (International Series), 1,174. Oxford: Archaeopress.

——, Forel, B., Monna, F., Naudin, A., Losno, R., Piningre, J. F., Mordant, C., Dominik, J., and Brugier, O. (2009). 'Influences atlantiques dans les productions métalliques de Bourgogne et Franche-Comté au Bronze moyen', in A. Richard, A. Daubigney, J.-F. Piningre, Ph. Barral, G. Kaenel, and C. Mordant (eds.), *L'Isthme européen Rhin-Saône-Rhône dans la Protohistoire: approches nouvelles en hommage à J.-P. Millotte*, Actes du Colloque Besançon, 2006. Besançon: Presses Universitaires de Franche-Comté, 149–59.

Gallay, A. (1996). 'Le Concept de culture du Rhône: repères pour un historique', in C. Mordant and O. Gaiffe (eds.), *Cultures et sociétés du Bronze ancien en Europe*, Actes du Colloque de Clermond-Ferrand, 1992. Paris: Comité des Travaux Historiques et Scientifiques, 271–86.

Giraud, J. P., Pons, F., and Janin, T. (eds.) (2003). *Nécropoles protohistoriques de la région de Castres (Tarn). Le Causse, Gourjade, Le Martinet*, Documents d'Archéologie Française, 94. Paris: Maison des Sciences de l'Homme.

Gomez, J. (1995). *Le Bronze moyen en Occident. La culture des Duffaits et la civilisation des Tumulus*, L'Âge du Bronze en France, 5. Paris: Picard.

Guilaine, J. (1972). *L'Âge du Bronze en Languedoc occidental*, Mémoire de la Société Préhistorique Française, 9. Paris: Klinsiek.

——, Rancoule, G., Vaquer, J., Passelac, M., Vigne, J. D. (1986). *Carsac. Une agglomération protohistorique en Languedoc*. Toulouse: Centre d'Anthropologie des Sociétés Rurales.

Janin, T. (2009). 'Jean Guilaine, Mailhac et le Mailhacien', in *De la Méditerranée et d'ailleurs. Mélanges offerts à Jean Guilaine*. Toulouse: Archives d'Écologie Préhistorique, 353–64.

Magny, M. and Peyron, O. (2008). 'Variations climatiques et histoire des sociétés à l'Âge du Bronze au Nord et au Sud des Alpes', in J. Guilaine (ed.), *Villes, villages, campagnes de l'Âge du Bronze*, Séminaires du Collège de France, 2007. Paris: Errance, 161–76.

Manem, S. (2010). 'Des Habitats aux sites de rassemblement à vocation rituelle. L'Âge du Bronze selon le concept de "chaîne opératoire"', *Les Nouvelles de l'Archéologie*, 119: 30–6.

Marcigny, C. and Ghesquière, E. (eds.) (2003). *L'Île de Tatihou (Manche) à l'Âge du Bronze*, Documents d'Archéologie Française, 93. Paris: Éditions de la Maison des Sciences de l'Homme.

—— and Ghesquière, E. (2008). 'Espace rural et systèmes agraires dans l'Ouest de la France à l'Âge du Bronze: quelques exemples normands', in J. Guilaine (ed.), *Villes, villages, campagnes de l'Âge du Bronze*, Séminaire du Collège de France, 2007. Paris: Errance, 256–78.

Mohen, J. P. and Bailloud, G. (1987). *La Vie quotidienne. Les Fouilles du Fort Harrouard*, L'Âge du Bronze en France, 4. Paris: Picard.

Monna, F., Petit, C., Guillaumet, J. P., Jouffroy-Bapicot, I., Blanchot, C., Dominik, J., Losno, R., Richard, H., Lévèque, J., and Château, C. (2004a). 'History and environmental impact of mining activity in Celtic Aeduan territory recorded in a peat bog', *Environmental Science and Technology*, 38/3: 665–73.

——, Galop, D., Carozza, L., Tual, M., Beyrie, A., Marembert, F., and Dominik, J. (2004b). 'Impact of local early metalworking in the Basque country pointed out by geochemical and pollen records in minerogenic peatlands', *Science of the Total Environment*, 327: 197–204.

Mordant, C. (2008). 'L'Habitat à l'Âge du Bronze en France orientale', in J. Guilaine (ed.), *Villes, villages, campagnes de l'Âge du Bronze*, Séminaire du Collège de France, 2007. Paris: Errance, 204–23.

—— and Mordant, D. (1970). *Le Site protohistorique des Gours-aux-Lions à Marolles-sur-Seine (Seine-et-Marne)*, Mémoire de la Société Préhistorique Française, 8. Paris: Société Préhistorique Française.

——, Mordant, D., and Prampart, J. Y. (1976). *Le Dépôt de bronze de Villethierry (Yonne) avec la collaboration de J. Bourhis, J. Briard et J. P. Mohen*, Supplément à Gallia Préhistoire, 19. Paris: CNRS.

——, Pernot, M., and Rychner, V. (eds.) (1998). *L'Atelier du bronzier en Europe du XXe au VIIIe siècle avant notre ère*, Actes du Colloque Bronze '96, Neuchâtel et Dijon, C.R.T.G.R. Université de Bourgogne et C.T.H.S., 3 vols. Paris: éditions du CTHS.

—— and G. Depierre (eds.) (2005). *Les Pratiques funéraires de l'Âge du Bronze en France*, Actes de la Table Ronde de Sens, 1998. Paris: Société Archéologique de Sens et Comité des Travaux Historiques et Scientifiques.

Moyat, P., Dumont, A., and Mariotti, J. F. (2005). 'Un Habitat et un dépôt d'objets métalliques protohistoriques découverts dans le lit de l'Hérault à Agde', Académie des Inscriptions et Belles-Lettres, Comptes Rendus des séances de l'année 2005, janvier–mars: 371–94.

Pennors, F. (2005). *Analyse fonctionnelle et pondérale des dépôts et trouvailles isolées de l'Âge du Bronze en France*, Thèse de Doctorat. Paris: Université de Paris 1 Panthéon-Sorbonne.

Piningre, J. F. and Grut, H. (2009). 'Dépôts et lieux de dépositions de bronzes dans la région salinoise au XIVe siècle av. J.-C.', A. Richard, P. Barral, A. Daubigney, G. Kaenel, C. Mordant, and J.-F. Piningre (eds.), *L'Isthme européen Rhin-Saône-Rhône dans la Protohistoire: approches nouvelles en hommage à J.-P. Millotte*, Actes du Colloque de Besançon, 16–18 Octobre 2006. Besançon: Presses Universitaires de Franche-Comté, 183–99.

Saligny, L., Nuninger, L., Ostir, K., Poirier, N., Fovet, E., Gandini, C., Gauthier, E., Kokajl, Z., and Tolle, F. (2008). 'Models and tools for territorial studies', *Colloque Archaedyn*, Dijon, 23–25 June 2008, prétirages. Dijon: Université de Bourgogne, 25–44.

Thevenot, J. P. (ed.) (1991). *L'Âge du Bronze en Bourgogne. Le dépôt de Blanot (Côte-d'Or)*, Supplément à la Revue Archéologique de l'Est, 11. Dijon: Université de Bourgogne.

Véber, C. (2009). *Métallurgie des dépôts de bronzes à la fin de l'Âge du Bronze final (IXe–VIIIe s. av. J.C.) dans le domaine Sarre-Lorraine. Essai de caractérisation d'une production bronzière au travers des études techniques*, British Archaeological Reports (International Series), 2,024. Oxford: Archaeopress.

Vital, J. (1999). 'Identification du Bronze moyen-récent en Provence et en Méditerranée nord-occidentale', *Documents d'Archéologie Méridionale*, 22: 7–115.

—— (2008). 'Architectures, sociétés, espaces durant l'Âge du Bronze. Quelques exemples dans le bassin rhodanien', in J. Guilaine (ed.), *Villes, villages, campagnes de l'Âge du Bronze*, Séminaire du Collège de France, 2007. Paris: Errance, 179–201.

—— (2009). 'L'Âge du Bronze en moyenne vallée du Rhône: quelques enseignements et perspectives', in A. Richard, P. Barral, A. Daubigney, G. Kaenel, C. Mordant, and J.-F. Piningre (eds.), *L'Isthme européen Rhin-Saône-Rhône dans la protohistoire: approches nouvelles en hommage à J.-P. Millotte*, Actes du Colloque Besançon, 2006. Besançon: Presses Universitaires de Franche-Comté, 241–54.

Wirth, S. (2006). 'Le Mystère de la barque solaire: quelques considérations à propos des décors sur les situles de type Hajduböszörmény et sur une situle inédite du Bronze final', in L. Baray (ed.), *Artisanats, sociétés et civilisations. Hommages à J. P. Thevenot*, Supplément à la Revue Archéologique de l'Est, 24. Dijon: Revue Archéologique de l'Est, 331–45.

CHAPTER 33

BRONZE AGE IBERIA[1]

VICENTE LULL, RAFAEL MICÓ, CRISTINA RIHUETE HERRADA, AND ROBERTO RISCH

The Iberian Peninsula is a territory covering nearly 600,000 square km (around 230,000 sq miles) in the extreme south-west of Europe. Its sheer size, the variety of its landscape, and its location between the Mediterranean Sea and Atlantic Ocean afford it considerable ecological diversity, though it can be divided into three broad geoclimatic zones (Fig. 33.1). The eastern and southern coast enjoys a warm, Mediterranean climate with little rainfall, while that in the far south-east consists of areas of semi-desert. On the Atlantic coast and along the Bay of Biscay a wetter, cooler oceanic climate is prevalent. Inland, the peninsula is a vast highland plateau (*Meseta*) divided in two and separated from the coast by mountain ranges with peaks that rise to above 2,500 m (over 8,000 ft). These interior regions have a continental climate characterized by warm summers and cold winters, and by moderate and irregular rainfall. The biggest rivers—the Duero, the Tagus, the Guadiana, and the Guadalquivir—cut across the centre and south of the peninsula in an east-west direction before flowing into the Atlantic, while the Ebro is fed largely by rainfall on the eastern end of the Cantabrian Mountains and on the southern slopes of the Pyrenees and runs into the Mediterranean Sea.

The Bronze Age in the Iberian Peninsula represents the period of time from c.2200 to 900 cal BC. In general terms its beginnings were marked by the onset of the crisis of the Copper Age societies of the Bell Beaker tradition, while its end coincided with the beginning of Phoenician colonial activity in the western Mediterranean. However, these two historical junctures did not affect every community in the same way and there was a considerable variety of forms of social organization during these approximately thirteen hundred years. More abundant and diverse archaeological evidence for the start of the Bronze Age has been found in the southern regions. Particularly outstanding is the El Argar group in the south-east of the peninsula, whose stratified sites and numerous funeral contexts have made it a fundamental chronocultural reference point and a source of constant interest for scholars.

---

[1] In this chapter, and in the following one on the Balearic Islands, there are no in-text references; a basic bibliography of important items is provided at the end.

FIG. 33.1 Map of Iberian sites mentioned in the text. 1. Cádiz, 2. Castillo de Alange, 3. Los Tolmos de Caracena, 4. Peña Negra, 5. La Traviesa, 6. El Trastejón, 7. El Castañuelo, 8. Marroquíes Bajos, 9. Ría de Huelva, 10. El Milagro, 11. Morro de Mezquitilla, 12. Cerro del Cuchillo, 13. Muntanya Assolada, 14. Mola d'Agres, 15. Mas de Menente, 16. Las Saladillas, 17. Acinipo, 18. Cazalilla, 19. Paranho, 20. Quinta de Água Branca, 21. Senhora da Guia, 22. Vale Ferrerio, 23. Cerro de la Encina, 24. Peñalosa, 25. Qurénima, 26. La Bastida, 27. Barranco de la Viuda, 28. Gatas, 29. El Argar, 30. El Oficio, 31. Cerro de las Viñas, 32. Castellón Alto, 33. Fuente Álamo, 34. El Rincón, 35. Los Cipreses, 36. Lorca, 37. Los Tolmos, 38. La Venta, 39. La Plaza de Cogeces, 40. Carretelà, 41. Castellets II, 42. Genó, 43. Ecce Homo, 44. Llanete de Los Moros, 45. Cuesta del Negro, 46. El Parpantique, 47. Aldeagordillo, 48. Loma del Lomo, 49. Santa María de Retamar, 50. Azuer, 51. Cabezo Redondo, 52. Setefilla, 53. Cerro de la Campana, 54. El Acequión, 55. Fuente Olmedo, 56. Can Roqueta II, 57. Terlinques, 58. Lloma de Betxí, 59. Hoya Quemada, 60. El Recuenco, 61. Orpesa la Vella, 62. Mas d'Abad, 63. Moncín, 64. Pic dels Corbs, 65. Morra de Quintanar, 66. Los Palacios, 67. Torrelló d'Onda, 68. Caserío de Perales, 69. Valdevimbre, 70. Castro de Ardón, 71. Can Missert, 72. Minferri, 73. Carricastro, 74. El Castillo de Cardeñosa, 75. Teso del Cuerno, 76. Capilla I, 77. Solana de Cabañas, 78. Torrejón de Rubio II.

Map: S. Gili and authors.

That less is known about other contemporary societies and about the rest of the peninsula during the Bronze Age in general is due to the fact that there is less well-preserved evidence of how its inhabitants lived and what happened to them when they died, compounded by the fact that investigation in this field has been less intensive or is still at the incipient stage. These gaps, coupled with disagreements over terminology among traditions of research, make periodization and inter-regional comparisons more difficult. Despite these problems, with more than eight hundred radiocarbon dates available the chronology of Bronze Age Iberia is one of the most solid in Europe, even if the quantity and quality of absolute dates and stratigraphic sequences in each region prove very different. The periodization of Bronze Age Iberia also varies from region to region and its evolution does not always match up with the sequence used in the rest of western Europe, which, even so, is used to draw typological parallels, particularly of metals. The best-documented sequences from the south of the peninsula suggest a tripartite subdivision of the Bronze Age. In the knowledge that it sidesteps disagreements and deficiencies at a general level, we shall use the following chronology:

- *Early Bronze Age* (c.2200–1550 cal BC). In some regions its beginnings are marked by a continuation of elements of the Bell Beaker culture, while in others such as the south-east there is a clear break. El Argar is the best-known archaeological group, on a par with the classic societies of the European Bronze Age such as Únětice, Wessex, or the Armorican tumuli. In the peninsula this period is often divided into two stages (Early Bronze Age and Middle Bronze Age).
- *Late Bronze Age* (c.1550–1300 cal BC). The fall in the number of stable settlements makes it difficult to identify sociopolitical groups with clear territorial boundaries. From this time on and throughout the following stage, new developments in Bronze Age metallurgy and pottery set the standard for defining archaeological groups and phases.
- *Final Bronze Age* (c.1300–900 cal BC). In the centuries leading up to the Iron Age, the peninsula communities appear to be more linked, both among one another and with the outside world, as suggested by the Atlantic, Mediterranean, and continental connections (Final Atlantic Bronze Age, Urnfield culture), based above all on the proliferation of common metal objects. The first evidence of Phoenician colonization on the southern coast is usually taken to mark the end of the Bronze Age.

The Early Bronze Age (c.2200–1550 cal bc)

The Argaric South-East

At the end of the nineteenth century the Siret brothers announced the discovery of numerous finds of pottery, metals, lithic material, and bones from their excavations at some ten sites in the south-eastern Iberian Peninsula (see Fig. 33.1). At the time of their maximum expansion, the Argaric communities occupied a territory covering some 33,000 sq km, from the coastal plains of Almería, Murcia, and south of Alicante to the high ground of Granada and Jaén (Fig. 33.2). Currently, this region is one of the driest in Europe. Annual rainfall is around 200–300 mm and is not sufficient to maintain permanent rivers.

Until recently, the general perception was that the climate during recent prehistory was similar to the present. In turn that led to the assumption that in the Copper and Bronze Ages subsistence must have been based on systems of intensive production (irrigation, forestry). However, the results of recent analyses of fruits and seeds, charcoal, fauna, and

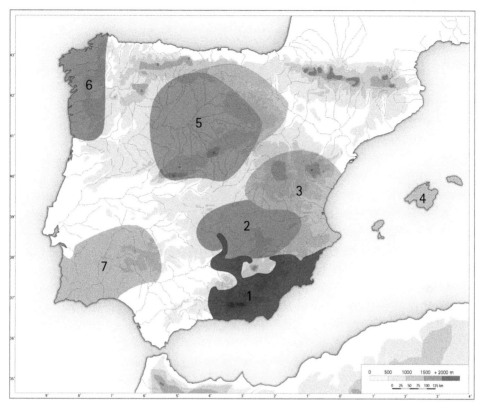

FIG. 33.2 Archaeological groups and artefact styles of the Iberian peninsula between c. 1900 and 1500 BC. 1. El Argar and its territorial frontiers; 2. La Mancha Bronze Age; 3. Ibero-Levantine Bronze Age; 4. Dolmenic phase; 5. Protocogotas style; 6. Vilavella/Atios facies; 7. Bronze Age of the south-west.

Map: S. Gili and authors.

pollen indicate that during the third millennium cal BC the climate was wetter than today and there was a notable presence of scrubland and Mediterranean forest in the lowlands, of mesophytic tree species in the hills, and even riparian vegetation. Thus, Argaric society began to develop in more favourable ecological conditions than today, although the same investigations also indicate that the human impact—in the shape of the clearing of farmland, agricultural over-exploitation, the creation of pasture, and the gathering of fuel—had a serious effect on the vegetation and soil, thus contributing to the crisis that spelt the end of Argaric society.

The majority of known Argaric settlements were located on steep hills at the foot of mountain ranges, separated from the fertile plains but commanding views of these areas and of communication routes (Fuente Álamo, Gatas and El Oficio in Almería; La Bastida in Murcia; Cerro de la Encina and Castellón Alto in Granada; San Antón in Alicante). They usually occupied between 1 and 2 hectares, though some were bigger (La Bastida and Lorca) (Fig. 33.3). It has also been suggested that some of the smaller, strategically placed upland settlements (Barranco de la Viuda and Cerro de las Viñas in Murcia) could have been defensive, or controlling enclaves servicing more highly ranked centres. Not so well documented (due to

FIG. 33.3 The upland settlement of La Bastida (Murcia). The plan shows the urban lay-out of one part of the lower mountain slope to the south-east.

Photo and plan: authors (La Bastida Project).

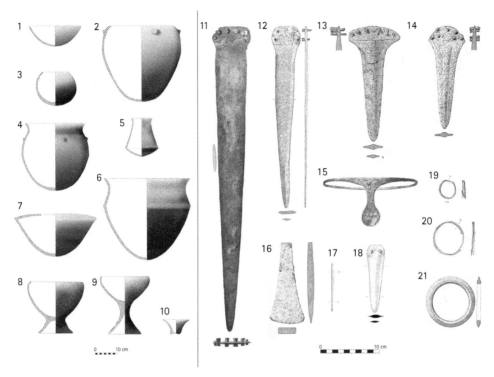

FIG. 33.4 Ceramic and metal types typical of El Argar.

Source: Lull et al. 2011.

more intense erosion) but probably plentiful were small and dispersed hamlets located on the plains and rich lowland areas (El Rincón and Los Cipreses in Murcia).

All the Argaric settlements shared the same funerary ritual, characterized by burial underneath the living area. These were almost always individual tombs, though sometimes they contained two bodies and, exceptionally, three or more. The bodies were placed in small artificial caves (*covachas*), stone cists, pottery urns, or simple pits.

The grave goods that were often placed alongside the body are a vital source of information for understanding the nature of the Argaric culture (Fig. 33.4). One of the most striking aspects is the standardization of pottery shapes and capacities, and of metallurgical production. The variety of the former can be divided into eight main styles, created from a combination of three simple geometric forms. Characteristic for El Argar are the large *pithoi* with a capacity of between 100 and 200 litres, and the goblets—bowls above a long stem—which were perhaps used in ceremonial events.

The inventory of metal objects includes weapons and tools (halberds, swords, axes, daggers, knives, awls, chisels) and ornaments (diadems, bracelets, earrings, rings, necklace beads). Most were manufactured in copper, often with significant percentages of arsenic already present in the mineral. As of 1800–1700 cal BC objects made of tin-bronze begin to appear. Silver and, occasionally, gold were used to produce ornaments, probably made from largely locally sourced metals.

Despite the abundance of copper mineralization, the sources of supply were few. The most unequivocal and extensive evidence of mining, smelting, and the production of ingots comes from the Peñalosa settlement in the foothills of the Sierra Morena (Jaén). From the centres of primary production the metal arrived at a small number of workshops in the main settlements, the only ones with the tools to proceed to the melting, forging, finishing, and maintenance of the objects. Finally, the objects were distributed, although not all strata of the population had access to these in the same conditions, as is shown by their unequal distribution inside the settlements and among grave goods. Argaric metallurgy was a centralized activity under strict and asymmetrical control as regards production, distribution, use, and consumption.

The production of lithic objects was remarkably rich and varied. The major settlements accumulated a large number of grinding stones, hammers, smoothing tools, and sharpeners. It appears that each central settlement organized the exploitation of the lithic resources available in a territory of between 10 and 50 sq km, while it inhibited the exchange of raw materials related to the manufacture of tools for everyday use. This practice, which would be unlikely without the restrictive effect of some kind of political structure, caused differences in productivity among neighbouring territories.

One of the main applications of the lithic industry was for the harvesting and milling of cereals. Wheat was ever-present, but almost without exception in quantities well below barley, which exceeds 90 per cent of the cultivated seeds recovered in the final phases of El Argar. Legumes (lentils, peas, and, above all, broad beans) barely reached 2 per cent. The small size of the barley seeds in the lowlands of Almería and the results of carbon-isotope analyses suggest extensive dry-farming strategies. That must have had a severe ecological impact owing to the intense ploughing of extensive areas on the plains. Meanwhile, legumes could have grown in plots on the lowlands, perhaps helped by small-scale irrigation systems.

Stockbreeding was standard practice in Argaric territory. In terms of the amount of meat they supplied, cattle and sheep or goats had a similar importance, between 30 and 50 per cent, followed some way behind by pigs and members of the horse family. There is also evidence of the use of secondary products. Hunting, fishing, and shellfishing played a secondary or minor role.

Initial Argaric Society (*c*.2200–1950 cal BC)

The origins of El Argar cannot be understood without an appreciation of the general changes that affected southern Copper Age societies coinciding with the Bell Beaker phenomenon (reduction in the size of settlements, increase in violence), nor without an appreciation of some economic and political transformations in different regions of western Europe at the end of the third millennium cal BC (changes in the technology and organization of metallurgy; the concentration of wealth; proliferation of weapons; and displays of violence and individualized power). The material remains of El Argar stand in marked contrast to those of the Copper Age Millares culture: large settlements on high ground versus villages on the plains; long, tightly packed dwellings on terraces versus circular huts separated by open areas; individual intramural burial versus interment in collective graves outside the settlement. There are also significant typological and organizational changes in the production of metal goods and pottery. To what extent the contrast between Los Millares and El Argar can be explained by an internal process or as the effect of outside intervention remains an open issue. What does seem clear is that from the outset Argaric society had an expansionist dynamic which caused it to spread from its original sources in the eastern lowlands of Almería and Murcia to the high ground inland.

During these initial centuries the Argaric buildings were huts erected using adobe and wooden posts (Gatas, La Bastida). Only a small proportion of the adult population was buried in cists, *covachas*, and pits. The social pyramid would have been topped by men interred with halberds, biconical cups, and in some cases short swords, while the women were buried with a knife and an awl, as well as other items of pottery and metalwork (see Fig. 33.3). Below this group, we find individuals either with some kind of metal tool, cup, or ornament, or with nothing.

The Structure of the Argaric State (*c*.1950–1550 cal BC)

At the beginning of the second millennium cal BC, El Argar brought to a close a significant phase of territorial expansion inland and embarked upon an exceptional stage of architectural, economic, and political development (Fig. 33.5). A fresh phase of construction brought

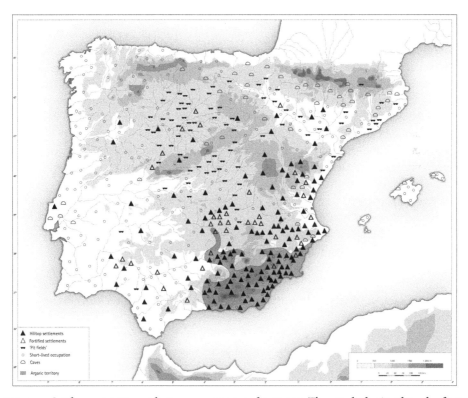

FIG. 33.5 Settlement patterns between *c*. 2200 and 1550 BC. The symbols simulate the form and density of settlement based on information derived from survey and excavation rather than indicating real locations.

Map: S. Gill and authors.

systematic terracing to the slopes of hilltop settlements and the planning of a dense network of stone and mud-brick structures of different shapes and sizes. The living quarters were built on apsidal, trapezoidal, or rectangular ground plans of up to 70 sq m. An exceptional quantity of productive capacity and storage were concentrated in large buildings standing several storeys high—evidence of activities carried out by groups of ten or more. The main function of these workshops appears to have been the processing of cereals and textile production, as well as the repair of different types of tools.

As well as living areas and workshops, cisterns, grain deposits, stables, possible raised granaries, towers, walls, and bastions were erected. Spaces to circulate between buildings were few and narrow, and open areas were uncommon.

As regards burials, burial rights were extended to children and, perhaps, other groups. In addition, the value and diversity of grave goods increased, which enabled a clear distinction of new social differences in an increasingly standardized ritual. Around 1750 cal BC a social and political model that would last until the end of El Argar was implemented. At this time men from the dominant class were buried with a long sword and the women were interred with a diadem as artefacts to distinguish them, as well as with a wide range of metal ornaments and tools, and pottery containers (see Fig. 33.4). A large part of social production and, seasonally, outside labour gathered in the central hill-settlements, in spite of their distance from the best arable land and the main sources of raw materials. In addition the buildings located on these hills stand out on account of their architecture (towers and bastions) and because of the means of production accumulated there (metallurgy), the available means of consumption (pottery vessels, remains of horses and cattle), and because of the wealth contained in their graves.

Beneath the dominant class was one formed by individuals with political rights and which was recognizable by the presence of metal implements at their burial sites—a dagger or knife and an axe for men and an awl for women, along with a certain number of metal ornaments and pottery vessels. The association of axes with men and awls with women does not indicate an attempt to identify gender, rather, and above all, to identify socioeconomic class, since only around 40 per cent of the women and just 25 per cent of the men were buried with these items. A third sector comprised individuals with very modest grave goods (pottery, necklace, or a single ornament); and lastly a group with no offerings.

Differences in funerary consumption seen in the adult and elderly population applied too in burials of infants or subadults, which indicates mechanisms for the hereditary transfer of property. Age played a secondary role in the access to wealth: although some items such as swords, diadems, or axes are exclusive or significantly associated with adults or the elderly, only one segment of society had the actual means to deposit them alongside their deceased elderly members.

In short, a dominant class that owned the land and the basic means of production (metal, food) was in a position to place objects of great social value in their graves, as well as to enjoy better living standards. This class used weapons to maintain its privileges by means of violence and costly ornaments to exhibit them. Its members exercised direct control over local political units, which were linked together to form the extensive Argaric territory, impervious to the outside yet capable of exerting influence beyond its borders, as suggested by Argaric influences in metal and pottery production and in funerary ideology. Such an economic and political structure fits the Marxist definition of a state.

The Beginning of the Bronze Age on the Periphery of El Argar

El Argar is remarkable not only because of the rapid establishment of a new model of habitat and burial that broke with the Copper Age tradition, but also because of a combination of easily recognizable social practices and material features that were present for almost seven hundred years. It is precisely this recurrence that has led to talk of an Argaric 'norm' or 'border' (see Fig. 33.2). Outside the Argaric boundary other archaeological groups have been defined on the basis of geographical criteria and certain material elements, but their limits in area and time are often vague or non-existent. It is also possible to recognize some characteristic features of El Argar beyond its territory, though generally in a distorted, impoverished manner and never representing a standardized programme of distinctive social practices.

The establishment of El Argar and of the neighbouring societies of the Early Bronze Age spelt the end of the social relations characteristic of the third millennium cal BC. One of the distinctive factors of that period had been the broad movement of goods, information, and possibly people. However, the interruption of that extensive network of relations gave way in the south-east to a policy of expansion and aggression. El Argar achieved a dominant position over certain resources and communication routes and in one way or another determined the way of life of the neighbouring societies. Its impact is apparent above all in the preference for settlements on protected promontories, a socially selective burial ritual within the living space, and the movement of important raw materials like copper, silver, or ivory. In all these aspects, the influence of the south-east appears to have been decisive, whether because of emulation or because of resistance (see Fig. 33.5).

Thus, the regions to the north of the Argaric territory share with it the practice of stone architecture and the establishment of numerous hilltop settlements. However, the two elements do not necessarily go together. The clearest example is to be found in La Mancha, where fortified settlements on high ground called *morras* and *castillejos* (Morra de Quintanar and Cerro del Cuchillo in Albacete) often existed alongside settlements on the plains with spectacular stone architecture—the *motillas* (Azuer, Los Palacios, and Santa María de Retamar in Ciudad Real, El Acequión in Albacete). Irrespective of their location, these settlements rarely cover more than 1 hectare and most of them vary between 0.01 and 0.5 hectares. One of the best-known *motillas* is that of Azuer. It has a central, square-shaped stone tower with remains measuring 11 m in height and is surrounded by two concentric walled enclosures, the external one measuring some 35 m in diameter. The inner spaces were used to store cereals, hold cattle, and perform various food and textile-producing activities. There is also an impressive stone-walled well that reached water at a depth of 20 m. In fact, the geographical location of the *motillas* prioritized access to underground water resources. The settlement extends around the outer enclosure and is formed by oval or rectangular dwellings with stone bases and adobe walls.

As well as *motillas* and hilltop settlements, there are other low-lying settlements revealed only by hut floors (Las Saladillas in Ciudad Real). Despite this variety, all of them share the use of plain pottery (bowls, carinated, globular, or ovoid pots). The few flint objects recovered are linked to the processing of vegetables, as are the grinding stones found in the dwellings. A small number of knives, awls, axes, and arrow- or spearheads are the most common copper objects.

Graves have been found under some of the dwellings, most of which are pits lined with stones and sometimes urns for children. Their numbers and density are much lower than those found at Argaric sites. They contain individual burials, with no apparent restrictions on the grounds of sex or age. The grave goods—non-existent or very modest—do not indicate marked contrasts in the access to wealth. This hypothesis would be called into question if it were demonstrated that the *motillas* were the residences of a social sector capable of appropriating for its own exclusive benefit large amounts of food and raw materials produced by other groups. The data from El Acequión, Santa María de Retamar, or Azuer do not necessarily indicate anything to that effect, therefore it is possible they were centres of communal storage and production. The contemporary role of the high settlements remains uncertain, but in view of the size of the defences of the *motillas* it is difficult to imagine that the population of the former dominated that of the latter. Perhaps they were more or less autonomous communities with direct access to their own economic territories.

In the Valencia region, in areas on its western borders, and in the Iberian mountain range we also find upland settlements with well-developed stone architecture that were often fortified (Mola d'Agres and Mas de Menente in Alicante, Muntanya Assolada in Valencia, Torrelló d'Onda in Castellón, El Recuenco in Cuenca, Hoya Quemada in Teruel, Cerro de la Campana in Murcia). The most outstanding settlements cover small areas of land (between 0.1 and 0.3 hectares) and most follow the pattern of a farm or small village (between 0.01 and 0.1 hectares). Generally speaking, the density of the settlements does not appear to have been lower than in the Argaric zone, but their average size is indeed smaller, which indicates a lower demographic density. The population was completed with small villages scattered across the plains (Cases de Montcada in Valencia), coastal enclaves (Orpesa la Vella in Castellón), and caves (Mas d'Abad in Castellón).

There is a considerable variety of construction types over time and space. In Phase I (*c*.2150–1900 cal BC) of the hilltop settlement of Terlinques (Alicante), a large building was erected that was the site of a variety of production and storage activities, while in Phase II (*c*.1700–1500 cal BC) the area was occupied by a dozen buildings lining both sides of a central passageway and which served different purposes. In Lloma de Betxí (Valencia), two large multi-purpose buildings, one of them measuring 24 by 10 m, occupy the top of the site, where two cisterns have also been discovered. Given the number of grinding stones and means of storing grain, and the evidence of textile production, the productive power of some of these buildings is not very dissimilar to those recorded in Argaric workshops. However, this centralization of economic activity was not on the scale of that present in El Argar, nor did it have the same social and political implications.

Funerary practices were almost always performed outside the settlements, using natural hollows that housed individual burials or those of small groups (Mola d'Agres in Alicante). The inventory of artefacts found is dominated by pottery: carinated or curved bowls, pots and vessels of different sizes, some of them with flat bases. Metal production (knives, awls, axes, arrow- or spearheads) are concentrated in the areas closest to Argaric territory, which has traditionally been indicated as the source of economic and political influences that were also expressed in isolated cases of burials within the settlement.

Finally, in the upper Guadalquivir region the Cazalilla II-Albalate archaeological horizon maintained high settlements in the local Copper Age tradition (Cazalilla in Jaén), but at the end of the third millennium cal BC low-lying settlements underwent an acute transformation. Thus, in Marroquíes Bajos (Jaén) the enormous Copper Age settlement covering more than 100 hectares and with five concentric pits was abandoned around 2200–2100 cal BC, to be replaced by small farms that testify to the fragmentation of the previous economic collectivism. The seductive hypothesis that the combination of upland settlements devoted to political control, and peasant villages devoted to agricultural production, reflects a state structure from at least midway through the third millennium cal BC, requires confirmation from more excavation.

The North and West of the Peninsula

Moving towards the west and the north of the peninsula, permanent settlements on high ground are scarce (see Fig. 33.5). Sometimes evidence of settlement is practically non-existent and where it does appear, it is usually on level ground or gentle slopes characterized by collections of underground structures. In fact, these 'pit fields' (*campos de hoyos*) constitute the most common type of settlement in a good part of the peninsula from the Neolithic until the end of the Bronze Age. They comprise structures of varying size, shape, and distribution that were used as silos to store grain, rubbish dumps, sites to place offerings, homes, graves, or dwellings (*fondos de cabaña*). They formed part of open settlements that were occupied temporarily or seasonally, whose development sometimes produces very extensive horizontal stratigraphies. They could have been inhabited by dozens of people and may have enjoyed a high degree of productive autonomy, as indicated by the availability of tools related to the processing, storage, and consumption of food, and to the production of pottery, stone and bone tools, and metal objects. They are common in the north-east and the basins of the upper and middle Ebro, Duero, Tagus, Guadiana, and Guadalquivir (Minferri in Lleida, Can Roqueta II in Barcelona Province, Loma del Lomo in Guadalajara, Caserío de Perales in Madrid Province). Even so there are also a significant number of hilltop settlements (El Castillo de Cardeñosa in Ávila, El Parpantique in Soria, Moncín in Zaragoza, and Castillo de Alange in Badajoz). In both cases, they are generally non-permanent sites occupied by small communities and almost always linked to the seasonal exploitation of certain resources more than to the centralized accumulation of products.

The economy revolved around stockbreeding and an increasingly developed agriculture, as is shown by the specialization of the flint-working industry for the preparation of sickle teeth and the communities' greater storage capacity. In general there is a clear rise in the number of silos per settlement and their size (with a capacity for between 500 and 2,000 litres and up to 4,000 litres) in comparison with the Copper Age.

Metallurgy probably gained ground in the production of tools, though in fact the pieces recovered remain scarce and are a continuation of previous models (flat axes, awls, tanged knives and daggers, and Palmela-type arrowheads). This scarcity of artefacts contrasts with the existence of mines, particularly in the Picos de Europa (El Milagro in Asturias). The complexity and size of these mines, which were opened in the Copper Age, are unparalleled in the rest of the Iberian Peninsula. However, this extensive extraction of ore took place in an archaeological context where there is little evidence of economic centralization and political hierarchy. Throughout the centre and north of the peninsula, metalwork was not limited to certain settlements and workshops, as appears to be the case in El Argar. Evidence of the melting and casting of metal appears in both pit settlements on the plains and in hilltop settlements.

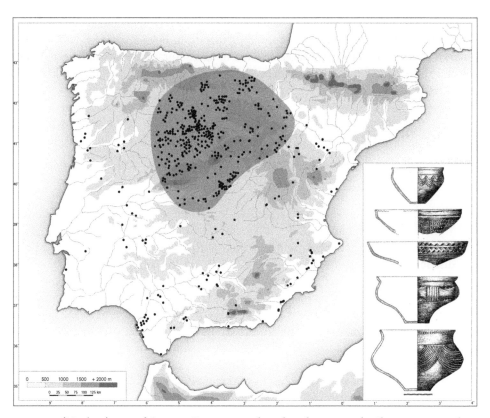

FIG. 33.6 'Nuclear' area of Cogotas I pottery and its distribution in the Iberian peninsula.
Source: S. Gili and authors, after Abarquero 2005, pottery after Fernández-Posse 1998.

The pottery of the new period is also marked by the predominance of plain vessels: open, carinated bowls and dishes and large vessels, often with a flat base and abundant applied plastic elements (corded impressions, tabs, knobs, and handles). However, it is common to find local elements coming from late Bell Beaker culture and regional takes on Bell Beaker developments (Ciempozuelos, Silos-Vaquera, Pirenaico, Salomó, Arbolí-Nordeste), which coexisted for a certain time with the new output. Around 1700 cal BC in the northern *Meseta* a Protocogotas decorative style began to emerge (La Plaza de Cogeces in Valladolid, Los Tolmos in Soria), characterized by the application of motifs using incisions or impressions (ears of wheat, triangles) in simple compositions on the upper part of the vessels. The Protocogotas horizon was the precedent of the Cogotas I style, which from the mid second century cal BC would spread across a large part of the peninsula (Fig 33.6). The Middle Bronze Age, whose beginnings in different regions coincided with the last two centuries of the Argaric world, did not bring about clear or significant changes in many of these zones.

Funerary customs did not break with Copper Age practices, as collective burial and the use of natural caves and megalithic tombs remained commonplace alongside the new practices. There is a remarkable diversity of grave forms in some zones. Thus in Catalonia, for example, burials in pits, caves, hypogea, mounds, and megalithic tombs, some of them newly built and small in size (cists, pseudo-dolmens, and chambers with vestibules), all coexisted. However, it appears that generally speaking the collective rite tended to become more restricted in view of the small size of the tombs and the few bodies they contained. In fact, the tendency towards the reduction of collective burial, which started in the Bell Beaker culture, crystallized in the practice of individual burials (Fuente Olmedo in Valladolid, Aldeagordillo in Ávila), sometimes with very rich grave goods, which are usually the only evidence of the development of social inequalities in these territories.

Individual burials are particularly frequent on the Atlantic seaboard, where they provide the bulk of the evidence of the start of the Early Bronze Age. In the north-west (Galicia and northern Portugal) this period is defined by the Montelavar-Atios horizon, characterized by individual burials in pits or cists. Among the grave goods are plain pottery vessels and metal objects in the Bell Beaker tradition (tanged daggers, Palmela arrowheads, and gold ornaments at sites in Quinta de Água Branca in Viana do Castelo and Vale Ferrerio in Braga), along with new developments such as Carrapatas halberds, which are usually interpreted as a sign of relations with the Atlantic area.

Further south the crisis of the flourishing Copper Age societies of the lower Tagus and the south-west brought about a drop in population and a change in social and other relations. From Spanish Extremadura to the mouth of the Tagus the majority of the Copper Age settlements and cemeteries were abandoned. Little is known about the new ways of living, although in some areas the occupation of caves and natural shelters prevailed. Prominent further south, as in the north-west, were cist cemeteries with Bell Beaker-influenced metal grave goods that define the Ferradeira culture. The development of these cemeteries is connected to the Bronze Age proper in the south-west, whose first phase, Atalaia, is characterized by cists under mounds of circular stones, plain carinated pottery, and copper tools. The presence of cemeteries made up of several dozen cists in central-western Andalucía and Extremadura (El Castañuelo in Huelva), the poverty of their grave goods, and the scarcity of data on the settlements mark a contrast to the Argaric south-east. However, the presence of some burials under settlements situated in strategic positions (Setefilla in Seville or El Trastejón in Huelva), the dominant position of some male graves with weapons at the heart of cist cemeteries (La Traviesa in Huelva), and the results of recent excavation in little-explored regions (Cerro de Capellanía in Málaga), may reduce the sharpness of that contrast. In short, towards the west as well, some groups appear to have tried to impose funerary practices and political relations similar to those of El Argar, although without attaining their intensity or stability.

The Early Bronze Age: Social and Economic Developments

The Iberian Peninsula between 2200 and 1550 cal BC was marked by striking social contrasts. In El Argar the bigger and more densely populated centres functioned as capitals of territories that included subordinate settlements on the plains. The marked differences in burial customs, in the control of and access to food, stone and metallurgy production, and in the use of physical coercion, are characteristic of a society divided into socioeconomic classes and organized into a state. The communities of La Mancha, the east coast, and western Andalucía do not display a comparable degree of social exploitation, although without doubt violence played a prominent role to judge from the effort devoted to the erection of fortifications and other defensive measures (see Fig. 33.5). It is not unreasonable to think that the expansionist and militaristic nature of Argaric society had some influence on its neighbours, who felt the need to erect fortifications for their own defence.

If in the south-east the break with the Copper Age gave way to a greater stabilization of settlement and, probably, to an increase in population and production, in the western peninsula there was a drastic reduction in the number of settlements and a profound reorganization of social relations. Meanwhile, in the central and northern regions the changes do not appear to have been so abrupt and took place within the framework of still relatively mobile communities, with only sporadic signs of socioeconomic inequalities.

Above and beyond these differences, the first centuries of the Bronze Age brought about an intensification of stockbreeding and, above all, of arable agriculture, as compared to the Copper Age. The increase in storage capacity in pottery vessels and silos, the predominance of barley and wheat remains in palaeobotanical records, the orientation of flint-working towards the production of sickle teeth and, at least in the south-east, a new type of grinder that made milling more efficient, are indicators of the importance now assumed by cereal growing. That led to a reduction in forest and a proliferation of open land, bordering on steppe in the driest areas and meadow-type terrain in wetter zones.

These changes spelt the end of the Copper Age socioeconomic structure based on the production of an exceptional variety of exchangeable goods with a high symbolic value, whose large-scale circulation transformed collective surpluses into reciprocal exchanges instead of private excess. From the third millennium cal BC on, forms of power would depend more on the control of the productive forces of increasingly demarcated economic territories than on the circulation of objects among communities. With production heading in this direction, new forms of settlement and architecture made sense as strategic elements in the storage and management of agricultural wealth. However, social and political developments varied, from the centralized appropriation of goods seen at El Argar, to the trusted method of storage spread across 'pit fields', and including the collective protection of crops in upland settlements or *motillas*. For centuries in many northern and western regions, mechanisms of resistance and social cooperation even stood in the way of subjugation to strategies of profit extraction, and the emergence of specialized control groups.

These differences are also reflected in the organization of metallurgy. If in El Argar the production and circulation of metal was organized on a regional scale and controlled by the dominant class, in the rest of the peninsula the places and means of production do not appear through outstanding architectural or burial contexts, the quality and effort invested, or topographic prominence. At the start of the Bronze Age the same copper ores continued to be employed as those used during the Copper Age. The real novelties were in the means and processes of production, with the introduction of casting and the perfection of forging, which improved metallurgical production and the quality of the objects. These and other technical innovations, such as the use of rivets to hold blade implements, enabled the development of specialized weapons such as halberds and, as of c.1800 cal BC, swords measuring more than 50 cm long. Their greater prevalence in the south-east suggests that social violence had taken a firmer hold here.

In short, the El Argar people reached a level of economic development that was far superior to the rest of the Iberian Peninsula and had a direct influence on their neighbours as a social and productive model from which to defend themselves collectively and, at the same time, to be emulated by emerging local elites. Around 1550 cal BC this focal point of hegemonic power was eliminated, apparently by internal forces as suggested by the suppression of its ideological superstructure (the end of the traditional funerary practices) and its economic system. Certain archaeological and environmental factors indicate that the ultimate cause of this 'revolutionary' event was an acute subsistence crisis, brought on by over-exploitation of the environment.

THE LATE BRONZE AGE (C.1550–1300 CAL BC)

From the point of view of population, in the centuries that followed the Argaric crisis it is possible to suggest the existence of three different social and economic environments in the Iberian Peninsula: 1. the southern half, in which El Argar and all the other groups more or less linked to it disappear; 2. the central zone, particularly the valleys of the middle Duero and Tagus, where the previous population continued without major changes, but acquired peninsula-wide importance as a result of the widespread distribution of the Cogotas I pottery style, which originated in those regions; 3. the Atlantic regions from Portugal to the Pyrenees, where data on settlements and cemeteries are very scarce.

The South of the Peninsula

In the southern half of the peninsula between 50 and 100 per cent of the most stable upland settlements were abandoned. Among the new societies, various economic and political paths can be discerned, from centres that tried to maintain the vertical system of production in the Argaric style, albeit on a local scale, to communities that returned to systems of self-sufficiency within the means offered by their respective environments. In some regions, such as south-western La Mancha, following the abandonment of their *motillas*, *morras*, and *castillejos*, there is no record of stable settlement structures until the Iron Age.

The hilltop settlements that remained in the south-east after El Argar, such as Gatas, Fuente Álamo, Cuesta del Negro, or Cerro de la Encina, retained the terraced layout of the living quarters, now quadrangular or rectangular, or simple huts. There are clear architectural differences between the settlements. In contrast to the previous period, the virtual absence of burial contexts indicates not just political and ideological changes, but economic ones too.

Although a large part of the Argaric means of production remained, the scarcity of large-capacity pottery vessels is significant, as is the disappearance of workshops specializing in the large-scale processing of cereals and textiles. Prominent among the new developments in the pottery repertoire are bottles, open dishes, and carinated bowls with vertical rims, often of high quality and with decorative motifs originally from the Meseta in the style of Cogotas I.

The dissolution of the Argaric state also brought with it the diversification of food production, by inference from the bone record in terms of hunted animals, from the significant regional differences in stockbreeding practices, and from the relative increase in the consumption of legumes and nuts compared to the overwhelming use of barley during El Argar.

Another sign of the decentralization of production was the relaxation of political control over metallurgy, with production sites appearing more regularly and with little regard to the size and location of settlements. The disappearance of the Argaric frontiers, both internally and externally, also triggered the participation of communities in medium and long-distance contacts and exchange. The circulation of volcanic rock for the manufacture of more effective grinding tools, the presence of vessels and decorative elements shared widely across the peninsula (Cogotas I), and the general appearance of trade in tin for the production of bronze, beyond the reach of centralized and institutionalized powers, reflect the dawn of a new type of social relations. Another indicator of the permeability of the peninsula's communities is the presence of wheel-turned pottery in the south of the peninsula, possibly of Mycenaean or Cypriot origin, around 1300 cal BC (Llanete de Los Moros in Córdoba, Cuesta del Negro in Granada, and Gatas in Almería).

In a social context characterized by greater autonomy of communities, diversification of production, and permeability in external relations, political and economic relations appear to have impeded levels of exploitation of the sort seen in the Argaric period. However, that does not stop us seeing concentrations of power in particular places, especially in the old Argaric periphery. El Cabezo Redondo (Alicante) is a prime example. This settlement occupied a hilltop site covering almost a hectare and located strategically above the natural corridor of the Vinalopó river, which connects the Mediterranean coast to La Mancha. To date, some 20 rooms have been uncovered, some measuring up to 14 by 5 m, and built with walls plastered with mud and stones, and roofs comprising wooden beams and thatch held up by tree trunks. Inside, evidence of workshops for the processing of cereals on a large scale, specialized textile production, and abundant signs of metallurgy have been documented. Both the architecture and the organization of production are without doubt reminiscent of Argaric workshops, as is the unusual survival of the burial ritual.

In this context, a novelty is the presence of gold ornaments. As well as the different objects that have appeared at Cabezo Redondo itself, on the eastern slope of the hill a child's grave was discovered in a cist along with a gold pendant and a hoard of 35 gold ornaments (diadem, pendants, bracelets, rings, and spirals, among other items). However, the most spectacular find—the Treasure of Villena—appeared in a nearby watercourse: a vessel buried in the gravel of the riverbed concealed a hoard consisting of 11 gold bowls and dishes, 2 bottles also made of gold and 3 of silver, 28 gold bracelets and 1 of iron, as well as several accessories, some with inlaid amber work. The total weight of the hoard amounts to almost 10 kg.

Bearing in mind the typically Argaric shape of the Treasure's pottery container, pottery pieces similar to the gold bottles, and the archaeological context of similar ornaments at Cabezo Redondo itself, this hoard cannot have been hidden much after the end of El Argar. Fresh excavations at Cabezo Redondo and radiocarbon dating confirm the date of the Treasure as prior to 1300/1200 cal BC, when the settlement was abandoned for good. In view of the organization of the forces of production in the settlement, it is not absurd to interpret the Treasure of Villena as evidence of a local, perhaps hereditary, aristocracy based on control over inter-regional communication routes and the centralization of local surpluses. However, such concentration of wealth and power was an exception for the period, which was dominated by small settlements that were relatively mobile but technologically well equipped. In addition to Cabezo Redondo, other centres of regional power in the south of the peninsula could have been Pic dels Corbs (Valencia) or Llanete de los Moros (Córdoba) (see above).

The North

Unlike the south, the societies in the north of the peninsula remained economically and politically stable during the turbulent sixteenth century cal BC. In fact, the new Cogotas I pottery style, defined by very characteristic techniques and decorative motifs, appears to have had its origin in the northern Meseta as a continuation of the Protocogotas decorations that marked the start of the Middle Bronze Age in the region (*c*.1800/1700 cal BC) (Fig. 33.6). Cogotas I defines a chronological horizon present over a geographical extent not seen since the Bell Beaker phenomenon. It would last until the turn of the millennium. Stylistically, it is characterized by the use of geometrical motifs (garlands of concentric semicircles, wolf's teeth, rows of spikes or circles) executed by means of linear incision techniques, *boquique* (dot and line decoration), 'sewn' decoration, and excision. There are various vessels on which these appear, though the emblematic pieces are the dishes with the lower part of the body being of truncated cone shape with high carination, open platters, and pots with prominent rim.

In the northern Meseta, the Tagus Valley, and the upper Ebro Valley, settlements continued to be divided between upland sites (Los Tolmos de Caracena in Soria, Ecce Homo in Madrid Province) and 'pit fields' in the lowlands (La Venta in Palencia, Teso del Cuerno in Salamanca, or Caserío de Perales in Madrid Province). The pits on these sites were sporadically used as tombs for individual interment with few or no grave goods. Before 1300 cal BC, there do not appear to have been any major differences in metallurgical production or in any other economic sector in relation to the previous period. Stability seems to have been the keynote of these societies.

This stability would have been reflected in communities that usually comprised a few dozen individuals, relatively high mobility, and a diversified economy. While the Cogotas I groups have traditionally been considered basically stockbreeders, the presence of grinding tools in many of the settlements points to a mixed economy in which more importance was given to arable agriculture or stockbreeding, depending on geographical conditions.

From the core zone of the Duero and upper Tagus, Cogotas I pottery spread across almost the entire peninsula, with areas of greater and lesser density. In the places where it appears, it signals the start of a new phase of the Bronze Age, even when it is not accompanied by other significant changes. In fact the general trend of continuity observed in the Meseta can also be seen in other western regions, where bronze objects, which were still not very abundant, indicate the maintenance of the Atlantic contacts registered centuries earlier.

THE FINAL BRONZE AGE (C.1300–900 CAL BC)

In general terms we only have patchy knowledge of the peninsula from *c*.1300 cal BC. The main gaps concern settlements, of which there is practically no record across entire regions, or which are characterized by traditional pits and hut floors, whether on the plains or on high ground. This situation is coupled with an increasingly intense and extensive circulation of products, particularly metal objects, throughout the peninsula—products that also have clear and frequent parallels on the Atlantic seaboard and in the Mediterranean basin. Given that economic power appears to have gradually moved back from the Atlantic and Meseta regions towards the Mediterranean and southern peninsula, this will be the order in which we approach the events of the final stage of the Bronze Age.

The 'Final Atlantic Bronze Age' takes in a broad series of relations maintained with societies from the rest of the European Atlantic seaboard and the British Isles. This archaeological expression has traditionally been defined on the basis of numerous discoveries of bronze weapons and tools, often gathered in hoards. They are distributed mainly in Galicia, Asturias, and in the middle and lower basins of the Duero and Tagus, but there is also a prominent presence in the south-west and even, in its final stages, on the Mediterranean coast. The main technological innovation is the frequent use of ternary bronzes (with three elements in the alloy) containing a low percentage of lead, but which over time went up to relatively high proportions. That could have facilitated the intensification of production of tools, weapons, and different ornaments, prominent among which are the first fibulae. Likewise, it is worth mentioning the occasional presence of iron objects prior to the turn of the millennium.

Despite the common character of the metal types, the Final Atlantic Bronze Age cannot be considered an archaeological entity that reflects a cultural or political unit. Behind those common objects, diverse regional developments can be observed. In any case, it is an indication that at the end of the second millennium cal BC the communities of the peninsula were not technologically backward nor had they stagnated; rather they were participating in inter-regional networks.

Recent research in Portugal and the northern Meseta is beginning to produce information about settlement modes and community economic organization responsible for this boom in metallurgy. Appearing in the central and northern part of Portugal from 1300/1200 cal BC were a series of hilltop sites, covering areas of between 0.05 and 1.5 hectares, which would reach their peak in the tenth century. At all excavated sites the remains of metallurgical production and in some cases as much as 18 kg of scrap, half-finished products, and finished bronze objects have been found (Senhora da Guia de Baiões in Beira Alta). Such a volume of production would have been achieved in basically domestic environments, of small communities with a diversified economy based on agriculture, stockbreeding, acorn gathering, and a little hunting. It is certainly remarkable that it should have been in this unfocused, relatively unspecialized economic and political context that the rich Baiões-Vénat horizon would subsequently arise (end of the ninth to the middle of the eighth century cal BC).

A greater degree of centralization of production, including of metallurgy, occurred in the Meseta, where the Cogotas I style still prevailed. New discoveries of moulds and metal objects from settlements and hoards confirm that this broad territory also participated in the production and circulation of Atlantic bronzes. Perhaps this metallurgy was dominated by specialists with a prominent social position, as the hoard of Valdevimbre (León) suggests. Within the large hilltop settlements and small low-lying villages, the most significant evidence of production is found in the former. While these settlements could cover up to 10 hectares, their architecture remained limited to huts and pits (Carricastro in Valladolid; Castro de Ardón in León; Ecce Homo in Madrid Province). Only occasionally were these prominent settlements delimited by ramparts intended for defence or demarcation (Los Castillejos de Sanchorreja in Ávila; Mesa del Carpio in Salamanca). The central importance of certain settlements is expressed by the concentration in the area of numerous querns, in contrast to a lesser presence on the plains, a situation that recalls the organization of productive forces of El Argar a few centuries earlier. Unfortunately, the extreme rarity of graves and the absence of a greater number of settlement excavations make it difficult to profile the social structure of these communities.

If the 'Final Atlantic Bronze Age' takes in a broad series of relations maintained with societies from the rest of the European Atlantic seaboard and British Isles, the Urnfields in the north-east of the peninsula demonstrate contacts between Iberia and central Europe. Here, the Segre-Cinca group defines the move from the initial wood and mud-brick-walled huts (Tossal de Solibert in Lleida) to rectangular dwellings with stone foundations set out in rows along a central street (Genó, Carretelà in Lleida). These communities used pottery vessels with fluted decoration that are linked to the emergence of the funerary phenomenon of the Urnfields (the cremation of the body and the deposition of the ashes in an urn). This, along with any grave goods, was then buried in a pit that was sometimes marked on the surface (Can Missert in Barcelona, Torre Filella in Lleida). Despite this practice being recorded at the same time in such distant regions as the north of Portugal (Paranho in Viseu) or the south-east (Qurénima in Almería), the greater density of graves in the north-east and their proximity to central European foci has led some scholars to link the new ritual to the arrival over the Pyrenees of populations or influences emanating from the Hallstatt culture. However, today there is a tendency to acknowledge the role of indigenous populations, given the continuation of previous forms of settlement and burial ritual, such as chamber or cist burial (Castellets II in Zaragoza).

Following the Mediterranean coast southwards, in the south-east of the peninsula most of the Late Bronze Age settlements were abandoned. In this part we find small settlements—some on hilltops, some not—comprising huts with oval bases made of stone or mud-brick (La Serrecica in Murcia, or Cerro del Real in Granada). The rarity of querns in these huts suggests these communities were more geared towards stockbreeding. Towards the end of the second millennium cal BC new hilltop centres began to appear, or existing settlements were reorganized around more stable structures, with evidence for specialized metallurgy (Peña Negra in Alicante or Acinipo in Málaga). Discovered at the Peña Negra hilltop settlement in Alicante was a workshop measuring 8 by 4.5 m and devoted to the production of Atlantic bronzes, such as carp's tongue swords, as well as textiles.

The Ría de Huelva hoard, carbon-dated to the tenth century cal BC, is the most outstanding example of the importance of the south-western corner of the peninsula as a producer and consumer of Atlantic metals at the beginning of the first millennium cal BC. It is composed of 400 pieces of bronze with a fairly uniform tin content, including carp's tongue swords and solid-hilted swords, spearheads, and ferrules, and Sicilian and Cypriot-type fibulae. Recent isotopic analyses indicate that the metal from these objects could have had as many as five different origins, among others Sierra Morena and possibly Sardinia.

It is no easy task to establish the characteristics of peninsular societies prior to Phoenician colonization. In addition to the previously mentioned scarcity of houses, except for those areas where urn cremation was the norm there is also a limited and irregular funerary record—burials in pits already used for other purposes, the reuse of previous graves, or unique monuments such as the tholos of Roça de Casal do Meio in Setúbal. The evidence that does exist largely consists of stone stelae, carved onto which are representations of weapons (shields, swords, spears, bows and arrows) and other objects (fibulae, mirrors, combs, razors, lyres, wagons) often, though not always, accompanied by a human figure (Brozas in Cáceres, Cabeza de Buey III in Badajoz). Recently, emphasis has been placed on the 'diadem stelae', which include a human figure, perhaps female, whose head may be crowned by a curved ornament (Torrejón de Rubio II in Cáceres, Capilla I in Badajoz). The stelae are particularly prevalent in the middle Guadiana Basin and the lower Guadalquivir, and are the last examples of figurative traditions dating back to the Early Bronze Age in the south of Portugal, the central mountain range, and the western Meseta (the so-called Alentejo stelae and pebble stelae). They could have been used as territorial markers or may have formed part of funerary and/or commemorative practices linked to distinguished figures. This idea would be particularly applicable to the stelae that show a human figure, perhaps a military leader, whether accompanied by weapons or other valuable objects or by a striking diadem. Similar funerary links have been attributed to hoards of gold (torcs, bracelets, rings), such as those from Sagrajas and Bodonal de la Sierra (Badajoz).

The concentration of wealth displayed in the metal hoards, the abundance of weapons, and the individualized symbolism of the stelae, suggest that some social groups held a degree of economic control, political power, and ideological hegemony. The base of this power could have lain precisely in the control of the circulation of metals and other goods, rather than in the productive processes themselves, given the abundance of raw materials available and the limited specialization of craftsmanship observed. Copper, tin, iron, ivory, and amber would have been just some of the materials and products that moved around a very dynamic network of circulation and communication by both land and sea. The discovery, for example, of many of these objects in the cemeteries of Menorca and Mallorca is an indication of the reliability of these supply routes, even to outlying islands with no raw materials of their own. It is not absurd to suppose that the very existence of such navigation and transport capability in the Late Bronze Age enabled the early appearance of Phoenician traders in the far west. It is just this discovery of a collection of Phoenician, Cypriot, Greek, and Sardinian pottery in Huelva, and its dating to around 915–850 cal BC, that would indicate the arrival of and route followed by the sailors from the east. The first Phoenician settlements in the south of the peninsula (Cádiz, Morro de Mezquitilla in Málaga) were founded around 900 cal BC. Their presence and the introduction of new exotic products could have led to a devaluation of Atlantic and Mediterranean traditions that resulted in the decline of the system of exchange of the Final Bronze Age. The emerging local elite would not have wasted the opportunities for further economic and political differentiation afforded by the new products of exchange and markets, thus facilitating the work of the colonizers. It was this period that witnessed the birth of the economic and social structures that were to mark a good part of the first millennium cal BC until the Carthaginian and then Roman conquests of the Iberian Peninsula.

Bibliography

Abarquero, F. J. (2005). *Cogotas I. La difusión de un tipo cerámico durante la Edad del Bronce*, Arqueología en Castilla-León, 4. Léon: Junta de Castilla-León.

Aranda, G., Fernández, S., Haro, M., Molina, F., Nájera, T., and Sánchez, M. (2008). 'Water control and cereal management on the Bronze Age Iberian Peninsula: La Motilla de Azuer', *Oxford Journal of Archaeology*, 27: 241–59.

Blasco, C., Blanco, J., Liesau, C., Carrión, E., García, J., Baena, J., Quero, S., and Rodríguez, MªJ. (2005–7). *El Bronce Medio y Final en la Región de Madrid—El poblado de la fábrica de Ladrillos (Getafe, Madrid)*, Estudio de Prehistoria y Arqueología Madrileñas 14–15, Número Monográfico. Madrid: Museo de los Orígenes.

Brandherm, D. (2003). *Die Dolche und Stabdolche der Steinkupfer- und der älteren Bronzezeit auf der Iberischen Halbinsel*, Prähistorische Bronzefunde, VI (12). Stuttgart: Franz Steiner Verlag.

Caja de Ahorros del Mediterráneo (ed.) (2001). *Y acumularon tesoros. Mil años de historia en nuestras tierras: Valencia, Murcia, Castellón, Alicante, Barcelona Valencia*. Alicante: Caja de Ahorros del Mediterráneo.

Castro, P. V., Lull, V., and Micó, R. (1996). *Cronología de la Prehistoria Reciente de la Península Ibérica y Baleares (c.2800–900 cal ANE)*, British Archaeological Reports, (International series), 652. Oxford: Archaeopress.

——, Chapman, R. W., Gili, S., Lull, V., Micó, R., Rihuete, C., Risch, R., and Sanahuja, Mª E. (1999). *Proyecto Gatas. 2. La dinámica arqueoecológica de la ocupación prehistórica*. Sevilla: Consejería de Cultura de la Junta de Andalucía.

Celestino, S. (2001). *Estelas de guerrero y estelas diademadas: la precolonización y formación del mundo tartésico*. Barcelona: Bellaterra.

——, Rafel, N., and Armada, X.-L. (eds.) (2008). *Contacto cultural entre el Mediterráneo y el Atlántico (siglos XII–VIII ane)—La precolonización a debate*, Serie Arqueológica, 11. Madrid: Escuela Española de Historia y Arqueología en Roma-CSIC.

Celis, J., Delibes, G., Fernández Manzano, J., and Grau, L. (eds.) (2007). *El hallazgo leonés de Valdevimbre y los depósitos del Bronce Final Atlántico en la Península Ibérica*. Leon: Junta de Castilla y León/Diputación Provincial de León.

Chapman, R. W. (1990). *Emerging Complexity: The Later Prehistory of South-East Spain, Iberia and the West Mediterranean*. Cambridge: Cambridge University Press.

—— (2003). *Archaeologies of Complexity*. London: Routledge.

Comendador, B. (1998). *Los inicios de la metalurgia en el noroeste de la Península Ibérica*, in *Brigantium*, 11. Concello de A Coruña: Museo Arquelóxico.

Contreras, F. (ed.) (2000). *Proyecto Peñalosa. Análisis histórico de las comunidades de la Edad del Bronce del Piedemonte meridional de Sierra Morena y Depresión Linares-Bailén*, Arqueología Monografías, 10. Seville: Junta de Andalucía.

Delibes, G. and Montero, I. (eds.) (1997). *Las primeras etapas metalúrgicas en la Península Ibérica. II. Estudios regionales*. Madrid: Fundación Ortega y Gasset.

Fábregas, R. (ed.) (1998). *A Idade do Bronce en Galicia: novas perspectivas*. Cuadernos do Seminario de Sargadelos, 77. Sada, Coruña: Do Castro.

Fernández-Posse, Mª D. (1998). *La investigación protohistórica en la Meseta y Galicia*. Madrid: Síntesis.

——, Gilman, A., Martín, C., and Brodsky, M. (2008). *Las comunidades agrarias de la Edad del Bronce en la Mancha Oriental (Albacete)*. Madrid: CSIC, Biblioteca Praehistórica Hispana, XXV.

Galán Domingo, E. (1993). *Estelas, paisaje y territorio en el Bronce Final del Suroeste de la Península Ibérica*. Madrid: Editorial Complutense.

García Huerta, M. and Morales, J. (eds.) (2004). *La Península Ibérica en el II milenio A.C.: poblados y fortificaciones*. Cuenca: Universidad de Castilla-La Mancha.

García Sanjuán, L. (1998). *La Traviesa*, SPAL Monografías, I. Seville: Universidad de Sevilla.

Hernández Alcaraz, L. and Hernández Pérez, M. (eds.) (2004). *La Edad del Bronce en tierras Valencianas y zonas limítrofes*. Alicante: Ayuntamiento de Villena.

Hernández Pérez, M., Soler, J. A., and López Padilla, J. A. (eds.) (2009). *En los confines del Argar. Una cultura de la Edad del Bronce en Alicante*. Alicante: Museo Arqueológico de Alicante.

Jorge, V. O. (ed.) (2000). *Pré-história recente da Península Ibérica*, Actas del 3º Congresso de Arqueología Peninsular, 4. Porto: ADECAP.

López, J., and Alonso, N. (1997–8). 'Minferri (Juneda, Garrigues): un nou tipus d'assentament a l'aire Lliure a la plana occidental catalana, durant la primera meitat del segon mil.lenni cal. bc', *Tribuna d'Arqueologia*: 279–306.

Lull, V. (1983). *La cultura de El Argar. Un modelo para el estudio de las formaciones económico-sociales prehistóricas*. Madrid: Akal.

—— (2000). 'Argaric society: death at home', *Antiquity*, 74: 581–90.

—— Micó, R., Rihuete, C., and Risch, R. (2010). 'Metal and social relations of production in the 3rd and 2nd millennia BCE in the southeast of the Iberian Peninsula', *Trabajos de Prehistoria*, 67: 323–47.

—— Micó, R., Rihuete, C., and Risch, R. (2011). 'El Argar and the beginning of class society in the Western Mediterranean', in S. Hansen and J. Müller (eds), *Sozialarchäologische Perspektiven: Gesellschaftlicher Wandel 5000–1500 v.Chr. zwischen Atlantik und Kaukasus*, Deutsches Archäologisches Institut. Berlin: Von Zabern, 381–414.

Nocete, F. (1994). *La formación del Estado en las campiñas del Alto Guadalquivir (3000–1500 a.n.e): Análisis de un proceso de transición*. Granada: Universidad de Granada.

Pavón Sodevilla, I. (1998). *El tránsito del II al I milenio a.c. en las cuecas medias de los ríos Tajo y Guadiana: La Edad del Bronce*. Cáceres: Universidad de Extremadura.

Risch, R. (2002). *Recursos naturales, medios de producción y explotación social. Un análisis económico de la industria lítica de Fuente Alamo (Almería), 2250–1400 ane*, Iberia Archaeologica. Mainz: Philipp von Zabern.

Ruiz-Gálvez, M. (1998). *La Europa atlántica en la Edad del Bronce. Un viaje a las raíces de la Europa occidental*. Barcelona: Crítica.

Schubart, H. (1975). *Die Kultur der Bronzezeit im Südwesten der Iberischen Halbinsel*, Madrider Forschungen, 9. Berlin: De Gruyter.

——, Pingel, V., and Arteaga, O. (2000). *Fuente Álamo. Las excavaciones arqueológicas 1977–1991 en el poblado de la Edad del Bronce*, Arqueología-Monografías. Seville: Junta de Andalucía.

—— and Ulreich, H. (1991). *Die Funde der Südostspanischen Bronzezeit aus der Sammlung Siret*, Madrider Beiträge, 17. Mainz: Philipp von Zabern.

Sesma, J. (1995). 'Diversidad y complejidad: poblamiento de Navarra en la Edad del Bronce', *Cuadernos de Arqueología de la Universidad de Navarra*, 3: 147–84.

Siret, L. and Siret, H. (1887). *Les Premières Âges du métal dans le sud-est de l'Espagne*, Antwerpen (1890) edition in Spanish online. Accessed online 11 May 2011 at http://www.arqueomurcia.com/index.php?a=pu_libro_siret.

Soler García, J. M., Hernández Pérez, M. S., and Soler Díaz, J. A. (eds.) (2005). *El Tesoro de Villena—Un descubrimiento de José María Soler*. Alicante: Museo Arqueológico de Alicante.

CHAPTER 34

THE BRONZE AGE IN THE BALEARIC ISLANDS

VICENTE LULL, RAFAEL MICÓ,
CRISTINA RIHUETE HERRADA,
AND ROBERTO RISCH

The Balearic archipelago consists of four main islands whose biogeographic variability has conditioned human population since prehistoric times. In antiquity the perception of these differences caused them to be differentiated as the Pine Islands and the Gymnesian Islands. The Pine Islands include Ibiza and Formentera, the southernmost and smallest islands, and those nearest the mainland (Fig. 34.1). Our archaeological knowledge of their prehistoric occupation is affected by some large gaps, as a result of research being focused traditionally on the abundant evidence of the Punic period and also perhaps due to a smaller initial human population.

The Gymnesian Islands include Mallorca and Menorca, the two largest islands, which are equally important in the current state of knowledge about Balearic prehistory. However, we should bear in mind the physical factors that differentiate them. Mallorca is by far the larger island (3,626 km^2) with a greater biogeographic diversity. This is partly due to its varied relief, including the Sierra de Tramuntana, a mountain range that is a prolongation of the Betic Systems in the Iberian Peninsula. These mountains follow the northern coast in a south-west–north-east direction, and reach altitudes of up to 1,445 m above sea level (Puig Major). The abrupt calcareous and dolomitic relief, and high rainfall, contrast with the central depression of *Es Pla* and the peripheral coastal plains (*Marines*). Their more gentle scenery is only broken by the mountains in the Sierras de Llevant, which run parallel to the eastern coast, and are no higher than 500 m above sea level. In contrast, the geomorphology of Menorca, with a surface area of only about 700 km^2, is simpler. The northern part of the island, beaten by the strong Tramuntana wind, combines Palaeozoic and Triassic rocks (slates and siliceous sandstones), while the southern half consists of calco-arenite sedimentary rocks divided up by a succession of parallel gorges that cut down to the coast. As a whole, Menorca is practically flat, which makes it invisible from other places, except from certain points on its neighbour Mallorca. The only small hill that stands out above the rest of the

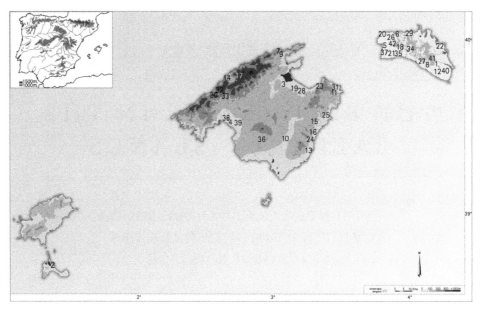

FIG. 34.1 The Balearic Islands with the principal sites mentioned in the text. 1. Binimaimut, 2. Ca Na Costa, 3. Ca Na Cotxera, 4. Ca Na Vidriera, 5. Cala Blanca, 6. Cala Morell, 7. Cala Sant Vicenç, 8. Calascoves, 9. Can Martorellet, 10. Can Roig Nou, 11. Canyamel, 12. Cap de Forma, 13. Closos de Can Gaià, 14. Cova de Moleta, 15. Cova des Bouer, 16. Cova des Moro, 17. Coval Simó, 18. Es Càrritx and Es Forat de ses Aritges, 19. Es Figueral de Son Real, 20. Es Mussol, 21. La Cova, 22. Mongofre Nou, 23. S'Aigua Dolça, 24. S'Hospitalet Vell, 25. S'Illot, 26. Ses Arenes de Baix, 27. Ses Roques Llises, 28. Son Bauló de Dalt, 29. Son Ermità, 30. Son Ferrandell-Olesa, 31. Son Jaumell, 32. Son Mas, 33. Son Matge, 34. Son Mercer de Baix, 35. Son Mestre de Dalt, 36. Son Mulet, 37. Son Olivaret, 38. Son Oms, 39. Son Sunyer, 40. Trebalúger, 41. Torralba d'en Salord, 42. Tudons.

Map: authors (drawing Sylvia Gili).

island is Monte Toro (357 m above sea level), in the centre of Menorca. It is also the furthest island from the mainland (200 km from the coast of Catalonia).

Our knowledge of the chronology and characteristics of the different prehistoric periods has changed radically in the last two decades. Until only a short time ago, the so-called 'Talayotic culture' held a central and almost omnipresent position. Its main diagnostic elements are monumental buildings with a circular or square floor plan (*talaiots*), built from large blocks of stone without any kind of mortar. They are very common in Mallorca and Menorca, but absent from the Pine Islands. It was assumed that these and other Cyclopean buildings, the houses and tombs with a floor plan in the shape of an upturned boat's keel (*navetas*), the sanctuaries, and the *taules*, were more or less synchronous, belonging to the same society that arose in the second millennium BC. The archaeological remains older than the *talaiots*, which were scarcer and less well known, were included within a heterogeneous period called the 'Pre-Talayotic'. One of the most important aspects of research into the remains from the time before the *talaiots* included the chronology and peculiarities of the human colonization of the archipelago. The range of theories about the age of the oldest population has been wide, from the Epipalaeolithic to the first Metal Age.

The current situation is very different thanks to systematic C14 dating programmes and the documentation of new stratigraphic sequences. In the first place, the chronology of the *talaiots* has been fixed clearly between the ninth and sixth centuries cal BC, and therefore the society that built them cannot be included in the Bronze Age, but in the early Iron Age, within European periodization. Secondly, not all the large stone buildings were synchronous. Thus, the *navetas* were built some centuries before the *talaiots*, whereas the construction of such well-known monuments as the *taules* in Menorca and the sanctuaries in Mallorca date, at most, from the last centuries before the Roman conquest.

Finally, the question of the first human colonization takes us back to the late third millennium cal BC, in other words, to a time not very different from the start of the Bronze Age in western Europe. This means that the traditional 'Pre-Talayotic' period lasted for over a millennium, longer than the Talayotic period, and is practically equivalent to the Bronze Age in Europe. In addition, recent research has differentiated a series of material assemblages within this period, so that the concept of 'Pre-Talayotic' itself has become obsolete. With the new data, the periodization in Mallorca and Menorca, from the first stable populations to the Talayotic society, has been established as follows:

- Bell Beaker (only Mallorca) (*c*.2300–2100/2000 cal BC)
- Epi-Bell Beaker–dolmen group (*c*.2100/2000–1600 cal BC)
- Naviform group (*c*.1600–1100/1000 cal BC)
- Proto-Talayotic period (*c*.1100/1000–850 cal BC)

The First Phase of Human Population in Mallorca and Menorca (c.2300–1600 cal bc)

Bell Beaker Archaeological Group (*c*.2300–2100/2000 cal BC)

According to the available evidence, Mallorca was the first island in the group to have a stable population. The most reliable radiocarbon determinations situate this colonization in the second half of the third millennium, probably about 2400–2300 cal BC. It seems these human groups lived in caves and rock shelters, some of which were occasionally used as burial sites (Son Matge rock shelter, Cova des Moro, Cova de Moleta, Coval Simó), or in small open-air settlements (Son Ferrandell-Olessa, Son Mas, Ca na Cotxera), consisting of huts where stone was rarely used as a building material. The characteristics of the settlements seem to indicate that they were occupied seasonally, a circumstance that, in turn, suggests the practice of subsistence strategies such as animal-herding or slash-and-burn agriculture. The role of fishing and shellfish gathering remains to be determined, although it was probably not important, according to the basically terrestrial components in the diet of Balearic populations throughout prehistory, as isotope analyses have shown. As regards hunting, an ongoing debate discusses the exploitation of *Myotragus balearicus*, a caprid endemic to the Gymnesian Islands. Although it is known historically how endemic species in certain island locations have become rapidly extinct as the direct or indirect consequence of human colonization, there is no evidence of the human consumption of *Myotragus*. In fact, it is not even possible to affirm that humans and goats lived together on the islands, as the latest dates obtained from bone samples of these animals are no younger than the first half of the fourth millennium cal BC. This means that it is possible to propose that their extinction was caused by purely ecological factors, and may have concluded over a thousand years before the first stable human settlements.

The most characteristic artefacts of the first occupations on Mallorca include ceramic vessels (bowls, carinated pots) decorated with incised designs in the Bell Beaker tradition. In fact, these objects have been used to define one of the regional styles in the later phases of the Bell Beaker phenomenon. However, this style may not have been fully autonomous, to judge by its affinities with the Pyrenean style, characteristic of the north-eastern Iberian Peninsula. We can also highlight the large ovoid-bodied, flat-based storage vessels, implements such as knives and sickle elements made from flint blades, and copper metallurgy, which probably benefited from local outcrops in the north-eastern part of the Sierra de Tramuntana.

Epi-Bell Beaker–Dolmen Archaeological Group (*c.*2100/2000–1600 cal BC)

In the transition between the third and second millennium BC, the archaeological record reveals a series of developments. In the first place, the presence of humans spread to Menorca and the Pine Islands. The settlements followed the same pattern as the first occupations, and consisted of open-air villages and the occupation of caves and rock shelters. Occasionally, as in the case of the settlements at Son Ferrandell-Olesa and Son Mas, the particularities of the formation of the deposit make it difficult to detect stratigraphic changes between this period and the previous occupations. Therefore, the vertical stratigraphic sequences at cave and rock-shelter sites, like Son Matge and Coval Simó, provide valuable information for the characterization of the material remains of the communities in the early second millennium BC in Mallorca and Menorca. The most striking artefacts include pottery decorated with incised designs, related in some way with late Bell Beaker styles, and which is usually described as 'epi-Bell Beaker'.

However, the clearest and most abundant data comes from funerary contexts. Although the use of natural caves continued in the early second millennium BC (Can Martorellet, Son Marroig, Sa Canova d'Ariany, Vernissa, Cova des Bouer), the use of new kinds of tombs is important. The first types were probably hypogea with a single circular or oval chamber, provided with a megalithic entrance and facade. The best-known examples are on Menorca (Biniai 1 and 2, Sant Tomàs, Cala Morell 11 and 12) and date back to the late third millennium BC, starting a style that lasted until the middle of the second millennium BC. Other simple hypogea, without a structure of orthostats, well documented in Mallorca (Ca na Vidriera 4, Son Sunyer 7, Rafal Llinàs, Son Mulet), were used briefly at the start of the second millennium BC.

The dolmens are another interesting new development. Their construction started in the nineteenth century cal BC, and they are found in the south of Menorca and on the Bay of Alcúdia in north-east Mallorca. They usually possess a small rectangular chamber, at most 3.5 x 2 m in size, accessed by a short corridor or vestibule (S'Aigua Dolça, Son Bauló de Dalt, Montplé, Binidalinet, Ses Roques Llises). The roof was probably made with a mixture of mud, small stones, and plant matter. The structure would have been covered by a mound of stones and earth about 7 or 8 m in diameter.

All these funerary spaces were used for dozens of primary burials deposited successively over two or three centuries. The human remains have occasionally stayed articulated in an orderly manner, but in most cases it is difficult to discern any pattern due to the apparent disorganization of the materials. The grave goods are usually scarce and are objects of everyday use, such as pottery (mostly open or slightly closed bowls, sometimes with a sunken base; pots with an out-turned rim and globular or carenated body; truncated conical vessels with lugs near the rim; and vessels tending to a cylindrical form with a flat base); copper and bronze daggers and awls; buttons made from bone or pig tusks of various types (prismatic and pyramidal with v-shaped perforations, discoidal or flat rectangular forms with double perforation, with a circular or oval body and 'tortoise'-type appendices, among others); simple adornments (pendants made from shells or pig teeth); and grindstones (wristguards).

Extra-Insular Connections and Social Organization during the Initial Occupation of Mallorca and Menorca

One of the most interesting topics in the prehistory of the Balearics is that of the beginning of human population. All the evidence suggests that the Balearics were not an attractive place for the settlement of Neolithic communities, unlike Corsica, Sardinia, Sicily, Malta, Crete, or Cyprus. The situation changed at the end of the third millennium and in the early second millennium BC, coinciding with the late Bell Beaker (Chalcolithic) period and the Early Bronze Age in south-west Europe. A careful examination of the archaeological record in Mallorca and Menorca suggests that the first communities to settle on the islands came from north-east Iberia and the shores of the Gulf of Lion (Roussillon and Languedoc). This hypothesis is supported by the similarities between the Bell Beaker pottery on Mallorca and the late Beaker style in Catalonia, as well as between undecorated vessels on the islands and the common types amongst the so-called *Begleitkeramik* ('accompanying pottery') in Bell Beaker and Early Bronze Age assemblages in north-east Catalonia and Mediterranean France. Other artefacts, like the prismatic and pyramidal bone buttons, and those related to the 'tortoise'-type, are common in Catalonia and south-east France. The funerary architecture also points in the same direction. The Balearic dolmens are similar to the generic type of megalithic tombs in Languedoc. In addition, the affinities are even greater if we take into account the fact that in the coastal strip of Languedoc and Provence monuments facing west and south-west predominate, the exclusive orientation of the Balearic examples. This common factor contrasts with the main trend in neighbouring regions, where the monuments mostly face south or south-east. Other architectural elements in the Balearics have parallels at sites in the north-west of the Mediterranean basin. Thus, the access system at Son Bauló de Dalt and S'Aigua Dolça displays similarities with that of the 'cists with entrance pit' documented in north-east Catalonia and dated to the final Chalcolithic and Early Bronze Age. Equally, the hypogea with or without megalithic entrances can be related to preceding and synchronous examples in the Catalan late Chalcolithic and Early Bronze Age.

In short, several elements coincide in indicating north-east Catalonia and much of Mediterranean France as the origin of the human groups who occupied Mallorca and Menorca, and as regions with which the islands continued to maintain contact and exchange during the first centuries of the second millennium cal BC.

Two questions are posed about the colonization: why? and why now? Several reasons can be given to explain the delay in the colonization of the Balearics compared with other Mediterranean islands. The relative distance of Mallorca and Menorca from other inhabited lands, combined with the absence of suitable raw materials for making polished stone tools, especially the axes and adzes needed to cut down the dense Balearic vegetation, might explain the absence of a stable Neolithic occupation of the islands. In addition, the geographical position away from the main routes for the circulation of obsidian from Sardinia and the Aeolian Islands would have a bearing on the lack of interest in the Balearics, even though communities on the shores of the Mediterranean may have been aware of their existence.

However, these limitations were overcome due to the conjunction of several factors. The first is connected with technological advances in the production of food and implements. By the late third millennium cal BC metallurgy had developed sufficiently for the exploitation of cupriferous minerals in Mallorca and Menorca. Recycling and recasting the metal also favoured productive autonomy, as the first peoples no longer depended on a continuous supply of raw materials, which would have been the case for harder igneous and metamorphic rocks (such as the jadeites, corneans, ophites, and amphibolites used extensively on the northern shores of the western Mediterranean). The first settlers' command of metallurgy has been shown by the discovery of a Beaker with copper adhering to its inner surface, at the rock shelter of Son Matge. Furthermore, the development of the so-called 'secondary products revolution' enabled an increase in productivity and the overall production of food. In practice, this could guarantee subsistence autonomy even in geographical environments that until then had been regarded as marginal. In short, by the late third millennium BC the material conditions had been met for the success of stable settlement on islands relatively far from the mainland.

However, it seems that these conditions were necessary but not sufficient. It is possible that the catalyst for the colonizing movement was the development of forms of economic exploitation and social violence in different parts of the mainland during the third millennium and in the early second millennium BC. In the face of tensions caused by this situation, certain groups from the area of the north-western Mediterranean migrated to lands that had previously been peripheral or marginal, where they could establish new social relationships, away from the conflicts experienced in their places of origin. If we take into account the lack of concern for defence in Balaearic settlements (scarcity of fortifications and preference for lowland locations), the absence of specialized weapons that became increasingly abundant in Europe, and on a symbolic level, the predominance of a collective burial rite that prevented shows of individual display, and the absence of gold and silver ornaments, we may propose that the new settlements stressed peaceful relationships and inhibited the development of permanent economic and political asymmetry.

THE NAVIFORM GROUP (C.1600–1100/1000 CAL BC)

About 1600 cal BC the archaeological record displays a series of new developments. The most significant element consists of large buildings with an elongated floor plan, Cyclopean stone walls, an entrance in the short side and a pointed end or apse (the 'naviform' plan), up to 15 m long and 6 m wide (Closos de Can Gaià, Son Oms, Can Roig Nou, S'Hospitalet Vell, Cala Blanca, Son Mercer de Baix) (Fig. 34.2). The finds documented inside them (hearths, benches, querns, bone, metal and stone implements, pottery for consumption and storage, food remains, and metallurgical production residues) are an indication of many activities associated with craft production, and only a moderate development of the division of labour between buildings. The naviform buildings may be individual structures or in groups of two or more units side by side. These detached or conjoined buildings may be found alone or grouped in open villages of varying density and size. In the second half of the second millennium BC, it becomes more common to find buildings that differ to a greater or lesser degree from the naviform pattern, although the custom of stone architecture is never abandoned (Es Figueral de Son Real, round hut at Torralba d'en Salord).

The naviform buildings extend over the whole of the Balearic Islands for the first time, although it is also true that there was a preference for low land with easy access to potentially fertile soil. The introduction of naviform settlements coincided with a reduction in the use of natural caves, which were only visited occasionally for ritual purposes (Es Càrritx, Es

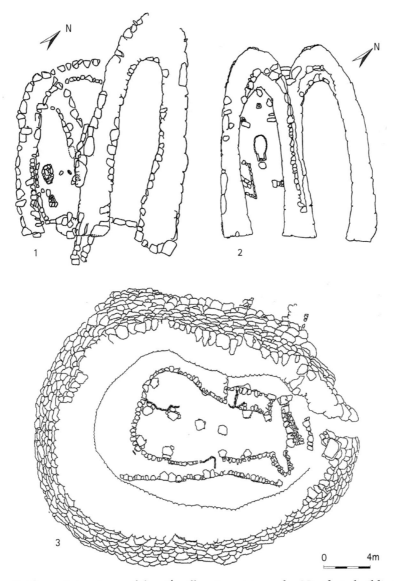

FIG. 34.2 Settlement structures of the 2nd millennium BC. 1 and 2. Naviform buildings from Canyamel and Son Oms; 3. Towerlike structure from Trebalúger.

Drawings: authors, redrawn after various sources.

Mussol). In the course of these subterranean ceremonies, between c.1600–1450 cal BC, fragments of stalactites were broken and piled up, sometimes in association with bones of human hands and feet; portions of meat and pottery vessels were deposited; and magic rites were acted out around hearths located tens of metres from the cave entrances. These customs have been interpreted in terms of chthonic cults that possibly linked the belief in an underground force, responsible for the renewal of fertility, and with life seen in the world outside.

The funerary contexts are noticeable because of their abundance and variety (Fig. 34.3). In addition to the occasional continuity of previous types (simple hypogea, dolmens, and caves), new kinds of structures are found: hypogea with elongated shapes and internal compartments (Cala Sant Vicenç, Son Sunyer, Son Jaumell, Son Vivó); round monuments with thick walls, like tumuli in appearance (only found in Menorca: Ses Arenes de Baix, Son Olivaret, Alcaidús, Son Ermità); and natural caves sealed off with Cyclopean stone walls (Es Càrritx, Es Forat de ses Aritges, Son Matge, Coval d'en Pep Rave, Calascoves LXXVII). All these monuments received varying numbers of burials over the course of several centuries.

Important new developments are seen in portable artefacts too (Figs. 34.4 and 34.5). Potters gradually began to add calcite as temper for the production of barrel-shaped storage jars with thickened rims, or with a globular or ovoid body and out-turned rim. Most of the kitchen and tableware consisted of globular and carinated pots with out-turned rims, of different sizes, and open or slightly in-turned bowls with flat base. They are mostly undecorated, apart from horizontal groups of finger impressions or incisions in certain areas of the upper part of the vessels.

The finds of moulds for making arm-rings, awls, axes, and knives inside some of the naviform structures (S'Hospitalet Vell), and the composition analysis of the metals, has shown that bronze artefacts were being manufactured on the islands. Their use increased until they reached their maximum frequency in the early first millennium cal BC. Bone working also achieved unusual vitality, seen in the abundance of awls, needles, and above all v-perforated buttons made from segments of the shafts of long bones or from pig tusks.

The occasional presence of querns and cereal grains suggests that agriculture was becoming more important in subsistence strategies. However, the abundance of the remains of domestic fauna and the first chemical and bio-archaeological studies of human remains indicate that animals made a substantial contribution to the diet. By contrast, the contribution of sea food was minimal.

The meticulous study of thousands of human remains in Chamber 1 at Cova des Càrritx (Fig. 34.6) has uncovered aspects of the socioeconomic organization of naviform communities in the middle and late phases. This funerary space received the bodies of some two hundred individuals of both sexes and all age groups, except foetuses and babies under three months. Chamber 1 was the tomb of a social unit formed originally by about 14 individuals, a number that is perfectly compatible with the size of a group that could live in a naviform house. The make-up of this social unit remained constant over the centuries, due to very low rates of incremental growth. There were more men than women (ratio of 1.4 to 1); life expectancy was lower for women than men, and there was clear sexual dimorphism in the post-cranial skeleton. As might be expected in a prehistoric society, child mortality was high, and only two thirds of the individuals reached the age of five. The low frequency of caries and, in contrast, the high proportion of plaque on the teeth, indicate that a large part of the diet consisted of food from land animals, and this interpretation has been supported by trace-element analysis. Furthermore, in this respect no difference can be seen between men and women. There

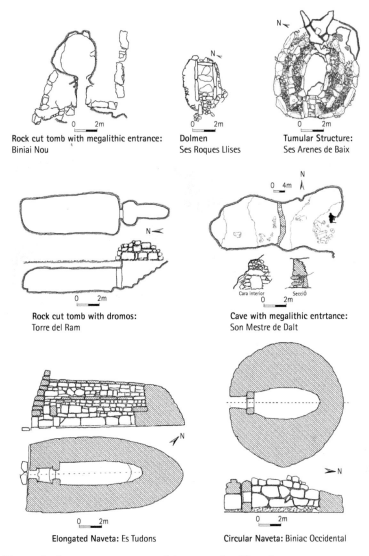

FIG. 34.3 The main funerary structures of the second millennium BC.

Source: Gili et al.

was a synergic relationship between anaemia and infections, and a high level of mobility for at least one sector of the community. This can be correlated with activities such as animal herding and the exploitation of resources over a wide area, characterized by its rugged relief.

One of the most interesting hypotheses suggests the practice of female infanticide, as a form of birth control. It is possible that the community which used Es Càrritx as a tomb employed a mechanism for regulating the population which kept the number of women lower than that of men, and that this infanticide took the form of poorer care and/or differential food during the first years of life. This hypothesis draws together a series of apparently unrelated data, such as the smaller number of adult women, the greater frequency of anaemia

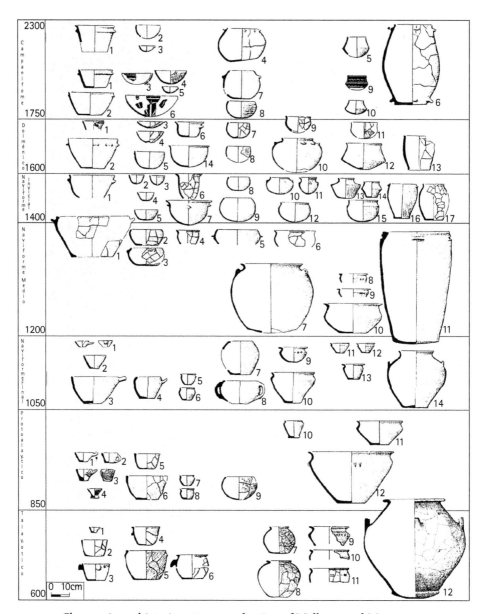

FIG. 34.4 Changes in prehistoric pottery production of Mallorca and Menorca.

Source: authors (modified after Lull et al. 1999).

amongst women, and noticeable differences in stature (sexual dimorphism). These differences would be maintained once maturity had been reached and would not disappear even when the diet was the same for men and women in adulthood.

The clear homogeneity reached in the production of artefacts occurred without the intervention of any form of politico-economic centralization or hierarchy. Society was organized in units that were basically autonomous in terms of subsistence production, as can be seen in the uniformity among the implements found in the houses. The groups who lived in the

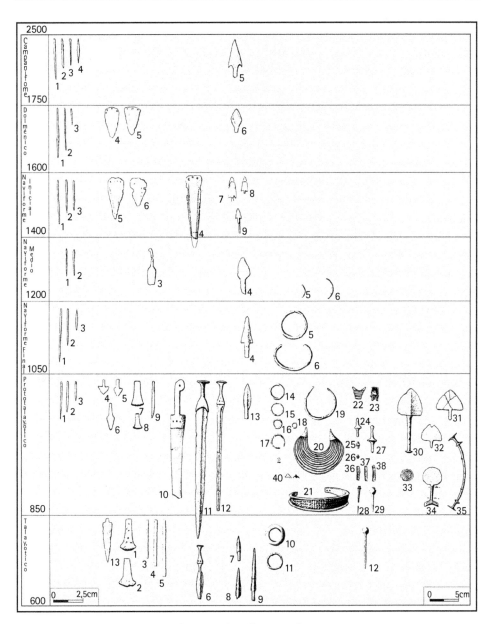

FIG. 34.5 Changes in metal production of Mallorca and Menorca.

Source: authors (Lull et al. 1999).

naviform houses cooperated in the building of the structures, the acquisition of raw materials (metals) and, perhaps, in herding the livestock and working in the fields.

Within a panorama characterized by the absence of political hierarchy, certain individuals have been identified who enjoyed a 'mediating' social position in the realm of politics and belief systems. This has been achieved through the analysis of the finds at Es Mussol, a cave located in an impressive cliff-face on the north-west coast of Menorca, whose access is extremely dangerous. A series of wooden objects, including two carvings in wild olive wood, were discovered in

FIG. 34.6 Digital photogrametric image of the funerary chamber of the cave of Es Càrritx prior to excavation.

Source: authors (Lull et al. 1999; photogrammetry by Sylvia Gili).

a small hidden interior chamber (Fig. 34.7). They each represent the head and neck of two beings, one of them anthropomorphic and the other zoo-anthropomorphic, whose meaning must lie within a discourse that combined mythological and metaphysical components. The place was visited during brief stays and was the scene of secret practices in which a small number of people took part. Cova des Mussol can be understood as a key stage in the initiation process through which Menorcan communities 'produced' a specific social category, formed by individuals responsible for social and politico-ideological mediation. These people would have acted out their social role in the late Naviform or even perhaps in the Proto-Talayotic phase.

The Proto-Talayotic Period (c.1100/1000–850 cal bc)

The two centuries on either side of the start of the first millennium cal BC are of key importance for an understanding of the end of naviform society and the rise of the Talayotic period. A series of material elements linked with the previous tradition, such as the naviform houses, began slowly to disappear. Some of the houses were still being occupied, occasionally after undergoing reorganization ('Naveta 1' at Closos de Can Gaià). However, in other cases, the settlements were organized in compact urban areas where a variable number of houses, of different floor plans, were gathered around a large, tall stone building that could have been ancestral to the *talaiots*. Es Figueral de Son Real, Cap de Forma, and S'Illot are the best-documented examples of a trend that in some ways foreshadowed the most common type of settlement in the Talayotic period.

FIG. 34.7 Anthropomorphic and zoo-anthropomorphic figures made of olive wood found in the cave of Es Mussol.

Source: authors (Lull et al. 1999; photo: Peter Witte).

In terms of funerary practices, the only trait shared by the communities of Mallorca and Menorca was the continuation of burials in natural caves sealed off by a Cyclopean wall (Es Càrritx, Son Matge, Mongofre Nou). However, unlike Mallorca, Menorca maintained the old habit of an abundance and diversity of funerary structures. The late second millennium and first millennium cal BC are characterized by the emergence of the *navetas* (Tudons, Binimaimut, Binipati Nou, La Cova). These are large stone buildings with a circular or apse-shaped plan, containing an elongated chamber occasionally divided into two levels. The excavation of the best-known site, Naveta des Tudons, showed that the larger tombs were used for the burial of hundreds of bodies (Fig. 34.3).

The practice of collective ritual, traditional on the island, is repeated in the hypogea with a simple floor plan, opening out in the walls of gorges and cliffs (Calascoves III, V, VII, IX, XI, and XXXV). It is also repeated in some natural caves, which may or may not have been modified, in similar locations (Cova des Pas).

The grave goods are more numerous and display greater variety than in previous centuries. Buttons made from bone and teeth, and small pottery vessels (s-shaped pots, conical vessels with a side handle), continued to appear. However, the most notable items are now bronze ornaments and tools ('pectorals', torques, biconical and cylindrical beads, knives, spearheads, awls, etcetera), occasional objects of iron (bracelets) or tin (beads), and also tubular wood or antler containers with a wood or bone lid to hold the hair that had been cut from certain individuals in the course of burial rites. The deposit inside Chamber 5 in Cova des Càrritx has yielded the most eloquent evidence of this ritual based on the post-mortem treatment of some people's hair (which was dyed, combed, cut, and deposited), and which might be linked to a new symbolic importance given to the human head. Although this individualized treatment was reserved for a small number of persons, there is no clear proof that it reflected politico-economic privileges.

Although the difference between Mallorca and Menorca is striking in terms of the variety of funerary spaces, it is less so if we consider the presence on both islands of a large number of artefact types (s-profiled pottery, carinated and globular vessels of different sizes, buttons with v-shaped perforations, 'mirrors', bronze knives and pins, etcetera). This suggests that the contacts between the communities in the early first millennium BC were still intense.

The use of all these types of tombs, as well as the burial practices that we assume they shared despite the diversity seen in the structures, came to an end in the late ninth century or, at the latest, in the early eighth century cal BC. It is probable that the time immediately before the final use of these tombs coincided with the ritual deposition of particularly valuable objects in places of difficult access inside natural caves (Es Càrritx, Mussol). They were symptoms of a society undergoing change, about to abandon ancient traditions and commence the Talayotic period, when the construction of social bonds would be based above all on the public affirmation of the community (construction of *talaiots*, compact settlements), rather than on the celebration of the past and the ancestors in the framework of funerary rites held some distance from the settlements.

Bibliography

Fernández-Miranda, M. (1978). *Secuencia cultural de la prehistoria de Mallorca*, Biblioteca Praehistorica Hispana, vol. XV. Madrid: Dibutación Provincial de Baleares, Instituto de Estudios Baleáricos.

Gili, S., Lull, V., Micó, R., Rihuete, C., and Risch, R. (2006). 'An island decides: megalithic burial rites on Menorca', *Antiquity*, 80: 829–42.

Guerrero, V. Mª. (ed.) (2007). *Prehistoria de las Islas Baleares*. British Archaeological Reports (International Series), 1690. Oxford: Archaeopress.

——, Calvo, M., and Coll, J. (eds.) (2003). *El dolmen de s'Aigua Dolça (Colònia de Sant Pere, Mallorca)*, Collecció La Deixa, 5. Palma de Mallorca: Consell de Mallorca.

Lull, V., Micó, R., Rihuete, C., and Risch, R. (1999). *La Cova des Càrritx y la Cova des Mussol. Ideología y sociedad en la prehistoria de Menorca*. Barcelona: Consell Insular de Menorca.

——, Micó, R., Rihuete, C., and Risch, R. (2002). 'Social and ideological changes in the Balearic Islands during the Later Prehistory', in W. H. Waldren and J. A. Ensenyat (eds.), *World Islands in Prehistory: International Insular Investigations*, British Archaeological Reports (International Series), 1,095. Oxford: Archaeopress, 117–26.

Micó, R. (2005). 'Towards a definition of politico-ideological practices in the prehistory of Minorca (Balearic Islands): the wooden carvings from the Cova des Mussol', *Journal of Social Archaeology*, 5/2: 276–99.

—— (2006). 'Radiocarbon dating and Balearic prehistory: reviewing the periodization of the prehistoric sequence', *Radiocarbon*, 48/3: 421–34.
Pericot, L. (1972). *The Balearic Islands*. London: Thames and Hudson.
Plantalamor, Ll. (1991). *L'arquitectura prehistòrica i protohistòrica de Menorca i el seu marc cultural*, Treballs del Museu de Menorca, 12. Maó: Museu de Menorca.
Pons i Homar, B. (1999). *Anàlisi espacial del poblament al Pretalaiòtic final i Talaiòtic I de Mallorca*, Col·lecció La Deixa, 2. Palma de Mallorca: Consell Insular de Mallorca.
Ramis, D. and Alcover, J. A. (2001). 'Revisiting the earliest human presence in Mallorca, Western Mediterranean', *Proceedings of the Prehistoric Society*, 67: 261–69.
Rihuete, C. (2003). *Bio-arqueología de las prácticas funerarias. Análisis de la comunidad enterrada en el cementerio prehistórico de la Cova des Càrritx (Ciutadella, Menorca)*, British Archaeological Reports (International Series), 1,161. Oxford: Archaeopress.
Roselló Bordoy, G. (ed.) (1992). *La Prehistòria de les illes de la Mediterrania occidental*, Jornades d'Estudis Historics Locals, 10. Palma de Mallorca, 29–31 October 1991. Palma de Mallorca: Institut d'Estudis Balearics.
—— (1973, 1979). *La Cultura Talayótica en Mallorca*. Palma de Mallorca: Cort.
Van Strydonck, M., Boudin, M., and Ervynck, A. (2002). 'Stable isotopes (13C and 15N) and diet: animal and human bone collagen from prehistoric sites on Mallorca, Menorca and Formentera (Balearic Islands, Spain)', in W. H. Waldren and J. A. Ensenyat (eds.), *World Islands in Prehistory: International Insular Investigations*. V Deia International Conference of Prehistory, British Archaeological Reports (International Series) 1,095. Oxford: Archaeopress, 189–97.
——, Boudin, M., Ervynck, A., Orvay, J., and Borms, H. (2005). 'Spatial and temporal variation of dietary habits during the prehistory of the Balearic Islands as reflected by ^{14}C, $\partial^{15}N$ and $\partial^{13}C$ analyses on human and animal bones', *Mayurqa*, 30: 523–41.
Veny, C. (1968). *Las cuevas sepulcrales del Bronce Antiguo de Mallorca*, Biblioteca Praehistorica Hispana, 9. Madrid: Consejo Superior de Investigaciones Científicas, Instituto Español de Prehistoria.
Veny, C. (1982). *La necrópolis protohistórica de Cales Coves, Menorca*, Biblioteca Praehistorica Hispanica, 20. Madrid: Consejo Superior de Investigaciones Científicas, Instituto Español de Prehistoria.
Waldren, W. H. (1982). *Balearic Prehistoric Ecology and Culture: The Excavation and Study of Certain Caves, Rock Shelters and Settlements*, British Archaeological Reports (International Series), 149. Oxford: Archaeopress.
—— (1998). *The Beaker Culture of the Balearic Islands: An Inventory of Evidence from Caves, Rock Shelters, Settlements and Ritual Sites*, British Archaeological Reports (International Series), 709; (Western Mediterranean Series), 1. Oxford: Archaeopress.

CHAPTER 35

PENINSULAR ITALY

ANNA MARIA BIETTI SESTIERI

Introduction

Despite its relatively limited extent, Italy is characterized by a considerable degree of diversity, and structurally the country can be divided into distinct regions. Peninsular Italy covers the whole land mass south of the Po plain (Fig. 35.1). Significant features include its central position in the Mediterranean and the extent of its coastline (8000 km), which make it a privileged destination for Mediterranean seafarers.

The main morphological component of the peninsula is the Apennine range, running longitudinally along its centre. This has been a limiting factor in the availability of settlement and agricultural space; moreover, it constituted a barrier between the Adriatic and Tyrrhenian sides. However, during the Bronze Age the Apennine passes were the medium for communication between them. Another inter-regional factor is the level morphology of the Adriatic coast, providing a route linking the peninsula to the north-east. The south Adriatic and east Ionian coasts are characterized by small peninsulas (Fig. 35.2), intensively settled from the late third–early second millennium BC. In this period coastal trade involved the peninsula along with Sicily and the small Tyrrhenian islands. The main deep metal ores are in the Alpine area and in Etruria (now divided into Tuscany and northern Lazio). Besides copper and iron, tin ores are a strategic resource in this region. Based on indirect evidence, it is also probable that the copper ores of Calabria were exploited from the time of the Final Bronze Age.

Italy's regional divisions, formalized by Emperor Augustus, constitute the foundation of the present system. From north-west to south-east, a comparatively wide natural region is Etruria, the only area of Italy where the Apennine range bends toward the Adriatic coast. Low hills and plains, with good agricultural soils, characterize this territory, which is also crossed by a network of minor rivers that provide a system of natural routes. Ancient Lazio (*Latium vetus*, between the Tiber and mount Circeo, and *Latium adiectum*, from the Circeo to the Garigliano) is a small region with a wide coastal plain, edged by the volcanic core of the Alban Hills, and the calcareous range of the Pre-Apennine mountains. Marche (ancient *Picenum*) is a narrow mountainous region, divided into three zones: the Apennine, joining Umbria to the west, the hilly zone, and the coastal plain. A specific feature of this area is a system of parallel river valleys. The central interior (including the coastal sections of Abruzzo

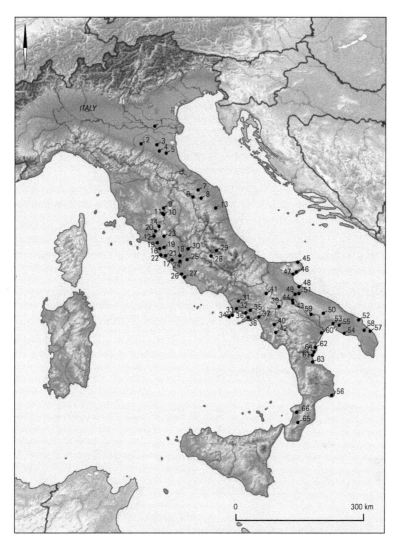

FIG. 35.1 Map of Italy showing sites mentioned in the text. The list includes the most important sites and those which are described in some detail. Drawing: Joanne Porc, Leiden University. 1. Frattesina, 2. Bologna, 3. Monte Castellaccio di Imola, 4. Calbana, 5. Verucchio, 6. Moscosi di Cingoli, 7. Pianello di Genga, 8. Matelica, 9. Chiusi, 10 and 11. Monte Cetona: Belverde cave and Casa Carletti, 12. Scarceta, 13. Fermo, 14. Bisenzio, 15. Vulci, 16. Tarquinia, 17. Caere, 18. Veii, 19. Luni sul Mignone, 20. Sorgenti della Nova, 21. Poggio La Pozza, 22. Coste del Marano, 23. Grotta Misa, 24. Roma, 25. Osteria dell'Osa (Roma) 26. Pratica di Mare (Lavinium), 27. Ardea, 28. Fucino, 29. Celano, 30. Cures, 31. Capua, 32. Carinaro, 33. Vivara, 34. Ischia, 35. Nola, 36. Sant'Abbondio, 37. Pontecagnano, 38. Poggiomarino, 39. Cairano, 40. Oliveto, 41. la Starza, 42. Sala Consilina, 43. Toppo Daguzzo, 44. Lavello, 45. Grotta Manaccora, 46. Monte Saraceno, 47. Coppa Nevigata, 48. Trinitapoli, 49. Madonna di Ripalta, 50. Laterza, 51. Canosa, 52. Punta Le Terrare, 53. Scoglio del Tonno, 54. Torre Castelluccia, 55. Taranto, 56. Capo Piccolo, 57. Roca Vecchia, 58. Surbo, 59. Timmari, 60. Incoronata- San Teodoro, 61. Francavilla, 62. Amendolara, 63. Torre Mordillo, 64. Broglio, 65. Castellace, 66. Torre Galli.

Map: Joanna Porc, Faculty of Archaeology, Leiden University.

and Molise) is marked by the highest Apennine mountains, alternating with confined inland plains and important river valleys. Campania is a wide territory, consisting of coastal plains separated by mountains, and accessible from the sea, from the north (the Sacco-Liri-Garigliano Valley), and from the interior (the Sele Valley). The volcanic system (Vesuvio-Campi Flegrei) provides rich agricultural soils. Except for the plain of Sybaris, Calabria is a mountainous area, continuing into the Ionian coastal plain of Basilicata and Apulia. Finally, Apulia is a wide region, characterized by a uniformly level morphology, except for the northern end (Monte Gargano), and the moderately high central section. Its position between two seas, at the end of the Adriatic corridor, was a decisive factor for the region's involvement in sea voyages from the eastern Mediterranean.

Throughout the Bronze Age the south Adriatic sea level was considerably lower than it is today. A climatic trend in peninsular Italy is an arid phase during the first half of the second millennium BC. Substantial data survive relative to natural catastrophes. The Vesuvian eruption of the Avellino pumices, c.nineteenth–eighteenth century cal BC, resulted in the abandonment of a wide area for several centuries. The natural factor that triggered the crisis of the Terramare settlements in the Po plain about 1200 BC was a steady lowering of the water table (Bernabò Brea and Cremaschi 2009).

The Bronze Age subsistence was based on cereals (wheats: *Triticum monococcum, dicoccum,* and *aestivum-compactum-durum*; barleys: *Hordeum distichum* and *haesasticum*); legumes (bean and chick-pea: *Faba minor, Lathyrus cicera/sativus*); fruits including acorns, figs, walnuts, hazelnuts, and wild berries. A steady trend towards olive and grape cultivation appears from the early second millennium BC.

FIG. 35.2 The peninsula of Roca Vecchia (Melendugno, Lecce), on the southern Adriatic coast. This is one of the main coastal sites in southern Italy, ranging from the Bronze Age to the Early Iron Age.

Photo: Laboratorio di Topografia Antica e Fotogrammetria, Università del Salento.

The three domestic animal species are present in different proportions, with a gradual increase of ovicaprines. Bovines were used mainly for secondary products and for traction. Horses are rare; donkeys appear in the Late Bronze Age.

The Cultural Sequence

The absolute chronology depends on the redefinition of the Italian Bronze and Early Iron Age chronology, based on calibrated radiocarbon dates from a number of contexts. However, many specialists would prefer to use the traditional chronology (Early Iron Age, c.900–730/720 BC), based on the reconstruction of Thucydides's dates for the earliest foundations of Greek colonies.

According to the relative chronology also in use, Bronze Age periods should coincide with distinctive archaeological cultures (Italian *facies*). The correspondence is far from precise. The main problems are the poor definition of the earliest part of the Early Bronze Age (c.2200–2000 cal BC) and the high absolute chronology (early second millennium BC) for the appearance of those archaeological aspects that should correspond to the initial Middle Bronze Age (c.1700–1500 BC).

Early Bronze Age and the So-Called Initial Middle Bronze Age (c.2200–1500 BC)

In central Italy Early Bronze Age complexes are identified from pottery features reminiscent of the Bell Beaker style, and similarities to the Polada repertoire.

The settlements include open-air sites—Tre Erici (Luni sul Mignone, Viterbo), Querciola and Lastruccia (Florence)—along with rock shelters and caves (e.g. Romita di Asciano, Fontino), that were used as dwelling places and for collective burial and cult practices. Pastoralism played an important role, along with breeding (cattle and pigs), agriculture, and hunting. The Copper Age *Laterza* facies continued throughout the final centuries of the third millennium BC in southern Italy, and up to southern Lazio.

The *Palma Campania* facies is documented in central and northern Campania. Its pottery comprises vessels on a high stand, hemispherical cups, bowls, and jars. Several Palma Campania villages were completely buried by a disastrous eruption of Vesuvius (the 'Avellino pumices'). The combined value of three radiocarbon dates on the bones of animals killed in the eruption is 3550 ± 12 BP, or 1920–1880 cal BC (68.2 per cent probability), 1950–1879 cal BC (89.7 per cent probability) (Nava et al. 2007).

Important information has been retrieved with the excavation (c.1,400 m^2) of the village at Croce del Papa (Albore Livadie and Vecchio 2005). Light fences divided the exposed area. Crossing of the settlement by animals and shepherds is indicated by human and animal footprints. Three elongated houses with apsidal end were built close together on the northern side; other features include wells, a small pond, and a cage with 13 pregnant sheep. The proximity of the three houses might indicate that the village space was divided among different kin-groups. Although locally the eruption produced a marked depopulation, there is evidence of continuity of the Palma Campania culture in adjacent areas.

An inhumation cemetery, probably dating from the final phase, has been excavated at S. Abbondio (Pompeii). The most notable burial, an adult man, was accompanied by an axe, three daggers, and a vessel decorated with a representation of daggers in relief.

The Pre-Apennine and Proto-Apennine Facies

Two similar aspects characterize the first half of the second millennium BC in central Italy: the *Pre-Apennine* facies, with specific elements in southern Etruria (Grotta Nuova), Tuscany (Candalla), and Emilia Romagna (Farneto). In southern Italy the *Proto-Apennine* is found in numerous settlements along the Adriatic and Ionian coasts. The high chronology for the beginnings of the Pre- and Proto-Apennine indicates that at the time of the earliest systematic sailings from the Aegean (seventeenth–sixteenth century BC) the south Italian coasts had been intensively settled for some centuries.

Pre-Apennine pottery includes carinated or rounded cups and bowls, biconical or ovoid jugs, ovoid jars, and truncated-conical bowls. Natural caves were used for both settlement and collective burial. Open-air villages are known along the Adriatic and Tyrrhenian coasts, and in connection with lakes (Mezzano, Bracciano, Baccano and Albano in Lazio, Velino between Umbria and Lazio). Grotta Nuova pottery also comes from the earliest settlement layers on the Capitoline Hill in Rome.

The best-known settlement is Monte Castellaccio, Romagna. The dwelling structures are small circular huts. The evidence includes spinning and weaving, clay weights, metallurgy, and the processing of antler, bone, and flint. The subsistence was based on cereals and legumes; the faunal sample includes the three domestic species plus horse, dog, possibly chicken, along with game. Radiocarbon dates indicate occupation around 3300 BP (1690–1490 cal BC at 95.4 per cent probability).

The funerary ritual was inhumation in natural caves, often associated with cult practices (e.g. Monte Cetona and Belverde, between Umbria and Tuscany). Subterranean multiple chamber tombs, e.g. Prato di Frabulino in southern Etruria, are considered exclusive to elite kin-groups. Seaborne activities are indicated by island and coastal settlements. Capo Graziano sherds from the Aeolian islands have been found at Luni-Tre Erici (Viterbo); a dagger of Italian type comes from a tomb of the north-western Balkan Četina facies.

The exploitation of the deep copper ores of Liguria, Tuscany, and southern Etruria begins in the Copper Age (Giardino 1995: 109–33; Maggi and Pearce 2005), and intensifies in the Early Bronze Age, as documented by several bronze hoards (Carancini and Peroni 1999: 9–11, tav. 2). The artefacts (axes, daggers, bun ingots) are usually whole. The distribution was probably carried out by metallurgists and craftsmen. The emergence of local workshops in the Early and Middle Bronze Age is indicated by the distribution of specific types.

Along the Adriatic and east Ionian coasts, Proto-Apennine settlements occupy small peninsulas, usually separated from the interior by a stone wall: a classic example is Roca Vecchia on the southern Adriatic coast (see Fig. 35.2). The average interval between sites is 20–40 km on the Adriatic and 3–5 km on the Ionian coast. On the west Ionian coast of Basilicata and Calabria, promontories are rare (e.g. Capo Piccolo), and some sites (e.g. Torre Mordillo) occupy low isolated plateaux (Trucco and Vagnetti 2001).

Throughout the second millennium the settlement system did not change significantly. The earliest imported Mycenaean (LH) I–II pottery occurs in the late Proto-Apennine layers of some Apulian coastal sites (Manaccora, Molinella, Punta Le Terrare, Santa Sabina, Giovinazzo). In the southern Tyrrhenian area maritime contacts concentrate in the Aeolian and Flegrean archipelagos, especially the settlements of Vivara (Cazzella and Moscoloni 1999). The earliest phase at Punta Mezzogiorno is documented by Palma Campania and Proto-Apennine pottery. An apsidal hut is associated with late Proto-Apennine and LH I–II pottery, and metallurgical activity. At Punta d'Alaca the association includes late Proto-Apennine and LH II and IIIA1 pottery. Interior Proto-Apennine sites include a few settlements in control of natural routes:

Madonna di Ripalta (Foggia), in the Ofanto Valley (Tunzi Sisto 1999), Tufariello, and La Starza. The settlement in Abruzzo concentrates around Lake Fucino. Rock shelters and caves were frequented for cult practices (Grotta Pertosa, Campania), permanent settlement (Grotta della Madonna and Grotta Cardini, Praia a Mare), and seasonal activities.

Inhumation and multiple or collective burial (from one to over two hundred) are the main features of the Proto-Apennine funerary practices in Apulia and Basilicata (Tunzi Sisto 1999; Cipolloni Sampò 1986). The burial complexes include caves (Grotta Manaccora), artificial caves (S. Vito dei Normanni, Crispiano), and underground chamber tombs (Trinitapoli, Terra di Corte, Toppo Daguzzo tomb 3, and Lavello tomb 743). Both natural caves and chamber tombs were initially used for the performance of cult practices. These tombs are seen as the correlates of the individual kin-groups of the local segmentary communities. The overall picture is one of relatively small communities, each comprising a few formally peer lineages. Around 1500 BC either all or some of the burials in these tombs were characterized by grave goods clearly hinting at a superordinate status: swords, daggers, arrowheads for the men, a variety of ornaments for the women; two small ivory figurines from one of the tombs in the Trinitapoli group. The evidence probably refers to those kin-groups that either had won, or were struggling to win, an elite status. The competition among the communities' component units might produce either a precarious balance or the exclusive, but structurally temporary, concentration of political control in the hands of one of them.

In the central section of Apulia (Bari) the tombs are megalithic rooms preceded by a long corridor and covered by a barrow. In the Salento Peninsula (Lecce) the funerary structures are megalithic chambers or cists (Fig. 35.3) covered by large barrows (*specchie*). The number of burials varies from one to ten. Burials in artificial caves are known from Santa Domenica di Ricadi, Calabria.

The evidence for metallurgical activity is relatively consistent (e.g. Vivara, Grotta Assergi in Abruzzo, Capo Piccolo in Calabria). This indicates a process of stabilization of metallurgical production, which until the end of the Middle Bronze Age was not an important structural component of the local economies. The pieces known are mainly axes. Metal artefacts from Proto-Apennine contexts are rare, and instead they feature in the transition to the final phase of the Middle Bronze Age. Their typological features indicate a wide range of interregional connections: swords of Pertosa type are specific to southern Italy and close to Sicilian types. Swords of Sacile type, arrowheads, daggers, razors, and pins derive from north Italian models. The intensity of trans-Adriatic contacts is exemplified by the widespread presence of bronzes in Apulian contexts, with parallels in Montenegro, Bosnia, and Albania. This evidence concentrates in northern Apulia, where Mycenaean pottery is almost absent from the indigenous contexts. This might indicate an autonomous role of the local communities in the exchange system activated by the sea voyages from the eastern Mediterranean. Some evidence of the production of purple dye has been found at Coppa Nevigata.

Final Phase of the Middle Bronze Age

This phase is characterized by the Apennine facies and dated c.1500–1350 BC. Recent dates from Roca, where seven people were suffocated in the fire which destroyed the fortification wall (Fig. 35.4), give a calibrated date range 1431–1399 BC (68.2 per cent probability), 1448–1379 BC (91.9 per cent). The Apennine facies is documented over the entire peninsula, with direct continuity from the Pre- and Proto-Apennine aspects. The pottery includes bowls, carinated and rounded cups, ovoid and biconical jars, with incised and engraved decoration.

FIG. 35.3 A Bronze Age megalithic tomb from Specchia Artanisi (Ugento, Lecce). A. the megalithic structure, a small rectangular room framed by slabs of local calcareous rock. B. the remains of the skeleton (a child), and two impasto vessels of Protoapennine type. The ^{14}C date from the bones ranges between 1980 and 1740 cal BC.

Photos: Laboratorio di Topografia Antica e Fotogrammetria, Università del Salento.

Coastal sites continue, as do the settlements in the Flegrean archipelago. In the Apennine area, there is an increase of lake settlements, for example around the Fucino and the Velino. Cave sites and shelters were still used in the Apennine regions, as well as in the coastal Tyrrhenian area. At Punta Le Terrare, on the Adriatic coast, there are circular huts with potsherd pavements, and horizontal pottery kilns, and at Madonna di Ripalta an apsidal hut around 7 m long. Ovens and hearths have been identified at Coppa Nevigata; at Ripalta a large oval kiln was used for both pottery firing and cooking, and metallurgical activity is also present.

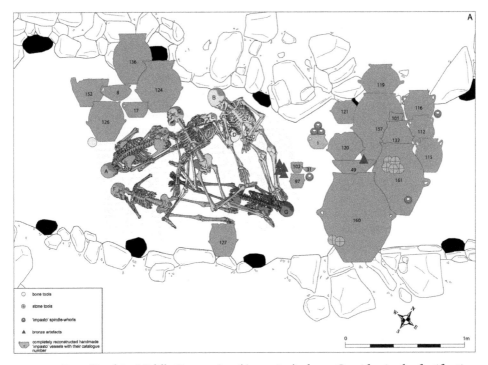

FIG. 35.4 Roca Vecchia, Middle Bronze Age (Apennine) phase. Corridor in the fortification wall of the settlement. The stone walls are reinforced by wooden poles. Seven individuals (two adults, an adolescent, three children and an infant) took refuge in this space, probably during a siege, and died of suffocation from the fire which destroyed the structure. The group was accompanied by numerous impasto vessels, and some personal items.

Drawing: T. Scarano.

On the Tyrrhenian coast of Calabria, the scarcity of Apennine settlements is combined with some sites characterized by the Sicilian-Aeolian Thapsos-Milazzese facies. This might indicate the deterioration of the local system of coastal trading, and the occupation of marginal areas of the peninsula by inhabitants from the Aeolian islands.

Overall the intensification of the Aegean presence is documented by the association of local *impasto* and imported LH IIIA and IIIB1 pottery, along the south Adriatic coast of Apulia, and also on the Ionian coast of Apulia, Basilicata, and Calabria. Apparently the indigenous-Aegean relationship in mainland Italy was not a colonization, nor did it depend on formalized political agreements. Rather, the Aegean sailors adjusted themselves to the local pattern of small autonomous polities. The general strategy was the integration of small groups of Aegean provenance within the individual communities, in order to participate in the local system of both trade and manufacture of metals, and amber. Two important sites, apparently differing from this pattern, are Scoglio del Tonno (Taranto), and Roca, on the coast of Salento (see Fig. 35.2).

In southern Italy there is continuity in the use of multiple or collective inhumation burials, whose specific feature is a marked ritual emphasis on weapon-bearers. There are some hints that similar funerary practices were also in use in central Italy. As we shall see in the following sections, the wide diffusion of cremation cemeteries, in which weapons were excluded from the funerary deposits, implies a radical change from the multiple elite graves that emphasize the paramount role of weapon-bearers. The earliest evidence, from the cemetery of Canosa (Bari), consists of urns with Apennine decoration.

The Late Bronze Age (*c*.1350–1200 BC)

The Late Bronze Age corresponds approximately to the Sub-Apennine facies. This is a time of radical changes, marking the beginnings of the structural transformations that developed in the Final Bronze Age and Early Iron Age. Radiocarbon dates from Sub-Apennine layers at Coppa Nevigata and Roca Vecchia range between about 1250 and 1000 cal BC.

Sub-Apennine pottery includes a variety of cups and bowls with plastic protrusions on the handles. It is often associated with LH IIIB2–IIIC early, which is mainly produced locally. Another local wheel-turned class is the grey ('Minyan') pottery.

The Sub-Appenine aspect is distributed over the whole area of peninsular Italy. In the southern Tyrrhenian area the Late Bronze Age coincides with a marked decrease in the overall number of settlements, which continues from the previous phase. At the end of the period, eastern Emilia (Bologna) and Romagna apparently experienced the demographic crisis of the Terramare, marked by depopulation of the plains, and settlement continuity in the Apennine area.

Settlement data are scanty. A large rectangular hut (*c*.15 by 7 m) has been found at Monte Rovello, southern Etruria, and a ditch-and-embankment system at Torre Mordillo. Oval structures have been identified at La Starza, small circular huts at Porto Perone. At Scoglio del Tonno two rectangular buildings and a third large apsidal one were possibly used for communal functions. There are also consistent indications of metallurgical activity. Metallurgical workshops include the large elliptical hut of Scarceta, in southern Tuscany (Poggiani Keller 1999), and the wooden platform at Moscosi di Cingoli, in the Marche.

Cremation cemeteries appear in Lazio (Cavallo Morto) and Apulia (Canosa and Torre Castelluccia). Throughout this period there is widespread evidence of relationships with the *Palafitte-Terramare* communities of the north, including the adoption of Peschiera bronzes (see Chapter 38). The circulation of Peschiera bronzes—violin-bow fibulae, Peschiera daggers, and flange-hilted swords—also took place in the Balkan Peninsula, the Aegean, Cyprus, and the Levant. Throughout peninsular Italy intensification in the use of metal produced radical changes in the local economies: bronze implements became a necessary support of all productive activities, leading to a structural interdependence among both the ore-rich and the other regions. In the central area, Tuscany, Umbria, and Marche, systematic contacts from northern Italy are indicated by formal features of northern type in the local pottery. Possible implications include an interest in the exploitation of the mining resources of Tuscany by the *Palafitte-Terramare* communities, who were probably also looking for a direct approach to the Adriatic. Rather than a pervasive formal influence, in southern Italy a small number of vessels of *Palafitte-Terramare* type appear in several contexts, both settlements and cremation cemeteries.

The period is also characterized by the main concentration of Aegean voyages to southern Italy. One of the most important sites is Scoglio del Tonno, at Taranto, probably an indigenous *emporion*, set on the best natural harbour of the Ionian coast. The abundant Mycenaean pottery consists mainly of imported closed vessels, probably traded for their contents. In the other important site, Roca, the Mycenaean pottery included a majority of open vessels, usually associated with individual consumption, along with the local production of bronze artefacts of Aegean type. This probably indicates the presence of a resident foreign group, a trend that continued in the Final Bronze Age.

Mycenaean pottery, mostly of south Italian production, is also found in the central and northern regions. The procurement of metal and amber were among the main goals of the intensive sailing to the central Mediterranean from the Aegean and eastern Mediterranean.

Another significant development was the invasion of the Aeolian islands and parts of north-eastern Sicily, starting from the southern Tyrrhenian coast. This episode, following the deterioration in the relationships between the islands and the Italian coast opposite, is the initial phase of a radical change in the political and economic setting in this area.

Final Bronze Age and Early Iron Age (c.1200–720 BC)

Together, the Final Bronze Age and Early Iron Age mark a definite change in territorial and sociopolitical organization: the Final Bronze Age facies may often be identified as the direct ancestor of regional Iron Age cultures. In turn, the consolidation of markedly regional aspects corresponds to processes of cultural and ethnic definition, which in the central Tyrrhenian area lead to the earliest emergence of city states.

The Final Bronze Age Facies, Chiusi-Cetona

In Tuscany, Umbria, Marche, and Romagna the Final Bronze Age facies ('Chiusi-Cetona') is characterized by formal similarities, indicating close relationships, with the north-eastern Po plain and Frattesina. The pottery includes the basic Final Bronze Age shapes—ovoid jars, biconical vessels, carinated cups and bowls, with decoration reminiscent of Terramare patterns. The regions involved are the same as those that in the Late Bronze Age were in contact with the *Terramare* communities. In the north-eastern Po plain, Frattesina, the paramount Final Bronze Age centre of both craftsmanship and trade, continued the *Terramare-Palafitte* tradition, though on a much larger scale. Thousands of glass and antler artefacts, hundreds of objects of bronze, faience, amber, and elephant ivory, along with huge quantities of unfinished pieces and discard, document the economic role of this site. The quantitative dimension of the production, and the distribution of some specific types (amber beads of Tiryns and Allumiere type, ivory combs, glass beads) from Sardinia to the eastern Mediterranean, probably indicate the involvement in this system of a Cypriot-Phoenician component (Bietti Sestieri 2010: 357).

In the Chiusi-Cetona area inland settlements are mostly on hills and plateaux, for example Chiusi and Casa Carletti in Tuscany, Calbana in Romagna (La Pilusa and Zanini 2007). Except for Vetulonia, there is no evidence of a Bronze Age occupation in the future Villanovan centres along the Tyrrhenian coast. Funerary practices are documented by small cremation cemeteries: Ponte S. Pietro and Sticciano Scalo (Tuscany), Panicarola and Monteleone di Spoleto (Umbria). The most important cemetery is Pianello di Genga (Ancona, Marche), with some 650 burials, and identified as corresponding to a 'tribal' community (Vanzetti 1999). The urns are frequently decorated with the *Vogelsonnenbarke* ('bird-sun-boat') or birds' heads pattern. Weapons are systematically excluded from the funerary outfit. The Chiusi-Cetona area participated in the circulation of some specific types of bronze artefact: pick-ingots, socketed shovels, and winged axes of Ponte S. Giovanni type. Between Frattesina and Tuscany, Umbria, and the coastal zone of Marche and Romagna, these types are found in a number of bronze hoards. Further east and north the Italian route merged into a wider international network, from Friuli to the northern Balkans, and Dalmatia, Switzerland, southern Germany, eastern and north-western France (Borgna 1992). A more localized metallurgical network emerged towards the end of the Final Bronze Age from northern Tuscany to the Alpine zone of France (Venturino Gambari 2009).

At the Final Bronze Age–Early Iron Age transition, different cultural and political entities emerged over the wide area of Chiusi-Cetona: in Emilia Romagna the northern Villanovan complex, with the main centres at Bologna and Verucchio, apparently the direct successors to Frattesina as central places of both production and trade. Other cultural and territorial entities that emerge in the adjacent regions are the *Piceni* (in the Marche), and *Umbri*, along with Villanovan centres at Fermo and Perugia.

The Early Iron Age Picene Culture (Marche)

The Iron Age facies in the Marche (Colonna and Franchi Dell'Orto 1999) is not clearly defined in the earliest phase; in the subsequent period the pottery is characterized by flamboyant elaborations of shapes in use on the peninsula. The local Villanovan (two cremation cemeteries and a settlement on an adjacent hilltop at Fermo) is connected to the Villanovan aspect of Chiusi, and to Bologna as regards the metal industry. Fermo preserves a Villanovan facies at least during the Early Iron Age. The initial phase of the Early Iron Age (Piceno I) is mainly documented by small groups of burials. In Piceno II a more substantial occupation concentrates in the Tronto, Tenna, Chienti, Potenza, and Esino valleys. Important hill settlements near the coast, often continuing from the Final Bronze Age, include Colle di Cappuccini (Ancona), Osimo, and Moie di Pollenza.

Recent excavations at Matelica (Macerata), in the upper Esino Valley, revealed a complex process that developed from the Early Iron Age to the Orientalizing period (Silvestrini and Sabbatini 2008): the sites comprise the settlements and cemeteries of Monte Gallo (Early Iron Age), and the later ones of Trinità and Crocifisso; from the seventh century BC a process of demographic growth is documented by small settlements and cemeteries along the valley.

After the earliest phase, in which there are only a few cremations, inhumation is the exclusive funerary ritual. During Piceno I the funerary goods consist of a fibula or a razor. In Piceno II some *impasto* vessels were given to the dead, along with personal ornaments, and weapons. A few pottery and bronze types (the so-called *cothon* and the spectacle and four-spiral fibulae) have close parallels on the eastern Adriatic coast, although the metal artefacts are mainly of Villanovan Bolognese type. The Early Iron Age–Orientalizing transition is marked by a process of social differentiation. The abundance of amber from Picene burials indicates the region's role in the amber trade towards peninsular Italy.

The Final Bronze Age Tolfa-Allumiere Group in Southern Etruria

The Final Bronze Age development in southern Etruria is the most important regional process towards sociopolitical complexity and territorial organization. The local Proto-Villanovan pottery (Tolfa-Allumiere facies) is characterized by engraved and plastic decoration.

The settlement system aims at territorial control, through the selection of isolated tuff plateaux (from 3–5 to around 20 hectares in extent). Formal burial is exclusive to a few individuals, probably those invested with superordinate social roles. From the earliest Final Bronze Age the ritual is based on the conception of the urn as the deceased's house, probably connected to the destruction of the body by fire, and its transition to a different physical dimension. This idea is expressed by modelling the urn lid as a miniature roof (Bietti Sestieri and De Santis 2004) and further elaborated in the successive phase by furnishing the deceased with a miniature outfit. Weapons are systematically excluded from burials. The only real cemetery (about one hundred tombs), at Poggio La Pozza, might mark the extension of formal burial to whole communities. Overall this ritual seems to indicate the centralization of political decision-making through the acceptance of the ideological implications of cremation.

The development of a sophisticated system of metal production is best exemplified by the bronze cups and stilted and foliate fibulae from Coste del Marano. Finished artefacts, and probably metal, were distributed from southern Etruria towards the interior and along the Tyrrhenian coast, from Lazio to Sicily. This trade line continued by sea towards the Aegean and eastern Mediterranean, as indicated by stilted fibulae of Italian inspiration from Attica and Cyprus (Dickinson 2006: 158, Fig. 5.22.10). There is also some evidence of trade with Sardinia. The Final Bronze Age-Early Iron Age transition is marked by the emergence of a distinctive metal industry ('Piediluco-Contigliano'; see Bietti Sestieri 2010: 258–60, Fig. 9).

The Early Iron Age in Etruria (Tuscany and Northern Lazio)

The Early Iron Age Villanovan is basically a unitary phenomenon, and the direct ancestor of the historical Etruscan culture. This is indicated by its overall cultural homogeneity, along with the synchronous emergence of both central and peripheral sites, and by the historical record. Ancient historians (Cato in Servius, *ad Aeneidem* xi.567; Livy i.2.3) hint at the Etruscans' early wide territorial power. The Villanovan facies is known mainly from cremation cemeteries: biconical urns with standardized decorative patterns, cups, bowls, vessels of specifically ritual significance; later classes include local imitations of Middle and Late Geometric Euboean-Cycladic skyphoi, and local Geometric pottery. The proto-urban centres of southern Etruria were established from the end of the Final Bronze Age on the large plateaux of Veii, Caere, Tarquinia, Bisenzio, and Vulci, all surrounded by several cemeteries; the emergence of a unified political organization took place according to the different local situations. In the interior and northern area of Etruria the settlements are smaller, and were mostly occupied from the Iron Age. Dwelling structures are known from the villages of Calvario (Tarquinia), and Grancarro on Lake Bolsena. From the Early Iron Age the Villanovan funerary ritual apparently reflects the centralization of political power, as indicated by the markedly limited number of men's funerary outfits containing a sword, probably relating to the community 'chiefs'. The appearance of princely figures, with outstanding funerary outfits, dates from the transition to the Orientalizing period. The rich metal industry produced arch and serpentine fibulae with disc-foot, lunate razors, 'italic' swords, spearheads, winged and socketed axes, bronze-sheet vessels, and defensive weapons. Villanovan bronzes were widely traded in Europe (e.g. Collis 1984: 58, Fig. 14).

The Final Bronze Age–Early Iron Age in Ancient Lazio

Radiocarbon dates fall around 1200–850 cal BC. During the earliest Final Bronze Age phase ancient Lazio was under the influence of southern Etruria, indicated by the similarity in material culture, ritual, and settlement patterns (Bietti Sestieri and De Santis 2008). The coastal plain, with major sites at Pratica di Mare (Lavinium) and Ardea, was involved in this connection. The formal features and ideological implications of the funerary ritual are identical to those seen in southern Etruria: small groups of cremations, with roof-lid urns, and no weapons. In the subsequent Final Bronze Age phase (Latial period 1) the influence of southern Etruria over Lazio faded, probably in connection with a process of consolidation of the region's cultural-ethnic identity. The evidence can be identified especially from the local elaboration of the funerary ritual: formal burial was still exclusive to a few individuals (the total for the whole region does not exceed 60 tombs), with miniature assemblages including the indicators of the main social roles: the sword, indicating military-political power; the knife, and a statuette in the form of an offerer apparently indicating a religious role. A few outstanding depositions include double shields, and, more rarely, a miniature cart drawn by two horses. In a few cases (Quadrato, Rome, tomb 1; Pratica di Mare tomb 21), the sword and the indicators of religious role appear in the same burial. Apparently the chiefs, priests, and possibly chiefly priests who were entitled to this exclusive ritual were also the agents of the region's assertion of cultural identity. In this period and the following one the region's acknowledged centre moved from the coastal plain to the Alban Hills.

The Early Iron Age (Latial periods 2 and 3, tenth–ninth century cal BC) is characterized by a process of territorial organization, including the emergence of proto-urban centres, that differs from the planned occupation of the plateaux of the future Etruscan cities seen in southern Etruria. Throughout period 2 the archaeological facies shows a connection to the Fossa-grave groups of Campania and Calabria.

With Latial period 3 the region's cultural-economic gravitation shifts from Campania to southern Etruria (Veii). The local development consists of the emergence of a number of territorial districts, around the central core of the Alban Hills, each comprising one of the future Latin city states: Rome, Gabii, Lavinium, Ardea, Antium, Satricum, Tibur. Rome, on the left bank of the Tiber and facing the Isola Tiberina, the best natural ford towards Etruria, was the first of these centres to be directly involved in the Villanovan connection, and to elaborate a process of urban formation. During period 2 it consisted of several small settlements and cemeteries, between the Capitoline and Palatine hills, and the Forum Valley. New evidence has been found on the Capitoline Hill and in Caesar's Forum. At the end of phase 2B a unified settlement occupied the central area, and the cemeteries were displaced on the adjacent hills (Esquiline, Quirinal, Viminal). This marked the beginnings of the process of Rome's urban formation.

The Early Iron Age funerary ritual involves both cremation and inhumation. A significant change from the Final Bronze Age is the generalized appearance of proper cemeteries, the correlate of whole communities, and organized by kin-groups.

In the earliest phase the cremation ritual with miniature outfit was still in use, for instance at Santa Palomba, Rome (Fig. 35.5); as is the case with the cemetery of Osteria dell'Osa, these burials are central to their group, and include the men invested with the main social roles. The communities were ruled by single 'chiefs'. Latial period 3 (Early Iron Age advanced-late) corresponds to the region's full involvement in the trade system of Etruria. The emergence of permanent social differences is documented by group N of Osteria dell'Osa.

The Final Bronze Age-Early Iron Age in Campania

Throughout this period different cultures coexisted in Campania. Despite limited evidence, distinctive archaeological aspects can be identified already in the Final Bronze Age: the miniature outfits in the cremation cemetery of Carinaro (Caserta) (Marzocchella 2004) are similar to those seen in Lazio, whereas the cremation ritual from a contemporary group of burials (S. Angelo in Formis) shows a close connection to southern Etruria. The distinctive features

FIG. 35.5 Santa Palomba, Rome, tomb 6, Early Iron Age cremation burial (adult man): urn and miniature vessels. Centre: urn with roof-lid. Left: three storage jars and four carinated bowls. Right: amphora, biconical jar, high stand, two carinated cups and two conical-truncated bowls.

Photo: A. De Santis.

of these two aspects may be identified as the direct ancestors of two main features of the local Iron Age: the Fossa-grave culture, and the southern Villanovan.

The Fossa-grave group is distributed along the Tyrrhenian coast and the adjacent areas of Campania and Calabria, with strong connections with Lazio. The overall homogeneity in the archaeological facies indicates intensive relationships over this wide territory. Fossa-grave cemeteries include Torre Galli (Pacciarelli 1999) and S. Onofrio in Calabria, Cuma, Suessula, and the Sarno Valley group in Campania. The main indigenous site is Cuma. The most important recent discovery, Poggiomarino in the Sarno Valley, is a specialized site set in an interior wetland (Albore Livadie and Cicirelli 2003). The structures are stratified platforms of earth, stone, and wood layers, with evidence of the processing of metal, antler, and bone, pottery, wood, possibly ivory, glass, and amber.

During the initial phase of the Early Iron Age a certain degree of similarity to the contemporary Villanovan facies of southern Etruria characterizes the Campanian aspects of Capua, Pontecagnano, Sala Consilina. In the subsequent period they were involved in processes of integration with the indigenous communities.

The third component, the Oliveto-Cairano group, consists of small inland settlements and inhumation cemeteries dating from an advanced phase of the Early Iron Age, and characterized by a distinctive material culture. This group was connected to the Adriatic coast, via the Ofanto and Sele valleys.

A further component to the picture of Early Iron Age Campania is the Euboean emporion of Pithecusa (Ischia), the predecessor of the Greek colonies of this region.

The Final Bronze Age–Early Iron Age in the Central-Southern Regions (Southern Umbria, Sabina, Abruzzo, Molise)

This section of the peninsula consists of a mountainous interior interconnected by river valleys; the eastern part includes the Adriatic coast. The Final Bronze Age/Early Iron Age facies is close to that of Lazio and southern Etruria. In the advanced phase of the Early Iron Age the inland Apennine and the Adriatic coastal areas show a systematic connection to the Picene facies of the Marche (Colonna and Franchi Dell'Orto 1999; *Atti IIPP* 2003).

The settlements are often on hills or small plateaux, as well as along lake banks and riverbanks. Important hill sites have been identified in the coastal zone of Abruzzo and Molise. A systematic connection to Apulia is indicated by the occurrence of Proto-Geometric and Geometric pottery, and of large dolia in coastal sites.

Inhumation is the exclusive funerary ritual in Abruzzo; individual burials are set within stone circles, and covered by mounds; rows of stone stelae, first documented in the Final Bronze Age group from Celano (Aquila), are specific to male burials. A recurrent feature is constituted by large cemeteries, continuing in use from the Final Bronze Age/Early Iron Age to the late republican period.

In Sabina the Early Iron Age cremation ritual is similar to the Latial one; in southern Umbria the local facies (Terni-Colfiorito) is related both to the regions further north and to Abruzzo, as indicated by the use of cremation along with inhumation, and of stone circles and stelae.

The Final Bronze Age and Early Iron Age in the Southernmost Regions

In Calabria, Basilicata, and Apulia distinctions between local aspects are nuanced. A Final Bronze Age facies characterized by the use of cremation is documented at Timmari (Basilicata). Some pottery of LH IIIC late is still present, while Sub-Mycenaean pottery is only represented at Roca. A functional and technological legacy of the Aegean/Near Eastern frequentation of these regions are the local Proto-Geometric pottery (mostly handmade from purified clay, and matt-painted) and the wheel-turned dolia. The Iron Age pottery includes a class of purified clay, with painted geometric decoration (Yntema 1990). The copper supply probably depended mainly on the resources of Calabria, although the abundance of spectacle and four-spiral fibulae are indications of trans-Adriatic contacts. The settlement system is still characterized by the occupation of coastal sites and of interior locations suited to the control of territory and long-distance communication. Both types are usually rather small (fewer than 5 hectares for Roca), and site hierarchy does not seem to exceed two levels. Apparently an autonomous development towards the emergence of local proto-urban and/ or Early State forms did not take place in these regions.

Calabria

Throughout the Final Bronze Age–Early Iron Age this region is connected to eastern Sicily and Lipari (*Atti IIPP* 2004); this is probably a direct sequel to the Late Bronze Age 'Ausonian' takeover. The abundance of bronze artefacts, combined with the development of local types and style, hints at the systematic exploitation of the Calabrian copper ores. Surveys in the Sybaris plain, the Poro promontory, and the Ionian coast indicate a limited demographic growth and the consolidation of a two-tiered settlement system; the extent of the plateaux occupied by major sites (Torre Mordillo, Amendolara) is 10–15 hectares. The Early Iron Age facies is similar to the Fossa-grave culture of Campania; in the Ionian area similarities to the adjacent sites of Basilicata include funerary mounds and painted geometric pottery. At Broglio the best-preserved Final Bronze Age building is a 7 x 3 m storage room with five large dolia, one of which probably contained olive oil (Peroni and Trucco 1994: 855, note 59). A contemporary feature is a smithy for the local manufacture of iron objects. Relatively complete elements have been recorded at Francavilla Marittima, on the Acropolis of Timpone della Motta:

these include a large Early Iron Age apsidal building, a hearth, and a group of loom-weights, along with *impasto* and geometric pottery, and metal artefacts. Radiocarbon dates from Early Iron Age structures range from 1040 to 800 cal BC at 95.4 per cent probability.

From the end of the Final Bronze Age inhumation was the exclusive ritual. A small group of inhumations, with weapons as part of men's funerary outfits, comes from Castellace (Oppido Mamertina). Early Iron Age inhumation cemeteries include Torre Galli and S. Onofrio di Roccella Jonica. At Torre Galli (Pacciarelli 1999) the tombs are organized by kin-groups, with weapons occurring regularly in men's burials. The cemeteries in the Sybaris plain (Castiglione di Paludi, Amendolara) are characterized by the wealth of bronzes; in the advanced phase of the Early Iron Age, the cemeteries of Torre Mordillo and Francavilla show some evidence of permanent social articulation. A different kind of cemetery, with parallels in eastern Sicily, is found in western Calabria: multiple burials in underground chamber tombs, associated with geometric pottery imitating Greek prototypes.

Calabria's rich metallurgy is also documented by hoards, for example Cerchiara and Cirò, mainly formed by whole but often unfinished shaft-hole axes. Iron was used at least from the Late Bronze Age. The participation in international trade is indicated by the local working of elephant ivory at Torre Mordillo, by the occurrence of Egyptian-style scarabs at Torre Galli, and of a Phoenician bronze bowl from Francavilla; moreover, spearheads of Albanian Pazhok type from Castellace, and spectacle and four-spiral fibulae, hint at a connection to the west Balkan coast.

Basilicata

The Final Bronze Age facies is not clearly defined; in the Early Iron Age a specific feature is the *tenda*-style geometric pottery. The main Final Bronze Age settlements, often continuing in the Early Iron Age, are hill sites in control of the coastal plain and of the natural routes towards the interior (Cipolloni Sampò 1999). Monte Timmari (Matera) is a system of small hill settlements with their cemeteries. Early Iron Age settlements occupy different locations (for example, Noepoli, Chiaromonte, in the Sinni Valley, S. Maria d'Anglona, between the Sinni and Agri valleys; Incoronata-San Teodoro, on an open terrace over the Basento Valley). Here an Early Iron Age phase is followed by a colonial phase, subsequent to the foundation of Metaponto.

Final Bronze Age cemeteries include different types. Some Bronze Age underground tombs are still in use. The cemetery of Timmari-Vigna Coretti (Cipolloni Sampò 1999), with 248 individual cremations, is organized by kin-groups. Anthropological examinations of a sample of 62 indicate the occurrence of both sexes and all age classes. Grave goods are rather rare and include fibulae, pins, glass beads, antler combs, and spindle-whorls or ornaments, and razors in men's burials.

The Early Iron Age cemeteries are formed by several hundred, and up to a few thousand, individual inhumation burials. Different cemetery cores are distributed around the settlements. Some differences, probably the correlate of varying degrees of social organization, have been observed. Around the settlement of Chiaromonte, in the cemeteries of Serrone and S. Pasquale, women's funerary outfits are especially rich in ornaments. At Sta. Maria d'Anglona differences in wealth are particularly clear: the Valle Sorigliano cemetery includes small groups of tumulus tombs with lavish sets of ornaments for the women, weapons and tools for some men (Frey 1991). In the nearby, slightly later cemetery of Cocuzzolo Sorigliano, tumuli are rare, and there is a generally smaller number of ornaments. The most important cemetery is Incoronata-San Teodoro (Chiartano 1996), where 532 Early Iron Age tombs have been excavated, divided into groups. The great majority of men have one or two spears/javelins, while only 14 have a bronze or iron sword, along with the most elaborate types of serpentine fibulae. An important indicator of ranking might be represented by two bronze sticks ('aste di comando'), along with a sword, from tomb 454. Personal ornaments in recurring combinations appear in nearly all women's burials, especially spectacle and four-spiral fibulae. An important female role is indicated by loom-weights associated with a painted askos in tombs 209 and 235. According to the excavator, the evidence from this cemetery indicates a relatively simple, kin-based social organization.

Inter-regional connections in the Final Bronze Age are mainly documented by the cemetery of Timmari, with parallels in the contemporary complexes of the same category in the Adriatic area (Pianello di Genga, Frattesina). In the Early Iron Age, Basilicata (ancient Enotria) was in contact with the Villanovan centres of Campania, especially Sala Consilina, where the Enotrian-style *tenda* pottery is quite popular. This site may have been the medium for the transmission of Enotrian-type artefacts and contacts to the Villanovan centres of Etruria.

Apulia

The Final Bronze Age facies is exemplified at Roca (Bietti Sestieri 2010: 27–30): the *impasto* pottery includes all the basic shapes of the period, along with matt-painted Proto-Geometric vessels, large corded dolia, and LH IIIC late and Sub-Mycenaean pottery. The main Final Bronze Age features are two unusually large buildings that were destroyed by a sudden fire. The largest one, a rectangular structure supported by wooden poles 40 x 15 m in extent, was used for a combination of ritual practices and craft activities. The finds comprise two hoards, one with bronzes of both local and north Italian type, and another with a group of gold-sheet sun discs; and a group of moulds for bronze artefacts of local and Aegean type (Guglielmino 2005). At Roca, and generally in the Salento, bronze artefacts of Aegean type, some of them of local manufacture, include pins, knives, double-axes, the Aegean short sword, and small hammers for the processing of bronze sheet, also of Aegean-Cypriot type, from Surbo (Macnamara 1970).

Other important settlements, mostly continuing in the Early Iron Age and later, are Monte Saraceno (Nava, Acquaroli, and Preite 1999) on the southern coast of Monte Gargano, with a ditch and a stone wall separating the settlement from its cemetery; also Coppa Nevigata, and Madonna di Ripalta (Tunzi Sisto 1999, 108–15), in the Ofanto Valley. Settlements on coastal promontories and interior hilltops are also known around Bari.

The Final Bronze–Early Iron Age settlement at Torre Castelluccia (Taranto) is characterized by a wall enclosing rectangular buildings and a central path. A small hoard of bronze objects and amber, glass, semi-precious stone, and bone ornaments was found beneath the floor of structure 7. In the Salento Iron Age layers have been found at Cavallino and Otranto, the latter including pottery of Albanian type.

Two hundred tombs, dating from the Final Bronze Age to the fourth century BC, have been excavated in the cemetery of Monte Saraceno. These are generally multiple-inhumation burials with an average use of around 50 to 75 years. The funerary outfit in the earliest phase consisted of a few ornaments; *impasto* pottery, and finally, in an advanced phase of the Early

Iron Age, Daunian-style painted pottery, arch, spectacle and four-spiral fibulae, and iron ornaments. Bronze weapons are rare; iron swords come from two tombs dating from the final phase of the Early Iron Age. Simple stone sculptures, evolving from geometric to anthropomorphic, are often connected to the tombs. Pit burials for adults and *enchytrismos* for children were in use at Salapia, while in the cemeteries of Ordona, Arpi, Lavello, and Banzi pit inhumations were covered by barrows. The numerous bronze hoards include local, Balkan, and Aegean components (Carancini and Peroni 1999). The hoards dating from the advanced Final Bronze Age and the Early Iron Age contain a large number of shaft-hole axes (Salapia), some trans-Adriatic imports, and various types of socketed axe of Balkan type from Manduria, Copertino, and Soleto (Carancini and Peroni 1999: plate 33 and table 34). The Balkan connection is also indicated by the occurrence of Italian bronzes in the coastal area of the Balkan Peninsula, and of large quantities of Daunian Geometric pottery from Istria, Dalmatia, and Slovenia.

Conclusion

An overview of the Italian Peninsula during this period shows a long-term sequence of local and regional processes, whose Final Bronze Age/Early Iron Age outcome may be considered on two different levels. On the one hand, there is the definition of specific ethnic-cultural identities, mainly corresponding to Italy's historical regions. On the other, these regional entities reveal the emergence of an overall structural difference between central and southern Italy.

Throughout the first half of the second millennium BC, and until *c.*1350–1300 BC (Middle–Late Bronze Age transition), the Pre- and Proto-Apennine, and Apennine, cultures that appear over the whole of the peninsula probably reflect a low degree of territorial and political organization. A system of coastal trade was active among the coasts and islands of southern Italy, and also involved the eastern Adriatic and central Tyrrhenian coasts. The social structure was based on kinship, with different lineages providing the basic units of the communities. Around the mid-second millennium BC, the funerary correlates of these formally peer kinship units are collective inhumation burials, in which weapon-bearers constituted the most important social component. Segmentary societies of this kind probably were not too different from those found in the same period over wide areas of Europe, including northern Italy.

A structural feature of these communities was their proneness to interior competition and conflict, which implies that effective political decisions might only be taken based either on the agreement among the component groups or on the temporary prevalence of one group over the others. This situation also involved those regions, mainly Apulia, which from the seventeenth century BC were reached by systematic sailings from the Aegean and the eastern Mediterranean. The aim of these voyages was probably the acquisition of resources, including local metals, and others, such as amber, which were channelled from Europe to the Adriatic corridor. The main processes of Aegean-East Mediterranean integration with the indigenous communities took place in Sicily and the Aeolian islands, which functioned as the territorial base for central Mediterranean trade.

From the Late Bronze Age new factors produced an acceleration in the processes that were already active in the peninsula: a steady trend of demographic growth, the increasing demand for metal, which had gradually become crucial and involved subsistence and craftsmanship activities, and the intensification of exterior contacts with northern Italy and the eastern Mediterranean. The latter were mainly mediated by the southern regions. Throughout the peninsula the Late Bronze Age repertoire of bronze artefacts depended almost entirely on the north Italian Peschiera metal industry. However, the relationship differed significantly between the central and southern regions. In the north-central area the widespread occurrence of *Palafitte-Terramare* features in the local *impasto* pottery indicates the circulation of individuals and groups between the two areas. In southern Italy, especially Apulia, the connection is more localized, and essentially consists of a few Late Bronze Age cremation cemeteries in which, along with the bronzes, at least some of the urns belong to specific north Italian types. Small groups of *impasto* vessels, also of north Italian type, are found in settlements, for example at Roca. Altogether, this new situation, marked by the intensification of inter-regional contacts and trade, probably sharpened the need for effective political control.

Cremation was the critical factor that provided a widely accepted solution to this problem. The evidence from northern and central Italy shows that this ritual was shaped and perceived in ideological opposition to the traditional inhumation of groups of socially representative men with their weapons. From the Late Bronze Age, and especially in the Final Bronze Age, cremation became the exclusive ritual. Weapons were systematically excluded from the men's funerary outfit. The only exceptions are single male burials, no more than one or two for each cemetery, whose grave goods include a weapon. A radical version of this ritual appears in southern Etruria and, mainly, in ancient Lazio, where Final Bronze Age cremation burial was exclusive to the few individuals holding the main male roles in each community. This probably indicates the transition from shared to centralized political power. Rather than depending on the spread of a new religion, this ritual change probably depended on the opportunistic adoption of a radical ideological innovation in a particularly favourable historical contingency.

The relationship between the use of cremation and the centralization of political decision-making was a basic factor of organization in the Late and Final Bronze Age in northern and central Italy, and apparently an essential condition for the Early Iron Age development of proto-urban processes in the Villanovan centres, from Emilia Romagna to Etruria and Campania, and in ancient Lazio.

As regards the southern regions, the rule in the Early Iron Age is a generalized return to inhumation, with large cemeteries organized by clearly identifiable groups, and weapons systematically present in men's graves. This situation probably corresponds to the traditional sharing of political power among the kinship units of each community. A relationship between this kind of political organization and the absence of local processes of Early State and proto-urban formation seems likely. In other words, in the Early Iron Age it is possible to recognize a permanent structural difference between central and southern Italy.

It is interesting to note that the main local trajectories toward social and political complexity did not develop in the regions of Aegean contact, but, rather, in northern and central Italy, where a Cypriot-Phoenician economic influence was probably operating from the time of the Final Bronze Age.

Bibliography

(For a more comprehensive bibliography see Bietti Sestieri 2010).

Albore Livadie, C. and Vecchio, G. (2005). *Il villaggio del Bronzo antico di Nola*. Pompeii: Istituto Italiano di Preistoria e Protostoria.

—— and Cicirelli, C. (2003). *L'insediamento protostorico di Poggiomarino. Nota preliminare*, La Parola del Passato LVIII.2 (CCCXXIX). Naples: Gaetano Macchiaroli, 88–138.

Atti IIPP (2003). *Atti della XXXVI Riunione Scientifica dell'Istituto Italiano di Preistoria e Protostoria (Chieti-Celano 2001*. Florence: Istituto Italiano di Preistoria e Protostoria.

—— (2004). *Atti della XXXVII Riunione Scientifica dell'Istituto Italiano di Preistoria e Protostoria (Scalea, Papasidero, Praia a Mare, Tortora 2002)*. Florence: Istituto Italiano di Preistoria e Protostoria.

Bernabò Brea M. and Cremaschi, M. (2009). *Acque e civiltà nelle terramare. La vasca votiva di Noceto*. Milan: Skirà.

Bietti Sestieri, A. M. (2010). *L'Italia nell'Età del Bronzo e del Ferro. Dalle palafitte a Romolo*. Rome: Carocci Editore.

—— and De Santis, A. (2004). 'Analisi delle decorazioni dei contenitori delle ceneri dalle sepolture a cremazione dell'Età del Bronzo Finale nell'area centrale tirrenica', in *Preistoria e Protostoria in Etruria*, VI. (Pitigliano–Valentano 2002). Milan: Centro Studi di Preistoria e Archeologia, 165–92.

—— and De Santis, A. (2008). 'Relative and absolute chronology of Latium vetus from the Late Bronze Age to the transition to the Orientalizing period', in D. Brandherm and M. Trachsel (eds.), *A New Dawn for the Dark Age? Shifting Paradigms in Mediterranean Iron Age Chronology*. Proceedings of the XV UISPP World Conference, Lisbon 2006. British Archaeological Reports (International Series), 1,871. Oxford: Archaeopress, 119–33.

Borgna, E. (1992). *Il ripostiglio di Madriolo presso Cividale, e i pani a piccone del Friuli-Venezia Giulia*, Studi e Ricerche di Protostoria Mediterranea, 1. Rome: Quasar.

Carancini, G. and Peroni, R. (1999). *L'Età del Bronzo in Italia: per una cronologia della produzione metallurgica*, Quaderni di Protostoria, 2. Perugia: Ali & No.

Cazzella, A. and Moscoloni, M. (1999). 'Vivara: le ricerche alla Punta di Mezzogiorno', in C. Giardino (ed.), *Culture marinare nel Mediterraneo centrale e occidentale fra il XVII e il XV sec. A.C.* Rome: Bagatto Libri, 216–26.

Chiartano, B. (1996). *La necropoli dell'Età del Ferro dell'Incoronata e di S. Teodoro (scavi 1978-1985)*. Galatina: Congedo Editore.

Cipolloni Sampò, M. (1986). 'La tomba 3 dell'acropoli di Toppo Daguzzo (Potenza). Elementi per uno studio preliminare', Annali di Archeologia e Storia Antica, 8: 1–36.

—— (1999). *L'Età del Bronzo Finale*, in D. Adamesteanu (ed.), *Storia della Basilicata*, 1. *L'antichità*, Bari: Editori Laterza, 130–6.

Collis, J. (1984). *The European Iron Age*. London: Routledge.

Colonna, G. and Franchi Dell'Orto, L. (eds.) (1999). *I Piceni, Popolo d'Europa*. Exhibition Catalogue. Rome: Edizioni De Luca.

Dickinson, O. (2006). *The Aegean from Bronze Age to Iron Age*. Cambridge: Cambridge University Press.

Frey, O. H. (1991). *Eine Nekropole der frühen Eisenzeit bei Santa Maria d'Anglona*, Quaderni di Archeologia e Storia Antica, 1. Le Galatina LE: Congedo Editore.

Giardino, C. (1995). *Il Mediterraneo occidentale fra XIV e VIII sec a.c. Cerchie minerarie e metallurgiche*, British Archaeological Reports (International Series), 612. Oxford: Tempus Reparatum.

Guglielmino R. (2005). 'Roca Vecchia (Lecce): testimonianze di attività metallurgiche in un sito costiero del Bronzo Finale', in B. Adembri (ed.), *Miscellanea di studi per Mauro Cristofani*, vol. I. Florence: Centro Di, 32–50.

La Pilusa, E. and Zanini, A. (2007). 'L'abitato di Ripa Calbana, San Giovanni in Galilea (FC)', *Padusa*, 43: 81–119.

Macnamara, E. (1970). 'A group of bronzes from Surbo, Italy: new evidence for Aegean contacts with Apulia during Mycenaean IIIB and C', *Proceedings of the Prehistoric Society*, 36: 241–60.

Maggi, R. and Pearce, M. (2005). 'Mid fourth-millennium copper mining in Liguria, northwest Italy: the earliest known copper mines in western Europe', *Antiquity*, 79/303: 66–77.

Marzochella, A. (2004). 'Dal Bronzo Finale all'inizio dell'Età del Ferro: nuove testimonianze dalla Campania', in *Atti della XXXVII Riunione Scientifica dell'Instituto Italiano di Preistoria e Protostoria (Scalea, Papasidero, Praia a Mare, Tortora 2002)*. Florence: Istituto Italiano di Preistoria e Protostoria, 616–20.

Nava, M. L., Acquaroli, G., and Preite, A. (1999). 'Monte Saraceno: aspetti insediativi e funerari dell'area garganica nella protostoria', in A. M. Tunzi Sisto (ed.), *Ipogei della Daunia. Preistoria di un territorio*. Foggia: Claudio Grenzi Editore, 48–63.

——, Giampaola, D., Laforgia, E., and Boenzi, G. (2007). 'Tra il Clanis e il Sebeto: nuovi dati sull'occupazione della piana campana tra il Neolitico e l'Età del Bronzo', in *Atti della XL Riunione Scientifica IIPP (Roma, Napoli, Pompei 2005)*. Florence: Istituto Italiano di Preistoria e Protostoria, 101–26.

Pacciarelli, M. (1999). *Torre Galli. La necropoli della I Età del Ferro (Scavi Paolo Orsi 1922–23)*, Soveria Mannelli (Catanzaro): Rubbettino Editore.

Peroni, R. and Trucco, F. (eds.) (1994). *Enotri e Micenei nella Sibaritide*. Taranto: Istituto per la Storia e l'Archeologia della Magna Grecia.

Poggiani Keller, R. (1999). *Scarceta di Manciano (Grosseto). Un centro abitativo dell'Età del Bronzo sulle rive del Fiora*. Manciano: Museo di Preistoria e Protostoria della Valle del Fiume Fiora.

Silvestrini, M. and Sabbatini, T. (eds.) (2008). *Potere e splendore a Matelica*. Exhibition Catalogue, Matelica 2008. Rome: L'Erma di Bretschneider.

Trucco, F. and Vagnetti, L. (2001). *Torre Mordillo 1987–1990*. Roma: CNR, Istituto per gli Studi Micenei ed Egeo-Anatolici.

Tunzi Sisto, A. M. (ed.) (1999). *Ipogei della Daunia. Preistoria di un territorio*. Foggia: Claudio Grenzi Editore.

Vanzetti, A. (1999). 'Osservazioni sulla composizione dei corredi e sull'assetto sociale e demografico del sepolcreto', in G. Colonna and L. Franchi dell'Orto (eds.), *I Piceni, Popolo d'Europa*. Exhibition Catalogue. Rome: Edizioni De Luca, 51–4.

Venturino Gambari, M. (ed.) (2009). *Il ripostiglio del Monte Cavanero di Chiusa di Pesio (Cuneo)*. Alessandria: LineLab Edizioni.

Yntema, D. (1990). *The Matt-Painted Pottery of Southern Italy*. Lecce: Dipartimento di Beni Culturali dell'Università di Lecce.

CHAPTER 36

THE BRONZE AGE IN SICILY

ANNA MARIA BIETTI SESTIERI

THROUGHOUT the Bronze Age, Sicily was characterized by two complementary features, often seen in association with insularity: an almost total autonomy from mainland Italy as regards both the formal traits of the local archaeological cultures and the structure and organization of the communities involved; and a concentration of foreign contacts, especially from the Aegean and the eastern Mediterranean, which produced specific forms of cultural, political, and economic integration that were far more pervasive than what is seen in the Italian Peninsula (Bietti Sestieri 2003). Both these features were radically altered by the closer relation with mainland Italy that was introduced in the thirteenth century BC with the so-called 'Ausonian' invasion.

The context of the historical process in Sicily and the Aeolian islands during the earliest phase of the local Bronze Age (c.2200–1800 BC) was a system of coastal trade probably extending over the greater part of the central Mediterranean, and involving both coastal sites and islands. The archaeological correlate of this system is an overall similarity in material culture (especially the general use of handmade *impasto* pottery with incised decoration, and many formal similarities in the basic repertoire). It seems rather likely that journeys to this area at the time of the earliest systematic sailings from the Aegean and eastern Mediterranean (c.seventeenth–sixteenth centuries BC) took place through participation in the local trade system.

The Sicilian territory is characterized by mountain ranges along the northern coast, and in the west-central zone, and by the volcanic peak of mount Etna (c.3,000 m a.s.l.), in the north-eastern zone. Relatively wide plains include the coastal strip, the area surrounding the Monti Iblei, from Catania to Gela, in the south-eastern corner, and the western zone between Trapani and Sciacca. The main rivers are the Belice, Platani, and Salso on the southern coast, the Tellaro, Anapo, and Simeto on the eastern coast, and several medium-range rivers along the northern coast. Natural resources include sulphur, salt, and alum in the south-central zone of Sicily, copper in the Monti Peloritani (the north-eastern corner), amber (simetite) from the western slopes of Etna, and obsidian from Lipari. Of the two archipelagos at a short distance from the Sicilian coasts, the Lipari/Aeolian and Egadi islands, only the former played an important role in the history of the region. Ustica and Pantelleria were culturally close to Sicily especially in the Middle Bronze Age; although probably autonomous, the Maltese islands were in continual contact with the much larger island, Sicily, to their north.

The Sicilian and Aeolian Bronze Age sequence, which is rather different from the Italian one, depends in the first place on the specific formal features and chronological length of the local archaeological cultures. It is worth mentioning that the main changes in the archaeological cultures apparently coincided with important historical processes and events. The relative and absolute chronology is based on stratigraphic evidence, especially from the Aeolian islands, recent calibrated radiocarbon dates, and Mycenaean pottery from local contexts, which is related to the Aegean Late Bronze Age chronology (1650–1050 BC). In Sicily the Early Bronze Age (c.2200–1500 cal BC) corresponds to the facies Naro-Partanna/Castelluccio, Rodì-Tindari-Vallelunga (RTV), and Moarda. The Aeolian Capo Graziano culture is divided into two phases, c.2200–1800, and c.1800–1430 BC. The earliest Aegean imports, (final MH and LH I-II-IIIA1) appear in phase 2. The Middle Bronze Age Thapsos-Milazzese facies (c.1500–1250 BC) is associated with LH IIIA and IIIB imports. To the Late Bronze Age belong the Sicilian Pantalica culture, probably beginning in the thirteenth century BC, and the roughly contemporary Lipari 'Ausonian', also present in north-eastern Sicily. From the twelfth century BC to the Iron Age the Sicilian archaeological evidence breaks progressively into an intricate picture of local facies that may be formally related either to the Ausonian or to the local Bronze Age tradition, or to both.

Our knowledge of the archaeological record depends mainly on the large-scale systematic excavations carried out by Paolo Orsi in Sicily (end of the nineteenth and early twentieth century), and by Luigi Bernabò Brea and Madeleine Cavalier in the Aeolian islands and on the Sicilian coast opposite them (second half of the twentieth century). Based on these works, the Bronze Age occupation in Sicily is thoroughly documented especially in the eastern and south-central zones, while more general information is available for the Aeolian archipelago (Fig. 36.1). Some recent studies have been devoted to the re-examination of old complexes and to a few recent excavations. Two syntheses, by Robert Leighton (1999) and Sebastiano Tusa (1999), provide accurate and useful overviews of the existing data.

The Early Bronze Age (c.2200–1500 bc)

Sicilian Styles

Based on recent research on the Sicilian Early Bronze Age, it seems clear that the Castelluccio culture was present over the whole territory of the region, whereas the other two more or less contemporary aspects, RTV and Moarda, were more locally significant.

The Castelluccio Culture

The Castelluccio facies is quite distinctive: its main feature is the handmade *impasto* pottery with matt-painted decoration in geometric patterns, usually in black-on-red. This type of pottery is clearly related to the local Copper Age tradition, as documented by the Serraferlicchio and S. Ippolito facies, but is also rather close to the Middle Helladic matt-painted pottery production. The repertoire includes different types of jars, high-handled

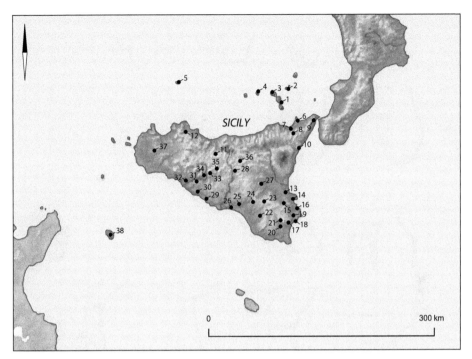

FIG. 36.1 Map of Sicily showing sites mentioned in the text. The list includes the most important sites and those which are described in some detail. Drawing: Joanne Porc, Leiden University. 1. Lipari, 2. Panarea, 3. Salina, 4. Filicudi, 5. Ustica, 6. Milazzo, 7. Tindari, 8. Rodì, 9. Messina, 10. Naxos, 11. Valledolmo, 12. Moarda, 13. Metapiccola, 14. Timpa Dieri, 15. Pantalica, 16. Thapsos, 17. Ognina, 18. Cassibile, 19. Grotta Chiusazza, 20. Cava Lazzaro, 21. Castelluccio, 22. Monte Tabuto, 23. Molino della Badia-Madonna del Piano, 24. Caltagirone, 25. Monte Dessueri, 26. Manfria, 27. Morgantina, 28. Sabucina, 29. Cannatello, 30. Monte Grande, 31. S.Angelo Muxaro, 32. Scirinda and Anguilla di Ribera, 33. Milena, 34. Caldare, 35. Polizzello, 36. Carcarella di Calascibetta, 37. Mokarta, 38. Pantelleria.

Map: Joanna Porc, Faculty of Archaeology, Leiden University.

carinated cups, and open vessels on a high conical stand (Fig. 36.2). Identified mainly by its decorative patterns, which are rather similar to the local Copper Age style, the Naro-Partanna group, located in the south-western interior and coastal areas of Sicily, is considered to be a marker of an early phase of Castelluccio. The Castelluccio facies from the Etna area has been divided into four phases in a recent study by Massimo Cultraro (1997).

The Rodì-Tindari-Vallelunga (RTV) Facies

Apart from a few sites of exclusively RTV facies on the northern coast (Boccadifalco (Palermo), Tindari, and Messina, three *grotticella* tombs from Rodì (Messina), and a small group of individual inhumations in large *dolia* (storage vessels) from Messina-Torrente

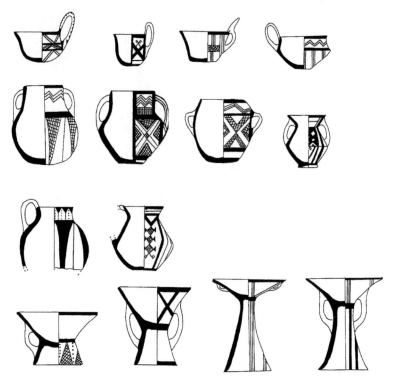

FIG. 36.2 The basic pottery shapes and decoration of the Early Bronze Age Castelluccio culture, in the area around Mount Etna. The pottery is hand-made, with matt painted decorations in black on red.

Source: Cultraro 1997.

Boccetta (Tusa 1999: 457), RTV pottery is systematically associated with Castelluccio material, for example at Serra del Palco, Ciavolaro di Ribera (Agrigento), and the *grotticella* tomb from Vallelunga (Caltanissetta) (Procelli 2004). The distinctive feature of RTV pottery is the absence of painted decoration. Its forms and functional features share some elements in common with the Castelluccio repertoire and, mainly, with the Palma Campania and Proto-Apennine pottery of the Italian peninsula (for example, conical stands, shallow high-handled cups, large carinated bowls, axe-shaped protrusions). Sites of RTV facies have been found on the Tyrrhenian coast of Calabria, while formal parallels with RTV pottery features appear as far as the Ionian and Adriatic coasts, at Capo Piccolo in Calabria and Cavallino in southern Puglia.

The Moarda Facies

Rather than an archaeological facies, this is a pottery style clearly related to Bell Beaker. It is found in limited quantities in the same area of western Sicily that in the late Copper Age was occupied by groups using Bell Beakers. Moarda pottery is usually found in association with Naro-Partanna and Castelluccio, and is sporadically present in the southern zone.

Structures and Organization in Early Bronze Age Sicily

Early Bronze Age society in Sicily was organized in small village communities, for example Manfria near Gela (Orlandini 1962) and La Muculufa near Licata (Holloway, Joukowsky, and Lukesh 1990), which joined together to form clusters, probably the equivalent of 'tribal' groups. A certain degree of functional specialization and interdependence may have been a specific feature of a settlement pattern of this kind. The territory of Sicily was intensively occupied along the coastal areas as well as in the interior. A considerable proportion of sites are on hills and small plateaux, but the plains were also occupied, in order to exploit their rich agricultural soils. Some specific environmental situations produced local adaptations. This is the case with the valleys in the Hyblaean area (*cave*), which provided a favourable environment for both settlement and farming. On the lower slopes of Etna and in the adjacent plain, the natural caves in the lava flows were used for both settlement and burial. The open-air dwelling structures are huts of circular or irregular plan, with a low base of pebbles or stones supporting a wattle-and-daub wall and conical roof. A single larger hut of oval or rectangular plan was present at Manfria, and also appears at other sites. Two settlements near Siracusa, Thapsos, and Timpa Dieri, were protected by a stone wall with semicircular towers along the outer face; at Monte Grande (Agrigento) there are circular stone enclosures. The centralization of some religious and economic activities appears both in the eastern and in the southern zone. At the eponymous site, Castelluccio (Siracusa), an interior settlement on a wide plateau in the Tellaro Valley, the highest terrace was occupied by an exceptionally large oval building (*c*.20 m long), partly cut into the bedrock. The performance of ritual functions is indicated by a concentration of large vessels in two holes in the floor, and by the repeated use of fire (Voza 1999: 17–23, Figs. 13–14). The important flint deposits of the Ippari Valley (Ragusa) were systematically exploited by the communities of a group of hill sites (Mounts Sallia, Raci, Tabuto, and Racello). The exploitation and trade of sulphur from the local deposits is attested at Monte Grande.

The earliest systematic Aegean presence in Sicily, which might be related to the acquisition of local raw materials, is indicated by a few LH II B–IIIA sherds in the area of Agrigento (Monte Grande, Madre Chiesa, Milena) (Castellana 1998). Some evidence is also present in the area around Mount Etna (Cultraro 1997). An important connection to the Maltese archipelago is documented at Ognina, a small island originally connected to the southern coast of Sicily, by an association of Maltese Tarxien cemetery, Castelluccio, grey *impasto*, and Capo Graziano pottery.

The funerary rite is inhumation, usually multiple or collective (up to 50 burials), in natural caves and more often in small chambers (*grotticelle*) cut horizontally in exposed rocky slopes. Megalithic funerary structures are rather rare, and usually associated with *grotticelle*. Special funerary features, possibly an indication of social competition between kin-groups in the same community, appear in the cemeteries of the Tellaro Valley (e.g. Cava Lazzaro): these are sculptured, probably figurative, patterns on some of the stone slabs that sealed the tombs' entrances, and rock-cut pillared porticos. The funerary outfits comprise pottery, flint blades, stone ornaments, clay figurines, and 'horns of consecration', some local amber, bone artefacts, including the bossed bone plaques, with parallels from Troy to Lerna, Apulia and Malta, bronzes with Aegean and Anatolian parallels (scale balances, tweezers, a flat spearhead) (Leighton 1999: 141, Figs. 70–1; Cultraro 1997 for Aegean imports from the Etna area). The subsistence economy as documented at Manfria was based on breeding (50 per cent cattle, ovicaprines, pigs, and a limited percentage of horse and dog) and on cereal cultivation. There is a limited evidence of a local production of bronze artefacts, mainly flat axes and small daggers. As regards trade activities, it is possible to hypothesize that a double system was in operation: local products, such as flint, stone ornaments, possibly amber, probably circulated domestically; exotic goods, some of them of Aegean origin, and possibly metal, reached Sicily through the coastal trade system that operated in this area of the Mediterranean.

The Aeolian Islands

The Early Bronze Age Capo Graziano Facies

According to Bernabò Brea and Cavalier (1980), in the earliest phase of the local Early Bronze Age the Aeolian settlements occupied open positions (e.g. Lipari, Contrada Diana, and Filicudi, Piano del Porto). The advanced phase is characterized by the shifting of the main settlements to naturally defended positions: the acropolis of Lipari, and Capo Graziano, the eponymous site, on a small promontory on the south-eastern side of Filicudi. Some traces are also known at Panarea: Punta Peppa Maria, Piano Quartara, and La Calcara. The cargo of a boat probably carrying pottery from Lipari to the other islands has been found in Lipari harbour, near Pignataro di Fuori. Some evidence is also known from Salina (Serro dei Cianfi) and Stromboli (Pianicelli di Ginostra and San Vincenzo). Capo Graziano pottery is an unpainted *impasto*, with black-grey surface. The forms are dolia, different types of jars, jugs, and cups with high handle, and a variety of carinated bowls. The incised decoration is relatively rare in the early phase, and quite frequent in the subsequent one. Early Mycenaean pottery (LH I, II, and IIIA) in considerable quantities is associated with Capo Graziano in the settlements of Lipari-Acropolis, Filicudi-Capo Graziano, and Salina-Serro dei Cianfi. In the advanced phase identification marks incised on local vessels make their first appearance (Marazzi 1997). The villages comprise some tens of circular and oval huts with stone foundation. In the village of Lipari Acropolis a larger oval structure was possibly used for cult activities. The only funerary evidence is a group of 30 cremations from Lipari, Contrada Diana. The subsistence was based on arable agriculture, pastoralism (along with cattle and pig breeding), fish, and molluscs. Lipari obsidian, and Sicilian clay for pot-making, were among the most important materials circulating in the archipelago.

The relevance of the Aeolian islands in the coastal trading system in this period is indicated by the occurrence of Capo Graziano pottery in the Tyrrhenian area, at Vivara-Punta di Mezzogiorno, in association with LH I–II material, at Luni sul Mignone in southern Etruria, and on the northern and eastern coasts of Sicily (Tusa 1999: 447, Fig. 76). Intense relations with Malta are indicated by the overall similarity between the Capo Graziano and Tarxien cemetery facies.

The Middle Bronze Age (c.1500–1250 BC)

A significant change from the Early Bronze Age, in which the Aeolian archipelago was culturally autonomous from Sicily, is indicated by the Middle Bronze Age Thapsos-Milazzese facies. This new archaeological culture extends over the whole territory of Sicily, the Aeolian islands including Ustica, and the Poro promontory on the adjacent coast of Calabria. This period coincides with the maximum intensity of sailings from the Aegean, with the participation of an east Mediterranean-Cypriot component. Calibrated radiocarbon dates from the Milazzese village at Portella di Salina range between 1525–1320 cal BC (1σ) and 1605–1260 cal BC (2σ) (Martinelli 2005: 289).

Thapsos-Milazzese pottery is a handmade *impasto*. The complete absence of painted decoration, and some formal and functional similarities, probably indicate a relationship to the RTV pottery repertoire. The forms are quite distinctive, with some local differences. In Sicily, and especially in the eastern zone, they comprise large dolia, ceremonial bowls/jars on a high flaring stand and with a horned plate, two-handled jars, narrow-necked jugs, bowls both plain and on a high stand, deep cups with high handle, decorated by engraved patterns and plastic cordons. The Aeolian repertoire does not include ceremonial vessels, and the most frequent decorations are plain plastic cordons. Imported LH IIIA and B pottery is found in considerable quantity in the Aeolian Milazzese settlements; in Sicily it is concentrated in the grave goods of some tombs in the eastern and southern area, and is also found in small quantities in the settlement of Thapsos and in some of the western sites (D'Agata 1997: 453). In the eastern area both form and decoration of Mycenaean and Cypriot pottery are imitated in the local unpainted *impasto* (D'Agata 2000). Maltese Borġ in-Nadur pottery is quite frequent in early Thapsos contexts on the eastern coast (Tanasi 2008a).

For Sicily, the marked decrease in the total number of sites compared to the Early Bronze Age probably indicates a more centralized political and territorial organization, with the main concentration in the east-central zone. Several sites are directly on the coast. The dwelling structures are circular or rectangular huts with stone foundations; the two types may also be combined. The tombs are plain *grotticelle*, with some more articulated structures with ante-chamber and lateral niches. A new feature of these tombs, usually considered as an imitation of the Mycenaean built or rock-cut tholos, is the ogival ceiling, often ending in a small circular cavity (Tomasello 2004). To this period belongs also a small cemetery of individual inhumations in large dolia found at Thapsos.

Thapsos is the eponymous site of this facies in Sicily, located on the small peninsula of Magnisi, some 10 km north of Siracusa (Fig. 36.3a). Although the settlement is still unpublished, and the only systematic information from the cemeteries are those relative to Paolo Orsi's excavations, this site has been the subject of several preliminary analyses and discussions. It seems rather well established that it was an *emporion*, structurally related to the international maritime trade system originating from the eastern Mediterranean and also involving the Aegean. The settlement extends over an area of *c*.1,000 by 300 m, with separate cemetery cores to the north and south (Paolo Orsi's excavations), and in the southern zone of the peninsula (more recent excavations by Voza).

Three phases have been identified by the excavator (Voza 1999: 23–31):

> Phase 1 (*c*.fifteenth–fourteenth century BC): northern settlement core, area A or 1. Circular huts associated with small rectangular structures and connected by narrow pathways. Earliest tombs imitate the tholos; the grave goods include local Thapsos pottery along with imported LH IIIA1–2, Cypriot White Shaved and Base Ring II pottery, glass, faience, and amber ornaments, probably also from the Aegean, and Maltese Borġ in-Nadur vessels.
>
> Phase 2 (*c*.thirteenth–twelfth centuries BC): central settlement core, area B or 2, organized by modules of rectangular rooms joining at right angles, with a central

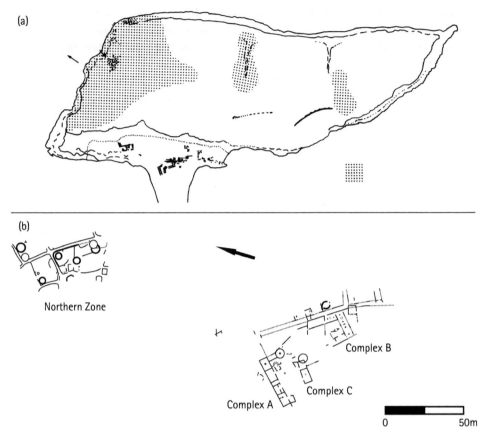

FIG. 36.3 (a) The peninsula of Thapsos, on the eastern coast of Sicily, north of Siracusa; (b) Plan of the Bronze Age settlement of Thapsos.

Source: Museo Archeologico Regionale "Paolo Orsi", Siracusa, by kind permission of the Assessorato dei Beni Cultarali e dell'Identità Siciliana della Regione Siciliana – Palermo. © All rights reserved.

open space or courtyard, and a few circular huts incorporated in the rectilinear structures (Fig. 36.3b). This kind of building plan and organization of space is not found elsewhere in this period in the central Mediterranean. It has been compared to the plans and corresponding spatial/functional organization of some Mycenaean palaces, and, more recently, to the organization in 'blocks' of the Cypriot Bronze Age cities (at emporia like Enkomi).

Phase 3 (c.eleventh–ninth centuries BC): there is no identifiable relation to the previous settlement organization. The main archaeological features include Maltese pottery (late Borġ in-Nadur and Bahrija), along with local bronzes of late 'Ausonian' and Cassibile type.

Other Thapsos sites in this area are Ognina, Cozzo Pantano (hill settlement and cemetery), Ortigia, Plemmirio, and Matrensa, in the area of the harbour of Siracusa, and Molinello di Augusta. Inland sites include grotta Chiusazza, Floridia, Buscemi, Caltagirone, Colle S. Mauro, Paternò, and a few settlements in the Ippari and Dirillo valleys. Coastal sites are also present near Capo Passero (grotta Calafarina) and in the gulf of Gela (Santa Croce

Camarina). In the Agrigento area the main sites are Milena-Serra del Palco, Madre Chiesa, Scirinda di Ribera, and S. Angelo Muxaro. A relevant role in Mediterranean trade may have been carried out by Cannatello, a coastal site dating from the advanced Middle Bronze Age and continuing in the Late Bronze Age. The buildings are circular and rectangular huts within a circular stone enclosure. The finds include Mycenaean and Cypriot pottery, and a fragment of oxhide ingot (De Miro 1999). Further west there are the settlements of Case Pietra, Erbe Bianche, Marcita, Ulina-Monte Castellazzo, and Thapsos layers from caves on the north-western coast. The funerary evidence consists of two tholos-type tombs (A and B) at Milena-Monte Campanella: the grave goods comprise Thapsos and LH IIIB or C, pottery, weapons, and a bronze bowl (La Rosa 1982). Combinations of possibly Cypriot bronze bowls, swords of the usual archaic type found in Sicily during the Middle and Late Bronze Age, and both local and imported pottery, come from a tomb at Caldare-Monte S. Vincenzo, from a burial in a natural cave at Capreria, and from the bronze hoard of Valledolmo (Palermo) (for the rather general Cypriot parallels for Sicilian Middle and Late Bronze Age swords see Tusa 1999: Fig. 47; for the possibly Cypriot bowls, and for the general problem of Cypriot material in the central Mediterranean see Vagnetti 1986; Graziadio 1997).

At Lipari the main Milazzese site is the village on the Acropolis, at Panarea it is the village of Punta Milazzese, at Salina it is La Portella, and Serro dei Cianfi; at Filicudi the main site is the final phase of the village of Montagnola di Capo Graziano. An important complex, systematically excavated in the last few years, is the Faraglioni village at Ustica (Holloway and Lukesh 2001).

The only cemetery of Milazzese facies, consisting of some 50 inhumation burials in large dolia, was found at Milazzo, Messina; two similar tombs have been found at Messina-Paradiso, and three at Naxos. Other finds in north-eastern Sicily include a dumping area from the hill settlement of Rometta Messinese, and Milazzese pottery from Naxos.

The Aeolian settlements are relatively small villages, whose average population probably did not exceed one to two hundred inhabitants. As regards both the selection of naturally defended situations, and the hut structures, they are quite similar to the earlier ones. One possible exception is Portella di Salina, on a steep crest on the island's northern coast, which was probably a specialized site for the collection of rainwater (Martinelli 2005). However, the Milazzese communities performed some important economic functions, as is implied by the increasing use of identification marks incised on different types of local vessel (Marazzi 1997). Probably the main such function of the archipelago was the establishment of trade relationships with the central and northern regions of the peninsula, aimed at the procurement of raw materials, and possibly of finished artefacts. The most important evidence is a group of discarded bronze artefacts from the Acropolis of Lipari, probably a founder's hoard, consisting of a collection of Italian Middle and, mainly, Recent Bronze Age Peschiera-type bronzes, along with Thapsos-Milazzese types and fragments of oxhide ingots (Moscetta 1988).

A different trend apparently developed in the southern Tyrrhenian area. From the advanced phase of the Early Bronze Age, and increasingly during the Middle Bronze Age, the role of Sicily and of the Aeolian islands in this maritime context seems to have undergone a radical change from the earlier system of intensive coastal trade. The main archaeological indicators are the shifting of the Aeolian settlements towards naturally defended positions, and the transformation of the previously autonomous archipelago into a northwards extension of Sicily. Moreover, two hints at increasingly hostile relationships in this area may be identified on the southern coast of Calabria and in the Aeolian islands: first, the establishment of settlement cores of Thapsos-Milazzese facies on the Poro promontory, which apparently coincided with a decrease in the local Apennine occupation; and, second, the occurrence of pottery of Apennine mainland type in limited quantity in Milazzese contexts both in Sicily and in the Aeolian islands. The analysis of the Apennine pottery from Portella di Salina indicates that it was made both locally and in mainland Italy (Martinelli 2005: 279). Thus, this pottery might be an indication of raids from the islands off the Italian coast, aimed at bringing back valuables, possibly including people.

THE LATE BRONZE AND EARLY IRON AGES (C.13TH–9TH CENTURIES BC)

From the thirteenth century BC a new connection between Sicily, the Aeolian islands, and mainland Italy, which expanded progressively until the Early Iron Age, radically changed the role of these islands in the Mediterranean context.

The Initial Phase: Lipari Ausonian I (c.1250–1050 BC)

The beginnings of this phase at Lipari, and in north-east Sicily (Cavalier 2004), can be dated around or somewhat before the mid thirteenth century BC, and are generally considered to be the result of a specific historical event: an invasion from the peninsula, probably from the coast of Calabria. The stratigraphic evidence on the Acropolis of Lipari is an extended fire, which produced the total destruction of the Milazzese settlement. The subsequent Ausonian I settlement was established in the same area. The new archaeological facies is a Sub-Apennine aspect of Italian mainland type, with handmade undecorated *impasto* pottery, a high percentage of carinated open shapes, and plastic protrusions over rims and handles. A small quantity of imported LH IIIB and IIIC pottery and a few local shapes of Sicilian Pantalica type (Tusa 1999: 556, Fig. 2, lower row) indicate a limited continuity of the earlier system of contacts and trade. The length of Ausonian I is marked archaeologically by the occurrence of a small amount of pottery of Final Bronze Age (Proto-Villanovan) type, along with the mass of Sub-Apennine. Ausonian I complexes in Sicily concentrate in the north-eastern zone: settlement evidence from Milazzo, Rometta Messinese, Barcellona, Messina, Naxos (Albanese Procelli 2003: 31), and a cremation cemetery at Milazzo, a typical Proto-Villanovan urnfield (Tusa 1999: 563). The earliest bronzes are a fibula with two knots of an intermediate violin-bow/stilted type, and narrow symmetrical razors of Pertosa type. The cemetery can probably be dated to the twelfth–eleventh centuries BC. The Ausonian I settlement at Lipari was destroyed by a new fire around the mid eleventh century BC.

The Initial Phase: The Sicilian Pantalica Culture, Early (c.13th–11th Century BC)

The Late Bronze Age Pantalica culture is structurally related to the Thapsos-Milazzese tradition involving the integration of Aegean groups, which were apparently still present and active in Sicily. Some significant changes include the shifting of the main centres from the eastern coast to the interior; at the same time the focus of the Mediterranean connection moved from the eastern to the southern coast. On a wider Mediterranean scale, at least from the thirteenth century BC, the east Mediterranean component of the international trade system gradually superseded the Aegean one, and the most important connections towards the Mediterranean far west were based in Sardinia. The Pantalica culture probably coincided with the final phase of Thapsos-Milazzese. The major centres in Sicily's eastern and southeastern zone are Pantalica, Caltagirone, and Dessueri; for each, a few minor sites have been identified in the adjacent territory (Tusa 1999: 575).

Pantalica, in the hinterland of Siracusa, occupies a wide plateau in the Anapo Valley; the only building known, the so-called *anaktoron*, is a rectangular ashlar structure, divided into seven rooms, one of which possibly contained a foundry. Around five thousand *grotticella* tombs cut in the rocky hill slopes are divided into several large groups, dating from the Late Bronze Age to the Greek colonization (Leighton 2011). Along with a majority of small rooms of circular plan, there are also some larger and multiple ones. Individual burials were rare. The cemeteries of Caltagirone (Catania) comprise around one thousand *grotticelle*, often with the ogival profile imitating the tholos. The main complex, Montagna di Caltagirone, has been recently re-examined (Tanasi 2008b). The settlement was in a strategic position relative to the main natural routes connecting the eastern and southern coast, and the interior. The third centre, Monte Dessueri, was on a steep hill (Monte Maio) on the Gela Valley, at a short distance from the southern coast. Some 1,500 *grotticella* tombs, divided into three cemeteries (Monte Canalotti, Monte Dessueri, and Fastucheria), were identified by Paolo Orsi (Panvini 1997).

FIG. 36.4 Some of the most common pottery shapes of the earliest phase of Pantalica. The pottery is wheel turned, and the majority of the shapes have Aegean and Cypriot parallels. The only possible import is the small painted jug in the lower row.

Source: Leighton 1999.

The funerary outfits from these sites comprise pottery, including some impressive ceremonial jars on high stands, rather similar to the ones used in the Thapsos period (Fig. 36.4), several bronze objects, including violin-bow, stilted, and arc fibulae with two knots, plain arc fibulae, mirrors, knives, razors, weapons, and golden rings, probably indicating important political roles.

The local pottery is mostly wheel-turned; overall the repertoire is close especially to LH IIIB and C, and, less precisely, to Cypriot forms (Leighton 1999: 174, Fig. 92; Tanasi 2005: Plates 129 and 130). As regards metal artefacts, the weapons and the mirrors are considered to be of Aegean or Cypriot inspiration, and golden rings have mainly Aegean parallels. The fibula series is probably an Italian contribution to Sicilian metallurgy: the earliest type, the violin-bow fibula with two knots, is among the most popular Peschiera bronzes, widely represented over the whole of Italy, and the Final Bronze Age stilted type is a specific product of the metallurgy of southern Etruria, distributed especially along the central and southern Tyrrhenian coast, and also present in the cemetery of Milazzo.

Pantalica sites in southern Sicily include the settlements of Sabucina and Montagna di Polizzello (Caltanissetta); around Agrigento, the earliest tombs in the cemetery of S. Angelo Muxaro, and the village of Scirinda with its rectangular buildings. In the cemetery of Anguilla di Ribera (Alonghi and Gullì 2009), in the Corno valley, 32 chamber tombs with rounded or ogival (tholos) ceilings and long corridors can be mainly attributed to the local Pantalica facies. The grave goods include a few combinations of Thapsos and Pantalica pottery, a majority of early Pantalica material, and a few groups dating from the Early Iron Age. Two golden rings were found in tomb 15. In the western zone one of the few published complexes, from Mokarta (Salemi, Trapani) is an interior hill site on the Fiume Grande Valley, with two settlement cores (Cresta di Gallo and Castello della Mokarta), which probably continued from the Middle Bronze Age to the Pantalica period, and two small cemeteries (Mannino and Spatafora 1995). The 37 tombs of the cemetery of Cresta di Gallo comprise both the plain and the ogival (tholos) type. The local Pantalica facies, also called Mokarta facies, is specific to central and western Sicily (Mannino and Spatafora 1995: Fig. 34). Although this facies is a simplified version of the eastern one, both the basic pottery and bronze types and the tombs' architectural features are rather specific to the Thapsos-Pantalica tradition. It also seems likely that the Late Bronze Age communities of central and western Sicily shared with the main eastern centres—Pantalica and Caltagirone—the formal correlates of the highest political roles.

The Final Bronze Age and Early Iron Age in the Aeolian Islands and Sicily (c.11th–9th Centuries bc)

The archaeological aspects that appeared at Lipari after the destruction by fire of the Ausonian I settlement on the Acropolis has been called Ausonian II by Bernabò Brea and Cavalier. The new facies is no longer dependent on the direct reproduction of Italian models, but rather on a local elaboration integrating formal and functional features of both Italian and Sicilian (Pantalica) origin. An important characteristic of the new facies is the systematic connection to the Italian mainland, especially Calabria, mainly as regards metal production. Ausonian II complexes at Lipari include the Acropolis village and the cremation cemetery of Piazza Monfalcone, with bronze, amber, and glass ornaments of Italian Proto-Villanovan type.

As regards Sicily, the new connection with Italy can be identified in different forms and areas (Albanese Procelli 2003: 31). A Final Bronze Age–Early Iron Age archaeological facies that seems to be directly linked to Lipari's Ausonian II has been identified, generally from surface finds, along the north-eastern coast. In eastern Sicily coastal sites include Monte di Giove, Giardini Naxos (Messina), and Punta Castelluzzo (Siracusa); the main interior ones are the hill settlement of Metapiccola di Lentini (Siracusa), the cemetery of Molino della Badia-Madonna del Piano (Catania), and the Early Iron Age hill settlement and cemetery of Morgantina (Enna). As regards the main Pantalica centres, Caltagirone apparently came to an end at the same time as the beginnings in the same region of the 'Ausonian' cemetery of Madonna del Piano. At Pantalica and Dessueri, in the Early Iron Age an Ausonian facies took the place of the traditional one. An Ausonian II facies is also present in the upper layers of the settlement of Scirinda di Ribera.

Another Final Bronze Age–Early Iron Age development, which is found in a few sites on the eastern coast of Sicily and in the interior, is a pottery repertoire of specifically local type, in the Thapsos-Pantalica tradition, combined with a rich metal industry of Ausonian character. This is found on the eastern coast at Cassibile (Turco 2000), south of Siracusa, possibly at Thapsos and Cozzo del Pantano, and at Carcarella di Calascibetta (Enna).

The continuity of the Thapsos-Pantalica tradition was confined to western Sicily and the S. Angelo Muxaro group (Spatafora 1996), from the Early Iron Age to the Archaic period. The uninterrupted link to the local Middle to Late Bronze Age cultural development is identifiable in the general formal and functional features of pottery production (Albanese Procelli 2003: Plate xix), along with the use of architectural features and role markers that had been adopted in Sicily as a result of the process of indigenous-Aegean integration: the ogival 'tholos' ceiling of the chamber tombs, and the golden rings still repeating Aegean patterns.

The economic implications of the Ausonian connection are rather clear, and are probably related to the intensive exploitation of the mining resources of Calabria: between the Final Bronze Age and the Early Iron Age the Sicilian metal industry in the Thapsos-Pantalica tradition was totally superseded by a new 'Ausonian' production, with strong links to Calabria. Throughout Sicily the new industry, which introduced significant technical and functional changes along with a quantitative increase in the use of metal artefacts, was universally adopted in both 'Ausonian' and 'local' contexts. Among the most important pieces of evidence are the Sabucina workshop, a group of stone moulds for the production of weapons and tools, mainly of 'Ausonian' type, and the generalized adoption of tanged and flanged swords and fibulae of the so-called Sicilian type (Albanese Procelli 2000; 2003: 88).

Bibliography

Albanese Procelli, R. M. (2000). 'Bronze metallurgy in protohistoric Sicily', in D. Ridgway, F. R. Serra Ridgway, M. Pearce, E. Herring, R. Whitehouse, and J. Wilkins (eds.), *Ancient Italy in its Mediterranean Setting: Studies in Honour of Ellen Macnamara*, Accordia Studies on the Mediterranean, 4. London: Accordia Research Institute, University of London, 75–90.

—— (2003). *Sicani, Siculi, Elimi*. Milan: Longanesi.

Alonghi, G. and Gullì, D. (2009). *La necropoli Anguilla di Ribera*. Agrigento, Palermo: Regione siciliana, Assessorato dei beni culturali, ambientali e della pubblica istruzione, Dipartimento dei beni culturali, ambientali e dell'educazione permanente.

Bernabò Brea, L. and Cavalier, M. (1980). *Meligunis Lipara IV*. Palermo: Flaccovio.

Bietti Sestieri, A. M. (2003). *Un modello per l'interazione fra Oriente e Occidente mediterranei: il ruolo delle grandi isole*, Atti della XXXV Riunione scientifica IIPP, Lipari 2000. Florence: Istituto Italiano di Preistoria e Protostoria, 557–86.

Castellana, G. (1998). *Il santuario castellucciano di Monte Grande e l'approvvigionamento dello zolfo nel Mediterraneo nell'Età del Bronzo*. Agrigento, Palermo: Regione Sicilia.

Cavalier, M. (2004). 'L'Ausonio I a Lipari', in D. Cocchi Genick (ed.), *L'Età del Bronzo Recente in Italia*. Atti del Congresso Nazionale di Lido di Camaiore, 26–29 ottobre 2000. Viareggio-Lucca: Mauro Baroni Editore, 185–90.

Cultraro, M. (1997). 'La civiltà di Castelluccio nella zona etnea', in M. Marazzi and S. Tusa (eds.), *Prima Sicilia*. Palermo: Regione Siciliana Assessorato al Turismo, 353–7.

D'Agata, A. L. (1997). *L'unità culturale e i fenomeni di acculturazione: la Media Età del Bronzo*, in M. Marazzi, S. Tusa, *Prima Sicilia*. Palermo: Regione Siciliana Assessorato al Turismo, 447–57.

D'Agata, A. L. (2000). 'Interactions between Aegean groups and local communities in Sicily in the Bronze Age: the evidence from pottery', *Studi Micenei ed Egeo-Anatolici*, 42/1: 61–83.

De Miro, E. (1999). 'Un emporio miceneo sulla costa sud della Sicilia', in V. La Rosa (ed.), *Epi ponton plazomenoi*. Simposio italiano di studi egei, Roma 1998. Rome: Scuola archeologica italiana di Atene, 439–49.

Graziadio, G. (1997). 'Le presenze cipriote in Italia nel quadro del commercio mediterraneo dei secoli XIV e XIII A.C.', *Studi Classici e Orientali*, 46/2: 681–719.

Holloway, R. R., Joukowsky, M., and Lukesh, S. S. (1990). 'La Muculufa. The Early Bronze Age sanctuary: the Early Bronze Age village (excavations of 1982 and 1983)', *Revue des Archéologues et Historiens d'Art de Louvain*, 23: 11–67.

Holloway, R. R. and Lukesh, S. S. (2001). *Ustica II—Excavations of 1994 and 1999*. Providence, Rhode Island: Brown University.

La Rosa, V. (1982). 'Milena', in L. Vagnetti (ed.), *Magna Grecia e mondo Miceneo. Nuovi documenti*. Taranto: Istituto per la storia e l'archeologia della Magna Grecia, 127–9.

Laffineur, R. and Greco, E. (eds.). *Emporia, Aegeans in the central and eastern Mediterranean*. Proceedings of the 10th International Aegean Conference: Italian School of Archaeology, Athens, 2004. Liège-Austin: Université de Liège.

Leighton, R. (1999). *Sicily before History: An Archaeological Survey from the Palaeolithic to the Iron Age*. London: Duckworth.

—— (2011). 'Pantalica (Sicily) from the Late Bronze Age to the Middle Ages: a new survey and interpretation of the rock-cut monuments', *American Journal of Archaeology* 115: 447–64.

Mannino, G. and Spatafora, F. (1995). *Mokarta. La necropoli di Cresta di Gallo*, Supplemento dei Quaderni del Museo Salinas, 1. Palermo: Regione Siciliana Assessorato dei Beni Culturali e Ambientali e della Pubblica Istruzione.

Marazzi, M. (1997). 'Le "scritture eoliane": i segni grafici sulle ceramiche', in M. Marazzi and S. Tusa (eds.), *Prima Sicilia*. Palermo: Regione Siciliana Assessorato al Turismo, 458–71.

Marazzi, M. and Tusa, S. (eds.) (1997). *Prima Sicilia*. Palermo: Regione Siciliana Assessorato al Turismo.

Martinelli, M. C. (ed.) (2005). *Il villaggio dell'età del Bronzo Medio della Portella a Salina nelle isole Eolie*, Collana Origines. Florence: Istituto italiano di Preistoria e Protostoria.

Moscetta, M. P. (1988). 'Il ripostiglio di Lipari. Nuove considerazioni per un inquadramento cronologico e culturale', *Dialoghi di Archeologia*, 3, 6/1: 53–78.

Orlandini, P. (1962). *Il villaggio preistorico di Manfria, presso Gela*. Palermo: Banco di Sicilia.

Panvini, R. (1997). 'Osservazioni sulle dinamiche socio-culturali a Dessueri', in M. Marazzi and S. Tusa (eds.), *Prima Sicilia*. Palermo: Regione Siciliana Assessorato al Turismo, 492–501.

Procelli, E. (2004). 'Una facies a cavallo dello stretto: Rodì-Tindari-Vallelunga e i rapporti fra Sicilia e Calabria nell'Età del Bronzo', in *Atti IIPP XXXVII, Calabria 2002*. Florence: Istituto Italiano di Preistoria e Protostoria, 381–92.

Spatafora, F. (1996). 'Gli Elimi e l'Età del Ferro nella Sicilia occidentale', in R. Leighton (ed.), *Early Societies in Sicily*. London: Accordia Research Institute, University of London, 155–65.

Tanasi, D. (2005). 'Mycenaean pottery imports and local imitations: Sicily vs southern Italy', in R. Laffineur and E. Greco (eds.), *Emporia, Aegeans in the Central and Eastern Mediterranean. Proceedings of the 10th International Aegean Conference: Italian School of Archaeology, Athens, 2004*. Liège-Austin: Université de Liège, 561–9.

—— (2008a). *La Sicilia e l'arcipelago maltese nell'Età del Bronzo Medio*, Koinè Archeologica Sapiente Antichita, 3. Palermo: Officina di Studi Medievali.

—— (2008b). *La necropoli protostorica di Montagna di Caltagirone*. Milan: Polimetric.

Tomasello, F. (2004). 'L'architettura "micenea" nel siracusano', in V. La Rosa (ed.), *Le presenze micenee nel territorio siracusano*. Padua: Aldo Ausilio Editore, 187–215.

Turco, M. (2000). *La necropoli di Cassibile*. Naples: Centre Jean Bérard.

Tusa, S. (1999). *La Sicilia nella preistoria*, 4th edn. Palermo: Sellerio Editore.

Vagnetti, L. (ed.) (1982). *Magna Grecia e mondo miceneo. Nuovi documenti*. Taranto: Istituto per la Storia e Archeologia della Magna Grecia.

Vagnetti, L. (1986). 'Cypriot elements beyond the Aegean in the Bronze Age', in V. Karageorghis (ed.), *Proceedings of the Symposium 'Cyprus between the Orient and the Occident', Nicosia 1985*. Nicosia: Department of Antiquities, 201–14.

Voza, G. (1999). *Nel segno dell'antico*. Palermo: Arnaldo Lombardi Editore.

CHAPTER 37

THE BRONZE AGE IN SARDINIA

FULVIA LO SCHIAVO

A Large Island: Almost a Continent

During the Bronze Age the process of social diversification, which had begun in the Copper Age, continued throughout Europe, leading to the formation of complex societies. In Sardinia (Fig. 37.1) this phenomenon was magnified by its being the second biggest island not only of Italy but also of the Mediterranean (about 24,000 square km) and because of the distances that separate it from other lands and islands (187 km from the Italian Peninsula, 270 km from north Africa), with the exception of Corsica (11 km over the Straits of Bonifacio); but these are distances that could be overcome by individual or collective choice and determination, above all in the Bronze Age. The possibility of access to Sardinia by chance can be discounted and, perhaps as a result, the island's absence of the need for fortification in the Bronze Age, as archaeological evidence increasingly demonstrates, is substituted by the evidence of control of resources, systems of internal communication, sea routes, and landing places.

This is certainly the reason why Sardinia, as well as other European regions, finds no place in a 'world system'. In fact it is practically impossible to apply to this large island rigid or previously established patterns. Research carried out so far largely confirms this fact and has investigated instead different forms and alternative solutions. Those currently identified, still using archaeological evidence, show peculiarities unique in Europe, among which are the island's privileged relationships, toward the eastern world with the Aegean and the east Mediterranean, and toward the western world with the Iberian Peninsula. These relations are not defined or uniform, but distinct and different in a surprising way, the result of specific choices based on substantial information and not generically determined.

All available sources should be studied together and comparatively: pot styles, the typology of metal objects, the extraordinary structure of the buildings, and the reciprocal links between them. This should apply even if one's intention is to offer a historical reading. One must use all the lines of evidence provided by archaeology, both directly from the data of material culture and indirectly from internal and external comparisons, and make use of the most recent discoveries.

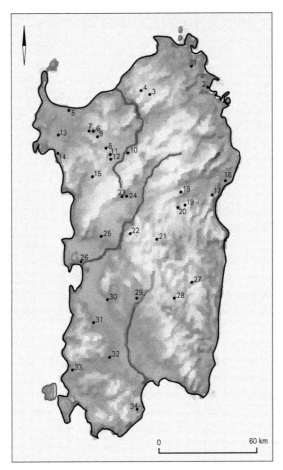

FIG. 37.1 Map of Sardinia with principal sites mentioned in the text; 1. Arzachena (SS); 2. Olbia (SS); 3. Calangianus (SS); 4. Tempio (SS); 5. Porto Torres (SS); 6. Muros (SS); 7. Ossi (SS); 8. Siligo (SS); 9. Florinas (SS); 10. Ittireddu (SS); 11. Bonnanaro (SS); 12. Torralba (SS); 13. Olmedo (SS), 14. Alghero (SS); 15. Mara (SS); 16. Orosei (NU); 17. Dorgali (NU); 18. Orune (NU); 19. Oliena (NU); 20. Fonni (NU); 21. Meana Sardo (NU); 22. Sorradile (OR); 23. Bortigali (NU); 24. Silanus (NU); 25. Paulilatino (OR); 26. Cabras (OR); 27. Esterzili (NU); 28. Orroli (NU); 29. Barumini (CA); 30. Mogoro (OR); 31. Gonnosfanadiga (CA); 32. Decimoputzu (CA), 33. Gonnesa (CA), 34. Sarroch (CA).

Legend: Cagliari: CA, Oristano: OR, Nuoro: NU, Sassari: SS. Map: Joanna Porc, Faculty of Archaeology, Leiden University.

Tribute is due to the great Sardinian archaeologist Giovanni Lilliu, who proposed and continually updated the complex cultural framework of prehistoric and protohistoric Sardinia over many decades (Lilliu 2003). His reconstructions and hypotheses have been modified and in some cases changed completely, but no one has been able to match his breadth of knowledge in Sardinian archaeology.

Issues of Chronology

The relative chronology of Bronze Age Sardinia is now based on the solid foundations of a reliable and continually re-analysed pottery typology (Campus and Leonelli 2000; 2006). On the one hand it is linked to nuragic pottery discovered at the harbour site of Kommos in Crete (Watrous 1989; Watrous, Day, and Jones 1998), at Cannatello near Agrigento in Sicily (Vanzetti 2004), and on the Aeolian island of Lipari. On the other hand it is associated with Mycenaean pottery of LH III A2 to IIIB and IIIC, found in the *nuraghi* (stone towers) Arrubiu-Orroli (Vagnetti and Lo Schiavo 1993), Antigori-Sarroch (Ferrarese Ceruti 1982), and others. This pottery comes from local contexts that relate it to the building and subsequent use of the monuments. The infrequency with which metal objects and pottery are found together, except for a few cases of bronze hoards in pots (Campus and Leonelli 1999), makes for considerable difficulties.

Strong support for the dating of metal objects derives from the similarities between Italian, Iberian, and Cypriot artefacts and the local typologies (Lo Schiavo, Macnamara, and Vagnetti 1985). Moreover, recent research on nuragic sanctuaries, which are the preferred sites for the deposition of bronze offerings (Nieddu 2007; Manunza 2008), provides valuable evidence of associations and stratigraphical details, particularly for the bronze figurines, parallel to Late Cypriot III production.

As far as absolute chronology is concerned, there are now good data and critical assessments (Tykot 1994), comparisons with Aegean chronology (Balmuth and Tykot 1998), and the results of research on material from stratigraphic surveys (Torres, Ruiz-Gálvez, and Rubinos 2004). However, as some analyses have shown, for crucial periods many uncertainties persist, and for these the best approach is still relative chronology, combining typology and find associations.

Since the earliest Mycenaean finds in Sardinia are associated with local pottery (surface finds at Mitza Purdia-Decimoputzu and stratified at the Arrubiu-Orroli nuraghe), there is confirmation that the Nuraghi Golden Age began between the end of the Middle Bronze Age and the beginning of the Recent Bronze Age. At Decimoputzu the surface association is with 'grey nuragic' pottery (or 'Antigori type'), whereas at Arrubiu-Orroli in the foundation layer of the central tower, in the courtyard and in tower C, the association is also with shallow bowls (*teglie*) and pyxides with flat, internal rim, decorated with impressed dots, of a type that is considered late by comparison with the *metope* pottery, and contemporary with the beginning of the *a pettine* pottery.

Different pottery styles of Recent Bronze Age 1 and 2 are increasingly being defined, as well as that between Final Bronze Age 1 and 2, which, with its link to monumental building, allows a subdivision of phases to be recognized, above all in the south and in the Oristano region. On the other hand, metallurgical production indicates the opposite. Throughout Bronze Age Sardinia, there is no local differentiation between or regional specialization in metal artefacts, as happened in the preceding period.

It is more difficult to fix the chronology of the end of the nuragic period. At present it is agreed that throughout the Recent Bronze Age there is a trend of development that includes at least the beginning of the Final Bronze Age (FBA 1). At the start of the final phase of the RBA no more nuraghi are being built, while restoration work seems to have stopped in the 'intermediate phase' of the FBA (FBA 2), yet this is not evidence of a final collapse in the culture but of important changes, the strengthening—if such a thing is possible—of an already thriving economy. In short, it is a socio-economic process, one that was growing fast and always looking for new markets, right up to the end in the Early Iron Age (Campus and Leonelli 2010).

The Early Bronze Age: An Age of Upheavals

Sardinia is no different from the rest of Europe when it comes to formulating an organic definition of the Early Bronze Age. The Chalcolithic culture of Monte Claro occupies roughly the second half of the third millennium BC, covering the whole island with strongly characterized living, funerary, and ritual aspects; pottery styles allow regional subdivisions. The subsequent events, which fall between the end of the third and the beginning of the second millennium, are still unexplained: there is the appearance of some of the material aspects typical of the Bell Beaker 'culture', with a widespread prevalence of pottery finds; and the spread of the so-called Bonnanaro A culture or archaeological facies of Corona Moltana, from the area situated in the historical region of the Meilogu in which the Domus de Janas ('House of the Fairies/Witches') appear, where for the first time typical materials of this culture were identified, perhaps datable between 2200 and 1900 cal BC (Early Bronze Age I).

In short, the evidence points to a wide cultural diffusion: the peculiar rituals amongst which burial in monumental tombs with reused anthropomorphic menhirs may be mentioned (in at least two cases, Nurallao-Aiodda and Isili-Murisiddi); the extensive distribution of the most typical pottery shapes; the appearance of metal; the spread of the practice of cranial trepanation; together with the small number of settlements, possibly small farms scattered over wide areas (Perra 2009). These factors lead to the conclusion that the archaeological facies of Bonnanaro A is 'formative', an ongoing process.

The consideration of these multiple factors may have inclined scholars in the past to speculate that in Early Bronze I an elaboration of the elements that subsequently constituted the nuragic civilization, including the erection of the first nuraghi, took place. At present this view is open to criticism, since it is not based on any typical finds, either in the nuraghi or in the Giants' tombs. By contrast, much progress has been made in identifying another archaeological facies, that of S. Iroxi, named from the artificial cave tomb of Decimoputzu where the majority of the finds have been made, and which have now been dated to the second phase of the Early Bronze Age (EBA 2). In this tomb around 60 indviduals were identified, some of them buried in a crouched position, together with objects made of arsenical copper such as a large number of rhomboid awls, pins, punches (*punteruoli*), and needles, as well as 5 daggers and 13 swords, whose shape is similar to the Argaric swords of the Iberian Peninsula (see Chapter 33). Metallurgical analysis has confirmed the presence of characteristic Sardinian copper, and therefore local manufacture. The analytical data are confirmed by the presence in the same hypogeum of weapons of various sizes, small and larger daggers, and short and long swords (Lo Schiavo 1992a).

In the Bingia le Monti-Gonnostramatza tomb, a S. Iroxi phase covers a collapse layer under which lie Bonnanaro deposits. Another interesting stratified sequence is in a tomb in the cemetery of the Domus de Janas at Montessu-Villaperuccio (unpublished excavations by E. Atzeni and R. Forresu).

In contrast to the abundant and distinctive production of metal, the pottery of the S. Iroxi phase is still scarce and not distinctive in shape. Yet it has nevertheless been identified in room *alpha* at Li Lolghi Arzachena, a chamber tomb made of orthostats and stone paving, preceding the Giants' tomb.

There are still no indications of settlement in the S. Iroxi facies. In the funerary rituals a difference can be seen from the preceding Bonnanaro A phase: the primary deposition is by crouched inhumation, with the grave goods showing stratification and a particular stress on weapons, pointing to the more important social role of the warrior.

In conclusion, it can be said for the Early Bronze Age that 'small groups dispersed throughout the territory to form single village groupings, organized along lines of kinship, which were apparently self-sufficient and autonomous' (Perra 2009: 360) were present in Sardinia; it seems possible to recognize the socio-economic forms of lineage societies. However, it is best not to force this idea too far, for various reasons. These include the wide distribution and differentiation of the pottery shapes, including contacts with the outside world that can be seen in the Bonnanaro A1 facies; the explosion of local metallurgical production, strongly influenced by Iberian models and identified in the S. Iroxi EBA 2 facies; and the fact that the following Sa Turricula MBA 1 facies, which inherited many Early Bronze Age cultural aspects, is also the immediate predecessor of the nuragic civilization. All of these factors indicate that the complexity and distinctiveness of the island's cultural evolution was greater than has been imagined hitherto.

The Nuragic Civilization

Formation

Originally the Bonnanaro culture was divided into two distinct aspects: Bonnanaro A, mentioned above, and Bonnanaro B or the Sa Turricula facies, from the name of the site (still largely unknown) in the district of Muros (Ferrarese Ceruti 1981a). Of the vast settlement located on the steep southern slope of Mount Tudurighe, only Hut no. 1 has been explored and published in a very preliminary way. The village was dominated by a nuragic tower, while the Funtana 'e Casu dolmen was located nearby at a lower altitude, in which a few sherds attributable to this facies (still unpublished) were apparently found.

In Sa Turricula there are elements of continuity such as a fragment of *cuenco* (hemispherical bowl) with Bell Beaker decoration, discovered in the hearth of Hut no. 1 (Ferrarese Ceruti 1978: Fig. 113), and a small simple dagger with round base and two rivet-holes, made of arsenical copper (Ferrarese Ceruti 1981a: Plate LXXIIb bottom left; analysis in Atzeni et al. 2005: 118–19), in addition to the survival of many Bonnanaro A shapes, such as the sharply angled bowls of truncated conical shape with 'elbow' handles. There are also new shapes destined to have a long life, such as shallow bowls. In addition, some sherds decorated with ribs and round bosses, the so-called *a nervature* ('ribbed') pottery (Middle Bronze Age 1/2), have been found.

From the point of view of bronze typology there is obvious continuity in some cultural elements between the Early Bronze Age and the full nuragic period, the strongest of which is represented by the large flanged axes. These tools, in their earliest form, characterized by a large size, straight sides, and very marked edges, are found throughout the island and are associated not only with the nuraghi but also with the Giants' tombs. They are very similar to a type found on the mainland in the Early Bronze Age in the Lazio area: the Sezze type (actually called the 'Sezze-Orosei type' from the first Sardinian site where it was identified: Carancini and Peroni 1999; Lo Schiavo 1992b). While the mainland axes quickly change, acquiring a notched base, sinuous sides, and developed flanged edges tending to small 'wings', in Sardinia the shape changes little and remains typical throughout the Bronze Age. The same phenomenon of contact with the Italian Peninsula is attested by the small disc-headed pin from the settlement site of Su 'e Predi Giaccu-Meana Sardo in the Barbagia of Ollolai, associated with pottery shapes that can be attributed to the final phase of the Middle Bronze Age (Perra: pers. comm.), while the much larger disc-headed pins on the mainland are dated to the Early Bronze Age (Carancini and Peroni 1999). The start of the relationship between Sardinia and the mainland should therefore be placed between the end of the Early Bronze Age and the beginning of the Middle Bronze Age, within the overall framework of the Sa Turricula culture, which during its long chronological and cultural evolution acquires and develops influences from both inside and outside Sardinia.

The 'ribbed' pottery, which hitherto—rather than an archaeological *facies* in itself—has been thought to represent a style of largely funerary use, has been found in the Giants' tombs of Gallura and Dorgalese, which suggests that the elaborate and monumental orthostatic architecture with an upright monolith could have been created in the first phase of the Middle Bronze Age. As for the nuraghi, the presence and density of them in Middle Bronze Age 3 leads to the tentative conclusion that the formation both of the 'corridor nuraghi' or 'proto-nuraghi', sometimes with an embryonic *tholos* chamber, and of the *tholos* nuraghi, together with or perhaps even preceded by villages, can be placed in the MBA 2 period, in parallel with the characteristic Giant's tombs (Ferrarese Ceruti 1981a).

The pottery style of S. Cosimo or of the *metope* 'pottery (MBA 3), from the Giants' tomb of Gonnosfanadiga, where it was named for the first time (Ugas 1981), has as its characteristic shape the so-called pyxis or large earthenware pot with a flat, internal rim, decorated on the rim and the shoulder with incised dotted triangles and plastic ribs, often in square-shaped or *metope* patterns. This pottery was found in, among other places, the nuraghi at Brunku Madugui-Gesturi, Sa Fogaia-Siddi, Su Mulinu-Villanovafranca, in the Giants' tombs of Marghine-Planargia, and on the Abbasanta plateau.

In metallurgy the simple forms of awl and rhomboid punch continue without typological changes in the Giants' tombs, where evidently they had the function of securing the shroud. Mention has already been made of the small disc-headed pin at Su 'e Predi Giaccu-Meana Sardo, and of the large flanged axes of the 'Sezze-Orosei' type found here and there throughout the island and concentrated in two sites, the first relating to the Sisine-Nule nuraghe and the second to an unidentified Giant's tomb at Ilbono (Lo Schiavo 1992b: the 'Nule-Ilbono type').

As for weapons, the few examples found so far are the simple daggers with rounded heel at Siniscola and Settimo S. Pietro, and the dirks at Su Mulinu-Villanovafranca (Ferrarese Ceruti and Lo Schiavo 1991–2). The find of the two tiny rat-tanged daggers with rivet-hole on the shoulder from the Giant's tomb at Is Lapideddas-Gonnosnò reinforces the assumption of local production, under the influence of central European Pépinville and Arco types, of at least one part of the weapons in the Ottana hoard, which still lacks a convincing provenance and classification (Lo Schiavo 2005a: 280–3).

The 'corridor nuraghi' or 'pseudo-nuraghi' (or even 'proto-nuraghi') have narrow internal rooms ('corridors') of limited extent when compared with the thickness of the stone walls and the covering of flat lintel blocks, the main function of which seems to be to create a powerful structure with good views from the top. Some maintain that these are the earliest forms of nuraghe, but this is not proven: these constructions are frequent mainly in granite environments, where the walled structure fits unevenly onto the rocky outcrop. There are also nuraghi of mixed shape, the result of successive additions, with corridors and tholos, for example the Talei-Sorgono, Cuccurada-Mogoro, Serucci-Gonnesa, Majore-Tempio nuraghi, or even with tholos and corridor as at Palmavera-Alghero, or Albucciu-Arzachena.

The basic shape of the so-called tholos nuraghe is that of a truncated cone topped by an overhanging walkway supported by stone brackets; in the commonest type, inside the circular chamber three niches open opposite the entrance; in the passage that runs through the thickness of the wall there is a niche on the right, and on the left a spiral staircase rises to the upper floor or to the walkway. There are numerous variations and exceptions for each of these features. The covering of the internal rooms is usually a cupola vault (tholos), or more exactly layered rings of stones placed one on top of the other with decreasing diameter. Detailed studies and structural and functional analyses have excluded the idea that Minoan-Mycenaean and nuragic *tholoi* are part of the same architectural tradition (Cavanagh and Laxton 1987).

From the technical point of view, it has now been established that, even in the case of the simplest structures, the construction of the nuraghi was a complex operation requiring precise planning and much organization of the workforce.

Giants' Tombs and Ceremonial Areas

The characteristic burials of the nuragic age are called 'Giants' tombs' because they are all collective tombs, often very large in size, the largest being about 30 m long and the smallest from 5 to 8 m (Fig. 37.2). They consist of an elongated and often paved burial chamber, the burial mound contained by a stone plinth, with an apsidal rear part and a ritual area opposite defined by a semicircular structure called the 'exedra'; and a large monolith or stele in the centre, in some cases reaching the spectacular height of 4 m, with a small entrance at the bottom (*portello*). These types of Giants' tombs are concentrated in central and northern Sardinia, although they are not unknown in the south. A peculiarity of nuragic Sardinia is the fact that in these monumental tombs the primary collective burials are always without grave goods of any kind; selected individual burials are never found and there is no apparent selection by age or gender, still less social or family distinction, in allowing admission to burial in the tomb.

On the other hand, from the Middle Bronze Age on, the Giants' tombs had a role as places of worship, both for their size and their visibility, and for the presence of the ceremonial area in front, dedicated to collective rituals for the dead, and a designated place for collective rituals that were intended to celebrate the ancestors and to single out the high descent of the local group. True temple structures are not known in this period; in fact the interpretation of the so-called 'little temple' at Malchittu-Arzachena has been disputed.

The nuraghi and the Giants' tombs are both territorial markers and contribute to the 'formation/transformation of the nuragic landscape' (Perra 2010). From communities based on kinship in the preceding period, a remarkable aggregating force takes shape, not just quantitative, as is evidenced by the spread of settlement nuclei, but above all qualitative, reflected in the concentration of a common effort to erect great monuments in dominant positions on natural outcrops and on the edges of the plateaux (*giare*), where the elevation provides wide visibility. To the Middle Bronze Age megalithic structures one may attribute first and foremost a function in territorial control–and thus also control of resources.

THE 'NURAGHI GOLDEN AGE'

I cannot find a more appropriate expression than 'Nuraghi Golden Age'.... The most outstanding and specific phenomenon of phase III consists in the origin and the development of the complex nuraghe... (Lilliu 2003: 413; translation Lo Schiavo)

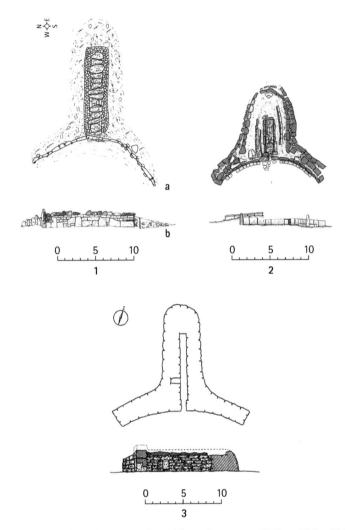

FIG. 37.2 Plans of Giants' tombs. 1. Pascharedda-Calangianus (SS); 2. Bidistili-Fonni (NU); 3. Domu 's Orku-Siddi (CA). Various sources.

General Characteristics

Despite the fact that earlier absolute chronologies are now out of date, the contents of Giovanni Lilliu's phase III correspond almost entirely to the period that is today placed between the end of the Middle Bronze Age (MBA 3B), the Recent Bronze Age (RBA), and the early part of the Final Bronze Age (FBA 1/2), in which the nuragic civilization reaches its height. His telling remark thus continues to hold true.

The nuraghi occur in a growing number of complex forms: multi-towered, polylobate, regular or irregular, with powerful stone enclosures and bastions (Fig. 37.3). The towers number from one to five, variously positioned, linked one to another by powerful bulwark walls inside which are passages and rooms. Between the central and the added towers, courtyards open off that allow communication between the various parts. This would have led to the construction of two-tower nuraghi (for example, at Orolo-Bortigali and many others), three-tower nuraghi (Santu Antine-Torralba, Madrone-Silanus, and others), four-tower nuraghi (Su Nuraxi-Barumini, Sa Serra-Orroli, and others), and multi-towered nuraghi (the only surviving one being Arrubiu-Orroli; Fig. 37.4). In some cases, an outer ring of towers are linked together by walls, forming an outer enclosure (*antemurale*). In the villages of this period, round huts with high stone foundation walls, often of remarkable thickness, and adapted to hold up a conical roof of poles covered with intertwined bundles of brushwood, are grouped around a central space, which sometimes encloses wells, cisterns, and places for collecting water (Serra Orrios-Dorgali; Su Putzu-Orroli). In the latest period (FBA 2–3) multi-chambered structures appear, placed around a courtyard (Su Putzu-Orroli; Serucci-Gonnesa).

Tombs retain their essential characteristic of a large chamber for collective burials, with an elongated mound with apsidal end and a semicircular area in front intended for collective rituals, but the building technique and the structure change.

Temple structures appear and increase rapidly, most frequently in the canonical form of Well-Temples and Sacred Springs (Fig. 37.5), but there are also *megaron* temples, 'rotundas', 'Rooms for making bread' (*Vani della Panificazione*), lustral basins with long stone channels, and paved ceremonial areas with benches. These forms spread rapidly all over the island, taking on elaborate and sophisticated shapes.

The characteristic building technique that appears in the Recent Bronze Age is the so-called 'isodomic' construction (in regular layers), with perfect joints, squared corners, vertical walls, straight sides, and smooth floors. This stoneworking, in basalt, trachyte, limestone, and sandstone, is widespread and not exclusive to the temple and funerary monuments, but also found in the upper structures of the nuraghi.

In this mature phase of nuragic cultural development, the full management of resources can be seen, through the visible and direct control of the territory, established by the continuous erection of complex nuraghi, by extending the villages, even independently from the nuraghi (for example, the territories of Oliena and Dorgali, or the hinterland of the Gulf of Cagliari), by locating and sometimes increasing the number of tombs in the most important spots (for example, the territory of Esterzili), and thus by unifying local communities in a concentrated and strategic building effort. This was not a random expansion, but one that was hierarchically planned within regional systems.

A fundamental part of the management of nuraghi is that of food resources. In the Recent and Final Bronze Ages cereal production increased exponentially, as can be seen by the erection of storage silos inside the nuraghi (as at Arrubiu-Orroli), and above all in the Final Bronze Age by the increase in the production of large containers and open-shape bowls that could have been used for measuring out quantities of cereals (Cossu et al. 2003). As far as wine is concerned, the recent and extensive excavations at Sa Osa-Cabras revealed the remains of grapes in such quantities and of such varieties as to indicate advanced cultivation during the Recent/Final Bronze Age transition (Usai 2010). Only a few years before, it had been hypothesized that the characteristics of Recent Bronze Age pottery would indicate a specific function of containers for highly prized liquids, for which a particular compactness and surface treatment was required. In fact, 'slate-grey' (*grigio-ardesia*) pottery (Ferrarese Ceruti 1981b) or 'nuragic grey' pottery appears, made from *impasto* and baked at very high temperatures, with metal-effect shiny-grey external surfaces. This pottery is characteristic of the Antigori-Sarroch nuraghe, where it is found in stratigraphic association with Mycenaean

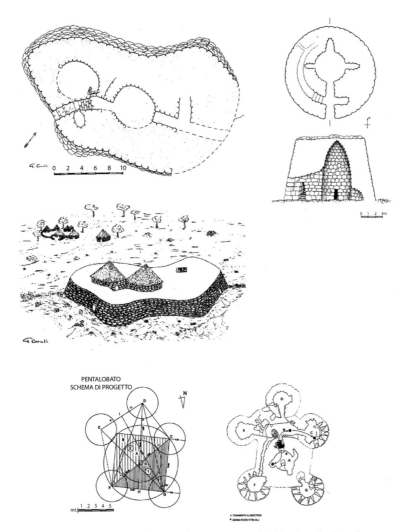

FIG. 37.3 Plans of nuraghi: 1. Brunku Madugui-Gesturi (CA), plan (1.1) and reconstruction (1.2); 2. S. Sabina-Silanus (NU); 3. Nuraghe Arrubiu-Orroli: projection (3.1) and plan (3.2).
Various sources.

pottery, but it is also spread through the whole of central-southern Sardinia. The high quality of the surfaces and the complete lack of porosity lead one to conclude that the pots must have been used to hold oil or wine. Between the RBA and the FBA the first types of pitchers or ewers also begin to appear.

Nuragic civilization is notably homogeneous from one end of the island to the other. This obviously does not indicate a lack of resources or cultural immobility but the contrary, richness and a considerable variety of local choices. The different pottery styles should undoubtedly be taken into account but not invested with too much significance, because such distinctions may depend on geography, the prevalent rock type, the presence of forest, soil characteristics, land use, and so on. All things considered, the cultural homogeneity of nuragic civilization is remarkable, lasting throughout the island until the final phase.

FIG. 37.4 Above: Nuraghe Arrubiu (excavated by the author). Below a reconstruction of the site.

Reconstruction: Ing. G. Todde.

From Simple Nuraghi to Complex Nuraghi

It was once thought that complex nuraghi were built simply by adding more towers to a central tower. In fact the excavation and detailed study of the Arrubiu-Orroli nuraghe (see Fig. 37.4), among others, has established the existence of real and complex planning, not only in the choice of location but also in the laying-out of the monument plan on the ground, the

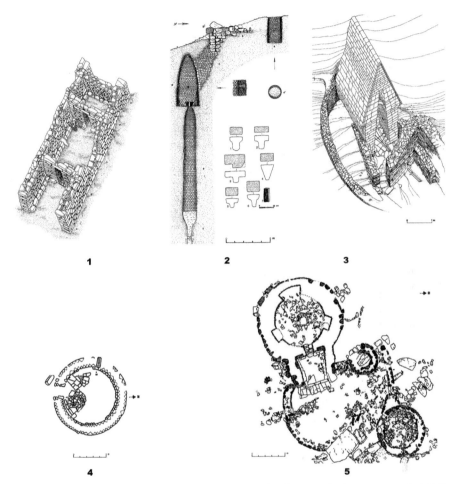

FIG. 37.5 Plans of Nuragic temples: 1. 'Megaron' temple of Domu de Orgia-Esterzili (NU); 2, Sacred Well of Cuccuru Nuraxi-Settimo S.Pietro (CA); 3. Sacred Spring of Su Tempiesu-Orune (NU); 4. 'Round' temple of Sa Corona Arrubia-Genoni (NU); 5. 'Round' temple of Su Monte-Sorradile (OR).

Various sources.

evaluation of the need for foundations, the research for and preparation of building materials, and the estimation of the workforce needed.

Above all, in this phase the reason for such a large number of imposing constructions (roughly eight thousand is no exaggeration), often close to one another in different geographical and topographical situations but with a considerable uniformity of general structural features and material culture, should be sought in the socio-economic context. This shows that environmental conditions were on average quite favourable; there was a raised and widespread level of well-being and a territorial community-based social organization, with a strong inherited awareness of earlier kinship traditions.

The nuraghi therefore would have been erected by means of a communal, concentrated effort by the local workforce and in quite a brief span of time, without the need to bother about subsistence resources, which were readily available. Importance and prestige within the social group might be linked to the size, number, and complexity of the nuragic towers, which functioned almost as status symbols, in a logical process of territorial occupation and control.

This hypothesis is confirmed during the Final Bronze Age (FBA 2/3), when in response to the end of nuraghi building, their symbolic value increases, as shown not only in the change in the use of the monuments (their transformation into centres for gathering in surplus production, as with Arrubiu-Orroli and Serucci-Gonnesa), but also in their sacralization (Su Mulinu-Villanovafranca), the reproduction in miniature of both simple and complex nuraghi in stone and bronze, and their location in sanctuaries or villages at the centre of *Capanne delle Riunioni* ('Reunion or Meeting Huts', for example Palmavera-Alghero, Punta 'e Onossi-Florinas).

The Mycenaean and Cypriot Connection

The nature of the relationship between Sardinia and the Aegean world is not yet completely clear. So far no finds have been made in the island relating to the earliest phases of Mycenaean expansion, as seen in the Aeolian islands and at Vivara (LH IA–LH IIB), and then spreading from the Adriatic to the Ionian islands, the Tyrrhenian Sea, and Sicily (LH IIC–LH IIIA1) (Vagnetti 2010). In Sardinia the earliest finds, dated to LH III A2, come from two southern regions, both inland (especially the second one), and some way from each other. They consist of valuable artefacts of different types: one being a small hippopotamus-ivory head with a boar's tusk helmet at Mitza Purdia-Decimoputzu; and an almost complete small *alabastron* found in fragments in the foundation level of the five-towered nuraghe at Arrubiu-Orroli, chemico-physical and mineralogical analysis confirming an Argolid provenance. While these are isolated instances, they nevertheless point towards the existence of previous relationships, now rapidly on the increase.

The change in the direction of Sardinia's relationship with other cultures that can be seen in the course of the eleventh century BC, from the close connections with the Cypriot and the Aegean world to that with the Iberian Peninsula, does not, however, indicate an interruption or a replacement of metallurgical traditions. The types of nuragic bronze tools, weapons, ornaments, containers, and miniature figurines continue with minor differences up to the end of the Bronze Age and beginning of the Iron Age. The Nuraghi Golden Age is thus both fundamentally homogeneous and culturally extraordinarily rich and varied.

The same type of socio-economic and organizational management that was necessary for the construction of the complex nuraghi in the context of a territorial system is needed to plan long- distance sailing and trading. For this reason evaluation of the building of the nuraghi cannot be separated from that of metallurgical production, nor should mastery of navigational techniques and knowledge of sea routes and landmarks be underestimated.

It is therefore to the period corresponding to the end of the Middle Bronze Age (MBA 3B), and to the elaboration of the complex nuraghe model, that we can date a change of course: from the adoption on Sardinia of models inspired by mainland Italy to those of the Aegean and—particularly for metallurgy—Cypriot models. On the other hand, the dating to the end of the fourteenth century BC of the Uluburun shipwreck, with its rich cargo, the major part consisting of copper and tin ingots but having on board a sword of Sicilian type (Pertosa B2 or C: Bettelli 2006), the presence of oxhide ingots at Cannatello and Thapsos in Sicily, and the presence of nuragic pottery at Cannatello (Sicily), Kommos (Crete), and at Pyla-Kokkinokremos on Cyprus, all show that at the end of the fourteenth century and in the thirteenth–twelfth centuries reciprocal Mediterranean connections were firmly established, and that nuragic Sardinia was an active partner in them.

The 'ox-hide' ingots (conventionally 'oxhide'), so-called because of their characteristic rectangular shape with more or less prominent 'ears', weigh on average between 25 and 30 kg and measure about 66 x 44 cm (Ozieri). Marks were stamped on the ingots while hot or chiselled when cold, identified as being pre-alphabetic and alphabetic marks of the eastern Mediterranean. In Sardinia, after the first discovery made at Serra Ilixi-Nuragus in 1857 by the great Sardinian archaeologist Giovanni Spano, the number of such finds has considerably increased. The places where the ingots have been discovered, either whole or as fragments, at present number 35 and are spread over the whole island, including the interior and the mountainous districts (Lo Schiavo 2009).

The distribution of oxhide ingots beyond Sardinia is extremely wide and includes the Levantine coasts, Asia Minor, the Black Sea, Cyprus, Crete, Greece, Sicily, the Aeolian islands, as well as a mould found at Ras Ibn-Hani in Syria, and pictorial representations on Egyptian tombs at Thebes, Karnak, and Medinet Habu. Fragments have been identified in a hoard in Baden-Württemberg, Germany. In the west, the highest concentration is in Sardinia, where the ingots are most frequently found in temples and sanctuaries. There are two complete ingots from Corsica and southern France. Production in Cyprus is dated from the fourteenth to the eleventh centuries BC. Since it has not yet been possible to prove local nuragic production, the conclusion that they are Cypriot products holds good for Sardinia as well as other areas, though obviously their use locally may have persisted somewhat longer.

It seems evident that in the Bronze Age nuragic Sardinia was a privileged market for Cypriot copper, prized not only for the advantage of having metal which was already refined but also for the opportunity to meet specialized artisans in order to learn about new technologies linked to the new quality of the copper, that is, highly purified (Cu 97 per cent to 99 per cent) copper from sulphide ores through a complex process of refining, already available in massive ingots. It is not unreasonable to suggest that together with copper, Sardinia also imported tin via Cyprus. It has been known for some time that this was the route along which the first knowledge of iron was acquired, although its use was not widespread (Lo Schiavo 2005b).

The arrival of oxhide ingots and tools for metalworking are not isolated episodes of trade and importation. On the contrary, the oxhide ingots were the carriers of the new metallurgical technology and at the same time of a 'new wave' in other spheres and techniques. It was not just a matter of similarities in the form of the equipment for working metal (hammers, shovels, tongs), but of the whole complex of metallurgical technology. This involved specific knowledge intimately bound up with the successive flourishing of an extraordinary level of production: the manufacture of tools, weapons, and ornaments, in both stone and clay moulds; the creation of bronze vessels either by the hammering of sheet metal or by shaping them using the lost-wax technique, and then applying massive handles to the sheet bronze; the early acquaintance with iron. These factors constitute the body of technological knowledge that nuragic Sardinia took from Cyprus, right from the earliest stages of contact between the two islands, which archaeological evidence increasingly puts at the beginning of the Recent Bronze Age (c.thirteenth to the first half of the twelfth century BC), a period during which local production improves exponentially and in a completely original way.

Despite the strong Cypriot influence in nuragic Sardinia, there was no break or radical change in the system of basic values: impressive monuments for the living and the dead, with highly visible, collective burials without grave goods; simple and largely undecorated pottery; no interest in personal ornaments or in the signs of rank; no attraction to gold or silver despite the presence of abundant supplies of silver (already known in prehistoric times); ivory hardly known and then only for functional uses such as handles; and other aspects of the local value system.

The Tomb, the Temple, and the Sword

The Giants' tombs in 'isodomic' construction are a development of older orthostatic tombs, and are distinctive for the careful working of the stone blocks that are set in regular courses, progressively overhanging one over the other inside the chamber. They are built in regular layers both in the chamber and on the facade of the exedra, at the centre of which the architraved entrance opens, either with no stele or with a stele *a dentelli* (scalloped or indented) (for example, Biristeddi-Dorgali and Seleni-Lanusei).

The nuragic structures intended for worship are varied, but those that occur most frequently are linked to springs: the Well Temples and the Sacred Springs (see Fig. 37.5). The Well Temples consist of a narrow staircase leading down to the level of the water, which is enclosed in the shaft of the well and covered by a tholos-type roof (Sa Testa-Olbia; in perfect isodomic style: S. Cristina-Paulilatino, Predio Canopoli-Perfugas, S. Vittoria-Serri, and many others). In the Sacred Springs the water is collected almost at surface level in a simple basin, sometimes covered with a small tholos. Both types of temple are preceded by a paved atrium and side benches. One of the most elegant and elaborate examples of Sacred Springs is Su Tempiesu-Orune.

Other sacred buildings are not linked to springs, even though large and small basins and channels can be found on all of them, indicating lustral rituals. The 'Megaron' Temples are so called because they have a rectangular plan sometimes divided up by internal partitions, and with *pronaos* and *opistodomos* (Serra Orrios-Dorgali, Domu de Orgia-Esterzili, S'Arcu 'e is Forros-Villagrande Strisaili, Su Romanzesu-Bitti, etcetera). Rotundas are round-plan buildings with a tholos covering a refined isodomic structure, of various kinds and dimensions (Cuccuru Mudeju-Nughedu S. Nicolò, Giorrè-Florinas, Sa Carcaredda-Villagrande Strisaili, Su Monte-Sorradile, etcetera). 'Huts for making bread'(*Vani della Panificazione*) are so called because of the large basin at the centre of a small circular room with a bench, next to a second large basin of water and one or more ovens (Sa Sedda e' Sos Carros-Oliena, Su Nuraxi-Barumini, S. Imbenia-Alghero, etc).

One aspect that the temples and Giants' tombs have in common is the presence of votive swords, with very long (on average 120 cm), narrow (on average 3–4 cm), and straight blades. These swords have been defined as votive because their shape, the composition of the alloy, and their small hilt do not make them a practical weapon. Votive swords are the earliest nuragic bronze production and form part of the offerings, since they are found tied together in bundles or inside large jars; above all they are linked to the construction phase of sacred buildings, stuck on the pediment of the temples (Su Tempiesu-Orune, Monte S. Antonio-Siligo), denoting the structure of the temple itself as both a symbol and an offering. The votive swords are found everywhere in sanctuaries together with the 'Offering Tables'. The swords are stuck in the cavities of the stones, fixed with lead, pointing upwards, and often represented in the hands of the bronze figurines of warriors and archers. They are sometimes combined with other symbolic objects or small bronze figurines, placed on their points and forming elaborate hunting magic. Their presence also in the Giants' tombs, complete or fragmentary, could indicate that from the beginning of the nuragic period weapon worship and ancestor worship had undergone changes of form and place, but not of intensity and importance.

Nuragic Metallurgical Production

The early flanged axe now becomes slender, with less-developed edges and polygonal cross section; it characterizes all hoards in Final Bronze Age 1 and 2 and remains in use in FBA 3 and the Early Iron Age, when it is even produced in miniature.

Among the offensive weapons, the types most frequently found, both in moulds and in bronze, are the daggers—daggers with gamma-shaped hilt are typical—leaf-shaped and tanged daggers, spearheads, and spear-butts. Swords of practical use are few in number, some of Iberian origin, from the eleventh century BC onwards, at first 'pistilliform' (widening in the lower third of the length and then thinning towards the tip); later on, Huelva-Saint Philbert swords and 'carp's tongue' swords. The Monte Sa Idda swords are solid proof of the exchange of goods between the Iberian Peninsula and Sardinia. Nothing remains of defensive weapons as shown on the bronze figurines; most must have been made from perishable materials: leather, animal skins, wood, and wickerwork.

Among the personal ornaments the most characteristic and frequently found are the pins, above all those with detachable head and often with a bead fastening the folds on the shank, stout and useful also as a dagger. There are a very few other decorative objects, such as necklaces of bronze beads, bracelets, and rings. The fibulae of the Recent and Final Bronze Age are for the most part imported from the Tyrrhenian region of the mainland, as are the objects for toilet and ritual use, like razors and tweezers (Fig. 37.6). The ritual objects are extremely interesting: mirrors, 'buttons', pendants, 'quivers', 'stool/rattles', 'two-branch torch-holders', and probably also collars with conical ends.

There are few associations between metal objects and pottery. As a result there is difficulty in establishing the chronology, which is usually done by means of typological studies and external comparisons. The hoards of the Recent Bronze Age are characterized by the presence of oxhide ingots (Lo Schiavo et al. 2009). The most relevant hoards of the Final Bronze Age are those of Pattada-Sedda Ottinnera, Ozieri-Chilivani, Torralba-S. Antine hut 1, Oliena-Costa Nighedda, etcetera. To this time are attributed hoards that contain objects both of the period and of earlier periods, such as the S. Maria in Paùlis-Usini hoard.

The Bronze Figurines and the Sanctuaries

The production of bronze figurines (Fig. 37.7) begins no later than the mature Final Bronze Age (FBA 2). It is now possible to add stratigraphic and contextual data from the sanctuary at Matzanni-Vallermosa (Nieddu 2007) and Funtana Coberta-Ballao (Manunza 2008). Humans, animals, wooden furniture, containers in basketry, pottery and bronze, weapons, monuments, ships, and chariots were reproduced in miniature by the lost-wax technique. The characteristics and dimensions of some of these bronzes are almost those of real statues,

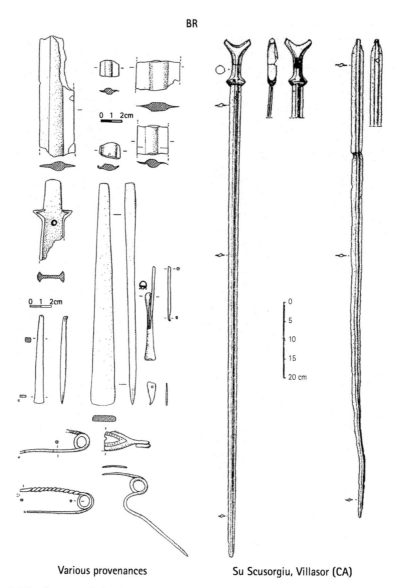

FIG. 37.6 Metal types of the Recent Bronze Age (RBA): Left: swords, chisels and fibulae fragments, various provenances. Right: two votive swords from the Su Scusorgiu-Villasor (CA) hoard.

Source: Lo Schiavo 2005a, Lo Schiavo et al. 2005.

as is now clear from comparison with stone sculpture: ox and ram protomes, single-tower and complex nuraghi as found in different temple structures, sometimes included in elaborate architectural ornamentation; and large anthropomorphic statues: boxers, archers, warriors, currently known only from the Mont'e Prama-Cabras *heroon*, in the Sinis region.

Rather than individual *ex votos*, the bronze figurines can be interpreted as ritual collective offerings, destined predominantly for the temples, which in the course of time developed into complex sanctuaries.

The End of the Bronze Age and Beginning of the Iron Age

Even more than in the preceding periods, the events of the final phase of the nuragic civilization need to be seen as parts of a complex whole, comprising territorial strategy, demographic increase, monument building (both civil and religious), pottery and metal production, and long-distance exchange, up to the time when an undisputedly new people, bringing an urban civilization, settled in Sardinia: the Phoenicians.

In general terms the collapse of a civilization in Sardinia, if there was one, is not to be found between the end of the Final Bronze Age and the beginning of the Iron Age. Instead, recent research has defined this period as a separate phase (Final Bronze Age 3/Early Iron Age 1A: Campus and Leonelli 2006; 2010). In this period the differences between the north, the centre, and the south-east of the island are underlined, and in the course of the Early Iron Age nuragic civilization dissolved both internally and externally into a new chapter of Sardinian history.

FIG. 37.7 Bronze statuette of a warrior, the so-called 'Great Bronze' in the Pigorini Museum, Rome.

Source: Pinza 1901.

From Sanctuary to Individual Burial

According to a recent review, from the climax of this phase during the eleventh century BC (FBA 2)—better viewed as a long period of elaboration—we witness the development of a new way of settling the landscape, with enlarged territorial systems and a greater cohesive force operating in the ceremonial and religious centres. This does not appear to be linked to warlike activity. There is an increase of the ritual or religious dimension as a means of expressing and overcoming conflicts, reaffirming social unity, and legitimizing the power of emerging groups (Perra 2009: 365–6).

The increasingly religious nature of the nuraghi is more and more evident, with the discovery of shrines in internal rooms or courtyards. These are characterized by ritual furnishings, such as carved basins (Su Mulinu-Villanovafranca), small stone 'tables' (*Tavolini*) (Funtana-Ittireddu), and most probably perishable structures (S. Pietro-Torpè). The presence of miniature four-towered nuraghi on the top of the *tutulus* 'buttons' that continued to be produced into the full Iron Age, apparently without losing their symbolic value, is evidence of this practice.

Throughout the island the 'strategy of the sanctuary' leads to an increase in the number and richness of places of worship, right up to the creation of complex 'federal' sanctuaries, places for gatherings and social meetings. These are almost always in elevated positions, but remain accessible and are never fortified. They became so large that in some cases it is possible to describe them as village-sanctuaries (Su Romanzesu-Bitti, Monte S. Antonio-Siligo, S. Vittoria-Serri). In some cases these structures—consisting of Well-Temples, one or more megaron temples and rotundas—are surrounded by large enclosures (Su Monte-Sorradile), which sometimes have monumental entrances (Gremanu-Fonni).

The expansion of the nuragic villages seems to have been uncontrolled, sometimes amounting to hundreds of huts, often organized in 'blocks' (S. Imbenia-Alghero), each with many rooms. In other cases the structures lean on each other and on the outer enclosure of the nuraghe (Palmavera-Alghero, Bau Nuraxi-Triei), overwhelming it (Genna Maria-Villanovaforru, Su Nuraxi-Barumini). It is a kind of deregulation recalling modern, disorderly house-building, and reflecting the demographic explosion that characterized the final phase of the nuragic civilization and caused its downfall.

At the beginning of the Final Bronze Age 3/Iron Age I period, funerary practice still included collective burials without grave goods, but collective burials in cist graves with grave goods, including ornaments (Motrox'e Bois-Usellus), begin to appear; there are individual inhumations in cist graves with grave goods (Senorbì, Sa Costa-Sardara), and shaft (*a pozzetto*) tombs with grave goods (Antas-Fluminimaggiore) or without them (Monti Prama-Cabras, Is Aruttas-Cabras). In Sardinia, which throughout its history had always preferred collective burials, this is a striking change that must, in one way or another, be connected to the Semitic peoples who, having known and practised these rituals in their country of origin, were now peacefully welcomed onto the island.

Nuragic Askoid Jugs and Votive Ships

Already in the Final Bronze Age, pottery production, which continued to produce the traditional shapes, has elegant, decorated forms ('pre-geometric', eleventh–tenth centuries, Final Bronze Age 2/3). These become more and more elaborate, in the style known as 'geometric', with incised, impressed, and sometimes relief or *a stralucido* decoration. The care accorded to, and decoration of, the pottery is another innovation, compared to earlier periods, which suggests not only a greater value assigned to the vessels, but also allowed immediate identification and, as a consequence, wider distribution of the pots. The most representative example of this are the askoid jugs with markedly eccentric neck, obliquely cut mouth, and an irregular globular body (Campus and Leonelli 2000: 392–400). These are the result of formal and exclusively local developments, which together with the contents provide an exclusive and distinctively Sardinian product, destined to be offerings in temples and sanctuaries throughout the island. This explains the increase in their distribution, which coincided with the earliest landfalls of the Phoenicians, and the very strong impact made on Tyrrhenian communities, principally those of Vetulonia, and its transmission to other centres in peninsular Italy during the Early Iron Age (Lo Schiavo 2005c).

A parallel phenomenon is observed in peninsular Italy in the late phase of production of a few bronze artefacts, whose origin is highly significant. These generally take the form of small amulets like *tutulus* 'buttons', with or without plastic decoration, 'pendulum' pendants and small 'quivers', which can be found both in Phoenician tombs in Sardinia and in Villanovan contexts in Etruria, *Latium vetus*, and Campania. Amongst these, the bronze boats stand out in quality and importance. These are reproductions in miniature of real boats, not so much technically faithful reproductions as symbolic and mythical representations, perfectly recognizable to the people of the time as an indication of the mastery of an essential resource, namely the sea routes. From the technical point of view of lost-wax production, the bronze boats and the nuragic bronze figurines are identical. As for the meaning they held, they are comparable; representative, each in their own way, of Bronze Age nuragic Sardinia, which in its final phase was transported beyond the island's boundaries. Up to that time the destination of the bronze figurines had been concentrated in the sanctuaries, whereas the distribution of the miniature boats seems to have been more 'personalized', linked to the head of the local group and his prestige. This explains the frequent discovery in Sardinia of the small boats in hoards, much more so than the bronze figurines, and in hoards, tombs, and shrines in peninsular Italy.

Many questions remain, the biggest of which is chronology. The little bronze boat at Su Monte-Sorradile offers many interesting perspectives; the assemblage with which it was found includes various bronze objects datable to the mature Final Bronze Age (FBA 1/2), and an askoid jug for which an overall date in the Final Bronze Age has been proposed.

The Coming of the Age of Iron

The close of the Bronze Age marked the end of an era in which the alloying of copper and tin dominated trade and technology. The Bronze Age was succeeded by the age of iron, already known in the west but not universally present. While iron artefacts from Elba and metals from Campigliese and Monte Amiata had not escaped the attention of Bronze Age Sardinians, there are no definitive traces of the systematic use of iron here before the Iron Age. With the introduction of a new material the nuragic civilization ended, without external traumas and, as far as archaeological evidence can tell us, without war or slaughter. On the contrary, the descendants of the nuragic civilization in the Final Bronze Age (FBA 2) must have led the search for new resources, markets, and trade partnerships.

The people of northern, central, and southern Sardinia were exceptionally skilled in the complex techniques of mineral exploitation and metallurgy, experts in the Mediterranean sea routes, and skilled traders, with contacts in both the Near East and the Far West. Northern Sardinians strengthened their relationship with the Tyrrhenian area, gravitating more and more towards the opposite shore and introducing ancient Sardinian customs to the local cultures of peninsular Italy. With this clear increase in contact between Sardinia and the mainland, the Tyrrhenian sea became a stage for joint naval ventures. Trade and piracy were linked in written sources, evidenced by the interconnected genealogies, mythologies, and common designations (*Trsha*, *Thyrsenoi*?). Piracy and trade dominated the Tyrrhenian sea until stronger land-based powers came to the fore in Sardinia, and fought over its seas.

The nuragic people living in the inland Nuoro region (*Barbaroi*, today *Barbaricini*) knew and participated in cultural developments throughout Sardinian prehistory and protohistory, such as changes in artefact form and rituals, and even acted as cultural intermediaries. Sanctuaries continued to be used for centuries, from the Final Bronze and Early Iron Age up to the medieval period, reflecting local reverence for early symbols and traditions (Sa Sedda 'e Carros-Oliena, Nurdole-Orani, Sa Carcaredda-Villagrande Strisàili, S. Vittoria-Serri, etcetera). This is confirmed by the letters of Gregory the Great to Ospitone (a Christian chief in sixth-century Sardinia), in which he complains about the persistent followers of ancient cults.

At the end of the Bronze Age the nuragic peoples living in the Oristanese and the south of the island (*Srdn*, *Shardana*?) shifted materially and ideologically towards cities on the coast. The new urban world marked a new way of life, with a new religion. Past rituals were transformed, as is evident from the new nuragic wheel-thrown *impasto* pots, the elbow-handled bowls in individual tombs, and iron pins with detachable bronze heads.

In the Early Iron Age the Phoenicians followed the Mediterranean routes of the Bronze Age, circulating copper in the form of oxhide ingots. The Phoenicians reached the far western regions of the Mediterranean. The Algherese area, among the most densely populated of nuragic Sardinia, and with a multitude of bronze finds in the temples (Camposanto-Olmedo) and hoards (Flumenelongu-Alghero), provides evidence of this cultural integration. The focus shifted from the nuragic village at Palmavera-Alghero to the new Phoenician emporium at the formerly nuragic village of S. Imbenia, a short distance away on the outskirts of Porto Conte bay. At S. Imbenia two hoards of copper ingots were gathered up and buried in amphorae, one a local *impasto* copy, the other Phoenician. Analysis of this copper has shown that it was from the nearby deposits at Calabona. Local amphorae carrying wine have been traced from Sardinia to Tyrrhenian Italy and to the Iberian Peninsula, as well as the Atlantic seaboard. The incentive for trade in the Bronze Age had been copper, but in the new Iron Age trade was driven not by metal, but by wine.

Bibliography

Albanese Procelli, R. M., Lo Schiavo, F., Martinelli, M. C., and Vanzetti, A. (2004). 'La Sicilia. Articolazioni cronologiche e differenziazioni locali', in D. Cocchi Genick (ed.), *L'Età del Bronzo recente in Italia, Atti Convegno Lido di Camaiore 2000*. Viareggio: Mauro Baroni, 313–34.

Atzeni, C., Massidda L., and Sanna U. (2005). 'Archaeometric data', in F. Lo Schiavo, A. Giumlia-Mair, U. Sanna, and R. Valera (eds.), *Archaeometallurgy in Sardinia from the Origins to the Beginning of the First Iron Age*, Monographies Instrumentum, 30. Montagnac: éditions Monique Mergoil, 111–83.

Balmuth, M. S. and Tykot, R. H. (eds.) (1998). *Sardinian and Aegean Chronology: Towards the Resolution of Relative and Absolute Dating in the Mediterranean*, Studies in Sardinian Archaeology, V. Oxford: Oxbow Books, 273–83.

Bettelli, M. (2006). 'Fogge simili ma non identiche: alcune considerazioni sulle spade tipo Thapsos-Pertosa', *Studi di Protostoria in onore di Renato Peroni*. Florence: All'Insegna del Giglio, 240–5.

Campus, F. and Leonelli, V. (1999). 'Considerazioni sui vasi-contenitori di lingotti di tipo oxhide e piano-convessi in ambito nuragico', in V. La Rosa, D. Palermo, and L. Vagnetti (eds.), *ΕΠΙ ΠΟΝΤΟΝ ΠΛΑΖΟΜΕΝΟΙ. Simposio Italiano di Studi Egei in onore di Luigi Bernabo Brea e Giovanni Pugliese Carratelli*. Rome: Italian School for Archaeology, 512–16.

—— (2000). *La tipologia della ceramica nuragica. Il materiale edito*. Viterbo: BetaGamma.

—— (2006). 'Sardegna fra l'Età del Bronzo finale e l'Età del Ferro. Proposta per una distinzione in fasi', *Studi di Protostoria in onore di Renato Peroni*. Florence: All'Insegna del Giglio, 372–92.

—— (2010). 'I cambiamenti nella civiltà nuragica', in F. Lo Schiavo, M. Perra, A. Usai, F. Campus, V. Leonelli, and P. Bernardini (2010). 'Sardegna: le ragioni dei cambiamenti nella Civiltà Nuragica', in M. Frangipane, R. Peroni, and A. Cardarelli (eds.), *Le Ragioni del Cambiamento: 'Nascita', 'Declino', 'Crollo' delle Società Antiche*, Atti del Convegno Internazionale (Roma 15–17 giugno 2006), *Scienze dell'Antichità*, 15/2009: 272–7.

Carancini, G. L. and Peroni, R. (1999). 'L'Età del Bronzo in Italia: per una cronologia della produzione metallurgica', *Quaderni di Protostoria*, 2. Perugia: Ali & No.

Cavanagh, W. G. and Laxton R. R. (1987). 'The mechanics of prehistoric corbelled buildings', in M. S. Balmuth (ed.), *Studies in Sardinian Archaeology, III: Nuragic Sardinia and the Mycenaean World*, British Archaeological Reports (International Series), 387. Oxford: British Archaeological Reports, 39–55.

Cossu, T., Campus F., Leonelli V., Perra M., and Sanges, M. (eds.) (2003). *La vita nel Nuraghe Arrubiu*, Arrubiu, 3. Comune di Orroli: Laboratorio della Conoscenza e della Memoria.

Ferrarese Ceruti, M. L. (1978). Notiziario–Sardegna, Provincia di Sassari, *Rivista di Scienze Preistoriche*, 33: 444–5.

—— (1981a). 'La cultura di Bonnànnaro', in E. Atzeni (ed.), *Ichnussa. La Sardegna dalle origini all'età classica*. Milan: Libri Scheiwiller, lxvii–lxxvii.

—— (1981b). 'Documenti micenei nella Sardegna meridionale', in E. Atzene (ed.), *Ichnussa. La Sardegna dalle origini all'età classica*. Milan: Libri Scheiwiller: 605–12.

—— (1982). 'Il complesso nuragico di Antigori (Sarroch, Cagliari)', in L. Vagnetti (ed.), *Magna Grecia e mondo miceneo. Nuovi documenti*. Taranto: Istituto per la storia e l'archeologia della Magna Grecia, 167–76.

Ferrarese Ceruti, M. L. and Lo Schiavo, F. (1991-2). 'La Sardegna', *Atti del Congresso: L'Eta del Bronzo in Italia nei secoli dal XVI al XIV* A.C, Rassegna di Archeologia, 10. Florence: All'Insegna del Giglio, 123–41.

Lilliu, G. (2003). *La Civiltà dei Sardi, dal Paleolitico all'età dei nuraghi*. Nuoro: Il Maestrale RAI—ERI.

Lo Schiavo, F. (1992a). 'Nota a margine delle spade argariche trovate in Sardegna', *Quaderni della Soprintendenza Archeologica per le Province di Cagliari ed Oristano*, 8: 69–85.

—— (1992b). 'Le più antiche asce a margini rialzati della Sardegna', *Rivista di Scienze Preistoriche*, XLII, 1989–90/1–2: 241–70.

—— (2005a). 'The first copper and bronze finds, from the beginning of the II millennium', in F. Lo Schiavo, A. Giumlia-Mair, U. Sanna, and R. Valera (eds.), *Archaeometallurgy in Sardinia from the Origins to the Beginning of the First Iron Age*, Monographies Instrumentum, 30. Montagnac: éditions Monique Mergoil, 279–87.

—— (2005b). 'The first iron in Sardinia', in F. Lo Schiavo, A. Giumlia-Mair, U. Sanna, and R. Valera (eds.), *Archaeometallurgy in Sardinia from the Origins to the Beginning of the First Iron Age*, Monographies Instrumentum, 30. Montagnac: éditions Monique Mergoil, 401–6.

—— (2005c). 'Le brocchette askoidi nuragiche nel Mediterraneo all'alba della storia', *Sicilia Archeologica*, 103: 101–16.

—— (2009). 'The oxhide ingots in Nuragic Sardinia', in F. Lo Schiavo, J. Muhly, R. Maddin, and A. Giumlia-Mair (eds.), *Oxhide Ingots in the Central Mediterranean*, Biblioteca di Antichità Cipriote, 8. Rome: Istituto di Studi sulle Civiltà dell'Egeo e del Vicino Oriente, 225–407.

Lo Schiavo, F., Macnamara E., and Vagnetti L. (1985). 'Late Cypriot imports to Italy and their influence on local bronzework', *Papers of the British School at Rome*, 53: 1–71.

Lo Schiavo, F., Giumlia-Mair, A., Sanna, U., and Valera, R. (eds.) (2005). *Archaeometallurgy in Sardinia from the Origins to the Beginning of the First Iron Age*, Monographies Instrumentum, 30. Montagnac: éditions Monique Mergoil.

Lo Schiavo, F., Muhly, J., Maddin, R., and Giumlia-Mair, A. (eds.) (2009). *Oxhide Ingots in the Central Mediterranean*, Biblioteca di Antichità Cipriote, 8. Rome: Istituto di Studi sulle Civiltà dell'Egeo e del Vicino Oriente.

Manunza, M. R. (ed.) (2008). *Funtana Coberta. Tempio nuragico a Ballao nel Gerrei*. Cagliari: Scuola Sarda Editrice.

Nieddu, F. (2007). 'Άριστον μεν ύδωρ. Il santuario nuragico di Matzanni: un tesoro ritrovato', *Villa Hermosa. Storia e identità di un luogo*. Monastir-Cagliari: Grafiche Ghiani, 13–55.

Perra, M. (2009). 'Osservazioni sull'evoluzione sociale e politica in età nuragica', *Rivista di Scienze Preistoriche*, LIX: 355–68.

—— (2010). 'La coropoiesi e la cenopoiesi alle origini della civiltà nuragica', in F. Lo Schiavo, M. Perra, A. Usai, F. Campus, V. Leonelli, and P. Bernardini (2010). 'Sardegna: le ragioni dei cambiamenti nella Civiltà Nuragica', in M. Frangipane, R. Peroni, A. Cardarelli (eds.), *Le Ragioni del Cambiamento: 'Nascita', 'Declino', 'Crollo' delle Società Antiche*, Atti del Convegno Internazionale (Roma 15–17 giugno 2006), *Scienze dell'Antichità*, 15/2009: 265–9.

Pinza, G. (1901). *Monumenti primitivi della Sardegna*, Monumenti Antichi dei Lincei, XI.

Torres, M., Ruiz-Gálvez, M., and Rubinos, A. (2004). 'La cronología de la Cultura Nuragica y los inicios de la Edad del Hierro y de las colonizaciones históricas en el Mediterráneo Centro-Occidental', in M. Ruiz-Gálvez (ed.), *Territorio nurágico y paisaje antiguo. La meseta de Pranemuru (Cerdeña) en la Edad del Bronce*, Complutum Anejos, 10. Madrid: Universidad Complutense de Madrid, 169–94.

Tykot, R. (1994). 'Radiocarbon dating and absolute chronology in Sardinia and Corsica', in R. Skeates and R. Whitehouse (eds.), *Radiocarbon Dating and Italian Prehistory*, Archaeological Monographies of the British School at Rome, 8. *Accordia Specialist Studies on Italy*, 3: 115–45.

Ugas, G. (1981). 'La tomba megalitica I di San Cosimo–Gonnosfanadiga: un monumento del Bronzo Medio (con la più antica attestazione micenea in Sardegna). Notizia preliminare', *Archeologia Sarda*, 2: 7–20.

Usai, A. (2010). 'L'insediamento prenuragico e nuragico di Sa Osa-Cabras (OR). Topografia e considerazioni generali', in A. Mastino, P. G. Spanu, A. Usai, and R. Zucca (eds.), *L'insediamento di Sa Osa-Cabras (OR) sul fiume Tirso*, Tharros Felix, 4. Rome: Carocci, 159–85.

Vagnetti, L. and Lo Schiavo, F. (1993). '*Alabastron* miceneo dal nuraghe Arrubiu di Orroli (Nuoro)', *Rendiconti dell'Accademia dei Lincei*, serie IX, IV/1: 121–48.

Vagnetti, L. (2010). 'Western Mediterranean', in E. H. Cline (ed.), *The Oxford Handbook of the Bronze Age Aegean*. Oxford: Oxford University Press, 890–905.

Vanzetti, A. (2004). *La Sicilia occidentale*, in R. M. Albanese Procelli, F. Lo Schiavo, M. C. Martinelli and A. Vanzetti A., *La Sicilia. Articolazioni cronologiche e differenziazioni locali*, in *L'età del Bronzo Recente in Italia*, Atti del congresso nazionale di Lido di Camaiore, 26–29 ottobre 2000, ed. Daniela Cocchi Genick. Viareggio (Lucca): M. Baroni Editore, 320–5.

Watrous, L. V. (1989). 'A preliminary report on imported "Italian" wares from the Late Bronze Age site of Kommos on Crete', *Studi Micenei ed Egeo-Anatolici*, XXVII: 69–79.

Watrous, L. V., Day, P. M., and Jones, R. E. (1998). 'The Sardinian pottery from the Late Bronze Age site of Kommos in Crete: description, chemical and petrographic analyses and historical context', in M. S. Balmuth and R. H. Tykot (eds.), *Sardinian and Aegean Chronology: Towards the Resolution of Relative and Absolute Dating in the Mediterranean*, Studies in Sardinian Archaeology, V. Oxford: Oxbow Books, 337–40.

Wertime, T. A. and Muhly, J. D. (eds.) (1980). *The Coming of the Age of Iron*. New Haven and London: Yale Univeristy Press, 151–83.

CHAPTER 38

NORTHERN ITALY

FRANCO NICOLIS

INTRODUCTION

The area covered in this paper includes the southern slopes of the central-eastern Alps and the central-eastern plain of the Po Valley, in particular eastern Lombardy (to the east of the River Adda), Trentino-Alto Adige/South Tyrol, Veneto, and Friuli-Venezia-Giulia. Despite the fact that it belongs to continental Italy, Emilia-Romagna is also taken into consideration, because the cultural dynamics in the Bronze Age, especially as regards the *Terramara/Palafitte* (pile-dwelling) cultures, are also applicable to this area (Fig. 38.1).

In this geographical context the most important morphological features are the Alps and the alluvial plain of the River Po. Since Roman times the former have always been considered a geographical limit and thus a cultural barrier. In actual fact the Alps have never really represented a barrier, but instead have played an active role in mediating between the central European and Mediterranean cultures. Some of the valleys have been used since the Mesolithic as communication routes, to establish contacts and for the exchange of materials and people over considerable distances. The discovery of Ötzi the Iceman high in the Alps in 1991 demonstrated incontrovertibly that this environment was accessible to individuals and groups from the end of the fourth millennium BC.

From the Early Neolithic period the plain of the Po Valley provided favourable conditions for the population of the area by human groups from central and eastern Europe, who found the wide flat spaces and fertile soils an ideal environment for developing agricultural techniques and animal husbandry. Lake Garda represents a very important morphological feature, benefiting among other things from a Mediterranean-type microclimate, the influence of which can already be seen in the Middle Neolithic. Situated between the plain and the mountains, the hills have always offered an alternative terrain for demographic development, equally important for the exploitation of economic and environmental resources.

As documented for previous periods, in the late and final phases of the Bronze Age the northern Adriatic coast would also seem to represent an important geographical feature, above all in terms of possible long-distance trading contacts with the Aegean and eastern Mediterranean coasts. However, the geographical and morphological characteristics and the river network in this area were very different to the way they are today, and the

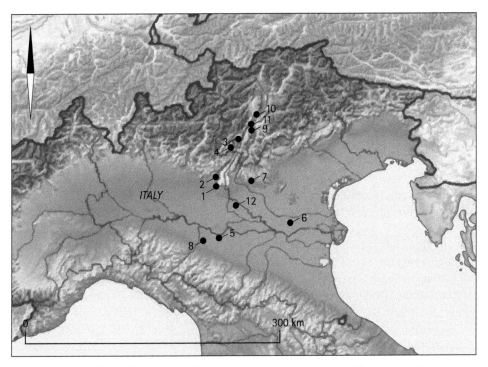

FIG. 38.1 Map of northern Italy showing places mentioned in the text. 1. Lavagnone, 2. Lucone, 3. Fiavè, 4. Ledro, 5. Santa Rosa di Poviglio, 6. Frattesina di Fratta Polesine, 7. Arano di Cellore di Illasi (VR), 8. Noceto (PR), 9. Romagnano, 10. Nogarole di Mezzolombardo, 11. Vela Valbusa, 12. Olmo di Nogara.

Map: Chiara Conci.

preferred communications routes must always have been the rivers, particularly the Po and the Adige.

Chronology

As with other areas, there has been progress in understanding the relative and absolute chronology of the Bronze Age in northern Italy, thanks to dendrochronological studies on lake-dwelling settlements by the small lakes in the morainic hills to the south of and along the banks of Lake Garda. However, there are still various aspects to be clarified, and the problems of interpreting the archaeological data remain, reflected above all in the subdivision of long chronological periods into phases and the attribution of individual complexes or archaeological levels to one phase rather than another (Fasani 2002: 148–9; Bietti Sestieri and Macnamara 2007: 27–30).

The sequence followed here is as follows:

Early Bronze Age (EBA) (*antica età del Bronzo*)
Middle Bronze Age (MBA) (*media età del Bronzo*)
Late Bronze Age (LBA) (*età del Bronzo recente*)

Final Bronze Age (FBA) (*età del Bronzo finale*)

Different phases in the Bronze Age have mostly been recognized and defined in northern Italy on the basis of pottery excavated from the most important stratified complexes. Raffaele de Marinis proposed the division of the EBA into four phases: IA, IB, IC, and II. The Lavagnone 2 phase and layer E of area D at Lucone di Polpenazze (Brescia), for which dendrochronological dates covering the period from 2077 to 1992 BC are available, have been attributed to EBA IA. This phase, to which the oldest Bronze Age hoards would appear to belong, is linked to the Bz A1 phase north of the Alps. During this phase copper was obtained from fahlore (*Fahlerz*). The Lavagnone 3 phase and layer D of area D at Lucone di Polpenazze (Brescia) have been attributed to EBA IB, for which dendro dating is available covering the period from 1985 to 1916 BC. The EBA IC phase has not been correlated to a definite period in Lavagnone but only in relation to the dumping of materials. It is also represented in the oldest cultural complex of the Canar settlement (Rovigo), which has dendro dating from 1869 to 1859 BC. The EBA IB and IC phases are linked to the Bz A2a phase north of the Alps, whereas EBA II, which corresponds with the Lavagnone 4 and Fiavè 3 phases, is linked to Bz A2b. According to Renato Perini, who carried out various excavations at Lavagnone in the 1970s, the Lavagnone 4 horizon corresponds to an initial phase of the MBA (De Marinis 1999; 2000: 93–175; De Marinis et al. 2005; Griggs, Kuniholm, and Newton 2002; Perini 1988).

De Marinis (1999) subdivides the MBA into I, IIA, IIB, and IIC. MBA I characterizes the Lavagnone 5–6 and Fiavè 4–5 phases and is linked to Bz B1 north of the Alps. The three MBA II phases are defined through the stratigraphy of different settlements including Fiavè 6, Muraiola, Castellaro del Vho, and the small *Terramara* village of Santa Rosa di Poviglio (Parma). According to De Marinis (1999) MBA IIA–IIB phases can be related to Bz B2/C1 north of the Alps, whereas MBA IIC can be linked to Bz C2.

Subdivision of the LBA into two phases (I and II) is based on stratigraphic data for the Ca' de' Cessi settlement (Mantua) and the large *Terramara* village at Santa Rosa di Poviglio. The two phases can be linked respectively to Bz D1 and Bz D2/Ha A1 (De Marinis 1999; 2006). As far as the final phases of the MBA and LBA are concerned, there are several differences between the De Marinis scheme and that proposed by Bernabò Brea and Cardarelli (De Marinis 1999: Fig. 50; Bernabò Brea and Cardarelli 1997: 299; De Marinis 2006).

Summarizing and integrating the various proposals for absolute chronology, it is possible to arrive at the following absolute chronology:

EBA 2300/2200–1650 cal BC
MBA 1650–1350/1300 cal BC
LBA 1350/1300–1200 cal BC
FBA 1200–900 cal BC

Cultural Development

In northern Italy the Early Bronze Age coincided with the sudden rise and subsequent development of the Polada culture, as defined by Laviosa Zambotti in 1939, from a lake-dwelling-type settlement near Lonato in the province of Brescia. The formation of this culture must have been affected by a substratum of local tradition, the cultural influence of the international Bell Beaker phenomenon, and perhaps an increase in population. The initial features therefore reflect both aspects of continuity and differences as compared to the previous Copper Age. As far as the differences are concerned, the Polada culture is characterized by strongly homogeneous characteristics, a large initial increase in population and settlement, and a remarkable expansion, leading it to cover large areas of northern Italy and also make its influence felt in neighbouring cultural regions. However, some elements of the material culture, often linked to the Bell Beaker culture but also to earlier aspects such as the Remedello culture, make it possible to glimpse a degree of continuity from the local cultural substratum, which would seem to have had a significant role in the transition between the two periods.

In the later phase the Polada culture was affected more significantly by contacts and relations with the Danubian cultures, already evident in the formative phase. The metallurgical products are more similar to those from the Únětice cultural area, but a real population influx can be suggested, given the evidence of relations with the Gata-Wieselburg group which can be noted at sites in eastern Veneto, in particular at Canar (Rovigo). The general demographic development at the beginning of the Early Bronze Age has indeed been interpreted by some as a genuine transfer of population groups (Fasani 2002: 108).

The centre of expansion for the Polada culture can be found around the southern banks of Lake Garda and the small lakes situated in the neighbouring morainic hills, many of which have been transformed into peat bogs today. The most important sites are Lavagnone, Lucone, Bande di Cavriana, and Barche di Solferino (see Fig. 38.1). However, the area over which the culture extended, sometimes with the presence of just a few cultural elements, is much larger: to the north it stretches up to the Val Venosta/Vinschgau (Bolzano), with some elements also found beyond the Brenner Pass, the two fundamental sites remaining, however, those at Ledro and Fiavè (Trento); to the south the Polada culture reaches the course of the Po; the eastern limits stretch up to the Berici and Euganean hills; whereas to the west it stretches up to Lake Pusiano (Lecco).

The fundamental features characterizing Bronze Age cultures in northern Italy were the two main settlement models: pile-dwellings and *Terramara* villages (*Palafitte* and *Terramare*). Both were the result of significant and rapid demographic development, as the areas concerned were little populated in previous eras (Fasani 2002: 108; Bernabò Brea and Cardarelli 1997: 296), although recent findings in Emilia-Romagna, still unpublished, suggest that the framework of cultural development in the EBA could be very different from that currently envisaged.

In terms of cultural interpretation there is no agreement regarding a definition of the relationship between pile-dwelling and *Terramara* complexes. According to some, they are separate and different (Fasani 1984: 566–7), whereas for others they are complementary and essentially unified; according to De Marinis, the cultural material of the *Terramare* derives from pile-dwellings, and the cultural aspects that define the MBA and LBA on the Po plain could be defined overall as the 'pile-dwelling/*terramara* culture' (De Marinis 1997: 415).

The pile-dwelling settlements in northern Italy were located in damp areas. In the initial phase of the EBA they existed on the southern banks of Lake Garda and the small lakes in the morainic hills, whereas in the later phase the first villages sprang up on the plain to the south of Lake Garda as far as the Po. They expanded to the southern Trentino, eastern Lombardy, and eastern Veneto, although they were significantly less common in these areas.

Excavations at the Fiavè peat bog, the site of Lake Carera in ancient times, made it possible to show that the pile-dwellings may have been built both in the water, on the lake bank, and on dry land. The best information about the evolution of the type of dwellings and the technical solutions adopted in the different phases of development again comes from Fiavè (Perini 1984). For example, the type of dwelling in phases Fiavè 3–5 (EBA II–MBA I), constructed in the water on isolated piles sunk deep into the lake mud and supporting the dwellings, was substituted in the Fiavè 6 phase (MBA II) by a technique based on the creation of a grid structure anchored to the bed of the lake with an efficient system of pairs of parallel beams resting on the lake bed, longitudinal supports and plinths (Fig. 38.2).

On the southern banks of Lake Garda and in the lakes in the surrounding morainic hills there was essentially continuity of settlement for the whole of the Bronze Age, despite a tendency for the areas inhabited to shift by a few dozen or a few hundred metres, towards shallower areas. On the eastern banks of Lake Garda the settlements were inhabited continuously up to the LBA. This period saw the maximum development of the pile-dwelling village at Peschiera, with genuine centres of production and commerce in bronze objects (several thousand have been found), also giving a name to a chronological period (the Peschiera phase) in which the standardization of types of objects and the circulation of metal products took on continental dimensions, the so-called metallurgical *koinè*.

During the central phase of the MBA the *Terramara* phenomenon took root, with the establishment of large settlements with banks and fortifications, widespread from the central part of the Po plain down to the Apennines. After a brief formative or pioneering phase between the seventeenth and sixteenth centuries BC, population and settlement development was so rapid that a form of genuine 'colonization' of the areas has been surmised (Bernabò Brea 2009: 11). This was probably supported by new techniques in arable and

FIG. 38.2 Structures of phase 6 of the pile dwelling settlement of Fiavè (Trentino).

Photo: Autonomous Province of Trento.

livestock agriculture, such as the use of the plough pulled by animals, crop rotation, and stabling.

By the middle of the sixteenth century BC the number of settlements had already increased considerably. These were still small (1–2 hectares), built on dry land, housing one to two hundred people. Some of the settlements had simple fences made of wooden posts, while others had a ditch and rampart. In this phase there are already traces of social organization, with the creation of elite areas within the individual settlements, but no hierarchical distinctions have been found between the various settlements. It is likely that there were 'confederations' of villages (Bernabò Brea 2009: 11). One of the sites providing the most information about this phase is the small village at Santa Rosa di Poviglio (Reggio Emilia) (Bernabò Brea and Cremaschi 2004). It is only later, between the fourteenth and thirteenth centuries BC and thus in the LBA, that one can see differentiation between settlements, within the context of population increase, and settlement and economic development. Some villages were abandoned and others extended, while others were constructed anew. Their size increased, until in some cases they reached 20 hectares and could house up to a thousand people. The layout of the villages saw the use of an essentially urban system, with regular rectangular spaces for roads, large houses, fencing, etcetera. The dwellings were structured like 'pile-dwellings on dry land' (Bernabò Brea 2009: 11). The fortifications became imposing: the large village at Santa Rosa di Poviglio was protected by a wooden fence structure which had gates aligned with the roads, but other villages had enormous earthwork ramparts (up to 20 m wide) and wide ditches.

The stability of the *Terramara* system, based on developed mechanisms for management of space, bartering, production, and social relations, deteriorated after 1200 BC and in a short time led to collapse of the system and the end of the *Terramare*. There has been much discussion about the causes of the collapse of the *Terramara* culture (De Marinis 2006: 452–4). Environmental decline or climatic changes are among the reasons suggested for this phenomenon. The latest theory suggests that the political instability of the whole Mediterranean in the twelfth century BC may have also had repercussions in northern Italy (Bernabò Brea 2009: 13).

The crisis of the pile-dwelling/*Terramara* system would not seem to have affected some areas, as for example the large valleys around Verona and the Po delta, where villages were relocated and economic strategies reorganized. Some of these large settlements were situated along the courses of the main rivers, and managed complex production systems and wide-ranging trading networks, demonstrated above all by the presence of Mycenaean pottery. The most important of these sites is Frattesina di Fratta Polesine (Rovigo). Founded in the LBA, the village of Frattesina extended over around 20 hectares along the 'Po di Adria', a palaeochannel of the Po (see Chapter 35). It experienced its greatest development between the twelfth and eleventh centuries BC, when it had a dominant economic role thanks to an extraordinary range of artisan production (metalworking, working of bone and deer horn, glass) and major commercial influence due to trading with the Italian Peninsula and the eastern Mediterranean. This is demonstrated by the presence of exotic objects and raw materials, such as Mycenaean pottery, amber, ivory, ostrich eggs, and glass paste.

For the Mycenaean sherds found in settlements in the Verona valleys and the Po delta, analysis of pottery fabrics has shown that some of them very probably come from centres in

Apulia where there were Aegean craftsmen and workers, whereas others would seem to have originated on the Greek mainland (Vagnetti 1996; Vagnetti 1998; Jones et al. 2002).

In this context a particular system of relations seems to link one specific Alpine region with the social and economic structure of the groups settling between the Adige and the Po and the eastern Mediterranean trading system. In eastern Trentino, at Acquafredda, metallurgical production on a proto-industrial scale has been demonstrated between the end of the LBA and the FBA (twelfth–eleventh centuries BC) (Cierny 2008) (Fig. 38.3). These products must have supplied markets stretching beyond the local area, linked to the Luco/Laugen culture typical of the central Alpine environment. According to Pearce and De Guio (1999), such extensive production must have been destined for the supply of metal to other markets, first of all to other centres on the Po plain, where transactions for materials of Mediterranean origin also took place.

The lake-dwelling/*Terramara* system represented the most widespread settlement model across northern Italy, but in some areas we find other models and cultural aspects with distinctive characteristics. In Trentino-Alto Adige, for example, one can find settlements on detrital cones such as the site at Mezzolombardo-La Rupe, attributable to the EBA (Bassetti, Degasperi, and Nicolis 2002), others on rocky spurs, as in the case of the fortified site of Sotciastel in Val Badia (BZ) (Tecchiati 1998). This site is situated at an altitude of around 1,400 m on artificial terraces. This is also true for Doss Gustinaci, attributable to the LBA, which was constructed in connection with the abandonment of the last settlement on the ancient lake of Carera di Fiavè (Fiavè 7) (Perini 1984: 164–93).

FIG. 38.3 The series of the Late Bronze Age smelting furnaces of Acquafredda site, Passo del Redebus (Trentino).

Photo: Soprintendenza per i beni librari archivistici e archeologici, Autonomous Province of Trento and Elena Munerati.

In the most easterly area of northern Italy (Friuli and Carso) the so-called *castellieri* settlements on hills, fortified with imposing defensive works, represent a settlement model that can be compared with Istria (see Chapter 46). These began to be established in the MBA and show partial continuity up to the final phases of the Bronze Age.

Funerary Rites

In contrast to the major developments in terms of population, settlement, culture, economy, and production in the EBA, archaeological evidence regarding funerary rites is paradoxically very scarce. Furthermore, this evidence is not evenly distributed over the area examined (De Marinis 2003; Nicolis 2004).

Most of the burial sites certainly belonging to the Early Bronze Age are concentrated in the foothills of the Alps and the Alpine area, both on the slopes and the valley floor, at altitudes between around 200 and 800 m above sea level. Known burial sites on the plain are less numerous, although the number has increased considerably in the last few years. The rites usually involve primary burial, although there is likely evidence of the use of secondary burial, possibly with partial removal of the flesh by means of fire. Various types of funerary site can be attributed to the Early Bronze Age. Simple graves have mainly been documented at sites on the plain. These burials are normally grouped together in small cemeteries. Those at Valserà in Gazzo Veronese (Verona) and Sorbara di Asola (Mantua), which are in some ways similar, have made it possible significantly to extend the picture for this type of burial. The recent finding of the Arano cemetery, at Cellore di Illasi (Verona), is of considerable interest. Sixty-two tombs were found, most of them single, but there are also examples of double and triple burials. The tombs are surrounded and covered by stones. The bodies were placed in a flexed position on one side, oriented in a north-south direction or vice versa. Grave goods were only found in 14 tombs and were mostly made up of ornaments. At Arano there are some indications that the tombs were plundered in ancient times (L. Salzani and P. Salzani 2009).

Trentino is a special case in funerary terms in northern Italy, firstly because of the large number of burials of this period, and secondly because the funerary rites are unique to the province. The sites are distributed above the whole Adige Valley, mostly situated in small caves or rock shelters or at the base of rock faces where crevices and recesses are sometimes used for burial. The most representative site is Romagnano Loc (sectors III and IV). Here the tombs mostly back onto the rock face and contain individual burials. The body of the deceased was generally placed tightly flexed on the right side, but there are some cases where it was extended. The tomb is usually marked by a perimeter ring of stones and covered with a small mound. One particular form of funeral rite, documented only in Trentino-Alto Adige to date, is reserved for immature children (foetuses or newborn babies), placed inside jars and protected by small mounds of stones. The secondary burial of the skull of a four or five year-old boy in a pot is probably linked to skull worship. Mezzocorona Borgonuovo, Mezzolombardo Nogarole, and Volano San Rocco provide further information on burial rites in Trentino during the EBA (Nicolis 2001).

Vela Valbusa is another burial site attributable to the EBA, situated just to the north of Trento. Here, inside an oval-shaped mound made up of large stones, a single female who had just reached adulthood was buried. The grave goods included numerous *Dentalium* shell beads, beads of bone and lignite, bone pendants, perforated animal teeth, and other elements that must have made up a decorative breastplate. This represents a very extensive range of ornaments compared with other EBA burials, so it is likely that they reflect the social status of the individual within the group (Nicolis 2001).

There is a clear distinction between the funerary rites at pile-dwelling/*Terramara* sites in the MBA and LBA in Emilia and eastern Lombardy, where cremation was used exclusively, and those in Veneto, where there was a progressive adoption of inhumation and the coexistence of the two rites within the same cemetery (Cardarelli and Tirabassi 1997; De Marinis and Salzani 1997; Salzani 2005).

For the *Terramara* culture the evidence for burial rites falls in a late phase of the MBA and LBA, whereas there is none for the preceding period. The remains of the dead were placed in urns, generally covered with a bowl and placed in small shallow pits, without burnt earth. Sometimes the remains of more than one individual were placed in the urn, usually one adult and one young child. The presence of grave goods is relatively rare and limited to a few ornaments or clothing attachments (pins, fibulae, etcetera).

One area that has provided important evidence for burial rites in the MBA and LBA is the Verona plain between the Adige and the Mincio. Seven large cemeteries have been excavated more or less fully: Povegliano, Bovolone, Olmo di Nogara, La Vallona di Ostiglia, Castello del Tartaro, Franzine Nuove, and Scalvinetto. Some of them must have belonged to settlements known from surface finds or excavation: Scalvinetto is linked to the settlement of Fondo Paviani, Franzine Nuove to Fabbrica dei Soci, and Povegliano to the settlement at Muraiola. A total of two thousand tombs is known. The cemeteries witnessed the use of both types of ritual, with the proportion of inhumations and cremations being quite variable. As in *Terramara* burial sites, the remains of cremated bodies, without grave goods, were placed in urns, usually covered with a bowl and placed in pits without burnt earth. In the case of inhumations, the bodies were placed in flat graves, usually in a supine position.

The Olmo di Nogara cemetery is the oldest and the one that has supplied the fullest information. It must have covered an area of around 14,000 sq m. With its 456 inhumation tombs and 61 cremation tombs it not only represents a significant demographic sample for analysis, representing an important segment of the population in the MBA and LBA on the Verona plain, but through the burial rite it also allows analysis of the social structure. In no fewer than 43 burial tombs a sword was found as one of the funerary objects (Fig. 38.4), often associated with a dagger (11 out of 16 cases). This demonstrates that the 'sword carrier' was a figure of considerable social significance for the groups making use of the Nogara cemetery. It also suggests that the presence of a sword in some burials was designed to illustrate, through a mechanism linked to the collective representation of death, the fact that the deceased belonged to an elite social group associated with warriors, within which the transmission of rank and power must have been hereditary. The female counterparts in this elite group would seem to be represented in the cemetery by tombs with grave goods including ornaments and exotic materials such as amber. The fact that most of the swords found in Nogara are pointed piercing swords suitable for close combat should be stressed, but some are slashing swords, probably also used for combat from chariots or horseback. Anthropological analysis has highlighted cut marks produced by blows made with pointed metal weapons on some males, clear evidence of social dynamics that provided for violence and armed conflict. Indicators of physical stress found on bones from some of the 'sword carriers' are compatible with bareback horse riding and therefore suggest the likely use of horses as mounts in this area (Salzani 2005).

In the rest of northern Italy few aspects appear to offer marked contrasts to the funerary rites in the MBA and LBA in *Terramare* and the Po Valley. We may mention the burial site at Stenico (Trento), attributable to Fiavè phase 6 (late MBA). This is a long mound, only partly dug out, covering six separate tombs delimited by stones. The encasing of a child between the age of seven and nine in a large pot in the Santa Croce cave (Trieste) is an isolated example, probably datable to the MBA or LBA (Nicolis 2004).

Certain villages developed in the Po delta area after the *Terramara* period. Of these the most important is Frattesina, covering more than 20 hectares (Bellintani 2000). Between the twelfth and ninth centuries BC the population of Frattesina made use of at least two burial areas, one situated around 500 m to the south-east of the settlement, the second around 700 m to the north. At the first, Fondo Zanotto, 150 tombs have been found, mostly cremation burials with a cinerary urn covered by a bowl and placed in a small pit with some of the burnt earth at the bottom (De Min 1986). The grave goods, placed inside the urn, consist of ornaments and many are damaged by fire. At the second cemetery, Narde, six hundred tombs have been found, mostly cremation burials, distributed over five superimposed levels forming an artificial mound around 30 m long by 1 m high (Salzani 1989; Salzani 1990–1). The structure of the funerary site is very similar to that used at Fondo Zanotto. Only two tombs offered exceptional elements, with the finding of grave goods including a sword. Recently 240 tombs, of which around 20 involved burial and the others cremation, were found in an area situated around 150 m to the south-east of Narde and known as Narde II (Salzani and Colonna 2010). An area used for the cremation of the dead has also been identified in this part of the site.

FIG. 38.4 Details of the swords found in Tomb 31, Tomb 24, and Tomb 410 of the Middle Bronze Age cemetery of Olmo di Nogara (Verona).

Source: Salzani 2005.

Ritual, Cult, and Religion

It is usually difficult to identify archaeological finds that may certainly be ascribed to the world of cults. In the context of the Bronze Age in northern Italy certain elements, often found in settlements, such as miniature terracotta objects, both small pots and anthropomorphic or animal figures, are usually linked to rituals, cults, and religious aspects.

In northern Italy the most widespread phenomenon assumed to be of ritual significance is the placing of weapons in water courses or in particular places such as mountain passes or peaks. The placing of swords in both the Sile and the Adige is well documented (Dal Ri and Tecchiati 2002). A recent find (2004), arguably of ritual import and belonging to the *Terramara* culture, is the wooden tank at Noceto (Parma) (Bernabò Brea and Cremaschi 2009). This was a large and complex construction filled with water, into which a large number of objects of various kinds were placed (pottery, miniature figures, wooden objects including some vessels and four ploughs, remains of wicker baskets, animal bones, etcetera). The complexity of the tank's construction (Fig. 38.5), which can be attributed to the late phase of the MBA, between 1420 and 1320 BC, involved the use of specific and significant skills, in terms of planning, engineering, geotechnology, carpentry, and the planning and organization of the work. The result was the creation of a 'singular archaeological monument' (Bernabò Brea and Cremaschi 2009: 242) that has no comparison elsewhere. The interpretation given to it by the excavators (although the excavations are as yet unfinished) is that it was related to rites within which water played a fundamental role. However,

FIG. 38.5 The Middle Bronze Age wooden tank of Noceto (Parma) during excavation.
Photo: Ministero per i Beni a le Attivitá Culturali – Soprintendenza per i Beni Archeologici dell'Emilia Romagna, by kind permission.

despite the complexity of the construction, which also suggests the existence of a complex social structure, the tank would seem to have been used for a relatively short period of time, just a few generations. This may be because it was not designed for activities linked to institutionalized rites but was rather related to a single historic event (Bernabò Brea and Cremaschi 2009: 244).

Conclusion

Overall in northern Italy the final phase of the Bronze Age shows a pattern characterized both by cultural elements that are different from other regions and by cultural traits that are common and shared with the Italian Peninsula. There is an absence of further demographic growth in comparison with the preceding periods, while there is also development of the production and circulation of the products of metallurgy, and increasing connections between the different regions, in particular along the Adriatic corridor that plays a fundamental role in connecting cultures.

Culturally speaking, the Protogolasecca culture predominates in the western regions while the so-called *Protovillanoviano padano* (the Protovillanovan of the Po plain), within which the Frattesina site plays a major role, predominates in the eastern regions, and shows several affinities with the Chiusi-Cetona group in Tuscany, Umbria, Marche, and Romagna.

The picture of the Final Bronze Age of these regions, which seems to be coherent with the development of the cultural setting of the Early Iron Age, shows that the birth of the proto-urban Villanovan centres of Bologna in Emilia and Verucchio in Romagna, at the beginning of the Iron Age, seems to follow a line of continuity starting with the role played by Frattesina in the Final Bronze Age (Bietti Sestieri 2008).

Bibliography

Bassetti, M., Degasperi, N., and Nicolis, F. (2002). 'Nuovi dati sulle modalità insediative in Trentino tra Età del Bronzo e Età del Ferro: il sito di Mezzolombardo–La Rupe', in *Atti della XXXIII Riunione Scientifica. Preistoria e Protostoria del Trentino Alto Adige/Südtirol*. Florence: Istituto Italiano di Preistoria e Protostoria, 131–40.

Bellintani, P. (2000). 'Il Medio Polesine tra la tarda Età del Bronzo e l'inizio dell'Età del Ferro', in M. Harari and M. Pearce (eds.), *Il Protovillanoviano al di qua e al di là dell'Appennino*. Como: New Press, 47–84.

Bernabò Brea, M. (2009). 'Le terramare nell'Età del Bronzo', in M. Bernabò Brea and M. Cremaschi (eds.), *Acqua e civiltà nelle terramare. La vasca votiva di Noceto*. Milan: Skira, 5–16.

—— and Cardarelli, A. (1997). 'Le terramare nel tempo', in M. Bernabò Brea, A. Cardarelli, and M. Cremaschi (eds.), *Le Terramare, la più antica civiltà padana*. Milan: Electa, 295–301.

—— and Cremaschi, M. (eds.) (2004). *Il villaggio piccolo della terramara di Santa Rosa di Poviglio. Scavi 1987–1992*. Florence: Istituto Italiano di Preistoria e Protostoria.

—— and Cremaschi, M. (eds.) (2009). *Acqua e civiltà nelle terramare. La vasca votiva di Noceto*. Milan: Skira.

Bietti Sestieri, A. M. (2008). 'L'Età del Bronzo finale nella penisola italiana', *Padusa*, XLIV: 7–54.

—— and Macnamara, E. (2007). *Prehistoric Metal Artefacts from Italy (3500-720 BC) in the British Museum*. London: The British Museum.
Cardarelli, A. and Tirabassi, J. (1997). 'Le necropoli delle terramare emiliane', in M. Bernabò Brea, A. Cardarelli, and M. Cremaschi (eds.), *Le Terramare, la più antica civiltà padana*. Milan: Electa, 677-82.
Cierny, J. (2008). *Prähistorische Kupferproduktion in den südlichen Alpen, Region Trentino Orientale*. Bochum: Deutsches Bergbau-Museum.
Dal Ri, L. and Tecchiati, U. (2002). 'I *Gewässerfunde* nella preistoria e protostoria dell'area alpina centromeridionale', in L. Zemmer-Planck (ed.), *Culti nella preistoria delle Alpi. Le offerte, i santuari, i riti. Parte I*. Bolzano: Athesia, 457-91.
De Marinis, R. C. (1997). 'L'Età del bronzo nella regione benacense e nella pianura padana a nord del Po', in M. Bernabò Brea, A. Cardarelli, and M. Cremaschi (eds.) (1997), *Le Terramare, la più antica civiltà padana*. Milan: Electa, 405-19.
—— (1999). 'Towards a relative and absolute chronology of the Bronze Age in Northern Italy', *Notizie Archeologiche Bergomensi*, 7: 23-100.
—— (2000). *Il Museo Civico Archeologico Giovanni Rambotti. Una introduzione alla preistoria del lago di Garda*. Desenzano del Garda: Comune di Desenzano del Garda.
—— (2003). 'Riti funerari e problemi di paleo-demografia dell'antica Erà del Bronzo nell'Italia settentrionale', *Notizie Archeologiche Bergomensi*, 11: 5-78.
—— (2006). 'Aspetti e problemi del Bronzo Recente nella regione benacense', in *Studi di Protostoria in Onore di Renato Peroni*. Florence: All'insegna del Giglio, 445-56.
—— and Salzani, L. (1997). 'Le necropoli del Bronzo Medio e Recente nella Lombardia orientale e nel Veneto occidentale', in M. Bernabò Brea, A. Cardarelli, and M. Cremaschi (eds.), *Le Terramare, la più antica civiltà padana*. Milan: Electa, 703-7.
——, Rapi, M., Ravazzi, C., Arpenti, E., Deaddis, M., and Perego, R. (2005). 'Lavagnone (Desenzano del Garda): new excavations and palaeoecology of a Bronze Age pile-dwelling site in northern Italy', in Ph. Della Casa and M. Trachsel (eds.), *WES'04: Wetland Economies and Societies*, Proceedings of the International Conference in Zürich, 10-13 March 2004. Zürich: Chronos, 221-32.
De Min, M. (1986). 'Frattesina di Fratta Polesine. La necropoli protostorica', in M. de Min and R. Peretto (eds.), *L'antico Polesine*. Padua: Museo Nazionale Archeologico di Adria, Museo Civico delle Civiltà in Polesine, 143-69.
Fasani, L. (1984). 'L'Età del Bronzo', in A. Aspes (ed.), *Il Veneto nell'antichità*, vol.2 Verona: Banca Popolare di Verona, 449-614.
—— (2002). 'Età del Bronzo', in A. Aspes (ed.), *Preistoria veronese. Contributi e aggiornamenti*. Verona: Museo Civico di Storia Naturale, 107-53.
Griggs, C. B., Kuniholm, P. I., and Newton, M. W. (2002). 'Lavagnone di Brescia in the Early Bronze Age: dendrochronological report', *Notizie Archeologiche Bergomensi*, 10: 19-33.
Jones, R. E., Vagnetti, L., Levi, S. T., Williams, J., Jenkins, D., and De Guio, A. (2002). 'Mycenaean pottery from northern Italy. Archaeological and archaeometric studies', *Studi Micenei ed Egeo-Anatolici*, 44/2: 221-61.
Nicolis, F. (2001). 'Il culto dei morti nell'antica e media Età del Bronzo', in M. Lanzinger, F. Marzatico, and A. Pedrotti (eds.), *Storia del Trentino. Volume I. La preistoria e la protostoria*. Bologna: Il Mulino: 337-65.
—— (2004). 'Le evidenze funerarie dell'antica Età del Bronzo in Italia settentrionale', in M. Besse and J. Desideri (eds.), *Graves and Funerary Rituals during the Late Neolithic and the Early Bronze Age in Europe (2700-2000 BC)*. Oxford: Archaeopress, 111-45.

Pearce, M. and De Guio, A. (1999). 'Between the mountains and the plain: an integrated metals production and circulation system in later Bronze Age north-eastern Italy', in Ph. Della Casa (ed.), *Prehistoric Alpine Environment, Society and Economy*, Papers of the International Colloquium PAESE '97 in Zürich. Bonn: Habelt, 289–93.

Perini, R. (1984). *Scavi archeologici nella zona palafitticola di Fiavé—Carera. Parte I. Campagne 1969-1976. Situazione dei depositi e dei resti strutturali*. Trento: Servizio Beni Culturali della Provincia Autonoma di Trento.

—— (1988). 'Gli scavi nel Lavagnone. Sequenza e tipologia degli abitati dell'Età del Bronzo', *Annali Benacensi*, 9: 109–54.

Salzani, L. (1989). 'Necropoli dell'Età del Bronzo Finale alle Narde di Fratta Polesine – Prima nota', *Padusa*, XXV: 5–42.

—— (1990–1). 'Necropoli dell'Età del Bronzo Finale alle Narde di Fratta Polesine – Seconda nota', *Padusa*, XXVI–XXVII: 125–206.

—— (ed.) (2005). *La necropoli dell'Età del Bronzo all'Olmo di Nogara*. Verona: Museo Civico di Storia Naturale.

—— and Colonna, C. (eds.) (2010). *La fragilità dell'urna. I recenti scavi a Narde Necropoli di Frattesina (XII–IX sec. a.c.)*. Rovigo: Museo dei Grandi Fiumi.

—— and Salzani, P. (2009). *Storie sepolte. Riti e culti all'alba del duemila avanti Cristo*. Verona: Museo Civico di Storia Naturale.

Tecchiati, U. (ed.) (1998). *Sotciastel. Un abitato fortificato dell'Età del Bronzo in Val Badia*. Bolzano: Soprintendenza Provinciale ai Beni Culturali di Bolzano.

Vagnetti, L. (1996). 'Ceramiche di tipo egeo dal Basso Veronese', in G. Belluzzo and L. Salzani (eds.), *Dalla terra al Museo*. Legnago: Fondazione Fioroni, 179–84.

—— (1998). 'Un frammento ceramico di tipo egeo da Montagnana-Borgo San Zeno', in E. Bianchin Citton, G. Gambacurta, and A. Ruta Serafini (eds.), *'presso l'Adige ridente'... Recenti ritrovamenti archeologici da Este a Montagnana*. Padua: ADLE, 329–30.

CHAPTER 39

SWITZERLAND AND THE CENTRAL ALPS

PHILIPPE DELLA CASA

ENVIRONMENT, CLIMATE, SETTLEMENT

The area discussed in this chapter covers a broad variety of regions, ecozones, and ecotopes. It ranges from the Prealpine lowlands around the major lakes and rivers of the Swiss Plateau, between Lake Constance to the north-east and Lake Geneva to the south-west, to the wide Alpine valley corridors of the rivers Rhine, Rhône (Valais), Ticino, and Inn (Engadine), and the mountain massifs of the Jura to the north and the Prealps and Central Alps to the south (Fig. 39.1). Absolute altitude ranges between 200 m above sea level in the Rhine Valley near Basel and more than 4,000 m for the highest peaks, while in terms of human activity the uppermost known sites are at around 2,300–2,500 m in the Alps (Hess et al. 2010; Reitmaier 2010).

The climatic zones roughly correspond to the geographic regions as detailed above, with a moderate continental climate for most of the Swiss Plateau, a more humid climate in the Prealps and the Jura, and a harsh sub-arctic climate in the Inner Alps, with the exception of the climatically favourable dry valleys such as the Valais and Engadine (*Atlas der Schweiz* 2008).

From this first overview a number of geographical zones emerge as predestined for settlement activity, in particular around the lakes and along the rivers of the Plateau, and in the broad valley bottoms of the major Alpine rivers such as the Rhine Valley between the Bodensee (Lake Constance) and Chur in the east-central Alps, the Rhône Valley between Lake Geneva and Sion in the Valais, and the lower parts of the Ticino Valley as well as the Insubrian lake shores south of the main Alpine ridges.

The Bronze Age starts off in a phase of optimum climatic conditions at the turn of the second to third millennium BC, when climatic and vegetational parameters—for example, the upper tree limit in the Alps—are believed to be equal to or even slightly better than nowadays. However, two mid-term events of climatic deterioration occur in the middle of the second and early first millennium BC—they have been named *Löbben* and *Göschenen 1* according to earlier observations, and are recorded through a number of climatic proxies such as pollen profiles, dendroclimatology, glacier advances, and sedimentological processes throughout the Alpine and Circumalpine zone (Burga and Perret 1998). These events had considerable effects on the

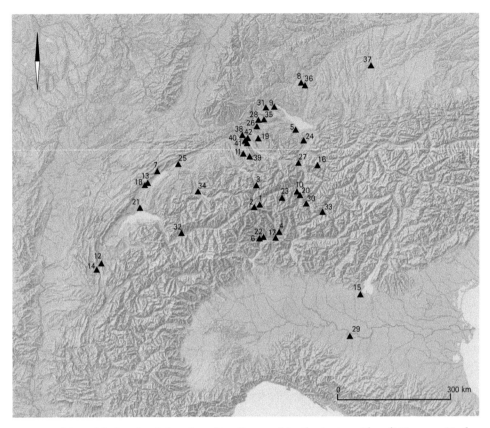

FIG. 39.1 Map of Switzerland showing sites discussed in the text. 1. Alpe di Tom, 2. Airolo-Madrano, 3. Amsteg-Flüeli, 4. Arbedo-Castione, 5. Arbon-Bleiche, 6. Ascona-San Materno, 7. Auvernier-Nord, 8. Bad Buchau-Forschner, 9. Bodman-Schachen, 10. Cazis-Cresta, 11. Cham-Oberwil, 12. Chindrieux-Châtillon, 13. Concise-Sous Colachoz, 14. Conjux-Pré Nuaz, 15. Desenzano del Garda-Lavagnone, 16. Friaga Wald-Bartholomäberg, 17. Giubiasco, 18. Grandson-Corcellettes, 19. Greifensee-Böschen, 20. Höhenrätien, 21. Lausanne-Vidy, 22. Locarno-San Jorio, 23. Lumbrein-Surin, 24. Montlingerberg, 25. Mörigen, 26. Neftenbach, 27. Ochsenberg-Wartau, 28. Ossingen-Im Speck, 29. Poviglio-Santa Rosa, 30. Savognin-Padnal, 31. Singen, 32. Sion-Petit Chasseur, 33. St. Moritz, 34. Thun-Renzenbühl, 35. Uerschhausen-Horn, 36. Wasserburg-Bad Buchau, 37. Wehringen-Hexenbergle, 38. Weiningen-Hardwald, 39. Zug-Sumpf, 40. Zürich-Alpenquai, 41. Zürich-Haumesser, 42. Zürich-Mozartstrasse.

Map: J. Bucher, Universität Zürich.

settlement and economic structure of both lowland and upland regions: around 1520 cal BC an abrupt shift towards cooler and wetter climatic conditions led to a rapid raise of the lake levels north of the Alps and a subsequent abandonment of the lakeshore and wetland settlements, the so-called 'pile dwellings' (Menotti 2001). In the Alps, at least in certain areas of the Inner Alps, the effects seem to have been the opposite: the Middle Bronze Age appears there as a major phase of settlement expansion and intensification, probably due to specific environmental and societal settings (Della Casa 2000: 172–7) (Fig. 39.2).

It is also believed that a climatic event, probably a major period of drought, triggered the collapse of the *Terramare* settlement system of the Po plain around 1150 BC (Bernabò Brea,

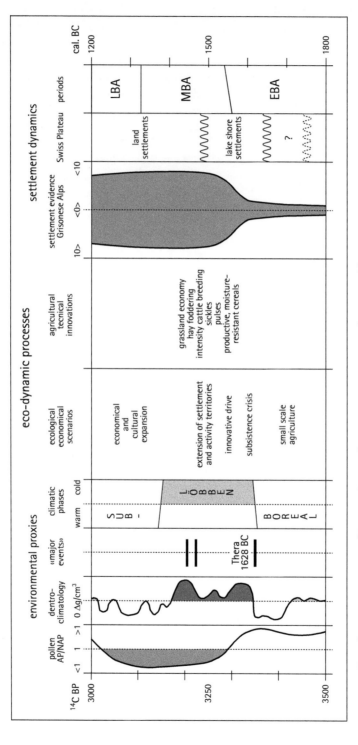

FIG. 39.2 Eco-dynamic scenario of Bronze Age settlement expansion into the Inner Alps.

Source: author.

Cardarelli, and Cremaschi 1997: 745–50). At the end of the Bronze Age, shortly before 800 BC, yet another climate crisis, with lake-level transgressions, led to the final abandonment of the wetland settlements, while in the Alps this event is marked by a noticeable absence of archaeological data, also due to environmental and behavioural changes within the ecological system.

To what extent cultural evolution can be understood as dependent on climatic events is a controversial matter, and it is not my aim here to advocate simplistic socio-environmental correlations. However, the Alpine and Circumalpine regions do offer—due to their specific ecological and cultural history, and the abundance of relevant (proxy) data—a particularly suitable setting for research into behavioural ecology, even more so as with the investigation of the so-called Little Ice Age (c. AD 1560–1860) a historical analogy can be provided. From this analogy, we can see that it is wetter and/or cooler weather conditions during the growing season that would have the strongest impact on subsistence economy, a scenario that is readily conceivable for certain parts of the Bronze Age as well.

CHRONOLOGY AND CHOROLOGY

As with the regions further to the north, a chronological subdivision into early, middle, and late is usually applied to the Bronze Age in the geographical areas covered by this chapter, and most commonly the terminology is that of the Reinecke system, with the phases Bz A1/A2 (Early Bronze Age), Bz B/C1/C2 (Middle Bronze Age), Bz D1/D2 and Ha A1/A2/B1/B2/B3 (Late Bronze Age). The phases Hallstatt (Ha) A1–B3 are often referred to as the Urnfield period, following German terminology. Alternative phasings have been proposed for the north Alpine Bronze Age, but are not commonly used. To the west the French terminology of *Bronze ancien* (BA I–II), *moyen* (BM I–III), and *final* (BF I–III) is sometimes used, whereas south of the Alps the Italian system with *Bronzo antico* (BA), *medio* (BM), *recente* (BR), and *finale* (BF: Protogolasecca I–III = Ha A1–B2) appears in parallel to the Reinecke system. The correlations of the various chronological phasings are well established, even if detailed discussions persist with respect to west, north, and south.

Various groups sharing common cultural traits have been defined for the areas under consideration, some of regional importance, others with clearly supra-regional relationships. In the Early Bronze Age (EBA) archaeological sources are not very prolific in the area studied here, and many regions totally lack settlement evidence. Two groups play major roles in the discussion of cultural entities: to the north-east the *Bodenseegruppe* (also called *Singen* and *Arbon group*; Schmidheiny 2011) concentrates in the zone between the Bodensee (Lake Constance) and Lake Zürich. It belongs to the EBA of southern Germany along with the Straubing, Neckar, and Oberrhein subgroups, and in the early phase—represented by the Singen cemetery near Konstanz (Krause 1988)—still bears many elements of the preceding Late Copper Age in its material culture, along with typical markers of the *Blechstil* (phase of sheet-metal ornament production) such as racket-head pins with incised decoration and pins of Horkheim type. Wide-ranging connections are indicated by tin-plated triangular daggers of Armorican type present in the assemblages of some of the richest graves in Singen. The later phases are illustrated by the abundant material from lakeshore dwellings such as Arbon-Bleiche 2 and Bodman-Schachen IC on Lake Constance, the characteristic material traits being richly decorated pottery, bronze daggers, various pins, and flanged axes of Langquaid type (Hochuli, Niffeler, and Rychner 1998: 32–42).

To the south-west the *Rhône group* is well attested in graves of the Bernese Oberland, Valais, and Lake Geneva region (Hafner 1995; Hochuli, Niffeler, and Rychner 1998: 20–31). Again, there is much that recalls Late Copper Age material in the earlier assemblages, for example in Sion-Petit Chasseur I, along with first metal items such as decorated racket-head pins. In Bz A2 pins with disc, wing, or massive globular heads, flanged axes of various types, and solid-hilted triangular daggers are counterparts to the material culture further east. The extent of supra-regional connections becomes most evident in the context of the Thun-Renzenbühl grave, with a rich inventory that places it in the small series of EBA *Überausstattungen* ('over-endowed [graves]') (Hansen 2002), known across and beyond the continent, from Únětice in the Czech Republic to Wessex in England. The grave goods— among other things two lozenge-head pins, a dagger, a long flanged axe with gold inlay, and several neck-rings of the *Ösenhalsring* type—speak in favour of long-distance relations, to the ore-producing zones of the north-eastern Alps, and beyond that to the spheres of Mycenaean influence, to be seen in the gold-inlay technique on the axe.

Material culture similar to the Rhône group is also known from the Swiss and French Jura (the *Saône group*) while—with the exception of the Arbedo-Castione hoard of pins and ornaments with Transalpine connotations (Hochuli, Niffeler, and Rychner 1998: 46–7)— there are very few EBA finds from the southern Swiss Alps (though the wetland settlements of the north Italian lakes with abundant material of the *Ledro group* are not far away: see Chapter 38). We can thus speak of mainly two areas of influence touching Switzerland in the EBA: one of north-eastern orientation (Germany, the Danube, as far as Únětice), and one of south-western orientation (the Rhône Valley).

At a later stage in the EBA specific Alpine forms emerge in the material culture in particular of the Valais and Grisons, the most characteristic being wing-head pins (*Flügelnadeln*), a variant of the disc-head pins, known for example from the necropolis of Lumbrein-Surin, and pottery with plastic cordon applications as in the early strata of Savognin-Padnal. An increase of such specific elements in the Middle Bronze Age (MBA) has led some scholars (e.g. Rageth 1986) to advocate an *Inner Alpine group* (*Inneralpine Bronzezeitkultur*) centred on the east-central Alps, mostly the Grisons and surrounding areas. The criteria for the definition of such a group are, however, still a matter of debate. There is a noticeable influence from the south where the rich *Terramare complex* of the Po plain existed for most of the MBA and early Late Bronze Age (LBA).

The north Alpine forelands show a MBA material culture much related to the *Hügelgräberbronzezeit* (Tumulus Bronze Age) of central and southern Germany, which is particularly visible in grave assemblages with metal items, such as pins with perforated shaft and spiral sheet ornaments, for example in the barrows of Weiningen-Hardwald (Hochuli, Niffeler, and Rychner 1998: 57–60). Though further to the west the influence of the Rhône group persists, the cultural traits are quite alike those across the Swiss Plateau. This trend persists into the LBA, with a noticeable increase of bronze objects in hoards and graves from Bz D onwards (C. Fischer 1997: 122), many of them international types such as the poppy-head pins (*Mohnkopfnadeln*), also to be found in northern Italy and the Ticino, where grave contexts begin to be known from this phase (Locarno-San Jorio, Giubiasco). The strongest affinities of the south Alpine valleys at the beginning of the LBA, however, are with the *Canegrate group* of the Po plain, and the subsequent *Protogolasecca* facies (Hochuli, Niffeler, and Rychner 1998: 98–102). The typical carinated, grooved, and smoothed black ware and the first bow fibulae are to be found, for example in the cemetery of Ascona-San Materno. There is a lack of evidence for the later LBA in this area, but the Pont-Valperga group defined by Francesco Rubat Borel (2006) for north-western Piedmont certainly shows strong Transalpine connections.

While the Inner Alps remain exposed to various cultural influences from the south, north, and east (for example, typical decorated pottery of the *Laugen-Melaun group* of the Inn and Adige valleys), the Swiss Plateau and Jura are commonly seen as an entity belonging to the *Urnfield culture*, and more precisely the *RSFO group* (Rhin-Suisse-France orientale) as defined through the well-stratified series of swords, knives, bracelets, pins, and pottery from wetland sites, among others Greifensee-Böschen, Zug-Sumpf, or Auvernier-Nord (Hochuli, Niffeler, and Rychner 1998: 70–92), and cremation burials such as those of Lausanne-Vidy (Moinat and David-Elbiali 2003), or Ossingen-Im Speck for the later phase. There are regional variations, but the material culture, both pottery and bronzes, shows strong affinities from the lakeshore settlements in the Zürich area to those of the Jura mountain foothills.

The absolute chronology relies on radiocarbon dates, and where and when available, dendrochronological dates, mostly from wetland settlements (Fig. 39.3). North of the Alps these do not start before 2000 BC or the transition Bz A1/A2 in the Lake Constance region (radiocarbon dates of Bodman-Schachen IA, and Zürich-Mozartstrasse 1a/b: Schmidheiny 2011), the oldest dendrodates in the Jura lake region being those of Concise-Sous Colachoz around 1800 BC for a subphase Bz A2a (Primas 2008: 5–6). Yet earlier radiocarbon dates around 2300/2200 cal BC measured on bone collagen are known from the Singen cemetery, with material attributed to Bz A1 (Krause 1996). However, some think these dates are too old. The majority of dendrodates for EBA wetland settlements on the eastern and western Swiss Plateau fall within the eighteenth/seventeenth centuries BC.

Dendrodates of the twenty-first century BC (*Bronzo antico I*) are reported from lakeshore dwellings in northern Italy, for example Desenzano del Garda-Lavagnone 2 (De Marinis 2005) where they mark the onset of the EBA sequence. In the western Alps and the Valais continuity from the Late Copper to the EBA is attested through graves in Dolmen MXI of the cemetery of Sion-Petit Chasseur, with radiocarbon dates between 2400 and 2000 cal BC (Bz A1) and a group of contemporaneous graves in the Bernese Oberland (Hafner 1995: 169–85).

Within the Alps no isolated finds or settlements are known prior to 2000 BC or the Bz A1/A2 transition. Remeasured radiocarbon dates for the initial phase E of the Savognin-Padnal dwelling in the Grisons cover the span 2000–1800 cal BC, corresponding to traces of earliest EBA human activity elsewhere in the Central Alps, for example on Alpe di Tom at 2000 m above sea level in the Gotthard Pass area (Hess et al. 2010). Settlements became more abundant in the Alps during the Bz A2 phase, however, and even more so in the subsequent MBA when the dendrodate of 1466 BC from the well built of larchwood at St Moritz (Seifert 2000) is a secure chronological marker for late Bz C1.

Secure absolute dates for the onset of the MBA are scarce, as wetland settlement activity mostly stops in the sixteenth century BC due to climatic variations (see above). Usually a date around 1550 BC is stated, as the younger dendrodates of 1510/1480 in Bad Buchau-Forschner D and Zürich-Mozartstrasse 1c3 seem to be correlated already with MBA (Bz B) material (Schmidheiny 2011). Overall the MBA appears as a rather short interlude of not much more than two hundred years, but again, the beginning of the LBA (phase Bz D1) is still a matter of debate. Della Casa and Fischer (1997) have advocated a date around 1325 BC using AMS dates from the Neftenbach-Steinmöri cemetery near Zürich and cross-European comparisons, while the few available dendrodates seem to be slightly younger (Primas 2008: 6–7).

To the south a series of radiocarbon dates from the *Terramara* Poviglio-Santa Rosa offers a sound chronological setting for the *Bronzo recente* and *finale*, in other words the fourteenth

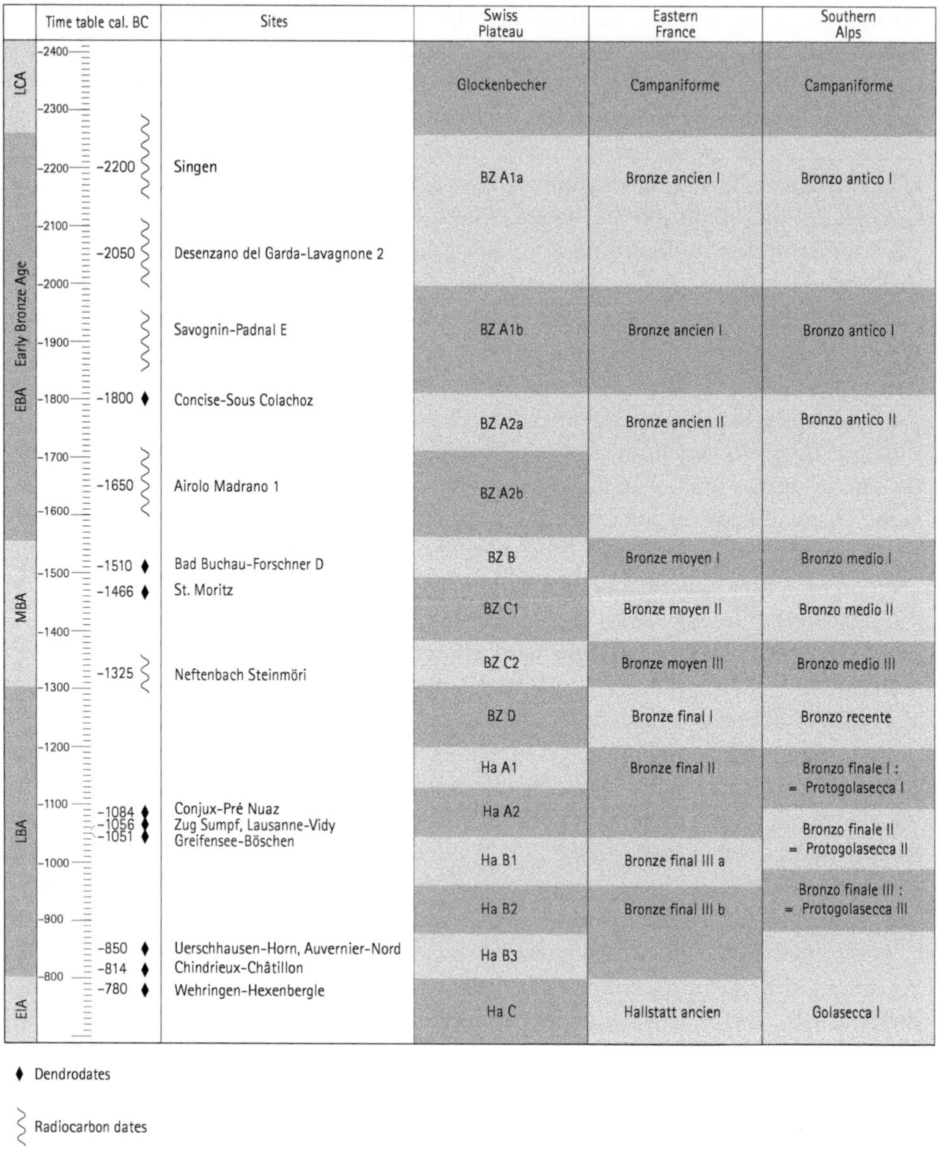

	Time table cal. BC	Sites	Swiss Plateau	Eastern France	Southern Alps
LCA	-2400 / -2300		Glockenbecher	Campaniforme	Campaniforme
EBA Early Bronze Age	-2200 ≈ -2200 / Singen	Singen	BZ A1a	Bronze ancien I	Bronzo antico I
	-2100 / -2050 ≈ / -2000	Desenzano del Garda-Lavagnone 2			
	-1900 ≈	Savognin-Padnal E	BZ A1b	Bronze ancien I	Bronzo antico I
	-1800 ♦ -1800	Concise-Sous Colachoz	BZ A2a	Bronze ancien II	Bronzo antico II
	-1700 / -1650 ≈ / -1600	Airolo Madrano 1	BZ A2b		
MBA	-1500 / -1510 ♦ / -1466 ♦ / -1400	Bad Buchau-Forschner D / St. Moritz	BZ B	Bronze moyen I	Bronzo medio I
			BZ C1	Bronze moyen II	Bronzo medio II
	-1300 / -1325 ≈	Neftenbach Steinmöri	BZ C2	Bronze moyen III	Bronzo medio III
	-1200		BZ D	Bronze final I	Bronzo recente
LBA	-1100 / -1084 ♦ / -1056 ♦ / -1051 ♦ / -1000	Conjux-Pré Nuaz / Zug Sumpf, Lausanne-Vidy / Greifensee-Böschen	Ha A1	Bronze final II	Bronzo finale I : = Protogolasecca I
			Ha A2		Bronzo finale II = Protogolasecca II
			Ha B1	Bronze final III a	
	-900		Ha B2	Bronze final III b	Bronzo finale III : = Protogolasecca III
EIA	-850 ♦ / -800 / -814 ♦ / -780 ♦	Uerschhausen-Horn, Auvernier-Nord / Chindrieux-Châtillon / Wehringen-Hexenbergle	Ha B3		
			Ha C	Hallstatt ancien	Golasecca I

♦ Dendrodates

≈ Radiocarbon dates

FIG. 39.3 Chronological phases, dates, and events in Switzerland.

Source: author (drawing J. Bucher, Universität Zürich).

to twelfth centuries BC (Bernabò Brea and Cremaschi 2004), prior to the abandonment of the *Terramare* dwellings in the Po plain. In the Alpine Ticino Valley stratified radiocarbon dates covering the late EBA to early LBA sequence (1650–1150 cal BC) are available from the Airolo-Madrano dwelling (Della Casa, Jochum Zimmermann, and Jacquat 2009).

From 1056 BC onwards, with the first dendrodates in Zug-Sumpf 1, there is again an abundance of dendrochronological dates from moor and lakeshore settlements around the Alps. On the Swiss Plateau terminological problems have been solved if the relevant phase is agreed to be Ha B1 (illustrated for example through material from the short-lived settlement of Greifensee-Böschen at 1051–1042 BC: Eberschweiler, Riethmann, and Ruoff 2007: 258), followed by phases Ha B2 around 960 BC and B3 around 880 BC (Primas 2008: 7). The last tree-ring dates pertaining to Ha B3 are around 850 BC for Uerschhausen-Horn and Auvernier-Nord. In eastern France the LBA sequence of occupation is slightly longer, from 1084 BC (BF IIb/IIIa) in Conjux-Pré Nuaz to 814 BC (BF IIIb) in Chindrieux-Châtillon on Lake Bourget.

The end of the LBA is commonly set at 800 BC, with reference to the 778 ± 5 BC dendrodate for the oak central chamber in the Wehringen-Hexenbergle Early Iron Age (Ha C1) barrow (Primas 2008: 8).

SETTLEMENT TOPOGRAPHY, SETTLEMENT STRUCTURES

As for the preceding Neolithic and Copper Age, wetlands and lakeshores were among the favourite locations for settlements on the Swiss Plateau and in the Prealpine zones. To what extent the landscape was already free of woodland and transformed by humans at the beginning of the Bronze Age is not an easy question to answer, given the scarcity of data available for the second half of the third millennium BC. This was, however, certainly the situation at the end of the Bronze Age, and many new ecotopes, in particular reed belts along the lakeshores and open grassland for pastures, are believed to originate in the period under consideration. In any case wetland areas offered many advantages for settlement: open space, proximity of woodlands, agricultural soils, and aquatic resources on the one hand, and natural protection as well as easy access to water communication routes on the other.

There is no standard size of wetland settlement. Some are small villages with just a few houses—as in the case of *Zürich-Mozartstrasse 1*—others are, already in the EBA, agglomerated settlements of considerable surface areas, up to 5000 and more sq m, and sometimes fortified, as in the case of the *Forschner* settlement in the Federsee area (Billamboz et al. 2010). Few villages have been comprehensively studied, *Greifensee-Böschen* (Fig. 39.4) being one spectacular exception, due to a remarkable underwater excavation in 1984–95 (Eberschweiler, Riethmann, and Ruoff 2007). This short-lived LBA settlement was destroyed by fire, which led to the preservation not only of a great number of wooden architectural features such as pile 'shoes', wooden house stands (*Ständerbauten*), timbers from log houses, wall boards, roof beams, and shingles, but also nearly complete inventories of household contents including metal, pottery, and other small finds, as well as biological macroremains that allow for a detailed reconstruction of the daily life in a dwelling around 1050 BC.

There is a clear trend towards increased settlement size in the LBA, some large settlements covering well over 10,000 sq m and displaying complex organizational structures in buildings, access paths and roads, open places, and defensive devices (Seifert *et al.* 1996). Many of these large settlements have, however, only been partially excavated, or were already looted with heavy mechanical devices in the nineteenth century during the 'pile dwelling fever' period, as with *Mörigen* on Lake Biel, *Grandson-Corcellettes* on Lake Geneva, or the sites of *Alpenquai* and *Haumesser* in the city of Zürich, from which rich collections of pottery and metal finds are known. *Zug-Sumpf* is a good example of such a large,

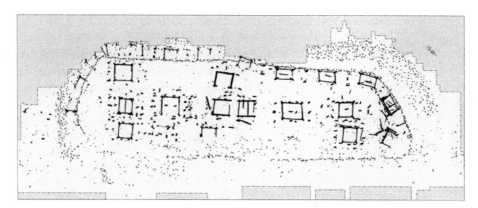

FIG. 39.4 Ground plan of the Greifensee-Böschen LBA lakeshore settlement near Zürich. Plan from Eberschweiler *et al.* 2007, by permission of Kantonsarchäologie Zürich.

quasi-proto-urban LBA settlement with complex structures (Seifert *et al.* 1996), while the *Wasserburg* of *Bad Buchau* in the Federseemoor is an archetype for the highly fortified villages (Schöbel 2000).

Zug-Sumpf 1, with a surface area of 15,000 sq m, comprised up to 120 houses arranged in 24 regular rows, and thus a considerable population of several hundred people. Spatial analysis has revealed many elements of social and economic organization, in particular concerning trade, as well as pottery and metal crafts. The moor settlement of *Bad Buchau* covered a surface area of 120 x 150 m and was encircled by three rows of wooden palisades. While in an earlier phase, some 30 houses of roughly 5 by 5 m in wattle and daub architecture formed a clustered village, the latest phase of the ninth century BC seems to be characterized by large complex buildings. Again, there are plentiful finds of many activities and crafts, in particular bronze objects, and evidence of on-site metalworking. As has been argued by Schlichtherle and Strobel (2001), Bad Buchau could have played the role of a central place within a defined territory starting from the MBA, along with other fortified settlements on the upper Danube, all of them however of the hill-fort type.

Naturally defended sites such as promontories and hilltops were selected for settlement during the entire Bronze Age, both in the Prealpine lowlands and the Alpine valleys. The phenomenon becomes particularly visible in those periods when additional fortification structures such as stone walls, ramparts, and ditches were fashionable, which is the case at the end of the EBA and in the evolved LBA (Primas 2008: 41–3).

The Alpine Rhine Valley between Chur and Bregenz displays a considerable number of fortified settlements, usually situated on large hillocks along the edges of the valley, as in the case of the Ochsenberg at Wartau. The latter is a typical *longue durée* site, repeatedly occupied over a long period of time. The full archaeological sequence starts with a Copper Age seasonal occupation around 3000 cal BC, followed by an EBA fortified village, an LBA settlement that expands well beyond the hilltop (Primas et al. 2004), an Iron Age ritual site of the *Brandopferplatz* type (see below), a Roman occupation, and again a fortified farmstead of the Early Medieval period. The Rhine Valley has always been an important route of communication, from north to south due to its geography, but also from east to west, connecting through the Seeztal to Lake Zürich, and through the Walgau and Montafon to the Inn Valley and the eastern Alps. Wartau-Ochsenberg holds an excellent strategic position in this system of communication, which must have been a key factor in the settlement process.

The importance of topo-strategic locations in the organization of space becomes even more tangible at the *Montlingerberg* near Oberriet further down in the valley, and close to Lake Constance. The extensive hilltop was settled from the LBA (Ha B1–B3), when a massive fortification system with rampart and ditch was built that eventually encircled a surface of more than 10,000 sq m. The archaeological excavations, mostly of the mid twentieth century, yielded rich material of pottery, metal, and remakably amber, testifying to the importance of the site and its many supra-regional connections (Hochuli, Niffeler, and Rychner 1998: 384).

In the mountainous regions of the Alps exposed topographic situations were used for dwelling as well as for territorial and transit control from the beginning of permanent settlement in the fourth and third millennia BC (Della Casa 2002; 2007). The term *Höhensiedlung* ('settlement on a height') has been applied incautiously to many differing situations, from proper hill forts to sites on simple ridges or morainic hills. As the valley bottoms would be seasonally flooded, Alpine settlements are almost inevitably located on river terraces or hills. The few houses, often not more than 10–20 units, were built of wooden stands or beams, usually on a dry stone base. Classic situations are more or less pronounced morainic structures such as the *Padnal* of Savognin in the Oberhalbstein Valley at 1,200 m above sea level (Rageth 1986). The site was inhabited over a long span of time from c.1800 to 1000 BC, subdivided into five settlement phases (E–A) though the exact duration of each phase is unknown. Some dwellings could be on hills, but intentionally placed out of view, as in the case of the equally long-lived village of *Cazis-Cresta* located in a depression (Hochuli, Niffeler, and Rychner 1998: 375).

Many sites had fortifications added during the Bronze Age, which underlines their function as territorial markers more than habitation sites. A good example is the *Friaga Wald* hill fort in Bartholomäberg in the Montafon Valley (Fig. 39.5), situated on a rather small hilltop, not more than 1000 m^2 in extent, which was artificially terraced and fortified with a dry stone wall 80 m long and 2–3 m wide in the sixteenth century BC; only five to eight log houses stood on the hill (Krause 2007). Slightly later, a much larger and open settlement was built nearby on the *Platta* terrace close to the agricultural zones of the valley slopes.

The precise function of these fortified places is not always evident, besides the fact that they correspond to quasi-European trends. For Bartholomäberg, Rüdiger Krause has argued in favour of an element of socio-territorial marking related to ore extraction and early copper and bronze metallurgy, as the valley yields many traces of metallurgical activities going back from the medieval period possibly as far as the EBA (see below). Other sites are evidently related to traffic connections and routes of communication, in particular trans-Alpine pass routes. Several examples can be cited from the central Alps, all of them sharing a common set of topographic features: they are placed along major axes, in other words valley and pass routes, and are situated on natural obstacles such as promontories and barriers, in order to control access and transit (Della Casa 2007). Some have an agricultural environment and respond also to criteria of settlement, for example in *Amsteg-Flüeli* and *Airolo-Madrano*, respectively north and south of the Gotthard Pass; while others have a pronounced defensive character, as on the castle rock of *Hohenrätien* at the entrance to the Viamala gorge on the San Bernardino route. As elsewhere, the site was

FIG. 39.5 Digital reconstruction of the Friaga Wald early MBA hill fort in Bartholomäberg, Montafon.

Drawing: R. Krause, Universität Frankfurt a.M., ArcTron 3D.

repeatedly occupied, in the LBA, EIA, and Roman period. In many cases, medieval weir systems or towers occupy the same locations.

It is still hard to get a complete understanding of regional settlement systems in the Bronze Age, as archaeological discoveries usually occur by chance or rescue interventions, and not through systematic research. Investigations also tend to be focused on specific settings or environments, for example wetland sites. On the Swiss Plateau dry-land settlements are far less well known than lakeshore or hilltop sites, though discoveries of the last two decades—such as the village of post buildings in *Cham-Oberwil*—tend to redress the balance. Several examples show that there were systemic relationships between lakeshore dwellings, hill forts, and open-land settlements on alluvial terraces, at least in the LBA (Primas 2008: 33–5).

In the southern valleys the settlement system corresponded essentially to the one described for the north and central Alpine regions, while in the Po plain, a specific type of dwelling emerged at the beginning of the MBA: the *Terramare* (Bernabò Brea, Cardarelli, and Cremaschi 1997) (see Chapter 38). These settlements are often counted as wetland settlements, which they are not—however, water management was an important subsistence issue in the *Terramare*. The earlier villages were rather small, around 1000–1500 sq m, but tend to become much larger in the *Bronzo recente* phase, as is the case at *Santa Rosa di Poviglio* (Bernabò Brea and Cremaschi 2004). Most *Terramare* had circular ditches, palisades or embankments, pile constructions, and cisterns, as well as silos for grain storage.

Economic Background

Thanks to the excellent conditions of preservation in waterlogged wetland settlements, the amount of data relating to economic activities, in particular subsistence economy—agriculture, cattle breeding, woodland economy—but also material production and various crafts, is considerable, even exceptional on a European scale. Wood remains from architecture and aspects of daily life, and biological macroremains, both vegetal and faunal, form the core body of data. The most important categories are piles and wooden construction elements, seeds and fruits from cultivated and wild plants, and animal bones, along with many other organic finds linked to daily activities such as tools and objects made of wood and antler, textiles or basketry. Crafts are of course also well attested through inorganic materials such as stone, pottery, and metals—to name the most important (Hochuli, Niffeler, and Rychner 1998: 232–306).

Piles and beams from wooden house constructions are not only essential for the dendrochronological sequencing (see above), but they also yield rich information pertaining to climate evolution (dendroclimatology) on the one hand and woodland management (dendroecology) on the other. Tree-ring growth is an important proxy for the reconstruction of past regional and supra-regional climate trends, and contributes—together with other proxies such as residual radiocarbon and pollen-based vegetation history—to the understanding of climatic evolution, particular climatic events such as the *Löbben* or *Göschenen 1* oscillations (see above), and their relationship to settlement and thus economic processes. On a local scale, tree-ring growth is a good marker of woodland ecology and woodland management, because trees tend to react rapidly to ecological changes in their immediate vicinity, for example through slash-and-burn activities or selective tree cutting for house construction. In the Lake Constance area, the cycles of woodland management—from the cutting of large trees in primary forests to the use of coppice forest for later expansion and reconstruction in the settlements—have been well observed, both for the Early Bronze Age and the Late Bronze Age (Billamboz 2005). These show that woodland management was an essential economic task to maintain a successful and sustainable colonization. Seifert et al. (1996) have calculated a quantity of 8,500–9,000 large trees for construction over the lifespan of the Zug-Sumpf 1 settlement, to which one has to add 600 tonnes of clay for hearths, wattle and daub architecture, and pottery production.

Primary (subsistence) economy in Bronze Age lakeshore dwellings was essentially based on crops, mostly cereals (different wheats, barley, millet), but also pulses (beans, lentils) and oleaginous plants such as flax und poppy. In addition to cultivation, the gathering of wild plants, berries, and fruits was common (Jacomet, Brombacher, and Dick 1989). Animal proteins came from the breeding of cattle, pigs, sheep, and goats—there is usually only a small amount of hunted animals such as deer, boar, or birds in the bone assemblages (Schibler et al. 1997). Fish were certainly an important dietary element, but are difficult to detect in the sediments, even when sieved and floated. Taken all together, the situation was not fundamentally different from the preceding Neolithic periods, though some important shifts and innovations can be noted: new cereals were added to the spectrum of crops, in particular spelt (resistant to wet and cold), and a grassland economy led to intensification in cattle breeding.

In the Alps the subsistence economy was adapted to specific needs in the often harsh climatic and topographic environment: barley is by far the most common crop in Alpine settlements of the Bronze Age, and sheep/goats appear to have been most suitable to the local ecology. Though the central Alps seem to be lacking the typical animal-dung strata in caves and rock shelters as known further to the west (*grottes bergeries* of the French Alps), vertical transhumance must have played an important role in the economic system. There is an increasing number of sites in the Alpine altitudinal range (2,000 m above sea level and more), including open and sheltered camps as well as stone-built structures, that can be related to the seasonal use of Alpine meadows in the context of agro-pastoral economy. Many of these are sited within or in the vicinity of medieval to recent Alpine pastures, which in itself is a clear indicator of the long-term use of purposeful locations for economic needs, in other words for an Alpine economy (*Alpwirtschaft*). Recently discovered and documented examples can be found in the Silvretta region (Reitmaier 2010) and the upper Leventina Valley and Gotthard pass area (Hess et al. 2010).

Besides the agro-pastoral economy, mining for metal ores—in particular copper—is the most common Alpine economic *topos* in the Bronze Age. By analogy with the situation further east, in North Tyrol and the Inn Valley, it has been postulated that the ore-rich regions of the central Alps such as the lower Valais and specifically the Oberhalbstein provided copper to the Prealpine lowlands, for example the Lake Constance region, possibly as early as the EBA. Though this scenario is not unlikely, one must acknowledge that there is no secure evidence for it: it has so far neither been possible to recognize an early production of central Alpine copper (for the most part chalcopyrite) by means of trace element or isotopic signatures, nor is there sufficient proof of metallurgical activity in the area prior to the LBA. Even in the settlement of Savognin-Padnal, where copper/bronze metallurgy is attested during the EBA, the relationship to the surrounding ophiolitic ores of the upper Oberhalbstein could not definitely be proven (Schaer 2003)—as the analyses show, some of the worked fahlore (*Fahlerz*) copper was certainly not of local origin. However, slag heaps, tuyères, and other finds do confirm the smelting and production of local copper in the LBA and EIA.

Society and Ideology

Information relating to the structure of society and its ideological background comes mainly from funerary sites, as well as from contexts of ritual activity such as deposits and offerings. Though recurring finds like the well-known crescent horns (*Mondhörner*) or the large bronze keys decorated with water birds (as at *Zürich-Alpenquai*) may indicate ritual activity within settlements, no specific buildings of cultic function have yet been identified. Whether the many and sometimes clustered finds of bronze objects within settlements, in particular lake dwellings, are to be interpreted as ritual deposits, is still a matter of debate (Hochuli, Niffeler, and Rychner 1998: 335; V. Fischer 2011).

There is abundant evidence for the use of 'sacred' natural places for ritual activities and depositions, in particular flowing waters, lakes, and ponds on the one hand, and from mountain and pass regions on the other. Conspicuous are the many isolated or sometimes paired finds of bronze objects—mostly daggers, axes, and pins—from Alpine locations such as the daggers from *Vals-Valserberg* and from the *Chringenpass*, both situations around 2,000 m above sea level (C. Fischer 1997: 85–95). Important depositions of axes, pins, and swords are known from the rivers *Limmat* in Zürich and *Rhône* in Geneva, as well as from a number of lakes in the Prealpine and Alpine area. While these are usually seen as the results of cultic or social rituals, there are other contexts, such as the hoard of 66 finished bronze axes from *Sennwald-Salez* (Hochuli, Niffeler, and Rychner 1998: 388) that appear to be more closely related to the production and circulation of bronze items.

Springs are peculiar locations for the deposition of votive offerings, as in the case of the Mauritius spring in St Moritz (Seifert 2000). The carbonated mineral water of the spring was used for medical purposes in the Middle Ages, but already during the MBA it was tapped using larchwood tubes, and a series of metal items (three swords, a pin, and a dagger) were deposited within the tubes, obviously as votives to a numinous world.

Though the Alpine burnt-offering places (*Brandopferplätze*) are often understood as a phenomenon of the Iron Age, the tradition clearly starts in the Bronze Age, as evidenced through the abundant finds of calcined domestic animal bones and pottery on the promontory of *Spiez-Eggli* in the Bernese Alps (Hochuli, Niffeler, and Rychner 1998: 325).

From the onset, and following Copper Age traditions in central Europe, there is a clear gender subdivision in funeral rituals and grave deposits in the Bronze Age. In the EBA tombs of the *Singen* cemetery this is evident in the position of the bodies (right/left crouched position for females/males), and in the assemblages—female inhumations mostly reveal elements of costume and ornament whereas male inhumations feature weapons, in particular daggers (Krause 1988). Though there are local and regional variations, it is possible to create a 'standard' or norm of gender-related grave deposits (Hafner 1995: 90–2) (Fig. 39.6). From an analysis of the situation in Singen, and in comparison to similar EBA cemeteries such as those of the Traisental in Austria (Gemeinlebarn, Franzhausen), it becomes evident that these are elite standards—only superseded by single burials with *Überausstattungen*, as in the case of the *Thun-Renzenbühl* tomb (see above). Tentatively, social structuring may also be inferred in the MBA from the number and importance of metal items in the graves (C. Fischer 1997: 80–5).

In Singen as in other EBA cemeteries, and more specifically in the MBA tumuli (for example, Weiningen-Hardwald, Birmensdorf-Rameren; see above), the inhumation graves are set in spatial clusters reflecting social entities, probably descent groups. One must, however, turn to more substantial contexts to the north (Schwäbische Alb, southern Germany) or east—such as the bi-ritual necropolis of Pitten in Lower Austria—to get a better understanding of the demographic and social organization of these cemeteries.

In the LBA, finally, just as in other regions of the Urnfield complex, cremation becomes the dominant burial rite, and the vertical social structures—argued from the wealth of bronze objects (swords for males, jewellery for females)—are more often marked by sets of drinking vessels. This is the case in grave 8 of the LBA necropolis of *Lausanne-Vidy*: the find contained a large jar, two medium-sized vessels, and a series of nine identical drinking bowls. This exceptional assemblage recurs in a small number of cremation graves throughout the Swiss Plateau—for example, in Möhlin-Niederriburg, Rafz-Im Fallentor, and Anselfingen near Konstanz (Moinat and David-Elbiali 2003: 194)—reflecting a common set of rituals and beliefs, and a wish to mark a specific person, function, or status within the society. It can be presumed that these persons were engaged in commensal activities as part of their elite social situation.

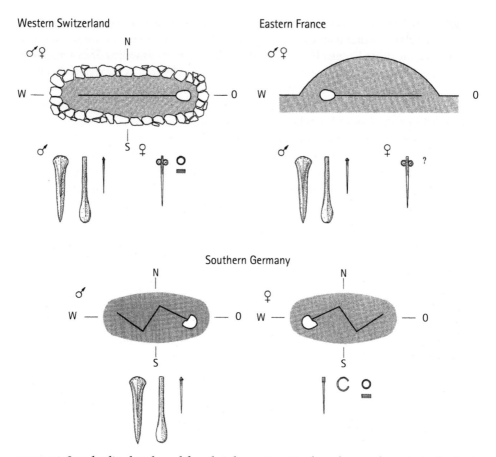

FIG. 39.6 Standardized male and female inhumation rituals and grave deposits in the Early Bronze Age for three distinct areas.

copyright A. Hafner 1995, Bern

Bibliography

Atlas der Schweiz 2.0 (2008). Edited by Institut für Kartografie ETHZ, ETH-Rat, Bundesamt für Statistik (BFS) and Bundesamt für Landestopografie (swisstopo).

Bernabò Brea, M. A., Cardarelli, A., and Cremaschi, M. (eds.) (1997). *Le Terramare, la più antica civiltà padana*. Milan: Electa.

—— and Cremaschi, M. (eds.) (2004). *Il villaggio piccolo della terramara di Santa Rosa di Poviglio. Scavi 1987–1992*. Florence: Origines.

Billamboz, A. (2005). '20 Jahre Dendroarchäologie in den Pfahlbausiedlungen Südwestdeutschlands. Bilanz und Perspektiven', in Ph. Della Casa and M. Trachsel (eds.), *WES'04: Wetland Economies and Societies*, Proceedings of the International Conference Zürich, 10–13 March 2004. Collectio Archaeologica, 3. Zürich: Chronos, 47–56.

——, Köninger, J., Schlichtherle, H., and Torke, W. (2010). *Siedlungsarchäologie im Alpenvorland XI. Die früh- und mittelbronzezeitliche 'Siedlung Forschner' im Federseemoor. Befunde und Dendrochronologie*, Forschungen und Berichte zur Vor- und Frühgeschichte in Baden-Württemberg, Band 113. Stuttgart: Theiss.

Burga, C. and Perret, R. (1998). *Vegetation und Klima der Schweiz seit dem jüngeren Eiszeitalter*. Thun: Ott.

Della Casa, Ph. (2000). *Mesolcina Praehistorica. Mensch und Naturraum in einem Bündner Südalpental vom Mesolithikum bis in römische Zeit*, Universitätsforschungen zur Prähistorischen Archäologie, 67. Bonn: Habelt.

—— (2002). *Landschaften, Siedlungen, Ressourcen—Langzeitszenarien menschlicher Aktivität in ausgewählten alpinen Gebieten der Schweiz, Italiens und Frankreichs*, Préhistoires, 6. Montagnac: Éditions Monique Mergoil.

—— (2007). 'Transalpine pass routes in the Swiss Central Alps and the strategic use of topographic resources', *Preistoria Alpina*, 42: 109–18.

—— and Fischer, C. (1997). 'Neftenbach (CH), Velika Gruda (YU), Kastanas (GR) und Trindhøj (DK)–Argumente für einen Beginn der Spätbronzezeit (Reinecke Bz D) im 14. Jahrhundert v. Chr', *Prähistorische Zeitschrift*, 72: 195–233.

——, Jochum Zimmermann, E., and Jacquat, C. (2009). 'Eine alpine Siedlung der Bronze- und Eisenzeit in Airolo-Madrano (Kt. Tessin, Schweiz)–archäologische und paläoökologische Grundlagen', *Archäologisches Korrespondenzblatt*, 39: 193–211.

Eberschweiler, B., Riethmann, P., and Ruoff, U. (2007). *Das spätbronzezeitliche Dorf von Greifensee-Böschen*, Monographien Kantonsarchäologie Zürich, 38. Zürich: Baudirektion ARV.

Fischer, C. (1997). *Innovation und Tradition in der Mittel- und Spätbronzezeit: Gräber und Siedlungen in Neftenbach, Fällanden, Dietikon, Pfäffikon und Erlenbach*, Monographien der Kantonsarchäologie Zürich, 28. Zürich/Egg: Fotorotar.

Fischer, V. (2011). 'The deposition of bronzes at Swiss lakeshore settlements: new investigations', *Antiquity*, 85: 1,298–311.

Hafner, A. (1995). *Die frühe Bronzezeit in der Westschweiz: Funde und Befunde aus Siedlungen, Gräbern und Horten der entwickelten Frühbronzezeit*, Ufersiedlungen am Bielersee, 5. Bern: Staatlicher Lehrmittelverlag.

Hansen, S. (2002). '"Überausstattungen" in Gräbern und Horten der Frühbronzezeit', in J. Müller (ed.), *Vom Endneolithikum zur Frühbronzezeit: Muster sozialen Wandels? Tagung Bamberg 14–16 Juni 2001*. Universitätsforschungen zur Prähistorischen Archäologie, 90. Bonn: Habelt, 151–73.

Hess, T., Reitmaier, T., Jochum Zimmermann, E., Ballmer, A., Dobler, I., and Della Casa, Ph. (2010). 'Leventina–Prähistorische Siedlungslandschaft. Archäologisches Survey im Alpinen Tessintal und entlang der Gotthardpassroute in 2007–08: kommentierter Katalog', *Jahrbuch der Archäologie Schweiz*, 93: 173–92.

Hochuli, S., Niffeler, U., and Rychner, V. (1998). *SPM: Die Schweiz vom Paläolithikum bis zum frühen Mittelalter. III: Bronzezeit*. Basel: SGUF.

Jacomet, S., Brombacher, C., and Dick, M. (1989). *Archäobotanik am Zürichsee: Ackerbau, Sammelwirtschaft und Umwelt von neolithischen und bronzezeitlichen Seeufersiedlungen im Raum Zürich*, Berichte der Zürcher Denkmalpflege (Monographien), 7. Zürich: Orell-Füssli.

Krause, R. (1988). *Die endneolithischen und frühbronzezeitlichen Grabfunde auf der Nordstadtterrasse von Singen am Hohentwiel*, Forschungen und Berichte zur Vor- und Frühgeschichte in Baden-Württemberg, 32. Stuttgart: Theiss.

—— (1996). 'Zur Chronologie der frühen und mittleren Bronzezeit Süddeutschlands, der Schweiz und Österreichs', in K. Randsborg (ed.), *Absolute Chronology: Archaeological Europe 2500–500 BC*, Acta Archaeologica, 67. Copenhagen: Munksgaard, 73–86.

—— (2007). 'The prehistoric settlement of the inneralpine valley of Montafon in Vorarlberg (Austria)', *Preistoria Alpina*, 42: 119–36.

Marinis, R. C. de (2005). 'Lavagnone (Desenzano del Garda): new excavations and palaeoecology of a Bronze Age pile-dwelling site in northern Italy', in Ph. Della Casa and M. Trachsel (eds.), *WES'04: Wetland Economies and Societies*, Proceedings of the International Conference Zürich, 10–13 March 2004. Collectio Archaeologica, 3. Zürich: Chronos, 221–32.

Menotti, F. (2001). *The Missing Period: Middle Bronze Age Lake-Dwellings in the Alps*, British Archaeological Reports (International Series), 968. Oxford: Archaeopress.

Moinat, P. and David-Elbiali, M. (2003). *Défunts, bûchers et céramiques: la nécropole de Lausanne-Vidy (VD) et les pratiques funéraires sur le Plateau suisse du XIe au VIIIe s. av. J.-C*, Cahiers d'Archéologie Romande, 93. Lausanne: CAR.

Primas, M. (2008). *Bronzezeit zwischen Elbe und Po. Strukturwandel in Zentraleuropa 2200–800 v. Chr*, Universitätsforschungen zur prähistorischen Archäologie, 150. Bonn: Habelt.

——, Della Casa, Ph., Jochum Zimmermann, E., and Huber, R. (2004). *Wartau-Ur- und frühgeschichtliche Siedlungen und Brandopferplatz im Alpenrheintal (Kanton St. Gallen, Schweiz). Band II. Bronzezeit, Kupferzeit, Mesolithikum*, Universitätsforschungen zur prähistorischen Archäologie, 108. Bonn: Habelt.

Rageth, J. (1986). 'Die wichtigsten Resultate der Ausgrabungen in der bronzezeitlichen Siedlung auf dem Padnal bei Savognin (Oberhalbstein GR)', *Jahrbuch der Schweizerischen Gesellschaft für Ur- und Frühgeschichte*, 69: 63–103.

Reitmaier, T. (2010). 'Neues Altes aus den Alpen. Archäologie in der Silvretta, ein Zwischenbericht', *Bündner Monatsblatt*, 2/2010: 107–41.

Rubat Borel, F. (2006). 'Tra Protogolasecca e cultura RSFO: il gruppo Pont-Valperga e il Bronzo Finale nel Piemonte nord-accidentale', in D. Vitali (ed.), *La Préhistoire des Celtes*, Actes de la Table Ronde de Bologne, 28–29 mai 2005. Bibracte, 12/2. Glux-en-Glenne: Bibracte, 197–202.

Schaer, A. (2003). 'Untersuchungen zum prähistorischen Bergbau im Oberhalbstein (Kanton Graubünden)', *Jahrbuch der Schweizerischen Gesellschaft für Ur- und Frühgeschichte*, 86: 7–54.

Schibler, J., Hüster-Plogmann, H., Jacomet, S., Brombacher, C., Gross-Klee, E., and Rast-Eicher, A. (1997). *Ökonomie und Ökologie neolithischer und bronzezeitlicher Ufersiedlungen am Zürichsee: Ergebnisse der Ausgrabungen Mozartstrasse, Kanalisationssanierung Seefeld, AKAD/Pressehaus und Mythenschloss in Zürich*, Monographien der Kantonsarchäologie Zürich, 20. Zürich/Egg: Fotorotar.

Schlichtherle, H. and Strobel, M. (2001). 'Ufersiedlungen–Höhensiedlungen', in B. Eberschweiler, J. Köninger, H. Schlichtherle, and C. Strahm (eds.), *Aktuelles zur Frühbronzezeit und frühen Mittelbronzezeit im nördlichen Alpenvorland*, Hemmenhofener Skripte, 2. Freiburg: Janus, 79–92.

Schmidheiny, M. (2011). *Zürich «Mozartstrasse». Neolithische und bronzezeitliche Ufersiedlungen. Die frühbronzezeitliche Besiedlung*, Monographien der Kantonsarchäologie Zürich, 42.

Schöbel, G. (2000). 'Die spätbronzezeitliche Ufersiedlung "Wasserburg Buchau", Kreis Biberach', in W. Schmid, H. Beer, and B. Sommer (eds.). *Inseln in der Archäologie*, Internationaler Kongress, Starnberg 1998. Archäologie unter Wasser, 3. Munich/Freiburg: Janus, 85–106.

Seifert, M. (2000). 'Vor 3466 Jahren erbaut! Die Quellfassung von St. Moritz', *Archäologie der Schweiz*, 23/2: 63–75.

——, Jacomet, S., Karg, S., Schibler, J., Veszeli, M., and Kaufmann, B. (1996). *Die spätbronzezeitlichen Ufersiedlungen von Zug-Sumpf. Band 1: Die Dorfgeschichte*. Zug: Kantonsarchäologie.

CHAPTER 40

GERMANY IN THE BRONZE AGE

ALBRECHT JOCKENHÖVEL

Introduction

The cultural diversity of Germany during the Bronze Age can be understood only against the background of the country's geology, geography, and climate. From south to north, Germany can be divided broadly into the following regions: the Bavarian Alps (to *c*.3,000 m) and Alpine foothills, the southern *cuesta* landforms (plateaux and mountains), the hills and low mountains of the Mittelgebirge (400–1,000 m), and the flat north German lowlands (to *c*.200 m), with the North Sea and Baltic Sea coastlines and offshore islands. The north is marked by sandy expanses and glacial moraines with lakes and bogs. The landscapes of the Mittelgebirge and southern Germany form many small, distinct areas with fertile soils, whereas the Alpine foothills are characterized by gravelly moraines and mountain landscapes. There are mineral deposits (copper, tin, and gold), but it is still unclear whether they were exploited at that time; this is in contrast to Bronze Age salt production.

The great river systems (rivers with tributaries) of the Danube, Rhine, Weser, Elbe, and Oder form physical networks for communication, by which common cultural elements and contacts were established. The south of Germany has always had strong connections with the Alpine countries (Switzerland, northern Italy) as well as Bohemia, Moravia, Austria, and Hungary. To the west are links to France, Belgium, and the Netherlands, as well as the British Isles. Eastern Germany has close connections with Poland, while the north (Lower Saxony, Schleswig-Holstein, Mecklenburg) has ties with Denmark and southern Sweden.

Consequently, there exist a large number of archaeological groups ('cultures') within an extremely complex timeframe (Fig. 40.1). From the south to the northern edge of the central uplands, the chronological system in use is that devised by Paul Reinecke (1872–1958) (*Bronzezeit* A–D; Hallstatt A and B), while the system introduced by the Swedish scholar Oscar Montelius (1843–1921) (Periods I–VI) is applied to the Nordic Bronze Age. Dendrochronology and radiocarbon dating have essentially confirmed previous absolute dates.

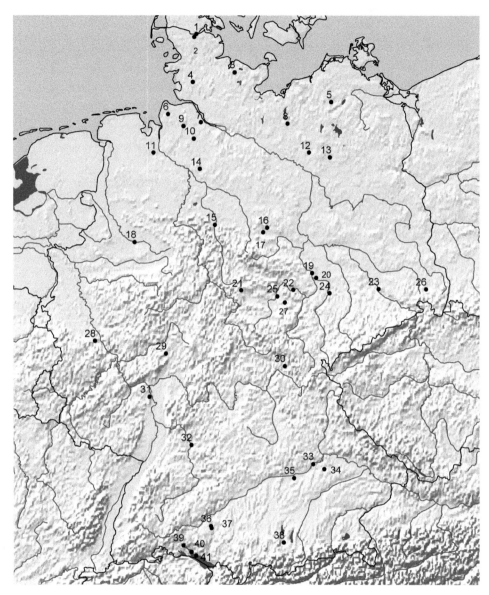

FIG. 40.1 Map of Germany showing sites discussed in the text. 1. Harrislee, 2. Handewitt, 3. Rastorf, 4. Albersdorf, 5. Thürkow, 6. Krempel, 7. Stade, 8. Peckatel, 9. Alfstedt, 10. Anderlingen, 11. Moordorf, 12. Seddin bei Groß Pankow, 13. Herzsprung, 14. Schafwinkel, 15. Schulenburg, 16. Schöningen, 17. Hünenburg bei Watenstedt, 18. Warendorf-Neuwarendorf, 19. Halle-Giebichenstein, 20. Dieskau, 21. Helmsdorf, 22. Mittelberg bei Nebra, 23. Heinrichsburg bei Seußlitz, 24. Zwenkau, 25. Leubingen, 26. Niederkaina, 27. Großbrembach, 28. Wachtberg-Fritzdorf, 29. Butzbach, 30. Heunischenburg bei Kronach, 31. Dexheim, 32. Neckarsulm, 33. Frauensberg bei Weltenburg, 34. Langquaid, 35. Ingolstadt-Zuchering, 36. Wasserburg Buchau am Federsee, 37. Forschner, 38. Weilheim, 39. Bodman, 40. Unteruhldingen, 41. Hagnau.

Map: author with M. Uckelmann.

The German Bronze Age is usually divided into an Early Bronze Age (EBA) (from the end of the third/beginning of the second millennium BC to around 1600 BC), a Middle Bronze Age (MBA) (1600–c.1300 BC), and a Late Bronze Age (LBA), also called the Urnfield period (1300–c.800 BC). The most important distinguishing features are the burial customs and grave forms: the Early Bronze Age is characterized by flat graves with bodies buried in the crouched position, the Middle Bronze Age by inhumations beneath mounds, and the Late Bronze Age by the deposition of urns containing cremated remains in burial places known as urnfields.

Central and Southern Germany

Early Bronze Age

In Germany, as an integral part of central Europe, there are numerous cultural manifestations in the EBA, which, although having their own regionally specific character, when taken average rich single graves and their associated together show distinct common features. These are evident in the appearance of above-votive depositions and hoards with new kinds of ceremonial weapons, such as solid-hilted daggers (*Vollgriffdolche*) and halberds, as well as various kinds of axe. From this it can be inferred that around 2000–1800 BC a leading social group ('chieftains') emerged, in farming communities that stretched from the lower Danube to southern Scandinavia, the south of England (Wessex culture), and Brittany, and were in close contact with one another. Their common features are evident not only on the physical level, as seen cross-regionally in very similar object forms and burial rites, but also in the spread of new technologies, like the introduction of tin-bronze, and the advent of complex metalworking techniques. EBA cultural groups are like 'islands' in central Europe, particularly near important deposits of copper, tin, and salt. Between these 'islands' are wide stretches of land that still continued in the Late Neolithic tradition. The most distinctive culture group is the Aunjetitz or Únětice culture (named after Únětice near Prague) (2300–2200 to 1600–1500 BC). Of more than just regional significance, this culture spreads from the middle Danube (south-west Slovakia, northern Lower Austria) across Moravia and Bohemia to central Germany, and as far away as Silesia and Great Poland. Flat cemeteries, some quite extensive, in which the graves contain crouched bodies oriented south-north, are predominantly situated near rural settlements—which, however, are still hardly known (e.g. Schöningen, with longhouses: Maier 1996). Beside simple burials there are occasionally graves with stone walls (*Mauergräber*) or graves holding tree-trunk coffins. Men and women are all buried lying on the right side and facing east. Children are occasionally buried in large storage jars (*pithoi*). Sometimes several people, probably members of one family, are buried in a single grave. The most important Únětice cemeteries are at Großbrembach and Nohra (Thuringia) and Wahlitz (Saxony-Anhalt), Burk bei Bautzen (Saxony) (Zich 1996). In the largest known central German site, Grossbrembach, single families were buried. It was also possible to demonstrate the people's supposed Bohemian origin from epigenetic markers on the skeletons (Ullrich 1972).

The roots of the early phase of the Únětice culture (Proto-Únětice phase), which largely lacks metal, are found in the outgoing Late Neolithic (Corded Ware culture, Bell Beaker culture). The Únětice culture reaches its peak in the later ('classical') phase. Characteristic artefact forms in the early phase are globular and narrow-necked pots with fringed decoration and small ornaments made of copper as well as bone and shell (Zich 1996; Bartelheim 1998).

The later phase, whose beginning has been dendrodated at the latest to the twentieth century BC, is characterized by its distinctive pottery forms. Burials from this time yield considerably more grave goods made of a copper alloy that is unusual for its higher tin content (Rassmann 2005). Most burials contain few other grave goods; however, there are exceptional richly furnished tumuli from this time. These are the isolated burial mounds, visible from afar, which are usually referred to as 'princely graves'. Such graves occur at Helmsdorf, Leubingen (the 'Leubingen Group' was named after the enormous mound there), Dieskau, Nienstedt, Sömmerda, Lochau, and Österkörner (Meller 2004). There are no such monuments elsewhere in the broad Únětice culture area, apart from comparable tumuli at Łęki Małe (Poland) (see Chapter 42). The two large mounds at Leubingen and Helmsdorf, which are strikingly similar, have been dated by dendrochronology (Leubingen: excavation 1877: 1942 [± 10] BC; Helmsdorf: excavation 1906–7: 1840 [± 60] BC; Becker, Krause, and Kromer 1989). According to the lavish grave goods, only one person was laid to rest in the burial chamber of these large mounds. Many grave goods were provided, some of gold. Altogether, the weight of all the gold objects from these 'princely graves' amounts to c.1 kg in the form of tools (flanged axes), pins, bracelets, diadems, and finger-rings. There are also bronze weapons such as axes, daggers, halberds, chisel-like tools, a cushion stone, and a large Middle Neolithic stone axe. The halberd, a pan-European weapon presumed to be of Irish origin, the stone axe, and the golden ceremonial axes (like the Dieskau axe), must also have functioned as insignia of status. The building of these burial monuments required a huge investment of labour. Rich hoards of metal objects from the same time and, to some extent, with the same forms were also found around several of the giant mounds (e.g. Bennewitz, Dieskau, Halle-Kanena, and Neunheiligen).

In comparison with the generally modestly furnished flat graves of the Únětice culture, the few princely graves of the 'Leubingen Group' convey a clear social differentiation, with concentration of wealth and power in a few—almost without exception—male personages. What brought about this almost unique social differentiation is still unclear. Certainly, close proximity to the copper deposits in the Harz foothills (e.g. Helmsdorf) was important on the one hand, just as the rich finds around Halle/Saale (e.g. Dieskau) can be explained, on the other hand, by the evidence of salt extraction at this time in Halle-Giebichenstein. However, there might be another explanation: a possible control of the exchange of metals (copper from the Alpine region [Krause 2003]; source of tin unknown), amber (from the western Baltic Sea), and salt (from Halle) on the trade route from the Danube to Scandinavia, which dates back to the Neolithic. Even today, however, there is no definite proof of the exploitation of central German copper and tin deposits at this time (Rassmann 2005).

Comparable burials are rare north of the central German Únětice culture. Rich hoards (Bresinchen I, II; Melz I, II) have been recorded in Brandenburg and Mecklenburg. The later Únětice culture reaches its north-eastern border in eastern lower Saxony, where it affects the Late Neolithic *Riesenbecher* ('Giant Beaker' group).

There are hardly any recorded graves from the end of the Únětice culture. It seems that the situation must be understood through the emergence of fortifications or small hill forts, which show strong connections to the middle Danube area (Maďarovce, Věteřov). At Zwenkau (Saxony) there is a low rampart surrounding large longhouses (Huth and Stäuble 1998), as well known from other areas (e.g. Schöningen) (Maier 1996). The end of this once-powerful culture is still unclear. It disappeared at the start of the Middle Bronze Age.

There are other pockets of EBA groups in the southern German region between the Alps and the Rhine and Main, mainly from flat cemeteries (crouched inhumations) with burials oriented according to sex (following the tradition of the Bell Beaker culture); some of the graves are furnished with tree-trunk coffins and/or stone covers. The groups are linked by the modesty of their copper grave goods, and a parallel is drawn between them and the earlier Únětice culture (Bz A1). The Straubing group is spread through southern and south-eastern Bavaria (e.g. cemeteries at Straubing and Alteglofsheim), and adjoins the Ries group to the west (Nähermemmingen cemetery). There are also the Singen group on the upper Rhine, the Hochrhein-Oberrhein group on the northern upper Rhine (Singen cemetery), and the Neckar group (Remseck-Aldingen cemetery) further north. In Weilheim, home of the Neckar group, a 4.5 m-high stone stele was found, with images of halberds and an oval disc or crescent moon depicted in relief. Adjoining these Early Bronze Age groups to the north is the Adlerberg group, which spreads across the northern upper Rhine and lower Main region (cemeteries at Worms-Adlerberg, Hofheim, and Trebur). There are scarcely any known settlements. The graves are provided mostly with small pieces of copper ornaments made from sheet-metal and wire, including cross-regional types of pins (oar and disc-headed: *Ruder-* and *Scheibenkopfnadeln*) with a geometric decoration that is also seen on other objects, such as triangular dagger blades. Bone and shell ornaments continue to be widespread.

The period Bz A2 produces the first burial mounds and weapon hoards containing solid-hilted daggers (Gaubickelheim and the Ingolstadt halberd hoard) and tools (axes) made of classic tin-bronze. Finds from this Langquaid stage include the first socketed spearheads and flanged axes with a strongly curved cutting edge, as well as pins with a perforated spherical head. These are spread across broad regions of central Europe and represent a cultural 'equalizing' process at the end of the Early Bronze Age (Vogt 2004).

Intensive copper mining was undertaken in the Alpine area from this time (certainly in the eastern Alps; and probably on the headwaters of the Rhine in modern Switzerland: Krause 2003). The mined metal circulated in the Alpine foothills in the form of ring ingots (*Ösenhalsringe*) or bars (*Rippen- und Spangenbarren*), as well as flanged axes (Neyruz type, Salez: Krause 2003). Thousands of these bars are recorded as the sole or major component of large hoards (Mauthausen, Austria, weighing *c.*150 kg: Lenerz-de Wilde 1995).

There are only a few noteworthy EBA findspots north of the Rhine-Main line and west of the northern and eastern boundaries of the Únětice culture. Between the lower Rhine and Elbe there are various regional forms of the so-called *Riesenbecher* group (Pot Beaker, Bentheim Beaker), which are recorded from both cemeteries and settlement sites. They are in the Late Neolithic tradition, and in their twisted cord-decorated pottery (*Wickelschnurkeramik*) they fit into the transition to the Middle Bronze Age (Sögel-Wohlde Period) (Vogt 2004). Probably also belonging to this phase, which is difficult to differentiate, are the leaf-shaped flint daggers, like those recorded in their thousands from Period I of the Nordic Bronze Age and seen as stone substitutes for metal daggers. There are several striking objects that are imports from other regions (in particular the British Isles): the Wachtberg-Fritzdorf (Rhineland) gold beaker, gold lunulae from Schulenburg (Lower Saxony) and Butzbach (Hessen) (and their copper imitations?), the golden disc from Moordorf (near Aurich, Friesland, Fig. 40.2), and Anglo-Irish axes. Numerous single finds of flat axes with curving blade and early trapezoid flanged axes, some with a raised tin content, possibly indicate imports. These axes partially compensate for the apparent absence of finds in other areas.

Middle Bronze Age

The transition from Early Bronze Age to the Middle Bronze Age or Tumulus period (*Hügelgräberbronzezeit*) was very fluid in the different landscapes of central Europe. The

FIG. 40.2 The gold disc from Moordorf near Aurich (Lower Saxony) found in 1910, dm. 14.5 cm and metal thickness 0.14 mm.

Source: Niedersächsisches Landesmuseum Hannover.

Tumulus culture occupied a rather large area characterized by inhumations beneath large mounds, which were grouped together in cemeteries that range in size from fairly small to quite large. The multitude of preserved mounds and the often rich graves recorded in them make this short period one of the most distinctive periods in central Europe. The cemeteries, which often include dozens of mounds, convey an impressive and lasting picture of the prehistoric landscape and even today make it to some extent a visible 'landscape of the dead'.

The roundish-oval mounds are still about 1–2 m high. They are built of soil, sand, turf (sod), stone, or a combination of these materials (e.g. Görner 2002; Geschwinde 2000). Their architecture is very varied, depending on the resources available in each particular region. The mounds are often bounded by a stone setting, a ring ditch, or rings of wooden posts (especially in Westphalia and the Netherlands). Modern anthropological investigations indicate that the burial under the mound begins with that of one man (Geschwinde 2000). There is no doubt that each mound belongs to a small family group (Ripdorf: Geschwinde 2000). Single burials predominate; however, cremations begin and increase during the Middle Bronze Age. The body is usually buried prone and oriented north-south or east-west in graves that are often protected by stones or burial chambers with wooden fittings. The central burial is then joined by any number of additional burials at the same or—more frequently—a higher level in the mound. Sometimes there are flat graves between the mounds or, especially in north-western Germany, long parallel rows of posts that lead to the mounds.

The dead were buried with their personal equipment. Men were provided with weapons (comprising—infrequently—sword, dagger, axe, and spearhead) and ornaments (usually a pin or bracelet) (Fig. 40.3a). Women's grave goods consisted of rich costume ornaments (Fig. 40.3b). 'Baltic' amber ornaments were very popular (spacer plates), and there are sites with hundreds,

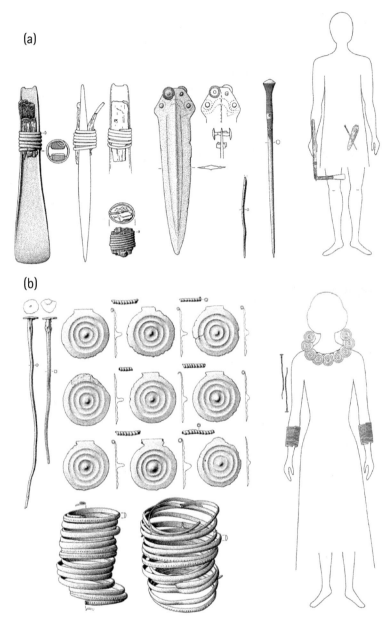

FIG. 40.3 (a) Wolnzach-Niederlauterbach (Bavaria), tumulus 1, grave 1: male burial of the earlier Tumulus culture (Bz B and later) with axe, dagger blade and pins, and a reconstruction of how they were worn; (b) Wolnzach-Niederlauterbach (Bavaria), tumulus 1, grave 2: jewellery of a female burial of the earlier Tumulus culture (Bz B and later) with pins, and neck ring with discs and spiral roll ornaments, as well as arm spirals and a reconstruction of how they were worn.

Source: U. Wels-Weyrauch.

even thousands, of amber beads in Württemberg (Hundersingen) and southern Bavaria (the Ingolstadt hoard has around 2,800), far more than in Nordic Bronze Age graves (see Chapter 41).

At the start of the Middle Bronze Age several innovations spread quickly and with lasting effect across central Europe, including Germany: swords (based on influences from the Danube region) and spears (socketed spearheads) appear as new weapons, while two-edged razors, tweezers, knives, and sickles are the new tools. Many small axes (flanged axes, *Absatzbeile*) might also have served as weapons. The use of the horse as a transport animal (for wagons and battle chariots) is particularly significant, and evidence for this is seen specifically in decorated bridle or cheek-pieces made from antler and bone. The grave goods reveal only very slight social ranking. In all, a largely egalitarian, or homogeneous, society can be inferred (Geschwinde 2000; Görner 2002).

The Middle Bronze Age can be divided into a number of short phases, each of which lasts only a few generations. While the older phase (Bz B or Lochham period) is characterized by certain bronze forms in widespread use, including the oldest solid-hilted swords (*Vollgriffschwerter*) (Spatzenhausen type) and rapier-like swords with organic hilt, in the following period (Bz C1–C2) it is possible to identify several regional groups by the distinctive metal fittings worn on their clothing. The regional groups of southern Germany up to the northern edge of the Mittelgebirge are distinguishable primarily by their grave goods: the southern Bavarian group, Alb group (Swabia), Haguenau group (Alsace), Rhine-Main and Fulda-Werra groups, Thuringian group, and Upper Palatinate group (closely linked to the western and southern Bohemian groups). To the north of the Mittelgebirge is the Lüneburg group, which is very closely related to the south German groups, particularly the Fulda-Werra group (north and east Hesse), but also has features of the Nordic Bronze Age (Period II). These groups had a range of about 50–100 sq km and were in close neighbourly contact. They also exchanged their women (the so-called *fremde Frauen*, foreign women phenomenon). As in the preceding EBA, the cultural forms grew weaker as one travelled down the Rhine, both in the middle and lower Rhine lands and in Westphalia. Here there are close cultural ties with the Low Countries, as evidenced particularly in the construction of burial mounds ringed by wooden posts and an already significant proportion of cremation burials (see Chapter 31).

During the MBA most bronzes were made inside Germany. It is often postulated that the Mittelgebirge copper deposits were exploited; however, to date this has not been proved (Jockenhövel 1983). MBA settlements are not well known. Rural settlements were probably close to the burial mounds and consisted of only a few houses or just a single farmstead. There are hill forts at the beginning and end of the period. For reasons that are not yet understood, the societies of the MBA pushed ahead with 'colonization' in the Mittelgebirge. This could have been driven by population pressure or social conflict. However, economic special interests, such as the as yet unproved mining of local copper, salt production, or regional transhumance, could also have been behind this development (Görner 2002).

Late Bronze Age

In the Late Bronze Age (Urnfield period) cremation gained acceptance in central Europe, from the thirteenth century BC onward. These ritual burials differed from one culture group to another. Not until around 1100 BC (Ha A2) was urn burial the common and standardized burial practice in much of southern Germany (Wiesner 2009). The dead were burned on a pyre, then the remains of their bones and ashes were picked out, scattered in graves, or interred in clay pots. Burials differ depending on time and region, with graves ranging from the very simple to constructions protected by stones. The urn is placed in the grave together with other clay vessels, which sometimes form complete table services (Wiesner 2009). As such cremations were already occurring in no small number in the MBA, a regional continuity of ritual is to be assumed, rather than a possible foreign innovation brought from the Danube region in the course of a migration. The move to cremation, which also leads to the general disappearance of burial mounds, was probably due to a change in religious beliefs based on social status and identity, burial rites, and a new range of symbols (water birds) (Primas 2008). Beside cremation burial there were still inhumations, which, because they were often richly equipped, involve both a tradition coming from the Tumulus culture and a social element.

The Urnfield period is generally divided according to its bronze forms into a number of phases that span Bz D/Ha A1, Ha A1 and Ha A2, Ha B1, and Ha B2/3, and lead into the Early Iron Age (Hallstatt period) (Müller-Karpe 1959; Sperber 1987). Iron was still an expensive metal in central Europe in the later Bronze Age; occasionally it was used to make ornaments and to decorate sword blades (especially damascening) (Primas 2008: 126–7).

In the LBA greater cultural standardization followed the geographical splintering of the MBA. Many metal forms (especially weapons and tools) appeared across large areas; however, there are also many regional variations in ornaments (especially fibulae) and pottery. From these the following local culture groups can be distinguished in southern Germany: the southern Bavarian group in the Alpine foothills (with connections to the Alpine Hötting-Morzg group [Tyrol] and the southern Alpine area) (Schütz 2006); the Franconia-Palatinate group in eastern Bavaria (with strong echoes of the western Bohemian groups: Knovíz, Milavče); westwards to the Rhine is the lower Main-Swabian group (Kreutle 2007); and the Rhenish-Swiss-Eastern France group (RSFO, see Chapters 32 and 39) occupies the left side of the upper and middle Rhine, and the Mosel and Saarland. The Lausitz group extends through central and eastern Germany and also influences the frontier areas (Thuringia, Harz Mountains, Brandenburg, and Mecklenburg), where a great many small groups develop (the Saale Mouth group, Unstrut group, Helmsdorf group, Elb-Havel group, etcetera).

LBA pottery and bronzes show less differentiation north of the Mittelgebirge zone, between the lower Rhine and the Saale and Elbe. From around 1000 BC these landscapes are increasingly influenced by the later Nordic Bronze Age (Periods IV and V). The LBA lasts until Period VI (c.600 BC), but it is visible in some imported objects (swords, razor-knives, bronze vessels, fibulae) from the Early Iron Age in southern Germany. The appearance of the Jastorf culture around 600–550 BC signals the end of the Bronze Age in this region.

All in all, there is a greater range of burial rituals in the Urnfield period than in the Tumulus period. The custom of cremation limits the possibility of reconstructing clothing. The grave goods only faintly reflect the actual lifestyle or function, in other words status, of the dead: Margarita Primas (2008: 95) speaks of a 'veiled, foggy' hierarchy. Many areas like lower Bavaria have only a few weapons among hundreds of graves. Nevertheless, clear signs of a vertical hierarchization of Urnfield society begin to emerge. There are few 'rich' graves, compared with masses of 'simple' ones (Sperber 1999; Clausing 2005; Wiesner 2009).

The majority of Urnfield burials are provided only with pottery grave goods; next are the graves that contain a few ornaments and decorative objects (pins and small ornaments). The 'richer' graves have knives and/or razors, and some have simple weapons (bows and arrows). The wealthiest graves are furnished with larger weapons (swords, spearheads), and bronze drinking vessels, or wagon parts, as well as high-quality bronze and gold ornaments (Clausing 2005). Most are the graves of adult men, conventionally described as 'chieftains' or 'nobles'. Graves of women are rare, though sometimes they followed the men in death, as shown by double (male with female) burials. The central figure in LBA society is the sword-bearer (Sperber 1999).

Warriors now bore swords with leaf-shaped blades that were used to cut or slash, whereas the earlier blades were used as thrusting weapons. The sword types found are solid-hilted (*Vollgriffschwerter*), or rod-tanged (*Griffangelschwerter*), and grip-tongue or flanged (*Griffzungenschwerter*) with an organic hilt. The warrior had a spear for throwing or thrusting at his side. In most cases the spear shafts were made of ash. Arrows with specially shaped heads were used as projectiles or for hunting and kept in a quiver of organic material with bronze fittings. Double buttons belong to a weapon-belt made of leather or fabric. More simply furnished male graves frequently also contain bronze knives and razors. Whetstones were used to sharpen both tools and weapons.

Female graves are identifiable from grave goods consisting of rich ornaments and dress fittings, especially head ornaments, neck-rings and wide anklets, as well as bracelets, fibulae, and one to two pins. Beside delicate hair-rings, headbands, and earrings, rich female attire includes neck ornaments (either a solid neck ring or a chain of spirally rolled beads called *Spiralröllchen*, some with amber and/or blue glass beads, and gold discs), and different kinds of pins, fibulae, bracelets, etcetera. They wore rings with a ribbed pattern on their fingers and occasionally wide, richly decorated ankle bands. On the whole, however, female graves are less richly furnished than male graves. The size of the graves and the urns used as containers for cremated remains reflect the age and sex differences between men and women, and boys and girls (Falkenstein 2006).

Children's graves are characterized by small bracelets, amulets, miniature vessels, and feeding vessels. Their grave goods are usually similar to those provided for women (their mothers?) (Wiesner 2009: 481).

Occasionally the rich graves contain vessels made of beaten bronze: mostly small cups, sometimes buckets, cauldrons, and sieves as parts of a complete drinking service (Jacob 1995: Fig. 4) (Fig. 40.4). Items of bronze body armour (helmets, corslets, greaves, shields) are totally unknown as grave goods. Such objects are, however, recorded from wet places (rivers, bogs) or from hoards, where they have been deposited in fragments.

The graves of an upper social stratum stand out from the simply furnished graves. They are identified by their construction (stone blocks, dry walls, or chambers of wooden beams, oriented with striking regularity in a north-south direction in south-western Germany: Falkenstein 2006); by the type of burial (sometimes cremated lying on a wagon [Clausing 2005] or a double interment of man and woman [Sperber 1999], at times also uncremated); and by the grave goods (weapons, bronze vessels, and gold ornaments). Sometimes it is possible to infer different generations from the position of such graves in relation to one another. These unusually rich graves include wagon-graves of the Poing/Hart an der Alz type. Such warrior graves spread through the Alpine foothills from eastern France to upper Austria (Clausing 2005) and are characterized by a ceremonial chariot (always with four-spoke wheels), together with grave goods of small bronze weights and raw metal (see Chapters 22 and 29).

The largest known cemetery from the LBA is in southern Bavaria at Ingolstadt-Zuchering near the Danube (Schütz 2006). Here around 580 graves (out of c.800–1,000) have been excavated, documenting use of the cemetery for almost 500 years, from around 1300 BC to 800 BC. The population of the accompanying settlement is estimated at about 30 people.

FIG. 40.4 The vessels from the cremation burial at Unterglauheim (Blindheim, Bavaria), dating to the later Urnfield period (Ha B1). The cremated remains were kept in the two gold cups which were placed on top of each other and lay between the two bronze basins, which were placed in the bronze bucket with bird-sun-boat-motifs.

Photo: H. Hollo, Augsburg.

An unusual site is the Neckarsulm cemetery (Württemberg), which consists exclusively of inhumation burials, about 50 in all (Knöpke 2009), in single, double, and multiple graves. All are males, many were sword-bearers; arguably they form a 'male band' (*Männerbund*). They all have remarkably good constitutions, which sets them apart from the rest of the population.

The extensive necropolis at Warendorf-Neuwarendorf (Westphalia), with about 350 graves, can be considered the most important reference cemetery of the north-western German Bronze Age (Jockenhövel 2003). It can be divided into five main occupation phases, which lasted more than 1,500 years and spread from west to east on both sides of an unpaved road that can still be followed for a length of 140 m. The route of the ancient road determines the orientation of the early grave enclosures, the so-called 'long beds' (*Langbetten*) (see Chapter 22). The oldest graves date to the Eneolithic and only one grave dates from the EBA. Two large burial mounds from the Tumulus period are distinctly visible in the landscape and form the starting point for a continuous occupation of the cemetery. The LBA graves that follow take their dimensions from one of these mounds. Most of the burials date from this phase, when the gradual transition from inhumation to cremation occurs. The foundation grave (Grave 105) lies in a *Langbett* and is identified as a male grave by a dagger and spearhead. Graves shaped like a keyhole (*Schlüssellochgräber*) follow, and there are ring ditches as well as unenclosed graves, with cremated remains in small pits. The vast majority of individuals buried in the long graves and keyhole-shaped grave enclosures are males, as in the Netherlands. In contrast to many south German cemeteries, occupation here continues into the Iron Age. The graves contain only one or two pots and very rarely small ornaments (mostly small pins).

Eastern Germany: The Lausitz Culture

The successor to the Únětice culture, and several smaller groupings that were still trapped in the Late Neolithic milieu, was an extensive culture complex which developed in eastern central Europe at the beginning of the Middle Bronze Age. Defined as the Lausitz (Lusatian) culture (after Rudolf Virchow in 1880), it nevertheless divides up into numerous smaller groups. The very distinctive pre-Lausitz culture in eastern central Germany, Silesia, and Great Poland is a fringe group of the central European Urnfield culture (Gedl 1992), which, however, at the start of the LBA, acquired a cultural independence that lasted about nine hundred years. It is a large region, spanning the great river systems of the Elbe, Oder, and Vistula. Poor in raw materials, yet always acting as a kind of mediator between south and north, it is therefore open to many stimuli. In their burials and particularly in their pottery traditions and clothing, the Lausitz groups in north-eastern Bohemia, northern Moravia, northern Slovakia, central Germany, and central and southern Poland distinguish themselves clearly from their neighbours (see Chapters 42 and 43); possibly there was quite a strong ideological or political structure behind a number of these groups.

The western Lausitz culture can be broken down into several smaller subgroups between the Oder and the Elbe, indicating that there were impediments to the spread of particular burial features, pot styles, and costume habits (Schunke 2004). A number of regional groups formed on the western edge of the culture. They include the Saale Mouth group, the Unstrut group, and the Helmsdorf or Elb-Havel group (Schunke 2004).

The periodization of the culture is made possible by the pottery typical of each phase (Buck 1989). The pre-Lausitz phase 1 (Bz B–C) is identified by pots ornamented with 'warts'; phase II (Bz C–D) by pots with rings of bosses; phase III (Bz D–Ha A1) by sharply angular, fluted pots; and phase IV (Ha A2–Ha C1) by pots with horizontal grooves. The late development is seen in the Billendorf phase, where strong influences from the eastern Alpine Hallstatt culture become apparent (Buck 1989). It is difficult to establish a correlation with hoards from the same region, as the graves contain few bronze objects (von Brunn 1968). The often very rich hoards with various bronze objects (also originating in the Danube area) complete the picture of an interlinking system of communication.

The large urnfields typical of the Lausitz culture were occupied over many generations, so they often contain thousands of graves (e.g. Tornow, Niederkaina, Liebersee, Saalhausen, Klein Lieskow, Neuendorf). The grave goods comprise almost exclusively large numbers of pots, with only few and small metal objects, such as pins, ornaments, and metal tools (knives, single-edged razors). As there are no graves with weapons and rich ornaments, the social hierarchy of these large groups is obscure. There are weapon burials, particularly in the Elbe-Saale region, which functions as a corridor between the Danube and the western Baltic, especially in the older phases of the LBA (Bz D to Ha B1) (von Brunn 1968).

In the Lausitz area, as in central Europe at the same time, a dense network of fortified settlements arose, some on high ground and plains, others on marshlands and islands. They functioned as centres where metalwork was particularly concentrated (e.g. Niederneundorf, Senftenberg, Dresden-Coschütz). Bronze-workers evidently enjoyed high standing, since a fair number of burials include casting moulds as grave goods (Jockenhövel 1990). Assemblages of metal objects—weapons especially—were deposited as supplies or as votive or sacrificial offerings. The Lausitz culture drew to an end with its late manifestations (Billendorf group, Aurith group, and Göritz group) around 500–400 BC, in a changing world of worsening climatic conditions, soil erosion, indigenous and exogenous factors (strong influences from the eastern Hallstatt culture group), as well as the emergence of iron technology. Probably the 'Scythians' or other mounted nomads also contributed to the Lausitz decline. Evidence of these people (the gold hoard at Witaszkowo, formerly Vettersfelde, lower Silesia) is found as far away as the Oder.

Northern Germany: The Nordic Bronze Age

The so-called Nordic Bronze Age, or Nordic culture area *(Nordischer Kreis)*, has represented one of the most striking developments of the European Bronze Age ever since the early days of systematic research. The culture stretches across the north German and south Scandinavian region, especially in the western Baltic area. Building on the Late Neolithic foundation of the Single Grave culture, an Early Bronze Age culture develops during a lengthy transition phase from around 2200 to 1700–1600 BC. In many respects this culture continues Stone Age traditions. This is especially evident in the thousands of flint daggers (which gives it the alternative name 'Dagger Period'). However, this culture must be seen in connection with the metal-using cultures that shared its southern boundaries, especially the Únětice culture. The metal finds, in particular the flat axes and flanged axes, are at first imported from both central and western Europe (so-called Anglo-Irish axes), but they increasingly assume their own native forms in a different craft tradition, which depended throughout the Bronze Age on a metal supply from central Europe (Krause 2003). There are rich metal hoards (Melz, Malchin) with halberds and solid-hilted daggers from the zone of contact between the Únětice culture of central Germany and the EBA in Mecklenburg. One example of the local metal craft is the Malchin-type dagger, cast in one piece (Wüstemann 1995).

Tin-bronze becomes established at the beginning of the following period, which is initially marked by a widely distributed set of forms consisting of flanged axes, early spearheads, and pins with perforated spherical head. They are influenced by the south German and Swiss culture area. The Sögel-Wohlde culture leads to a distinct cultural development that spreads from the eastern lowlands across Westphalia to Jutland. It is characterized particularly by inhumations in burial mounds and at this stage—unlike the contemporaneous Tumulus culture of central Europe—is only known from male graves. They are identified by their grave goods: short swords or daggers, flanged axes, heart-shaped flint arrowheads, pins, and occasionally small rings formed of spirally wound gold wire.

The Rastorf (east Holstein) burial mound, raised over a megalithic grave, represents a short-lived development at the start of the Nordic Bronze Age. The oldest male grave with its triangular dagger belongs to the EBA; above it there is an early solid-hilted sword (of Sögel or Apa type); the latest burial contains a Wohlde short sword.

If the find circumstances and context are reliable, the Mittelberge assemblage near Nebra (with Sögel-Wohlde swords and axes) (Sachsen-Anhalt) is datable to the beginning of the Middle Bronze Age. The large mysterious sheet-gold 'Sky Disc', with its astral symbols (sun, moon, stars), a boat (?), and two 'horizon arcs', was reworked several times in the ancient past (see Chapter 14). It is widely considered to be the oldest concrete representation of the heavens, or a kind of calendar, a 'memogram' (as is also presumed for the gold 'hats', mostly dating to the MBA). At present it is impossible to reach a definitive conclusion about its function and significance (Pernicka et al. 2008).

There is no doubt that the Sögel-Wohlde forms stand at the beginning of the flourishing Bronze Age culture (Periods II–III: c.1450–1250 BC; 1250–1100 BC), which is recorded north of the Elbe (including the district around Stade) and also in Schleswig-Holstein. Magnificent finds of high technical and artistic quality come from large burial mounds with stone cist graves, with or without oak coffins, which still mark the landscape today. The mounds, as in central Europe, contain several graves, often a man and woman placed together simultaneously, or sometimes successively, and possibly with a distinction between generations (e.g. the Galgenberg near Itzehoe). Thus the mound as a whole can be viewed as the family burial site of an egalitarian society, belonging to an agriculturally oriented single farm.

In all of its stages the Nordic Bronze Age absorbed stimuli from the central European region, most of all early in the period as shown by early swords (of Apa type), the first spearheads, and the spiral ornamentation that was later transformed into a local artistic style. Local forms were developed: the first fibulae (two-part fibulae) as clothing fasteners, and the razor-knife with a carved horse-head hilt. The bronzes were usually cast with little reforging. Nevertheless, as well as cast-bronze vessels, there are some early vessels made of gold and sheet bronze, which were probably of local manufacture. Some assemblages, for example of sickle-sword weapons, double-axe ornaments, and wooden folding chairs with bronze hinges (Daensen find from the Stade group) are reminiscent of Mycenaean, Near Eastern, and Egyptian models. Finds of Baltic amber in the eastern Mediterranean region (the Qatna Kings' Graves, the Uluburun shipwreck, and the Mycenaean Shaft Graves) suggest they may be exchange gifts through direct or indirect connections, via land or sea. Other items, like furs or stockfish, might also have been exchanged.

Several regional groups in Schleswig-Holstein and western Mecklenburg can be identified by specific weapon combinations. Examples are the western Holstein group (sword, spearhead), the Segeberg group (sword, palstave, like the Stade group), and the western Mecklenburg group (sword, palstave, dagger).

In male burials there is an unmistakable emphasis on fighting, so chiefs and warriors are referred to as representatives of a prosperous, rurally structured community, which was not, however, very large in number. Near the burial mounds are the isolated farmsteads that have only been investigated in recent decades, identified as early house-and-barn buildings, where a byre is provided for the cattle. This house form, so well adapted to its surroundings, continued to exist in the region until the pre-modern period. The site of Handewitt (Schleswig-Flensburg district) is revealing, because it shows the instability of Bronze Age settlements. Within a short period there were, in turn, farmland (plough traces), a house-and-barn (*Wohnstallhaus*), and a burial mound on this site.

Among the valuable finds, the so-called *Trachthügel* (costume-mounds) are important as they preserved objects that otherwise would have decayed, such as wooden vessels decorated with tin studs in star-like shapes (from the Stade group: Heerstedt), and the remains of woollen clothing (e.g. Harrislee). Of particular note in this region are cast bronze vessels (Jacob 1995; Martin 2009), which partially resemble the wooden vessels.

Period III saw the inclusion of other areas in this independent cultural region, in particular, Mecklenburg-Vorpommern (von Brunn 1968), indicating a dynamic process whose sequence of events cannot be fully understood. The first imports of bronze vessels from the Danube-Moravia-Bohemia region appear, giving rise to local imitations. Particularly striking are the cauldron-wagons from Peckatel (Mecklenburg) and Skallerup (Zealand), which, as cult equipment, bear the symbols of a new religious movement that quickly takes hold in central Europe (e.g. Skallerup with its bird symbolism). This movement also brings the change from inhumation to cremation, which predominates from now on in the north, and is practised exclusively from Period IV. Cemeteries may contain up to several hundred urn burials (urnfields), as in southern Germany. Often they are placed around older grave monuments (megalithic graves, older Bronze Age tumuli) (memorials?) and they are occupied until the Early Iron Age (eg. Schwanbeck, district Mecklenburg-Strelitz). If anything, they contain only a few small grave goods (for example, razors, tweezers, pins, awls), while larger objects, such as swords, now occur in miniature form. Often the bronzes are placed together in hoards and deposited outside the graves as 'treasures of the dead' (*Totenschätze*). Many ritual bog depositions contain collections of male or (mainly in the later phase) female ornaments, which correspond to grave goods. In the Late Bronze Age pots are used more often than before as containers for cremated remains; however, the variety seen in southern German or the Lausitz area is never reached. Clay urns shaped like houses (*Hausurnen*) or human faces (*Gesichtsurnen*) are a special form from the end of the Bronze Age. At the same time, certain stone implements become important, like the axes known as *nackengebogene Äxte*.

During Periods IV and V there was a further expansion of the cultural (and political) influences of the Nordic Bronze Age. Regionally specific bronzes characteristic of the north (single-bladed razor-knives, often with boat decoration, tweezers, brooches or *Plattenfibeln*, and cast bronze bowls) are spread in burials and hoards across Lower Saxony as far as the lower Rhine, and from eastern Holland through the entire German lowlands to Pomerania. A few magnificent graves stand out from the mass of relatively modestly furnished graves, such as Albersdorf (Dithmarschen district, Holstein) or the 'King's Grave' at Seddin (parish of Gross Pankow, Prignitz district, Brandenburg), which indicate a similar social evolution to contemporaneous central European cultures (Hostomice, Bohemia; St-Romain-de-Jalionas, Western Alps).

There are still many hypotheses for the amassing of such wealth in the 'King's Grave' (Period V) at Seddin, which was excavated in 1899. An enormous amount of work was also expended on the construction of the grave that contained three cremation burials. The primary burial in a chased bronze amphora is that of a warrior (sword, axe, razor-knife, comb, etcetera), the secondary burials contain the cremated remains of two women who died with him. Other relatively richly furnished graves are found in the region around Seddin. They are also notable for their grave goods of wagon parts (bronze wheels, fittings) and horse harness (cheek-pieces).

During Period V many bronzes from the south-western German-Swiss area were imported into the north and east of Germany. They are evidence of a line of cross-regional communication that replaces the older route from the Danube region via the Elbe and Oder. Some examples from Periods III and IV are the bronze vessels. Of pan-European significance are the four LBA bronze spoked wheels from Stade (total weight $c.45$–50 kg). They belong to one or two ceremonial wagons and prove cultural links as far away as the Pyrenees (see Chapter 22).

High-quality large bronzes are still created, like the hanging-bowl, whose function remains unclear, and in particular the trumpet-like lurs, played in pairs (see Chapter 41). Other large objects made of beaten sheet bronze, such as round shields of Herzsprung type (named after examples from a site in Brandenburg), or bronze amphorae of the Seddin/Herzsprung/Rørbæk type, are most probably made in a few highly skilled workshops.

The end of the Nordic Bronze Age occurs in Period VI. Although the custom of urn burial continued, this period produces few bronzes. As well as objects of local production, there are also imports from central Europe from the Early Iron Age Hallstatt culture (swords and razors). Period VI leads into Jastorf culture of the later Iron Age, which is one of the archaeological groups for which there are sound reasons to see a connection with the Germanic tribes first mentioned in ancient sources in the first century BC.

The numerous hoards in the bogs of northern Germany are very important. The bronze objects in particular add to the stock of forms in the Late Bronze Age, because only a small number of forms have been recorded from graves. A votive deposit of imported bronzes (a helmet of the Biebesheim type, and swords), recovered from the Lesum (near the Weser at Bremen), is comparable to the south German river finds.

Settlement

There are essentially three settlement types that can be distinguished during the Bronze Age in central Europe, including Germany: open settlements without fortifications, fortified settlements (hill forts), and settlements on damp ground (lakeside sites or pile dwellings).

Open Settlements

The traditions that applied to Neolithic settlements continued into the Bronze Age. This is particularly so for the areas where self-sufficient farming settlements dominate (Assendorp 1997; Schefzik 2001). For the most part they are located on or near fertile soils, especially on lowland sites which are not flood-prone, or on slopes or hilltops, so that they have access to the valley meadows on the one hand and economically productive lands on the other. Proximity to water is the crucial factor. Some settlements ensured their water supply by building wells, which at times also served as places of sacrifice (e.g. Berlin-Lichterfelde; Atting, Lower Bavaria; Grossschkorlopp, Saxony). The houses lasted only a short time because they were made of wattle and daub, but the lifespan of the settlement itself was no longer than three to five generations. It seems that when the soil was exhausted of nutrients for cultivation, people moved on, within the same region.

Germany has produced few EBA settlements, but that near Ingolstadt-Zuchering (Upper Bavaria) serves to convey the basic 'village' structure: five trapezoidal houses spread over an area of about 2 hectares (Fig. 40.5). All that remains are the postholes for their timber uprights. The houses are uniformly oriented (north-south). The house size varies, with a length of 20–25 m and a width of 6–10 m; the floor area is approximately 120–250 m^2. Inside, storage vessels were set into the floor. Such EBA longhouses have now been found elsewhere in south and central Germany; they are typical of almost all central European culture groups (Schefzik 2001).

FIG. 40.5 Reconstruction of the Early Bronze Age settlement of Zuchering-Ingolstadt (Bavaria).

Source: A. Wimmer, Poing.

Few house floor-plans are known from the following MBA; settlements are mostly domestic sites with pottery. It was long the view that there were scarcely any permanent settlements, due to the apparent dominance of pastoralism in the economy of the period. Today, however, it is known that there were settlements in almost all areas and landscapes during the MBA, and that this period stands out as a time of settlement expansion. Besides the fertile lowlands, that is the productive loess soils, higher areas and hill sites were also sought out. Thus the Alps were widely settled during the period, and a system similar to a mountain pasture economy was in operation. These settlements would have been involved to some extent with the Alpine copper mining that took place in the Inn Valley in Austria until the LBA.

During the LBA settlements in many places again appear to be concentrated on the fertile soils. The huge number of finds is proof of a very dense settlement. Excavations of some of the larger settlements of this time convey an impression of their physical structure (for example, Unterhaching, Bavaria; Zedau, Sachsen-Anhalt; Berlin-Buch) (Schefzik 2001). They measured some 10–20 hectares in extent, but were not intensively occupied. The houses were mostly oriented north-south. Empty spaces indicate open areas within the village.

From the position of the posts it is possible to reconstruct relatively small (4–6 m by 4–6 m), rectangular, one-storey, predominantly one- and two-aisled, sometimes three-aisled buildings of $c.20$–40 m^2. The walls are mostly wattle and daub. The painting of internal walls was widespread, even if it has only rarely been preserved—white and red have been verified—and/or some form of plastic decoration was also carried out. As the floors of the houses have suffered from erosion, there is seldom evidence for hearths or ovens inside, but they do appear outside the houses, where perhaps they were shared by several families.

Smaller four- or six-post structures are identified as stores raised on stilts, for grain and other farm products. Probably the base was set high above ground level so that animals could not reach the supplies.

The settlement area was generally strewn with many pits of varying size and shape, which also had a partly ritual function. Grain was stored underground in them, while a number served as tanners' pits, others held soil or clay for building, or clay for ceramic production. These had a protective cover if necessary. Heavy looms were set up in pit houses.

Most of the rural settlements had no particular protection. It has been established that a few had palisades and/or thorn fences, which might have been meant to keep the animals out of the settlement, or else to hold them inside it (e.g. Berlin-Lichterfelde). In southern Bavaria a particular form of settlement emerged towards the end of the Bronze Age: a single farmstead set inside a rectangular system of palisades and ditches. These were the forerunners of a popular Iron Age settlement form called the leader's compound (*Herrenhof*).

The single farmstead is the typical settlement form for the north-west German region, and consisted of a *Wohnstallhaus* with small ancillary buildings. A characteristic of this zone is that to date there are no known fortified settlements; simple fences were their only protection. Another characteristic is the wide distribution of mostly long (up to 20–40 m by 10–15 m), three-aisled *Wohnstallhäuser* (house-and-barn), especially towards the end of the LBA. These rural settlements were largely self-sufficient apart from supplies of sought-after raw materials (copper, tin, amber, glass, etcetera). As a rule they numbered no more than 50–80 persons; thus a settlement would consist of only five to eight families. Rarely did it last longer than three or four generations.

Fortified Settlements

A dense network of fortifications protected by walls, gates, and outer defence ditches dot the central European landscape in the Bronze Age (Jockenhövel 1990). Even here, however, there are regional differences. The hill forts multiply over time in particular 'stronghold horizons'. The first horizon occurs in the transition from Early to Middle Bronze Age, the second in the transition from Middle to Late Bronze Age, and the third at the end of the Bronze Age. This cyclical fluctuation is evidently connected to prevailing social, economic, and ecological conditions and to changes in them (Jockenhövel 1990).

Nevertheless, the Bronze Age enthusiasm for fort building did not affect every part of Germany. In the EBA it is confined to the regions that are influenced by the Middle Danube culture. There, it is native especially to the Mad`arovce/Věteřov culture, a dynamic group that influences the late phase of the EBA of south and central Germany.

During the MBA fort building almost completely disappears in Germany, as it does in the rest of central Europe. It reappears only at the start of the LBA, when it is highly developed, particularly in south Germany and in central and eastern Germany, the home of the Lausitz culture. There are well over a hundred of these constructions, not all of which were built at the same time. Most of the forts in eastern south Germany belong to the early and middle phase of the Urnfield period, those in the west almost exclusively to the late phase, while the Lausitz culture forts in many cases extend into the earlier Iron Age, some only being constructed in this period.

While the early fortifications have a relatively small internal surface area of up to 3 hectares, later fortifications are considerably larger: up to 30 hectares or more. Unfortunately larger-scale excavation inside such sites, which might elucidate their function, has yet to take place.

The forts are mostly situated on prominent and naturally protected sites: on hilltops, on plateau-like flat-topped hills (*mesas*), or land that is protected by loops of river bends in the south German hill country and Mittelgebirge areas, and on sand ridges surrounded by marshland in eastern Germany. The hilltops and mountain tops are fortified with solid ramparts, the river sites with rows of embankments. Usually the defensive walls are adapted to the natural conditions. The fortified area varies in size from 1 to more than 30 hectares: smaller hilltops are 1–1.5 hectares, embanked sites 2–6 hectares, the combined systems 10–17 hectares, and the flat-topped hills 10–30 hectares, with exceptional cases of more than 100 hectares (e.g. the Bullenheimer Berg).

The population of such forts is estimated at up to one thousand. From the location of fortified settlements and their distance apart in certain well-researched regions, the circumference and area of such 'territories' can be determined: they covered about 50–150 km^2. From certain finds it can also be assumed that they had an additional function as cult places.

The ramparts that are still visible today are really walls that have collapsed. Their construction is very varied, the local variations depending on the building materials available. Outside the walls there was a ditch. The few entrances, the gates, were simple openings with barriers that could easily be moved together. There is a remarkable strongly fortified gate at Heunischenburg near Kronach, a fort which, to judge from the many weapons found, must have served as a kind of military base (Abels 2002).

Almost all the Bronze Age fortified settlements have a wealth of often valuable finds, including status-specific bronzes of the elite (weapons, horse harness, bronze vessels). Within the forts there are traces of dense occupation that indicate an increased population, and longer and permanent occupation of the site. These fortified settlements were 'suburbs' of the unfortified agrarian settlements that belonged to them. They can be regarded as specially protected 'concentration centres' for the political, social, economic, and religious life of the local community, the group that regarded them as centres of safety. A hierarchy of fortified highland settlements, unfortified highland settlements, and open lowland settlements must have existed. It has not yet been possible, however, to provide information about the interior of the residential buildings of the upper social classes in these forts.

Extensive research into the Hünenburg near Watenstedt (eastern Lower Saxony), and its Urnfield cemetery, has opened up a whole LBA landscape (from the twelfth century BC), with a fortified settlement and a large annexe (*Vorburg*) (15 hectares), an unfortified outer settlement (with houses), as well as a cemetery (Beierstedt). Evidence of a local metal workshop is significant—objects cast there include swords and high-quality hanging bowls—as also are signs of the very early cultivation of winter cereals (Heske 2008).

Large hoards have been discovered in many forts (e.g. Bullenheimer Berg; Bleibeskopf, Dresden-Coschütz). This accumulation served both profane and religious purposes. High-quality craft production, in particular of fine metal products, was concentrated in the forts. Numerous workshops are examples of this (e.g. Hesselberg; Runder Berg near Urach; Niederneundorf). It can be assumed that there were specialist craftsmen in the forts who worked for an elite or were dependent on it.

Settlements on Damp Ground and Pile Dwellings

A particular form of settlement was continued from the Neolithic into the Bronze Age; but ended around 850 BC. This was the pile dwelling (*palafitta*), or lakeside settlement (Schlichtherle 1997) (see Chapters 38 and 39). Early debate on whether these settlements were permanently on platforms above the water surface, as the well-known reconstructions of Unteruhldingen on Lake Constance would suggest, has since been settled in favour of settlements built close to the shore or occasionally in the soft muds close to the lake. Long and recurring periods of high water levels prevented continuous settlement of the lakeshore, which was possible only in dry periods. Such settlements thus existed mainly in the transition phases between the Early and Middle Bronze Age, and the early and middle Urnfield period, and at the end of the Urnfield period. The best-known sites on Lake Constance are the settlements of Bodman, Hagnau, and Unteruhldingen-Stollenwiesen (Schöbel 1996), on the Federsee in Upper Swabia, the Forschner settlement (Billamboz et al. 2009), and the Wasserburg settlement, both near Bad Buchau (see Chapter 39).

In spite of all the differences in timber architecture, there emerges a standardized type of settlement that was decided by its specific location and which differed from the contemporary forts and open settlements. Typical of these settlements is a systematic layout, with mainly circular, oval, or rectangular ground-plans. They were surrounded by breakwaters, strong palisades of protective posts. The Forschner settlement, for example, was accessible by a wooden bridge (Billamboz et al. 2010). In the settlements there were rows of houses and lanes set out either parallel or at right angles to one another. A kind of ring road inside the palisade provided access. The houses, with up to three aisles, were built as pile dwellings or log houses on posts or low mounds. The floor area varied in extent from 10 to 50 m^2. The settlement at Unteruhldingen-Stollenwiesen had up to 85 houses (Schöbel 1996). With an occupancy of four to eight persons per house, the settlement would have numbered approximately 340–680 people. Thus there are real villages, in contrast to the small open settlements on the mineral soils and the large fortified settlements of this region.

The economy of the damp-ground settlements was certainly oriented towards using the resources of the rivers and lakes. Mainly, however, like the dry-land settlements, they had a mixed agricultural economy. Cereal was cultivated and cattle were raised in their hinterland.

Bibliography

Abels, B.-U. (2002). *Die Heunischenburg bei Kronach. Eine späturnenfelderzeitliche Befestigung*, Regensburger Beiträge zur prähistorischen Archäologie, 9. Regensburg: Universitätsverlag Regensburg.

Assendorp, J. J. (ed.) (1997). *Forschungen zur bronzezeitlichen Besiedlung in Nord- und Mitteleuropa*. Internationales Symposium vom 9–11 Mai 1996 in Hitzacker. Internationale Archäologie, 38. Espelkamp: Marie Leidorf.

Bartelheim, M. (1998). *Studien zur böhmischen Aunjetitzer Kultur. Chronologische und chorologische Untersuchungen*, Universitätsforschungen zur prähistorischen Archäologie, 46. Bonn: Dr Rudolf Habelt.

Becker, B., Krause, R., and Kromer, B. (1989). 'Zur absoluten Chronologie der frühen Bronzezeit', *Germania*, 67/2: 421–42.

Billamboz, A., Köninger, J., Schlichtherle, H., and Torke, W. (2009). *Die früh- und mittelbronzezeitliche 'Siedlung Forschner' im Federseemoor. Befunde und Dendrochronologie*. Siedlungsarchäologie im Alpenvorland, XI. Forschungen und Berichte zur Vor- und Frühgeschichte in Baden-Württemberg, 113. Stuttgart: Theiss.

Brunn, W. A. v. (1968). *Mitteldeutsche Hortfunde der jüngeren Bronzezeit*, Römisch-Germanische Forschungen, 29. Berlin: De Gruyter.

Buck, D.-W. (1989). 'Zur chronologischen Gliederung der Lausitzer Gruppe', *Veröffentlichungen des Museums für Ur- und Frühgeschichte Potsdam*, 23: 75–95.

Clausing, Chr. (2005). *Untersuchungen zu den urnenfelderzeitlichen Gräbern mit Waffenbeigaben vom Alpenkamm bis zur Südzone des Nordischen Kreises. Eine Analyse ihrer Grabinventare und Grabformen.* Oxford: Hedges.

Falkenstein, F. (2006). 'Aspekte von Alter und Geschlecht im Bestattungsbrauchtum der nordalpinen Bronzezeit', in J. Müller (ed.), *Alter und Geschlecht in ur- und frühgeschichtlichen Gesellschaften. Tagung Bamberg 20–21 Februar 2004*, Universitätsforschungen zur prähistorischen Archäologie, 126. Bonn: Dr Rudolf Habelt, 73–90.

Gedl, M. (1992). *Die Vorlausitzer Kultur*, Prähistorische Bronzefunde, XXI, 2. Stuttgart: Steiner.

Geschwinde, M. (2000). *Die Hügelgräber auf der Großen Heide bei Ripdorf im Landkreis Uelzen*, Göttinger Schriften zur Vor- und Frühgeschichte, 27. Neumünster: Wachholtz.

Görner, I. (2002). *Bestattungssitten der Hügelbronzegräberzeit in Nord- und Osthessen*, Marburger Studien zur Vor- und Frühgeschichte, 20. Rahden/Westf.: Marie Leidorf.

Heske, I. (2006). *Die Hünenburg bei Watenstedt, Ldkr. Helmstedt. Eine ur- und frühgeschichtliche Befestigung und ihr Umfeld*, Göttinger Schriften zur Vor- und Frühgeschichte, 29. Neumünster: August Lax.

Huth, Ch. and Stäuble, H. (1998). 'Ländliche Siedlungen der Bronzezeit und älteren Eisenzeit. Ein Zwischenbericht aus Zwenkau', in H. Küster, A. Lang, and P. Schauer (eds.), *Archäologische Forschungen in urgeschichtlichen Siedlungslandschaften. Festschrift für Georg Kossack zum 75. Geburtstag*. Regensburg: Universitätsverlag, 185–230.

Jacob, Ch. (1995). *Metallgefässe der Bronze- und Hallstattzeit in Nordwest-, West- und Süddeutschland*, Prähistorische Bronzefunde, II, 9. Stuttgart: Steiner.

Jockenhövel, A. (1983). 'Kupferlagerstätten und prähistorische Metallverarbeitung in Nordhessen: zum Stand der Forschung', *Archäologisches Korrblatt*, 13: 65–73.

—— (1990). 'Bronzezeitlicher Burgenbau in Mitteleuropa. Untersuchungen zur Struktur frühmetallzeitlicher Gesellschaften', in Römisch-Germanisches Zentralmuseum, *Orientalisch-ägäische Einflüsse in der europäischen Bronzezeit. Ergebnisse eines Kolloquiums 16–19 Oktober 1985*, Römisch-Germanisches Zentralmuseum Monographien, 15. Bonn: Dr Rudolf Habelt, 209–28.

—— (2003). 'Von der Bronzezeit zur Eisenzeit: Bemerkungen zur Kontinuität und Diskontinuität auf ausgewählten Gräberfeldern Westdeutschlands', in R. Vasić (ed.), *Burial Customs in the Bronze and Iron Age*. Symposium Čačak, 4–8 September 2002. Čačak: Narodni Muzej Čačak, 91–100.

Knöpke, St. (2009). *Der urnenfelderzeitliche Männerfriedhof von Neckarsulm. Mit einem Beitrag von Joachim Wahl*, Forschungen und Berichte zur Vor- und Frühgeschichte in Baden-Württemberg, 116. Stuttgart: Theiss.

Krause, R. (2003). *Studien zur kupfer- und frühbronzezeitlichen Metallurgie zwischen Karpatenbecken und Ostsee*, Vorgeschichtliche Forschungen, 24. Rahden/Westf.: Leidorf.

Kreutle, R. (2007). *Die Urnenfelderkultur zwischen Schwarzwald und Iller. Südliches Württemberg, Hohenzollern und südöstliches Baden. 1. Auswertung (Text und Katalog). 2. Tafeln und Beilagen*. Büchenbach: Dr Faustus.

Lenerz-de Wilde, M. (1995). 'Prämonetäre Zahlungsmittel in der Kupfer- und Bronzezeit Mitteleuropas', *Fundberichte Baden-Württemberg*, 20: 229–327.

Maier, R. (1996). 'Siedlungs- und Grabfunde der Aunjetitzer Kultur aus dem Braunkohletagebau Schöningen, Ldkr. Helmstedt', *Die Kunde, Neue Folge*, 47: 111–25.

Martin, J. (2009). *Die Bronzegefässe in Mecklenburg-Vorpommern, Brandenburg, Berlin, Sachsen-Anhalt, Thüringen und Sachsen*, Prähistorische Bronzefunde II/16. Stuttgart: Steiner.

Meller, H. (ed.) (2004). *Der geschmiedete Himmel. Die weite Welt im Herzen Europas vor 3600 Jahren. Begleitband zur Sonderausstellung Landesmuseum für Vorgeschichte Halle (Saale) vom 15. Oktober 2004 bis 24. April 2005, Dänisches Nationalmuseum Kopenhagen 2005, Reiss-Engelhorn-Museen Mannheim 2006*. Stuttgart: Konrad Theiss.

Müller-Karpe, H. (1959). *Beiträge zur Chronologie der Urnenfelderzeit nördlich und südlich der Alpen*, Römisch-Germanische Forschungen, 22. Berlin: De Gruyter.

Pernicka, E., Wunderlich, Chr.-H., Reichenberger, A., Meller, H., and Borg, G. (2008). 'Zur Echtheit der Himmelsscheibe von Nebra–eine kurze Zusammenfassung der durchgeführten Untersuchungen', *Archäologisches Korrblatt*, 38/3: 331–52.

Primas, M. (2008). *Bronzezeit zwischen Elbe und Po: Strukturwandel in Zentraleuropa 2200–800 v. Chr*, Universitätsforschungen zur prähistorischen Archäologie, 150. Bonn: Dr Rudolf Habelt.

Rassmann, K. (2005). 'Zur Chronologie der Hortfunde der Klassischen Aunjetitzer Kultur. Eine Auswertung von Metallanalysen aus dem Forschungsvorhaben "Frühe Metallurgie im zentralen Mitteleuropa"', in B. Horejs, R. Jung, and E. Kaiser (eds.), *Interpretationsraum Bronzezeit. Bernhard Hänsel von seinen Schülern gewidmet*, Universitätsforschungen zur prähistorischen Archäologie, 121. Bonn: Dr Rudolf Habelt, 463–80.

Schefzik, M. (2001). *Die bronze- und eisenzeitliche Besiedlungsgeschichte der Münchner Ebene. Eine Untersuchung zu Gebäude- und Siedlungsformen im süddeutschen Raum*, Internationale Archäologie, 68. Rahden/Westf.: Marie Leidorf.

Schlichtherle, H. (ed.) (1997). *Pfahlbauten rund um die Alpen*. Archäologie in Deutschland, Sonderheft. Stuttgart: Konrad Theiss.

Schöbel, G. (1996). *Die Spätbronzezeit am nordwestlichen Bodensee: Taucharchäologische Untersuchungen in Hagnau und Unteruhldingen 1982–1989*, Siedlungsarchäologie im Alpenvorland, 4. Stuttgart: Konrad Theiss.

Schütz, C. (2006). *Das urnenfelderzeitliche Gräberfeld von Zuchering-Ost, Stadt Ingolstadt. Mit Beiträgen von Antja Bartel und Manfred Kunter*, Materialhefte zur bayerischen Vorgeschichte, Reihe A, 90. Kallmünz/Opf.: Lassleben.

Schunke, T. (2004). 'Der Hortfund von Hohenweiden-Rockendorf, Saalkreis, und der Bronzekreis Mittelsaale. Ein Beitrag zur jungbronzezeitlichen Kulturgruppengliederung in Mitteldeutschland', *Jahresschrift mitteldeutsche Vorgeschichte*, 88: 219–337.

Sperber, L. (1987). *Untersuchungen zur Chronologie der Urnenfelderkultur im nördlichen Alpenvorland von der Schweiz bis Oberösterreich*. Antiquitas, Reihe 3 = Abhandlungen zur Vor- und Frühgeschichte, zur klassischen und provinzial-römischen Archäologie und zur Geschichte des Altertums, 29. Bonn: Dr Rudolf Habelt.

—— (1999). 'Zu den Schwertträgern im westlichen Kreis der Urnenfelderkultur: Profane und religiöse Aspekte', in Römisch-Germanisches Zentralmuseum Mainz (RGZM) (1999), *Eliten in der Bronzezeit. Ergebnisse zweier Kolloquien in Mainz und Athen*. Mainz: Römisch-Germanisches Zentralmuseum, 605–59.

Ullrich, H. (1972). *Das Aunjetitzer Gräberfeld von Großbrembach 1: Anthropologische Untersuchungen zur Frage nach Entstehung und Verwandtschaft der thüringischen, böhmischen und mährischen Aunjetitzer*, Veröffentlichungen des Museums für Ur- und Frühgeschichte Thüringens, 3. Weimar: Böhlau.

Vogt, I. (2004). *Der Übergang von der frühen zur mittleren Bronzezeit in Mittel- und Nordeuropa unter besonderer Berücksichtigung der Griffplattenklingen*, Saarbrücker Beiträge zur Altertumskunde, 79. Bonn: Dr Rudolf Habelt.

Wiesner, N. (2009). *Grabbau und Bestattungssitten während der Urnenfelderzeit im südlichen Mitteleuropa. Ein Beitrag zur Entwicklung der Grabsitten in der späten Bronzezeit*, Internationale Archäologie, 110. Rahden/Westf.: Leidorf.

Wüstemann, H. (1995). *Die Dolche und Stabdolche in Ostdeutschland*, Prähistorische Bronzefunde, VI, 8. Stuttgart: Steiner.

Zich, B. (1996). *Studien zur regionalen und chronologischen Gliederung der nördlichen Aunjetitzer Kultur*, Vorgeschichtliche Forschungen, 20. Berlin, New York: De Gruyter.

CHAPTER 41

SCANDINAVIA

HENRIK THRANE

INTRODUCTION

Scandinavia stretches from the Barents Sea to the Baltic and North Sea, and the sea played a decisive role for the economy and culture of the Nordic Bronze Age, whose characteristics are best seen in the metalwork, the burial mounds or cairns, the longhouse or farm, and the rock carvings. While the south of Scandinavia was inextricably linked with the Bronze Age of continental Europe, the north, from the time of the earliest human settlement, formed part of a circumpolar zone with a Stone Age way of life. Finland and central Sweden had close ties with the Baltic countries and Russia. The Nordic Bronze Age constantly received innovations from abroad, copied and transformed them into a special, unmistakeable local mould, best expressed by metalwork, decoration styles, and rock carvings (Fig. 41.1).

In this area the term 'Early Bronze Age' usually refers to Montelius Periods I–III (equivalent to Bz A2–Ha A in Germany) while 'Late Bronze Age' comprises Periods IV–VI (Ha B1–C). An exhaustive corpus of publication is available for periods I–III for Denmark and

FIG. 41.1. Map of Scandinavia, showing sites mentioned in the text. Map: Joanne Porc, Faculty of Archaeology, Leiden University.
Norway: 1. Alta, 2. Høstad, 3. Mjeltehaugen, 4. Reg, 5. Viste Cave, 6. Forsandmoen, 7. Vestby
Sweden: 8 Nämforsen, 9. Håga, 10. Skälby, 11. Apalle, 12. Hallunda, 14. Hassle, 15. Fröslunda, 16. Tanum, 17. Norrköping with Ekenberg & Pryssgården, 18. Svartarp, 19. Grimeton, 20. Sagaholm, 21. Uggårda röir, Gotland, 22. Blåa röir, Öland, 23. Stockhult, 24. Lugnaro, 25. Hälsingborg, 26. Fogdarp, 27. Bromölla, 28. Malmö with Fosie, 29. Pile, 30. Kivik, 31. Köpinge, 32. Simris, 33. Balkåkra
Finland: 13. Otterböte, Åland Islands, 34. Kokemäki
Denmark: 35. Understed, 36. Bjerre, 37. Fragtrup, 38. Borremose, 39. Hohøj, 40. Fårdal, 41. Broddenbjerg, 42. Dystrup, 43. Hemmed, 44. Muldbjerg, 45. Engedal, 46. Borum Eshøj, 47. Spjald, 48. Håg, 49. Egtved, 50. Trindhøj, 51. Skelhøj, 52. Guldhøj, 53. Trappendal, 54. Maltbæk, 55. Dragshøj, 56. Højgård, 57. Skrydstrup, 58. Mariesminde, 59. Voldtofte with Lusehøj & Kirkebjerg, 60. Korshøj, 61. Trundholm, 62. Maglehøj, 63. Asnæs, 64. Rørby, 65. Ejby, 66. Viksø, 67. Hvidegård, 68. Smørumovre, 69. Karlstrup, 70. Valsømagle, 71. Boeslunde with Borbjerg, 72. Skallerup, 73. Grevensvænge, 74. Sværdborg, 75. Hårbølle, 76. Budsene.

SCANDINAVIA 747

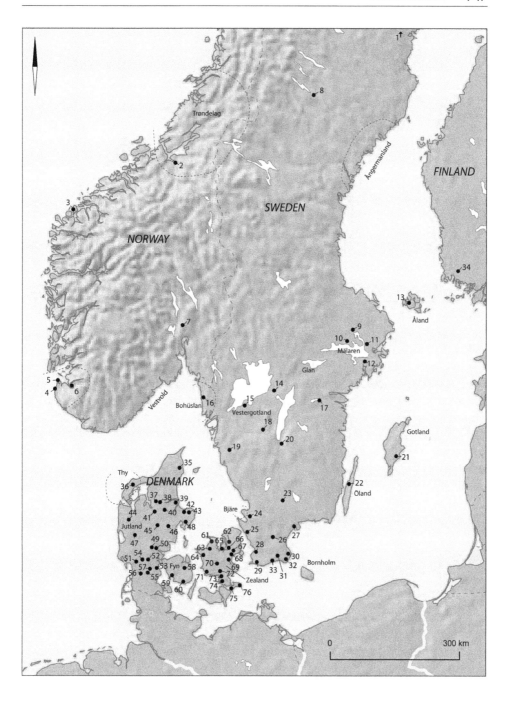

contiguous German provinces (Aner and Kersten 1973–2009), and another for Sweden (Oldeberg 1974). For Periods IV–VI only the Danish island of Fyn and Schleswig-Holstein are published (Schmidt 1993; Thrane 2004). The Late Bronze Age was surveyed by Evert Baudou (1960) but there is no exhaustive treatise. Denmark has an up-to-date treatment of the entire Bronze Age, fully referenced (Jensen 2002).

A rough division into three geographical zones is useful:

1. South (Denmark, Scania, and Blekinge, and the Swedish west coast): mainly deciduous forest and the best conditions for agriculture;
2. Central parts of Sweden and southern Norway (from Småland northwards to Dalarna, and along the west coast as far north as Trondheim): arable zones along the sea and the Swedish lakes, but pine forest dominant north of the Mälaren region;
3. North and the inland mountain zone: very limited possibilities for agriculture with conifers, birch, and taiga vegetation. The Caledonian mountain zone and the forests of the north favoured a continuing Mesolithic economy with hunting and fishing as the main ingredients.

These divisions have cultural significance. A simple count of bronzes shows a strong prevalence in the south and an equally marked scarcity in the north, while the central zone had (late) periods with rich metal finds. Whereas the Nordic Bronze Age may be seen from a central European perspective as a periphery, with the north and Baltic regions as marginal, south Scandinavia may be regarded as the centre of Nordic culture, with the central parts as more peripheral and the north as marginal. Although much emphasis has been placed upon the role of metals as a means of demonstrating and maintaining the status and ideology of the elite, this concept can have little relevance in the large tracts in the north and the mountaineous region, where metal is scarcely known at all. The dichotomy between the bronze culture of the central and southern regions and the inland lithic culture, so prominent in Norway, is equally relevant in Norrland and Finland, and further east. The metal objects and technology must have seemed just as fabulous to these foresters or tundra hunters as when bronze was first introduced in the south.

Cultural Development and Diversity

Nordic Bronze Age culture is best expressed by its bronzes which already in the earliest phase had their own characteristics vis-à-vis other Bronze Age cultures (Vandkilde 1996). The south is probably the richest zone in Europe in terms of the density of bronzes per km^2. Proper Nordic bronzes have been found as far north as 68.10° N, but did not penetrate much further south than the Baltic shores. The richness of the metal finds is somewhat paradoxical, as intensive prospection in Sweden has not yet located any copper deposits that were exploited during the Bronze Age; in other words every gram had to be imported—mainly from central Europe. Equally, gold had to be imported, and is greatly over-represented in south Scandinavia as compared to central Europe. While the Nordic bronzes have a clear common style making them easily recognizable, bronzes of eastern (Ananino) type are known from the north, where finds of moulds indicate a production that is otherwise difficult to spot because of the scarcity of finds.

The second characteristic is the existence of burial mounds, which are even more ubiquitous than the bronzes. In the south they are built of turves, while further north boulders were used to form cairns, probably thirty thousand cairns matching the hundred thousand tumuli in the south. The majority are still contextually unknown. They tend to form lines along land routes and coasts, with clusters indicating centres of population (Johansen, Laursen, and Holst 2004).

The third characteristic element is rock carvings, which the Swedish scholar Mats Malmer saw as a substitute for metalwork. The distribution is dependent upon the existence of suitable rock surfaces, which are absent in the south with the exception of eastern Scania and the present-day Danish island of Bornholm. The Bronze Age carvings are best expressed by the ship depictions, which reach as far north as the Alta Fjord.

The longhouse may be used as a fourth criterion. However, it is part of a geographical and chronological tradition extending beyond Scandinavia.

Chronology and Regional Differentiation

The chronology still uses the six periods defined by Oscar Montelius (1885), albeit modified by typology, especially for Periods I–III (Randsborg 1968; Vandkilde 1996), and by dendrochronology for the oak coffins of Period II (Randsborg 2006). Radiocarbon dating plays a minor role, but is more important in the centre and north of the region.

The circumpolar north was hardly Nordic in the same sense as the south but rather a sphere where southern and eastern cultures met, as expressed by the common appearance of hunter and farmer carvings on the rocks of Alta and Nämforsen. This phenomenon is repeated in Trøndelag (Sognnes 2001).

Regional differences are to be expected under such varied conditions. The north, with its eastern connections and Mesolithic way of life, used quartz for the flat-based points and scrapers between 1500 and 500 BC. Small huts at 45 m above sea level represent coastal activities. Asbestos-tempered (50–60 per cent) pots and containers used in pyrotechnology (iron smelting) are a northern speciality. The few axes of eastern (Ananino) type are outnumbered by moulds showing a wider production than the bronzes seem to indicate. Seal oil was produced at Kökarr/Otterböte on the Åland islands in the Baltic (Meinander 1954). The burials show southern acculturation with man-size stone cists and later smaller cists in the cairns along the coast. A border ran through Ångermanland in northern Sweden, coinciding with the more recent border between the subarctic nomads and the Swedish-speaking population further south. Here farming and agriculture began during the Late Bronze Age, which is hard to distinguish from the Early Iron Age. The relations with the Mälar region of Sweden coloured this southern group, but this group was not an integral part of the central region. In the highly segmented fjord landscapes of Norway, and along the big rivers and lakes of Sweden, local variability had natural causes. Inland landscapes like Småland in southern Sweden differ from the more open coastal landscapes.

The transition to the Bronze Age was long and gradual (Vandkilde 1996), many elements being carried over from the preceding period, such as longhouses, flintwork, metalwork, and burial rites. The transition to the Iron Age also took time and several elements continued, notably longhouses and hoard deposition. Period VI with its Hallstatt elements marks a break with the preceding centuries—expressed by the introduction of new types of pin, razors, and the absence of native weapons. Thus important changes took place at the transitions Period I–II, Period III–IV, and Period V–VI.

Regions developed at different speeds, so that zone 2 took the lead in Period III while Period II lingered on in zone I (according to Randsborg 1968); and Period III continued in the north-west when Period IV had already begun in the east. For the Late Bronze Age, Period VI presents similar problems, being well represented on Gotland, but little visible in other regions.

Settlement

Until 1955 settlement was identified only by rubbish pits, and the absence of proper houses led to speculation that the lifestyle was nomadic. It was a great surprise when longhouses of the same tradition as the Danish (and north-west German and Dutch) Iron Age houses at Fragtrup turned out to characterize the Bronze Age as well. In Sweden this type became known with the excavation of Fosie IV in 1979 (Björhem and Säfvestad 1993) and in Norway with that of Forsandmoen in 1987.

The use of mechanical equipment led to the uncovering of groups of houses and associated pits and cooking pits in large-scale excavations from the 1960s onwards. No village has yet been identified except Apalle in Sweden. The settlement structure is taken to be one or two farms, each with a longhouse supplemented by four-post structures for holding fodder. The longhouse started off two-aisled, continuing the Neolithic tradition, but changed to three-aisled during Period II, thus marking the beginning of a 2,000-year-long tradition. This innovation must be seen as connected with the regions south and west of the Baltic (P. O. Nielsen 1999). The houses had wooden posts supporting the roof and the walls, which were either of wattle and daub or plank-built, occasionally half timbered. Walls could be whitewashed (Apalle) or even painted (Kirkebjerg, in Denmark). As the posts were dug into the ground they would rot with time. The duration of a longhouse would rarely have exceeded 30–40 years (S. Nielsen 1999).

The orientation is nearly always west-east, the entrance on the long side, with living quarters in the west (P. O. Nielsen 1999; Bech and Mikkelsen 1999; Fig. 41.2). From Period III onwards byres are occasionally observed, but they did not become the norm. The length of the houses varies from an upper extreme of 50 m down to 10 m (giving an internal area of between 500 and 50 m^2). There are three sizes: roughly 50–70 m^2, 85–130 m^2, and 200–300 m^2. The largest are named 'halls' by some and taken to be chiefly residences by analogy with constructions in the Late Iron Age. Local sequences are known from Hemmed and Højgård (DK), Forsandmoen (N) and Apalle, Fosie IV, Köpinge and Pryssgården, all in Sweden. No fortification or palisade is known to have surrounded a Nordic Bronze Age settlement, Vistad in Sweden being the strange exception.

Small huts, resulting from seasonal settlement, are known from central Scandinavia and the northern coasts. Broad shallow multiple pits dug for raw materials are typical of the Late Bronze Age in the south. Potsherds and animal bones from these sites are important evidence for subsistence practices; wells occur occasionally. Casting refuse appears on most settlements, indicating that simple bronze production took place everywhere in the south, but also further north (see Prescott 1995). Specialized products like swords, belt-bowls, and lurs were cast at few sites like Kirkebjerg and Håg in Denmark (Jantzen 2008: 73). The majority of the casting indicators are stray finds of soapstone moulds.

Large settlements in the Mälar region of Sweden, like Apalle with its five phases, Pryssgården in the midst of one of the largest rock-carving concentrations at Norrköping, and Hallunda, show a lengthy site continuity (Ullén 2003). Apalle was one of two settlements

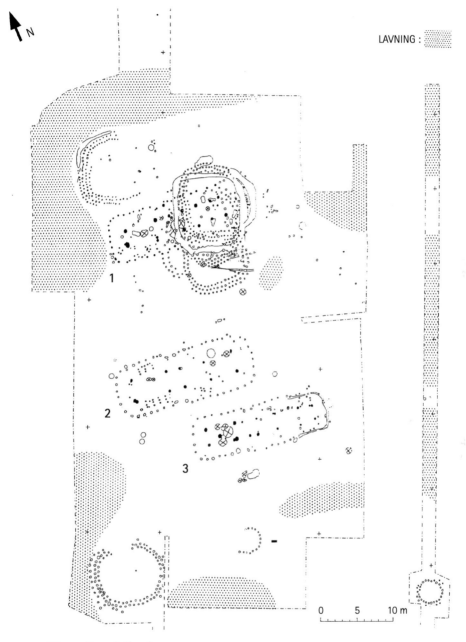

FIG. 41.2 Bjerre site 2, Jutland.

Source: Bech 1991.

on an island in the Mälar. Half of the 79 houses had burned down. The rubbish layers gave a stratigraphy and good preservation for wells, hearths, cooking stone, and constructional details such as walls, whitewash, wattle, and a rich and varied bone material including human bones. Pig, dog, ox and horse jaws and skulls were deposited beside the walls. Thick rubbish layers rarely survive; Kirkebjerg at Voldtofte, which is seen as a central settlement, is an exception. None of these sites has been completely excavated.

Centres are inferred from concentrations of rich burials and/or monumental mounds (Kivik, Albersdorf, Seddin, Håga), hoarded gold and bronzes, large longhouses (Skrydstrup), and rock carvings (Tanum and Ekenberg by Lake Glan in Sweden). In Period V, Voldtofte remains the only case with more than one source group as evidence of a hierarchical settlement and a social structure interpreted as a chiefdom.

Earlier stone-built longhouses in central Sweden are now seen as cult houses (Victor 2002). Certainly the stone-framed house at Sandagergård, with three standing stones and four boulders with carvings of hands, merits such an interpretation. Another sort of cult house is known from Jutland where square or oval enclosures were added to mounds (Jensen and Bech 2004).

Agriculture and Land Use

Sand has covered settlements and fields on Mols and Thy and on the west coast of Jutland (Bech 2003). Fields are known as small irregular plots (c.40 x 30 m). They could be ploughed several times but did not become permanent until the end of the Bronze Age. The criss-cross furrows left by the ard are well known when covered by wind-blown sand or burial mounds (Bech 2003). Barley was the main cereal along with emmer and spelt (see Chapter 19), cattle and sheep the main domestic animals, bovids playing a special role as draught power and a source of wealth (see Chapter 18). In Thy cattle enclosures were found near the house (Bech 2003).

The shifting use of the landscape is stratigraphically documented, for instance at Fragtrup and Lusehøj on Fyn, where a settlement was ploughed and barrows placed on the abandoned field (Thrane 1984). The settlement system is regarded as mobile, in other words the settlement or farm moved within a territory. Various attempts have been made to define such territories by natural borders that may now only be recognized theoretically—or indirectly by marginal depositions. Some scholars use barrows to define the centre of territories, others see them as defining borders. The size of the proposed territories varies from 0.5–6 km^2 (Sognnes 2001). A problem is to decide how many farms could exist within a given territory. One approach is to estimate the size of the arable land necessary for feeding a family. Using a number of economic and geographical variables, a radius round the settlement of half a kilometre was deemed sufficient if mixed farming was practised. For Norway 800 m^2 per person has been proposed.

Mounds

The Nordic burial mounds number thousands, probably one hundred thousand from the Bronze Age, most of them under plough and therefore continually being eroded. The vast majority may be dated to Periods II–III. Their size ranges from mini—0.5 m high and less than 5 m in diameter—to mega, more than 6 m high and 35 m in diameter (Fig. 41.3). Normally small mounds are defined as less than 10 m in diameter, big mounds as more than 25 m (Jensen 2002: 143), the average mound measuring 2.5 m high and 25 m in diameter. The mounds of the south are constructed of layers of grass sods, sometimes rather elaborately laid, as best documented at Skelhøj in Jutland (see Chapter 6). Both a circular and a radial principle were

FIG. 41.3 A row of Bronze Age barrows that overlook the bog where the Trundholm Sun Chariot (Fig. 41.6) was found.

Source: National Museum Copenhagen.

applied, sometimes assisted by radial wooden structures as at Lusehøj in Jutland (Thrane 1984). The Bjäre peninsula in Sweden has a density of eight mounds per km². Hohøj in East Jutland measures 12 m high and 72 m across and has been radiocarbon dated to 1380 cal BC.

The cairns of Scandinavia probably number around thirty thousand. Along the coasts they normally contained a central cist; large cairns in Sweden, like Uggårda röir on the island of Gotland and Blåa röir on the island of Öland, and Bredarör/Kivik in Scania (diameter 75 m, unknown height), are among the biggest monuments in Scandinavia. In the south Early Bronze Age primary burials were quite often covered by a small cairn, which would be covered by the turves of the mound. Occasionally Late Bronze Age cairns appear in Denmark too. In Odsherred on Zealand the Early Bronze Age mounds sit on the highest hills while the Late Bronze Age mounds and cairns lie on lower land, and a similar situation prevails on Bjäre. This implies that it was important that the barrows could be seen from a distance.

Apart from the rare long barrows and those with a flat top, barrows look pretty much alike, with their hemispherical shape, no matter how large or small. Once excavated, however, it becomes clear that no two barrows are identical. The graves may vary, and the perimeter varies from a single row of stones to complicated constructions, the most complicated being Hohøj in Denmark (Early Bronze Age). The most striking is Sagaholm at Lake Vättern in Sweden, whose rock-carved slabs feature men and horses (see Chapter 15).

A barrow may have one or more phases, extensions, and additions (see Chapter 6). A mound would be built over a single burial and subsequently enlarged to accommodate more graves. On the other hand, even big mounds may contain just a single burial (as at the Swedish sites of Håga, near Uppsala, and Kivik). The sequence normally covers no more than two successive periods. Late Neolithic mounds could be reused in the Early Bronze Age. Bronze Age mounds could become integrated into a field system. They could form the nucleus of Early Iron Age mini mound cemeteries, or much later burials. Late Bronze Age urns would be inserted into existing mounds. Not only small mounds, sometimes in cemeteries as at Hårbølle in Denmark (Jensen 1997), but even big mounds like Lusehøj and Lerbjerg, also in Denmark, were still being built during Periods V and VI (Thrane 2004). As a rule it is safe to say that a primary phase with Early Bronze Age inhumations was succeeded by secondary burials from the Late Bronze Age—or even later.

A special type of small to medium cairn was built of fire-cracked stones. The material came from the use of fire in cooking pits (earth ovens) at Late Bronze Age settlements. The stones were sometimes deposited in layers (Apalle) or reused in these stone cairns. They look like burial mounds and may have one or more stone rings on the bottom but rarely any proper burials, just settlement debris. Their purpose has been hotly debated. They are so closely related to settlements that they act as proxies in landscapes where settlements are difficult to locate, typically central Sweden but also southern Norway, and even occasionally in Denmark. They seem to show a ritual use of fire elements. The cooking pits were sometimes placed inside longhouses but are normally found in clusters away from the houses, sometimes systematically organized in single or multiple rows. These occur around the West Baltic Sea. Around the Bay of Bottnia large cooking pits are interpreted as being for seal oil production.

Burials

Unlike other European societies the Nordic Bronze Age left a continuous record of its burials, albeit with the majority during Periods II–IV. Inhumation was the rule until some time during Period II, when cremation began to appear sporadically. Period III and the rest of the Bronze Age simply used cremation, with Gotland as an exception at the end of the Bronze Age.

The earliest burials continue the earlier tradition, with stone cists concentrated in large areas of central and north Scandinavia, and in north-west Jutland in Period III, perhaps because suitable trees had been used up. On the other hand, tree-trunk coffins were nearly ubiquitous in Denmark and Scania. A few large cists had carvings on the slabs, the most famous being Kivik in Sweden (Randsborg 1993), and Mjeltehaugen and Rege in Norway.

The wooden coffins were normally hollowed-out oak trunks that have rotted away, leaving only faint traces. They were sometimes shaped on the spot, as shown by wood chips from palstave blows. The coffin could be supported by just a few stones or by regular stone frames or trough-shaped heaps. The corpse is always extended on its back, head to the west. In Period III the direction changes to north–south. An ox hide was laid out in the hollowed-out bottom half of the cist, with a woollen 'blanket' 2.15 x 1.2 m in extent covering the deceased (Fig. 41.4).

Mortuary houses may occur over the coffins and longhouses may be found under barrows, indicating a functional connection, for example at Handewitt and Trappendal in Denmark. Funeral pyres are hardly known except for the pit next to the burial under a barrow at Damgård, Thy, in Period III, and under Late Bronze Age barrows on Fyn with three-post constructions (Thrane 2004).

A small group of mounds in central Jutland with wet cores have yielded well-preserved coffins (see Fig. 41.4) with a unique collection of clothes, though there are no children's clothes. They give us an exceptional insight into details of clothing in the period. Details of hairstyle, manicure, and occasionally the bodies, were also preserved in the anaerobic conditions created in the wet cores of these mounds (see Chapter 6). The wet cores are only known from a small part of Jutland. While the wetness and the ensuing preservation were long considered the result of natural processes, recent research has indicated that it must result from human actions, which make them all the more remarkable. The phenomenon is strange, as it is restricted to a few generations, as demonstrated by the dendro dates from 1396 to 1268

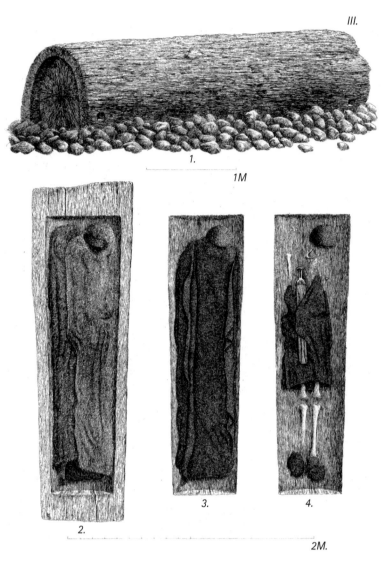

FIG. 41.4 The oak coffin burial grave A from the wet core mound Muldbjerg, Hover parish in west Jutland excavated 1883 by Henry Petersen. It stood in the eastern of two joined mounds, each with a coffin. The flange hilted sword is the only one with preserved organic hilt from period II.

Drawing: A.P. Madsen after Boye 1896.

BC (Randsborg 2006). Sometimes, when the bark is preserved, precise dates for a burial can be obtained. For instance, all three coffins in Guldhøj in Denmark were of wood felled in the same year (1389 BC), two of them cut from the same tree.

Four fully dressed women are known, all in Denmark: from Egtved, Skrydstrup, and two from Trindhøj (Jensen 2002). They wore a blouse and skirt. The 16 to 18-year-old Egtved girl with her short hair wore a miniskirt 38 cm long. A rather strange long skirt is also known.

Round the waist a long belt with tassels would be worn. The Skrydstrup girl was the same age, tall, with a very elaborate coiffure with hairnet and long skirt.

Four men all wore the same dress: piled cap, kidney-shaped cloak, and 'kilt', with belt and shoulder-strap. Much work went into making the round caps look like fur. The Trindhøj man from Denmark had an extra, tall cap in a bark 'hatbox'. Their clothes were cut from the same lengths of cloth as those in the women's coffins. The wool was normally brown, but occasionally white belts or cloth can be recognized.

The coiffures are very varied, the hair either short, or long and elaborately put up (Skrydstrup and Egtved). The men could have a 'Beatles' style like the young Borum Eshøj man from Denmark, or the hair cut short on the forehead and sides with a long ponytail down the neck, as at the Danish site of Dragshøj.

Tools, furniture, wooden bowls, and the indications of grave robbing also result from these remarkable chemical conditions. Stools are the only furniture known. Bronze fittings for the four ends of the seat are known from graves concentrated north of the mouth of the River Elbe, northern Germany. Carved bowls with star pattern made of fine tin studs have a bronze counterpart from Bornholm. The hafted palstave and a spoon from Guldhøj remain unique. Scabbards for the swords were pattern-carved from broad boards in Period II, or made of thin boards bound and lined by leather in Period III.

The graves changed gradually during Period IV when they became smaller because of the cremation rite, which demanded less space. Consequently swords and other large artefacts were no longer put in the graves. During Periods IV–VI urns took over as containers of the dead, but stone cists and cremation pits occur, in numerous varieties, down to simple nests of bones. A consequence was a severe limitation in the type of grave goods, men now being characterized only by their toilet equipment—razor and tweezers, awl or double button. Most cremation burials are without any metal objects, few containing more than three (Thrane 1984).

Age and Sex

Little is known of the population in spite of the many burials. The grave goods show that men and women were buried with the same rites, but men received more grave goods. While the population of the preceding period is well studied, few Bronze Age skeletons are preserved in a measurable state. The lack of well-preserved skeletons plus the difficulty of determining age and sex on cremated bone necessitates the use of bronzes as determinants of the sex of the deceased, but sometimes curious results occur. A determination of the age and sex of cremated bone sometimes disagrees with that made archaeologically (from grave goods); thus sword graves have occasionally been considered as those of females.

The absence of children's graves is notable. In the Late Bronze Age cremated adults may be accompanied by a child, while in the Early Bronze Age the 6 to 8-year-old cremated child in the Egtved grave is an exception. Any estimate of population size on the basis of the mounds is hampered by the varying number of burials per mound. Apparently not everyone had access to burial in a mound, but the few burials without mounds do not differ from those in mounds. In Schleswig-Holstein, and further south, quite extensive cemeteries existed in the Late Bronze Age, and smaller ones are known from Scania (Stjernquist 1961), and now also from Denmark, mainly in Period VI. Single flat graves are only found by chance (Björhem and Säfvestad 1993).

While the graves that we know represent only a part of the population, this part may be grouped socially according to the grave goods. The mound burials show social stratification and Period III Thy looks like an exceptionally close cluster of wealth. Certain ornaments were worn as sets but the composition of the grave goods is highly individual.

The wealthiest social stratum might be buried with gold. Gold armlets occur with weapons in Period III, for instance at Skallerup on southern Zealand, and in Period V on south-west Fyn (Thrane 1984: 163). A lower social level might have special knives and richly decorated razors and tweezers, while further down the scale the majority of graves have one or no metal objects. The Late Bronze Age shows the strongest contrast between normal (poor) and rich graves (Lusehøj, south-west Fyn, or Seddin in Mecklenburg, northern Germany).

Princely Burials

Kung Björn's mound at Håga near Uppsala in Sweden was excavated in 1903 (Fig. 41.5). The primary burial under a cairn was an oak coffin with a charcoal layer on which a flanged sword with gold-studded pommel and hilt, gold-plated fibula and five double buttons, two razors, two tweezers, rattle pendants, and gold wire lay with the cremated bones of an adult man of slender build. In the cairn and in the covering mound were bones of domestic animals and deer, plus two men and a woman, all the bones having been split for marrow extraction.

The two burials from Lusehøj on Fyn are the richest of Period V in the whole of Scandinavia. In 1862 a stone cist was excavated rather crudely. In it stood an imported bronze vessel, with a flat lid smeared with resin and inlaid pieces of amber. Three beakers were attached to the outside of the bucket by a woollen rug and the obligatory ox hide. The bones were inside the bucket along with an oath ring and two gold toggles, two bronze toggles, and two razors, while a unique socketed axe lay outside the urn. The bones were wrapped in fine textile woven from nettle bast.

When the mound was re-examined in 1973–5 another grave was found. A simple pit contained a funeral pyre with three stake-holes round it. The pit was covered by a reed mat surrounded by a rectangular wattle construction measuring 2.85 by 1.50 m, still preserved as holes lined with iron-pan up to 85 cm deep. The pit contained a few bones, 52 litres of charcoal (giving a date in the ninth century cal BC), and hundreds of partly or completely burnt gold and bronze remains, plus a simple iron finger ring, fragments of a sword, a chain, tiny buckles for a leather belt, many nails and other pieces from a wagon, rings, and other objects (Thrane 1984: 78). Both burials were covered by a great turf mound.

Special Graves

In some burials the selection of objects indicates that the individual buried was special. The Hvidegård mound outside Copenhagen, excavated in 1843, contained a Period III inventory with a sword in a stone cist (Aner and Kersten 1973: no. 399). Most curious was a leather purse which, apart from the usual men's toilet set, contained what looks like a sorcerer's or shaman's utensils: pieces of a red stone, an amber bead, a flint chip, a perforated Mediterranean shell, a small dice, roots and bark all of fir, the tail of a snake, a falcon's claw, and a smaller leather pouch with the lower jaw of a squirrel and small stones in a bladder (from a bird's crop?): hardly essential items for an ordinary individual. Moreover, a woollen textile fragment has

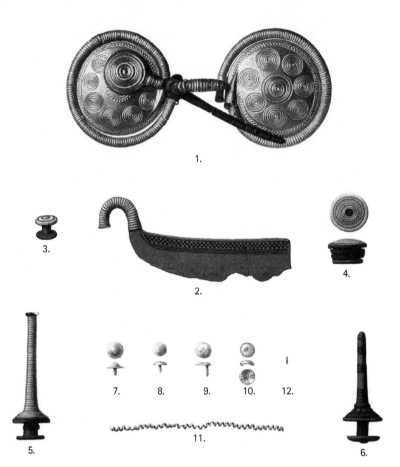

FIG. 41.5 Selection of finds from one of the richest Scandinavian period IV burials, Håga near Uppsala, Sweden, excavated 1903 by Oscar Almgren.

Source: Almgren 1904 and author (Thrane 2004).

been interpreted as the 'tail' of a hood like those worn by the men in the Grevensvænge hoard (see below)—another abnormal feature.

A contemporary cist tomb from Maglehøj in North Zealand, probably a female burial, contained among other things a hanging vessel in which lay the worked teeth of two horses, bones from a weasel and a lamb, part of a lynx claw, a bird's windpipe, snake vertebrae, a rowan twig, a piece of charcoal, small stones, two pieces of pyrites, and bronze wire (Aner and Kersten 1973: no. 183A).

Ship-shaped stone settings became popular during the Late Bronze Age, stretching from Halland in Sweden (Lugnaro) to Latvia, with a concentration on Gotland. They contain urns and their size varies considerably.

Arts and Crafts

The lost-wax casting process (*à cire perdue*) was the main way of making Nordic bronzes. Even complicated objects like the hangings bowls of the Late Bronze Age, the Trundholm wagon from Zealand (Fig. 41.6), and the lurs were made over clay cores, small iron tags being used to hold the inner and outer moulds in place. Lurs are the biggest cast bronzes (Lund 1987) and along with bronze chains are a Nordic invention.

Nordic metal production began with the copper axes, a hoard of Early Bronze Age metalwork from Pile in Sweden. Recent analyses of impurity patterns suggest that the majority of the metal used in a given period came from one source, beginning with the Mitterberg mines of Austria, changing to probably the Inn Valley by Period IV. A dominance of Swiss metal in Period V agrees with the usual archaeological interpretation (Liversage 2000; Thrane 1975: 230). Bronzes from Period VI show several impurity patterns, none being dominant.

The sword is the emblem of the Bronze Age, and thanks to the burial rite of Periods II–III it is nowhere more numerous than in south Scandinavia. From the south alone derive more than 2,700 swords. The earliest Nordic swords are from the Valsømagle hoard in Denmark, along with heavy swords/scimitars with curved tip from late Period I (Vandkilde 1996). Imported Apa swords, from south-east and central Europe, reached as far as Uppland, eastern Sweden, and the short swords of Sögel and Wohlde type (named after German finds),

FIG. 41.6 No treatise of Nordic Bronze Age can be without the Trundholm wagon. It is a unique combination of foreign elements like the horse and the chariot with four-spoked wheels—turned into a wagon for the disc, one side having gold plated spiral decoration, the other concentric circles. New techniques and elements are combined into a genial solution of the problem of creating a moveable medium for the horse drawn sun (and moon). It was deposited in the extensive, then dry, Trundholm bog in Odsherred, north-west Zealand, Denmark and found 1902. The decoration places it in sub per. II.

Photo: National Museum Kopenhagen.

initiated local production. The Valsømagle long sword represents the start of *Vollgriffschwerter* (solid-hilted swords) in the north, continuing into Period II. Tumulus-culture types like the octagonal-hilted (Von Quillfeldt 1996) and flange-hilted swords were imported in Period II. Most of the northern swords are copies. The Nordic bronze-hilted swords may be attributed to three or four regional workshops (Ottenjann 1969).

In Period IV flange-hilted swords from eastern Denmark sometimes have gold-plated hilts. They continued do be used as grave goods, but later swords were only exceptionally buried in graves (Thrane 1984). Late Urnfield types like antenna, Mörigen, and Auvernier swords indicate a more limited importation in Period V (Thrane 1975). Periods IV–V saw a development of local types with kidney and horned pommels and a monotype with reinforced tip in Period V. From Period VI a handful of Hallstatt swords survive (Jensen 1997).

Weapons like axes and spearheads form an important group (arrowheads are only of flint or bone). Spearheads were a characteristic element from all the periods. This starts in Period I with the Bagterp type (Vandkilde 1996) and ends in Period V with the big West Baltic type. A succession of axe types developed, from the flanged axes of Period I through the palstaves of Period II to the socketed axes that dominate the Late Bronze Age, in increasingly small versions (Baudou 1960). Against the approximately 2,600 bronze axes around 870 stone (shaft-hole) axes are known (Baudou 1960: 141). Another special group of massive bronze shaft-hole axes with spiral decoration are the supposed cult axes, found in pairs and deposited as hoards (Periods II–V). This looks like a continuation of Neolithic rites. Axes with extra high flanges and fine bronze handle terminals must also have had a non-practical purpose (Vandkilde 1996: 126). The ubiquitous palstaves of Period II had a heavy version used as a tool, and a finer, decorated version used as a weapon, but in later periods utility took over and the socketed axes just have simple grooves or ribs. The average Late Bronze Age axe weighed more than 100 g.

Knives were introduced in Period II and Urnfield types were copied, in Period IV via the Oder. A multitude of large and small knives developed locally, the small ones found with the male toilet set. The razor with animal or spiral handle is a Nordic invention and the tweezers also took on a local form.

The two-piece fibula is a Nordic invention of Period II and it developed into huge creations during the Late Bronze Age (Baudou 1960). Another invention is the small bronze container carried at the belt, with bronze or wooden lid. Presumably bark containers gave the model for the cylindrical Period III type, which developed into the big, heavily decorated Late Bronze Age type in Denmark and Mecklenburg in northern Germany. Although pins were introduced from abroad in Period I, local types mainly developed in the Late Bronze Age. Toggles and double buttons also developed locally. The belt discs, tutuli (small discs with projecting point), and collars arose from Tumulus-culture types. Arm-rings and anklets show a similar development from foreign to sometimes baroque local types, for instance the Period IV anklets, up to 7 cm wide, or the golden oath rings (Baudou 1960).

Flint remained in use and it is hard to distinguish daggers and sickles of Periods I–II from the Late Neolithic products. Asymmetrical sickles were produced and distributed from a few sites in Thy. Late Bronze Age flintwork was a rather messy affair that used very poor-quality flint, but an exception were some heavy-backed blades in four variants, used for reaping grain and reeds, obviously the products of specialized production on Stevns, Zealand, and in Scania and Rügen during Periods V–VI (Högberg 2009, 198). They were distributed all over

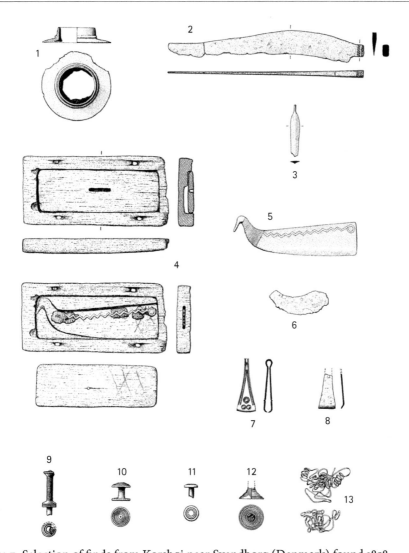

FIG. 41.7 Selection of finds from Korshøj near Svendborg (Denmark) found 1858.

Source: author (Thrane 2004).

the south but only occasionally reached the central region. At Apalle and Hallunda in Sweden southern flint was worked locally (Högberg 2009). In the north, apart from reused Scandinavian flint, quartz and quartzite provided the local tool material (Baudou 1992; Lavento 2001).

Woodwork is rarely attested but provides indications of a high level of proficiency. The carved bowls from the oak coffins, the stool from Guldhøj, the razor box from Korshøj on Fyn (Fig. 41.7), and the carved headrest from Høstad in Norway give us occasional glimpses. This is equally true of leatherwork, where only the Hvidegård burial near Copenhagen with its pouch and sword belt shows the quality of work.

Pottery

Nordic pottery is not very striking, carries little decoration, and therefore is difficult to arrange in typo-chronologies. The early group of pots continues the Late Neolithic *Kummerkeramik* and is poorly known. During Period II Tumulus and Lausitz pottery began to influence southern Scandinavia with new types (small amphorae with two small handles), and a new smoother appearance. The mottled surfaces show poorly regulated oxygen control. The Late Bronze Age pottery corpus is large, thanks to the Urnfield rite, but characterized by a somewhat indistinct morphology, making chronological division difficult.

In central Sweden a group of pots with a completely different decoration and technique indicates connections across the Baltic to Finland via Åland during the Late Bronze Age (Ambrosiani 1986). Pottery in the subarctic region, with asbestos temper and textile imprints, is specific to the north (Lavento 2001).

Very occasionally the pots may carry decoration, like the horseheads on a face urn from Vallby in Sweden. Face urns vary from the simplest addition of 'eyes' or lugs to well-modelled eyebrows and mouth.

Ornamentation

A chief characteristic of Nordic culture was the decorative styles and elements, clearly inspired by and imitating continental styles. It begins with the south-eastern geometric style on the Period I Valsømagle axes and Bagterp spearheads (Vandkilde 1996). Period II has the spiral as its main motif with, in addition, the *Schlingband* (pulley motif) of central European origin. The spirals were replaced by concentric circles late in the period, and in Periods III–IV stars or radial motifs became dominant, reflecting Urnfield styles. While the south-western *Ribbe-Rillenstil* adorned spearheads and other weapons and tools in Period V, a different style was developed for the large cast hanging bowls and belt buckles, with a revival of the concentric order. Multiple wavy motifs were used in this style in the same way as the spiral had been previously. Although most of the motifs are geometric, the occasional addition of horse heads or ship features indicates that symbolic aspects were not ignored. The Urnfield *Vogelsonnenbark* (bird-sun-boat) was copied from imported bronze vessels. On the Early Bronze Age scimitar from Rørby in Zealand, and especially on Late Bronze Age razors, tweezers and neck-rings, ships are quite frequent, some with a twin crew, underlining the symbolic value of objects and decoration (Kaul 1998). Decoration and tumuli alike testify to the use of the circle as a basic element, and the use of compasses and simple geometry must have been well known.

Figurines

Modelled figurines are known during Periods II–VI, starting with the horse-head razor handles and Trundholm wagon, and the similar lost pair of horses from the Hälsingborg hoard in Sweden (Oldeberg 1974: no. 96). The Stockhult hoard, also in Sweden, contained cult axes and palstaves plus three sets of women's ornaments and two identical figurines of men, 14.7 cm tall, unfortunately without their arms (Oldeberg 1974: no. 463). The Grevensvænge and Fårdal hoards in Sweden contain human and animal figurines meant to sit in an organic substructure, perhaps miniature ships. They show men wielding axes and horned helmets like those from Viksø in Denmark, and the Fogdarp yoke mountings, female acrobats in short skirts, snake and horned animal protomes, also from Denmark. Also in later periods representations of animals (horses, birds) and even females, occur on bronze objects, especially knives.

Rock Carvings

While cup-marks are ubiquitous in the Nordic rock art, proper carvings on the ice-smoothed rock surfaces cluster in the landscape, with remarkable concentrations in Bohuslän, western Sweden, and neighbouring south Norway. Our knowledge of them is far from complete, and each year brings new discoveries. Two main traditions have been recognized, a hunters' or northern Stone Age tradition focusing on big game and fish motifs, located on rocks in the north and along the inland rivers; and a farmers' or southern tradition, where ships dominate but cattle and other domestic motifs also occur. This subject is treated in more detail in Chapter 15.

Trade and Transport

The sea must have been the main means of communication in Bronze Age Scandinavia, as shown by the distribution of burial monuments and the hundreds of ship depictions. Strangely enough, no actual ship has been found in Scandinavian waters apart from log canoes, which are very similar to Stone Age boats. Fish-hooks indicate deep-water fishing (e.g. Karlstrup, Period III, with line preserved). Speculation about the existence of skin boats has not been confirmed, and predecessors of the Iron Age plank-built Hjortspring war canoe in Denmark remain unknown.

Land transport can hardly have equalled the importance of seafaring in Scandinavia. Bronze parts for prestige vehicles are known from the Late Bronze Age, however. Like the miniature spoked wheels of the Trundholm wagon and the wheeled cauldrons from Skallerup, they indicate an influx of martial and ritualistic vehicles like those depicted in the Kivik cist. They remain exceptions and their role in local society is open to interpretation. Furthermore horse bones are infrequent on settlements. We know from bronze sculptural art (Trundholm; see Fig. 41.6) and rock carvings that the horse functioned as a draught animal, while cheek pieces for harness have also been found. Riding, however, is not attested at this period.

Communication lines are inferred from the linear patterns of the mounds best observed in Jutland, where traffic lanes may be seen leading to the North Sea. A main line running south along the central watershed in Jutland functioned in historical times, because people used the most favourable land. The routes would usually be simple tracks without any constructional elements, but tracks with a paving of small stones are known from the Malmö area in southern Sweden. Otherwise Bronze Age roads are only found at fords. The 300-m-long Danish road in the Speghøje bog required 1,500 oak trunks (*c*.1450 cal BC), while the Skalså track in Denmark was 250 m long, ending in the middle of the river valley (*c*.800

cal BC). At the Danish site of Kvorning a construction reminiscent of Flag Fen near Peterborough in England is dated c.800 cal BC.

The often-proposed trans-European amber route from Jutland hardly reflects reality. The amount of amber in Scandinavian finds is quite small. Amber was collected on the coast of Jutland. A small hoard on its east coast lay in a house at Bjerre site 7, where 1,800 pieces were found (Bech 2003). Unlike in the Neolithic no large hoards are known, other than the 3.3 kg hoard at Understed (Period II) on Jutland's north-east coast. Instead the odd bead or small unworked piece appears in Late Bronze Age burials, the most remarkable being the Lusehøj tomb on the Danish island of Fyn discovered in 1862 (Jensen 1966; Thrane 1984). As the term 'Baltic amber' covers amber from the North Sea as well as the Baltic, we cannot assume that Denmark was the place of origin for the European amber finds, or those at Mycenae. The vastly bigger deposits on the Samland coast in the south-eastern Baltic represent a better candidate.

HOARDS AND VOTIVE DEPOSITS

Hoards and votive deposits are covered in a more theoretical way in Chapter 7. Here I will simply mention the special character of Nordic bronze hoards. Nowhere have such masses of objects been deposited, and nowhere has such a variety of intricately made objects been found. Hoards may contain weapons or tools, ornaments, or a mixture of both, plus occasionally casting refuse or ingots, as is the case with the biggest of all: Smørumovre, near Copenhagen. Especially eye-catching are objects like the twin solid ceremonial axes, the paired lurs (trumpets; see Lund 1987), or twin gold bowls like the three sets from the Borbjerg hill in Jutland. At Mariesminde, on Fyn, as many as 11 bowls were placed in an amphora of south-eastern origin. And of course there are weapons too, like the cauldron and two Hallstatt swords from Hassle (Sweden); the Viksø helmets (Denmark); the 16 Herzsprung shields from Fröslunda (Sweden); and collections of swords like the six from Asnæs or the eight swords of Apa type from Dystrup (both Denmark).

All of these special finds show the high level of craftsmanship on the one hand, but also the special ritual meaning of many of these objects. The fact that several objects have been placed in sets has provoked many speculative interpretations (e.g. Kristiansen and Larsson 2005).

CONCLUSION

The Nordic Bronze Age proper is well defined compared with other European Bronze Ages, but it is not synonymous with 'Scandinavian Bronze Age'. Regional diversity and different orientations towards the outside world changed in intensity and direction over time. Recent research has successfully concentrated on settlements, but the study of burials also remains a rewarding field. A permanent process of acceptance and renewal of foreign influences determined the development of the period throughout the Nordic area.

Bibliography

Almgren, O. (1904). *'Kung Björns Hög', och andra fornlämningar vid Håga*. Stockholm: Wahlström & Widstrand.

Ambrosiani, B. (ed.) (1986). *Die Bronzezeit im Ostseegebiet*. Stockholm: Almqvist and Wiksell International.

Aner, E. and Kersten, K. (1973–2009). *Die Funde der älteren Bronzezeit in Dänemark, Schleswig-Holstein und Niedersachsen I–XII*. Neumünster: Karl Wachholz.

Baudou, E. (1960). *Regionale und chronologische Einteilung der jüngeren Bronzezeit in Skandinavien*. Stockholm: Almqvist and Wiksell.

—— (1992). *Norrlands forntid*. Umeå: Wiken.

Bech, J.-H. (1991). 'Et bronzealderlanskab ved Bjerre i Nordthy. Om arkæologiske udgravninger forud for en planlagt motorbane', *Miv. Museerne i Viborg amt*, 16: 41–8.

—— (2003). 'The Thy archaeological project – Results and reflections from a multinational archaeological project', in H. Thrane (ed.), *Diachronic Settlement Studies in the Metal Ages*. Højbjerg: Jutland Archaeological Society, 45–60.

—— and Mikkelsen, M. (1999). 'Landscapes, settlement and subsistence in Bronze Age Thy, NW Denmark', in C. Fabech and J. Ringtved (eds.), *Settlement and Landscape*. Proceedings of a Conference in Aarhus, Denmark, 4–7 May 1998. Højbjerg: Jutland Archaeological Society, 69–77.

Björhem, N. and Säfvestad, U. (1993). *Fosie IV*. Malmö: Malmö Museer.

Fabech, C. and Ringtved, J. (ed.) (1999). *Settlement and Landscape*. Aarhus: Jutland Archaeological Society.

Högberg, A. (2009). *Lithics in the Scandinavian Bronze Age*, British Archaeological Reports (International Series), 1,932. Oxford: Archaeopress.

Jantzen, D. (2008). *Quellen zur Metallverarbeitung im Nordischen Kreis der Bronzezeit*, Prähistorische Bronefunde, XIX/2. Stuttgart: Franz Steiner.

Jensen, J. (1966). 'Bernsteinfunde und Bernsteinhandel der jüngeren Bronzezeit Dänemarks', *Acta Archaeologica*, 26: 43–86.

—— (1997). *Fra bronze- til jernalder*. Copenhagen: Det Kongelige Nordiske Oldskriftselskab.

—— (2002). *Danmarks Oldtid Bronzealderen*. Copenhagen: Gyldendal.

Jensen, B. H. and Bech, J.-H. (2004). 'Bronzealderens kulthuse i Thy', *Kuml*, 2004: 129–60.

Johansen, K. L., Laursen, S. T., and Holst, M. K. (2004). 'Spatial patterns of social organization in the Early Bronze Age of South Scandinavia', *Journal of Anthropological Archaeology*, 23: 33–55.

Kaul, F. (1998). *Ships on Bronzes*, vols. 1–2. Copenhagen: National Museum.

Kristiansen, K. and Larsson, T. B. (2005). *The Rise of Bronze Age Society*. Cambridge: Cambridge University Press.

Lavento, M. (2001). *Textile Ceramics in Finland and on the Karelian Isthmus*, Finska Fornminnesföreningens Tidskrift, 109. Helsinki: Suomen Muinaismuistoyhdistys.

Liversage, D. (2000). *Interpreting Impurity Patterns in Ancient Bronze: Denmark*. Copenhagen: Det Kongelige Nordiske Oldskriftselskab.

Lund, C. (ed.) (1987). *The Bronze Lurs: Second Conference of the ICTM Study Group on Music Archaeology*, vol. ii: *The Bronze Lurs (1986–7): The 'Phenomenal' Bronze Lurs*, Kungl. Musikaliska Akademiens Skriftserie. Stockholm: Kungl Musikaliska Akademien.

Malmer, M. P. (1981). *A Chorological Study of North European Rock Art*. Stockholm: Kungliga Vitterhets Historie och Antikvitets Akademiens handlingar, Antikvariska serien 32.

Meinander, C. F. (1954). *Die Bronzezeit Finnlands*, Finska Fornminnesföreningens Tidskrift, 54. Helsinki: Helsingfors.

Montelius, O. (1885). *Om tidsbestämning inom bronsåldern*. Stockholm: På Akademiens Förlag.

Nielsen, P. O. (1999). 'Limensgård and Grødbygård. Settlements with house remains from the Early, Middle and Late Neolithic on Bornholm', in C. Fabech and J. Ringtved (eds.), *Settlement and Landscape, Proceedings of a Conference in Aarhus, Denmark, 4–7 May 1998*. Højbjerg: Jutland Archaeological Society, 149–65.

Nielsen, S. (1999). *The Domestic Mode of Production*. Copenhagen: Det Kongelige Nordiske Oldskriftselskab.

Oldeberg, A. (1974). *Die ältere Metallzeit in Schweden I*. Stockholm: Kungliga Vitterhets Historie och Antikvitets Akademien.

Ottenjann, H. (1969). *Die nordischen Vollgriffschwerter der älteren und mittleren Bronzezeit*, Römisch-Germanische Forschungen, 30. Berlin: De Gruyter.

Quillfeldt, I. von (1996). *Die Vollgriffschwerter in Österreich und der Schweiz*, Prähistorische Bronzefund, IV, 11. Stuttgart: Franz Steiner.

Prescott, C. (1995). *From Stone Age to Iron Age*, British Archaeological Reports (International Series), 603. Oxford: Tempus Reparatum.

Randsborg, K. (1968). 'Von Periode II zu III', *Acta Archaeologica*, 49:1–142.

—— (1993). 'Kivik: archaeology and iconography', *Acta Archaeologica*, 64: 1–147.

—— (2006). 'Opening the oak-coffins—new prospects', *Acta Archaeologica*, 77: 1–162.

Schmidt, J.-P. (1993). *Studien zur jüngeren Bronzezeit in Schleswig-Holstein und dem nordelbingischen Hamburg*, vols 1–2. Bonn: Habelt.

Sognnes, K. (2001). *Rock Art in Stjørdal, Trøndelag, Norway*, British Archaeological Reports (International Series), 998. Oxford: Archaeopress.

Stjernquist, B. (1961). *Simris II: Bronze Age Problems in the Light of the Simris Excavations*. Lund: C. W. K. Gleerup.

Thrane, H. (1975). *Europæiske forbindelser. Bidrag til studiet af fremmede forbindelser i Danmarks yngre broncealder (periode IV–V)*. Copenhagen: Nationalmuseet.

—— (1984). *Lusehøj ved Voldtofte*. Odense: Odense Bys Museer.

—— (2004). *Fyns yngre broncealdergrave 1–2*. Odense: Odense Bys Museer.

Ullén, I. (2003). *Bronsåldersboplatsen vid Apalle i Uppland*. Stockholm: Riksantikvarieämbetet.

Vandkilde, H. (1996). *From Stone to Bronze*. Aarhus: Jutland Archaeological Society.

Victor, H. (2002). *Med graven som granne*. Uppsala: Department of Archaeology and Ancient History.

CHAPTER 42

THE BRONZE AGE IN THE POLISH LANDS

JANUSZ CZEBRESZUK

Introduction: The Natural Environment

With the exception of its southern reaches, the entire landscape of Poland, which lies in central Europe, was transformed by glacial activity in the Late Pleistocene. Along the north–south axis, distinct geomorphological zones can be distinguished. The Baltic coastline constitutes the northern border, delimiting a broad belt of plains and lakes extending for 400 to 500 km. Further south stretch uplands and a low mountain range (the Świętokrzyskie, or Holy Cross Mountains) that widens towards the east. Mountain ranges also make up the southern limits of the territory: the Sudeten mountains to the west and the Carpathians (Tatra Mountains) to the east, reaching c.2,500 m above sea level. The majority of the country is drained by two large rivers: the Oder and the Vistula. Because the two watershed regions are not clearly demarcated, there were no natural barriers to impede cultural exchanges. The river system facilitated free interactions among people; the southern mountain ranges, with a series of convenient passes and depressions, such as the Moravian Gate separating the Sudeten and the Carpathian mountains, were never an obstacle.

The presence of fertile soils was critical for prehistoric settlement. Black earth derived from loess is found mainly in the upland belt. The most extensive portion of the lowlands contained enclaves of black earth of hemihydrate origin (soils formed from the slow drying of peat bogs). The largest of these pockets are located in Kuyavia, along the lower Oder, and in a few places in Great Poland.

The scarce natural resources that were accessible in the Bronze Age were not evenly distributed across the country. The choicest flint pieces come mainly from the uplands (Jura flint, banded flint, and chocolate flint) and from the lower Oder basin (so-called Rügen flint). Salt deposits and brine sources were exploited within a wide belt covering Pomerania, Kuyavia, the eastern part of Great Poland, and the western part of Little Poland. There is evidence that brine wells existed in the region as early as the Neolithic.

In this region during the Bronze Age the key natural resource was abundant amber. It was found mainly along the coast, especially in the Vistula delta, where deposits were the richest and culturally most significant (Czebreszuk 2009).

One of the most distinct climate boundaries also passes through Polish territory, roughly following the Vistula river, separating the continental climate zone (to the east) and the Atlantic climate zone (to the west).

Historic Regions of Polish Territory

Poland can be divided into several historical regions (Fig. 42.1a), the most significant of which have seen important archaeological research. The northern regions comprise Pomerania, with a western part (principal city: Szczecin) and an eastern part (Gdańsk), and Masuria, which extends eastwards. Great Poland (capital Poznań), Kuyavia, and Masovia (Warsaw) occupy the central part of the country, whereas the south is divided into Lower Silesia (Wrocław) and Upper Silesia (Katowice), and Little Poland, with principal cities Kraków (in the west) and Rzeszów (in the east).

Cultural Chronology

In Poland the Bronze Age extends from 2300/2200 to 800 cal BC. Since there is cultural continuity, the period overlaps with the early phases of the Iron Age (Hallstatt period, 800–400 cal BC).

The Bronze Age is associated with the emergence of new forms of social organization characterized by internal stratification (Czebreszuk 2001; Kadrow 2001), with a military aristocracy constituting the ruling class. Communities of this type relied on extensive cultural contacts and placed high value on prestige. Their value system created a demand for goods made of 'strategic' or even 'exotic' materials of distant provenance, such as metals or amber. These communities possessed stable settlement structures, often with a central fortified settlement. They had developed well-organized agricultural and diversified manufacturing systems that used metal tools as standard.

Nevertheless, it must be noted that in the Bronze Age not all communities inhabiting Poland can be considered representative of Bronze Age culture. The Polish territories were split along a cultural divide, which corresponded to the regional divisions of Europe at the time. The main boundary ran from the Moravian Gate in the south to the Bay of Gdańsk in the north (see Fig. 42.1a). A secondary line of division ran parallel to the northern edge of the uplands and split the eastern half of the territory into northern and southern parts. Polish territory can thus be divided into three cultural zones: western, south-eastern, and north-eastern.

The western zone belonged to an area that was key throughout the duration of the European Bronze Age. It constituted the north-eastern or eastern border of such cultural complexes as the Únětice culture, the Tumulus culture, and the Hallstatt culture. The upland regions in south-eastern Poland formed the northernmost reaches of the Carpathian Basin cultures. The societies inhabiting the north-eastern zone followed a different rhythm of life, and remained isolated from the cultural processes that defined the Bronze Age elsewhere.

The littoral zone extending from the Oder delta to the Vistula delta have a particular character because of the diverse ecological niche of the coastline, which helped to stabilize settlement

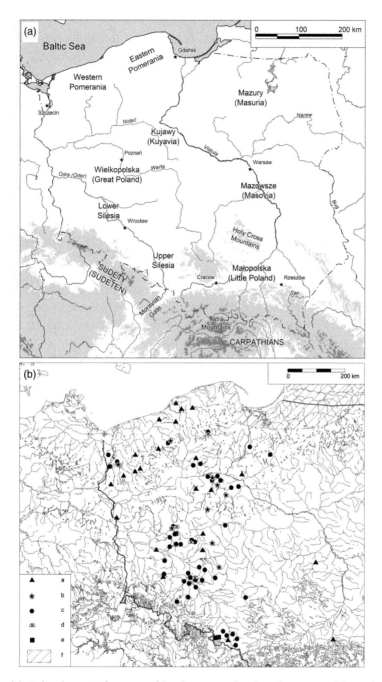

FIG. 42.1 (a) Poland: main features of landscape and cultural regions; (b) Finds used to trace the coastal route and the first amber route in the Early Bronze Age: a. imported bronze objects; b. gold objects, c. amber, d; 'princely kurgans'; e. fortified settlements; f. Sambia, centre of amber extraction.

Map: author.

throughout prehistory, and because of its extensive network of cultural exchanges, stretching across the Baltic shore and further west to the North Sea. The littoral zone owed its privileged character in the Bronze Age to abundant deposits of amber (Czebreszuk 2009), which had become a commodity in great demand across Europe.

The basic division of the Bronze Age into early, middle, and late is valid above all in the western part of Poland. However, this represents a schematic approach that obscures the specifics of the area. Furthermore, absolute dating techniques, including radiocarbon dating and dendrochronology, have made chronometric dating widely applicable.

The Cultural Sequence

The earliest period of the Early Bronze Age may be designated as the proto-Bronze phase and extended from 2300/2200 to 2000 cal BC. In the western and south-eastern zones it is associated with the Bell Beaker culture. Three distinct centres of Bell Beaker provenance have been traced: Jutland and north-eastern Germany were the source of Pomeranian and Kuyavian Bell Beakers (Czebreszuk 2001); those found in Lower Silesia originated in the Czech lands (Makarowicz 2003); whereas those in Little Poland came from Moravia (Budziszewski and Włodarczak 2010). The presence of Beaker features in western Poland attests to the participation of the population in a wide network of cultural exchanges and in the transformation of the social structure (Czebreszuk 2001). Little Poland, on the other hand, is one of the rare examples of indisputable migration from Moravia of a small group of representatives of the Bell Beaker culture (Budziszewski and Włodarczak 2010).

The presence of the Bell Beakers was always a catalyst for cultural change. In western Poland, around 2300/2250 cal BC, they form the context of the earliest traces of the Únětice culture (proto-Únětice phase), which first appeared in Lower Silesia (Machnik 1977). Over time, clusters of the Únětice culture reached Kuyavia and the lower Oder (Kośko 1991). At the same time, the Mierzanowice culture started to flourish in Little Poland (Kadrow and Machnik 1997) and reached its heyday during that period (see the early Mierzanowice phase: Kadrow and Machnik 1997: 29–53). Around 2000 cal BC significant changes occurred in both regions. The Mierzanowice culture increasingly cut its contacts with the West, whereas the watershed of the upper Oder and Vistula rivers became a real cultural barrier.

The Únětice culture itself followed more than one course. Toward the end of the third millennium BC it was characterized by the scarcity of metal objects, and its settlement structures and social organization were rather simple. Around 2000 cal BC—in the lowlands earlier (before 2000 cal BC, Rassmann and Schoknecht 1997) than in Lower Silesia (after 2000 cal BC)—the Únětice culture underwent a substantial transformation. Metal objects showing the specific Únětice style began to be manufactured using local ore deposits from the Harz Mountains and the eastern Alps, located directly south-west of the region (Krause 2003). Significantly, tin-bronze also started to be widely used. Highly developed metallurgy ushered in social stratification. This is confirmed by the finds of rich barrows (kurgans; the so-called princely tumuli) (Fig. 42.2c); prestige objects, including bronze weapons, and especially halberds and fluted stone mace-heads; imports testifying to a broad network of cultural contacts, including gold, amber, and foreign bronze objects; and complex settlements with stable, fortified centres (Fig. 42.2a).

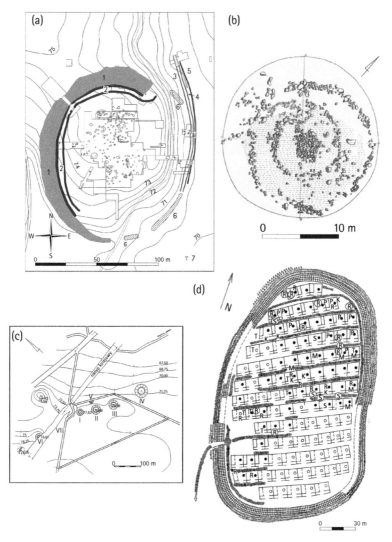

FIG. 42.2 (a) Plan of the Early Bronze Age settlement at Bruszczewo (Great Poland). 1 – moat 2 – palisade, 3 – inner fascine (bundle of brushwood) 4 – outer fascine, 5 – wall of double vertical pillars and horizontal planks wedged between them, 6 – fortifications traces found by magnetometry (Müller, Czebreszuk, and Kneisel 2010); (b) Ludgierzowice (Lower Silesia), kurgan of the Tumulus culture (Butent 1992); (c) Plan of the barrow cemetery at Łęki Małe (Great Poland), including reconstructed kurgans (Kowiańska-Piaszykowa 2008); (d) Plan of Biskupin (Kuyavia), including the location of artefacts related to: M. metallurgy, T. weaving, K. parts of harness, R. farming, S. bone-working, P. fishing (Niesiołowska-Wędzka 1991).

The situation east of the divide after 2000 cal BC was radically different. The Mierzanowice culture still existed in Little Poland (classic and late phases), and its development was increasingly fragmented, as evidenced by a diversity of local styles during the late Mierzanowice phase (Giebułtów, Szarbia, Pleszów, and Samborzec groups: Kadrow and Machnik 1997).

Throughout the Early Bronze Age north-eastern Poland was, on the other hand, home to evolving para-Neolithic societies (Józwiak 2003). Although their pottery showed evidence of contacts with the population of western Poland (Manasterski 2009), their way of life, dependent on gathering and fishing and only marginally on agricultural activity, remained unaltered.

After 2000 cal BC, a new cultural phenomenon, the Trzciniec culture, began to spread from the west (Kuyavia and Great Poland) to the east (Masovia, and beyond the borders of today's Poland), and to the south (Little Poland). The Trzciniec culture, derived from late Bell Beaker groups (Czebreszuk 2001), attained its most distinct archaeological form east of the Vistula (Makarowicz 2010). The arrival of the Trzciniec culture in Little Poland is considered an example of southward migration (Górski 2007: 99–100), estimated to have taken place around 1650/1600 cal BC (Górski 2007: 91).

THE MIDDLE BRONZE AGE

The decline of the Early Bronze Age was marked by the arrival of new cultural trends from the north-west (the Nordic culture: Fogel 1988) and from the south-west (the Tumulus culture: Gedl 1992). The former was the first to appear: the earliest traces of the Nordic culture in western Pomerania date to some time after 1700 cal BC. The Tumulus culture, on the other hand, appeared in Lower Silesia and Little Poland a little later, most likely post-1600 cal BC. Despite visible differences in material culture (in particular, differing styles of metal objects), both these cultural groups maintained cultural contacts and were part of a unified cultural sphere, extending over the same regions as in the Early Bronze Age. Settlement stabilized in this period. Both groups were initially known for their graves, especially kurgans (Fig. 42.2b), and hoards of metal objects. Over time, their cemeteries grew larger and their settlements longer lasting (Makarowicz 2010).

Eastern Poland was still home to a complex of internally diverse phenomena of the Trzciniec culture. Strong connections to earlier prehistoric periods were still visible in Masovia. The region is known mainly for its dune settlements, and an economy that relied only on farming. In Little Poland the Trzciniec culture was in turn characterized by stable settlements whose inhabitants focused on agricultural activity and used kurgan cemeteries, thereby continuing the practices of earlier groups (the Corded Ware and Mierzanowice cultures; see Górski 2007).

THE LATE BRONZE AGE/HALLSTATT PERIOD

The Late Bronze Age in Poland is synonymous with the expansion of the Lausitz or Lusatian culture, which constituted the north-easternmost branch of the Urnfield cultures. The oldest Lausitz artefacts found in Silesia and Great Poland date to after 1400 cal BC (Harding 2000: 18). The Lausitz culture brought the stabilization of settlement, with societies coming to inhabit particular micro-regions permanently. The cemeteries, such as Kietrz in Upper Silesia, were utilized over long periods of time, starting with the Tumulus period and ending with La

Tène (Gedl 1980). The eastward expansion of the Lausitz culture was rather complex. In Little Poland the process consisted mainly in a gradual migration of populations from Silesia. The migrations began around 1300 cal BC (Górski 2007: 91) and were a major step in overcoming the cultural barrier separating the river basins of the upper Vistula and upper Oder. The presence of the Lausitz culture in north-eastern Poland is more difficult to explain, since there is no doubt that it differed significantly from its counterparts in Lower Silesia, Great Poland, Kuyavia, and Little Poland. For instance, finds of bronze objects became more abundant (Dąbrowski 1997; Blajer 2001), and the anthropogenic component in palaeobotanical data has been shown to be smaller (Dąbrowski 1997: 101–4). At the same time the south-eastern part of Poland, in the San River Basin, constituted a distinct cultural sphere, formed by the Tarnobrzeg group that was open to influences both from the steppes as well as from Carpathian Ruthenia to the south (Czopek 1996). As a civilization, the Lausitz culture constituted a period of uninterrupted prosperity lasting nearly a thousand years (from c.1400/1300 to 400 cal BC).

After 800 cal BC the influence of the Hallstatt culture reached Lower Silesia, which has been confirmed by recent archaeological finds (recent research by Boguslaw Gediga: Gediga 2007). The traces of the Hallstatt culture are concentrated in Lower Silesia and scattered throughout a wide belt extending from Great Poland to Kuyavia. The Hallstatt C phase is associated with a new phenomenon, the construction of fortified settlements such as Biskupin (Fig. 42.2d).

Settlement and Economy

Open settlements, composed of rectangular post-built houses surrounded with multi-function pit features, are the most common in Poland and can be found throughout the Bronze Age. The number of settlements known from the Middle Bronze Age is smaller, which may be the result of insufficient research on this period.

In the Early and Late Bronze Age, and the Hallstatt period, there were stable micro-regions often with fortified settlements at the centre. The earliest examples have been found in Bruszczewo in Great Poland (see Fig 42.2a: fortifications dating back to the twentieth century cal BC—Czebreszuk and Müller 2004). In the Carpathian foreland strongholds of the Otomani-Füzesabony culture dating back to the seventeenth and sixteenth centuries cal BC have been uncovered (Gašaj 2002: Fig. 10) (see Chapter 44).

A complex of fortified settlements located on the border of Kuyavia and Great Poland, and comprising several settlements, was particularly important to settlement practices in the Late Bronze Age and the Hallstatt period. Biskupin is the most systematically researched of these settlements: it forms a compact group of 13 rows of houses (see Fig. 42.2d), each composed of up to a dozen identical houses (Niesiołowska-Wędzka 1991). In Lower Silesia the remains of at least two complete homesteads (Wrocław-Milejowice 19 and Stary Śleszów 17) have been excavated. They were enclosed by palisades and thus intentionally isolated, which may indicate that their residents enjoyed a privileged status (Gediga 2007).

From a broader perspective of the evolution of settlement practices and variations in population density, the Bronze Age was characterized by dynamic changes. Increasing settlement density has been observed in the Early Bronze Age, in the settlement area of the Únětice and Mierzanowice cultures. The most significant population growth was noted in the Late Bronze Age and the Hallstatt period (Kurnatowski 1992), when networks of micro-regions, or stable rural communities composed of multiple villages, were formed in many regions, in particular in western and southern Poland.

Fortified settlements located in wet environments have yielded detailed insights into the economy. Farming was developing on three fronts: extensive cereal cultivation; leguminous plant cultivation; and small horticultural plots. In the Early Bronze Age there is evidence of the cultivation of barley (*Hordeum vulgare*), emmer wheat (*Triticum dicoccum*), and einkorn (*Triticum monococcum*) (Czebreszuk and Müller 2004: 263–72). There are also indications that millet (*Panicum miliaceum*) may have been sown on a small scale in the Early Bronze Age (Müller et al. 2010: 262). Leguminous plants known already in the Early Bronze Age include peas (*Pisum sativum*) and lentils (*Lens culinaris*). In addition, seeds of cultivated poppy (*Papaver somniferum*) and dill (*Foenicum vulgare*) were found in Bruszczewo (Müller et al. 2010: 260–4).

The range of plants differed significantly in the Late Bronze Age and Hallstatt period (Harding et al. 2004: 67–119; Müller et al. 2010: 250–87). Millet gained in importance alongside wheat and barley. Oats (*Avena*) were also grown. The most popular leguminous plants included peas, broad bean (*Vicia faba*), and lentils. There are also traces of flax (*Linum usitatissimum*), gold of pleasure (*Camelina sativa*), poppy, field mustard (*Brassica rapa*), and turnip rape (*Brassica rapa* subsp. *oleifera*).

Animal husbandry was intensive at the time, as indicated by large deposits of post-consumption bone waste, as well as layers of manure (Early Bronze Age finds in Bruszczewo; Czebreszuk and Müller 2004: 264–6). A system of tree exploitation was also in place, which may indicate that some species were used for winter grazing (Müller et al. 2010: 576–661). Cattle were the chief livestock, whereas pigs and sheep/goats were of secondary importance. The presence of the horse should also be noted (Müller et al. 2010: 288–314).

The quantities of pig and sheep/goat bones in the Late Bronze Age/Hallstatt period were comparable (Biskupin: Kostrzewski 1950: 39–71). In the Sobiejuchy settlement, however, sheep/goats were found in larger numbers (Harding et al. 2004: 120–64).

The material recovered contained relatively small quantities of fish bones (Makowiecki 2003). This does not necessarily reflect the importance of fishing as a food source; the situation of most Bronze Age settlements, which were located on lake islands and peninsulas, must suggest that fish formed an important component of the diet; in addition, fish bones do not survive well on archaeological sites. Gathering was another way of obtaining food. Acorns, hazelnuts, wild strawberries, and apples/pears were an important part of the diet (Müller et al. 2010: 250–87).

The first instances of anthropogenic pressure, which led to a number of localized ecological disasters, are also associated with the Early Bronze Age. Land exploitation around Bruszczewo may serve as an example. The area was settled uninterruptedly from c.2100/2000 to c.1600 cal BC, with a central fortified settlement present at least in the twentieth and eighteenth centuries BC. The steady and intensive occupation of the land had a significant impact on the environment. Wooded areas in the immediate vicinity of the settlement (2–3 km), composed mainly of small, scattered groups of trees (Müller et al. 2010: 232–7), were drastically depleted (Müller et al. 2010: 78). Human activity (farming) and cattle grazing led to the degradation of the top humus layer and intensified erosion (Müller et al. 2010: 270). The consequences of the changes in water composition in the adjacent lake were even more serious. Studies have showed the presence of algae, eggs of human and animal parasites, and spores of coprophilous fungi. It is very likely that during some periods in the Bronze Age the water in the lake was undrinkable, or even toxic to humans and animals. In the case of Bruszczewo we can assume that the destruction of the environment by humans was the chief reason for the abandonment of the settlement.

Burials

The shift from inhumation to cremation during the Middle to Late Bronze Age transition is among the most significant cultural changes to occur in the period. This does not mean, of course, that burial customs before and after the transition were homogeneous. On the contrary, funerary practices have always varied across time and space. In the Early Bronze Age three types of burial practice mean that three geographical areas can be identified: the northwest, the south-west (the northern and southern part of the Únětice culture settlement area respectively), and the south-east (the Mierzanowice culture).

In the south-east, men and women were buried in positions that were the mirror image of each other. The deceased were placed on their side, aligned west-east with the face to the south. Males lay on their right side, with heads facing west, females on their left side, with heads facing east (Machnik 1977). Gender differentiation was not clearly marked in burial practices in the south-west. The dead were buried in the same posture: on their left side, in the foetal position, oriented on a north–south axis, with the head pointing south and face turned to the east.

In the north-west, or in the northern part of the Únětice settlement area, cemeteries, although less numerous, were more spectacular, for instance Łęki Małe (see Fig. 42.2c; Czebreszuk 2001: 84–8), as well as in Brusy and Przysieka Polska (Czebreszuk 2009). This may be due to an unequal distribution of the right to burial which, in the north, was granted mainly to members of the upper class. This hierarchy indicates greater social stratification in the Únětice culture in the north than in the south. It should also be noted that the rare extended burials, apart from a few isolated finds such as one found at Bruszczewo where a mat made of osier was used to wrap the body of the deceased (Müller et al. 2010: 724–9), diverged from the burial positions that were a feature of the south. The Bruszczewo male was placed on his right side on an east-west axis, with his head pointing west, and face turned south.

By the Middle Bronze Age the custom of constructing barrows (kurgans) became widespread, and is characteristic of the Tumulus culture (see Fig. 42.2b). Kurgans are most often mounds of heaped rocks arranged in the form or stars, rings, or paved areas (Gedl 1992). In eastern Poland kurgans were only one among a great variety of elements characteristic of the Trzciniec culture (Makarowicz 2010). This diversity is undoubtedly a sign of a low level of cultural integration of the population inhabiting the area.

Cremation—the new practice of depositing the ashes of the cremated dead in a cinerary urn—grew in popularity during the Middle to Late Bronze Age transition. In large, long-lived cemeteries utilized from the Tumulus to the Lausitz cultures, inhumation burial was gradually replaced by cremation. The shift was documented, for example, in the large cemetery at Kietrz which was among the largest in the entire Urnfield zone, with approximately four thousand excavated graves (Gedl 1980: 82). The cemeteries were used continuously from the Middle Bronze Age up to the later stages of La Tène. This continuity constitutes a major socio-religious characteristic, and proves not only the stability of settlement structures but also the existence of a universal right to burial which is not evident in earlier periods.

Material Culture

In the Bronze Age pottery plays a key role, not just in terms of utilitarian production but as an important cultural identifier. Next to pottery, however, a new group of objects begin to emerge. Metal products become a marker of individual and group identity, especially among the elites in the western part of the area. The artefacts fall into four stylistic categories, characteristic of Únětice, the Tumulus cultures, the Urnfields, and the Hallstatt culture.

Pottery

Bronze Age pottery displays a variety of styles that can be divided into a few basic groups. The sequence of stylistic transformations can be best observed in western Poland, and particularly in Lower Silesia and Great Poland. It opens with a series of Únětice styles that are technologically highly developed (thin walls despite the frequently large size of the vessels, and very carefully detailed body) and diverse in form. The most characteristic trait of the Únětice style after 2000 cal BC was carination (angular profiling of the body), more evocative of the shape of metal than clay vessels (Fig. 42.3, A2).

After 1500 cal BC, following an interval, a new pottery style emerged that can be defined as knobbed ware of the late Tumulus and the early Lausitz periods (Fig. 42.3, A1). Its main feature, besides its high technological standard, is its specific ornamentation: knobs were applied to the surface or shaped as protrusions from inside the body of the vessel.

In the Late Bronze Age an array of Lausitz styles developed, characterized on the one hand by regional diversity and on the other by shared features, including a clear division into cooking ware and table ware, a high technological level (especially in table ware), and a great variety of pot types, including zoomorphic and miniature vessels, rattles, and shoe-shaped containers (Figs 42.3, A3–6).

Recent Hallstatt-period finds in Lower Silesia (Gediga 2007; 2009), and in particular the increasingly frequent discoveries of painted pottery, have allowed a specific Hallstatt style to be identified. The importance of the cemetery at Damasław, Lower Silesia (Gediga 2009), must be noted in this context. One of its wealthy chamber graves (no. 4270) yielded a unique find (Fig. 42.3, B): a ritual clay cart with painted ornaments (Gediga 2007: Fig. 9; 2009: Fig. 9).

The development of the northern (Pomerania) and the north-eastern (Masuria, Masovia) regions followed a different course. Pottery styles show less stability and inferior craftsmanship. The 'Trzciniec style', the most typical of the region, is the best exam-

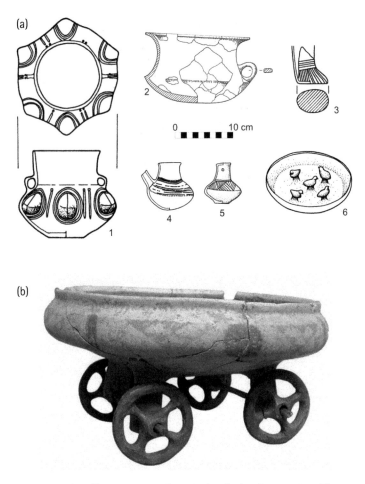

FIG. 42.3 Bronze Age/ Hallstatt pottery from Poland. A1. Swarzynica (Kaczmarek 2002: table 2: D9); A2. Łęki Małe (Kowiańska-Piaszykowa 2008); A3. Biernatki (Kaczmarek 2002: table 31: B1); A4-5. Śródka (Kaczmarek 2002: table 24: B2-3); A6. Wartosław (Kaczmarek 2002: table 22:14). B. Damasław (Lower Silesia), grave 4270 (Gediga 2009).

ple. A single form of pottery was very common in the early phases of the Trzciniec group: a large pot with an S-shaped profile and a decorative strip running from the neck of the pot across the body (Czebreszuk 2001). Other ceramic features were strictly regional. It is therefore difficult to speak of any unifying Trzciniec style in Poland (Makarowicz 2010). Similarly, in the Late Bronze Age, the so-called Lausitz pottery (Dąbrowski 1997) greatly diverged in style from the technological standards and stylistic patterns used in the west.

In south-eastern Poland a group of Early Bronze Age Mierzanowice styles has been recorded. Initially mugs, jugs, and amphorae were the most popular; later on jars (Kadrow and Machnik 1997). The Mierzanowice style became increasingly fragmented until, in the late phase of the culture, there were as many as four distinct stylistic units corresponding to four discrete groups that emerged within the Mierzanowice culture. Trzciniec styles were also present in the area, and quickly took on a distinctly regional character (Górski 2007). Their specific nature was also the result of influences from the Carpathian Basin (Otomani-Füzesabony and Piliny cultures). In the Late Bronze Age, starting *c*.1300 cal BC, Lausitz styles reached Little Poland (Górski 2007).

Metallurgy

Stylistic transformations in metallurgy in Poland have been the subject of many detailed studies (Blajer 1990; 2001). Metal was widely and continuously exploited through the Bronze Age only in western Poland. In the east there are only intermittent periods when metal objects were common. This tendency is particularly evident in south-eastern Poland and has been observed in the Middle and beginning of the Late Bronze Age (objects stylistically reminiscent of the Carpathian Basin cultures: Blajer 2001: 268–79), as well as at the close of the Hallstatt period (Blajer 2001: 293–7).

The area was home to three major stylistic groups of metal products, namely Únětice (Blajer 1990), Tumulus (Blajer 2001), and Lausitz. Experts have further subdivided them into a number of specific styles. It has been widely accepted that the metallurgy of the Lausitz culture in the Hallstatt period (especially in Lower Silesia) already possesses the key features of the metallurgy of the Hallstatt culture (Blajer 2001: 289; Gediga 2007).

Nordic metalworking was continuously present in the north-western part of Poland, starting in the Middle Bronze Age (Fogel 1988), which confirms the hypothesis that western Pomerania belonged within the Nordic cultural zone. There is some evidence that a local metallurgical industry was present in Poland already in the Early Bronze Age. Recent research indicates the long-term presence of metallurgical activity at Bruszczewo. Metallurgical analysis of artefacts from there has identified them as corresponding to metal types of Rüdiger Krause's III–IV horizon (Krause 2003; later modified by Rassmann: Müller et al. 2010:713–22). As early as the second millennium BC bronze metallurgy was a major element in the culture of the societies inhabiting western Poland, despite the fact that the region was remote from any known metal deposits. In the Middle Bronze Age there are indications of metallurgical production, for example in the Szczepidło settlement in the middle Warta Valley (Makarowicz 2010). Regional styles of metal objects testify to the presence of a local industry, a continuing phenomenon in western Poland from the Early Bronze Age on (Blajer 2001).

INDUSTRIES BASED ON OTHER RAW MATERIALS

The stabilization of settlement observable in the Bronze Age favoured the manufacture of a variety of objects. Research at Bruszczewo, as well as in Late Bronze Age/Hallstatt period settlements on the border of Kuyavia and Great Poland, has uncovered the evidence of horn- and bone-working, carpentry, quarrying, a flint industry, weaving and basketry, as well as amber-working.

Bone and horn artefacts have been preserved in large quantities in peat environments. These raw materials were used to manufacture various implements, such as chisels, pickaxes, flat hoes, hammers, pins, many types of handle attachment, and (especially popular) awls or needles (Müller et al. 2010: 662–99). Bone was also used, among other things, to fashion hoes and weaving blades made of scapulae, characteristic of the Early Bronze Age (Müller et al. 2010: 662–99). Antler and bone were also widely used in manufacturing various tools in Hallstatt settlements (Drzewicz 2004).

The varied Early Bronze Age flint industry has received much attention in the literature (recent studies: Libera 2001). The flint industry was particularly well developed in southeastern Poland (Kadrow and Machnik 1997; Libera 2001). In western Pomerania, on the other hand, flint was important in the manufacture of Scandinavian daggers (Czebreszuk 2001). These were prestige rather than utilitarian objects. With the Únětice culture metal began to replace flint and stone tools. This phenomenon is even more pronounced in the Late Bronze Age when stone implements had become rare, in particular in western Poland.

The use of metal tools in carpentry had a big influence on the development of this industry. This is true in the Bruszczewo settlement, in the construction of houses and defensive structures, dated by dendrochronology to the early eighteenth century cal BC, built entirely using metal tools (Müller et al. 2010: 576–661). Carpenters made use of elaborate wood joints (Müller et al. 2010: 166–231). Similarly, a whole range of building techniques were known in the eighth century cal BC at Biskupin (Kostrzewski 1950: 238–85).

There is also evidence to support the existence of other areas of production. Numerous weaving implements document the development of the textile industry (Kostrzewski 1950: 132–60), as does pottery with imprints of woven fabric. Traces of wattle were preserved in peat deposits, including the spectacular wicker walls at Bruszczewo, dating to the early eighteenth century cal BC (Müller et al. 2010: 166–231).

Amber production, known since the Neolithic, continued to flourish in the Bronze Age. In the Early Bronze Age manufacturing centres were concentrated along the coast, in particular in the lower Vistula Valley (Czebreszuk 2009). Over time, amber workshops spread inland and are found, for example, in the Komorowo settlement (Bukowski 2002). The daily use of amber objects has been confirmed throughout the Bronze Age, especially in the western part of the country. In the Únětice culture two distinct styles can be distinguished: northern and southern. Stunning disc-shaped artefacts were uncovered in large quantities in the north, especially in cemeteries (kurgans with many imported bronze objects, gold, complex wood and stone constructions: Czebreszuk 2009). Beads dominate in the south, as part of composite necklaces (most frequently with coiled copper-wire ornaments). Beads are also the main product in the Middle Bronze Age, and especially in the Hallstatt period, when amber production and exchange intensified (Bukowski 2002).

Other Aspects of Social Life in the Bronze Age

An analysis of the Polish Bronze Age cannot ignore certain phenomena that are local variants of larger, Europe-wide tendencies (such as hoard deposition, or the establishment of communities along major trade routes), or the result of specific processes that have no equivalent elsewhere on the continent (e.g. structures of Bruszczewo-Łęki Małe type, or the network of settlements with Biskupin as the most spectacular).

The Deposition of Hoards

The practice of depositing hoards of bronze objects was common throughout the Bronze Age, in Poland as elsewhere (Blajer 2001) (see Chapter 7). It was most frequent in western Poland and, during certain periods, in the south-east. The local practice is part of a widespread phenomenon observed in Early Bronze Age groups, the Tumulus, Urnfield, and Hallstatt cultures. Wojciech Blajer's detailed analysis has shown that the reasons for depositing metal objects were multifold (Blajer 2001: 253–8). Wet areas seem to have been the preferred location throughout the Bronze Age, as can be observed in Pomerania (Blajer 2001: Fig. 39).

Trade Route Communities

Among the cultural innovations of the Bronze Age was the development of extensive socio-cultural contacts. This in turn entailed different cultural structures from those of the Neolithic: Bronze Age communities are found not only in clusters (forming what was known as the 'archaeological group' in traditional scholarship), but can also take on a linear character. Communities started to concentrate along trade routes. In the Early Bronze Age (Fig. 42.1b) and the Hallstatt period (Bukowski 1993: Fig. 2), Poland was part of an extensive network of contacts. Maps representing the distribution of finds for both periods show a belt roughly 100 km wide extending from the Moravian Gate in the south, through Lower Silesia, Great Poland, Kuyavia, to the Vistula delta. The Early Bronze Age finds recorded in this area include amber, gold artefacts, bronze objects imported from remote regions of Europe, as well as remarkable 'princely kurgans' (see Fig. 42.2c) and fortified settlements (see Fig. 42.2a). During the Hallstatt period amber becomes more abundant in this zone (Bukowski 2002: Map IV), as do Hallstatt imports (Bukowski 1993: Fig. 2).

The cultural structures that developed along the lower Vistula constituted the northern stretches of what can be termed the first and second amber routes. In the Early Bronze Age (the first half of the second millennium cal BC) the first amber route in Europe (Czebreszuk 2009) ran from the Bay of Gdańsk through Kuyavia, Great Poland, Silesia, and the Moravian Gate to the upper Tisza, and then from the Middle Danube to the Adriatic and beyond to the Peloponnese. The second route, used in the Hallstatt period, overlapped with the earlier one along the Polish stretch. From the Moravian Gate, however, it headed for the eastern Alps, then to the Caput Adria, and terminated in central Italy. The modification of this southern stretch of the route (when it stopped in Italy) took place after 1200 cal BC. It is worth noting that a large concentration of house-urns and face-urns dating to that period were found in the Gdańsk area; they are analogous to similar finds made in Italy.

In addition to the amber route, seaways were becoming increasingly popular trade routes (see Fig. 42.1b). One of them connected the lower Vistula region, Pomerania, and Mecklenburg with Jutland, and further away, with the North Sea, the British Isles, and Atlantic Europe.

Case study 1: Bruszczewo- Łęki Małe Type Structures

The best example of the transformations that affected Únětice society after 2000 cal BC is the cluster known as the Kościan group (Czebreszuk 2001: 149–50). It covers an area 50 km long (north-south) by 20 km wide (west-east), located on the main route connecting Lower Silesia and Kuyavia, and continuing to the amber-rich Vistula delta. This small region yielded a particularly large number of Early Bronze Age finds. The structures uncovered included a fortified settlement in Bruszczewo; at least two kurgan cemeteries of so-called princely tumuli (Łęki Małe and Przysieka Polska); hoards (among others those from Czempiń, Granowo, Nacław, Poniec, and Szczodrowo); and other settlements. The stability of settlements in this region has been confirmed by excavations at Bruszczewo (see Fig. 42.2a). According to the earliest radiocarbon date, the main defensive structures (two palisades and a moat separating the settlement from the higher ground to the north) were erected in the twentieth century cal BC (Czebreszuk and Müller 2004: 293–310). On the other hand, palynological data shows that a settlement (most likely unfortified) existed as early as the twenty-first century cal BC (Müller et al. 2010: 66). Dendrochronology was used to determine the age of supporting defensive structures in the eastern part of the site (two wicker walls and a dividing wall made of double vertical pillars and horizontal planks wedged between them), and vestiges of buildings. They were constructed between 1797 and 1779 BC (Müller et al. 2010: 244–7). The fortifications were most likely destroyed in the seventeenth century BC, as the latest fills of rubbish pits indicate (Czebreszuk and Müller 2004: 293–310). Bruszczewo was home to a metallurgist's workshop. Other artefacts documented on this site included a tuyère, crucibles, clay stands, a stone mould for bracelets, finished products in the form of daggers, axes, and ornaments at different wear stages (one of the dagger blades was shortened by repeated sharpening), as well as metal scraps collected for remelting, and droplets from the casting of liquid metal. Metal analyses have shown that metal objects made of types of copper characteristic of horizons III and IV, according to Rüdiger Krause and Knut Rassmann, were manufactured and used locally, which suggests an extended period of metallurgical activity at Bruszczewo, spanning the period 2000 to 1600 cal BC (Müller et al. 2010: 712–22). The intensive exploitation of the natural environment included cultivation of cereals, legumes, vegetables, and other domesticated plants; cattle and pig husbandry, and the breeding of small herbivores, which brought about the localized ecological disaster discussed above.

In the direct vicinity of the Bruszczewo settlement on the other side of the Samica river, there was a large cemetery of tumuli, of which only the chance discovery at Przysieka Polska survives (Czebreszuk and Müller 2004: 317–29). Another better-preserved barrow cemetery was located several kilometres north at Łęki Małe (see Fig. 42.2c) (Kowiańska-Piaszykowa 2008). It was composed of a row of at least 14 tumuli extending along the edge of the valley of the Mogilnica river. Excavations in five of them revealed complex stone and wood structures, richly equipped inhumation burials, with bronze, gold, and amber objects, and much pottery. Such a large number of linearly aligned tumuli indicates the long-term use of the cemetery, which undoubtedly served as the burial ground of the elite or ruling class. The cultural importance of this site has been confirmed by the concentration of bronze hoards in the area, associated with the Kościan group (Blajer 1990).

Significantly, the area occupied by the Kościan group constituted a small enclave isolated from both the Głogów and Wrocław clusters on the Oder, and from the Kuyavia cluster to the north-east, while acting as a bridge between the two. Its location along a trading route was a key factor in the emergence within the Kościan group of settlement and cultural structures that can be called 'Bruszczewo-Łęki Małe structures'. They were typically characterized by a stable situation that lasted a few centuries, which was evidenced both in the (central) settlement and in the cemeteries containing the remains of members of the elite.

This hierarchical funerary practice signals the presence of a well-established and most likely hereditary ruling class, at the head of an efficiently functioning community that was capable both of constructing a spectacular complex like Bruszczewo and of maintaining it in good order for a few hundred years. The community owed its long-term prosperity in great measure to its location along the amber route, which has been confirmed by the find of a well-preserved amber bead at Bruszczewo in a cultural layer dated to the nineteenth century cal BC (Müller et al. 2010: 696).

Phenomena such as Bruszczewo-Łęki Małe may be interpreted in terms of proto-state structures possessing a stable governing body, an extensive network of extra-regional contacts, varied artisanal production, and a well-organized food economy. This entity lasted for at least two hundred years and its decline dates to the seventeenth century cal BC.

Case Study 2: The Biskupin Settlement Network

A complex of over a dozen contemporaneous fortified settlements on the border of Kuyavia and Great Poland was particularly important for Bronze Age/Hallstatt settlement (Harding and Rączkowski 2010). Biskupin is the most extensively researched among these sites (see Fig. 42.2d). Designed and constructed as a compact settlement, Biskupin comprises 13 rows of buildings each composed of up to a dozen or more identical houses (Niesiołowska-Wędzka 1991). Each settlement most likely functioned as a centre for a particular community unit within a network of territorial structures. As a whole, the settlement complex dates to the eighth century cal BC. Dendrochronological data has helped us narrow down the chronology of some of the settlements. Wood used in construction in Biskupin was cut between 750 and 708 BC (Ważny 2009: 63). Individual timbers at Sobiejuchy have been dated to c.750 BC (Harding and Rączkowski 2010). The date of a piece of timber used in a construction in Izdebno was determined as 'circa or after' 729 BC (Ważny 2009: 72). Wood sampled in Ostrowite Trzemeszeńskie was dated to 'circa or after' 706 BC. In summary, it can be said that a network of territorially organized units extended across the border region between Kuyavia and Great Poland. Communities belonging to that network were internally well-organized, and functioned on the basis of division of labour. They undoubtedly possessed governmental structures capable of mobilizing collective effort. Significantly, however, there is no evidence of this type of elite within the settlement structure of Biskupin, where all houses are identical and traces of specialized activity (metallurgy, weaving, use of draught animals, etcetera) are fairly evenly distributed among many households (see Fig. 42.2d) (Niesiołowska-Wędzka 1991: Fig. 3).

There can be little doubt about the existence of a widespread network of small units concentrated around fortified settlements in the eighth century cal BC. The presence of this type of settlement structure opens up a number of questions. To what extent were these territorial units independent of one another? What was their political status? These and other questions should be the subject of further research. The potential information resource of these Hallstatt period fortified settlements cannot be overemphasized. The remains of wooden fortifications have been preserved in all the sites, and are suitable for dendrochronological dating, which might enable us to reconstruct a detailed chronology of construction in each settlement, that is, to create a specific micro-history of the region covering the eighth century cal BC. Moreover, each of these (peat-based) settlements contains a wealth of potential data relating to human-environment relationships, as well as an abundant collection of artefacts of organic materials.

Conclusion

During the Bronze Age the territory of Poland constituted the eastern fringes of the culturally most advanced region of Europe. It was divided along a major cultural border into two parts: east and west. Throughout the period, the south-west (Lower Silesia and Great Poland, along with the narrow zone leading through Kuyavia to Eastern Pomerania) belonged to a zone delimited by the Harz, the Rudawy (Erzgebirge), and the Eastern Alps (Harding 2000: Fig. 13.1, bottom). It saw a sequence of cultural transformations: Únětice culture–Tumulus culture–Urnfield cultures–Hallstatt culture. The north-west (western Pomerania), on the other hand, remained longest within the Nordic cultural sphere of influence (the sequence here being Únětice culture–Nordic culture). Both the north-western and the south-western parts of Poland continued to interact; this can be traced through cross-cultural borrowing and imports.

The eastern half of Poland was isolated from the mainstream transformations of Bronze Age Europe. Little Poland played a particularly significant role as the northern fringe of the Carpathian Basin culture, and gained in importance especially after 1700 cal BC. Societies occupying the north-eastern part of Poland had a different lifestyle, rooted in earlier periods of prehistory.

The 'civilizational geography' outlined here was shaped by two major factors. The first, social, consisted of changes leading to increased internal group stratification. These processes predate the Bronze Age, and are marked by the appearance of Bell Beakers. It is no coincidence that the area they occupied underwent a sweeping cultural transformation in the Bronze Age.

The second factor derives from the first: in an internally stratified society, military aristocracy plays a key role. The need to reassert its position dictates its activity; and the principal means of satisfying this need is material culture, and in particular the acquisition of goods, especially products made of exotic materials ('strategic raw materials'). This in turn contributed to the creation of a Europe-wide network of exchanges. Poland was home to amber deposits of the highest quality, and in the Bronze Age amber became one of the raw materials most sought after in Europe, including the Mediterranean zone.

From the diachronic point of view, the Bronze Age in the Polish territory can be divided into two long periods of prosperity, separated by a relatively short interval. The first period of steady growth spans the Early Bronze Age (c.2300–1600/1500 cal BC) and is associated with the Únětice culture. The second period of uninterrupted growth is the Late Bronze Age/Hallstatt period (c.1400/1300–400 cal BC), during which the Lausitz culture initiated an unprecedented process of cultural transformation (the stabilization of settlement and increased population density). The intervening Middle Bronze Age (c.1600/1500–1400/1300 cal BC), associated with the Tumulus culture, saw a crisis in settlement practices, although there was no disruption to cultural contacts, which persisted, especially among the inhabitants of the western half of the country.

Bibliography

Blajer, W. (1990). *Skarby z wczesnej epoki brązu na ziemiach polskich*. Wrocław: Ossolineum.

—— (2001). *Skarby przedmiotów metalowych z epoki brązu i wczesnej epoki żelaza na ziemiach polskich*. Kraków: Jagiellonian University.

Budziszewski, J. and Włodarczak, P. (2010). *Kultura puchara dzwonowatych na Wyżynie Małopolskiej*. Kraków: Institute of Archaeology and Ethnology PAS.

Bukowski, Z. (1993). 'Über die früheisenzeitliche sog. Bernsteinstrasse im Flussgebiet von Oder und Weichsel', in C.W. Beck and J. Bouzek (eds.), *Amber in Archaeology*, Proceedings of the Second International Conference on Amber in Archaeology, Libice 1990. Prague: Univerzita Karlova, 117–28.

—— (2002). *Znaleziska bursztynu w zespołach z epoki brązu i z wczesnej epoki żelaza z dorzecza Odry oraz Wisły*. Warsaw: Institute of Archaeology and Ethnology PAS.

Butent, B. (1992). 'Zagadnienie kurhanów w Niedarach i Ludgierzowicach, gm. Trzebnica, woj. Wrocław', *Studia Archaeologiczne*, XXII, 35–83.

Czebreszuk, J. (2001). *Schyłek neolitu i początki epoki brązu w strefie południowo-zachodniobałtyckiej (III i początki II tys. przed Chr.). Alternatywny model kultur*. Poznań: Adam Mickiewicz University.

—— (2009). 'The northern section of the first amber trail. An outline of significance for civilization development', in A. Palavestra, C. W. Beck, and J. M. Todd (eds.), *Amber in Archaeology*, Proceedings of the Fifth International Conference on Amber in Archaeology, Belgrad 2006. Belgrade: National Museum, 100–9, 284–5.

—— and Müller, J. (eds.) (2004). *Bruszczewo. Ausgrabungen und Forschungen in einer prähistorischen Siedlungskammer Grosspolens/Badania mikroregionu z terenu Wielkopolski. Band/Tom I. Forschungsstand—Erste Ergebnisse—Das östliche Feuchtbodenareal/Stan badań—Pierwsze wyniki—Wschodnia, torfowa część stanowiska*. Poznań-Kiel-Rahden (Westf.): Verlag Marie Leidorf.

Czopek, S. (1996). *Grupa tarnobrzeska nad środkowym Sanem i dolnym Wisłokiem*. Rzeszów: Rzeszów University.

Dąbrowski, J. (1997). *Epoka brązu w północno-wschodniej Polsce*. Białystok: Białostockie Towarzystwo Naukowe.

Drzewicz, A. (2004). *Wyroby z kości i poroża z osiedla obronnego ludności kultury łużyckiej w Biskupinie*. Warsaw: State Archaeological Museum.

Fogel, J. (1988). *'Import' nordyjski na ziemiach polskich u schyłku epoki brązu*. Poznań: Wydawnictwo UAM.

Gašaj, D. (2002). 'Chronologia/Chronology', in J. Gancarski (ed.), *Między Mykenami a Bałtykiem. Kultura Otomani-Füzesabony*. Krosno-Warsaw: Muzeum Podkarpackie, 94–101.

Gediga, B. (2007). *Problemy obrazu kultury wczesnej epoki żelaza na Śląsku w świetle nowych badań terenowych*, *Śląskie Sprawozdania Archaeologiczne*, vol. 49, 123–46.

—— (2009). 'Refleksje o problematyce badań nad dziejami społeczeństw tarnobrzeskiej kultury łużyckiej', in S. Czopek (ed.), *Tarnobrzeska kultura łużycka—źródła i interpretacje*. Rzeszów: Rzeszów University, 119–37.

Gedl, M. (1980). 'Studia nad periodyzacją kultury łużyckiej w południowej części Śląska', *Archaeologia Polski*, 25:1, 79–129.

—— (1992). *Die Vorlausitzer Kultur. Prähistorische Bronzefunde*, vol. XXI/2. Stuttgart: Franz Steiner.

Górski, J. (2007). *Chronologia kultury trzcinieckiej na lessach Niecki Niedziańskiej*. Kraków: Archaeological Museum.

Harding, A. (2000). *European Societies in the Bronze Age*. Cambridge: Cambridge University Press.

—— Ostoja-Zagórski, J., Rackham, J. and Palmer, C. (2004). *Sobiejuchy: A Fortified Site of the Early Iron Age in Poland*. Warsaw: Institute of Archaeology and Ethnology PAS.

—— and Rączkowski, W. (2010). 'Living on the lake in the Iron Age: new results from geophysical survey and dendrochronology on sites of Biskupin type', *Antiquity*, 84: 386–404.

Józwiak, B. (2003). *Społeczności subneolitu wschodnioeuropejskiego na Niżu Polskim w międzyrzeczu Odry i Wisły*. Poznań: Institute of Prehistory AMU.

Kaczmarek, M. (2002). *Zachodniowielkopolskie społeczności kultury łużyckiej w epoce brązu*. Poznań: Wydawnistwo Naukowe UAM.

Kadrow, S. (2001). *U progu nowej epoki. Gospodarka i społeczeństwo wczesnego okresu epoki brązu w Europie Środkowej*. Kraków: Institute of Archaeology and Ethnology PAS.

—— and Machnik, J. (1997). *Kultura mierzanowicka. Chronologia, taksonomia i rozwój przestrzenny*. Kraków: Wydawnictwo PAN w Krakowie.

Kostrzewski, J. (ed.) (1950). *III Sprawozdanie z prac wykopaliskowych w grodzie kultury łużyckiej w Biskupinie w powiecie żnińskim. Za lata 1938–1939 i 1946–1948*. Poznań: Poznań University.

Kośko, A. (1991). *Ze studiów nad kujawską enklawą naddunajskiej cywilizacji wczesnobrązowej*, Poznań-Inowrocław: Institute of Prehistory AMU.

Kowiańska-Piaszykowa, M. (2008). *Cmentarzysko kurhanowe z wczesnej epoki brązu w Łękach Małych w Wielkopolsce*. Poznań: Archaeological Museum.

Krause, R. (2003). *Studien zur kupfer-und frühbronzezeitlichen Metallurgie zwischen Karpatenbecken und Ostsee*, Vorgeschichtliche Forschungen, 24. Rahden/Westf.: Verlag Marie Leidorf.

Kurnatowski, S. (1992). 'Próba oceny zmian zaludnienia ziem polskich między XIII w. p.n.e. a IV w. n.e.', in K. Kaczanowski, S. Kurnatowski, A. Malinowski, and J. Piontek, *Zaludnienie ziem polskich między XIII w. p.n.e. a IV w. n.e.—materiały źródłowe, próba oceny*. Warsaw: Wydawnictwo SGPiS, 15–99.

Libera, J. (2001). *Krzemienne formy bifacjalne na terenach Polski i zachodniej Ukrainy (od środkowego neolitu do wczesnej epoki brązu)*. Lublin: Maria Curie-Skłodowska University.

Machnik, J. (1977). *Frühbronzezeit Polens. Übersicht über die Kulturen und Kulturgruppen*, Wrocław: Ossolineum.

Makarowicz, P. (2003). 'Northern and southern Bell Beakers in Poland', in J. Czebreszuk and M. Szmyt (eds.), *The Northeast Frontier of Bell Beakers, Proceedings of the symposium held at the Adam Mickiewicz University, Poznań (Poland), 26–29 May 2002*, British Archaeological Reports (International Series), 1,155. Oxford: Archaeopress, 39–49.

—— (2010). *Trzciniecki krąg kulturowy—wspólnota pograniczna Wschodu i Zachodu Europy*. Poznań: Wydawnictwo Poznańskie.

Makowiecki, D. (2003). *Historia ryb i rybołówstwa w holocenie na Niżu Polskim w świetle badań archeoichtiologicznych*. Poznań: Institute of Archaeology and Ethnology PAS.

Manasterski, D. (2009). *Pojezierze Mazurskie u schyłku neolitu i na początku epoki brązu w świetle zespołów typu Ząbie-Szestno*. Warsaw: Institute of Archaeology WU.

Müller, J., Czebreszuk, J., and Kneisel, J. (eds.) (2010). *Bruszczewo II. Badania mikroregionu osadniczego z terenu Wiekopolski/Ausgrabungen und Forschungen in einer prähistorischen Siedlungskammer Grosspolens*. Bonn: Dr Rudolf Habelt.

Niesiołowska-Wędzka, A. (1991). 'Procesy urbanizacyjne w kulturze łużyckiej', in J. Jaskanis (ed.), *Prahistoryczny gród w Biskupinie. Problematyka osiedli obronnych na początku epoki żelaza*. Warsaw: State Archaeological Museum, 57–80.

Rassmann, K. and Schoknecht, U. (1997). 'Insignien der Macht—Die Stabdolche aus dem Depot von Melz II', in A. Hänsel and B. Hänsel (eds.), *Gaben an die Götter. Schätzen der Bronzezeit Europas*. Berlin: Museum für Vor- und Frühgeschichte, 43–7.

Ważny, T. (2009). 'Dendrochronologia drewna biskupińskiego, czyli co drzewa zapisały w przyrostach rocznych', in L. Babiński (ed.), *Stan i perspektywy zachowania drewna biskupińskiego*. Biskupin: Archaeological Museum, 63–76.

CHAPTER 43

THE CZECH LANDS AND AUSTRIA IN THE BRONZE AGE

LUBOŠ JIRÁŇ, MILAN SALAŠ, AND ALEXANDRA KRENN-LEEB

Introduction: Natural Environment and Landscapes

The Czech lands, consisting of Bohemia and Moravia, and Austria, constitute a very varied natural environment. The territory of Bohemia makes up an enclosed geographical unit, wreathed by chains of mountains. The landscape is broken up by numerous hilly areas and depressions, and threaded by countless streams and rivers associated with the lower-lying parts. The main watercourses are the Vltava (Moldau), which runs through Bohemia from south to north, and the Labe (Elbe), which on Czech territory flows from north-east to north-west Bohemia. Also significant is a left-bank tributary of the Labe, the Ohře (Eger), which is a major axis in the north-west, running along the foothills of the Ore Mountains (Erzgebirge). Moravia also has a dense network of rivers and streams. The main rivers—the Morava (March), Bečva, and Svratka—run basically north to south, and jointly were part of the hugely important prehistoric route across Europe that linked the Mediterranean to the shores of the Baltic Sea. The left-bank tributaries of the Morava also provided natural lines of communication, joining Moravia eastwards to the Carpathian Basin via passes through the Carpathian Mountains (Fig. 43.1a).

Because of the marked geomorphological zoning of Bohemia and Moravia, the climate is not uniform across the territory. The warmest areas are the lowlands along the Labe, Ohře, and the lower reaches of the Vltava, Morava, Dyje, and Svratka. Rainfall is distributed evenly across the four seasons. The driest areas lie to the south-east of high mountain ridges, which create a rain shadow, as in the case of the Ore Mountains and the Drnholec Hills (*Drnholecká pahorkatina*). During the Bronze Age a major role was played by soil conditions, with settlements preferring black earths, which are usually associated with underlying loess.

In contrast to Bohemia and Moravia, Austria is much more taken up by mountain ranges, covering nearly 70 percent its territory. Lowlands of any size are to be found in the east of the

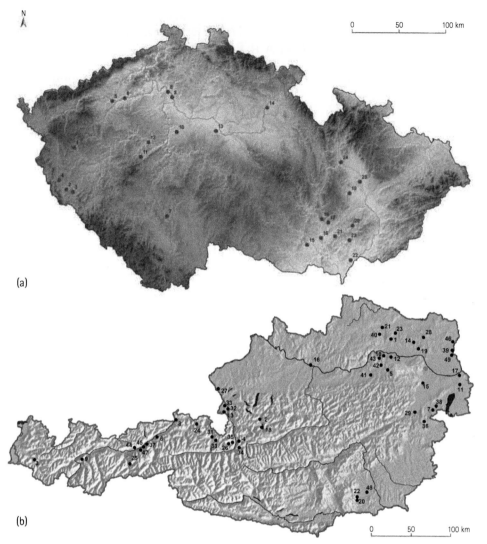

FIG. 43.1 (a) Map showing Bohemian and Moravian sites mentioned in the text. Bohemia: 1. Konstantinovy Lázně (district Tachov), 2. Meclov-Březí (district Domažlice), 3. Milavče (district Domažlice), 4. Svržno-Černý vrch ((district Domažlice), 5. Žatec (district Louny), 6. Březno (district Louny), 7. Hosty (district České Budějovice), 8. Horní Počaply (district Mělnik), 9. Vliněves (district Mělnik), 10. Prague-Hostivař (district Prague), 11. Plešivec hillfort (district Beroun), 12. Tetín (district Beroun), 13. Skalka near Velim (district Kolín), 14. Skalice district Hradec Králové. Moravia: 15. Šumice (district Znojmo), 16. Blučina (district Brno-venkov), 17. Velatice (district Brno-venkov), 18. Brno-Obřany (district Brno-město), 19. Čehovice (district Prostějov), 20. Dobročkovice (district Vyškov), 21. Lovčičky (district Vyškov), 22. Lužice (district Hodonín), 23. Věteřov (district Hodonín), 24. Moravičany (district Šumperk), 25. Olomouc-Slavonín (district Olomouc).

Map: authors.

(b) Map showing Austrian sites mentioned in the text. 1. Baierdorf (Lower Austria), 2. Bad Goisern-Arikogel (Upper Austria), 3. Bartholomäberg-Friaga (Vorarlberg), 4. Bischofshofen (Salzburg region), 5. Böheimkirchen (Lower Austria), 6. Brixlegg (Tyrol), 7. Drassburg (Burgen-

country. Nonetheless, the Alps themselves are interlaced with numerous fertile valleys following the course of the larger rivers. The more northerly parts of Austria are watered by the west-east flowing Danube, which constituted both a natural regional boundary and a major line of communication. It provided a link between this area and the more advanced Carpathian Basin from the start of the Bronze Age, and indeed before. The climate of the northern, eastern, and southern regions of Austria favoured the uninterrupted development of settlement by early farmers. The eastern regions are drier, with harder frosts in winter, but higher temperatures in summer (Pannonian climate) (Fig. 43.1b).

Cultural Sequence and Chronology

Throughout the area the Bronze Age is divided into four basic periods: the Early (EBA), Middle (MBA), Late (LBA), and Final Bronze Age (FBA). In Austria for the EBA several distinct entities can be discerned. North of the Danube, the Proto-Únětice (Aunjetitz) culture continues to evolve from its Eneolithic foundations analogously to the Únětice culture of Moravia and Bohemia. The emergence of the Proto-Únětice culture is due in part to impulses from the Carpathian Basin (the Nagyrév culture). Contemporary with the Proto-Únětice culture and early Únětice, but to the east of the River Morava, is the Nitra group, of which the late Eneolithic Chłopice-Veselé type is taken to be an early phase (see Chapter 44).

South of the Danube and east of the Vienna Woods (Wienerwald) we find, at the start of the Bronze Age, the Leithaprodersdorf group, which is followed—clearly influenced from the south-east—by the Wieselburg culture. The Unterwölbling culture left its mark south of Vienna and to the west of the Wienerwald as far as the rivers Enns and Traun in the foothills of the Alps in Lower and eastern Upper Austria. In the western part of Lower Austria, reaching as far as the Tyrol and beyond, the EBA is represented by the Straubing culture, which was centred on Bavaria (see Chapter 40) (Neugebauer 1994; Lauerman 2003; Leeb 1987).

land), 8. Ebbs-Tischoferhöhle (Tyrol), 9. Fließ-Moosbruckschrofen (Tyrol), 10. Franzhausen (Lower Austria), 11. Gattendorf (Burgenland), 12. Gemeinlebarn (Lower Austria), 13. Grödig (Salzburg region), 14. Großmugl (Lower Austria), 15. Guntramsdorf (Lower Austria), 16. Gusen (Upper Austria), 17. Hainburg an der Donau-Teichtal (Lower Austria), 18. Hallstatt (Upper Austria), 19. Haselbach-Michelberg (Lower Austria), 20. Hörbing (Styria), 21. Horn (Lower Austria), 22. Leibenfeld (Styria), 23. Limberg-Heidenstatt (Lower Austria), 24. Mühlau (Tyrol), 25. Mühlbach-Gschleirsbühel (Tyrol), 26. Mühlbach am Hochkönig-Mitterberg (Salzburg region), 27. Obereching (Salzburg region), 28. Oberleis-Oberleiserberg (Lower Austria), 29. Pitten (Lower Austria), 30. Saalfelden-Taxau (Salzburg region), 31. Saalfelden-Wiesersberg (Salzburg region), 32. Salzburg-Maxglan (Salzburg), 33. Salzburg-Morzg (Salzburg), 34. St. Johann im Pongau (Salzburg region), 35. Schernberg (Salzburg region), 36. Schwarzenbach (Lower Austria), 37. Schwaz (Tyrol), 38. Siegendorf (Burgenland), 39. Stillfried an der March (Lower Austria), 40. Thunau am Kamp (Lower Austria), 41. Unterradl (Lower Austria), 42. Unterradlberg (Lower Austria), 43. Unterwölbling (Lower Austria), 44. Volders (Tyrol), 45. Vomp (Tyrol), 46. Waidendorf-Buhuberg (Lower Austria), 47. Weer (Tyrol), 48. Wohlsdorf (Styria), 49. Zwerndorf an der March (Lower Austria).

Map: author and K. Kalser/ASINOE, www.ginkomaps.com.

As the EBA came to an end, Moravia, and to an extent Bohemia as well, fell under particularly strong influences from the south-east, which gave rise to the quite separate Věteřov culture. This represents the most north-westerly outpost of the proto-urban civilizations of the middle Danube and the Carpathian region, which were typified by their close contacts with south-eastern Europe and even the eastern Mediterranean.

Parallel to the Věteřov culture, other new cultures took shape on Austrian soil as successors to the Únětice culture: the Unterwölbling culture was followed by the Böheimkirchen group, while the Drassburg group and late Wieselburg culture, associated with the Pannonian culture and its encrusted pottery, emerged in the east, and the Attersee group in the Salzkammergut (Neugebauer 1994; Willvonseder 1963–8).

During the MBA Moravia underwent a cultural split. In central and northern Moravia the Věteřov culture lived on, its specific elements contributing to the genesis of the Moravian group of the Lausitz (Lusatian) culture. By contrast, as the MBA began, the south of Moravia, almost the whole of Bohemia and the eastern half of Austria witnessed the establishment of the Middle Danubian Tumulus culture. The Tumulus culture of western Austria subsequently had more in common with its congeners in southern Germany (Willvonseder 1937; Neugebauer 1994).

In Bohemia cultural diversification occurred later, around the turn of the Middle to Late Bronze Age. Most of the area cohered with the range of Urnfield groups of the upper Danube, the easternmost representative of which is the Knovíz culture. By contrast, settlements of the Lausitz culture in northern and eastern Bohemia belong within the cultural orbit of the northern Urnfield groups. The polycultural picture of settlement is further enhanced in the far west by the unique Cheb (Eger) Urnfield group, which is clearly linked to the quite different cultural developments on the territory of modern Germany.

Over the period covering the latest stages of the Bronze Age (*Spät- and Jungbronzezeit*), Austria was fairly uniform in cultural terms (Early, Older, Middle, Younger, and Late Urnfield periods), although in the eastern part of the country and beyond, in Slovakia and Hungary, the Čaka culture (named after the eponymous village in Levice district in Slovakia) lived on into Ha A1 (Lochner 1991a; 1994). Further west we distinguish the Middle Danubian Urnfield group and in the western half of Austria the Upper Danubian Urnfields. One group marked out by finds of a distinctive kind of pottery lies to the south of the central Alps, stretching from the Vorarlberg to Styria, and evincing clear links to the south-west (Urban 2000: 210–11).

At the turn of MBA and LBA southern Moravia fell culturally within the orbit of the Middle Danubian Urnfields, while northern Moravia was, in Urnfield terms, an integral part of the area covered by the Lausitz culture. A division of these groups chronologically into Late or Final Bronze Age is represented by the Velatice and Podolí phases for Middle Danubian groups in Moravia, and as the Lausitz and Silesian phases for the Lausitz culture area.[1]

In Bohemia the Final Bronze Age is represented by the Štítary stage of the Knovíz culture in the centre, south, and north-west of the province, the Silesia-Platěnice culture in the eastern quadrant, and the Nynice culture in the west. In the north the Lausitz culture continued to evolve, and at the very end the earliest phase of the Billendorf culture, which was centred on Saxony, began to make itself felt.

---

[1] It should be noted that it is customary in the Czech Lands to describe the period Bz D–Ha A2 as the 'younger' = 'late' Bronze Age, while the period Ha B1–B3 is known as the 'late' = 'final' Bronze Age.

Settlement and Settlements

In Bohemia settlement was focused on a fair number of self-contained regions. The climate and soil conditions in these preferred regions suggest that agriculture was the main means of subsistence. The altitude of sites selected for settlement is around 200–300 m above sea level, rising exceptionally (in southern Bohemia) to 650–800 m. Settlement is clearly linked to watercourses, which doubtless also served as lines of communication.

In Moravia settlement was concentrated in valley bottoms with streams or rivers and on the lower slopes of adjacent uplands. It exploited fertile black earths with underlying loess at altitudes of c.180–300 m, but avoiding floodplains.

Despite being predominantly mountainous, today's Austria was also heavily settled in the Bronze Age, especially in the foothills of the Alps, river basins, and valleys, and also in the larger lowland areas. Thus we find concentrations of settlements in the area between Salzburg and the Wienerwald, in the hills of eastern Styria, and in the region of fertile loess soils in Lower Austria and the Burgenland, which offered optimum conditions for successful agriculture. The dense network of rivers surrounded by forests made for good hunting and fishing.

The higher-altitude Alpine regions were also settled as early as the final phase of the EBA, though this might well have been seasonal only. The *raison d'être* for settlements in such places must certainly have been herding and activities associated with copper mining (in the Mitterberg region and elsewhere in Salzburg region) and salt extraction (Hallstatt, Upper Austria) (Stöllner et al. 2006; Kern et al. 2008).

Throughout the Bronze Age we find two basic types of settlement: those on level plains and those in upland, exposed positions. Level-ground settlements preferred plateaux or gentle slopes close to rivers. Many were several hectares in extent. Their greatest density was achieved by settlements of the Urnfield period. Urnfield settlements in Franzhausen-Neumühle and Gemeinlebarn (Lower Austria) appear to have been built up into something like streets, which indicates a measure of planned development (Blesl 2001). From the end of the EBA we find, in the area of the Attersee group and the south-east Alpine region, a special kind of settlement in waterlogged terrain in the form of so-called pile villages (Urban 2000: 174–7).

Settlements in exposed locations go back to the EBA. They might be on promontories and even on the tops of hills; some offer no evidence of any real fortification, whereas others were fortified on a grand scale. In the Alpine region such settlements were often constructed close to sites of mineral extraction. Finds at such sites have frequently included tools and equipment for processing metals (moulds, tuyères). River terraces were also settled, the dispersal of the various centres within the overall settlement structure clearly reflecting how they were tied in to a system that provided for the processing and transportation of raw materials and for inter-regional exchange.

Throughout the area under discussion large numbers of hill forts are found, especially in the final phases of the EBA and in the FBA. Some forts in Austria lasted on beyond the EBA into the MBA to become centres of economic and social dominance. A case in point is the one at Bartholomäberg-Friaga in the Montafon (Voralberg), a massive fort on a terrace reinforced by a defensive dry-stone wall some 80 m long and 3 m wide, with a ditch hacked out of the rock (see Chapter 39) (Krause 2011). This fort did not just offer strategic protection to the area round about, but was also a centre of influence and authority whose populace enjoyed a higher status than the inhabitants of the smaller open settlements on other terraces nearby.

Important evidence of architectural maturity comes from the heavily fortified Urnfield forts. Some had been settled during the MBA, but now they expanded to cover an area of many hectares. Austrian examples include, among others, Thunau am Kamp, Stillfried an der March, and Oberleiserberg (Urban 2000: 199–205). There is evidence that crafts, especially metalworking, were concentrated at these sites, but also in their immediate environs, suggesting that they played an important role economically.

Ramparts were constructed using a variety of techniques depending on the configuration of the terrain and the specific demands of particular stretches of defences. There are stone-and-soil cores reinforced with a timber construction (sometimes faced with a dry-stone wall) and fortifications made up of two rows of stakes or large stones, the space between being filled with smaller stones and soil. These massive ramparts were accompanied by deep ditches, sometimes with a berm between ditch and rampart. The elaborate nature of these fortifications indicates not only their defensive function, but also points to an advanced economic, political, and social structure of the period and area.

There are also special types of settlement, such as Cezavy hill near Blučina in Moravia with its numerous, often incomplete human skeletons, a quantity of bronze artefacts, often deposited together, and evidence of metalworking. Activity here peaked in the early LBA and the site has been interpreted as a religious centre on a commanding height, where cult rituals were repeatedly carried out in association with the production of metal goods. There is a similar site, from the turn of the MBA and LBA, at Skalka near Velim in Bohemia (Hrala, Šumberová, and Vávra 2000; Harding et al. 2007), where there is a system of apparently defensive works (ditches), with what some have interpreted as human sacrificial victims in them, hoards of gold and bronze, and evidence that unusual rites took place.

The basic unit of a settlement was the house. Bronze Age houses could be above-ground structures based on upright poles with walls of wattle and daub between, or structures with a shallow foundation trench, houses with a sunken floor (semi-underground structures), and even pile dwellings (Attersee group).

During the EBA above-ground houses constructed of upright posts clearly predominate. The most striking feature of houses of the Únětice culture is their length: one house discovered at Březno in Bohemia measured 32 m in length (Pleinerová 1992). A building of the Věteřov culture at Šumice in Moravia, with a length of 56.6 m, could not have been a normal house, and in view of its situation in a circular space enclosed by a ditch we prefer to interpret it as belonging to the socio-religious sphere (Stuchlík and Stuchlíková 1999).

The larger houses identified on Austrian territory also reach 20 m in length and 7 m in width. Smaller structures close by were probably outhouses connected with farming. The settlements are readily identified thanks to the large number of sunken pits serving various purposes. Only recently have houses of the Wieselburg culture been identified. At Schwarzenbach (Lower Austria) and Gattendorf (Burgenland) houses constructed in the technique known as *Schwellriegelbau* ('swelling beam construction') were erected on large wooden beams set in shallow foundation trenches (Krenn, Hölbling, and Mittermann 2008). This advanced construction technique was certainly more stable than simple post structures and even allowed for upper floors to be added. One large example of this type of building is at Gattendorf, which was 17.5 m long and 7.5 m wide.

Another dominant type of dwelling in the MBA and LBA were above-ground post-built houses. In the MBA we find, throughout the region, long, beam-built structures with smaller buildings nearby constructed by the pillar-building method. Some finds in eastern Austria suggest the existence of small settlements or groups of separate farmsteads (Fig. 43.2; Blesl 2001; Urban 2000: 184–7).

Post structures from the Urnfield period can be divided by size as follows: large—rectangular and consisting of two or three 'rooms'; medium-sized—up to 10 m in length and requiring

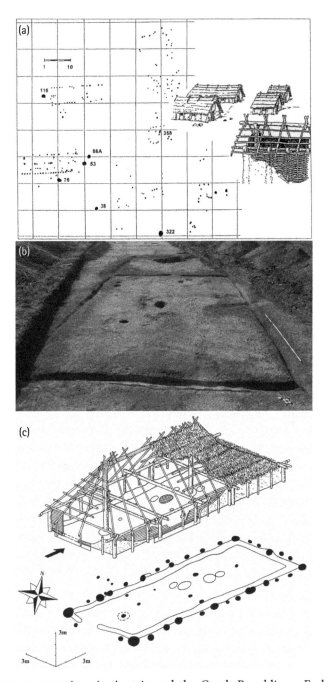

FIG. 43.2 House constructions in Austria and the Czech Republic. a. Early Bronze Age house of the Unterwölbling Culture from Franzhausen/Lower Austria. b. Early Bronze Age house of the Wieselburg Culture from Gattendorf/Burgenland. c. Middle Bronze Age house from Olomouc–Slavonín.

Source: a. after Neugebauer 1994; b. R. Mittermann AS-BDA; c. Vlastivědné muzeum v. Olomouci 2001.

fewer timber posts; and small and square, measuring up to 5 m², having four posts and probably not intended as dwellings. At a level settlement of the Middle Danubian Urnfields near Lovčičky 48 ground plans of surface post structures, including some dwellings, were found; they were placed in a planned manner around a central open space (Říhovský 1982).

At Unterradlberg (Lower Austria) over 50 structures have been documented. There are buildings of various sizes from the Bz D–Ha A1 phase, some of them with remnants of fencing, proving that the settlement was divided into several enclosed compounds. During the FBA settlement here took on the form of independent farmsteads, which were typical of the period.

For most of the Bronze Age semi-underground structures are a less usual dwelling type, though they ultimately come into their own in the FBA. Most are single-room dwellings with a hearth either inside or in close proximity to the house. The habitable area of these structures was around 7–10 m², and it is not until the Urnfield period that we also find houses up to twice as big, or more.

Settlements consist not just of houses, but also of farm buildings and, especially, huge numbers of pits, predominantly for storage. Most typical are storage pits with a narrow neck, widening downwards towards a flat bottom.

Funerary Archaeology: Implications for Society and Identity

In the area of the Únětice culture funerary rites were conducted according to fixed rules. These determined how the body was to be placed in the grave, what the grave pit had to be like, and where it should be sited within the cemetery. The only differences concern the basic form of graves. In the more northerly regions of Bohemia, but also in Moravia and adjacent parts of Austria, cemeteries are mostly on level ground, while in southern and western Bohemia graves beneath mounds predominate. The mounds were constructed with a central stone core and an overlay of clay, the core construction covering the actual inhumation, which was sunk below ground level. All these mounds obviously belong to the later parts of the EBA. Earlier Únětice graves are found throughout Moravia, adjacent parts of Austria, and the northern half of Bohemia. Classical Únětice burials went straight into bare ground, though the arrangement of the grave pit often suggests some effort at creating an insulated space for the dead. Not only were the sides walled with stones, but sometimes the floor was paved as well. Another indication of insulation was the use of wooden coffins made from tree trunks or planks. The chambers of tombs were hollow, covered over with beams or stone slabs, and sometimes made secure by an infill of stones. The graves could also be covered by wooden post constructions, as was evidenced for example at Vlíněves in central Bohemia (Fig. 43.3).

In Únětice burial practice we usually find individual inhumation graves with the body lying on its right side in a crouched position, mostly oriented south-north, irrespective of the sex of the deceased. Equally frequent is burial with the body supine and only the legs turned sideways. Graves containing the remains of two, three, or even more individuals are less common. In some the burials clearly took place simultaneously, whereas in others the subsequent interment took place after a short interval, with care being taken not to disturb

FIG. 43.3 Various grave constructions of the Únětice Culture (1–3) and the Wieselburg Culture (4).

Source: 1–3: Institute of Archaeology, Prague; 4: Neugebauer/BDA 1994.

the earlier burial. There are also successive burials in which the remains of previously buried individuals are disturbed and pushed aside. Graves of the Únětice culture were often disturbed secondarily by acts of robbery, which probably occurred at the tail end of the EBA. At some burial grounds in Moravia as many as three-quarters of all graves were so affected (Stuchlík and Stuchlíková 1996).

The dead were buried in clothing held together with pins of various shapes, and with personal ornaments. Sometimes metal weapons are present (daggers, axes, and axe-hammers). The graves of certain individuals also contain prestige artefacts made of less usual, more exclusive, materials (gold, amber, faience). Nevertheless, pottery represents the main grave offering. For the earlier period graves usually contain quite a number of vessels, some of them fairly large. Later on we find mostly small or very small items, whether classical cups or, especially, bowls, beakers, and miniature amphorae. Stone objects include flaked blades and arrowheads, flint daggers, and, rarely, flint axes. Animal bones have also been found, though in some cases only those that had no use as food: an aurochs tooth, a shoulder-blade and part of the horn of an aurochs, and a pig's jaw.

Some graves exhibit peculiarities that contrast with the strict observation of funerary ritual. There are instances of buried body parts, apparently with their ligaments still attached, and others where a grave was dug up and the remains removed to a different one. Another odd rite is setting the deceased's head in a bowl or encasing the head within flat stones. Cenotaphs may even be present.

Finds of mass deposits of human bodies in pits are surprisingly common on settlements. They start during the Únětice culture and run on into the Tumulus culture and even the Urnfield period. These are not burials, but the simple dumping of whole bodies or their parts. It is interesting that such mass depositions of skeletons are often found at the edge of settlements, where manufacturing and storage areas were located.

Changes in the funerary rite came at the end of the Únětice culture as its development fell under the influence of the Věteřov culture. One new feature was the appearance of child skeletons buried in vessels. A general trend towards variation of practice can be discerned, culminating in the MBA with bi-ritual burial.

The Austrian Leithaprodersdorf group exhibits great variability in how uncremated bodies were positioned, though with women a south-north orientation predominates, the body lying on its right side in a crouched position, whereas men lie north-south on their left side facing east. The arms and neck areas of the bodies often carry ornaments. Necklaces are made of shells and bone. Copper grave goods often include simple spiral bangles, oar-shaped pins with bent neck and disc-headed pins, and strips of thin copper sheet, which might be interpreted as bands from headgear. It is quite usual to find triangular daggers and awls.

People of the Wieselburg culture also buried their dead in the crouched position, oriented according to sex. Women lie mostly oriented south-west–north-east, on their right side facing east, whereas men lie on their left side facing west. The crouched posture is sometimes so extreme that the corpses must have been bound in some way.

We find graves lined with stones and burials in tree-trunk coffins. Social status was accentuated not only by the usual provision of weapons and prestigious metal, glass, and amber objects, but also by the number of pots. New shapes appear, especially amphorae with from one to four handles, which are frequently part of a large and careful arrangement of pots. The best-known burial ground is at Hainburg-Teichtal with some 350 burials (Krenn-Leeb 2011).

Burial sites of the Unterwölbling culture had on average 30 to 70 graves and lay close to settlements. The best-known site is at Franzhausen, where over two thousand graves have been uncovered in three large groups (Neugebauer and Neugebauer 1997). Differentiation by sex was strictly observed, and the way the graves are fitted out is striking for its highly standardized composition. Women were buried oriented south-north, crouched, on their right side and facing east. Men were oriented north-south, crouched, on their left side and also facing east. The bodies were placed in wooden coffins from hollowed-out tree trunks within a space separated off by being lined with stones or stone slabs. The usual furnishings of graves were richer than in the case of neighbouring EBA cultures, with numerous objects made of sheet bronze.

Bracelets, pins, and necklaces are frequently found, the latter in more decorative form in female graves. Both sexes often have massive neck-rings. Women and girls usually had whole collections of pots, such as bowls or dishes, cups, beakers, or pots, while men received weapons in addition to pottery. Male graves had a higher value proportion of metal artefacts than female ones.

Cemeteries further west in Upper Austria have suggested that there was considerable contact between peoples of the Unterwölbling and Straubing cultures, though the funerary rites of the latter within Austria remain unclear. Although large numbers of occupied sites and hoards indicate that the Salzburg region north of the Alps was heavily settled, no graves have been found. However, Straubing culture graves in Bavaria use the same burial patterns as those of the Unterwölbling culture.

To the south, in the Alps, a mere two finds suggest that the funerary rite might have been inhumation. Skulls and long bones from at most 20 children and 7 adults (all of them young women) were discovered in Ebbs-Tischoferhöhle cave in the Tyrol (Harb 2002). However, in this case there is no way of telling whether it was a regular burial ground. The finds have been dated to the end of the EBA.

In the area of the inner Alps, where the local cultural base was heavily influenced from the Straubing culture, there is a gradual change in funerary rites: cremation becomes the norm. No EBA graves at all have been found in the south-eastern Alps.

During the MBA the universal norm is burial beneath a barrow, the basis of which is a solid ring of stones, or just single stones laid out to mark the circular perimeter. The actual mound was mostly simple, made of soil, or a mixture of soil and stones with no particular internal structure. The space within the perimeter ring may be broken up by stone constructions tied to burials. Both inhumation and cremation were used throughout the duration of the Tumulus culture; initially inhumation graves predominate, but with the passage of time cremations come to the fore. In the case of inhumations, pots were placed by the feet or head; bronze and other dress ornaments were placed where the occupant had worn them, and weapons and tools alongside the body. With cremation, grave goods were not put into the fire, but added to the burial before it was covered over. The range of grave goods reflected the sex of the occupant. Men's graves contain weapons (dagger, sword), but also sometimes tools and gold spirals, less often razors and/or pins. Women's graves are typified by dress decoration, ornaments, necklaces, and pairs of pins. This gender pattern is adhered to even in the case of burials of juveniles. The size and contents of barrows exhibit no correlation with wealth, nor can we identify any rules in the manner of construction.

Barrow burial sites survive today especially in southern and western Bohemia and in Austria. One of the best-known and most important sites in the Middle Danubian region was discovered at Pitten (Lower Austria; Hampl et al. 1978–81; Benkovsky-Pivovarová 1991). Locations where finds have been made have been well preserved and provide evidence of variation in the structure of burial chambers within individual barrows containing many richly endowed burials. Roughly two-thirds of the graves contained cremation burials, mostly of women. Among male graves inhumation predominates.

In western Austria the influence of the south German Tumulus culture is much in evidence. At Grödig (Salzburg region), barrows with a ring of stones were found to contain inhumations with the deceased lying on their backs. Cremation graves in pits partially covered by stones contained burnt metal objects and pottery (Urban 2000: 186). The rare MBA finds from the inner Alps are of individual ground-level cremation graves with the ashes contained in a pot or a case made of organic material. No grave goods have been found.

At Schernberg (Salzburg) calcified bones were placed in urns; these have been found inside small cists or under an overlay of stones inside a low mound, graced with just a single beaker or a bow. Sometimes the remains were placed in wooden cists bordered with stones (e.g. Saalfelden-Taxau). These cremation graves were marked at the surface by stone stelae (Moosleitner 1991).

In terms of regular funerary customs, the Urnfield period is uniform: here the custom was to place the ashes of the dead in urns in flat graves within cemeteries that were often quite large. Observation of the details of the funerary rite, the arrangement of the grave, the position of the occupant, and the repertoire of grave goods clearly indicate that there were differences in the ideology and social structure of the various groups.

Whereas in the milieu of the Lausitz and Silesia-Platěnice cultures cremation is practically universal, in the Knovíz culture and the Middle Danubian Urnfields, where cremation graves predominate, isolated inhumation graves have also been attested. In all Urnfield cultures, graves beneath mounds are also found sporadically. The highest density of these is in western Bohemia and eastern Moravia, but also in easternmost Austria, where the Čaka culture, typified by its greater variety of funerary ritual, survives until Ha A. Mounds also covered the isolated large chambered graves, which contained bronze vessels, swords, axes, and even on occasion a cart and horse skeletons.

Ordinary cemeteries are much alike across all Urnfield cultures. Graves with the ashes placed in vessels predominate. Urns have often been found to contain not just burnt human bones, but also burnt animal bones. Bronze goods were mostly knives to go with the food placed in the bowls, then razors, fragments of bangles, and pins that were part of the deceased's personal possessions and clothes. While the tools—knives and razors—were mostly added to the bodily remains after cremation, personal ornaments passed through the fire of the pyre. The number of vessels in these graves is highly variable—rising to several dozen in the Lausitz and Silesia-Platěnice cultures. A departure from the uniformity of cremation graves of the Urnfield period in Bohemia are graves of the west-Bohemian Nynice culture. Here it has proved possible to trace the stylistic evolution of their construction over time.

Many cemeteries that originated in the MBA were still in use in the early phases of the Urnfield period. The early and middle Urnfield periods are typified by cremation burials placed in large stone cists containing not just the ashes, but also grave goods in urns, made of organic material or loosely scattered about the whole grave. Stone cists of human dimensions remain common. There are also rectangular and oval grave pits.

Typical of the late Urnfield period in western Austria are simple pit graves with urns and other pots for grave goods, with or without stone reinforcements, as at Obereching (Salzburg) (Höglinger 1993). A regular feature is their poor grave goods and the absence of weapons. The situation is similar in eastern Austria, confirming the view that funerary rites in the early and middle Urnfield period in Salzburg and Upper Austria were influenced from more westerly areas. Conversely, in the later Urnfield period eastern influences clearly predominate.

Some cemeteries at the tail end of the Bronze Age, especially in the inner Alps, reached their peak in the Early Iron Age, as at Bischofshofen (Salzburg) (Urban 2000: 216). Several late Urnfield graves in the southern Alps have been found to contain pottery of the north-Italian Laugen-Melaun culture (Urban 2000: 222–3).

Material Culture

Pottery

Typical of the early period of the Únětice culture is the limited range of vessels, of just a handful of basic shapes: jugs, pots with horizontal handles, little amphorae, and bowls of various shapes. These oldest types evolve smoothly into later stages of Únětice pottery. Jugs acquire fringe-like embellishments, sometimes with zigzags. The surface of coarse pots often shows fingerprint decoration. The most typical shape is that known as the Únětice cup (Fig. 43.4, 1). The main shape in the Unterwölbling culture comes in the typical long-necked jug-like cups that frequently have a decorative moulding running round them (Fig. 43.5, 26). Wieselburg culture pottery has a similar range of shapes, but with more moulding and incised decoration, and the typical handles in the shape of hourglasses on jugs and amphorae. The pottery of the Drassburg group, which partly exists parallel with and follows on from the Wieselburg culture at the very end of the EBA, represents the north-west part of the Pannonian complex of Encrusted Pottery. It has a special decoration consisting of parallel textile impressions, hence its occasional designation as *Litzenkeramik*.

Major changes come at the end of the EBA in connection with the rise of the Věteřov culture. Typical shapes include, in particular, amphoras, barrel-shaped mugs on legs (Fig. 43.6, 5), little cups with a chalice-shaped widening of the rim (Fig. 43.6, 6), and conical bowls with the edge trimmed away horizontally and widened. The full range of pot forms included such specialized products as strainers, spoons, and funnels. We occasionally find impressed decoration, sometimes bearing signs of white encrustation. Types of plastic ornamentation include the application of pointed protuberances and short horizontal or vertical ribs; very typical are incised triangles covered with indentations. Certain clay objects have no identifiable purpose and are known as *Brotlaibidole* (loaf-of-bread idols) (Fig. 43.5, 35; 43.6.3); they are about 10 cm long, decorated with incised lines and stamped with such motifs as a sun disc, a cross, but also sometimes shell impressions.

Vessels of the classical Únětice and Věteřov cultures tend to have perfectly smooth surfaces, often with a 'metallic' sheen, while with those of the MBA Tumulus culture there was a preference for ornament, whether incised or plastic. The main ornament types are triangles, ladder-like bands, fir tree-like ornaments, and concentric or multiple circles. Deep grooves were commonly filled with a white encrustation. In the later period of the Tumulus culture the preference was smooth surfaces and knobs, the latter usually outlined with circular or horseshoe-shaped grooves (Fig. 43.4, 13; Fig. 43.7, 4). Various kind of plastic protrusions are also quite common (Fig. 43.6.10; 43.7, 5, 10). The pottery shapes most typical of the Tumulus culture are small amphorae, with or without a foot, footed bowls (Fig. 43.4, 12; 43.6.12), and small jugs (Fig. 43.6, 10). For the MBA pottery hoards become more common, suggesting that they form a kind of ritual drinking set.

The shapes, typology, and ornamentation of pottery are *de facto* criteria by which the separate cultural groups within the largely homogeneous milieu of the Urnfield period are distinguished. Nonetheless the range of pottery types and their morphology are both fairly uniform. There are biconical vessels, amphorae, storage vessels, mugs, jugs, bowls, cups, and beakers. Only the two-tiered vessels of the Knovíz culture in Bohemia (Fig. 43.4, 21)—exaggerated variants of amphorae—are absent from other cultures. Specific to the early phase of

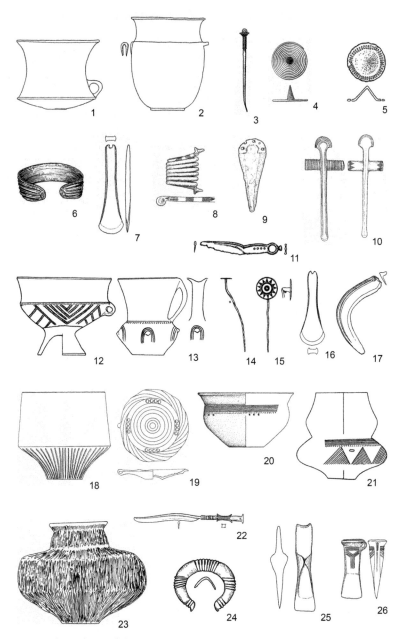

FIG. 43.4 Typical artefacts of the Bronze Age from Bohemia. 1–10 Early Bronze Age, 11–17 Middle Bronze Age, 18–26 Late and Final Bronze Age.

Drawings: L. Jiráň.

the Middle Danubian Urnfields are some elegant cups with banded or longitudinally bevelled handles drawn up high above the rim (Fig. 43.6, 17).

The delicate and less refined vessels of the Urnfield cultures usually have their surfaces blackened with graphite and polished, or smoothed and polished with a fine clay slip. In the decoration of Lausitz pottery an evolutionary pattern can partially be observed: initially

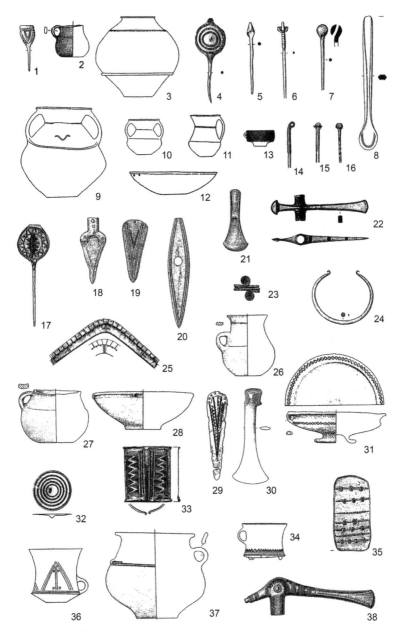

FIG. 43.5 Typical artefacts of the Early Bronze Age from Austria. 1–3 Leithaprodersdorf Group. 4–16 Wieselburg Culture. 17–28 Unterwölbling Culture. 29–30, 32–33, 36–37 Únětice Culture. 31, 34–5, 38 Věteřov horizon.

Source: Neugebauer 1994.

(Bz D) they were still using decorative plastic knobs outlined with channels or grooves, the later period (Ha A1–2) being typified by continuous vertical striation, and later still (Ha B1) these were broken into 'bundles'. In terms of the morphology of vessels there is a general evolutionary trend from sharply contoured forms towards soft, flowing profiles associated with a reduction in the height of certain forms.

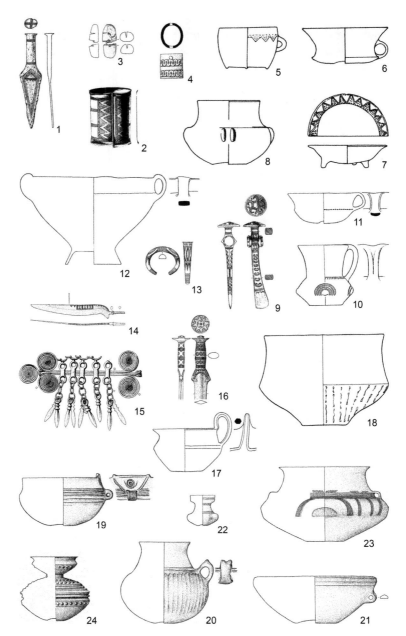

FIG. 43.6 Typical artefacts of the Bronze Age from Moravia. 1–7 Early Bronze Age, 8–10 Middle Bronze Age, 11–21 Late and Final Bronze Age.

Drawings: M. Salaš.

A greater diversity of shapes in the pottery of individual cultures is not apparent until we reach the FBA. Clear differences are to be seen both between the Podolí phase of the Middle Danubian Urnfields and the Silesian phase of the Lausitz culture or the Štítary stage of the Knovíz culture, and especially the Nynice culture. The finer vessels of the Silesia-Platěnice and of the Silesian phase of the Lausitz culture in Moravia generally have a well-smoothed

FIG. 43.7 Typical artefacts of the Middle Bronze Age (1-12), Late and Final Bronze Age (13-25) from Austria.

Source: Neugebauer 1994.

surface, often finely polished or graphited. Richly ornamented rattles and so-called drinking horns have been found.

Pottery of the Štítary stage of the Knovíz culture is limited to large storage vessels, amphorae, pots, cups, and bowl shapes. Squared profiles emerge gradually. Graphiting of finer vessels is widespread, sometimes similar to black polishing. The main ornaments are combed bands of delicate furrows and fine grooves. Coarse decoration is done by combing or smoothing with a wooden spatula (Fig. 43.4, 23).

Nynice pottery is akin to the output of the south German urnfields. Graphiting to produce a metallic sheen is favoured, as is the application of a fine film of black colour to give a leathery surface sheen. The main decorative elements are a combination of horizontal incised grooves supplemented with furrows and fringes—a line of short oblique strokes made mechanically, by means of a little wheel with oblique incisions. During the later phase we find a double garland of shallow grooves or narrow furrows (Fig. 43.4, 19).

Pottery of the Podolí phase of the Middle Danubian Urnfields has flowing, rounded profiles, though with a tendency towards sharper lines by the end of the Ha B stage; this anticipates the three-part segmentation of vessels of the Hallstatt period. Typical Podolí shapes are primarily amphorae and bowls with the rim drawn out flat above the handles and with incised decoration (Fig. 43.6, 19). The dominant form of ornamentation is vertical furrowing, combined in the case of amphorae with horizontal furrows below the neck.

In Austria, too, there are discernible regional distinctions in pottery of the Urnfield period. For example, Carinthian pottery differs in certain details from the FBA ware of eastern Austria, Salzburg, or the Tyrol. However, regional subdivisions in the forms of pottery are not so striking as in Bohemia and Moravia. The one exception in the LBA is where the Čaka culture penetrates into eastern Austria; its marked channelling and the tapered edges of vessels of almost 'baroque' proportions set it apart from all other Urnfield production within Austria (Urban 2000: 207–10).

Metalwork

Objects made of gold, copper and, later, bronze appear from the very beginning of the Bronze Age. In the fully fledged EBA environment we encounter metal both in graves, on settlements, and in hoards dating to the whole range of cultures in Bohemia, Moravia, and Austria. Besides ornaments (pins, earrings, bracelets, rings, diadems) we also find tools (awls, chisels, axes), weapons (hammer-axes, daggers, spearheads), and raw copper. A specific form of sheet-metal ornament is the usually richly decorated cuff-like bracelets of the so-called Borotice type (Fig. 43.6, 2; Fig. 43.5, 33).

The production of bronze goods in Bohemia, Moravia, and Austria was affected by the existence of two types of production technology whose impact reached here from outside. For the more southerly regions—the source of the raw copper—the main types of products are made of sheet metal—diadems, pins with head beaten flat, discoidal (Fig. 43.5, 4) and paddle-shaped needles, discoidal earrings—as in the *Blechstilkreis*. The more northerly regions, bordering the Elbe-Oder production area, provided mainly cast goods: daggers with solid cast handle (Fig. 43.6, 1), bar-shaped bracelets, oval leg-rings, pins with an annular head, pins of Únětice type (Fig. 43.4, 3; Fig. 43.5, 15), rosettes with chains made of cast links, etcetera.

Crude copper was transported from the Alpine region in the form of ring or rib ingots. Ring ingots are round, fatter at their centre, and with the ends beaten flat, then bent round in eyelet form. Their surface is roughly hammered. Their weight varies between 185 g and 200 g. Rib ingots are widespread in the Upper Danube area, less so in Austria and Bohemia; their incidence declines further north, and they do not occur at all in Moravia (see Chapter 23).

In the MBA there is a vast increase in the range of metalwork, with new kinds of artefacts appearing (Fig. 43.7, 2, 3), knives (Fig. 43.4, 11), sickles, razors, tweezers, as well as new ornamentation and production techniques (e.g. clay-core casting, recasting). The shape of these artefacts is clearly linked to the Middle Danube region and the Carpathian Basin. Even in the earlier period we find some technically advanced forms from that area, for example band-like arm-rings. For obvious reasons locally made products are more common, albeit designed to south-eastern patterns, as in the case of discoidal or heart-shaped pendants. The production and use of bronze objects reached its peak in the Urnfield cultures of the LBA and FBA. This is when we find the first metal vessels (Fig. 43.6, 24; Fig. 43.7, 19) and armour (helmets, corslets, greaves).

Much the biggest sources of Bronze Age metal artefacts are cemeteries and hoards. In the case of the MBA grave finds predominate, whereas hoards are dominant in the EBA and Urn-field period. The area under discussion has yielded hundreds of hoards of metal. The EBA has revealed hoards both of raw metal and of finished products (tools, weapons, ornaments), but also mixed finds, with both elements. In southern Bohemia hoards of raw metal follow the course of the River Vltava, while in central and northern Bohemia the more frequent hoards of finished goods indicate links to central Germany. Similarly, in the Moravian Únětice culture there is a notable concentration of raw-metal hoards, sometimes with hundreds of ring ingots, along the lower reaches of the major rivers of southern Moravia, or in the important traffic corridor of the Vyškov Gate. This spatial relationship says something about lines of communication, but also about the source and distribution of the raw metal from the Alpine area, which is further demonstrated by the distribution of similar assemblages in Austria. New research shows that different types of deposits existed in the EBA, differentiated as pottery hoards (the remains of ritual feasts), hoards with a large metal value (offerings to the gods), and equipment hoards (the remains of legitimation processes) (Krenn-Leeb 2010).

The incidence of hoards drops perceptibly during the MBA. While they may be found for the entire duration of the Tumulus culture, they are, for most of that period, rather rare and meagre in content. The situation is different at the southernmost tip of south Moravia: the Bz B1 stage has revealed a group of hoards that are somewhat akin to those in the Carpathian Basin of Koszider type (see Chapter 44). Their contents include numerous copper ingots and the entire group is conspicuous for the sheer numbers of non-functional, fragmentary artefacts.

By contrast, bronze hoards of Urnfield date are very numerous and contain thousands of artefacts. Their composition varies over time and space. For Bz D and Ha A1 the hoards mostly contain a great variety of fragments: personal ornaments and their broken parts, together with fragments of weapons and tools, notably axes and sickles, and fragments of copper ingots. From the Lausitz culture milieu a different kind of hoard occurs, consisting of just one type of artefact. This took the form especially of bracelet hoards, but sickles, axes, neck-rings, and leg-rings also appear as single-type hoards.

In Moravia there is a regional group of hoards along the middle reaches of the River Morava, dating back as early as the end of the MBA. They are mostly distinguished by their complete personal ornaments and items of clothing, all of local provenance, which also matches most hoards of the subsequent Lausitz culture. In a later regional group of hoards in south-east Moravia (Bz D) we find an unprecedented concentration of Carpathian imports. Carpathian influence also shows in some hoards of the north Moravian Lausitz culture, while large hoards of fragments from the Middle Danubian Urnfields in south-western Moravia betray influences coming from the west. Their composition is similarly fragmentary and heterogeneous, with a general prevalence of sickle fragments and broken metal ingots. By contrast, the north Moravian Lausitz hoards have a higher proportion of whole ornaments, especially annular ones.

In Austria large pottery hoards with only a few types, and bronze equipment hoards with a very large number of objects, indicative of high prestige, dominated in the MBA.

Hoards of fragmentary objects were succeeded by those containing more impressive products, especially ornaments and metal vessels, and in the FBA, weapons. Yet at the same time there are hoards consisting of a single type, and others with a mix of new and damaged objects, sometimes also including bits of copper ingot. Hoards from the final phase of the Urnfield period see the appearance of the first iron artefacts. Moravia is strikingly asymmetrical in the spatial distribution of hoards by culture, since in the Lausitz culture of north Moravia there are four times as many hoards (often with whole bronze vessels and magnificent personal ornaments) as in the southern area of Middle Danubian Urnfields.

The main copper source area lies north of the main Alpine ridge, where four mining districts are known (Mitterberg region, two districts in the Inntal Valley in Schwaz/Brixlegg, Montafon). No mining area in the eastern Alps or further afield offers as much information as the Mitterberg region in Salzburg province, located between Mühlbach am Hochkönig, Bischofshofen, and St Johann im Pongau. This is because of the size of the copper ore deposit, probably the richest in the eastern Alps (Goldenberg et al. 2011).

Gold

Gold is generally present in even the earliest graves from the turn of the Eneolithic and the EBA, and with the same workmanship as in the preceding Eneolithic cultures. Subsequently, gold does not appear until the later part of the EBA. Gold objects of that period have been found at nearly 50 sites in Bohemia, and 17 gold artefacts come from 11 sites in Moravia. Graves have usually produced gold-wire ornaments, while hoards have produced more massive items, including two cuff-like bracelets from the Minice hoard. In Moravia the pattern of small gold ornaments is similarly broken by two massive gold pendants from Dobročkovice. In Austria gold objects have been documented in EBA graves and in a hoard. In Hainburg-Teichtal there is also an earring of silver (Krenn-Leeb 2011).

The MBA has also produced gold finds, the vast majority of the Bohemian ones dating from the final stage in the evolution of Tumulus culture. This phenomenon appears slightly earlier in western Bohemia, but a little later in eastern Bohemia, where, however, it lasted longer. West Bohemian finds are confined to graves, east Bohemian to hoards. Typical finds were single or double spirals of gold wire as recorded over a large area of central and northern Europe and the western Balkans. In the pre-Lausitz period of eastern Bohemia the so-called 'figures-of-eight' appear—entwined double strands of gold, usually tied with a fine gold wire at the point where they cross (as at Hradec Králové). Another shape consists of strips of beaten sheet gold with eyelets at the ends. In western Bohemia there are ornaments made of single or double strands of gold, broader or narrower strips of gold, and plastically decorated discs of extremely fine gold sheet or foil. Those from western Bohemia certainly take their inspiration from from the Carpathian Basin, while the foils and strips are unique and unrecorded in other regions.

In the Middle Danubian Tumulus culture in Moravia and Austria, gold artefacts are quite rare. An exception is the gold hoard from Čehovice in Prostějov district, where some gold discs and pieces of gold wire were placed inside a hollow bronze casting. Gold threads and wires were also part of the find at Lužice in Hodonín district.

The Urnfield period in Bohemia has also revealed a number of gold artefacts. Forged products predominate, but cast artefacts also occur. The former include typical wire spirals, small spiral tubes, bracelets, neck-rings and finger-rings, spectacle-pendants, and items made of sheet gold, for example diadems and various bands and thin foil strips. By contrast, items made by casting include an axe from Sokoleč (Hellich 1913: 32, Table III: 6) and a gold pin, whose head is shaped like a tiny vase, from Hradec Králové (Duška 1898: 4, Table I: 1).

The Urnfield period in Moravia has produced gold only rarely, and always as small forged personal ornaments (spirals, pendants, beads). It is none the less remarkable that it is just such small items (beads, small tubes) that are found quite frequently in individual inhumation graves.

Gold objects of the Urnfield period in Austria have been discovered in deposits in the Alpine region, for example Arikogel in Bad Goisern, Upper Austria (Gruber 2008).

Amber

Necklaces made of variously shaped perforated beads and decorative plates of amber (sometimes combined with bronze spirals, shells, and so on) are typical of graves from the (later) EBA. Amber ornaments achieved their greatest popularity during the Tumulus culture. Most are beads of various shapes and sizes, and analysis has shown that the vast majority, like those of all earlier periods, were of Baltic origin. There are no amber finds from the Urnfield period, which may be due to the practice of cremation. However, amber has occasionally been found with bronze hoards.

Glass and Faience

Artefacts akin to glass begin to appear in the area already in the Bell Beaker milieu and continue in the EBA. All are small, opaque, blue-green beads, generally termed 'faience'. MBA beads, of light-blue, blue-green, or sky-blue glass, translucent and opaque, are technologically more advanced and are the first true glass (Venclová 1990: Plate 4). In the Urnfield period we find annular blue or blue-green beads and the gradual appearance of polychrome beads, the first prior to classical antiquity. They are assumed not to be local, but imports from the Mediterranean, though production centres in the northern Tyrol have been conjectured (Venclová 1990: 42).

Stone

Stone was a widely used material. It was roughly quarried in the case of quernstones, crushers, strikers, and whetstones. Smooth-ground stone objects include, for example, slender wristguards from the early phase of the EBA. For the later period, stone worked by grinding and polishing or delicate chipping is chiefly represented by unperforated axe-hammers, grooved hammer-stones, and by small polished stone axes. Evidence of the knowledge of grinding and polishing stone, and perforating it with small holes, is provided by cylindrical marble beads from a necklace (Dvořák 1932: 10, Table II). Knapping was carried out on siliceous materials (e.g. flint). The early period of the Únětice culture has yielded surface-retouched triangular arrowheads and leaf-shaped spearheads. Nordic imports are rarely found; they consist of chipped and retouched flint daggers complete with handle. We also encounter miniature chipped stone in the shape of small knives, blades, side-scrapers, and end-scrapers. Other stone artefacts are moulds, mostly made from sandstone, the use of which continued throughout the Bronze Age. From the MBA onwards there are special spherical objects with a central, conically bored hole that enabled it to be mounted on a wooden handle.

Stone artefacts are also common in the LBA and FBA. Knapping was occasionally used to produce tools for use as strike-a-lights, or knives and scrapers.

Aspects of Craft Production

The production of foodstuffs, pottery, textiles, and stone and metal artifacts, and the processing of organic materials, are all attested chiefly by secondary infill finds in pits or dwellings (loom-weights, quernstones, bone implements, casting moulds). Besides these ordinary activities, we can also take it for granted that various raw materials were exploited.

The mining and processing of copper ore in the Alpine region was very important, the evidence going back to the EBA, along with associated activities relating to the transport and exchange of the product. We assume that as processing technologies evolved, deforestation of the area would have occurred to meet the need for timber for the construction of mine galleries and especially the mass production of charcoal.

Since the MBA at the latest, the Alpine Salzkammergut saw the developed exploitation of salt mines in the Salzberg at Hallstatt (Upper Austria). Special antler tools show us that salt springs had probably been known since the Neolithic (Kern et al. 2008). It is no accident that salt and copper mining achieved an almost comparable degree of professionalisn at the same time at the end of the EBA and beginning of the MBA, with all the same features in mining and distribution. But mining technology and conditions were different in the mountains. For extracting salt, wooden constructions were always needed in salt mines. Salt mining was a feature of especial importance for the producing societies. Special fields of technology had to be developed, while at the same time social differences can be presumed to have characterized the groups of people involved. Maybe one thing above all shows the different consequences of salt and copper mining. The people of Hallstatt had specialized knowledge of salt mining technology, and used it to profit from the resulting exchange.

The acquisition of tin by panning in watercourses running down the Erzgebirge (Ore Mountains) is considered likely by some scholars, given that these deposits are the only ones in central Europe.

Another raw material to consider is graphite in the form of nodules, mined or collected on the surface in southern Bohemia and Austria; it was used predominantly for the surface treatment of pottery. Graphite could also have been used in inter-regional exchange (one outcome of which are the bits of graphite found on Cezavy hill near Blučina).

Most of what we know about craftwork is connected with the production of bronzework. Activities associated with metalworking are attested at settlements going back as far as the EBA; the main evidence is in the shape of clay tuyères, such as are found in all central

European EBA cultures. Crucibles have been found at, for example, Hosty (Beneš 1984: 18, Table XI: 3). Other reliable evidence of metallurgy is represented by the flat clay slabs used in the casting of tongue-shaped ingots, as well as by other moulds, mostly of stone, but also of clay. The technique of lost-wax casting was probably also used. Metal processing is further indicated by the tools required to finish the end product, such as the little hammer found at Prague (Hájek and Moucha 1985: Fig. 3: 37) or the sandstone whetstones used to trim the surface of metal objects. Other tools were used to decorate objects: narrow-bladed bronze chisels for engraving, or bronze points for stamped decoration (e.g. Hosty: Beneš 1984: Fig. 12: 2, 3, 4).

Most information on the manufacture of bronze objects in the MBA is provided by hoards of Bz C2 (e.g. a hoard of smithing tools, bronze mould, copper ingots, etcetera). For the Urnfield period we have convincing evidence of the production of bronzes in the shape of tuyères, crucibles, and above all moulds. Of these there is no shortage: there have been 140 found in Bohemia alone (Blažek, Ernée, and Smejtek 1998: 9, 11). To date we have few finds showing direct evidence of bronze smelting, though at a Knovíz settlement in Prague-Hostivář an extraordinary assemblage of bronze artefacts was found along with a fragment of smelt. Also, an area among the rocks of the Bohemian Paradise that was in use in the period of the Silesia-Platěnice culture has revealed small crucibles, fragments of sheet bronze, and, most importantly, numerous droplets of bronze. Signs of metal founding have also been discerned at certain upland sites, such as the fort at Svržno-Černý vrch (Chytráček 1992: 65–9). Similar activities can be inferred at Plešivec and Tetín hill forts, in Moravia at, for example, Hradisko in Brno-Obřany, and within the upland cult site at Cezavy hill near Blučina (Salaš 1985; 1995); and in Lower Austria at the Heidenstatt at Limberg (Lochner 1994).

Ceramic production is evinced by finds of crude graphite or nodules of ochre used in decorating the surface of pots and hoards of ceramic balls, deposited for use as potting clay. Kilns have also been found, if rarely. The quality of the pottery produced, especially in the case of finer ware, was of a high standard throughout the Bronze Age. Technical proficiency peaked in the Únětice cups that appear to imitate metal models, the richly decorated MBA footed bowls, or in the LBA storeyed vessels (Fig. 43.4, 21) and high-handled Velatice cups (Fig. 43.6, 17).

Considerable dexterity in the working of bone and horn is evinced by artefacts from as early as the EBA. This applies in particular to various types of pin, but also such components of decorative necklaces as cylindrical bone beads, small tubes made from animal bones and perforated animal teeth. Animal bones were also worked into various kinds of awl and point, also flat chisels or handles for bronze awls. True craftsmanship is revealed by an ornamental bone object from Malé Číčovice (Hnízdová 1954: Fig. 12) or the bone artefacts with 'Mycenaean' pulley motifs from Blučina and Věteřov in Moravia (Tihelka 1960), and Waidendorf-Buhuberg, Guntramsdorf, and Pitten in Austria (Neugebauer 1994). A unique find from the Urnfield period is a workshop for making horn artefacts discovered at Pečky (central Bohemia). It turned up a variety of semi-finished goods such as awls, engraving tools, and a horse bit, as well as discarded scrap material (Justová 1965).

Finds of clay spindle-whorls, weights and, more rarely, textile impressions in the patina of metal artefacts are evidence of the development of textile production. Woven linen textiles go back as far as the EBA, as shown by an impression in the patina of a cuff bracelet found in a grave at Tursko (Schránil 1921: Fig. 10:3).

Bibliography

Beneš, A. (1984). *Pravěká osada z doby bronzové na soutoku Lužnice a Vltavy. Předstihový archeologický výzkum v Hostech 1981–1983.* Týn nad Vltavou: Městské muzeum.

Benkovsky-Pivovarová, Z. (1991). *Das mittelbronzezeitliche Gräberfeld von Pitten in Niederösterreich Bd. 3,* Mitteilungen der Prähistorischen Kommission, 24. Vienna.

Blažek, J., Ernée, M., and Smejtek, L. (1998). *Die bronzezeitliche Gussformen in Nordwestböhmen,* Beiträge zur Ur- und Frühgeschichte Nordwestböhmen, 3. Nordböhmische Bronzefunde, 2. Most.

Blesl, Chr. (2001). 'Früh- und mittelbronzezeitliche Siedlungsstrukturen im Unteren Traisental (Niederösterreich)', in B. Eberschweiler, J. Köninger, H. Schlichtherle, and Chr. Strahm (eds.), *Aktuelles zur Frühbronzezeit und frühen Mittelbronzezeit im nördlichen Alpenvorland,* Hemmenhofener Skripte, 2. Gaienhofen-Hemmenhofen, Freiburg: Janus, 11–16.

Chytráček, M. (1992). 'Doklady metalurgie v pozdní době bronzové na Černém vrchu u Svržna (okres Domažlice) a otázka možného využívání místních zdrojů nerostných surovin', *Historie,* VIII. *Sborník Západočeského muzea v Plzni,* 59–73.

Duška, J. (1898). *Nálezy předhistorické v kraji Královéhradeckém.* Hradec Králové: Historické a průmyslové museum v Hradci Králové.

Dvořák, F. (1932). 'Nálezy únětické kultury na Kolínsku III', *Památky archeologické,* 38: 8–14, Table I, II.

Goldenberg, G., Töchterle, U., Oeggl, K., and Krenn-Leeb, A. (eds.) (2011). 'HiMAT. Neues zur Bergbaugeschichte der Ostalpen'. *Archäologie Österreichs Spezial,* 4. Vienna.

Gruber, H. (2008). 'Schätze aus Gold. Die urnenfelderzeitlichen Depotfunde vom Arikogel und aus dem Koppental', in Chr. Farka (ed.), *Schätze. Gräber. Opferplätze Traunkirchen. 08. Archäologie im Salzkammergut,* Fundberichte aus Österreich Materialhefte, Sonderheft 6: 72–7.

Hájek, L. and Moucha, V. (1985). 'Nálezy ze Zámků u Bohnic v Národním Muzeu v Praze. II', *Archaeologica Pragensia,* 6: 5–76.

Hampl, F., Kerchler, H., and Benkovsky-Pivovarová, Z. (1978–1981). *Das mittelbronzezeitliche Gräberfeld von Pitten in Niederösterreich* Bd. 1. Mitteilungen der Prähistorischen Kommission, 19/20. Vienna.

Hampl, F., Kerchler, H., and Benkovsky-Pivovarová, Z. (1982–1985). *Das mittelbronzezeitliche Gräberfeld von Pitten in Niederösterreich* Bd. 2. Mitteilungen der Prähistorischen Kommission, 21/22. Vienna.

Harb, I. (2002). *Die Ausgrabungen in der Tischoferhöhle bei Kufstein in Tirol,* Praearchos, 1. Innsbruck: Konrad Spindler, Golf-Verlag.

Harding, A., Šumberová, R., Outram, A. K., and Knüsel, C. (2007). *Velim: Violence and Death in Bronze Age Bohemia: The Results of Fieldwork 1992–95, with a Consideration of Peri-Mortem Trauma and Deposition in the Bronze Age.* Prague: Institute of Archaeology.

Hellich, J. (1913). 'Poklady předvěkého zlata z Poděbradska', *Památky archeologické,* 25: 27–36, 67–79.

Hnízdová, I. (1954). 'Otázka věteřovských tvarů v české únětické kultuře', *Památky archeologické,* 45: 193–218.

Höglinger, P. (1993). 'Das urnenfelderzeitliche Gräberfeld von Obereching, Land Salzburg', *Archäologie in Salzburg,* 2. Salzburg.

Hrala, J., Šumberová, R., and Vávra, M. (2000). *Velim: A Bronze age Fortified Site in Bohemia.* Praha: Institute of Archaeology.

Justová, J. (1965). 'Knovízská dílna na výrobu parohových předmětů v Pečkách', *Archeologické rozhledy,* 17: 790–5, 801–9.

Kern, A., Kowarik, K., Rausch, A., and Reschreiter, H. (2008). *Salz-Reich. 7000 Jahre Hallstatt*, Veröffentlichungen der Prähistorischen Abteilung, 2. Vienna.

Krause, R., Bechter, D., Lutz, J., Oeggl, K., Pernicka, E., Schwarz, A. St., Tropper, P., and Würfel, F. (2011). 'Prähistorische Siedlungen und mittelalterlicher Bergbau im Montafon, Vorarlberg', in G. Goldenberg, U. Töchterle, K. Oeggl, and A. Krenn-Leeb (eds.), HiMAT. Neues zur Bergbaugeschichte der Ostalpen. *Archäologie Österreichs Spezial*, 4. Vienna.

Krenn, M., Hölbling, E., and Mittermann, R. (2008). 'KG Gattendorf', *Fundberichte aus Österreich*, 47: 13–14.

——, Hölbling, E., and Mittermann, R (2008). KG Gatterndorf'. *Fundberichte aus Österreich* 47:13–14.

Krenn-Leeb, A. (2010). 'Ressource versus Ritual – Deponierungsstrategien der Frühbronzezeit in Österreich', in F. Bertemes and H. Meller (eds.), Der Griff nach den Sternen. Wie Europas Eliten zu Macht und Reichtum kamen. *Tagungen des Landesmuseums für Vorgeschichte Halle*, 05/1: 281–315. Halle (Saale).

Krenn-Leeb, A. (2011). 'Zwischen Buckliger Welt und Kleinen Karpaten: Die Lebenswelt der Wieselburg-Kultur', in A. Krenn-Leeb (ed.), *Lebenswelten—Archäologische Spurensuche in der Region Hainburger Pforte/Römerland*, Archäologie Österreichs, 22/1: 11–26.

Lauermann, E. (2003). *Studien zur Aunjetitz-Kultur im nördlichen Niederösterreich*. Universitätsforschungen zur prähistorischen Archäologie, 99. Bonn.

Leeb, A. (1987). 'Überblick über die Chorologie, Typologie und Chronologie der Wieselburgkultur. 100 Jahre Forschungsstand', in W. Hicke (ed.), *Hügel- und Flachgräber der Frühbronzezeit aus Jois und Oggau*. Wissenschaftliche Arbeiten aus dem Burgenland, 75: 231–283.

Lochner, M. (1991). *Studien zur Urnenfelderkultur im Waldviertel*. Mitteilungen der Prähistorischen Kommission, 25. Vienna.

—— (1994). 'Späte Bronzezeit, Urnenfelderzeit. Aktueller Überblick über die Urnenfelderkultur im Osten Österreichs', in J.-W. Neugebauer (ed.), *Bronzezeit in Ostösterreich*, Wissenschaftliche Schriftenreihe Niederösterreich, 98–101. St. Pölten-Vienna: Verlag Niederösterreichisches Pressehaus.

Moosleitner, F. (1991). *Bronzezeit im Saalfeldener Becken*, Archäologie in Salzburg, 1. Salzburg: Amt der Salzburger Landesregierung (Landesarchäologie).

Neugebauer, J.-W. (1994). *Bronzezeit in Ostösterreich*, Wissenschaftliche Schriftenreihe Niederösterreich, 98–101. St. Pölten-Vienna: Verlag Niederösterreichisches Pressehaus.

Neugebauer, Chr. and Neugebauer, J.-W. (1997). *Franzhausen. Das frühbronzezeitliche Gräberfeld I. Teil 1: Materialvorlage, Textteil, Tafelteil*, Fundberichte aus Österreich Materialhefte, 5/1-2. Vienna: Verlag Berger.

Pleinerová, I. (1992). 'Les Habitats et les maisons du Bronze Ancien en Bohême du Nord-ouest', in C. Mordant and A. Richard (eds.), *L' Habitat et l' occupation du sol a l âge du Bronze en Europe*. Paris: éditions du Comité des Travaux Historiques et Scientifiques, 383–90.

Říhovský, J. (1982). 'Hospodářský a společenský život velatické osady v Lovčičkách', *Památky archeologické*, LXXIII: 5–56.

Salaš, M. (1985). 'Metalurgická výroba na výšinném sídlišti z doby bronzové u Blučiny', *Časopis Moravského muzea*, LXX: 37–56.

—— (1995). 'Bemerkungen zur Organisation der urnenfelderzeitlichen Metallverarbeitung unter Berücksichtigung des mitteldonauländischen Kulturkreises in Mähren', *Archeologické rozhledy*, XLVII: 569–86.

Schránil, J. (1921). *Studie o vzniku kultury bronzové v Čechách*. Prague: V. & A. Janata.

Stöllner, Th., Breitenlechner, E., Eibner, C., Herd, R., Kienlin, T., Lutz, J., Maass, A., Nicolussi, K., Pichler, Th., Pils, R., Röttger, K., Song, B., Taube, N., Thomas, P., and Thurner, A. (2011). 'Der Mitterberg – Der Großproduzent für Kupfer im östlichen Alpenraum während der Bronzezeit', in G. Goldenberg, U. Töchterle, K. Oeggl, and A. Krenn-Leeb (eds.), HiMAT. Neues zur Bergbaugeschichte der Ostalpen. *Archäologie Österreichs Spezial*, 4. Vienna.

Stuchlík, S. and Stuchlíková, J. (1996). 'Aunjetitzer Gräberfeld in Velké Pavlovice. Südmähren', *Prähistorische Zeitschrift*, 71: 123–69.

—— (1999). 'Šumice, okr. Znojmo', in V. Podborský (ed.), *Pravěká sociokultovní architektura na Moravě*. Brno: Masarykova univerzita v Brně, 95–114.

Tihelka, K. (1960). 'Moravský věteřovský typ', *Památky archeologické*, LI: 27–135.

Urban, O. H. (2000). *Der lange Weg zur Geschichte. Die Urgeschichte Österreichs, Österreichische Geschichte bis 15 v. Chr.* Vienna: Verlag Ueberreuter.

Venclová, N. (1990). *Prehistoric Glass in Bohemia*. Prague: Archeologický Ústav ČSAV.

Willvonseder, K. (1937). *Die mittlere Bronzezeit in Österreich*. Bücher zur Ur- und Frühgeschichte, 4. Vienna-Leipzig.

Willvonseder, K. (1963–1968). *Die jungsteinzeitlichen und bronzezeitlichen Pfahlbauten des Attersees in Oberösterreich*. Mitteilungen der Prähistorischen Kommission, 11/12. Vienna.

CHAPTER 44

SLOVAKIA AND HUNGARY

KLÁRA MARKOVÁ WITH GÁBOR ILON

SETTING AND NATURAL CONDITIONS

Slovakia is characterized by the mountain ranges of the western and northern Carpathians. Lowlands lie in both the south-west (the Danubian lowlands) and the south-east (east Slovak lowlands), an extension of the Little Hungarian Plain (Little Alföld) in the west, and the Great Hungarian Plain (Great Alföld) in the east, itself forming a large part of Hungary. In the south-west the River Drava and in the south-east the Maros roughly outline the territory under discussion. Both countries are part of the space known in the archaeological literature as the Carpathian Basin (Fig. 44.1).

The cultural development of Slovakia and Hungary has been substantially affected by the Danube and Tisza rivers, flowing from north to south, the modern appearance of which results from vast drainage works at the end of the nineteenth century. These rivers determined geographical and cultural boundaries and vegetation, the climatic borders between the mid-European, mixed, and sub-Mediterranean zones in the west of the area and the steppe zone in the Alföld and Mezőföld regions (Gál, Juhász, and Sümegi 2005; Zatykó, Juhász, and Sümegi 2007). The Danube and Tisza with their tributaries were also the main communication routes that together with mountain passes in the north allowed people to move across the European landmass not only in a north-south direction, but also east to west. In the Bronze Age the Carpathian Basin was a crossroads where west and central European cultural traditions met eastern steppe manifestations or traditions from the northern Balkan world.

Natural Resources

In Slovakia copper and gold deposits of European importance were still exploited in the medieval period. The most important were those in the Low Tatras, Slovenské Rudohorie, Malá Fatra, Malé Karpaty in Slovakia, and in the Mátra Mountains in Hungary. Both oxide and sulphide ores are present. No direct evidence of mining, in other words mining or ore-roasting installations, has been found, since it has been destroyed by later activity. Indirect evidence exists in the form of finds of waisted stone hammers (*Rillenhämmer*) at Špania dolina. In chemical terms, Slovak copper falls within the wider south-eastern Carpathian circle. The first Eneolithic hoards are usually connected with the Nógrádmarcal-type raw material. During the classic phase of the Únětice culture production was oriented towards Alpine raw-material deposits, also true for a part of the Encrusted Pottery culture. In the Koszider horizon, deposits from the wider Carpathian region were used (Novotná 1982).

Václav Furmánek (2005: 16) has suggested the use of local tin deposits, pointing to cassiterite accumulations in deposits at Hnilec and vicinity, and elsewhere, exploited by panning. Apart from cassiterite, stannite occurs in Slovakia, containing copper and iron together with tin.

Along with gold from Transylvania, recent research has shown that local deposits of gold were exploited. Finds of moulds in houses at Nižná Myšľa and Spišský Štvrtok show that gold ornaments were cast.

Chronology

Different chronological systems are used in the literature of the two countries. Both come from the traditional basic subdivision of the Bronze Age into Early, Middle, Late, and Final Bronze Age. Hungarian archaeologists use their own chronological system, which is based on the stratigraphy of the tell settlement at Tószeg, as modified by Istvan Bóna. It is also used in other regions of the Carpathian Basin, where, unlike south-west Slovakia, west and central European cultures do not occur. The Slovak chronology follows a modified Reinecke system.

A better interlinking of the Hungarian and central European chronological systems is helped by attempts to classify the Late Eneolithic as a transitional period overlapping with the Early Bronze Age in Slovakia, which finds from southern Moravia also confirm. In this connection one of the first waves of eastern origin is relevant—the Pit Grave and Catacomb cultures in the Tisza Basin, which are dated in Hungary to the Early Bronze I period, and in Slovakia as a result of recent finds perhaps to Late Eneolithic I.

The data needed for the absolute chronology of the area, mostly obtained from radiocarbon dates, are still limited, and what does exist has usually been published without find context (Barta: forthcoming).

The Early Bronze Age
(c.2500/2300–1500/1450 cal bc)

The start of the Bronze Age in Slovakia and Hungary was characterized by a culturally miscellaneous and territorially fragmented picture. The richly diverse cultural picture comes from environmental variation, the different incoming cultures and economies, and their differing degrees of adaptation to local conditions; maybe also from coexistence or integration with the local inhabitants. Metals are rarely present. The start of the Bronze Age was connected with both the local cultures of the preceding period (Late Eneolithic to Early Bronze Age [Bz A0] in the modified Reinecke system) (Lichardus and Vladár 1996; Bátora 2000: abb. 692)—in the Hungarian literature referred to as the Early Bronze Age II and III (Meier-Arendt 1992: 40–1)—and with the penetration of several foreign cultures from different directions.

SLOVAKIA AND HUNGARY 815

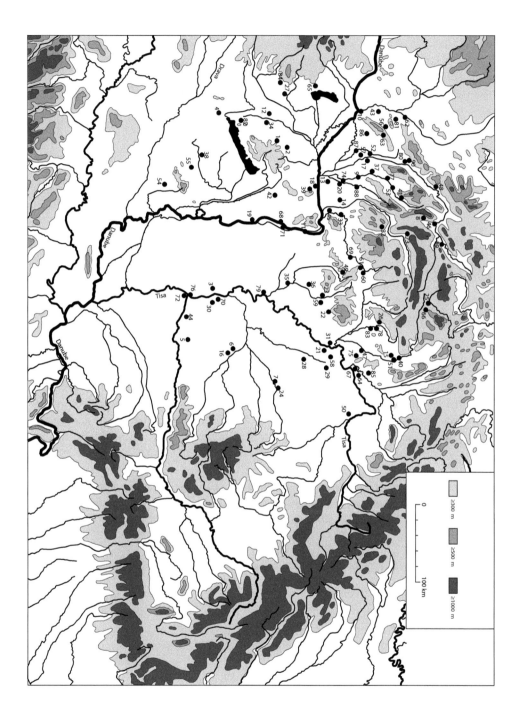

FIG. 44.1 (*previous page*) Map of Hungary and Slovakia showing sites mentioned in the text. 1. Bakonyjákó, 2. Bakonyszűcs, 3. Baks, 4. Balatonmagyaród; Barca—see Košice, 5. Battonya, 6. Békés, 7. Berettyóújfalu, 8. Blatnica-Plešovica, 9. Branč, 10. Bratislava, 11. Budapest, 12. Celldömölk-Sághegy, 13. Chotín, 14. Čaka, 15. Čaňa, 16. Doboz, 17. Ducové, 18. Dunaalmás, 19. Dunaújváros-Kosziderpadlás, 20. Dvory n. Žitavou, 21. Egyek, 22. Felsőtárkány, 23. Füzesabony, 24. Gáborján, 25. Gánovce, 26. Gemer, 27. Gór, 28. Hajdúbagos, 29. Hajdúböszörmény, 30. Hódmezővásárhely 31. Igrici, 32. Ilja-Sitno, 33. Ipeľský Sokolec, 34. Jánosháza 35. Jánoshida, 36. Jászdózsa, 37. Jelšovce, 38. Kaposvár, 39. Környe, 40. Košice, 41. Lužany, 42. Lovasberény, 43. Lozorno, 44. Makó, 45. Malé Kosihy, 46. Martin, 47. Megyaszó 48. Mikušovce, 49. Nagybátony, 50. Nagydobos; Nitriansky Hrádok see Šurany-Nitriansky Hrádok, 51. Nižná Myšľa, 52. Očkov, 53. Partizánske, 54. Pécs-Nagyárpád, 55. Pécsvárad, 56. Plavecké Podhradie, 57. Pobedim, 58. Polgár, 59. Poroszló, 60. Radzovce, 61. Sálgótarján-Zagyvapálfalva, 62. Skalica, 63. Smolenice, 64. Somotor, 65. Sopron-Burgstall, 66. Spišský Štvrtok, 67. Streda nad Bodrogom, 68. Százhalombatta, 69. Szécsény-Benczúrfalva, 70. Szentes-Nagyhegy, 71. Szigetszentmiklós, 72. Szőreg; Šafárikovo—see Tornaľa, 73. Špania dolina, 74. Šurany - Nitriansky Hrádok, 75. Taktabáj, 76. Tápé, 77. Topoľčany, 78. Tornaľa, 79. Tószeg, 80. Trenčianske Bohuslavice, 81. Unín, 82. Várvölgy-Felsőzsid, 83. Včelince, 84. Velemszentvid hill, 85. Veľké Raškovce, 86. Veľký Grob, 87. Veselé, 88. Vráble, 89. Vyšný Kubín, 90. Zemianske Podhradie.

Map: authors.

Gradually, during the early phase of the Early Bronze Age (Bz A1 or EBA III to MBA I in Hungarian terms), the situation changed and new, typically Carpathian, cultures emerged.

The later phase of the Early Bronze Age (end of Bz A1, Bz A2, Bz B1 in Slovak terminology, Middle Bronze Age II and III in Hungary) was a time of continuous development, expressed by the further stabilization of settlement, the formation of larger cultural entities with an increased density of settlement, economic and social growth, and social differentiation. Metals were widely used, and tin-bronze appeared. A developing social structure is also reflected in settlement structure. Settlement continuity and the settled way of life are indicated by a number of cemeteries and by numerous tell settlements. Long-distance contacts and exchange within the Carpathian Basin were intensified; influences from the eastern Mediterranean region are also possible.

Slovakia and Hungary in the Early Bronze Age can be divided into three basic geographical areas, each with its own cultural development: the Danubian region, the Danube and Tisza interfluve, and the Tisza region.

Danubian Region

The local roots of Bronze Age cultures are represented by the local late Eneolithic cultural substrate, surviving up to Bz A0 and in some places as late as Bz A1. The geographically extensive Makó-Kosihy-Čaka culture is understood to be a complex of local expressions over virtually the whole area under discussion (Kulcsár 2009). Most archaeological sites are settlements with indistinct occupation layers in varying geographical environments, with a small number of scattered features (as at Makó or Čaka). Graves are isolated, the cremation rite being used both in scattered graves and in urns. Sporadic inhumation graves occur at the end of the culture. Metallurgy is documented mostly by artefacts and moulds for copper shaft-hole axes, where connections with the Circumpontic metallurgical area can be suggested.

In the mountains and hills of Slovakia and northern Hungary other late Eneolithic local cultures continued, such as the Bošáca culture in the west.

Several streams of external influence arrived in the Carpathian Basin at the start of the Bronze Age. For Transdanubia, the Somogyvár-Vinkovci culture from the north and north-western Balkan area was the most important. In southern and north-western Transdanubia these influences manifested themselves by specific regional and chronological differences. Excavations here indicate dispersed, short-lived, open settlements, rarely with any indication of differentiated internal structure, as at Pécs-Nagyárpád. A few fortified settlements with multiple ditches on defensible hills (e.g. Nagygörbő) have been found. Post-built or semi-subterranean houses of various sizes occur. Sporadic graves have varying funeral rites: usually inhumations, less often urned cremations. Some graves are in mounds, some are flat, some have a stone packing. The number of rich grave goods, common in the south, decreases as one goes northwards (Kulcsár 2009). In south-west Slovakia and in west-central Slovakia this Bz A0 phase is only sporadically known from graves (e.g. Čaka: Bátora, Marková, and Vladár 2003: Abb. 5, 6).

From the west the Bell Beaker culture came through southern Moravia to the outer Carpathian part of Slovakia in Bz A0. The culture here is represented by the limited occurrence of inhumation graves in Beaker settlement pits (Skalica). The Bell Beaker culture probably came down the Danube to the Budapest area (Budapest-Albertfalva), where it is known as the Csepel group (Endrődi 2003). These cremation graves are different from the Beaker inhumation cemeteries of western Europe: inhumation graves are rare. Recently more extensive riverbank settlements with typical boat-shaped buildings and pits with ritual connotations have been discovered. The wider occurrence of accompanying material in the Carpathian part of Slovakia is supposed to be connected with the Csepel group (Bátora, Marková, and Vladár 2003), where it participates in further development during the Early Bronze Age, as in western Europe.

Western Slovakia was affected by the expansion of the Corded Ware culture from the northwest. The expansion of groups of the epi-Corded complex from Little Poland through Moravia led to adjoining south-west Slovakia. These groups did not penetrate far southwards into Transdanubia. The cultural borderline they formed remained through the rest of the Early Bronze Age. The oldest of them, the Chłopice-Veselé culture dating to Bz A0, is known predominantly from flat inhumation graves in south-west Slovakia (Veselé). Settlement finds are very rare. Copper-wire artefacts and willow-leaf ornaments are found; the origin of the shape is to be sought in the Caucasus region and is characteristic for the whole epi-Corded cultural complex.

In south-western Slovakia, as far as the Váh river, these components of the Chłopice-Veselé, Makó-Kosihy-Čaka, and Bell Beaker cultures led to the appearance of the Nitra culture in Bz A1, known also in Moravia (see Chapter 43). In Slovakia the culture is represented predominantly by grave finds (Nitra, Branč, Jelšovce); settlement finds are exceptional (Nitra). Elements of eastern origin gradually faded out in the course of its existence (copper willow-leaf ornaments, chipped stone in the form of shouldered points, aspects of the funeral rite). Local artefacts include copper 'Cypriot' pins, rings made of double wire, triangular daggers, and antler artefacts. Faience beads occur sporadically. Bodies in inhumation graves are usually in the crouched bipolar position with a basic east-west orientation. The construction of the grave pits and post-built houses (*Totenhäuser*) indicate social ranking—the graves of hunters, medicine men, and craftsmen have been identified. Elements from the expanding Únětice culture in the west started to appear towards the end of the Nitra culture. Metal analysis also indicates copper with high arsenic and nickel, similar to material of the Únětice culture and the Singen group (Bátora 2000: 579–80). Radiocarbon dates suggest a 300–500 year timespan for graves with specific Nitra material (Barta: forthcoming).

The expanding Únětice culture entered south-western Slovakia at the end of Bz A1 and formed a regional variant on its south-eastern boundary at the beginning of Bz A2 (Jelšovce, Veľký Grob: Bátora 2000). The usual orientation of bodies becomes less common with increasing distance from the centre. In Slovakia, the Carpathian part of the Únětice culture, bipolar west-east or east-west orientations often survive in graves of Nitra tradition. Social differences in grave goods and grave constructions occur to a lesser extent (e.g. stone lining of the grave), and they did not reach the level of the Leubingen-type princely burial mounds in Poland and Germany (Chapters 40 and 42). Metal analysis shows that Alpine ore was still used, while tin-bronze is infrequent (Bátora 2000: 579–80). Slovakia represents the border of the spread of raw material in the form of ring ingots (*Ösenringe*) and rib ingots (Bratislava, Skalica) (see Chapters 20 and 23). Unlike several adjacent cultures with a sheet-bronze industry (e.g. Wieselburg, Kisapostag), the Únětice culture preferred casting to hammering, as in the Carpathian region. There have been few excavations of the single-culture, single-layer settlements in Slovakia, while on tell settlements there are mixed settlement layers with material from contemporary Carpathian cultures, such as those of the Únětice-Hatvan or Únětice-Maďarovce horizons (Vráble, Nitriansky Hrádok). Settlement micro-regions and relationships between different settlement layers have not yet been defined.

Futher to the south-east only Únětice imports occur. They extended into other regions of the Carpathian Basin and beyond (e.g. neck-rings, *Dolchstaben*). The development of metallurgy particularly brought the Carpathian Basin into European long-distance exchange. From the classic phase on, this is also shown by the occurrence of Baltic amber in Slovakia and Hungary, as far as the cultures of the Maros Basin. To judge from the pottery of the Kisapostag and Hatvan cultures, the contacts were reciprocal.

In south-western Slovakia during Bz A2–Bz B1 there was an unbroken evolution from the Únětice culture to the Maďarovce culture. There it represents the eastern part of the Maďarovce-Věteřov-Böheimkirchen cultural complex, also found in Austria and Moravia (see Chapter 43). Unlike the preceding cultures in the Danube region there are numerous settlements sites (Veselé, Vráble). They are characterized by open settlements usually situated on level ground, relatively frequent fortified settlements, and sporadic tells. Among them the systematically excavated fortified tell settlement at Nitriansky Hrádok, which was divided into two parts, is worthy of mention. The fortified area included constructions with between one and three rooms, either built of posts (dwellings) or of logs (maybe storerooms). This part has evidence for craft production: stoneworking, the processing of antler and bone, potting and dedicated metallurgical workshops. Human skeletons, whole or partial, found in settlement pits and layers, are evidence of cult practices. Several hoards of bronze artefacts were found, generally of the Koszider horizon (e.g. Nitriansky Hrádok) (Fig. 44.2). A new range of ornament forms appears along with a new bronze implement (the sickle) and weapons (socketed spearheads and short swords).

The Maďarovce culture favoured casting technology and brought in real tin-bronzes that use, in the main, two new kinds of fahlore (*Fahlerz*) copper. One of the ores used was probably from the eastern Alps (Bátora 2000: 579–80). The culture participated in long-distance exchange or trade that became more intense towards the end of the period, particularly in its eastern group, where many finds belong to the North-Pannonian and Otomani cultures. Exchange has been proved in a north-south direction (amber). Jugs of Maďarovce type, together with Encrusted Pottery jugs, were imported and imitated in regions reaching from Little Poland in the north to the Iron Gates in the south. Long-distance contacts in an east-west direction are probably proved

FIG. 44.2 Koszider-type hoard from the settlement at Včelince–Lászlófala, Slovakia.
Photo: M. Novotná, Archaeological Institute of the Slovak Academy of Sciences, Nitra.

by the so-called *Brotlaibidole* ('loaf-of-bread' idols). In the late Maďarovce culture pits with *Litzenkeramik* pottery are found in settlements. This decorative technique occurs in several cultures in Austria, Slovakia, and Hungary in Bz A2–Bz B1 (see Chapter 43). The funerary rite of the Maďarovce culture was flat inhumation, with tumuli and cremation burials at the end (Dolný Peter, Jelšovce: Bátora 2000). The Maďarovce culture disappears at a time of increasing exchange and mobility, by means of a gradual acculturation into Bz B1.

The western entrance to the Carpathian Basin was, for a short time, part of the development in north-eastern Austria. This was an area of expansion, both of the Leithaprodersdorf culture (Bratislava, Devínska Nová Ves) (with intrusions into the region of the Nitra culture), and of the Wieselburg culture (Mosony, Bratislava-Rusovce, in Hungarian literature known also as the Gáta or Mosony culture), with intrusions northwards into the Únětice cultural milieu (Branč, Jelšovce).

In Transdanubia, south-west of the Danube, the Kisapostag culture (Bz A0–Bz A1, earlier phase) was based on the Makó-Kosihy-Čaka culture, with contributions from the late Somogyvár culture. The cremation funerary rites of the Kisapostag culture used both urns and scattered graves; inhumation graves are rare. Artefacts of the copper-sheet industry (e.g.

pendants, tubes, diadems) are typical. Imports ascribed to this culture have been documented as far east as the Tisza region and to the west in the upper Danube region.

The Kisapostag culture was succeeded by the Transdanubian Encrusted Pottery (North Pannonian culture in Slovak terminology). Two basic geographical groups are distinguished: northern and southern, with further representatives at Esztergom and Veszprém in the north and Szekszárd and Pecica/Pécska in the south (Bóna 1975). At first only short-lived settlements and cattle breeding were suggested. New excavations have shown the existence of long-lived settlements as well, but no tells are documented. The settlements differ in size and a hierarchy is presumed. More semi-subterranean houses with small numbers of postholes have been documented (Dunaalmás-Foktorok), characterized as production locations. At the settlement at Kaposvár, where a shallow ditch delineates the site, the above-ground rectangular post constructions are thought to be dwellings. In the hoards of Tolnanémedi type, jewellery is represented by, for example, comb-shaped pendants and disc or anchor-shaped pendants of tin, shown analytically to be of eastern Transalpine or Harz origin. Casting moulds and the graves of metalworkers (Környe) indicate local production, different from that of the contemporary Tisza-region cultures. The finds are connected with social ranking, as elite objects were deposited in a cultic manner (Kiss 2009), which is reflected to a lesser extent in the cemeteries. Cremation graves are in both pits and urns, and are situated in groups. Inhumation graves occur sporadically.

The Danube-Tisza Interfluve Region

The territory between the Danube and Tisza featured its own specific development in the Early Bronze Age. At first western influences from Transdanubia prevailed; later the links to the Tisza region are more striking.

The Nagyrév culture arose in the Danube-Tisza region in Bz A0–Bz A1; its extension to the north in Slovakia is unclear (Malé Kosihy). Settlements of the Nagyrév culture are situated in both the lowlands and uplands. Different chronological and geographical variants can be distinguished (e.g. Kőtörés, Ökörhalom, Szigetszentmiklós). Settlements with only one layer predominate and were usually short-lived. In tell settlements deep layers were formed. In contrast to the cultures of the following period, those of Nagyrév are unfortified and sparse, frequently located near the Danube (Százhalombatta, Dunaújváros), more rarely near the Tisza (Tószeg). Fortifications appeared towards the end of the period. Houses had a rectangular ground plan, two rooms, with a post construction and gabled roof. The outer sides of the walls had relief ornamentation, which is repeated in the pottery decoration. Burials are scattered graves and urned cremations; at larger cemeteries it seems probable the graves form family groups (Szigetszentmiklós). The use of isolated inhumation graves occurs in the formative phase.

The Vatya culture was formed from the background of the Nagyrév culture together with influences from the Kisapostag culture. Cemeteries of a range of sizes comprise several hundred urn burials (e.g. Dunaújváros-Kosziderpadlás). Burials of the Vatya culture followed a consistent rite, with cremations laid out in a structured manner, sometimes bounded or covered by stones. Initially, cremation urns were ordered in clan groupings. Social differentiation was reflected in the grave goods recovered from the final phases of the cemeteries. Settlements were formed at former Nagyrév sites (Százhalombatta) and were also established in previously unsettled sandy locations. Fortifications were built on naturally defensible sites with good visibility; they consisted of ditches and other earthworks, enclosing areas dedicated to particular functions, such as at Lovasberény where a metallurgical workshop was situated in the lower part of the site. The appearance of fortified settlements in the Vatya culture is thought to reflect the formation of a social hierarchy rather than a response to external threats.

Bronze artefacts are abundant: at first small sheet tubes, diadems, and tutuli, later cast massive objects, for example hammer-axes of Țufalău (Cófalva) type, spearheads. A hoard, after which the entire Koszider horizon was named (finds of bronze and sometimes gold), was found on a Vatya site in the upper layer of the Dunaújváros-Kosziderpadlás settlement. These hoards in the Carpathian Basin are dated to the end of the Early and beginning of the Middle Bronze Age, and are connected with the final stage of the Early Bronze Age cultures, in other words the final Rákospalota-Alpár phase of the Vatya culture (Bóna 1975; Bóna 1992: 24–6, 32; Vicze 1992: 92). Various kinds of jewellery, weapons, and implements, for example developed *Nackenscheibenäxte* (axes with disc butt), bar-shaped bracelets, heart-shaped arm-rings, crescent-shaped pendants, etcetera, are present. In this period the first sickles, spearheads, and massive *Absatzbeile* (axes with stop-ridge) occur in Slovakia and Hungary, with influences reaching the upper Danube.

The Tisza Region

The Tisza river Basin had been settled by migrants during the early stages of the Bronze Age and they influenced its further development in a remarkable way.

The Beba Veche/Óbéba-Pitvaros culture from the beginning of the Bronze Age (Bz A0, in Hungarian terminology EB II, EB III), which was situated in the lower Tisza Basin in Hungary, Romania, and Serbia, was influenced from the south (the northern Balkans) (Bóna 1992: 18–19). The culture introduced the rite of crouched inhumation (bipolar north-south orientation) with rich grave goods. Attractive personal ornaments were made of copper or bronze (e.g. 'Cypriot' pins, neck-rings with eyelet terminals, copper-wire jewellery, diadems made of panpipe-shaped plates), gold (*Lockenringe*), tin (ornamental plates), or faience.

Another wave of migrants is represented by the Periam/Perjámos-Szőreg culture (also known under other names: Pecica/Pécska, Mokrin or Maros/Mureș/Moriš culture). Although the population lived mostly on the same territory as the Beba Veche/Óbéba-Pitvaros culture, it gave rise to its own new settlements. Usually they were tells, where huge layers were formed (e.g. Periam/Perjámos, Pecica/Pécska, Klárafalva). Post-built houses (6–8 by 4–5 m) with floor and hearth were arranged in narrow lanes. A range of metal artefacts were created, for example *Rollenkopfnadeln*, *Hülsenkopfnadeln*, neck-rings, triangular short daggers at first; later tutuli, crescentic and heart-shaped pendants; and finally flat axes, long daggers, spearheads, Țufalău-type axes, hammer-axes of Gaura and Křtenov types. Beads of faience and amber are also present, indicating a wide range of long-distance contacts. The burial rite consists of skeletons in crouched or sitting position, with the appearance of pithos burials as well. Social differences are observable from the third phase. In Hungary the sites at Szőreg, Deszk, and Battonya are important (Bóna 1975).

From the Eneolithic and the start of the Bronze Age, the Nyírség-Zatín culture manifested itself by a great density of sites in the north-eastern part of Hungary (Tisza-Körös Basins), east Slovakia, and the adjacent parts of Romania. Settlement pits and layers in the different environments in both the lowland and upland settlements have produced shallow ditches and floors indicating the remains of huts. The settlements were single-phase, or else they formed the lower layers of tells (Gáborján, Polgár). Burial was cremation mostly in an urn. The Andrid transitional group represents a smooth passage to the Ottomani culture, which occurs in lower parts of tell sites (Berettyóújfalu-Szihalom, Sz. Máthé 1988: Fig. 21). Settlements were concentrated around larger sites, situated some way from each other. It is presumed they consisted of farmers and stockbreeders. The cremation rite, the ashes placed in pits or urns, gave way to both inhumation and cremation after influences from the Otomani-Füzesabony cultural complex arrived in the area.

In the western part of the former Nyírség area (the basins of the upper Tisza, the Slaná, and other tributaries) the extensive and long-lasting Hatvan culture was formed. The culture is mainly known from settlements. Several settlement forms were present, including tells and tell-like settlements (Jászdózsa, Tószeg, Törökszentmiklós, Včelince). On some sites Hatvan layers succeed those of the Nagyrév culture (Tószeg), but new tells are formed as well. Fortified settlements were built on higher ground up to 100 m, as well as in lowland locations. The fortified area is small, often with a ditch around, sometimes with a rampart. The unfortified part forms an annexe, or satellite settlements may be added on (Kalicz and Kalicz-Schreiber 2006: 107–24).

In the settlement structure of the Early Bronze Age in south-western Slovakia circular enclosures are found, some of them probably belonging to the Hatvan culture. Rectangular houses of post construction with an earthen bench along the wall were large at first. Some cemeteries probably for family use were situated around the settlement (Hatvan). Cemeteries are small, with scattered cremation and urn graves in groups. In metallurgy the eastern origin of the culture was reflected in the casting technology (axes of Tószeg type). Isolated imports or imitations of its pottery have appeared as far as the upper Danube region. The cultural development reflects three basic phases: the independent development of the culture; interaction with the Otomani-Füzesabony complex; and the final phase, supported also by radiocarbon dates (Včelince). Later house rooms were smaller; in pottery the Otomani-Füzesabony influenced new shapes and decoration techniques in its later phase. In some places the culture survives together with the cremation rite up to Bz B1 (Jászdózsa, Aszód).

The influence of Corded Ware from the north-east can be detected in the north and east of the area, as shown by tumuli with inhumation and cremation burials of the east Slovakian Tumulus culture (Šapinec). Tumuli are low (0.5–1.5 m high), with a ditch around the grave. A Transcarpathian component can be detected in the raw materials of the chipped-stone industry. No copper or bronze artefacts have yet been found. The short-lived settlements are probably connected with the life of migrating shepherds.

The epi-Corded complex expanded from the north into eastern Slovakia. The oldest culture of this complex, the Chłopice-Veselé culture, came from Little Poland not only to Moravia and south-west Slovakia, but also through the Lower Beskidy mountains to eastern Slovakia. Another constituent part of this complex is the Košťany culture in the northern part of the region. Until now it has been known only from inhumation graves in flat cemeteries. They are accompanied by the usual eastern copper industry shapes: willow-leaf-shaped jewellery, *Noppenringe*, *Lockenringe*, bone pins, and a chipped stone industry. Recent excavations have found the first indications of an unfortified site. In Hungary the only cemetery of the culture is at Nagydobos. Finds from Košice are relevant for the proto-Košťany phase (Bz A1 early). The character of the final Košťany-Otomani phase (Bz A1/Bz A2 early, cemeteries at Nižná Myšľa, Čaňa) implies continuity in the development of the region, as it became a core for further cultural evolution.

The Otomani-Füzesabony cultural complex covers an area beyond the frontiers of present-day Hungary and Slovakia, notably to north-western Transylvania. However, there are regional differences, which are observable particularly in pottery forms. The results of several settlement analyses show a complicated relationship with the neighbouring Hatvan culture. In some tells there is a period where the Hatvan culture becomes more Füzesabony-like, but the proper Füzesabony culture is not present in these sites (e.g. Jászdózsa, Tószeg III–VI, Ároktő: Fischl 2006: 164–6).

Analysis of cemeteries has delineated the inner development of the cultures within the Otomani-Füzesabony cultural complex, as well as details of their social structure (Nižná Myšľa, Hernádkak, Megyaszó, Streda nad Bodrogom: Olexa 2002: 53–85; Bóna 1975: 151–3). Large cemeteries encompassing hundreds of graves (e.g. Tiszafüred) show strict burial rites: inhumation burials in crouched position with bipolar orientation—either on their left side (for females) or their right side (for males). The Nižná Myšľa cemetery has more than 750 graves, and is thus the largest cemetery of the period in the Carpathian Basin, and illustrates continuity in burial. In the Košťany-Otomani phase bipolar east-west and related orientations are predominant. In two subphases of the classic stage, north-south and related orientations occur. The remarkably varied grave goods reflect social differences (wealth and social status). Individuals were interred in a variety of wooden coffins or just laid in the earth with or without a grave lining or shroud, depending on their status in society. Items of personal jewellery were found, such as pins, *Lockenringe*, heart-shaped and crescentic pendants made of copper, bronze, gold, faience, and amber (Fig. 44.3). Little rectangular tabs of gold for securing the ends of strings, or bands, were found only in the graves of rich women. Some graves had no grave goods.

The end of the culture is characterized by sporadic cremation burials, such as those at Streda nad Bodrogom in phase Bz B1. This stage of the culture saw the earliest urnfields (Otomani-Piliny horizon and Otomani-Suciu de Sus horizon).

Some aspects of social and economic distinctions within this community are seen in settlement patterns where there is evidence of craft production of gold and bronze. Bronze hoards of the Koszider horizon are found in upper settlement layers, which are connected with the late phase of the Otomani-Füzesabony cultural complex (Streda nad Bodrogom stage). Grave goods consist mostly of jewellery, such as heart-shaped and lunular pendants, sickle-shaped pins, rod bracelets, arm-rings, and less often weapons, such as axe-hammers with disc butt, or implements such as sickles.

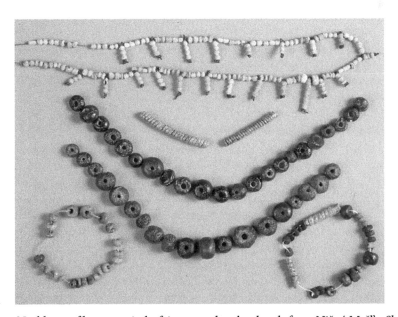

FIG. 44.3 Necklaces of bronze spirals, faience, and amber beads from Nižná Myšľa, Slovakia.

Photo: A. Marková, excavation of the Archaeological Institute of the Slovak Academy of Sciences, courtesy L. Olexa.

FIG. 44.4 Burial pit with human sacrifices from Nižná Myšľa, Slovakia.

Photo: L. Olexa.

Human skeletons and fragments found in settlement pits and layers have been seen by some as cultic in nature (Fig. 44.4) (Nižná Myšľa: Gancarski 2002: 89–93).

Two fortified settlements are of great importance. At the tell settlement of Barca I there are one- to three-roomed huts, maybe workshops, which are laid out on a street system with paving. Further north, at Spišský Štvrtok, there were fortifications different from those on other sites. They included a stone-reinforced rampart with bastions and berm, and inner segmentation. The site was divided into four parts: an 'acropolis' containing different types of one or two-roomed houses with stone foundations, and including several finds of hoards of gold and bronze objects, separated from other parts by a cross-rampart; a cult area with human and animal sacrifices; and two specialized craft areas, for bronze casting and stone-working in the south, and production of pottery, antler and bone artefacts in the north. At the cult well at Gánovce, an iron knife with bronze rivets was found—perhaps the first local iron object, indicating links with distant lands in the eastern Mediterranean (Vladár 1973; Lichardus and Vladár 1996).

The Gyulavarsánd culture was situated east of the Tisza in the river basins of the Körös and Berettyó. Although the origin of this culture is not clear, southern influences are evident, in particular from the Vatina culture. Similarly, some of the ornamental elements are identical with the Füzesabony culture, and imports from the Wietenberg culture in Transylvania also had an effect. There is ample evidence that gold was worked, but there is less documentation for the casting of bronze. The famous hoard from Hajdúsámson, dating to an advanced phase of the culture, included the earliest Carpathian solid-hilted sword with engraved ornament, accompanied by axes of different types and origin (the Gaura type with disc butt, axes with comb-shaped butt, an axe of the Křtěnov type). Similar artefacts occur mainly in cultures of the Tisza Basin (e.g. the Apa hoard). The interpretation, cultural relations, and ornamentation of these artefacts, which resemble Mycenaean spiral and wavy ornaments, have been much discussed.

The dead were buried in a crouched position in inhumations. Tell settlements were founded at new locations, such as the tell at the eponymous site of Gyulavarsánd-Laposhalom. Sites were levelled prior to construction (Békés). There are open settlements with post-built houses. Fortified tells are often 'islands'. Large timber houses encircled by farm buildings might represent the dwellings of a higher social class.

Settlements

Settlements of the final Eneolithic up to Bz A1 are documented only sporadically in the north. Settlements and buildings indicate cattle rearing and agriculture. More permanent settlements were built at the end of Bz A1 and developed in Bz A2 and early Bz B1. Settlements were permanent and there is evidence for increasing settlement density. This led to economic and social growth with different settlement types (temporary, permanent, tells, fortified or unfortified).

Tells in the Early Bronze Age occur mostly in the Tisza Basin and also throughout the interfluve region. Slovakia represents the northern border of their occurrence. Tells have not yet turned up in Transdanubia (Hungary west of the Danube).

Fortified settlement played a significant role in all settlement areas. The rise and fall of particular settlements varies (Kovács 1982). This variety of settlements is concentrated in the cultures of the Tisza basin, but also in the Vatya and Maďarovce cultures. The size of sites varies; small sites (up to 1 hectare) predominate. Other fortified settlements, maybe later, are bigger and more complicated, with a small separate fortified part (acropolis) that is connected to other fortified areas (Spišský Štvrtok, Vráble, Malé Kosihy, Lovasberény). Fortification structures vary as well. These fortified settlements vary in function: they may be places of defence, control centres, or centres for craft activity, exchange, and cultic practice. At particular sites some functions dominate, at others they can be absent.

Agricultural implements and grain-storage pits indicate the importance of farming. The range of plants cultivated in the region increased markedly during the Late/Final Bronze Age (Gyulai 1993). Animal breeding in the Early Bronze Age has been described by Sándor Bökönyi (1992: 69–72) (see Chapter 18).

Both the tell settlements that indicate a peaceful lifestyle and the large number of graves in the cemeteries point to a significant demographic development at the end of the Early Bronze Age and beginning of the Middle Bronze Age. This was a period of great population increase compared to previous times. The basic reason was presumably the availability of sufficient food. From archaeobotanical and archaeozoological data, we can say that advanced cultivation skills (grain cultivation supplemented with horticulture) and cattle breeding were the basis of the economy. Besides riverine transport, finds of spoked wheels and horse cheek-pieces (part of the harness) indicate the use of animal power in transport over land.

The Middle Bronze Age (c.1500/1450–1200/1150 cal bc)

Burial rites in the Early Bronze Age in Slovakia and Hungary were not uniform. Contact between cultures that practised inhumation and those that practised cremation in the Early Bronze Age had vanished by the start of the Middle Bronze Age, when the Tumulus cultures used both rites, in different areas.

The Early to Middle Bronze Age transition is reflected also by bronze artefacts in hoards of the Koszider type, and in grave inventories. However, there are different opinions about how to define this transition and establish its cause. One view sees these artefacts as a marker of the end of the Early Bronze Age in the Carpathian Basin as a result of incoming Tumulus culture people from the west (Mozsolics 1957; Kőszegi 1988). The same artefacts are seen by others as partly connected to the Early Bronze Age but indicating the gradual spread of cultural influences from the east (Hänsel 1968; Furmánek, Veliačik, and Vladár 1999).

The Middle Bronze Age in this region is a rather short period, from the end of Bz B1 up to Bz C, or in Hungarian literature, the earlier phase of the Late Bronze Age. In this period metallurgy developed in both quantity and quality, as seen in hoards (Dreveník I, Dreveník II, Ožďany, or Forró and Ópályi in Hungary). Hoard contents vary in the frequency of ornaments, weapons, and tools.

The Danube Region

The Middle Danubian Tumulus culture in Slovakia and north-western Transdanubia appears very similar to that in other parts of central Europe. Funeral rites are bi-ritual and graves are under tumuli (Buková, Smolenice), in grave pits or on the ground surface. Open settlements are frequently found in low-lying positions (e.g. Veselé, Bratislava-Mlynská dolina, Bratislava-Rusovce: Bartík 2004) and on elevations in defensible positions (Unín). No fortification has so far been documented in Slovakia. Some settlements continue through several phases of cultural development, while others did not last long enough to create a significant cultural layer. Large open settlements with a considerable distance between features are typical. Rectangular post-built houses were found scattered over a large area (Bratislava-Rusovce). Pottery hoards from the late and final phases also suggest a connection with agricultural ritual practices (Lozorno). There is so far no chronological scheme that ties the dominant pottery types in with the sequence of bronze artefacts.

The Middle Danubian Tumulus culture is assumed to have come to Transdanubia from adjacent parts of Austria, Moravia, or western Slovakia. This shift is evident in the older phases of the Middle Bronze Age (Nagydém-Középrépáspuszta). Open settlements are known from this region (Balatonmagyaród), and judging by cemetery finds social differentiation was expressed through large social units. The culture was transformed into the Middle Danubian Urnfield cultures in Bz D, but continuity in burial practices at Zohor-Nová Štrkovňa suggests little change.

The Danube-Tisza Interfluve and Tisza Region

In Slovakia the Dolný Peter phase (a transitional Maďarovce-Tumulus horizon) appears during Bz B1 and later developments are represented by the early Tumulus phase (Nové Zámky), the classic phase (Salka), and the final phase (end of Bz C). The appearance of the Carpathian Tumulus culture is not uniform. The Tápé group in the Szeged region around the Körös river mouth extended to the mouth of the Maros, and continued through Bz B1 and Bz C. This group is represented by a bi-ritual flat burial ground in Tápé, with inhumation burials in which the dead are either crouched or in extended positions; cremation burials are less frequent. The Egyek and Hajdúbagos groups in the north-eastern Tisza Basin had urned cremation burials but only sporadic settlement finds.

Apart from the groups of Tumulus cultures, the Piliny culture also existed in this region in the Middle Bronze Age. It developed from the local Otomani and Hatvan cultures in the end of Bz B1 (the Otomani-Piliny horizon).

The Late and Final Bronze Age (c.1250/1150–800/750 cal bc)

In the Late Bronze Age the cultural development of Slovakia and Hungary was divided into three basic areas: 1. The Tisza Basin and and Tisza-Danube interfluve regions; 2. The valleys of the mountainous north of Slovakia; 3. The Danube region. The high mountainous north of Slovakia is now settled more continuously for the first time.

Apart from a typical cremation funeral rite, mostly using urns, the most significant features of the Urnfield groups are the development of bronze metallurgy in production centres, along with a wide range of bronze tools, and extensive trade. We find groups of armed chieftains and prominent women, buried with much pomp and circumstance in rich barrow. In the Müller-Karpe classification (1959), and as used in the Prähistorische Bronzefunde series, the beginning of the urnfields can be dated to Bz D, but that applies only to the south-western and mid-Danubian urnfields. If this approach was applied to the south-eastern urnfields and the Lausitz culture in Slovakia, the sequence would be interrupted by an artificial division (Furmánek, Veliačik, and Vladár 1999: 70, 90).

The Tisza and Tisza-Danube Interfluve Regions

The South-Eastern Urnfields

The earliest urnfields are observable in the north-eastern area. No Tumulus cultures existed on these territories in the Middle Bronze Age, or were only a marginal expression of the cultural and historical development, for example in the upper Tisza Basin, south-central Slovakia, and the hilly areas of northern Hungary. As far as geography and chronology are concerned, the south-eastern urnfields can be divided into western and eastern parts, and earlier and later phases. The western region saw the rise of the Piliny and Kyjatice cultures, while the Suciu de Sus, Berkesz-Demecser, and Gáva cultures occupied the eastern part.

If we ignore the earlier cremation burials of the Vatya and Hatvan cultures, the Piliny culture is the earliest Urnfield culture in central Europe, running from Bz B1 to Ha A1. The large urn cemeteries, exceptionally scattered graves, are known from Tornaľa (formerly Šafárikovo), Radzovce (Furmánek and Mitáš 2010) in the west, and Košice-Barca II, Nagybátony (Kemenczei 1984) in the east. Their frequency in the north-east (Spiš) is also fairly dense.

Taking into account both settlements (Včelince) and cemeteries (Tornaľa) of the early period (Bz B1, the Otomani-Piliny horizon), the area over which the culture crystallised was small. In the course of its development large settlement agglomerations at both upland and lowland sites served as administrative and economic centres (e.g. Gemer-Tovaš with six hoards, Ožďany, Kisterenye, Szécsény-Benczúrfalva). Excavations at Radzovce and Zagyvapálfalva show that open settlements are similar.

High-altitude settlements may be surrounded by ditches and ramparts, as at Szécsény-Benczúrfalva-Majorhegy. The intensive production of bronzes is typical (hoards at Veľký Blh, Rimavská Sobota, Ožďany). In metallurgy swords of Riegsee-Ragály type, with elaborated decorated hilts and pommels, are notable; some of these productions also appeared in the Lausitz culture area.

The Kyjatice culture existed in the Northern Medium Mountains (Északi-középhegység, the hills running from the Danube Bend to the Upper Tisza region), and in their foreland. This culture started in Ha A1 and survived into the Early Iron Age. Its ritual sites have been identified in caves (Aggtelek-Baradla, Majda Hraškova caves, with skeletons). Sites are on plains (e.g. Sajószentpéter), and in higher areas (Szécsény-Benczúrfalva-Majorhegy). The latter were fortified in many cases. At the site of Felsőtárkány-Várhegy the dimensions of the post-built houses were 3.2 by 5.5–6 m. There is an extremely high proportion of hunted animal bones in these settlements. Domestic animals were cattle, sheep/goat, and pig. In the case of the well-studied settlement of Radzovce, where houses with stone foundations and many artefacts relating to advanced metallurgy were found, wild game comprised only 10 per cent. Of their cemeteries, Radzovce (72 per cent Piliny, 20 per cent Kyjatice graves) is noteworthy.

As regards differences between male and female burials, no differences were found in the quantity and shape of the urns, but there were variations in non-ceramic equipment. Social ranking is reflected in extraordinarily rich grave goods or the occurrence of cremation burials with built constructions (Furmánek, Mitáš, and Pavelková 2010). Demographic analysis suggested one hundred individuals lived in the neighbouring site in the Piliny period, while during the Kyjatice phase their number decreased by 50 per cent.

There are numerous bronze hoards, of which Krasznokvajda, Bükkszentlászló, and Gyöngyössolymos are noteworthy. Of the typical metallurgical products, the Liptov-type swords (e.g. Bükkaranyos) and the bronze cauldrons (e.g. Vácszentlászló) may be mentioned.

The Suciu de Sus culture in north-eastern Hungary (Hungarian Felsőszőcs), better known in north-western Romania and present also in Ukraine, represents the easternmost central European Urnfield group. Artefacts from its early phases include imports from the Otomani or Maďarovce cultures. At Veľké Raškovce an amphora depicting a wagon was found.

On the Great Hungarian Plain the Middle Bronze Age cultures in Ha A1–2 were replaced by the Gáva culture, so the late tumulus burials in the cemetery of Csorva (Szabó 1996) exemplify a transitional phase; in fact, they indicate accelerating changes in the culture. Cattle husbandry was one of the main subsistence elements. The most important metallurgical production, while at the same time the ritual centre of the culture, might have taken place at Szentes-Nagyhegy in the Great Hungarian Plain. Slovakia represents the north-western extent of its distribution. Finds are known mostly from lowland settlements and fortified sites (Somotor), continuing into the Hallstatt period. At the majority of sites traces of craft production and farming were found; and concentrations of hoards indicate a connection with the trade route from north-eastern Hungary to Poland.

Research on settlements of this culture has been much more extensive than that on Transdanubia and northern Hungary. The central settlement site of Baks-Temetőpart and its surrounding sites, as well as the settlement networks of Hódmezővásárhely-Szakálhát and at the northern boundary of Makó, are of great importance. The excavation at Polgár in the Upper Tisza region is equally important because of the well found there (Szabó 2004b; Ilon 2007b: Fig. 44.5). Although research is ongoing, the long house at Jánoshida (26 by 6.5 metres) appears

FIG. 44.5 The well of the Polgár (Hungary) M3/29 rescue site, showing a vessel *in situ*.
Photo: G. Ilon.

to be unique; normally houses in this culture measure 5–10 m in length and 4–6 m in width, and are equipped with built hearths (e.g. Doboz and Poroszló), perhaps derived from tell traditions. Pot hoards were found on the settlements of Igrici and Tiszacsege (Ha A1), as well as in Hódmezővásárhely (Ha A2/B1) (Szabó 2004a). Up to now, burials of this culture have been under-represented in Hungary: the only site, with 17 urn burials, is at Taktabáj. Of the bronze hoards, those at Nagykálló (Ha A1), Szentes-Nagyhegy, and Hajdúböszörmény are the most significant. The culture lived on at certain sites (e.g. Hódmezővásárhely), into the Mezőcsát phase, with elements of the Basarabi culture at Hodmezővásárhely-Gorzsa.

The Region of Mountainous Northern Slovakia

The Lausitz Culture in Slovakia

The expansion of the Lausitz culture in the north-western mountainous part of Slovakia represents the southern border of the European northern Urnfield complex (Veliačik 1983). The culture is characterized by settlements on elevated positions in hilly terrain, avoiding flat open country; it concentrates on brown soils and their variants. In the Final Bronze Age (Ha B) the Lausitz culture moved to chernozems, which in this warm and dry period had a steppe character, more suitable for animal breeding, the main activity of the culture (Romsauer and Veliačik 1998). Since settlement had previously been sparse, it is supposed that many of these sites were of local origin. In the early period Lausitz finds are sporadic and isolated (Martin).

The development of the Lausitz culture in Slovakia is characterized by three evolutionary stages (Veliačik 1983). The first is formative; the second (Ha A1–2) shows increasing settlement density, increasing production of bronzes (in hoards the local component predominates), while towards its end fortified settlements on spurs occur. In the late stage, at the transition from the Final Bronze Age to the Early Iron Age, a second horizon of fortified settlements occurs. Intertribal conflict used to be blamed for the end of the culture, as well as economic depression and the invasion of foreign groups. In some regions settlement lasted into the Hallstatt period (Ha C and D) and in the Orava region down to La Tène. The so-called migration of the Lausitz culture southwards, in the sense of an expansion to the area of the south-eastern urnfields, or as an expansion leading to the rise of the Kyjatice culture, has not been borne out by recent finds. The finds suggest instead a genetic continuity of the Kyjatice culture with the Piliny culture.

For the Lausitz culture in Slovakia, flat urn burial is characteristic. From its beginning the funeral rite also includes tumuli, sometimes with several burials, indicating social differentiation. Tumuli with stone rings are gradually substituted by a full stone covering, and later by small mounds. Settlements are both open and fortified. In the Lausitz area there is more evidence of metallurgical activities, with a high concentration of such finds at Pobedim, which seems to have been a cross-cultural production centre. Considering the mixed character of the material, it seems likely that it supplied part of the Velatice settlement area in Slovakia, which had no production centre of its own. At Vyšný Kubín-Tupá skala a smith's workshop with hearth was excavated. Finds of casting moulds and cores under a mound at Vyšný Kubín come from burials of specialized metallurgists, while those from Trenčianske Bohuslavice can be regarded as coming from workshops: witness the presence of tools and semi-products or waste.

The Danube Region

The Middle Danubian Urnfield Complex

During Bz D–Ha A1 two cultures of the Middle Danubian urnfields are found in south-western Slovakia: the Velatice culture, developing from the Middle Danubian Tumulus culture in the west, and the Čaka culture based on the Carpathian Tumulus culture in the east. The Váh river forms the border between the two. In excavation above-ground post constructions of rectangular ground plan and rather small size, with an area of $9-17$ m^2, come in unagglomerated plans, and tended be oriented the same way. The remains of two buildings at Bratislava-Rusovce indicate a possible arrangement around a courtyard (Bartík 2004).

In Transdanubia the situation is similar. The central European Urnfield complex here has two main phases, and various subgroups such as the north-western Transdanubian (Velemszentzid, Celldömölk-Sághegy), similar to the east Alpine group, the south Transdanubian group (Lengyel-Pécsvárad), and the north-eastern group (Vál culture). Settlements on hills appear in a late phase, such as Várvölgy-Felsőzsid, Velemszentzid, Celldömölk-Sághegy, and Pécsvárad-Aranyhegy. Of the lowland sites, noteworthy are the rescue excavations of the palisaded site of Balatonmagyaród, and of the so-called Kápolnadomb in Gór from the end of the period, which contain abundant metallurgical artefacts (moulds) (Ilon 2007a). There are post-built houses, but also others with stone foundations. Important cemeteries are those at Bakonyszűcs, Bakonyjákó, Celldömölk-Sághegy, and Sopron-Burgstall (Ilon 2007b; Kőszegi 1988). In some hoards like those from Velem, Sághegy, Várvölgy-Felsőzsid, and Nagy-Lázhegy gold also occurs (Fig. 44.6).

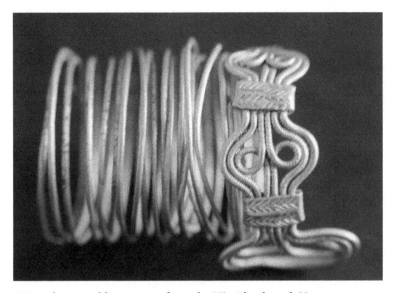

FIG. 44.6 Wound-wire gold ornament from the Várvölgy hoard, Hungary.

Photo: G. Ilon.

The Velatice culture came to an end in Ha A2, perhaps because of a worsening climate and consequently deteriorating agricultural conditions. Its influence was then felt in the Lausitz culture area and in part further south (Romsauer and Veliačik 1998), for instance in the vicinity of Bratislava and Esztergom (Bándi 1982: 81–9), based on control of the trade to the west and north. The Podolí culture (Chotín), for instance, represents a development from the Velatice culture, contemporary with the Stillfried phase in Austria and Vál II in Transdanubia. Bronze artefacts arrived in south-west Slovakia mainly by trade from production centres in Transdanubia (Velemszentzid, Celldömölk-Sághegy), and from centres of the Lausitz culture (Pobedim). The smaller workshops were particularly active (Bratislava-Devín, Plavecké Podhradie).

Hill Forts

The hill forts that appeared at the end of the Late Bronze Age, and became common in the Final Bronze Age, were a typical phenomenon. They occurred in all three Urnfield areas (Nováki, Czajlik, and Holl 2006). In Slovakia they emerged in three phases: the earliest in the Late Bronze Age, when they are not common; the second dates to the beginning of the Final Bronze Age; the third to the end of the Final Bronze Age and earliest Iron Age, when particularly large hill forts were built.

The earliest hill forts lie in the south-eastern Urnfield group. In Hungary they appear at the beginning of the Late Bronze Age (Szécsény, Bükkaranyos), while in the Middle Danubian urnfields in Slovakia they are relatively rare but appear in both the upland (e.g. Ducové, Velatice culture), and lowland areas (settlements of the Čaka culture, e.g. Dvory nad Žitavou, Ipeľský Sokolec: Furmánek, Veliačik, and Romsauer 1982). The most numerous fortified settlements appear in the Lausitz culture area. The primary aim of these sites was probably to provide a safe haven in the area during a period of settlement stabilization. Those built upon promontories were intended to guard communication routes and important microregions (e.g. Vyšný Kubín-Tupá skala, Mikušovce).

Fortified settlements on hilltops in upland areas had massive surrounding fortifications and were often divided into subareas according to their economic or social purpose, indicating a variety of functions (e.g. Zemianske Podhradie). Apart from this they were also power and trade centres, and in some cases ritual sites. Such fortified sites might have been sacred hills (Blatnica-Plešovica). Bearing in mind the presence of foreign goods on them, they could be of inter-regional and intercultural importance (Blatnica-Plešovica: at least 9 hoards; Trenčianske Bohuslavice: 16 hoards; Veliačik 2004). From the Late Bronze Age metallurgical centres appear at fortified settlements. During the Middle Danubian Urnfield period Bratislava-Devín and Plavecké Podhradie had similar status, though not as remarkable as Velemszentzid in Transdanubia, Sitno-Ilija in the Lausitz area, or Somotor in the south-eastern Urnfield area.

In areas of wider contact, particularly Urnfield sites in Slovakia, a mixture of finds occurs. The contact between the Velatice and Lausitz cultures is visible on settlements (Pobedim, Partizánske), in burials, and also in prominent tumuli at Očkov, in the Čaka culture warrior chieftains, prominent women (Lužany), or in the use of the same ritual features by the Velatice and Lausitz cultures (Pobedim) or the Čaka and Lausitz cultures (Topoľčany). The armed warrior elite were equipped with swords (both flange-hilted and solid-hilted), spears, and armour (helmet, breastplate, greave, shield).

Hundreds of hoards containing bronze artefacts (ornaments, weapons, tools, and raw copper) occur in the Middle Bronze Age (Tumulus cultures) and the Late and Final Bronze Ages (Urnfield cultures) (Mozsolics 1967; 1973; 1985; 2000). Nearly 450 Late Bronze Age hoards have been found in Hungary during the past 150 years. The fact that the number has increased in the last decade, following the discovery of the Nagykálló hoard (with good excavation context), represents progress in research on hoards. The excavation between 2003 and 2006 on the upland settlement at Várvölgy-Nagy-Lázhegy prior to quarrying, a site covering 160 hectares, recovered 12 bronze hoards and 1 gold one. Gábor Szabó (2009) documented as many as 16 bronze and 2 gold hoards on 12 sites east of the Danube between 2006 and 2009, in competition with illegal treasure hunters.

The so-called sun-bird-boat (*Sonnenvogelbark*), which has been identified on sword grips, greaves, diadems, belt-plates, and bronze vessels, is crucial to an understanding of the religious life of the period.

The End of the Bronze Age

The closing phase of the Urnfield culture can be related to steppe and pre-Scythian (Cimmerian) influences coming from the east (the Hajdúböszörmény hoard, and later the hoards of Bükkszentlászló type). The assemblage of the latter belongs to the Mezőcsát culture. At cemeteries associated with it in the westernmost part of the steppe belt (Mezőcsát, Füzesabony) inhumation graves are found, with the remains of horse harness in bronze and iron, bone plates with typical ornamentation, and cattle and sheep bones (Kemenczei 2005; Romsauer 1999; Stegmann-Rajtár 2004). Increasing Cimmerian influence is reflected in numerous changes in metal production, warfare, horse harness, animal breeding, religion, and long-distance trade and exchange. The culture occupied the territory of the Gáva culture and pushed the bearers of the Kyjatice and Lausitz cultures up into the hills. In the western regions of Hungary and Slovakia this period is represented by hoards of Románd type, following which the evolution of the eastern provinces of the Hallstatt culture began.

Bibliography

Bándi, G. (1982). 'Spätbronzezeitliche befestigte Höhensiedlungen in Westungarn', in *Beiträge zum bronzezeitlichen Burgenbau in Mitteleuropa*. Berlin: Zentralinstitut für Alte Geschichte und Archäologie; Nitra: Archeologický Ústav Slovenskej Akadémie Vied, 81–90.

Barta, P. (forthcoming). *Absolute Dating of the Bronze Age in East-Central Europe: Methods and Applications*, British Archaeological Reports. Oxford: Archaeopress.

Bartík, J. (2004). 'Ku kolovým stavbám strednej a mladšej doby bronzovej na západnom Slovensku', *Študijné zvesti AÚ SAV*, 36: 75–91.

Bátora, J. (2000). *Das Gräberfeld von Jelšovce/Slowakei. Ein Beitrag zur Frühbronzezeit im nordkarpatischen Karpatenbecken. Teil I., II*, Prähistorische Archäologie in Südosteuropa. Bd. 16. Kiel: Verlag Oetker/Voges.

——, Marková, K., and Vladár, J. (2003). 'Die Glockenbecherkultur im Kontext der kulturhistorischen Entwicklung in der Südwestslowakei', in J. Czebreszuk and M. Szmyt (eds.), *The Northeast Frontier of Bell Beakers*. Proceedings of the symposium held at the Adam Mickiewicz University, Poznań (Poland), 26–29 May 2002, British Archaeological Reports (International Series), 1,115. Oxford: Archaeopress, 255–64.

Bökönyi, S. (1992). 'Jagd und Tierzucht', in W. Meier-Arendt (ed.), *Bronzezeit in Ungarn. Forschungen in Tell-Siedlungen an Donau und Theiss*. Frankfurt am Main: Museum für Vor- und Frühgeschichte Frankfurt am Main, 69–72.

Bóna, I. (1975). *Die mittlere Bronzezeit Ungarns und ihre südostlichen Beziehungen*. Budapest: Akadémiai kiadó.

—— (1992). 'Bronzezeitliche Tell-Kulturen in Ungarn', in W. Meier-Arendt (ed.), *Bronzezeit in Ungarn. Forschungen in Tell-Siedlungen an Donau und Theiss*. Frankfurt am Main: Museum für Vor- und Frühgeschichte Frankfurt am Main, 9–39.

Endrődi, A. (2003). 'The late phase of the Bell Beakers–Csepel Group in Hungary', in J. Czebreszuk and M. Szmyt (eds.), *The Northeast Frontier of Bell Beakers*. Proceedings of the symposium held at the Adam Mickiewicz Univewsity, Poznań (Poland), 26–29 May 2002, Oxford British Archaeological Reports (International Series), 1,115. Oxford: Archaeopress, 146–51.

Fischl, K. (2005). 'Stav poznania pravekej prospekcie a ťažby neželezných kovov na Slovensku', in *Montánna archeológia na Slovensku: 25 rokov výskumu lokality Glazenberg v Banskej Štiavnici*. Banská Štiavnica: Slovenské banské museum, 15–18.

—— (2006). *Aroktő-Dongóhalom bronzkori tell telep. Bronzezeitliche Tell-Siedlung in Arokto-Dongohalom*, Borsod-Abauj-Zempen Megye Regeszeti emlekei, 4. Miskolc: Hermann Otto Muzeum.

Furmánek, V., Mitáš, V., and Pavelková, J. (2010). 'The burial ground of the Kyjatice culture in Cinobaňa, Slovakia', in Sz. Guba and K. Tankó (eds), *Régről Kell Kezdenünk'. Studia Archaeologica in Honorem Pauli Patay*. Szécsény: Nógrád County Museums, 125–36.

Furmánek, V., Veliačík, L., and Romsauer, P. (1982). 'Jungbronzezeitliche befestigte Siedlungen in der Slowakei', in *Beiträge zum bronzezeitlichen Burgenbau in Mitteleuropa*. Berlin: Zentralinstitut für Alte Geschichte und Archäologie; Nitra: Archeologický Ústav Slovenskej Akadémie Vied, 159–75.

Furmánek, V., Veliačík, L., and Vladár, J. (1999). *Die Bronzezeit im slowakischen Raum*, Prähistorische Archäologie in Südoseuropa, Bd. 15. Rahden/Westfahlen: Verlag Marie Leidorf.

Gál, E., Juhász, I., and Sümegi, P. (eds.) (2005). *Environmental Archaeology in North-Eastern Hungary*, Varia Archaeologica Hungarica, XIX. Budapest: Archaeological Institute of the Hungarian Academy of Sciences.

Gancarski, J. (ed.) (2002). *Wystawa. Miedzi Mykenami a Baltikem. Kultura Otomani-Füzesabony. Exhibition Between Mycenae and the Baltic Sea. The Otomaqni- Füzesabony Culture*. Krosno-Warsaw: Muzeum Podkarpackie w Krośnie, Państwowe Muzeum Archeologiczne w Warszawie.

Gyulai, F. (1993). *Environment and Agriculture in Bronze Age Hungary*, Archaeolingua Series, 4. Budapest: Archaeological Institute of the Hungarian Academy of Sciences.

Hänsel, B. (1968). *Beiträge zur Chronologie der mittleren Bronzezeit im Karpatenbecken. Teil I,II*, Beiträge zur Ur- und frühgeschichtlichen Archäologie des Mittelmeer-Kulturraume, Band 7, 8. Bonn: Dr Rudolf Habelt GmbH.

Ilon, G. (2007a). 'Über die Zusammenhänge zwischen Siedlungsnetz und Metallurgie im Gebiet Nordwesttransdanubiens in der Spätbronzezeit', *Acta Archaelogica Academiae Scientiarum Hungaricae*, 58: 135–44.

—— (2007b). 'Houses of the Late Tumulus/Early Urnfield culture—based on the excavations at Némebánya', *Ősrégészeti Levelek, Prehistoric Newsletter*, 7: 135–45.

Kalicz, N. and Kalicz-Schreiber, R. (2006). 'Befestigunganlagen der frühbronzezeitlichen Hatvan-Kultur in Ungarn', in A. Krenn-Leeb (ed.), *Wirtschaft, Macht und Strategie. Höhensiedlungen und ihre Funktionen in der Ur- und Frühgeschichte*, Archäologie Österreichs Spezial, 1. Vienna: Österreichische Gesellschaft für Ur- und Frühgeschichte, 107–24.

Kemenczei, T. (1984). *Die Spätbronzezeit in Ungarn*. Budapest: Akadémiai Kiadó.

—— (2005). *Funde ostkarpatenländischen Typs im Karpatenbecken*, Prähistorische Bronzefunde, XX/10. Stuttgart: Steiner Verlag.

Kiss, V. (2009). 'The life of Middle Bronze Age artefacts from the western part of the Carpathian Basin', in T. L. Kienlin and B. W. Roberts (eds.), *Metals and Societes: Studies in Honour of Barbara S. Ottaway*, Universitätforschungen zur Prähistorischen Archäologie, Bd. 169. Bonn: Verlag Dr Rudolf Habelt GmbH, 328–35.

Kőszegi, F. (1988). *A Dunántúl története a későbronzkorban. The History of Transdanubia during the Late Bronze Age*, Budapesti Történeti Múzeum, Műhely 1. Budapest: Budapesti Történeti Múzeum.

Kovács, T. (1982). 'Befestigungsanlagen um die Mitte des 2. Jahrtausends v. u. Z. in Mittelungarn', in *Beiträge zum bronzezeitlichen Burgenbau in Mitteleuropa*. Berlin: Zentralinstitut für Alte Geschichte und Archäologie; Nitra: Archeologický Ústav Slovenskej Akadémie Vied, 279–92.

Kulcsár, G. (2009). *The Beginnings of the Bronze Age in the Carpathian Basin: The Makó-Kosihy-Čaka and the Somogyvár-Vinkovci Cultures in Hungary*, Archaeolingua, XXIII. Varia Archaelogica Hungarica. Budapest: Archaeological Institute of the Hungarian Academy of Sciences.

Lichardus, J. and Vladár, J. (1996). 'Karpatenbecken-Sintašta-Mykene. Ein Beitrag zur Definition der Bronzezeit als historische Epoche', *Slovenská Archeológia*, 4: 25–93.

Meier-Arendt, W. (ed.) (1992). *Bronzezeit in Ungarn. Forschungen in Tell-Siedlungen an Donau und Theiss*. Frankfurt am Main: Museum für Vor- und Frühgeschichte Frankfurt am Main.

Mozsolics, A. (1957). 'Archäologische Beiträge zur Geschichte der Grossen Wanderung', *Acta Archaelogica Academiae Scientiarum Hungaricae*, 8: 119–56.

—— (1967). *Bronzefunde des Karpatenbeckens. Depotfundhorizonte von Hajdúsámson und Kosziderpadlás*. Budapest: Akadémiai kiadó.

—— (1973). *Bronze und Goldfunde des Karpatenbeckens. Depotfundhorizonte von Forró und Ópályi*. Budapest: Akadémiai kiadó.

—— (1985). *Bronzefunde aus Ungarn. Depotfundhorizonte von Aranyos, Kurd und Gyermely.* Budapest: Akadémiai kiadó.

—— (2000). *Bronzefunde aus Ungarn. Depotfundhorizonte von Hajdúböszörmény, Románd und Bükkszentlászló,* Prähistorische Archaeologie in Südosteuropa, 17. Kiel: Velag Oetker/Voges.

Müller-Karpe, H. (1959). *Beiträge zur Chronologie der Urnenfelderzeit nördlich und südlich der Alpen.* Römisch-Germanische Forschungen, 22. Berlin: Walter de Gruyter and Co.

Nováki, Gy., Czajlik, Z., and Holl, B. (2006). 'Kataster der prähistorischen Erdburgen Ungarns—Versuch einer umfassenden Datenerfassung zum Schutz des kulturellen, archäologischen und naturräumlichen Erbes' in A. Krenn-Leeb (ed.), *Wirtschaft, Macht und Strategie. Höhensiedlungen und ihre Funktionen in der Ur- und Frühgeschichte*, Archäologie Österreichs Spezial, 1. Vienna: Österreichische Gesellschaft für Ur- und Frühgeschichte, 125–39.

Novotná, M. (1982). 'Metalurgia medi a bronzu v dobe bronzovej na Slovensku', *Archeologia Polski*, XXVII: 359–68.

Olexa, L. (2002). 'Burial grounds and funeral ceremonies', in J. Gancarski (ed.), *Wystawa. Miedzi Mykenami a Baltikem. Kultura Otomani-Füzesabony. Exhibition. Between Mycenae and the Baltic Sea. The Otomani- Füzesabony Culture.* Krosno-Warsaw: Muzeum Podkarpackie w Krośnie, Państwowe Muzeum Archeologiczne w Warszawie, 52–88.

Romsauer, P. (1999). 'Zur Frage der Westgrenze der Mezőcsát-Gruppe', in E. Jerem and I. Poroszlai (eds.), *Archaeology of the Bronze and Iron Age.* Proceedings of the International Archaeological Conference, Százhalombatta 1,999. Archaeolingua, 9. Budapest: Archaeolingua, 167–76.

—— and Veliačik, L. (1998). 'Der Umweltanteil an der Siedlungsstrukturgestaltung während der Urnenfelder- und Hallstattzeit in der WestSlowakei', *Przegląd Archeologiczny*, 46: 59–72.

Stegmann-Rajtár, Z. (2004). 'Die slowakisch-deutschen Ausgrabungen auf der befestigten Höhensiedlung Štitáre-Žibrica, Kr. Nitra. (Slowakei)', in J. Hrala (ed.), *Popelnicová pole a doba halstatská: príspevky z VIII. konference, Ceské Budejovice 22.–24.9.2004,* Archeologické výskumy Jižní Čechy, Suplementum 1. České Budějovice: Jihoceské muzeum, 503–19.

Sz. Máthé, M. (1988). 'Bronze Age tells in the Berettyó valley', in T. Kovács and I. Stanczik (eds.), *Bronze Age Tell Settlements on the Great Hungarian Plain, I,* Inventaria Praehistorica Hungariae, 1. Budapest: Magyar Nemzeti Múzeum, 27–122.

Szabó, G. (1996). 'A Csorva-csoport és a Gáva-kultúra kutatásának problémái néhány Csongrád megyei leletegyüttes alapján. Forschungsprobleme der Csorva-Gruppe und der Gáva-Kultur aufgrund einiger Fundverbände aus dem Komitat Csongrád'. *A Móra Ferenc Múzeum Évkönyve, Studia Archaeologica*, II.: 9–110.

—— (2004a). 'A tiszacsegei edénydepó. Das Gefäßdepot von Tiszacsege. Neue Angaben zur Sitte der spätbronzezeitlichen Gefäßdeponierung in der Theißgegend', *A Móra Ferenc Múzeum Évkönyve, Studia Archaeologica*, X: 81–114.

—— (2004b). 'Ház, település és településszerkezet a késő bronzkori (BD, HA, HB periódus) Tisza-vidéken. Houses, settlements and settlement structures in the Tisza region of the Late Bronze Age (periods BD, HA, HB)', in E. G. Nagy, J. Dani, and Z. Hajdú (eds.), *MΩMOΣ II. Őskoros Kutatók II. Összejövetelének konferenciakötete.* Debrecen: Hajdú-Bihar Magyei Múzeumok Igazgatósága, 137–70.

—— (2009). 'Kincsek a föld alatt. Elrejtett bronzkori fémek nyomában', in A. Anders, M. Szabó, and P. Raczky (eds.), *Régészeti dimenziók.* Budapest: L'Harmattan, 123–35.

Veliačik, L. (1983). *Die Lausitzer Kultur in der Slowakei,* Studia Archaeologia Slovaca Instituti Archaeologici Acadaemiae Scientiarum, III. Nitra: Slovaca Instituti Archaeologici Acadaemiae Scientiarum.

—— (2004). 'Nové poznatky ku štruktúre hradísk lužickej kultúry na severnom Slovensku', *Študijné zvesti AÚ SAV*, 36: 57–74.

Vicze, M. (1992). 'Die Bestattungen der Vatya Kultur', in W. Meier-Arendt (ed.), *Bronzezeit in Ungarn. Forschungen in Tell-Siedlungen an Donau und Theiss*. Frankfurt am Main: Museum für Vor- und Frühgeschichte Frankfurt am Main, 92–5.

Vladár, J. (1973). 'Osteuropäische und mediterrane Einflüsse im Gebiet der Slowakei während der Bronzezeit', *Slovenská Archeológia*, 21: 253–75.

Zatykó, C., Juhász, I., and Sümegi, P. (eds.) (2007). *Environmental Archaeology in Transdanubia*, Varia Archaeologica Hungarica, XX. Budapest: Archaeological Institute of the Hungarian Academy of Sciences.

CHAPTER 45

THE WESTERN BALKANS IN THE BRONZE AGE

BIBA TERŽAN

Introduction: Geography and Environment

The western Balkans are a mainly mountainous region, given special emphasis by the high massif of the Dinaric Mountains, the dividing line between the Mediterranean and continental zones. Only in the north does it give way to the lowlands of southern Pannonia, part of the Carpathian Basin (Fig. 45.1). In the west it runs into the south-eastern slopes of the Julian Alps across the pre-Alpine uplands, while in the east the Morava and Vardar river basins and the Stara Planina uplands form the border with the central and eastern Balkans.

Two main regions can be distinguished. The first is the eastern coast of the Adriatic and its hinterland. The second comprises the continental areas of the western Balkan Peninsula, which fall within the Danube Basin. This survey will deal primarily with the continental section of the western Balkan Peninsula, in other words the Danube Basin, and less with the hinterland of the Adriatic Sea (see Chapter 46).

A hydrological map of the Carpathian Basin depicting the water conditions prior to the major regulation activities undertaken before 1900 clearly shows that there were very extensive inundated and marshy areas along most watercourses (Hänsel and Medović 1991: 50 ff., Plate 1), which were quite unsuitable for settlement. It can be hypothesized that similar conditions very likely existed in the Bronze Age, which must certainly have affected the choice of areas for permanent settlement. Hence it comes as no surprise that the majority of Bronze Age settlements were positioned on the edges of elevated river terraces or on dominant heights that were protected from floods, and were also suitable for defence.

Among the significant natural factors that encouraged settlement in the Bronze Age, particularly in the hilly sections of the western Balkan Peninsula, the rich ore deposits should be mentioned. This is an extensive ore-bearing region that extends from Stara Planina (the Bor metallogenic zone with the famous Majdanpek mine) across the central Bosnian mountain massif (Vranica-Komar) all the way to the Zasavsko and Cerkljansko Mountains and the

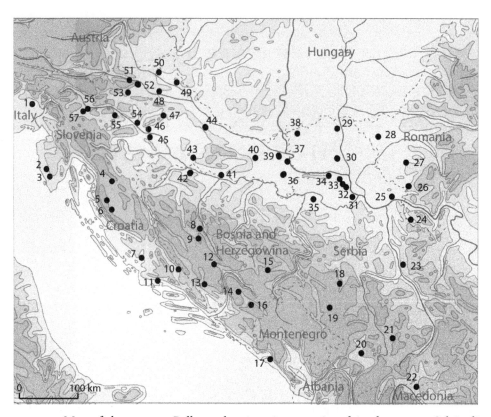

FIG. 45.1 Map of the western Balkans showing sites mentioned in the text: 1. Selvis di Remanzacco, Udine (Videm), 2. Maklavun, 3. Monkodonja, 4. Bezdanjača, 5. Lićki Osik, 6. Gospić, 7. Škarin Samograd, 8. Pod by Bugojno, 9. Kupreško polje, 10. Čitluk, 11. Vučevica, 12. Gradina na Varvari, 13. Posušje, 14. Rabin, 15. Glasinac, 16. Orah, 17. Velika and Mala Gruda, 18. Mojsinje and Ivkovo Brdo, 19. Pešter, 20. Iglarevo, 21. Donja Brnjica, 22. Ključka, 23. Paraćin, 24. Žuto Brdo, 25. Dubovac, 26. Dupljaja and Židovar, 27. Vatin, 28. Mokrin, 29. Senta, 30. Feudvar, 31. Zemun–asfaltna baza, 32. Belegiš, 33. Kalakača by Beška, 34. Perovaradin, 35. Belotić, 36. Vinkovci, 37. Dalj, 38. Sombor, 39. Bijelo Brdo, 40. Josipovac Punitovački, 41. Mačkovac-Crišnjevi, 42. Barice, 43. Građani, 44. Virovitica, 45. Velika Gorica, 46. Zagreb, 47. Kalnik, 48. Ormož, 49. Oloris, 50. Za Raščico, 51. Ruše, 52. Rogoza and Pobrežje, 53. Brinjeva gora, 54. Dobova, 55. Loka, 21 Loka near Ruhna vas, 56. Ljubljana, 57. Založnica on Ljubljana Moor.

Map: author.

Pohorje-Kozjak Heights in Slovenia, with ore deposits of various types of copper and other ores (silver, gold, lead, mercury, iron, etcetera); while deposits of cassiterite are known from the Cer region in western Serbia, Srebrenica in the Drina Valley, and the Fojnička river in the Vranica Massif. Although there is no direct evidence of the exploitation of these ore deposits as early as the Copper and Bronze Ages, nonetheless there are indications—despite scepticism as a result of a number of spectrographic analyses of elemental or chemical composition of objects—that they had been utilized in the pre-Roman period.

The State of Research and Chronology

The most recent synthesis of the Bronze Age in the western Balkan Peninsula was published in the fourth volume of *Praistorija jugoslavenskih zemalja* (*Prehistory of the Yugoslav [South Slavic] Lands*) (Benac and Čović 1983), which gives a general chronological division into Early, Middle, and Late Bronze Ages, and is mostly synchronized with the central European chronological scheme according to Reinecke and his followers (Early: Bz A 1–2[3]; Middle: Bz B1–C2; Late: Bz D, Ha A1–Ha B1–2[3]). The main characteristics of the regional cultural groups as well as the dynamics of their individual chronologies are also discussed there. In this connection it is important to note that in the chronological system of Milutin Garašanin for Serbia, the Ha A–B phases belonged to phase I of the Iron Age (Garašanin 1973: 404 ff.). The chronological system of Bernhard Hänsel (1968) for the Carpathian Basin must also be mentioned: this divided individual phases of the Bronze Age in more detail (Early Danubian I–III, Middle Danubian I–III, Late Danubian I–II, in the sense of the Minoan and Helladic chronological periods), thereby creating a correlation between the chronological systems for the central European and Aegean Bronze Ages. These works are now quite old and in the meantime a series of new studies have been published that provide significant supplementary information. Along with this, one should note that for the absolute dating of individual chronological stages of the Bronze Age, and particularly the Early Bronze Age, significant changes have occurred as the result of advances in dating methods, particularly as a result of radiocarbon and dendrochronological dates.

SETTLEMENTS AND THEIR SOCIAL IMPLICATIONS

With Snježana Karavanić

Only in the last decades of the twentieth and beginning of the twenty-first century have a number of larger-scale excavations been conducted, which addressed the problems of settlement in the Bronze Age. One such important research project in the former Yugoslavia took place between 1959 and 1983 under the direction of Borivoj Čović at the upland settlement of Pod near Bugojno in central Bosnia (Čović 1965: 48 ff.; 1991). Other important investigations that have led to vital new knowledge about Bronze Age settlement dynamics and the organization of the settlement as well as its immediate surroundings—the microregion—were carried out between 1986 and 1990 as part of a Yugoslav-German project under the leadership of Hänsel and Predrag Medović on the Titel Plateau, where large-scale excavations were undertaken at the settlement of Feudvar near Mošorin, accompanied by intensive field survey of the plateau and its immediate vicinity. Unfortunately, the excavations were not completed because of the outbreak of war (Hänsel and Medović 1991; 1998; Falkenstein 1998). Large-scale settlement investigations also took place at the strongly fortified settlement of Monkodonja in Istria (1997–2008; Figs. 46.3, 46.4), which led to the striking discovery of a proto-urban layout and construction, as well as the hierarchical organization of the settlement and its territory (see Chapter 46). In addition to these systematic archaeological investigations, in the last two decades extensive rescue excavations have taken place, primarily in advance of motorway construction in Slovenia and in Croatia, which have brought to light unexpectedly large amounts of data about the occupation of various regions and the character of settlements, chronologically spanning the entire Bronze Age.

One characteristic element of the Early Bronze Age in the southern parts of the Pannonian plain, extending all the way through northern Croatia to central Slovenia, and to Lake Balaton in Hungary, was the Somogyvár-Vinkovci culture. It was tied to the traditions of the Vučedol culture, and hence some authors treated it as a transitional cultural phenomenon between the Late Copper and Early Bronze Ages. More recent dendrochronological and radiocarbon dating from the site of Založnica in the Ljubljana Moors indicate its existence in the middle of the third millennium BC.

The settlements were located as a rule on elevated positions in the vicinity of water, whether on high river terraces or on more or less dominant heights, and often also on artificial heights such as 'tells', which was true of the eponymous site of Vinkovci (Ložnjak 2001: 33 ff.). Pile-dwelling settlements are known only from the Ljubljana Moor region (Velušček and Čufar 2003). It seems that the majority of settlements were not specially fortified, while some of them, such as the Petrovaradin Fortress in the foothills of the Fruška Gora Mountains just above the Danube, had immense earthen banks. In the present state of research it is difficult to say anything about the interior layout of the settlements, but several more recent excavations (e.g. Za Raščico pri Krogu, Josipovac Punitovački) indicate that the buildings were not closely spaced beside each other, but rather in groups, perhaps in the sense of individual households (or farms) with structures of various types. Buildings with load-bearing wooden beams, from which numerous postholes were preserved, along with daub, indicate more or less rectangular plans of above-ground houses of various dimensions, to a certain extent standardized and mostly single-roomed. 'Dug-in' structures of larger dimensions are also common, and some authors consider that these were pit-dwellings, in other words residential structures dug into the ground, while others have interpreted them as cellars or storage pits, or some other kind of outbuilding; the identification of smaller pits as refuse or storage pits seems unarguable (see Šavel and Sankovič 2010: 28 ff., fig. 22, 23 A-E, 64 ff.; Hirschler 2009: 147 ff., add.). One can only speculate on the economic foundation of these villages and hamlets, since the available data are still very modest. Analysis of animal bones at several sites has shown that no role was played by hunting, while the bones of domesticated animals consisted primarily of cattle in addition to pigs and small animals, leading to the conclusion that stock-raising was a very important part of the economy (Hirschler 2009: 156). Even less information is available about arable agriculture, although given the presence of numerous large pots and storage vessels for food, a sedentary way of life can be presumed (Šavel and Sanković 2010: 48 ff., Figs. 26–8).

Notable advances in the Early Bronze Age, with significant cultural shifts, occurred around 2000 BC, which so far has been best documented by research at the site of Feudvar near Mošorin in the Bačka region (Hänsel and Medović 1991; 1998). Feudvar is one of the most important sites of the Vatina culture, particularly widespread in Vojvodina, while its twin in the Banat region is the site of Židovar (Lazić 1997). The cultural influences of the Vatina culture extended into the neighbouring areas, all the way to central Serbia, to Slavonia in Croatia, and to central Bosnia. At Feudvar, a tell-type settlement, all four chronological phases of the Vatina culture are represented stratigraphically with seven construction phases, corresponding to Early Danubian I–II and Middle Danubian I–II, and radiocarbon dated between the twenty-first and the sixteenth/fifteenth centuries cal BC (Hänsel and Medović 1991: 66 ff., Figs. 5, 7; Hänsel et al. 1992). This Early Bronze Age settlement is located on the northern edge of the Titel Plateau, which at c.55 m in height towers over the lowland area along the confluence of the Tisza and Danube, and with its geostrategic position visually controlled traffic along both rivers as well as the flatlands of the Bačka and Banat regions. At the same time the Titel Plateau, extending over 17 by 8 km, protected from floods and with exceptionally fertile blown loessic soil, offered ideal conditions for settlement, representing a classic example of a 'settlement area' (*Siedlungskammer*).

Although the settlement was not completely preserved because of erosion, working out its dimensions and potential number of inhabitants (up to about one thousand) can be done by simple arithmetic. All the analyses indicate a synoecistic origin process as a central-place settlement. The settlement was fortified with a defensive ditch and earthen bank (with palisade), with some kind of 'suburb' or outlying settlement outside the defences. The settlement displayed a proto-urban organization in the interior. Through all the construction phases of the Early Bronze Age, at least seven of them, an orthogonal settlement plan was preserved. It was created by rectangular buildings with dimensions in the range of 9–12 m by 5–6 m, arranged along narrow streets 1 m wide, and in places also broader streets representing main corridors (Fig. 45.2). It is clear that a settlement organized in this manner could not have arisen completely by chance; rather it must have been carefully planned and strictly organized from the very beginning. The individual houses, mostly with one room, had a somewhat standardized form, with the entrance on the longer side, while their interior fittings indicated a relatively high level of living style. The load-bearing wooden beams, some 90 cm from one another, the postholes of which were sometimes preserved, as well as in places the clay bases, formed the framework for wattle walls of interwoven branches or reeds, which were then coated with clay. Fragments of clay stucco were also found, and hence the interiors of the houses were not merely coated but also skilfully decorated (Fig. 45.3a, b). As a rule the floors were of stamped earth. Each house had a rectangular hearth or an oval oven, usually facing the entrance. On the other hand, loom-weights as indicators of looms, and other implements related to weaving (an indication of the women's areas), were as a rule located in the corner sections of the house, those furthest from the entrance. Despite the uniformity of the buildings, certain individual features can be noted, as shown on the one hand by collections of domestic vessels of varied provenance, and on the other by the food: in one house they consumed more fish, in another more meat, in a third they brewed beer. This must be more closely connected with individual tastes than with social differentiation (Hänsel 2002: 80 ff.; Kroll 1998; Becker 1998). The only evident exception was a building of somewhat smaller dimensions, but with two or three rooms, that stood adjacent to a small courtyard or square. It belonged to an artisan—a metal-caster, as it contained large quantities of multivalve moulds and fragments resulting from the lost-wax technique, along with clay cores of various sizes, chaplets, crucibles, stone slabs, etcetera. Considering the form of the moulds, which were used to cast axes, spearheads, tools, and ornaments, and in view of the fact that such products can be found over quite a broad geographical area, it can be concluded that this was a specialized professional craftsman, whose prestigious products additionally support the image of Feudvar as a central-place settlement (Hänsel and Medović 1991: 82 ff., Plates 11–12; 2004).

The central importance of Feudvar is also emphasized by the fact that in the Early Bronze Age, the period of the developed Vatina culture, this site was almost the only large fortified settlement on the entire Titel Plateau. Such a picture of the occupation of the Titel Plateau in the Early Bronze Age differs greatly from that of the previous Copper Age/Eneolithic settlement pattern, as well as that of the subsequent Middle Bronze Age, since on the plateau those two periods were characterized by large numbers of smaller, mostly unfortified hamlets

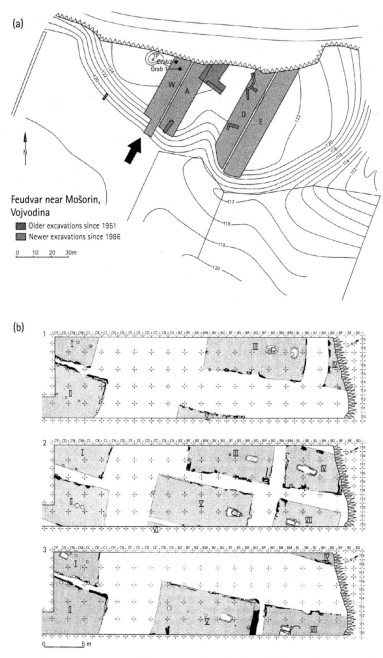

FIG. 45.2 Feudvar near Mošorin: (a) topographical plan of the settlement with excavated areas; (b) three successive settlement phases with the rectangular plans of buildings along right-angled streets, dated to the Early Bronze Age.

Source: Hänsel and Medović 1991.

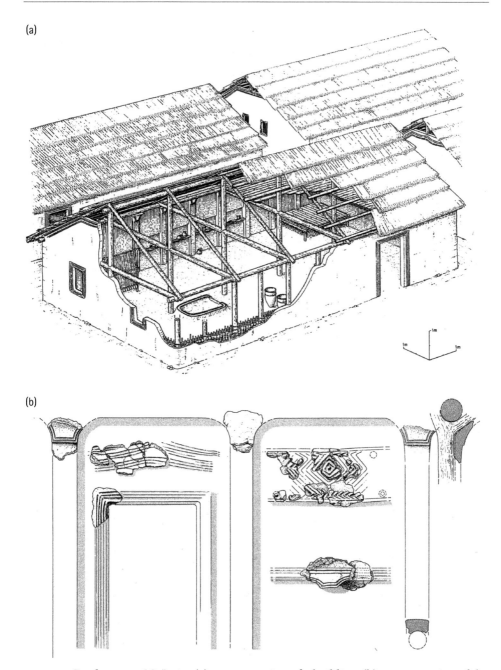

FIG. 45.3 Feudvar near Mošorin: (a) reconstruction of a building; (b) reconstruction of the wall stucco.

Source: Hänsel and Medović 1991.

(Falkenstein 1998: 264 ff., Figs. 234–6). At the transition to the Middle Bronze Age, specifically in its early phase (MD II or Bz B1), the highly organized proto-urban settlement of Feudvar met its end, as was also the case with Židovar and indeed the entire Vatina culture, although this represents part of a wider event that took place in the Carpathian Basin, as is also shown by 'central'-type settlements such as Barca and Spišsky Štvrtok in Slovakia.

West of the Danube in the lowlands along the Drava and Sava rivers all the way to central Slovenia, as the main cultural feature of the period following the Somogyvár-Vinkovci culture, a group emerged with *Litzenkeramik*, a style similar to Corded Ware pottery. Its decorations are carried out in various styles and hence different authors refer to it either as a local group of the Kisapostag culture or as the brushed or wire-brushed pottery culture (*Litzenkeramik*) (several phases of which can be distinguished: Marković 2002; Guštin 2005). As is indicated by the most recent radiocarbon dates, this pottery belongs to the period between about the twenty-first and seventeenth centuries cal BC (Guštin 2005: 94; Sanković 2010: 96; Črešnar 2010). So far, mainly lowland settlements have been discovered on low elevations and river terraces near watercourses, and pile-dwelling settlements have been found in the Ljubljana Moors, while elevated upland sites such as Brinjeva gora in the foothills of Pohorje Mountain (in the immediate vicinity of ore deposits) are rarer. Even today, very little is known about settlement and buildings.

Completely different settlement forms can be found in the mountainous parts of the western Balkans. It is interesting that a similar developmental dynamic to Feudvar can also be found at the site of Pod near Bugojno in central Bosnia, the best-excavated settlement of the Early Bronze Age within the so-called 'transitional zone' according to Borislav Čović, defined as the region between the valleys of the upper Vrbas, Neretva, and Bosna rivers, where contacts and synthesis occurred between the Mediterranean and areas of Carpathian-Danubian culture. At the same time one should remember that the settlements in this zone lie in the middle of ore-bearing areas, and at most of them traces of metallurgical activities have been found (Čović 1983: 170 ff.; 1991). It seems significant that most were elevated settlements or hill forts, of small dimensions and with defences that are primarily natural in character, placed at important strategic points. The settlement at Pod near Bugojno lies on a height above a fertile valley of the Vrbas river, one of the main communication routes between Pannonia and the Adriatic. The position of Pod is hence above all important in a strategic sense. The beginning of the settlement was dated by Čović to Bz A2, *c.*2000 BC, with its end *c.*1600 BC, with habitation divided into two phases (Pod A1–A2). Numerous postholes for load-bearing beams were documented in the excavated areas, arranged quite regularly in straight lines, from which rectangular house structures can be presumed. They were accompanied by pits of other purposes, and in places also hearths and ovens, indicating a very dense occupation of the area and also multiple repairs made to the buildings (Čović 1991: 13 ff., add. 1, 7–9). The entire arrangement of the building remains at Pod is reminiscent of the proto-urban organization of the settlement and construction phases of Feudvar, which retained the concept of its original layout, as was also indicated by the density of the posthole rows at Pod. This leads one to suggest that the settlement at Pod also represents a central-place settlement, constructed according to the same 'proto-urbanistic principles' as Feudvar. A similar layout can also be suggested for the site of Gradina at Varvara above the source of the Rama river, even though the excavation trenches there were smaller in scale. The outlines of a rectangular building dating to Bz A2–B1 were uncovered here, whose plan, construction, and dimensions were all reminiscent of Feudvar (Čović 1978: 41 ff., plan 2, 4–5). At both Pod and Varvara traces of metallurgical activity were found (Čović 1991: 16, Plates 3, 4; 4, 18–20), similar to the finds at Feudvar, in this case not surprisingly given the proximity of ore deposits.

In the Early Bronze Age the Posušje culture (Čović 1989), also called the Dinaric culture (Govedarica 1989), was formed in the area of the Dalmatian hinterland and Herzegovina extending from the Zrmanja river to Montenegro. Čović dated its beginning to Bz A1, although in contrast to Pod near Bugojno it did not end with Bz A2/B1, but rather, as at Velika Gradina at Varvara, it continued into the Middle Bronze Age. It is characterized by elevated settlements (hill forts), as a rule fortified with powerful walls and in some places also bastions, made in the dry-stone technique. These were usually small settlements with a diameter of 50–100 m, only a few reaching around 150 m. The latter usually have an interior with additional dividing walls, indicating a complete fortification with an acropolis. Considering both the topographic and structural characteristics of the hill forts of the Posušje culture, as well as its chronological span, parallels can be drawn with the *Castellieri* culture of Istria and the northern Adriatic, where (mainly on the basis of the Monkodonja findings) a better understanding of the structure and organization of settlements of the hill-fort type has been reached (see Chapter 46). Another interesting theory, suggested by Čović (1989: 93 ff.), was that in the Early Bronze Age the Posušje and Cetina cultures would have coexisted in the same geographical area, but people in the Cetina culture area would have been nomadic herders, as their settlements (other than cave shelters such as Škarin Samograd) remain unknown, whereas those in the Posušje culture area would have been sedentary farmers, primarily involved with agriculture.

Major changes occurred throughout the area under consideration in the Middle Bronze Age, with the exception of the region along the Adriatic. As noted above, Bronze Age settlements of the central type, such as Feudvar near Mošorin or Pod near Bugojno, as well as numerous other settlements of various cultural groups, mainly in the lowlands, were abandoned during or at the end of Bz B1. There are still very few traces of newly created settlements, so we know next to nothing about their appearance. The best insights into the events in question are again offered by the excavations on the Titel Plateau, notably Feudvar. In the developed Middle Bronze Age settlement conditions on the plateau change completely: in place of the central fortified settlement of Feudvar, a series of smaller unfortified settlements appear along the edges of the plateau and also on lower-lying terraces, which were placed at roughly equal distances from one another, indicating a new, purposefully organized, colonization of the area. These were primarily small hamlets with two to six buildings, which could also be up to 50 m from one another, indicating individual farms. As Frank Falkenstein has shown, such a settlement structure was retained through several horizons dating to Bz B2/C1–D (Falkenstein 1998: 269 ff., Figs. 237–239). It is apparent that this was a new form of settement with a different economic base and spatial utilization. At Feudvar itself the settlement levels of the period are so modest that a brief hiatus could perhaps have existed before the Belegiš II–Gava horizon (Hänsel and Medović 1991: 66 ff., Fig. 4).

Another element of the Middle Bronze Age to the west of the middle Danube was the Virovitica culture (Bz B2–C–D), which spread along the Drava and Sava from its eponymous site in Croatia all the way to central Slovenia and Lake Balaton on one side and to northern Bosnia on the other, where it is also called the Barice-Građani group (Vinski-Gasparini 1973: 57 ff.; Teržan 1995: 324 ff., Fig. 1; Karavanić 2009: 43 ff.). Despite the numerous documented settlements, few have been excavated, and most were located in plains on low elevations in the vicinity of watercourses. As indicated by the most thoroughly excavated settlement to date, at Oloris pri Dolnjem Lakošu (Dular, Šavel, and Tecco Hvala 2002), the settlement was encircled by a stream, consisting in part of a natural bend in the stream and perhaps also with a dug channel, which would mean that additional construction activities were undertaken in building the defensive ditch that was additionally fortified with a palisade. The interior was occupied mainly in two places in the middle of the settlement area, where the elevation was highest. The building plans, which were defined by postholes and distinct concentrations of house daub, indicate relatively small rectangular houses with wooden beams and wattle walls. The houses were arranged in groups around a courtyard area that also contained several hearths or ovens. A similar situation can also be noted at the settlement of Mačkovac-Crišnjevi on the Sava river (Karavanić 2009: 4 ff.). This has led to the hypothesis that relatively small, mostly single-roomed buildings were characteristic of the Virovitica culture, joined into small densely grouped farming settlements, sometimes fortified with a defensive ditch and palisade.

The Late Bronze Age (Bz D/Ha A–B) again saw changes, both in terms of the spatial pattern and the types of settlement. The settlement on the Titel Plateau will again best serve as an illustration. A large number of Middle Bronze Age settlements were abandoned, and new ones created, only rarely exhibiting continuity as at Feudvar. They were arranged along the edges of the plateau, only 2.5 to 4 km apart, so that they could be intervisible. The settlement of Feudvar again became important, particularly in the so-called Kalakača horizon (Ha A/B1–2), probably because of its strategic position, as even its defensive system was reactivated (Falkenstein 1998: 274 ff., Fig. 240; Hänsel and Medović 1991: 68 ff., Figs. 4–5). Although in this period the settlement of Feudvar was not so strictly organized and densely inhabited, nonetheless the arrangement of the relatively small and mostly rectangular buildings was more fluid and irregular. Several buildings and the accompanying frequent circular storage pits were arranged in small groups that are considered to represent individual farming households. Both narrow and broad paths rans between them in some kind of pattern. Given the numerous circular storage pits—for storing grain—there is no doubt that these were mainly agricultural communities, although stock-raising was also well developed, and hunting and fishing also played a significant role in the diet (Hänsel and Medović 1991: 144 ff.; Kroll 1998; Becker 1998). This settlement phase reached its end in the Ha B3/C1 phase (the late ninth–early eighth centuries BC), when Feudvar remained the only settlement on the plateau. Its cultural-chronological identity is defined by the appearance of Basarabi-type pottery. Falkenstein connected this demographic breakdown, and the reduction of settlements to only one, fortified position on the Titel Plateau, with an invasion of nomadic horsemen from the east European steppes (Falkenstein 1998: 275 ff., Fig. 241).

Structural characteristics in the organization of settlements and the construction of buildings similar to Feudvar can be seen at several other contemporary settlements along the Danube, such as Kalakača near Beška (Medović 1988) and Zemun-Asfaltna Baza (Petrović 2010). In contrast to Feudvar, both examples were single-layer settlements on high river terraces just above the Danube, settled only in one short chronological period, in the horizon of the Kalakača Bosut culture (Ha A2–B2), whose end coincided with the changes to settlement on the Titel Plateau, in other words with the appearance of Basarabi pottery.

New settlement phases occurred further along the Sava and Drava, extending all the way to central Slovenia during the Urnfield period (Ha A–B), as shown by a greater intensity of occupation, particularly in the lowlands along watercourses, and sometimes also in hilly areas, such as at Kalnik (Karavanić 2009: 17 ff.) and Špičak (Pavišić 2001), and at Brinjeva gora (Teržan 1999: 101 ff.). As is indicated by excavations in the Slovenian Drava basin, one of the better-investigated regions, settlements of various types existed, on the one hand distinctly rural settlements of the so-called open or scattered type, and on the other hand settlements of the central type with proto-urban characteristics. Such differences in the plans of the settlements indicate innate social differentiation in the occupation of the region. Settlements of the open or scattered type had no defensive system, and the buildings were arranged in small groups around a courtyard, sometimes with a hearth, some tens of metres between each; hence one may assume that these were individual farmsteads. Their dispersed structure and traces of varied activities suggest these were the settlements of small rural communities (e.g. Rogoza near Maribor: Črešnar 2010: 59 ff., add. 2–3).

In addition to rural settlements, around 1000 BC (Ha B1–3) new proto-urban centres were created, located primarily on elevated outcrops or high river terraces. One characteristic example would be Ormož on the Drava, where a relatively large area was investigated in excavation (Lamut 1987; Dular and Tomanič Jevremov 2010). The settlement was encircled by an earthen bank (and probably also a palisade) and a deep defensive ditch, while the interior was densely occupied (Fig. 45.4). In addition, occupation was discovered at Ormož beyond the fortified settlement, indicating the existence of some kind of ancillary settlement ('suburb'), similar to that at Feudvar. At Ormož this indicates a clear differentiation between the fortified town with its regular, orthogonal plan, where traces of various craft activities, including metal smelting and casting (Lamut 1987: 52 ff.), were discovered, along with the suburb, and the settlement of scattered rural type at Hajndl just a few kilometres away. Hence it can be concluded that in the Late Bronze Age the formation of proto-urban agglomerations occurred, accompanied by a differentiated organization of individual regions. However, their prosperity, particularly in lowland areas, was relatively short-lived, as with rare exceptions they gradually died off in the Early Iron Age. Significant changes took place in the settlement pattern: for the most part new fortified settlements, hill forts, were formed at elevated spots, leading to a new territorial organization.

Certain similarities are also evident in central Bosnia, both in terms of the type of settlement as well as the chronology, again best illustrated by the site of Pod (see above). After a lengthy gap following the Middle Bronze Age, the site was again inhabited in the Late Bronze Age (Ha A–B). The newly established settlement was fortified by stone walls and a rampart, and probably also a wooden palisade, while the interior was densely settled and strictly arranged. From the beginning, two main streets were established, one running north-west/south-east and the other north-east/south-west, in this manner dividing the settlement into quarters. Rectangular buildings of fairly uniform size lined both streets in orderly rows, with smaller streets or paths between them, creating a net-like settlement layout. It is significant that despite repairs, renovation, and rebuilding, the buildings survived in the same places through all settlement phases, both in horizon Pod B (eleventh–eighth centuries BC according to Čović), and later in the Early Iron Age, so that the basic features of the original settlement layout were preserved throughout its existence, indicating an exceptional preservation of traditions and a strict organization of the settlement, probably an expression of a distinctly hierarchical social structure. The traces of metallurgical activity discovered for the production of both bronze and iron, as well as other crafts, indicate that the settlement played a prominent role in the manufacture of metal products for a broad region between Pannonia and the Adriatic. The exceptional strategic position, proto-urban layout, and economic potential in terms of trade surely define Pod as a central settlement that retained its leading role throughout the Early Iron Age, in contrast to other sites discussed above.

In conclusion, it seems evident that a remarkable advance in metallurgical production took place in the Late Bronze Age, as indicated not merely by the numerous hoards of bronze objects, from which an exceptionally diverse repertory of local products can be perceived,

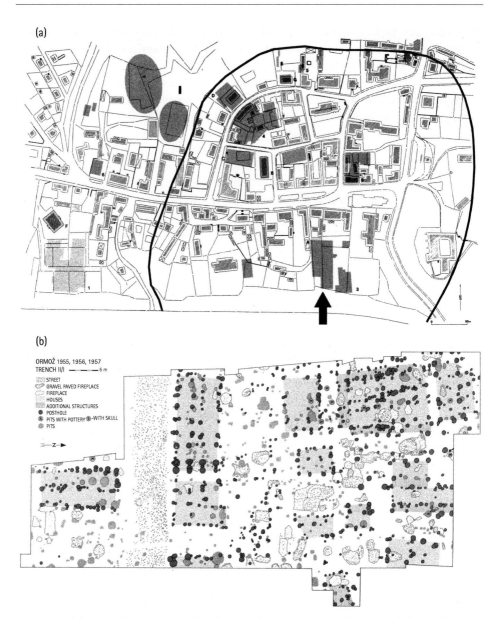

FIG. 45.4 (a) Ormož: a. topographical plan showing excavated parts of the settlement; (b) plan of the excavated part of the settlement.

Source: author (Teržan 1995; Lamut 1987).

along with the existence of extensive exchange and trade; but also by the settlement finds of metallurgical material, such as moulds, clay cores, and chaplets, as well as a range of ingots and half-finished products. It seems significant that they are found not only on settlements of central type but also on smaller settlements. This probably points to an extensive market, while at the same time raising a series of questions related, for example, to the interactions between central-type settlements and their hinterland or periphery, to the transmission of technological knowledge, and to the possible existence of travelling prospectors and master artisans—specialized craftsmen such as are described in the myth of Daedalus.

Burial Rites and their Social Implications

The Adriatic and its Hinterland

Along the Adriatic coast and its mountainous hinterland, from the Early Bronze Age onwards the main funerary rites involved interring the dead in mounds, mainly stone cairns, though earthen tumuli also occur. Inhumation was the main rite, though in some places cremation was also used. Systematic excavations have taken place on only a few of the tumuli, and grave goods proved scarce, which often makes dating difficult.

The so-called Cetina culture, centred on Dalmatia, is an important Early Bronze Age phenomenon (Marović and Čović 1983). Its influence can be traced along the Adriatic on the one side all the way to Istria and the karst hinterland of Trieste, and on the other side to the Peloponnese and the southern Apennines in Italy; on the third side its influence extends to the continental hinterland as far as the cultural groups of Glasinac in Bosnia and Belotić-Bela Crkva in western Serbia. Its dating is reckoned to be contemporary with Early Helladic III, thus in the last centuries of the third millennium BC. The Cetina cultural identity can be recognized primarily through grave structures, specific pottery types and decorative styles (Fig. 45.5a), and grave goods, especially weapons. Tumuli, primarily of stone, between 4 and 26 m in diameter and preserved up to a height of 3 m, usually contain one grave, rarely more. The tumuli can have a kerb of large stones; dry-stone circle constructions or circular platforms have turned up only in rare cases. In the centre of the tumulus there was a rectangular cist grave generally made of stone slabs, with a stone-covering slab. As a rule only one person was buried in the cist, generally in a contracted position on the right or left side. There are rare instances of individual body parts or skulls alone being placed in the grave. In cases where the deceased was cremated, their remains were put in urns placed in the central part of the tumulus. There is a relatively large number of tumuli in which no graves or remains of buried individuals were found: Ivan Marović believes these to have been cenotaphs. The tumuli generally contained fairly large quantities of broken pots, indicative of special funerary rites. Given that there is an approximately equal number of contemporaneous inhumations and cremations, one may conclude that a bi-ritual burial practice was used, though rather specific to individual local social groups within the Cetina culture (Marović and Čović 1983: 205).

An extensive mound cemetery dating from the Early Bronze Age is also known in the central Dalmatian hinterland, at Kupreško polje, but this does not belong to the Cetina culture. Its characteristics led Alojz Benac (1986) to link it with the nomadic peoples of the eastern European steppes. Tumuli of various sizes are clustered in larger and smaller groups or separately along both banks of the river that meanders through the plain. Excavations of four tumuli, two smaller and two larger, showed that these were built of regularly shaped blocks of turf taken from the mossy ground in the immediate vicinity. The burials were made directly on the well-trodden earth, and were well-preserved, especially in one or two cases. The present

FIG. 45.5 (a) Pottery of the Cetina culture (Dalmatia), After Čović and Marović 1983; (b) Three wheeled cult-wagon from Dupljaja (Vojvodina).

Source: Benac and Čović 1983.

state of knowledge suggests that the grave furniture, that is, the coffin and grave goods, were primarily made of wood, and therefore mostly not preserved. The finds in one of the tumuli are of particular interest (Fig. 45.6): the upper part of an exceptionally finely worked wooden sledge was used as a bier or coffin, roofed with a wooden lid and secured with cross-pieces, which were pushed through wooden pegs wedged into the ground. An elderly male, wrapped in a skilfully woven woollen shroud or cloak, was laid on an animal skin on the bottom of the coffin, in a crouched position on his right side. The entire coffin and grave surroundings, to a diameter of around 5.5 m, were first covered with sheaves of grass, then blocks of turf were piled on top to make the tumulus. Another large tumulus built in a similar way, Dokanova

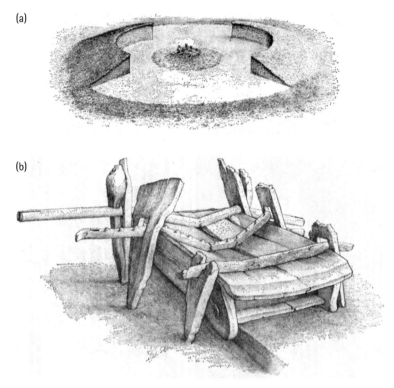

FIG. 45.6 Kupreško polje (Bosnia-Hercegovina): (a) Pustopolje, tumulus 16, picture of the excavated mound; (b) the wooden sledge used as a coffin.

Source: Benac 1986.

Glavica, was found to feature a separate structure in the middle of the tumulus, with two wooden daggers plunged into the ground. In addition, incinerated remains and ash, animal bones, and pottery fragments were found in several places in the mound, suggesting that there were specific funerary rituals, though these are still difficult to interpret.

The present state of research indicates that funerary rituals were quite varied, but it seems probable that due to its particular geographical and climatic position, the Kupreško polje represented a special cult area where various pastoral communities buried individuals of greater importance in skilfully built tumuli, or put up cenotaphs to them (Benac 1986).

Although tumuli are known in Istria from the Early Bronze Age onwards (Codacci-Terlević 2006), recent research into the fortified settlement at Monkodonja, a prominent representative of the *Castelliere/gradina* culture, revealed a specific form of burial. Two tombs had been integrated into the monumental architecture of the labyrinth-like main entrance to the settlement (Fig. 45.7). Both contained rectangular stone cist graves. The first, north of the entrance, surrounded by a rectangular platform, contained the selected bones of more than ten individuals of both genders and various ages, suggesting some sort of family tomb. The other, which was integrated into the entrance tower, contained a young female, while in the corner of the grave the bones of a child were also preserved. The dominant position of the two tombs at the entrance to the fortified settlement indicates that these were special burials of selected members of the local elite. These tombs may be considered to have

FIG. 45.7 Monkodonja, Istria (Croatia): two tombs integrated into the main entrance into the fortified settlement.

Source: Hänsel *et al.* 2009.

had cult significance, probably as a *memento mori*, honouring founding forefathers who perhaps functioned at the same time as guardians of the settlement (Hänsel, Teržan, and Mihovilić 2007: 35ff.; Hänsel et al. 2009).

Other specific features of burial practice and tomb architecture can be observed in Istria. A large stone tumulus was excavated on the summit of Maklavun hill near Karastak, not far from Rovinj. This was found to be a tumulus of tholos type (Hänsel and Teržan 2000).

Although only a few grave goods were preserved, the tholos can be tentatively dated to the Middle Bronze Age.

The tumuli on Mušego hill, an elite cemetery of the hill fort of Monkodonja, recently excavated, also belong to the Middle Bronze Age. They are arranged over the hillside in a number of clusters, with some isolated larger ones. The mounds are 11 m and more in diameter, made up of large stones in the form of a low cone and surrounded by a circuit of large stone blocks. A stone cist grave holding the remains of selected bones of the deceased, usually of several individuals, was in the centre of each tumulus. Some had been used for repeated burials, so they had built up, though always in conical form with the cist located in the middle of the cone. Anthropological analysis of the bones has shown that there could have been special funerary rituals, probably involving lengthy exposure of the deceased and only later burial, not of the whole skeleton but of selected bones only, together with jewellery (amber and faience beads, bronze bracelets, etcetera) and sherds of deliberately broken vessels. Radiocarbon dating of bones from three tumuli has put the cemetery into the period 1500–1300 cal BC (Mihovilić et al. 2009: 50 ff.).

Tumuli as the dominant form of grave monument in the Middle Bronze Age are also present elsewhere in the western Balkans, although their construction and the manner of burial differ from those in Istria. Stone tumuli are to be found in the Lika area (Croatia), but these are less monumental and arranged in smaller groups, for example those in Lički Osik. Each of them contained just one grave, and the deceased were buried in an extended position (Drechsler-Bižić 1975). Grave goods are rare, though prestige weapons have been found, such as a bronze axe or a sword of the Sauerbrunn-Boiu type. Although only a few tumuli were excavated in Dalmatia and Hercegovina, they show similarities in the way the tumuli were constructed and the manner of burial, but inhumation burials in a crouched position in stone cist graves predominate. Although grave goods are exceptionally scarce, weapons are again noteworthy; these are indicative of customs similar to those in Lika, where the warrior cult is manifested through weaponry. This suggests that social communities along the eastern Adriatic were similar in their social differentiation, with a leading warrior stratum at the head, probably in the tradition of the Early Bronze Age Cetina culture.

The great tumulus Velika Gruda near Tivat in Boka Kotorska (Montenegro) is an exception to this. The top layers of the tumulus, which originally housed the central grave of a prominent individual from the Late Copper Age (Primas 1996), was found to contain a cemetery from the Middle and Late Bronze Age, with radiocarbon dates between 1400 and 1200 cal BC (Della Casa 1996). These are mostly collective graves. They had pebble floors and were surrounded with large stones and covered with stone slabs or boulders. In some graves several individuals, from 2 to as many as 22, were buried in a contracted position. Just one burial was also cremated. Human bones were also deposited in several places round the edge of the tumulus, in no anatomical order, giving rise to the interpretation that these are the remains of bones from older burials, removed from their original positions during successive burials in the collective graves. In addition to the collective graves, a large number of pithoi and large vessels in which children and infants had been buried were also discovered in the tumulus. Grave goods here too were rather scarce, mostly pieces of small bronze jewellery. In the mound there were graves of males and females of all ages, at least 125 individuals. This seems to indicate the cemetery belonged to a relatively small social community, the main nucleus of which was most probably a family of five to six members, perhaps living in five or six contemporaneous households.

Burials in karst caves represent a particular type of cemetery in the Adriatic hinterland. Most research has been done in the Bezdanjača cave near Vrhovine in Lika, dated to the Middle Bronze Age and the transition to the Late Bronze Age (Bz B/C–Bz D/Ha A1) (Drechsler-Bižić 1979–80; Malinar 1998). The entrance to the cave is on the side of a cliff and can only be accessed using climbing equipment such as a rope or ladder. In the cave a cemetery was found, with several graves placed on the bedrock floor. Skeletons were variously arranged in the cave, from group burials of several individuals to double burials, as well as individual ones; in all the remains of more than 200 individuals were found. Indicative of special funerary rites and cults is the large number of hearths discovered near the buried individuals, around which were found whole vessels and sherds, in addition to many bones of domestic and wild animals, including, notably, deer. These last are probably animal sacrifices. There were also numerous finds of wooden tapers, probably for illuminating the cave. The remains of ochre used both as a grave good and as a colouring for the bodies was a further interesting indication of special ritual practices. Noteworthy grave goods found were jewellery and other clothing accessories, weapons and tools. Given the comparative rarity of such a wide range of goods in the graves of this period in the western Balkans, Bezdanjača is a most significant find and shows some affinity with contemporary hoards.

The picture that emerges in the central part of the western Balkans in the Middle and Late Bronze Age is rather different and more highly differentiated. Burial in tumuli, just as in the tradition of Early Bronze Age funerary rites, is a characteristic of the so-called Glasinac culture, as defined by Benac and Čović (1956). This continues into the Early Iron Age. It extends from the Glasinac plateau in central Bosnia through the Drina river basin to regions of western Serbia. Milutin Garašanin (1983b: 736 ff.) attributed these last to 'a west Serbian variant of the Vatina culture' but with specific local features in funerary rites and accompanying grave goods. The tumuli, which are mainly earthen and on average have a diameter of 8 to 12 m, are mostly found in larger groups. Recent excavations have shown that the graves often had pebbles on the base and were lined and covered with stones (Kosorić 1976: 19 ff., t. 9–14). The individual mounds usually contain several graves. Inhumation burials predominate, placed in an extended or slightly contracted position, but there are also cases of cremation. Graves of the Glasinac culture are relatively rich in metal artefacts, primarily bronze jewellery and other adjuncts to clothing, and also amber beads (Benac and Čović 1956; Kosorić 1976), but there are also graves, albeit few in number, containing weapons, which point to the leading social role of the warrior stratum (Kosorić 1976; Zotović 1985: 27 ff.). The number of graves in individual tumuli belonging to one or two generations suggests that the majority are tumuli for family burial. The size of individual social communities can be deduced from the number of tumuli in individual cemeteries, though such calculations can be misleading because burials continued in one and the same cemetery from the Late Copper Age to the Iron Age. We can nevertheless suppose that these were relatively small communities whose 'wealth' was manifested within the funerary ritual through prestige ornaments.

In the central and eastern areas of Serbia, east of the region outlined above where the Glasinac culture extended, burial monuments in the form of tumuli are equally customary, but cremation predominates. This applies to the so-called cultural group of the western Serbian variant of the Vatina culture to which we attribute the mound cemeteries in the eastern Morava river basin, best illustrated by the recently excavated tumuli around Užiška Požega near Mojsinje and Krstac-Ivkovo Brdo (Nikitović, Stojić, and Vasić 2002; Nikitović 2003). Its beginnings fall into the late Early Bronze Age and are thus linked to an earlier tradition. The tumuli each contained several cremation graves, with only one in the central place in the tumulus. Some graves were dug into the original surface, others were placed there and encircled and covered with stones. In some tumuli there were also remains of the pyre, ritually covered with pebbles. Anthropological analyses have shown that there are female, male, and also children's graves, which suggests that individual tumuli formed the burial grounds of small social communities, as was the case in the Glasinac culture. Interestingly, the grave goods attest to very diverse cultural links: the majority of the urns and vessels are related in form to the pottery of the Vatina culture, which was centred on Vojvodina; bronze jewellery originally belonged to the Glasinac cultural area; while the bronze knives and stone pseudo-wristguards or whetstones are male attributes that point to links with the Adriatic or Aegean region (Nikitović, Stojić, and Vasić 2002: 110 ff., Plate 10, 58–9; 14, 115; Hänsel and Teržan 2000: 172 ff., abb. 19). This suggests that this regional cultural group represents a contact area between the continental-Danubian, western Balkan, and Aegean cultural spheres.

Two further very closely linked cultural groupings that had their beginnings in the Middle Bronze Age and continued into the Late Bronze Age are the so-called Paraćin group around the middle and southern course of the Morava river (Garašanin 1983b: 727 ff.; Della Casa 1996: 162 ff.); and the Donja Brnjica-Gornja Stražava group (Garašanin 1983b: 773 ff.), extending from south-western Serbia through Kosovo to the Skopje Valley in northern Macedonia (Mitrevski 1992–93). Cremation and urn burial is characteristic of the funerary ritual of both groups, though cremation graves without urns are also found. Results published so far indicate that the manner of burial was quite complex: special constructions built of stone slabs and circuits of stones have often been discovered, and the grave pits could be lined and covered with stones and/or pebbles, which suggests there were graves or clusters of graves under smaller stone tumuli (Srejović 1959–60; Luci 1984). In some places too inhumation burials occur in the same cemeteries, such as for example in Donja Brnjica, Iglarevo, and Pešter, suggesting a bi-ritual funerary cult. Because graves are often found in groups and within stone constructions, stone circles, or small tumuli, we may assume that these are burials of persons belonging to smaller social nuclei, probably in the sense of individual families. Apart from pottery, grave goods are rather scarce, though the weapons are of particular note. For instance in Donja Brnjica and Iglarevo inhumation graves were provided with swords, while a small number of spear and arrowheads originate from cremation graves or from their immediate vicinity. Particularly noteworthy too are bone plates, probably parts of a boar's-tusk helmet, from one of the graves in the Ključka cemetery near Skopje (Mitrevski 1992–3: 115 ff., Fig. 2, 1–6; 11). Weaponry obviously had a special significance amongst the grave goods, for warriors with weapons, especially swords, were treated differently in the funerary ritual from most others who were cremated, which suggests that we can see them as representatives of a social elite, and perhaps even of foreign origin.

The chronology of the two groups, particularly the Donja Brnjica-Gornja Stražava group, has been the subject of lengthy discussion. The original dating to Ha B in the Reinecke system (Garašanin 1983b: 773 ff.) was first moved back to Bz D–Ha A, whereas it is now supposed that its beginnings go back to the Middle Bronze Age, to the Bz B period.

Continental Region

In the Early Bronze Age several different cultural groups had already formed in the continental region of the western Balkans and the southern Carpathian Basin, such as the Moriš or Mokrin group in northern Banat (see Chapter 44), and the Vinkovci or Somogyvar-Vinkovci group (Garašanin 1983a: 471 ff.), which stretched from Vojvodina (Bačka, Srem) across Slavonia along the Drava and Sava rivers to Prekmurje (Šavel 2005) and central Slovenia, as far as Lake Balaton. However, with the exception of the large flat cemetery of Mokrin, exceptionally few graves are known, so that it is difficult to get an idea of funerary rituals and the manner of burial in the early phases of the Bronze Age in southern Pannonia as a whole.

Inhumation was an important characteristic of burial practice in the Moriš group, which was spread primarily through the Moriš/Maros/Mureș river valley. One prominent cemetery of this grouping was studied at Mokrin, near Kikinda in Banat, and is dated to Bz A1 and the transition to early Bz A2. More than 300 inhumation graves were discovered, some of which had also been cremated (Girić 1971). The majority are burials in a crouched position, mostly oriented north-south. It is noteworthy that in the grave rite there were strict rules determining the position and grave goods of the deceased, depending on their gender and social status. Females were placed as a rule on their right side with their head towards the south; males were on their left side with their head towards the north, thus both were facing east, towards the rising sun. The relatively rich grave goods indicate differences in clothing, primarily in the head ornament, depending on the gender, age, and status of individuals. Women's dress is characterized by rich bronze or copper head ornaments, bone and faience beads, plain torcs, and spiral bracelets. Weapons in particular, such as daggers and axes, were important as status symbols in the graves of prominent men. Pottery is common in all graves, not only the richer ones. As recent research has shown, the Mokrin cemetery reflects a complex stratified society, a society that was not static but rather evolving dynamically (Primas 1977; Wagner 2005).

Little is known about the cemeteries of the Somogyvar-Vinkovci group (Bz A1) or of subsequent groups such as the southern Pannonian variant of the Kisapostag group and the Litzenkeramik ('braided pottery') group (Bz A2 and transition to B1), which were spread throughout Pannonia (Transdanubia) and in the areas along the valleys of the Mura, Drava, and Sava to central Slovenia. The exceptionally few, scanty graves indicate that the funerary practices were bi-ritual (Garašanin 1983a: 473).

In the Vatina culture too, the characteristic phenomenon of the developed Early Bronze Age and initial phase of the Middle Bronze Age in Vojvodina, relatively few significant graves are known. As is evident from what is still the best review of the funerary evidence (Hänsel 1968: 238 ff., Taf. 13, 22–3; 15; Beilage 14), cremation burial predominated from the very beginning, although there were also individual inhumations, which suggests that bi-ritual funerary customs were practised here, too. The pithos burials at the cemetery in Ostojićevo, containing children or newborn infants in a crouching position, represent on present knowledge a somewhat isolated case in this area.

It should be noted in particular that most of the inhumation graves have weapons in them, mainly swords and battle-axes, so are the graves of warriors, as for example at the Vatin site near Vršac, at Senta, and probably also at Sombor (Hänsel 1968: 238 ff., taf. 15, 23–5; 38, 1–5, 19). The fact that these warrior graves fall into the Middle Bronze Age (Bz B1–2), but do not belong to the central European Tumulus culture, indicates that we are dealing here with a 'convergence phenomenon', as in the Donja Brnjica-Gornja Stražava group: the social elite manifests itself through the funerary rite—inhumation—and through weaponry as prestige grave goods, and in this way establishes difference to and distance from the rest of the population.

During the Middle Bronze Age cremation of the deceased and the placing of the ashes in urns dominate in the funerary ritual throughout southern Pannonia. Burial took place in flat cemeteries. For the most part these are burial sites with a large number of graves, from which we may conclude that the majority of members of individual social communities were buried, not just selected individuals. Grave goods include a rich repertoire of pottery, both in terms of the forms of the vessels and of the decoration, as well as small figurative sculptures, especially anthropomorphic figurines, which cast light on the religious beliefs of social communities in the region. One of the most famous originates from Dupljaja (see Fig. 45.5b), a model of a three-wheeled cart drawn by water-fowl, on the base of which is carved a sun symbol, and which bears an anthropomorphic statuette, probably the image of a deity (Letica 1973; Schumacher-Matthäus 1985; Şandor-Chicideanu 2003). The local stylistic features in pottery enable us to distinguish between a number of cultural groups, named after the eponymous sites in the central Danube Basin, such as Dubovac-Žuto Brdo-Gîrla Mare, Szeremle-Bijelo Brdo, and Belegiš (I–II), which extend along the Danube from Hungary across eastern Slavonia, Srem, and Banat, and also beyond the Đerdap (Iron Gates) as far as Oltenia in Romania. At the end of the Middle Bronze Age, or during the transition to the Late Bronze Age, these groups received many influences from the Gáva culture in the eastern regions of the Carpathian Basin. This is reflected in new forms of pottery and ornamentation, primarily fluting (channelled pottery), while funerary customs continued to feature cremation and burial in flat urn cemeteries (Hänsel 1968: 133 ff., Beilage 12–14; Tasić 1983: 99 ff.; Hänsel and Medović 1991: 61 ff., abb. 4).

West of the cultural groups along the middle Danube, with their richly ornamented encrusted pottery, in the Middle Bronze Age (Bz B2–C/D) the so-called Virovitica group, as defined by Vinski-Gasparini (1973: 37 ff.; see Teržan 1995: 324 ff., abb. 1; Karavanić 2009: 43 ff.), made itself felt in the area between the Drava and Sava, from Slavonia to central Slovenia as far as Lake Balaton on one side and northern Bosnia on the other. In the Sava Basin in northern Bosnia this is also known in a local variant, named the Barice-Gređani group, which Čović conjectured had linked up to a local Early Bronze Age tradition (Čović 1988: 60 ff.). Cremation of the deceased and burial in flat cemeteries is also characteristic of that group, although a number of local particularities can be noted in the funerary ritual. Within the Barice-Gređani group, cremation graves were customary, where the cremated remains of the deceased were placed either on the ground or in shallow pits and covered with pots, primarily large bowls (*Brandschüttungsgräber*). In the early phase small tumuli occur, then flat cemeteries predominate. Different funerary customs were established in the more northerly areas of this group, for example in the Virovitica cemetery, where there are urns covered with a bowl or broken pottery. The grave pottery is very uniform, simple, and for the most part without decoration. In general, the graves were very modest, with metal grave goods such as items of clothing or jewellery being rare; there were no weapons as grave goods at all, which indicates that this was a taboo within the funerary rite. The burial sites of this group discovered so far suggest relatively small communities, in social terms barely stratified.

In the period of the classic Urnfield culture—Ha A2–B1 according to Hermann Müller-Karpe—new cultural groups settled southern Pannonia right up to the foothills of the eastern Alps. Characteristic of these groups were large flat urnfields with hundreds of graves. Only the most significant will be mentioned, such as the Dalj group in the central Danube Basin (Baranja, eastern Slavonia, and Bačka: Vinski-Gasparini 1973: 159 ff.), the Zagreb-Velika Gorica-Dobova group in the Sava river basin (Vinski-Gasparini 1973: 68 ff.; Karavanić 2009: 54 ff.), the Ruše group in the Drava river basin (Müller-Karpe 1959: 115 ff., taf. 108–23; Pahić 1972; Črešnar 2006), and the Ljubljana group in central Slovenia (Stare 1954; Puš 1971; Gabrovec 1973; Puš 1982: 52 ff.).

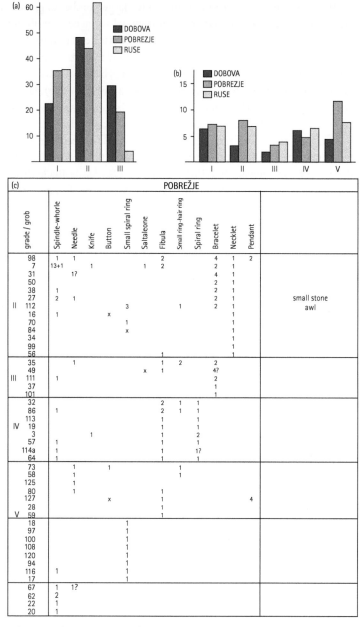

FIG. 45.8 Dobova, Pobrežje, Ruše (Slovenia), comparison between the grave-goods of the cemeteries: a. I – graves with metal grave-goods, II – graves with pottery, III – graves without grave-goods; b. groupings of graves with metal grave-goods, differentiated into dress-sets: I (men), II–V (women); c. Pobrežje near Maribor, graves with female dress-sets of variants II–V.

Source: author (Teržan 1995, 1999).

Analysis of funerary customs, above all of grave goods at some of these cemeteries, (Teržan 1987: 65 ff.; Teržan 1995: 338 ff.), has given us an insight into the social structure of the communities involved. The funeral of each individual appears to have been undertaken according to a strict ritual, manifested through a recurring model of dress combinations (metal items and jewellery), tools, and pottery (Fig. 45.8).

There exists in both male and female graves a division regarding grave furniture on the one hand and on the other a differentiation within the grave group, based on the attributes of jewellery and dress and utensils. This suggests that by comparison with the preceding periods of the Bronze Age, society became more complex in structure and more markedly stratified during the Urnfield period.

Bibliography

Becker, C. (1998). 'Möglichkeiten und Grenzen von Tierknochenanalysen am Beispiel der Funde aus Feudvar', in B. Hänsel and P. Medović (eds.), *Feudvar I. Ausgrabungen und Forschungen in einer Mikroregion am Zusammenfluss von Donau und Theiss. Das Plateau von Titel und die Šajkaška/Titelski plato i Šajkaška*. Kiel: Verlag Oetker/Voges, 321–32.

Benac, A. (1986). *Praistorijski tumuli na Kupreškom polju*, Djela 64. Centar za balkanološka ispitivanja 5. Sarajevo: Akademija nauka i umjetnosti Bosne i Hercegovine.

—— and Čović, B. (1956). *Glasinac I. Bronzano doba/Bronzezeit*. Sarajevo: Izdanje Zemaljskog muzeja u Sarajevu/Verlag des Landesmuseums in Sarajevo.

—— and Čović, B. (eds.) (1983). *Praistorija jugoslavenskih zemalja IV. Bronzano doba*. Sarajevo: Akademija nauka i umjetnosti Bosne i Hercegovine, Centar za balkanološka ispitivanja.

Codacci-Terlević, G. (2006). 'Prilog poznavanju brončanodobnih pogrebnih običaja u Istri—stanje istraženosti istarskih tumula te rezultati istraživanja tumula iz uvale Marić kod Barbarige', *Histria archaeological*, 35/2004: 41–74.

Čataj, L. (ed.) (2009). *Josipovac Punitovački—Veliko polje I. Eneolitičko, brončanodobno i srednjovjekovno naselje. Zaštitna arheološka istraživanja na trasi autoceste A 5/Rescue archaeological excavations on the route of the highway A 5*. Zagreb: Hrvatski restauratorski zavod.

Čović, B. (1965). 'Uvod v stratigrafiju i hronologiju praistorijskih gradina u Bosni', *Glasnik Zemaljskog muzeja*, NS 20: 27–145.

—— (1978). 'Velika Gradina u Varvari—I dio (slojevi eneolita, ranog i srednjeg bronzanog doba/Velika Gradina im Dorf Varvara, I. Teil', *Glasnik Zemaljskog muzeja Bosne i Hercegovine*, NS 32/1977: 5–81.

—— (1983). 'Regionalne grupe ranog bronzanog doba', in A. Benac and B. Čović (eds.) (1983), *Praistorija jugoslavenskih zemalja IV. Bronzano doba*. Sarajevo: Akademija nauka i umjetnosti Bosne i Hercegovine, Centar za balkanološka ispitivanja, 114–90.

—— (1988). 'Barice-Gredjani—Kulturna skupina', *Arheološki leksikon Bosne i Hercegovine*, 1: 60–1.

—— (1989). 'Posuška kultura', *Glasnik Zemaljskog muzeja Bosne i Hercegovine*, NS 44: 61–127.

—— (1991). *Pod kod Bugojna, Naselje bronzanog i željeznog doba u centralnoj Bosni. Sveska 1: Rano bronzano doba*. Sarajevo: Zemaljski muzej Bosne i Hercegovine.

Črešnar, M. (2006). 'Novi žarni grobovi iz Ruš in pogrebni običaji v ruški žarnogrobiščni skupini', *Arheološki vestnik*, 57: 97–162.

—— (2010). 'New research on the Urnfield period of Eastern Slovenia. A case study of Rogoza near Maribor', *Arheološki vestnik*, 61: 7–119.

Della Casa, Ph. (1996). *Velika Gruda II. Die bronzezeitliche Nekropole Velika Gruda (Opš. Kotor, Montenegro)*, Universitätsforschungen zur Prähistorischen Archäologie, 33. Bonn: Dr Rudolf Habelt GmbH.

Drechsler-Bižić, R. (1975). 'Istraživanja tumula ranog brončanog doba u Ličkom Osiku', *Vjesnik Arheološkog muzeju u Zagrebu*, 3/9: 1–22.

—— (1979–80). 'Nekropola brončanog doba u pećini Bezdanjači kot Vrhovina', *Vjesnik Arheološkog muzeja u Zagrebu*, 3/12–13: 27–88.

Dular, J., Šavel, I., and Tecco Hvala, S. (2002). *Bronastodobno naselje Oloris pri Dolnjem Lakošu*, Opera Instituti Archaeologici Sloveniae 5. Ljubljana: Založba ZRC.

—— and Tomanič Jevremov, M. (2010). *Ormož. Utrjeno naselje iz pozne bronaste in starejše železne dobe*, Opera Instituti Archaeologici Sloveniae 18. Ljubljana: Založba ZRC.

Falkenstein, F. (1998). *Feudvar II. Die Siedlungsgeschichte Titeler Plateaus*, Prähistorische Archäologie in Südosteuropa, 14. Kiel: Oetker Verlag.

Gabrovec, S. (1973). 'Začetek halštatkega obdobja v Sloveniji', *Arheološki Vestnik* 24: 338–85.

Garašanin, M. (1973). *Praistorija na tlu SR Srbije*. Beograd: Srpska književna zadruga.

—— (1983a). 'Podunavsko-balkanski kompleks ranog bronzanog doba', in A. Benac and B. Čović (eds.), *Praistorija jugoslavenskih zemalja IV. Bronzano doba*. Sarajevo: Akademija nauka i umjetnosti Bosne i Hercegovine, Centar za balkanološka ispitivanja, 436–83.

—— (1983b). 'Centralnobalkanska regija', in A. Benac and B. Čović (eds.), *Praistorija jugoslavenskih zemalja IV. Bronzano doba*. Sarajevo: Akademija nauka i umjetnosti Bosne i Hercegovine, Centar za balkanološka ispitivanja, 703–98.

Girić, M. (1971). *Mokrin—nekropola ranog bronzanog doba*, Dissertationes et monographiae, 11. Belgrade: Arheološko društvo Jugoslavije.

Govedarica, B. (1989). *Rano bronzano doba na području Jadrana*, Centar za balkanološka ispitivanja Djela 67/Knjiga 7. Sarajevo.

Guštin, M. (2005). 'Starejša bronasta doba v Prekmurju. Horizont pramenaste (litzen) keramike', *Zbornik soboškega muzeja*, 8: 85–98.

Hänsel, B. (1968). *Beiträge zur Chronologie der mittleren Bronzezeit im Karpatenbecken I-II*, Beiträge zur ur- und frühgeschichtlichen Archäologie des Mittelmeer-Kulturraumes, 7–8. Bonn: Rudolf Habelt Verlag GmbH.

—— (2002). 'Stationen der Bronzezeit zwischen Griechenland und Mitteleuropa', *Bericht der RGK*, 83/2002: 69–97.

—— and Medović, P. (1991). 'Vorbericht über die jugoslawisch-deutschen Ausgrabungen in der Siedlung von Feudvar bei Mošorin (Gem. Titel, Vojvodina) von 1986–1990. Bronzezeit-Vorrömische Eisenzeit', *Bericht der RGK*, 72: 45–204.

—— and Medović, P. (eds.) (1998). *Feudvar I. Ausgrabungen und Forschungen in einer Mikroregion am Zusammenfluss von Donau und Theiss. Das Plateau von Titel und die Šajkaška/Titelski plato i Šajkaška*. Prähistorische Archäologie in Südosteuropa, 13. Kiel: Verlag Oetker/Voges.

—— and Medović, P. (2004). 'Eine Bronzegiesserwerkstatt der frühen Bronzezeit in Feudvar bei Mošorin in der Vojvodina. Parerga Praehistorica. Jubiläumsschrift zur Prähistorischen Archäologie 15 Jahre UPA', *Universitätsforschungen zur Prähistorischen Archäologie*, 100. Bonn: Verlag Dr Rudolf Habelt GmbH, 83–111.

—— and Teržan, B. (2000). 'Ein bronzezeitliches Kuppelgrab ausserhalb der mykenischen Welt im Norden der Adria', *Praehistorische Zeitschrift*, 75: 161–83.

—— Teržan, B., and Mihovilić, K. (2007). 'Radiokarbondaten zur älteren und mittleren Bronzezeit Istriens', *Praehistorische Zeitschrift*, 82: 23–50.

—— Medović, P., Roeder, M., and Görsdorf, J. (1992). 'C 14-Datierungen aus den früh- und mittelbronzezeiltichen Schichten der Siedlung von Feudvar bei Mošorin in der Vojvodina', *Germania*, 70: 251–91.

—— Matošević, D., Mihovilić, K., and Teržan, B. (2009). 'Zur Sozialarchäologie der befestigten Siedlung von Monkodonja (Istrien) und ihrer Gräber am Tor', *Praehistorische Zeitschrift*, 84: 151–80.

Hirschler, I. (2009). 'Vinkovačka kultura', in L. Čataj (ed.), *Josipovac Punitovački—Veliko polje I. Eneolitičko, brončanodobno i srednjovjekovno naselje. Zaštitna arheološka istraživanja na trasi autoceste A 5/Rescue archaeological excavations on the route of the highway A5*. Zagreb: Hrvatski restauratorski zavod, 142–71.

Karavanić, S. (2009). *The Urnfield Culture in Continental Croatia*, British Archaeological Reports (International Series), 2s036. Oxford: British Archaeological Reports.

Kosorić, M. (1976). *Kulturni, etnički i hronološki problemi ilirskih nekropola Podrinja*, Dissertationes et monographiae, 18. Belgrade: Association des Sociétés Archéologiques de Yougoslavie/Museum of Eastern Bosnia.

Kroll, H. (1998). 'Die Kultur- und Naturlandschaften des Titeler Plateaus im Spiegel der metallzeitlichen Pflanzenreste von Feudvar', in B. Hänsel and P. Medović (eds.), *Feudvar I. Ausgrabungen und Forschungen in einer Mikroregion am Zusammenfluss von Donau und Theiss. Das Plateau von Titel und die Šajkaška/Titelski plato i Šajkaška*, Prähistorische Archaeologie in Südosteuropa, 13. Kiel: Verlag Oetker/Voges, 305–17.

Lamut, B. (1987). 'Ormož, podoba prazgodovinskega naselja', in *Bronasta doba na Slovenskem*. Ljubljana: Narodni muzej Slovenije, 46–57.

Lazić, M. (1997). 'Židovar in the Bronze Age', in M. Lazić (ed.), *Židovar—Bronze Age and Iron Age Settlement*. Belgrade-Vršac: Filozofski fakultet u Beogradu—Narodni muzej u Vršcu, 22–35.

—— (ed.) (1997). *Židovar—Bronze Age and Iron Age Settlement*. Belgrade-Vršac: Filozofski fakultet u Beogradu—Narodni muzej u Vršcu.

Letica, Z. (1973). *Antropomorfne figurine bronzanog doba u Jugoslaviji*, Dissertationes et monographiae, 16. Belgrade: Filozofski fakultet.

Ložnjak, D. (2001). 'Nalazišta brončanog doba na vinkovačkom području', *Prilozi Instituta za arheologiju u Zagrebu*, 18: 33–61.

Luci, K. (1984). 'Nova grupa grobova na praistorijskoj nekropoli u Donjoj Brnjici', *Glasnik Muzeja Kosova*, 13–14: 25–34.

Malinar, M. (1998). 'Brončanodobni lokalitet špilja Bezdanjača—novi material i interpretacija', *Opuscula Archaeologica*, 22: 141–62.

Marković, Z. (2002). 'O genezi i počecima licenskokeramičke kulture u sjevernoj Hrvatskoj', *Opuscula Archaeologica*, 27: 117–50.

Marović, I. and Čović, B. (1983). 'Cetinska kultura', in A. Benac and B. Čović (eds.) (1983), *Praistorija jugoslavenskih zemalja IV. Bronzano doba*. Sarajevo: Akademija nauka i umjetnosti Bosne i Hercegovine, Centar za balkanološka ispitivanja, 191–231.

Medović, P. (1988). *Kalakača, naselje ranog gvozdenog doba*. Novi Sad: Vojvođanski muzej.

Mihovilić, K., Hänsel, B., Matošević, D., and Teržan, B. (2009). *Monkodonja i Mušego. Izložba, Rovinj, Zavičajni muzej Grada Rovinja 18.06.-30.19.2009. Katalog 79*. Pula: Arheološki muzej Istre.

Mitrevski, D. (1992–3). 'A Brnjica type necropolis near Skopje', *Starinar*, NS 43–4: 115–24.

Müller-Karpe, H. (1959). *Beiträge zur Chronologie der Urnenfelderzeit nördlich und südlich der Alpen*, Römisch-Germanische Forschungen, 22. Berlin: Walter de Gruyter & Co.

Nikitović, L. (2003). 'Krstac-Ivkovo brdo. Nekropola sa humkama iz bronzanog doba. Sahranjivanje u bronzano i gvozdeno doba', in *Simpozijum, Čačak, 4–8. septembar 2002.* Čačak: National museum Čačak, Archaeological Institute Belgrade, 11–22.

——, Stojić, M. and Vasić, R. (2002). *Mojsinje—nekropola pod humkama iz bronzanog i gvozdenog doba/A bronze age and iron age mound necropolis*. Čačak: National Museum Čačak, Archaeological Institute Belgrade.

Pahič, S. (1972). *Pobrežje*, Katalogi in monografije, 6. Ljubljana: Narodni muzej Slovenije.

Pavišić, I. (2001). 'Die spätbronzezeitliche Siedlung Špičak in Hrvatsko zagorje', in A. Lippert (ed.), *Die Drau-, Mur- und Raab-Region im 1. vorchristlichen Jahrtausend*, Universitätsforschungen zur Prähistorischen Archäologie, 78. Bonn: Habelt, 165–79.

Petrović, B. (2010). *Asfaltna baza u Zemunu. Naselje ranog gvozdenog doba*, Monografije, 15. Belgrade: Belgrade City Museum.

Primas, M. (1977). 'Untersuchungen zu den Bestattungssitten der ausgehenden Kupfer- und frühen Bronzezeit', *Bericht der RGK*, 58: 4–160.

—— (1996). *Velika Gruda I. Hügelgräber des frühen 3. Jahrtausends v.Chr. im Adriagebiet— Velika Gruda, Mala Gruda und ihr Context*, Universitätsforschungen zur Prähistorischen Archäologie, 32. Bonn: Dr Rudolf Habelt GmbH.

Puš, I. (1971). *Žarnogrobiščna nekropola na dvorišču SAZU v Ljubljani*, Razprave I. razreda SAZU, 7/1. Ljubljana: Slovenska akademija znanosti in umetnosti.

—— (1982). *Prazgodovinsko žarno grobišče v Ljubljani*, Razprave I. razreda SAZU, 13/2. Ljubljana: Slovenska akademija znanosti in umetnosti.

Şandor-Chicideanu, M. (2003). *Cultura Žuto Brdo—Gârla Mare I-II*. Cluj-Napoca: Editura Nereamia Napocae.

Sanković, S. (2010). 'Začetki bronaste dobe v Prekmurju', *Zbornik soboškega muzeja*, 15: 91–105.

Schumacher-Matthäus, G. (1985). *Studien zu bronzezeitlichen Schmucktrachten im Karpatenbecken. Ein Beitrag zur Deutung der Horfunde im Karpatenbecken*, Marburger Studien zur Vor- und Frühgeschichte, 6. Mainz am Rhein: Verlag Philipp von Zabern.

Srejović, D. (1959–60). 'Praistorijska nekropola u Donjoj Brnjici', *Glasnik Muzeja Kosova i Metohije*, 4–5: 83–132.

Stare, F. (1954). *Ilirske najdbe železne dobe v Ljubljani. Dela 1. Razreda SAZU*, 9. Ljubljana: Slovenska akademija znanosti in umetnosti.

Šavel, I. (2005). 'Najdišče za Raščico pri Krogu—naselbina kulture Somogyvár-Vinkovci', *Zbornik Soboškega muzeja*, 8: 39–84.

—— and Sanković, S. (2010). *Za Raščico pri krogu*, AAS—Arheologija na avtocestah Slovenije, 13. Ljubljana: Zavod za varstvo kulturne dediščine Slovenije.

Tasić, N. (1983). *Jugoslavensko Podunavlje od indoevropske seobe do prodora Skita*, Balkanološki institut SANU. Posebna izdanja, 17. Belgrade: Novi Sad.

Teržan, B. (1987). 'Verovanje in obredi', in *Bronasta doba na Slovenskem*. Ljubljana: Narodni muzej Slovenije, 65–78.

—— (1995). 'Stand und Aufgaben der Forschungen zur Urnenfelderzeit in Jugoslawien. Beiträge zur Urnenfelderzeit nördlich und südlich der Alpen', in *Ergebnisse eines Kolloquiums*, Römisch-Germnisches Zentralmuseum Mainz. Monographien, 35. Bonn: Dr Rudolf Habelt GmbH, 323–72.

—— (1999). 'An outline of the Urnfield culture period in Slovenia', *Arheološki vestnik*, 50: 97–143.

Velušček, A. and Čufar, K. (2003). 'Založnica pri Kamniku pod Krimom na Ljubljanskem barju—naselbina kulture Somogyvár-Vinkovci', *Arheološki vestnik*, 54: 123–58.

Vinski-Gasparini, K. (1973). *Kultura polja sa žarama u sjevernoj Hrvatskoj/Die Urnengräberkultur in Nordkroatien*. Zadar: Filozofski Fakultet.

Wagner, J. (2005). 'Muster sozialer Differenzierung im frühbronzezeitlichen Gräberfeld von Mokrin/Vojvodina', *Mitteilungen der Berliner Gesellschaft für Anthropologie, Ethnologie und Urgeschichte*, 26: 111–46.

Zotović, M. (1985). *Arheološki i etnički problemi bronzanog i gvozdenog doba zapadne Srbije*. Dissertationes et monographiae, 26. Beograd, Titovo Užice: Zavičajni muzej Titovo Užice, Savez arheoloških društava Jugoslavije.

CHAPTER 46

CASTELLIERI-GRADINE OF THE NORTHERN ADRIATIC

KRISTINA MIHOVILIĆ

THE term *castelliere* or *gradina* has been used by archaeologists since research began into these fortified hill settlements in the nineteenth century. Numerous variations of the terms *castelliere* (Italian; pl. *castellieri*) and *gradina* (Croatian; pl. *gradine*) occur locally in traditional toponyms in Caput Adriae, Istria, the northern Adriatic, and along the whole of the eastern Adriatic coast, and throughout the western Balkans. The term usually signifies the sites of abandoned fortresses, most often high up and isolated, and generally corresponding to the location of prehistoric settlements (Bronze and Iron Age), where medieval fortresses or settlements developed, in continuous use up to the present day (Fig. 46.1).

Although this type of settlement can also be found elsewhere, there is an exceptionally large concentration of them in the northern Adriatic, especially in Istria and the karst hinterland of Trieste. The term *Cultura dei castellieri* or *Kašteljerska kultura* is used to denote the Bronze Age cultural facies clearly characteristic of Caput Adriae (Peroni 1983: 66; Gabrovec 1983: 46–51, Fig. 5: 11–22).

The northern Adriatic area encompasses the Kvarner islands, the Istrian Peninsula, and the zone towards the north, including Kras (the karstland), present-day Notranjska and Primorska, and the Soča river valley. The terrain is one of mainly gentle relief, the easily accessible limestone karst manifesting typical geological phenomena such as sinkholes and numerous caves. Only in central and north-western Istria are there flysch deposits which are subject to severe erosion, so that the *gradine* have been poorly preserved. There is a mild Mediterranean climate throughout the area, which is located at the crossroads of east-west and north-south routes that have always been important, a factor influencing the shape of cultures from the Palaeolithic onwards.

A HISTORY OF RESEARCH

The first map and description of 321 *gradine* appeared in the mid nineteenth century, the work of Trieste historian Pietro Kandler. Focusing on Istria and the Kvarner islands, Kandler regarded the *gradine* as Roman forts used to control Roman communication routes (Amoroso 1884: 54).

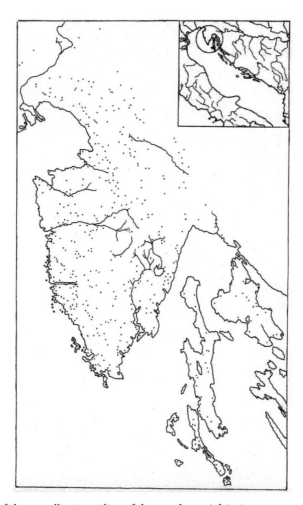

FIG. 46.1 Map of the *castellieri–gradine* of the northern Adriatic.

Source: Marchesetti 1903, with additions.

The first scientific work to describe *gradine* as prehistoric settlements is thought to be that written by Richard Francis Burton, then British consul in Trieste, under the title 'Notes on the Castellieri or Prehistoric Ruins of the Istrian Peninsula' and published in London in 1874, in *Anthropologia* (Italian translation: Burton 1877). Travelling alone or with local researchers who directed his attention to the phenomenon (Tommaso Luciani, Antonio Scampicchio, Carlo De Franceschi, Antonio Covaz), Burton visited a number of Istrian *gradine*. In his opinion, evidence that the remains were prehistoric rather than Roman included the finds of pottery, stone weapons, and tools, dry-stone ramparts surrounding the settlements, and inside, levelled-off plateaux and distinctly black soil. He noted that the *gradine* were sited on the tops of isolated hills and on the edges of promontories, overlooking deep valleys, which had been artificially levelled and surrounded by ramparts. He drew ground plans and showed the details of construction of Kunci *gradina* near Labin (Burton 1877: T. 8) and of Monkaštel near Červar (Poreč) (Burton 1877: T. 5–6). He visited many other sites, which he described separately.

After Burton, the physician and naturalist Carlo Marchesetti carried out seminal work. He was for many years director of the Museo Civico di Storia Naturale in Trieste. His first visit to a fortified settlement was in 1874, actually with Burton and a number of other historians (Ruaro Loseri 1983). Soon afterwards, from 1883, Marchesetti started systematically researching and going out in the field, carrying out many more or less extensive excavations which in 1903 resulted in the publication of the synthesis *I Castellieri preistorici di Trieste e della Regione Giulia*. The area covered by his work encompasses the Kvarner islands, Istria, stretching north-east as far as Rječina, and in the north including the present region of Notranjska, then Primorska and the Soča river valley, that is, the area of the former Küstenland province of the Austrian empire. In this area he recorded 455 *gradine*. Alongside a list of fortified settlements, giving a short description of the location and the altitude above sea level, he described his observations about the construction of the ramparts, how the space within the ramparts was organized, house types, population, finds, and chronology. His observations still form the foundation for studying the phenomenon.

Apart from Marchesetti there was Alberto Puschi, known for his research at Nesactium (1900–13), who was for many years director of the Museo Civico di Storia ed Arte in Trieste. Gathering data for an archaeological map of Istria for the needs of the Società Istriana di Archeologia e Storia Patria, Puschi visited and sketched numerous sites and carried out limited excavations. His work has been preserved in manuscript form and is in the Trieste and Rijeka archives; only a small part has been published (Benussi 1927–8: 243–82; Buršić Matijašić 2007: 83–4).

As conservator for the Austrian littoral, Anton Gnirs carried out important research in southern Istria at the beginning of the twentieth century, working especially on *gradine* on Veliki Brijun, in Vintijan, and on Mali Majan (in Italian: Monte Magnan piccolo) (Gnirs 1925: 28–39, 99–112). Between the two World Wars Raffaello Battaglia and Bruna Tamaro Forlati, working on behalf of the Soprintendenza of Padua and Trieste, carried out excavations of the *gradine* Kas, Glavica (Boncastel), and Vrčin, obtaining fresh data on the way the ramparts and gateways were built, the type of houses, and the cemeteries (Battaglia 1958).

After the Second World War, Boris Baćić did important work, starting to revise Marchesetti's list by re-surveying the terrain in Istria and on the Kvarner islands. A selection of the data from his reports, held in the archives of the Archaeological Museum of Istria in Pula, has been published (Buršić Matijašić 2007). He undertook a number of important excavations, revealing new data about the details of the fortifications (Baćić 1970) and the buildings inside the *gradine* (Baćić 1978a: 32–4; Čović 1983: 123).

In addition to Marchesetti (1924), Vladimir Mirosavljević (1974) did important work on the Kvarner islands, drawing and carrying out test excavations on a whole series of *gradine*.

In the karst hinterland of Trieste there was a revival of interest in the *gradine* in the mid twentieth century thanks to excavations carried out first by Benedetto Lonza (1977) and Dante Cannarella (1968) (Elleri, Cattinara, Montedoro, Monrupino, Rupin Piccolo), and then by Giorgio Stacul (1972). Excavating Slivia *gradina*, Stacul obtained the first radiocarbon date. With this, the foundation of the *gradina* was generally accepted as dating to the Middle Bronze Age.

Franca Maselli Scotti carried out both preventive and systematic excavations on *gradine* around Trieste, especially on flysch terrain (Elleri, Montedoro, Cattinara) (Maselli Scotti 1997). The research of Paola Cassola Guida and a number of colleagues into the fortified settlements in the central Friuli lowlands provides an important comparison with the better-known *gradine* on the karst terrain of the northern Adriatic. In the Friuli lowlands settlements are surrounded by a defensive system constructed in a different way, using earthen embankments, stones, and trenches (Cassola Guida and Vitri 1997).

Small trial excavations were carried out at Punta Kašteja *gradina* near Medulin in southern Istria and at Gradac-Turan *gradina* above Koromačno (central area of the eastern coast of Istria), where a stratigraphy as well as constructional elements were elucidated (Mihovilić 1979; 1997). In his review of *gradine* settlements in the area between Rovinj and Bale, and between the Lim channel and the Barbariga area, Luka Bekić (1996) threw fresh light on specific *gradine*, working out and publishing ground plans of the *gradine* he examined, in addition to other material collected on the surface.

Marchesetti's monograph has been used as the basis for a number of compilations, with a survey of *gradine* for the territory of Istria and interpretations of specific characteristics (Karoušková Soper 1983; Škiljan 1979–80; and in particular detail Buršić Matijašić 2007).

Systematic research on Monkodonja *gradina* near Rovinj over a number of years (1997–2008) has yielded major results, providing the basis for explaining the key characteristics of *gradine* (Mihovilić, Hänsel, and Teržan 2005).

The Characteristics of *Castellieri-Gradine*

Gradine were sited in strategic positions that could be easily defended, but that often do not look especially dominating. Monkodonja *gradina*, for example, occupies a characteristic location, sited at between 71 and 81 m above sea level, and surrounded by a whole series of higher hills. The *gradine* are defended by dry-stone ramparts adapted to the terrain. Sites on conical hills are encircled by a circuit of one or more walls (Monkodonja, Gradina on Veliki Brijun, Picugi, Sv. Anđeo, Sv. Juraj). On the edges of high plateaux (Jašmovica, Monte Grisa, Limska *gradina*), on tongue-shaped promontories over valleys (Nezakcij, Valaron, Prezenak, Šiljar) and by the sea (Punta Kašteja, Sv. Ivan Kornetski), the walls are more distinct or are built only in the more accessible places. In areas where there are no prominent hills, drystone walls were built for defence, and karst valley sites surrounded by sinkholes were used, such as in the central part of southern Istria, for example (Vrčin, Novi grad [Cittanova] near Čabrunići, Bale etcetera) (Fig. 46.2).

At first glance they look like simple protected areas, with the internal space not being organized in any obvious way. Extensive research at Monkodonja *gradina* near Rovinj in Istria revealed a series of essential elements indicative of a well-structured, stratified society capable of organizing the founding and construction of a settlement with proto-urban characteristics. Monkodonja is one of the more extensive *gradine*, with ramparts enclosing an oval plateau 160 by 250 m in size. Prominent within this area is the central, separately fortified space of a citadel or acropolis 80 by 100 m in size, where there are large structures and numerous smaller areas, covered doorways, and narrow passageways. Special artefacts confirm that this was an area inhabited by the ruling stratum, the elite of the settlement. West of the citadel, an area named the upper town slopes gently downwards: this was probably inhabited chiefly by artisans, to judge particularly from the remains of bronze smelting. This area was separated, by a not particularly significant wall, from the terraces which followed the

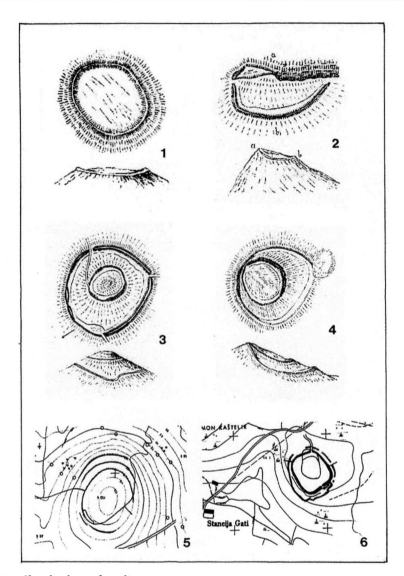

FIG. 46.2 Sketch-plans of *gradine*.

Source: Marchesetti 1903, Bekić 1996.

line of the outer rampart, that is, the lower town. Here smaller buildings were strung closely together along the rampart, leaning up against its inner face, as well as along the inner edge of the sloping terraces. Houses and other buildings in this section are sometimes separated from one another by narrow passageways. Geophysical prospection of the whole site has shown that the entire area surrounded by the rampart was intensively settled (Hänsel et al. 2009: 153) (Fig. 46.3).

The tops of hills or other selected sites were levelled, stone being broken up and extracted to create a plateau and often also terraces on the slopes, on which dwellings and other buildings were erected (Marchesetti 1903: 116; Čović 1983: 123). The sedimentary limestone in most of Istria and the wider area of the northern Adriatic, and the flysch foundation of central and

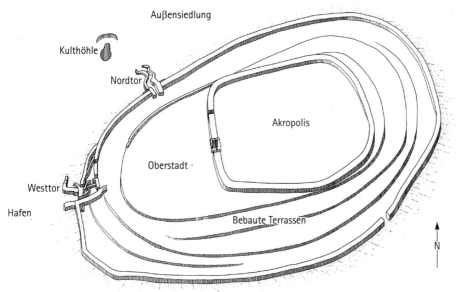

FIG. 46.3 Monkodonja *gradina*: aerial view and diagrammatic plan of the site.

Source: Mihovilić et al. 2005.

north-western Istria, are easily broken up by using wooden levers and wedges (Roglić 1975: 5–18). There is evidence of extensive stone-breaking at Monkodonja *gradina*, where the originally conical hill was levelled off and a spacious oval plateau created. Traces of deposits of crystalline calcium carbonate have been found in the central part of Monkodonja, indicating that there were previously small cave formations inside the hill which were destroyed when the plateau was created (Hänsel 2002: 84–5; abb. 13; 14). The broken and segregated stone was used in the construction of the ramparts, which were built from the two faces of selected blocks, or massive slabs placed vertically (the size of the blocks depends on the local geological conditions), while the space between was filled with gravel, small stones, and the fragments left from breaking up the larger blocks. Thus, for example, the ramparts at the *Gradina* on Veliki Brijun island, at Vrčin and Limska, are built mainly of regularly disposed small stones, interspersed with larger blocks, while the walls of the *gradine* of Monkodonja (Fig. 46.4), Karaštak, or Kunci are made up of mostly larger blocks, which look almost megalithic (Marchesetti 1903: 115–18; Gnirs 1925: 28–37; abb. 19–21; 109–12; abb. 64; Teržan, Mihovilić, and Hänsel 1998: 166–7; abb. 9, 10a).

The ramparts are most often 2 to 3 m wide, but sometimes, as at Gradišće Kunci, almost 10 m wide. At Monkodonja the ramparts were found to have been constructed, reinforced, and repaired in several phases, with new walls added from the inner side of the terrace or even on the external face of the walls, for example on the north-western section of the citadel rampart. In this section of the rampart there is also evidence of a section built using a 'coffer' system: in front of the first phase of the section, another face was built in parallel, and the space between them partitioned with transverse walls and then filled in with smaller stones (Mihovilić, Hänsel, and Teržan 2005: Fig. 8; 12). Judging from what is left of the stone ruins of ramparts at some *gradine*, the rampart may have been around 6 or even 10 m high. At Monkodonja the height of the ramparts, judging from the section between the western and northern gateways that has been studied, was from 3 to 4 m, suggesting that there was some sort of wooden superstructure like a parapet.

The security of the settlement was strengthened by the complicated system of entrances or passageways through the ramparts. At Monkodonja research has been done on the western entrance to the main rampart of the settlement, which took on a labyrinthine appearance

FIG. 46.4 Monkodonja: detail of the rampart.

Photo: O. Thiel.

after various reconstructions, with concealed passages and the main passageway being narrowed to a width of about 1 m. Four main phases of reconstruction have been documented, the last encompassing and concealing two tombs (Hänsel et al. 2009: abb. 17) (see Fig. 45.7).

In the first building phase, the gateway to the *gradina* was a simple staggered opening through the end of the rampart circuit. In many *gradine* such entrances can be recognized without excavation. In the case of settlements with several rampart circuits, the entrance through the next internal rampart is staggered from the outermost one. Several phases of reinforcement, or narrowing and remodelling of the passageways, has been documented at some other *gradine*. The main entrance at Vrčin *gradina* underwent at least three phases of remodelling and narrowing, until a passageway about 1 m wide was created. An entire cemetery was formed in front of the main entrance there, with walls built between the tombs to form a winding approach (Battaglia 1958: 423, 428–30). At Gradina on Veliki Brijun island, four phases of building were carried out to build on a massive reinforcement in front of the basic entrance through the main rampart, creating a new, staggered entrance and a narrow corridor before the main gateway (Gnirs 1925: 31–2; abb. 18; 21; Vitasović 2005: 411, Fig. 3). At Karastak *gradina* the eastern gateway was reinforced by a special structure with a rectangular ground plan and a narrow passage built at a diagonal to the passageway through the rampart (Baćić 1970: 220–1; Sl. 7). At Elleri *gradina*, which is built on flysch terrain, the earliest phase of the fortification involved building a massive circular rampart enclosing the plateau on which the settlement is sited, and a special fortification, like a projecting external turret, was built alongside the simple gateway (Degrassi 1997: 95–8; Fig. 17). Rupinpiccolo, built on karst, has one passage through the *gradina* rampart which was originally 3 m wide, but which at an unknown period was completely walled up, whilst a narrow corridor led to another, very narrow entrance. There is a similar entrance at Kolombanija *gradina* (Lonza 1977: 38–40; Fig. 1; 2). At Kunci *gradina* one of the passageways through the strong rampart was rebuilt to make it narrower before a narrow corridor was constructed (Baćić 1970: 218–9; Sl. 5).

At some sites there is evidence of an additional defensive construction (Vrčin, Gradac-Turan, Gradina on Veliki Brijun, Vintijan). About 10 m in front of the rampart circuit there is an earthwork 4–10 m wide, with sharp upright stones, slabs and blocks 0.5–1 m high densely inserted in it, creating a separate barrier hampering the approach to the actual walls. The stratigraphy established during protective excavations at the Gradac-Turan *gradina* above Koromačno suggested that the outer circuit of sharp upright stones could have been created in the Late Bronze Age (Gnirs 1925: 103; Battaglia 1958: 425, 430; Mihovilić 1997: 42–3; Sl. 7; 10).

Settlements founded on ridges above valleys, mostly surrounded by steep natural slopes, may have preserved a defensive earthwork like a high embankment on their weakest side. A construction like this is present on the western edge of Nesactium. The embankment that defends the western approach to the settlement remains mostly intact today: the average height is between 3 and 4 m and its width (from the external to the inner dry-stone wall) 23 to 27 m. Excavations in 1965–7 revealed a dry-stone wall of irregular width lying north to south that proved to be the western edge of an Iron Age cemetery (Puschi 1905: 14), and behind which two further parallel walls stretch to the external rampart. Josip Mladin is of the view that the parallel walls separate various constructions and passageways linked with an Iron Age cremation cemetery which seems to have arisen on the site of the previous Bronze Age cemetery (Mladin 1977–8: 7; T. XVIII; XXII). Similar earthworks, which look like high embankments, in some places preserved to a height of about 10 m, are to be found on the accessible sides of other sites as well, such as for example Šiljar and Prezenak above the Raša channel or Valaron above the Mirna river valley, Kaštelir near Dvori above Izola (Sakara Sučević 2004: 10–2; Sl. 3; Baćić 1957: 395; Boltin Tome 1967: 166–73).

As the first researchers noted, a well-organized society and knowledge of building methods were needed to construct such large defensive systems. Borivoj Čović also suggested that construction would have had to take place in a single phase (Čović 1983: 128). At Monkodonja this has been confirmed by a series of radiocarbon dates, which place the construction of the main rampart round the settlement, as well as of the citadel rampart, at around 1800 cal BC, or even a little earlier (Hänsel, Teržan, and Mihovilić 2007).

Before the wide-ranging research at Monkodonja, various hypotheses were put forward on the basis of smaller studies about the internal organization, the 'urbanism' of the settlements, and the social organization of the community. There is evidence of houses built with rectangular stone foundations, which, depending on the method of construction, could reach a height of around 1 m, while the superstructure could be of wood, branches, etcetera, as shown by finds of daub bearing plant impressions (Marchesetti 1903: 132). Fragments of painted plaster and relief ornament show that some buildings were internally decorated. At Kas (Mon Cas) *gradina* near Bale, Bruna Tamaro Forlati pointed out that the floors of rectangular houses are partly cut into the bedrock (Battaglia 1926: 42–3; Fig. 1). At the same *gradina* Baćić researched a number of other features, of which he left similar descriptions, while at Tondolon-Sv. Petar *gradina* near Savičenta, initial work suggested that one site was a house with an apse, but this has not been confirmed (Buršić Matijašić 2007: 259).

Buildings within the settlement at Monkodonja made abundant use of wood over drystone foundations, as indicated by the large number of recesses carved into the level foundation of the bedrock, and the remains of stone slabs by which the bearing beams were wedged into the walls, or which were used to support the roof constructions, were also found. Branches, shingles, straw, and various reeds were used to cover the roofs, traces of which have been found at Monkodonja, as well as thin stone slabs (Mihovilić, Hänsel, and Teržan 2005: 396; Fig. 7; 8; Degrassi 1997: 96).

The dwellings within the rampart were arranged along the defensive circuit of the settlements, leaning right up against the wall of the rampart, with passageways arranged accordingly, as Marchesetti suggested (1903: 115). The hypothesis was based on the characteristics of certain settlements that have been continuously settled from the Bronze/Iron Age right up to the present day, particularly in Istria.

Being mostly a karst landscape, the northern Adriatic has a problem of water supply. Surface waters and springs were of particular importance when choosing a settlement site. There are also likely to have been numerous clay-lined pools, such as those that served until quite recently for collecting and conserving rainwater in these regions. At Monkodonja *gradina* a number of fairly large cavities hollowed out from the bedrock, among other things, have been found, which when lined with clay might have been used as receptacles for collecting rainwater from the house roofs.

Gradine similar in size to Monkodonja (over 100 m in diameter) can be assumed to have organized the space within the settlement in the same way, this being indicative of the social divisions in the community. Such *gradine* represented centres to which surrounding smaller *gradine* (up to 100 m in diameter) gravitated, creating specific communities. The great density of *gradine* suggests the existence of alliances based upon mutual interest in using arable lands, pastures, or controlling scarce water sources and communications; individual settlements may have specialized in certain activities. Such speculations are difficult to prove, because Monkodonja is virtually the only *gradina* where research has been carried out that would yield data about the foundation, duration, or importance of the *gradina* within the community (Hänsel et al. 2009).

In the northern Adriatic area caves and rock shelters continued to be inhabited in parallel with and at the same time as the numerous *gradine*, but less intensively (numerous caves have been excavated in the karst hinterland of Trieste, in Istria, and on the islands of Cres and Lošinj, and fragments of Bronze Age pottery have been collected on the surface in many of them) (Montagnari Kokelj 1992; Stacul 1971–2; Baćić 1956; 1978b). There is also evidence of the existence of contemporary settlements outside the *gradine* fortifications, along the entire eastern shore of the Adriatic and in the hinterland. These are sites that have no great depth of stratigraphy, so they were probably used from time to time and for short periods (Čović 1983: 143–4; Batović 1990: 116, 135; Mihovilić 2007–8: 47–50).

Economy

The *gradine* that have been studied so far provide evidence of the importance of cattle-breeding; the bones of domestic animals predominate. Remains of game are less common, but large fish, sea snails, and shellfish feature (Riedel 1978–81; Becker 2001). Numerous grinding stones confirm the importance of agriculture. Botanical analysis of samples from Monkodonja revealed cereals, legumes, and a large proportion of grape pips, indicating that a vine-growing area existed here as early as the Bronze Age.

The geographical location of the area meant that cooperation in trade and exchange was important. Particularly significant in this respect are the finds of loaf-of-bread idols (*Brotlaibidole*) at Monkodonja, finds of amber beads in graves (Monkodonja, Mušego, Vrčin, Žamnjak, Krmedski Novi grad), and finds of bronze weapons of very varied origins (Aegean, Rhône, Italic regions) (Vinski 1961; Hänsel and Teržan 2000).

Chronology

At various *gradine* isolated objects have been found belonging to various periods between the Early Neolithic and the Late Eneolithic, indicating that the sites had been occupied sporadically since those times. On the basis of other phenomena in the western Balkans and the available find material, Čović placed the start of *gradine* in the northern Adriatic at the end of the Early Bronze Age (Bz A2), designated it Istra II (Čović 1983: 117, 123–32). This is confirmed by a number of radiocarbon dates from Monkodonja (Hänsel et al. 2007):

Construction of the acropolis rampart: 3430 ± 27 BP: 1766–1687 cal BC (1σ); 1875–1640 cal BC (2σ)

Building of the rampart around the site: 3490 ± 30 BP: 1881–1826 cal BC (1σ); 1910–1740 cal BC (2σ)

Upper levels of the site, near the northern gate (latest date): 2964 ± 31 BP: 1258–1128 cal BC (1σ); 1297–1049 cal BC (2σ)

The period ends with the emergence of cremation as the burial rite in Istria, Kras, and Notranjska, as opposed to the Bronze Age custom of inhumation in stone cists, covered with stone tumuli or in small cemeteries beside the main entrances to settlements. This period also approximates to the new wave of *gradina* settlement proposed by Marchesetti (1903: 151–5), when in some *gradine* life stops altogether, as at Monkodonja, whereas in others it continued, and new *gradine* were established. The appearance of cremation and the development of a new culture in the *gradine* of Istria occurred during the central European Late Bronze Age Urnfield period, the emergence of Proto-Villanovan in Italy (see Chapter 35), and Late Helladic IIIC in the Aegean. Components of all these cultures appear in the earliest urn cemeteries in Istria, which are usually ascribed to the Histri, and which then continue until the period of Romanization (Gabrovec and Mihovilić 1987: 293–308; 334–5). The situation was similar in the *gradine* of the karst hinterland of Trieste, present-day Primorska and Notranjska (Cardarelli 1983; Montagnari Kokelj 1997; Guštin 1979), but not on the Kvarner islands. There, the life of the *gradine* continued without any abrupt interruptions (Osor, Krk), as was also the case with the *gradine* of northern Dalmatia (Asseria, Bribir, Nadin, etcetera), where the Liburnian culture formed and developed through the Iron Age up until the Roman period (Batović 1983; 1987).

Bibliography

Amoroso, A. (1884). 'I castellieri istriani e la necropoli di Vermo presso Pisino', *Atti e memorie della Società istriana di archeologia e storia patria*, 1: 53–74.

Baćić, B. (1956). 'Arheološko iskopavanje spilje Cingarela kod Momjana', *Jadranski zbornik*, 1: 323–64.

—— (1957). 'Ilirsko žarno groblje u Kaštelu kraj Buja', *Jadranski zbornik*, 2: 381–432.

—— (1970). 'Prilozi poznavanju prethistorijske gradinske fortifikacije u Istri', In *Adriatica praehistorica et antiqua: Zbornik radova posvećen Grgi Novaku*, eds. V. Mirosavljević, D. Rendić-Miočević and M. Suić: 215–26. Zagreb: Arheološki institut Filozofskog fakulteta.

—— (1978a). *Prapovijesna zbirka*, Arheološki muzej Istre, Vodič [Guide] III, 28–44. Pula: Archaeological Museum.

—— (1978b). 'Trogrla pećina. Rezultati arheološkog istraživanja 1974. god', *Jadranski zbornik*, 10: 161–72.

Batović, Š. (1983). 'Kasno brončano doba na istočnom jadranskom primorju', In *Praistorija jugoslavenskih zemalja IV, bronzano doba*, 271–373. Sarajevo: Svjetlost.

—— (1987). 'Liburnska grupa', in *Praistorija jugoslavenskih zemalja V, željezno doba*, 339–90. Sarajevo: Svjetlost.

—— (1990). 'Novija istraživanja prapovijesti u biogradskom kraju', *Biogradski zbornik*, 1: 85–195.

Battaglia, R. (1926). 'Ricerche paletnologiche e folcloristiche sulla casa istriana primitiva', *Atti e memorie della Società istriana di archeologia e storia patria*, 38/2: 33–79.

Battaglia, R. (1958). 'I Castellieri della Venezia Giulia', *Le meraviglie del passato*, 2, Milan: A. Mondadori, 419–34.

Becker, C. (2001). 'Monkodonja in Istrien. Konsumverhalten in einem bronzezeitlichen Kastelliere', *Mitteilungen der Berliner Gesellschaft für Anthropologie, Ethnologie und Urgeschichte*, 22: 25–41.

Bekić, L. (1996). 'Sustav gradina na rovinjskom području', *Histria archaeologica*, 27: 19–92.

Benussi, B. (1927–8). 'Dalle annotazioni di Alberto Puschi per la carta archeologica dell'Istria', *Archeografo Triestino*, 14/III: 245–82.

Boltin Tome, E. (1967). 'Poročilo o raziskovanju na srednjem prečnem nasipu Kaštelirja pri Dvorih nad Izolo', *Arheološki vestnik*, 18: 163–77.

Buršić Matijašić, K. (2007). 'Gradine Istre', *Povijest Istre*, 6. Pula: Zavičajna naklada Žakan Juri.

Burton, R. F. (1877). *Note sopra i castellieri o rovine preistoriche della penisola Istriana*. Capodistria: Redazione della Provincia (Reprint Trieste 1970: Libreria internazionale Italo Svevo).

Cannarella, D. (1968). *Il Carso*. Trieste: Il nostro Carso.

Cardarelli, A. (1983). 'Castellieri nel Carso e nell'Istria: Cronologia degli insediamenti fra media Età del Bronzo e prima Età del Ferro', in *Preistoria del Caput Adriae. Trieste, Castello di S. Giusto*. Udine: Istituto per l'Enciclopedia del Friuli Venezia Giulia, 87–104.

Cassola Guida, P., and Vitri, S. (1997). 'Gli insediamenti arginati della pianura friulana nell'età del bronzo', in M. Bernabò Brea, A. Cardarelli, M. Cremaschi (eds.), *Le Terramare, la più antica civilta Padana*. Milan: Electa, 257–62.

Čović, B. (1983). 'Regionalne grupe ranog bronzanog doba', in *Praistorija jugoslavenskih zemalja IV, bronzano doba*, 114–90. Sarajevo: Svjetlost.

Degrassi, V. (1997). 'Il sito archeologico di Elleri: la periodizzazione', in *Il Civico Museo Archeologico di Muggia*, ed F. Maselli Scotti, 95–8. Trieste: Civico museo archeologico (Muggia).

Gabrovec, S. (1983). 'Jugoistočno alpska regija', in *Praistorija jugoslavenskih zemalja*, IV, *bronzano doba*, 21–96. Sarajevo: Svjetlost.

—— and Mihovilić, K. (1987). 'Istarska grupa', in *Praistorija jugoslavenskih zemalja V, željezno doba*, 293–338. Sarajevo: Svjetlost.

Gnirs, A. (1925). *Istria praeromana*. Karlsbad: Verlag von Walther Heimisch.

Guštin, M. (1979). *Notranjska. K začetkom železne dobe na severnem Jadranu*, Katalogi in Monografije, 17. Ljubljana: Narodni Muzej.

Hänsel, B. (2002). 'Station der Bronzezeit zwischen Griechenland und Mitteleuropa', *Bericht der Römisch-Germanischen Kommission*, 83: 69–97.

—— and Teržan, B. (2000). 'Ein bronzezeitliches Kuppelgrab außerhalb der mykenischen Welt im Norden der Adria', *Praehistorische Zeitschrift*, 75: 161–83.

——, Teržan, B., and Mihovilić, K. (2007). 'Radiokarbondaten zur älteren und mittleren Bronzezeit Istriens'., *Praehistorische Zeitschrift*, 82/1: 23–50.

——, Matošević, D., Mihovilić, K., and Teržan, B. (2009). 'Zur Sozialarchäologie der befestigten Siedlung von Monkodonja (Istrien) und ihre Gräber am Tor', *Praehistorische Zeitschrift*, 84: 151–80.

Karoušková Soper, V. (1983). *The Castellieri of Venezia Giulia, North-Eastern Italy (2nd–1st millenium B.C.)*, British Archaeological Reports (International Series), 192. Oxford: Archaeopress.

Lonza, B. (1977). 'Appunti sui castellieri dell'Istria e della provincia di Trieste', *Società per la Preistoria e Protostoria della regione Friuli-Venezia Giulia*, Quaderno, 2. Trieste: Edizioni 'Italo Svevo'.

Marchesetti, C. (1903). 'I Castellieri preistorici di Trieste e della regione Giulia', *Atti del Museo Civico di Storia Naturale di Trieste*, 4. Trieste: Edizioni 'Italo Svevo'.

—— (1924). 'Isole del Quarnero—Ricerche Paletnologiche', *Notizie degli scavi*, 21: 121–48.

Maselli Scotti, F. (ed.) (1997). *Il Civico Museo Archeologico di Muggia*. Trieste: Ministero per i beni culturali e ambientali, Soprintendenza per i beni ambientali architettonici archeologici artistici e storici del Friuli Venezia-Giulia, Comune di Muggia, Provincia di Trieste.

Mihovilić, K. (1979). 'Gradina Punta Kašteja kod Medulina', *Histria archaeologica*, 10/1: 37–56.

—— (1997). 'Fortifikacija gradine Gradac-Turan iznad Koromačna', *Izdanja Hrvatskog Arheološkog Društva*, 18: 39–59.

—— (2007-8). 'Gropi—Stari Guran: Analiza prapovijesne keramike', *Histria archaeologica*, 38–39: 37–79.

—— Hänsel, B., and Teržan, B. (2005). 'Moncodogno—Scavi recenti e prospetive future', Carlo Marchesetti e i castellieri 1903–2003, G. Bandelli and E. Montagnari Kokelj (eds.), *Fonti e studi per la storia della Venezia Giulia*, 9: 389–407.

Mirosavljević, V. (1974). 'Gradine i gradinski sistemi u prahistorijsko i protohistorijsko doba, I dio, Nalazišta: (otoci Cres i Lošinj)', *Arheološki radovi i rasprave*, 7: 259–91.

Mladin, J. (1977-8). 'Geneza čovjeka u likovnim spomenicima iz prapovijesti Nezakcija', *Histria archaeologica*, 8–9: 5–115.

Montagnari Kokelj, E. (1992). 'La Grotta dei Ciclami nel Carso Triestino (Materiali degli scavi 1959-1961)', *Atti della Società per la Preistoria e Protostoria del Friuli-Venezia Giulia*, 7: 65–162.

Peroni, R. (1983). 'L'Età del Bronzo', in *Preistoria del Caput Adriae. Trieste, Castello di S. Giusto*. Udine: Istituto per l'Enciclopedia del Friuli Venezia Giulia, 65–7.

Puschi, A. (1905). 'La necropoli preromana di Nesazio. Relazione degli scavi eseguiti negli anni 1901, 1902 e 1903', *Atti e memorie della Società istriana di archeologia e storia patria*, 22: 3–202.

Riedel, A. (1978–1981). 'Cenni sulle prospetive delle ricerche archeozoologiche', *Atti della Società per la Preistoria e Protostoria del Friuli—Venezia Giulia*, 4: 209–16.

Roglić, J. (1975). 'Prirodna osnova', *Geografija SR Hrvatske*, 5: 5–28. Zagreb: Školska knjiga.

Ruaro Loseri, L. (1983). 'Nascita della Mostra', in *Preistoria del Caput Adriae. Trieste, Castello di S. Giusto*. Udine: Istituto per l'Enciclopedia del Friuli Venezia Giulia, 11–16.

Sakara Sučević, M. (2004). *Kaštelir. Prazgodovinska naselbina pri Novi vasi/Brtonigla (Istra)*. Koper: Univerza na Primorskem, Znanstveno-raziskovalno središče, Inštitut za dediščino Sredozemlja.

Stacul, G. (1971-2). 'Scavo nella grotta del Mitreo presso S. Giovanni al Timavo', *Atti dei Civici Musei di Storia ed Arte di Trieste*, 7: 35–60.

Stacul, G. (1972). 'Il castelliere "C. Marchesetti" presso Slivia', *Rivista di Scienze Preistoriche*, 27/1: 145–62.

Škiljan, M. (1979-80). 'L'Istria nella protostoria e nell'età protoantica', *Atti Centro di ricerche storiche—Rovigno*, 10: 9–73.

Teržan, B., Mihovilić, K. and Hänsel, B. (1998). 'Eine älterbronzezeitliche befestigte Siedlung von Monkodonja bei Rovinj in Istrien', in H. Küster, A. Lang, and P. Shauer (eds.), *Archäologische Forschungen in urgeschichtlichen Siedlungslandschaften*, Festschrift für Georg Kossack zum 75. Geburtstag. Regensburg: Universitätsverlag Regensburg, 155–84.

Vinski, Z. (1961). 'O oružju ranog brončanog doba u Jugoslaviji', *Vjesnik Arheološkog muzeja u Zagrebu*, series 3, 2: 1–37.

Vitasović, A. (2005). 'La cultura dei castellieri sulle isole Brioni', in *Carlo Marchesetti e i castellieri 1903–2003*, eds. G. Bandelli and E. Montagnari Kokelj, 409–18, Fonti e studi per la storia della Venezia Giulia, 9. Rome: Edizioni Quasar.

CHAPTER 47

ROMANIA, MOLDOVA, AND BULGARIA[1]

NIKOLAUS BOROFFKA

THE three countries considered in this chapter have varying histories and traditions of research, as well as differing environments and archaeological cultures. Figure 47.1 shows the main regions and sites discussed.

A History of Research

Interest in the archaeological remains of Romania goes back to the eighteenth century, mostly concentrating on the Roman period in a search for the ancestors of modern Romanians. After Aiud (1796) and Sibiu (1817), most major museums became active during the later nineteenth century. Archaeological site catalogues were first published for Transylvania, and a first general sketch of the pre-Roman history of Romania was published in 1880. The most important milestone and the first systematic discussion of prehistory was the extensive study by Ion Nestor published in 1932, where the major Bronze Age cultures were named for the first time and placed in a systematic order (Glina III = Schneckenberg [dated to the Eneolithic], Periamuş [also known as Periam-Pecica or Mureş/Maros], Otomani, Wietenberg, Monteoru, Tei, Vattina, Bordei-Herăstrău).

It was only from 1960 onwards, starting with the *History of Romania* (Nestor 1960), that the Bronze Age in general, in specific regions or individual cultures of the period (some newly identified), was again treated in comprehensive studies. While the foundations had thus been laid, after the political changes at the end of the 1980s, new views on many aspects of the Bronze and Early Iron Age were presented and site catalogues became accessible online (see, for example, http://www.cimec.ro/scripts/ARH/RAn/sel.asp).

Research in the Republic of Moldova (the term 'Moldavia' should strictly speaking embrace both the Republic and the eastern province of present-day Romania) was initially closely connected to that in Romania, with a focus on Greek and Roman antiquities of the Black Sea coast, as well as on the spectacular monuments of the Eneolithic Cucuteni-Tripolye culture.

---

[1] In this chapter in-text references are mostly not given; the Bibliography includes the most important items for the Bronze Age in the countries concerned.

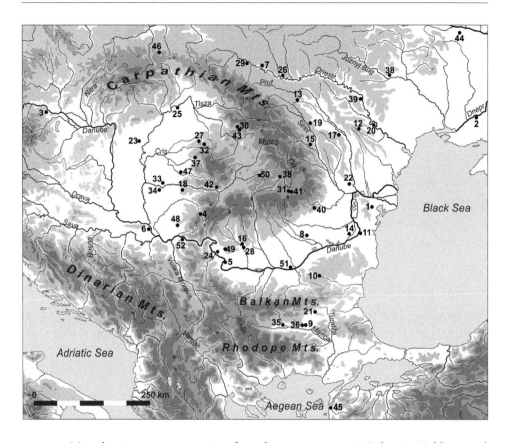

FIG. 47.1 Map showing eponymous sites for cultures or groups in Bulgaria, Moldova, and Romania: 1. Babadag, 2. Babino, 3. Baden, 4. Balta Sărată, 5. Basarabi, 6. Belegiš, 7. Biały Potok, 8. Bordei-Herăstrău /Bucureşti (Bucharest)/Glina /Popeşti/Tei, 9. Čatalka, 10. Čerkovna, 11. Cernavodă, 12. Chişinău, 13. Corlăteni, 14. Coslogeni, 15. Costişa, 16. Coţofeni, 17. Cozia, 18. Cruceni, 19. Cucuteni, 20. Delacău, 21. Ezero, 22. Folteşti, 23. Füzesabony, 24. Gîrla Mare, 25. Gáva, 26. Holihrady, 27. Igriţa, 28. Işalniţa, 29. Komarov, 30. Lăpuş, 31. Noua, 32. Otomani, 33. Pecica, 34. Periam, 35. Plovdiv, 36. Pšeničevo, 37. Roşia, 38. Sabatinovka, 39. Saharna, 40. Sărata Monteoru, 41. Schneckenberg, 42. Şoimuş, 43. Suciu de Sus, 44. Tripolye, 45. Troy, 46. Trzcinica, 47. Vărşand (Gyulávarsánd), 48. Vatina, 49. Verbicioara, 50. Wietenberg, 51. Zimnicea, 52. Žuto Brdo (Gray-scale stages are at 500, 1000 and 1500 m above sea level).

Map: author.

After World War II the influence of Soviet Russia dominated; the results of research on the Bronze Age of Moldova since the 1950s were viewed more in an eastern context and primarily published in Russian, but here too new views were published after the political changes of the late 1980s. A database of archaeological sites and materials is in progress at the National Museum (Muzeul Naţional de Arheologie şi Istorie a Moldovei), but not yet available online.

In modern Bulgaria, founded as a monarchy only in 1878, early archaeological research was initially carried out by foreigners, since the Ottoman empire had no institution specifically occupied with historical research. The National Museum originated from a permanent exhibition in 1892 in the Büjük Dzhamija mosque in Sofia, and by 1921 the Archaeological Institute had been founded. In the 1920s and 1930s Bulgarian archaeologists drew up catalogues of prehistoric sites and these are still valuable today.

Chronology and Terminology

The number of radiocarbon dates available in these countries is still insufficient, nor do they cover all phases or cultures, so that it is mainly relative chronologies that are used, absolute dates usually being provided through comparison with neighbouring regions (Fig. 47.2).

A specific feature of Romania is the 'transition period', represented mainly by the Coţofeni group of central and southern Romania, which also spread into part of northern Bulgaria. In the west its neighbour is the Baden complex, to which it is so closely related that Coţofeni

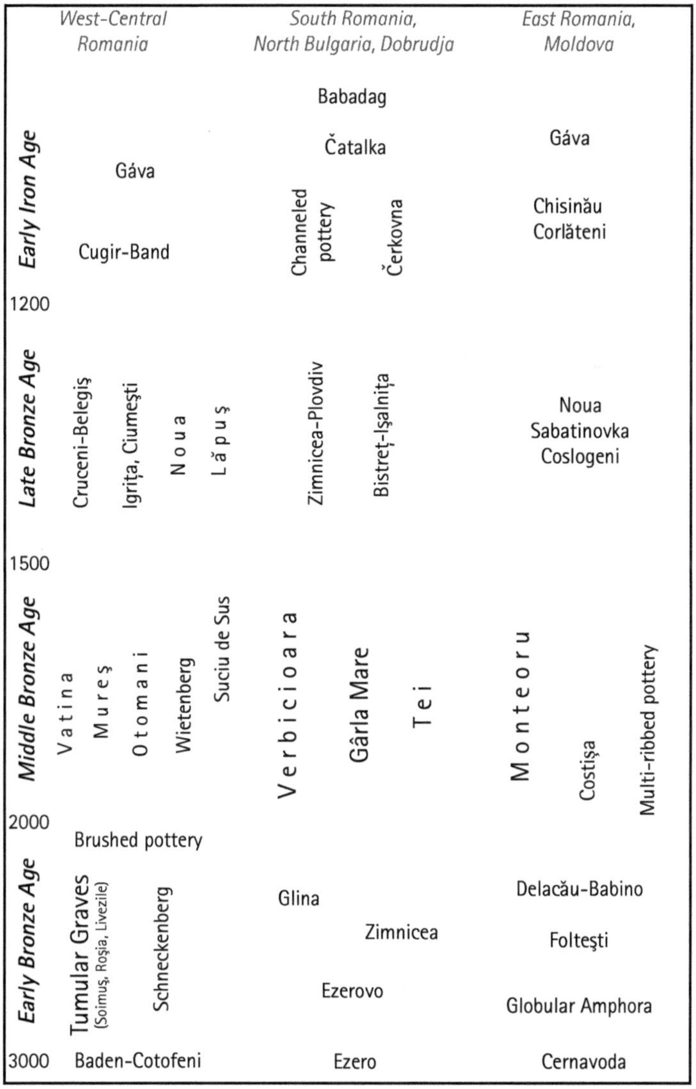

	West-Central Romania	South Romania, North Bulgaria, Dobrudja	East Romania, Moldova
Early Iron Age	Gáva Cugir-Band	Babadag Čatalka Channeled pottery / Čerkovna	Gáva Chisinău Corlăteni
1200			
Late Bronze Age	Cruceni-Belegiš Igriţa, Ciumeşti Noua Lăpuş	Zimnicea-Plovdiv Bistreţ-Işalniţa	Noua Sabatinovka Coslogeni
1500			
Middle Bronze Age	Vatina Mureş Otomani Wietenberg Suciu de Sus	Verbicioara Gârla Mare Tei	Monteoru Costişa Multi-ribbed pottery
2000	Brushed pottery		
Early Bronze Age	Tumular Graves (Soimuş, Roşia, Livezile) Schneckenberg	Glina Zimnicea Ezerovo	Delacău-Babino Folteşti Globular Amphora
3000	Baden-Coţofeni	Ezero	Cernavoda

FIG. 47.2 Chronological table of the main Bronze Age/Early Iron Age cultures in Romania, Bulgaria, and Moldova.

could be considered as the eastern variant of Baden, while it is unclear what phenomena correspond to this in the east. The later Coțofeni phases, datable in absolute terms to the first half or middle of the third millennium BC, have more recently been included by some authors in the Early Bronze Age. If the Bulgarian chronology (see below) becomes more widely accepted, then the Baden complex, including the Coțofeni group, as well as the partially present Beaker and Globular Amphora groups, would fall into the Early Bronze Age. This may be justified by the general cultural changes (pottery, metallurgy, transport, etcetera), but would have nothing to do with the naming of the period, since 'bronze' in the strict sense of tin-copper alloys, does not actually appear before the Middle Bronze Age in local terminology.

The 'classical' Early Bronze Age is accepted as beginning with the Glina-Schneckenberg culture and early Zimnicea. These are followed by the well-established Middle Bronze Age cultures, for which the stratigraphic sequences of Sărata-Monteoru, Periam, and Derșida may be considered as the most important. The Romanian Late Bronze Age begins with phenomena such as Igrița in the west and the widespread Noua-Coslogeni complex ranging from Moldova to central Romania and into Bulgaria. Early Hallstatt cultures, closely connected to the central European Urnfield societies, mark the beginning of the Iron Age in Romanian terminology. At present the Bronze Age can thus be placed roughly between *c*.3000/2500 BC and 1200/1100 BC, although it should be mentioned that (tin) bronze becomes widely used only from the Middle Bronze Age, beginning around 2000/1900 BC onwards. While the central European periodization of Paul Reinecke and Hermann Müller-Karpe (especially for the Early Iron Age or Hallstatt period) is still often used for bronzes, the pottery-defined cultures are usually only placed within in a relative chronological framework.

The Moldovan research tradition was originally close to the Romanian one, then influenced strongly by the Soviet Union, but is now rebuilding its own identity. Although many aspects of the Early Bronze Age in eastern Romania and Moldova are still unclear, eastern elements (Yamnaya, Katakombnaya; see Chapter 48) together with some late Eneolithic/Early Bronze Age north-western influences (e.g. Globular Amphora or Trzciniec culture) are present. The Moldovan Bronze Age has an intermediate position between that of Romania and that of Russia, with some local phenomena especially in the Middle Bronze Age (e.g. Mnogovalikovaya pottery), and can principally be dated in accord with Romanian chronology.

The Bulgarian Bronze Age has in recent times been classified in a similar way to the Romanian, the principal difference being an earlier absolute date for the beginning of the Early Bronze Age, justified by radiocarbon dates from the type site of Ezero, around 3200/3100 cal BC, in other words almost half a millennium earlier than further north. Here too the period after 1200/1100 BC is considered as Early Iron Age, ending around the ninth/eighth century BC.

Cultural Evolution

First it must be stressed that most so-called archaeological 'cultures', 'groups', or 'cultural aspects' in the region have not generally been precisely defined, and are mainly identified by pottery shapes and decoration styles, while features such as burials or settlement structures have rarely been included. Any theoretical discussion of the terminology used is completely lacking. Internal or foreign parallels are largely limited to single-shape or ornament analogies, while statistical comparisons, for example of the frequency of ceramics, are hardly possible given the very selective publication of materials that exists at present.

The Eneolithic cultural basis of the Bronze Age in the region discussed here is largely provided by widespread phenomena such as the Baden-Cernavodă-Coțofeni complex (if this is not included as the beginning phase of the Bronze Age) for the western and southern part, and the late Cucuteni-Tripolye complex in the east. Local features of the Early Bronze Age may sometimes be explained by this background. Some influences from Greece and Turkey are visible in the south.

Early Bronze Age (*c*.3000/2500–2000/1900 BC)

A general characteristic of Early Bronze Age pottery in this region, in contrast to the preceding Eneolithic, is the disappearance of incised and incrusted (e.g. Coțofeni) or painted (Cucuteni-Tripolye) decoration and a dominance of plastic knobs and ribs (cultural groups: Șoimuș, Roșia, the Tumulus grave group of western Transylvania, Glina-Schneckenberg, Foltești, Delacău-Babino, early Zimnicea, Ezero) (Fig. 47.3, lower part). Another widespread common characteristic, derivable from early western cultural groups (e.g. Ljubljana, Mondsee), are vessel-rims with exterior sleeve-like thickening. Among other older traditions, small footed bowls, the foot sometimes in the shape of a cross, may be mentioned, which may be derived from the Bell Beaker culture (see Chapter 3), and which are found in Glina and Ezero contexts far to the south and as far east as Romanian Moldova (e.g. in Bogdănești and Corlăteni), often together with cord-impressed decoration. Wide, open, angularly profiled bowls, sometimes with rims containing a channelled interior, were already a feature of the Baden complex and continue into the pottery of the Transylvanian Tumulus group and the Foltești phenomenon of Moldova (Fig. 47.3, lower part). In the latter, monochrome painting still occurs sporadically, recalling the final phase of the preceding Cucuteni-Tripolye communities (Fig. 47.3, lower right). A feature considered specific to the southern Glina variant of the Glina-Schneckenberg complex are so called hole-knobs under the vessel-rims, produced by impressing a small blunt round point into the soft clay. New shapes, presumably originating in the south, are asymmetrical jugs and *askoi*, which are found in Ezero and Ezerovo (Bulgaria), the Early Bronze Age cemetery at Zimnicea (southern Romania), Foltești (Romanian Moldavia), and as far north as the Schneckenberg group (south-east Transylvania) (Fig. 47.3, lower, centre and right), a specific form continuously developed throughout the Middle Bronze Age Monteoru culture of eastern Romania (Fig. 47.3, Monteoru). In southeastern Bulgaria influences from the Troad in Turkey have become clear, although the potter's wheel, well established in Troy itself, was not adopted—the very few wheel-thrown fragments are most probably imports.

In the developed Early Bronze Age, vessels with brushed or combed lower body (Fig. 47.3, Ezerovo, Foltești), in Transylvania also with textile impressions, are a chronological indicator, well known from the Early Bronze Age of Hungary. This feature may again be observed as far south as Bulgaria (e.g. Ezero, Dyadovo) and up to Moldova in the east (e.g. Bogdănești, Iacobeni), and continues in the early phases of some of the classical Middle Bronze Age cultures (e.g. Mureș, Otomani, Wietenberg). It may have had the technical aim of enlarging the outer surface (microstructure) of cooking vessels for better heat absorption and/or higher porosity for the cooling of liquid contents by evaporation through the walls.

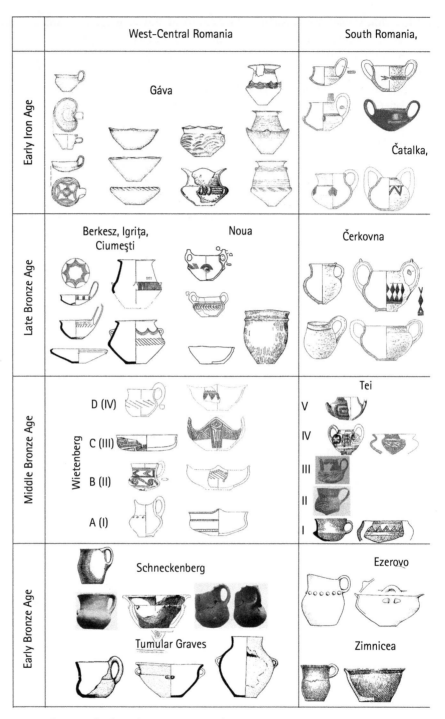

FIG. 47.3 Evolution of selected pottery types for some important Bronze Age/Early Iron Age cultures in Romania, Bulgaria, and Moldova. Various scales.

Source: various (illustration R. Boroffka).

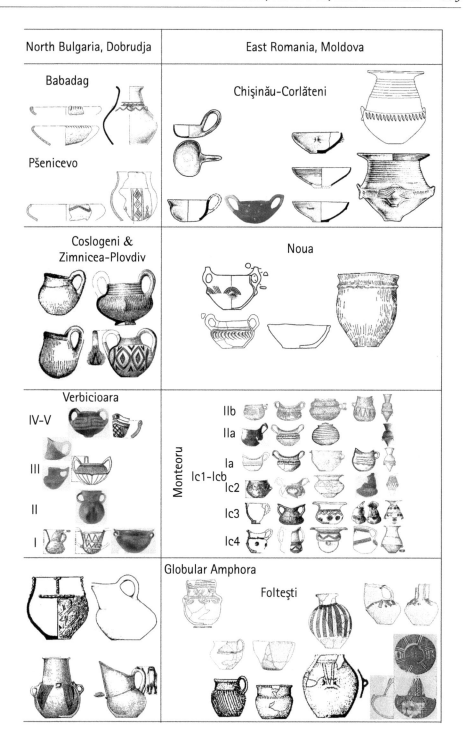

Some metal finds, such as the massive golden lock-rings known from Ampoiţa in Transylvania, Tărnava in Bulgaria, Mala Gruda in Montenegro, and on the western Greek island of Levkas, or silver spiral lock-rings known from several sites in southern Romania, Bulgaria, and far to the east in Moldova or Ukraine, illustrate a system of wide-ranging exchange networks in high-status goods. Similar long-distance contacts are also expressed in some zooarchaological material, such as the bones of fallow deer, at that time native to Turkey east of the Bosphorus but found as imports as far north as Poiana Ampoiului (Romania), Feudvar (Vojvodina), or Ripač (Bosnia-Herzegovina).

Burials of this period are mostly inhumations and found in fairly small groups, as large cemeteries so far are not known. Funerary structures are rather varied: mounds with earthen or stone covering are frequent in western Transylvania (Fig. 47.4, below left; Fig. 47.5), stone slab cists are found in eastern Transylvania, Moldova, and large parts of southern Romania (Fig. 47.4, below right). On the northern Danube shores, the flat inhumation burial cemetery near Zimnicea should be noted. In southern Romania and Bulgaria we also know of earthen mound-burials of 'ochre' or Yamnaya-type. The eastern slab-cist graves could possibly be derived from the Globular Amphora tradition documented in Romanian Moldova and south-eastern Transylvania.

Most settlements have not been extensively excavated, so that no reliable data are available either on house structures or the internal structure of habitation sites. In southern Romania and Bulgaria, however, some older tell sites were still used in the Early Bronze Age (e.g. Glina, Yunatsite), although it is not clear whether this is a continuation from the late Eneolithic or a resettlement after an interruption.

Middle Bronze Age (*c*.2000/1900–1500/1400 BC)

Regional differences, visible during the Early Bronze Age in spite of the common features, are accentuated in the following Middle Bronze Age cultures. Although some groups either continue features or evolved from the later Early Bronze Age (Monteoru, Mureş, Otomani, Tei, Wietenberg, possibly Verbicioara), pottery shapes and decoration display much higher variety in the Middle Bronze Age (see Fig. 47.3, lower middle row).

In the earlier part of the period, pottery shapes already present in the Early Bronze Age become a frequent and characteristic shape common to most cultures (Otomani, Wietenberg, Mureş/Maros/Periam-Pecica, Verbicioara, Tei, Monteoru, Costişa), varying only in details. Besides common elements, each culture may be defined by its own ceramic forms (see Fig. 47.3). The pottery is generally the main defining criterion, more comprehensive definitions (including burial rites, settlement structures, economics, or ritual elements) not usually being taken into account. This has obviously led to a rather unsatisfactory characterization of 'cultures' and 'groups', some of which have their centre of gravity in neighbouring regions (Otomani, in Hungary under the name of Füzesabony and Gyulavarsánd; Vatina, in former Yugoslavia; Costişa, often included in or connected to Biały Potok-Komarov from Ukraine and south-eastern Poland). While for southern Romania and northern Bulgaria the Middle Bronze Age includes Tei and Verbicioara and later Gîrla Mare/Žuto Brdo (see Fig. 47.3, lower middle centre), this period is still largely unknown in southern Bulgaria.

Pottery becomes more and more decorated, sometimes over the entire surface including even the base. Most decoration, especially in the earlier Middle Bronze Age, is incised by various techniques (simple incision, cord, impression, lines of pricked decoration) or

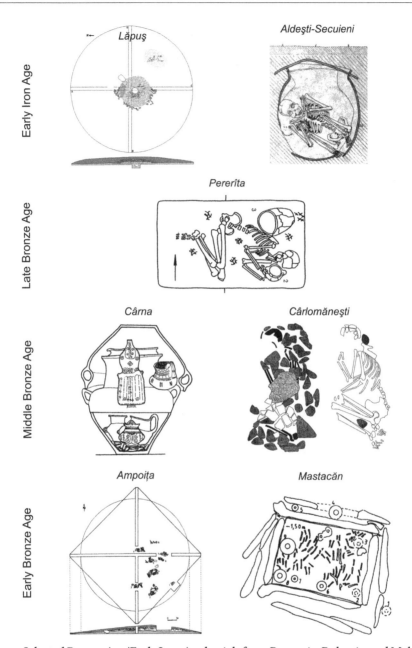

FIG. 47.4 Selected Bronze Age/Early Iron Age burials from Romania, Bulgaria, and Moldova. Various scales.

Source: various (illustration: R. Boroffka).

stamped (e.g. comb-stamps in Wietenberg, concentric circle stamps in Gîrla Mare/Žuto Brdo), and probably held incrusted material, which is, however, seldom preserved (though it is well documented in Gîrla Mare/Žuto Brdo and Tei). Decoration techniques or ornaments may be specific to particular cultural groups (see Fig. 47.3, lower middle row) and can generally be described as spiral-meandroid.

FIG. 47.5 Early Bronze Age burial mounds at Meteş, western Transylvania. Note the typical situation on high hill crests.

Photo: author.

Further east, in Monteoru, a quite different development takes place: cups and *kantharoi* were in use together throughout the evolution. These, as well as the bowls, offering vessels, and *askoi* were initially decorated by finely incised zigzags and 'solar' circles filled by fine concentric lines, and then mainly with zigzag motifs produced by fine applied ribs, changing to finely incised 'stitched' patterns, often accompanying shallow channelling, in the later phases (see Fig. 47.3, lower middle row, right). Neighbouring Costişa (north) and Mnogovalikovaya (east) are less clearly characterized by elongated hatched triangles and applied rib ornaments respectively, although they are present only on a low percentage of the ceramic production.

Generally some overall tendencies may be observed: 1. there is an evolution from spiral to meander motifs; 2. channelled decoration, usually oblique, but sometimes following spiral shapes, appears in the developed phases of most Middle Bronze Age cultures; and 3. a replacement of one-handled cups by other vessel shapes, all presumably for drinking, takes place. Characteristically in Tei and Verbicioara the cups are replaced by *kantharoi*, while in Wietenberg, and to some extent in Otomani and Suciu de Sus, they are replaced by weakly profiled, shallow open bowls, often with an *omphalos* instead of a handle (see Fig. 47.3, lower middle row). Exceptions to this are Mureş/Maros/Periam-Pecica in the south-west and Monteoru in the east (Costişa is probably later replaced by a Monteoru expansion to the north). While the *kantharoi*, in spite of continuity in Mureş/Maros/Periam-Pecica and Monteoru, may be a southern influence, especially since very similar shape and ornament combinations are widely known in southern Romania, Bulgaria, and northern Greece, it is less clear where the shallow *omphalos* bowls originate. At present, one may only remark on the apparent change in drinking habits.

High-status goods probably belonging to the Middle Bronze Age are represented, for example, by the golden daggers and silver axes from Perşinari. They do not occur in settlements or graves, but are deposited separately in hoards. Long-distance connections are indicated by bone psalia (bridle parts), with round plate-shaped variants of the cheek-piece (as in Monteoru and Wietenberg) probably originating far to the east in the steppes, while bar-shaped cheek-pieces appear to be a local development in the Carpathian Basin. Some of these bone objects are ornamented with spiral-based motifs (so-called 'pulley-ornament'), which may be followed as far east as the Ural region, or south to Mycenaean Greece, where they are later in date.

Just like the pottery, burial rites show great variation. For Otomani (mostly known from Hungary), Mureş/Maros/Periam-Pecica (known from Hungary and former Yugoslavia), Monteoru (crouched inhumations; see Fig. 47.4, lower middle row, right), and Gîrla Mare/ Žuto Brdo (cremation; see Fig. 47.4, lower middle row, left), larger cemeteries have been excavated, which may include over a hundred and up to more than a thousand graves (e.g. Cîndeşti, with over 1,500 claimed burials, although still very insufficiently published). Geographically in between, only small cemeteries (not more than 50 graves) are known in the Wietenberg area, while for others, for example Tei and Verbicioara, our knowledge is still extremely scanty. The actual burials also vary: crouched inhumations with vessels, jewellery, and sometimes tools or weapons are characteristic for Otomani and Mureş/Maros/Periam-Pecica; simple cremation burials in urns, rarely with supplementary grave goods, are specific to Wietenberg; cremation and deposition in urns with complex arrangements of vessels, clay figurines, or miniature axes (only in children's graves) are the rule in Gîrla Mare/Žuto Brdo (see Fig. 47.4, lower middle row, left); and crouched inhumations, with vessels, jewellery, and some tools or weapons are encountered in Monteoru (see Fig. 47.4, lower middle row, right). However, for the latter group cremation is also documented and the funerary environment may be complicated, ranging from simple pits, stone cists, stone rings on the old ground surface, to catacomb-like subterranean structures. Further east the Mnogovalikovaya culture practised inhumation burials in large rectangular pits, often with wooden structures and sometimes under earthen mounds (kurgans). Bone belt-buckles, circular with a large central and, sometimes, a small lateral hole, are characteristic grave goods besides pottery.

Settlement structures appear to be determined by landscapes rather than the pottery-defined cultural groups that inhabited them. In the western plains we find multilayer tell sites (e.g. Periam and Pecica for Mureş/Maros/Periam-Pecica, or Derşida for Wietenberg), which are also known in the south-west (e.g. the eponymous site of Verbicioara). For the western sites combined wood-clay architecture is documented (better known from Hungary) and this may hold true for the south-west too, although published excavations over large areas are still lacking. Most sites in Transylvania are not stratified, although some of them were settled for longer periods, judging by the finds. This is also the case in the south-east of Romania, where a single stratigraphic sequence from Popeşti is known for the Tei culture, although no clear house plans are published. Similarly, several sites of the Monteoru culture (e.g. Sărata Monteoru, Bogdăneşti) show many layers (see Fig. 47.6), but house plans or interior settlement structures cannot be reconstructed. Fortification of sites is rare. Further east the Mnogovalikovaya culture is known mainly from burials, and in Bulgaria no well-excavated Middle Bronze Age settlement is known, most finds being either from caves (e.g. Devetaki) or without clear context. The explanation offered for this in these eastern areas is a nomadic way of life based mainly on a mobile pastoralist economy, which left few settlement traces identifiable archaeologically. For the Wietenberg and Monteoru cultures, in fact, a few posthole-plan sites have been published, which together with burnt wattle-and-daub remains have led to the idea of mainly wood-based houses built with supporting posts.

However, a look at traditional buildings in the region today indicates that posts fixed in the earth are rarely used—a more likely possibility are block-houses or houses built on (raised) foundation beams, in both cases the gaps in the wooden structure being sealed by twigs and clay (wattle and daub). These would also leave few traces, even in the case of fire, and would be difficult to identify archaeologically.

Late Bronze Age (*c.*1500/1400–1200/1100 BC)

The Late Bronze Age is marked by two cultural groupings, a south-eastern (Noua-Sabatinovka-Coslogeni) and a western (channelled pottery). Both have roots in the developed Middle Bronze Age, with which they partly overlap chronologically, but become much more unified and widely distributed. In the west and south-west this is to some extent the result of less variation in vessel shape (see Fig. 47.3, upper middle row, left). Characteristic forms are bowls with rims turned inwards, hemispherical cups with high strap-handles, and larger biconical vessels, and firing technology now aims at a black exterior on vessels, sometimes combined with red interiors. Simultaneously the incised decoration is largely replaced by channelling, typical motifs being oblique or garland-shaped channelling (e.g. Ciumeşti, Lăpuş I, Igriţa, Belegiš-Cruceni, Bistreţ-Işalniţa). This change is often described as 'Hallstattization' in the local terminology and continues into the Early Iron Age. In the east and the south *kantharoi* become the characteristic shape, widespread in the Noua-Sabatinovka-Coslogeni complex of Moldavia (both Romanian and Moldova), Transylvania, the Dobrudja and north-eastern Bulgaria, and in the related Čerkovna/Zimnicea-Plovdiv group of central and western Bulgaria (see Fig. 47.3, upper middle row, centre and right). In the latter, a revival of older pottery shapes may also be observed and a special mention should be made of the fact that at Čerkovna and Plovdiv groups of complete vessels were intentionally deposited in wells which had ceased to function. A similar situation may have existed at Govora (late

FIG. 47.6 Sărata Monteoru, eponymous site of the Monteoru culture. Excavation situation in 1995 with complex stone structures and multi-layer stratigraphy.

Photo: author.

Verbicioara), where a contemporaneous group of vessels was discovered as a hoard. While in Čerkovna/Zimnicea-Plovdiv (and late Tei and Verbicioara), the pottery remains decorated with incised, originally encrusted, ornaments, similar to those found in northern Greece, the material of Noua-Sabatinovka-Coslogeni is usually undecorated or sparsely provided with channelling or incisions.

The western and south-western 'Hallstattization' is often explained by western influences, first from the Tumulus cultures, then from early Urnfield phenomena, although vessel shapes can be derived from the larger Middle Bronze Age repertoire, and channelling, although not predominant, was already present in most cultures.

In the south we see a continuous and natural evolution from the late Tei and Verbicioara phases, possibly with an expansion southwards as far as northern Greece. On the other hand, Noua-Sabatinovka-Coslogeni in Moldavia (both Romania and Moldova) and Transylvania is usually considered an eastern intrusion, reaching far back into the Ukraine and southern European Russia, where it may be connected to the Srubnaya culture (see Chapter 48). The reduction of the repertoire of vessel forms, together with specific settlement structures and a presumed pastoralist stock-breeding economy spreading westwards (see below), are interpreted as proof of a highly mobile nomadic society, although this rather simple model has been contested in recent works. While the Noua ceramic repertoire does not have precursors in Transylvania and may indeed be intrusive there, most pottery shapes (and ornaments) can be derived from the preceding Monteoru culture of western Moldavia.

Long-distance connections are illustrated by 'Mycenaean' rapiers discovered in Bulgaria and Romania, mostly belonging to the Late Bronze Age. Stone sceptres of phallic shape (probably originating in the east), or in the shape of axe-sceptres with inward curled tip and mushroom-shaped butt (Drajna, Lozova II, Ljulin, Pobit Kamăk), have good analogies in the example found in the Bronze Age shipwreck of Uluburun off the south Turkish coast. Gold vessels similar to Late Bronze Age shapes, such as those from Vălčitrăn (Bulgaria), Rădeni (Romanian Moldavia), and Kryžovlin (Ukraine), illustrate a high-status exchange network oriented roughly south-west to north-east. Characteristic pins (with perforated head and knobs on the neck) of the Noua group have, conversely, been found as far south as northern Greece.

In the western early channelled pottery groups, the dead were cremated and buried in urns (e.g. in the Belegiš-Cruceni and Bistreț-Ișalnița groups of south-western and southern Romania), although for some groups no clearly defined burials are known (Ciumești, Igrița). In Lăpuș (north-western Romania) the cremation graves were also covered by complex earthen mounds, and a similar situation may have existed in the south-west at the possibly slightly later site of Susani, where, however, in the partly disturbed mound no human bone remains were identified. The Noua-Sabatinovka-Coslogeni communities, in contrast, practiced inhumation in a crouched position, with few vessels, and (rarely) jewellery and tools or weapons as grave goods; apart from minor details, this situation occurs fairly uniformly throughout Moldavia (Romania and Moldova) and Transylvania (see Fig. 47.4, upper middle row, centre). The cemeteries sometimes included burials in or on older tumuli, but mounds were not raised anew. To the south crouched inhumation burials are also documented from Zimnicea and Krušovica, while cremations under mounds with Čerkovna/Zimnicea-Plovdiv pottery were excavated at Batak.

Fortified settlements, some of enormous size (e.g. Cornești, with an inner rampart enclosing an area of 72 hectares and the fourth outer one encircling 1,722 hectares: Szentmiklosi et al. 2011), are known from south-western Romania. However, the houses and the internal structuring of these sites are as yet unexplored. In the large open site of Dridu in south-eastern Romania (unfortunately still largely unpublished), mainly settled in the Belegiš II period (the transition between Late Bronze Age and Early Iron Age), several dozen loosely strewn shallow pit houses were excavated. In southern Romania and Bulgaria, Late Bronze Age and Early Iron Age layers are encountered in tell settlements, but there are generally no preceding Middle Bronze Age traces and the houses or interior structures remain largely unknown. In north-eastern Bulgaria (Durankulak) rectangular stone foundations have been attributed to the Coslogeni group. To the east, in Moldova and Ukraine, a specific settlement type of the Noua-Sabatinovka-Coslogeni complex is the so-called ash-mound (*zolnik*), usually round or oval low mounds with whitish-grey soil showing up against the darker surroundings. They are often found in groups and may contain pits and fireplaces, but their formation and function is still controversial. The unusually large quantity of animal bones they contain, their presumed temporary use, and the limited ceramic repertoire, have been interpreted as indicating a mobile pastoralist society (see above). Such ash-mounds are still unknown for the western Noua group in Transylvania, the traces of which are often found together with late Wietenberg pottery.

Early Iron Age (*c*.1200/1100–800/700 BC)

The Early Iron Age sees the disappearance of the steppe influence (Noua-Sabatinovka-Coslogeni) and the spread eastwards of the early Hallstatt channelled pottery groups, closely connected to the Urnfield groups further west. A large northern block, represented by the Gáva-Holihrady culture, extends from eastern Hungary through the whole of Transylvania to Moldova (see Fig. 47.2, top row, left). Belegiš II-type pottery spreads in the Romanian Banat, throughout southern Romania and into Moldova, including a slightly later eastern variant, the Chișinău-Corlăteni group. Both groups are characterized by channelled pottery, usually fired black on the exterior and reddish inside. A major difference between the two groups may be observed in the larger vessels, which in Gáva-Holihrady are often provided with exaggerated large hypertrophic upwards-curving knobs on the body (see Fig. 47.3, top row, left), while the Belegiš II urns bear smaller paired knobs pointing both upwards and downwards (see Fig. 47.3, top row, right). Some ceramic shapes and decorations clearly show continuity from the Late Bronze Age (see Fig. 47.3, top row). In the Dobrudja, Bulgaria and, somewhat later in parts of Moldova, the channelled pottery may be combined with stamped and incised decoration (Babadag, Čatalka, Pšeničevo, Cozia, Saharna) (see Fig. 47.3, top row, centre), which may represent the origin of the widespread later Basarabi culture. Interestingly, the Bulgarian channelled pottery, apart from the generally common features, displays connections to the Gáva-Holihrady group of the north, rather than to the immediately neighbouring Belegiš II types of southern Romania. Traces of these elements may also be found further south in Troy VIIb or in the so-called 'Barbarian Ware' of Greece.

The Belegiš II society disposed of their dead by cremation and burial in cemeteries (e.g. at Belgrade-Karaburma, Serbia) and this was probably the case throughout the extensive territory where this type of pottery is distributed, although we know only isolated graves from the region discussed here. Similarly the burials of the Gáva-Holihrady complex are known only from isolated finds, also by cremation and deposited in urns. Cremation graves are also mentioned for the pottery groups with channelled and stamped/incised ware from Bulgaria, but none has been excavated professionally. Inhumation in large typical Gáva-Holihrady vessels is also known (see Fig. 47.4, top, right), but again only in a few cases. Several inhumation graves in settlement pits, crouched or extended on the back, have been excavated in Babadag sites, but it is not clear wether this was the regular burial practice. The Lăpuș group still raised earthen mounds over the burials (see Fig. 47.4, top left), but this may be a local tradition also observed in the pottery. However, in southern Romania (e.g. Meri) and Bulgaria (e.g. Sboryanovo) inhumation graves under tumuli are also known from the Early Iron Age.

Some of the fortified sites from western Romania (e.g. Sântana) were erected or still in use in this period and similar settlements are known starting from the early Gáva period in Transylvania (e.g. Teleac). At Teleac wooden beams had been built into the rampart and the location of houses could be determined by roughly rectangular patches of burnt wattle and daub, presumably from collapsed walls, but there are few data on the actual construction of these houses and the excavated surfaces are too small to allow conclusions on the general interior layout of the site. Fortified sites, and rectangular pit houses or patches of burnt wattle and daub have also been documented in Moldavia (Romania and Moldova) (e.g. Grăniceşti, Trinca, Saharna), but large areas in settlements have not been exposed. From Bulgaria we know Early Iron Age layers from several tell sites, but here too preservation or the extent of excavations do not allow a proper reconstruction of interior structuring.

Metal

Metal finds have so far hardly been mentioned: they are known in fairly large quantities, rarely from graves or settlements, often from hoards, a phenomenon already well known from the Eneolithic period, and from isolated finds. Copper, gold, and silver were widely available in Romania and Bulgaria, but had to be imported to Moldavia (Romania and Moldova). Tin deposits are known from the Transylvanian Carpathians, although their possible prehistoric exploitation is not certain (Boroffka 2009: 120, Fig. 1; list of minerals by site, 141–6).

For the Early Bronze Age, hoards of torcs with curled ends (*Ösenhalsringe*), for example at Deva, or of shaft-hole axes, for example at Vâlcele (Fig. 47.7, bottom right), may be cited as representative, the latter types even going back to Eneolithic precursors. In both cases mainly a single type of object was deposited, complete and not fragmentary, indicating a specific selection of objects that is difficult to reconcile with the purely materialistic explanation that hoards were a form of wealth accumulation (see Chapter 7). From settlements and/or graves, flat axes, early leaf-shaped daggers, often with grip-tongue or spike, pins, spiral spectacle pendants, the earliest forms of crescentic pendants with inward curling ends, and gold and silver lock-rings (see above) are also known, so that tools/weapons and jewellery are all present. The various shaft-hole axes especially continued to develop in a characteristically Carpathian manner throughout the Bronze Age (see Fig. 47.7, right columns). All analysed objects from this period have proved to be of copper, sometimes with added arsenic, while tin-bronzes appear only from the Middle Bronze Age onwards.

The Middle Bronze Age sees the appearance of several new features, besides the introduction of tin-bronze. Bracelets with large protective spirals may be connected to the

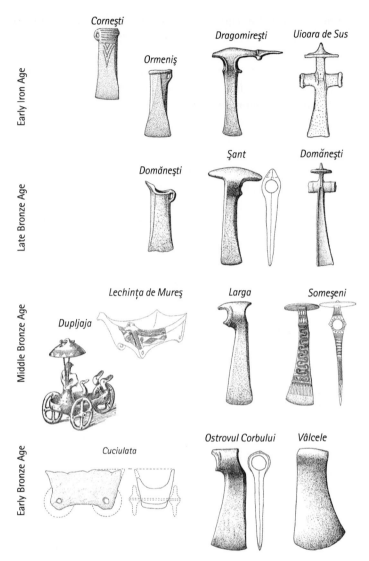

FIG. 47.7 Outline evolution of clay vehicle models, metal shaft-hole axes and axes with disc (and spike) in Romania, Bulgaria, and Moldova. Various scales.

Source: various (illustration: R. Boroffka).

introduction of swords and daggers with riveted grips, all of which may be richly decorated with spiral motifs reminiscent of the dense and complex ornaments encountered on the pottery of this period. Socketed spearheads also occur for the first time, as do metal knives and sickles. Pins and pendants are more frequent and closely connected to types widely spread through central Europe, such as those with perforated globular head, or the so-called Cypriot pins. The lock-rings evolve to shapes with boat-shaped solid or hollow ends, which are very widespread throughout the Old World, including the Near East and Asia. Most metal objects are again known from hoards, with mainly jewellery being represented in the burials of some cultures (e.g. lock-rings, frequent in Monteoru graves), while settlement finds are generally rare. We know of few hoards datable to the later Middle Bronze Age and the transition to the Late Bronze Age, but since the typological evolution, for example of shaft-hole axes and axes with disc or pointed butt, appears to be continuous up to the Early Iron Age (see Fig. 47.7, right column), this may rather be a problem of correctly dating the hoards, which often contain only one type of object and thus cannot always be cross-dated. On closer inspection, swords and spearheads are actually quite rare, whereas traditional shaft-hole axes (now with more profiled shaft-hole) and newly developed axes with disc butt are very common. They are also often decorated with complex spiral motifs of the Apa-Hajdúsámson style, echoing the pottery, although this is gradually reduced in the course of time. While the function of the shaft-hole axes may theoretically have been as tools or weapons, the disc-butted axes, later also those with pointed butt, were more probably used as weapons, presumably also with representative and/or symbolic meaning. Thus we observe here a major difference in weaponry, and presumably fighting tactics, from central Europe to the northwest and Greece to the south—in those regions daggers and swords are used, while in the Balkan-Carpathian region 'battle-axes', if we can call them that, were the preferred weapon, both in fighting and as objects of display. The sword, adapted to local taste by decoration and other details (e.g. Apa), in spite of rare local developments (e.g. the Boiu-Keszthely type), may have been more important in demonstrating high-status 'foreign' contacts. In Moldova, and to some degree in Bulgaria, the evolution of the dagger especially is more connected to the eastern tradition with grip-tongue or spike, rather than to the western one with riveted grip, and combinations of the two methods may even occur.

In the Late Bronze Age and the Early Iron Age, hoards, which can individually include around 1,000 kg of metal (e.g. Aiud, Şpălnaca II, Uioara), are the main find category for bronze objects. Several object types continue a logical evolution: sickles, diversifying into many variants, shaft-hole axes with more and more baroque elongations, axes with disc and spike butt (see Fig. 47.7, right column) (both axe shapes gradually becoming rarer), and the latest types of lock-ring. Besides these, a large number of new forms begin to replace traditional ones. In the first place socketed axes, mainly the Transylvanian type and the 'beaked' type (with asymmetric socket mouth), both occasionally already present in the last phases of some classical Middle Bronze Age cultures, become frequent and widely distributed (see Fig. 47.7, top, left). Later they develop in various ways, and become decorated with triangular ribs that have many variations. Two further aspects of the socketed axes may be mentioned: 1. the inner-Carpathian examples are usually provided with an 'ear' near the socket for fixing, whereas those outside the Carpathians, in Moldova and Bulgaria, often lack this ear and are perforated on one of the broad sides instead; 2. the eastern axes seem, on present knowledge, to be the oldest and may go back to Eurasian roots (the Sejma-Turbino culture area), now dated as far back as the turn of the third to second millennia BC (see Chapter 48).

A further category, specific to the region, is represented by the large and richly decorated belts made from sheet bronze. Besides these local developments, during the Late Bronze Age a strong eastern influence may be observed, especially in the shape of the daggers, but also on some sickles and pins. This, however, does not persist long into the Early Iron Age. At that time, similar to the central European connections visible in the Urnfield-related pottery, strong relations to the west or north-west predominate, represented for example by swords, jewellery of all kinds, and metal vessels, of types well known and very widespread in central Europe. Although iron is present in the Early Iron Age, in isolated instances also in Bronze Age contexts, it is still rare and can hardly be considered a material in common use.

Transport and the Symbolic Meaning of Vehicles

The exploitation of animal traction had major consequences for transportation, communication, and warfare. The Carpathian region, among others, is known for early clay models of four-wheeled carts from the Baden complex, probably drawn by bovid pairs (see Chapter 22). They do not appear to have any direct connection to a specific phenomenon of the Carpathian Basin, where in the Bronze Age clay models of vehicles again occur frequently, in contrast to other parts of Europe. These are mostly of rectangular shape and four-wheeled, with few indications of having been drawn by bovids (shown by horned protomes, e.g. on those from Derșida and Lechința de Mureș) (see Fig. 47.7, middle, left). The earliest such models, undecorated, are known east of the Carpathians from Glina-Schneckenberg context (see Fig. 47.7, lower left), and they remain in use throughout most of the Middle Bronze Age in Hungary, Transylvania, and along the lower Danube (Otomani, Wietenberg, Gîrla Mare/Žuto Brdo), but disappear from the record in the Late Bronze Age. These models, as well as the bone cheekpieces, indicate both transport and the use of horses as traction animals. The domesticated horse is documented since the Early Bronze Age from bone material found on both sides of the Carpathians (e.g. Poiana Ampoiului, Năeni), so that the connection is further corroborated.

A use in warfare, even of the four-wheeled carts, cannot be completely excluded. In the Near East similar heavy vehicles, indeed pulled by equids (possibly onagers), are clearly shown in the context of fighting. The Middle Bronze Age wagon models of the Carpathian Basin, often with a raised front, formally correspond well to some of these early fighting wagons of the Orient.

Models of light spoked wheels are also present in almost all these cultures and may be connected to the light chariot. Clay models, not just of spoked wheels but also of chariots, are only known from the Gîrla Mare/Žuto Brdo culture (see Chapter 22), where they are also combined with bird-headed figurines and sometimes have water-bird protomes as well. One model from Dupljaja carries a bird-figure on the front edge of the vehicle body and two bars projecting forwards, ending in bird heads and with a third spoked wheel placed in between them for stability (see Fig. 45.5b; Fig. 47.7, lower left). This is the earliest indication of a forked pole, inside which the traction animal would have stood. Although harnessing by a yoke is possible in principle, collar-harnessing would transmit power more effectively and be more likely, even though collars are otherwise not known before the first millennium BC, even in the Near East.

It is likely that the cart and chariot had not only a practical function for transportation, but also bore ideological meaning. The models, as symbols of real wagons, carry a transcendental meaning as transport for the transition to another world from as early as the Baden culture, where such finds come exclusively from graves. This aspect later peaks in the European wagon graves of the Hallstatt and La Tène periods, and actually continues to the present day in the form of especially ostentatious hearses or car-shaped coffins. Besides this, they probably mark a special social position of the buried individuals, since not everyone could afford to keep a vehicle, along with the animals required to pull it.

Although such a symbolic-ritual aspect is not so clear for the Bronze Age models from the Carpathian Basin, which come mostly from settlements, it is not entirely absent. Most of the Middle Bronze Age models of the Otomani culture were discovered in tell settlements, which must be considered as 'central sites'. The Middle Bronze Age in the Carpathian Basin, from which most wagon models are known, is a phase when an elite social class had achieved a dominant social position and was concerned to demonstrate it, amongst other things by valuable treasures and by fortifications. Part of these demonstrations of power also featured the ownership and display of vehicles, which are reflected in the concentration of wagon models at the 'central sites'. The cart depiction from Veľke Raškovce (see Chapter 44) belongs in a funerary context, and wagon models or their parts were found in funerary contexts at Nižná Myšľa (Slovakia), as well as in the Gîrla Mare/Žuto Brdo and Wietenberg cultures. Representations of animals in Wietenberg are found only on wagon models or as bird-shaped vessels. During the Late Bronze Age and Early Iron Age these models disappear from the archaeological record (see Fig. 47.7, left column), to reappear only in the Hallstatt B3/C period as cauldron-wagons, again in combination with water-bird protomes, both in funerary contexts (Bujoru) and in hoards (Vaidei/Orăștie).

Conclusion

Widespread uniformity may be observed in the Early Bronze Age of this region in ceramic shapes and decoration styles. Local differences in this aspect are largely due to influences from neighbouring regions (Hungary in the west, Poland and western Ukraine in the north, the steppes in the east, Greece and Turkey in the south). Settlement structures and details of settlement sites are insufficiently known, while burial practices underline regional differences, and could be more extensively used to define cultural groups than has been the case so far. Prestige goods with wide-ranging parallels are especially important for underlining long-distance interconnections.

The Middle Bronze Age of this area too may in a way be bound up with greater regional variety of pottery shapes and a general tendency for spiral-based ornamentation. However, the rich ornaments also make geographically restricted development more evident. Prestige goods are still present, but display fewer long-distance connections, probably with the exception of the horse gear. Again settlement structures and details of houses are largely unknown. Funerary practices underline the regionalization visible in the pottery styles. Outside influences are still present from the adjacent areas, but appear less striking—the period could actually be characterized as one where local groups reached their high point.

In the Late Bronze Age the western margin of the region discussed here continues a local development, characterized by western influences. Much of the east and the south are, in contrast, dominated by eastern and southern elements visible in pottery and metal objects, to some degree even in settlement types (*zolniki*) or burials. Long-distance interconnections seem to reinforce the eastern and southern orientation.

This dramatically changes in the Early Iron Age, although some local traditions continue. The eastern and southern orientation is markedly reduced, while western elements penetrate as far east as the steppes or western Turkey. Some antecedents are present (channelled decoration, some metal types) and combine to form cultures connected to the central European Urnfield tradition, also visible in new bronze objects brought in to the area from outside. This is also supported by the appearance of very large fortifications, though the inner structure of these is still little known due to a lack of large surface excavations. Few graves are known, but besides some local continuity, appear to follow the same westerly trend towards cremation and burial in urns.

Bibliography

Burtănescu, F. (2002). *Epoca timpurie a bronzului între Carpați și Prut cu unele contribuții la problemele perioadei premergătoare epocii bronzului în Moldova*, Bibliotheca de Thracologie, 37. Bucharest: Institutul Român de Tracologie.

Boroffka, N. (1994). *Die Wietenberg-Kultur. Ein Beitrag zur Erforschung der Bronzezeit in Südosteuropa*, Universitätsforschungen zur Prähistorischen Archäologie, 19. Bonn: Habelt.

—— (2009). 'Mineralische Rohstoffvorkommen und der Forschungsstand des urgeschichtlichen Bergbaues in Rumänien', in M. Bartelheim and H. Stäuble (eds.), *Die Wirtschaftlichen Grundlagen der Bronzezeit Europas/The Economic Foundations of the European Bronze Age*, Forschungen zur Archäometrie und Altertumswissenschaft, 4. Rahden/Westfalen: Verlag Marie Leidorf.

Cavruc, V. and Dumitroaia, G. (eds.) (2001). *Cultura Costișa în contextul epocii bronzului din România*. Piatra Neamț: Muzeul de Istorie Piatra Neamț.

Chernykh, E. N. (1978). 'Gornoe delo i metallurgiya v drevneyshey B'lgarii'. Sofia: Izdatel'stvo B'lgarskoy Akademii Nauk.

Ciugudean, H. (1996). *Epoca timpurie a bronzului în centrul și sud-vestul Transilvaniei*, Bibliotheca Thracologica, 13. Bucharest: Institutul Român de Tracologie.

Dergachev, V. A. (1986). 'Moldaviya I sosednie territoriy v epokhu bronzy (analiz i kharakteristika kul'turnikh grupi)'. Kishinev: Shtiintsa.

—— (2002). *Die äneolithischen und bronzezeitlichen Metallfunde aus Moldavien*. Prähistorische Bronzefunde XX,9. Stuttgart: Franz Steiner.

Florescu, A. C. (1991). *Repertoriul culturii Noua-Coslogeni din România. Așezări și necropole*, Cultura și Civilizația la Dunărea de Jos, 9/Biblioteca Thracologica, 1. Călărași: S. C. Alcor Impex SRL.

Georgiev, G. I., Merpert, N. Y., Katincharov, R. V., and Dimitrov, D. G. (eds.) (1979). 'Ezero. Rannebronzovoto selishche'. Sofia: Izdatel'stvo na B'lgarskata Akademiya na Naukite.

Gogâltan, F. (1999). *Bronzul timpuriu și mijlociu în Banatul Românesc și pe cursul inferior al Mureșului. Cronologia și descoperirile de metal*, Bibliotheca Historica et Archaeologica Banatica, 23. Timișoara: Editura Orizonturi Universitare.

Gumă, M. (1993). *Civilizația primei epoci a fierului în sud-vestul României*, Bibliotheca Thracologica, 4. Bucharest: Institutul Român de Tracologie.

—— (1997). *Epoca bronzului în Banat. Orizonturi cronologice și manifestări culturale/The Bronze Age in Banat: Chronological Levels and Cultural Entities*, Bibliotheca Historica et Archaeologica Banatica, 5. Timișoara: Editura Mirton.

Hänsel, B. (1976). *Beiträge zur regionalen und chronologischen Gliederung der älteren Hallstattzeit an der unteren Donau*, Beiträge zur Ur- und Frühgeschichtlichen Archäologie des Mittelmeer-Kulturraumes, 16–17. Bonn: Rudolf Habelt Verlag GmbH.

Jugănaru, G. (2005). *Cultura Babadag*, I, Biblioteca Istro-Pontică, Seria Arheologie, 7. Constanța: Ex Ponto.

Krauss, R. (2008). 'Die deutschen und österreichischen Grabungen in Bulgarien', *Bulgarien-Jahrbuch*: 67–89.

László, A. (1994). *Începuturile epocii fierului la est de Carpați. Culturile Gáva-Holihrady și Corlăteni-Chișinău pe teritoriul Moldovei*. Bibliotheca Thracologica 6. Bucharest: Institutul Român de Tracologie.

Leahu, V. (2003). *Cultura Tei. Grupul cultural Fundenii Doamnei. Probleme ale epocii bronzului în Muntenia*, Bibliotheca Thracologica, 38. Bucharest: Institutul Român de Tracologie.

Leshchakov, K. (1992). Izsledovaniya vărchu bronzovata epokha v Trakiya I. Sravitelna stratigrafiya na selishchnite mogili ot rannata bronzova epokha v Yugoistochna Bălgariya. *Godishnik na sofiiskiya Universitet" Sv. Kliment Okhridski", Istroricheskii fakultet* 84-85/1999-2000: 5–119.

Levițki, O. (1994). *Cultura Hallstattului canelat la răsărit de Carpați*, Bibliotheca Thracologica, 7. Bucharest: Institutul Român de Tracologie.

Morintz, S. (1978). *Contribuții arheologice la istoria tracilor timpurii, I. Epoca bronzului in spațul carpato-balcanic*, Biblioteca de Arheologie, 34. Bucharest: Editura Academiei Republicii Socialiste România.

Motzoi-Chicideanu, I. (2011). *Obiceiuri funerare în epoca bronzului la Dunărea Mijlocie și Inferioară*, I–II. Bucharest: Editura Academiei Române.

Nestor, J. (1932). 'Der Stand der Vorgeschichtsforschung in Rumänien', *Bericht der Römisch-Germanischen Kommission*, 22/1933: 11–181 and pl. 1–27.

—— (1960). 'Începuturile societății gentilice patriarhale și ale destrămării orînduirii comunei primitive. Epoca bronzului', in C. Daicoviciu, E. M. Condurachi, and J. Nestor (eds.), *Istoria Romîniei*, 1. Bucharest: Editura Academiei Republicii Populare Romîne, 90–132.

Nicic, A. (2008). *Interferențe cultural-cronologice în nord-vestul Pontului Euxin la finele mil. II—începutul mil. I a. Chr*, Bibliotheca 'Tyragetia', 15. Chișinău: Muzeul Național de Arheologie și Istorie a Moldovei.

Nikolova, L. (ed.) (1999). *The Balkans in Later Prehistory: Periodization, Chronology and Cultural development in the Final Copper and Early Bronze Age (Fourth and Third Millennia BC)*, British Archaeological Reports (International Series), 791. Oxford: Archaeopress.

Panayotov, I. (1995). 'The Bronze Age in Bulgaria: studies and problems', in D. W. Bailey and I. Panayotov (eds.), *Prehistoric Bulgaria*, Monographs in World Archaeology, 22. Madison: Prehistory Press, 243–52.

Petrescu-Dîmbovița, M. (1977). *Depozitele de bronzuri din România*, Biblioteca de Arheologie, 30. Bucharest: Editura Academiei Republicii Socialiste România.

—— (1978). *Die Sicheln in Rumänien. Mit Corpus der jung- und spätbronzezeitlichen Horte Rumäniens*. Prähistorische Bronzefunde XVIII,1. München: C. H. Beck.

Prox, A. (1941). *Die Schneckenbergkultur*. Kronstadt: Verlag Burzenländer Museum.

Roska, M. (1942). *Erdély régészeti repertóriuma I. Őskor/Thesaurus Antiquitatum Transsilvanicarum I. Praehistorica*. Kolozsvár: Nagy Jenő és fia Könyvnyomdaja.

Șandor-Chicideanu, M. (2003). *Cultura Žuto Brdo-Gârla Mare. Contribuții la cunoașterea epocii bronzului la Dunărea Mijlocie și Inferioară, I-II*. Cluj-Napoca: Editura Nereamia Napocae.

Sava, E. (2002). *Die Bestattungen der Noua-Kultur. Ein Beitrag zur Erforschung spätbronzezeitlicher Bestattungsriten zwischen Dnestr und Westkarpaten, mit Katalogbeiträgen von N. Boroffka, L. Dascălu, Gh. Dumitroaia, E. V. Jarovoj, and T. Soroceanu*, Prähistorische Archäologie in Südosteuropa, 19. Kiel: Verlag Oetker/Voges.

Savva, E. N. (1992). 'Kul'tura mnogovalikovoi keramiki Dnestrovsko-Prutskogo mezhdurech'ya (po materialam pogrebal'nogo obryada)'. Kishinev: Shtiintsa.

Szentmiklosi, A., Heeb, B., Heeb, J., Harding, A., Krause, R., and Becker, H. (2011). 'Cornești-Iarcuri—a Bronze Age town in the Romanian Banat?', *Antiquity*, 85: 819–38.

Tončeva, G. (1980). *Chronologie du Hallstatt ancien dans la Bulgarie de Nord-Est*, Studia Thracica, 5. Sofia: Academia Litterarum Bulgarica.

Ursulescu, N. (1998). *Începuturile istoriei pe teritoriul României*. Iași: Demiurg.

Vulpe, A. (1970). *Die Äxte und Beile in Rumänien I*. Prähistorische Bronzefunde IX,2. München: C. H. Beck.

—— (1975). *Die Äxte und Beile in Rumänien II*. Prähistorische Bronzefunde IX,5. München: C. H. Beck.

CHAPTER 48

UKRAINE AND SOUTH RUSSIA IN THE BRONZE AGE

HERMANN PARZINGER

The cultural relationships in the regions north of the Black Sea, between the Carpathian Mountains in the west and the Urals in the east, were always strongly shaped by the natural features of this area (Fig. 48.1). To the far south stretches the steppe belt, following the northern shore of the Black Sea. In the north, its border lies slightly north of the Dnieper bend; further west, it narrows towards the junction of the Prut with the Danube. The forest-steppe zone, which runs roughly parallel to the steppe belt, adjoins it to the north; in the west, however, it spreads into the region north of the curve formed by the Carpathians. The mixed forest zone finally begins in the area around Kiev and extends far to the north, taking in large parts of the East European lowlands, in what are today central Russia and Belarus. These forest regions had brown and grey forest soils (*Rasenpodsolböden*), and the diverse flora and fauna of the forest offered hunters and gatherers an almost ideal environment, which is why it was important to these economies longer than elsewhere. The forest-steppe zone broadly coincides with the extremely fertile black-earth belt, which is best suited to agriculture. Towards the south, the black earth turns into less moisture-retentive chestnut-coloured soil, which covers the largest part of the steppe belt. There, agriculture is almost impossible without artificial irrigation; however, the dominant herbaceous plants have important nutrients for grazing animals, which is why the steppe was always the preferred terrain for animal husbandry.

The climatic changes over the last five thousand years can be observed in the fluctuating water levels of the Black Sea and the rivers, lakes, and peat-bogs, and also in the differing plant cover. Each climate change had immediate and lasting consequences in the steppe, whereas it affected the forest-steppe only slightly, and the forest zone was scarcely touched. The forest forms a self-contained, stable ecosystem, which could only be altered by major, widespread climatic shifts.

During the Early Bronze Age, in the late fourth and early third millennia BC, eastern Europe had a dry, temperate, continental climate. The boundary between steppe and forest-steppe ran somewhat further north of its present position. In the regions with lower rainfall far to the south, semi-arid landscapes developed, and the forests in the gorges and on the

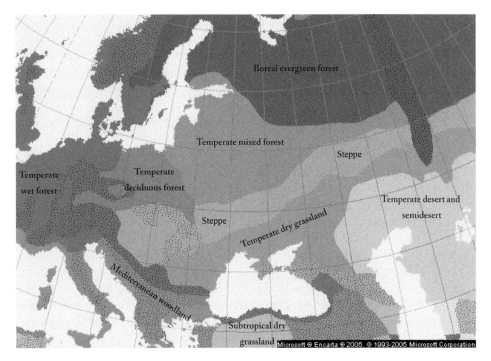

FIG. 48.1 Map showing the extension of the different vegetation zones in Russia and Ukraine.

rivers receded sharply, at times disappearing altogether. A distinct improvement in climatic conditions returned only at the start of the seventh century BC, towards the close of the Bronze Age, when bands of settlers from the steppe were replaced by groups of horse-borne nomads of the earlier Iron Age, and the first Greek settlers had already established themselves on the north coast of the Black Sea.

THE FOUNDATIONS OF BRONZE AGE CULTURAL DEVELOPMENT: THE ENEOLITHIC

Any description of the Bronze Age should start with an examination of the Eneolithic that preceded it, a period in which metalworking emerged, gradually assumed importance, and began to shape cultural and social structures ever more strongly. During the Eneolithic, the gradual process of shaking off the Neolithic chains also occurred in Ukraine and southern Russia, as an entirely new cultural period dawned with the Bronze Age.

Soon after the middle of the fifth millennium BC fundamental changes occurred in the North Pontic area, particularly affecting the steppe belt and the eastern forest-steppe belt. The Late Neolithic cultures of this area (Seroglazov, Rakushechny Yar, Dnieper-Donets, and Sursk) came to an end almost simultaneously and were replaced by new cultural groups of a different nature, which were already processing copper. For that reason this is designated a new period—the Eneolithic. At the same time, the Neolithic Bug-Dniester culture was replaced in the western forest-steppe by the developed Tripolye culture, whose easternmost sites are scattered almost as far as the middle Dnieper. Farming life, with agriculture and animal husbandry, had already begun in the western forest-steppe—probably in response to a stimulus from the Carpathian zone—in the sixth millennium BC, and remained unaltered in the Eneolithic; then, after the middle of the fifth millennium BC, systematically laid-out large settlements, reflecting considerable numbers of inhabitants, appeared in the area occupied by the Tripolye culture.

Quite different conditions prevailed in the steppe belt at the same time. In the area between the Dnieper and the Don, the Eneolithic arrivals are combined as the Sredni Stog culture, which corresponds to the Novodanilovka culture further west towards the southern Bug, and to the Khvalynsk culture in the east on the Volga (Parzinger 1998: 460–2, Fig. 2). This picture has become even more complex now, with the identification of numerous other Eneolithic groups (Rassamakin 1994; 2004). Soon after the middle of the fifth millennium BC climatic conditions became optimal between the Volga and the Dnieper, with mild summers and winters and less precipitation. The steppe grass-cover improved and the vegetation as a whole became more varied. These changes favoured the importance of animal husbandry, which had intensified in the Eneolithic. Fundamental innovations also occurred in burial customs, because the supine position was widely replaced by the crouched position, and kurgan burials appeared beside flat graves for the first time. Grave goods now reveal social stratification; the richer burials in Khvalynsk, for example, contain stone clubs and axes, animal-head sceptres, long flint blades, and ornaments for clothing, not least those made of copper.

In the North Pontic area, the metal objects are predominantly of pure copper. E. N. Chernykh used spectral analysis to determine that the metal came mostly from Balkan and Carpathian mines; the deposits in Ukraine, the Caucasus, and the Urals were evidently not yet being mined in the fifth millennium BC (Chernykh 1992: 42–5). If Chernykh's thesis is supported by current research, this would establish a dense network of extensive trading links.

The changes described in burial customs indicate that tightly structured social groups had already formed in the North Pontic steppe belt during the Eneolithic period after the middle of the fifth millennium BC. Dominant persons identified themselves by means of their grave goods and grave construction (the first kurgans), and marked their status through their clothing (copper jewellery) and symbols of power (mace and sceptre). They alone had the opportunity to access the Carpathian copper that had apparently reached the Volga area. Since even children's graves echo this differentiation in burial customs, membership of social groups appears to have been determined by birth.

Of course it is only certain aspects of a fundamental cultural change that are apparent to us. Yet its temporal coincidence with the advancing steppe landscape of the regions north of the Black Sea on the one hand, and the demonstrably greater impetus towards animal husbandry on the other, is clearly no accident; rather, there must be a causal relationship. The constant pressure to defend herds and grazing lands could have led to the emergence of a warrior class, whose members were social leaders and directed the community settlement. An obviously ritual burial of horses' heads in the Dereivka site appeared to fit this image very well, and was seen as evidence for the domestication of the horse and its use as a riding mount by the late fifth millennium BC. However, this find has not yet been dated. Moreover, the remains could be those of wild, rather than domestic horses; there is still no evidence for their use as riding mounts at this early time.

All of these innovations, however, remained confined to the steppe and forest-steppe belts. Spread across the mixed forest regions of northern Ukraine and the central Russian lowland plain to the Volga area and the Kama Valley, there were groups of late pricked and comb-stamped ceramic cultures, for example the Volosovo culture. Settlement sites with partially sunken earth-houses or dugouts (*poluzemlyanki*) yielded simply formed, round- and pointed-based vessels with imprint-decorated outer surfaces, as well as an extensive range of implements, including harpoons, made of flint, bone, and horn. These deposits obviously belong to an older Mesolithic-Neolithic tradition (Krainov 1987a: Pl. 1–7). Copper objects appear only in isolation; however, animal figures, associated with the forest fauna (bears, fish, beavers, and so on) and made of bone or stone, are typical. The difference from the world of the steppe and forest-steppe could not be clearer.

Arsenical Bronzes, Wagons, and Domestic Horses: The Beginnings of the Bronze Age

Soon after the middle of the fourth millennium BC, the Yamnaya—or Pit Grave culture, with its characteristic graves (Fig. 48.2)—developed in the steppe between the southern Bug and lower Volga on the foundation of Eneolithic cultures, such as Sredni Stog and Khvalynsk. In an early phase its range stretched from the western reaches of the Urals initially only as far as the southern Bug; then, in a later phase, it extended considerably farther west (Parzinger 1998: 468, Fig. 7.1). Despite regional peculiarities, the material culture becomes remarkably standardized within this area (Chernykh 1992, 83–5; Rassamakin 1994). The first arsenical bronzes appear in the Yamnaya context, although most metal artefacts are still made of copper. The beginning of the Yamnaya culture coincides approximately with the beginning of other early Bronze Age cultures, such as Kura-Arax, Maikop, Kemi Oba, Ezero, and Troy I. Calibrated radiocarbon dates place Yamnaya in the late fourth and first half of the third millennia BC, corresponding to the still Eneolithic cultures of Botai in North Kazakhstan and Afanasevo in southern Siberia, east of the Urals. Occasionally the survival of a remnant Yamnaya culture is recognized up to the second half of the third millennium BC, by which time the succeeding Katakombnaya (Catacomb) culture had already developed (Pustovalov 1994).

The close connections between the Yamnaya culture and preceding culture groups of the Eneolithic are particularly apparent in pottery. The same is true further east, in the Volga region, where the grave goods in the Eneolithic burials of Khvalynsk barely differ from those in early Yamnaya burials. These observations show that the bearers of the Yamnaya culture had not migrated from the east; rather, their origins were in various Eneolithic regional groups (Shaposhnikova 1985). Although the early Yamnaya only occasionally reached the forest-steppe further north, a later phase of this culture saw them firmly settled there. At the same time there was an influx into the North Caucasian steppes and areas in the northern Balkans, where solitary Yamnaya kurgans appear. Larger bands penetrated into the eastern

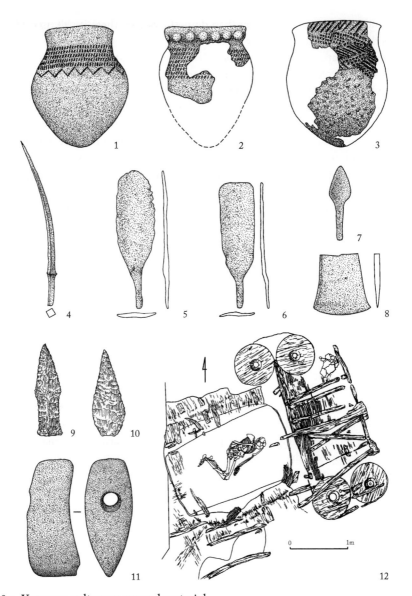

FIG. 48.2 Yamnaya culture grave and material.

Source: redrawn from Shaposhnikova 1985 (1–11) and Gei 2000 (12).

Carpathian basin, where they found living conditions comparable to the North Pontic steppe. Regional groups of Yamnaya culture arose in all of these landscapes.

Little is known about the Yamnaya settlements in the absence of larger-scale excavations of settlement sites. Important insights came from Mikhaylovka on the lower Dnieper, where the transition from Eneolithic to the Early Bronze Age was easily discernible. The lowest stratum, Layer I, still belongs to the Eneolithic Sredni Stog period, Layer II dates to the early Yamnaya culture, while Layer III represents the developed Yamnaya, or early Catacomb, cultures (Rassamakin 1994). Both Layers I and II yielded only a few elongated oval domestic pits; however, in Mikhaylovka III, the settlement area increased, reaching across a valley to a neighbouring elevation to the south-west. At this time the site was enclosed by up to two rings of stone-wall fortification, inside which stood rectangular buildings with stone foundations.

The innovations that appeared only occasionally in the North Pontic Eneolithic burial customs (kurgans, crouched supine position, socially differentiated grave furnishings) were the rule in the Yamnaya culture. Most striking are the particularly richly furnished male burials, with weapons among the grave goods. One example given is that of Kurgan 1 at Utevka on the Volga, an earth mound of at least 110 m diameter and 3 m high. A dagger, shaft-hole axe, flat axe, and awl, made of copper or bronze, as well as two gold rings, pottery, and a stone axe were found in the burial chamber, which had been covered with timber beams. Graves furnished with wagons or wagon parts (wooden wheel rims), which are ascribed to socially prominent personalities, only occur in isolated instances in the Yamnaya culture, but they are very numerous in the Novotitarovka group on the Kuban river, where almost every fourth burial contained wagon parts (Gei 2000). This suggests that the custom had spread from the Kuban area to other parts of the steppe belt. In some cases the grave occupants were identified as metalsmiths by the grave goods of casting moulds and bronze tools (Chernykh 1992: 84). Pieces of copper-containing sandstone from the southern Urals (Samara, Belaya) were found in Kurgan 2 at Utevka (Chernykh 1992: 86). Chernykh has identified large-scale copper-ore mining in the Kargaly area, which had already begun in the third millennium BC, although it flourished in the second half of the second millennium BC (Chernykh 2002).

Contacts in the Caucasus must have been important for the supply of ore to the North Pontic region during the Early Bronze Age, as is shown by numerous arsenical bronzes (Chernykh 1992: 83–5). According to radiocarbon dating, the Maikop culture occupied the Kuban region from the second quarter of the fourth to the start of the third millennium BC. Maikop imports to the Yamnaya territory emphasize their influence on the North Pontic area. This even allows for a migration of Maikop groups into the steppe, which can be argued from the emergence of a new burial custom, in which the body lay on its side in a contracted position (Rassamakin 2004). On the other hand, Maikop elements can also be identified in the Kemi Oba culture in the Crimea, whose characteristic burials were in stone cists beneath grave mounds. Some of these Kemi Oba cists, like those in Maikop territory, show decoration on their inner walls, and certain strikingly similar decorations are also found on stone cists in the central German area, for instance in Leuna-Göhlitzsch (Rezepkin 2000: Fig. 8).

The Maikop culture is characterized by rather large burial grounds, with stone cists and dolmen-like structures amongst the kurgans. The lavishly furnished elite graves are a distinctive feature; they show large numbers of objects made of arsenical bronze, as well as gold and silver: vessels, weapons, tools, implements, and clothing attachments (Rezepkin 2000; Kohl 2007: 72–5). There are also settlements, both fortified central places (Galyugai, Mashoko) and open village-like areas (Kohl 2007: 75–6). Arable agriculture is probable, although it has not been definitely established. The livestock are predominantly cattle and pigs, which is also typical of the Tripolye culture (Kohl 2007: 75). Connections with the Near East are obvious, among other things because of the occasional cylindrical seals (*Rollsiegel*) in Maikop assemblages (Kohl 2007: 86).

The climate became drier during the Early Bronze Age. The forests in the river valleys receded markedly, and semi-arid landscapes appeared in the areas with the lowest rainfall to the south of the Pontic lowlands. The steppe grass-cover changed and pastoral productivity fell by approximately 50–60 per cent, as modern research shows (Rassamakin 1994: 62). This must have affected the lives of the Yamnaya culture bearers and led to the development of specialized and mobile types of animal husbandry, unimaginable without the horse as a pack and riding animal. The general consensus is that the domestication of the horse occurs at this time in the North Pontic area (Kohl 2007). On the other hand, there was probably another Eurasian centre of horse domestication in the north Caucasian steppe (Botai). Places like Mikhaylovka show that permanent settlements arose simultaneously in the river valleys. Their inhabitants, besides hunting and fishing, evidently also practised agriculture sporadically, as evidenced by occasional grain impressions inside their vessels (Kohl 2007: 143). Among domestic animals, herd animals predominated (cattle, then sheep and goats, followed by horses); however, pig bones also appear consistently, indicating a sedentary way of life (Pustovalov 1994: 113).

While the early Yamnaya culture was emerging in the steppe between the southern Bug and lower Volga, the Tripolye culture was disintegrating into a multitude of regional groups in the forest-steppe and southern forest region between the Prut and the Dnieper (Parzinger 1998: 464–5, Fig. 5). Although these groups still show traditions from the Tripolye period, such as painted vessels and anthropomorphic clay figurines, in their settlements, economy, and burial customs they have less in common with Tripolye culture. In particular, the systematically laid-out central places with their radial arrangement of buildings no longer appear (Dergačev 1991). These post-Tripolye groups (Tripolye C2 phase) were more mobile and extended their range considerably compared with Tripolye culture: some are found in the western forest-steppe (in the heartland of the preceding Tripolye culture), whereas the Gorodsk-Troyanov and Lukashi-Sofieva groups advanced further north into the adjoining forest belt, while the Serezlievka and Usatovo groups reached the steppe between the southern Bug and the Danube delta, an area in the south that the early Yamnaya culture had not penetrated.

The Usatovo culture group encompassed a tightly defined area to the north-west of the Black Sea (Dergačev 1991: Pl. 1; 2). In their cemetery sites flat graves can be distinguished from kurgans. As a rule, the kurgans contain a primary grave and from two to six secondary burials; often there are stone rings or stone cairns, also ochre scatters. Contracted inhumations, with the body lying on the side, predominate, and there are occasional supine burials. However, the supine-with-raised-knees position, so typical of the steppe cultures (Yamnaya) since the Eneolithic, is absent. The grave goods include metal objects (pieces of jewellery, awls, chisels, flat axes, and daggers); many of these objects are already made of arsenical bronze (Chernykh 1992: 95). It is striking that the bulk of these bronze objects were not found in flat cemeteries, but in the primary graves of kurgans. Thus, social differentiation appears to be emerging in burial customs here too, just like in the Eneolithic groups (Sredni Stog, Khvalynsk) in the neighbouring steppes to the east. Little is known about the Usatovo settlements (Usatovo-Bolshoy Kuyalnik, Mayaki, and others). There are no indications of house construction, although there are occasional defensive ditches (Mayaki). The crucial economic factor was animal husbandry, since 95 per cent of the animal bones belong to domestic animals (mostly cattle and up to 14 per cent horses).

Consolidation and Further Development: From the Catacomb Culture to the Srubnaya Culture

Around the middle of the third millennium BC at the latest, the Yamnaya culture was replaced right across the North Pontic steppe area by the Katakombna (Catacomb Grave) culture (Fig. 48.3), which was dispersed in roughly the same region. Radiocarbon dating puts the Catacomb culture in the period between 2500 and 1950 BC (Kaiser 2003). It thus coincides exactly with the older phase of the Early Bronze Age in central Europe (Reinecke Bz A1). It is assumed though that the eastern Catacomb burials in the area between the Don, Volga, and Caucasus foothills appeared even earlier and went back to the late Yamnaya culture there.

Regional groups can be distinguished within the Catacomb culture, as in the Yamnaya period (Bratchenko and Shaposhnikova 1985; Kaiser 2003). Common to all the groups are the so-called catacomb grave complexes—kurgans with an entrance shaft and burial niches in its side walls. The dead were buried in both crouched and supine positions. Graves that contained wagons with two, or even four, disc wheels represented members of an elevated social stratum (Pustovalov 1994: Fig. 11), as in the Yamnaya and Novotitarovka periods. Smiths' graves appear, with casting moulds, crucibles, and clay nozzles (Pokrovka Mound 4/Burial 3, Novoalekseyevka Mound 1/Burial 6) (Pustovalov 1994: Fig. 5; 6). Otherwise, graves and grave gifts are largely similar across the Catacomb territory, and only occasionally do individuals stand out.

Characteristic bronze artefacts are slender shaft-hole axes, adzes, bodkins, chisels, daggers with flanged hilts, a range of blades, little spirals, beads, and hair rings. Other small finds encountered are bone hammerhead nails, stone clubheads, axes, and arrow heads, and flint spears and arrowheads (Bratchenko and Shaposhnikova 1985; Chernykh 1992: 124–7). The ceramics, on the other hand, show local differences more clearly, although cross-regional style elements are also in evidence. Pots with funnel or cylinder necks, deep bowls with short rims, and *Räucherschalen* (incense burners) are the typical vessel forms. The incised and impressed ceramic decoration consists of concentric circles, triangles, crescents, zigzags, and herringbone patterns (Bratchenko and Shaposhnikova 1985).

A dry climate and the resulting partial aridity of further parts of the North Pontic steppe area had already set in during the Yamnaya period, but they also shaped the Catacomb culture. Relatively little is known about the nature of their settlements. In many places no intact layers were preserved and house remnants and other objects (pits, postholes) are largely absent. Many would have been regarded as only seasonally visited camps, with tent-like shelters at most. Such places varied in size, but rarely exceeded 100 sq m, and no powerful cultural strata emerged there (Pustovalov 1994: 103–4). These settlements are found not only on river flats, but also in valleys that had become steppe and in the steppe itself, which indicates that they lasted from spring to autumn, when cattle breeders drove their herds out onto the steppe. Part of the population remained behind in the permanent river valley settlements, to engage in agriculture and pig-breeding, as proved by upper Layer III at Mikhaylovka, which had even reached the early Catacomb period (Parzinger 1998: 468).

FIG. 48.3 Catacomb Grave culture grave and material.

Source: redrawn from Bratchenko and Shaposhnikova 1985.

Three oval- to circular-shaped earthworks, indicative of cattle pens, were found next to some pits and small graves in Mateevka 1 (Pustovalov 1994: Fig. 13). In Malaya Khortitsa, on the Dnieper island of Bayda near Zaporozhe, there was a fortification of several stone walls encircling houses with stone foundations; doubtless such sites were central places of greater importance (Pustovalov 1994: Fig. 20). The same also applies to the Molochansk site, for which the bearers of the Catacomb culture had erected a kurgan-like cult site consisting of at least 30,000 m³ of stone and earth. The construction underwent several extension phases and was an enormous communal achievement (Pustovalov 1994: Figs. 24–6).

While the Catacomb culture was concentrated on the North Pontic steppe and southern forest-steppe zone (Parzinger 1998: Fig. 9.1), the northernmost part of the forest-steppe, in particular the mixed forest area, was occupied by late Corded Ware groups. The Middle Dnieper culture was one of these regional groups, whose territory spread across central and eastern Europe, stretching far north from around Kiev to the central Russian lowlands with the Dnieper tributaries. The parallelism of the Middle Dnieper and Catacomb cultures rests not only on common features in their material culture but also on radiocarbon dates, putting both in the period 2370–1670 BC (Kaiser 2003). Adjoining the Middle Dnieper culture to the north are the sites of the Fatyanovo-Balanovo culture, which stretched from the Volga area and the Kama Valley in the east to Pripet and the Bug in the west (Krainov 1987b). Besides a few settlements, this culture is exemplified primarily by grave finds: rectangular pits with single burials lying in the side-contracted or supine-with-raised-knees position, and grave goods of clay pots, animal-tooth pendants, and, rarely, bronze jewellery. Male graves are identified in particular by stone battleaxes.

In the North Pontic area, the period following the Catacomb culture is characterized by ceramics with cord-marked decorations on their upper surfaces; not only horizontal lines, but also complex patterns (diagonally hatched triangles). From this derived the name *kul'tura mnogovalikovoi keramiki* ('multi-cordoned ware' culture), or KMK. Stratigraphy of the kurgans showed that the KMK must have been younger than the Catacomb culture and older than the Srubnaya (Timber Grave) culture (Berezanskaya et al. 1986: 35–9). The KMK occupies the whole former range of the Catacomb culture and spreads even further north as far as the southern forest area, where it replaces the Middle Dnieper culture.

The KMK also divides into several regional groups, which are recognizable primarily by their pottery (Berezanskaya et al. 1986). Its eastern deposits reveal clear links with the Abashevo culture in the forest areas west of the Urals (Pryakhin and Khalikov 1987). The Abashevo culture forms an important chronological bracket between the KMK in the west and the Sintashta culture, which spread immediately to the east of the Urals with its carefully laid-out circular-shaped settlements (Sintashta, Arkaim, and many others) and prominent warrior graves furnished with weapons and chariot grave goods (Fig. 48.4) (V. F. Gening, Zdanovich, and V. V. Gening 1992; Zdanovich 1995). The synchronicity of the Abashevo and Sintashta cultures pushes the KMK into the late third and early second millennium BC. This is also supported indirectly by the fact that the Srubnaya culture that followed the KMK was contemporaneous with the Andronovo-Fedorovka culture in western Siberia, which has been radiocarbon dated to c.1850–1450 BC (Parzinger 2006).

The KMK metalware forms differ only slightly from those of the Catacomb culture; they are, however, rather more developed. The bronze adzes are longer, slimmer, and more curved, as are the bronze shaft-hole axes and flange-hilted daggers. The same applies to polished stone axes. Round disc-toggles and extensively retouched flint arrowheads of various forms are also characteristic (Bratchenko 1985: Fig. 123; Berezanskaya et al. 1986: Fig. 2, 1–3). Together with the flange-hilted daggers and shaft-hole axes, they allow a correlation with the Sintashta burials. The leading KMK form is the outwardly round, in cross-section curved, bone disc with a large centre hole and an additional hole bored in the side (Bratchenko 1985: Fig. 123, 10; 124, 7), which likewise occurs in the Abashevo culture (Pryakhin and Khalikov 1987: Fig. 60).

There have been numerous KMK grave finds. The kurgan earth-banks are not very high; as a rule they contain from one to three burials in a pit with vertical walls. Occasionally

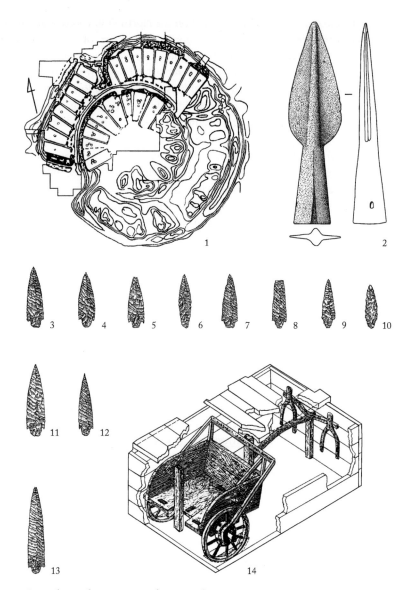

FIG. 48.4 Sintashta culture sites and material.

Source: redrawn from V. F. Gening, Zdanovich, and V. V. Gening 1992, Zdanovich 1995.

burials are also found in side niches. Stone cists as well as timber fittings in building-block fashion already anticipate the constructions of the following Srubnaya culture. Body placement (supine and also contracted position on the side) and orientation are not uniform and show neither chronological nor regional differences. A feature of the KMK burial ritual is the striking scarcity of grave goods. Ceramics, especially, are decidedly rare, which often makes it difficult to identify KMK graves (Bratchenko 1985: 453).

The number of settlement sites from the KMK period clearly increases in comparison with the earlier cultures. They occur primarily on river terraces; now and again there are fortified settlements on elevations (Knyazha Gora, Donetskoe gorodishche) (Bratchenko 1985: 451). The hill fort at Liventsovka, one of the most important sites of the Kamensko-Liventsovka group of the KMK in the eastern Crimea, has been best researched. Among the house forms, partially sunken earth-houses (*poluzemlyanki*) and ground-level wooden-post buildings with a predominantly rectangular plan can be distinguished there (Bratchenko 1985: 451–4). Animal husbandry plays a leading role in the economy (cattle before sheep and goats, then horses, and a strikingly higher proportion of pigs), while there is no evidence of cultivation. Finds of bridle cheek-pieces (*psalia*) have led to the conclusion that the horse was not only a source of meat but was also used for transport. As a riding animal, the horse made it possible to cover great distances and travel to pasture further afield.

The Abashevo culture, which was largely contemporaneous with the KMK, stretched across the middle Volga area to the upper reaches of the Don in the forest regions of the Urals (Pryakhin and Khalikov 1987). As indicated above, the Abashevo culture, in view of its contemporaneity with the Sintashta culture east of the Urals, dates to the late third and early second millennium BC. Small finds of bronze, flint, stone, and bone have many parallels in the Sintashta, as well as the KMK, area (Pryakhin and Khalikov 1987: Figs. 60–4). The same applies to ceramics, even if this is where the typical features of the Abashevo culture may be seen most clearly. Thus, for example, the different variants of pots with deep belly and prominent funnel-shaped neck have not been proven beyond the Abashevo range (Pryakhin and Khalikov 1987: Fig. 60a; 63; 64). On the other hand, the multi-cordoned decoration so characteristic of the KMK is absent from the Abashevo ware.

The multi-strata Silovskoe site in Voronezh shows that the Abashevo culture also had central, fortified settlements. The site, 7,500 m^2 in extent, was enclosed by a ditch, inside which there was a wall of two parallel rows of posts. Inside were eight strikingly large storage pits (14–20 m long and 10–14 m wide) (Pryakhin and Khalikov 1987: 124, Fig. 59). Animal husbandry was important, with cattle predominating over sheep and goats (Pryakhin and Khalikov 1987: 125). There is, however, no definite evidence of agriculture.

Coinciding with this, the Sosnitsa culture, which had succeeded the Middle Dnieper culture, was spread across the mixed forest zone of the middle and upper Dnieper area. Its beginning and end have yet to be more closely correlated with cultural developments further south in the steppe and forest-steppe, as radiocarbon dates are not available. Most finds come from graves; both kurgans and flat graves with inhumation and cremation remains are found. Vessel forms and ornamentation (in particular, horizontal beaded decoration on the neck and shoulders) reveal links not only to the Abashevo culture and the KMK but also to the subsequent Srubnaya culture (Artemenko 1987a: Pls. 50–2). The range of bronze finds (spiral bracelets, spiral pendants, socketed axes, etcetera) shows connections westwards and into eastern central Europe. This east-central European character is seen in the cultures to the west of the Sosnitsa culture: in the Trzciniec (especially East Trzciniec) culture between the Pripet and Vistula, and also, even more clearly, in the Komarovo (Komarów) culture in the upper Dniester Basin (Artemenko 1987b: Pl. 53). The Komarovo culture, particularly in pottery and bronze forms, has features in common with late Early Bronze Age find assemblages in southern Poland and in the northern Carpathian Basin (Otomani, Madarov'ce).

All of these east-central European-influenced culture groups in the mixed forest zone of the upper Dnieper and westwards may also have entered the following period by the time the Abashevo and Srubnaya (Timber-grave) cultures, which followed the KMK, had developed in the North Pontic region, at the latest in the second quarter of the second millennium BC. The Ural river, which flows from the north into the Caspian Sea, roughly marks the boundary between the Srubnaya culture in the west and the related Andronovo-Fedorovka cultures, which spread through western and southern Siberia, in the east. Srubnaya culture sites are distributed from the Volga area to the Crimea, appearing in equally large numbers in the steppe and forest-steppe.

To date it has been very difficult to determine the internal structure of the Srubnaya culture and its absolute dating. Occasionally a distinction is made between an early and a late phase, each with two stages (Berezanskaya and Cherednichenko 1985; Berezanskaya et al. 1986). The reliability of this fine distinction, however, remains doubtful, because it relies primarily on typological considerations. At present it is only certain that the Srubnaya culture followed the KMK, as evidenced by countless settlement site stratigraphics (Osipovka, Chernetchina, Staroe Selo). Elsewhere, however, the Srubnaya culture strata overlay the Abashevo culture (Beregovskoe I, Silovskoe, and Maslovskoe). As the period connecting the KMK, Abashevo, and Sintashta cultures dates to the closing third and early second millennia BC, a beginning date for the Srubnaya culture in the second quarter of the second millennium BC is probable, as with the Andronovo-Fedorovka culture. However, whereas the Andronovo-Fedorovka culture was replaced by Late Bronze Age groups in western and southern Siberia soon after the middle of the second millennium BC, the date of the end of the Srubnaya culture is still uncertain, since no radiocarbon dates are available.

Srubnaya pottery comprises round to hour-glass shaped cups, bowls, and pots. The shoulders are decorated with triangles, diamonds, and zigzag bands, which can be either carved, pricked, or impressed. Both vessel shape and ornamentation reveal numerous features in common with Andronovo-Fedorovka ware, and there are also traditions from earlier times (Abashevo, KMK) (Berezanskaya et al. 1986). On the whole the Srubnaya ceramics are very homogeneous and show little variation, making regional and chronological differentiation difficult to spot. They have this in common with Andronovo-Fedorovka wares.

Spearheads, hooked sickles, flange-hilted daggers, narrow shaft-hole axes, and bracelets with spiral ends are characteristic bronze objects (Berezanskaya et al. 1986: Fig. 17). The copper could have come from the Urals where there was then intensive copper mining in the region around Kargaly (Chernykh 2002). Whereas tin bronzes predominated in the Andronovo-Fedorovka areas, only about 25–30 per cent tin-bronze is found in Srubnaya contexts, which could be due to the distance from the central Asian tin deposits. Instead, arsenical and antimony bronzes predominate to the west of the Urals and Volga (Chernykh 1992: 206). Bone bridle attachments are also important, as are bone discs with wavy ornamentation. This is indicative of connections with the Mycenaean Shaft Graves, as well as the Late Bronze Age Carpathian Basin cultures (Otomani, Madarov'ce).

The Srubnaya culture is named for the timber-lined grave chambers beneath kurgans (burial mounds). Now, however, we know that these timber constructions only occur in 2–5 per cent of Srubnaya burials, and therefore are the exception rather than the rule. Usually the dead rested in simple earth pits that were, if necessary, covered with branches before the earth mound followed. The dead were buried in a contracted position on the side, with the head often oriented to the north. The few grave goods comprised only one or two clay vessels at most, occasionally some bronze objects; quite a few inventories are completely empty. A leadership stratum is not marked in the burial ritual, and slightly richer graves furnished with weapons (spearheads, axes) were seldom encountered (Berezanskaya et al. 1986).

In the meantime, hundreds of Srubnaya culture settlement sites have been found, mostly in the forest-steppe, but they also appear in the steppe; there have been occasional large-scale investigations (Ilichevka, Rubtsy, and others). Some places were fortified, either with embankments (Kapitanovo) or trenches (Ilichevka, Usovo Ozero). Both farmstead-like clusters and rows of houses appear inside the settlements: buildings with partially sunken areas (*poluzemlyanki*), earth-houses, or dugouts (*zemlyanki*) as deep as 1.2 m, and ground-level wooden-post buildings. Places like Mosolovka on the Don show that there were also specialist metalworking settlements, with workshops as well as casting moulds, crucibles, and other casting equipment (Chernykh 1992: 208).

At the beginning of the Bronze Age the Srubnaya culture not only overlay the KMK in the steppe and forest-steppe zone of southern Russia and Ukraine, it also advanced into southern and south-western parts of the Abashevo range. Somewhat further north, however, in the forest region between the Oka and Vetluga rivers, the Abashevo culture was replaced by the Pozdnyakovo culture (Bader and Popova 1987). The Pozdnyakovo bronze forms (well-developed flange-hilted daggers, spearheads, axes, sickles, and solid bracelets with spiral ends) suggest an extensive synchronization with the Srubnaya culture further south and the Andronovo-Fedorovka culture east of the Urals. This is supported by pot form and decoration, even though local distinctive features are clearly apparent (Bader and Popova 1987: Figs. 65–71). Although the Pozdnyakovo culture is one from the southern forest zone, it owes its characteristic forms to enduring southern influences from the steppe and forest-steppe regions; in other words, without the Srubnaya culture, the Pozdnyakovo culture would have been inconceivable.

The Heyday of Bronze Age Cultural Relationships: From Sabatinovka to Belozerka

The younger Srubnaya culture continued to occupy the steppes and forest-steppes between the Volga and the Dnieper after the middle of the second millennium BC. There are no reliable radiocarbon dates for the end of the culture. Adjoining the later Srubnaya to the west was the Sabatinovka culture, which was bounded by the steppe zone; its archaeological sites are scattered from the Sea of Azov across the lower Dnieper area to the lower Danube Valley (Berezanskaya and Sharafutdinova 1985; Gerškovič 1999). Sabatinovka burial and hoard finds (Fig. 48.5) suggest extensive connections as far as the Caucasus.

Sabatinovka ceramics have dishes, pots, and storage vessels with conical or slightly curved sides, and simple bowls, as well as single and double-lugged vessels (Berezanskaya and Sharafutdinova 1985: Fig. 134; Gerškovič 1999). Beaded decoration on the neck and shoulders links the Sabatinovka culture (Berezanskaya and Sharafutdinova 1985: Fig. 134, 13; Gerškovič 1999: Fig. 11j) with the Sargary-Alekseevskoe culture east of the Urals and other western Siberian groups from the second half of the second millennium BC. Socketed narrow-blade spearheads, socketed axes, sickles, and daggers with lancet blades are prominent among the bronze objects, as are late variants of Danubian axes (*Nackenkammäxte* and *Nackenscheibenäxte*) (Klochko 1995). These allow a synchronization of the Sabatinovka culture with neighbouring cultures and tie in to the eastern-central European chronology,

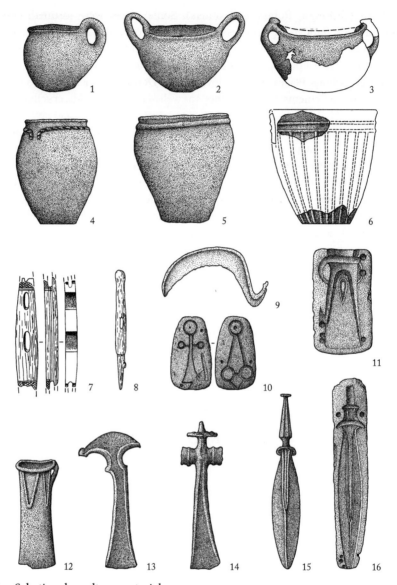

FIG. 48.5 Sabatinovka culture material.

Source: redrawn from Berezanskaya and Sharafutdinova 1985.

which puts its beginnings in the fifteenth–fourteenth to the thirteenth–twelfth centuries BC (Gerškovič 1999: 82–3). It is striking, moreover, that in this time horizon, which links the Sabatinovka, Noua, and late Srubnaya cultures, the custom of depositing bronze objects in hoards also gained acceptance in the North Pontic steppe and forest-steppe areas (Leskov 1981). Thus the regions between the Carpathians and Urals were now also following ritual rules that had already applied for generations in much of 'Old Europe', although they likewise increased in significance there during the second millennium BC.

After the middle of the second millennium BC there was a marked increase in settlements in the entire steppe and forest-steppe zone northwards from the Black Sea, and it is clear that their sizes also grew. This trend is already traceable in the KMK period; however, it is particularly obvious in the Sabatinovka culture, with over seven hundred settlement sites. Rows of houses and also larger, multi-roomed complexes with living and working quarters are found in the settlements, and in the building itself, greater use was made of stone and lime (Berezanskaya and Sharafutdinova 1985; Gerškovič 1999). Relevant finds show that the bearers of the Sabatinovka culture lived from agriculture and animal husbandry (Berezanskaya and Sharafutdinova 1985: 498). The dead were buried both under kurgans and in flat cemeteries, lying mostly on the left side, less often on the right, and with the head oriented to the east. Social differences are scarcely discernible in the treatment of the dead, with the exception of the occasional, somewhat more richly furnished warrior grave (e.g. Borisovka, Kurgan 3) (Berezanskaya and Sharafutdinova 1985; Gerškovič 1999).

The Noua culture, which spread across the forest-steppes from the Dniester to Transylvania, is closely related to the Sabatinovka culture. Besides settlement sites there are also extensive cemeteries. In Ostrovets more than 180 crouched inhumations were unearthed in simple rectangular graves. The grave goods were limited to a few vessels; bronze jewellery, bone implements, and stone objects remained rarer. Hoards appear (Derzhev, Viktorov, Isakovo, Sidorovo), which broaden the spectrum of metal forms compared with the settlement and burial finds. The close similarities between Noua and Sabatinovka ceramics are extensive, although the Danubian-Transylvanian curvilinear decorative patterns, which are absent from the Sabatinovka range, appear occasionally on Noua vessels. The absolute chronology of the Noua culture, based on radiocarbon dating and synchronisms with the Carpathian Basin, fits in the fourteenth to thirteenth/twelfth centuries BC. To a large extent this corresponds to the beginnings of the Sabatinovka culture and emphasizes the contemporaneity of the two cultures.

Around 1200 BC fundamental changes occurred in the North Pontic steppe and forest-steppe, as in other parts of Europe and the Mediterranean region, and led to the emergence of new cultures (Belozerka, Belogrudovka, and Bondarikha). This time is called the close of the Bronze Age. The Belozerka culture belongs in the eleventh–ninth centuries BC (Otroshchenko 1985: 519). Their sites are scattered across the entire steppe belt, from the Don in the east to the Danube in the west. Despite certain traditions, the ceramics are clearly distinguishable from Noua, Sabatinovka, or late Srubnaya ceramics. Typical of the Belozerka culture are rounded or biconical vessels with cylindrical necks, and funnel- and cylinder-neck bowls; jugs, conical dishes, and the numerous variants of cord-decorated pots were already known (Otroshchenko 1985: Fig. 141). Pot decoration includes engraved, incised, and pricked diagonally hatched bands, as well as multi-line zigzag patterns, so far unknown in the Sabatinovka culture.

Most small finds (wire rings, little spools, and simple pins, as well as bronze knives, bone arrowheads, and flint knives) are chronologically undiagnostic. Socketed axes with side loops, spearheads with semicircular blades, and grip-tongue daggers with lancet-shaped blades are also in the Sabatinovka tradition (Otroshchenko 1985). One- and two-looped curved brooches made of fine wire are new, so far the oldest known brooch type in the northern Black Sea area generally, dating close to 1000 BC. Connections with Hallstatt A in east-central Europe, and the Sub-Mycenaean period in Greece, place the Belozerka culture in the twelfth–tenth centuries BC (Otroshchenko 1985).

The preferred Belozerka settlement sites lay on high terraces above rivers and estuaries. Excavations found both rectangular partially sunken earth-houses (*poluzemlyanki*) (Belozerka,

Babina IV, Tudorovo) and ground-level wattle-and-daub houses with stone cladding (Zmeevka I, Kirovo), which were in quite another building tradition (Otroshchenko 1985). While there is evidence of animal husbandry (cattle, sheep, goats, horses, even pigs, and camels in the Crimea), agriculture cannot be shown to have been important with any certainty (Otroshchenko 1985: 524). Burials in the Belozerka culture occurred in flat inhumation cemeteries as well as kurgans, with the right- or left-side crouched position predominant. Usually the grave goods include, at most, a few vessels and occasionally a little bronze jewellery in female graves. The burial ritual was thus not fundamentally different from that of the Sabatinovka culture.

Contemporaneous with the Belozerka culture in the steppe, the Belogrudovka culture was spread in the forest-steppe between the Dnieper and the Dniester (Berezanskaya 1985). The burials—inhumation and cremation in kurgans or flat cemeteries—once again held few grave goods (some pottery and a little bronze jewellery), which do not contribute greatly to solving questions of chronology. Double-lugged vessels and jugs remain in the Noua and Sabatinovka traditions, while the other finds are later and compare with the Belozerka culture in the steppe (Berezanskaya 1985: Fig. 137). The small finds also repeat the spectrum familiar from the Belozerka culture (Berezanskaya 1985: Fig. 136). The Belogrudovka culture is thus also datable to between 1200 and 1000 BC.

The eastern parts of the North Pontic forest-steppe between the Dnieper and the Don, as well as the adjoining northern forest areas to the south of the central Russian lowlands, are occupied at this time by the Bondarikha culture, whose beginnings probably go back to the time immediately following the middle of the second millennium BC. Items of pottery found in graves and settlements are, on the one hand, recognizably in the pricked- and comb-stamped traditions. On the other hand, the round-bellied cylindrical-necked vessels and biconical pots with hatched triangles and angular multi-lined patterns show connections with Belozerka and Belogrudovka wares (Berezanskaya and Ilinskaya 1985). The end of the Belozerka, Belogrudovka, and Bondarikha cultures can thus be considered largely contemporaneous, and the assumption is that the Bondarikha culture outlasted the Belozerka and Belogrudovka cultures (Berezanskaya and Ilinskaya 1985). The Prikazanskaya culture corresponds to it in the Volga-Kama region.

The End of the Bronze Age and Beginnings of Horse-Borne Nomadism

According to Herodotus, the steppes immediately to the north of the Black Sea are the original home of the Scythians, who, in the course of a mass movement east of the Urals, migrated into the North Pontic area. The centuries that followed the Late Bronze Age, but preceded the beginning of the Scythian culture in the early seventh century BC, are referred to as the 'proto-Scythian' period. The finds from this time were already characterized as those of horse-borne nomads; however, since they were not associated with the early Scythian culture, they are interpreted instead as 'Cimmerian' assemblages. Tradition holds that the Cimmerians reached the northern Black Sea region before the Scythians. A. I. Terenozhkin later allocated the Chernogorovka kurgan graves and the Novocherkassk hoard to this horizon and divided the pre-Scythian time between an older Chernogorovka and a younger

Novocherkassk group, which demonstrated certain differences in grave construction, deposition of the dead, and artefact form. Based on associations with the Near East, the Novocherkassk types are today dated to the late ninth and eighth centuries BC (Kossack 1994); thus they correspond chronologically to the early Scythian period (Arzhan 1) in southern Siberia. The type group prior to Novocherkassk, Chernogorovka, must accordingly be placed earlier. Since the Belozerka culture is linked with the eleventh–tenth centuries BC by early wire-shaped loop brooches, this dates the Chernogorovka culture to the tenth–ninth centuries BC (Kossack 1994).

Towards the end of the Late Bronze Age the Belogrudovka culture was situated in the Dnieper forest-steppes. It was replaced there by the Chernoles culture, which ran synchronously with the Chernogorovka group in the steppe. The Chernoles culture was then followed by the Zhabotin I culture, which was contemporaneous with the Novocherkassk culture. The settlement sequence of the fortified site of Zhabotin is critical for the transition to the Early Scythian period in the forest-steppe. One of the oldest levels there, Zhabotin I, contains pottery that has a connection with the late Chernoles culture, and also the Cozia-Sakharna and Bessarabi I cultures on the lower Danube, and therefore it dates to the later ninth and early eighth centuries BC. Fluted ware is typical of the younger Zhabotin II, forming a bridge to Bessarabi II and to the second half of the eighth century BC. Finally, Zhabotin III can be linked with the early Scythian period, which began in the first half of the seventh century BC, because the first Greek imported ceramics from the middle of the seventh century BC appear towards the end of this stage (Daragan 2005). This tallies with Georg Kossack's argument (1994) that the beginnings of the early Scythian culture in the northern Black Sea steppes and the Kuban region lie in the early seventh century BC.

Further east on the Volga the transition from the Bronze Age to the Iron Age, a period characterized by horse-borne nomads, cannot be divided so reliably into phases, for the source materials are discontinuous. The Late Bronze Age ended there at the start of the first millennium BC, prior to the emergence of a so-called pre-Savromatian level, whose lower time limit is set, in turn, in the early seventh century BC by the start of early Savromatian finds (Dvornichenko and Korenyako 1989). Weapons, horse harness, clothing, and pottery from this pre-Savromatian level (Dvornichenko and Korenyako 1989: Figs. 61–2) show associations with the early Ananino culture on the middle Volga and the pre-Scythian assemblages in the North Pontic steppe (Chernogorovka, Novocherkassk), as well as the Zhabotin I level in the middle Dnieper forest-steppe. Thus this horizon belongs in the late ninth and eighth centuries BC (Kossack 1994). This earliest horizon, characterized by groups of horse-borne nomads, no longer has much in common with the Bronze Age cultures of the preceding millennia. It already stands on the threshold of early history.

Conclusion

The Bronze Age development in the steppe, forest-steppe, and forest regions, between the Carpathians in the west and the Urals in the east, showed that the crucial changes in economic forms and social systems, which continued in varying intensity right through the Bronze Age, had already appeared in the Eneolithic. Moreover, during the Bronze Age, there was an unchanging connection between culture and natural environment, since the development in the landscapes on the upper Dnieper and northwards followed a completely different rhythm from that in the southern forest-steppe and steppe regions. It was the steppe belt, in particular, that on the one hand constantly adopted new stimuli and impulses, and on the other reacted most sensitively to climatic changes. With some qualifications, this also affected the forest-steppe cultures, yet the mixed forest zone took scarcely any notice of it, and at least in its western part followed the pattern set by east-central Europe.

When we look at the economy of Bronze Age cultures in the steppe and forest-steppe, the period from the middle of the fourth millennium BC (Yamnaya culture) to the end of the Bronze Age in the early first century BC appears a gradual process, during which animal husbandry assumed ever greater significance. After the Yamnaya period, at the latest, agriculture played a constant, if secondary, role and achieved only sporadic importance. Concurrently, the Maikop culture maintained close relations with the Near East, which resulted in the emergence of a social leadership stratum in the Kuban that found archaeological expression in burials richly furnished with precious metals. Though the Maikop culture influenced Early Bronze Age relationships in the North Pontic steppe, the phenomenon of elite burials was unknown there until horse-borne nomads appeared.

Further development from the third to the early first millennium BC was marked in the steppe and forest-steppe by a continuous process that affected equally the nature of settlement, the manner of burial, and the form of the economy. The number of settlements clearly increased, particularly during the second millennium BC, and sites also became larger and more permanent, with central towns and village settlements more clearly differentiated. Through almost the entire Bronze Age, grave construction and goods—despite apparently extensively furnished graves in the Late Bronze Age—express only limited social differences, which implies a fairly egalitarian society, insofar as this can be reliably assessed on current knowledge. However, even the lavishly furnished graves of the Late Bronze Age are far removed from the graves of Scythian princes and kings, something that clearly conveys the fundamental cultural change accompanying the beginning of the period of Early Iron Age horse-borne nomads.

The increase in the number of bronze objects, and the almost contemporaneous custom of depositing metal objects in large quantities in hoards, emphasize that, at the latest in the second half of the second millennium BC, bronze mining and processing occurred on a grand scale. There is still too little known about the details of this 'pre-industrial' metallurgy, yet it must certainly have affected Late Bronze Age society. Despite the systematically laid-out settlements of the Sintashta-Arkaim type east of the Urals from around 2000 BC, each domestic unit there carried on metalworking for its own requirements. From the Noua, Sabatinovka, and late Srubnaya horizon onward, this can scarcely have been the case any longer, because production had vastly increased.

The animal husbandry that was predominant throughout the Bronze Age, with agriculture sporadically appearing, over time developed ever more effective forms of stock-raising, in which transhumance probably also played an important role. Animal husbandry, combined with climatic changes, laid the foundation for the emergence of the Early Iron Age horse-borne nomads. The roots of this nomadism lie in the North Pontic area, at a time that pre-dates the appearance of the earliest Scythian elements, in the ninth and eighth centuries BC. Near Eastern influences were probably also of crucial significance, as there are Assyrian-influenced finds in warrior elite graves of the Novocherkassk group (Kossack 1994). The Bronze Age ended with this development, and a new period began in the history of the steppe.

Bibliography

Artemenko, I. I. (1987a). 'Sosnitskaya kultura', in O. N. Bader, D. A. Krainov, and M. F. Kosarev (eds.), *Epokha bronzy lesnoi polosy SSSR. Arkheoloiya SSSR*. Moscow: Izdarelstvo Nauka, 106–13.

Artemenko, I. I. (1987b). 'Komarovskaya kultura', in O. N. Bader, D. A. Krainov, and M. F. Kosarev (eds.), *Epokha bronzy lesnoi polosy SSSR. Arkheoloiya SSSR*. Moscow: Izdarelstvo Nauka, 113–16.

Bader, O. N. and Popova, T. B. (1987). 'Pozdnyakovskaya kultura', in O. N. Bader, D. A. Krainov, and M. F. Kosarev (eds.), *Epokha bronzy lesnoi polosy SSSR. Arkheoloiya SSSR*. Moscow: Izdarelstvo Nauka, 131–6.

Berezanskaya, S. S. (1985). 'Belogrudovskaya kultura', in *Arkheologiya Ukrainskoy SSR*, 1. Kiev: Naukova dumka, 499–512.

—— and Cherednichenko, N. N. (1985). 'Srubnaya kultura', in *Arkheologiya Ukrainskoy SSR*, 1. Kiev: Naukova dumka, 473–81.

—— and Ilinskaya, V. A. (1985). 'Bondarikhinskaya kultura', in *Arkheologiya Ukrainskoy SSR*, 1. Kiev: Naukova dumka, 512–19.

—— and Sharafutdinova, I. N. (1985). 'Sabatinovskaya kultura', in *Arkheologiya Ukrainskoy SSR*, 1. Kiev: Naukova dumka, 489–99.

——, Otroshchenko, V. V., Cherednichenko, N. N., and Sharafutdinova, I. N. (1986). *Kultury epokhi bronzy na territorii Ukrainy*. Kiev: Naukova dumka.

Bratchenko, S. N. (1985). 'Kultura mnogovalikovoy keramiki', in *Arkheologiya Ukrainskoy SSR*, 1. Kiev: Naukova dumka, 451–8.

—— and Shaposhnikova, O. G. (1985). 'Katakombnaya kulturno-istorichaskaya obshchnost', in *Arkheologiya Ukrainskoy SSR*, 1. Kiev: Naukova dumka, 403–19.

Chernykh, E. N. (1992). *Ancient Metallurgy in the USSR: The Early Metal Age*. Cambridge, MA: Cambridge University Press.

—— (2002). *Kargaly I-II*. Moscow: Yaziki slavyanskoi kultury.

Daragan, M. N. (2004). 'Periodisierung und Chronologie der Siedlung Žabotin', *Eurasia Antiqua*, 10: 53–145.

Dergačev, V. A. (1991). *Bestattungskomplexe der späten Tripolje-Kultur*, Materialien zur Allgemeinen und Vergleichenden Archäologie, 45. Mainz: Verlag Philipp von Zabern.

Dvornichenko, V. V. and Korenyako, V. A. (1989). 'Predshestvenniki savromatov v Volgo-Donskom mezhdurechye, Zavolzhye i yuzhnom Priuralye', in A. I. Moshkova (ed.), *Stepi evropeiskoi chasti SSSR v skifo-sarmatskoe vremya. Arkheologiya SSSR*. Moscow: Izdatelstvo Nauka, 148–52.

Gei, A. N. (2000). *Novotitarovskaya kultura*. Moscow: Rossiiskaya Akademiya Nauk, Institut Arkheologii.

Gening, V. F., Zdanovich, G. B., and Gening, V. V. (1992). *Sintashta*. Chelyabinsk: Yuzhno-Uralskoe knizhnoe izdatelstvo.

Gerškovič, Ja. P. (1999). *Studien zur spätbronzezeitlichen Sabatinovka-Kultur am unteren Dnepr und an der Westküste des Azov'schen Meeres*, Archäologie in Eurasien, 7. Rahden: Verlag Marie Leidorf GmbH.

Kaiser, E. (2003). *Die Katakombengrabkultur zwischen Dnestr und Prut*, Archäologie in Eurasien, 14. Mainz: Verlag Philipp von Zabern.

Klochko, V. (1995). 'Zur bronzezeitlichen Bewaffnung in der Ukraine. Die Metallwaffen des 17.–10. Jhs. v. Chr.', *Eurasia Antiqua*, 1: 81–164.

Kohl, Ph. L. (2007). *The Making of the Bronze Age Eurasia*, Cambridge World Archaeology. Cambridge: Cambridge University Press.

Kossack, G. (1994). 'Neufunde aus dem Novočerkassker Formenkreis und ihre Bedeutung für die Geschichte steppenbezogener Reitervölker der späten Bronzezeit', *Il Mar Nero*, 1: 19–54.

Krainov, D. A. (1987a). 'Volosovskaya kultura', in O. N. Bader, D. A. Krainov, and M. F. Kosarev (eds.), *Epokha bronzy lesnoi polosy SSSR. Arkheoloiya SSSR*. Moscow: Izdarelstvo Nauka, 10–28.

—— (1987b). 'Fatyanovskaya kultura', in O. N. Bader, D. A. Krainov, and M. F. Kosarev (eds.), *Epokha bronzy lesnoi polosy SSSR. Arkheoloiya SSSR*. Moscow: Izdarelstvo Nauka, 58–76.

Leskov, A. M. (1981). *Jung- und spätbronzezeitliche Depotfunde im nördlichen Schwarzmeergebiet*, Prähistorische Bronzefunde, 20/5. Munich: Verlag C. H. Beck.

Otroshchenko, V. V. (1985). 'Belozerskaya kultura', in *Arkheologiya Ukrainskoy SSR*, 1. Kiev: Naukova dumka, 519–35.

Parzinger, H. (1998). 'Kulturverhältnisse in der eurasischen Steppe während der Bronzezeit', in B. Hänsel (ed.), *Mensch und Umwelt in der Bronzezeit Europas. Die Bronzezeit, das erste goldene Zeitalter Europas*. Kiel: Oetker-Voges Verlag, 457–80.

—— (2006). *Die frühen Völker Eurasiens. Von der Jungsteinzeit bis zum Frühmittelalter*. Munich: Verlag C. H. Beck.

Pryakhin, A. D. and Khalikov, A. Kh. (1987). 'Abashevskaya kultura', in O. N. Bader, D. A. Krainov, and M. F. Kosarev (eds.), *Epokha bronzy lesnoi polosy SSSR. Arkheoloiya SSSR*. Moscow: Izdarelstvo Nauka, 124–31.

Pustovalov, S. Z. (1994). 'Economy and social organization of Northern Pontic steppe-forest steppe pastoral populations: 2700–2000 BC (Catacomb culture)', *Baltic-Pontic Studies*, 2: 86–134.

Rassamakin, Y. Y. (1994). 'The main directions of the development of early pastoral societies of the Northern Pontic zone, 4500–2450 BC (Pre-yamnaya cultures and yamnaya cultures)', *Baltic-Pontic Studies*, 2: 29–70.

Rassamakin, Y. Y. (2004). *Die nordpontische Steppe in der Kupferzeit. Gräber aus der Mitte des 5. Jts. bis Ende des 4. Jts. v. Chr*, Archäologie in Eurasien, 17. Mainz: Verlag Philipp von Zabern.

Rezepkin, A. D. (2000). *Das frühbronzezeitliche Gräberfeld von Klady und die Majkop-Kultur in Nordwestkaukasien*, Archäologie in Eurasien, 10. Rahden/Westf.: Verlag Marie Leidorf.

Shaposhnikova, O. G. (1985). 'Yamnaya kulturno-istoricheskaya obshchnost', in *Arkheologiya Ukrainskoy SSR*, 1. Kiev: Naukova dumka, 336–53.

Zdanovich, G. B. (1995). *Arkaim*. Chelyabinsk: Trudy zapovednika.

Index

Note: Page numbers in *italics* indicate references to figures and those in **bold** indicate tables.

Abashevo culture 907, 909, 911
Abbasanta plateau, Sardinia 673
Abkhazian dolmens 143
Acinipo, Spain 595
acorns 612, 634, 774
Acquafredda, Italy 698
Adlerberg group 727
Adriatic, Northern
  burial rites 874
  castellieri/gradine of the 864–76
  caves and rock shelters 873
  chronology 873–4
  climate 864
  coast 692
    burial rites along the 849–55
  economy of 873
  region 864
Adriatic sea 54, 634, 837
  see also Northern Adriatic
Aegean 3, 370, 649
  arsenical copper and bronze 429
  Bronze Age 454
  'International Spirit' period in 48–9
  pottery 379
  precision weighing 509
  shipwrecks in 371
Aeolian Islands 636, 641, 649, 653, 654, 658, 661, 664–5
aerial ground surveys 312
Afansevo, Siberia 901
Afghanistan 375
African blackwood 385
Agde, France 589
agriculture 535, 538, 580, 624, 916
  arable agriculture 543, 608
  crop cultivation 364
  crop rotation 363
  intensive agriculture 325
  in the Low Countries 556–7
  mixed farming 96, 331
  mixed-herd 329
  in North and West of Iberia 605
  pastoral 543
  in Scandinavia 752
Agris, 'Grotte des Perrats', weighing equipment *518*
Ai Bunar, Bulgaria 440
airborne laser scanning 312
Airolo-Madrano, Switzerland *707, 712, 712, 715*
Akeret, Örni 360
Akkadian period 48
Akrotiri, Thera 386, 510
alabastron 680
Albania 50, 57, 155, 378, 482, 483, 637
Albersdorf, Schleswig-Holstein, Germany 458, *724*, 737
Alberti, Maria Emanuela 511
Aldeagordillo, Ávila, Spain 595, 607
Alderley Edge, near Manchester, England 445
Alentejo stelae, Portugal 147
Alfstedt, Germany *724*
Alghero, Sardinia 669
Almagro Gorbea, Martin 36
Almería, Andalucia, Spain 354, 601
Almgren, Oscar 279
almond 352, 363
Alpe di Tom, Switzerland *707*, 711
Alpenquai, Zürich, Switzerland *707*, 713
Alpine
  copper mining communities 421–5
  'Iceman' 187, 692
  rock carvings and statue-menhirs 291–310
  swords 378

INDEX

Alpine foreland 360, 421, 710
  Bronze Age villages in 92
  house size during the Bronze Age 88
Alps 8, 692
  barley in 360
  burnt-offering places 719
  non-cereals in Eastern Alps 356
  non-cereals in Western 357
  plant cultivation in the Eastern Alps 356
  plant cultivation in Western 357
  RI values of non-cereals in the archaeobotanical record of Eastern Alps **356**
  RI values of non-cereals in the archaeobotanical record of Western Alps **357**
  settlement during the Middle Bronze Age 707
  subsistence economy in 718
Alta, Norway 746-7
Altân Tepe, Romania 51
amber 62, 95, 375-7, 459, 464, 614, 649, 726, 767, 780, 783, 807
  amber-working 778
  Baltic amber 375, 582, 736, 764
  beads 93, 376, 582, 730, 779, 873
  jewellery 588
  necklaces 206, 535
  pendants 200, 582
  production of 779
  trans-European route 764
Amboise, France 574
Amendolara, Italy 633
Amesbury Archer, Wiltshire, England 11, 59, 172, 173, 179, 187, 380, 382, 398, 454, 534, 545
Amesbury, Wiltshire, England 162, *533*
Amiens-Le Plainseau, France 574
amino acids, analysis of 193
amphorae
  bronze amphorae 738
  Canaanite amphorae 385
Ampoița, Transylvania, Romania 884
AMS radiocarbon dating 21
Amsteg-Flüeli, Switzerland 707, 715
amulets 57, 338, 406, 687, 732
anaktoron 663
Ananino culture 915

Anatolia 51, 481, 484
  clay idols 51
  red slipware 51
Andalusia, Spain 147
Anderlingen, Germany 724
Andrid transitional group 821
Andronovo-Fedorovka culture 907, 910
Angelslo, the Netherlands 90, 336, 566
Anguilla di Ribera, Sicily 664, *655*
animal bones 809
  distribution of assemblages of *331*
  for mining copper 448
  see also bone(s)
animal-fat lamps 449
animal husbandry 329, 909, 916
animal stalls 84
animals 192, 328-47
  animal skulls 92
  bone and stone figures of 901
  carbon isotopic data 190
  at Durrington Walls 169
  exploitation of 330-1, 342
  as a means of transport 364, 401, 411, 894
  nitrogen isotopic data 190
  skeletal data from 184
  use of animal canines as ornaments 484
  see also caprines; cattle; dogs; goats; oxen; pigs
anklets 760
Anselfingen, Switzerland 719
antimony bronzes 910
antler(s) 340-1, 779
  balance-beam 517
  ornaments 483
  picks 448
  tools 483, 808
anvils 464
Apa swords 759
Apalle, Sweden 89, 746-7, 750, 761
Apennine culture pottery 473, 475
Apennine facies 637
Apennine Peninsula 334
Appenwihr, France 573
apples 774
  see also fruit
Apulia, Italy 59, 634, 637, 648-9, 698
Arano di Cellore di Illasi, Italy 693, 699
Arbedo-Castione, Switzerland 707, 710

Arbon-Bleiche, Switzerland 707
Ardea, Italy 633, 643
Ardnacross, Scotland 149
Argaric culture 37, 61, 239, 244, 594, 596–600, 597
　beginning of the Bronze Age 603–5
　burial rights 602
　ceramic and metal types typical of 599
　El Argar B burials 472
　funerary rituals 599
　grave goods 599, 602
　harvesting and milling of cereals 600
　jar burials in houses 108
　metal objects 599
　metallurgy in 600
　origins of 600
　production of lithic objects 600
　settlements 597
　sources of copper 600
　structure of the Argaric state (c.1950–1550 cal BC) 601–2
Arikogel, Bad Goisern, Upper Austria 807
arm ornaments
　from the Late Bronze Age hoard of Villena, Alicante, Spain 463
　from Lockington, Leicestershire, England 455
arm-rings 760
Armenochóri, Macedonia 54
Armorica, France 21, 571
armour 587, 805
Arpi, Italy 649
arrowheads 237, 637
Arrubiu-Orroli, Sardinia 670, 678
arsenic 430
arsenical copper 419, 425, 430, 599, 672, 901, 910
art *see* rock art
artefacts
　arrangement in graves 207
　deposited in bogs and rivers 209
　from epi-Bell Beaker-Dolmen archaeological group 620
　interpretation of artefact assemblages in burials 107
　using to date fields 315
　see also grave goods; hoards
artificial caves 599

Arzachena, Sardinia 669
Ascona-San Materno, Switzerland 707, 710
ash-mounds 890
Asiatic steppe 336
Asnæs, Denmark 746–7, 764
ass 337, 635
Assara, Bulgaria 51, 53
astragali, from Hungary 484
Asva, Saaremaa Island, Estonia 339
Atalaia, Portugal 607
Atkinson, Richard 160, 161
Atlantic Europe *see* Atlantic Zone
Atlantic exchange network 551, 557
Atlantic Zone
　Clava Cairns 143
　menhirs 147
　round barrows 144, 145
　seafaring and riverine navigation in 387–90
　small circular enclosed spaces 155
　stone circles and ovals 150
　stone pairs 149
　stone rows/post rows 149
Attersee group 790, 791
Auga dos Cebros, Spain 389
Aunjetitz culture *see* Únětice culture
aurochs 92, 340
Austria 474, 787–812, 818
　amber 807
　barrows 797
　cemeteries in 797
　copper in 438, 441, 450
　craft production in 808–9
　cultural sequence and chronology in 789–90
　distribution of Urnfield swords in rivers and hoards in 132
　Early Bronze Age artefacts from 801
　Early Bronze Age in 789
　faience 807
　funerary archaeology 794–9
　glass in 807
　gold in 806–7
　hill forts 791
　Late and Final Bronze Age artefacts from 803
　Leithaprodersdorf group 796
　life expectancies of Early Bronze Age community in 113
　map of 788
　material culture in 799–809

922 INDEX

Austria (cont.)
　metalwork in 804–6
　Middle Bronze Age artefacts from 803
　natural environment of 787–8
　pottery in 799–804, 806
　production of bronze goods in 804
　settlement and settlements in 791–4
　simple pit graves with urns 798
　stone 807–8
　swords 236
　Urnfield forts 791–2
　Urnfield period pottery 804
Auvernier-Nord, Switzerland 707, 711, 713
Avanton gold cone 587
Avebury, Wiltshire, England 150, 159
Avon, River 159, 168, 170
awls 416, 417, 482, 484, 673
axe-adzes 416
axes 128, 170, 211, 212, 220, 237, 293, 419, 562, 564, 565, 725, 737, 749, 760
　Anglo-Irish axes 727, 735
　axe heads 128
　bronze axes 536, 719, 760
　ceremonial axes 764
　cupellated silver 54
　deposited in southern Netherlands 136
　disc-butted axes 893
　double axes 379
　from Early Bronze Age barrow at Leubingen, Germany 200
　Eneolithic/Copper Age and Bronze Age axes 429
　flanged axes 460, 587, 672, 683, 727, 735, 760
　flat axes 416, 417, 427, 585, 727, 735, 891
　Geistingen type 563
　Late Neolithic Altheim-type flat axes 427
　movement of 378
　palstave axes 38
　Sezze type 672
　shaft-hole axes 891, 892, 893
　silver axes 54, 886
　small axes 730
　socketed axes 38, 760, 893
　spatula axes 294
　Valsømagle axes 762
　winged axes 563
　see also hammer-axes

Ayia Irini, Chios 510
Azuer, Spain 595, 603, 604

Babadag, Romania 878, 891
Babino, Ukraine 878
Bačić, Boris 866
Bad Buchau, Germany 707, 711, 712
Bad Goisern-Arikogel, Austria 788
Baden complex 47, 879, 881, 894
Baden, Austria 878
Baden-Württemberg, Germany 357
Baierdorf, Austria 788
Băile Figa, Beclean, Romania 505
Bailey, Douglass 416
Bailleul-sur-Thérain, France 573
Bakke, Norway 279
Bakonyjákó, Hungary 815–6
Bakonyszűcs, Hungary 815–6
Baks, Hungary 815–6
Baks-Temetőpart, Hungary 828
balance beams 511, 517
Balatonmagyaród, Hungary 815–6, 830
Balearic Islands 617–31
　epi-Bell Beaker-Dolmen archaeological group (c.2100/2000-1600 cal BC) 620–1
　first human colonization of 619
　map of Bronze Age sites 618
　monumental buildings in 618
　Navetas 143
　see also Formentera; Ibiza; Mallorca; Menorca
Balinghem, Pas-de-Calais, France 456
Balkåkra, Sweden 746–7
Balkans 49–59, 361, 416, 486
　chronological correlation of archaeological cultures, groups and key site stratigraphies in the third millennium BC for the 52
　Eastern Balkans 50, 51–4
　tell sites in 96
　see also Western Balkans
Ballybrowney, County Cork, Ireland 208
Balme Gontran, France 353
Balta Sărată, Romania 878
Baltic amber 375, 582, 736, 764

Baltic countries 63, 746
  see also Estonia; Finland; Lithuania
Baltic 'stone ships' 389
Banzi, Italy 649
bar-torcs 456
Barbed Wire Beaker culture 553, 566
Barbey, France 574
Barbuise-Courtavant/La Saulsotte/La Villeneuve-au-Châtelot, France 574
Barca I, Slovakia 824
Barfield, Lawrence 496
Bargeroosterveld, Drenthe, the Netherlands 156, 563, 565
Bargrennan Graves, Scotland 143
Bari-Taranto Tombs, Italy 143
Barice, Bosnia and Herzegovina 838
Barice- Gređani group 845, 857
barley 359–60, 538, 600, 608, 752, 774
  and Bronze Age Alpine settlements 718
  in central and nothern Italy 351
  in the Eastern Alps and their Foreland 356
  free-threshing barley 356, 359, 360
  in Greece and southern Bulgaria 350
  hulled barley 350, 352, 353, 354, 355, 356, 359, 360, 364, 538
  in Mediterranean Spain 353
  naked barley 350, 352, 353, 359, 538
  in the Pannonian Basin 355
  in southern France 352
  in west-central Europe 358
  in the Western Alps and their foreland 357
Barleycroft Farm, Cambridgeshire, England 149, 322, 533, 538
Barnstorfer Moor, Germany 403
Barranco de la Viuda, Spain 595
Barrel and Bucket urns 539
Barrow Hills, Radley, Oxfordshire, England 115, 210
barrows 92, 96, 102, 103, 108, 322, 534, 540, 550, 557, 775
  in Apulia 649
  in Bohemia and Austria 797
  bowl barrows 145
  in Britain 84
  cemetery in Warendorf-Neuwarendorf, Germany 410
  fancy barrows 145
  individual barrows 145

  in Jutland, Denmark 114
  long barrows 143, 159, 162
  in the Low Countries 561
  in the Netherlands 199, 557
  at Oss-Zevenbergen 559
  in Poland 781
  round barrows 144–6, 157, 173
  in Scandinavia 753
  in Skelhøj, Jutland, Denmark 110, *111*
  see also kurgans
barter 523
  and trade 49
Bartholomäberg, Austria 424, 715, *788*, 791
Barumini, Sardinia 669
Baruya, New Guinea 309
Basarabi, Romania 878
Basarabi-type pottery 846
Basilicanova, Italy 475
Basilicata, Italy 647–8
basket weave/basketry 479, 778
Bass, George 385
Battonya, Hungary 815–6
Baume Layrou, Gard, France 353
Bayesian statistical methods 21, 39
Beacon Hill, England 161
beads 416, 492, 700
  amber beads 93, 376
  glass beads 95
Beaghmore, County Tyrone, Northern Ireland 150
Beaker
  burial rite 534, 545
  Folk 70, 73
  groups 382, 880
  package' 73, 75
  pottery 36, 315, 443, 537
  'Beaker People Project' 187, 188–9
  beans 538
Beba Veche/Óbéba-Pitvaros culture 821
Bedd Branwen, Anglesey, bone pommel from burial at 206
Bedeni, Russia 144
beef 330
Begleitkeramik ('accompanying pottery') 621
Bègues, Spain 572
Behre, Karl-Ernst 362
Behy, County Mayo, Ireland 316
Békés, Hungary 815–6

Bekić, Luka 867
Belarus 63, 898
Belderg, County Mayo, Ireland 316
Belegiš, Serbia 838, 878, 890
Belgium 462, 550
    barrows in Belgian Flanders 557
    Belgian Ardennes 557
    Bronze Age in 30–1
    burials in Flanders 550
    chronological systems for 18–9, 28–9
    deposition practices in 199, 564
    Late Bronze Age metalwork hoards in 125
    Late Bronze Age pottery styles 553
    round barrows in 145
Bell Beaker culture 22, 25, 38, 48, 61, 170, 172–3, 216, 220, 294, 380, 454
    burials 172
    centres of 770
    chronological chart **296**
    and copper metallurgy 75
    culture-history research 70–2
    daggers 306
    in the Danubian region 817
    distribution map of 69
    domestic horses and 337
    gold neck-rings 58
    graves 59
    in Iberia 594, 596, 606
    influence in Northern Italy 695
    interpretative themes of 77
    in the Low Countries 553
    in Mallorca and Menorca 619–20
    and metallurgy 419
    Moarda pottery 656
    network 62–4
    pan-European distribution of 70
    research from 1970s to early 1990s 72–4
    research from the late 1990s to present 74–6
    selective deposition of 205
    settling in Wessex or Scotland 11
    and Singen metal 562
    in Slovakia 817
    theories on 68–81
    tombs 308
    treatment of the dead 558, 566
    use of low-tin bronzes 420
    see also Beakers

Belogrudovka culture 914
Belotić-Bela Crkva, central Serbia 54, 838, 849
Belozerka culture 913–4, 915
belt disc 760
belts 589, 893
Belverde cave, Italy 633
Benac, Alojz 849
Benecke, Norbert 339
Béniguet, Côtes-d'Amor, France 153
Berettyóújfalu, Hungary 815–6
Bergerbrant, Sophie 237
Bernabò Brea, Luigi 654, 658, 664
Bernese Alps 719
Bernese Oberland, Switzerland 711
Bernières-d'Ailly, France 574, 589
Bernstorf, Bavaria 456
berserker tradition 237
Berwick-upon-Tweed, Northumberland, England 460
Berzé, France 572
Bessarabi I culture 915
Besse, Marie 74
Bestwall Quarry, England 533, 538
Bezdanjača, Croatia 838, 854
Biały Potok, Poland 878
Biconical urns 539
Bidistili-Fonni, Sardinia 675
Biernatki, Poland 777
Bignan, France 573
Bijelo Brdo, Croatia 838
Billendorf phase 734
Bingia è Monti, Sardinia 58
Bingia le Monti-Gonnostramatza tomb, Sardinia 671
Binimaimut, Menorca 618
biography of objects 6
birds 343
Birkendegaard, Kalundborg, Denmark 153
Bischofshofen, Salzburg, Austria 788, 798
Bisenzio, Italy 633
Biskupin, Poland 240, 483, 773, 782–3
bison 340
bitter vetch **350**, 351, 352, 353, 354, 355, **356**, 358, 363
Bjäre peninsula, Sweden 753
Bjerre, Jutland, Denmark 746–7, 751, 764
    longhouses at 85
Blåa röir, Öland, Sweden 746–7, 753

INDEX 925

Blajer, Wojciech 780
Blanot, France 574, 588
Blatnica-Plešovica, Slovakia 815–6
Blechstil phase of sheet-metal ornament production 709
Blučina, Moravia 244, 788
Bluestonehenge, West Amesbury, England 151, 159, 164, 165, 171
boar tusks 483
boats 380
  boat crews 238
  boat models 385–6
  Brigg logboat 390
  hide-covered 389, 393
  images of 385
  logboats 389, 390–1, 393
  plank boats 389, 390
  rock carvings of 388–9
  sewn-plank 387–8, 393
  skin boats 763
  see also ships
Bodenseegruppe group 709
Bodman, Germany 707, 724
Bodmin Moor, England 319
body armour 198, 220, 732
Boeslunde with Borbjerg, Denmark 746–7
bog burials, in eastern England 535
bog depositions 737
Böheimkirchen, Austria 788, 790
Bohemia 787, 790
  artefacts from 800
  barrows 797
  Final Bronze Age in 790
  funerary archaeology in 794
  gold artefacts from the Urnfield period 807
  gold objects 806
  hoards of raw metal 805
  map of 788
  Middle to Late Bronze Age in 790
  production of bronze goods in 804
  settlements in 791
  Urnfield period 807
Bohuslän, Sweden 275, 279
  rock carvings of boats in 388
Bökönyi, Sándor 332
Bologna, Italy 633
Bóna, István 814
Bondarikha culture 914

bone(s) 482–7, 779
  animal skulls 92
  artefacts 778
  balance-beam 517
  beads 700
  bone working 624, 778, 809
  bossed bone plaques 58
  buttons 621
  collagen 180, 181, 186
  dating of cremated 21
  links to other crafts 487
  materials selection and manufacturing process 486–7
  objects 482–4, 887
  organization of production of 487
  pendants 700
  plates 855
  regional and temporal variation of 485–6
  rib-based scrapers 482–3
  scale-beams 517
  tools 482, 484
Bonnanaro, Sardinia 669, 671, 672
Borbjerg hill, Jutland, Denmark 764
Bordei-Herăstrău, Romania 878
Bordjoš, Serbia 517
Borel, Francesco Rubat 711
Borġ in-Nadur pottery 659
Borgbjerg hoard 459
Bornholm, Denmark 282
bornite 442
Borremose, Denmark 746–7
Bortigali, Sardinia 669
Borum Eshøj, Jutland, Denmark 104, 237, 746–7
  inhumation burial 105
Bosnia 54, 637, 839, 840, 844, 845, 847, 849, 854, 857
Botai, Kazakhstan 336, 901
Bouco-Payrol, Aveyron, France 442
Boulder Burials 143
Boulder Dolmens 143
Bourbriac, France 572
Bouzek, Jan 8
Bovenkarspel, West Frisia, the Netherlands 561
  Bronze Age cultural landscape 556
  nucleated settlement at 91
bovids 399, 752
bovines 635

bow and arrow 220
Bowen, Collin 312
Bowl Tradition 536
bowls 881
   elbow-handled 688
   fineware bowls 91
bracelets 59, 200, 456, 537, 587
Bradley, Richard 154, 200, 253, 277, 314, 388
Brančˇ, Slovakia 815–6
Bratislava, Slovakia 815–6, 830, 831
bread 364
Brean Down, Somerset, England 502
Bredarör cairn, Kivik, Sweden 279, 284, 753
Breton burial mounds 461
Březno, Bohemia 788, 792
Briard, Jacques 1
bridges 409
Brill, Robert 498
brine 502, 504, 767
Brinjeva gora, Slovenia 838
briquetage technique 377, 501, 502, 503
Britain 21, 135, 312
   barrows 84, 145
   Beaker burial rite 534
   Bronze Age in 22–5, 531–49
   chronological systems for 18–9
   copper in 372, 443–5
   Early Bronze Age ceramics 471
   hill forts 240
   house foundations and abandonment deposits in 86–7
   house-landscape in 96
   interpretation of hoards in 123
   landscape 532
   linear landscapes in southern Britain 320–2
   lock-rings and hair-rings 462
   logboats in 392
   metalwork depositions in 125
   in the mid second to early first millennium BC 537–43
   in the mid third to early second millennium BC 533–7
   pottery production in 476
   round barrows 145
   roundhouses in 84, 90
   settlements in 534
   synchronized version of the relevant chronological systems for 23–4

   treatment of dead bodies and objects in Middle and Late Bronze Age in 208
   victims of violence 244
   z-plied yarns 479
British Isles
   barrows in the 144
   burials in the 106
   Galician-style rock art 154
   gold lock-rings 460
   replacement of arsenical copper with tin-bronze 429
   round barrows in the 144–5
   stone and post circles 150
   stone rows/post rows 149
   twenty-second and twenty-first centuries BC in 61
   see also Britain; Ireland
Brittany 571
   Early Bronze Age 'princely graves' 207
   menhirs 147
   round barrows 145
   stone pairs 149
   stone rows 150
   see also France
Brixlegg, Austria 417, 788
Brno-Obřany, Moravia 788
broad beans 774
Broddenbjerg, Denmark 746–7
Brogar, Orkney Islands 151
Broglio, Italy 633, 646
Bromölla, Sweden 746–7
Brongers, Ayolt 312
bronze 38, 804
   amphorae 738
   antimony bronzes 910
   arrowheads 237
   arsenical bronzes 901, 910
   axes 536, 719, 760
   balance beam 511
   body armour 732
   and the Bronze Age 419–20
   cast bronze vessels 736
   cauldron-wagon, from Acholshausen, Ldr. Würzburg, Germany 408
   chains 759
   cups 379
   daggers 461, 535

deposition 7, 202, 540, 544
discs 251, 255, 263
exchanges involving 387
figurines 128, 481, 683–4, 687
fragments, Salins Valley 583
goods 798
halberds 200
hardness of 431
jewellery, found in the river Hérault 588
keys 718
objects 93, 780
picks 448
points 809
production in France 586–7
production of goods in Bohemia, Moravia and Austria 804
razors 263, 458
sickles 563, 565
smelting 809
spheres 511
spoked wheels 404, 737
supply of 198
ternary 612
in the Tisza region 823
tools 612
use in chronological markers 20
vessels 58, 737
weapons 612, 649, 873
Bronze Age 291
animals in the 328–47
burial traditions 103–6
changes through the 226–331
chronological schemes 20
chronology of Western Europe 17–46
communities 544
cosmology 248–65
economics 210–2
farmsteads 90–1
house architecture in the 84–7
identities 218–22
introduction to 1–13
see also Early Bronze Age; Final Bronze Age; Final Bronze Age-Early Iron Age; Late Bronze Age; Middle Bronze Age
Bronze Age archaeology
chronology 7–8
debates in 7–10

future of 10–1
world systems 8–10
Bronze Age in Barbarian Europe, The (Briard) 1
Bronze Age in Europe, The (Coles and Harding) 1
bronzesmiths 219
Broodbank, Cyprian 385
Broom Quarry, Bedfordshire, England 208
Brotlaibidole (loaf-of-bread idols) 799, 819
Broussy le Grand, Marne, France 155
brown bear 92, 340
Brunku Madugui-Gesturi, Sardinia 673, 677
brushed or wire-brushed pottery culture 844
Bruszczewo- Łęki Małe type structures 780–2
Bruszczewo, Poland 95, 358, 773, 774, 775, 778
metallurgical activity at 778
plan of Early Bronze Age settlement at 771
Bruteigsteinen, Norway 279
Bubanj Hum III, Serbia 54
Buchberg, Switzerland 426
Buckskin Barrow, Hampshire, England 146
București (Bucharest) 878
Bucy/Missy-sur-Aisne, France 572
Budapest, Hungary 815–6
Budsene, Denmark 746–7
Bug-Dniester culture 900
Bulford, England 159, 173
Bulgaria 51, 420, 877–97
archaeological research 878
axes with discs 892
barley in 359–60
burials in 884, 885, 887, 889
chronology and terminology 879–80
clay vehicle models 892
copper production in 440
cultural evolution in 880–91
Early Bronze Age in 881–4
Early Iron Age in 890–1
einkorn in 360
Late Bronze Age in 888–90
Lefkandi I-Kastri pottery 53
map of 878
metal in 891
metal shaft-hole axes 892
Middle Bronze Age in 884–8
oil plants in 363
plant cultivation in 349–51
pottery from the Early Bronze Age in 881

Bulgaria (*cont.*)
   pottery types from Bronze Age/Early Iron
      Age cultures in 882–3
   transport and vehicles in 894–5
bullae 466
Bullenheimer Berg, Bavaria, Germany 94, 741
bullocks *see* oxen
Buoux, Vaucluse, France 583
Burgess, Colin 122
burial monuments 277, 544
burial mounds 534, 535, 540
   in France 581, 582
   sod-built 115
burial pits, with human sacrifices from Nižná
      Myšľa, Slovakia 824
burial practices
   in Britain and Ireland 535
   in Romania, Moldova and Bulgaria 895
burial rock art 283–5
burials 102–20
   in barrows 108
   Boulder Burials 143
   burial traditions 103–6
   of chieftains 561
   clusters of 112–3
   in the Early Bronze Age in Romania,
      Moldova and Bulgaria 884
   as an event 109–12
   gender and 107–8
   in Germany during the Late Bronze Age
      730–1
   individual burials 71, 106–8
   interpretations of 102–3
   jar burials 108
   in karst caves 854
   objects and materials presence in 545
   in Poland 775–6
   research into 117
   in Scandinavia 754–8
   setting of 114–6
Burl, Aubrey 151
burnt mounds (*fulacht fiadh*) 535
burnt stones 125
Burren, County Clare, Ireland 316
Burton, Richard Francis 865
Bussy-Saint-Georges, France 573
buttons 629, 760
Butzbach, Germany 724, 727

Ca Na Costa, Formentera *618*
Ca Na Cotxera, Mallorca *618*
Ca Na Vidriera, Mallorca *618*
Cabezo Redondo, Villena, Alicante, Spain
   332, 595, 610
Cabras, Sardinia *669*
Cabrières, France 442
Cádiz, Spain 595
Caere, Italy 633
Cahagnes, Normandy, France 95, 578
Cairano, Italy 633
cairnfields 318, 319
cairns 150, 277, 318
   clearance cairns 318
   made from fire-cracked stones 754
   in Scandinavia 753
Čaka culture 790, 798, 804, 815–6, 830, 832
   smelting furnaces 698
Čakovice, Prague, Czech Republic 156
Cala Blanca, Menorca *618*
Cala Morell, Menorca *618*
Cala Sant Vicenç, Mallorca *618*
Calabona, Mallorca 688
Calabria, Italy 646–7
Calangianus, Sardinia *669*
Calascoves, Menorca *618*
Calbana, Italy 633
Caldare, Sicily 655
Caldas de Reyes, Pontevedra, Spain 457,
   459, 465
Caltagirone, Sicily 655, 663
Camp de Laure, France 572
Campania, Italy 634, 644–5
Can Martorellet, Menorca *618*
Can Missert, Spain 595
Can Roig Nou, Mallorca *618*
Can Roqueta II, Spain 595
Čaňa, Slovakia 815–6
Canaanite amphorae 385
Canegrate group of the Po plain 710
Cannarella, Dante 866
Cannatello, Sicily 655, 661, 670, 680
Canosa, Italy 633, 639
Canyamel, Mallorca *618*, 623
Cap de Forma, Menorca *618*, 628
Cap Hornu hoard 586
Cape Gelidonya shipwreck 370, 383, 385
capeduncola (one-handled cup or bowl) 473

Capelle, Torsten 389
Capilla I 595
Capo Graziano culture 654
Capo Graziano pottery 636, 657, 658
Capo Piccolo, Italy 633
caprines 330, 334–5, 483
   see also animals
Capua, Italy 633
Caput Adriae 59, 502, 780, 864
carbon 180
   analytical fraction, dietary input and
      interpretation of **183**
   from collagen samples 191
carbon isotopic data 182, *185*, 190
Carcarella di Calascibetta, Sicily 655
Carinaro, Italy 633
Carn Goedog, Wales 165
Carn Menyn, Wales 165
Carnac, Morbihan, France 150
Carpathian Basin 144, 156, 337, 416, 419, 813,
      837, 887
   bone and antler manufacturing 486
   ceramics 472
   clay figurines from 224
   clay models of four-wheeled carts 894
   gold objects 462
   Late Bronze Age vessels 473
   Middle Bronze Age fineware bowls 470
   Middle Bronze Age in 895
   organization of settlements 61
   role of specialist potters in 476
   vessel-forming techniques 474
Carpathian Tumulus culture 826
carpentry 778, 779
Carrapatas halberds 607
Carretelà, Spain 595
Carricastro, Spain 595
Carsac, France 574
Carschenna, Switzerland 154, 401
Carter, Stephen 315
carts 399, 411
   see also wagons
Casa Carletti, Italy 633
Casal Sabini, Bari, Italy 58
Caserío de Perales, Spain 595
Casone San Severo, Italy 56
Cassibile, Sicily 655
Cassola Guida, Paola 866

Castellace, Italy 633
Castellets II 595
castellieri-gradine 699
   characteristics of 867–73
   chronology 873–4
   economy and 873
   map of the Northern Adriatic *865*
   of the Northern Adriatic 864–76
   sketch-plans of *868*
Castellón Alto, Spain 595
Castelluccio culture 654–5
   facies from the Etna area in Sicily 655
   pottery *656*
   vessels from Santa Croce Camarina, Sicily *53*
Castelluccio dei Sauri, Italy 149
Castelluccio, Sicily 58, 59, 511, 517, 655, 657
   weighing equipment *518*
castillejos 603
Castillo de Alange, Spain 595
casting 430
   and working 427–31
casting jets 128
Castlekelly, County Galway, Ireland 460
Castlerigg, Cumbria, England 151
Castro de Ardón, Spain 595
catacomb grave complexes 905
Čatalka, Bulgaria 878
Catalonia, burials in 606–7
cattle 96, 170, 190, 331–3, 342, 364, 483, 752, 774
   bones 330
   height of 332
   horns 332, 333
   prevalence in ceremonial pits and funerary
      practices 534
   shoulder-blade bones for copper mining
      448–9
   stalls 90, 553, 555, 566
   see also animals
Caucasus 143
cauldron-wagons 407, 737
Caulfield, Seamus 316
Cauria, Corsica 150
Cava Lazzaro, Sicily 655
Cavalier, Madeleine 654, 658, 664
caves 581
   artificial caves 599
   cave burials in northern England 535
   funerary use in southern France 583

Cazalilla II-Albalate, Spain 604
Cazalilla, Spain 595
Cazis-Cresta, Switzerland 707, 715
cedarwood 385
Čehovice, Moravia 788, 806–7
Céide fields, County Mayo, Ireland 316
Celano, Italy 633
Celldömölk-Sághegy, Hungary 815–6
'Celtic fields' 312, 322–4, 556–7, 566
cemeteries 112–3
   age and gender distribution in 113
   in Germany in the Nordic Bronze Age 737
   see also barrows; cremation
Cernavodă III-Boleráz 47
Central Alps, Switzerland and 706–22
Central Europe 145
   Bronze Age villages in 92
   chronological systems for 18–9, 26–7, 28–9
   copper mines in the eastern Alps
      and 440–1
   enclosures in 156
   house architecture in 84
   precision-weighing equipment 520
   rock art sites in 154
   round barrows 146
   statue menhirs 147
   weighing in 511–4
   see also Europe
Central Zone see Central Europe
Centre-Periphery relations see World Systems
ceramics 20, 95, 469–77
   attaching handles to 477
   colour of 475
   links to other crafts 476–7
   materials selection and manufacturing
      process 473–5
   production of 475–6, 809
   regional and temporal variation of 470–3
   in Romania, Moldova and Bulgaria 895
   types of objects and use of 470
   vessels 470, 474, 539, 620
cereals 349, 634, 717
   cultivation of 331
   grains 624
   in Sardinia 676
   in Southern Scandinavia and the North Sea
      coast 359
   see also barley; non-cereals; rye; wheat

ceremonial enclosures 84
ceremonial monuments 544
Čerkovna, Bulgaria 878
Cerkovna/Zimnicea/Plovdiv group 888, 889
Cernavodă, Romania 878
Cerro de la Campana, Spain 595
Cerro de la Encina, Spain 235, 595
Cerro de la Vinas, Spain 595
Cerro de la Virgen, Granada, Spain 332
Cerro del Cuchillo, Spain 595
Cetina, Croatia 54, 63
Cetina culture 55, 845, 849
   pottery 850
Chagford Common, Dartmoor, England,
   Bronze Age landscape on 97
Chalandriani, Greece 58
Chalcolithic 33, 157, 291, 298, 531
   copper mining in the 446
   fort sites 239
   use of copper and gold during the 437
chalcopyrite copper ores 424
chalk uplands, Marlborough Downs,
   Salisbury Plain 320
Chalon-sur-Saône, France 574
Cham-Oberwil, Switzerland 410, 707, 716
Champlay-La Colombine, France 574
Chancellorsland, County Tipperary, Ireland 91
Channel-North Sea group 591
Chapman, John 136
Charente, France 517
chariots 401, 405, 411, 894
Charnham Lane, West Berkshire, England 151
Chemin des Collines, Switzerland 300
Cherna Gora, Bulgaria 51
Chernogorovka culture 914, 915
Chernoles culture 915
Chernykh, E. N. 900
Chiaromonte, Italy 647
chickpea 350, 351, 352, 363
chiefdoms 197, 201, 216
Childe, Gordon 7, 71, 122, 129, 197, 330
children
   enchytrismos for 649
   graves of 732
   skeletons buried in vessels 796
Chindrieux-Châtillon, Switzerland 707,
   712, 713
Chinflón mine, Huelva, Spain 443

chisels 200, 416, 486, 684, 809
Chișinău-Corlateni group 890
Chișinău, Moldova 878
Chiusi-Cetona area 641–2
Chiusi, Italy 633
Chłopice-Veselé culture 63, 789, 817, 822
Choisy-au-Bac, Oise, France 464, 574, 579
Chotín, Slovakia 815–6
Choyke, Alice 483
Chringenpass, Switzerland 719
chthonic cults 624
'Cimmerian' assemblages 914
cist cemeteries 607
cist-grave art 154
cists 582, 758
Čitluk, Bosnia and Herzegovina 838
Cladh Hallan, Scotland 90, 533, 543
Clarke, David 73
clasp-ingots 514
Clausis, France 442
Clava Cairns 143
clay 469–70
  Aegaeo-Balkanic anchors 57
  figurines from the Carpathian Basin 224
  models of four-wheeled carts 894
  moulds 586
  objects 470
  spindle-whorls 809
  urns 737
  wheel models 402
Cloghbreedy, County Tipperary, Ireland, house at 86
Clones, County Monaghan, Ireland 460
Closos de Can Gaià, Mallorca 618
cloth 225, 228
clothing 477–8
  see also dress
Cocuzzolo Sorigliano, Italy 647
coffins, log-coffins 392
Cogotas I pottery, Iberia 476–7, 606, 611, 612
coins, Iron Age and Roman 128
Coles, John 2, 277, 388
collagen 180, 186, 193
collared urns 173, 536, 537
collars 760
Colmar, France 574
commodification 510
  weighing and 522–4

common vetch 352, 355, 358, 363
communities 112–3, 544
Concise-Sous Colachoz, Switzerland 707, 712
Conelle, Adriatic Basin 63
Coneybury Hill, England 159, 162, 164
Conjux-Pré Nuaz, Switzerland 707, 712, 713
Continental Europe
  division of houses in 88
  logboats 391
Continental Zone see Continental Europe
cooking pits 754
Coolaghmore, County Kilkenny, Ireland, lunula from 210
Coppa Nevigata, Apulia, Italy 55, 511, 633, 638, 640, 648
copper 38, 72, 197, 261, 372–4, 599, 614, 688, 694, 718, 748, 804
  alloy objects 4
  alloy weights 517
  arsenical copper 419, 425, 430, 599, 672
  artefacts 416, 418
  axes 170, 205, 448, 759
  bars 727
  beads 417
  clasp-ingots 523
  Cypriot copper 681
  daggers 205
  east Alpine copper 424
  from Germany 726
  from Hungary 813
  ingots 516
  in Italy 636, 646
  metallurgy 75
  objects in Ukraine and South Russia 901
  'ox-hide' ingots 385
  pure copper 430
  rib ingots 374
  ring-ingots 374, 523, 727
  rings 417
  in Romania, Moldova and Bulgaria 891
  from Sardinia 671
  search for 446–7
  sheet objects 58
  from Slovakia 813, 814
  smelting 416, 450
  smelting slag 450
  sources in the Czech lands and Austria 806
  spirals 417

copper (cont.)
    supply in prehistoric Europe 446
    use before bronze 414
    use during the Chalcolithic 437
    wire artefacts 817
Copper Age 332, 454, 594, 719
    chronological chart **296**
    Laterza facies 635
    Millares culture 600
    settlements 604
    societies of the lower Tagus and the south-west of Iberia 607
'Copper Man' 449
copper mines/mining 437–53, 791
    in the Alpine area of Germany 727
    in the Alpine region 808
    approaches to 447–8
    in cental Europe and the eastern Alps 440–1
    in Chalcolithic and Bronze Age Europe 446
    distribution of 437
    in the East Mediterranean 438–9
    flooding in 449
    in France and the Western Alps 441–2
    in Iberia 442–3
    in Ireland and Britain 443–5
    in Kargaly 903, 910
    in south-east/eastern Europe 439–40
    techniques used 448
copper ores 416, 446–7, 532
copper sulphides 261
Corded Ware culture 47, 71, 84, 220, 419, 817, 822
    beaker 64
Cordoned Urns 536, 537, 539, 540
core-periphery theory 2, 9
Corfu 57
Cork, Ireland
    copper mining in 443–5
    stone circles 151
Corlăteni, Moldova 878
Corlea bog, County Longford, Ireland 409
Cornwall, England 143, 372, 445
    stone pairs 149
Corona Moltana, Sardinia 671
Corran Bog, Northern Ireland 209
'corridor nuraghi', Sardinia 673
Corrstown, Northern Ireland 92, 533, 538
Corsica 143

menhirs and statue menhirs 149, 150
Cortaillod-Est, Lake Neuchâtel, Switzerland 92
Coslogeni, Romania 878, 890
cosmology 248–65, 288
    and Bronze Age landscape 253–5
Coste del Marano, Italy 633, 643
Costişa, Romania 878, 886
Coţofeni group 878, 879, 880
Couchey La Rente Neuve, France 573
counter-gifts 263
Cova de Moleta, Mallorca 618
Cova des Bouer, Mallorca 618
Cova des Càrritx, Menorca 624, 630
Cova des Moro, Menorca 618
Cova des Mussol, Menorca 628
Coval Simó, Mallorca 618, 620
Cozia, Romania 878
Cozia-Sakharna culture 915
craft production 95, 469–91
craft specialization 432–3
Cranborne Chase, England 159
crannogs 542
Crawford, O.G.S. 312
cremated bones, dating of 21
cremation 8, 103, 106, 146, 173, 230–1, 535, 540, 558, 575, 700, 731
    burials 108, 711
    cemeteries 581, 582, 640
    cremation burials and evidence of bronze working 129
    Hvidegård cremation burial from Sjælland, period III *105*
    in the Late Bronze Age in Switzerland and the Central Alps 719
    in Peninsular Italy 650
    pits 756
    in Poland 775
    in Scandinavia 754
    in the Tumulus culture 797
crescent horns 718
Crestaulta, Graubünden, Switzerland 95
Crete 383, 385, 386, 506
Crévéchamps, France 573
Crimea 903
Croatia 54, 474
    burial practice and tomb architecture in Istria 852
    inlaid vessels 476

Croce del Papa, Nola, Italy 88–9, 635
Croft Moraig, Scotland 533, 540
Crow Down hoard, West Berkshire, England 458
Cruceni, Romania 878
crucibles 128, 809
Csepel group 817
Cuccuru Nuraxi-Settimo S.Pietro, sacred well 679
Cuckoo Stone, England 159
cucumber 355
Cucuteni, Romania 878
Cucuteni-Tripolye complex 881
cuenco (hemispherical bowl) 672
Cuesta del Negro, Spain 595
cult houses 130, 156, 258
cult-wagon, from Dupljaja 850
cultivated fruit *see* fruit
cults 702–3
Cumbria, England 318
cup marks 270, 283
cups
　bronze cups 379
　fineware cups 91
Cures, Italy 633
cursus monuments 162
Curwen, Eliot and Cecil 312
Cwmystwyth, Wales 445, 449
Cycladic 'frying pans' 385
Cycladic graves 58
Cycladic pottery 383
cynophagy 338
Cypriot pottery 385, 659, 661
Cyprus 372
　colonization of 383
　as a metal source 438
　production of oxhide ingots in 681
Czech lands 787–812
　amber 807
　climate 787
　craft production in 808–9
　cultural sequence and chronology in 789–90
　faience 807
　funerary archaeology 794–9
　glass 807
　gold in 806–7
　material culture in 799–809

　metalwork in 804–6
　pottery in 799–804
　settlement and settlements in 791–4
　stone 807–8
　see also Bohemia; Czech Republic; Moravia
Czech Republic 483
　house constructions in 793
　plant cultivation in 358

daggers 65, 200, 220, 235, 293, 298, 379, 417, 419, 637, 672, 673
　bronze daggers 461, 535
　Early Bronze Age 220
　in female graves 237–8
　flint 279
　gold 460
　leaf-shaped 891
　Malchin-type 735
　in male graves 237
　in Moldova and Bulgaria 893
　in Sardinia 683
　Sicilian riveted 58
　solid-hilted 725, 727
　tanged copper daggers 62
　tin-plated triangular 709
　triangular riveted 59
dairy products 543
Dalj, Croatia 838, 857
Dallet, France 572
Damasław, Poland, pottery from 777
Damgård, Thy, Denmark 754
Dampierre-sur-le-Doubs, France 574, 578
Danube region 826
　Early Bronze Age in 816–20
　gold objects 462
　Middle Danubian Urnfield complex 830–1
Danube river 54, 789, 813
Danube-Tisza interfluve region 820–1, 826–7
Danubian culture 456
Dartmeet, Devon, England 320
Dartmoor, south-west England 311, 322, 538
　Bronze Age landscape on 97
　co-axial fields 320
　field systems in 313–4
Darvill, Timothy 152, 166

Darwin, Charles 329
date (*Phoenix dactylifera*) **354**
dating
  of the Bronze Age 39
  of cremated bones 21
daub chaulking 85
de Lumley, Henri 301
de Marinis, Raffaele 298, 694
dead, treatment of the 108, 227, 558
deben 509
Decimoputzu, Sardinia 669, 670, 671
defended sites 239–40
Delacău, Moldova *878*
dendrochronology 8, 20, 21
Denmark 135, 220, 245, 253, 261, 312, 359, 555, 746–8, 756
  barrows in Jutland 114
  clothing from 223, 226, 229
  cult houses 258
  cult houses in north-east Jutland 156
  daggers in 235
  farmsteads in northern 90
  gravhøj 145
  large houses in northern 87
  oak-log coffins 108, 226, 481
  quartz pebbles in pottery in 473
  razors from 252
  rock art 154
  spoked wheels 403
  standing stones 147
  study of hoards in 124
  sword burials 206
  terpen 329
Dentalium shell 699
dentine collagen 181–2
depas amphikypellon (two-handled drinking cup) 61, 509
  from Michalich-Baa Dere, Assara and Gŭlŭbovo 53
  from Niš -Bubanj (Serbia) 53
deposition
  practices in southern Netherlands and Belgium 564
  selective deposition 198–200
deposits
  contexts and contents 123–9
  in wetlands 136
  see also artefacts; hoards

Dereivka, Ukraine 336
  ritual burial of horses' heads at 900
Derrinboy, County Offaly, gold hoard at 458
Derryoghil bog, County Longford, Ireland, trackways in 409, *410*
Desenzano del Garda-Lavagnone, Switzerland *707, 712*
Deva, Romania 891
developer-funded archaeology 2
Deverel-Rimbury, England 539, 573
Devil's Arrows, near Boroughbridge, North Yorkshire, England 148, 149
Devon, England 372
Dexheim, Germany *724*
diachronic trend 339
diadem stelae 613–4
diadems 461
Dieskau, Germany *724*
  princely grave 459
diet studies 184–7, 189–91
dikes, Cotentin Peninsula in La Hague, France 580
dill 774
Dinaric culture 845
Dinorben, Wales 240
dirks 236, 673
Disa's Ting, Svarte, Skåne, Sweden 153
disc wheels 402
discreet art 304, 304–5, 306, 308
discs, bronze 251, 255, 263
Disgwylfa Fawr, Ceredigion, Wales 392
distaffs 480
distribution maps 7
Ditchling Common, England 125
DNA studies 11
Dobova, Slovenia *838*
  grave goods *858*
Doboz, Hungary 815–6
Dobročkovice, Moravia *788*
dogs 337–8, 343
Dokanova Glavica, Western Balkans 850–1
Dolmenic phase 597
dolmens 143
  Abkhazian Dolmens 143
  Boulder Dolmens 143
  on Corsica 143
  in Mallorca and Menorca 620, 621
  on Sardinia 143

Dolný Peter phase 826
domestic architecture *see* house(s), architecture
domestic hens 338–9, 342
Dömmestorp, Sweden 389
Domu de Orgia-Esterzili, 'Megaron' temple, Sardinia 679
Domus de Janas ('House of the Fairies/Witches'), Sardinia 671
Domu's Orku-Siddi, Sardinia 675
Donja Brnjica, Bosnia and Herzegovina 838, 855, 856
donkeys 337, 635
Dorchester-on-Thames, England 159, 235
Dorgalese, Sardinia 673
Dorgali, Sardinia 669
Doss Gustinaci, Italy 698
Doucier, Chalain, France 572
Dover, England 533, 540, 541
Dragshøj, Denmark 746–7
Drassburg group 788, 790
  pottery 799
Drenthe, the Netherlands 88, 311
dress 216, 218, 223–4
  see also clothing
drinking horns 803
drinking water 181
Dromatuk, County Kerry, Ireland, stone rows 150
Drombeg, County Cork, Ireland 151, 152
drop spindles 480
Drouwen, the Netherlands 206, 565
  Søgel burial 560
drystone walls 85
Dubovac, Serbia 838
Ducové, Slovakia 815–6
Duffaits culture 573
Dumfries, Scotland 143
Dunaalmás, Hungary 815–6
Dunaújváros-Kosziderpadlás, Hungary 470, 815–6, 821
Dupljaja, Serbia 857, 894
  cult-wagon from 850
  model chariot from 474
Durankulak, Bulgaria 340
Durrington Walls, Wiltshire, England 142, 159, 160, 162, 168, 169, 170, 171
'Dutch Model' 72

Dvory n. Žitavou, Slovakia 815–6
dyeing/dyes 225, 229, 480
Dystrup, Denmark 746–7, 764

Earle, Timothy 2
Early Bronze Age 48, 84, 216, 330
  barrows 461
  burials 21, 205
  Capo Graziano facies 658
  ceramics 471, 472
  chief graves 207
  chronological chart **296**
  circum-Aegean exchange and trade network and its cultural peripheries in the Balkans and central Mediterranean in the 50
  cist-grave art 154
  climate during the 898
  copper mining in France 585
  daggers 220, 430, 460
  defended sites 239
  in Germany 725–33
  grave goods 206, 461
  handled cup 461
  hoards in France 587
  jar burials 108
  jet and amber necklaces 206
  Leubingen, Germany burial at 205
  in the Low Countries 566
  metal ingots 211
  monuments 141
  phases of 694
  pins 430
  pottery 25
  quartz pebbles in pottery 473
  site at Durrington Walls, England 142
  transition between Middle Bronze Age and 250
  Únětice burials 107
  use of token money in 514
  vessels 459
  weapons 294
  west European barrow tradition 103
  wristguards 460
Early Bronze Age I 671
Early Catacomb culture 902
Early Helladic-Cycladic-Minoan II period 48

Early Helladic IIb 56
Early Iron Age 404, 688, 890–1
    in Etruria, Italy 643
    goldworking 466
    Hallstatt culture 738
    picene culture (Marche) 642
    in Romania, Moldova and Bulgaria 895
    urnfields 557
    Wehringen-Hexenbergle barrow 713
Early medieval period 136
earplugs 462
East Anglia, England 321
East Mediterranean
    copper mines in 438–9
    developments in weighing in the Late
        Bronze Age in 510–1
East Slovakian Tumulus culture 822
East Yorkshire Wolds, England 188
Eastern Zone
    enclosures 156
    megalithic tombs 143
    Pontic Steppes 144
    rock art 154
Ebbs-Tischoferhöhle, Austria 788–9, 797
Eberswalde hoard, Germany 459
ebony 385
Ecce Homo, Spain 595
economics 210–2
economy, of damp-ground settlements in
        Germany 742
Egtved, Skrydstrup, Denmark 746–7, 755
Egyek, Hungary 815–6, 827
Egypt 365, 383, 405, 508
    Pharaonic 481
    primary production of glass in 495
einkorn 350, 351, 352, 353, 354, 355, 356, 357,
        358, 359, 360, 774
Ejby, Denmark 746–7
Ekaryd, Småland, Sweden, stone rows 150
Ekenberg, Sweden 746–7
Ekkersrijt, the Netherlands 566
El Acequión, Spain 595, 604
El Aramo, Spain 443
    Chalcolithic/Early Bronze Age copper
        mine at 444
El Argar culture *see* Argaric culture
El Argar, Spain 595, 607
    production and circulation of metal 608

El Cabezo Redondo, Alicante, Spain 610
El Castanuelo, Spain 595
El Castillo de Cardeñosa, Spain 595
El Milagro, Spain 443, 595
El Oficio, Spain 595
El Parpantique, Spain 595
El Recuenco, Spain 595
El Rincón, Spain 595
El Trastejón, Spain 595
Elba 687
Elbe-Saale region 734
electron microscopy 463
elephant ivory 647
elk 340
Elleri, Italy 871
Elp, the Netherlands 555, 561
    fenced stock pens at 91
    houses at 90
    pottery 553
Emenska Peshtera, Bulgaria 51
Emilia Romagna, Italy 642, 692, 695
emmer
    see also cereals; wheat
emmer wheat 360, 538
    in Central and Northern Italy 351
    in the Eastern Alps and their Foreland 356
    in Greece and southern Bulgaria 350
    in Mediterranean Spain 353
    in the Pannonian Basin 354, 355
    in Poland 774
    in Scandinavia 752
    in Southern France 352
    in Southern Scandinavia and the North Sea
        coast 359
    in west-central Europe 358
    in the Western Alps and their foreland 357
Emmerhout-Angelslo, the Netherlands 555
Ems group 553
enamel data, from Neolithic and Bronze Age
        barrows on the Yorkshire Wolds 186
enchytrismos, for children 649
enclosures 155–6
    cremation cemeteries 155
    settlements 542
Encrusted pottery jugs 818
Eneolithic 881, 891
Eneolithic/Copper Age, hammer-axes and
        axe-adzes 417

Engedal, Denmark 746–7
England 312
  copper mines at 445
  four-poster stone circles 153
  houses in southern 86, 87
  Late Bronze Age ceramics 471
  sewn-plank boats 387
  stone rows in 150
  tin in south-west 38
  weapons found in 125
English Channel, shipwrecks in 371
English Heritage 161
Enigma of the Gift, The (Godelier) 256
Enkuizen, the Netherlands 566
Ensisheim, France 574
Entrance Graves 143
Eogan, George 122
epi-Bell Beaker-Dolmen archaeological group, in Mallorca and Menorca 620–1
epi-Corded complex 822
equal-arm balance 508, 517
Erzgebirge mountains, Central Europe 38, 374–5, 808
Es Càrritx, Menorca 618, 625, 628
Es Figueral de Son Real, Mallorca 618, 628
Es Forat de ses Aritges, Menorca 618
Es Mussol, Menorca 618, 627
  figures made of olive wood in the cave of 629
Eshøj, Denmark 145
Eskiyapar, Turkey 58
Essai sur le Don (Mauss) 256
Esterzili, Sardinia 669
Estonia
  barbed and tanged arrowheads 483
  bone objects 486
Esztergom, Hungary 831
Etaules, France 579
Étigny, France 517, 519–20
Etruria, Italy 632
  Early Iron Age in 643
  Final Bronze Age cremation burials in 650
  Final Bronze Age Tolfa-Allumiere group in 642–3
Euboean emporion of Pithecusa 645
Europe
  barley in western central 360
  Bronze Age chronology of Western 17–46
  Bronze Age villages in south-east 92

  at c.2500 BC 47–8
  ceramics in central and eastern 472
  chronological systems for Western 18–9
  copper mines in south-east/eastern 439–40
  fortified and aggregated sites in 96
  house architecture in 84, 92
  linen tabbies in West-Central 479
  longhouses in northern 84
  monument-building zones in 142
  plant cultivation in West-Central 357–9
  RI values of non-cereals in the archaeobotanical record of Western Central **358**
  rock art in Northern 270–90
  ship-setting burials in 104
  see also Central Europe; Continental Europe; north-west Europe
Evans, France 574
Evershed, Richard 10
Extremadura, Spain 147
Ezero, Bulgaria 878, 901

Fabbrica dei Soci, Italy 700
face urns 762, 780
fahlore copper 422, 424, 426, 430, 440, 446, 818
faience 62, 492–500, 807
  archaeological sites 492
  beads 492
  conical buttons 496, 497
  description of 493
  in northern Italy 496–8
  occurrence of 492
  production zones of 494–5
Falkenstein, Frank 845
fallow deer 884
Falun, Sweden 373
families 83
Fårdal, Denmark 746–7
  hoard 762
Farébersviller, France 586
farming *see* agriculture
farmsteads 4, 90–1, 576
  in Germany 740
  located near barrows 92
  in the Low Countries 555

Fatyanovo-Balanovo culture 907
feet (footsole) images 286
Felsőtárkány, Hungary 815–6, 828
female graves in Germany 732
female infanticide 625
female jewellery 588, 589
Fengate, Peterborough, Cambridgeshire, England 321, 322
Fermo, Italy 633
Feudvar, Serbia 341, *838*, 840–1, 845, 846
   settlement *842, 843*
Fiavè, Italy 693
   peat bog 696
   pile dwelling settlement at 696
fibulae 736
   Recent Bronze Age fragments of *684*
   two-piece 760
Fidvár, Vráble, Slovakia 93, *94*
field and land divisions 311–27
field bean **350**, 351, **352**, 353, 354, 355, **356, 357**, 358, **359**, 363, 364–5
field mustard 774
field systems 314, 544
   aggregate and cohesive 314
   co-axial 314
fields
   in Britain and Ireland 538
   chronology and history of 315–6
   classification of 314–5
   co-axial fields 320–2
   landscape and society 324–5
fieldstone 319
fig 351, 352, 354, 363
figurative art 270, 274, **350**
figurines, from Scandinavia 762–3
Filicudi, Sicily 655, 661
filigree 466
Final Bronze Age 670
   facies 641–2, 646
   Tolfa-Allumiere group, in Southern Etruria 642–3
Final Bronze Age-Early Iron Age 641–9
fineware cups and bowls 91
finished goods, movement of 378–9
Finistère, France, stone circles in 153
Finland 63, 746, *746–7*
   see also Scandinavia
firesetting 448, 449

fish 190
fish bones 774
fish-hooks 416, 763
Flag Fen, Peterborough, England 156, 408, *533*, 538
Flagstones, Dorchester, England 164
flanged axes *see* axes
flat axes *see* axes
flat cemeteries 535, 725, 904
flat graves 756, 909
flax 349, **350**, 351, **352**, **353**, **354**, **355**, **356**, 357, **358**, 359, 479–80, 774
Fleming, Andrew 96, 313, 320
Fließ-Moosbruckschrofen, Austria 788–9
flint 532, 562, 760, 761, 767
   arrowheads 242
   burnt flint 91
   daggers 279, 535, 727, 735
   objects 207
   in Sicily 657
flint industry 778, 779
flint mines 536
flint-working 608
Flintsbach, 'Rachelburg', weighing equipment *518*
floors, in Bronze Age settlements 85
Florinas, Sardinia 669
Fogdarp, Sweden 746–7
   yoke mountings 763
Fokkens, Harry 555
Foltești, Moldova *878*, 881
Fondo Paviani, Italy 700
Fondo Zanotto, Italy 701
Fonni, Sardinia 669
Fontanalba, Mont Bégo, France 301, *304*, 305
Fontijn, David 6, 136, 550, 564
food vessels 173, 471, 537
Foppe di Nadro, Valcamonica, Italy, weapons as engravings on natural rock slabs 295
Forêt de Haguenau, France 582
forge, as woman in disguise 260
Forlati, Bruna Tamaro 872
Formentera 617
Former Yugoslavia
   density of swords in the 236
   gold and silver finds from the 56
Forsandmoen, Norway 746–7, 750
Forschner, Germany 713, 724, 742

Fort Harrouard, France 580, 586
fortified settlements 825
  hoards discovered in 741
  in the Late Bronze Age in Romania,
    Moldova and Bulgaria 889–90
  of the Northern Adriatic 864–76
  in Romania, Moldova and Bulgaria 891
  see also settlements
Fosie IV, Sweden 750
Fossa-grave culture 645
Fossum, Bohuslän, Sweden 238
fowl 338–9
Fragtrup, Denmark 746–7, 752
  Iron Age house 750
Francavilla, Italy 633, 646, 647
France 31, 32
  archaeological cultures in 33
  arrangement of settlements 576–9
  Bronze Age cultural zones in 572, 573
  Bronze Age in 31–3, 571–93
  Bronze Age villages 579
  bronze production in 586–7
  chronological systems for 18–9, 28–9
  controlled land and territories in 579–81
  copper mines in the western Alps and 441–2
  copper-trading networks 586
  distribution of Bronze Age hoards in
    589, 590
  Early Bronze Age in 571
  enclosed cremation cemeteries in 155
  funerary practice and beliefs in 581–5
  geographical and cultural regions of 571–5
  gold lock-rings 460
  hoards 123, 587–90
  house-landscape in 96
  individual burials in 581
  ingots and semi-finished products 585–6
  inhumation rituals and grave deposits in
    the Early Bronze Age in 720
  Late Bronze Age cultural zones in 574
  Late Bronze Age weights from 521, **522**
  menhirs in 147
  metal production in 585–90
  metalliferous resources 585
  rock art in 154
  round barrows 145
  roundhouses in 84
  sacred places in 583

  sanctuaries and ritualized cult
    practices 583–5
  settlements and the use of space 575–81
  stone circles in 153
  upland settlements 579
  wood and earth constructions 576
  see also Brittany; Normandy; southern
    France
Franche-Comté, France 581
Franconia-Palatinate group 731
Franzhausen, Austria 211, 788–9, 796–7
Franzine Nuove, Italy 700
Frattesina, Italy 492, 496, 498, 633, 641, 693,
    697, 701, 703
  glass industry at 497–8
Frauensberg bei Weltenburg, Germany 724
freshwater fish 190
Friaga Wald-Bartholomäberg,
    Switzerland 707
  hill fort 715, 716
Frøjk, Denmark 237
Fröslunda, Sweden 746–7
fruit 349, 363–4, 634
  Representatives Index of cultivated fruit **350**
  see also apples; grape; plum; pomegranate
fruit trees 352, 354, 356, 363–4
Fucino, Italy 633
Fuente Álamo, Almería, Spain 93, 353,
    361, 595
Fuente Olmedo, Castile, Spain 59, 595
fulacht fiadh 535
Fulda-Werra group 730
funeral monuments 582
funeral pyres 754
funerary practices
  in Apulia and Basilicata 637
  and beliefs in France 581–5
  Early Iron Age picene culture
    (Marche) 642
  in Etruria in the Early Iron Age 643
  in Final Bronze Age-Early Iron Age in
    Lazio 644
  Kisapostag culture 819
  in the Low Countries 557
  in North and West of Iberia 606
  in Northern Italy 699–701
  in Romania, Moldova and Bulgaria 895
Funnel Beaker culture 552, 553

Funtan Coberta-Ballao, Sardinia 683
Funtana 'e Casu dolmen, Sardinia 672
Furmánek, Václav 814
Füzesabony, Hungary 815–6, 824, 878
Fyn, Denmark 757, 764

Gáborján, Hungary 815–6
Gaggio, Italy 511
Galician-style rock art 154, 238
Gallay, Alain 292
Galloway, Scotland 143, 340
Gallura, Sardinia 673
Gánovce, Poprad, Slovakia 155, 815–6
Garašanin, Milutin 839, 854
garden pea 350, 351, 352, 354, **355**, 356, **357**, 358, 363
Gatas, Spain 595
Gattendorf, Austria 788–9
    houses 792
Gáva-Holihrady culture 828, 833, 857, 890
    burials of the 890
    inhumation in vessels 891
Gáva, Hungary 878
Gayhurst, Buckinghamshire, England 332, 533, 535
Gelidonya shipwreck 510
Gemeinlebarn, Austria 788–9
    male and female burials at 227
Gemer, Slovakia 815–6
gender
    and dress 222
    identity and 217–8
Génelard, France 574
Genlis, France 577
Genlis-Izier, France 572, 576
Genó, Spain 595
Georgia 464
Germany 8, 135, 245, 253, 361, 723–45
    archaeological groups 723
    barrows at Lower Saxony 105
    Bavaria 358
    division of the Bronze Age in 725
    Early Bronze Age in 725–33
    Early Bronze Age settlements 738, *739*
    fortified settlements in 740–1
    interpretation of hoards as votive offerings 123
    Iron Age settlements in 740
    lake villages 96
    Late Bronze Age in 730–3
    Late Bronze Age settlement in 739–40
    Lausitz culture in 734–5
    map of *724*
    Middle Bronze Age in 727–30
    Middle Bronze Age settlements 739
    Northern *261*, 358
        hoards from bogs in 738
        metal hoards in 735
        Nordic Bronze Age in 735–8
        oak-log coffins 108
        ship-setting burials 104
        sword burials 206
    open settlements in 738–40
    prehistoric wooden trackways in 408
    regional groups in 730
    regions 723
    river systems 723
    selective deposition in 199
    settlements in 738–42
    south German Bronze Age 4
    southern Germany 129
    terpen 329
    weapon finds in 125
    western 211
    see also northern Germany
Giants' tombs, Sardinia 671, 672, 673, 674, 675, 682
gift exchange 202
gifts 256, 263
Gîrla Mare/Žuto Brdo culture 475, 878, 894, 895
Giubiasco, Switzerland 707
Glasinac, Bosnia and Herzegovina 838
Glasinac culture 849, 854, 855
glass 492–500, 807
    archaeological sites 492
    beads 492
    glass beads 95
    mixed-alkali 494, 496, 498
    occurrence of 492
    opaque 493
    plant-ash and mixed-alkali 495
    production of 493–4
    production zones of 495–6
    raw glass 385
    types of 498

Glina, Romania *878*
Glina-Schneckenberg culture 880, 881, 894
Glob, Peter 284
Globular Amphora group 880
Glüsing, Schleswig-Holstein, Germany 461
Gnirs, Anton 866
Gnisvärd, Gotland, Sweden 389
goats 330, 334–5, 619, 718, 774, 909
Godelier, Maurice 256–7, 309
gold 372, 377, 515, 519, 520, 523, 540, 599, 726, 748, 757, 804
   acquisition of 463–4
   armlets 757
   artefacts 780
   Avanton gold cone 587
   bar casts 465
   beakers 727
   blades 460
   boats 459
   bowls 764
   bracelets 54, 460, 462
   cast gold dress-fasteners 462
   ceremonial axes 726
   ceremonial hats (cones) 459
   chasing 466
   combs 460
   cones 459, 461
   cups 537
   daggers 54, 886
   decorative techniques 466
   deposition of objects 544
   diadems 54
   discs 212, 459, 466, 727, 728
   dust, as money 514
   figures of eight 806
   finishing 466
   forging sheets, rods and wire from gold bars 465
   function of gold objects 458–61
   gold finds from the Former Yugoslavia 56
   and gold working 454–68
   granulation of 466
   grave goods 461
   hair ornaments 93
   hair rings 203, 206
   hoards 457–8
   from Hungary 813
   ingots 458
   from Ireland and Wales 532
   jewellery 54, 200, 458, 460, 589
   lock-rings 460, 462, 884, 891
   lunulae 209
   oath rings 760
   objects 587
   ornaments 200, 205, 565, 610
   plastic deformation 465
   from Rathgall, County Wicklow 95
   rings 461, 664
   ritual objects 459
   in Romania, Moldova and Bulgaria 891
   Schulenburg lunulae 727
   sheets 460, 461, 462
   from Slovakia 813
   smelting, alloying and casting 465
   sources of 464
   stamping 466
   technology 464
   as a textile material 479
   thread inlay 460
   in the Tisza region 823
   torcs 458
   touchstone 464
   from Transylvania 814
   tweezers 460
   typo-chronologies in 25
   use during the Chalcolithic 437
   vessels 459, 462, 463, 466
   weapons 459
   wire 462
   wound-wire gold ornament from Várvölgy hoard 831
gold-of-pleasure 349, **350**, 351, 355, 356, 357, 358, 359, 363, 774
Goldhahn, Joakim 129, 130
goldsmiths 454
goldworking
   in Britain and Ireland 537
   after the Bronze Age 466–7
   chronological development of 461–2
   investigation methods 463
   research into 455–6
Gondelsheim, Germany, rectangular weights 518
Gönnebek, Schleswig-Holstein, Germany 461
Gonnesa, Sardinia 669
Gonnosfanadiga, Sardinia 669, 673
Gór, Hungary 815–6, 830

gorgets 460, 462
Gorodsk-Troyanov group 904
Góry Kościuszki, Ślęża, Poland 156
Göschenen I 706, 717
Gospić, Croatia 838
Gosselain, Olivier 6
Gotland, Sweden, barrows 144
Götschenberg, Bishofshofen, Austria 441
Gotthard Pass area 711
Gourjade, France 574
Govora, Romania 888
Gowland, William 160
Gradac-Turan, Croatia 867, 871
gradine, of the Northern
    Adriatic 864–76
Gradišče Kunci, Slovenia 870
grain 517
Granadan Bronze Age 244
Grand Menhir Brisé, near Carnac, Morbihan,
    France 149
Grandson-Corcellettes, Switzerland
    707, 713
Granges-sous-Grignon, France 573
Gransha, Northern Ireland 533, 540
grape 351, 352, 353, 354, 356, 363, 634
grapevine 350, 352, 353, 354, 355, 356,
    357, 358
graphite 808
grass pea 350, 351, 352, 353, 355, 357, 363
grave goods 7, 75–6, 558, 581, 604, 650, 699,
    701, 726, 731–2, 797, 854, 857, 900
  bell beakers as 173
  in cemeteries in Dobova 858
  copper 796
  daggers as 235
  deposition of 3
  El Argar culture 599
  gold grave goods 461
  Lausitz culture 734
  in the Low Countries 558–61
  during the proto-talayotic period 629
  Sicilian Pantalica culture, Early 664
  Thun-Renzenbühl, Bern 710
  Tisza region 823
  in the Western Balkans 853
  see also artefacts
grave jewellery 458
grave markers 146

graves 54, 603–4
  balances found in 511
  communal graves in the southern central
    Mediterranean area 55
  in the Low Countries 558–61
  two-wheeled chariots in 405
gravhøj, in Denmark 145
Great Britain *see* Britain
Great Orme, North Wales 533, 536–7, 539
  copper mine 444, 445, 447, 451
Great Poland 734
Greater Stonehenge Cursus, Wiltshire,
    England 159, 162
Gređani, Croatia 838
Greece 3, 334
  amber in 377
  barley in 359
  Bronze Age lion finds from 340
  copper mining in 438
  domestic horses 337
  einkorn in 360
  later third millennium BC Italian finds of
    the Aegean origin in 60
  oil plants 363
  plant cultivation in 349–51
  roles of animals in 328
Green Park, Berkshire, England 91, 208
Greifensee-Böschen, Switzerland 707, 712,
    713, 714
Grevensvænge, Denmark 746–7, 758, 762
grey seal 341
greylag goose 339
Grimes Graves, England 533, 536
Grimeton, Sweden 746–7
grinders 608
Grinsell, Leslie 392
Gristhorpe, Yorkshire, England 187, 392
Grödig, Austria 788–9, 797
Grooved ware pottery 534, 537
Großbrembach, Germany 724
Großmugl, Austria 788–9
Grotta Cappuccini, south Apulia, Italy 57,
    58, 63
Grotta Chiusazza, Sicily 655
Grotta del Pipistrello Solitario, Taranto,
    Italy 58
Grotta della Monace, Calabria, Italy 439
Grotta Manaccora, Italy 633

Grotta Misa, Italy 633
Grotta Nuova, Italy 511
Grotte des Perrats, near Agris, France 517
grotticella tombs 655, 656, 657, 659, 663
ground surveys 312
Gué-des-Piles, Chalon-sur-Saône, France 579
Guernsey 147
Guido, Peggy 492
Guînes, Pas-de-Calais, France 456, 460, 589
  jewellery from 455
Guldhøj, Denmark 746–7, 755
Gŭlŭbovo, Bulgaria 51
Gundestrup cauldron 379
Guntramsdorf, Austria 788–9
Gusen, Austria 788–9
Gwithian, Cornwall, England 319
Gymnesian Islands 617
Gyulavarsánd culture 824

hafted palstaves 756
Håg, Denmark 746–7
Håga, Sweden 746–7, 753, 757
  finds from 758
Hagendrug, Zealand, Denmark, headpiece 459
Hagnau-Burg, Lake Constance 357, 362, 724
Haguenau, France 573
Hainburg-Teichtal, Austria 788–9, 796
hair ornaments 93
hair-rings 582
Hajdúbagos, Hungary 815–6, 827
Hajdúböszörmény, Hungary 236, 815–6
Hajdúsámson, Hungary 824
halberds 38, 59, 205, 235, 293, 725, 726
  bronze halberds 200
  Carrapatas halberds 607
  solid-hilted halberds 294
Halle-Giebichenstein, Germany 724, 726
Halle (Saale), Sachsen-Anhalt, Germany 501
Hallstatt A1 135
Hallstatt, Austria 400, 479, 788–9
Hallstatt culture 709, 773, 880, 890, 894
  swords 764
  use of antler and bone in settlements 779

Hallstatt salt mine 400, 480, 506, 808
  Bronze Age salt mining at 503–4
  Iron Age mining at 504
  source of Bronze Age textiles 478
Hallstattization 889
Hallunda, Stockholm, Sweden 746–7, 750, 761
  workshops 259
Hälsingborg, Sweden 746–7, 762
hammer-axes
  shaft-hole 416, 417
  see also axes
hammers 445, 809
  waisted stone 813
Hamneda, Sweden 315
Han-sur-Lesse, Belgium 565
Hänsel, Bernhard 839
Handewitt, Germany 724, 736, 754
Hårbølle, Denmark 746–7, 753
harbour seal 341
Harding, Anthony 1, 236, 494
Harold's Stones, near Trelleck, Monmouthshire, Wales 148, 149
harp seal 341
Harrislee, Germany 724
Hart an der Alz, Germany 406
Hartshill Copse, near Bucklebury, England 149, 533, 543
Haselbach-Michelberg, Austria 788–9
Hassle, Sweden 746–7, 764
Hassloch, Germany 404
Hatt, Gudmund 312
Hatvan culture 822
Haumesser, Switzerland 707, 713
Hauterive-Champréveyres, Lake Neuchâtel, Switzerland 339, 475, 492
Hawkes, Christopher 248
Hawley, William 160
hazelnuts 634, 774
hearths 91
Hebrides, the 149
Hedeager, Lotte 255
Heinrichsburg, Seußlitz, Germany 724
Hellenistic Greece 365
helmets 236, 586
Helms, Mary 130, 393
Helmsdorf, Germany 206, 724, 726
Hemmed, Denmark 746–7
hemp 349, 479

Herbert, Eugenia 260
Hernádkak, Hungary 235
Herzogenburg, Austria 475
Herzsprung, Germany 724
Hesse, Germany 357
Het Noordse Veld, Zeijen, Drenthe, the
    Netherlands, Celtic fields at 321
Heunischenburg, Kronach, Bavaria,
    Germany 240, 724
  fortified gate 741
Hildebrand, Bror Emil 274
hill forts 94, 239–40, 329, 791
  associated with the production and supply
    of copper 441
  Friaga Wald, Bartholomäberg 715, 716
  in Germany 740
  in Hungary 831–2
  in Slovakia 831–2
hilltop settlements 95, 603
  in Iberia 605
Hilversum tradition 553
hippopotamus 385
  hippopotamus-ivory head with a boar's
    tusk helmet 680
Hjordkjaer, Jutland, Denmark 144
Hjortekorg cairn, Sweden 284
hoarding traditions 96
hoards
  and the deposition of metalwork 121–39
  and the development of prehistoric
    archaeology 122
  dry land 124, 125, 131, 136
  'Founders' hoards' 123
  in France 587–90
  in Iberia 36
  interpretation of 122–3
  'merchants' hoards' 123
  'mixed' hoards 134
  'non-ritual' hoards 124, 128, 130
  ornament hoards 132, 588
  relationships between finds from rivers and
    graves and the occurrence of similar
    artefacts in scrap hoards 134
  'ritual' hoards 124
  scrap hoards 128–9
  and single finds 131
  'utilitarian' hoards 124
  and votive deposits in Scandinavia 764

wetland 124–5
see also artefacts; deposits
Hochrhein-Oberrhein group 727
Hódmezővásárhely, Hungary 815–6, 828
Höhenrätien, Switzerland 707, 715
Höhensiedlung ('settlement on a
    height') 715
Hohøj, East Jutland, Denmark 746–7, 753
Højgård, Denmark 746–7
Holihrady 878
Holland see Netherlands, the
Holme-next-the-Sea, Norfolk, eastern
    England 533, 536
  timber circle at 21
Holocene 551
Hoogkarspel, the Netherlands 323
Hörbing, Austria 788–9
horn artefacts 778, 809
Horn, Austria 788–9
Horní Počaply, Bohemia 788
Hornstaad-Hörnle, Lake Constance 417
Horridge Common, Dartmoor, England,
    co-axial fields 321
horse(s) 335–7, 342, 399, 483, 635, 700, 774,
    894, 900–1, 909
  bits 401
  domestication of 904
  harnesses 401, 485
  horse-borne nomads 915, 916
  horse-head razor handles 762
  nose reins 401
  walking speed 401
Høstad, Norway 746–7
Hosty, Bohemia 788, 809
house(s)
  architecture 83, 84–7
  and households 83–4
  landscapes 95–6
  mud-bricks 85
  organization of household space 88–90
  post-built structures 85
  reconstruction at Százhalombatta,
    Hungary 87
  size differences between 87–8
  uses of large buildings 88
Hoya Quemada, Spain 595
hubs 402
Huelva, Spain 443

Hügelgräberbronzezeit (Tumulus Bronze Age) 710, 558
human enamel data, from Neolithic and Bronze Age barrows on the Yorkshire Wolds *186*
human mobility 75, 398
human remains, deliberate placing in roundhouses and ditches 544
human skulls 91
humans, as bearers 400
Humphrey, Caroline 523
Hünenburg, Watenstedt, Germany *724*, *741*
Hungary 197, 338, 378, 460, 474, 486, 790, 813
   agriculture in 825
   burial rites in 825
   chronology 814
   Early Bronze Age in 814–25
   end of the Bronze Age in 832–3
   hill forts 831–2
   Late and Final Bronze Age in 827–32
   Late Bronze Age hoards 832
   map of *815–6*
   Middle Bronze Age cooking and storage vessels *473*
   Middle Bronze Age in 825–7
   natural resources 813–4
   salt importation 506
   setting and natural conditions 813–4
   settlements 825
   tells 473
   use of red deer antlers 485
hunter-gatherer communities 270
hunting 339–41
Hüsby, Schleswig-Holstein, Germany 459
   barrows at 105
Hvidegård, Denmark 104, 222, 746–7, 757
hydrogen isotope data *180*, *181*
   analysis of collagen *193*
   /deuterium, analytical fraction, dietary input and interpretation of *183*

Iberia 21, 239, 334, 594–616
   archaeological groups and artefact styles between *c.* 1900 and 1500 BC *597*
   area of Cogotas I pottery and its distribution in *606*
   Argaric south-east 596–600
   Atlantic Coast and Bay of Biscay 594
   beginnings of the Bronze Age in 594
   Bronze Age in 33–8, *597*
   chronological systems for *18–9*, 34–5
   climate during the Early Bronze Age 596–7
   construction types 604
   copper mines in 442–3, 600
   decorations and surface finishes to ceramic vessels *474*
   Early Bronze Age 596–609
   eastern and southern coast 594
   end of the Bronze Age in 594
   Final Bronze Age in 596, 611–4
   funerary practices 604
   geoclimatic zones 594
   gold jewellery 462
   goldworking in 462
   hilltop settlements 609
   hoards in 36
   individual burials along Atlantic seaboard of 607
   initial Argaric society (*c.*2000–1950 cal BC) 600–1
   inland region 594
   Late Bronze Age in 596, 609–11
   map of Bronze Age sites *595*
   metal hoards 614
   North and West of 605–7
   pottery *470*, *472*
   rivers 594
   settlement patterns between *c.*2200 and 1550 BC *601*
   social and economic developments in Early Bronze Age 607–9
   stelae 239
   urnfields in 613
   victims of violence 244
   weapons and weaponry as grave goods 245
   western Iberia 38
Ibero-Levantine bronze age 597
Ibiza 617
'Iceman' 187, 692
identities/identity 204, 216, 218–22
   and dress 223
   and gender 217–8
idols, loaf-of-bread 873

Iglarevo, Metohija *838*, 855
Igrici, Hungary *815–6*
Igrița, Romania *878*, 880
Ilja-Sitno, Slovakia *815–6*
Ille-et-Vilaine, France, four-poster stone circle 153
Iliad 371
imported goods 398
Incoronata-San Teodoro, Italy *633*, 647–8
Indonesia 212
information sources 3–7
Ingolstadt-Zuchering, Germany *724*, 738
  cemetery 732
  Early Bronze Age settlement of 739
ingot weights 513–4
ingots 128, 562
  hoards 515
  plano-convex 586
  and semi-finished products 585–6
Ingram, Rebecca 492
inhumations 8, 104, 146, 535, 558, 646, 719, 754, 797
  Borum Eshøj, Jutland, Denmark *105*
  in Calabria 647
  in Germany during the Middle Bronze Age 728
  Moriš group 856
  in southern Italy 639
Inner Alpine group 710
Inner Alps
  Bronze Age settlement expansion into the *708*
  funerary rites 797
Insoll, Tim 141
Inventaria Archaeologica 5
Ipelský Sokolec, Slovakia *815–6*
Iran, arsenical copper and bronze 429
Ireland 462, 471
  Beaker burial rite 534
  bowls and vases 537
  Bronze Age in 22–5, 531–49
  chronological systems for *18–9*, 23–4
  copper in 372, 443–5
  cremation 540
  dolmens in 143
  Early Bronze Age pottery in 25, 471
  Entrance Graves or Scilly-Tramore tombs in 143
  entrances to stone circles in Cork and Kerry 151
  flat axes 378
  four-poster stone circles in 153
  gold lunulae 209
  hearths in settlements in 91
  house foundations and abandonment deposits in 86–7
  house-landscape in 96
  landscape 532
  Late Bronze Age gold objects 460, *462*
  Late Bronze Age gorgets 460
  logboats in 392
  metalwork depositions in 125
  in the mid third to early second millennium BC 533–7
  recumbent stone circles in 151
  round barrows in 145
  roundhouses in 84, 90, 96
  settlements in 534
  stone cairns 145
  stone pairs 149
  stone rows 150
  swords in 236
  trackways in 409
  victims of violence 244
  wedge tombs in 143
  see also Britain
iron 563, 614, 647, 731, 893
ironworking 22, 543
  objects 543
  pins 563, 688
  in Sardinia 687–8
  swords 649
Iron Age 136, 240, 596, 719
  coins 128
  garments 231
  pottery from Italy 646
  ritual site 714
Irthlingborough, Northamptonshire, England 332, 535
Is Lapideddas-Gonnosnò, Sardinia 673
Ișalnița, Romania 878
Ischia, Italy 633
Island of Nias, Indonesia 309
Isle of Man 143
  gold casting mould 465
Isleham, Cambridgeshire, England 125

Isles of Scilly 492
isotope analyses 10, 11, 179–96
   limitations and problems of 191–2
   techniques of 180
Italy 632–52
   Adriatic sea level during the Bronze
      Age 634
   Aegean pottery 379
   Bari-Taranto Tombs in 143
   Bell Beaker culture in 63
   central and northern 351–2
   coastal plain 632
   einkorn in 360
   emmer wheat in 360
   later third millennium BC Italian finds of
      Aegean origin in 60
   map of 633
   Middle Bronze Age glass from 494
   non-cereals in 352
   Northern 692–705
      Bronze Age chronology of 693–4
      cultural development of 694–9
      final phase of the Bronze Age in 703
      funerary rites 699–701
      lake villages of 96
      map of 693
      pottery 694
      ritual, cult and religion in 702–3
      settlement models in 695
      statue menhirs 147
   Otranto Tombs 143
   Peninsular 632–52
      coastal trade 649
      cultural sequence in 635–49
      domestic animals 635
      Early Bronze Age in 635–7
      Final Bronze Age and Early Iron Age in
         641–9
      final phase of the Middle Bronze Age in
         637–9
      funerary practices 649
      inhumation burials in 639
      inhumation cemetery 635
      from the Late Bronze Age 650
      Late Bronze Age in 640–1
      Middle Bronze Age in 635–7
      pre-Apennine and proto-Apennine
         facies 636–7
      settlements 635, 638, 640
      social structure 649
      subsistence 634
   regional division 632
   salt production in 502
   terramare 473
   third millennium BC finds with Aegean
      connections from 57
   weighing in 511–4
   see also Northern Italy; Peninsular Italy;
      southern Italy
Itford Hill, Sussex, England 87
Ittireddu, Sardinia 669
Ivkovo Brdo 838
ivory of elephant 385, 614
Izdebno, Poland 782

Jaegerborg Hogn, Copenhagen,
   Denmark 461
Jánosháza, Hungary 815–6
Jánoshida, Hungary 815–6, 828
jar burials 108
Jastorf culture 738
Jászdósza-Kápolnahalom, Hungary 92, 93,
   815–6
Jelšovce, Slovakia 815–6
jet 62, 532
   beads 209
   necklaces 206, 535
   vessels 459
jewellery 62
   anklets 760
   bronze jewellery, found in the river
      Hérault 588
   from France 455, 588
   gold jewellery 200, 458
   Tolnanémedi 820
   willow-leaf 822
   see also necklaces
Jockenhövel, Albrecht 378
Jones, Carlton 316
Josipovac Punitovački, Croatia 838
jugs 799
   Maďarovce culture 818
   two-handled 58
Jumièges, France 580
Just, Ille-et-Vilaine, France 150

Kalakača, Beška, Serbia *838*, 846
Kalnik, Croatia *838*
Kamensko-Liventsovka group 909
Kandler, Pietro 864
Kanligeçit, Turkish Thrace 51
Kápolnadomb, Gór, Danube Region 830
Kaposvár, Hungary 815–6, 820
Karastak, Northern Adriatic 871
Kargaly, Russia 440, 910
Karlstrup, Denmark 746–7
karst caves 583, 854
Kas, Northern Adriatic 872
Kaštelir, Croatia 872
Kašteljerska kultura 864–76
Katakombnaya kultura (Catacomb Grave culture) 47, 336, 905–7
Kaul, Flemming 156, 251, 275, 389
Kazakhstan 483
Kemi Oba culture 901, 903
Kendall, David 519
Kerbschnitt decoration 477
Kernonen en Plouvorn, Finistère, France 145
Kerzerho, France 150
Kettlasbrunn, Austria 244
keys, bronze 718
Khvalynsk culture 900, 901
Kilmartin valley, Scotland *533*
kilns 475, 809
King Barrow Ridge, Wiltshire, England 162, 164
'King's Grave', Seddin, Germany 737
King's Stables, County Armagh, Ireland 155
kinship 432
Kirkebjerg, Voldtofte, Denmark 746–7, 751
Kisapostag culture 819–20, 844, 856
Kitchen, Willy 319
Kivik, Sweden 156, 221, *746–7*, 763
Klinglberg, St Veit, Austria 441
Ključka, Macedonia *838*, 855
KMK period *see kul'tura mnogovalikovoi keramiki* ('multi-cordoned ware' culture) (KMK)
Knackyboy, Isles of Scilly 492
knapping 808
knives 730, 760
  tin bronze 54
Knocksaggart, County Clare, Ireland 208

Knörzer, Karl-Heinz 358
Knovíz culture 798
  pottery 799
  settlement in Prague-Hostivař 809
  Štítary stage of 790, 803
Koarum, Skåne, Sweden 156
Kokemäki, Finland 746–7
Kola Peninsula, Russia 154
Kolombanija, Croatia 871
Komarovo culture *878*, 909
Kommos, Crete 670
Komorowo settlements, Poland 779
Konstantinovy Lázně, Bohemia 788
Köpinge, Sweden 746–7
Környe, Hungary 815–6
Korshøj, near Svendborg, Denmark 746–7
  selection of finds from *761*
Kościan group 780, 781
Košice, Slovakia 815–6
Kossack, Georg 915
Košťany culture 822, 823
Koszider-type hoard, from Včelince - Lászlófala, Slovakia *819*
Krause, Rüdiger 715
Krempel, Germany 724
Kristiansen, Kristian 2, 9, 220, 236, 339
Kroll, Helmut 364
Kronoberg, Sweden 286
Krušovica, Bulgaria 889
Kuban culture 916
Kulm, Trofaiach, Austria 356
kulthused see cult houses
kul'tura mnogovalikovoi keramiki ('multi-cordoned ware' culture) (KMK) 907, 910, 913
  grave finds 907–8
  metalware 907
  regional groups 907
  settlement sites 908–9
Kunci, Northern Adriatic 871
Kung Björn's mound, Sweden 757
Kupreško polje, Bosnia and Herzegovina *838*, 849, *851*
Kura-Arax culture 901
kurgans 115, 144, 775, 781, 900, 904, 905, 909
  see also barrows
Kuyavian Bell Beakers 770
Kville, Sweden 238

Kvorning, Denmark 764
Kyjatice culture 828, 830

La Bastida, Murcia, Spain 595
　upland settlement 597, 598
La Chapelle du Bois-de-Faulz, France 573
La Chapelle-sous-Furieuse, Salins,
　　France 572
La Côte-Saint-André, France 404
La Cova, Mallorca 618
La-Lède-du-Gurp, France 573
La Mancha, Spain 240, 597, 603, 607, 609
La Muculufa, Sicily 657
La Plaza de Cogeces, Spain 595
La Profunda, León, Spain 443
La Rochefoucault, France, karst caves 583
La Starza, Italy 633, 640
La Tène period 480, 894
La Traviesa, Spain 595
La Venta, Spain 595
La Vierge, France 442
labour, division of 400
Lake Annecy 579
Lake Biel, Switzerland 338
Lake Bourget 579
Lake Carera 696
Lake Constance, woodland management
　　in 717
Lake Garda 692, 695
　settlements 696
Lake Léman 579
Lake Onega, Russia 154
lake villages, of southern Germany,
　　Switzerland and northern Italy 96
lallemantia **350**, 351, 363
lamps, animal-fat 449
land division
　early 316–8
　prehistoric 311–4
land transport 398–413
Langbetten 410
Langdon Bay, England 125, 533, 539
　shipwrecks in 372, 388
Langgraben (long ditched graves) 583
Langquaid, Germany 724
Languedoc, France 576, 579
Langweiler, Germany 358, 362

Lannion, La Motta, France 572
Lanting, Jan 390
Laprade, Vaucluse, France 576, 577
Lăpuș, Romania 878, 889, 891
Larnaud, France 574, 586
Laroche-Migennes, France 586
Las Cogotas pottery, Meseta group 474
Las Saladillas, Spain 595
Late Bronze Age 271, 283, 517
　arm ornaments 463
　bar-torcs 456
　barrows 105
　bone scale-beams 517
　bronze figurines from Scandinavia 128
　burial traditions 103
　Carpathian Basin cultures 910
　ceramics 471
　cremation in 230
　cult houses 156
　cylinder-necked urns 472
　developments in weighing in the East
　　Mediterranean 510–1
　in Germany 730–3
　gold bowl from Zürich-Altstetten 459
　gold jewellery 462
　gold objects 460
　gorgets 460
　grave goods 206, 561
　graves and grave goods in the Low
　　Countries 561
　hill forts 239–40
　hoards in western Europe 211
　mud-brick houses in France 85
　phases of 694
　razors 252
　in Romania, Moldova and Bulgaria
　　888–90, 895
　scrap hoards 128
　spearheads 235
　specialized tableware 91
　swords 236
　Urnfield pottery 472
　urnfields 557
　vessels 472
　warrior graves 206
　weights and weighing 520, 521
Late Chalcolithic/Early Bronze Age, copper
　　mining in the 446

Late Corded Ware groups 907
Late Neolithic 84, 144, 329, 417, 558, 725
    Altheim-type flat axes 427
    cremation burials 168
    houses 169, 554
    timber circles 170
    wagons and carts 399
Laterza-Cellino San Marco culture, Italy 63
Laterza, Italy 63, 633
Lauermann, Ernst 88
Laugen-Melaun group 711
Lausanne-Vidy, Switzerland 707, 712, 719
Lausitz culture 240, 407, 474, 477, 731, 772–3, 783, 790, 798, 831, 832
    decline of 735
    in Eastern Germany 734–5
    flat urn burials 830
    fortified settlements 734, 740
    grave goods 734
    hoards 805
    metal products 778
    pottery 762, 800
    Silesian phase of 802
    in Slovakia 829–30
    urnfields 734
    vessels in graves 798
    western Lausitz culture 734
Lavagnone, Italy 693
Lavello, Italy 633, 649
Lazio, Italy, Final Bronze Age-Early Iron Age in 643–4
Le Bourget, France 574
Le Noyer, France 573
lead 180, 181, 182, 612
    analytical fraction, dietary input and interpretation of **183**
    boat models 385
lead isotope analysis 193
leather 225, 761
    leather-working tools 483
    pouch 761
    purse 757
    thong-smoothers 483
Lède-du-Gurp, Gironde, France 580
Ledro, Italy 693
Lefkandi-I-Kastri pottery 51, 61
legerplaatsen 311
legumes 349, 362–3, 600, 774

Leibenfeld, Austria *788–9*
Leighton, Robert 654
Leirvåg, Norway 277
Leithaprodersdorf culture 789, 796, *801*, 819
Łęki Małe, Great Poland *771*, *777*, 781
Lenerz-de Wilde, Majolie 512, 513, 514
lentils **350**, 351, 352, 354, 355, **357**, 358, 363, 774
Les Duffaits La Rochette, France 573
Les Neuf Bouches, France 442
Leskernick Hill, Bodmin Moor, England 317, 319
Lesser Cursus, England 159, 162
Leubingen, Germany 146, 200, 205, *724*, 726
    arrangement of the bodies and grave goods 208
    Early Bronze Age barrow at *201*
    'princely grave' 454, 726
Levantine-eastern Mediterranean region 48
Levkas (Ionian island) 54, 884
Levy, Janet 124
Li Lolghi Arzachena, Sardinia 671
Libiola, Italy 441
Lichfield, Staffordshire, England 464
Lički Osik, Croatia *838*
life expectancies 113
lignite 95, 700
    beads 700
Liguria, Italy 441
Lilliu, Giovanni 669, 675
Limberg-Heidenstatt, Austria *788–9*
Linear B tablets 517
linear landscapes 320–2, 543
Linearbandkeramik 552
linen 225
Ling, Johan 275
linseed 351, 352, 353, 354, 355, 356, 358, 359, 363
Linz-St Peter, Austria 417
lions 340
Lipari, Sicily 655, 658, 661, 662, 670
lipid analysis 10, 11
Lithuania 483
Little Ice Age 709
Little Poland 63, 770, *771*
    Lausitz culture in 773
Litzenkeramik ('braided pottery') 819, 844, 856

Liventsovka, Crimea 909
Ljubljana, Slovenia 338, *838*, 857
Llandegai Henge A, Wales 164
Llanete de Los Moros, Spain 595
Llanmaes, Wales 533, 543
Llo-Ladre, France 574
Lloma de Betxí, Spain 595
loads, speed of transport and 400–1
Löbben climatic event 706, 717
Locarno-San Jorio, Switzerland 707
lock-rings 466, 892
Lockington, Leicestershire, England 456, 537
  arm ornaments from 455
log cabins 85
log-coffins 392
Loka near Ruhna vas, Slovenia 838
Loma de la Tejería, Albarracín, Teruel, Spain 443
Loma del Lomo, Spain 595
long barrows *see* barrows
long beds 733
longhouses 84, 96, 554–5, 738, 749
  at Bjerre site 2, northwest Jutland 85
  in north-west Europe 89–90
  in Scandinavia 750
Lonza, Benedetto 866
loom-weights 480, 648
looms 480
Loose Howe, Yorkshire, England 392
Lorca, Spain 595
Lorraine, France 357
Los Cipreses, Spain 595
Los Millares, Spain 143, 600
Los Palacios, Spain 595
Los Tolmos de Caracena, Spain 595
lost-wax casting process 759, 809
Lovasberény, Hungary 815–6, 817–8, 820
Lovčičky, Moravia 788
Lovech, Bulgaria 51
Low Countries 82, 211, 550–70
  agriculture in the 556–7
  British imports to 563
  Bronze Age farmers 551
  cemeteries 566
  chronology and cultural traditions 552–3
  Early Bronze Age traditions 553
  farmsteads 90, 92, 555
  funerary archaeology in 557
  graves and grave goods 558–61
  house plans 554, 566
  house size during the Bronze Age 88
  house types in 554
  house walls 555
  houses in 86
  Late Bronze Age farm buildings 566
  Late Bronze Age settlements and architecture 555
  in the Late Neolithic 553
  map of the 552
  maritime connections 563
  metalwork depositions in the 563–5
  Middle Bronze Age settlements and architecture 554
  Middle Bronze Age traditions 553
  natural environment and palaeogeography 551
  networks 563
  pottery traditions 553
  river deltas 552
  settlement structure 555–6
  settlements and architecture 553–7
  treatment of the dead 558
  urnfields 557
  see also Belgium; Luxemburg; Netherlands, the
Lower Main-Swabian group 731
Lower Rhine Urnfield culture 553
Lozorno, Slovakia 815–6
Lucone, Italy 693
Ludgierzowice, Poland, Tumulus culture kurgan 771
Lugnaro, Sweden 746–7
Luine site, Valcamonica, Italy 304
Lukashi-Sofieva group 904
Lumbrein-Surin, Switzerland 707
Lüneburg group 730
Luni sul Mignone, Italy 633
Lunigiana, Italy 300
lunulae 59, *210*, 466
lurs 221, 738, 759, 764
  lur-blower 223
Lusatian culture 772 *see also* Lausitz culture
Lusehøj, Denmark 105, 752, 753, 757, 764
Lutry, Switzerland 299
Luxemburg 358
Lužany, Slovakia 815–6

Lužice, Moravia 788
lynchets 320
Lyon-Périphérique Nord, France, Early Bronze Age settlement 577
Lyon Vaise, France 572
Lyshøj, Zealand, Denmark 460

Macedonia 54, 340, 378, 855
Mačkovac-Crišnjevi, Croatia 838, 846
Maďarovce culture 740, 818
   funerary rites 819
Maďarovce -Věteřov- Böheimkirchen cultural complex 818
Madonna di Ripalta, Italy 633, 638, 648
magic 287
Magdalenenberg, Germany 105
Maglehøj, Zealand, Denmark 262, 746–7
   cist tomb 758
Maikop, Adygeja, Russia 144, 901, 903, 916
Mailhac, France 574, 582
Maizières-les-Metz, France 574
Majorca *see* Mallorca
Maklavun, Western Balkans 838, 852
Makó, Hungary 815–6, 828
Makó-Kosihy-Čaka culture 816, 817, 819
Mala Gruda, Montenegro 54, 460, 838, 884
Mälar, Sweden 253, 750, 751
Malaya Khortitsa, Ukraine 906
Male Číčovice, Czech Republic, ornamental bone object from 809
Malé Kosihy, Slovakia 815–6
Mali Sturac, Serbia 440
Malleville-sur-le-Bec, France 574, 578, 578
Mallorca 156, 614, 617, 618
   artefacts from the first occupation of 620
   Bell Beaker group in 619–20
   epi-Bell Beaker-Dolmen group in 620–1
   extra-insular connections and social organization during the initial occupation of 621–2
   first phase of human population in 619–22
   funerary practices 629–30
   metal production in 627
   Naviform group in 622–8
   prehistoric pottery production in 626
   Proto-Talayotic period 628–30
Malmer, Mats 749

Malmö, Sweden 746–7, 763
Malta 55, 57, 58, 63, 653, 658
   colonization of 383
   dolmens on 143
   menhirs on 149
Maltbaek, Denmark 746–7
Mandt, Gro 277
Manem, Sébastien 6
Manfria, Sicily 655, 657
Mannheim-Wallstadt, Germany 517
Maoris, New Zealand 256
Mara, Sardinia 669
Maran, Joseph 49
Marche region, Italy 59, 632, 642
Marchesetti, Carlo 866
Marden, England 159
Marghine-Planargia, Sardinia 673
Mariesminde, Denmark 746–7
   hoard 458, 459, 764
marine fish 190
Maritime Bell Beaker 382
Markt, Bavaria 59
Marmesse, France 589
Marolles-sur-Seine, France 517, 574
   'Gours aux Lions', grave, weighing equipment 518
   graves 519
   'La Croix de la Mission', grave, weighing equipment 518
Marroquíes Bajos, Spain 595, 604
Martin, Slovakia 815–6
Marx, Karl 523
Mas d'Abad, Spain 595
Mas de Menente, Spain 595
Masada de Ratón, Spain 353
Maselli Scotti, Franca 866
mass spectrometers 11
Massif Central, France 442
Mateevka, Ukraine 906
Matelica, Italy 633, 642
Mathay hoard, France 588
Matzanni-Vallermosa, Sardinia 683
Mauritius spring, St Moritz, Switzerland 719
Mauss, Marcel 256, 307
Meana Sardo, Sardinia 669
Mecklenburg-Vorpommern, Germany 243, 736, 737
Meclov- Březí, Bohemia 788

medicine bags 262
Mediterranean Europe
  bronze arrowheads 237
  seafaring and riverine navigation 383–6
Mediterranean Sea, shipwrecks in 371
Mediterranean Zone
  late passage graves in 143
  menhirs in 147, 150
  production of salt in the 502–3
  statue menhirs in 147, 150
  stelae in 147
  stone rows/post rows 149
Médoc phenomenon 587
Medović, Predrag 839
megalithic circles, at Stonehenge, Wiltshire, England 141
megalithic tombs 143, 293
  from Specchia Artanisi 638
megalithic tradition 557
megalithic wedge-tombs 534
'Megaron' temples 682, 686
Megyaszó, Hungary 815–6
melon 350, 351, 363
Melos, Greece 383
Mengen, Königsbronn, Germany 406
menhirs 146, 147, 157
  on Corsica 149
  on Malta 149
  pairs and rows 149–50
  at Rhos-y-Clegyrn, Pembrokeshire, Wales 148
  on Sardinia 149
  in southern Italy 149
Menorca 156, 614, 617–8
  Bell Beaker group in 619–20
  epi-Bell Beaker-Dolmen group in 620–1
  extra-insular connections and social organization during the initial occupation of 621–2
  first phase of human population in 619–22
  funerary practices 629–30
  metal production in 627
  Naviform group in 622–8
  prehistoric pottery production in 626
  Proto-Talayotic period 628–30
Merveilles 301, 305
Meseta, Spain 606, 611, 612
Mesolithic period 161–2, 270

Mesopotamia 48, 481, 508
  production of glass in 495
Messina, Sicily 655
metal-detecting 532
metal production
  in France 585–90
  in Mallorca and Menorca 627
  metal products 776
metallurgy
  in the Danubian region 818
  evidence for 809
  in France 571–2
  in Iberia 605
  in Italy 637, 640, 698
  in Mallorca and Menorca 622
  origins of 415
  in Poland 778
metal(s)
  from the Alpine region 726
  artefacts, belonging to Archbishop Michael Ramsey 121
  diadems 59
  from the Early Bronze Age in Romania, Moldova and Bulgaria 891
  goods 49
  grave goods 581
  hoards in Germany 735
  and indicator of type and status of individuals 591
  ingots 211
  knives 892
  from the Middle Bronze Age in Romania, Moldova and Bulgaria 891–3
  in Romania, Moldova and Bulgaria 891–3
  vessels 805
  weighing metals as currency 520
metalsmiths 285
Metalwork Assemblages 25
metalwork depositions 34–5, 198, 540
  by-products 128
  content of 125–9
  contexts of 124–5
  distribution of 134
  on dry land 124
  hoards and 121–39
  in the Low Countries 563–5
  in natural and watery places 565

metalwork depositions (*cont.*)
  from Petters Sports Field, Thames Valley 123
  relationship between Bronze Age
    settlements, burnt mounds, freshwater
    streams and 126
  sitings in south-east England 127
  in wetland locations 124–5
Metalwork Stages I-XIII 25
metalworking 219, 414–36, 725
  in the Low Countries 562–3
  organization of 431
  regional traditions of 122
  and society 431–3
  tools 200
Metapiccola, Sicily 655
Metaponto, Italy 340
Meteş, western Transylvania, Early Bronze
    Age burial mounds at 886
Mezőcsát culture 832
Mezzolombardo-La Rupe, Italy 698
Michalich-Baa Dere, Bulgaria 51
middens 543
Middle Bronze Age 4, 8, 270, 271, 283,
    294, 517
  barrow at Oss-Zevenbergen 559
  barrows in the Netherlands 206
  bone tools 484
  burial traditions 103
  cist-grave art 154
  deposition of swords 199
  female graves in Germany 203
  fine-ware bowls 470
  in Germany 727–30
  gold jewellery 462
  hoard at Voorhout, the Netherlands 211
  hoards in France 587
  Koszider period bowl, Százhalombatta,
    Hungary 472
  metallurgy in France 572
  phases of 694
  replacement of daggers with swords 220
  in Romania, Moldova and Bulgaria
    884–8, 895
  royal kurgans 144
  sea level 280
  settlements 91, 323
  at Stonehenge, Wiltshire, England 175
  Thapsos-Milazzese facies 654, 658
  transition from Early Bronze Age to 250
  twill 479
  warrior graves 206
Middle Danubian Tumulus culture 740,
    790, 826
  gold artefacts 806
Middle Danubian Urnfield complex 790, 798,
    805, 830–1
  Podoli phase 802
  pottery 800, 804
Middle Dnieper culture 907
Middle Neolithic 156, 162, 270, 283, 306
Mierzanowice culture 770, 771, 774
Migennes, France 519–20, 574
  graves 519
  plan of Late Bronze Age burial at 584
migration studies 184–7
Mikhaylovka, Ukraine 902, 903, 904, 905
Mikušovce, Slovakia 815–6
Milavče, Bohemia 788
Milazzo, Messina, Sicily 655, 661
Milena, Sicily 655, 661
millet 190, 354, 359, 361–2, 364, 774
  broomcorn millet 350, 351, 352–3, 355,
    356, 357, 358, 359, 361
  foxtail millet 351, 353, 355, 357, 358,
    361, 362
  see also cereals
Milston 12, Silk Hill, England 145
Milton Keynes, Buckinghamshire,
    England 456
Minferri, Spain 595
mining
  and metal production 449–50
  and society 450–1
  see also copper mines/mining
Minoan Crete/Minoans 197, 383
  figurines 222
  weight system 510
Minorca *see* Menorca
Minos of Crete, King 383
Miosgán Meadhbha, Knocknarea Mountain,
    County Sligo, Ireland 145
Mirosavljević, Vladimir 866
Misy-sur-Yonne, France 573
Mittelberg bei Nebra, Germany 724, 735
Mittelgebirge copper deposits, Germany 730
Mitterberg, Salzburg, Austria 373

Mitza Purdia-Decimoputzu, Sardinia 680
Mjeltehaugen, Norway 284, *746–7*
Mnogovalikovaya culture 886, 887
Moarda, Sicily 655
   facies 656
   pottery 656
mobility studies 10, 187–8
Moel Goedog, Gwynedd, Wales 208
Mogoro, Sardinia 669
Möhlin-Niederriburg, Switzerland 719
Mojsinje, Serbia *838*
Mokarta, Sicily 655
Mokrin, Serbia 113, *838*, 855, 856
Mola D'Agres, Spain 595
Mold cape, North Wales 459, 461, 466, *537, 533*
Moldova, Republic of 63, 378, 877–97
   burials in 884, *885*, 887, 889
   chronology and terminology 879–80
   clay vehicle models 892
   cultural evolution in 880–91
   Early Bronze Age in 881–4
   Early Iron Age in 890–1
   Late Bronze Age in 888–90
   map of *878*
   metal in 891
   metal shaft-hole axes 892
   Middle Bronze Age in 884–8
   pottery from the Early Bronze Age in 881
   pottery types from Bronze Age/Early Iron Age cultures in *882–3*
   research into the Bronze Age in 877
   transport and vehicles 894–5
Molina di Ledro, Italy 481
Molino della Badia-Madonna del Piano, Sicily 655
Molochansk, Ukraine 906
Moncín, Spain 595
money 510, 522–3
   marine shells as 514
   'primitive money' 514
   weighed metals used as a form of 524
Mongofre Nou, Menorca 618
Monkodonja, Istria, Croatia *838*, 839, *851*, 853, 867, 870–1, 872, 873
   aerial view and plan of the site *869*
   ramparts 870
   tombs integrated into fortified settlement *852*

Mont Bégo, France 291, 300–3, 305, *572*, 583
   rock art 154, *302*
Montagna di Caltagirone, Sicily 663
Montagnola di Capo Graziano, Sicily 661
Monte Castellaccio di Imola, Italy 633
Monte Castellaccio, Romagna, Italy 636
Monte Cetona, Italy 633
Monte Claro Chalcolithic culture 671
Monte Dessueri, Sicily 655, 663
Monte Grande, Sicily 655, 657
Monte Loreto, Italy 441
Monte Rovello, Etruria, Italy 640
Monte Saraceno, Italy 633, 648
Monte Tabuto, Sicily 655
Monte Timmari, Matera, Italy 647
Monte Toro, Menorca 618
Monte Venere, Taormina, Sicily 57
Montelavar-Atios horizon 607
Montelius, Oscar 4, 723, 749
   Period II 251
   type table devised by 5
   typology 275
Montenegro 853
Monteoru culture 886, 887
Montgomery, Janet 187
Montgomery toggles 64
Montjovet-Chenal, Italy 299
Montlingerberg, Switzerland *707*, 715
Montou, France 572
monumental art 294, 304, 305, 306–8
monumental barrows 557
monumental burial 102
monuments
   change over time in design, construction, purpose and meaning of 141
   late chambered tombs 143
   location of 140
   and monumentality 140–58
Mooghaun, County Clare, Ireland 95
Moor Sands, Devon, England 388
Moordorf, Germany 724, 727
   gold discs from *728*
Morava river 55, 787, 789, 805, 837, 854, 855
Moravia 63, 244, 770, 787, 790, 818
   Bronze Age artefacts from *802*
   distribution of hoards in *806*
   gold objects 806, *807*
   graves in *794, 795*

Moravia (cont.)
　hoards 805–6
　map of 788
　Middle Bronze Age in 790
　production of bronze goods in 804
　raw-metal hoards 805
　settlements in 791
　see also Czech Republic
Moravičany, Moravia 788
Moray Firth, Scotland 143
Moray, Scotland 315
Morbihan, France, stone circles in 153
Mordant, Claude 128
Morgantina, Sicily 334, 655
Mörigen, Switzerland 707, 713
Moriš group 855
Morra de Quintanar, Spain 595
morras 603
Morro de Mezquitilla, Spain 595
mortuary houses 754
Morvan, Bibracte, France 585
Moscosi di Cingoli, Italy 511, 633
Mosolovka, Russia 911
motifs 154, 461, 762
Motilla del Azuer, Spain 240
motillas 240, 603, 604
moulds 128, 624
Mound of the Hostages, Ireland 533
Mount Etna 653, 657
Mount Gabriel, County Cork, Ireland 445, 533, 537
　copper mine 447, 448, 451
Mount Tudurighe, Sardinia 672
Mudrets, Bulgaria 51
Mühlau, Austria 788–9
Mühlbach am Hochkönig-Mitterberg, Austria 788–9
Mühlbach-Gschleirsbühel, Austria 788–9
Muids, France 573
Muldbjerg, Denmark 746–7
　oak coffin burial graves 755
Müller, Sophus 114, 237
Müller-Karpe, Hermann 6, 857, 880
Müller-Wille, Michael 312
mummification 108
Muntanya Assolada, Spain 595
Muraiola, Italy 700
Murcia, Spain 601

Mureş /Maros/Periam-Pecica 886
Muros, Sardinia 669
Mušego hill, Croatia 853
Mycenae, Greece 21
　Shaft Graves 910
Mycenaean
　culture 456
　Greece 197, 481
　pottery 379, 520, 636, 640, 654, 659, 661, 670
Myhre, Lise 277, 279
Myotragus balearicus 619
Myrhøj, Jutland, Denmark, stone rows 150

Nagybátony, Hungary 815–6
Nagydobos, Hungary 815–6, 822
Nagykálló hoard 832
Nagyrév culture 229, 820
Nämforsen, Sweden 746–7
Nantes, France 574
Naro-Partanna group 655
natural places 153–5
natural springs 155
Navetas 143
Naviform group (*c.*1600-1100/1000 cal BC)
　buildings from Canyamel and Son Oms 623
　funerary practices 624
　funerary structures 625
　in Mallorca and Menorca 622–8
　potable artefacts 624
navigation skills 393
Naxos, Sicily 385, 655, 661
Near East 330, 335, 492, 509, 894
　faience 494
　roles of animals in 328
　trade in 370
Nebelsick, Louis 129
Nebra, Germany 208, 251, 255, 263
　Sky Disc 221, 266–9, 393, 431, 459, 460, 461
neck ornaments 59
neck-rings ('ring-money') 58, 422, 512, 762
Neckar group 727
Neckarsulm, Germany 724, 733
necklaces 200, 206
　composite necklaces 59, 200
　Exloo necklace 563
　from Nižná Myšľa, Slovakia 823
Needham, Stuart 8, 123

Neftenbach, Switzerland 707, 712
Nenquin, Jacques 501
Neolithic period 136, 157, 270, 454
  artefacts of native copper 427
  use of split boar's tusks as scrapers 483
  wheels 402
Nesactium, Croatia 871
Nestor, Ion 877
Netheravon Bake, Wiltshire, England 162
Netherlands, the 21, 25–30, 136, 253, 312, 339
  barrows in 105, 144, 145, 199
  Bronze Age settlements 550–1
  chronological systems for 18–9, 26–7, 28–9
  deposition practices in 199, 564
  pottery traditions 553
  sword burials in 206
  terpen 329
  upstanding barrows 145
Neuvy-sous-Barangeon, France 574
Newgrange, Ireland 533, 534
nickel 422
Niederkaina, Germany 724
Niederrheinische Grabhügelkultur 561
Nin-Privlaka, Dalmatia, Croatia 54
Nine Ladies, Stannon Moor, Derbyshire, England 151
Niš-Bubanj, Serbia 55
Nitra culture 244, 789, 817
Nitriansky Hrádok, Slovakia 818
nitrogen 180, 181, 182, 186, 191
  analytical fraction, dietary input and interpretation of 183
  isotopic data
    for animals 190
    for Early Bronze Age and Iron Age humans and herbivores 185
Nižná Myšľa, Slovakia 244, 815–6
  burial pit with human sacrifices from 824
  cemetery 823
  necklaces from 823
Noceto, Italy 693, 702–3
Nogarole di Mezzolombardo, Italy 693
Nola, Italy 633
nomads, horse-borne 915, 916
non-cereals
  in the Eastern Alps and their Foreland 356
  in Italy 352
  in Mediterranean Spain 354

Representativeness Index of 350
  RI values in the archaeobotanical record of central and northern Italy 352
  RI values of non-cereals in the archaeobotanical record of Southern Scandinavia and the north sea coast 359
  RI values of non-cereals in the archaeobotanical record of Western Central Europe (outside the Alps) 358
  in Southern Scandinavia and the North Sea coast 359
  in West-Central Europe (outside the Alps) 358
  in the Western Alps and their foreland 357
  see also cereals
Nonant, France 573, 578
Noppenringe (knobbed rings) 59
Nordbladh, Jarl 277
Nordic Bronze Age 4, 8, 228, 364, 748
  artefacts 736
  bronzes 748
  burials 8
  cult houses 156
  dendro-dating on oak coffins of the 8
  end of 738
  gold objects 462
  male burials in Northern Germany 736
  metalworking 778
  network 551, 557
  in Northern Germany 735–8
  periods II-III 217
  rock art 154, 405
  standing stones 147
  stone and timber circles 153
  stone rows 149, 150
  tumuli 145
  Zone 145, 735–8
Normandy 571
  moated systems and boundaries in 579
  roundhouses in 84
  see also France
Normanton Down, England, barrow group 115, 116
Norrköping, Sweden 282, 746–7, 750
Nors, Jutland, Denmark 459
North Pontic Eneolithic burial customs 903
North Pontic steppe 900, 907

North Sea coast
  barley in 360
  and Southern Scandinavia 359
north-west Europe
  houses in 89
  longhouses in 89
  lowlands 96
  settlements 88
  see also Europe, Germany, Italy
Northton, Isle of Harris, Outer Hebrides 533
Norway 253, 747
  rock art in 154
Noua culture 878, 913
  ceramics 913
  pins 889
Noua-Sabatinovka-Coslogeni 888, 880
  inhumation 889
  pottery 889
  settlements 890
Novocherkassk culture 914, 915
Novodanilovka culture 900
Novotitarovka group, grave goods 903
Nuraghe Arrubiu-Orroli, Sardinia 677, 678
nuraghi (stone towers) 239, 670, 671, 674–84
  building technique 676
  construction of 673–4
  general characteristics of 675–7
  management of 676
  plans of 677
  religious nature of 686
  tombs 676
Nuragic culture 351, 672–4
  askoid jugs 686–7
  bronze figurines, Sardinia 239
  formation of 672–4
  pottery 670, 681
  temples 679
nuts 609
Nyírség area, Hungary 822
Nyírség-Zatín culture 821
Nynice culture 790
  pottery 804

oak coffins 108, 477–8, 755
  Borum Eshøj, Jutland, Denmark 105
oats 350, 352, 353, 355, 356, 357, 358, 362
  see also cereals

Obereching, Austria 788–9, 798
Oberhalbstein Valley, Switzerland 715
Oberleis-Oberleiserberg, Austria 788–9
Oberwilflingen, Germany 524
objects
  biography of 6
  found outside their place of
      manufacture 372–9
  and relational identity 206–7
  relationships between people and 207–9
obsidian 58, 383, 622, 653, 658
ochre 854
Ochsenberg, Wartau, Switzerland 707, 714
Ockenhausen-Oltmannsfeh, Ldkr. Leer,
      Germany, Late Bronze Age trackway
      from a bog near 409
Očkov, Slovakia 815–6
Odsherred, Zealand, Denmark 753
Oeversee, Germany 389
Ognina, Sicily 655
oil plants 354, 356, 363
oilseeds 349, 351, 353, 357
  Representativeness Index of 350
Olbia, Sardinia 669
Oliena, Sardinia 669
olive **350**, 351, 352, 354, 363, 634
olive oil 351
Oliveto-Cairano group 633, 645
Olmedo, Sardinia 669
Olmo di Nogara, Italy 693
  cemetery 700
  swords found at cemetery 701
Olomouc-Slavonín, Moravia 788
  Middle Bronze Age house 793
Olorid pri Dolnjem Lakošu, Slovenia
      845–6
Oloris, Western Balkans 838
Olympia, Greece 64
Onzain, France 574
open settlements
  in the Danube region 826
  in Germany 738–42
  in Poland 773
  in Tisza and Tisza-Danube interfluve
      regions 827
  see also settlements
opium poppy 349, **350**, 351, 353, 354, 355, **356**,
      357, 358, 363

Optical Stimulated Luminescence dating 315
Ör, Sweden 284
Orah, Western Balkans 838
oral discourse 288
Ordona, Italy 649
Orkney 149, 534
Ormož, Slovenia 838, 847, 848
ornaments 228, 599
    willow-leaf 817
Orolik, Croatia 54
Orosei, Sardinia 669
Orpesa la Vella, Spain 595
Orroli, Sardinia 669
Orsi, Paolo 654, 659, 663
Orune, Sardinia 669
Ösenringe 210, 211, 212, 440
Ösenringkupfer 422
Osgood, Richard 235
Oss-Zevenbergen, Low Countries, Middle Bronze Age barrow 559
Ossi, Sardinia 669
Ossingen-Im Speck, Switzerland 707
ostentation 306–9
Östergötland, Sweden 286
Österholm, Sven 389
Osteria dell'Osa, Roma, Italy 633, 644
Østfold, Norway 279
    rock carvings of boats in 388
ostrich eggshells 385
Ostrov-Zápy, Prague, Czech Republic 339
Ostrovets, Belarus 913
Ostrowite Trzemeszeńskie, Poland 782
Otomani-Füzesabony culture 156, 474, 773, 821, 822, 823
Otomani, Romania 878
Otranto Tombs 143
Otterböte, Åland Islands, Finland 746–7
Ötzi the Iceman 187, 692
Ouroux, France 579
Over, Cambridgeshire, England 322
Over-Vindinge, Denmark 235, 242
oxen 331, 332, 401
    see also animals
oxhide ingots 373, 661, 680, 681, 683, 688
oxygen 180, 182
    analytical fraction, dietary input and interpretation of **183**
oxygen isotope analysis 75, 181, 184, 193

palace civilizations 197
Palafitte-Terramare communities 640, 650
Palaggiu, Corsica 150
Palagonia, Sicily 58
Palma Campania facies 635, 636
Palmavera-Alghero, Sardinia 688
palstaves 38, 586, 587, 760
Panajot Hitovo, Bulgaria 51
Panarea, Sicily 655, 661
Pannonian Basin 363
    barley in 360
    einkorn in 360
    plant cultivation in 354–6
    RI values of non-cereals in the archaeobotanical record of **355**
Pannonian complex of Encrusted Pottery 790, 799
Pantalica culture 654, 663, 655
    funerary practices 664
    metal artefacts 664
    pottery 663, 664
Pantelleria, Sicily 655
para-Neolithic societies 772
Paračin, Serbia 838, 855
Paranho, Portugal 595
Paris, France 574
Parker Pearson, Mike 152, 236
Partizánske, Slovakia 815–6
Pascharedda-Calangianus, Sardinia 675
Paulilatino, Sardinia 669
paved paths 410
pears 774
peas 354, 355, 774
    see also garden pea
Pecica, Romania 878
Peckatel, Mecklenburg, Germany 407, 724, 737
Pečky, Bohemia 809
Pécs-Nagyárpád, Hungary 815–6, 817
Pécsvárad, Hungary 815–6
Peña Negra, Alicante, Spain 595
    hilltop settlement 613
Peñalosa, Spain 595, 600
Penard, south Wales 131
pendants 892
pens, fenced stock 91
Periam/Perjámos-Szöreg culture 821
Periam, Romania 878
Perovaradin (Petrovaradin), Serbia 838

Perry Oaks, Middlesex, England 316, 321
Perşinari, Romania 460, 886
personal items, movement of 378
personhood 204
Peschiera, Italy 640, 696
Pešter, Serbia 838
Peter-Röcher, Heidi 244
Petit-Chasseur 293
Petrovaradin Fortress, Serbia 840
Petters Sports Field, Thames Valley, England, metalwork depositions from 123
Pfäffikon-Irgenhausen, Switzerland 480
phalanges 484
Phoenician colonization 594, 596, 614, 688
phosphate analysis 11
Pianello di Genga, Italy 633, 641
Pic dels Corbs, Iberia 595
Picardt, Johan 311
Piceno 642
pickaxes 200
picks, bronze 448
Picos de Europa, Spain 605
Piding hoard, Germany, ingots 513
Piggott, Stuart 8, 160
pigs 169, 333, 483, 774
   bones 330
Pile, Sweden 746-7, 759
pile-dwellings 695, 696, 697, 707, 713
   Ljubljana moor region 840
pile villages 791
Piliny culture 827, 830
Pine Islands 617, 618, 620
pins 125, 136, 228, 637, 672, 683, 735, 760, 809, 889, 892
   disc-head 673
   poppy-head 710
   wing-head 710
pit burials 535, 649
pit cemeteries 540
pit fields, in Iberia 605
pit inhumations 649
pithoi (large jars) 472, 599
Pitigliano, Etruria, Italy 339
Pit Grave culture 901
pits 91, 599
Pitten, Austria 470, 788-9, 797
Pittioni, Richard 422
Pitvaros, Carpathian Basin 63

plant cultivation 348-69
   in the Eastern Alps and their Foreland 356
   methods 348-9
   in the Pannonian Basin 354-6
   in West-Central Europe (outside the Alps) 357-9
   in the Western Alps and their foreland 357
Plavecké Podhradie, Slovakia 815-6
Pleistocene 551
Plešivec hillfort, Bohemia 788, 809
Pliny the Elder 517
plough marks 329, 556
Plouvorn, France 572
Plovdiv, Bulgaria 878
plum **352**, 352, 363
   see also fruit
Po, River 692
Pobedim, Slovakia 815-6
Pobrežje, Slovenia 838
Pod, near Bugojno, Bosnia 838, 839, 844, 847
Podgorica- Tološi, Montenegro 54
Podolí culture 802, 831
Poggio La Pozza, Italy 633, 643
Poggiomarino, Italy 633, 645
Poiana, Romania 340
Poing, Upper Bavaria 407
   weighing equipment 518
Point Iria shipwreck 383
points, bronze 809
Polada culture **296**, 694-5
Poland 63, 474, 767-86
   animal husbandry in 774
   Bronze Age/Hallstatt pottery from 777
   burials in 775-6
   cultural chronology of 768-70
   cultural sequence in 770-2
   cultural transformations in 783
   cultural zones 768
   deposition of hoards in 780
   farming in 774
   finds from 769
   fortified settlements 774
   historic regions of 768
   industries 778-9
   landscape and cultural regions 769
   Late Bronze Age in 772-3
   Lower Silesia 770
   material culture in 776-8

metallurgy in 778
Middle Bronze Age in 772
natural environment of 767–8
natural resources 767
pottery in 776–8
prosperity in 783
settlement and economy in 773–5
social life in 779–83
trade route communities 780
tree exploitation in 774
zones 768, 783
Polanyi, Karl 523
Polgár, Hungary 815–6, 828
  wells 829
Poliochni, Greece 58
political economy 7
Polizzello, Sicily 655
pomegranate 350, 351, 363
  see also fruit
Pomerania 770
Pont-Valperga group 711
Pontecagnano, Italy 633
Pontic Steppes, Eastern Zone 144
Popești, Romania, 878
poppy 353, 354, 355, 356, 774
population history 78
porcelain plates 212
Poroszló, Hungary 815–6
portages 393
Portal Vielh, Langudeoc, France 95
Portella di Salina, Apennine pottery from 662
Porto Perone, Italy 640
Porto Torres, Sardinia 669
Portugal 147
  Alentejo stelae in 147
  Galician-style rock art in 154
  metallurgy during the Final Bronze Age in 612
  tombs in 143
post rows see stone rows
Posušje, Bosnia and Herzegovina 838, 845
pots 737, 762
potter's wheels 474
pottery 59, 558, 776
  Aegean pottery 379
  analysis of 6, 11
  Andronovo-Fedorovka culture 910
  in Austria 799–804

Beaker pottery 36, 315, 443, 537
Begleitkeramik ('accompanying pottery') 621
Borġ in-Nadur 659
of the Cetina culture 850
in the Czech lands 799–804
Early Mycenaean pottery 658
Elp pottery 553
from Gŭlŭbovo, Bulgaria 53
Hallstatt style 776
Hilversum pottery 30
in Iberia 606
impasto pottery 648, 650, 654, 657, 658, 659, 662
knobbed ware 776
Kummerkeramik ('sorrow-pottery') 553
Las Cogotas pottery of the Meseta group 474
Lausitz 776, 777
Lefkandi-I-Kastri pottery 49, 51, 61
Litzenkeramik ('braided pottery') 819, 844, 856
in Mallorca and Menorca 626
metope pottery 673
Mierzanowice 777
movement of 378–9
a nervature ('ribbed') pottery 672
Palma Campania pottery 636
Pantalica culture 663, 664
in Poland 776–8
pre-Lausitz phase pottery 734
proto-Apennine 636
Proto-Geometric 646
Proto-Villanovan 642
ribbed pottery 673
rilled-ware pottery 575
from Romania, Moldova and Bulgaria 881, 884–5, 888–9, 895
S. Cosimo, pottery 673
from Sardinia 670, 676, 677
from Scandinavia 762
settlement and cemetery material 470
Sub-Apennine pottery 640
Thapsos-Milazzese pottery 659, 664
Trzciniec style 776, 777–8
Tumulus pottery 762
twisted cord-decorated 727
Únětice style 776
Urnfield pottery 472, 475, 553

pottery (*cont.*)
  urns 599
  vessels 608
  wheel-made 49, 610
Povegliano, Italy 700
Poviglio-Santa Rosa, Switzerland 707, 711
Pozdynakovo culture 911
Prague- Hostivař, Bohemia 788
Prähistorische Bronzefunde (PBF) 5, 6, 249, 378, 839
Pratica di Mare, Lavinium, Italy 633, 643
pre-Apennine and proto-Apennine facies 636–7
pre-Apennine pottery 636
pre-Lausitz phase pottery 734
Pre-Roman Iron Age 270
pre-Savromatian level 915
precision balances 523
precision weighing 508, 509, 517, 519, 582
Prehistory of the Netherlands 30
Preseli Hills, north Pembrokeshire, Wales 141, 151, 152
preservation 82
prestige goods 7, 73, 74, 255–6, 263, 379, 387
  see also hoards
Preuschen, Ernst 422
Prezenak, Northern Adriatic 871
Price, Douglas 10
priests 218, 221–2
Prikazanskaya culture 914
Primas, Margarita 515, 516, 731
princely burials 146
  in Scandinavia 757
'princely grave', Dieskau, Germany 459
princely tumuli 781
Progress in Old World Palaeoethnobotany (Van Zeist, Wasylikowa, Behre) 348
proto-Bronze phase 770
'proto-Scythian' period 914
Proto-Talayotic period, in Mallorca and Menorca 628–30
Proto- Únětice culture 789
Protocogotas style 597, 606
Protogolasecca culture 703, 710
Protovillanoviano padano culture 703
Pryor, Francis 322, 535
Pryssgården, Sweden 746–7, 750
Przeczyce, Poland 106

Przysieka Polska, Poland 781
Pšeničevo, Bulgaria *878*
'pseudo-nuraghi' 673
Pulak, Cemal 520
pulses 349, 356, 358, 362–3, 364
  Representativeness Index of **350**
Punta d'Alaca, Italy 636
Punta Kašteja, Croatia 867
Punta Le Terrare, Italy 633, 638
Puschi, Alberto 866

Quantal Analysis 519
quarrying 263, 778
quartz 261–2, 263, 473, 749, 761
quartzite 761
Quaternary 551
querns 624
Quimperlé, France 572
Quinta da Água, Branca, Portugal 461, 595
Qurénima, Spain 595

Rabin, Western Balkans *838*
radiocarbon dating 7, 20, 33, 39, 71, 315
radiography 463
Radunia, near Sobótka, Wrocław, Poland 156
Radzovce, Slovakia *815–6*, 828
rafts 393
Rafz-Im Fallentor, Switzerland 719
Ragelsdorf 2 hoard, Austria, ingot weights 513
Rahmstorf, Lorenz 509
ramparts 792
Ramsey, Archbishop Michael 121, 137
Rancogne, France 574
Randsborg, Klavs 237
rapiers 236, 379, 545, 889
Rastorf, Germany 724, 735
Rathgall, County Wicklow, Ireland 95, 492
raw materials 372–9
razor-knives 736
razors 203, 206, 222, 252, 253–4, 255, 257, 637, 760, 762
  bronze 263, 458
  two-edged 730
Reading Business Park, Berkshire, England, roundhouses in 91

Reardnogy More, County Tipperary,
    Ireland 209
reaves 311
Recent Bronze Age 670
    metal types of the 684
recumbent stone circles 151
red deer 340–1, 342, 483
    antler 483, 485
Reg, Norway 746–7
Regional Research Frameworks 532
regulations, relating to archaeological
    fieldwork 531–2
Reinecke, Paul 4, 709, 723, 880
reins 401, 411
Remedello culture 63, 294, **296**, 298
    cemetery 308
    daggers 306
Renfrew, Colin 48
Representativeness Index 349
    of non-cereals 350
Republic of Ireland *see* Ireland
research traditions 82
Rhin-Suisse-France Oriental tradition
    (RSFO) 553, 557, 575, 582, 591, 711, 731
Rhine-Meuse delta 550
Rhine-Switzerland-eastern France culture *see*
    Rhin-Suisse-France Oriental tradition
    (RSFO)
Rhine Valley 714
Rhodanian Bronze Age 581
rhomboid punch 673
Rhône culture 571, 710
Ría de Huelva, Spain 125, 595
    hoard 613
rib ingots 422, 562, 804, 818
Richemont-Pépinville, Moselle 518
Ridala, Estonia 333, 341
Ries group 727
Riesenbecher group 727
Rillaton, Cornwall, England 461
Rinaldone, Italy 63
ring-cairns 155, 536
ring ditches 31, 145, 155
ring-ingots (*Ösenringbarren*) 440, 512, 514,
    562, 804, 818
ring-works 542
ringed seal 341
Ringlemere, Kent, England 456, 533, 537

Ripač, Bosnia 341
Ripalta, Italy 638
Ripdorf barrows, Lüneburg, Germany 113, *114*
Rise of Bronze Age Society, The (Kristiansen
    and Larsson) 2
ritual enclosures 156
rivers 390–2
    finds in 136
    transport along 411
rivets 58, 235, 294, 460, 608, 824
Rixheim, France 574
roads and paths 407–11
Robin Hood's Ball, England 159
Roca Vecchia, Italy 633, 634, 636, 639, 640,
    646, 648, 650
rock art 149, 238–9, 258, 262, 328, 534
    along Norwegian west coast 277
    in burial monuments 271
    Camunian rock art 306
    chronology 274–5
    dating 275
    excavation of 282–3
    figurative art 274
    formal interpretation 272
    images and interpretative trends 272–4
    and landscape 275–7
    in Northern Europe 270–90
    on open-air panels 271
    and picturing the dead 283–5
    on portable slabs 271
    practice and cosmology 286–7
    rock art ships from Tanum, Bohuslän,
        Sweden 276
    rock outcrops and 153–4
    in Scandinavia 253, 271, 272, *278*
    and seascapes 277–82
    ships 286
    as social format 287–8
    in the Tanum area in western Sweden *281*
    themes of 274
    theories about 285–6
    wagons and carts in Nordic rock art 405
rock carvings 291–310
    anthropomorphs 301
    archaeological context 293
    chrono-cultural attributes 293–7
    dating of 295–7
    form and content 303–5, 306

rock carvings (cont.)
    geometric figures 301, 305
    harness 301
    horned figures 301
    human figures 301
    iconographic variations of 305–9
    in Scandinavia 763
    sites 297–303
    superimposition of 295
    visibility of 303
    of weapons 293–5, 301
rock faces 303–4
rock salt 502, 506
rock-smiths 285
Rodenkirchen-Hahnenknooper Mühle, Lower Saxony, Germany 88, 359, 362, 363
Rodì, Sicily 655
Rodi-Tindari-Vallelunga (RTV) facies 655–6
roe deer 483
Rogaland, Norway 272, 284
Rogoza, Slovenia 838
Roma, Italy 633
Romagnano Loc, Italy 693, 699
Roman coins 128
Roman period 136
Románd type hoards 833
Romania 59, 63, 338, 339, 506, 877–97
    axes with discs 892
    burials in 884, 885, 887, 889
    chronology and terminology 879–80
    clay vehicle models 892
    cultural evolution in 880–91
    Early Bronze Age in 881–4
    Early Iron Age in 890–1
    Late Bronze Age in 888–90
    map of 878
    metal in 891
    metal shaft-hole axes 892
    Middle Bronze Age in 884–8
    pottery from the Early Bronze Age in 881
    pottery types from Bronze Age/Early Iron Age cultures in 882–3
    research into the Bronze Age in 877–8
    salt production in 378, 504
    transport and vehicles 894–5
Rongères cup 587

Rørby, Zealand, Denmark 746–7, 762
Roşia, Romania 878
Rosières-les-Salines, France 574
Rosnoën, France 574
Ross Island, Killarney, County Kerry, Ireland 443, 533, 534
rotundas 682, 686
Roughaun Hill (Roughan Hill), County Clare, Ireland 316–7, 533, 535
roundhouses 84, 538, 542
    in Britain and Ireland 90, 96
    deliberate placing of objects in 544
    entrances to 90
    placing of special deposits in 539
    in Reading Business Park, Berkshire, England 91
    in western France 96
Rove, France, Laure settlement at 579
Rowlands, Michael 10, 432
royal kurgans 144
Royal Museum of Nordic Antiquities, Denmark 17
Roynac, Le Serre, France 572
Rubín, Czech Republic 339
Rückstrom theory 71
Rudna Glava, Serbia 416
    copper mines in 439
Rügen, Germany 760
Ruggles, Clive 150, 160
Rullstorf, Germany 362
Rupinpiccolo, Italy 871
Ruše, Slovenia 838, 857
Russia 336, 746
    beginning of the Bronze Age in 901–4
    Bronze Age development in 915–6
    bronze objects 916
    cultural relationships in 911–4
    economy in 916
    end of the Bronze Age in 914–5
    Eneolithic in 899–901
    influence on Moldova after World War II 878
    south Russia 898–918
    vegetation zones in 899
Rütimeyer, Ludwig 329, 338
Rychner, Valentin 586
rye 355, 356, 357, 358, 362, 538
    see also cereals

S. Abbondio, Pompeii, Italy 635
S. Angelo Muxaro, Sicily 655
S. Imbenia, Sardinia 688
S. Iroxi, Sardinia 671
S. Pasquale, Italy 647
Sa Corona Arrubia-Genoni, Sardinia, 'round' temple 679
Sa Fogaia-Siddi, Sardinia 673
Sa Turricula facies 672, 673
Saalfelden-Taxau, Austria 788–9
Saalfelden-Wiesersberg, Austria 788–9
Saalkreis, Germany 460
Saaremaa Island, Estonia 341
Sabatinovka culture 878, 911, 913
    ceramics 911, 913
    material 912
    settlements 913
Sabina, Italy, Early Iron Age cremation rituals in 646
Sabina-Silanus, Sardinia 677
Sabucina, Sicily 655
Sachkere, Russia 144
Sacred Springs 676, 682
saddle quern 208
safflower **350**, 351, 355, 363
Sagaholm, Sweden 746–7
    barrow 145, 284–5, 753
Saharna, Moldova 878
S'Aigua Dolça, Mallorca 618
Saile, Thomas 501
sailing 393
Saint-Brieuc-des-Iffs, France 574
Saint-Denis-de-Pile, France 574
St Florian, copper clasp-ingot 513
St Johann im Pongau, Austria 788–9
St-Léonard, rock carvings 300
St-Martin-de-Corléans 299
St Mary's, Isles of Scilly 147
St Moritz, Switzerland 156, 707, 712
    Mauritius spring 719
Saint-Paul-sur-Ubaye, France 300
Saint-Priest, France 574
St Romains-de-Jalionas, France 585
St-Valéry-sur-Somme, France 572, 586
St Veit-Klingberg 424
St Véran, France 442, 572
Sala Consilina, Italy 633
Sălacea (Marghita), Romania 156

Salanova, Laure 74
Salapia, Italy 649
Salcombe, England 375, 533, 540
Salento Peninsula, Italy, funerary structures 637
Salgótarján-Zagyvapálfalva, Hungary 815–6
Salina, Sicily 655, 658, 661
Salisbury Plain, England 151, 159, 315, 322
salt 377–8, 543, 726, 767
    Bronze Age 505–6
    extraction 791
    lagoons 503
    mines/mining 503–5, 808
    as money 514
    production 501–7
    in the Mediterranean 502–3
    using briquetage 502
    in wooden troughs 504–5
    uses of 501
'Salt Mountain', Cardona, Catalonia, Spain 503
Salzberg, Hallstatt, Austria 808
Salzburg-Maxglan, Austria 788–9
Salzburg-Morzg, Austria 788–9
Salzkammergut, Austria 790, 808
Samson, Alice 125
San Biagio della Valle, Umbria, Italy 58
sanctuaries, on Sardinia 688
Sandagergård, Sjælland, Denmark 156, 752
    cult houses 258
sandstone 151
sandstone whetstones 809
Santa Croce Camerina, Italy 58
Santa Croce cave, Italy 701
Santa Domenica di Ricadi, Calabria, Italy 637
Santa María de Retamur, Iberia 595, 604
Santa Palomba, Rome, Italy 644
    Early Iron Age cremation burial artefacts 645
Santa Rosa di Poviglio, Italy 693, 697, 716
Sant'Abbondio, Italy 633
Sărată-Monteoru, Romania 878, 888
Sardinia 142, 351, 668–91
    bronze figurines 683–4
    cereal production in 676
    ceremonial areas 674
    chronology of the Bronze Age in 670–2
    copper mining in 438

Sardinia (cont.)
  dating of metal objects from 670
  dolmens on 143
  Early Bronze Age in 671–2
  end of the Bronze Age and the beginning of the Iron Age in 685–7
  food resources in 676
  funerary practices in 686
  Giants' tombs 674, 682
  and iron 687–8
  map of 669
  menhirs on 149
  metallurgy 673
  mineral exploitation in 688
  Mycenaean and Cypriot connections to 680–2
  Nuraghi golden age 674–84
  nuraghi (stone towers) 239
  Nuragic askoid jugs and votive ships 686–7
  Nuragic bronze figurines 239
  Nuragic civilization 672–4
  Nuragic metallurgical production 683
  pottery 670, 676, 677
  sanctuaries on 683–4
  social diversification in 668
  springs 155
  temple structures 676
  Tombe di Giganti 143
  tombs 676
Sargary-Alekseevskoe culture 911
Sarroch, Sardinia 669
sarsen circle 171
Sava river 54
Savognin-Padnal, Graubünden, Switzerland 85, 707, 710, 711, 712, 715, 718
scabbards 756
scale pans 511
Scalvinetto, Italy 700
Scandinavia 258, 746–66
  agriculture and land use in 752
  arts and crafts in 759–63
  barley in 360
  barrows in 753, 753
  bronze figurines from 128, 225
  bronze razors from 222
  burial mounds in 749
  burials in 106, 749, 754–8
  cairns 753
  children's graves 756
  chronological systems for 26–7
  chronology and regional differentiation 749–50
  cultural development and diversity in 748–9
  deposits in 764
  Early Bronze Age in 746
  figurines 762–3
  geographic regions 748
  hoards in 123, 132, 764
  house size during the Bronze Age 88
  land transport 763
  Late Bronze Age ceramics 471
  Late Bronze Age in 746
  logboats in 392
  longhouses 84, 749
  map of 747
  mounds 752–4
  non-cereals in the North Sea Coast and 359
  ornamentation in 762
  pottery 762
  princely burials 757
  research on prehistoric settlements 82
  RI values of non-cereals in the archaeobotanical record of Southern Scandinavia and the north sea coast **359**
  roads in 763
  rock art in 238, 253, 270–1, 405
  rock carvings 749, 763
  settlements in 750–2
  ship-setting burials 104
  soapstone 261
  solid-hilted swords from 236
  special graves in 757–8
  spindle-whorls 480
  textiles 479
  trade and transport 763–4
  transitions to the Bronze Age and the Iron Age in 749
  use of quartz in 749
  warfare research 245
  weaving 480
Scania, Sweden 272, 279, 286, 389, 405, 749, 753, 754, 756, 760
Scarceta, Italy 633
Schafwinkel, Germany 724
Schernberg, Austria 788–9, 798

Schleswig-Holstein, Germany 736, 756
Schneckenberg, Romania 878–9
Schöningen, Germany 724
Schulenburg, Germany 724, 727
Schwarzenbach, Austria 788–9, 792
Schwaz, Austria 788–9
Scilly-Tramore Tombs 143
Scirinda, Sicily 655
Scoglio del Tonno, Italy 633, 639, 640
Scord of Brouster, Shetland 317
Scotland
   Early Bronze Age pottery in 25
   four-poster stone circles 153
   mummification in 108
   placement of the cremated dead 540
   recumbent stone circles in north-eastern 151
   stone pairs in southern and central 149
   stone rows in 150
scrap hoards 128–9, 200, 211, 212
Scythian period 915
sea food 624
sea level 280
seafaring and riverine navigation 382–97
Seahenge, Norfolk, England 151
seal oil 749
seals 341
seascapes 277–82
Seddin bei Groß Pankow, Germany 724
Segre-Cinca group 613
Seille Valley, Lorraine, France 501
selective deposition 198–200, 205
self, the 204
Selimpaşa Höyük, Turkey 51
Selvis di Remanzacco, Udine (Videm), Italy 838
Semitic peoples 686
Senhora da Guia, Portugal 595
Sennwald-Salez, Switzerland 719
Senta, Serbia 838
Serbia 54
   burial monuments in 854
   Lefkandi I-Kastri pottery 53
Serezlievka group 904
Seribaus, France 442
Serjeantson, Dale 339
Serlingsholm, Sweden 389
Sermizelles, France 586
Serra Ilixi-Nuragus, Sardinia 681

Serres, Thierry 303
Serrone, Italy 647
service tree **352**
Ses Arenes de Baix, Menorca 618
Ses Roques Llises, Menorca 618
Setefilla, Spain 595
settlements 82–101, 538, 542
   architecture of 84–7
   circular 538
   evidence from 4
   farmsteads 90–1
   floors 85
   in Germany 738–42
   hierarchies 93–5
   house architecture 84–7
   house landscapes of 95–6, 97
   houses and households 83–4
   in Hungary 825
   in Iberia 611
   nucleated 91
   organization of household space 88–90
   organization of household space in 88–90
   in Romania, Moldova and Bulgaria 895
   in Scandinavia 750–2
   size differences between 87–8
   in Slovakia 825
   villages 91–3
   see also fortified settlements
Shaft Graves, Mycenae 377
shafts 155
shaman 221–2
   bags 262
Shap, Cumbria, England 392
sheep 330, 334–5, 342, 480, 543, 718, 752, 774, 909
shekels 370, 509, 510
shell armlets 212
shellfish 533, 535, 600, 619
shells 62, 484
Shennan, Stephen 72–3, 424
Sheridan, Alison 536
Sherratt, Andrew 2
Shetland 149, 317
shields 235
   Nipperwiese type 235
   round shields, Herzsprung type 738
   Yetholm type 235
ship-setting burials, in northern Europe 104

ships 762
  Baltic 'stone ships' 389
  ship-shaped stone settings 758
  see also boats
shipwrecks 371–2, 392, 540
  in British waters 388
  Kefalonia 55
shore displacement 275
S'Hospitalet Vell, Mallorca 618
Shovel Down, England 320
'shrine franchising' 141
shrines 155–6
Siberia 336
Sicily 55, 56, 383, 649, 653–67
  Bell Beaker culture in 63
  bronze artefacts 658
  connections with Italy in the Final Bronze Age-Early Iron Age 665
  Early Bronze Age in 654–8
  excavations in 654
  Final Bronze Age-Early Iron Age in 664–5
  funerary practices in 657
  Late Bronze Age and Early Iron Age in 662–4
  Lefkandi I-Kastri pottery 53
  Lipari Ausonian I 662
  Maltese architecture in 657
  map of Bronze Age sites 655
  Middle Bronze Age in 658–62
  natural resources 653
  Pantalica culture 662–4
  role in Mediterranean trade 661
  subsistence 657
sickle teeth 608
sickles 128, 136, 378, 515–6, 730, 760, 805, 892
  bronze 563, 565
Siedlung Forschner, Federsee, Baden-Württemberg 92
Siegendorf, Austria 788–9
Sierra de Tramuntana 617
Sierra Morena 600
Sierras de Llevant 617
Sigmaringen, Germany 515
Silanus, Sardinia 669
Silbury Hill, Wiltshire, England 146, 172
Silesia- Platěnice culture 790, 798, 809
  vessels 798, 802
silica 494

Siligo, Sardinia 669
Šiljar, Northern Adriatic 871
S'Illot, Mallorca 618, 628
silos 608
Silovskoe site, Voronezh 909
silver 459, 509, 523, 599
  axes 54, 886
  finds 56, 58
  grave goods 58
  lock-rings 891
  in Romania, Moldova and Bulgaria 891
  spiral lock-rings 884
Simris, Sweden 746–7
Simrishamm, Sweden 279
Singen group 727, 817–8
Singen, Germany 707, 709, 712, 719
  cemetery 711
  copper 422, 424, 440
Single Grave culture 552, 553, 557
Sintashta culture 336, 907, 908
Sion group 299
Sion-Petit Chasseur, Switzerland 147, 707, 710
  cemetery 711
Sjælland, period III, cremation burial 105
Skälby, Sweden 746–7
Skalica, Slovakia 815–6
Skalice district, Bohemia 788
Skalka, Velim, Bohemia 788, 792
Skallerup, Zealand, Denmark 737, 746–7, 757
Skalså track, Denmark 763
Skara Brae, Orkney 169
Škarin Samograd, Croatia 838
skates 483
Skeldal, Jutland, Denmark, gold objects found at 457
skeletal fractions 181–2
skeletal isotope analysis 179–96
Skelhøj, Jutland, Denmark 746–7
  Early Bronze Age barrow at 110, 111
skeuomorphism 476
Skjødstrup, Jutland, Denmark 132
Skrydstrup, Jutland, Denmark 478, 746–7
sky disc of Nebra 266–9, 735–6
slag 128
Slovakia 63, 197, 244, 790, 813, 829–30
  agriculture in 825
  burial rites in 825

chronology 814
Early Bronze Age in 814–25
end of the Bronze Age in 832–3
hill forts 831–2
Late and Final Bronze Age in 827–32
Lausitz culture in 829–30
map of 815–6
Middle Bronze Age in 825–7
natural resources 813–4
setting and natural conditions 813–4
settlements 95, 825
Slovinsky, Slovakia 440
Småland, Sweden 316
smelting 425–7
smiths 218, 219, 255, 256, 258, 260, 285
   and cosmology 257–62, 263
   graves 905
   in Norse saga 259
   role of 129–30
   social position of 259
   wandering smiths 75
Smolenice, Slovakia 815–6
Smørumovre, Denmark 237, 746–7, 764
snaffle-bits 401
soapstone 260, 261, 262, 263, 285
Sobiejuchy settlement 774, 782
social hierarchy 197
socketed axes 38, 760, 893
   eastern axes 893
   inner-Carpathian 893
socketed spearheads 483, 892
Sögel burial, Drouwen 560, 561
Sögel warrior graves 206, 565
Sögel-Wohlde culture 735, 736
Sognnes, Kalle 277
Șoimuș, Romania 878
Solana de Cabañas, Spain 595
Sollières, France 574
'Sologne', weighing equipment 518
Sombor, Serbia 838
Somerset Levels, England, trackways in 409
Somogyvár culture 819
Somogyvár-Vinkovci culture 817, 840, 844, 855–6
Somotor, Slovakia 815–6
Son Bauló de Dalt, Mallorca 618
Son Ermità, Menorca 618
Son Ferrandell-Olesa, Balearic Islands 618, 620
Son Jaumell, Mallorca 618
Son Mas, Mallorca 618, 620
Son Matge, Mallorca 618, 620
Son Mercer de Baix, Menorca 618
Son Mestre de Dalt, Menorca 618
Son Mulet, Mallorca 618
Son Olivaret, Menorca 618
Son Oms, Mallorca 618, 623
Son Sunyer, Mallorca 618
Sonnenvogelbark (sun-bird-boat) *see* sun-bird-boat
Sopron-Burgstall, Hungary 815–6
Sorbara di Asola, Italy 699
Sorel-Moussel, Frod Harrouard, France 572, 573, 574
Sørensen, Marie Louise 200
Sorgenti della Nova, Italy 633
Sorradile, Sardinia 669
Sosnitsa culture 909
Sotteville-sur Mer, France 125
South Cadbury, England 235
South Downs, England 320
south German Tumulus culture 797
South Lodge Camp, Dorset, southern England 91
south Russia, Ukraine and 898–918
southern Bavarian group 731
southern central Mediterranean area 51, 55–9
southern France 31, 32
   barley in 360
   non-cereals 353
   plant cultivation in 352–3
   RI values in the archaeobotanical record of **353**
   see also France
southern Italy 49–59
   Aegean voyages to 640
   menhirs 149
   statue menhirs 149
   see also Italy
southern Scandinavia *see* Scandinavia
Spain 332
   barley in 360
   bronze arrowheads 237
   copper mines in 443
   copper smelting 450
   daggers in 235
   El Argar culture 61

Spain (cont.)
  Galician-style rock art in 154
  gold hoard of Caldas de Reyes,
    Pontevedra 457
  Guadalquivir region 604
  non-cereals in 354
  plant cultivation in 353–4
  production of salt in 502, 503
  RI values of non-cereals in the
    archaeobotanical record of
    Mediterranean Spain 354
  rock art in 154
  wheat in 360
Spălnaca II hoard 516
Špania Dolina, Slovakia 440, 815–6
Spano, Giovanni 681
spatulae/scrapers 58
spear-butts 683
spearheads 95, 235, 379, 683, 735, 736, 760
  Aegean-Anatolian slotted spearheads 57
  Bagterp spearheads 762
  hollow-cast 235
  from Romania, Moldova and Bulgaria 893
  socketed spearheads from Lithuania 483
spears 131, 136, 237, 545, 565, 730
Specchia Artanisi, Italy, Bronze Age
    megalithic tomb from 638
Speghøje bog, Denmark 763
spelt 350, 351, 352, 353, 354, 355, 356, 357, 358,
    359, 360–1, 364, 538, 752
sphendonoids (sling-shot) 509, 510, 520
Spiez-Eggli, Bernese Alps, Switzerland 719
spindle-whorls 480
spinning 480
Spišský Štvrtok, Slovakia 240, 815–6, 824
Spjald, Denmark 746–7
Split-Gripe, Croatia 54
spoons 756
spotted dolerite 165
Springfield Lyons, Essex, England 542
springs 155, 719
Sredni culture 900
Sredni Stog culture 901, 902
Srodka, Poland, pottery from 777
Srubnaya (Timber-grave) culture 907, 908,
    909, 910–1
Sta. Maria d'Anglona 647
Stackpole Warren, Pembrokeshire, Wales 147

Stade, Germany 724, 737
Staffordshire, England 205
standing stones 146–7, 536
Stari Jankovci, Croatia 54
statue menhirs 146–7, 149
  Castel, Guernsey 148
  Filetto-Malgarte 300
  Pontevecchio type 300
  as a social marker 308
  in southern Italy 149
status 7, 93, 212
Stavanger, Norway 279
Stein group 553
Steinfurth, weighing equipment 518
stelae 146–7
Stele Torrejón el Rubio II, Portugal 148
Stenico, Italy 701
Stenness, Orkney Islands 151
Steno, Levkas 54, 57, 58
Stevn, Zealand, Denmark 760
Stillfried an der March, Austria 244, 788–9
stockbreeding 600, 605, 608, 613
Stockhult, Sweden 746–7, 762
stone
  artefacts in Czech lands and Austria
    807–8
  axeheads 448
  axes 726
  cairns 145
  exploitation of 532
  hammer 445
  implements 737
  monuments 535
  pickaxes 200
  sceptres 889
  ships 389
  tools for metalworkers 586
  weights 509
stone circles 150–3, 536
  Drombeg, County Cork, Ireland 152
  early circles 151
  entrances to 151
  four-poster stone circles 153
  history of circle building 151
  late-period circles 151
  middle-period circles 151
  in northern France 153
  raw materials for 151

recumbent stone circles 151
see also Stonehenge, Wiltshire, England
stone cists 535, 599, 754, 756, 757
Stone, J.F.S. 160
stone rows *148*, 149–50
Stonehenge, Wiltshire, England 141, 151, *152*, 159–78, *533*, 534
    Altar Stone 151, 165
    Aubrey Holes 162
    Avenue 159, 163
    chronological schemes for 161
    Early Neolithic, 4000-3600 BC 162
    environs of *160*
    Environs Project 160
    Greater Cursus 167
    Heel Stone 167
    history of the research of 160–1
    Mesolithic period before building of 161–2
    Middle Neolithic, 3600-3000 BC 162
    North Barrow 167
    Palisade Ditch 174
    Riverside Project (SRP) 160, 164
    Slaughter Stone 167
    South Barrow 167
    Southern Circle 172
    Stage 1 (3015-2935 BC) 162–5
    Stage 2 (2620-2480 BC) 165–71
    Stage 3 (2480-2280 BC) 171–3
    Stage 4 (2270-2020 BC) 173, *174*
    Stage 5 (1630-1520 BC) 174–5
    Station Stones 167
    Stonehenge Archer 171
    Trilithon Horseshoe 151
Stora Kopparberget, Falun, Sweden 373
Straubing, Bavaria, Germany 472
Straubing culture 727, 789, 797
Streda nad Bodrogom, Slovakia 815–6
Stromboli, Sicily 658
strontium 180, 181, 182
    analytical fraction, dietary input and interpretation of **183**
    in bone and dentine 191
    concentration of 180
strontium isotope analysis 10, 75, 182
Studien zu den Anfängen der Metallurgie (SAM) project 422, *423*, 456
Su 'e Predi Giaccu-Meana Sardo, Sardinia 672, *673*

Su Monte-Sorradile, Sardinia, 'round' temple 679
Su Mulinu-Villanovafranca, Sardinia 673
Su Nuraxi di Barumini, Sardinia 239
Su Scusorgiu-Villasor, Sardinia, votive swords from 684
Su Tempiesu-Orune, Sardinia, sacred spring 679
Sub-Apennine
    facies 640
    pottery 640
subsistence 534–5
Substantivist school 523
Suciu de Sus culture 828
Suciu de Sus, Romania *878*
Sucy-en-Brie, France *573*
sulphur 180, 181, **183**, 187, 193, 426, 657
Sumerian Early Dynastic III period 48
Šumice, Moravia 88, *788*
sun-bird-boat 584, 641, 762, 832
sun chariot *see* Trundholm sun chariot/wagon
sun discs 209, 251
'sun drum' 379
sun-symbolism 144
Sund, Norway 241, 245
Šurany - Nitriansky Hrádok, Slovakia 815–6
Surbo, Italy 633
Sutton Hoo, England 315
Sværdborg, Denmark 746–7
Svartarp, Sweden 746–7
Svržno-Černý vrch, Bohemia 788, 809
Swalecliffe, Kent, England 155
Swarzynica, Poland, Bronze Age/Hallstatt pottery from *777*
Sweden 245, 359, 746
    cult houses 258, 752
    map of *746–7*
    rock art in 154
    standing stones in 147
    stone and timber circles in 153
    see also Scandinavia
sweet chestnut **354**, 357
Swifterbant group 552
Switzerland 8, 338, 360
    animal remains in 329
    Bronze Age copper mining 423
    inhumation rituals and grave deposits in the Early Bronze Age in *720*

Switzerland (*cont.*)
  lake villages of 96
  Late Bronze Age weights from 521, **522**
  map of 707
  rock carving sites 299–300
  sheep and goat remains 334
  see also Switzerland and the Central Alps
Switzerland and the Central Alps 706–22
  chronological phases, dates and events in 712
  chronology and chorology 709–13
  climatic zones 706
  dry-land settlements 716
  economic background 717–8
  environment, climate and settlement in 706–9
  funerary sites 718
  gender subdivision in funeral rituals and grave deposits 719
  geographic regions 706
  mining for metal ores in 718
  promontory and hilltop settlements 714–5
  sacred natural places in 718
  settlement size in the Late Bronze Age 713
  settlement topography and settlement structures in 713–6
  society and ideology 718–9
  wetland settlements 713
  see also Switzerland
sword belts 761
swords 203, 205, 206, 209, 219, 220, 236, 245, 378, 545, 562, 565, 582, 637, 644
  Alpine swords 378
  Apa swords 759
  carp's-tongue swords 38
  deposition in burial mounds 199
  distribution of Urnfield swords in Austrian rivers and hoards 132
  distributions of Mindelheim and Thames swords in rivers and graves 133
  dry land hoards containing 131
  flange-hilted swords 760
  found at Olmo di Nogara cemetery 701
  in Germany 730, 737
  as grave goods 732, 760
  Gündlingen swords 563
  Hallstatt swords 764
  as indicator of warrior role 108
  in male graves 237
  Monte Sa Idda 683
  movement of 378
  Mycenaean 378
    in northern Italy 700
  octagonal-hilted 760
  placement in water courses or particular places 702
  as prestige item 198, 201
  produced at Rathgall workshop 95
  Recent Bronze Age 684
  river finds of 136
  from Romania, Moldova and Bulgaria 893
  short swords 759
  solid-hilted swords 236, 760
  in south Scandinavia 759
  Valsømagle long sword 760
  votive swords 682
Sybaris plain, Italy, cemeteries in 647
Sylt 364
symbolic strategies 304–5
symbolism 7
Syria 508
Szabó, Gábor 832
Százhalombatta, Hungary 89, 92, 93, 229, 360, 476, 815–6
Szczepidlo settlement 778
Szécsény-Benczúrfalva, Hungary 815–6, 828
Szentes-Nagyhegy, Hungary 815–6, 828
Szeremle group 474
Szigetszentmiklós, Hungary 815–6
Szőreg, Hungary 815–6

Taburles-en-Avançon, France 572
Taktabáj, Hungary 815–6
talaiots 618, 619
'Talayotic culture' 618
Tanum, Bohuslän, Sweden 280, 746–7
Tápé, Hungary 815–6, 826
Taranto, Italy 633
Tărnava, Bulgaria 884
Tarquinia, Italy 633
Tarxien Cremation cemetery 58, 657
Tatihou, France 573
taula, of Menorca 156
teeth 181
  animals 484, 700
  see also tooth enamel

Tei, Romania 878
Teleac, Romania 891
Tell Ezero, Bulgaria 51
tell settlements 92, 328–9, 473, 820, 840, 894
   in the Balkans 96
   in northern Greece and Albania 482
   in the Tisza Basin 825
Tellaro Valley, Sicily 657
Tempio, Sardinia 669
terebinth resin 385
Terenozhkin, A. I. 914
Terlinques, Alicante, Spain 595, 604
Termitito, Italy 337
terpen 329
Terramara/Terramare 329, 473, 475, 485, 487, 496, 511, 692, 696, 697, 707, 716
   access to metal tools 487
   burial rites 700
   masses of stone weights 512
   points and bevelled-edged tools 486
   stone weights 512
   villages 695
   weights 517, 524
Teso del Cuerno, Spain 595
Tetín, Bohemia 788
   hill fort 809
textiles 225, 228, 477–81, 779, 809
   from Hallstatt 481
   links to other crafts 481
   materials selection and manufacturing process 479–80
   north European lowlands 479
   production of 229, 481
   regional and temporal variation of 478–9
Thames River, England, weapons deposited in 131
Thames swords, distribution of 133
Thapsos-Milazzese tradition 639, 659, 662
Thapsos-Pantalica tradition 665
Thapsos, Sicily 655, 660, 680
   pottery 664
tholos nuraghe, Sardinia 673
Thom, Alexander 150
Thomsen, Christian Jørgensen 17, 328, 414
Thrace 53
Thucydides 383
Thumby, Germany 389

Thun-Renzenbühl, Bern, Switzerland 460, 707, 710, 719
Thunau am Kamp, Austria 95, 788–9
Thürkow, Germany 724
Thy, Jutland, Denmark 359, 752
Ticino Valley, Switzerland 712
Tilley, Chris 277
timber circles 150, 151, 168, 536
timber monuments 147
Timmari, Italy 633, 648
Timmari-Vigna Coretti cemetery 647
Timpa Dieri, Sicily 655
tin 197, 374–5, 419–20, 437, 445, 610, 614, 808, 814
   approximate dates of the transition to the use of 421
   deposits of 421, 585
   from Germany 726
   ingots 372, 385
   ore 539
   sources of 38, 532
   from Transylvanian Carpathians 891
tin-bronze 420, 428, 429, 536, 563, 599, 725, 727, 735, 770, 818, 910
   alloying 22
   Andronovo-Fedorovka culture 910
   knives 54
Tindari, Sicily 655
Tisza-Danube interfluve region 827–9
Tisza region 821–5, 826–7
   cemeteries 822–3
   cremation burials 823
   fortified settlements 824
   gold and bronze production 823
   grave goods 823
   Late and Final Bronze Age in 827–9
   settlements in 822
   tell in 825
Tisza river 813
Tiszaug- Kéménytető, Hungary 84, 85
Titel Plateau, Western Balkans 840–1, 845, 846
Tobø, Jutland, Denmark 145
toggles 760
token cremations 540
Tombe di Giganti, Sardinia 143
tombs 620
   late chambered tombs 143
   wedge tombs 143, 535

Tomnaverie, Aberdeenshire, Scotland 151, 533
Tondolon-Sv. Petar, Northern Adriatic 872
Tonnerre, France 574
tools 599, 727
   bevel-ended tools 482, 484
   bronze tools 612
   for metallurgy 586
   movement of 378
   radius-based faceted 484
tooth enamel 180, 181, *186*
   see also teeth
Topoľčany, Slovakia 815–6
Toppo Daguzzo, Italy 633
Torbhlaren, Argyll and Bute, Scotland 154
Torbrügge, Walter 131
torcs 891
Tormarton, Gloucestershire, England 243
Tornaľa, Slovakia 815–6
Torralba d'en Salord, Menorca 618
Torralba, Sardinia 669
Torre Castelluccia, Italy 633, 648
Torre Galli, Italy 633, 647
Torre Mordillo, Calabria, Italy 334, 633, 640, 647
Torrejón de Rubio II, Spain 595
Torrelló d'Onda, Spain 595
Torsbo, near Kville, Bohuslän, Sweden 154
Torsted, Denmark 237
Tossene parish, Sotenäset, Bohuslän, Sweden 282
Tószeg-Laposhalom, Hungary 338, 814, 815–6
Trachthügel (costume-mounds) 736
trade
   and exchange 370–81
   meaning of 370–1
   sources of evidence for 371–2
   and transport in Scandinavia 763–4
Traisental, Austria 719
Transcaucasia 144, 360
Transdanubia 817, 819, 830
Transdanubian Encrusted pottery culture 475, 820
transhumance 718
transport
   means of 399–400
   over land 398–413
   speed of 400–1
Transylvania, Romania 378, 516, 824, 877, 887

   burials in 889
   patterns on womens' skirts in 224
Transylvanian Tumulus group 881
Trappendal, Jutland, Denmark 90, 746–7, 754
Trebalúger, Menorca 618, 623
Tréboul-en-Douarnenez, France 572, *573*
tree-ring growth 717
tree-trunk coffins 754
Treherne, Paul 224
Trenčianske Bohuslavice, Slovakia 815–6
Trentino-Alto Adige, Italy 297, 698, 699
Trethellan Farm, Cornwall, England 87
tribal societies, transformation into chiefdoms 216
Trindhøj, Denmark 746–7, 755
Trinitapoli, Italy 633
Tripolye culture 878, 900, 903, 904
Troad, Turkey 881
Trøndelag, Norway 270, 286, 749
Trou de Han, Belgium 125
Troy 58, *878*, 881, 901
Trundholm sun chariot/wagon 251, 255, 263, 401, 403, *459*, 746–7, *753*, *759*, 759, 762
Trzcinica, Poland 878
Trzciniec culture, Poland 477, 772, 775, 909
Tsnori, Georgia 144
Tudons, Menorca 618
tumuli 144, 145, 571, 647, 719, 726, 781, 822
   in the Adriatic coast 849
   of Lausitz culture in Slovakia 830
Tumulus culture 103, 145, 217, 475, 558, 573, 591, 728, 772, 775, 783, 797, 825
   metal products 778
   pottery 762, 799
Túrkeve-Terehalom, Hungary 92
Turkey 361
turnip rape 774
Tusa, Sebastiano 654
tutuli 760
tuyères and soapstone moulds, from Scandinavia 261
tweezers 206, 730, 760, 762
twill 479, 480
Tyrrhenian sea 688

Ubaye Valley 300
überausstattete (over-equipped) burials 107

Überlingen, Lake Constance 417
Uerschhausen-Horn, Auvernier-Nord, Switzerland 707, 712, 713
Uggårda röir, Gotland, Sweden 746-7, 753
Ukraine 378, 504, 890, 898-918
  beginning of the Bronze Age in 901-4
  Bronze Age development in 915-6
  bronze objects 916
  Catacomb culture and the Srubnaya culture 905-11
  climate in 898
  cultural relationships in 898, 911-4
  economy in 916
  end of the Bronze Age in 914-5
  Eneolithic in 899-901
  forest regions 898
  vegetation zones in 899
Uluburun shipwreck 370, 371, 379, 383-5, 392, 492, 510, 520, 680, 889
  amber 377
  oxhide ingots 438
  tin ingots on 375
Understed, Denmark 746-7, 764
Únětice culture 244, 457, 725-6, 770, 773, 775, 783, 801, 814, 817, 818
  amber objects 779
  artefacts from 725
  burials 107, 200, *201*, 206
  cemeteries 725
  cups 799, 809
  daggers in 235
  funerary rites 794
  graves 726, 795
  'hour-glass' cup 472
  houses 792
  metal products 778
  pottery 799
  stone artefacts 808
  vessels 799
ungulates 340
Unín, Slovakia 815-6
Unneset, Norway 277
Unterglauheim hoard, Germany 458, *733*
Unterradl, Austria 788-9
Unterradlberg, Austria 788-9, 794, 724, 741
Unteruhldingen-Stollenwiesen, Bodensee, Germany 92, 742, 724, 741

Unterwölbling culture 788-9, 789, 790, 797, *801*
  burial sites 796
  Early Bronze Age house 793
  pottery 799
Upper Danubian Urnfield group 790
Uppland, Sweden 275
Ural Mountains 337
Ural piedmont area 335
urn burials 730, 738
urnfield barrows 561
Urnfield culture 217, 557, 711, 827, 857
  burials 31, 106
  cemeteries 113, 155, 741
  forts 791
  in Slovakia and Hungary 832
Urnfield period 8, 240, 406, 407, 558, 709
  basket weave 479
  in Bohemia 807
  bronze hoards 805
  funerary customs 798
  in Germany 731
  gold as a textile material in an Austrian grave from 479
  pottery 472, 475, 553, 799, 800
  sites 358
  swords, distribution in Austrian rivers and hoards 132
  tuyères and crucibles 809
  vehicles 411
  vessels 474
urnfields 557, 561, 566, 575, 823
  grave goods 565
  in Iberia 613
  Lausitz culture 734
  in the Tisza region 827-9
  in Vledder, Northern Netherlands 562
urns 471, 561, 798
  Barrel and Bucket urns 539
  Biconical urns 539
Usatovo group 904
Ustica, Sicily 655
Utevka, Russia 903
Užiška Požega, Western Balkans 854

Vaassen, Epe, the Netherlands 312, 323
Val Camonica, Italy, rock art 154
Val d'Aosta, Italy 299

Valaron, Northern Adriatic 872
Valcamonica, Italy 291, 297–9, 305, 306
Vâlcele, Romania 891
Valdevimbre, León, Spain 595, 612
Vale Ferrerio, Portugal 595
Valencia, upland settlements 604
Vallarade, France 442
Valle Sorigliano, Italy 647
Valledolmo, Sicily 655
Vals-Valserberg, Switzerland 719
Valserà, Gazzo Veronese, Italy 699
Valsømagle, Denmark 746–7, 759
  axes 762
  long sword 760
Valtellina, Italy 297–9, 305
van Giffen, A. E. 312, 550
Vardar-Axios river 55
Varna cemetery, Bulgaria 454
Vărșand (Gyulavarsánd), Romania 878
Várvölgy- Felsőzsid, Slovakia 815–6
Varvara, Bosnia and Herzegovina 838, 844
Várvölgy-Nagy-Lázhegy, Hungary 832
Várvölgy, wound-wire gold ornament from hoard at 831
Vase Tradition 536
Vatin, Serbia 838, 856
Vatina culture 824, 840, 841, 855, 856, 878
Vatya culture 475, 820
Vatya tell settlement, Százhalombatta, Hungary 476
Vaudrevanges, France 574
Včelince - Lászlófala, Slovakia, Koszider-type hoard from 815–6, 819
Veii, Italy 633
Velika Gorica, Western Balkans 838
Vela Valbusa, Italy 693, 699
Velatice culture 788, 830, 831, 832
Velemszentvid hill, Hungary 815–6
Velika Gruda, Montenegro 54, 838, 853
Veliki Brijun Island 870, 871
Velim, Bohemia, Czech Republic 240–1, 244
Veľké Raškovce, Slovakia 405, 815–6, 828
  cart depiction from 895
Velký Grob, Slovakia 815–6
Veneti 393
Venice region, Italy 297
Verbicioara, Romania 878, 886
Verucchio, Italy 633

Veselé, Slovakia 815–6
vessels 587
  cast bronze 736
  chalice-shaped 472
Vestby, Norway 746–7
Vestra Fiold, Orkney Islands 151
Vesuvius 635
Věteřov culture 788, 790, 796, 801
  pottery 799
  vessels 799
victims of violence 240–5
Videlles, France 573
Viksø, Denmark 746–7, 763
Vila Nova da Cerveira, Portugal 460
Vilavella/Atios facies 597
Vilhonneur, France, 'Cave Chaude', weighing equipment 518
Villafáfila, Zamora, Spain 503
Villafranca Veronese, Veneto, Italy 58, 59
villages 91–3, 96
Villanovan facies 643
Villena, Alicante, Spain
  gold hoard 459
  Late Bronze Age precious-metal hoard 458
Villeneuve St-Vistre vessels 587
Villethierry, France 128, 574, 586
  jewellery 589
Vinča culture pottery 440
Vinkovci, Western Balkans 54, 838, 855
violin idols, Piano Conte site, Camaro, Messina, Sicily 55
Virovitica, Croatia 838, 845, 846, 857
  cemetery 857
Viste Cave, Norway 746–7
Vital, Joel 580
Vivara, Italy 633
Vlaardingen culture 552, 553, 557
Vledder, the Netherlands, urnfield in 562
Vliněves, Bohemia 788
Vogelsonnenbark (sun-bird-boat) *see* sun-bird-boat
Vojvodina, Serbia 856
volcanic rock 610
Volders, Austria 788–9
Voldtofte with Lusehøj, Denmark 746–7
Volosovo culture 338, 901
Vomp, Austria 788–9

Voorhout, the Netherlands 211
    scrap axe hoard 562
votive deposits 91, 92, 123, 124, 136
    in Scandinavia 764
votive ships 686–7
votive swords 682
    from Su Scusorgiu-Villasor hoard 684
Vráble, Slovakia 815–6
Vrčin, Northern Adriatic 871
Vučedol culture 54, 840
Vučevica, Croatia 838
Vulci, Italy 633
Vyšný Kubín, Slovakia 815–6, 830

Wachtberg-Fritzdorf, Germany 724
    gold beaker 727
wagons 399, 402–11
    ceremonial wagons 737
    drawn by draught animals 401
    four-wheeled wagon 405–6
    functions of wheels and 406–7
    as funerary gifts 407
    in graves 903
    as hearse 407
    see also carts
Waidendorf-Buhuberg, Austria 788–9
Wainwright, Geoffrey 152
Wales
    copper mining in 445
    four-poster stone circles 153
    Late Bronze Age ceramics 471
    Mold 'cape', North Wales 461
    sewn-plank boats 387
    stone pairs 149
Wallerstein, Immanuel 9
walls 319
walnuts 352, 634
Warendorf-Neuwarendorf, Germany
    724, 733
warfare 76, 198, 203, 234–48, 545
warrior graves 200, 203, 206, 561, 589, 732
warriors 198, 218, 219–21, 234, 237, 245,
    545, 685
Wartau-Ochsenberg, Switzerland 715
Wartosław, Bronze Age/Hallstatt pottery
    from 777
Wassenaar, the Netherlands 242, 245

Wasserburg, Bad Buchau, Germany 402, 707,
    714, 724
waterways 411
wattle 779
wax-turning 586
weapons 76, 125, 209, 220, 234–8, 564, 565,
    599, 643, 650, 760, 893
    bronze weapons 612, 649, 873
    burials 237–8
    carvings of 305
    deposited in the River Thames 131
    as engravings on natural rock slabs 295
    in graves 221, 565
    hoards 727
    movement of 378
    in Sardinia 673
    single finds of 131
    solid-gold 459
Wear, River 121, 137
weaving 480, 778
weaving patterns 225
wedge tombs 143, 535
Weer, Austria 788–9
Wehringen-Hexenbergle, Germany 707,
    712, 713
weighing
    in Bronze Age Europe 514–21
    and commodification 522–4
    and the development of complex
        metalworking 509
    earliest evidence for 508–10
    equipment 517, 518
weights 809
    disc-shaped weights 510
    found in high-status graves 523
    from France and Switzerland 521, **522**
    and measures 370
    rectangular **519**
Weilheim, Germany 724, 727
Weiningen-Hardwald, Switzerland 707
Well-Temples 676, 682, 686
Welland Bank Quarry, England 322
wells 155, 538, 829
Wels-Weyrauch, Ulrike 228
Welsh bluestones 165
Weser-Ems, Germany, wooden
    trackways 408
'Weltbild' by Karol Schauer 249

Wessex culture 25
Wessex, England 21
West Frisia, the Netherlands 323, 551, 555, 556, 557, 566
West House, Akrotiri, Thera 386
West Row Fen, Suffolk, England 332
West Siberian Sintashta culture 405
Western Balkans 50, 54–5, 837–63
   burial rites and their social implications 849–59
   continental region 855–9
   Early Bronze Age characteristic element in 840
   geography and environment 837–9
   grave goods in the 853
   Late Bronze Age in 846
   map of 838
   metallurgical production in 847–9
   ore deposits 837–8
   regions 837
   research and chronology 839
   settlements and social implications 839–49
   tumuli in 853
   urban centres 847
   see also Balkans
wheat 360–1, 364, 608
   club wheat 355
   free-threshing wheat 350, 351, 352, 353, 355, 356, 357, 358, 359, 361
   glume wheat 355, 361
   naked wheat 351
   Timopheev 361
wheel-symbolism 144
wheels 399, 411
   bronze 404
   cross-bar 402
   Danish spoked wheels 403
   disc wheels 402
   light spoked 894
   metal spoked 404–5
   spoked 402–3
   strutted 402
whetstones 200
Wickstead, Helen 314
Wieselburg culture 789, *801*, 819
   Early Bronze Age house 793
   funerary practices 796
   grave constructions of *795*
   houses 792
   pottery 799
Wietenberg culture 824, 895, *878*, 887
wild boar 92
wild horses 336
wild oats 358
wild pigs 333
wild strawberries 774
Wilsford Shaft, Wiltshire, England 155
Wirth, Stefan 584
Wohlsdorf, Austria *788–9*
Wohnstallhaus 740
Wolnzach-Niederlauterbach, Bavaria, Germany, tumulus I male and female burials 729
women
   daggers found in burials of 235
   movement of 378
wood
   clubs 243
   coffins 754
   disc wheels 402, *403*
   and earth constructions 576
   shovels 448
   tanks 702–3
   tapers 854
   troughs 505
   wellheads 90
Woodhenge 159, 160, 162, 168–9
woodwork 761
wool 225, 479, 480
worked bone *see* bone(s)
workshops 95
world systems 2, 8–10
Worms-Herrnsheim, Germany 237
wrist bracers 209
wristguards 62, 64, 460

X-ray fluorescence 10

Yamnaya culture 47, 51, 144, 901, 904, 905, 916
   burials 903
   grave and material 902
   grave goods 901
   settlements 902

yarn 479
Yates, David 313, 538
Yates, Timothy 285
Yellow River Valley, China 361
Yonne region, France 520, 523

Za Raščico, Western Balkans 838
Zagreb, Croatia 838
Zagreb-Velika Gorica-Dobova group 857
Zakro, Crete 506
Zalkin, Veniamin Iosifovich 332
Založnica on Ljubljana Moor, Western Balkans 838, 840
Zambotti, Laviosa 694
Žatec, Bohemia 788
Zealand, Denmark 104, 251
Zemianske Podhradie, Slovakia 815–6
Zemun–Asfaltna Baza, Western Balkans 838, 846
Zhabotin, Ukraine 915
Židovar, Serbia 838
Zijderveld, Utrecht, the Netherlands 323
Zimnicea, Romania 878, 880, 889
Zug-Sumpf, Switzerland 357, 361, 707, 712, 712, 713, 714
Zürich-Mozartstrasse, Switzerland 337, 707, 711, 713
Zürich, Switzerland 713
Žuto Brdo, Serbia 838, 878
Zwenkau, Germany 724, 726
  wooden wellhead at 90
Zwerndorf an der March, Austria 788–9